THE INDIAN
ANNUAL REGISTER

THE INDIAN
ANNUAL REGISTER

An Annual Digest of Public Affairs of India

Recording the Nation's Activities each year in matters Political, Economic, Industrial, Educational, Social Etc.

1919–1947

(In 58 Volumes)

Volume I 1936

(Volume 36)

By

H.N. Mitra

N.N. Mitra

Introduction by

Bipan Chandra

GYAN

The Indian Annual Register
An Annual Digest of Public Affairs of India Recording the Nation's
Activities each year in matters Political, Economic, Industrial, Educational, Social Etc. 1919–1947

ISBN : 978-81-212-0213-8 (Set)
ISBN : 978-81-212-0364-7 (Vol. 36)

First Published 1990, reprint 2015 in India by
Gyan Publishing House
23, Main Ansari Road, Daryaganj,
New Delhi - 110002
Phones : 23282060, 23261060
Fax : (011) 23285914
E-mail: books@gyanbooks.com
website: gyanbooks.com

Printed at : Sagar Color Scan, New Delhi.

THE INDIAN
ANNUAL REGISTER

JANUARY—JUNE 1936

TABLE OF CONTENTS

CHRONICLE OF EVENTS

JANUARY—JUNE 1936

Chronicle of Events

JANUARY—JUNE 1936

JANUARY 1936

1st. *Split in the Hindu Mahasabha Session* at Poona, where a new party was formed styled as the Sarvadeshik Hindu Sabha to work purely on nationalistic lines and to co-operate with all Indian political parties. The split had its origin in the anti-national and communal aspect of the Mahasabha which was obsessing a few of its adherents.

Temple-Entry Satyagraha :—Mass Satyagraha for temple-entry by Depressed Classes was apprehended in several cities in the United Provinces. Two of the Depressed Classes leaders in Lucknow issued an appeal for recruiting 120 volunteers, who would be sent out in batches to offer Satyagraha at the various Hindu temples in the province, where members of their community were refused admission. This decision was arrived at following a meeting of several panchayats of Balmiki sweepers, Bhagat "Raiedas" and Chamars, three different sections of the Depressed Classes. An appeal for volunteers was issued on behalf of these sections. It was pointed out in the manifesto that though the Hindu Mahasabha had recognised the right of temple-entry by Depressed Classes, the right had not been conceded by the custodians of the great Hindu temples.

2nd. *Bengal Congress Tangle settled* :—The Congress Working Committee in Bombay authorised the Congress President to nominate, after consulting Mr. Sarat Chandra Bose, a provisional Bengal Provincial Congress Committee in order to carry out the work of the Congress in Bengal until a proper Congress Committee was duly elected. This had the effect of satisfying both the rival Congress groups in Bengal.

Baroda Ruler's Diamond Jubilee :—Gorgeous scenes marked the celebration of Diamond Jubilee of His Highness the Maharaja Gaekwar, the most important part of the crowded programme, the Durbar for receiving the address of the people by the Maharaja. After the presentation of the address, the Maharaja in his message to his people, announced that in commemoration of the Diamond Jubilee he had decided to set apart a fund of one crore of rupees, the income from which would be devoted to improving the conditions of life of the rural population, especially those of the poor and depressed classes. A science and technological institute was opened at Baroda on the occasion by H. E. the Viceroy.

Indian Science Congress :—His Highness the Maharaja Holkar of Indore inaugurated the 23rd session of the Indian Science Congress in Indore before a gathering of scientists from all over the country and visitors, including Sir S. M. Bapna the Prime Minister, other ministers, high officers and prominent citizens of Indore State. Dr. P. Basu, Vice-Chancellor of the Agra University, welcoming the delegates, surveyed the great scientific discoveries in various fields in recent years and their effect on practical life. After the address of the president Sir U. N. Brahmachari, sectional meetings were held.

Indian Economic Conference :—Khan Bahadur M. Azizul Haque, Minister of Education, Bengal, opened the nineteenth session of the Indian Economic Conference at Dacca. India's fiscal position under the new Constitution was discussed at the Conference.

3rd. A hint to police officers not to ask for increased salaries in view of the great poverty of the ryot was made in the presidential address at the conference of the Assam Police Association.

Pandit Malaviya paid a fine tribute to H. H. the Gaekwar of Baroda in a speech at a special darbar held in connexion with the ruler's diamond jubilee celebrations.

'h. *Calcutta Khilafat Conference* :—The political ideal of the Moslems was described as equal status with other communities in a self-governing India, by the Nawab of Dacca in his presidential address at the Khilafat Conference in Calcutta.

5th. At a conference of landholders held in Calcutta, resolutions were passed demanding seats on the proposed Debt Conciliation Boards and requesting the authorities not to countenance agitation which would have the effect of interfering with the Permanent Settlement.

A striking tribute to the Maharaja Gaekwar of Baroda was paid by His Excellency the Viceroy on the occasion of a State banquet.

6th. "The Congress during the next ten years" was the subject of an address delivered by Dr. Kitchlew to the students of a Lahore college.

8th. *House-Searches in Bombay* :—The Bombay Police carried out simultaneous house searches and raids and arrested 4 persons with the assistance of the Lahore Police. It was stated that the raids and arrests were prompted by the suspicion that the arrested persons were carrying on Communist activities in the city and distributing Communist literature. The Police seized large quantities of Communist literature, hundreds of copies of "The Communist", cyclostyle machines and other paraphernalia used for multigraphing copies. The arrested persons hailed from Northern India.

11th. The Congress attitude on the acceptance of Office was in itself the best proof that India had accepted the reforms, said Sir Mohammad Yakub in a speech at Bombay.

16th. *U. P. Unemployment Committee Report* :—The Report of the U. P. Unemployment Committee, appointed by the Government in October 1934, with Sir Tej Bahadur Sapru as Chairman, was released for publication. The Committee held 18 public sittings in various educational centres of the Province and examined 127 witnesses, including 30 officials, besides a number of memoranda submitted to it. The report laid great emphasis on the reorganisation of all stages of education, primary, secondary and higher, and said that the remedy for the evil of unemployment did not lie merely in stiffening the University standard so as to restrict the number of entrants. Apart from educational reform, the report advocated the development of vocational education on modern lines. There could not be one single remedy which could solve the question of unemployment, added the report, nor could the problem of unemployment be solved immediately, but if it was attacked systematically, on a well-conceived plan, with the resources available to the Government, great relief could be given to the unemployed among educated men.

Sir Otto Niemeyer arrived in India to conduct his inquiry into the finances of the coming Federation.

17th. Dr. Subbaroyan of Madras revealed that India lost the chance of better Constitution at the second Round Table Conference in London owing to Mr. Gandhi's motives being misunderstood by Indian politicians.

18th. The service facilities offered to the minority communities and the measures undertaken to fight road competition were described in the annual administration report of Indian Railways for 1934-35.

19th. The Congress Socialists, it was understood, proposed to remain in the Congress in order to be in a position to fight the Reforms.

A trenchant attack on the Hindu majority in the Calcutta Corporation and praise for the resignation of Moslem Councillors were made at a Moslem meeting in Calcutta.

20th. The Calcutta Corporation passed a resolution reiterating its policy of recognizing the claims of qualified Moslems to a fare share in the Corporation services.

The Socialist Conference of Meerut concluded after passing several resolutions, including one indicating the line of action Congressmen should take in the Legislature on behalf of the masses.

Death of King George the V:—The death of His Majesty King George V at Sandringham at 11-55 p. m. (G. M. T.) in the presence of the Royal Household. The King suffered no pain. Wonderful world-wide tributes were paid by all shades of opinion throughout the world to the late King.

22nd. *Andhra Youth Conference* :– Resolutions demanding the release of all political prisoners, condemning the attitude of the Congress towards the Native States and opposing acceptance of offices under the new Constitution were passed by the Andhra Provincial Youth Conference, held at Cocanada under the presidency of Mr. J. Ramalingiah. Most of the resolutions evoked heated discussion.

The late King's deep concern for the welfare of his millions of subjects in India was referred to by His Excellency the Viceroy in an All-India broadcast message.

One hundred and thirty Sikhs were arrested in Lahore for defying the *kripan* ban.

23rd. *Harijans and Sanatan Dharma* :—The All-India Sanatan Dharma Conference, held at the Kumbha Mela, Allahabad, arrived at an unanimous decision that Harijans being the followers of Sanathan Dharma, it should be the duty of all Sanatanists to assist them in the enjoyment of privileges which the followers of Sanathan Dharma were entitled to. The Conference recorded resolutions to allow Harijans "Devadharshan" wherever they were disallowed till now, as also the use of wells and tanks, gardens, schools etc., without any interference or hindrance. The Conference enjoined its Committee to arrange for Brahmins to give the "Shiva Mantra" of five syllables on the occasion of the coming Shivaratri to the so-called untouchables also as was done to the Sanatanists.

A section of Lahore Moslems launched a "civil disobedience movement" in connection with the Shahidgunj mosque dispute.

25th. *Tamil Nad Provincial Conference* :—"Now that the Congress has been successful in getting the majority in all the newly elected District Boards and Municipalities and has also succeeded in getting its own men elected as Presidents and Chairmen respectively, it must be our endeavour to see that the good name of the Congress is maintained at any cost and that we do not fall victims to those very mistakes for which the party in power to-day is being condemned. Let these local bodies serve as a means to further local welfare as well as national interest", observed Mrs. Rukmani Lakshmipathi, in the course of her address in presiding over the thirty-seventh session of the Tamil Nad Provincial Conference held at Karaikudi.

The name of Pandit Jawharlal Nehru was recommended for the presidentship of the Lucknow session of the Congress by a large number of provincial Congress Committees.

The C. P. Tobacco Taxation Bill was thrown out by a two to one majority in the C. P. Council.

One of the most important measures adopted in the Midnapore district to fight terrorism was the formation of anti-terrorist leagues with watch and ward committees.

26th. *Sikh Muslim Clash* :—Report of a serious clash between the Sikhs and Moslems was received from the village of Dhutial in Jhelum District, about 50 miles from Rawalpindi. It appears the trouble arose recently over the attempt to construct a shop facing the Gurdwara to which the Sikhs objected. The matter was reported to the Police, who intervened and arrested a dozen persons who were subsequently bound down to keep the peace. But a large number of Moslems, it was stated, attempted to take possession of the site which was resisted by the Sikhs, leading to a serious encounter lasting for several hours, when axes, lathis and lethal weapons were alleged to have been freely used and which resulted in injuries to about 20 persons. Simultaneously, it was stated, another party of Moslems came into clash with Sikhs at the Gurdwara Gurusingh Sabha, in which one man who died fell from the roof of the Gurdwara during the scuffle.

Funeral of King George :—The funeral of His late Majesty King George V took place at St. George's Chapel, Windsor. King Edward and his brothers walked behind the coffin through London to Paddington station. All were in uniform, as well as the foreign Kings and Princes attending. Churches of all denominations throughout Britain were thronged, it being estimated that at least 1,000,000 persons attended the services. More than five hundred thousand persons filed through Westminster Hall where King George's body was lying in State. Patient queues, sombrely clad, stretched for miles. Moving forward at a snail's pace, those at the rear took four hours to reach the entrance to the Hall.

27th. In a broadcast talk on "Some of the dying industries of Bengal," the Government's Industrial Surveyor gave an account of the endeavours of the Department of Industries to rehabilitate those small and cottage industries of the province.

28th. Scenes of unexempled solemnity were witnessed in Calcutta on the occasion of the funeral of His Majesty King George V in London. An impressive memorial service at the Church of the Redemption, New Delhi, was the Imperial Capital's last tribute to King George.

30th. The Joint conference of the International Council of Women and the National Council of Women in India began in Calcutta.

Several persons were killed in a colliery explosion at Loyabad (Bihar). It was officially stated that five Europeans and 32 Indians were killed.

31st. Presiding at the annual meeting of the Indian Jute Mills Association, Mr. H. H. Burn gave a warning that unless an agreement was arrived at regarding the restriction of jute output a trade war with disastrous consequences to the industry was inevitable.

FEBRUARY 1936

4th. The Assembly voted for a Joint Standing Army Committee of members of both Houses to advise on India's defence policy.

5th. *Search for Proscribed Literature* :—The C. I. D. with the assistance of the Police carried out searches in Lucknow. The police were maintaining the strictest secrecy as to the cause of these searches, but it was believed that these were the continuation of those conducted on January 30 last when several hundred copies of proscribed literature, it was alleged, were seized. It was reported from Allahabad that a number of searches were conducted by the Police in connection with Communist literature. The persons involved, it was alleged, were mostly students. Some pamphlets and other printed matter were taken possession of by the police. The police also searched three houses and a shop in quest of alleged Communist literature and seized certain books and papers.

6th. The Opposition in the Assembly defeated a Government motion regarding the closure on Clause 2 of the Criminal Law Amendment Act.

It was stated in the Assembly that the Government of India were alive to the need of drastic action regarding the Jharia coalfields where 45 separate fires were said to be raging.

7th. The opening of cottage industries as a cure for unemployment in Bengal was suggested by Mr. D. P. Khaitan in a speech in Calcutta.

8th. The Indian Chamber of Commerce, Calcutta, urged the Government of India to terminate the Ottawa Trade Agreement without delay.

9th. *Andhra Provincial Conference* :—The fifteenth Conference was held at Cocanada under the presidentship of Mr. C. Ramalinga Reddy. A large number of delegates from all over the province, including ladies, attended. Dr. Subrahmanyam, Chairman of the Reception Committee, welcoming the President and delegates, commended the triple programme of boycott of councils preparing the country for direct action and carrying on village reconstuction work. Mr. T. Prakasam, declaring the Conference open, advocated council-entry and acceptance of office, as there was no suitable atmosphere in the country for direct action. While rejecting the new C nstitution, the Lucknow Congress should lift the ban on acceptance of office, was the opinion expressed by the Conference, by a majority of 93 votes to 35. Mr. T. Prakasam was the principal supporter of the resolution, while Dr. Pattabhi Seetharamayya opposed it vigorously.

Calcutta Moslems held a demonstration and asked Moslems to boycott the municipal elections until the community's grievances in the Corporation were redressed.

11th. The assembly passed without a division Mr. Azhar Ali's resolution urging the Government to take over control of the B. and N. W. and M. and S. M. Railways.

Sir Henry Craik stated in the Assembly that the detention of the present number of State prisoners was necessary in the public interest.

12th. *Death of Mr. Bardaloi* :—Death occurred of Mr. Nabin Chandra Bardaloi, member of the Legislative Assembly and a devoted Congress workers and patriot of Assam.

13th. The Assembly rejected Mr. B. Das's Bill to amend the Criminal Law Amendment Act by 67 votes to 66.

A proposal for fixing minimum prices for agricultural produce was rejected in the Bengal Council.

The measures contemplated by the Madras Government to help handloome weavers in the province was explained by Sir Zafrullah Khan in the Assembly.

14th. Lieut. Misri Chand, one of the competitors of the Viceroy's Trophy Air Race, was the first to arrive in Bombay. Lieut. Chand won the Viceroy's Cup Air Race at New Delhi.

Whipping for offences against women :—The Bengal Council passed without division the Whipping Bill providing whipping as punishment for some offences against women. Mr. Suhrawardy's motion for circulation of bill was defeated.

16th. *All India Moslem Conference* :—The political development and aspirations of the Moslem community in India were outlined by the Aga Khan when he addressed a meeting of the All-India Mosle m Conference.

17th. The Railway Budget was presented in both Houses of the Central Legislature in New Delhi.

The Burma Council by 44 votes to 33 rejected the Criminal Law Amendment Act Bill sponsored by the Government.

18th. *Death of Sir D. Wacha* :—Sir Dinsha Wacha, the oldest Congress President died at his residence in Bombay. Sir Dinshaw was 91 years old and was keeping indifferent health for some months past. Mr. Gandhi issued the following statement regarding him :—"In the death of Sir Dinshaw Wacha, the country has lost a great patriot. The very first Congress, I had the privilege of attending, was presided over by him at Calcutta. I have vivid recollection of his great industries and unfailing co urtesy to all. I remember well how much his fearless criticism of Government measures and his grasp of financial questions were admired by all Congressmen."

The Assembly accepted a non-official resolution recommending the extension of reforms to the backward tracts.

20th. His Excellency the Governor of Bengal, speaking at the dinner of the Calcutta Trades Association, declared that members of the Association should play a bigger role in public affairs.

The Imperial Council of Agricultural Research constituted two standing committees on rice and wheat which would consider the marketing facilities and general improvement of the two crops.

21st. In opening the ryots' conference in Serajganj, Nawab Sir Mohiuddin Faroqui made suggestions for increasing the income of agriculturists.

The scheme of relief outlined in the Bengal Agricultural Debtors' Bill was explained by Mr. H. S. Suhrawardy at a conference of agriculturists at Serajgunj.

A striking tribute to the services rendered by the Aga Khan was paid by the Nawab of Rampur at the All-India Moslem Educational Conference at Rampur.

22nd. *Hitler's insult to India* :—At an urgent meeting of the Bombay Medical Union, the following resolution was unanimously passed by members of the Union against Herr Hitler's recent speech to the Nazi University students, Munich :—"This urgent meeting of the Bombay Medical Union resents the insult gratuitously hurled by Herr Hitler on the people of India in a recent speech, and unanimously resolves to recommend to the members of the Union and the medical profession in India to boycott German goods generally and all medical and surgical requisites particularly, wherever and whenever possible, until an 'amende honourable' is made." It was further hoped that various Associations, medical as well as others in the country, would take up this question of national self-respect and pass similar resolutions and act upon them.

The Burma Council, for the second time, rejected the Criminal Law Amendment Bill.

24th. The Congress Party's token cut on the Railway Budget Estimates was carried in the Assembly by 62 votes to 45.

26th. Sir M. Zafrulla Khan, in the Assembly, denied that the claims of Bengali candidates for cadetships in the Dufferin were superseded by those of Anglo-Indians.

Exclusion of other provincials from the motor driving trade in Bengal was proposed in the Bengal Council.

27th. *Ferozabad Riots sequel* :—Thirty-three Muslims were sentenced to transportation for life by the Sessions Judge of Agra on charges of rioting and committing arson and murders in Ferozabad in May last in a communal frenzy. Nineteen other accused were acquitted. It may be recalled that communal rioting occurred at Ferozabad, when Muslims set fire to several Hindu houses, particularly the house of Dr. Jivaraj Mehta, who perished with his three children in the blaze. Eight other Hindus were also burnt to death.

The Assembly passed all the railway demands for grants.

Terrorist activities had not been absent from Bengal for a considerable time, said Sir Robert Reid in the Bengal Council.

28th. *Hunger-strike of a political prisoner* :—The condition of Jogesh Chatterjee, the Kakori Conspiracy Case prisoner, who was on hunger-strike in the Lucknow Central Jail, for more than 3 months, was reported to have taken a bad turn. His voice was reported to have become almost inaudible. "Hunger-strike or no hunger-strike, the question is whether his demands are reasonable, and we find they are so," said Mr. Ramananda Chatterjee presiding over a largely attended public meeting at Albert Hall, Calcutta, to consider Mr. Jogesh Chatterjee's fast. A resolution was passed supporting the demands of Mr. Jogesh Chandra Chatterjee regarding the political prisoners and urging on the Government the imperative need of conceding Mr. Chatterjee's demands, so as to prevent the threatened act of self-immolation, and further urging on Mr. Chatterjee to abandon the fast, as he had succeeded in enlisting public sympathy with the cause of political prisoners.

Sir Jame's Grigg's Budget for 1936-37, presented to the Assembly showed a surplus of over Rs. 2 crores.

A survey of trade conditions in Bengal was made by Mr. M. A. Ispahani at the annual meeting of the Calcutta Muslim Chamber of Commerce.

The death took place at Geneva of Mrs. Kamala Nehru.

The Punjab Government granted an amnesty to "Shahidgunj prisoners" following an abandonment by Moslems of civil disobedience.

Sir G. Campbell, presiding over the meeting of the Bengal Chamber of Commerce, said that there was a feeling abroad that if the Agents of State Railways were allowed to manage their own lines, without control from the "unwieldy" Railway Board, the present deficits may be converted into surpluses.

MARCH 1936

1st. *Lahore Peace Talks* :—Success crowned Mr. M. A. Jinnah's efforts to restore the peaceful atmosphere among Moslem ranks, as a preliminary to the restoration of communal harmony. While Muslims endorsed and accepted his advice for stopping civil disobedience and confiding agitation to lawful means, Government, on their part, fully met Moslem demands as far as concern them, by declaring amnesty to Shahidganj prisoners and restoring forfeited securities. Mr. Jinnah had before him the bigger problem of settlement with Sikhs. The Punjab Government decided to release all prisoners convicted of offences directly connected with the Shahidgunj agitation and not involving serious violence to person or property, or abetment of such violence. They also decided to withdraw the pending cases falling within the same category. They also revoked the action taken under the Indian Press Act, where this action was directly in connection with the Shahidgunj agitation.

2nd. The report of the Hammond Delimitation Committee was published.

The evil effects of the Meston Award on the finances of Bengal and the need for the allocation to the province of the entire jute duty were stressed during Budget discussions in the Legislative Council.

3rd. The Federation of Indian Chambers of Commerce and Industry urged retrenchment in railway expenditure with a view to augmenting the revenues.

4th. *The Aga Khan's Advice to Muslims* :—A warning against the formation of parties on a communal basis in the coming Reformed Councils and advice that forming political groups should only be on principles for raising the economic condition of the masses were given by H. H. the Aga Khan, speaking at the dinner party given in his honour by Sir Rafiuddin Ahmed, ex-Minister, Bombay Government. Putting forward a strong plea for the uplift of the depressed and backward classes, be they Muslims or Hindus, the Aga Khan said that he favoured the rich being taxed for the benefit of the poor.

5th. *Censure Motion Against Police* :—Without division, the C. P. Council carried Mr. K. P. Pande's adjournment motion, in respect of "the assault with lathis and batons on and arrest of 43 persons by the Khandwa Police, including several respectable persons of high social status at Khandwa on February 27." The Home Member, Mr. Raghavendra Rao, said that though the case was technically sub-judice, it would become sub-judice any moment. He, therefore, asked the House to treat the matter as such. The evidence on record showed, he said, that when the Sub-Inspector and constables went to make investigations at the Ashram, where strange and suspicious characters were staying, and also asked the driver of Dhunivale Dadaji about the licence for driving the car, they were assaulted by the inmates and the Sub-Inspector confined to custody. When another police party went for their rescue, a mob of 300 attacked them with lathis. Rifles were tampered with and 15 policemen sustained injuries. As regards attack on women and other allegations regarding interviews with and legal assistance to prisoners, the matter was engaging the Government's attention and enquiries would be made.

7th. A committee of fifty leading Moslems of Calcutta was set up to conduct successfully the boycott of the Corporation elections.

A survey of the Punjab communal situation was made by the Governor in a speech at the European Association dinner.

8th. *Sadhus Sack a Village* :—An orgy of rioting, arson and looting was reported to have been committed by a gang of 400 Sadhus (mendicants) at Chandravali, a village in Sitapur District, U.P. It was dark, it was stated, when the gang of mendicants arrived at the village on their way to Musrikh, a place of pilgrimage. They decided to spend the night at the village and the villagers were approached for the free supply of at least fore cart-loads of fuel for the Sadhus to warm themselves. The villagers did not comply with the request whereupon the gang surronded the village to block any-body from escaping, and a party, armed with lathis and brickbats, forcibly broke open every house, dragged out the inmates and beat them mercilessly. Some houses were also set on fire, and cattle let loose and chased out. This rioting was reported to have lasted for several hours, in the course of which even standing crops on the outskirts of the village were destroyed.

No agreement was reached regarding the Shahidganj dispute, and Mr. Jinnah's retirement was considered a "startegic retreat."

10th. *Government defeats in the Assembly* :—The Congress party's cut motion in the Assembly, moved by Mr. Asaf Ali, relating to the foreign and Political Department grant, to discuss the Frontier policy of the Government of India, was carried by 72 votes against 47. Another cut motion moved by Mr. S. Satyamurthi, reducing demand for the Executive Council to one rupee, which was meant as a refusal of supplies with a view to showing that the House had no confidence in the Government, was carried by 68 votes against 62. The Opposition scored another victory, when the Independent Party's cut motion refusing grant to the Defence Department, moved by Mr. K. L. Gauba, was carried by 79 votes to 46.

Review of commercial and political problems affecting Europeans in India was made at the annual meeting of the Bombay Chamber of Commerce.

11th. Assam's administrative problems were reviewed by the Governor in a striking address to the Legislative Council.

The Budget estimates for Assam, presented in the Council revealed that expenditure next year would be Rs 57,12,000 above the receipts.

The Council of State rejected a resolution demanding the formation of a non-official committee to advise on Defence affairs.

12th. *Mr. Jawharlal Returns to India* :—Pandit Jawharlal Nehru returned to India by air. He was accorded a warm reception at Karachi and at Allahabad. He also brought with him the ashes of Mrs. Kamala Nehru which were immersed in the Ganges with due ceremony. A spontaneous hartal was observed in Allahabad in memory of Mrs. Nehru.

Assam Land Revenue Re-assessment Bill was accepted in the Legislative Council.

The Assembly passed Mr. M. S. Aney's motion censuring the Government's "policy of repression" and rejected Sir L. Hudson's motion demanding the abolition of the surcharge on incomes.

The smaller States of Gujerat and Kathiawar were in favour of a confederation of their own instead of their amalgamation with larger Indian States.

13th. The abolition of the Permanent Settlement in Bengal was demanded by the Bengal Council during the debate on a cut motion on budget grants under the head "Land Revenue."

The Council of State recommended that women be admitted to its membership.

14th. *West Kistna Political Conference* :—That this country should not be stampeded into accepting a Socialist State, but should be permitted to consider calmly whether such a state would accord with the genius of the country, was the plea made by Dr. D. S. Ramchandra Rao, in his address welcoming the delegates to the West Kistna Political Conference, held at Bezwada. Srimathi Rukmani Lakshmipati, presided. Delegates from all over the district were present in large numbers. The conference passed a number of important resolutions among which one recommended drastic changes in the constitution of the Congress and another reiterated the goal of the Congress as Purna Swaraj, which could be achieved only by Civil Disobedience.

Pandit Malaviya advised Harijans not to break away from Hinduism and stated that no other religion had claims on the community as it was a domestic quarrel among Hindus.

15th. *Pandit Malaviya in Nasik* :—A rousing reception was accorded to Pandit Malaviya when he arrived at Nasik in connection with Harijan propaganda. Led by bedecked horses and Hindu scouts, with bands playing the Pandit was taken in procession through the gaily festooned streets of the city to the bungalow on the river-bank. Huge crowds greeted the Pandit when he entered the city from the railway station, where he and party were welcomed by the Reception Committee members. Three hundred associations representing all communities garlanded him. Later, addresses on behalf of the Hindu Sabha and citizens were presented at a mammoth meeting near Holy Ramkund. The addresses stressed Pandit Malaviya's services to the country in educational, social, religious and political spheres.

Pt. Jawaharlal's exhortation :—"Discipline should be our sheet anchor," said Pt. Nehru addressing the Volunteer Corps at Motinagar, Allahabad, when he opened the second battalion of the Congress Volunteer Corps. He asked them not to be disheart ened by the lull in political atmosphere but be ready to respond to the country's call whenever it came. He deprecated the idea of people thinking of Mr. Gandhi as an Avatar and that Swaraj would fall from Heaven and appealed to everyone, irrespective of caste, or creed or sex, to think independently, weigh every proposals before them, appreciate such proposals in the true perspective and arrive at independent judgment, prior to giving assent to every call for sacrifice made on them.

16th. The Commander-in-Chief made an important statement in regard to the Indian Military Academy in the Council of State

The Government of Bengal's irrigation policy was explained in the Legislative Council during the debate on the demand for a grant of Rs. 34,29,000 under this head.

17th. *Agricultural Training for Detenus* :—"Experiments in connection with the scheme of industrial and agricultural training for detenus are distinctly hopeful," said the Home Member of the Bengal Government, moving a demand a Rs. 1,10,51,000 under General Administrrion, in the Bengal Council. The centres were run virtually on boarding house lines with minimum restrictions, he added. Fifteen detenus were receiving instructions in each of the four camps and 25 were working in the Agricultural Centre. Arrangements had been made to open six more industrial centres, giving 90 men instructions and another Agricultural Centre would be opened to provide instruction for 45 men.

A strong plea for the industrialization of India was made by Sir H. Mody speaking on the Finance Bill in the Assembly.

A suggestion for centralizing under one committee the phases of the health welfare activities was made by Sir John Anderson at a meeting of the Bengal and Calcutta Health Welfare Week Committees in Calcutta.

18th. *Military Route Marches in Bengal* :—In order to discuss the military route marches in various districts of Bengal a motion was made in the Bengal Council, to reduce the demand for Rs. 12,000 under the head Executive Council by Rs. 100. The mover, Mr. P Bannerjee, alleged that the marches were arranged in those villages which were either politically advanced or where Congress workers lived.

Mr. N. K. Basu urged that the allegations of Mr. Bannerjee called for swift and immediate enquiry. The Home Member, replying, said that none of the representatives of Midnapore District in the Council came forward to represent the grievances. He had absolute faith in the man on the spot. Since 1932, there had been very few extraordinary cases of indiscipline among troops in Bengal. As regards saluting the Union Jack Government did not force anybody to salute it against his wishes. It was a travesty of truth that troops were terrorising the countryside. The motion was lost.

The suggestion of the Fiji Government that the method of selecting Indian representatives in the Fiji Council should be by nomination and not election was opposed in the Council of State.

The administation of the Calcutta Corporation was criticized by Mr. H. S. Suhrawardy in the Bengal Council.

19th. *Anti-Constitution Conference* :—An Anti-Constitution Conference of Congressmen held at Bombay passed resolution on the question of office acceptance under the new constitution and declared that the Conference was emphatically of opinion that acceptance of offices under the constitution was direct contravention of the goal of the National Independence and declared policy of rejecting the Reforms. Acceptance of offices. for whatever purposes, amounted to working the reforms and co-operation with the Government in carrying on the administration which had exploited and would continue to exploit the country. It was the considered opinion of the Conference that Congressmen should under no circumstances accept offices and should resolve to carry on an intensive struggle against the policy of office acceptance. The resolution also called on the Bombay delegates to the Lucknow session of the Congress to vote against any proposal which might lead directly or indirectly to a policy of accepting offices.

20th. *The Finance Bill rejected in Assembly* :—Pandit Nilkantha Das moved in the Assembly that to Clause 2 of the Finance Bill relating to salt duty the following be added : "And the said provisions shall, in so far as they enable the Governor-General-in-Council to remit any duty so imposed, be construed as if with effect from April 1, 1936, they remitted duty to the extent of the said one rupee and four annas and such remission shall be deemed to have been made out of the leviable duty by Rule made under that section." Dr. Bhagwan Das supported the amendment, saying that for people whose daily income was calculated by the Central Banking Enquiry Committee as seven pice daily, the salt tax was cruel. Sir James Grigg, the Finance Member, opposed the amendment on the ground that it would involve loss of revenue to the extent of eight crores. The amendment was carried by 52 votes to 41, members of the Independent Party remaining neutral. The Assembly passed the amendment of Dr. Banerji to the Finance Bill, reducing the price of a post card to half anna, by 83 votes to 44. Mr. Pallival moved that the quarter anna postage should carry registered newspapers weighing up to 10 tolas instead of 8 as now. Mr. G. V. Bewoor, opposing the motion, said that the change would cost the Government Rs. 74,000. The rate was already the smallest compared with the rates in other countries and had not been increased since 1898. The motion was passed by 64 votes to 41. The Finance Bill was recommended by His Excellency the Viceroy in its original form, excepting the amendment with regard to the postal rate for newspapers. The Assembly rejected the recommended Bill by 68 votes to 51.

Sind Hindus Conference :—The fears of the Hindu minority under separated Sind were voiced at the All-Sind Hindu Conference held at Karachi. The Conference urged on the Government the necessity of introducing into the new Constitution proper safeguards and system of Joint Electorates, with reservation of seats with sufficient weightage and equitable adjustment of franchise in the local Assembly. The Conference, disagreeing with the neutral attitude of the Congress on the Communal Award, opined that the Award was a negation of the elementary principle of democratic Government. The Conference further developed the reported attitude of the Bahawalpur State authorities to the Hindus and sympathised with their brethren and appealed to the Government of India to intervene and bring about reconciliation.

22nd. *Boycott of Calcutta Municipal Elections* :—A largely attended meeting of Calcutta Moslems was held in the Calcutta Maidan, the Nawab Bahadur of Dacca presiding, to vetilate Moslem grievances in connection with the City Corporation affairs. Small processions of Moslems carrying posters shouting, "Boycott Corporation elections," were taken out from different parts of the City, terminating at the meeting place. The meeting condemned the conduct of Moslems, since declared elected to the Corporation who "deliberately flouted the will of the entire community" by not resigning their seats and resented the attitude of indifference on the part of the Moslem members of the Bengal Legislature in this connection and demanded of them that the interest of Moslems should be properly safeguarded and also reiterated the decision to boycott the ensuing Corporation election and not to accept Government nomination or appointment or seek election to Corporation as Alderman untill Moslem grievances were redressed.

Anti-ministry day :—A public meeting held at Khalikdina Hall, Karachi, in connection with the Anti-Ministry Day resolved that in view of the fact that the Government of India Act is a denial of India's inalienable right of self-determination and is reactionary and retrograde, the Lucknow Congress should decide to make a warning that the Constitution is impossible of being worked. It further opined that acceptance of Ministerial office by Congressmen is undesirable and would prove disastrous to Congress and for freedom. The Anti-Ministry Day was observed in Benares also.

23rd. *Censure motion Re : Ban on Mr. Bose* :—In the Assembly, Mr. Nilkantha Das moved an adjournment motion to censure the Government for the decision conveyed to Mr. Subash Chandra Bose that if he returned to India he could not be expected to remain at liberty. The motion was carried by the House by 65 votes to 56. Some Independents including Mr. Jinnah remained neutral.

Company Law Amendment :—Sir N. N. Sircar, Law member, introduced in the Assembly the Bill amending the Company Law, which had been hammered into final shape, as the result of discussions with commercial leaders. Opinions received disclosed the demand for deal with mush-room and fraudulent companies, for changes in the provisions relating to issue and contents of prospectuses, for increased disclosure to shareholders of the financial position of companies and for increased right to shareholders in connection with management of companies for modification of the present law applicable to Managing Agents, for changes in provisions applicable to winding up, for special provisions to govern banking companies and for numerous other improvements. The Bill retains the existing form of the Indian Act. The English Law had been followed where possible.

Compulsory Primay Education for girls :—The Government of the United Provinces sanctioned the introduction, with effect from April 29, 1936, of compulsory primary education of girls whose ages were not less than six and not more than eleven years (in the case of Muslim girls not less than five and not more than nine years) in the Itaunja and Kakori village areas of the Lucknow district. This was the second district board whose scheme had been sanctioned by the Government under Section 3 (2) of the United Province District Board Primary Education Act, 1926.

24th. *University for the Frontier Province* :—The Frontier Council carried a non-official resolution, recommending the establishment of a Unitary University at Peshawar. Dr. Gill, Director of Education, said that the Local Government submitted a strong case for a grant to the Government of India, hoping it would include it in the subvention. Sir Abdul Quaiyum, Minister, said that the new University would cater to the needs of the tribal area forming half the Province. It was not their intention to transmit to the tribal area ideas imported by Section from South India.

25th. The U. P. Unemployment Committee's report was discussed in the Council it State.

The Finance Bill, as recommended by the Governor-General, was rejected by the Legislative Assembly.

26th. *Import duty on Wheat* :—The Punjab Council unanimously passed a Council of resolution, recommending to the Government to convey to the Government of India that in view of the prevailing low prices, the import duty on wheat should be raised to Rs. 2 per hundred-weight. Nawab Muzaffar Khan, Revenue Member, supporting the resolution said that the Punjab had already strongly represented the matter to the Government of India and promised to further convey the wish of the House to them.

28th. *Uplift of Muslims* :—The All-India Moslem Conference, held at New Delhi, under the presidency of Haji Abdullah Haroon, among other things, discussed the question of the uplift of the masses, especially the Muslims. The Conference was of opinion that it was imperative to adopt a programme for their moral, intellectual, social and economic betterment. The Conference authorised the Working Committee to execute and popularise the programme and frame definite lines of action at the earliest possible mom ent and devise effective meaures most likely to reform and ameliorate the condition of the poor and unemployed cultivators and starving masses of India.

The Madras Government passed orders on the report of the special officer appointed to inquire into agricultural indebtedness in the province.

In criticizing India's protection policy Sir H. P. Mody made a plea for the setting up of a new fiscal commission.

The Maharaja of Darbhanga gave one lakh of rupees to the Bihar Memorial to His late Majesty King George V.

The creation of local self-government institutes was advocated at the first All-India Local Self-Government Conference at Delhi.

The Legislative Assembly adopted the report of its Committee on the findings of the Indian Delimitation Committee.

29th. The All-India Moslem Conference at Delhi passed a resolution condemning the renewed attacks on the Communal Award.

An agreement was reported to have been reached on the Nizam's claim for a symbolic expression of his sovereignty over Berar.

Addressing Bombay journalists, Sir Stanley Reed said that to be a successful journalist, one must first become a reporter.

There had been a fall in the number of industrial strikes in Bombay in 1934-35 as a result of the Government's efforts for conciliation.

30th. *Assembly's Verdict on Ottawa Pact* :—The Assembly accepted by 70 to 65 votes Mr. Jinnah's amendment urging immediate termination of the Ottawa Pact and recommending to the Government to examine the trend of trade for entering into bilateral treaties with foreign countries, including the United Kingdom. Sir Cowasji Jehangir and Sir H. P. Mody voted for the Government. The nominated members Mr. D'Souza and Mr. N. M. Joshi voted in favour of Mr. Jinnah's motion. The two Burman members voted for the amendment in spite of Sir Mahomed Zafrulla's appeal that the rejection of the Ottawa Pact would have repercussions on the Indo-Burma Agreement.

Punjab Debtors' Protection Bill :—The Punjab Debtors' Protection Bill which was passed by the Council last session was sent back to the Council for re-consideration. It would be recalled that certain vital Government amendments proposed to the Bill during the last session were not accepted by the House. The Bill in the form recommended by the Governor, sought to make exemption of ancestral property from attachment conditional, among other things, on the determination of the liability of such land by the court as if this section had not been expressly charged by way of mortgage on the ancestral individual property by the predecessor in interest, whereas the Bill as passed, made the exemption unconditional.

A municipality's responsibilities in regard to the education of its citizens was the subject of an address at the Local Self-Government Conference at Delhi.

An appeal to the Government to revise their railway coal purchase policy was made at the annual meeting of the Indian Mining Federation.

A Bill proposing abolition of local boards was introduced in the Bengal Council.

The Assembly accepted Mr. M. A. Jinnah's amendment demanding the termination of the Ottawa Agreement.

The Council of State passed the Finance Bill as certified by the Governor-General by by 32 votes to 10..

31st. *Gandhiji on Temple-entry Campaign* :—In a communication to the "Harijan" on temple-entry, Gandhiji wrote : "Local Sanghs should make a sustained effort to have the existing temples thrown open, and even to build new ones, not for Harijans only, but for all. Care must be taken that where temples are opened to Harijans, no discrimination is made against them. They must be opened on precisely the same terms as they are opened to other Hindus. It is hardly necessary to state that in different localities different methods may be adopted for securing the desired end. Perfect non-violence must, of course, be maintained in all cases. An All-India, simultaneous movement of the same type, is not contemplated. It will vary in intensity and methods, according to the circumstances of each locality. Nowhere should temples be opened, where there is an active minority opposed to the opening. Practical unanimity should be secured before a temple is opened. Thus what is required is sustained effort to convert local public opinion in favour of temple-entry."

APRIL 1936

1st. *Sind a New Province* :—The inauguration of the new province of Sind took place. Sir Lancelot Graham, the Governor, entered upon his duties on 1st April. The Mayor of Karachi, Kazi Khuda Bux, presented His Excellency with an address of welcome to which His Excellency replied suitably. The message of H. E. the Viceroy, conveying His Majesty the King-Emperor' message, was read by His Excellency.

2nd. Mr. Rajendra Prasad, Congress President, appealed to different political parties in India to adopt a tolerant attitude to one another.

4th. A resolution supporting the Assembly vote regarding the Ottawa Agreement was passed at the annual meeting of the Federation of Indian Chambers of Commerce.

6th. *Inauguration of Orissa Province* :—His Excellency Sir John Hubback was installed as the first Governor of the newly constituted Province when at the Durbar Hall of Ravenshaw College, Cuttack, Mr. P. T. Mansfield' Chief Secretary-designate of Orissa read the warrant of appointment and Sir Courtney Terrel, Chief Justice of Patna High Court, administered oaths of allegiance and office to His Excellency. Immediately following his installation, His Excellency was the recepient of a joint address from deputations representing Oriya Peoples' Association, Orissa Landholders' Association, Orissa Chamber of Commerce, Orissa Mahomedan Association and All-Orissa Domiciled Bengalees' Association. Replying to the address, His Excellency, in the course of his speech, read a special message from his Majesty the King-Emperor, which he had sent through the Viceroy together with Viceroy's own message.

His Excellency Sir John Anderson invested the Maharaja of Cooch Behar with rulling powers at a durbar held at Cooch Behar.

7th. The Legislative Assembly rejected are solution urging the release of detenus, the Congress Party declining to take part in the voting.

8th. *H. E. Lord Willingdon's Address* :—His Excellency the Viceroy addressed both Houses of the Central Legislature. He surveyed at length the political and economic situation in the country and the position of Indians overseas, appealing to other parts of the Empire to realise India's status in the British Commonwealth of Nations. He concluded his address by drawing a vivid picture of the future of the country under the new Constitution and wished all good wishes to the new Viceroy.

Mr. S. C. Bose was arrested on landing at Bombay.

The Government Bill to amend the Indian Mines Act so as to provide against the danger of fires in collieries was referred by the Assembly to a Select Committee.

Several changes, including the abolition of the manual labour clause and the method of election of delegates and President of the Congress, were adopted by the Congress Working Committee.

9th. *The Lucknow Congress* :—Mr. Satyamurthi was the only speaker in the Assembly on his Bill to repeal or amend repressive Laws. He spoke for 3 hours and his speech was unfinished.

Socialists suffered a defeat in the Subjects Committee meeting of the Congress over proposed changes in the constitution.

11th. Criticism of the new Reforms in India was made by Rai Bahadur Thakur Hanuman Singh, presiding at the U. P. Liberal Conference at Fyzabad.

The need for public help in effecting educational reforms in India was emphasized at the College and University Teachers' Conference.

The goal of the All-India Muslim League was responsible self-government for India, declared the President.

The Subjects Committee of the Congress accepted the Working Committee's resolution, condemning the India Act and postponing office issue.

12th. The new Constituti on was condemned by Mr. M. A. Jinnah in a resolution which was accepted by the Muslim League at Bombay.

The United Provinces Liberal Party continued their conference at Fyzabad.

Government measures for the relief of unemployment were discussed by the Hon. Nawab Sir Mohiuddin Faroque, Bengal Minister.

The Congress session opened in Lucknow.

13th. *Guntur Audhra Conference* :—The Guntur District Andhra Mahasabha Conference was held at Tenali, with the Raja of Challapallo in the chair. Nearly a thousand persons, including delegates from Ganjam, attended the function. The Conference arged that a separate Andhra Province be formed with 12 Telugu districts of the Madras Presidency. Another resolution demanded that the Ceded Districts be included again in the jurisdiction of the Audhra University. The Mahasabha requested the Government to give representation to Andhras in the public services either on the basis of population or on the basis of revenue derived from the Andhra area. Another resolution called upon the electors of this district and of this province to give their votes only to those who supported the formation of a separate Andhra Province and who would agitate for the recovery of Andhra tracts now annexed to Grissa.

The Congress passed the official resolution, rejecting the new constitution and postponing the issue of acceptance of office by its members.

Women for the first time held a conference of their own in the Congress camp at Lucknow.

The scope for industrial expansion in the North and South Arcot districts and adjacent areas as a result of the Mettur Scheme, was outlined in a Note sumitted to the Madras Government.

The goodwill rather than political machinery built up the strength of the nation was the view expressed by Mr. Ranganadhan, presiding over a conference of South Indian Christians at Madras.

14th. The legislative Assembly passed two Bills prohibiting loans and credits to Italy and extending the additional import duty on Salt at a reduced rate.

The Congress session concluded at Lucknow after drafting an agrarian programme.

15th. Sir N. N. Sircar moved in the Legislative Assembly for a select committee on his Bill to amend the Indian Campanies Act.

A reference to the clash of ideas in the Congress was made by Pandit Nehru before the meeting of the All-India Committee at Lucknow.

16th. *Congress Nationalist Party* :—The failure of unity talks with Congress leaders and the decision of the Lucknow Congress to fight the next election on its own ticket made the Con gress Nationalist Party organise themselves on a permanent basis and begin their campaign in right earnest and put up a strong fight against the Congress in the forthcoming elections to the Provincial Legislatures. This was the purpose of the Provincial Hindu Conference held at Patna under the presidentship of Kumar Ganganand Sinha and another held at Agra under the presidentship of Raja Sir Rampal Singh. The party, whatever its local name and origin will, under affiliation, be called the Nationalist Party for All-India purposes. Nationalists, at their meeting at Birla house on April 16, arrived at two main conclusions, the first regarding contesting the forthcoming elections and the second that they should for that purpose form a coalition with other parties such as Liberals, Landholders and others, who have been affected by the Communal Award or who feel its adverse effects on national life and outlook. This party believed that all avenues of honourable compromise having been closed by the Congress, they must form a party on a permanent basis.

18th. Lord and Lady Willingdon left for England.

The Marquess of Linlithgow was installed as Viceroy at New Delhi and made his first broadcast to the people of India.

Questions regarding the termination of the Ottawa Agreement were asked in the Legislative Assembly.

Problems relating to the tea industry were discussed by the chairman of the Indian Tea Planters' Association at its annual general meeting held at Jalpaiguri.

19th. Their Excellencies the Viceroy and the Marchioness of Linlithgow fed the poor of Delhi to commemorate their arrival and their silver wedding.

20th. Italy's "high-handedness" in Abyssinia was condemned in the Council of State when the House passed the Bill banning credit to Italy.

The Legislative Assembly passed the Validating Bill removing certain doubts and establishing the validity of certrin High Court proceedings.

22nd. The preferential margin on United Kingdom imports of fents would be considerably reduced as a result of an amendment to the Tariff Bill accepted by the Assembly.

24th. *Hindu-Muslim Riot in Poona* :—There was serious Hindu-Muslim rioting in front of the Maruthi temple, in Poona, necessitating British Military being called out. Three hundred police, under officers, rushed to the scene and restored order. One Inspector was injured. The authorities then called out the Military. Over 200 persons were injured. The Bombay Government issued a communique on the riots, in the course of which they said: The Sonya Maruthi Temple, which was formerly on the wall of a house in Raviwarpeth, was reconstructed last year in a small area on the public road, because the house was pushed back owing to the broadening of the road. Prior to the change, Hanuman Jayanti used to be celebrated in the shrine with music. When reconstruction of the shrine on the public way was sanctioned by the District Magistrate, it was laid down that there should not be obstruction to the public and that the trustees should give a written undertaking that music would not be played before the shrine. This written undertaking, pointed out the communique, however was not received, and when the time for celebrating Hanuman Jayanti approached, the District Magistrate, on receipt of request for permission to play music from April 6 to 23 prohibited under Sub-Section 42, Bombay District Police Act, playing music at the shrine, or any public place within 30 yards. Later, the trustees of the shrine approached the District Magistrate for permission for worship with music, on the last day of the festival only, representing that the feelings of the Hindus had been seriously stirred by the prohibitory order. The District Magistrate invited prominent Mahomedans and discussed the situation with them. They admitted that no objection was offered by their co-religionists in the past probably because the shrine had not been in such a prominent position. After further discussion and careful consideration, the District Magistrate issued an order on April 23, permitting worship with music on April 24 from the shrine with restriction as to the times of play and on condition that no obstruction was caused to traffic. At 9 p. m., on April 24. when Hindus commenced worship, Mahomedans collected near the shrine in increasing numbers, but were kept moving by the police. Later another crowd of Mahomedans came towards the shrine, shouting "Din, Din." On their being pushed back, other Mohamedans arrived and commenced flinging stones and bricks at the shrine. More Hindus came on the scene and retaliated by throwing stones. The rival crowds were separated and pushed back by the Police. Members of both parties had lathis, and several Police were injured. Eventually, the Hindus were prevailed upon to discotinue worship and the crowds to disperse. At noon the situation became more serious as Mahomedans began damaging the property of Hindus.

26th. Rao Bahadur M. C. Rajah appealed to the Scheduled Castes to work the new Reforms, and to form election boards in each province to contest the coming elections.

27th. ***More Communal Riots*** :—One Hindu was killed and several were injured, including one Mahomedan, in a communal riot which occurred in front of a mosque at Jamalpur, Monghyr District, while a Hindu wedding procession was passing along the main road in Jamalpur. When a Marwari marriage procession was going past a mosque at Jalpaiguri, with music and band, Mahomedans, it was alleged, came out of the mosque and demanded immediate stoppage of music. The Police, in charge of the procession, had the music discontinued, but in the meantime, it was alleged, missiles were hurled at the processionists as the result of which one was injured. A report from Khanpur, Belgaum District, said that a Hindu-Moslem fracas occurred there last week. Three on each side were injured. It was alleged that a Mahomedan attacked members of a procession who were taking out the portrait of Basheswar which led to the fracas.

29th. ***Mr. Nehru's Appeal*** :—Mr. Jawaharlal Nehru, Congress President, addressed a public meeting of over 10,000 people at Chitnavis Park, Nagpur. Mr. Nehru said: "I will not ask you to cast a single vote in favour of Congress if you do not wish to vote for independence."

30th. Sir Otto Niemeyer's report on the allocation of finances under the new Constitution was published.

MAY 1936.

2nd. A claim for Government recognition of Ayurvedic system of medicine in Bengal was made at a conference held in Calcutta.

Lord Linlithgow visited two villages near Dehra Dun and had informal talks with the inhabitants.

To implement the recommendations of the Sapru Committee the Lucknow University proposed the starting of a school of dentistry and a veterinary science department.

3rd. Sir K. V. Reddi was appointed to act as Governor of Madras during the absence, on four months' leave, of Lord Erskine.

7th. The Marwari Association claimed that Bengal had been most ungenerously treated by the Niemeyer settlement.

Authoritative circles in the Punjab were disturbed by the "niggardly treatment" meted out to the Province in the Niemeyer Report.

The appointment of Sir Firoz Khan Noon as High Commissioner for India was officially announced.

9th. Resolutions expressing sympathy with Abyssinia and criticizing the action of Italy were passed at meetings held in many places in India.

Efforts were being made for closer co-operation between the Congress and Trade Union movement.

10th. ***Dr. Ansari's end*** :—The death occurred of Dr. M. A. Ansari, ex-President of the Congress, in train, while he was travelling from Dehra Dun to Delhi.

That Congress unity in Madras would be replaced by warring factions, each greedy for power, if the ban on acceptance of Ministerial responsibility were raised, was the fear expressed by S. Subramanian at the Villuparam Pol. Conference.

The Calcutta Corporation adjourned as a protest against the arrest and detention of Mr. Subhas Bose.

12th. ***Socialist Houses Raided*** :—The C.I.D. Police raided the office of the Punjab Socialist Party at Bradlaugh Hall, Lahore, in the early hours and searched the belongings of four workers. Searches were also carried out in the houses of President of the Press Workers' Union and of another student. Certain papers and books were seized. No arrests were made. Searches were carried out simultaneously in about a dozen places, including the houses of the General Secretary of the Punjab Socialist Party and other office-bearers and prominent members of the party. It was stated that the searches were a sequel to the alleged distribution at a meeting held in observance of the Subash Bose Day on May 10, of a proscribed leaflet relating to Communism. Reports from Amritsar showed that similar searches of houses of members of the Socialist Party were carried out there also.

The comments of the Provincial Governments together with the Government of India's views on the Niemeyer Report were published.

Four hundred and fifty agricultural farms were established in Bengal with the help of the rural development grant of the Government of India.

One of the biggest fires that ever occurred in Bombay, caused damage estimated at Rs. 25 lakhs.

14th. "Not a hell on earth but a prisoners' paradise" was how Sir Henry Craik described the Andamans on his return from a visit of inspection.

15th. In a talk with Bombay journalists Pandit Jawaharlal Nehru said that while he remained convinced that socialism was the only political panacea for India's ills he would not seek to force this view on Congress.

The death occurred in Calcutta of Sir R. N. Mookerjee. Sir Rajendra was one of Calcutta's foremost commercial magnates. He was senior partner of Messrs. Martin & Co.

16th. India's formal notice to terminate her participation in the terms of the Ottawa Pact was acknowledged by the Board of Trade.

Pandit Jawaharlal Nehru was trying to bring about unity in trade union ranks in Bombay.

Mr. E. Raghavendra Rao took the Oath of Office as Acting Governor of the Central Provinces at Pachmarhi.

17th. ***Trade Unions and Congress*** :—The 15th Session of the All-India Trade Union Congress opened at Bombay in the presence of a large gathering of workers and Trade Union leaders. Mr. Jawaharlal Nehru, Congress President, together with other local Congressites and Socialists were present. Addressing the Congress, Mr. Jawaharlal appealed to the working classes and the Trade Union Congress to establish closer contact with the Congress. The Congress was the only organisation in the country, he said, which had attempted to bring about a revolution. "You claim to be revolutionaries and raise revolutionary slogans, but they will not bring freedom," he added. Although there is fundamental difference in the ideology and methods of working of the Indian National Congress and the Trade Union Congress, I firmly believe these two bodies can still work in unison in regard to many matters." Therefore he emphasised the need for closer contact.

The death occurred at Bangalore of Sir M. Ramachandra Rao, a director of the Reserve Bank of India.

18th. *Business-men and Socialism* :—The apprehensions created in the minds of Indian businessmen by Mr. Jawaharlal Nehru s advocacy of a Socialistic form of Government for India found expression in the issue of a joint manifesto by 21 leading businessmen of Bombay. The signatories said: Pandit Jawaharlal, in his presidential speech at Lucknow Congress, said: "I see no way of ending the poverty, vast unemployment, degradation and subjection of the Indian people, except through Socialism. That involves vast revolutionary changes in our political and social structure, ending vested interests in the land and industry as well as the feudal, autocratic Indian States system. That means ending private property, except in a restricted sense and replacement of the present profit system by the higher ideal of co-operative service."

Moving tributes were paid at a meeting of the Calcutta Corporation to the qualities that made the late Sir R. N. Mookerjee's career unique in the annals of Indian National life.

Because of his uncompromising attack on the Hindu caste system, a Hindu mandal cancelled the annual session over which Dr. Ambedkar was to have presided.

Indian Labour's attitude towards the new Constitution was outlined in a resolution passed at the Trade Union Conference.

Five persons were killed and 20 injured in a clash between parties of Moslems, Christians and Ezhawas near Trivandrum.

Two Moslems were injured in a clash between Sikhs and Moslems at Lahore.

20th. Deploring the growth of socialism in India a leading Indian merchant suggested that economic regeneration was the best way to counter the "evil"; meanwhile Pandit Nehru told a Bombay audience that they despaired of bridging the gulf between "Big Business" and socialists.

Mr. Subhas Chandra Bose was brought to Kurseong under escort and was detained in his brother's home.

21st. Mr. S. Satyamurthi, at a meeting in Kumbakonam, was reported to have stated that if he became a Minister under the new Constitution he would provide the police with Khaddar uniforms.

Rapid progress was being made with the scheme for the industrial and agricultural training of Bengal detenus.

22nd. The younger section of Bombay merchants supported Pandit Jawaharlal Nehru's Socialist programme.

23rd. That India had vast untapped resources which it would require the services of skilled engineers to place at the country's service was the subject of the Minister of Education's address to students of the Shibpur Engineering College.

24th. The Minister for Education, Bengal, speaking at a Hoogly function, described the unemployment problem as "a national crisis."

25th. *All India Depressed Classes Conference* :—A resolution urging the members of the Depressed Classes not to embrace any other religion till the question was finally decided at the next All-India Conference was passed at the All-India Adi-Hindu Depressed Classes Conference held at Lucknow under the presidentship of Dr. Rasiklal Viswas of Calcutta. The Conference also passed a resolution expressing full confidence in Dr. Ambedkar and supporting the Yeola decision taken under his presidentship regarding change of religion.

The Shahidganj Civil dispute was dismissed. There was tense excitement in Lahore on the eve of the judgment.

The uneconomic competition between the road and railway services in India was condemned by the general secretary of the Transport Development Association.

26th. Pandit Jawaharlal Nehru made another effort to induce Sir Tej Bahadur Sapru to join his proposed Civil Liberties Union.

The Congress launched its foreign campaign for the overthrow of Imperialism.

The Federation of Indian Chambers of Commerce and Industry submitted their view on the Niemeyer report to the Government of India.

27th. A resolution for the constitution of a special committee to consider the question of appointment of Moslems was considered by the Calcutta Corporation.

28th. The Chairman of the Tata Iron and Steel Company announced that it was intended to explore the possibilities of developing the steel industry in this country.

29th. The need for a clearer perspective so that trifles do not present the appearance of insurmountable obstacles in India's progress was urged by Pandit Nehru in a speech at Lahore.

30th. Presiding at the Bombay Presidency Mahars Conference Mr. B. S. Venkata Rao discussed the question of Harijans' leaving Hinduism.

In an address to the Punjab Political Conference at Gujranwala, Pandit Jawaharlal Nehru reiterated his faith in Socialism as the panacea for all India's ills.

The charge that the Congress President's faith was not in Socialism but in Communism was made by Sir Cowasji Jehangir of Bombay. Sir Cowasji accused Pandit Nehru of using Socialism as a smoke screen for Communist propaganda.

31st. At a meeting where Punjab peasants presented Pandit Nehru with a banner bearing the Communist emblems of the hammer and sickle, he made the significant remark that he did not wish them to copy everything in Russia.

Punjab merchants told Pandit Jawaharlal Nehru that his socialist views, including the cancellation of debts, were dangerous doctrines to preach to illiterate villagers.

JUNE 1936.

1st. Mr. Satyamurti, in a speech at Madras, said that while there were valuable elements in Socialism, he was opposed to expropriation of property and private rights.

3rd. Lahore merchants expressed their apprehensions about Pandit Nehru's Socialist doctrines and vainly endeavoured to persuade him that his propaganda was inopportune.

A powerful plea for the constitution of an Indian Bar, so as to remove the present grade distinctions among lawyers, was made by the President of the Bengal and Assam Lawyers' Conference at Barisal.

The announcement of the decision of the British Medical Council to recognize Indian degrees was received with mixed feelings in Indian medical circles in Calcutta.

6th. Pandit Jawharlal Nehru's over-emphasis on Socialism had, it was reported, caused some dissatisfaction to his colleagues in the Congress.

Heavy rain in Assam continued to swell the Brahmaputra's waters, resulting in floods, while many towns in Bengal experienced severe storms.

7th. The Political Conference at Unao passed a resolution that, in the event of an Imperialist war, India should be no party to it.

9th. Several persons were killed following a clash between tribal chieftains and their followers across the N. W. F. border.

10th. Sir Henry Gidney deplored the tragic apathy of Anglo-Indians as evidenced by poor support of the Association safeguarding their interests.

The Moslem League's Central Parliamentary Board published a manifesto devising its aims.

12th. Although far from satisfied with the measure of autonomy granted in the new constitution the Moslem League would use the scheme to further their objective of full and complete Home Rule in India.

15th. Three persons were killed when the Jaipur police fired on a mob of Gujars.

Dr. R. K. Mukherjee of Lucknow University suggested the introduction of a system of inter-communal marriages with a view to settling the differences between Hindus and Moslems.

Following demonstrations by students a strong police guard was posted outside the Bombay University building.

16th. The Government of India decided to dispense with the Tariff Board and orders communicating this decision were sent to the President and members of the Board.

17th. The Madras Government constituted a Provincial Economic Council to advise the various Government departments regarding the economic and educational advancement of the people.

The need for trained teachers in Bengal was stressed by Mr. S. P. Mookerjee, Vice-Chancellor of the Calcutta University, when he addressed a number of teachers who had completed their training course.

19th. The value of research work in India was stressed by the Viceroy when he opened the first meeting of the Nutrition Advisory Board at Simla.

20th. The Government of India consulted all local interests concerned as to the advisability of widening the scope of control of the mining industry to conserve the country's coal assets and more economical working.

22nd. Orthodox and Socialist Congressmen at Bombay expressed diametrically opposite views in a report advocating ways of establishing contact with "the masses."

Mr. Jinnah was severe in his criticism of U. P. Moslem leaders who changed their minds about serving on the Central Parliamentary Board he planned to set up.

A vigorous defence of the new Moslem United Party was made by the Hon. Sir Khwaja Nazimuddin, Member of the Executive Council, when he addressed a Moslem meeting in Darjeeling.

23rd. In celebration of His Majesty the King-Emperor's birthday, a parade was held in Simla when the Viceroy took the salute. A Birthday Parade was also held on the Calcutta maidan.

25th. The Government of India accepted the recommendations of the Special Tarriff Board in regard to the reduction of duty on certain types of cotton piecegoods.

26th. Bengal Hindus sent a memorial to the Secretary of State for India, urging greater representation for their community in the new legislatures.

An attack on the Justice Party was made by Mr. S. Satyamurthi in a speech at Congress House, Madras.

27th. A scheme calculated to improve the quality of recruitment to the University Training Corps and to promote enthusiasm among students of the University for military training was adopted by the Senate of the Calcutta University.

29th. Serious floods occurred at many centres in North India and the rainfall at Delhi established a record for this period of the year.

The Government of India decided to create a Central Dairy Husbandry Department and outlined plans to develop the Industry.

Suggestions for relieving unemployment amongst the educated classes were made by Mr. J. Aiman at the conference of Secretaries of the Y. M. C. A. held at Madras.

Administration of India 1936

Reigning Sovereign—Edward the VIII

INDIA OFFICE

Secretary of State

The Most Hon. the Marquess of Zetland, P.C., G.C.S.I., G.C.I.E.

Perm. Under-Sec. of State

Sir Findlater Stewart, G.C.I.E., K.C.B.

Parliam. Under-Sec. of State

R. A. Butler, M.P.

Deputy Under-Secretary of State

Sir L. D. Wakely, K.C.I.E., C.B.

Assistant Under-Secretary of State

Sir Cecil H. Kisch, K.C.I.E., C.B.
S. K. Brown, C.B., C.V.O.

Council

Sir Henry Wheeler K.C.S.I., K.C.I.E.
Sir Denys de S. Bray, K.C.S.I.
Sir Henry Strakosch, G.B.E.
Sir Reginald I. R. Glancy, K.C.I.E.
Sir Charles A. Tegart, C.S.I., C.I.E.
Sir Atul C. Chatterjee, G.C.I.E.
Sir A. A. L. Parsons, K.C.I.E.
Sir Abdul Qadir.
Sardar Bahadur Mohan Singh.

Govt. of India

His Excellency Victor Alexander John Hope, Marquess of Linlithgow, K.T., G.M.S.I., G.M.I.E., O.B.E., D.L., T.D., Viceroy and Governor-General of India.

Members of the Executive Council

H. E. General Sir Robert A. Cassels, G.C.B., C.S.I. D.S.O., (*Commander-in-Chief in India*).
The Hon'ble Sir Frank Noyce, K.C.S.I. (*Industries and Labour*)
The Hon'ble Sir N. N. Sircar, (*Law*)
The Hon'ble Sir James Grigg, K.C.B. (*Finance*)
The Hon'ble Sir Henry Craik, Bart, K.C.S.I. (*Home*)
The Hon'ble Kunwar Sir Jagadish Prasad, K.T., C.S.I., C.I.E., O.B.E. (*Education Health and Lands*)
The Hon'ble Sir Zafrullah Khan, (*Railway and Commerce*)

Govt of Bengal

His Excellency The Right Hon'ble Sir John Anderson, G.C.I.E. Governor of Bengal

Members of the Executive Council

The Hon'ble Sir John Ackroyd Woodhead, K.C.S.I., C.I.E. I.C.S.
The Hon. Khwaja Sir Nazim-ud-Din
The Hon'ble Sir Robert Niel Reid
The Hon. Sir Brojendra Lal Mitter

Ministers

The Hon'ble Nawab Sir Mohi-ud-din Faroqui
The Hon'ble Sir Bijoy Prasad Singh Roy
The Hon'ble Khan Bahadur M. Azzizul Haque

Govt. of Bihar

His Excellency Sir James David Sifton, K.C.S.I., K.C.I.E., C.S.I., C.I.E. I.C.S., Governor of Bihar.

Members of the Executive Council,

The Hon. Mr. Nirsu Narayan Sinha
The Hon'ble Mr. P. C. Tallents

Ministers

The Hon. Sir Ganesh Datta Singh
The Hon. Mr. Saiyid Abdul Aziz

Govt. of Bombay

His Excellency The Right Hon'ble Michael Herbert Rudolf Knatchbull, Lord Brabourne, G.C.I.E., M.C., Governor of Bombay.

Members of Executive Council

The Hon. Sir Robert Duncan Bell
The Hon. Khan Bahadur D.B. Cooper

Ministers

The Hon. Diwan Bahadur S.D. Kambli
The Hon'ble Sir Ali Mahomed Khan Dehlavi

Govt. of C. P.

His Excellency Sir Hyde Clarendon Gowan, K.C.S.I., C.I.E., V.D., I.C.S., Governor of Central Provinces.

Members of Executive Council

The Hon. Mr. E. Raghavendra Rao
The Hon'ble Mr. Eyre Gordon

Ministers

The Hon'ble Mr B. G. Khaparde
The Hon Rai Bdr. K. S. Nayudu

Govt. of Madras

His Excellency John Francis Ashley, Lord Erskine, G.C.I.E., Governor of Madras

Members of Executive Council

The Hon'ble Rai Bahadur Sir Kurma Venkata Reddi

The Hon'ble Rao Bahadur A. T. Pannireselvam
The Hon'ble Sir Charles Souter
The Hon. Mr. G.T.H. Bracken

Ministers

The Hon'ble The Raja of Bobbili
The Hon'ble Mr. P. T. Rajan
The Hon'ble Diwan Bahadur S. Kumaraswami Reddiyar

Govt. of Orissa

His Excellency Sir John Austen Hubback K.C.S.I., I.C.S., M.A., Governor of Orissa.

Administration

Chief Secy. : G. T. Mansfield
Develop. Secy. : A. F. W. Dixon
Law Secretary : Diwan Bahadur C. Govindan Nair.

Govt. of Punjab

His Excellency Sir Herbert William Emerson, K.C.S.I. C.I.E., Governor of the Punjab.

Members of Executive Council

The Hon'ble Sir D. J. Boyd
The Hon'ble Khan Bahadur Nawab Muzaffar Khan

Ministers

The Hon'ble Sir Jogendra Singh
The Hon. Sir Firoz Khan Noon
The Hon'ble Dr. Sir Gokul Chand Narang

Govt. of U. P.

His Excellency Sir Harry Graham Haig, K.C.S.I. C.I.E., C.S.I., Governor of the U. P.

Members of Executive Council

The Hon'ble Kunwar Sir Maharaj Singh
The Hon'ble Mr. J. M. Clay

Ministers

The Hon. Nawab Sir M. Yusuf
The Hon. Sir J. P. Srivastava

Govt. of Burma

H. E. the Hon. Archibald Douglas Cochrane, D.S.O., Governor of Burma.

Executive Council

The Hon'ble Sir Maung Ba K. S. M.
The Hon'ble Mr. Geoffrey Lloyd

Ministers

The Hon. U. Ba Pe.
The Hon. Dr. Ba Maw

Govt. of Assam

H. E. Sir Michael Keane, K. C. S. I. C.I.E., I.C.S., Governor of Assam

Executive Council

The Hon. Rai Bdr. P. C. Datta
The Hon'ble Mr. W. L. Scott,

Ministers

The Hon'ble Maulavi Abdul Hamid
The Hon. Rai Bdr. Kanak Lal Barua

Govt. of N. W. F. Pr.

H. E. Lieut. Col. Sir Ralph Griffith, K.C.S.I., C.I.E., Governor of N. W. F. Pr.
The Hon'ble Sir George Cunnigham, Executive Councillor
The Hon'ble K. B. Nawab Sir Abdul Qayum Khan, Minister

Govt. of Sind

His Excellency Sir Lancelot Graham, K.C.S.I. K.C.I.E. I.C.S., Governor of Sind
Chief Secy. Mr. H. K. Kripalani
Revenue Commsr. Mr. S. Ridley
P. W. Secy. Mr. W. L. C. Trendh
I. G. of Police Mr. D. Healy
President—Sir Ghulam Hussain Hidayatullah

Members.—Khan Bahadur Alla Bakhsh wd. Khan Saheb Haji Mahomed Omar, O. B. E.; Sir Shah Nawaz Khan Ghulam Murtaza Khan Bhutto, Kt., C.I.E., O.B.E.; Khan Bahadur Shore Muhammad Khan Karam Khan Bijarani; Mr. Mahomed Hashim Gazdar; Mr. Ghulam Hyder Shah Sahibdino Shah; Khan Bahadur Ghulam Nabi Shah Moujali Shah Sayed, M.B.E.; Mr. Gover Rora; Diwan Bahadur Hiranand Khemsing, Khan Bahadur Ghulam Muhammad Abdulla Khan Isran; Diwan Bahadur Issarsing Tiloksing; Sardar Bahadur Jam Jan Muhammad wd. Muhammad Sharf Junejo; Khan Bahadur Jan Muhammad Khan wd. Khan Bahadur Muhammad Ayub Shah Muhammad; Mr. H. K. Kirpalani, I.C.S.; Syed Miran Muhammad Shah Zaunlabdin Shah; Khan Bahadur Muhammad Kamil Shah Kabul Muhammad Shah; Mukhi Gobindram Pritamdas; Mr. Parmanand Kundanmal; Mr. G. H. Raschen; Mr. S. Ridley, I.C.S.; Sheikh Abdul Majid Lilaram; Sardar Bahadur Haji Mir Alladad Khan Mir Imam Baksh Khan Talpur; Mir Bandehali Khan Mir Muhammad Hassan Khan Talpur; Mr. Satraamdas Sakhawatrai Tolani.

To assist the Governor "in such manner as may be prescribed by him in that behalf"—Sir Shah Nawaz Khan Ghulam Murtaza Khan Bhutto Kt, C.I.E., O.B.E., and Diwan Bahadur Hiranand Khemsing.

Notes on Indian History

and

India in Home Polity

Notes on Indian History

It has truly been said that a history of India that reveals the whole panorama of the vast millenia of her distinctive life and civilisation in its actual shade and colour and due proportion and perspective, still remains to be written. The materials for drawing such a vast outline and making such a comprehensive and connected sketch are not yet in hand. A fairly definite outline and connected sketch which gives the promise of being some day developed into what is called "scientific history" has, however, been steadily emerging out of the mist that veils the immensity of India's past--a mist which (thanks to the labours of the investigators) has perceptibly thinned without being as yet actually lifted as far as one can now make one's incursion into the age that saw the birth of Budhism and Jainism in India in the sixth century B. C. Beyond that there is still only "cosmic nebulae" relieved here and there by a few stray constellations of lucidly distinct historical facts. These "nebulae" have, probably, a depth and density to be measured only in terms of millenia. But from the position where we can now make our historical prospecting, these vast remote dark spaces of Indian history recede and shrink and fold up and, at last, look like a far-away blank, black spherule beyond the galaxy of human remembrance.

Ancient Indian history is, apparently, "full" of such gaps and blanks. Beyond the time when Alexander the Great invaded the Punjab (326 B. C.), the galactical system of detailed and authentic Indian history does not far extend. There are too many unexplored blank spaces and unformed, chaotic nebulae beyond that time still. Beginning approximately with that period, we are furnished, sometimes in abundance, with fairly trustworthy material in the shape of contemporary Greek testimony bearing on Indian history, and also, as time rolls on, with inscriptional and other kinds of decipherable and dependable domestic evidence. Of course, an immense mass of "documentary" evidence and evidence in the more or less fluid, volatile state of tradition, hearsay and folk-lore (written or unwritten) have always lain by the side of the historian hitherto busy with his inscriptions, plates, coins, artefacts and any corroborative evidence that may be forthcoming from outside And that mass of ancient Indian documentary evidence and tradition has, generally, lain neglected by his side. Is has been, generally, of little help to him in reconstructing, "on scientific lines", the missing skeleton of ancient Indian history. It has been, however, of great use to the comparative mythologist, phylologist and anthropologist.

But even the historian who seeks to reconstruct on scientific lines the missing skeleton of ancient history, whether of India or of any other country, should do well to remember that the dry bones of the skeleton he may have been able to put together will not be true, living history unless they can be made instinct with the touch of life which literature, art, tradition, 'myths', folk-lore, religious and social institutions in their earlier and later forms alone can give. From coins, tablets etc. we can build a possible or even probable frame-work of chronology into which we can put our little bits of tested facts according to one possible plan or other. Such a mosaic of dates and facts (mainly relating to dynastic succession, wars and conquests) is of course important as a necessary ground-plan of history. But it is not the completed structure of history. It is not history as an organic process of evolution. So we have to distinguish beween structural or morphological history and organic, "physiological" history.

Now, India has been so far poor in comparison with some other ancient countries like Egypt, Babylonia and China in her "materials" for writing the first kind of history, and the available materials, as we saw, do not carry us much beyond the time of Budha and Mahavira in the sixth century B. C. Recently, however, a very old and, apparently, a high order of civilisation has been unearthed in the Indus Valley in the Punjab and in Sind, which, according to current official beliefs, is of the Sumerian pattern. The buried cities now discovered bring to light not only very interesting features of a civilisation thriving in the western part of India in so remote a past (when the Indo-Aryans had not, according to the common view, yet migrated into India), but they even put into our hands interesting clues that may eventually help us to unravel many of the riddles of our Vedic and post-Vedic history. The Tantrik cult, for instance, may have older and deeper roots in the soil of India than have so far been granted or suspected. Nothing contemporaneous with or earlier than the Indus Valley civilisation has yet been unearthed in other parts of the subcontinent. So the present trend of speculation is to regard the Indus Valley civilisation as sort of wedge driven into western India—the whole of which was still at the low level of aboriginal darkness (with the possible exception of some parts that might have risen to the Dravidian 'light' level)—probably by the races and civilisation of Sumer.

We are still in the duskland of probabilities or even less than probabilities as to the dates, origins, early habitats and earlier forms not only of the Indus Valley but also of the Dravidian and Indo-Aryan peoples. We do not know for certainty when and from where the Indo-Aryans came into India. The fact of Aryan immigration into India itself, though generally accepted, is still disputed. And if immigration be admitted, we have, probably, to admit not one but several successive streams of immigration. Such a theory, apparently called for to account for some of the critical turnings and "sudden mutations" in our ancient historical evolution, will lead to many unexplored avenues of enquiry as to ages and dates, origins and characteristics.

The Rigveda

The Rigveda—the earliest and the most informing (and instructive "documentary" evidence that we possess—appears to set the stage amidst scenes which show the Aboriginal, Dravidian and Indo-Aryan factors fighting for supremacy first in the land of "Five Rivers" and in the Ganges Valley, and then gradually, beyond the Vindhya Range which with its impenetrable forest mantle, stood as a barrier between Northern India (Aryyavatta) and Deccan. Gradually we find the aborigines cornered and driven to the hills and forest where their descendants, more or less Aryanised, still continue to live. In considerable parts, they were also absorbed into the fold of Aryan society and culture. And in being absorbed they did not fail to impart some little part of their own character to the Aryan complex. There was not so much of racial or even linguistic fusion as of cultural assimilation. This process of Aryanisation in language, culture etc. has been a process admitting, naturally, of different shades and degrees, leaving at the one end aboriginal races that have almost kept aloof from Aryan influence and having at the other others that have become part and parcel of the Aryan system. The Aryanisation of the Dravidian peoples, especially in religion, culture and civilisation, has been a much more perfected process. But, on the other hand, the Dravidian impress on the Aryan system is also, in many places, deep and unmistakable. The Dravidian is co-ordinated or even subordinated to the Aryan but not lost in the latter. This power of assimilation of alien races and cultures without losing the individuality of its own essential Type or Pattern and without at the same time making the diverse elements assimilated lose whatever is essential in them—has been a special characteristic of the Indo-Aryan race and culture-complex. This has meant organic unity or unity in diversity of a more fundamental and abiding nature than can, perhaps, be claimed for the political or national unity with which historians are commonly familiar. Historians, accordingly, commonly miss the unity which lies deep and sees only the diversity which lies on the surface. India to them is thus a veritable chaos of jarring elements of races, languages, religions, castes, sects and culture which have never known unity before the days of the unitary political rule of the British. Of course the introduction, in later times, of the Semitic religions—Mahammedanism and Chirstianity—disturbed to some extent the ages-long unity and balance of the Aryo-Dravidian culture and social system in India. But even these elements were in the process of being slowly drawn into the sphere of influence of what we may call the Genius of India. In other words, a slow but sure process of cultural assimilation even of these "militant" factors was going apace. Buddhism, which had risen as a "revolt" against orthodox Hinduism—but yet as a revolt from within—and which dominated the situation in India for several centuries, ended in the land of its birth by being eventually absorbed and assimilated into the parent religion. Jainism and many other old or latter "revolts" have thus "squared their accounts" with the same parent religion, and have been for many centuries living peaceably side by side with one another and with the latter.

This power of assimilation and co-ordination in which all the components make their own contributions and are permitted to live side by side as members of a commonwealth of cultures, has been the secret of the wonderful resisting and staying power of the Indian culture-complex against such disintergrating forces as have smashed up many an old and glorius civilsation of the world. And it can be easily shown from facts that this staying power has been in evidence not only in the realm of cultural contacts and impacts but also in that of social and political ones. There have been many raids into India and invasions before and after Christ, but it is a travesty of facts to imagine that Indian resistance has always been weak and short-lived and that such invasions are typically like the raids of the Mahmud of Gazni which ever swept away Indian armies and Kingdoms like cobweb or a house of cards. Before her final subjugation by the Mahammedan Power—and the final subjugation of the whole of India was anything like an accomplished fact only for a time during the reign of the great Mogul Emperors—India had been, it should be borne in mind, a mighty Power and a Model of civilisation and culture for at least three thousand years. And it should be remembered further that, when the British in India turned from trade to conquest (always with native help and alliance) they had to settle their accounts with Haidar Ali and Tipu Sultan in the South, but mainly the Maharatta and Sikh Powers which had risen on the ruins of the Mahammedan Powor in India.

Unitary Indian Empire

But there were and still have been other factors which, to some extent, operated against India developing a compact and coherent political and military organisation, except occasionally, like, for instance, the great Roman Empire of old or the British Empire in modern times. We possess, apparently, no connected retrospect of the remote past of which the Vedas, Epics and Puranas speak. But as far as appearances go, an unitary, centralised Indian Empire was the exception and not the rule. In later times also, an Empire like that of Asoka was not a common achievement. As we said, India has possessed deep-laid cultural and institutional unity beneath all her diversities. India has fought, and fought bravely, for the integrity of her sacred Land, her sacred Religion and Tradition, and for their sacred visible Symbols and Embodiments. But she has rarely fought for the "State" as such or an Empire as such. The spirit of her culture did not favour the formation and consolidation of Nationalism in the sense it is commonly understood, and her basic institutions would hardly consist with many form of centralised State control. The all-controlling and co-ordinating Principle was *Dharma* (the Principle of human Values and Conduct) rather than any State agency. Each village, for example, was a self-contained commune and autonomous unit owing permanent allegiance to the reign of Dharma and only temporary allegiance to any kingship that might function for the time being. So the village communities continued to live though kingdoms after kingdoms rose and fell. They were but little affected by the accidents and exigencies of politics.

Again, the spirit of Dharma (which should not be translated as religion) has definitely and systematically favoured all human or even all-living values and tendencies and a cosmopolitan outlook, and has opposed militant, aggressive "predatory" nationalism. The old Upanishads are clear and courageous in their conception of those higher values; and the Dharmashastras (or Codes laying down social and individual conduct) were bold and consistent in their execution of those ideas. Later, Budhism and Jainism and other "reforming" movements have tended only to stress such values as non-violence and fellowship with all men and all living beings. These forces operating through the ages tended to produce in the Indian classes and masses a common disposition not quite favourable to the formation and consolidation of an unitary military state for purposes of offence and defence.

Of the immense back-ground of Indian History which is represented by the Vedas (Samhitas, Brahmanas, Aranyakas and Upanishadas), the various Sutras (or Digests), Philosophies, Epics (the Ramayana and Mahavarata), Puranas and Tantras (our statement here is not anything like full), we possess (unless one is prepared to grant the claim of the Puranas recently put forth in their behalf that they do contain materials for reconstructing a fairly connected chronological history beginning with the very earliest times) very little precise and connected information for the purpose of writing a political history both copious and correct as to facts and their chronological order. But of the ideals and ideas, practices and institutions of the times we do possess a very full, informing and instructive presentation. And, after all, what is real history but this? Scholars have been busy with their sketches and drawings of the ancient orders and specimens of ideas, beliefs and practices that existed in India. But oftener than not their reviews and retrospects have been made from modern standpoints, with modern notions, criteria and standards of testing facts and appraising values. This has not enabled us, in any just measure, to understand much less appreciate a Civilisation (not confined to India but, possibly, reaching some of its greatest heights in this country) which was essentially of a different kind, and cannot, therefore, be represented as only the first uncertain and timid steps taken on the road which has, through a long, long march, at last brought us to our present advanced stage. The ideology, plan and methods of that ancient civilisation we have yet not seriously studied and rightly understood. Much of that civilisation we still regard, without understanding, as consisting of "savage" magic, meaningless ritualism, theological twaddle" and crude superstition. Side by side with all this we find, however, the highest philosophy, deepest mysticism and purest ethics. There is also much that is of original and genuine value from the point of view of human material and mundane progress. This seems to us a curious medley of what is nearly the highest and what is about the lowest. But let us pass on.

Coming to "historical" times we find that the invasion by Alexandar the Great of India proved in the result to be little more than a brilliant raid. His victorious armies could only cut off a small slice of North-Western India, and this little slice the Macedonian would ingest, but could not digest. His steam-roller of conquest speedily developed "war-weariness" on the plains of the Punjab, and he had to go back only adding a bit of India to his vast Empire. He had won some of his battles in India, but it had not been an "easy walk-over" with him.

Chandragupta and Asoka

After his death shortly afterwards, the vast Macedonian Empire practically went to pieces. Chandragupta, who became the king of Magadha, proved himself too powerful for the Greek invaders who had violated the sanctity and integrity of the sacred Land of the Five Rivers. As the result of the formidable opposition by the armies of Chandragupta, a treaty was concluded between him and the Greek which made him the supreme, undisputed lord and sovereign of the Indian Empire. Megasthenes, who was sent by Seleucus as an ambassador to the court of Chandragupta, left a very valuable record of the times, of the customs and morals of the people, and of the administration, which, though unfortunately fragmentary, bears an eloquent and admiring testimony to the high order of material and moral civilisation attained by the Hindus centuries before the Christian era. And this high civilisation was evolved in India not in isolation but in commerce with other civilisations that flourished in ancient times such as the Babylonian, Greek, Persian and Chinese. Chandragupta's son was Bindusara who was succeded by Asoka (260—231 B. C.), who was, undoubtedly, one of the greatest rulers of men holding their sway for the material and spiritual good of mankind. Numerous edicts and inscriptions record the noble and glorious achievements of his reign which, in its later stages, left the bloody path of war and conquest and devoted itself to the much more noble and fruitful task of the moral and spiritual conquest and redemption of ourselves and our fellow-beings. With commendable catholicity and tolerance, not seeking to impose it upon others by his great imperial authority and power, he exercised that authority and power for the purpose of transforming Budhism, which had been more or less a local sect in the Ganges valley, into one of the greatest and most potent living world religions. Asoka's reign is therefore rightly held to be an epoch in the history of the world. His edicts also show the man, his ideals and his methods. But all this had not allowed or favoured the cement of the great Mauryya Empire setting into the requisite hardness. Independent kingdoms like Bacteria and Parthia took their rise in the border land, and the Greeks renewed their incursions. New races (the Yuen-chi) came in a surge of migration which swept all before them, and in the first century A. D. a considerable portion of North-west India came under their influence.

Gupta Dynasty

Kanishka, who made Peshawar his capital, proved great as a ruler and as a patron and missionary of the Buddhistic religion. Under him the Kushan branch of the Yuen-chi reached the zenith of its power. But this power fell as another power in middle India rose—the Andhra dynasty. A peak like Amaravati or Ujjain would, sometime, rise and shine in the midst of the moving vastness of Indian waters. In the beginning of the fourth century the centre of political influence in India was again shifted to Pataliputra in Magadha as the Gupta dynasty emerged into power. Samudragupta, who ruled for fifty years, and his son Chandragupta, greatly distinguished themselves not only in war but in the sphere of peaceful and fruitful administration, promoting general prosperity and giving liberal encouragement to art and literature, a glorious tribute to which was paid by the Chinese pilgrim Fa-hien. According to his testimony, their Empires were vast and their administration just, enlightened. Towards the end of the fifth century—when the White Huns from Central India began to pour themselves into India—the sun of the Gupta dynasty set (during whose regime, it should be noted, there had been a revival and reconstruction of ancient Brahmanism and Brahmanical culture as evidenced especially by the literature of the Puranas ; but this reviving process was, very largely, a process of quiet adaptation and peaceful assimilation). More than a century had elapsed after the fall of the Gupta dynasty before there rose another great and enlightened monarch who could emulate with no mean success the greatest of the Indian rulers in historical times—Asoka. Emperor Harsha, who consolidated his authority practically over the whole of Northern India in the beginning of the seventh century, was famous equally for his great prowess, his high intellectual attainments and for the broad catholicity of his religious outlook. An account of his times has been left by a Chinese, Huen Tsiang by name. In that, India is still painted in generally bright and even glowing colours.

Mediaeval India

After the death of Harsha, and gradually, with the emergence of India into what may be called the mediaeval period, the conditions which had made the political unification of India sometimes possible in the past, nearly disappeared, and India was thrown into a state of political confusion and chaos in which petty kingdoms rose like mushrooms and constant internecine strife prevailed. Some outstanding figures like Vikramaditya would occasionally appear on the stage ; but such events were few and far between. In the South of India was being enacted a very interesting but involved drama in which the Andhras, Pallavas, Chalukyas and Cholas were the principal actors. Kashmere in the north, Kanauj in the Doab and Bengal in the east were also alive with many vivid and vital scenes and events of political, cultural and social interest. But we shall not try to make a review of them here. One outstanding event in the confusion and complexity of the general Indian situation which deserves notice even in passing was the rise of the Rajput power upon which the mantile of the old caste of Kshatriyas (the warrior and ruling caste) fell, and which was the chief opposition that the waves of Mahommedan invasion coming one after another ever since the second quarter of the 7th. century had to encounter and ultimately bear down. Guzarat, Malwa, Ajmer, Kanauj and Delhi were the principal scenes of the new drama of Rajput ascendency—a darma so full of episodes of superhuman bravery, noble heroism and sacrifice for the sacred cause of religion and liberty that they have ever since lived in human memory as models which future generations of patriots in any country might well try to emulate. Though Rajput opposition was borne down in Northern India by the end of the twelfth century, Rajput bravery and the spirit that animated it survived the crash of the Hindu Empire of Delhi and Ajmere over which Prithvi Raj, the hero, the last of the Hindu emperors, though not the last of the Hindu rulers, had held sway. Rajput bravery and Rajput love of independence were still factors to reckon with in the days of the great Moghuls—Akbar, Jahangir, Shahjahan and Aurangzib. Col. Todd and some others have narrated the story, and it constitutes one of the proudest annals in the vast archives of the Hindu glory in India. As to the conquest of Northern India by the Mohammedans, it should be noted, the great prize was not very easily or quickly won ; that the first Mohammedan impact was in the seventh century shortly after the passing away of the Prophet, and a Mohammedan kingdom in Northern India came into being towards the end of the 12th century. Even this did not mean either a complete or a final subjugation of India. And there is another thing to be noted. Hindu Power fell not because its resistance was weak and its opposition timid, but because it did not possess sufficient compactness, and its bravery and heroism in the field was not backed by adequate tact, strategy and discipline in diplomacy, planning and preparation.

The centuries of the mediaeval age in India were marked by a conspicuous lack of political unity and solidarity. But they were by no means unimportant and barren. It was not a "dark" Age. In the Gupta period and in the centuries before and after, a marvellous process of social, cultural and religious reconstruction was going apace. The old Vedic scheme of social economy (involving as it did the four Varnas or "castes" and the four Ashramas or "stages" of life) was being transformed through a process of adaptation, assimilation and multiplication which made society more comprehensive and at the same time more complex. The influence of Buddhism, Hellenism and that of the Mongoloid races also led to adaptations and assimilations in many important directions in the older order of Indian customs and institutions. The gradual assimilation of Budhism itself was a phenomenon of the greatest importance. The Vedic religion survived but it was transformed. The Puranas and Tantras renewed and gave a new expression to the Sanatana Dharma. In the domain of literature, art (both useful and fine), science and mathematics, philosophy and metaphysics, these centuries were also productive of fruits that were and still are of the greatest interest and value. Great poets like Kalidas and Bhavabhuti, and great philosophers like Shankaracharyya and Ramanuja, and also other pioneers and masters in other fields, formed a galaxy of men of genius and talents which showed that an age of political dis-equilibrium and confusion in India was yet not necessarily an age of cultural depression and darkness and social disruption. The soul of India could, apparently, function to its best advantage in spite of her troubled politics.

But whilst this was true for some time it could not be true for all time. Her politics at last began to tell on her constitution. We do not, however, propose to continue the story through the Mohammedan and British periods. The history of these periods is more settled and definite in features, and these are, generally, well-known. One special feature, which is not always clearly recognised and to which we should like to draw attention, is this. From the twelfth century right up to the eighteenth, or even for some time later, the Hindu power of revival and regeneration, of initiation and execution, was never like dead or even dying. Independent and often powerful kingdoms like Vijayanagar in the South, those of Pratab, Shivaji and the Peshwas in the west (we do not mention some others e. g. those in Bengal) would, now and then, proudly lift their heads and challenge the authority of the great Moslem emperors. Under that authority, too, there flouished many great Hindu administrators, ministers, governors, generals and financiers. In short, during the Mohammedan era the Hindu genius was not at its best, but it was not quite decadent.

The Mohammedan Rule

The Mohammedan conquerors, again, from Mahomed Ghori who wrested the sceptre of the kingdom of Delhi from Prithviraj after a first unsuccessful attempt, came to India as foreigners but they did not remain here as foreigners. India was the land of their adoption. Raids like those by Chengis Khan or Nadir Shah were rare and they did not represent the normal course of events. India suffered, and sometimes badly, no doubt, from the effects of the conquering ardour and proselytising zeal of some of the Mohammedan rulers. But the Great Moghuls were as much "children of the soil" as the humblest of the Hindu "heathens". And this sharing together by the Hindus and Mussalmans of a common "hearth and home" naturally tended to breed a consciousness of community of interests in both as India's offspring. There was a steady assimilation of the Semitic and Indo-Aryan cultures also and even a growing understanding and appreciation of one religion by the other. The religions touched and even blended with each other at their highest points—e. g. in Sufism and Vedantic mysticism. They also met and evolved a broad common "shrine" to which folk beliefs, practices and institutions would bring their united homage. Even a common dialect (Urdu or Hindusthani) was evolved between the two in Northern India which gradually blossomed into a fine literature. The patronage extended by the Mohammedan emperors to Music, Architecture etc. was also fruitful of very fine results: India's wealth attracted the trade and commerce of the whole civilised world. In fact, America or the West Indies was discovered in an attempt to discover an western route to the Indian market. British, French, Dutch and Portugese traders all came and scrambled for market, and eventually, for political power in India. It is also worthy of note that even under the sway of such masterful monarchs as Sher Shah, Akbar or Aurangzeb, the government of the country was in the main, decentralised, allowing provincial and local autonomy—down to the autonomy of the village units—to adequately function. Even petty local chiefs—like the feudal lords of the mediaeval West—never unlearnt the art of fighting and governing. So it was always possible for a man of ambition and ability, like Shivaji for example, to evolve sanctions whereby he could implement his high political aspirations. It was the very large measure of local autonomy and local initiative that existed that rendered possible the rise of the Marhatta and Sikh Powers and also of the kingdoms of Hyder Ali and the Nizam in the south. And British Power in India in its rise to paramountcy found its most formidable rivals or powerful allies in them.

In 1599, during the reign of Queen Elizabeth, some merchants of London formed an association for the purpose of trade with India, and this association was granted a royal charter of incorporation. At first this Company was purely a trading concern establishing factories in the east and west coasts of India and in Bengal and administering its affairs in the three "presidencies", which were at first independent of one another but subordinate to the Board of Directors at home. In course of time, however, chiefly with a view to preserving and consolidating its growing and extensive trade in India, in the face of the French rivalry and intrigue and the prevailing political anarchy and unrest in the land, it established military garrison of defence which soon became involved in hostilities that saddled it with territorial responsibilities. It fought some decisive battles in Madras and in Bengal, which raised a trading company to the status of a political Power in India. French intrigue failed and French rivalry practically died down in India. One of the most decisive battles fought was the battle of Plassey in 1757. The battle was won with the aid of faithful native battalions, and with the active or passive support of the generals and noblemen of the unfortunate young Nawab of Bengal. It is worthy of note that the path of British supremacy in India, and often, its influence and prestige abroad, has been paved, amongst other things, with the consent, alliance and willing co-operation of the Natives of India. It was so even during the critical period of the Sepoy Mutiny, one hundred years after the battle of Plassey. It was again so during the "ordeal" of the last Great War. The machinery of administration by the East India Company was from to time modified by Acts of Parliament (1773, 1784; and the Charter Acts of 1793 and 1833). By these a Governor-General-in-Council was made the supreme administrative authority in India subject to a Board of Control at home. By the last Act, the Company ceased to be a commercial concern and became a political and administrative body only. After the Sepoy Mutiny another Act was passed by which the Government of India was transferred from the Company to the Crown, and henceforth, the Governor-General was also the Viceroy of India. The functions of the Government of India are wide and its responsibilities heavy. But its responsibilities are to the Crown and the Parliament. It has not rested on an elective popular basis. There have been legislative bodies, but its motions, resolutions and votes have not, except as regards certain matters of secondary importance under the Act of 1919, a binding effect on the Government.

India's contributions and sacrifices in the Great War were great, but the "reward" that came in the shape of the Parliamentary Declaration promising her "a progressive realisation of responsible government", the stages and times of which were to be determined by the Parliament alone, was not comforting to her nationalist aspirations. And the Government of India Act of 1919, which is still in actual function though it has been, apparently, broadened and amplified in some directions by a recent Parliamentary Statute, did not meet the wishes or expectations of India. By that Act dyarchy or a kind of dual responsibility was established in the provinces, where the "nation-building" subjects were "transferred" to Ministers (not responsible however to the legislatures), whilst the more important subjects were "reserved". In practice the transference of certain subjects to Ministers (who were appointed by, held office under the pleasure of, and were responsible to, the Governor) meant little more than a complication of the administrative machinery which became, in consequence, more cumbrous and expensive. The Central Government continued to remain unitary under the scheme. The legislative bodies, both provincial and central, were expanded with non-official majorities, but this placed little power, for construction or even for obstruction, in the hands of the popular parties. Whilst the liberals proceeded to work the scheme, the main body of nationalist forces, as represented by the Indian National Congress, would not at first even look at it. But some time later, under the guidance of Mr. C. R. Das and Pandit Motilal Nehru, a Swaraj Party, analogous to the present Congress Parliamentary Party, was formed which entered the legislatures, both provincial and central, in telling numbers, and by its obstructionist tactics caused not a little embarrassment to those entrusted with the work of day to day administration. In some provinces it was even able to "wreck" dyarchy for a time. Generally, however, the system has worked, though not satisfactorily even according to official appreciation. We need not in particular refer to the unwelcome labours of the All-White Statutory Simon Commission, to which even the habitually co-operating liberals refused to lend their co-operation. Meanwhile the Congress ideology was becoming bolder day by day, and the Lahore session adopted a resolution setting as the goal of India complete Independence or Purna Swaraj. A campaign of civil disobedience followed to create "sanctions under the leadership of Mahatma Gandhi who has been really at the helm of Congress affairs since the early twenties. The Round Table idea was broached rather too late; but Mahatma Gandhi, after concluding what is known as the Gandhi-Irwin Pact, joined the Conference subsequently. The results of the deliberations of that body fell short of the Congress demand. And the Congress again withdrew its offer of co-operation.

INDIA IN HOME POLITY

INTRODUCTION

"Golden Jubilee" of the Congress

On the 28th. December, 1935, the Indian National Congress completed fifty years of its life. On that date in 1885, 72 men from different parts of India, speaking different languages, wearing different dresses, guided by differing traditions, assembled in the Gokuldas Tejpal Pathsala Hall in Bombay to evolve an unity of life, thought and conduct out of the diversities of Indian life—an India, one, whole, and indivisible. Starting out as a thin stream like unto that which one witnesses at the Gongotri in the heart of the Himalayas, the Indian Renaissance of the 19th. century, precipitated by methods of British administration and enlightenment, has broadened out, as the Ganges has done, into a mighty stream by contributions from various movements of awakening and uplift from right and left. And, from out of the abundant flow of its sweeping life newer channels of activity have been cut to irrigate and enrich hitherto untapped and unorganized centres of life. The Indian National Congress represents one such channel of awakened life.

On the occasion of the "Golden Jubilee" of the Congress the story of its rise and growth has been broadcasted far and wide both in and outside the country. Leaders of thought, orators and speakers, minis-trels of nationalism, authors and journalists have sought to bring out of the storied past the life-work of the men and women who laid out the roads on which the present generation walk with more assurance and intrepidity. This new courage and wider vision has been generated and acquired as the result of the spade work of men and women, Indian and European, who are to-day only a memory of far-off things, but to whom belonged the credit of the New India that has risen over the consciousness of our people.

British Conquest of India

Some glimpses of the developments that have culminated in the Indian National Congress should find a place in the pages of the "Indian Annual Register", if the problems which at present confound the intelligence of men in our country were to be understood and properly handled and solved. For this purpose it would be necessary to hark back to the early days of "John" Company, and trace the processes and effects of the various measures of consolidation and enlightenment adopted by the new rulers of the country. Rajput and Marhatta had wrecked the Moghul empire, but were themselves wrecked when they clashed against the might and wit :of the British. This process had been completed by 1818. The Moslem Nawabs and governors of provinces who offered less than lip-service to the Emperor at Delhi and set up practically independent kingdoms did not show better stamina or fight. The Khalsa organized by the Sikhs was as unsuccessful. The conquest of India was almost a walk-over, if we are to trust to the words of

Sir John Seeley who said that the British acquired India in a "fit of absent-mindedness". However, an organisation of traders, of "factors and clerks" became rulers of the country. Capture of political power by a foreign people is no mere transfer of ruling authority from the hands of one set of people to those of another. It entails revolutionary changes in every department in the life of the subject population. With all the good-will in the world the new rulers cannot help affecting and influencing the life and thought of the ruled, in undermining, unknowingly and imperceptibly perhaps, their social usages, economic institutions and organizations. The self-interest of the ruling race may also consciously work to this end. Their conceit of superiority and contempt for the subject people and for the weaknesses of their social life that had led to their defeat—both these feelings impel them instinctively to ignore or minimise any virtue that may inform the thought and conduct of the people under their rule. This has been the universal experience in the relationship between the rulers and the ruled when they happen to be aliens to one another. The foreign rulers are ignorant ; the subject people is ever afraid. Ignorance and fear give a twist to the relation between the two which no generosity or good-will can straighten out or set right. This unnatural state of things causes material and spiritual losses to both the parties which it has been the duty of statesmanship to seek to make good. Indo-British relation has been passing through this test these one hundred and seventy-five years.

From Trader to Ruler

When the East India Company got a foot-hold in the country as rulers of particular patches in it, their officers had no time to think of anything else than "getting rich quick". The result is expressed in Dean Inge's words :

> "The first impetus (to the industrial revolution in Britain) was given by the plunder of Bengal which, after the victories of Clive, flowed into the country in a broad stream for about thirty years. This ill-gotten wealth played the same part in stimulating England's industries as the "five milliards" exhorted from France did for Germany after 1870".

While enriching themselves by all manner of means, the Company's officers did not bother themselves with the internal administration of the country. The first shock that roused the British people to their responsibilities as rulers in India was the famine of 1769-70 which swept away more than a crore of people, a third of the entire population of the province of Bengal. The famine played havoc in the western districts of Bengal proper and the eastern districts of Bihar. The decrease in the population did not lower the land-revenue demands of the Company ; and from Warren Hastings to Lord Cornwallis, for about twenty years, it was one long-drawn effort to make the Zamindar and "farmers" of revenue pay up—proof of which is indirectly afforded by Sir William Hunter's description of an ideal Collector—"The realization of revenue formed the Collector's paramount duty, and on his success in this respect rather than on the prosperity of the people, his reputation as an officer depended". The administrative policy indicated above was changed by the Permanent Settlement of land revenue with which is associated the name of Lord Cornwallis. It precipitated a revolution in the social and economic life of the province which has come home to roost after more than one hundred and thirty years.

The famine of 1769-70 had caused 'the ruin of two-thirds of the old aristocracy of Lower Bengal'. To the rest, somehow existing, Lord Cornwallis' land settlement dealt a death-blow, so to say. In the Bengal Administration Report of 1872-73, the then Lieutenant-Governor, Sir George Campbell, recalls these facts :

Disintegration of Economic Life

"The Government demand was then one which left a margin of profit, but small compared with that given to Zemindars in modern days. There was wide-spread default in the payment of the Government dues, and extensive consequent sales of estates or parts of estates for recovery of arrears under the unbending system introduced in 1793. In 1796-97, lands bearing a total revenue of sikka Rs. 14, 18, 756 were sold for arrears of revenue, and, in 1797-98, the revenue of land so sold amounted to sikka Rs. 22,74,076. By the end of the century the greater portions of the estates of the Nadiya, Rajshahi, Bishanpur, and Dinajpur Rajas had been alienated. The Burdwan estate was seriously crippled, and the Birbhum Zamindari was completely ruined. A host of smaller zamindars shared the same fate. In fact, it is scarcely too much to say that within the ten years that followed the Permanent Settlement a complete revolution took place in the constitution and ownership of the estates which formed the subject of the settlement'".

The smaller fry fared no better. The resumption of "Lakheraj" lands formed part of the Cornwallis Settlemant (1793); in 1819 the net was drawn tighter, the process completing in 1828, when the smallest of the spawns could not and did not escape.

The same story of dispossession and relinquishment can be found in the Ryotwari tracts in Madras and Bombay. Letters and remonstrances from the Company's officials addressed to the Court of Directors in London bear witness to the havoc created all over. Colonel Munro (later Sir Thomas, Governor of Madras) is credited with being the inaugurator of the Ryotwari system of land revenue settlement. His opinion on his own system should be regarded as final judgment. He said that the Ryotwari assessment was "considerably higher than it ought to be, and higher than it ever had been, or than could be realized as long as there are bad crops and poor Ryots"; to protect the interest of the Government in the assessment involved "continual interference with the cultivators, and a constant exercise of domiciliary control." In a particular report (dated 25th August, 1805) he stated that "if every restraint on their (Ryots') inclination were removed, they would probably throw up one-fourth of the land in cultivation."

Thus between the Zemindari and the Ryotwari settlements was the economic life of the people, based on land, disorganised.

Side by side, the industries of the country were being submerged under the flood of machine-made goods entering the country under the aegis of an administration which was a trading and profiteering institution as well. The Indian indigenous textile, ship-building and other "luxury" industries were ruined. Cotton piece-goods sent from India to Great Britain fell from 1,266, 608 pieces in 1814 to 356,086 in 1835; while British cotton exports to India rose from 8,18,208 yards in 1814 to 5,17,77,277 yards in 1835. The same story of fall and rise is registered in the value of cotton goods exported and imported. In 1815 India sent cotton goods of the value of above 2 crores rupees to Britain, and in 1832 of the value of 15 lakhs only. As against

Ruin of Indian Arts and Industries

this, Britain exported to India in 1815 cotton goods to the value of 4 lakhs only; in 1832 the figure rose to rupees 60 lakhs. Deprived of State patronage or protection the ship-building industry in India could not stand the competition of Britain. Ramesh Chandra Dutt records in his "India in the Victorian Age" the progressive decline of the industry.

"In 1795-'96 six ships were built in Calcutta with tonnage of 4105 tons, and five large vessels of 500 to 600 tons were on the stocks.
In 1797-'98 several vessels were launched from the dock-yards of Calcutta.".

By the middle of the 19th. Century the industry had become subject for historical research in Calcutta and Chittagong, the other part of the province.

The ruin of Indian industries through the pressure of the "new industrialism" of the ruling power in the country is illustrative of the tendency of things and not exhaustive of the full story. The statistics that have been quoted above appear so precise and natural. But it requires an effort of imagination at this distance of time to translate them into terms of flesh and blood, to recapture the condition of unemployment, misery, sickness of body and soul of millions of men, women and children. Speaking of an identical development in Britain itself as a result of the first onslaught of Industrialism on her institions, a historian writes: "It is a piteous story, this of the quick, unprepared, unsoftened transformation of a people's life..........." But in the case of Britain the law of compensation had opportunity to work in "the wealth and glory of the few and the misery of the many". As pioneer in the use of steam in the textile and iron manufacturing industries, and its application to land and sea carriage, Britain became the greatest imperial nation in the world, which position she held unchallenged almost to the cataclysmic years of the Great War (1914-1918). The grandeur and glory of an imperial destiny secured by a tiny island in North Atlantic reconciled the many to the deprivations and privations of their lives, and blinded the privileged few to the "England of the poor", to the "black abyss which lay under the surface of England's wealth". Both the few and the many in India had none of these consolations and compensations.

Identical Developments in Britain and India

The revenue and economic policies pursued by the East India Company under the inspiration of British ideas and the dictation of British interests disrupted India's social and economic institutions. A certain measures of breakdown was inevitable under the circumstances. And, to the historian passing in review these developments a hundred years after, both the rulers and the ruled appear to be helpless victims of the impersonal forces of social and economic evolution. In the case of our rulers, however, they could not build better than they knew. Thinking British institutions the best for the purpose of an ordered society, they imported them wholesale, ignorant of, and ignoring and disturbing the social equilibrium and the hierarchy of economic arrangements that held up society in India. The men of the generation who pioneered these measures in this country knew not or had forgotten how in their own country "the commonwealth of farmers" had been usurped by

landlords enclosing "common lands", entailing great social changes, thus described by Prof. Ramsay Muir :

"The big landlords were adding field after field, the small holders were slowly disappearing. English rural society was ceasing to be the homogenous society without sharp cleavages between class and class,..............a gulf was gradually opening between a mass of landless labourers on the one hand, and on the other a group of great landholders and class of capitalist farmers."

The social effect of the Cornwallis Settlement partakes of something of this character, as recognised as early as 1820 by Sir Edward Colebrooke :

"The errors of the Permanent Settlement were two-fold ; first, in the sacrifice of what may be denominated the *yeomanry*, by merging all village-rights, whether of property or of occupancy in the all devouring recognition of the Zamindar's permanent property in the soil ; and, secondly, in the sacrifice of the peasantry by one sweeping enactment, which left the Zaminder to make his settlement with them on such terms as he might choose to require".

The breakdown in the "communal" system of economic organization that had prevailed in our country and which had been represented by the craft-guilds, threw men on their own resources, deprived them of the protection of the joint family system which was a sort of non-official unemployment provision ; it exposed the people to the competition of all the world, a world of industries, employing a new and un-understood technique of production and distribution, the ramifications of which few could understand, and fewer control or regulate. Faced by such a situation Indian arts, industries and crafts dwindled silently, and the artisans followed the same fate without protest. The social and economic effects of the measures started under the auspices of our new rulers stare us in the face to-day ; and rulers and ruled loudly lament the decay of industry and increasing pressure on the land, speak of rural disintegration as major problems of India's economic and social life. This is how history revenges herself on men's pretensions to wisdom. This is the rhythm of history.

Policy of Enlightenment

The economic break-down had repurcussions on the social life of the people. Some of these measures were inevitable for purposes of consolidation of the power and interests of the new rulers. But even for that purpose, not only was the supine and passive acquiescence of the subject population necessary, their enlightened co-operation was sought to be enlisted as well. To this problem of enlightenment the East India Company turned their attention with great hesitation and much misgiving. Till 1813, they "did not recognize the promotion of education among the natives of India as part of its duty or concern". For, to quote Monier-Williams, "the rulers feared the evil consequences of education for the ruled, and the ruled anticipated no good results for themselves". The rulers and the ruled could not forget that they were "separated by almost every conceivable circumstance of alienation", to quote the words from an address presented to Lord William Bentick. They ruled over them and "trafficked" with the people, but did not understand them. nor did the ruled understand the character of the rulers. In circumstance like these "the dangerous consequence to our power in this country from imparting instruction to the natives" was hotly debated among Englishmen, in Britain and India. Apart from political considerations the authorities were apprehensive that any system of education initiated by them or conducted by missionaries eager to utilize educational institutions as a potent means of conversion to Christianity might create irremediable dissatisfaction and complications. But the time forces were fighting against their fears and policies. On the occasion of the renewal of the Company's Charter in 1813, a clause was inserted in the Act which is regarded as "the first legislative admission of the right of education in India to participate in the public revenues". For, by this time the rulers had been able to persuade themselves that they had a mission to carry out in this country, the mission of opening out the minds of the people of India to the great truths of their faith and culture to the mutual advantage of both the peoples. This faith finds expression in the following words found in the Charter Act of 1813 :

"It is the duty of this country to promote the introduction of useful knowledge and of religion and of moral improvement, and that facilities be offered by law to persons who are desirous of going to and remaining in India to accomplish this benevolent design".

Logic of Defeat

The people of India had also by that time acknowledged the superiority of the ruling race in every department of action and knowledge. The upholders of the older native traditions among Hindus and Muslims could not throw up from among themselves any one who could challenge the pretensions of the ruling race ; they retired to their huts, leaving the moulding of the life and thought of their people to these new-comers. They nursed a conceit of superiority, it is true, but it lacked any strength of conviction, and was not supported by knowledge. The Hindus were the first to capitulate, body and soul ; the Moslems took another half a century to throw up their hands. On the threshold of this development stands Raja Ram Mohun Roy. The evolution of his mind and attitude towards British rule and all that it stood for may be accepted as representative of the generation that made India what it to-day is. That evolution is expressed in his own words :

"........I proceeded on my travels, and passed through different countries, chiefly within, but some beyond, the bounds of Hindoostan, with a feeling of great aversion to the establishment of British Power in India. When I had reached the age of twenty, my father recalled me,.................. ; after which I first saw and began to associate with Europeans, and soon after made me tolerably acquainted with their laws and form of government. Finding them generally more intelligent, more steady and moderate in their conduct, I gave up my prejudice against them, and became inclined in their favour, feeling persuaded that their rule, though a foreign yoke, would lead more speedily and surely to the amelioration of the native inhabitants......................".

That generation accepted the logic of defeat, and agreed to be docile and apt pupils of the system introduced by the ruling race so that disciplined, organized, and regimented by it, they might in the fulness of time outgrow that system. The English biographer of Raja Ram Mohan Roy accepted this interpretation of the acquiescence of the natives of India in British rule, when she (Miss Collet) wrote :

"The prospect of an educated India, of an India approximating to European standards of culture, seems to have never been long absent from Rammohun's mind ; and he did, however vaguely, claim in advance for his countrymen the political rights which progress in civilization inevitably involves. Here, again, he stands forth as the tribune and prophet of New India.

Political tutelage under Britain

The opinion that British domination of India was a period of political tutelage persisted as far down as 1905. In Bankim Chandra's *Ananda-Mutt* this feeling and this opinion is expressed in vivid and compelling language ; in Gopal Krishna Gokhale's Servant of India Society British rule was accepted as a dispensation of Providence. Something of such a belief impelled Lord Macaulay to throw his weight and prestige to the initiation of the policy of Anglioizing education in India which, he hoped, would produce a race "Indian in blood and colour, but English in tastes, in opinions, in morals, and in intellect", who would, by the bond of obligation and gratitude, be the pillars of Britain's far-flung empire, the dusky standard-bearers of her mission to the East.

What he said in depreciation of the learning and intellectual heritage of the East—of a shelf of European books containing more knowledge than the whole host of Eastern manuscripts—has kept up an estrangement which must have been his purpose to bridge over. The maiden belief of the early British Liberals in the supreme efficacy of European science and culture and their right of free entrance to every country irrespective of the wishes and inclinations of the peoples concerned was still green when Macaulay perpetrated that bombast; he forgot that the Indian mind was not "a blank sheet of paper on which anything could be written by any man". A century later the effects of that forgetfulness is being sought to be neutralized by proposals of educational reconstruction which are "designed...........to adapt the whole system (of education) in (to ?) the social and economic back-ground of the people", to quote the words of a Bengal Government Resolution 1935, presaging a new orientation to popular education in the province. But when in 1835 Lord William Bentick's government declared that "the great object of the British Government ought to be the promotion of European literature and science amongst the natives of India" and that "all the funds appropriated for purposes of education would be best employed on English education alone", they believed that the education of the higher classes must have precedence over that of the masses ; it was hoped that the former, their minds illumined by the new enlightenment and liberalised by it, would carry and transfer the light that they had received and benefitted from to the cottages of their neighbours. Sir Charles Wood's Despatch of 1854 which historians call the "charter" of education in India called for a re-consideration of Indo-British education policy by acknowledging that there had been "too exclusive a direction of the efforts of the Government towards providing the means of acquiring a very high degree of education for a smaller number of natives of India drawn for the most part from what we should here call the higher classes." Since that time Indian education has zig-zagged between the claims of the classes and the needs of the masses.

Pre-British Indian Education

We have been taught to believe that the initiation of what may be called the Macaulay-Bentick scheme of education was a great step forward in popularizing modern education in India. Rather, it should be regarded as a few steps backwards, perhaps with the intention of a bigger jump forward. For history, facts recorded in the "Journals" and reports of the early British historians and enquirers show that when the British were laying the foundations of their rule in this country in the second half of the 18th. century and the first two decades of the 19th., the whole country was studded over with institutions for primary and higher education. "The English found in India a wide-spread system of elementary and higher education, of which the former was mainly practical, and the latter mainly literary, philosophical and religious", writes F. W Thomas. Results of enquiries initiated by Sir Thomas Munro, as Governor of Madras in 1821, show that "in a population of 1, 28, 50, 941, there were actually 1,84,170 students (......probably about 10 per cent of the population of school-going age) attending schools, besides those who received instruction at home". These enquiries were held at a time when "the earlier tradition of national education was almost dead". In a Minute by Lord William Bentick dated 20th January, 1835, suggesting the desirability of an enquiry into "the actual state of Native education, that is, of that which is carried on, as it probably has been for centuries, entirely under Native management", appears the following: "...........that in 1823 there existed in the Madras territories no less than 12,498 institutions for education, supported partly by the endowments of Native Princes, but chiefly by the voluntary contributions of the people". Bengal and Behar had a similar tale to tell. Mr. W. Adam was commissioned to take a survey of educational facilities in Bengal and Behar. In his first report submitted in 1835, he speaks of "Indigenous Elementary Schools" as follows:

"By this description are meant those schools in which instruction in the elements of knowledge is communicated, and which have been originated and supported by the Natives themselves, in contra-distinction from those that are supported by Religious or Philanthropic Societies, The number of such schools in Bengal is supposed to be very great. A distinguished member of the General Committee of Public Instruction in a minute on the subject expressed the opinion that if one rupee per mensem were expended on each existing village schools in the Lower Provinces, the amount would probably fall little short of 12 lakhs of rupees per annum. This supposes that there are 1,00,000 such schools in Bengal and Behar, and assuming the population of those two provinces to be 4,00,00,000 there would be a village school for every 400 persons".

In the absence of any available data to determine the proportion of school-going children, or of children capable of going to schools, or of children of the age at which, according to the custom of the country, it is usual to go to school, the writer of the report instituted a comparison between conditions in Prussia where a census had been taken, and those in Bengal and Behar to arrive at some reliable figures of the juvenile student population of the latter. He found that in a population 1,22,56,725 in Prussia, the number of children capable of receiving education was 19,23,000, three-sevenths of the number of children under fourteen years of age. This gives for Bengal and Behar on an average a village school for every 63 children of the school-going age, including boys and girls. Mr. Adam found no "indigenous girls' school", and deducting the number of girls from those of the school-going age, he reached the conclusion that there was "an indigenous elementary school for every 31 or 32 boys". The estimate of 1,00,000 such schools in Bengal and Behar was confirmed by the consideration of the number of villages in those provinces, which had been officially estimated at 1,50,748. The writer concedes that the figures he enumerates were only "distant approximations" to the real state of things. But he asserts that—

> "................ it will still appear that the system of village schools is extensively prevalent; that the desire to give education to their male children must be deeply seated in the minds of parents even of the humblest classes; and that these are the institutions, closely interwoven as they are with the habits of the people and the customs of the country, through which primarily, although not exclusively, we may hope to improve the morals and intellect of the Native population."

Thus were the foundations of enlightenment as a buttress of imperial consolidation sought to be strengthened by spreading it amongst the widest commonalty. Mr. W. Adam came into touch with all sorts and conditions of men, in the rural parts of the province in course of his enquiry, and he could well gauge the innermost mind of the people in relation to the administration. He advised "wary treading" even in measures of uplift and sincere help; he put it down that "the utmost that can be said of native society in general, even in its most favourable aspect, is that there is no hostility, but in place of it a cold, dead, apathetic indifference which would lead the people to change masters to-morrow without a struggle or a sign". The conqueror's spirit, the pride of domination, on the one hand, and the fears and prejudices of native society on the other had between them combined to raise a barrier of suspicion. This barrier could be pulled down only by the Government initiating "comprehensive measures for the promotion and right direction of national education", education in consonance with national prepossessions, traditions and prejudices. This education would enlist the services of the young men of the higher classes who were being turned out of the colleges in ever-increasing numbers. Wisely handled, the extension of vernacular education would place the Government in friendly relations with every city, town and hamlet, with every head of a family, with every instructor of youth, and with the entire juvenile population gradually developing into the adult population of the country; it would constitute a chain the links of which would be found in every village and at every hearth. This, in brief, was the prospect which Mr. W. Adam called up before the Government in pressing for the acceptance of his proposals.

Growing Consciousness of rights

The apostles of enlightenment, of the reconstruction of life and thought of an ancient people in the moulds imported from Europe, had hoped that Western education would confirm the then political and social order, strengthen British rule and the leadership of the native aristocracy. This hope very soon proved vain and futile. The spirit of criticism and revolt against traditional life and conduct which the new enlightenment had encouraged, soon learnt to spare no authority, sacred or profane. The socio-religious revolt and revolution presaged an order and quality of mind which would be less disposed to regard an executive order as a decree of Providence, and would be more conscious of positive rights secured by statutes and enforceable in law. Though this habit of mind might speak of these rights as inherent in British citizenship, the rights of men did not take long to crop up and assert their individuality and indefeasibility. It took three quarter of a century to complete this full cycle of evolution. As in other fields of activity so in helping to evolve a watchful public and political life in India, open and organised, Raja Ram Mohun Roy acted as the pioneer. Around him gathered men who fought for justice and equity in society and state, and organised themselves for the redress of the grievances of their people and the assertion of their rights as citizens—Dwarkanath Tagore, Romanath Tagore, Prasanna Kumar Tagore, Tara Charan Chakravorty, succeeded by Ram Gopal Ghosh, Dakshminaranjan Mukherjee, Harish Chandra Mukherjee and Rev. K. M. Banerjee. Raja Ram Mohun Ray was a realist in politics; he recognized and acknowledged the need of "many years of British domination" in India. But he could imagine a time when it would serve the British empire better to have India "as a willing province, an ally of British empire or troublesome and annoying as a determined enemy". He could think of such a possibility:

> "Supposing that hundred years hence the Native character becomes elevated from the constant intercourse with Europeans and the acquirement of general and political knowledge as well as of modern arts and sciences, is it possible that they will not have the spirit as well as the inclination to resist effectually any unjust and oppressive measures serving to degrade them in the scale of society".

The men who followed the foot-steps of Raja Ram Mohun Roy in his endeavours and strivings for social and political reform and progress worked under the impulse of hope and faith that in process of time the rulers would redeem their promises to efface "all distinction between conqueror and conquered"; they laboured, encouraged by the teachings of their own interpretations of British history. And they could work and labour in all charity and equanimity of temper. For more than two generations they trod their self-chosen path of appealing to the good sense and the better nature of their rulers.

Indo-British co-operation in Politics

This dependence on the good-will of the rulers for the realization of their hopes of political reform and advance had for its corollary the attempt to invite and enlist the sympathy and support of individual British men and women in their cause, both in India and Britain. The name of Mr. J. Crawford needs mention in this connection, for he was entrusted by Ram Mohun Ray, in 1829, with petitions, signed by Hindus and Muslims, for presentation to both the Houses of Parliament against the Jury Act passed two years before in the British Parliament. This Act introduced "religious distinctions into the judicial system of the country". "Any Natives, either Hindu or Mahomedan, are rendered............subject to judicial trial by Christians, either European or Native, while Christians, including Native converts, are exempted from the degradation of being tried by a Hindu or Mussalman juror, however high he may stand in the estimation of society"; the Act denied to both the Hindus and Moslems "the honour of a seat in the Grand Jury even in the trial of fellow Hindus or Mussulmans." Mr. Crawford seems to belong to that fraternity who roam over the world, succouring distress, and fighting injustice, thus justifying the faith of man in man. The ideas of Liberty, Equality and Fraternity, associated with the French Revolution, had released a liberality of spirit which desired and strove for equality of human relations all over the world, irrespective of colour or creed. The abolition of slavery in the British empire was owing to some such impulse. In their attitude towards the people of India many a British politician and administrator shared this humanitarianism. The Marquis of Hastings is generally known as a military governor-general; he broke the back of the Marhatta confederacy. He also could think of "a time not very remote" when England will "on sound principles of policy wish to relinquish the domination which she has gradually and unintentionally assumed over this country, and from which she cannot at present recede." This was in 1818. In 1824 Sir Thomas Munro, Governor of Madras, could look forward to a time when "it will probably be best for both countries that the British control over India should be gradually withdrawn." Lord William Bentick, governor-general in the early thirties of the last century, was fully conscious of the drawbacks of British rule in this country. Appearing as a witness before a House of Commons Committee (1837) he declared:

"In many respects the Mahomedans surpassed our rule; they settled in the countries which they conquered; they intermixed and intermarried with the natives; they admitted them to all privileges; the interests and sympathies of the conquerors and conquered became identified. Our policy, on the contrary, has been the reverse of this...............

About 1838, Dwarkanath Tagore organised an agitation against the resumption of *lakheraj* (rent free) lands, in which we find European names, Messrs. Dickens and Turton, leading lawyers. In the same year was started the "Landholders' Society"; Dwarkanath Tagore was President, Prasanna Kumar Tagore and W. C. Hurry, the then Editor of the "Englishman" were Secretaries. But one British name stands out at that period of Indo-British co-operation for the redress of Indian grievances and the advancement of the political status of the Indian people—that of George Thompson. In 1838 there was dire famine in the "Upper Provinces"; the news of the ravages of starvation and death reached Britain. And George Thompson heard India "a-calling". Through his exertions the British India Society was started in London in 1839 with Lord Brougham as President. Thompson's writings and speeches on behalf of the Indian people brought on his head the thunders of the "Edinburgh Review" and other Jingo periodicals. To meet these attacks and to make the cause of India more known to the British public, he started a monthly—the "British Indian Advocate". In 1842 he came to Calcutta on the invitation of "Prince" Dwarkanath to study personally on the spot the questions and problems that waited solution to make the life of the Indian people self-respecting, contended, and happy under the British Crown. An Indian admirer, the editor of some of his Indian speeches, called him "the Father of Political Education in India". Well did he deserve the title. For, he taught "Young Bengal" the technique of political agitation, of the study and discussion of public questions. Under his inspiration was inaugurated the Bengal British India Society in 1843, the object of which was proposed to be "the collection and dissemination of information, relating to the actual condition of the people of India, and the Laws and Institutions and the Resources of the country, and to employ such other means of a peaceful and lawful character, as may appear calculated to secure the welfare, to extend the just rights, and advance the interest of all classes of our fellow subjects". Two European gentlemen, Messrs. Speed and Crow, are found among those who proposed or seconded the resolutions at the inaugural meeting. It was decided also that the new Society would co-operate with that under Lord Brougham for the promotion of Indian interests. The possibilities of this co-operation did not suit the taste or interests of a section of Europeans in India whose press-organ stigmatized the London Society as "admirably adapted as a receptacle for the resentments of Native Land-holders". The amalgamation of the Landholders' Society and the British India Society paved the way of the British India Association (1851).

Racial Estrangement

Indo British co-operation in politics, however, was getting difficult. Young India, nurtured in the colleges, were being rendered unstable with the introduction of the fumes of the "New wine of Western Learning" into its head; it was learning to look the dominant race straight in the face; it began to assert claims to equality with the ruling race' in the scheme of the State-organization of the country. These claims put up the back of Anglo-India, and rendered it sensitive to the premonitory disturbances in the atmosphere in India. An occasion was offered by the Government for a burst up of racial arrogance. In 1849 they published four "Draft Acts", touching the rights and privileges of the European and Christian subjects of the Crown in India, distinct from those of the Natives of the land. They were;

(1) An Act for abolishing exemption from the jurisdiction of the East India Company's courts, hitherto enjoyed by Europeans in India;
(2) an Act declaring the law as to the privileges of Her Majesty's European subjects in India;
(3) an Act for trial by Jury;
(4) an Act for protection of judicial officers.

The European community raised a great hue and cry; there were gatherings of all the clans at which their "class privileges" were angrily asserted; Indian jurors and judges who might, under the proposed amendments, sit in judgment on European and Christian culprits, were, in anticipation, roundly denounced; and the character of the natives of the country was traduced, a group of Europeans in Behar declaring that under the proposed laws no one would "find security against accusation in the inoffensiveness of his own character in this country, where the immorality of the population is extreme and universal"; the Natives of the country were reminded anew that they were a subject race, and that it was not in the power of men "to make unequals equals". This agitation of the Europeans against the "Black

Acts" roused responsive angry feelings in the hearts of educated Indians; and Ram Gopal Ghosh as tribune of the people denounced the agitators as a "new breed of Brahmins" who refused to be made amenable or subject to the ordinary laws of the land. This denunciation was a symptom of the rising temper in the educated community in India.

Liberalism halted Half-way

The gulf that separated the Native inhabitants of India and the British community sojourning here for purposes of administration as also those who came as traders, merchants, planters, captains of industries, missionary proselytisers and educators, had been thinly covered up by good-will on the part of the latter and a sense of gratitude on that of the former. The education that the former had been receiving had created in them a bias in favour of the new rulers and all that they stood for as evangelists of modernism and progress. Liberalism was in the air in the West; it was wafted to the East. In religion and society the rulers, and the resident European community encouraged this liberalism as a solvent of the weaknesses and corruptions of Indian life. But they were not prepared to allow it to intrude into the fields of administration and politics. This policy of reticence finds its best expression in the words Sir Alfred Lyall who may be accepted as the representative of the better mind of the ruling authority. Said he in one of his articles since published in the book—"Asiatic Studies":

"We may hope that all reflecting and far-sighted natives of the class, which we are rapidly training up in large towns in political knowledge and social freedom, will perceive that England's prime function in India is at present this, to superintend the tranquil elevation of the whole moral and intellectual standard. Those who are interested in such a change in the ethics of their country, in broadening the realms of the known and the true, must see how ruinously premature it is to quarrel with the English Government upon details of administration, or even upon what are called constitutional questions".

Consistent Opposition to Equality

But the mischief which started with the Anglo-Indian agitation in 1849, rending the thin cover from over the gulf between the two peoples, was not precipitated by any limited State policy against which the subject population had any wide-awake grievance. The British community in India by their arrogance and the language in which they expressed it raised this insignificant problem to a wider and higher plane—the plane of racial self-respect. The educated Indian community felt compelled by their new ideas of personal and racial honour, induced by the new enlightenment, to refuse to compromise on the matter. The administration might retreat in face of the intransigience of their nationals, as they did in 1849, as also eight years later on the eve of the "Sepoy Mutiny". In the latter year the Government attempted to carry out the same reform, and was met with the same clamour and opposition; the country was treated to the same exhibition of racial arrogance. A public meeting was held, and resolutions were passed defamatory of Indian character. A petition to the British Parliament was drawn up in which the following words found place:—

"Your petitioners boldy and confidently assert, that *no class* of Natives is fit to be entrusted with criminal powers over Europeans, being *wholly disqualified* for the due exercise of such powers, by antagonistic feelings, *inveterate prejudice of caste*, utter want of *independence of mind*, and *of freedom from improper influences* of all kinds."

Thus and then was the foundation of estrangement between Indian and Briton laid in the middle of the last century. The "Sepoy Mutiny" with its brutalities and terrorisms worsened conditions. It was thought and hoped, however, that the outburst being an abnormal episode in a long-drawn political maladjustment, the tension of feeling generated thereby would have but a temporary tenure. We find Lord Lawrence as governor-general writing to his friends in Britain about this bitterness, his helplessness in face of it, and of his hopes of a better time. Irritation of feelings roused by frankly political considerations do not give rise to permanent bitterness. But the feeling that was stirred by the Government attempt at bringing European culprits to the judgment seat of Indian Magistrates and Judges had elsewhere its rise, as manifested by the doggrel when the first Indian was appointed a judge of the High Court at Calcutta:

"A sop to the Bengali,
to English minds a wrench.
Our rulers thought it right to raise,
One native to the Bench".

This attitude of the British community in India the administrators found themselves unable to control or regulate. Both these factors imparted the first astonished shock of repulsion felt by the educated Indian against the order of things, educational and cultural, that had followed British rule in India. The disillusionment reached its climax nearly thirty years after at the time of Lord Ripon when what is known in history as the "Ilbert Bill" was before the Legislative Council. It was introduced by Sir Courtney Ilbert on the 2nd February, 1883. And the storm burst. Not clearing the atmosphere. But darkening the prospect of Indo-British amity for a long day. Men of the generations that have followed inherited the memories of those days, making things difficult, if not almost insoluble. What those memories were and what have they meant to educated Indians, we will let an Anglo-Indian writer to describe, before a narration of those excited events is attempted. Lord Ripon's Government failed to pass the Bill in its integrity. This failure was regarded by Indians as a "surrender", and by Anglo-Indians, official and non-official, as a "triumph". Soon after Lord Ripon left India, amidst the frigid civility of his countrymen. As a counter-blast the Indian community showered on him addresses, and other marks of exuberant friendliness. The unanimity of these demonstrations almost startled all, testifying to the emergence of an all-India feeling. A Calcutta paper wrote an article on the lesson of these demonstrations, entitled—"If it be real, what does it mean?" The *Pioneer* of Allahabad, the newspaper that reflected the mind of the Anglo-Indian bureaucracy, published an article from an anonymous correspondent, almost as a sort of a reply to the question asked in the Calcutta paper. In Sir Surendra Nath Banerjee's speeches, and in his autobiography—"A Nation in the Making"—the article has been ascribed to Sir Auckland Colvin, who as lieutenant-governor of

Ilbert Bill Agitation

the United Provinces in 1887 helped to organize an opposition to the Indian National Congress headed by Sir Sayyad Ahmmad and Raja Shiv Prasad. The impression seems to be wrong. For, we find the article reprinted in the life of Sir Sayyad Ahmmad, written by Lieutenant-Colonel Graham, a Superintendent of Police in the province. Though occupying a not very high position in the official hierarchy, the writer appears to have held a high position in his society.

"If it be real what does it mean"?

He traced the evolution of the awakening in Indian society as a result of British connection, and accepted its reality. While the Indian mind had moved responsive to the new forces,.................

"............... the English mind in India has been tempted to stand still, arrested by the contemplation of the fruits of its own efforts in former times, and by the symmetry of the shrine, the pride of its creation, in which it lingers to offer incense to its past successful labours, the Indian mind has been marching on, eager and anxious, to expand its own sphere of action. and to do what it, for its own part, has to do............... it has succeeded at length in waking to the consciousness of its own powers and the assurance of its own success. The breath has come into the bones, and they are about to live and stand up upon their feet, an exceeding great army..............."

But the full awakening had yet to come, waiting on events and the realisation of their full significance, waiting for the destined impetus.

"........while the native mind is still in this mood, half day-dawn and half chaos, has occurred the catastrophe of March, 1883. The sudden declaration of the English in India that they would recognise in the Indian nothing but simply a subject race, has brought the issue clearly and without possibility of self-deception before all classes and races in the country. The dry bones of the children of activity, their opponents have urged, shall not live, nor again stand up upon their feet. There shall be subordination ; there shall not be citizenship. Nevertheless the prophet has said that the bones shall live ; that the spirit of their Maker shall be in them ; that He would place them in their own land ; and that then they should know that He has spoken it and performed it."

The miracle of the awakening had been implicit in the developments of the fifty years previous to Lord Ripon ; for, to use the words of Sir William Hunter, "the Queen's Government had deliberately accepted the risks of a united India".

"The incident of the Criminal Procedure Bill may no doubt have brought about abruptly, brutally, and of force, what would otherwise, in the ordinary course of events, have arrived in the consummation of time. But the time, in truth, was ripe ; the hour of the new birth was a narrow question. Whether it were by Ripon or another, the charm which had held the sleeper bound was to be broken, and the time for breaking it was at hand................"

Genesis of the "Ilbert" proposals

The days of the old system that "made for mere repression" were numbered. The rank and file of the European community in India were not prepared to acknowledge the inevitability of the process. And in trying to prolong the influence of the charm that held India bound, they hastened "the time for breaking it". How they did this by their ignorance and violence, by their unconsciousness to the march of human progress, may here be narrated. Such a recital is necessary to understand the evolution of political thought and life in India which has been slowly revealing to the world these fifty years and more.

The Bill for an amendment of the Criminal Procedure Code proposed "to confine the office of justice of the peace, and with it the power of trying European British subjects, to those persons, whether European or native, who have received a training that may be presumed to guarantee the possession of the qualities required for the proper disposal of such cases...........all district and sessions judges should be vested with the powers in question in virtue of their office, and by a definite provision in the law;...............to empower the Local Governments, outside the Presidency towns, to confer these upon those members (a) of the covenanted Civil Service, (b) of the Native Civil Service constituted under the statutory Rules, and (c) of the non-Regulation Commissions, who were already exercising first class magisterial powers, and, in their opinion, fit to be entrusted with these further powers". In a letter to Lord Hartington (Secretary of State for India) (Sept. 8, 1882), Lord Ripon explained the genesis of these proposals.

"The Native members of the Civil Service...........both those who have got in by competition at home, and those who are being admitted every year out here under the system established in Lytton's time -will ere long be rising to positions in which, although they are in all other respects on an equal footing with their English colleagues, they will, under the provisions of the existing law, be precluded from trying Europeans in the Mofussil. In the Presidency towns, by a strange anomaly, natives are allowed to exercise over Europeans jurisdiction.............. It is clear that an invidious distinction of this kind between members of the same service cannot be maintained. When we were passing the Bill for amending the Criminal Procedure Code........... last winter, one of the leading members of the Council, Maharajah Sir Jatindra Mohan Tagore, was anxious to bring the subject forward and move amendments in the Bill with a view to giving Native Civil Servants jurisdiction over Europeans...... I pointed out that it would be impossible for the Government to make so important a change ...... at such short notice...... very shortly afterwards Sir Ashley Eden (lieutenant-Governor of Bengal) sent us a letter saying that in his opinion the existing law on the subject could not be maintained, and explained the manner in which he thought it should be altered. We, therefore, sent a circular letter to the Local Governments generally,.........and they have, with the insignificant exception of Coorg, decided in favour of the alteration to the present law".

Supported by these approvals of the local Governments, Sir Courtney Ilbert, the Law Member, proceeded with the draft, and presented the Bill to the Council on the 2nd February, 1883. What followed may well be described in the words of Lucien Wolf, Lord Ripon's biographer :

New Method of Agitation

"Within a few weeks the whole of the British community in the Peninsula was swept by a tornado of violent denunciation of the Bill. A monster indignation meeting took place in the Calcutta Town Hall, at which the speeches were of an intemperance beyond all limits of decency. Similar meetings were held all over the Presidency, and the Anglo-Indian press, notably the *Englishman*—became utterly hysterical. An 'Anglo-Indian and European Defence Association' was formed...... Among other features of their campaign, the volunteers were openly incited to resign in a mass, and certain persons even 'sounded opinions in the canteens' ...... in other words attempted to seduce the Army. The non-official community boycotted Ripon's levees, and there was a proposal to boycott the Government loan. On his return to Calcutta in the winter, the Viceroy was openly insulted in the streets by planters brought down from the Mofussil for the occasion...... The wife of the Chief Justice showed her appreciation of the responsibility attaching to her husband's official position by getting up a 'Ladies' Petition' against the Bill. Ripon gives a quotation f.om the letters of a certain Britannicus, (Sic !) who wrote to the *Englishman* regularly on the subject : 'The only people who have any right to India are the British : the so-called (Sic !) Indians have no right whatever'. The behavior of the natives in face of this campaign was, on the whole, surprisingly moderate, though of course the extreme newspapers on their side replied in kind to the European attacks".

A conspiracy was set on foot to get hold of Lord Ripon, put him on board a steamer and send him to Britain via the Cape of Good Hope. Mr. Rivers Thompson, lieutenant-governor of Bengal, was cognisant of the fact, says Buckland in his book—"Bengal under the Lieutenant-Governors."

Inner History of the Agitation

Lord Ripon explained the inner history of the agitation as follows in a private letter :

"The bar have been very sore about the reduction of the Judges' pay and Mitter's (Ramesh Chandra) appointment as Acting Chief Justice, and were only too glad of an opportunity to do the Government an injury, if they could ; and the idea of an opposition to the Bill was started in the Bar Library by some of the English barristers. Communications were entered into with the *Englishman* office, and circulars in the shape of letters were sent to the Planters and settlers up-country suggesting their opposition to the Bill, and I fancy, putting a strong fanciful case before them"

How fanciful these could be was shown by a letter of Meredith Townsend, author of "Asia and Europe", to a friend saying :

"Would you like to live in a country where at any moment your wife would be sentenced on a false charge of slappidg an Ayah to three days' imprisonment, the Magistrate being a copper-coloured Pagan, who probably worships the *Linga*......"

Wilfrid Blunt in his book—"India under Ripon"—has another explanation of the agitation.

"Lord Ripon in the spring of 1883, when after two years of unwearied labour in the attempt to gain over the Anglo-Indian officials to some practical measure in accordance with the Queen's Proclamation, he decided to give battle on what is called as the Ilbert Bill of that year, knew himself already to be a beaten man ; he felt that he was championing a lost cause".

The Lesson of the Agitation

The lesson of the Anglo-Indian agitation against the Ilbert Bill was unmistakable. It was hinted at in Lieutenant-Colonel Graham's article in the *Pioneer*, extracts from which have been quoted above. A British historian, Prof. Dodwell, puts it tersely : "The passionate claim of the European to predominance was to be answered by the passionate claim of the Indian to equality". The London *Punch* had a cartoon "representing Ripon driving an elephant (India), while a party of Anglo-Indians threatened him and molested him from the howdah". The cartoon had the characterization,

"The Anglo-Indian Mutiny...... a bad example for the elephant".

Conscious Adaptation to new influences

The disharmony between the two peoples which the Ilbert Bill agitation had laid bare was the final stage of a development that had begun years earlier. It partook something of the character of the evolution of a natural process, slowly revealing itself in successive stages and stratifications. The world have been taught to believe that the East was a static body which bowed low before the blast of European aggression, political, religious and cultural, not in fear or from a sense of helplessness, but "in patient deep disdain" ; and that it "plunged in thought again", letting the legion thunder past. It is difficult to say whether this picture was meant, or should be accepted, as a commendation or a condemnation, and how far it is true. If it carried the impression that the East "plunged in thought again" unconscious of the threat that the new-comer from the West held to the integrity of its life, it would not be true. In one sense the portrait may be accepted as true, in the sense that the East plunged into thought to plumb the depths of the soul of her culture and to draw up from it the waters of life with a view to irrigate and fertilize the varied fields of her social life. In no other sense was it true to facts or to the experiences of the time we have been dealing with.

True it is that in India the generations that slowly and painfully learnt to accommodate themselves to the order of things introduced by the British rulers had succumbed in complete political helplessness. With these defences going down, they seemed to lie helpless face to face with a triumphant and aggressive civilization and culture. The ruling authorities very soon convinced themselves that this country not only needed their political control, but also that the acceptance of the higher social ethics represented by them was the only lever which could rescue the subject populations from their degradation. Alexander Duff may be taken as a representative of this type of mind. "He visualized the utter destruction of Indian culture and social institutions. In his suggestive figure, he was laying a mine which would one day rend Hinduism from its foundations". On the side of administration, Dalhousie was "the tool and fashioner" of "the new spirit of eager, masterful, inventive Anglicism" which hoped to force its ways through "the last barriers of Eastern prejudice, sluggishness and self-content". An American author of a book on the influence of Christian missions on the evolution of Indian nationalism, speaking of Duff's hopes and their failure, says that "the years have revealed Hinduism as a far more organic structure than he (Duff) recognized it to be". Years of self-organisation have enabled Indian culture and social life to win this recognition of its strength and vitality. The history of the years we have been dealing with is the history of a social organization that had become alive to the dangers that threatened the norms and forms of its life, and that consciously adopted measures for their safety.

Distinguishing characteristic of British Rule

India in the milleniums of her life-history have met with many a stranger who came to her as a scourge and remained to strengthen her life by the assimilation of their virility into the life and conduct of this country. Persians, Greeks, Sakas, Huns came as conquerors and are to-day undistinguishable as separate entities, consciously asserting a separate individuality of their own. The Moslem came professing a faith different from that of the subject Hindu population. There were iconoclastic outbursts and attempts at suppression of Hindn faith and practices. But in course of time, as they came to settle down into peaceful social life and learnt to adapt themselves to the physical and mental atmosphere of the country as neighbours of an unbelieving "majority" community, a synthesis of cultures and interests was worked out. In the general economic life of the country Hindu and Moslem did not come into conflict. Economic organisation and arrangements, based on "easy-going, self-sufficing agriculture and handicrafts", came in easily and naturally to both the rulers and the ruled. Race or religion ceased to be considered or recognised as a "bar sinister" to the legitimate ambition of partnership in the enjoyment or exercise of the powers of the State. But with the advent of British rule "a system of specialized machinery and communication" was introduced into the country forcing out of existence or reducing to a pale imitation of life, India's multifarious industries. Ignorance of India's basic principle of proprietorship of the soil led the new rulers to adopt a land policy which disrupted social life. In certain tracts of the country, in Bombay and Madras, the Government decided to deal with every individual cultivator as regards the payment of revenue, the tendency of which was "to break up the village community". In other parts, in Bengal, Behar, Orissa and the U. P. they converted "farmers" or collectors of revenue into proprietors of land, with a similar result. As stated by Sir Thomas Maine, in a state of society where the rights of individual members are determined by customs, more or less vague, by status and not by contract, the question as to whom the Government makes responsible for the payment of its dues, practically determines what type of society it shall assume. The disruption of village communities had begun in the anarchy that intervened between the weaknesses and curruptions of Hindu and Moslem rule and the secure establishment of British rule. By their land-policy the new rulers only hastened their destruction.

Scepticism of "Young India"

In the thirties of the last century the leaders of the Indian communities were confronted with this disruption, rather they awoke to the full realization of the danger that lurked behind and before them. They found the old idols fallen from the tripods ; and new idols presented by the ruling race for adoption and worship. From an article by Girish Chandra Ghosh, the founder and first editor of the *Bengalee*, one can get an idea of the mind of that age.

"They have learned to disbelieve the old religion, it is true, but they are not ignorant of the tenets of the Christian faith but in many instances have studied the subject deeply—though having escaped from the trammels of one class of prejudices (at least in idea) they are not willing to be entangled in the snares of any other class."

Composite character of Reforms

This scepticism had reference not only to the religious life but also to other departments of society. The old social polity had failed to protect and ensure an independent, coherent and equitable life in the country, and there were very few to do it sincere reverence. Faced by attacks from without and defection from within, Indian society felt the need, moved by the impulse of self-preservation, of a re-examination and re-interpretation of life in the light of universal experience and in response to the demands of modern life. Reform of social life became thus urgent, and there was great, keen, and varied controversies with regard to the methods of carrying it out. The methods discussed, and adopted by men, temperamentally or intellectually differing from one another, were :

(i) The traditional method, i. e. which sought to carry out reforms by showing that they are not innovations at all, but they faithfully carry out the spirit and even the letter of ancient scriptures which are the repositories of the experiences of men in different countries ;

(ii) The legislative method, i, e, which sought to carry out reforms with the help of decrees from the authority of the State ;

(iii) The conscience method, i, e, which sought to carry out reforms by appealing to the sense of right and wrong, native to every human being, which, deadened or clouded by custom, manages to assert its authority in crises of individual and social life ;

(iv) Rebellion method, i, e, which sought to carry out reforms by separating from conservative orthodox people and forming a new camp, breaking with the historic continuity of social life.

In none of the apostles of the new life in India, beginning with Raja Ram Mohun Roy and continued by Mahatma Gandhi, can one find any of them adopting one single method. They combined one or the other or one after another as the necessities of the case demanded. Ram Mohun Roy in eastern India, and Dadoba Pandurang in Western India anticipated and paved the way of almost all the social reforms that are still with us. The latter founded in 1840 the *Paramhansa Mandali*—Divine Society—with the following objects : abolition of caste ; re-introduction of the custom of widow re-marriage ; and the renunciation of idolatry. Particular items of social reform, such as widow-remarriage, enlisted the services of eminent scholars—Vidyasagar (Iswar Chandra) in Bengal, Vishnu-Sastri Pandit in Bombay, Kandukuri Veerasalingam Pantalu in the Andhra-Desha, Behramji Mehta Malabari and Kursundas Mulji in Guzerat, and Dayaram Gidumal in Sindh. Swami Dayananda Saraswati, the founder of the Arya Samaj, in the maturity of his youth, received from Virajananda the mission of his life, bound by an oath which demanded that he "would carry increasing war against the dogma and idolatry of the Puranic faith, and establish education in accordance with the ancient Brahmanic traditions." The Prarthana Samaj in Bombay (1867) inaugurated "amid the wave of religious enthusiasm that marked the second visit to Bombay of......Keshab Chandra Sen," was the expression of the type of practical intellectuality for which Maharashtra is famous. Mahadev Gobind Ranade was the leading spirit of this development seeking to apply and realize "the love of God in the service of men."

Hindu Reformers

Among Indian Moslems Sir Sayyad Ahmmad was the pioneer in the British period of rationalistic thought ; his "Commentaries on the Bible" showed the way in which he wanted his community to move. Wilfrid Blunt calls him a "Deist," and reports that by his community he was regarded as nothing better than a "nature worshipper." His biographer says that he saw

Moslem Reformers

"the weakness that had crept over the Mohamedans through their estrangement from the thoughts and aspirations of the 19th. century, and he proposed to himself the great task of making Mohamedans change, not their dogmas, but their policy, so that independence and political liberation should no longer be accounted as symptoms of heterodoxy."

For his troubles in this behalf he was denounced as a "lieutenant of the Evil One." When he took the lead in founding the Mohammedan Anglo-Oriental College (1875) the Ulemas of Mecca whose *futwa* had been invited by opponents of the scheme issued the curse—"May God destroy it and its founder" ; one of them declaring that "Shere Ali (the murderer of Lord Mayo)......could have ensured Paradise for himself by killing Sayyad Ahmmad" !

The results of Sir Sayyad Ahmmad's work prove that he represented "the future." Nawab Abdul Lateef and his generation of English educated Moslems had started on their mission of reform years before Sir Sayyad, when they tried to "break down prejudices and exclusiveness, and to interest their community in present-day politics and modern thought learning." But they lacked the vision of the Aligarh reformer, and an English admirer of theirs lamented that they would go down before the school represented by Sayyad Ameer Ali. The rational and liberal interpretation of Islamic life and culture initiated in India by Sir Sayyad Ahmmad was carried on by the school of modern educated Moslems of whom the Bengali Shia Moslem, Sayyad Ameer Ali, was the most prominent member. His writings on Moslem history and kindred subjects first opened the eyes of his community to the glories of of their heritage, confirmed them in their self-repect, and played the pioneer part of the awakening of Moslems in India. He was a child of the 19th. century, and his historical work had a deep significance for his community, for it nursed and encouraged that spirit of separatism with which Indian statesmanship finds itself wrestling even to-day. This process is a stage in self-realization, whether individual or social. The ferment of new thought that had begun to stir life in India has penetrated the dour conservatism of Indian Moslems, and custodians of traditional culture are found to-day trying to cut a way through the mazes of hair-splitting subtleties. Moulana Abul Kalam Azad in his *Turzaman-i-Koran* attempts a liberal interpretation of Islam which will bring it into line with the other theologies of the world. And the centres of traditional learning of Islam in India such as those at Nadva, and Deobund in the U. P. are face to face with the same problem of how to reconcile the spirit of their creed and its injunctions with the thoughts and needs of the modern world. Hindu society had been challenged fifty years earlier by similar problems, more intricate in their nature, because Hinduism and its social polity are weighted down with a longer tradition and a more complex hierarchy of relations ; and that society has been moving forward consciously in advance, step by step, into new difficulties, new experiences, new accommodations to new environments. Moslem society in India cannot escape the travails of this experience, whereby only can it throw out the loads of traditional life that clog its movements.

Protective measures through Education

In discussing the first introduction of British Education into India we pointed to the political motives of its initiation. In earlier ages in all countries conquerors adopted the rougher and readier methods of physical coercion to secure and retain the allegiance of their subjects. In modern times the subtler method of "education in citizenship" is thought to be the better method of the two. All governments consciously direct and utilize their powers towards this objective, because newer ideas of state-craft have with vividness brought to view the "importance of education and its organisation in relation to political and constitutional conditions and potentialities of progress", to quote the terms of reference to the Simon Commission. British rulers in India had realized the importance of this issue a hundred years back. Christian missionaries in India had their own ambitions to realize which in the ultimate analysis was found to be not incompatible with the purposes and inclinations of the "Christian Power" in the country. It was Christian missionary education as represented by Duff in Bengal, Wilson in Bombay, Anderson in Madras, Noble in the Andhra Desa, that first came into clash with the feelings and interests of the Indian community. That generation of Christian missionaries were triumphantly declaring their intentions and proclaiming the coming of the day of their victory. It was Hindu Society that first woke up to the dangers of these activities. It saw that the education that had received the imprimatur of the ruling authority could not be rejected without detriment to material interests, and to that extent it was prepared to welcome it, tolerate and promote it. But education under Christian control, with conscious and deliberate Christian bias instilled into the students, was another and a different proposition. Realizing this, it decided to give battle to the foreign education, not by rejecting it, but by getting control over it and neutralizing its anti-Indian bias. This was the psychology of wide-spread educational activities that started on the initiative of Hindu Society even as early as the twenties and thirties of the last century. In Bengal, in Bombay, in Maharashtra, in Madras, in the Andhra Desa, in the Punjab, educational institutions were started by Hindus, individually and collectively, under their own control, teaching the official curricula, but shorn of any bias that offended the customs and usages of the country. The biographies of Bengalee celebrities of whom Bhudev Chandra Mukherjee was the best constructive type record these activities. In Bombay we find Gokuldas Tejpal maintaining a string of schools and a Sanskrit College ; the Bombay Students' Literary and Scientific Society maintaining a number of Hindu Girls' Schools and a Hindu Boys' School. In Maharashtra the fullest flowering of these efforts was the Deccan Education Society (1881), the first members of which were Vishnu Sastri Chiplunkar, Balwant Gangadhar Tilak, Gopalrao Agarkar and Madhorao Namjoshi and their friends. We read in their biographies that these youngmen were dissatisfied as early as 1875, hardly twenty years after the establishment of British universities in the country, with the system of alien values introduced through education. They wanted and sought to modify them by making education racy of the soil, making it cheap in consonance with the economic condition of the country. In Madras the Triplicane High English School was preceded by the Pachhyappa's Foundation, the major part of whose income was devoted to education, as was that founded by the great Moslem philanthropist, Haji Mohammad Moshin, in Bengal. In the Andhra Desa the Pithapuram Raja's College (Coconada) and the Vizianagram Raja's College have developed from very small beginnings started in the middle of the last century. The Hindu High School at Masulipatam started on the initiative of two Deputy Magistrates who begged from door to door for boys as well as for funds, and the Theistic High School at Rajahmundry owed their inauguration to the same impulse. In Northern India, in the Punjab specially, the colleges and the *Gurukulas* started under the auspices of the Arya Samaj in fulfilment of the mission of its founder, are a triumphant culmination of the same tradition. The Moslem community in India had at this period retired into its shelf. But by 1875 it decided to come out of it and play its legitimate part in the ordering of the destiny of the country, the symbol of which was the Mohammedan Anglo-Oriental College.

As a product of educational activities, carried on by foreign or native agency, there grew up a new sense of self-respect in the Indian community. The researches of Sir William Jones, Colebrooke, Max Muller, Weber and others opened before India the glories of the past which could be reproduced in the future. The Theosophical Society contributed its share in the awakening of this self-respect. All these influences worked in the educated Indian and helped him to throw oft the apologetic attitude he had been cultivating with regard to his social institutions and religious life ; they made the educated Indian "less submissive in tone and language than formerly, more erect in mental and moral stature in the presence of Europeans", to quote the words of Sir Temple. Raj Narayan Basu, the grand-father of Sri Aurobinda, in his Bengali autobiography, has recorded for us the history of this evolution in Indian mind. Speaking of one of the apostles of the Brahmo Samaj, Maharshi Devendra Nath Tagore's studied avoidance of Europeans, he says :

Revival of National Self-respect

"Devendra Babu is by nature averse to intimate relation with Europeans, because there existed a difference of opinion between him and Europeans in relation to matters pertaining to India. It is possible to acquire name and fame in India, and Britain if one said ditto to British opinion ; but Devendra Babu is not at all anxious to secure this approbation. Principal Lobb of the Krishnagore College once wrote to a newspaper—"The proud old man does not condescend to accept the praise of Europeans".

This new self-respect in the educated Indian found its echo in what has been called the "return movement" in Indian society in the British period. Some call it "a revival", others characterize it "a reaction". Reaction or revival, the educated Indian, the product of English education, was the first to stand up on behalf of his creed and his customs. Emboldened by his example, the custodians of orthodoxy came forward to lead the counter-attack on alien ways of life and thought. Dayananda Saraswati, Sasadhar Tarkachuramani and Sri Krishnaprasanna Sen in Bengal, and Vishnuboa Brahmachari in Bombay represent this phase of life. The Indian community had had placed in their hands proofs of the glories of their past ; more intimate knowledge of European life enabled them to start comparison between the two ; a comparative study showed them that they had no reason to be apologetic or shamefaced when confronted with European values of life. The last quarter of the 19th. century shows us this development in its aggressiveness.

This outline of the beginnings of resurgent self-respect and self-assertion in India would be incomplete if the awakening among Indian Moslems were not given its proper place in it. It is a generally-accepted view that Sir Sayyad Ahmad was the inaugurator of the "new departure" in the life of his community. This view circumscribes the back-ground, and is not true to facts. The awakening among Indian Moslems is not due to British inspiration and administration alone ; it was part of the awakening that had its rise in Arabia, associated with the name of the founder of the Wahhabi movement, Mohommed Ibn Abd-el Wahhab, who lived and propagated his ideas of reform and reconstruction in the middle of the 18th. century A. D. A return to early Islam in its primitive purity and sim-

Moslem Awakening

plicity, and a reform of the abuses that had crept into, and the deviations from, the original faith and conduct—abuses and deviations that had laid Islam low in the comity of faiths and cultures—this was the objective of Abd-el Wahhab. A stern Puritanism characterized the reformer and his followers. All luxury in habitation, dress, and daily life was proscribed; "all decorations were removed from mosques; minarets, a Turkish innovation, and the rosary, adopted from Buddhism, were abolished." A Jewish writer assessing the ideal of the movement, initiated by Abd-el Wahhab, says :—

"The primitive moral purity and simplicity of the desert religion was to be restored and the influence of city civilisation on the development of Islam was to be eradicated. In this respect the Wahhabi movement resembles certain tendencies in ancient Jewish religious history which centred in the sect of Rechabites and the circles influenced by the early prophets............at the same time this early prophetic movement involved a national protest against alien ways."

Wahhabism in India

Amongst the most prominent of the followers of Abd-el Wahhab was Sheik Mohammed Ibn Saud of Deraya in the territory of Nejd in central Arabia, the ancestor of the present King of the Hedjaz. He and his son succeeded in bringing all the central Arabian tribes under unified political control and came to be regarded as the spear-head of the new dispensation. By 1801 A. D., the grandson of Mohammed Ibn Saud felt himself strong enough to go forth in his career of agression against those Arabs who had lapsed into heathen superstition and the worship of saints. The holy cities of Islam were regarded with intense hatred, for there had taken root all manner of abuses and abominations. Kerbala, the sacred city of the Shias in Mesopotamia, felt their first fury; the inhabitants were killed, the holy sepulchre destroyed, treasures collected in course of centuries plundered, and all sacred relics dishonoured. The next year (1802) Mecca was captured, the tombs of saints and objects of worship destroyed. Two years later Medina fell; the monument erected over the Prophet's grave was destroyed; and the hoarded treasnres carried away. These atrocities called forth reprisals at the hand of the Turkish Government who cruelly suppressed the reformers' zeal and activity. They were wise in their apprehensions and persecutions. For the Wahhabi movement proved itself to be the precursor of Nationalism in Arabia, disrupting the Turkish Empire, and in other Moslem countries which were threatened by European Imperialism or were under it.

This intensification of religious feeling and political sentiments soon stepped over the boundaries of Arabia, and was imported into India by the numerous Indian Moslem pilgrims to Mecca. No records are available to trace the development of Wahhabism at this period. One Indian Moslem name, however, emerges out of the obscurity of these tangled happenings, that of Haji Shariyat Ullah, a native of Faridpur (Bengal). His followers are known to this day as "Ferazis" whose differences with other Sunni Moslems in our rural tracts have come to be attenuated with the passage of time. Shariyat Ullah's teachings prepared the minds of Moslems in India to receive and accept the tenets of Abd-el Wahhab. The man who encompassed this was Sayyad Ahmmad of Rae Bareilly in the United Provinces. In his early life he entered the services of Amir Khan Pindari, the founder of the Nawab family of Tonk. A little before 1817, when Amir Khan's bands were dispersed, Sayyad Ahmmad came to Delhi and became a disciple of Shah Abd-ul Aziz, the most learned Moslem theologian of the time, whose name and fame had spread beyond Hindusthan, and had earned for him the title which translated meant "Sun of India" from the Arab divines. Considering the time in which he lived, and the wreckage of Moslem power and prestige amidst which he moved, he seems to have been a realist, ready to compromise with the alien governing authority in the country, and the new order of things they had introduced here. A writer in an English-edited Indian monthly writing of him, says: "He recognized the propriety of learning English and taking service" with and under the British. This can be regarded as the first intimation of the Moslem acceptance of the regime started under British auspices in this country.

To return to Sayyad Ahmmad. After a discipleship of a few years, he started, on his own account. He claimed that he had been vouchsafed divine revelation in a dream "to take up the position of a *murshid*, and enrol disciples" When he developed a revised version of Wahhabism his former religious guide, Shah Abd-ul Aziz, repudiated him, as also his own nephew Mohammed Ismail and son-in-law Abdul Hai, who had become Sayyad Ahmmad's disciples. The adherence of these two learned divines sent up Sayyad Ahmmad's prestige in his community. In 1820 he asked his followers to take up the organization of a *jihad* against the Sikhs who were rulers and masters of the Punjab up to Peshawar. He started on a tour throughout northern India to propagate his ideas on religion and politics, secure forces and resources for the proposed war against the Sikhs. He came down to Calcutta (1821) where he was acclaimed by the Moslems as a deliverer. It is recorded that the Moslem population "of Baraset flocked to him in numbers". Among these was Titu Mir who in 1831 organized an *emuete* against the ruling authority. This attempt has become a byword of blind, ignorant and ineffective fanaticism.

In 1822 Sayyad Ahmmad went on pilgrimage to Mecca wherefrom he returned the next year with a new halo of sanctity and authority. He passed through Bombay, enlisting disciples. He was a honoured guest at Tonk where his old commander's son and heir to the throne became his disciple. At Khairpur in Sindh, yet an independent country, he gained the ears of Moslem rulers and their subjects. From 1826 to 1831 he kept working at his project of a holy war against the Sikhs ; but the best he could organize was desultory skirmishes, unproductive of any tangible advantage. In May, 1831, he and his followers were surprised and routed by the Sikhs at Balakot where Sayyad Ahmmad and Mohammed Ismail fell in the action.

This in brief was the life-history of Sayyad Ahmmad, the positive achievement of which was next to nothing. But in the realm of the spirit, in the widening of ideas, the movement initiated by him breathed "new life into the torpid existence of Indian Mohammedans." Its followers preached a return to the purity of Islam of the days of their Prophet, as a preliminary to the renewal of its life of spiritual glory and secular empire. It is said that soon after his return from Mecca,

Sayyad Ahmmad called a conference of his *caliphs* (lieutenants or agents) at Patna, and "parcelled out" India among them. Religious awakening led to a revival of the ideas of political hegemony from which the Moslems had been displaced only three-quarters of a century back. Sayyad Ahmmad's principal followers toured the country rousing these hopes in the heart of the community. Records of certain of these are available. Keramat Ali of Jaunpur travelled through Chittagong, Noakhali, Dacca, Mymensingh, Faridpur and Barisal; Inayat Ali of Patna through central Bengal, Pabna, Rajshahi, Maldah and Bogra; his elder broth r Vilayat Ali's mission lay chiefly among the people of central India, Hyderabad (Deccan) and Bombay. It is recorded that in the Deccan "the people were stirred up to such a pitch of religious enthusiasm that even women were found to be selling their jewelleries and devoting the proceeds to the support of the movement." The special attention that was devoted to the Bengali Moslems did not at first reap a harvest of men and money. But in course of time the movement became, we are told, "a Bengali-Mahommedan revival", due to the "intellectual superiority" of Bengali Moslems. The death or disappearance of Sayyad Ahmmad did not damp the fervour and enthusiasm of his followers, the most active among whom were Vilayat Ali and Inayat Ali of Patna. For, two decades after, when the Punjab had ceased to be a Sikh Kingdom, and had come to form a part of British India. the two brothers are found organizing an attack on India from their retreat in the hills beyond the Indus at a certain place called Sittana, and getting recruits and monetary contributions from Bengal and Behar. One of their disciples, Zain-ul Abdin of Hyderabad (Deccan) was a successful Wahhabi missionary, the number of his disciples even in Dacca and Sylhet testified to the religious and inchoate political appeal of Syyad Ahmmad's version of Wahhabism.

Dar-ul-Islam & Dar-ul-Harb

The doctrinal differences that separate Indian Wahhabis from the main bodies of the Sunni Moslems in India, and agitate Moslems, even those living in our rural tracts, are not of importance to the other communities in India, or to the ruling power in the country. Even fanaticism learns after a while to make concession to the needs and demands of ordinary human relationships which are not equal to the strain of continuous ecstacies or exaltations of thought and activity. Wahhabism and its by-products have not escaped this experience. Hans Kohn in his "history of Nationalism in the East" traces the streak of liberalism that has evolved out of the fanatically inspired beginning. Says he:—

> "On the other hand, reforming zeal aimed at a revival of the basic ethical code of Islam in a new liberal and humanistic form, not shunning the influence of other religións. These aspirations found ex pression principally in Babism (Persian in origin) and the Ahmadiya movement"

In the controversies among different sectaries of Islam, precipitated by the Wahhabis, there is one theory in which both the government and the other communities are vitally interested—the theory which divided the world into *Dar-ul-Islam*, the "country of safety" comprising all Moslem Kingdoms, and *Dar-ul-harb*, the "country of enmity" including all non-believing nations. According to the doctrines of the Hanafi sect, three conditions condemn a country to be regarded as *Dar-ul-harb* :

(i) The public exercise of infidel authority, and the non-exercise of Moslem authority within it ;

(ii) Annexation to the *Dar-ul-harb* without the interposition of any Moslem city or community ;

(iii) The non-existence in it of a true believer.

Was India Dar-ul-Islam?

The second and the third conditions do not apply to India for it touches countries under Moslem domination, and the Moslem population of India count one-fifth of the total population. The first condition condemns India to a "country of enmity" if it be rigidly interpreted ; for the ruling authority in India is in "infidel" hands, non-Moslem. There is a lack of unanimity among Moslem jurists in their attitude to India. And the prospect of a democratic responsible self-government based on majority vote or voice cannot be welcome to the upholders of this theory, for, so far as human calculations go, the ruling authority will still be non-Moslem. Here is the source and root of the apparently insoluble problems of majority and minority representation, separate electorates, Moslem provinces, reservation and weightage. India does not satisfy conditions of orthodox statehood beloved of Hanafi doctrinaires. It is true that a section of Moslem jurists were or are prepared to waive objections to India being considered as *Dar-ul-Islam* considering the immense size of the Moslem population of the country. But the Hanafi theorists, under the influence of Wahhabism, as preached by Mohammed Ismail, one of the first and foremost of the disciples of Sayyad Ahmmad, held that India cannot be regarded as *Dar-ul-Islam* as and when it is under "infidel authority". They called the testimony of Jewish history to the support of the condition of Indian Moslems under the British comparing it to that "of the Israelites in Egypt", hoping and praying for a second Moses who would lead them out of servitude and destitution to freedom and plentitude. Under the influence of this belief the followers of Sayyad Ahmmad levied war against the British Government in India. That the general body of the Indian Moslem *intelligentsia* do not hold or stand by the strict interpretation of the Hanafi-cum-Wahhabi theory of state is all too apparent. But while conscious reason rejects as absurd many a theory or doctrine, the unconscious soul of nations or societies hugs them to heart. Therefore it is that Indian Moslems are torn by divided loyalties, one to their country and the other to their creed. This conflict stands in the way of their thought-leaders giving a right lead to their community ; it has clouded their counsels and encouraged them to cultivate a conceit of a separate and inviolate entity. How far this could go was expressed by Maulavi Kootb-ud-din, a successor of Shah Abdul Aziz, in his book *Tama Tafasar* published at Delhi in 1867. The following quotation is pertinent to the point under discussion :—

"The prophet said, 'I am displeased with every one of those Mussalmans who live among "*Mushriks*" (a term applied to Christians in India). The companions of the prophet asked him......'O Messenger of God, why are you displeased' ? Then the prophet replied, 'Because it is essential to faith, that *Mushriks* and *Mussulmans* should not be able to see each others' fires, i. e. it is necessary for a Muhammedan to keep himself at such a distance and so far aloof from a *Kafir*, that they may not be able to see each others' fire. Living amongst them is out of the question, for it produces weakness in Islam. This weakness is caused by looking at their custom".

Theodore Morison was Principal of the Mohammedan Anglo-Oriental College at Aligarh during the last years of the last century. In his book—"Imperial Rule in India"—published in 1899 he opined that the Mohammedans did so little regard "India as their own country" that their great poet Altaf Hossain Hali, one of the ministrels of Moslem Renaissance in India, "compared his people to guests who had outstayed their welcome and lamented that they had left their native homes for India". And he quotes the following stanzas from Hali's poem—*Shikwah Hind*, to confirm his contention:

"Morning and evening our eyes now behold that which we thought would be the end of thy gracious acceptance."

"Quickly hast thou broken all thy promises and pledges; O India! we were told a-right that thou wast faithless."

"From every side we hear thee say that the guest is unwelcome who tarries long."

* *

"Hast thou ever beheld the men of Islam in this plight before? Was this the Islam which we brought with us from Arabia?"

"Oh Mill of Revolving Time! thou hast ground us small; enough; have done; What boots thee to grind us further?

* *

As the host of the Greeks turned back from thy (India) border, would that in like manner, we had turned back baffled from thy door."

The words quoted above may be characterized as the cry of a defeated people. But it did not represent the better mind of Indian Moslems which refused to be shut behind glass doors. But before it could assert itself fully and decidedly and take command of the community's destiny from the hands of short-sighted men it had to go through a prolonged penance. The secret Wahhabi movement reached its open climax by 1870 in the abortive attack on India referred to in a previous paragraph. The *Dar-ul-harb* theory and its logical corollary, the imperative duty of a *jehad* imposed on the faithful and pious Moslem, intruded themselves into public view with all their menace to the peace and prosperity of a country inhabited by a composite population. Leaders of Moslem opinion hastened forward to repudiate the logic of the Wahbabi interpretation of Moslem jurisprudence. Maulvi Keramat Ali of Jaunpur, one time Wahhabi missionary and one of the most celebrated Moslem religious teachers of the day, proved that British India was *Dar-ul-Islam*, and that as such it was "unlawful and irreligious" for Indian Moslems to preach a *jehad* against the British government established in the country. The up-heaval that is known in history as the "Sepoy Mutiny", was not caused by any appeal to exclusive religious bigotry; it was a frank attempt of "the supporters of the lost cause of the Marhattas and Moghuls" to regain control of the machinery of the State in India.

Moslem Separatism

The repudiation of the *Dar-ul-harb* theory in its application to India through the pen and voice of Moulvi Keramat Ali of Jaunpur was the ultimate stage of the process of penance, the deliverance of the Moslem mind in India from the thraldrom of an exclusive religious bigotry out of tune with mid-19th century rationalism, and fraught with danger to a country where men of different faiths must learn to live peacefully as neighbours, where "each other's fire" cannot but be visible to each other, and where they must pull their full weight if the country were to evolve into an equal among equals in the comity of nations. This is an aspiration unrealized yet. More so was it so when the Moslem community were sulking in their tents while the surging tide in the national life was sweeping over India in the middle of the last century. Intensely conservative, with a conservatism seeking to protect their communal life by the adoption of what is called in Hindu social theory as *Kurma-Niti*—the attitude of withdrawing into itself as a turtle does when it scents or apprehends the approach of a stranger —"unaccustomed to competition", and not understanding that the pre-eminence they had always held in legal and administrative posts could ever be questioned or threatened, they failed to advance with the times. In 1839 Persian ceased to be the court language of British India, and the Moslem *intelligentsia* lost the monopoly which they had hitherto held, eighty years after political power had passed out of their hands, in service under the government. After the "Mutiny" Moslems in general and the inhabitants of the tract of the country extending from round about Delhi in the West to Behar in the east "lost caste" with the British Government for their leadership in organizing it. The result was an economic break-down, and dispersal of men, east and west, in search of occupations. The initiation of Western methods of industrialism coincided in time with this disintegration in the social and economic life of northern India, and many among the masses belonging to these districts found work in the rising and growing port of Calcutta, in the railway lines, in mines, and factories. A host of Moslem *intelligentsia* sought and found asylum and livelihood in the Nizam State and other Moslem courts. This was the period of penance when the Moslem community was slowly but surely throwing off the apathy and indifference which seemed to have settled like a pall upon them. The world knows that Sir Sayyad Ahmmad, who had flirted at one period of his life with the doctrinal rigidities of Wahhabism, was the representative man among Indian Moslems, throwing off all the conceit of superiority and the spirit of irreconcilable separatism, and accepting the new light from the West; he represented the "young Moslem" in India who dared meet all on equal terms and was not afraid to see the "others' fire." But he had precursors represented by Nawab Abdul Lateef (Bengal) Nawab Amir Ali (Behar). They frankly accepted the advantages and limitations of the conditions introduced into India by British rule, and bent all their energies to the task of educating their community to a like acceptance and adoption. The National Muhammedan Association was started in Calcutta (1855) with the object of uniting all classes of Moslems for work for the furtherance of the common good. For reasons which one can understand though he may regard them as short-sighted, these Moslem leaders stood out for "separate consideration" for Moslem interests. In the field of education also they chose to play a lone hand. The benefactions left by Haji Mohammed Moshin (1806) were not circumscribed by any consideration of creed. Nearly fifty years after, Moslem leaders woke up to the fact that—"a Fund founded by a Muhammedan primarily for Muhammedans" should be benefitting the Hindus, who had been more prompt to take advantage of the educational facilities afforded by the Fund. This spirit of separatism flourishes under various disguises, and expresses itself in political discussions sometimes as possessing a special importance as the gate-keepers of India; sometimes as still capable of carrying on the traditions of imperial rule, sometimes calling in the aid of Pan-Islamism to restore the balance disturbed by Moslem weakness in India. Sayyad Jelal-ud-din Afghani, born in Iran and educated at Bokhara, was the prophet of this new orientation in Islam's world-policy. Sultan Abdul Hamid supported this movement as a barrage erected to intercept the aggression of European Imperialism. Sir Sayyad Ahmmad gave expression to the current Mosl m feeling on the second contention in a historic speech as follows :—

"We the Mohammedans are those who ruled India for six or seven hundred years. From our hands the government was taken by the English. Is the Indian Government so foolish as to suppose in seventy years we have forgotten all our grandeur and our Empire" ?

The mentality that diverts and deflects national energies from the main current of building up a composite national life in India had its birth a century back. It has been exercising the heart and intellect of the country to find a way out of this impasse. As a preliminary to a right understanding of the problem and its right solution some such historical presentation must be attemped as has been done above.

The many forces that were generated by methods of British administration and enlightenment have been traced above. These have disrupted many centres of our community life, but have also helped to create new ones round which have gathered and consolidated the sentiments and interests of the people.

Synthesis of Efforts

In the realm of the spirit, in the region of invisible things there was unrest; new dogmas challenged the old that had satisfied the cravings of the human heart and mind in India. This challenge gave birth to the Wahhabi movement, the Brahmo Samaj, the Prarthana Samaj, the Arya Samaj, the Theosophical Society, and the brotherhood that emanated from Ram Krishna Paramhansa Deva. All these stirrings of the human spirit were born responsive to the questionings precipitated by the failure of Indian institutions to the stand up to the new-comer from the West with his new values of human personality and fellowship. These called for new groupings of thought and life incarnated in the new institutions of our associated effort. British administration and enlightenment offered solutions for the new problems raised in the country. The Indian mind winnowed them out, guided by the wisdom of centuries, rejecting some, accepting others. The synthesis of these rejections and acceptances is embodied in the various institutions that have been working in our midst these hundred years and more.

British Promises of Equal Status

This synthesis of efforts have contributed in no small measure to the deepening and broadening of what is generally called the public life of the country. In the fields of administrative and political developments the new rulers initiated policies and raised hopes that demanded fulfilment. Promises, parliamentary and royal, declared for the ending of inequalities and distinctions between the rulers and the ruled. The earliest of such promises were made as far back as 1833 when it was declared :

> "That no native of the said territories, nor any natural-born subject of his Majesty, resident therein, shall, by reason only of his religion, place of birth, descent, colour, or any of them, be disabled from holding any place, office, or employment under the said Company."

When the East India Company handed over the administration of India to the British Crown, Queen Victoria in her proclamation dated the first of November, 1858, declared :

> "We hold ourselves bound to the natives of our Indian territories by the same obligations of duty which bind us to all our subjects, and those obligations by the blessing of Almighty God, we shall faithfully and conscientiously fulfil."
>
> "............It is our further will, that so far as may be, our subjects, of whatever race or creed, be freely and impartially admitted to offices in our service, the duties of which they may be qualified by their education, ability, and integrity duly to discharge."
>
> "............We do strictly charge and enjoin all those who may be in authority under us, that they abstain from all interference with the religious belief or worship of any of our subjects."

These promises were considered by the first few generations of English educated Indians as the Magna Charta of their rights and liberties ; they learnt to read into them a new spirit of governance. This new spirit inspired them to launch into those open and organised political struggles, the first stirrings of which have been indicated above. For the redress of grievances, removal of abuses and promotion of political interests, the technique of public meetings, protests, petitions, prayers and deputations have been a new development in the history of the world, East and West, since the third decade of the 19th. century. Where it had been the custom to break into disturbances and rebellions to draw the attention of the ruling authorities to popular grievances, it became the custom to organize public demonstrations of wordy revolt to secure the same object. Our ancestors took to these with an avidity and an innocence of belief in their efficacy that appear pathetic to-day. The grievances which first moved them to record protest and petition for redress were concerned with particular acts and activities of the government. What they were in Bengal have been discussed in a previous paragraph.

Beginings of Political Agitation in Madras

In Madras we find Guzulu Lakshminarasu Chetty, as early as 1843, financing and starting a paper— *The Crescent*—with one Mr. Harley as editor. The editor has served in the army, and brought to the conduct of the paper the spirit of his former life. The object of the paper was declared to be "the amelioration of the condition of the Hindus". Lakshminarasu Chetty was a self-made man, self-educated ; his biographer summed up his life by saying that he "lived in days when he had not merely to educate himself, but educate the people" in their duties to society, in their rights and privileges. The first question that brought him to public life against the government of the Marquis of Tweeddale, the then governor of Madras, was the proselytizing practices of the missionaries and "the countenance openly given to their cause by not a few of the English functionaries". In Lionel J. Trotter's "History of the British Empire in India" is described the dissatisfaction of the people with the state of affairs :which broke out into riots, that at Tinnevelly (1846) being specially mentioned. Mr. Lewis, judge of the Sadr Court, was removed from office for opposition to executive high-handedness. Commenting on this the historian says:

"Mr. Lewis' treatment at the hands of the Madras Government for his bold defence of the judgment passed by himself and his brethren of the Sadr Court seemed to justify the charge rife against that Government of using its high powers as a missionary partisan, not as the ruler of a non-Christian realm."

Lakshminarasu Chetty carried this agitation to the notice of the Court of Directors at London. The memorial signed by over twelve thousand people was shelved. But the publicity given to the matter in the press and the platform curbed the zeal of the missionaries. In this fight Lakshminarasu Chetty was helped by George Norton, Advocate-general of Madras, and John Bruce Norton, another leading lawyer. On the eve of the renewal of the Company's Charter (1853) Mr. Danby Seymour M. P. came to India to personally enquire into the grievances of the Indian people. The Madras public man accompanied him in his tour through certain districts, and both of them were witnesses to the "tortures" that were inflicted on ryots failing to pay their revenue dues timely to the State-landlord. On a motion by Mr. Seymour in the British House of Commons (1854), a commission of enquiry was set up, and the practice "condemned". The Madras Native Association was founded in 1852, and under Lakshminarasu Chetty's guidance a petition was presented to Parliament detailing the grievances of the people. The petition premised by saying:

"That the grievances of your petitioners arise principally from the excessive taxation and the vexations which accompany its collections, and the insufficiency, delays and expenses of the Company's Courts of Law; that their chief wants are the construction of roads, bridges and works for the supply of irrigation, and a better provision for the education of the people; they also desire a reduction of public expenditure, and a form of local government more generally conducive to the happiness of the subjects and the prosperity of the country".

The Madras Native Association sent a representation suggesting the transfer of the government of India to the British Crown. The British Indian Association, and also the Bombay Association sent representations making identical suggestion, and putting forth similar demands. In the first annual report of the British Indian Association of Calcutta, the Committee of the Association specially drew attention to the correspondence that they had opened with prominent men of other provinces, and noted "the formation at Poona, Madras and Bombay successively of Associations of a similar character which, though they have elected to carry on operations independently of each other, cannot but largely contribute towards the important end of acquainting the British public with the state of feeling in India with regard to its past and future administration". Here do we notice the germs of that all-India sentiment which took shape nearly thirty years later in the Indian National Congress. The heroic and successful fight of the Bengal indigo ryots against the indigo planters was keenly watched by people in other provinces; when the Revd. James Long, the friend of the royts, was passing through Madras on his way to Britain (1862), the citizens honoured him by presenting an address to him, headed by

Hafiz Sadrool Islam Khan, B.A., M. Venkataryoloo Naidu and V. Rajaratanam Moodelly. The end of the Lytton regime finds Madras pulsating with a new life—Rangiah Naidu, G. Subramanya Iyer, S. Viraraghavachariar, Salem Ramaswami Mudaliar, and Chakravarty Vijayraghavachariar leading public life. The last is still happily with us. His solution of the Indian political tangle is the elimination of the British Parliament from Indian concerns, the symbol of British connection being the King of Britain as he is of the other Dominions.

A parallel movement of reform and reconstruction was proceeding in Bombay and Maharashtra. The first products of British education "Young Bombay" as they were called, were forging ahead with their watch-word of Reform, religious, social, intellectual and political. Naoroji Furdunji popularly known as "Naoroji Master" to distinguish him from Dadabhai Naoroji who was known as "Naoroji Professor", and Dr. Bhau Daji—these were the leading spirits in starting the Bombay Association (1852) under the auspices of which the organization and conduct of "the first political movement" in the Presidency was set on foot. The *Rast-gofter* (Truth-Teller) started in 1851 carried their message to the country. Soon after Dadabhai Naoroji transferred his activities to London where in 1866 he founded the East India Association "for the independent and disinterested advocacy and promotion by all legitimate means of the interests and welfare of India generally". Many British public men, and retired Anglo-Indian officials are found connected with it. Young men from India who had increasingly begun to go out of the country for education in British universities and in the Inns of Courts found in Dadabhai their guide, philosopher and friend in more than one sense. At a meeting of the Association (1867) we find the first president of the Indian National Congress to be, Mr. W. C. Bonerjee, reading a paper on "Representative and Responsible Government for India" and the second, third and the sixth presidents of that organization, Dadabhai Naoroji, Badr ud din Tyabji, and Pherozeshah Merwanji Mehta taking part in the discussion. In what a minor key were the proposals in support of the claims of India pitched, and how warily did the young Indian speakers walk, every minute fearful of treading on the corns of British conceit or interests! The class represented by the names given above accepted the superiority of the British values of life, and were sincerely vigorous in their convictions and utterances. With all their limitations they were the builders of the New India as we have it to-day. The class included lawyers and doctors, journalists, educationists, the school master "abroad", and government servants. This class professed and possessed a unity of feeling greater than anything existent in any other section of the Indian people. They were the first to transcend the particularisms that divided the country, provincial, caste, and occupational. They became "consciously Indian". And they reacted as Indians to any attack on the honour or interests of their country. In the time dealt with here they formed only a "microscopic minority" of the more than two hundred millions that inhabited India. But they were the leaven that leaveneth the whole lump.

In Bombay & Maharashtra

Mahadev Gobind Ranade, "the prince of graduates", may be accepted as a representative of this class. More than one writer, Indian and foreign, have said that no Indian in the British period reached the height of Ram Mohun Roy's intellectual perceptions and the breadth of his vision, the imperturbability of his temper, and persistence in the path of duty as God had given him to understand it, except it be Mahadev Govinda Ranade and Sir Sayyad Ahmmad. Mahadev Govind Ranade's social and political thought and conduct was based on (1) a frank rec gnition of the weaknesses of his country, (2) hearty approval of the British connection, (3) recognition of the "inevitable drawbacks" of that connection. What they were was indicated by Sir Richard Temple who closed a long and distinguished official life in India as governor of Bombay:

"...... although political talent, statesmanlike ambition and administrative power fail to be fostered under British rule, still there are ample fields for learned research, for literary taste, for social reform, for poetic culture, for philosophic meditation –, in short, for general culture, both varied and comprehensive".

Of particular value in this process of "culture" opened out by the new education was the scientific research into many lines of intellectual, social, religious, historical, archeological and aesthetic interest in which ancient and mediaeval India xpressed itself. In the days of Sir William Jones, it was called the "discovery of Sanskrit." Mahadev Govind Ranade and his class appreciated, and availed themselves fully of, the opportunities and advantages of this "discovery." Raja Rajendra Lal Mittra, Sir Ram Krishna Bhandarkar are outstanding pioneers in this line of development.

By the time Mahadev Gobind Ranade had entered service under the Government in the Judicial Department he had settled down to his life's work also—reform of society and reform of the State. Ganesh Vashudeo Joshi had founded at Poona the Sarvajanik Sabha (1870). But Mahadev Gobind Ranade was the power behind the activities of this organisation, for which he enjoyed much "Irish promotion" into the outlying districts of the presidency, as he had become "politically suspect with the Lytton administration." As a result of these activities Poona carved out a new place for herself as a competitor with Bombay in the leadership of all progressive movements. Bombay was cosmopolitan, Poona was nationalist. And in this evolution of Poona, Vishnu Sastri Chiplunkar played the dominant part. The "historic" role played by him is thus expressed by Narasimha Chintamon Kelkar in his biography of Lokamanya Tilak:

"If it be contended that Tilak got the torch from Chiplunkar's hands, it was he, without the shadow of a doubt, who kept it burning and shining in his day with a brighter flame. If it be said that Tilak borrowed the brick from Chiplunker, it must be equally conceded that he left it marble. And both these pioneers are revered by posterity, Chiplunkar as the father of Nationalism in Maharashtra, and Tilak as a more illustrious son who spread the patriotic spirit to all quarters of the country".

The London *Graphic* in an obituary notice of Vishnu Sastri's spoke of him as "one of those pioneers of progress, who, if they become numerous enough, will some day make India a self-governing community."

All-India Sentiment

People had by this time been recovering from the demoralization of the "Sepoy Mutiny". Quicker methods of communication were erasing distances, physical and cultural. The famines that devastated Orissa, Behar and north Bengal, Madras and the Deccan had called forth sympathy wide and deep from all parts of India. The north-west frontier had been sucking mints of Indian money into the erection of a stable and scientific frontier. Lord Northbrook had not been many months in the country before he had convinced himself of the existence of an "uneasy and dissatisfied feeling" in the country. And all over the country open and organized expression to this feeling was being given. Keshab Chandra Sen by his All-India tours (1864 and 1867), in furtherance of his religious and social ideas, had pointed out to the possibility of bringing men belonging to different provinces and speaking different languages on one common platform. The "unity of India" was a topic of constant discussion in the press which could be given concrete shape only by starting an all-India association holding its sessions in cities in different provinces. In Lord Lytton's time the order of the Secretary of State reducing the age of aspirants to the Indian Civil Service from 21 to 19, evoked an all India protest, and Surendra Nath Banerjee helped to widen and consolidate the feeling by his tours through the provinces, all moved by a "common grievance and the inspiration of a common resolve". In course of this tour in the Punjab Surendra Nath drew to public life and public service Sardar Dayal Singh Majethia, who by his benefactions made it possible for progressive and liberal movements to function in the Province. The Delhi Durbar on the occasion of the proclamation of the assumption of the title—Empress of India—by Queen Victoria brought many representatives of educated India to it where they had an opportunity of common deliberation. It is on record that Mahadev Gobind Ranade and Ganesh Vashudeo Joshi canvassed among their fellow-guests the practicability of forming an all-India institution for the discussion of all-India problems and the adoption of all-India measures for their solution.

Apprehensions of mass revolt

While the educated community were thus feeling their way to rearing up an all-India organisation competent by its prestige and authority to direct popular grievances into open and constitutional channels of expression and lawful methods of redress, there appeared evidences that the minds of the masses were moving towards outbreaks of physical violence. For some reason or other Lord Lytton's administration seemed to have brought matters to a head; "the state of things at the end of Lord Lytton's 'reign' was bordering upon revolution. Armed bands were beginning to go about; having the sympathy of the people", said William Wedderburn who was for a time chief secretary to the Government of Bombay. In a pamphlet published by the Bengal National League (Maharaja Sir Jatindra Mohun Tagore was the president of this organisation) appear words that confirm the statement made by Sir William Wedderburn. When "heaven sent us a genius for a Viceroy"………

"...... when matters were almost at their worst, when British supremacy was scarcely worth six months' purchase, that an hitherto unrecognized agency working for peace and goodwill among men, first entered the sphere of practical politics...... when, however, the crisis grew to be really acute, they resolved that more overt measures should be resorted to in order, if possible, to avert what to them seemed an immediately impending and incalculably disastrous calamity".

"Then began they to preach...the doctrine that expression must be given to the hitherto repressed and imprisoned national feelings......, and that this expansion could only safely take the form of overt constitutional agitation, no matter how noisy, or even at first childish, if only it afforded due vent for those bitter and vindictive feelings".

Lord Lytton's Vernacular Press Act and the Arms Act are explained by the apprehensions of revolutionary outbreaks. The growing body of educated public men must have sensed the dangers of the situation and they felt called upon to throw themselves into the breach to avert the calamity of a bloody conflict between an organised government and disorganized masses of people. Allan Octavian Hume, a retired civilian, had knowledge of the dissatisfaction that had been seething in the mass mind of India, and of the desperate measures which a hopeless and helpless mass of people were being driven to adopt in Lord Lytton's time. For the good of the British empire in India upheld by the contentment and self-respect of a people, he invited the co-operation of educated India in his "Open Letter" dated the 1st. March, 1883, to "the graduates of the Calcutta University".

On the eve of the Congress

In December of that year the first session of the Indian National Conference was held in Calcutta, in the organization of which the Indian Association and the Central Mohammedan Association had co-operated. It was attended by delegates from almost all the provinces. Next year at Adyar (a suburb of Madras) the delegates to the Theosophical Convention, Indian officials and non-officials, after the close of their advertized work, conferred among themselves at Dewan Bahadur Raghunath Row's place, and resolved to meet in a Indian National Union at Poona in the Christmas week of 1885. This version is taken from Mrs. Besant's book—"How India wrought for Freedom". Another version appears in Ambica Charan Mazumdar's book—"Indian National Evolution". Therein it is stated that Allan Octavian Hume followed his "Open Letter" to the graduates of the Calcutta University by correspondence and interviews with Indian reformers and high officials. He approached Lord Dufferin and put before him his concrete proposal of an organization holding annual sessions in different provincial capitals with the provincial satrap as president. Reform of India's social institutions and the methods of carrying it out would form the agenda of these conferences. Lord Dufferin, however, suggested instead a responsible political organization holding its public sessions "through which the Government might be kept informed regarding the best Indian public opinion", no government officer having had anything to do with it in public, and the Government observing a sort of "benevolent neutrality" towards it. Hume went to Britain to enlist the sympathy and support of liberal-minded and progressive men in behalf of this venture. The preliminaries thus settled, the leaders of Poona working under the auspices of the Sarvajanik Sabha seriously and enthusiastically took in hand the arrangements for the Indian National Congress, for thus has the name been changed in course of a year's discussion. Why was Poona preferred to all other cities in the country for the honour of holding the first session of the Congress, and not Calcutta the capital of the empire where Surendra Nath Banerjee and his fellow-workers had anticipated it by two years, not Madras which took the initiative in taking a definite step in the matter, and Bombay, the capital of the western presidency? This preference must have been intended as a compliment to the virile and watchful public life that had grown up round Mahadeo Govind Ranade, Kashinath Trimbak Telang, and Ganesh Vashudeo Joshi. Almost at the last moment owing to the out-break of cholera at Poona the venue of the Congress was hastily shifted to Bombay where it held its first session on the 28th. December, 1885, at the Gokuldas Tejpal Pathsala.

Hopes of early Congress Workers

Thus was the Indian National Congress born, with very modest objects: (1) to enable all the most earnest labourers in the cause of national progress to become personally known to each other; (2) to discuss and decide upon the political operations to be undertaken during the ensuing year. In the speeches of the early workers in the Congress field loyalty to the British connection was reiterated: "I am patriotic because I am loyal; I am loyal, because I am patriotic"—words like these were received with cheers and acclamation: the same speaker lived to write in 1906 of the political ideal of India as — "absolute autonomy free from British control"—marking the march of ideas and of events. What they are to-day the world knows. "The more progress people made in education and material prosperity the greater would be their insight into political matters, and keener their desire for political advancement"—this was the hope that W. C. Banerjee predicted. To-day material adversity has added a keener edge to the demand for radical reform in the country. The Indian National Congress would work "to mitigate, if not to eradicate, race prejudices, to disarm creed antipathies, and to remove provincial jealousies"— this had been Ananda Charlu's aspiration for his National organization. That aspiration remains unrealized. Perhaps things must grow worse before they can get better.

Evolution of Political Thought

A panoramic view of Indian life and thought antecedent to 1885 has been presented above. It showed us a people who were consciously reacting against the pressure of an administrative system based on the assumption and acceptance of racial and cultural supremacy; it showed us a people who were consciously repudiating that assumption; it showed us a people the leaders of which had begun to employ "western machinery to overthrow western predominance"; it showed us also that these leaders depended for the success of their efforts and the fulfilment of their hopes on the righteous instincts of their rulers, on their declarations of policy and their promises; it showed us that these leaders had no faith in the organized public spirit of their own people for the assertion of their rights and liberties dependant not on human promises but received from on high from their Maker. But these leaders lived to see their methods criticized and decried as "political mendicancy", and the pioneer of them, Dadabhai Naoroji, glad and proud that he had lived to see that day. It is curious, however, that it was not the politician that first awoke to the unnaturalness of these methods and this politics. It was reserved for people who are called "literary men" to recall the politician from the pursuit of futility, the futility of expecting a ruling authority to divest itself of power under the pressure of "petition, protest and prayer". Vishnu Sastri Chiplunkar in Maharashtra through his monthly the "*Nibandh Mala*", and in Bengal Bankim Chandra Chatterjee through his "*Banga-Darshan*" and Dr. Rabindra Nath Tagore through his essays and poems, first drew the attention of their countrymen to methods of self-help. And among politicians, the first to repudiate the ideology of imperialism was Balwant Gangadhar Tilak, This ideology has always sought to cite science in its support. The skin of a people, their nasal index and the girth of their head-piece, the supporters of imperialism have averred, ought to be entered into the assessment of a people's right and eligibility to self-rule. Social usages and disabilities, such as idol worship, child-marriage, interdict on widow re-marriage, illiteracy, untouchability, unapproachability and such other crudities stand as so many bars to self-rule. And a people whose life was tortured and disfigured by such usages, cruel and demoralizing, could never hope to attain self-rule. These were the dominant thoughts which ruled the life and conduct of the early reformers among our people during the British regime. Balwantrao Tilak very early in life, under the impulse of a conviction, born natural in him and not by any ratiocinative process; refused to accept the logic of any such ideology, or its truth and validity. And his conviction flared forth thirty years later in the declaration—"Swaraj is my birth right". Dadabhai Naoroji first brought the word "Swaraj" into currency in modern Indian politics. Since then the word has found place in a royal proclamation.

In the opening years of the present century Bipin Chaudra Pal in Bengal appeared as the protagonist of the ideas of self-help and self-respect in politics. His English weekly — "*The New India*" was the organ voice of the development. A social and religious reformer who grew under the inspiration of Keshab Chandra Sen and Shiv Nath Shastri, he had lost faith in the religious and social institutions of his people as a centre and citadel of progress. He combined in himself two contradictory qualities, a rugged individuality and a sensitiveness to developing mental and moral disturbances in the atmosphere around himself. The spirit of the reformer kept him at a distance from sympathy with the day-to-day strivings of his people for a better life ; his psychological insight into the soul of these strivings brought him nearer to them, and made him their tribune. He was moved, all inspite of his prepossessions, by the triumphant march of Swami Vivekananda through the West asserting the hegemony of Indian thought in the modern world. A kindred soul to the makers of modern India was Brahmabandhab Upadhyaya whose Catholic Christianity found nothing incompatible in loyalty to his country and his country's culture. These were the men who moulded the minds of people for the mighty transformation that India witnessed in 1905 and the succeeding years, prepared the field in which came Aurobinda Ghosh, who is best described in the words of a fellew-worker of his of that period:

"...... The other leaders of the movement have left their life behind them: Aurobinda has his before him. Nationalism is their last love: it is his first passion. They are burdened with the cares and responsibilities of large families or complex relations: Aurobinda has a small family and practically no cumulative obligations. His only care is for his country—the mother, as he always calls her...... Nationalism, at the best a concern of the intellect with some, at the lowest a political cry and aspirations with others, is with Aurobinda a supreme passion of his soul. Few, indeed, have grasped the full force and meaning of the Nationalist ideal as Aurobinda has done. But of these very few—though their vision may be clear, their action is weak....To see the vision of truth and yet not to be possessed by the supreme passion for it which burns up all other desires and snaps asunder, like ashen bands, all other ties and obligations—this is the divine tragedy of most finer natures....But blessed are they for whom this tragic antithesis between the ideal and the real has been cancelled; for whom to know the truth is to love it; to love the truth is to strive after it, and to strive after the the truth is to attain it: in whom there is no disparity, either in time or degree, between the idea and its realization: in whom the vision of the ideal, by its own intrinsic strength at once attunes every craving of the flesh, every movement of the mind, every motion of the heart, and every impulse of the will to itself: .... These are so to say the chosen of God...Their towering optimism, and the Grace of God, turn every evil into good, every opposition to help, every loss into a gain. By the general verdict of his countrymen, Aurobinda stands to-day among these favoured sons of God".

In Memorium

Chittaranjan Das (Deshabandhu) who successfully defended Aurobinda Ghose in the Alipore Bomb case, carried on the tradition of the cumulative protest of India, first registered in Bengal in 1905; the abandon of his sacrifice was the urge of a rich nature which knew how to live, and how to deny life. It is noteworthy that his two most forceful colleagues and disciples—Jatindra Mohun Sen Gupta and Birendra Nath Sasmal—should have had the qualities of their leader—qualities that enabled them to grasp the joys of life and drink them to the lees, the qualities that made it easy for them to offer these at the altar of their motherland. Syam Sundar Chakravarty whose nationalism came to him as the natural and instinctive conservatism of a people, with his concrete patriotism rooted in the strength and the weakness of his people, found his highest self-expression in the days of Non-co-operation when his daily, the *Servant*, was a pillar of the movement.

The terrorist movement that had its birth in the turmoil of the Bengal anti-partition agitation has created problems that exercise the statesmanship of both the rulers and the ruled. The former seek to solve it by repression. Mahatmaji's non-violent *Satyagraha* offers a constructive substitute for violence, individual and national, asserts the right and the duty to do and dare, to "die in one's *dharma*", in the fulfilment of the law of one's own being.

Subramanya Bharati and Chidambaram Pillai, the former by his songs and the latter by his practical Swadeshi gave the first hint of the potentialities that have reached fruition to-day in the ebullient life of Tamil Nad, guided by the cool intellectuality of a culture more Indian than in any other part of the country.

The Andhra movement did not exhaust itself simply by rationalizing the plea of linguistic provinces in India. The Andhra Jatiya Kalasala of Masulipatam made an effort to direct energies to the higher reaches of thought and life. Hanumantha Rao spent himself in building up this institution.

Lala Lajpat Rai in the Punjab, Aswini Kumar Dutta in Bengal were the two most outstanding constructive leaders of public life in their respective provinces. Things were more difficult for the former for reasons, which were some of them social, implicit in the aggressiveness of the Arya Samaj of which Lalaji was one of the first proponents; the other reasons were administrative due to the semi-military regime in the province; its contiguity to the north-west frontier with the menace of Russia ever present to the foreign office at Simla is responsible for "methods of suppression" of which the world had the best demonstration at Jallianwala Bagh in April, 1919.

Mukhtar Ahmmad Ansari tested his patriotism in the fire of his community's disapproval, and proved it before all the world as pure gold. Beginning as a Pan Islamist, his faith in the world message of Islam did not stand in the way of his fight for the freedom of his country.

Hakim Ajmal Khan, one of Nature's noble man, brought to the 20th century the graces of the 16th. His personality, avoiding limelight, was one of the silent forces of Moslem awakening in India.

Mrs. Annie Besant as president of the Theosophical Society was one of the most potent personal influences in our national awakening. Her leadership in the Home Rule Movement (1915-'17) was the fulfilment of a great career working for international fellowship, the last desperate attempt of a British thought-leader to erect a bridge of reconciliation between India and Britain.

Vithalbhai Patel's demonstration of an Indian politician using the resources and limitations of British laws in India to weaken and paralyse British administration in the country.

Babu Mahesh Narayan was one of the unknown makers and builders of modern Behar—unknown to the wider public life of India. He belonged to the type who narrowed their view, so that their sight might be sharpened. Bihar to-day is in the fore-front of India's many fronted battle-line. This proud position has been made possible by the life-work of Babu Mahesh Narayan among others.

Nabin Chandra Bardoloi of Assam and Acharya Gidwani of Sindh came to the national movement carried to it by the swell of new life that flowed into the creeks and corners of India when the flood-gates were opened by Mahatma Gandhi. Their lives, cut short, are a record of promises unfulfilled, and an inspiration to their countrymen.

Ethics of Individuality

With ups and downs the movement of Indian thought and activity had been progressing towards a fuller realization of the meaning of human personality, perfecting itself in a life of co-operative effort in the bosom of society. The early reformers had drawn their inspiration from European social and political experiences. These had laid emphasis on the rights of the individual, society and State being regarded as existing solely to secure respect for these rights. An interpretation of European history has it that 18th. century British liberty was incarnated in a parliament controlling the aristocracy and the monarchy; the paradox resulting therefrom was that the basis of society was not to obey those who governed but to disobey them, control them and make things difficult for them; the economists, Adam Smith and Richardo, and their propagandists, Cobden and Bright, extended the scope of British liberalism by making the State practically 'evanescent' through the bold idea of reducing its functions to as little as possible, giving the State nothing to do but simply allow individuals to exchange the products of their respective labours; this freedom reached its acme in the forties and fifties of the last century. This liberty of person sanctified the institution of private property, thereby securing the ultimate good of society and State. In social ethics the enrichment of human personality was accepted as the ideal end, the reason for existence of society and State. The society and State that did not afford opportunity for this development deserved to be broken. This philosophy had played its part in the evolution of our social and political thought and conduct also in the last quarter of the 19th century. Social usages that barred this claim—the claim of the human personality for free and unfettered development—came in for condemnation and demanded their abolition. As the fight for political freedom widened, and grew intense, recruits from newer stratas of society were drawn to it, the habits of centuries of a social discipline were disturbed, directing a new insight into traditional life.

Ethics of Mass Awakening

The Non-co-operation movement revealed the strength of our social polity by the wide-spread response of the mass-mind, and its weakness by quick relapse into listlessness and indifference. The Khilafat movement has introduced a complexity into Indian life, in so far as it has encouraged the spirit of separatism among Indian Moslems; Moulana Mohammed Ali was the leading spirit in the enunciation of this dual patriotism for Indian Moslems. And the trials and travails of the last fifteen years have not been able to evolve a unity out of this duality. The non-Brahmin movement in southern and westeren India was the fore-runner of a development which proved that the Hindu methods of social reform had failed to satisfy and conciliate normal human feelings—methods that paid homage to spiritual elevation but maintained the rigid distinctions between men and men. In the Maharashtra we find its protagonist in Jotirao Fule (born 1827), the founder of the "*Satya Sodhak* Samaj". He was a remarkable personality, the pioneer of education among non-Brahmins of the lower stratum of society, a prolific writer whose books form "the scripture" of the Samaj. Regarded as an anti-Brahmin, his appreciation of the life and labour of Balwantrao Tilak was sincere, evidence of which he gave by arranging for security for the accused, Balwantrao Tilak and Gopalrao Agarkar, in the Sholapur case. His insight into the economic basis of Indian life was proved by his erecting at his own expense the statue of a peasant at the main gate-way of the Poona Congress (1895). To-day that movement has widened its scope, quickened by the inspiration of Mahatma Gandhi's fight for the down-trodden. The adi-Dravida and the Adi-

Andhra movements in southern India, the Adi-Hindu and their companion activities in other parts of the country, have given rise to particularistic demands and conceits that stand in the way of evolving a coherent and united life in the country. Linguistic provinces are one such factor. They are, however, a necessary and healthy growth. And in the evolution of this idea Madhusudhan Das, the grand old man of Utkal, was one of the pioneers, as rugged an individualist as ever lived. Pandit Gopabandhu Das affiliated this provincial patriotism to the composite nationalism of India under the inspiration of Mahatma Gandhi. After centuries of neglect, of frustrations, liberal concessions fail to make any appeal to men ; in removing conscious causes of grievances, social distinctions and such other inequalities, men do not secure peace. Therefore it is that men propose that the other cause of grievance rampant to-day, the inequalities of wealth, should be removed to secure this peace. This uneasiness and unrest has become world-wide. And India finds itself to-day fighting on two fronts, one against the inequalities of the British rule, the other against the social and economic inequalities of Indian life.

Men *versus* State

The classes of educated Indians who had taken the lead in fighting the former had been taught to respect individual liberty and private property. In the old-world Indian polity individuality in the life spiritual was recognised and encouraged, while in social life and economic arrangements it was sought to be canalized into co-operative efforts, upholding a peculiar balance and harmony. This balance and harmony was maintained by the theory of re-incarnation of souls in a series of lives, beginningless and endless, taking shelter in bodies belonging to different stratas of society, according to their merits and demerits. These beliefs afford no consolation to men to-day. The old oracles are either dumb, or their messages are incomprehensible. The modern oracles are with us. Our discipleship to British theorists still retains its loyalty. The news of the harmony that is being worked out in Britain between the claims of the individual and the needs of State, "recantation" as some would call it, has reached us. Socialism, rather State Socialism has been called a product of the German mind, a product of Bismarckian methods of harnessing the services of the needy to the chariot-wheel of the State, the State that demands the whole of man, and suffers no rival near or about itself. But we in India have not yet been able to fully realize the logic of this development or accept its validity. This is the psychology of the opposition that Pandit Jawahar Lal Nehru's ideology has met with even from his colleagues in the Indian National Congress. The evolution from the idea of State at the service of the individual to that of the State suppressing the individual has not taken a very long time to come its full circle. As they say in the story book, a time came when industrialism, directed and controlled by the individual profit-making instinct, brutalized the poor by over-working them, and men called upon the State to intercede. Thus did the doctrine of *laissez faire* (let alone) come to be regulated. To-day it finds none to do it reverence. And the State has come to its own, as the ruler of men, of their thoughts and activities.

In our country there is only the beginning of industrialism. But there is poverty. And this poverty seems irremovable except by eliminating the instinct for personal and private profit and greed, except by dividing the existing wealth of the country. Men as sensitive to the sufferings of others advise that the need of the hour is the production of more wealth, and not its division here and now. The tumult and the shouting, heard all round the world, are evidences of a wide-awake consciousness that a social and economic adjustment must be worked out if civilized life is to be continued.

Test for India

Thus does India's "home polity" find itself merging into world polity. In India the polity is more complicated; she is the battle-ground of nationalism and socialism. Capture of political power is in many parts of the world a fact realized in the life of the people; they are free to bend their energies to the capture of economic power. In our country both these developments have forced themselves to public view, and demand to be led to their natural culmination. The test for India is more difficult, and more penetrating.

Women's Movement in India

The woman's cause was man's, sang the mid-Victorian poet-laureate of Britain. To-day women have lost faith in that chivalry; men also do not find strength and inspiration in it. As a result, women have decided to claim and have a determining voice in making a new thing of the mis-shapen, man-made world. Science has placed at our hands mighty instruments for making a better world—man has failed to do it. So it was time that woman should take a hand in the affair. The women's movement in India, as represented by the All-India Women's Conference and the innumerable sectional and communal organisations, as a separate activity, gives shape and form to this aspiration on the part of Indian women to play their legitimate and rightful part in building up New India. Individual women in India have gone forth as pioneers, and have proved the possibility of women taking part in public movements and organizing them. The first Indian name that appears of these pioneers, was that of Pandita Ramabai, a Marhatta lady. Mrs. Annie Besant's many-sided activities must have been an inspiration to many women, the products of modern education in India. Education had been accepted as the very lever of all progress, and in this activity women's contributions have been many and varied, both in quantity and quality.

All-India Women's Conference

To-day all these are found synthesized in the All-India Women's Conference. Its history is an interesting story. As in other parts of the world so in India time-forces, to use a hackneyed phrase not quite explanatory of the many developments in social life, have compelled men to call in women to council, on the principle, perhaps, that two heads are better than one. The latest report of the All-India Women's Conference has it that the "original stimulus" of the idea was

> "an appeal made by the Director of Public Instruction, Bengal, at a prize-giving function of the Bethune College, Calcutta, in which he called on Indian Women to '*tell us with one voice what they want, and keep on telling us till they get it.*' Mrs. A. L. Huide-koper, an ex-Principal of Bethune College,.........made use of this appeal

as the basis of two articles which were published in *Stri Dharma*, the monthly magazine of the Women's Indian Association............"

This appeal and the two articles in the *Stri Dharma* led Mrs. Margaret E. Cousin, Secretary of the Women's Indian Association, Adyar (Madras) to address an appeal in the autumn of 1926 to women all over the country "to form local committees and hold Constituent Conferences in each of the provinces and in certain other clearly defined districts and Indian States, for the purpose of declaring their views on problems of education." In response to this appeal Constituent Conferences were held in 22 places during the months of September to December 1926. And the wide and lively enthusiasm evoked by these conferences was solidified in the 1st. session of the All India Women's Conference held at Poona on the 5th to 8th January 1927, with Her Highness Maharani Chimnabai Gaekwad, Maharani of Baroda as President. The resolutions passed related to matters educational only, except the resolution on early-marriage, and another in support of Sir Harising Gour's Age-of-consent Bill. This extension of interest has widened at every session, till to-day no subject of national interest is outside the purview of the Conference, as its "sections" and "sub-committees" testify. There are the educational and social "sections"; there are the Sarda Act sub committee, the Indigenous Industries Sub-Committee, Rural Reconstruction Sub-Committee, and the Sub-Committee on Labour. Women's education in all its stages, social usages that stand in the way of individual and social development, and women working in mines, and factories and mills are the concern of the appropriate committees which study the problems connected therewith and deal with them.

There have been ten sessions of the Conferences, the last held being at Trivandrum, the capital city of Travancore in the last week of December 1935. The second session (1928) was held at Delhi, Her Highness the Begum mother of Bhopal presiding; the third (1929) at Patna, Her Highness the Dowager Rani of Mandi presiding; the fourth (1930), at Bombay, Mrs. Sarojini Naidu presiding; the fifth (1931) at Lahore. Dr. (Mrs.) Muthulakshmi Reddi presiding; the sixth (1932) at Madras, Mrs. P. K. Ray presiding; the seventh (1933) at Lucknow, Lady Ramanbhai Neelkanth presiding; the eighth at Calcutta, Lady Abdul Quadir presiding; the ninth at Karachi, Mrs. Rustomji Furidonji presiding. The tenth session was presided over by Her Highness Maharani Setu Parvati Bayi of Travancore.

Significance of Travancore Conference

There was an appropriateness in the All-India Women's Conference holding its session in Kerala, of which Travancore forms an important unit,—Kerala which is known as "Penmalayam"—"Women's Malayalam." The social polity based on the matriarchal system makes woman the head and fountain of all power and beneficence; succession is traced through her. The tenth session was thus held in the right atmosphere where woman's experience as the head of a State, as the head of family and social life could point out to lessons of efficiency and on equity which ought to be the guide and ideal of the woman's movement in India. These the Maharani-President brought out vividly in her address.

The All India Women's Conference is a non-party and a non-partisan organization. Fortunately for itself it had not to struggle for the political recognition of women in India; that recognition had been won by the great war for British women, and their Indian sisters enjoy the fruits of the labours of the Despards and Pankhursts. The principle that woman has of right a place in the making of laws as she has in the making of the home has been recognized. Indian women have now to work for details some of which they embodied in their Memorandam to the Franchise Committee set up in connection with the Hoare scheme of constitutional changes for India. The claim of Indian women "to fight elections on equal terms with men, in mixed general electorates," as also that with regard to "adult suffrage," and for "no reservation of seats for women as such"—none of them has een accepted by the Government. The "communal decision" of the "National Government" of Britain has disappointed these "clear" demands of Indian women.

Political Affiliation of the Conference

The activities of the Conference are coming into contact with centres of Indian life hitherto neglected by educated women. Dirt, disease and ignorance smother healthy growth in India; when educated women come face to face with them, their removal will become possible and the "life beautiful" will emerge out of them. Then will Indian women contribute "their due share in the task of Nation-building" as they do to-day in building and keeping up homes.

The Future

We have tried to trace India's evolution in course of a hundred years of British rule. The immediate past, the last fifteen years, has witnessed an upheaval, the "high audacity" of which has been an eye-opener to both the rulers and the ruled. The period which is covered by the present volume of the "Annual Register" is marked by calm after a storm—the storm that blowed on the wake of the two Civil Disobedience Movements. The first started under Mahatma Gandhi's personal direction; after his incarceration the momentum received from him carried it through to almost the end of 1930; during the latter months the driving force was imparted by Pandit Matilal Nehru, one of the patricians of an earlier generation with its faith in British generosity and statesmanship intact through many disappointments. To Matilalji the Punjab under Sir Michael O'Dwyer was a revelation. Since then the old man knew no respite from fight, and he died fighting. His contemporary, Pandit Madan Mohan Malaviya, stands as a rock, the symbol of India's eternal quest of freedom and of peace. The Gandhi-Irwin Pact secured a temporary truce; it was valuable as an indication of the true path to reconciliation between the rulers and the ruled, not for any immediate and tangible gain.

Gandhi Irwin Pact & After

What this path is has been sketched by J. Coatman in his book —"Years of Destiny".

"As long as the Indian feels that they are being treated not only fairly, but as equals, they are not a difficult people to deal with, and Lord Irwin's unprecedented action had given the Indian people the strongest possible assurance that he, at any rate, was not going to allow any false notion of prestige to stand in the way of his dealing with any of their leaders on terms which they could accept without any possible feelings of resentment"

Lord Willingdon succeeded to the Irwin method. He spoke of his ambition to go down to history "as the first constitutional Governor-general" in India. But fate decreed otherwise. He was not, to quote the words of an American author, perhaps temperamentally, perhaps forced by imperial policy, "one to adopt the Conference method in the manner of his predecessor". Therefore do we find him rejecting Mahatma Gandhi's offer as carried in his wire of 29th. December 1931—"whether you expect me to see you and receive guidance from you as to the course I am to pursue in advising the Congress". The historian of India need not go further than the American writer in his judgment on Lord Willingdon's regime.

Lord Linlithgow

His Excellency Lord Linlithgow does not come to the country as a "stranger". He came to India as Chairman of the Royal Agricultural Commission, and got to know something of the "real life" of the people. His interest in agricultural life and progress in his own country finds outlets and opportunities for wider service to the teeming agricultural population in India. His meeting a batch of Deccani agriculturists on landing in Bombay as Governor-General is significant of developments in rural life. In his first speech broadcasted to all parts of India and addressed to all classes he exhorts the "Civil Service" to "know your villages", and offers a new interpretation of their duties in eloquent words—"For you in your own generation it remains abundantly true that the tent is mighter than the pen". These words of Lord Linlithgow convey to us hints of a new policy which he desires to pursue in India. Whether this policy is inspired by personal inclination or by the necessities of a State where agriculturists form the majority of the population, it is not necessary to enquire now. In the long role of British administrators in India one other name only emerges who was sincerely interested in agricultural life and progress ; it is Lord Mayo's. During his tenure of office the Department of Commerce and Agriculture was inaugurated. The State in India was the biggest landlord, a "great forest proprietor," and a "great mineral proprietor". The exploitation of these riches was part of the duty of the administration co-operatively with British enterprise. Lord Mayo was the first to realise the importance, financial and political, of this dual function. His insight into India's agricultural condition, and methods of its improvement, is acutely expressed in his notes :

> "I do not know what is precisely meant by 'amoniac manure' If it means guano, super-phosphate or any artificial product of the kind, we might as well ask the people of India to manure their ground with champagne"

Again, in another note, he writes

> "In connection with agriculture we must be careful of two things. First, we must not ostentatiously tell native husbandmen to do things which they have been doing for centuries. Second, we must not tell them to do things which they can't do, and have no means of doing. In either case, they will laugh at us, and they will learn to disregard really useful advance when it is given"

We do not know if these warnings of Lord Mayo's were called forth by "experts" or enthusiasts in his time in India. The same warnings have need of repetition by Lord Linlithgow to the "experts" and enthusiasts who have been crowding into India at the invitation of the Government.

"The cultivator tilling his fields remains as ever the backbone of this country and the foundation of her prosperity", said Lord Linlithgow in reply to the address of the Bombay Corporation. The peasantry of India on whose shoulders rest the huge fabric of a modern government are, however, unequal to maintaining this burden. Long ago Lord Cromer (he was then Evelyn Baring) recognized that India could support at best a cheap despotism. And British rule, however benevolent, is a very costly despotism, or bureaucracy if one must have it so. Over and above this, a debt of Rs. 1,800 crores is crushing all hope and all initiative out of him whose "life is a long-drawn question between a crop and a crop". And the government of Lord Linlithgow must look on helpless faced by a poverty as wide as this, and a distress which centuries have taught the trick of remaining mute and silent. Other countries may do brave things for the relief of unemployment ; we in India have nothing better than the vaguest of idea of unemployment figures in the country. The government cannot show any better knowledge in the matter. Rural decay is a fact and continues to be so, for men flee from decay. The Imperial Council of Agricultural Research which hopes to successfully battle with this decay by reviving rural industries, by its "planned campaign for the uplift of the ryot," will need the goodwill and the co-operation of all. The conditions of successfully enlisting that good-will and co-operation have yet to be fulfilled. Debt Redemption and Conciliation Acts can touch but the fringe of the problem. Rural credit has been shaken by these Acts, and Land Mortgage Banks under State-control will take decades to take shape and be able to meet even a moiety of the whole demand for agricultural short-time credit. Co-operative banks play a very insignificant part in offering facilities to the peasantry in need of cash. The Indian Central Banking Enquiry Committee's majority report present certain figures which are revealing in this connection. In Bombay the financial requirement of the agricultural population was Rs. 32 crores 50 lakhs ; the co-operative organisations supplied about Rs. 2 crores 20 lakhs. In Bengal the short and medium term need was for Rs. 96 crores, as against Rs. 4 crores supplied. In Madras no provincial estimate was forthcoming ; in its absence the estimate of the Tanjore district helped to arrive at an idea ; the cost of one crop of paddy in the wet delta area was Rs. 3 crores 50 lakhs ; the co-operative societies supplied Rs. 17 lakhs 50 thousand. In face of these needs, and the widening responsibilities that provincial governments are preparing themselves to assume, the controversies over the Niemeyer report and the heart-burning and provincial jealousies developed, appear how unreal and how petty !

Rural Indebtedness

Economists, administrative or theoretical, have been trying to stir up public opinion to the danger of over-population in the country. They assert that by 1941, the population will number 40 crores which the present national income will be unable to maintain. The pessimist among them say that the problem of "relieving the growing pressure on the soil is insoluble" and that the fullest industrial development cannot hope

Over-population & Unemployment

to absorb more than 30 lakhs of workers, that is making provision for the maintenance of one crore and a half of men, women and children. In 1921 an estimate showed that there were about 5 crores agriculturists who have been forced out of their lands. How few of these have found employment? A question which none can give a satisfactory reply to. Indian Society has never cared to consciously trouble its head over this problem, depending on nature and nature's God to establish a satisfactory relation and proportion between feeding mouths and provision for food. To such a society these warnings and exhortations—what are they but "bourgeoise" economics, inspired by communal considerations! When the political future of the country is to be ruled by communal votes, every community must strive to return an increasing number at each successive census' to the confusion of all economists. Communal cries will fill hungry mouths. How does his Excellency Lord Linlithgow propose to cure this madness? In a letter of his addressed to the heads of provincial governments appear the words: "........... there is no point in trying to improve the breed of cattle if the fodder is not there for their nourishment". The same question with the substitution of the word "men" for "cattle", is writ large over India, waiting for a reply.

Political Prospect

Lord Linlithgow has succeeded to a political stale-mate in the country. The Indian National Congress may cease from troubling, and may be at rest from weariness. But the dissatisfaction that the Congress voices, has it ceased or has it sought rest? Reply to this question must be the quest of his Excellency. What the Government of India Act of 1935 was intended to secure for British interests Lord Linlithgow knows, for it is partly his handi-work. What it secures to India we can imagine. The British Parliament is anxious to endow Indians with "real responsibility for Indian social conditions". Social conditions to-day are incapable of divorce from economic and political factors. These economic and political factors have not been made amenable to Indian initiative and Indian control. How Lord Linlithgow proposes to shape these within the frame-work of the Government of India Act only the future can show. It would be unjust to anticipate developments and pass judgment thereon. Lord Linlithgow also is not free; he must fit himself into the system which has passed through many transformations. But the spirit of domination that has informed its activities in connection with the "dependent" parts of the empire remains, retaining its old-time vigour. This is the meaning of the "safeguards" which Lord Linlithgow must defend in the interests of Britain. Bearing in mind even all this, there will be few Indians who cannot respond to his appeal to remember him in their prayers. (*Specially contributed by Sj. Suresh Chandra Deb.*)

King George the V's Reign

Early Life

His Most Excellent Majesty George V, King of Great Britain and Ireland and the British Dominions beyond the Seas and Emperor of India was the only surviving son of King Edward VII and Queen Alexandra. He was born at Marlborough House, London on June 3, 1865, and when four years old he and his elder brother, Prince Albert Victor, who was two years his senior, were placed under the tutorship of the Rev. John Neale Dalton, the curate of Sandringham.

In the year 1877, Prince George was sent with his elder brother the late Duke of Clarence to the *Britannia*, there to be trained for a naval career. The brothers were as dissimilar in appearance as in temperament—the elder fragile of frame, thoughtful and pensive ; the younger (Prince George) though not very robust physically, full of vigour, high-spirited with an under-current of mischievous humour. They were placed in the tutorial charge of Mr. Lawless, and except for the fact that they were berthed in separate cabin, shared the ordinary life and routine of the ship. It was not an easy routine by any means, for the lads were on deck at half-past six, and had to use their muscles as well as brains. They were taught the humbler arts of seamanship—the management of sailing boats, sail-making, rope-splicing and other duties essential for a naval career. The two Princes remained on the *Britannia* for about two years, and during the whole of the time the vessel was stationary in the River Dart.

Their course on the *Britannia* completed, the two Princes were sent to H. M. S. *Bacchante* to learn their business in great waters and see the wonders of the world, especially those of the British Empire. Prince George was then just over fourteen, and was a lively dashing lad with a reputation among his comrades for dash and masterfulness. They went first to the West Indies, crossed back to the island off West Africa, rounded the Cape, went south to Australia, and thence to Fiji, Yokahama Hongkong and Singapore, returning home via the Suez Canal, with an excursion ashore into the Holy Land. Thus by the time he was sixteen Prince George had seen far more of the world and its divers races than had ever any Prince of the West or the East

Prince George took to the life with a zest that was to make him one of the best naval officers of his time, and he was an excellent mathematician, with the makings of a senior wrangler.

At the close of this tour in 1882 the brothers separated. Prince George, who remained in the naval service was appointed to H. M. S. *Canada*, commanded by Captain Durrant, on the North American and West Indian Station, and was promoted sub-lieutenant. On his return home he passed through the Royal Naval College at Greenwich and the gunnery and torpedo schools, being promoted lieutenant in 1885.

A year later he was appointed to H. M. S. *Thunderer* of the Mediterranean Squadron, and was subsequently transferred to H. M. S. *Dreadnought* and H. M. S. *Alexandra*. In 1889 he joined the flagship of the Channel Squadron, H. M. S. *Northumberland* and in that year was in command of torpedo boat No. 79 for the naval manoeuvers. In 1890 he was put in command of the gunboat H. M. S. *Thrush* for service on the North American and West Indian Station. After his promotion as Commander in 1891 he commissioned H. M. S. *Melampus*, the command of which he relinquished on the death of his brother, Albert Victor, the Duke of Clarence, in January 1892, since his duties as eventual heir to the Crown precluded from devoting himself exclusively to the Navy. He was promoted Captain in 1893, Rear-Admiral in 1901, and Vice-Admiral in 1903.

The Prince obtained his promotion to the *Thrush* by a fine bit of semanship during the naval manœuvres of 1899, when he was in charge of one of the torpedo boats and in a driving gale off the Irish coast succeeded in rescuing a disabled consort.

In November, after a visit to Ireland, he was stricken by an attack of enteric fever. The Princess of Wales was in Russia at the time, and the Prince took upon himself the superintendence of his son's nursing, and hardly left his bedside till the Princess arrived. Happily Prince George recovered, but he had hardly done so when a terrible blow fell on the happy family at Sandringham. The Duke of Clarence

(Prince Eddy) caught a chill early in January, which quickly took a serious turn, and he passed away on January 14.

This sad event placed Prince George in direct succession to the throne, and he assumed his new responsibilities with a seriousness for which he was hardly credited during his breezy sailor days. It also meant giving up his active career in the Navy, which was a great disappointment to him, for although he occasionally got to sea again, it was only at irregular intervals.

After his brother's death Prince George was created Duke of York, and his marriage became a question of great importance and interest, not only to the Royal Family, but to the nation at large.

There was a universal feeling of satisfaction when it was announced that he was engaged to an English Princess, the only daughter of the Duke and Duchess of Teck. Of all the ladies of the Royal Family there was none more popular and beloved than Princess Mary of Cambridge, Duchess of Teck. Her good nature, sympathy, and untiring work in the cause of charity endeared her to all classes. Her daughter, Princess Victoria Mary—Princess "May", as she was then called—brought up in the simple home life of White Lodge, Richmond, entered society with a strong claim on the affections of public as her mother's daughter, and made the claim good by her own personal charm and attractiveness. It is not surprising therefore, that the wedding caused intense pleasure and enthusiasm. It was celebrated at the Chapel Royal, St. James, on July 6, 1893, in the presence of Queen Victoria. Ten princesses, all granddaughters of the queen, attended the bride as bridesmaids. After the wedding the Duke and Duchess of York took up their residence at York Cottage, Sandringham, and at York House, St. James's.

Later in the year, they made some thing like a royal "progress" to Edinburgh and York, and on their return commenced that busy public life as representative of the Crown, which fitted them so admirably for the exalted position they were destined to occupy in the future. Every year was a continual round of laying foundation-stones, opening buildings, and attending public functions in London and the large manufacturing towns of England, varied by visits to Ireland, Scotland and Wales.

Meanwhile a new generation was growing up at York Cottage. On June 33, 1894, Prince Edward was born at White Lodge. Prince Albert, now Duke of York, was born on December 14, 1895, and Princess Mary came to grace the Queen's Diamond Jubilee in 1897. But a great grief came upon the family before the end of the Jubilee year, when the Duchess of Teck died at White Lodge on October 27. In 1900 a third son Prince Henry, was born to the Duke and Duchess of York.

For some time before the death of Queen Victoria the idea of the Duke of York making a tour of the British Colonies had been under consideration and in the year 1900 the plan took definite form. The loyal rally of the colonies to the help of the mother country in her hour of need in South Africa seemed to demand some recognition from the Sovereign, and the opening of the first Parliament of the Australian Commonwealth was a fitting opportunity for the Duke of York to visit Australia. All the arrangements had already been made when Queen Victoria passed away in January 1901, but as it was by her express desire that the Duke of York was undertaking the tour, it was not abandoned. On March 16, escorted by two cruisers, the Duke and Duchess of Cornwall and York set sail in the Orient liner *Ophir* commanded by a crew of the Royal Navy. At Gibraltar, Their Royal Highnesses were welcomed by Sir George White, and at Malta by Sir John Fisher. In Ceylon they were shown the sacred tooth of Budha, and the Duke was able to perform an act of of clemency by securing the return of the exiled Arabi to his native land of Egypt. At Singapore the Duke received the Malay Sultans and the Duchess received their wives. On coming to the equator the Duke, although he had crossed the line before, good-humouredly submitted to the attentions of King Neptune, and took his "saving" and his ducking with a smile, *pour encourager les autres*.

The real business of the tour began at Melbourne. On May 9, in the great Exhibition building the Duke opened the first Parliament of the Australian Commonwealth and the Union Jack was run up over every school in Australia. From Melbourne the Royal party proceeded to Ballarat, Sydney, and Brisbane. They inspected the mines, visited the stockmen in the up-country stations, and in Queensland witnessed a boomerang-throwing performance by the aborigines. At all the large towns, both in Australia and New Zealand, the chief feature of their welcome was the parade of the school children and cadets. How many of these sturdy school boys were to give their lives for the King and Empire fifteen years later in Gallipoli, France and Palestine !

The Duke had many reminders of his *Bacchante* visit, such as the trees he and his brother planted at Melbourne; but perhaps the one which appealed most to his sporting instincts was the quail shooting, reminiscent of the policeman's "quail call."

From Australia the *Ophir* steamed to New Zealand, and on June 4 arrived at Auckland, where the Duke and Duchess were welcomed by Mr. Seddon, the premier. Perhaps the most interesting event in New Zealand was the visit to the native settlement when the Maori chief returned to the Duke all the presents they had received from Queen Victoria, to show how carefully they have kept them. Of course he gave them back again. Then followed a great demonstration of native songs and dances, which Their Royal Highnesses witnessed wearing the kiwi mats or mantles which had been presented to them.

From New Zealand the *Ophir* returned to Tasmania and Adelaide, and a cross-country railway journey was made to Perth and the mining district of Coolgarde.

The voyage was continued *via* Mauritius to South Africa, where Natal and Capetown were visited, and then across the Atlantic to Canada. Great receptions awaited them at Quebec, Ottawa and Montreal, and at these Canadian cities, as in Australia and New Zealand, war medals were presented to the troops who had fought in South Africa, and now and then a Victoria Cross was pinned on a proud and gallant breast. After a day spent in shooting the rapids with the "lumberman" came the long railway journey to Winnipeg, and a visit to the Red Indian chief near Calgary, then across the Rocky Mountains (the Duke riding on the "cow-catcher" of the engine), to British Columbia and Vancouver Island. The return journey gave the Royal party a change of seeing Toronto and the Falls of Niagara.

On October 31, the *Ophir* left Halifax for home, and soon after arrival—on King Edward's birthday, November 9—the Duke of Cornwall and York was created Prince of Wales and Earl of Chester.

A banquet was given at Guildhall on December 5 to welcome Their Royal Highnesses at home. In the course of his speech the Prince startled the assembly with that famous phrase "Wake up, England !" which next day was on everybody's lips.

As Duke of Cornwall, the heir to the throne had already done a great work in strengthening the bonds of union between the British Colonies and the motherland, and had widely increased his personal knowledge of that great Empire over which he was destined to rule. As Prince of Wales he began a career of usefulness at home as the right-hand man of the King. His position differed somewhat from that of his father during the long reign of Queen Victoria. There was not now a monarch living in semi-retirement at Balmoral and Osborne, but a real live King and Queen holding a brilliant court at Buckingham Palace and Windsor. But there was no rivalry of opposition between the King and the Prince. The latter had his own private circle of friends, chiefly his old companions in the Navy, but he and the Princess liked to be with the King and Queen when their engagements permitted, and were frequently to be seen at Sandringham and Windsor, and in the Highlands.

To the Fleet also the King paid several visits, and though here he did not find the excitement and the same sense of nearness to the actual conflict, his old associations with the Navy and his intimate knowledge of the life of the Senior Service invested these visits with special interest for him. Moreorer, though for long periods the perilous and unpretentious service of the Navy was receiving little attention from the general public, the King followed all its doings with close attention and an understanding eye. The sea Lords who had audience of the King had always to take great care that they were well-informed.

In every activity in which the Queen could collaborate with the King, Her Majesty was his indefatigable supporter. But there were some feminine movements, like Queen Mary's Army Auxiliary Crops and the Needle-work Guild which were particularly the Queen's care. Her interest in such movements was so real that she contrived to make their leaders feel that they were personally answerable to their Queen for the efficient discharge of their duties, and that achievement had a remarkable influence on the organisations to which she lent her name or patronage.

At about three o'clock on the morning of 7th May, 1910, the Admiralty yacht "*Enchantress*," making for Plymouth from the coast of Spain, received a wireless message of such a nature that it was taken at once to the cabin in which the Prime Minister, Mr. Asquith, was sleeping. It was a message which fully justified the urgency with which it was transmitted.

"I am deeply grieved," it ran, "to inform you that my beloved father, the King, passed away peacefully to-night.

George

After receiving such news it was impossible for the Prime Minister to resume his rest. He dressed and went up on the deck to reflect upon the meaning of these tidings, which had fallen upon him with shocking suddenness. Such an event had been so little anticipated that, barely a week ago, Mr. Asquith had set out with the First Lord of the Admiralty (Mr. Reginald McKenna) for a visit to Gibraltar. The first intimation that the King's health was anything but normal had been received the previous day. For a first bulletin it was distinctly alarming, for it was described the King's condition as "most critical." At once the yacht had been turned about, and it was making for England with all speed when the fateful news was received.

On his meditations under the stars as the ship cut its way through calm waters, the Prime Minister recorded later: "I felt bewildered, and indeed stunned. At a most anxious moment in the fortunes of the State we had lost, without warning or preparation, the Sovereign whose ripe experience, trained sagacity, equitable judgment and unvarying consideration counted for so much...His successors, with all his fine and engaging qualities, was without political experience. We were nearing a crisis without example in our constitutional history."

Asquith, never a man to use the language of sensation, did not exaggerate the gravity of the political situation in which King George came to the throne.

It was, as Asquith said, "a crisis without example." At no time had the House of Lords rejected the Budget and thus challenged the right of the Commons to control the finances of the country.

Challenge to Lords

The Lords had previously rejected some measures put forward by the Liberal Government, and Liberals had begun to feel that the right of the Lords to thwart the elected Government of the day should be challenged in decisive fashion. Because the Peers had always looked upon the Budget as something exempt from their veto, the Government chose the Budget as the measure that would provide the test case. They planned it to goad the Peers, and it succeeded. Once the Lords began to talk of rejecting it, the only anxiety of the Liberals was lest the Peers should change their minds and thus deprive the Ministry of an issue upon which they could dissolve Parliament and ask the country as to whether this veto of the Peers was consistent with a system of democratic government.

There were wise Conservatives who saw the peril in which the Lords were placing themselves. Better swallow the Budget now than be obliged later to wash with a cup of hemlock. To invite an election, they argued, would be to give a new lease of life to a Government whose popularity was already suffering after four years of office. But the Lords did not heed these advisers. They rejected the Budget. Parliament was dissolved and, in January 1910, the Liberals came back to office; but dependent for their majority upon the Irish Nationalists who did not care for the Budget and were interested only in self-government for Ireland. Still the Liberals maintained that they had secured a mandate to abolish the veto of the House of Lords.

After that, of course, the lords let the Budget pass. But worse was to come, so far as they were concerned. They would be faced by a Bill which would limit very drastically their power over all future legislation. In other words, as an effective Chamber, they would be invited to commit suicide.

And suppose they refused ?

That was where King Edward was drawn into this very dangerous situtation. He would be advised by his Ministers to create a sufficient number of new peers (about 300) to overwhelm the conservative majority in the Lords and thus ensure the passage of the measure.

Before the January election the possibility of his receiving that advice was considered by King Edward, but he cherished the hope that if the Liberals were returned, the House of Lords would not allow the situation to drift to a deadlock that could be solved only by such a fantastic procedure. But should the worst come to the worst he would not take the decisive step unless another election were held in which the terms of the Bill for reforming the Lords was before the country.

The Liberals having come back, and the Lords having passed the Finance Bill, the question of curbing the power of the Peers became the next issue. At this stage in the development of the crisis King Edward died.

What would be the attitude towards this grave problem of the new Monarch who, "with all his fine and engaging qualities was without political experience." Much hung upon his personal view and handling of the situation, because there was no categorical pledge from King Edward that could be considered binding upon his successor.

The accession of King George improved the atmosphere somewhat. Everyone concerned in the controversy showed a sportsmanlike sympathy with him in the inheritance of this thorny problem. In such an atmosphere it was possible, with the King's active encouragement, to bring the parties into conference on the subject with a view to an agreed solution.

For part of the summer, and again after the vacation, on into the late autumn, representatives of the parties laboured in secret to find a way out of the impasse, but in November Asquith was obliged to report to the King that agreement was impossible. The crisis, after subsiding, had attained another peak. The King was informed that his Ministers were not willing to continue under the old conditions of veto, nor could they advise him to dissolve Parliament unless they had the "reasonable assurance" of the King that, if necessary, he would use his powers of peer-making to swamp the resistance of the House of Lords.

It was an unhappy situation for the new Sovereign, but observed Asquith, "I have never seen the King to better advantage." What impressed the Prime Minister was the way in which the King listened to reasoned argument, recognised that for neither his Ministers nor himself was there any course but the one advised. At the King's wish, the new Parliament Bill was put before the House of Lords before the dissolution, and in December the country was in the throes of a general election for the second time in that eventful year.

In theory, the plan was simple. If the Liberals were returned, it would mean that the Bill for reforming the Lords had been considered and approved by the country; and, after that, surely the Lords would submit without compelling the King to make Peers by the hundred. If the Conservatives came back, then the Bill had been killed by the people; and no peer-making would be necessary.

What happened was that the parties returned in the same numbers as previously. The election did not show that swing of opinion in one way or the other which would have made for peace. So the wrangle continued with even greater asperity.

Worst of all, the King's name was bandied about the political arena. A lesser man might have been tempted to intervene personally, to breathe the spirit of compromise and endeavour to find a formula of agreement. It seemed the natural thing for the King to do. But it would have beeen constitutionally improper.

There were many, very many, outside the ranks of the Government who would have liked audience of the King with a view to advising him. But the King has only one set of political advisers—the Government. Not until he had ascertained that there would be no objection from the Prime Minister did His Majesty receive even Lord Lansdowne, the Leader of the Conservatives in the House of Lords, and then only to obtain a first-hand report of the views of the dissentient Peers and not to hear advice.

The Lords fought to the last. So probable did it seem that the King would have to act, that Asquith drew up a list of those who would provide the reinforcements for the Upper house. Nevertheless, to the cry of, "Shall we perish in the dark by our own hands, or in the light, kindled by our enemies?" the Peers gave way, and, in the words of one commentator, disappointed three hundred commoners who were "trembling on the brink of ennoblement."

Six years later when the solution of another vexatious problem had been reached, the King wrote to his Prime Minister, "You and I have passed through some strenuous and critical times, and once again, thank God, we have "weathered the storm." The political upheaval of 1910-11 was the first of those crises; and, for the King, it must have been the most difficult, not only because he was new to his responsibilities, but also because the stress of it fell where human nature is weakest. The situation called not so much for action, but for infinite patience and restraint. The natural instinct of a man called to an exhalted office is to exercise his powers. In this the King was required, right at the outset of his reign, to show an unfailing awareness of the limitations of his authority, to tread very closely to the boundary of his powers without ever setting a foot over the line. And that he did with supreme success.

Later, the King's relationship towards his Ministers was different in one important respect from what it was in those earlier times. Then he was a new Sovereign surrounded by Ministers who had long experience of statesmanship. Afterwards he had the experience of a quarter of a century at his command. Because of the King's aloofness from party interests people did not think readily of the unique store of knowledge, of measures and of men, which informed his mind when he dealt with affairs of State.

The conception of a Prime Minister who had been continuously in office for twenty-five years afforded an estimate of the accumulated experience which was at the King's disposal. During the period a succession of statesmen of differing schools of thought, each an expert in political matters, discussed with the King—intimately, privately and without reservation—the problems of the country. Overseas statesmen whose names would make a formidable catalogue had similar talks with the King, while foreign Sovereigns, statesmen and envoys laid before him their view of the problems of the work at large. Having no sectional interests to serve, no last ditch of party pride or policy to defend, His Majesty had a freedom of mind which many of his political visitors envied and respected. His influence at times when party passions ran high was of unestimable value to the country and the empire.

Time and again statesmen testified to the King's conscientious study of all the matters submitted to him, and to his remarkable grasp of the essentials of every piece of business which they were required to discuss with him. The late Lord Brentford (Sir William Joynson-Hicks) had a lawyer's mind quick to appreciate whether the person with whom he was conferring had mastered his case. It was he who said that the Minister who went to the Palace with his case inadequately prepared would soon find himself in a dilemma.

Lord Bentford revealed, also, that inspite of the mass of papers which the King had to read, His Majesty lost no time in dealing with them. At a morning audience, the King discussed a certain matter with his Home Secretary. "Sir," said "Jix," in surprise, "I sent the paper on that matter to the Cabinet only yesterday afternoon." "Quite true," replied the King, "but I read it yesterday evening."

That an audience of the King was a strictly business-like proceeding was obvious from the news of the King's daily round. The time of His Majesty and of the statesmen concerned was too valuable to be spent in dealing with subjects which could be disposed of by action between their respective secretaries.

Eve of Great War

At times of crisis the King adopted his routine to meet the exigencies of the situation. On the eve of the War he came from his bed in the small hours of the morning and, clad in a dressing gown, had a consultation with the Prime Minister and Lord Tyrrell (then Private Secretary to Sir Edward Grey) about an eleventh-hour telegram to Russia that might turn the scales in favour of peace.

Every considerate person recognized that the lives of the King and Queen would become intolerable were visitors to retail details of their private conversations. If their Majesties had always to be on their guard, always thinking of the possibility of publication before they uttered a word, there would have been an end to that natural conversation with visitors which made it possible for the King and Queen to keep themselves informed of all that was going on in the workaday life of the country. But a trickle of anecdotes inevitably escaped, and of these none was more characteristic of the King than the story told of the first visit to the Palace of a newly appointed Overseas Governor (now dead) who was to receive a knighthood. He was a Labour man of humble beginnings who had been a worker in the furniture trade, of which fact the King was aware. The visitor had regarded the visit with trepidation, and when the investing ceremony was over he found himself tongue-tied with nervousness and emotion. Whereupon, said the report, the King took his arm in the most friendly fashion, and led him to a more intimate room with the remark : "Come along Sir James, let us talk of cabinet-making—not my sort, but your's." And they did.

"Alone on the terrible height !" exclaimed Tennyson, after a conversation with Queen Victoria. King George occupied that same terrible height, and he sustained the spectacular duties and individual responsibilities of that eminence with simple dignity and admirable correctness. But he knew the way down, and the actions that won for him the warm affection of a race which does not give its affection readily, was achieved on that plane where one touch of nature and human understanding make the whole world kin.

Visit to India

King George has unique distinction among British sovereigns of having visited India twice—once as Prince of Wales in 1905-06—when he laid the foundation stone of the Victoria Memorial Hall in Calcutta—and again as King-Emperor, when his coronation was celebrated at the never-to-be-forgotten Delhi Durbar of 1911.

Both these visits were made, so to say, before the Flood—before the catastrophe of the Great War and the profound changes in the social and political atmosphere which have resulted from the Montagu-Chelmsford Reforms.

It is difficult to realize the comparative tranquillity which prevailed in India. especially at a time of the first visit. Discontent was practically non-existent. Political agitation had not advanced beyond the mildest constitutional methods, and this despite the fact that the partition of Bengal had produced an excitement greater than had been witnessed since the Ilbert Bill. Boycott, it is true, had been born..............

First Calcutta Visit

Elaborate precautions were of course taken in 1905-06 for the protection of Their Royal Highness all over India, but, like other members of the Royal Family the Prince (as he then was) and even the Princess (now Queen Mary) defied the police measures and came into close contact with their subjects. This was actually the case in 1912, when a brilliant Pageant was staged on the Calcutta Maidan in honour of Their Imperial Majesties. There was an enormous concourse numbering anything up to 500,000 people ; and after the Pageant the Royal carriage moved off as if to return to Government House.

To the general consternation, however, it suddenly turned and made the entire circuit of the amphitheatre, driving along the edge of the cheering crowds. This unrehearsed effect was Their Majesties' own idea, and it made a marked impression on public opinion, which had been violently stirred by the transfer of the capital to Delhi and by the sudden rearrangement of provinces announced in connextion with that change. The spectre of anarchist outrages had also been present for several years, and there was a real concern for Their Majesties on this account.

The excitement created in Bengal by the Impertial visit in 1911-12. was extraordinary. At least a million people from the districts flocked into Calcutta—some of them the poorest and most ignorant of their kind—all eager to obtain *Darshan*—that is, a glimpse of the face of the *Badshah* (Emperor)—for they believed that it would wipe away the sins of a life-time. The writer recollects talking to a poor old woman on the Maidan who had come to Calcutta from a great distance for this purpose, and was waiting to see Their Majesties when they came out from the service at the Cathedral.

Great Delhi Durbar

The great Durbar at Delhi was an unforgettable experience For nearly a month at least two million people were encamped in and round the Ridge, and every day there were feasts, tournaments and other *tamashas* leading up to and away from the great Durbar. The Durbar itself was a gorgeous spectacle, which has been recorded by pen and brush in a thousand descriptions. Its most sensational feature was the unexpected announcement that the capital was to be changed from Calcutta to Delhi —a surprise which had been prepared in secret by Lord Hardinge and Lord Crewe and was now thurst into the mouth of His Majesty. It was a masterstroke of diplomacy for the change having been announced by the King-Emperer in person there could be no undoing it. But the indignation and excitement which it aroused increased the anxieties of those responsible for Their Majesties' safety. How necessary were the precautions taken at Delhi in 1911, was proved a year later, when Lord Hardinge himself was bombed and nearly killed while riding up the Gandhi Chowk on an elephant during what was intended to be his first triumphant entry into the new capital.

King George, it may be mentioned, made his entry on horseback and surrounded by such a crowd of generals that it was a little difficult to pick out His Majesty from the red-coated horse-men surrounding him.

While both the King and Queen enjoyed their visits to the great centres, there can be no doubt that King George's happiest hours in India were spent in the jungles of Nepal, where he shot tiger and lived the simple life of the hunter for a fortnight. The select party which accompanied the King found him delightful company and said his reputation as a marksman was well sustained.

In an article on political development in India during the late King's reign, the *Times* points out that in another way the Durbar was pregnant with meaning.

When King George returned from his earlier visit to India, he had laid great stress on the need of approaching Indian problems with sympathy and understanding. How seriously he had meant those words was emphasized by the announcement of 1911. The men of the Indian Army became eligible for the most highly prized of all military decorations. Large grants were to be made for the promotion of popular education. Above all the capital of British India was to be transferred from Calcutta, emphatically the creation of British blood and energy, to the most famous of all the capitals of India—to Delhi, the city of Indian Imperial tradition.

Many missed at the time the true significance of the decision; but event after event has since driven it home. It meant the coming transformation of that all-British Government which had dominated India for over a century, which had recognized the administration, which had suppressed internal wars, which had secured the highways for unarmed travellers, and which, by the precept of education and the example of high ideals, had breathed new spirit into a great country, exhausted, impoverished, and demoralised by the collapse of its Government and the conflicts of its peoples.

The development of the ideas implicit in his Majesty's announcements at Delhi forms the outstanding feature of the King's reign in India. It is needless to recite the details of the measures taken all those years ago, or of those since taken. But the multiplication of Indians in the Services, the progressive limitation of the numbers of Englishmen recruited, the formation of exclusively Indian military units, the revival of the old Indian Marine under the proud title of the Royal Indian Navy and the creation of an Indian Flying Corps are all striking evidences of the changed attitude, while the recognition on all hands of Dominion status as the goal of British statesmanship makes the King-Emperor's reign the most remarkable period of Indian political history.

While on the political side the developments of the last quarter of a century have been of outstanding importance, the physical memorials are no less striking. Foremost among them must always be reckoned the creation of the new capital. Not very long ago the visitor would have regarded Delhi as a city belonging together to the past. Perhaps no spot on earth has been more often soaked in blood, or offers more reminders of the vanity of riches and the transience of power.

Of Mogul might there remain one splendid and many deserted tombs; of past magnificence of the only living emblems are the golden-crested hoopoes playing on the lawns of the palace. But all the old cities of Delhi grew up under the shadow and protection of fortresses. The new one lies open to the world, cunningly planned, a superb monument to the power which an unnumbered multitude of Indians helped to establish, and which they would not willingly see fall. Here at all events is an answer to those critics who used to complain that the memorials of British rule in India were utilitarian only, for the New Delhi is an unquestioned work of genius.

And yet ought we have been ashamed if our memorials had after all been merely useful? Dalhousie planning the first railways of India and laying out its lines of telegraphs, was accomplishing work of which the greatness, as measured by results, we can still hardly estimate. Nothing more closely affects the lives of men and the nature of society than the ease with which persons can move from place to place and make contact with others. Despite the cultural unity of ancient India, its distances most effectively prevented the development of economic or political union. In that sense Dalhousie was more truly the founder of Indian nationalism than any other individual. The influences which he brought to bear have in our own days become yet more intensively powerul. To the railway succeeds the aeroplane, and the telegraph is supplemented by wireless broadcast.

The consequences of developing communications are both moral and economic. But in the narrower economic sphere results of the first importance have been achieved. The development of means by which natural forces may be harnessed in the service of man has made great strides in the last quarter of a century, and in India progress has been relatively enormous. The extension of the use of electric light and power, with improvement in the conditions of factory work and reduction of both the effort and danger of mining, has meant much. Twenty-five years ago electricity was new in India; to-day it lights and cools all the larger centres. The disappearance of the inconvenient, ineffective, and dangerous oil-lamp, the advantage of the electric fan over the tired and sleepy punkah-coolie, the ease with which air-conditioning plants can be installed and operated, all have tended powerfully to relieve the strain and temper the influence of an enervating climate. Over large regions, too, hydro-electric schemes have been, or are being, brought to fruition. The Tata hydro-electric scheme in Western India and the other great hydro-electric scheme which has done much to transform a wide tract of Northern India are outstanding memorials of this development.

In all these ways, and many more the influence and ideas of the Western world have been pressing hard on the ancient land of India. Even when all allowance has been made for that perspective time which exaggerates the extent of the changes which a man has personally witnessed, India has changed more rapidly and more greatly than even during the 63 years of the reign of Queen Victoria. The truth seems to be that for a long time the results of a continuing movement are slow and small. It attacks the fringes, it affects individuals but it seems to leave the great mass inert and unaltered. So it has been in India. There until the close of the nineteenth century it was possible to believe the Western influence while evident in the cities, had not actually touched those endless plains of villages and fields which form the real India. The good, in fact, had only reached the top of the bund and here and there begun to slip over, carrying with it a few grains of earth. That was the state of affairs when King George ascended the throne. Since then the bund of long established custom has been breached. The result in a way has been a period of stress confusion, and uncertainty. But it has been marked throughout by the pressure of one consistent policy. The King, his Ministers, his Viceroys, and his people have desired and sought to modernize India.

Britain's Entry into the War

Of the causes of Great Britain's entry into the Great War—which is likely to remain incomparably the most historic event of the reign of King George the Fifth, much has been written. The diplomatic documents relating to British intervention are voluminous, and the comments of contemporary writers would of themselves make a library.

But no one has given a better summing-up of the situation in which Great Britain found herself, and the mood in which the nation assented to war, than did the King himself a few days after the fateful fourth of August. His Majesty had been talking earnestly with the American Ambassador, Walter Hines Page, for half-an hour, explaining the events that led up to the war when, according to Page's own account, the King threw up his hands and explained: "My God, Mr. Page, what else could we do?" Such, in less concise form, is likely to be the historian's verdict on Britain's entry into the European War of 1914-1918.

During the days immediately preceding the war the King collaborated closely with his Ministers in their desperate efforts to avert the catastrophe. From the 28th July, Lord Oxford's biographers tell us, the Prime Minister was in "constant oral communication with the King." This process involved consultations at all hours, and, as has been related, necessitated a call upon the King in the middle of the night. The business that brought him from his bed was a German complaint that Russia, by mobilizing, was forcing war on Europe; and with the Prime Minister the King arranged for a personal appeal to be telegraphed from himself to the Tsar to "remove the misapprehension which I feel must have occurred.

"If," said the King to the Tsar, "I can in any way contribute to that all-important purpose (peace), I will do everything in my power to assist in reopening the interrupted conversations"

By that time, however, the die was cast. Perhaps neither Russia nor Germany could regain control of the forces that they had unleashed; perhaps those who governed Germany had determined upon war and had no intention of being deflected from the great gamble upon which clearly their minds had been concentrated for many years. Whatever might be the prospect which were presented to them, King George's view of it was not concealed. He described it as a "terrible calamity, the evil of which could not be remedied."

But once the decision was taken His Majesty had, of necessity, to fill his role as the head of the armed forces. Not for him the old monarchial privilege of leading his armies in the field; nor yet to step aboard a flagship as the Commander-in-Chief of the Grand Fleet. Such spectacular roles are now constitutionally forbidden to the Sovereign.

Even for the restricted part permitted to him, the King was not, in one respect, well-equipped. Though highly-trained as a sailor, His Majesty had never served professionally as a soldier. So little is the British sovereign regarded as a War Lord that King George had never been given the military rank which was essential to his position as head of the Army. Thus, on his accession, he was obliged to contemplate the farcical situation of promoting himself to the rank of Field-Marshall and of presenting himself with the baton. His senior military officers, however, relieved him of the dilemma. A number of Field-Marshals sought audience of him and petitioned him to take the rank.

Thereafter His Majesty lost no opportunity of extending his knowledge of the army, and inspections, reviews and manœuvres found in him an eager student of the practical side of soldiering. On one occasion, in 1912, the King remained with his generals to the end of some manoeuvres near Cambridge and then attended the conference which it was customary to hold to discuss the lessons of such exercises. As head of the Army the king took the chair at the conference, and listened to the debate, which was opened by Sir Douglas Haig.

A few days after the declaration of war, the King visited Aldershot to bid farewell to the divisions stationed there, a considerable proportion of the "Contemptible Little Army." On the parade ground where those superbly disciplined and highly trained men marched past for the last time on British soil, the King was on several subsequent occasions to see, springing into life and into military effectiveness, that army millions which was created by Kitchener.

Few men saw so much of the making of that army as did His Majesty. His visit to training camps were innumerable, and he saw the hardships of those early volunteers in something like their harsh realities. It was impossible to conjure uniforms and equipment out of the air, and the King more than once inspected soldiers dressed in the manner in which they had gone to enlist. Their clothes bore testimony to the way in which men of all classes and conditions had responded to the call to arms. Men in shabby piebald suits, with mufflers round their necks, side by side with young gentlemen whose Savile Row trousers still retained a suggestion of a crease and with straw-hatted clerks who were soon to show that courage and endurance are not the monopolies of any grade or class.

There is evidence in his speeches later in the war that the King never forgot the realities that lay behind the uniform, not only the uniform of khaki, but also of those suits of bright blue which were the costume of wounded men who were not bedridden.

With the creator of this, the greatest army that Great Britain had ever put in the field, the King had long been acquainted. They had met in various places—in south Africa towards the close of the South African War, and on Egyptian soil—and at the King's command Kitchener came from the East to take charge of the troops at the Coronation.

On Kitchener's appointment as Secretary of state for War, the King gave the Field Marshal the use of York House which was, indeed, Kitchener's last home, for from there he set out to meet his doom in the icy waters off the Orkneys. During his anxious tenure of the war Office, Kitchener was frequently at Buckingham Palace, not always for formal audiences as a Minister, but sometimes, late in the evening, when the "weary Titan" found relaxation and understanding friendship in the King's study.

Though the King was not permitted to lead his soldiers in the field, he soon discovered that there was no reason why he should not pay visits to them, and so in December 1914, when conditions were far from being congenial, His Majesty paid his first visit to the Western front, "to gain," as he said in a message to his men, "a slight experience of the life you are leading." Thus, for the first time in 170 years, a King of England joined his army on the fields of France. Five times, in all, he repeated that experience, and though naturally the generals took such steps as they could to ensure that the enemy did not have the satisfaction of killing the King, his desire to see certain battle fronts took him under shell fire on more than one occasion, while the risk of aerial bombardment was ever present. The last Royal head to be annointed in the Abbey Church of Westminster knows the feel of a steel helmet, worn under conditions that made it a necessity.

The King knows also what it is to be loaded into an ordinary military ambulance as a casualty and to be driven in pain over the wartime roads of Northern France. His Majesty had been inspecting some airmen and was mounted on the horse of a distinguished general. Cynics might find material for comment in the fact of a general's horse being unaccustomed to the sound of hearty cheers, but it is undeniable that the animal, on hearing the rousing acclamation of the soldiers, reared three times. The King sat the horse perfectly during two of these jolts, but the third was exceptionally violent, with the result that his Majesty was thrown, and sustained injuries which necessitated his transfer to England on a stretcher and an absence from public duties for some weeks.

JUBILEE CELEBRATIONS IN INDIA

There were amazing scenes in Calcutta on the occasion of the Silver Jubilee celebrations. It seemed that the whole of Calcutta's million and a quarter population had turned out, and that every private car, taxi, bus, *gharry* and rickshaw was in commission.

Main roads, particularly those running in the vicinity of the large number of brilliantly illuminated buildings, were blocked from kerb to kerb with vehicular traffic, and pavements were no less congested with pedestrians.

The following message from His Excellency Sir John Anderson to the school children of Bengal was read in almost every school in the province to-day :

"I invite Young Bengal to study the life of His Majesty and to strive to emulate the example he has set to his subjects."

The Governor pointed out that the King's life is one "characterized by qualities which are indeed kingly unselfish devotion to duty ; service to others, courage which has supported him through trials well-nigh unsupportable and has flowed from him to inspire his people the bearing of greatness with modesty and simplicity."

In Calcutta the celebrations began in the morning when thousands of poor people were fed on the maidan.

Seldom has St. Paul's Cathedral accommodated such a large congregration as that which attended the Thanks-giving Service held there the previous morning.

His Excellency the Governor of Bengal in full uniform, Ministers and Members of His Excellency's Executive Council, the Chief Justice of Bengal, Judges of the High Court, military officers representing various units, the Commissioner of Police, Calcutta, and prominent members of almost every community in Calcutta were present.

Owing to the great demand for accommodation the Cathedral had to be entirely re-seated, but even so, half-an-hour before the service began the body of the church, the aisles and even the gallery wore fully occupied.

Under the command of Lt.-Col. C. H. Gotto, 100 officers and men of the 1st Battalion, Devonshire Regiment, attended the service. There were also present detachments from St. John's Ambulance Association and the Nursing Divisions, and troops of Boy Scouts and Girl Guides.

His Excellency the Governor, accompanied by his staff, also attended a special Thanksgiving Service at St. Andrew's Church, conducted by the Rey. W. S. Urquhart, Principal, Scottish Churches College, the Rev. John Wood of Wellesley Square Church and the Rev. R. E. Lee, Presidency Senior Chaplain and Moderator of the Presbytery of Bengal who delivered the address.

A special Thanksgiving Parade Service was held in the Garrison Church of St. Patrick, Fort William. Pontifical High Mass was by the Rt. Rev. Mgr. J. Fernandes, Administrator of the Archdiocese assisted by the Rev. J. Weaver. S. J., and S. Gomes, S. J. After the Gospel of the Mass the Rev. J. Weaver delivered an address.

Thanksgiving services were held in all the other Calcutta Churches and at the leading temples and mosques.

All over India the same generous demonstration of the people's affection was made apparent in whole-hearted participation in the Jubilee celebrations.

At Simla His Excellency the Viceroy and the Countess of Willingdon drove in state to the Cathedral, the streets of the Summer Capital presenting a gaily decorated appearance and the scene at night, when a million lights twinkled in an artistic scheme of illuminations, beggars description.

At Bombay, too, as also in Madras, the people's joyous tribute of affectionate loyalty was everywhere apparent. Lord Brabourne, the Governor of Bombay, was present in the Capital of the Presidency, but Lord Erskine, Governor of Madras, was in Ootacamund, the summer headquarters where the Jubilee celebrations added to Nilgiri's seasonal gaiety.

In the Indian States the Jubilee was celebrated with equal loyalty and devotion.

Traditional splendour marked the festivities in Mysore, Travancore, Cochin, Hyderabad, the Punjab and Kathiwar States, Kashmir, and the Eastern Agency.

The following was the text of the Viceroy's broadcast Silver Jubilee mesage : "On behalf of the Princes and the people of India I beg to send to His Majesty the King-Emperor our respectful and joyful greetings on this auspicious day and express our profound hope that he may be spared for many years to contine to rule this great country. Loyalty to the King-Emperor has always been the abiding faith of the Indian people and while it is impossible in these days of change and development to expect that many millions in India will be free from all the stress and strain which comes with the desire for political advancement, His Majesty can rest assured that his hold will be above and apart from such movements and that we are all devotedly loyal to the King-Emperor's Throne and person.

"We gratefully thank him for the constant and abiding interest that he has always taken in the welfare, proserity and progress of all his subjects in India.

"When we who live in India look back on these 25 years, we can put aside all our temporary disputes and differences and agree that the close association of our two races has brought immense advance and development in all branches of our public life, with a higher standard of comfort and prosperity, for all classes and communities in this country.

"Never has the devotion and loyalty of the Princes and the people of India to their Sovereign been shown to greater advantage than during the four years of the Great War, when they shared to the full all the terrible sacrifices made to secure the safety and security of the Empire, and so to-day in the privileged position which I hold as His Majesty's personal representative in India I ask all my fellow-citizens who proudly claim his as their ruler to join with me in gratefully thanking His Majesty for the splendid example of courage and fortitude he has always shown to us in guiding the destinies of our Empire in the past, in assuring him of our loyalty and devotion and in sending up a prayer to Providence that he may long be spared to reign over us."

Their Majesties' Silver Jubilee Fund met with a generous response in India and on September 16, the following telegrams were exchanged between Their Excellencies and the King-Emperor.

From Lord and Lady Willingdon : "We are indeed happy to inform Your Majesties that Your Majestys' Silver Jubilee Fund in India which closed yesterday, reached the splendid figure of just over £1,000,000 thus ensuring that Your Majesty's Silver Jubilee will live in the memory of your Indian subjects by extended and improved means of medical relief which that great occasion has enabled them to be provided with."

From the King-Emperor : "The Qneen and I are delighted to hear of the magnificent response to the Silver Jubliiee Fund in India by which the medical resources of the country will so greatly benefit. We heartily congratulate you on the splendid success of your efforts."

In a broadcast message to his farflung Empire His Majesty said :

"I dedicate myself to your service for the years that may be given to me. I look back on the past with thankfulness to God. My people and I have gone through great trials and difficulties together and they are not yet over. In the midst of this day's rejoicings I grieve that numbers of my people are still without work. We ought to think of them and also of those who are suffering from any form of disablement, of the sympathy and help that we can give them."

Lord Linlithgow's Broadcast Speech

His Excellency, Lord Linlithgow, the Viceroy broadcasted the following address on April 18 on the assumption of his office :—

A few moments ago you listened to a brief but profoundly significant ceremony when you heard me take the oaths of allegiance and of office. Now speaking to you in your homes with those you love about you, I wish you to know that as I promised my true allegience to his Majesty and dedicated myself to the service of India I was conscious that I spoke not only for myself but also for you all. By the eager manifestations of your loyalty to the throne and person of the King-Emperor forthcoming last year at the jubilee of his late Majesty King George V and by your grief and sympathy in the sad hour of his late Majesty's demise you have given fresh proof of your constant devotion to the imperial throne. I am confident too that everyone of you will wish on this solemn occasion with me to pledge yourselves anew to the service of your motherland and of your fellow men.

Law And Order

You know well the heavy responsibility that rests upon the Viceroy—a responsibility which has been discharged with such signal success over a long period of years by the illustrious public servant whom I have the honour to follow in that great office. Amongst the manifold duties of the Viceroy none is more vital than that for the maintenance of peace and good order throughout India. Believe me, my friends, that I can do you no greater service than by the vigilant and effective discharge of this duty. The long story of progress and political evolution throughout the world proves beyond all question that of all the factors that may make for retrogression and reaction none is more powerful than civil disorder to inflict irreparable hurt upon the body politic. This and all other duties and responsibilities laid upon me by law and by the Instrument of Instructions which the King-Emperor has been graciously pleased to bestow upon me. I will discharge without fear or favour, affection or ill-will including that to do right to all manner of people after the laws and usages of India.

Personal Knowledge of British India

Most of you know that I am no stranger to this lovely land and to its kindly peoples. During the tour of the Royal Commission on Agriculture in India I saw not only a great part of the countryside in many provinces but also many of your cities and towns and met not a few persons whose kindness to me I can never forget and whose friendship I greatly value.

The Indian States

The terms of our appointment upon that commission confined the scope of our enquiry to British India. I did not have the pleasure except during the brief period of a holiday of visiting the territories of any Indian rulers. This omission, I hope, by the kindness of their Highnesses to repair at an early date. Let me at once assure you that I have ever in mind that the constant and devoted loyalty to his Majesty the King-Emperor of the princes and people of the Indian States and here affirm my profound admiration for their proud record of constant and undeviating service to the throne and empire both in peace and war.

To the services of the Crown in India, I give my greeting.

Royal Indian Navy

The Royal Indian Navy, young in years, yet the heir of ancient and glorious traditions of service at sea will, I am confident, vie in loyalty and efficiency with the other armed forces of the Crown in India. As one who has occupied the office of Civil Lord of the Admiralty, I can claim some familiarity with naval matters. My hope is that during my viceroyalty I may find it possible to witness in person something of the life and work of the service.

Army in India and the R. A. F.

To the army in India and the Royal Air Force I speak as one who in his time has shared their life both in peace and in war and whose happiest days have been spent with the colours. I recall with pride and pleasure that in northern France in 1915 I witnessed the loyalty, discipline and valour of units of the Indian army. Of the decorations that his Majesty has been graciously pleased to confer upon me there is none that I prize more highly than the long service medal of that branch of the army in which I had the honour to serve. Of my own knowledge then I can vouch for your loyalty to the throne and person of the Sovereign and to your devotion to duty. I look forward with keen pleasure to those occasions upon which I shall be with you, whether on the parade ground or during field training.

Indian Civil Service

The fame of the Indian Civil Service is acknowledged throughout the British Empire and beyond. I look to the members of that service throughout India to give me during my viceroyalty the help and support that they have been wont at all times to extend to my predecessors. The glorious traditions of your service require that you should give to the people of India, whose servants you are, the best that is in you to the limits of your strength. I have every confidence that you will do no less than this in the difficult years to come. Some among you there may be who have felt honest doubts as to this or that element in the plan of constitutional reform which Parliament last year approved. Now that this matter is no longer in issue and the new constitution is upon the statute book I call upon you to banish doubt and to eschew half-heartedness and with me and the Governors of your provinces to go forward in faith and courage to put into effect and to make to work this body of reforms which with your help has been shaped by the joint wisdom of Britain and India after labours which for care and scope have in matters of the kind no parallel in the history of the world.

The District Officer

Let me add this word to those of you occupying the immensely responsible position of district officer. Be sure that I will bear constantly in mind the vital import of your work as the senior representative of the Crown in your district. You constitute the essential link between Government and the rural population. The cultivators of India look to you for guidance, help and comfort. I am well aware that you do your utmost to serve them. I appreciate the extent to which in recent times and in growing degree the ever rising tide of office work has hampered you in the performance of your first and foremost duty—that of maintaining yourselves in close personal touch with your villages. It is a question as to which I propose to take an early opportunity to consult Governors of provinces and my advisers whether means cannot be discovered whereby you may be relieved at least in the touring season of some part of your desk work and thereby be given the opportunity (of which I am certain you would eagerly avail yourselves) to devote more of your time to touring. But in any event I conjure you, whatever the difficulties, to strive your utmost to know your villages. It is true that contemporary standards and traditions of administrations must inevitably lay upon you more desk work than your predecessors were accustomed to perform. Remember nevertheless that the traditions of your service and its greatest glory have their origin in the camps of your predecessors. For you in your own generation it remains abundantly true that the *tent* is mightier than the pen.

Remaining Civil Services of Crown

All India I am sure desire, as I do, that during the forthcoming period of constitutional change there may be no stay in those beneficent activities of Government in India designed to ameliorate the lot of the people. Knowing them as well as I do and having indeed worked with not a few, I am sure that I may count implicitly upon the members, whatever their standing, of all those other civil services of the Crown in India, which through so long a period have in their various capacities helped to sustain the burden of Government, resolutely to perform the duties with which they are severally charged. You may count upon me to support your labours. I know well the difficulties which in certain fields confront you and the trials and disappointment which inevitably you are called upon to bear. I am confident too that I speak for you all when I say that those difficulties exist not to deter you but to be boldly and cheerfully faced and as soon as may be overcome.

The Police

Of all those who serve the public none perform more invaluable services, than do the police, the friends and guardians of all persons who are concerned within the law of the land to proceed upon their lawful occasions. You may be sure that in the performance of your arduous duties, sometimes difficult, at moments dangerous and always delicate, you may count upon my stead support.

If I am aware of the hard times which farmers have had to face I have also in mind the difficulties through which industrialists and the urban populations have passed during the period of world-wide depression. Indeed engaged as I myself have been in commerce and finance, I am able to extend to them my understanding sympathy but great and real as may have been those difficulties, to those of you engaged in any capacity in commerce, finance and industry, I would say that you can at this time render no greater service to your country than by going quietly, yet confidently, about your business.

I know too that the difficulty of finding employment, particularly, in the case of young men of education has saddened and embittered many youthful lives. Nothing could give me greater pleasure than that, after due consideration and enquiry, I may find it to be within my power in some degree to mitigate this cruel burden of quite undeserved hardship.

Amongst those responsibilities in Great Britain that I had perforce to forego when I undertook my present charge were the chairmanships of the Medical Research Council, of the Privy Council and of the governing body of the Imperial College of Science and Technology. I hope greatly, that I may find the means during my viceroyalty to forward in India the cause of medicine and of all other branches of science and technology.

It will be in keeping with the experience in many countries and in many ages, if it should emerge, that the present phase of intense political activity is to be followed by a quickening of the creative impulse in the field of indigenous art and literature, nothing could give me higher satisfaction than that I should be privileged to foster and encourage a movement of that nature.

Now, let me say a word or two as one who has ever experienced the greatest happiness from his relations with his own family to those young people who may hear me to-day. Children, I speak to you, as your King Emperor's Viceroy and as your friend. Remember that when you grow up it will be with you that the honour of your country will rest. Remember that no man or woman can be a good citizen and a true patriot who does not, first of all, learn and govern and subdue his own nature. That is never easy but take to heart of grace and believe me that if you try hard and long to be good you will in the end succeed. I shall very often think of you to fear God, honour the King Emperor and obey your parents.

I turn now to a matter of the highest importance. I would have you know that I am incapable of preferring any one community before another. Let me bring home to you my inflexible resolution in this matter by a homely illustration. God has indeed been good to me for He has given me five children. They came into the world each one with a nature and with characteristics different from their brothers and sisters. I have tried my utmost to understand those differences and to deal with each one of my children in a fashion appropriate to his or her nature, to give support where support has seemed to me to be needed and in each to cultivate the natural gifts and good qualities. I have sought too to encourage them at all times to be tolerant of each other. I love them all most dearly but among my children I have no favourite.

PROVINCIAL AUTONOMY

In a few months you may expect to see inaugurated the system of provincial autonomy laid down in the Government of India Act of 1935. This, as you are aware, will mark the first stage towards the completion of that constitutional structure whose natural crown and summit will be the All India Federation as now prescribed in the same statute. The consummation of constitutional changes so profound cannot, in the nature of things, be simple of achievement. The success of this signal endeavour rests very largely with you and must, in a great degree, depend upon your steadiness and forbearance. It will be my duty throughout this anxious period to tender to you such counsel as may seem to me to be within my proper function and to be calculated to assist you in discharging the responsibilities of citizenship under representative government. In no circumstances can it be for me to advise you how to vote, for it is of the very essence of this system of Government that in that matter you should decide of your own individual and unfettered judgment where it is that your duty lies. Therefore the leaders of political parties, by whatever name they are known, competing within the ambit of the constitution for the suffrage of the provincial electorates, may rely implicitly upon me, never wittingly to use language calculated to prejudice their lawful interests.

It is quite true that at the centre, as at present constituted, my Government finds itself opposed from time to time by substantial elements in the central legislatures. The conditions of that opposition and the fact that in no circumstances can those who compose such opposition be called upon by me to form part of an alternative Government constitute in my considered view, as indeed they did in the opinion of the Joint Select Committee of Parliament which considered the Reforms, the best of all reasons for the constitutional changes at the centre adumbrated in the recent Act of Parliament. Meantime let me only say that in my judgment the appropriate forum for the exposition and where necessary the defence of Government policy is upon the floor of the legislatures. The circumstances then (and I speak to you as I intend always to do with the utmost frankness) which must exist upon the inauguration of provincial autonomy and before the setting up of the Federation will inevitably lay upon me to inconsiderable difficulty. You may rest assured that my constant endeavour throughout the period shortly to be entered upon will be to contribute to the best of my opportunities towards the successful working of self-Government in the provinces and at the same time to prepare the way for the changes at the centre implicit in the setting up of an All India Federation.

The successful working of representative government, particularly in the formative period shortly to be entered upon, requires amongst other things that I should as far as practicable be in touch with the leaders of all political parties as well as with the trend of opinion in the electorates. It is highly important that you should understand plainly that when I grant an interview to the leader or leaders of this or that political party, this in no way signifies that I favour such leaders of their parties. The rule and convention is well understood in Great Britain as between the Crown and political leaders in that country. Its general acceptance in India is in my judgment essential to the successful working in this country of representative self-Government.

It is within the power of the press of all democratic countries to make the most material contribution towards the successful working of public institutions and the development of an informed and responsible body of opinion. But like the rest of us newspaper men cannot be expected to make bricks without straw. If they are to discharge their responsible duties towards the public and to comment effectively upon current affairs, they require, whatever their editorial policy, to be informed as far as practicable upon the facts at issue. As one well accustomed to their requirements in this regard I intend to do my utmost to give them such assistance as properly I may and both they and their readers may rest assured that such help as my officers may find it possible to give to the press will be confined to facts, that these will be presented in a fashion entirely objective and that the material available will be at the disposal of the press as a whole without distinction or discrimination.

It has occurred to me that there may be those amongst you who may wish to hear in the Hindustani language the words which I have spoken to you to-day. I have therefore given my instructions that a full and exact translation into Hindustani of my speech is to be broadcast immediately I have finished speaking.

In conclusion, let me say to you that of all those conditions which in great endeavours make for a happy and successful issue none is more essential than that those who participate in them should both trust and respect each other. All men are liable to error. I do not ask or expect that all of you will at all times find yourselves in agreement with me. Nevertheless you may be sure that I shall never doubt your sincerity or the integrity of your minds. I ask no more than that you should favour me with the same whole-hearted trust that I have promised to extend to you for the next five years without let or stay. I will devote my mind, my heart and such health as Providence may vouchsafe to me to the service of your country. For this I ask you to remember me in your prayers. Let us move boldly forward with faith and courage, you I. and with all our strength strive to better the lot of her peoples wheresoever they may be and to sustain in all its ancient fame and glory the great name of India over all the world.

Proceedings of the

COUNCIL OF STATE

LEGISLATIVE ASSEMBLY

and

PROVINCIAL COUNCILS

JANUARY—JUNE 1936

The Council of State

LIST OF MEMBERS

President :—The Honourable Sir Maneckji Byramji Dadabhoy

Nominated—Officials (11)

1. His Excellency General Sir Robert Cassels
2. The Hon'ble Kunwar Sir Jagadish Prassad
3. The Hon'ble Mr. T. A. Stewart,
4. The Hon'ble Sir Bertrand Glancy
5. The Hon'ble Mr. M. G. Hallett
6. The Hon'ble Sir Guthrie Russell
7. The Hon'ble Mr. A. De C. Williams
8. The Hon'ble Mr. A. J. Raisman
9. The Hon'ble Mr. A. G. Clow
10. The Hon'ble Mr. J. N G. Johnson
11. The Hon'ble Mr. E. F. Thomas

From Berar

The Hon'ble Mr. Ganesh Srikrishna Khaparade

Non-Officials (14)

1. The Hon'ble Sir David Devadoss,
2. The Hon'ble Diwan Bahadur Sir K. Ramuni Menon
3. The Hon'ble Khan Bahadur Dr. Sir N. Choksy
4. The Hon'ble Sir Josna Ghosal
5. The Hon'ble Prince Afsar-ul-Mulk
6. The Hon'ble Mr. Bijay Kumar Basu
7. The Hon'ble Maharaja Jagadish Nath Ray, of Dinajpur
8. The Hon'ble Khan Bahadur Sheikh Makbul Hosain
9. The Hon'ble Saiyid Ishrat Husain
10. The Hon'ble Raja Charanjit Singh
11. The Hon'ble Nawab Malik Sir Mohammad Hayat Khan Noon Kt.
12. The Hon'ble Maharajadhiraja Sir Kameshwar Singh,
13. The Hon'ble Khan Bahadur Shams-ud-din Haidar,
14. The Hon'ble Lieut-Colonel Nawab Sir Akbar Khan

Elected—Non-officials (33)

1. The Hon'ble Rajah Sir Annamalai Chettiyar,
2. The Hon'ble Mr. Yarlagadda Ranganayakalu Naidu
3. The Hon'ble Mr. V. C. Vellingiri Gounder
4. The Hon'ble Saiyad Mohamed Padsha Shahib Bahadur
6. The Hon'ble Sardar Shri Jagannath Maharaj Pandit
7. The Hon'ble Mr Santidas Askuran
8. The Hon'ble Sir Phiroze C. Sethna
9. The Hon'ble Sirdar Saheb Sir Suleman Cassum Haji Mitha
10 The Hon'ble Khan Bahadur Alli Buksh Mohamed Hussain
11. The Hon'ble Mr. R. H. Parker
12. The Hon'ble Mr. Jagadish Chandra Banerjee
13. The Hon'ble Kumar Nripendra Narayan Sinha, of Nashipur
14. The Hon'ble Mr. Satyendra Chandra Ghosh Maulik
15. The Hon'ble Khan Bahadur Said Abdul Hafeez
16. The Hon'ble Mr. Mahmood Suhrawardy
17. The Hon'ble Sir George Campbell
18. The Hon'ble Rai Bahadur Lala Mathura Prasad Mehrotra
19. The Hon'ble Rai Bahadur Lala Jagadish Prassad
20. The Hon'ble Pandit Prakash Narain Sapru
21. The Hon'ble Khan Bahadur Hafiz Muhammad Halim
22. The Hon'ble Shaikh Mushir Hosain Kidwai
23. The Hon'ble Rai Bahadur Lala Ramsaran Das
24. The Hon'ble Sardar Buta Singh
25. The Hon'ble Khan Bahadur Nawab Chauduri Muhammad din
26. The Hon'ble Raja Ghazanfar A Khan
27. The Hon'ble Rai Bahadur Radha Krishna Jalan
28. The Hon'ble Raja Raghunandan Prassad Singh
29. The Hon'ble Mr. Hossain Imam
30. The Hon'ble Mr. V.V. Kalikar
31. The Hon'ble Srijut Heramba Prosad Barua
32. The Hon'ble Captain Maung Aye
33. The Hon'ble Mr. W. T. McIntyre

Proceedings of the Council

Budget Session—New Delhi—15th February to 25th April 1936

The winter session of the Council of State opened at New Delhi on the **15th. February 1936** with *Sir Maneckji Dadabhoy* in the chair and adjourned after a brief session as a mark of respect to His late Majesty King George V.

Railway Budget Discussion

17th. & 20th. FEBRUARY :—The main business to-day was the presentation of the Railway budget by *Sir Guthrie Russell* after which the Council adjourned till the 20th when the general discussion of the Railway Budget was held.

The hon. Mr. *Hossain Imam* speaking on the budget, struck a new ground with the suggestion that the interest paid on provident fund by commercially run railways should not be higher than on short-term Government loans. This only helped to fill the pockets of the employees and the speaker opined that by reducing the rate by one per cent there would be a saving of two crores which might help to wipe out the deficit at least of commercial lines. The hon. Mr. *V. V. Kalikkar* wanted locomotives to be built in India with state aid. The hon. *K. B. Chaudhri Mohamed Din* and the hon. K. B. *Syed Abdul Hafeez* claimed 25 per cent representation of Muslims in railways and a greater scrutiny of the evil of corruption. The hon. Mr. *Parker* welcomed the proposal to amend the Railway Act against ticketless travelling and urged severe punishment of the staff who indulged in bribery and fraud. He agreed that road competition should be placed on a fair basis. Messrs. *Ramsaran Das*, *Banerji*, *Suhrawardy*, *P. N. Sapru*, *Padshah*, *Jagdish Prasad* and *Barua* further subjected the Railway Board to criticisms, to which *Sir Zafrullah Khan* elaborately replied in a speech which occupied over 75 minutes.

Payment of Wages Bill

24th. FEBRUARY :—The payment ot Wages Bill was passed to-day by the Council of State, with the amendment of Mr. *P. N. Supru*, which provided that for concerted absence of 10 or more workers without due notice as required under the terms of contract and without reasonable cause, only maximum of 8 days' wages (and not 13 days as provided by the Lower House) may be deducted.

Reduction of Military Expenditure

26th FEBRUARY :—By 31 votes to 17 the Council rejected to-day the resolution of *Lala Mathraprased Mehrotra* urging that the relation of military expenditure to the average income in India should be the same as in the Dominions. Lala Mathraprasad's main argument was that, as a result of the recent agreement between Britain and Russia the bogey of a Russian menace had largely disappeared. The Government of India could, therefore, reconsider their policy regarding military expenditure with a view to reducing it substantially and thus reduce taxation and spend more on nation-building departments. The *Commander-in-Chief*, opposing, said : "Rearmanent is the order of the day and His Majesty's Government in Britain and most of the Dominions are faced with the need for increases in strength". He pointed out that the effect of the resolution was that India's defence expenditure should be reduced from about forty-five crores to something in the neighbourhood of nine crores, from twenty-five per cent. of her national income on defence expenditure, as now, to five per cent as in the Dominions.

The Council then adjourned till the 28th when the Budget was presented whereafter it adjourned till the 6th March.

General Discussion of Budget

6th MARCH :—The Council held a general budget discussion to day. Twenty-two members participated. Opposition was launched by Sir *Phiroz Sethna* and the main criticism charged the Finance Member with under-estimating the budget and having offered no gesture of relief to the poor masses. Several members criticised the methods of carrying out of the rural uplift work with the help of Government grants. Mr. *Hossain Imam* accused the Government that most money was spent in propaganda intended to wean the masses from the Congress. *Raja Ghazanfar Ali* pointed out the fallacy of Government propagandists in urging the villagers to use mosquito nets with a view to ward off malaria when the people had not even a sheet of cloth to cover themselves against sun, rain and cold. *Lala Ram Saram Das* opined that the increased amenities provided by the radio and other luxuries increased the burden of the masses instead of relieving them of it. Several others criticised the unchecked export of gold and wished alteration in exchange ratio. The *Finance Member* replying said that it was better to under-estimate revenue than over-estimate it and then face disappointment. He opposed subsidising from revenues of the commercial department like posts and telegraphs as that would also lay the central Government's budget to a similar demand from the railways. Sir James Grigg opined that any embargo on gold would fall ultimately on the agriculturist who sold gold. Concluding, the Finance Member reiterated that he had done his best to frame the budget as circumstances required in view of the responsibilities of seeing that the provincial autonomy was given an undisturbed start next year. The Council then adjourned till 11.

Defence of India

11th. MARCH :—Mr. *P. N. Sapru* urged the Government to-day to constitute a joint standing committee of the central legislature for consultation and advice on problems connected with defence in India. He explained that if given effect to the resolution would only apply to conditions before the Federation for after the Federation the army would become the sole charge of the Governor-General when three Indian and three British members' advice would be taken.

Sir *Robert Cassels*, the Commander-in-Chief, stoutly opposed the resolution and said that those who wished to advice the Government must first study the army matters on which Government had been endeavouring their best to give all the available information. Members had not availed themselves of opportunities hitherto offered and indulged in same uniformed criticisms. The responsibility of armed forces rested on the executive and there could be no question of the executive being automatically called upon to consult the standing committee of the legislature before taking such action as it might consider necessary in public interest. It must remain for the executive alone to decide whether consultation with the legislature in any particular case was either necessary or feasible.

The speeches of non-official members that followed expressed indignation on the tone and temper of the Commander-in-Chief's reply which they contended was most unsatisfactory. Mr. *P.N. Sapru* described Sir Robert Cassel's speech as die-hardish and warned that if the legislators were treated as untouchables in army matters they would have to revolt against the defence department and could not be responsive to the Government. The resolution was negatived by 10 to 27 votes. The Council adjourned till 13th.

Parsi Marriages & Divorce Bill

13th. MARCH :—The bill amending the law relating to marriage and divorce among Parsis unanimously reported upon by the joint committee of both the Houses had an easy passage in the Council to-day. Certain, drafting amendments suggested by Sir David Devadas were accepted and one amendment moved by *Sir N. Chocksy* defining Parsees as Parsee Zorastrians was passed. The Mover, Sir Phirozo Sethna, thanked the House.

Removal of Sex-Disqualification

Similarly, *Sir Ramunni K. Menon* found an all-round support to his resolution for removing the sex-disqualification for election or nomination to the Council of State. Government Members remained neutral but other official members were given freedom to vote. Several speakers including Maung Aye, Mr. A. G. Clow (official), Pandit Prakash Narayan Sapru, Mr. Hossain Imam, and Sir David Devadoss joined in the support. The resolution was passed without a dissentent voice.

Youths for Military Academy

16th. MARCH :—In the Council to-day Mr. *V. V. Kalikar* in moving a resolution urging the appointment of a committee to advise the Government to secure the requisite type of Indian youths for admission to the Military Academy, criticised the policy of discrimination between martial and non-martial classes, which was the main cause for the present dearth of competent youths offering themselves for admission into the Academy. He also thought that the present course of training had proved very expensive, which Indian parents could not afford. If a committee were appointed these could be examined and. with enough propaganda in the country, the requisite youths would be forthcoming. He urged the Government to create feeder schools in those places where a University Training Corps did not exist and said that the Government should also assist and encourage private schools. Concluding, Mr. Kalikar pointed out that the present method of nominating the majority of the cadets of the Academy had created a heart-buring all over the country. On the *Commander-in-Chief* suggesting an informal conference, the resolution was withdrawn.

Indians in Fiji

18th. MARCH :—The Council unanimously adopted to-day Pandit *P.N. Sapru's* resolution protesting against the Fijian Government's recommendation to substitute the nomination of three Indian members to the Fizi Legislature instead of election. All sections of the House, elected and nominated, the European group and the Government whole-heartedly supported the resolution, characterising the recommendation as a retrograde step. Sir *Jagadish Prasad* said that the Government had agreed with the Opposition that adoption of the system of nomination would not give effective representation to over eighty thousand Indians in Fiji and if such a course were adopted, it would remain a source of constant irritation and there would be serious repercussions here.

Release of Detenus

The House then rejected without division the recommendation of Rai Bahadur *Mathura Prasad Mehrotra* for the appointment of a judicial committee of three High Court Judges to examine the cases of all political prisoners now under detention and the release of those prisoners recommended by the committee.

Mr. *M. G. Hallett* opposing reiterated Sir Henry Craik's speech made in the Assembly on Friday as to the care with which the evidence was tested before a person was detained and said the appointment of a judicial committee was expensive and unnecessary. In any case the question of release must rest with the Executive.

Unemployment Problem

25th. MARCH :—The Hon. Mr. *P. N. Sapru* moved to-day a resolution urging the Government of India to give effect to those recommendations which would relieve unemployment among the educated classes. Mr. Sapru reviewed the salient features of the report of the committee over which his father presided in the United Provinces and said that the problem of unemployment being essentially an economic one the Government of India could in the language of the Committee help and give relief by a coordinate effort from the centre. Firstly, the statistics regarding unemployment must be made up to-date and there should be also a survey of economic conditions throughout India as recommended by Professors Robertson and Bowley. Efforts should be made to organize production, the Government of India, themselves undertaking the financing of bigger undertakings like locomotive manufacture, motor manufacturing, mercantile marine, etc., through loans at a time when money was cheap. An organization should be started which would act as a thinking centre of economic matters and on whose findings Government's policy could be evolved. The fiscal policy of the Central Government also needed an urgent revision as the policy of discriminating protection laid down 15 years ago, appeared not satisfying the needs of India at present, especially in view of world conditions with important quotas, protective duties, bounties, subsidies, depreciated currencies, etc. The tariff procedure must be simplified and, furthermore, the development of social service must form another part of the Government's efforts to relieve unemployment. Education must be reconstructed with a view to give it a practical bias and, lastly, the legal profession needed reconstitution eliminating the evil of touching.

Mr. *A. G. Clow*, secretary of the Industries department, agreed with the tragedy of the situation and with the menance to society which unemployment meant. The report of the Sapru committee was confined in the first instance to the problem as viewed in the United Provinces though several aspects of the problem were common throughout India. The report had been published only a few weeks ago. The Government of India proposed to study it sympathetically to take such action as was desirable on it, but on the understanding they did not commit themselves to accepting every one of the recommendations of the committee (Cheers.) The report had suggested concerted action throughout India for an effective solution of the problem. But it had emphasized that the problem centred round the questions connected with education, agriculture and industries. All these subjects were provincial and transfered subjects. Still the Government of India had been playing increasing part in order to secure a coordinated development of these subjects. The agricultural Commission was followed by the establishment of the Imperial Council of Agricultural Research whose work done in respect of sugar establishment was well known. There was also the Pusa Research Institute which had been transferred to Delhi. The Industrial Research Bureau had recently been established whose assistance would be available to secure the fullest possibilities of industrial development.

Regarding the glass industry, the Government of India had deputed one special officer to make a survey of glass factories. His investigation had not yet been completed, but there were indications that in the technical sphere there were distinct possibilities of giving substantial help to the industry. Indeed the Government of India felt sure that the giving of technical assistance to scattered industries would be more helpful to manufaturers than arising revenue by a tariff wall.

Proceeding, Mr. Clow deplored the impression that in mere industrialisation lay the solution. On the other hand, the Sapru Committee had rightly pointed out that the starting point of any effort to solve the problem was overhauling the system of education so as to make the educated youth a useful member of society. As one who attended the meetings of the Central Advisory Board Education Mr. Clow paid a tribute to the work of Sir Tej Bahadur Sapru on it and said that the recommendations of the board has been forwarded to the provincial Governments for adoption. The difficulty there was one of finance. Mr. Hosain Imam had wanted infloation of currency. Mr. Clow maintained that it was another form of taxation. He reiterated Sir James Grigg's remarks on the subject of protection and said it was chimerical to suppose that by absolute protection India could solve her difficulties. Whatever the merits of protection, when it was viewed in relation to the question of employment the House should remember that if there was the possibility of creating employment in some cases there would be opposite effects in other cases. For as Sir James Grigg had pointed out to the Assembly unless India was prepared to import she could not export. Concluding, Mr. Clow said that there was not one single remedy for unemployment but several remedies to be adopted by all. Hence co-operation of all was needed and the Government of India welcomed the discussions.

Mr. *Prakash Narain Sapru* expressed satisfaction at the Government's attitude. The resolution was adopted unanimously.

Finance Bill Discussion

30th. MARCH :—The Finance Bill in the certified form came up for consideration to-day. Mr. *A. J. Raisman*, moving consideration of the Bill, said, "it is a matter of regret that the Bill comes once more in a certified form, but the House is aware of the circumstances which have rendered this step inevitable. The amendment carried by the Assembly were such as to make it impossible to balance the budget and the acceptance of those amendments would have resulted in a serious financial situation."

Mr. *Hossain Imam* led the Opposition. He reminded the House that this was the third time that a certified measure came up before them during one year. The last two instances were the Finance Bill, 1935-36, and the Criminal Amendment Bill. What was the use of the 'Executive every time ignoring the wishes of the Legislature, giving a handle to those who did not believe in constitutional progress? It was far better to abolish the Legislatures than every time impose an Executive decree. Worse still was the fact that the Council could not make any amendment to a certified measure. And the Government admitted in the Assembly that there was no transfer of power in finance, and all these budget discussions were a farce. Continuing, Mr. Hossain Imam dwelt at length on the financial aspect of the question and protested against the gold drain. He thought there was no necessity for a Controller of Currency after the establishment of the Reserve Bank. While industrialists in foreign countries like England and France could not stand the drain of war debts to America, was it any wonder that they did not want to saddle India with increased external payments. As an advocate of the poor he asked for removal of the surcharge on salt.

Raja Ghaznafar Ali strongly objected to the Government reducing the House into a dignified debating club. He had used the word "dignified" out of respect for the non-official President. Referring to the constitutional position of the certified bill, the speaker asked what was the necessity of the motion for consideration and the Government would have been more in order if they had straightway asked for the passage of the measure instead of wasting the valuable time of the Legislature. The attitude of the Government in this respect was the most unreasonable, defiant and insulting and this had already alienated the sympathy of well-meaning moderate opinion in the country who were always ready to help the Government. The Government ought to change their policy radically if they wanted their support.

Mr. *S. Askuran* regretted that the Government had not accepted the half-anna postcard also elimination of surcharge on supertax altogether. He criticised the fiscal policy and said that there had been much discrimination and too little protection. Referring to the Ottawa Agreement he suggested a tripartite conference between India, England and Japan for an equitable settlement.

The *Maharaja of Darbhanga* regretted the emergency taxes which still existed and thought a half-hearted measure for rural uplift would never succeed. He disapproved of the rebuilding of Quetta out of revenue. Referring to the Sugar industry the Maharaja stressed that both central and provincial Governments should keep a close watch on the interest of the agriculturist. While urging extension of postal facilities in rural parts he hoped the Government would sympathetically consider the half-anna postcard.

Mr. *P. N. Sapru* spoke with full knowledge of the limitations of the present constitution, which owed its responsibility to the British Parliament and the executive which was irremovable. Even then, he felt the course adopted was not conducive to the growth of a heavy Parliamentary mentality in this country, and the procedure adopted violated the spirit of law, cherished great hopes of new Viceroy, Lord Linlithgow, but the Government of India are not giving a fair start. Proceeding, Pandit Sapru quoted copious quotations of history to rebutt Sir James Grigg's conclusion from ancient history that British raj was really beneficial to India. Pandit Sapru pointed out that there were chapters in history in the days of East India Company, which were happily forgotten, in the interest of both races, but he hardly anticipated that responsible spokesman of the Government, as the Finance Member, would have thought it fit to refer to such obsolete passages.

31st. MARCH :—The final phase of the certified Finance Bill was gone through the Council with a somewhat thin attendance. Sir *James Grigg* said he was glad to be in upper air and calmer House. The complaint by many members yesterday was that even if it was necessary for the Governor-General to certify salt duty why did he restore the reduction made in postal rate. Sir James Grigg maintained that 50 lakhs was a substantial sum in a budget of eight crores and reminded the House how the Governor-General on a previous occasion had to restore salt duty when reduction had happened to encourage the belief that there would be any greater (?) in the budget as a whole in the year now closing than what had been forecast. On the other hand the revenues under sugar and salt showed a slight decline. Let the House remember that the Government of India had to see that provincial autonomy was given a sound financial start in 1937-38 and that in the succeeding years also the financial position in the provinces was at least equally sound. And, again, partly on account of separation of Burma and partly from liability on the Central Government under Sir Otto Niemeyer's proposals he calculated that there would be an additional burden of something like five crores a year. If Sir Otto Niemeyer's proposals were to place greater obligation on the Central Government than two crores the difficulty would be greater unless of course the economic condition in India improved more rapidly than it had. Reduction in the postcard rate would mean the recurring of a deficit postal budget seriously affecting the credit of the country.

Sir *Frank Noyce* confined himself to the vindication of the restoration of postcard rate from the departmental point of view. Fifty lakhs would mean a great gap and there was no recurrent surplus to meet it. The rural population used fewer postcards per head than the urban population and, therefore, the benefit of lower rate would not spread so much to rural areas. The department had been trying its best to reduce expenditure and any suggestion to give it an artificial stimulus by providing 50 lakhs from the general budget would not only result in checking the process of retrenchment but allowing the department a policy of drift, and not to talk of other departments like railways being given a chance to claim a similar artificial stimulus. The best policy was to let the half-anna postcard come in the normal way. Don't believe in an artificial stimulus. We are as keen as you are to have the half-anna postcard. But the time has not yet come.'

Referring to the criticism about subsidy to the Indian National Airways, Sir Frank Noyce emphasised that Government were giving subsidy to the company for a limited time and for a limited purpose only in exceptional circumstances. If the company were shut down the Government of India might have to give subsidy to another new company at a much greater cost.

Lala Ramsaran Das said that by no stretch of imagination could it be contended that the power of certification was meant for routine application as had been done year after year. Government could have at least accepted the vote regarding the postcard. While he considered communism as dangerous to India, he suggested that in a matter of economic planning India could well follow the example of Russia and Government should appoint central and provincial boards for the purpose. The question of financing agriculture and industry was also important. Co-operative banks had sufficient funds but had no adequate security to make advances. This defect should be remedied. As regards rural uplift grant, people would be benefitted better if instead of such grant taxes on the poor had been lowered. He feared that unless the army budget was reduced there would be no substantial relief and asked the Commander-in-Chief to show why the army budget was double than before the war and whether the army in India was kept in readiness for Mid-Eastern and Far-Eastern commitments. Finally, he said that though the recommendations emanating from the head of the Government would be treated with respect, he felt that as the popular wishes were not responded to he must dissociate himself from the proposal in the bill.

The motion was adopted.

At the final stage of the bill, Mr. *V. V. Kalikkar* declared that the executive distrusted the representatives of the people and by their attitude and action created an atmosphere not conducive to reforms and were playing into the hands of extremists who wished to boycott the reforms. Posterity would hold the present Government responsible for failure of reforms. (Applause.)

The motion for the passage of the bill was passed by 32 against 10 votes

I. L. O. Draft Conventions

15th. APRIL :—Mr. *Clow* moved the following resolution to-day :—

"The Council of State, having considered the draft convention limiting the hours of work in coal mines adopted by the 19th session of the International Labour Conference recommends to the Governor General-in-Council that he do not ratify the the convention. He pointed out that only a year ago the hours of work in mines had been reduced and it was not proper to make further radical reduction in the hours of work so soon, particularly as conditions in India were quite different.

The House adopted the resolution.

Mr. *Clow* moved another resolution urging the non-ratification of the draft convention concerning the establishment of an international scheme for the maintenance of rights under invalidity, old age and widows and orphans insurance adopted by the 19th session of the International Labour Conference. He emphasised that in India there was no system to coordinate these conventions which were largely designed to suit conditions in European countries. Further, India was separated thousand of miles away from those countries and there was no opportunity for working out mutual schemes of coordination.

The resolution was adopted and the Council adjourned till 17.

Non-official Resolutions

17th. APRIL :—The Council met today to dispose of non-official business.

Mr. *J. C. Banerji* moved a resolution urging that immediate steps be taken to bring forward legislation whereby all companies which will hereafter be floated with external capital for the purpose of opening factories in India for manufacturing any kind of articles either from raw materials available in India or from semi-finished parts imported into India would be compelled to take at least 50 per cent, of the total capital from natural born Indians. Mr. Banerji assured that he had no political or racial motive behind and that he was an unbeliever in the doctrine of expropriation of all external capital. His demand for the reservation of 50 per cent. of the capital of foreign concerns for natural born Indians was not new, but it was an accepted principle when protection was given to Tatas. He quoted in his favour the opinions of the External Capital Committee, which went into the question in 1925. He detailed numerous wealthy foreign concerns which had opened branches in India and entered into unfair competition with indigenous manufactures. He emphasised that the necessity had arisen to stop entirely foreign capital from deriving unrestricted advantage in draining out India's resources in the shape of middleman's profits for changing the raw materials of India into finished products within her own boundaries. If once the necessity was felt, it was but logical that legislation should be undertaken to achieve the desired end. Concluding, the speaker again assured that the resolution touched only such companies which would in future be floated with foreign capital. The penalties of forfeiture of shares purchased under benami transactions which was apprehended by the External Capital Committee if provided into future legislation would have sufficient deterrent effect to prevent such benami transaction by Europeans.

Mr. *Stewart*, Commerce secretary, opposed the resolution. He pointed out that section 113, Government of India Act, prevented such legislation being undertaken.

The *President* added: 'Even if such legislation were passed in India it would not override an Act of the British Parliament.' Mr. Banerjee's mention of sugar factories established in recent years only showed that the need for legislation was less than what it was eleven years ago, when the External Capital Committee reported. Again, a practical difficulty arose if there was 50-50 British and Indian capital, for there would be a double set of quotations in the stock exchange and purely Indian companies would be at a considerable discount.

No other member spoke on the resolution, which was rejected without a division.

RAILWAY FACILITIES TO SUGAR FACTORIES

Lala Mathura Prassad Mehrotra urged the railway authorities to grant special facilities to sugar factories by giving concession rates of freight and by providing an adequate supply of wagons for transport of cane, mollasses and sugar. His speech covered mostly factories established in the United Provinces. He alluded to the investment of Rs. 25 crores in the industry in recent years, with the growth in the number of factories from 32 to 154. Thus it was the second largest industry and employed one lakh of manual workers besides hundreds of graduates and others. The industry was faced with difficulties since the imposition of the excise duty and very few factories were paying proper dividends, while some had become losing concerns. Quoting from the letters of the Sugar Mills Association, Mr. Mehrotra complained of inadequate supply of wagons, partiality to certain companies for transport of molasses on the B. N. W. Railway and also the high freight rate.

Sir Guthrie Russell, Chief Commissioner of Railways, elaborately explained the freight concessions, as compared with the ordinary rate, given to the sugar industry over several sections of different railways and also detailed the facilities for transport of cane. As for molasses, he pointed out that its transport could not be further facilitated unless there was a large quantity sent. The resolution was withdrawn.

SEPARATE CIVIL MEDICAL SERVICE

Lala Jagdish Prasad (non-official, U. P.) moved that a separate civil medical service be established independently of the Indian Medical Service, which was primarily a military service. He wanted the Government to consider the needs of 33 crores of civil population and referred to the decades-old resolutions passed by the Indian National Congress in support of the contention that the system created in the time of the East India Company should now give place to modern conditions, especially when qualified medical practitioners were available in large numbers. The mover alluded in particular to the resolution passed almost every year by the U. P. Legislative Council as illustrative of the depth of feeling in the country against the present system and objected also to reserving certain districts to I. M. S. men.

Major General Sprawson, director general of I. M. S., explained that the present strength was the minimum possible and in fact there was room for a large number of British I. M. S. officers. He pointed out that various local Governments as well as centrally administered areas were required to appoint a certain number of British officers, for attending on British army and superior service officers and their families residing in respective areas. He had no doubt that as Indianisation progressed there would be fewer number of British I. M. S officers required. Almost all the local Governments expressed their inability to recruit officers on a short term basis and release them in case of war. He assured the House that it was not the intention of the Government to foist these officers on local Governments surreptitiously or with a dishonest motive. The resolution was withdrawn.

COASTAL TRAFFIC IN INDIA

Mr. *P. N. Sapru* introduced the Bill to Control the Coastal Traffic in India. (This measure was to have been introduced in the Assembly by Sir Abdul Halim Ghaznavi but he could not get a chance there.) Mr. Sapru stated that this was not racially discriminatory but merely intended to regulate the coastal traffic by empowering the Governor-General in Council to fix the minimum rates of fare and freight and to prohibit the grant of rebates or other concessions calculated to reduce such rates. The infringement of rules made under this bill was to be punishable with fine or refusal of entry into an Indian port. The bill was necessary as there was the fear that a well-established powerful company could easily put a new venture out of action by unfair competition such as rate cutting, grant of rebates etc. The bill was introduced without opposition in accordance with convention.

Italian Aggression in Abyssinia

20th. APRIL :—The Italian highhandedness in Abyssinia, carrying on the most barbarous methods of warfare, use of mustard gas, bombing of Red Cross equipment and the merciless bombing of undefended women and children of a Christian nation came for scathing criticism in the Council while discussing the motion of Mr. *Raisman* that the bill to prohibit the making of certain loans and credits to Italy be taken into consideration.

Sir *Jagadish Prasad* pointed out that the Government of India was not in a position to influence the international politics, and what was the use of such a wide discussion in which Government could not participate. *Raja Ghazanfar Ali* stressed that the bill was undertaken under the behests of the League and it was within their right to criticise that body. Sir *David Devadoss* also protested against the Italian war against a Christian nation. Mr. *P. N. Sapru* as a confirmed pacifist deeply sympathised with Abyssinia but at the same time he would not be a party to any action on the part of the League, namely the application of military sanctions which would ignite a world conflagration. He condemned the Italian adventure but felt that under the circumstances there was no other alternative left to the League except the policy so far adopted. Messrs. *Kalikkar* and *Hossain Imam* disagreed with Mr. Sapru and thought that the League should have adopted a firmer attitude from the beginning and could have even applied oil sanctions. The League as at present constituted, was a sham and quite different from that conceived by President Wilson for ensuring world peace. Rai Bahadur *Lala Ramsaran Das*, supporting, further emphasised the opposition view-point. Mr. *Raisman*, replying to the debate, refrained from entering into the rigmarole of international politics and stressed that the effectiveness of collective action must be judged in relation to the whole scheme of economic sanctions applied by all countries of the League. It is too early to estimate the extent of economic damages which have been inflicted on Italy. The bill was passed.

23rd. APRIL :—The Council after brief discussions passed five Bills which were passed by the Assembly. They were the Bills to remove certain doubts and establish the validity of certain proceedings in High Courts in British India, the Bill to make special provision for the administration of Cochin Port, the Bill; to amend the Aircraft Act, the Bill to amend the Factories Act and the Bill to amend the Lac Cess Act.

The Tariff Bill

24th. APRIL :—Mr. *Steward* moved consideration of the Tariff Bill regarding the import duty on wheat and rice. He said that the present world stock position of wheat was better than what had been for many years. Indian prices were in very close relationship with world parity and the reduction of duty to Re. 1 per cwt. would not adversely affect the Indian wheat. As for the duty on rice, the Government was convinced that the present duty had been effective but not excessive. Hence they decided to continue the same duty for another year.

A vigorous criticism of Government action in reducing the wheat duty came from unofficials, particularly from members of the wheat-growing provinces. The motion for consideration was adopted. During the discussion on clauses Messrs. Hossain Imam and Mehrotra were the only two speakers who spoke against the Bill. Thereafter, it was passed.

25th. APRIL :—The Tariff Bill regarding fonts was discussed for an hour on the motion of Mr. *Stewart*, Commerce Secretary. Messrs. Hossain Imam, Ramsaran Das, Padshah and Mehrotra expressed the opposition viewpoint in similar terms as those expressed by several members in the Assembly.

The bill was passed and the Council of State adjourned *sine die*.

The Legislative Assembly

LIST OF MEMBERS

President :—THE HONOURABLE SIR ABDUR RAHIM

Elected—Non-officials (105)

1. S. SATYAMURTI
2. V. V. GIRI
3. K. NAGESWARA RAO
4. PROFESSOR N. G. RANGA
5. M. ANANTHASAYANAM AYYANGAR
6. T. S. AVINASHILINGAM CHETTIAR
7. C. N. MUTHURANGA MUDALIAR
8. DR. T. S. S. RAJAN
9. P. S. KUMARASWAMI RAJU
10. SAMUEL AARON
11. UMAR ALY SHAH
12. MAULVI SYED MURTUZA SAHIB BAHADUR
13. H. A. SATHAR H. ESSAK SAIT
14. F. E. JAMES
15. RAJAH SIR VASUDEVA RAJAH
16. M. R. RY. SAMI VENCATACHELAM
17. DR. G. V. DESHMUKH
18. SIR COWASJEE JEHANGIR
19. DIWAN LALCHAND NAVALRAI
20. BHULABHAI JIVANJI DESAI
21. HOOSEINBHOY A. LALLJEE
22. KESHAVRAO MARUTIRAO JEDHE
23. N. V. GADGIL
24. S. K. HOSMANI
25. MAHOMED ALI JINNAH
26. NABI BAKSH ILLAHI BAKHSH BHUTTO
27. SETH HAJI ABDOOLA HAROON
28. W. B. HOSSACK
29. *Bombay European seats*
30. MATHURADAS VISSANJI
31. S. GHULAM HUSSAIN HIDAYATALLAH
32. SIR HORMUSJI PEROSHAW MODY
33. N. C. CHUNDER
34. DR. P. N. BANERJEA
35. BABU AMARENDRA NATA CHATTOPADHYAYA
36. PANDIT LAKSAMI KANTA MAITRA
37. SURYYA KUMAR SOM
38. AKHIL CHANDRA DATTA
39. SIR ABDUR RAHIM
40. HAJEE CHOWDHURY MOHAMMUD ISMAIL KHAN
41. SIR ABDUL HALIM GHUZNAVI
42. A. K. FUZLUL HUQ
43. MD. ANWAR-UL-AZIM
44. M. A. BAQUI
45. G. MORGAN
46. THOMAS CHAPMAN-MORTIMER
47. J. A. MILLIGAN
48. SRIJUT DHIRENDRA KANTA LAHIRI CHAUDHURY
49. BABU BAIJNATH BAJORIA
50. DR. BHAGAVAN DAS
51. CHOUDHRI RAGHUBIR NARAIN SINGH
52. PANDIT SRI KRISHNA DUTTA PALIWAL
53. PANDIT GOVIND BALLABH PANT
54. SRI PRAKASA
55. PANDIT KRISHNA KANT MALAVIYA
56. SHRI MOHAN LAL SAKSENA
57. SIRDAR JOGENDRA SINGH
58. MAULANA SHAUKAT ALI
59. QAZI MOHAMMAD AHMAD KAZMI
60. SIR MUHAMMAD YAMIN KHAN
61. MAULVI SIR MOHAMMAD YAKUB
62. DR. ZIA UDDIN AHMAD
63. MOHAMED AZHAR ALI
64. J. RAMSAY SCOT
65. MAHARAJ KUMAR VIJAYA ANANDA GAJAPATIRAJ
66. SHAM LAL
67. RAIZADA HANS RAJ
68. BHAI PARMA NAND
69. SYED GHULAM BHIK NAIRANG
70. K. L. GAUBA
71. H. M. ABDULLAH
72. NAWAB SAHIBZADA SAYAD SIR MOHAMMAD MEHR SHAH
73. KHAN BAHADUR SHAIKH FAZL-I-HAQ PIRACHA
74. KHAN BAHADUR MAKHDUM SAYAD RAJAN BAKHSH SHAH
75. SARDAR MANGAL SINGH
76. SARDAR SANT SINGH
77. M. GHIASUDDIN
78. SATYA NARAYAN SINHA
79. B. B. VARMA
80. B. DAS
81. PANDIT NILAKANTHA DAS
82. ANUGRAH NARAYAN SINHA
83. SHRI KRISHNA SINHA
84. BABU KAILASHBEHARI LAL
85. BABU RAM NARAYAN SINGH
86. MUHAMMAD NAUMAN
87. MAULVI BADI-UZ-ZAMAN
88. BADRUL HASAN
89. RAJA BAHADUR HARIHAR PROSAD NARAYAN SINHA
90. DR. NARAYAN B. KHARE

91. Seth Govind Das
92. Ghanshiam Singh Gupta
93. Khan Sahib Nawab Siddique Ali Khan
94. Seth Sheodass Daga
95. Srijut Nabin C. Bardoloi
96. Basanta Kumar Das
97. Abdul Matin Chaudhury
98. C. H. Witherington
99. U. Thein Maung
100. Dr. Thein Maung
101. U. Ba Si
102. F. B. Leach
103. M. Asaf Ali
104. Rai Bahadur Seth Bhagchand Soni
105. Dr. Khan Sahib
106. M. S. Aney

Nominated-officials (40)

107. The Hon. Sir Frank Noyce
108. The Hon. Sir Nripen Sircar
109. The Hon. Sir Percy James Grigg
110. The Hon. Sir Henry Craik
111. The Honourable Sir Muhammad Zafrullah Khan
112. Sir Girija Shankar Bajpai
113. Sir Aubrey Metcalfe
114 G. R. F. Tottenham
115. G. H. Spence
116. J. C. Nixon
117. A. H. Lloyd
118. A. G. Clow
119. P. R. Rau
120. A. S. Hands
121. M. R. Ry. Rao Bahadur A. A. Venkatarama Ayyar Avargal
122. M. R. Ry. Diwan Bahadur R. V. Krishna Ayyar Avargal
123. D. MacLachlan
124. Madhusudan Damodar Bhat
125. J. M. Chatterjee
126. P. J. Griffiths
127. J. F. Sale
128. *(Punjab Seat)*
129. Rai Bahadur Shyam Narayan
130. W. V. Grigson
131. Dr. J. H. Hutton
132. *(Burma Seat)*

Nominated—Non-officials (13)

133. Sardar Bahadur Sardar Sir Jawahar Singh
134. Rai Bahadur Sir Satya Charan Mukherjee
135. Rao Bahadur M. C. Rajah
136. R. S. Sarma
137. N. M. Joshi
138. Dr. R. D. Dalal
139. Dr. Francis Xavier DeSouza
140. Hony. Captain Rao Bahadur Ch. Lal Chand
141. Captain Sardar Sher Mohammad Khan
142. Major Nawab Ahmad Nawaz Khan
143. Khan Bahadur Nawab Malik Allah Bakhsh Khan Tiwana
144. J. H Blackwell
145. E. H. M. Bower

The Legislative Assembly

Budget Session—New Delhi—3rd. February to 23rd. April 1936.

SORROW FOR THE LATE KING

The Budget Session of the Legislative Assembly commenced at New Delhi on the **3rd. February 1936.** Black ties were worn by majority of the members and the usual exchange of greetings when a session opens were subdued. There was an atmosphere of solemnity occasioned by the decision to dedicate the sitting to the memory of the late King George.

The question hour having been dispensed with, *Sir Nripendra Nath Sarcar*, the Leader of the House, moved :

"This Assembly do place upon record an expression of its deep sorrow on the death of His Majesty King George V Emperor of India and of its heartfelt sympathy with His Majesty King Edward VIII Emperor of India and Her Gracious Majesty Queen Mary in their grievous loss and do convey to His Majesty loyal congratulations upon his accession and assurance of devotion to His Royal person."

The motion was passed all standing.

STANDING ARMY ADVISORY COMMITTEE

4th. NOVEMBER :—The Assembly passed a resolution, sponsored by Sir *Muhammad Mehr Shah*, recommending the appointment of a Joint Standing Army Committee, consisting of members of both Houses, to advise the Government on all matters connected with the defence of India.

Sardar Mangal Singh, who moved the resolution in the absence of Sir Muhammad, said that the origin of the resolution was the despatch of a contingent of troops to Addis Ababa without consulting the Legislature, the Government plea at the time being that the Legislature was not in session. Some members, he said, had raised the question at the last Simla session and asked for a Standing Committee that could be consulted in such an event in the future and the Commander-in-Chief had offered to consider any proposal agreed on by all parties.

Mr. *Asaf Ali*, the Congress whip, wanted to see the whole Defence Department controlled by an Indian Minister, but was prepared to accept a Standing Committee for the present.

Mr. Tottenham, replying on behalf of the Government, said he did not deny that the Government would welcome a closer liasion between themselves and the Legislature on defence matters and a greater knowledge of the Defence Department than was at present possessed by members of the Legislature. The Government's opposition was not based on a desire to oppose for the sake of opposing or to go back on pledges, but on the conviction that it would be a mistake to accept this resolution.

Mr. Tottenham referred to the origin of the resolution in the debate at Simla on the dispatch of troops to Abyssinia. He then said that although the Government had given an undertaking that they would consult the Legislature, so far as was possible, whenever the question arose of sending troops overseas for purposes other than the defence of India, yet even supposing that the sending of that small contingent to Addis Ababa for the defence of the Legation was not for Indian purposes, it would have been impossible to consult the Legislature as it was not in session and a decision had to be taken immediately.

The present resolution, Mr. Tottenham said, went far beyond anything that the Government had contemplated or any member had contemplated in the debates at Simla. It recommended a committee not for consultation on a limited question when the Legislature was not in session, which was what the Government undertook to consider, but the setting up of a committee to give advice on all defence matters without restriction. The Government had given no undertaking even to consider a proposal of that kind and therefore, could not be charged with any breach of faith. The promise to consider a more limited proposal had been discharged. The suggestion had been considered and could not be accepted for practical reasons.

Decisions to send troops overseas, he said, generally had to be taken on short notice as a matter of great urgency which further imposed the necessity of extreme secrecy until the move of the troops had taken place. Before deciding to send troops overseas the Government had to consider whether the situation in India permitted the despatch of troops and whether the despatch of troops was itself justifiable. The first question was one that the Government of India could decide for themselves and on which it required no advice. As regards the second question, there were circumstances in which the Government would be well aware that the proposal to send troops overseas would be opposed by Indian opinion and in other circumstances the Government would be aware that such a proposal would not be objected to. The committee urged by Mr. Navalrai could only confirm the correctness of the Governments views. Moreover, it was doubtful whether such a committee would reflect all shades of Indian opinion and it would take time to collect it when urgent decisions were needed. It would have been easy for the Government to accept the Committee and so gain a little cheap popularity. Then an occasion might have arisen when the Government found it impossible to consult the Committee in time, or such consultation would have been ruled out on the ground of secrecy. The Government would then have been rightly charged with setting up an "eye wash" Committee. The Government had therefore decided, said Mr. Tottenham, to be perfectly honest and to say that the practical difficulties were too great and that they did not propose to accept even such a limited proposal.

The Ministers would be able to arrange themselves as they wished in the departments under their own control, but in the Defence Department it would be wrong for the Governor-General to take views from a committee of parties in the Legislature. If the Governor-General choose to take advice it would be his clear duly to take that advice from his Ministers. When any question arose in connection with defence in which Indian opinion was interested, e. g., pensions, the Government would continue to appoint committees of the House to help them in deliberating on them. But that was no reason why they should accept the Standing Committee proposed by the mover.

Sir Cowasji Jehangir, who spoke after the Defence Secretary, supported the resolution. Federation was a good many years away, he said, and the resolution was designed to deal with the present situation. What the legislature suffered most from was ignorance in regard to the Defence Department; it only desired to be able to criticize it effectively and reasonably. They wanted education, but not in order to pry into confidential army matters. They did not want to know what type of aeroplane the Government had just ordered but what it would cost. If this resolution was rejected by the Government they would have great doubts about the "bona fides' of the Government in regard to the new constitution.

Dr. Deshmukh from the Congress benches condemned the Government pronouncement, saying that the defence of India was the Indian's concern. He referred bitterly to the recent speeches by Herr Hitler and Signor Mussolini and asked why no Englishman had protested against these Dictators' use of vulgar language about Asiatic and African peoples.

The resolution was however passed, the Government not challenging a division. The House then adjourned.

Adjournment Motions Disallowed

5th. FEBRUARY :—The President announced in the Assembly to-day that the Governor-General had disallowed the adjournment motion of Mr. *Akhil Chandra Dutt* about the Government's failure to issue instructions to Local Governments not to interfere with the celebrations of the Congress Golden Jubilee.

Similarly the adjournment motions about the hunger-strike of Jogesh Chatterjee Kakori Conspiracy case prisoner, were also disallowed by the Governor-General.

The Governor-General also disallowed the adjournment motion of *Sardar Sant Singh* about the forfeiture of the security of the "Abhyudaya" for publishing the speech of Pundit Krishnakanta Malaviya.

The *President* disallowed the adjournment motion of *Pundit Nilkantha Dass* about declaring hartal on January 28 on which day fell the important Hindu festival of Basanta Panchami on the ground that no orders had been issued by the Government to observe hartal.

Sir Girja Shanker Bajpai introduced a *bill* further to amend the *Indian Lac Cess Act.*

Payment of Wages Bill

The Payment of Wages Bill as reported by the Select Committee being taken up, Mr. *N. M. Joshi* moved a comprehensive amendment enlarging the scope of application of the Bill by including all factories, tramways, docks, mines and plantations. He contended that the Bill did not go even as far as the Labour Commissioner's recommendations. Sir *Frank Noyce* said that this legislation, unlike other labour laws, broke an entirely new ground and was purely of an experimental nature and its extension must be done after a careful consideration of the merits of each case by the local Government

Mr. *J. A. Milligan* said that in certain parts of the country payment in kind was an essential part of the terms of the engagement of labour. All such agreements would be illegal if Mr. Joshi's amendment were accepted. The amendment was rejected.

Mr. Milligan moved an amendment proposing to authorise the local Governments to extend the Bill subject to any relaxations that might be considered necessary. He held that this would enable a free use of the Bill to be made than was otherwise possible.

Sir *Frank Noyce* expressed sympathy with the object of Mr. Milligan. The speaker had reasons to believe that there might be a more rapid progress in the direction of extension of the Act if the amendment were accepted, but relaxation might also have dangers and, weighing the pros and cons, he opposed the amendment which was negatived.

Two other amendments of Mr. *G. Morgan* amending the same clause were rejected.

Mr. *Ghanshyam Gupta* proposed to exclude persons employed in agriculture. Sir *Frank Noyce* saw the force of Mr. Gupta's argument and offered to amend the Bill, including the same definition of plantation as appears in the Workmen's Compensation Act. Mr. *F. E. James* wanted time to consider the matter. Sir Frank Noyce agreed to take up the amendment on Friday.

Mr. *Leach* moved an amendment which would bring within the definition of the Bill motor omnibus companies run by tramway companies or railways or any private individual. Sir *Frank Noyce* accepted the amendment, extending the definition to the motor omnibus service, meaning any service run by a company or individual which is conducted on regular routes at regular intervals.

The two amendments of Mr. *A. G. Clow* making the object of the Bill clear, were adopted, but Mr. *Joshi's* amendment imposing obligation for payment of wages to temporary substitutes was defeated after Sir *H. P. Mody* and Sir *Frank Noyce* declared that the responsibility for the appointment of substitutes did not rest with the employers, but was a personal concern of the employed who absented himself. Mr. *Milligan's* amendment fixing the responsibility of the contractor in the terms of the Select Committee's remarks was accepted by the House.

Mr. *Joshi's* amendment providing for fortnightly payment of wages instead of monthly was criticised by Mr. *Clow* who opposed revolutionary changes. The amendment was rejected.

Mr. *Joshi* moved an amendment proposing that wages should be paid within seven days after the last day of the wage period and omitting the concession of an extra three days in the case of an establishment employing more than a thousand hands. Sir *H. P. Mody* opposed the amendment. Sir *Frank Noyce* said that the Select Committee formula struck a balance between the two viewpoints. The House divided and the amendment was rejected by 38 votes to 59, this being the first division during the session. The voting was not on party lines.

A series of other amendments moved by Mr. *Joshi* was similarly defeated. His motion that when an employer discharged a servant the latter must be paid promptly, was opposed by Sir *Cowasji Jehangir*, Mr. *Milligan* and Sir *Frank Noyce*, but was supported by Mr. *Pant* and Mr. *Giri*. As regards the practical difficulties pointed out, Mr. Pant retorted "Don't" turn him out until his dues have been calculated".

Sir *Cowasji* explained how this would be impossible in the case of piece-workers. Sir Homy Mody said that the services of an employee might be discharged only in exceptional cases like theft or misbehaviour, and it was therefore unjust that the employer should be asked to pay his dues immediately and not given time to settle the accounts. Mr. *Joshi* by another amendment wanted that in case an employee goes on leave and his services are terminated at that time or while he is on leave, then his wages should be paid on the day he proceeds on leave or his services are terminated. Sir *Frank Noyce* opposing said, "We Government servants are not paid before we go on leave"

Clauses 5, 6 and 7 were then passed. The only noteworthy change effected was on the motion of Mr. *Milligan* to clause 7 whereby deductions to be made from the amount due to an employee could include subscription to any provident fund approved by the local Government. This amendment met the support of Mr. Joshi and the Government.

Adjournment Motions Disallowed

6th. FEBRUARY :—The adjournment motion of *Sardar Sant Singh* relating to the Howrah Bridge contract was ruled out of order by the President on the ground that it was not a definite and urgent matter.

Sardar Sant Singh's second adjournment motion relating to the security demand from "Abhyudaya" for publishing the speech of Pundit Krishnakant Malaviya was also ruled out of order on the ground that it was not urgent and a matter of privilege (privilege of the Assembly members to publish their speeches in the Assembly) and could not be discussed under the rules through an adjournment motion.

Criminal Law Amend. Act Repeal Bill

The House next resumed consideration of the clauses of Mr. *B. Das's* Bill to repeal the Criminal Law Amendment Act. Mr. P. J. Griffths, who had not finished his speech last session, not being a member of the House now, Mr. Sri Prakash started the discussion by supporting the Bill.

Mr. *Sri Prakash* said that the ordinary law was quite enough to deal with the situation. That this law had not been of much use was clear from the fact that, after the passage of the Act of 1908, as many as 58 terrorist crimes had been perpetrated. Moreover, this law not only applied a ban on Congress organisations, but also such harmless educational institutions as the Kashi Vidyapith. This unfortunate institution had been searched a hundred and fifty times during the last fifteen years of its existence and several of its students had been detained for months in jail and then found to be innocent. On none of these occasions was a single incriminating article found in the Vidyapith premises. Continuing Mr. Sri Prakash gave an instance of how at midnight forty school children were turned out of the school and this building was seized by the police and how even now the Prem Mahavidyala had remained closed for three and a half years. The Hindustani Sevadal had been closed for the existence of a rifle not yet traced by the Home Member. He appealed to the Law Member, whose patriotism, sacrifice and knowledge the speaker acknowledged to be none the less than any member of the House. He criticised at length the District Magistrates, particularly the Indian officials, adding, "We want Europeanisation of the lower services", (Laughter) He asked why the Government were getting a bad name by retaining this law while under the ordinary law they could do anything.

The *Leader of House* and his followers rose almost in a body and moved the closure which the President accepted in view of the fact that fifteen members had already spoken on the motion.

Mr. *Desai* requested the Chair to reconsider his ruling in view of the fact that his predecessor had ruled when party leaders wished to speak, and closure was not accepted. In this case he and Mr. Aney wished to speak and others too.

Mr. *N. N. Sircar* recalled the ruling given by the President last session and said that clause 2 now under discussion embodied the principles of the Bill which had been discussed threadbare upon consideration of the motion and Mr. Desai and other leaders had spoken during the consideration stage. Moreover, the ruling quoted by Mr. Desai referred to a resolution under discussion. Sir N. N. Sircar submitted that the Chair had already given his ruling which should stand.

The *President* upheld the Law Member's view and said that clause 2 of the Bill was the whole Bill and leaders of all parties had spoken on that during the consideration stage. He accepted the closure and put it to vote.

The House rejected the motion by 60-58 votes. The Opposition received the announcement with cheers and cries of 'shame'.

Sardar Sant Singh (Nationalist Party) spoke for an hour criticising what he called the abuses of law during the last few years. He asked the Government to produce a single case in which any executive officer had been punished for his excesses committed under the law. If any case were forthcoming, then he would be prepared to reconsider his views on this Bill. In war Red Cross Societies were generally protected and there were provisions in international law that the civil population should not be bombed and that women and children should be protected. But in this war against people's organisations nothing was sacred. If the Act was not repealed then the atmosphere of the country would continue to be unfavourable to the new constitution which would therefore prove unworkable.

The discussion was adjourned at this stage.

Payment of Wages Bill (Contd.)

7th. FEBRUARY :—The Assembly started to-day consideration of the Wages Payment Bill. On the motion of Mr. *A. G. Clow*, the House agreed to the definition of the term 'plantation' for the purposes of the Bill as 'an estate which is maintained for the purpose of growing cinchona, rubber, coffee and tea and on which 25 or more persons are employed for that purpose'. Mr. *N. M. Joshi* attempted to extend the provisions of the Bill to workers in sugar plantations also, but the President disallowed the motion on the ground that sufficient notice of the amendment had not been given.

Mr. *Joshi* next moved an amendment in order to make a provision in the Bill that no fine should be imposed on a worker unless he had been given an opportunity 'through himself or through representatives, including an officer of the Trade Union of which he is a member to show cause against the fine.'

Mr. *J. A. Milligan* and Sir *Frank Noyce* opposed the motion on the ground that the imposition of a fine, which was such an ordinary matter, should not be converted into quasi-judicial proceedings. Sir Frank Noyce added that the Act provided that representatives of Trade Unions might intervene at a later stage when the fine was imposed in contravention of the provisions of the Act. The House divided on the amendment which was defeated by 49 to 44 votes.

Sir *H. P. Mody* moved the following amendment: "That subject to any rules made in this behalf by the local Government, if ten or more employed persons, acting in concert, absent themselves without due notice or reasonable cause, such deduction from any such person may include such amount not exceeding his wages for thirteen days as may under this contract of employment be due to the employer in lieu of notice."

He asked the House to hold the balance fairly between the employer and the employee. The latter was given the right of demand of salary for the notice period, so should the employer have the right of deduction. The Fawcett Committee in Bombay admitted such right. At present an employer could forfeit the salary of even an individual employee. Hereafter it should be done if only ten or more persons acted in concert. Again, with a view to meeting Congressmen who were now opposing him, he agreed to whittle down the proposal by including the words "giving employers the right of forfeiture if only the employer had reasonable cause to do so and subject to the rules made by the local Government.

Mr. *N. V. Gadgil* supporting said that, in an unequal fight between the organised and influential employer and the poor ill-organised employee, the right of strike earned, at great price by the employee, should not be taken away from him.

Sir *Frank Noyce* said that the Government were prepared to support the amendment. He was glad that the adjournment of the Bill from the Simla session had enabled them to ascertain the views of the Bombay Government which were reflected on Sir H. P. Mody's amendment. The amendment contained three safeguards and would give time to the employee to think twice before resorting to a lightening strike.

Mr. *Joshi*, in the course of a one-hour speech, said that if the employer wanted damages from the employee the former had the weapon of deducting the latter's wages. But the employee had to go to court for recovering his dues. Experience had shown that the court generally sympathised with the employer and gave a decree for payment by instalments. Even if ten employees absented themselves with a view to standing a funeral of their colleague their action could be deemed as a lightening strike and their wages deducted not for one day, but for thirteen days.

Sir *N. N. Sircar* suggested a modification with a view to emphasising that there should be not only due notice but also reasonable cause shown by the employees. Then it would not be regarded as a lightening strike and there would be no question of deduction of thirteen days' wages.

Mr. *Joshi* did not object to an amendment being made at this stage, but feared that it did not change the substance of Sir H. P. Mody's amendment.

The *President* ordered postponement of clause 9, pending receipt of a properly-worded amendment.

Clause 10 was then taken up and approved without change.

Mr. *Buss* moved an amendment that Inspectors should be entitled to examine not any register or document but only those "relating to calculation or payment of wages." He said that the power as it stood could be used by an Inspector to secure information having no connection with the payment of wages and which could be of value to a competing concern.

Sir *Frank Noyce* admitted that there was a good deal of substance in Mr. Buss' remarks, but he left the matter to the free vote of the House. Government officials and a majority of Opposition members remained neutral. The amendment was carried by 32 to 22 votes. All clauses of the Bill were passed except one to which Sir Homy Mody moved an amendment. The House at this stage adjourned till the 10th.

Adjournment Motions Axed

10th. FEBRUARY :—Three adjournment motions were ruled out of order by the President to-day.

The first was by Dr. *Khare*, which referred to "the misapplication and abuse" of the Legislative Rules in the disallowing by the Governor-General of the adjournment motion on the Benda incident. The reason adduced for ruling this motion out of order was that the conduct or action of the Governor-General could not be reflected on by the members of the Assembly.

The second motion was by *Swami Venkatachalam Chetti* regarding the abolition of direct mail service between Madras and Rangoon. This was ruled out on the ground of non-urgency.

The third was by Mr. *Abinashalingam Chettiar* relating to the loss of Indian life and property in the recent Zanzibar riots. This was disallowed as no information was available about the incident.

"Abhudaya" Case—Privilege of Speech

The President informed the House of *Sardar Sant Singh's* motion claiming that the right of freedom of speech had been encroached by an order of the U. P. Government demanding security from the paper *Abhudaya* for publishing Pandit Krishnakant Malaviya's speech on the Bill to repeal the Criminal Law Amendment Act of 1908, which was delivered in the last September session, and asked : "Was the speech published at the instance of the member who made the speech" ? (Laughter).

Pandit Malaviya : It is my own paper ? I did not send a copy.

President : Has Sardar Sant Singh got a copy of the paper ?—No Sir.

Sir *N. N. Sircar* said that the privilege claimed did not exist. But even assuming that it did, on the English analogy such a motion was required to be made without delay. This Sardar Sant Singh had failed to do on the opening day, or even after his adjournment motion had been disallowed. Secondly, the speakers in the House of Commons ruled out a motion if a member failed to produce the paper in which the matter complained of had appeared. Sardar Sant Singh had failed to produce the paper. The Law Member, exhibiting the paper to the Chair and the House, showed that it was not a case of reprinting, but the paper also contained an article commenting on the speech. Sensational headlines had been given to the speech and a poem put within an ornamentally bordered "box", which *inter alia* punned on the word "Azad," meaning both freedom, and following the example of "Azad", a terrorist.

Sardar Sant Singh could not therefore, he contended, claim that it was a case of mere reprinting. Further, the Legislative Assembly rules were mandatory in that no business except official could be placed on an official day, except with the consent of the Governor General-in-Council or by way of an adjournment motion. No discussion on a matter of general or public interest should take place except on a resolution moved with the consent of the President and the Government Member in charge of the Department concerned.

Sir Nripendra Nath said that only if a *prima facie* case of breach of privilege was established, could the matter be referred to a select committee. The standing order specially guaranteed freedom of speech in respect of an official report of the proceedings only.

Sardar Sant Singh said that his claim was based on the opinion given by the former Law Member of the Government of India that the Press Emergency Act did not make any change in the ordinary law of the land in the matter of publication in the Press or otherwise of a Legislature's proceedings.

Sir N. N. Sircar: I have not suggested that there has been a change.

The *President* asked how the publication of the speech of any member by the Press was a privilege and what the rules regulating business on official days were.

Sardar Sant Singh read out the Local Government's order showing that the action was taken for the publication of Pandit Krishnakant Malaviya's speech and not for any comments or poems. The Sardar contended that if there was freedom of speech, it extended to the publishing of it, so long as the reproduction of the speech was faithful. The privilege he claimed was inherent.

Pandit Govind Ballabh Pant said that the Law Member had now suggested that the proper method to raise a question was to bring forward a resolution. The speaker feared that this too would be disallowed as referring to an individual case and not being a matter of general and public interest.

The question, he said, was whether the Press could be penalised and molested by the Executive of the Government for publishing a speech. The rules relating to freedom of speech had as a corollary freedom of publication. Certain privileges must be deemed to be implicit in the Constitution itself. A vital question was involved and it would be unfortunate if discussions were to be ruled out.

Mr. *M. A. Jinnah* said that Sardar Sant Singh had not delayed in raising the matter, but had been actively pursuing remedy after remedy. Mr. Jinnah contended that the freedom of speech granted by the Government of India Act implied freedom of publication and whereas, if the matter of the breach of this privilege was taken to a court, he could take his stand on the act, he had no remedy against an executive order except to approach the House.

The Government of India Act in granting freedom from action in respect of publication in official reports, he said, did not exhaust the privilege, because unless a speech could be published by a member, the right of the freedom of speech was useless.

The *President* said that that was why he had allowed such a discussion with a view to ascertaining all viewpoints.

Mr. *Bhulabhai Desai* said that the rules regulated only public business, whether official or unofficial, but this was a matter of privilege which was outside public business and above it. Whether the House had or had not the power of punishing parties for a breach of the privilege, it could consider whether the privilege existed and whether it had been broken and the House could appoint a committee to go into that matter.

The *President* wished to know why the matter could not be brought within the rules, which enabled a resolution being moved with the consent of the Governor-General-in-Council or with the consent of the President and the member-in-charge.

Mr. *Desai* answered that they knew in fact what the Government view on the matter was and how they could exercise that right. In depending on these rules, the House would be invoking, in the matter of its privileges, the restrictions embodied in those rules in favour of the Executive and place the House at the mercy of the Executive.

Sir N. N. Sircar pointed out that the action against the *Abhudaya* was an executive action taken under Section 7 of the Press Emergency Act of 1931 and not an administrative action. The action being based on the statutory power given to the Executive, that power was open to examination by the High Court.

Sir N. N. Sircar added that unless it was a matter of great urgency, the House should discuss it only after complying strictly with the rules relating to the bringing up of any matter. At present the rule was mandatory that no business other than Government business could be transacted except with the consent of the Governor-General. It was open to the members of the House, if they felt that the matter was important, to jointly table a resolution. No question of privilege arose, because it had been laid down in the House of Commons that if a member published his speech, his printed statement become a publication unconnected with the proceedings of the Parliament. The House had no privilege outside the Statute, and it was only by the Statute of 1925 that the members got the freedom ensured to them as enjoyed by members of Parliament.

The *President* promised to give his ruling later.

PAYMENT OF WAGES BILL (CONTD.)

The House then resumed discussion on the Payment of Wages Bill and *Sir Homi Mody*'s amendment for preventing lightning strike was taken up.

Sir N. N. Sarcar moved an amendment substituting the following for Sir Homi Mody's amendment which was to be inserted as a fresh sub-clause: "Provided that subject to any rules made in this behalf by a local Government, if ten or more employed persons acting in concert absent themselves without due notice (that is to say without giving the notice which they are required to give either expressly by their contracts of employment or implied by the terms of their service) and without reasonable cause, such deduction from any such person may include such an amount not exceeding his wages for 15 days as may by any of such contracts or terms be due to the employed in lieu of due notice."

Mr. *V. V. Giri* opposed it on the ground that a new situation had been created in the Bill which firstly was not in the mind of the Government when the Bill was introduced. Secondly, Sir Homi Mody placed the text of the amendment before the select committee which did not accept it and, thirdly, at the Simla session the amendment did not find place in the Order Paper. nor did Sir Homi bring it forward.

Mr. Giri said that lightning strikes were declared by workers on provocation on the part of the supervising staff, who indulged in bribery and corruption. It was the inherent right of the workers to resort to such a strike, which right they were not prepared to give up.

Purchase of Two More Railways

11th. FEBRUARY :—The Assembly passed without a division a resolution by Mr. *Azhar Ali* urging the Government to take over control of the Bengal and North-Western and Madras and Southern Marhatta Railways.

Sir *Henry Gidney* opposed State control which, he said, has a history of failure. He added that if the two railways were taken over, they would merely add to the burden of the Railway Board.

Sir *Zafrullah Khan*, for the Government, said that the latter was entitled to acquire the Bengal and North Western Railway at the end of 1937 on 12 months' notice, or at the end of 1942. In order to purchase the two railways, however, the Government would have to find £17,000,000. Unfortunately, the Government's borrowing powers were limited during the transitional period before the new Constitution. Further, the taking over of the railways, if decided on, would synchronise with the setting up of the Federal Railway Authority. Would it be fair, he asked, to face the Authority with this as its first task ?

Excluded Areas

Towards the close of its sitting, the Assembly discussed a resolution moved by Mr. *Ram Narain Singh* on the Excluded Areas.

The *Law Member* explained how the draft Order-in-Council originated and agreed that the speeches in Parliament made it clear that M. P's realized that Indian opinion was hostile to any extension of these areas. The position now was that the House of Commons having on February 7 considered these draft orders, they stood over for the consideration of any amendments received from the House of Lords. Sir N. N. Sircar promised that any resolution passed by the Assembly would be cabled to Whitehall.

Mr. *N. V. Gadgil* from the Congress benches, castigated the order. He quoted Mr. Churchill as wishing to include the whole of Indih in the Excluded Areas.

Payment of Wages Bill (Contd.)

12th. FEBRUARY :—The Assembly to-day adopted, by 65 votes to 44, Sir *Homi Mody's* amendment to Clause 9 of the Payment of Wages Bill, penalizing lightning strikes. The House also passed the remaining clauses of the Bill.

Mr. *V. V. Giri* said that by the inclusion of such a provision the bill was regarded by the workers as an anti-stirke bill. Mr. Giri complained that the Government had not introduced the arbitration machinery as suggested by the Wolby Commission and now supported the proposal initiated by employers against employees, which was inequitable and unjust. Mr. Giri feared when employees felt strong they would combine and hit back employers.

Mr. *Ranga* opined that, if the amendment were carried, it would not only stop lightning strikes, but also irregular strikes, and thus deprive the workers of the only right which they now enjoyed. It would be a great hardship to penalise the worker for going on strike, for they suffered even without the existence of such drastic law as was sought to be passed.

Prof. *N. G. Ranga* accused the Government of being hand-in-glove with the Capitalists and declared that the amendment, if carried. would deprive the workers of the only weapon they possessed against unjust treatment.

Mr. A. G. Clow, speaking on behalf of the Government, poured scorn on the argument of the opposition. He said that the amendment, far from depriving the workers of any of their rights, would actually place them in a far more favourable position than they were at present. Mr. Clow said that to leave an employer, as had been suggested, to recover damages caused by breach of contract by filing suits was to give him an illusory remedy. The amendment was the merest justice to the employer. Mr. Clow assured the House that the amendment did not confer on the employer the right to withhold a single anna that was not his.

Criminal Law Repeal Bill (contd.)

13th. FEBRURRY :—*Sir Muhammad Yakub*, resuming his speech on Mr. B. Das's Bill seeking to repeal the Criminal Law Amend Act, 1908, said that abuse of the law was no reason for repeal. He asked whether the House knew the secret methods adopted by the Communists to poison the mind of the youth. Sir Muhammad read from a Gurmukhi pamphlet meant for tampering with the loyalty of the troops, telling them that Mr. Gandhi's peaceful movement had failed and that other methods should now be tried ; that, while outwardly remaining loyal, the troops should always work for the Ghadar Party.

Congressmen, said Sir Muhammad, were hankering after office and shortly Indians would sit on Treasury Benches and would need these powers to combat the growing forces of communism. As regards Mr. Sri Prakasa's speech, Sir Muhammad contended that the Prem Mahavidyalya and Vidyapeth had been made the hot-bed of Communist and terrorist propaganda. They taught seditious methods to the inmates of the institutions. Those who used these institutions and like cowards took cover behind the women and children working there, should thank themselves if the institutions had been declared unlawful.

Mr. Bhulabhai Desai amidst the cheers of his party dwelt on the provisions of the Criminal Law Act which was sought to be repealed and its legal meaning. This he did because he did not wish any member of the House to act in delusion, because certain words camouflaged the real meaning of the statute. The fact of the matter was that it was not open to any court to examine the question whether the Government had declared an association unlawful, because it interfered with the administration of law or dangerous to the public peace. These words were legally unnecessary and the clause would really read that the local Government could by a notification declare any association unlawful. They could not examine the opinion of the Government at all. If the Government wished to fight communism they could have amended the law and penalised associations which encouraged communism, but it did not suit the Government to have any definition. Captain Lalchand had warned them against exploiting young men. What about exploiting old men ? (Laughter and cheers). I wish and trust that a generation will now grow which whatever happened to the old men would make the exploitation of young men impossible.

As regards Sir M. Yakub and Sir Abdul Guznavi, they were the only fortunate beings to have received some red leaflets. Their source was apparent and they seemed to read them as if they were from approved genuine sources. The real question before the House was, "Should the executive continue to have power of the kind I have described, whereby the life and property of individuals who dare to stand for the freedom of the land is to be in their keeping and on behalf of those who believe that to be pro-Indian is not anti-British ? I ask the House to support the Bill (Cheers).

The House then divided on whether clause 2 of the Bill which was an operative clause would be passed. Keen excitement followed when whips found the scene was changing every second. Ultimately, the Government lost one vote down and the vote of *Khan Bahadur Rajan Baksh* equalised the votes, making it 66 on either side. Then Opposition whips tried to persuade Mr. *Lal Chand Navalrai* and Mr. *K. L. Gauba* to vote, but they remained neutral. Then the President declared that following the well-known principle of standing for status quo, he voted for the rejection of the clause. The result was received by the Government amidst cheers.

After clause two of Mr. Das's Bill had been rejected with the casting vote of the President, there was no other clause to be put and the Bill was thus killed.

Cr. Pr. Code Amend. Bills

Sardar Sant Singh secured an easy passage for his Bill to amend the Code of the Criminal Procedure, whereby the proviso to section 406 was deleted. He said that this section referred to proceedings for peace and good behaviour in the interests of law and order. Cases from Sub-Divisional Magistrates, who worked under District Magistrates were sent in appeal to District Magistrates, who being heads of districts were themselves prosecutors and judges. In many provinces such appeals were sent to Sessions Judges, but the practice was not uniform in all provinces. The omission of the proviso would ensure such cases going in appeal to Sessions Judges.

Sir Henry Craik, Home Member, said that though he did not append a minute of dissent in the Select Committee's report, he disliked the Bill still and was in fact opposed to it. Sir Henry informed the House that the Government did not oppose the Bill. The Bill was then passed.

Sardar Sant Singh's next Bill was then taken up. This also amends the Criminal Procedure Code by attempting to delete sections 30 and 34. The object is to abolish Magistrates, who are selected for their seniority and efficiency to deal with all cases in which the accused might be sentenced upto seven years' imprisonment. Sardar Sant Singh and Mr. Shamlal contended that these Special Magistrates worked under District Magistrates and their promotion depended on the latter's opinion There was the general impression that these "Section Thirty Magistrates" invariably convicted the accused persons. Mr. Shamlal said that this was the case at any rate in the Punjab. Sardar Sant Singh desired circulation of the Bill.

The House was discussing the Bill when further discussion was adjourned.

Payment of Wages Bill (contd.)

14th. FEBRUARY :—The final reading of the Wages Payment Bill was resumed today. *Sir Homi Mody* enumerated the labour measures passed and wished that Sir Frank Noyce and Mr. A. G. Clow would slacken a little. *Dr. P. N. Banerjee* wanted the House to hold the balance between capital and labour, but to be a little inclined towards the weaker party, namely, labour. Mr. *B. Das* wished Sir Homi Mody's amendments had not been moved and the goodwill disturbed. *Mr. Giri* hoped Sir Frank Noyce would get the Council of State to remove Sir Homi Mody's amendment to make the measure acceptable to labour. *Prof. Ranga* expressed the greatest dissatisfaction with the Bill and enumetrated the many directions in which legislation was still necessary.

Sir *Frank Noyce* continuing reminded Prof. Ranga that it was the motion of a Congress member backed by that party which had eliminated agriculture from the operation of the Bill. The difference between Mr. Joshi and Prof. Ranga and the speaker was that the former were men of war and he was a man of peace. (Cheers). He assured Mr. James and Mr. Joshi that if as a result of working the Act improvements were found desirable, the Government would not hesitate to bring an amending bill. Sir Frank Noyce thanked the members for the congratulations which really Mr. Clow deserved. (Applause).

The Wages Payment Bill was then passed.

Bill Prohibiting Loan to Italy

Sir James Grigg then moved for the consideration of the Bill prohibiting loans and credits to Italy. He said that it seemed possible and even probable that the war would last longer than Viceroy's Ordinance. It was, therefore, necessary to have the Act passed.

Mr. B. Das opposed the Bill because India's Foreign relations were entirely in charge of the British foreign office and also because the "old women" of Geneva did not act when Japan took away Chinese territory. He wished that the Government of India had taken similar steps against Zanzibar. He advised the House to take no responsibility for the measure.

Mr. *Satyamurti* analysed India's position vis-a-vis the League of Nations. He contended that whereas India was deemed an original member, she had no free voice and that the Assembly was debarred by a series of rules and standing orders from raising any question or debate on India's foreign relations. He asked Sir James Grigg as a member franker than the rest on the Treasury benches whether India had any voice or share in the matter of evolving sanctions. Why should then the House be asked merely to register a decree passed by Great Britain to whom India in the League meant one more vote for Great Britain ? The League had by her hesitancy encouraged Italy to launch on this campaign. India stood by Ethiopia and sent her a message of sympathy because she had not the power to fight on her side which she would have done had she been a free country. While the House could not oppose the bill, their attitude should not be misunderstood and he hoped it would be properly conveyed to the Secretary of State. Let the House send to Ethiopia a message of hope and cheer and to Italy "Bandit, thou shalt not go further" (applause).

Sir James Grigg, replying to the debate, said the speeches had been diffuse and spirited, but none except Mr. B. Das and Mr. Satyamurti had referred to the subject matter of the Bill. Mr. Satyamurti had enquired the position regarding mutual support and compensation among the members hit by the sanction policy. The Government had made full representation and would be represented on the committee which was to discuss the subject. It was difficult to prove that India had suffered very much damage because long before the sanctions against Italy became operative the trade with Italy had, owing to the economic difficulties, reduced to small dimensions.

The House then agreed to the motion for consideration, some members crying "no", but not challenging a division. The clauses of the Bill were taken up.

Mr. *M. A. Ayyangar* wished to move an amendment that nothing in the Act be construed to affect or prohibit the payment of insurance premia to any Italian company doing business in India with respect to policies taken before the passing of the Act. *Sir James Grigg* assured that the Bill did not affect such matters.

Discussion then arose whether assurance was enough for legal purposes. Some members wished the President to give ruling. Mr. *Bhulabhai Desai* said that the matter was not for the President to decide when based on any construction put on the clause by the Government. At this stage the proceedings concluded and the House adjourned till the 17th.

Railway Budget for 1936-37

17th. FEBRUARY :—The Railway Estimates presented by Sir *Zafrullah Khan* in the Assembly to-day forecast a final deficit in 1935-36 of about 2 and 2-3 crores more than originally estimated. For 1936-37 the budget anticipates a deficit on commercial and strategic lines taken together of nearly 3 and a half crores.

The revised estimate of deficit on railways in 1935-36 is 4 and a half crores against 5 crores of last year. The improvement is due mainly to the reduction of about half a crore in interest charges. Total traffic receipts of State lines are expected to reach 90 crores—a quarter crore less than last year. Total working expenses amount to 64 crores including 13 and one-fourth crores for depreciation, or the same as last year.

The total deficit of 4 and a half crores (of which 2 crores are for strategic lines) will be met by temporary loan from the depreciation fund which will stand at 9 crores at the end of the year.

Budget estimate for 1936-37 assumes receipts of 91 and one-fourth crores over current year based on slight increase in traffic anticipated and alterations in rates and fares made by railways. Total working expenses will amount to 64 and a half crores and will be half a crore more than in the current year. Deficits on all State lines in 1936-37 will be 3 and a half crores, including 2 crores on strategic lines. Balance of depreciation fund at the end of the year will be 11 and three-fourth crores. Loans from fund to meet deficits will stand at 35 and a half crores.

Works programme for 1936-37 is smaller than in recent years. Total sum provided is 10 and one-fourth crores after allowing for reduction of stores balances by half a crore. No new construction is proposed. Track renewals account for 5 crores, bridge work for three-fourth crore, other structural works for 2 and a half crores and rolling stock for 3 and one-fourth crores. Provision of 12 lakhs has been made for repairs of earthquake damages at Quetta. Programme includes provision of about 1,200 wagons to meet increase in traffic demands, of which 750 are broad gauge general service wagons to be added to the pool.

Sir Zafrullah pointed out that in the first six years after separation, railways had met all their liabilities, including the contribution to general revenues, and even in 1930-31, the first year of depression, they made the contribution to the general revenues, though from accumulations in the railway reserve fund. The total contributions to general revenues amounted to 42 crores. After 1930-31, though no contribution has been made to general revenues, railways had met the losses on strategic railways, about 2 crores per annum.

The main reasons for the falling off in earnings during the period of adversity, he summarised as :—

(a) world depression and general collapse of commodity prices ;
(b) striving after self-sufficiency by almost every country in the world, including India, and development of internal trade and production ; and
(c) increase in motor competition, and to a lesser degree, river and sea competition ;

to which should be added two factors tending to keep working expenses at a higher level than otherwise, namely ;

(i) labour legislation ;
(ii) improvement in service conditions of staff.

On the question of the striving of different countries after self-sufficiency and the development of internal trade and production, he said, "The general effect of this policy on railway earnings, so far as India is concerned, has been to replace long lead traffic to and from the ports by short lead internal traffic. With increasing prosperity and the further development of industries in the country, part of this loss may be made up, but it is apprehended that in the present state of world industry and international commerce, it will take a very considerable period of time for this happy consummation to be achieved.

On the competition of road-motor transport, he said, "It is estimated that to-day railways are losing three crores of revenue to the roads per annum. So far, the loss has mainly been on passenger traffic, but signs are not wanting that valuable goods traffic, such as piece-goods, is being lost to the roads. This process must continue unless there is a reconsideration of the present road and motor transport policy. At present, much of the money available for roads is being spent on the improvement, or reconstruction of roads in competition with railways, and yet there are in the aggregate vast areas in India which have no means of modern transport either by road or by rail. Then, apart altogether from road transport, river and sea competition has been intensified in the past few years. These interests, owing to the trade slump, have had to cut down their rates or go out of business. In some cases, it has been possible to retain traffic to the railways, but only by a reduction in rates with consequent loss in earnings."

As regards labour legislation, he pointed out that the application of the Washington and Geneva Conventions to railways had meant an increase of about half a crore of rupees per annum in working expenses. Increase of pay in pre-depression days to lower paid staff had cost a similar amount.

Turning to action taken by railways to improve position, he explained that during years of adversity railways had overhauled their expenditure, every item coming under their scrutiny. The result had been that working expenses had been reduced by about 6 crores per annum. Attempts had also been made by judicious increases or decreases in rates and fares to increase earnings.

He observed, "Till world conditions improve and there is a general rise in the prices of commodities there is little, if any, prospect of railways retaining the greater part of the traffic they have lost on this account. Though the signs may be faint, there are, I think, signs that the world conditions are improving. As regards the problem of self-sufficiency, the more outside countries become self-sufficient, the less will India export to them and unless there is a radical charge in general world policy, I am afraid there is little chance of regaining the traffic lost through this cause. As for the self-sufficiency of India herself, as her industries develop, presumably the country will become wealthier, and though we may have lost the larger portion of our long lead traffic, if there is more money to spend, it is bound to have its effect on railway earnings."

Returning to the subject of road motor transport, he considered it essential if the railways were to regain lost position or retain present position, that road transport should, so far as is possible, be placed on a fair competitive basis. He said, "The main difficulty, however, in the way of a proper and thorough co-ordination between rail and road transport, which is peculiar to this country, is that Railways are the concern of the Central Government, and the development of roads and the control of motor transport, that of the Provincial Governments. I fully appreciate the position of the Provincial Governments, whose policy is naturally influenced by a strong and often vocal public opinion. But there are certain fundamental facts which are sometimes forgotten.

It must be realised that over 750 crores of the taxpayer's money have been invested in railways in India, and in the last resort it is the Indian taxpayer who must pay the interest charges amounting to over 31 crores on this capital. Nor must it be forgotten that the success of the new system of autonomous provinces presupposes that the Central revenue will have a considerable surplus for distribution among the provinces. If the Central revenues are faced with the prospect of having to finance an unremunerative system of Railways their capacity to contribute towards the resources of the provinces will be correspondingly reduced. It will thus be seen that the financial prosperity of the provinces is intimately bound up with the prosperity of Railways, and it is to be hoped that Provincial Governments will assist the Centre in the adjustment of policy which now appear to be inevitable. We propose to discuss the question further with them in the near future."

With respect to labour legislation, he pointed out that a stage had been reached where a halt might be called, at least for some time more, especially having regard to the present financial position of railways, in the liberalisation of rules relating to the hours and conditions of work and the granting of further privileges to the railway staff.

He then referred to two factors which occasion considerable leakage in railway revenue for which early remedy was necessary—

(1) evil of ticketless passenger ; and

(2) under-charging of freight either by negligence or fraud of railway employees through under-weighment and misdeclaration of goods.

As regards the latter the necessity of a more rigorous check has been impressed on Agents. At the same time he made an earnest appeal to the members of the Assembly and, through them, to the general public to co-operate with railways in bringing to notice cases of such negligence or fraud so that a deterrent disciplinary action may be taken where the culpability of a railway employee can be established. As regards the ticketless passenger, he pointed out that the loss to railway revenues on this account was estimated to be half a crore per annum, and it is possible that it is considerably more. Government have been forced to the conclusion that stricter legislation than what exists at present is necessary, and it is proposed to place before the Legislature proposals for necessary amendment to the Indian Railway Act.

Comparing Indian railways with foreign railways with regard to the percentage yield of net revenue on capital invested, Sir Zafrullah said, "As against the rather gloomy picture of the present railways, we have at least the consolation that our position is no worse than the position of other railways throughout the British Empire and throughout the world ; in fact, it is considerably better than most other countries."

He concluded on a note of restrained hope and optimism, and said, "To sum up, the position, though causing anxiety and requiring ceaseless watchfulness, is not by any means desperate. Given a reasonable improvement in world conditions, regulation of motor transport on a fair competitive basis, a check on further concessions and privileges to railway staff, and legislation imposing effective check upon ticketless travel, there is a fair chance that the financial position of railways will gradually improve and that they will, within a reasonable period, achieve a sound financial position."

Reforms Extension to Backward Areas

18th. FEBRUARY :—The Assembly accepted to-day a non-official resolution recommending the extension of reforms to excluded and partially excluded areas as from January 1 next. Mr. *N. M. Joshi*, opposing exclusion, said that the idea emanated from interested parties, such as Civil Servants, who wanted some areas where they could escape from the "evils" of political reforms.

Although the resolution was not challenged to a division, there was some opposition from the European Group. Mr. *C. A. Witherington* (Assam) held that the people of the backward tracts were not ready for any change in the present form of administration. Dr. *J. H. Hutton*, on behalf of the Government of Assam, said that the cost of civilized administration in these tracts would be prohibitive. The primitive people were bound to resent legislation against their customs and rebellions were also a costly affair. Sir *Aubrey Metcalfe* explained the position in regard to British Baluchistan. It was maintained for strategic reasons at an administrative cost of 70 lakhs of rupees in excess of revenue. Introduction of reforms in this area would add considerably to the burden on the Central finances.

GENERAL DISCUSSION OF RAILWAY BUDGET

19th. FEBRUARY :—The general discussion of the Railway Budget commenced to-day. Mr. *B. Das* said that he had heard with a good deal of attention to the railway budget presented by the first non-official railway member, but confessed his disappointment. It had recorded a tone of optimism whereas the Public Accounts Committee as advised by the Auditor-General and under the chairmanship of Sir James Grigg had unanimously expressed alarm at the state railway finances. They were reaping the reward of extravagance of the days of Sir Charles Innes and Sir Clement Hindley. He would welcome an expert enquiry into the railways by men of the type of Sir Josiah Stamp and not by another Mr. Pope. The remedy did not lie in the direction of fighting the road-rail competition which would never end but by the abolition of Lee Concessions. This state management was really Europeanised management and perpetuated the sins of the past.

Sir *Leslie Hudson* on behalf of the European group said that the Railway Member's speech was one of the clearest statement of its kind heard in the House (hear, hear), particularly in respect of the frank manner in which the problems had been examined. If railways should be run on a commercial basis then much of the control and detail which were at present conducted from Simla and Delhi must be surrendered to the various railway administrations. Referring to the actual financial position, Sir Leslie Hudson drew attention to the fact that the Depreciation Fund had been reduced below nine crores and if the decreasing traffic revenues were to continue then he feared the railways would become an unexpected burden upon the resources of the country. The question of over capitalisation of the railways should be looked into and also the separation convention should be completely revised (hear, hear), as there was no prospect within a measurable distance of time of the railways contributing to the general finances.

Sardar *Mangal Singh* said that the administration always tried to discourage the export of raw materials but encouraged the import of manufactured goods which resulted in considerable reduction of traffic of the railways. The proposed raising of rates was most unpopular and would not result in any increase in earnings as they had already to face keen motor competition.

Dr. *Ziauddin* criticised the tendency of the Railway Board to overestimate the income and underestimate the deficits. He said that retrenchment had reached such dangerous limits that the low-paid staff resorted to backdoor methods, making the position of the travelling public intolerable. He suggested four methods, by which a saving of fourteen crores could be achieved; firstly the percentage of the amount debited to the Depreciation Fund was too high and they should reduce it at least by four crores; secondly, the defence department should take over the strategic railways giving the railways a relief of two crores; thirdly all railways in India should be amalgamated and divided into four zones which, according to his calculation, would result in a saving of three crores in overhead charges and fourthly, a saving of five crores could be made if the high rate of interest was reduced on the capital corresponding to the prevailing rate.

Sir *Ghulam Hussain Hidayatullah* said that the budget was very disappointing, because instead of providing amenities for the poorer classes it proposed to enhance third class fares. Examining the financial position of railways the speaker emphasised the need for a proper reserve fund. He warned against any increase in freight charges, or fares, as these "might be the last straw to break the camel's back," and urged, instead, that the two crores deficit on the strategic lines should be charged to the army budget.

Mr. *D. K. Lahiri Choudhury* opposed the idea of amending the law against ticketless travel, as it would only give one more handle to the police and railway servants to harass the public.

Mr. *Nauman* said that trade movement had been killed because freight charges stood to-day exactly at the same height as when the prices of commodities like hides were eight times they were to-day.

Sir *Zafrullah* expressed gratefulness for the temperate criticism, compared with the bitterness over a deficit budget. He assured that all the suggestions made would be examined and effect given to those which were practicable as early as possible, though it may not be within the space of twelve months. As regards ticketless travel, Sir Zafrullah did not admit that this evil could be completely abolished, but wanted the co-operation of all to check the evil, so that this might be reduced, and a bonafide passenger might obtain more convenience for his travels. Similarly, as regards corruption, the Railway Member appealed for specific instances for investigation and bringing the culprits to book. A system of check had already been introduced in certain stations wherefrom better traffic returns were noticeable, and this would be spread and continued. The Railway Member stressed the need for civility and courtesy by the staff to passengers. He informed the House that he had himself, whenever he found time during his travels, inspected the position of third class passengers without giving an appearance that he was prowling about. The House then adjourned.

Cr. P. Code Amend. Bill (contd.)

20th. FEBRUARY :—The House resumed to-day the consideration of the circulation motion concerning Mr. *Sant Singh's* Bill to amend the code of Criminal Procedure with a view not to give special powers to Magistrates to try accused charged with serious offences.

Sir Henry Craik, replying to the debate, said the case was completely demolished, that what was left was to give a decent burial. (voices : Oh). He contended that there was no popular demand for reform, except perhaps in the bar rooms, which he could well understand. Secondly, on the eve of provincial autonomy, would they be justified in imposing on the four provinces a system which would be costly and on provinces which were already having deficits ? It was not in the interest of witnesses to undergo the trouble of two trials. The unanimous opinions of local Governments and High Courts showed that a change was not in the interest of the accused. Now remained the lawyers, and all the speakers except one, who supported the Bill to-day, were lawyers. The Government would thus oppose the Bill at every stage, and the fact that he would not challenge a division on the circulation motion should not be taken to mean that he would not oppose the Bill at a later stage.

The motion for circulation of the Bill was then passed.

Repeal of Repressive Laws

Mr. *Satyamurthi* was cheered when he rose to move the Bill to repeal the repressive laws. He moved that the Bill be referred to a Select Committee. The Bill sought to amend section 124A I. P. C., section 144, Cr. P. C. and repeal fourteen acts ranging from 1818 to 1932, including the Madras and Bengal State Prisoners Regulations of 1818, Press Emergency Act, the Criminal Law Amendment Act and the Indian States Protection Act. He said that there was one common element among all, namely, mistrust of the judiciary and arming of the executive with powers to deprive the people of the elementary rights. The Bill, instead of increasing expenditure of provinces, would actually reduce it by doing away with certain unnecessary acts by the executive, such as detention of innocent persons. To the argument that it was undesirable on the eve of provincial autonomy to repeal the Acts, which might disturb the peace and order, his answer was that if that was a genuine fear the Government of India Act had made provision for all such contingencies. He challenged the Government to prove through any reliable source that public opinion was against the measure. He cited the judgments of Indian and British Courts to show that Section 124A I. P. C. was too wide in India. Mere expression of grievance against the Government and reference to the weakness and imbecility of the Government amounted to sedition, which was not the case in England. Continuing, Mr. Satyamurthi said that sedition was caused by causing disaffection against the Government established by law in British India. Under the new constitution that would mean the Minister in power. Supposing the speaker was a Minister, how would Sir N. N. Sircar, in the opposition, dislodge him except by words causing disaffection against the speaker's Government ? Mr Satyamurthi warned that this weapon would be dangerous in the hands of unscrupulous political parties in power. The irremovable executive in abstract had no interest in misusing the weapon, but a party Government would.

The House at this stage adjourned till the 24th.

Voting on Railway Budget Demands

24th. FEBRUARY :—Voting on Railway Budget demands commenced to. *Sir Zafarullah Khan* moved the Railway Board demand.

Pandit G. B. Pant moved a token cut of a hundred rupees in order raise a debate on the financial policy of the railways. He said that the budget speech had made no reference to the "Lee Loot" nor any regret been expressed for restoring the salary cut even when the estimates were not realised and the railways were running at a loss. Mr. Pant said that Sir Zafarullah had failed to face the problem in a spirit of scientific reality. The world was undergoing an economic revolution and, unless a solution was found courageously, there would be a political revolution in its wake. Sir Zafarullah had laid the blame at the door of the ticketless beggar and rail-road competition and had asked for an increase in the rates of fares. The losses were really under the goods traffic. Sir Zafarulla's predecessor had welcomed rail-road competition as conducing to maximum efficiency. He asked how Sir Zafarullah justified attributing the misfortune to this head. The entire mischief lay at the door of uneconomic rates and in this respect the policy of the Railway Board had been stupid, perverted and even wicked. Every foreign country in the world had reduced the rates and the salary bill as a result of the fall in prices, but in India, though the fall in prices was sixty to seventy per cent., there was an increase in the fares and rates of sixty to seventy per cent.

Sir Muhamed Zafarullah, replying to the debate, removed a number of misapprehensions and said that the experiment of lowering rates and fares had been tried but had only caused a drop in earnings. As regards salary cut, leaving out salaries below Rs. 100 there was only 9 crores left and he asked what was the scope for retrenchment even if the cut was imposed. He promised to give effect in the next year's budget to whatever suggestions made in the course of the debate were found to be practicable. The House divided and carried the cut motion of Pandit Pant censuring the Railway financial policy by 62 to 45 votes. The Assembly then adjourned.

25th. FEBRUARY :—Mr. *Sant Singh* moved an adjournment motion to-day with a view to discussing the action of the Finance Member in taking advantage of yesterday's question time in casting a reflection on the members of the House with regard to questions admitted by the President and thereby intending to deprive the members of their right of putting questions. After two hours' heated debate the motion was talked out, as the entire period of two hours allotted to the discussion on this motion was taken up by speeches of different members.

Mr. *A.C. Dutt* (Nationalist Party) then initiated the debate on the grievances of third class passengers on a token cut. He said that the grievances were as old as 1903 when the Government themselves publicly admitted them. He quoted the opinion of high Government officials that these grievances still continued despite the fact that third class passengers brought the largest revenue. In 1934 they had contributed nine times the amount contributed by all other classes of passengers. The main grievances was that the fare was high. The Government had gradually and systematically raised the fares.

Sir Zafarullah Khan, replying to the debate, said that the Government were at one with the members when they said that the passengers needed minimum amenities required from a purely human point of view and it was the duty of railways to provide such amenities (cheers). Then there could be no excuse on the part of railway officials for not offering all possible courtesy and attention towards passengers, who were in greater need of it. The grievances of railway workers were ventilated on a cut motion of Mr. *V. V. Giri*, who catalogued the omissions on the part of the Railway Board to implement the recommendations of the Whitley Commission in respect of the joint standing machinery for the prevention of disputes, establishment of employment exchanges, although this was pressed as essential so long as 1928, and also the non-observance of regulations under the Geneva and Washington conventions on several lines.

Mr. Dutt's motion was carried and the House adjourned.

26th. FEBRUARY :—After questions to-day, the debate was resumed on Mr. *V. V. Giri's* cut motion raising the grievances of the railway staff.

Sir *Zafarullah Khan*, replying to the debate, said that in the case of good many of the suggestions the difficulties of funds arose and he could not hold out a hope for the next two or three years. But in the case of other suggestions he would see what could be done. Shortage of funds stood in the way of setting up a machinery for settling the disputes. As regards Mr. Joshi's point, the speaker had not mentioned the Lee concessions in his speech. He had mentioned the amount spent on Labour not with a view to saying that the expenditure was undesirable. On the other hand, he had mentioned that if circumstances permitted, matters concerning Labour Legislation might be still further carried. As regards the question of passes, he gave details to show that in the case of the officers who were originally entitled to an unlimited number of passes the number had been reduced to twelve. But in the case of the subordinate staff the reduction had been very slight. As regards the recognition of Unions, the railways had all times encouraged the formation of recognised unions whose object was to obtain facilities for their members to bring their grievances to the notice of the Administration and on the whole to contribute to the welfare of the staff, and not to achieve personal ends. The cut motion was carried.

Mr. *Azhar Ali*, on behalf of the Independent Party, moved a token cut with a view to urging amalgamation of various railways.

Sir *M. Zafarullah*, replying to the debate, said that Mr. Sri Prakash's suggestions were all for standardisation, not for amalgamation and regrouping in the manner which might be feasible.

Mr. Ali's motion was carried.

Mr. *Essak Sait* moved a token cut motion to urge better Muslim representation on the M. and S. M. and E. I. R., and thanked the Independent Party for giving him time to ventilate the grievance. Mr. Sait said that there was almost no Muslim in Commercial Engineering, Traffic and Stores Departments of both Railways.

Sir *M. Zafarullah* said that so far as these two railways were concerned Government's orders had reached there only at the end of 1934, as a result of which these two railways had agreed to recruit twenty-five per cent Muslims in their superior services, as against eleven per cent in subordinate services, of the M. and S. M. and six per cent in the subordinate services of the S. I. R.

The cut motion was withdrawn and the House adjourned.

Abhudaya Case—Privilege of Speech

27th. FEBRUARY:—The *President* read out a considered ruling to-day running to over two thousand words on Mr. Sant Singh's claim that the breach of privilege caused by the U. P. Government's order in demanding a security from the *Abhyudaya* should be discussed on a motion in the Assembly, having priority over other business.

Towards the end of the ruling the President said that, whereas the new Government of India Act empowered the Federal Legislature to define the privileges of members of the Legislature, until that was done those privileges would be such as were enjoyed by members of the Indian Legislature at present. The extent of those privileges might be briefly indicated in general terms as being such as were necessary for the proper discharge of their duties by members in the Council Chamber. In addition to the President exercising such powers as had been conferred on him by the Rules and Standing Orders the House itself, when a breach of privilege was made out, could always upon a proper motion express its condemnation and in suitable cases make such recommendation to the Governor General in Council as it thought fit.

The motion of Mr. Sant Singh, for reasons mentioned in the ruling, was disallowed.

The President declared that privilege could not be raised through an adjournment motion as already ruled by President Patel. A non-official resolution was not the proper procedure as there was the risk of a ballot and urgency would be lost. Rule 24-A permits discussion of any matter of general public interest provided the President and the Government Member-in-charge consented. In interpreting the Rule he could not proceed on the assumption that either the President or the Home Member was likely to withhold consent in a proper case. The President therefore held that "the question of privilege of the nature involved in the notice given by Sardar Sant Singh can be discussed on a motion moved under Rule 24-A. Sardar Sant Singh having brought a motion without conforming to the requirements of that rule he disallowed the motion.

The President further said that when such a motion conforming to rules would be brought the Government might well be expected to find time for its discussion. The President before giving his consent to a discussion must be satisfied that a *prima facie* case of privilege had been made out. When such a case had been made out, it would be desirable to refer it to the Committee of privileges appointed at the commencement of each session and on its report the matter would be discussed by the House. The President after emphasising the importance of protecting the honour and privileges of the legislature suggested that the Assembly and the Government should consider whether the rules and standing orders should not suitably be amended so that the difficulties in the way of raising a question of privilege be removed.

Dealing next with the question of freedom of speech the President said that law did not protect publication of any such speech in other than official reports such as in a newspaper, however, faithful or bonafide such publication might be.

VOTING ON RAILWAY BUDGET (CONTD.)

Resuming the voting on Railway Demand for grants the European group initiated a debate on the urgent necessity of the co-ordination of communications throughout India and for this purpose the desirability of redistribution of the portfolios in the Viceroy's Executive Council so as to provide for a Minister of Communications. Mr. *F. E. James*, opening the debate with a cut motion, emphasised that rail and road were not antagonistic to each other. The legitimate competition which existed between the two was not a luxury as Sir Guthrie Russell stated at the Railway Conference. It was wrong for either one to impede the development of the other.

The European group was opposed to further taxation on road development or on road traffic. The railways had tended to hamper road development by raising the freights on road material. The proceeds from the ten annas of the petrol tax to the Central Government amounted to five crores and thirty lakhs. The consumption of petrol in Great Britain and other countries was much more than in India. Between eight and nine crores of rupees were collected on motor transport through the petrol tax and local duties. Fifty-five per cent. of this went to the Centre and remainder to the provinces. The Government's policy should be not to penalise one or the other form of transport. The railways must face competition on its own ground. The Government would do well to get the Bill ready. But, as for the railways, their solution lay not in restricting the other forms of transport, but in rejuvenating their own methods Co-ordination did non mean restriction. There should be co-ordination of authority in the centre with one member in charge.

Sir *Frank Noyce*, replying to the debate, said that the road development account had been run with a proper balance between the railway and road interests. There was the fullest co-ordination between him and the Railway Member, and if there had been a Ministry of Communications the railway losses would not have been less. He recalled that only eight years ago the Road Development Committee was set up by the House when no reference was made to rail-road competition, even as a distant danger, and the Railway Board's memorandum welcomed road construction and even road services parallel to railways. Within the last few years the competition had become serious. Sir Frank announced that the Transport Advisory Council would meet next July, and the Government had prepared a draft amending the Bill and the rules for consideration in July. The Bill on the subject would be introduced in the next Simla session. The Government were also reviewing the policy of the road account, and if changes were necessary, the House would be asked to amend the previous resolution at the next session.

Sir *Zafarullah Khan*, replying to the debate, said that certain general principles were accepted at the December conference between railway and shipping interests. It was agreed that both the interests should get together in order to adjust their differences in accordance with those principles. The Railway Member accepted the general principle mentioned by Mr. James that the different forms of transport were not antagonistic to one another. Unless the tendency was such that competition was wasteful and uneconomic the railways did not propose to interfere. Regarding the demand for one portfolio of communications, Mr. James must have realised that there was no agreement among all sections of the House. But the Government stood by the committed principle that a portfolio of communications should be set up. It was true that there had been some delay. This was because more difficulties had arisen than was originally thought.

Mr. James withdrew the cut motion.

Sir *A. H. Ghuznavi* moved a token cut to censure the Board for failure to provide money for the construction of the Dacca Aricha Railway in Bengal.

Sir *M. Zafarullah* said that three years ago the Bengal Government wrote to the Government of India quoting opinions of experts to the effect that if the railway was constructed that area's sanitation and harvest would suffer. Moreover, the Railway Board also found that the estimates of 1929, when it was found remunerative, if applied to the present conditions, the line would not be remunerative. The motion was rejected.

Mr. *Fazl-i-Haq Piracha* raised a debate on a cut motion and protested against the paucity of Muslims in railway employ. He gave figures which showed that Government orders had made no difference in the proportion.

Bhai Parmanand asked Muslims to be content with getting the Communal Award both politically and in the matter of the services. The speaker stood for defensive communalism and protested that a number of advertisements by the N. W. R. reserved posts for Muslims even above sixty per cent and gave the rest to the minorities, while not even a Hindu name was mentioned.

Mr. *Sant Singh* said that the Sikhs had not even a population proportion share in the services in the N. W. R. He wanted this cry to be called off or let the Government with one sweep retire and replace men on the population proportion everywhere rather than do injustice in case after case by supercession.

Sir *Zafarulla*, replying in a two-minute speech, said his responsibility was to see that Government orders were carried out. He had no desire to enlarge the scope of those orders and no amount of pressure would induce him to do so. He would take all possible steps to enforce Government order.

The motion was withdrawn. All railway demands for grants were passed under the guillotine at 5 p. m. The House then adjourned.

Financial Statement for 1936-37

28th. FEBRUARY :—The Assembly met to-day in order to hear Sir James Grigg perform the enviable task of disposing of the surpluses of three years' budgets. The public galleries were crowded and the House cheered him frequently as he unfolded his tale. The speech lasted for an hour and a quarter. The following are the principal proposals of the Budget :

No tax on income up to Rs. 2,000.

Income-tax and Super-tax Surcharge Halved ; now it becomes one-third of the Original Surcharge.

You may hereafter send one-tola letter (instead of half formerly) at an anna, and will have to pay additional half-anna for each additional tola.

The Finance Member had the satisfaction of providing for these taxation reliefs out of 205 lakhs surplus of 1936-37. The figures stand thus :

Revenue estimated at Rs. 87,35 lakhs.

Expenditure estimated at Rs. 85,30 lakhs.

Out of the realised surplus of 4,05 lakhs, items will be disbursed thus :

(1) 30 lakhs for agricultural research scheme.
(2) 10 lakhs for Research Fund Association.
(3) 20 lakhs for broadcasting.
(4) 108 and a half lakhs will be given to provinces on rural population basis for rural uplift schemes, to be approved by the India Government.
(5) 5 lakhs for cottage and rural industries.

As regards the surplus for the current year, Sir James Grigg proposed to allot 17 and a half lakhs for Sind and 27 and a half lakhs for Orissa for expenditure on buildings, leaving 197 lakhs which he would put into Revenue Reserve Fund to help out finances of the 1st year of provincial autonomy.

Sir James Grigg said, "I attached rather too much importance to the Cassandra-like prophecies of those who were concerned for one reason or other to proclaim that India was being ruined by its attachment to the British Empire and its adherence to sterling, and too little to the assurances of those who told me that India had a marvellous power of recuperation from economic troubles."

Last year the House decided to transfer the whole of the unallocated surplus to the Rural Development Fund. This surplus has turned out to be 2,81 instead of 1,13 as was expected. (*Figures are in Lakhs of rupees unless otherwise stated.*)

Revised estimate expect a surplus of 2,42 instead of 6. This is due to an improvement in revenue of 3,53, offset by an increase of 1,17 in expenditure.

Of this 3,53 improvement in revenue 1,55 comes from the import duty on sugar, 40 from Income Tax (duty to trade recovery being greater than expected), while duties on raw cotton, machinery, petrol, jute, sugar, and matches are "bearing for surpluses."

Expenditure increases were due to the Quetta earthquake (forty-one and half), interest on Ordinary Debt and other Obligations (10,63 instead of 10,49) and a number of items under Civil Administration in which Frontier Watch and Ward figures largely.

The Budget figure was 44,98. Substantial savings have accrued from unforeseen causes, for example, 10 as a result of troops being despatched beyond India, and the postponement of nine and half of new works in order to provide funds for emergency wore at Quetta. Against this has to be set expenditure in Baluchistan as a result of the earthquake and the cost of the Mohmand operations. These variations result in an under-spending of 4, which accrues to the Defence Reserve Fund.

Instead of loss of 13, a profit is expected of 6, due to lower interest rates, increased sales of stamps and higher receipts from trunk telephone calls.

The revenue forecast is placed at 87,35 an improvement of 83 over the revised estimate for the current year.

Receipts are estimated at 54,82. Allowance is made for 1,60 less from the sugar duty an improvement of 1,71 under other heads.

A yield of 17,60 is anticipated, an increase of 80.

Expenditure is estimated at 85,30, an increase of 1,20.

Ordinary Debt and other Obligations are estimated at 9.20, as against 10,63, a reduction of Rs. one and half crores.

These two new provinces start on April 1, 1936. Subventions of 1,08 for Sind and 50 for Orissa are intended only to enable the provinces to balance their budgets during their first year's working. They are not intended to prejudge the claims of these two provinces at the inquiry which Sir Otto Niemeyer is now holding.

An increase of 64 includes provision for two public health schemes in Delhi (18), the growing Broad-casting Service (4), Civil Aviation (5), and restoration of cuts in pay for the full twelve months instead of eleven months last year (11).

Estimates stand at 45,45 including 60 for Quetta. Excluding this and making allowance for a certain accounting change this means an increase of 21, including enhanced provision for ordinance stores 20.

In 1935-36 it is expected to spend from Civil Funds forty-one and half and from Army Funds 36, practically the whole of this being on relief, temporary housing, and salvage. Next year from Civil Grants 40 will be provided, 12 for clearance and special staff and 28 for reconstruction. Under Defence there will be 10 for replacement of stores and 50 for reconstruction.

The reconstruction both Civil and Military is expected to cost something over Rs. 7 crores spread over seven or eight years.

Sir James Grigg justified the payment for reconstruction of Quetta out of revenue on these grounds :—

It is contrary to strict financial orthodoxy to borrow for expenditure which does not yield a cash return equivalent to the interest and sinking fund charges on the amount borrowed. Sinking fund provision is at present only Rs. 3 crores per annum or one-fourth per cent on the total debt, and the charging of the cost of Quetta to capital would be equivalent to reducing this already inadequate provision by amounts of the order of 75 per annum.

Debiting the cost of Quetta to capital would entail a burden on the central budget in the early forties, when it would or should be distributing a substantial proportion of its income tax receipts to the provinces.

It is proposed to abandon the scheme for a depreciation fund in favour of one for renewals and minor improvements, to which 25 will be contributed next year. An enhanced provision of 2 is proposed for providing postal facilities in rural areas. A net surplus of 15 is forecast.

A surplus of 2,05, is, therefore, estimated for 1936-37, with revenue at 87,35 and expenditure at 85,30.

The Government of India received 43 as its share of profits of the Reserve Bank during its first nine months' working.

Next year's sterling requirements are estimated to be £41 millions, including the repayment of the five and half per cent Stock 1936-38 without fresh borrowing in London

Excess of Savings Bank deposits next year over withdrawals are estimated at 8,25. As regards Cash Certificates the reduction in the rate of interest in 1934 has been, of course, followed by larger discharges. Except, therefore a balance of receipts and discharges in 1935-36 and a net discharge of 50 in 1936-37.

Government have been able to take considerable advantage of the low market rates during the year, both in converting sterling and rupee maturities and in borrowing funds through Treasury Bills. Three per cent issues at 98 in London and ninety-six and half in India heavily over-subscribed.

I have now set out the final result for 1934-35, the revised forecast for 1935-36 and the first forecast for 1936-37. I now turn to the surpluses that have either accrued or are expected to accrue and the Government's proposals for dealing with them. They are, first, the balance of Rupees one hundred and seventy-three and half lakhs remaining over in the Rural Development Fund from the surplus of 1934-35 : secondly, an expected surplus of Rs. 2,42 lakhs for the current year and, finally an estimated surplus of 2,05 lakhs for the next year.

From the balance of Rs. one hundred and seventy-three and half lakhs available in the Rural Development Fund we propose to allocate, first, a grant of Rs. 30 lakhs for agricultural research. This will cover Rs. 10 lakhs still outstanding of the block grant promised to the Imperial Council of Agricultural Research when it was first established and a further Rs. 20 lakhs for financing other urgent schemes of research some of which will be under the direct control and supervision of the Government. These other schemes include sugarcane research and investigations in connection with the dairying side of animal husbandry. This branch of the peasants' activity has not received sufficient attention in the past. Experience, elsewhere, emphasises importance to cultivators both as means of supplementing his income and of adding to his diet elements that make for good nutrition and, therefore, for good health. Secondly, a grant of Rs. 10 lakhs to the Indian Research Fund Association. Health is the vital factor in a measure aiming at general improvement in the conditions of village life and to the rural population. The association will be required to devote the amount mainly to schemes connected with the prevention and cure of malaria. Thirdly, a grant of Rs. 5 lakhs for the benefit of cottage and small-scale woolen industries. Hon. Members are aware that the case of protection of the woolen industry was examined last year by the Tariff Board and that for certain reasons, including the refusal of evidence on the part of an important section of the mill industry, we were unable to accept its claim to protection. But woolen manufacture is also carried on in cottages and in small scale workshops and the Tariff Board's findings suggested that this branch of industry stood in greater need for assistance than others. Further, there was no reason why the action of the manufacturers should be allowed to prejudice its claims. But, as the Tariff Board pointed out in this case, cottage industry is likely to derive more benefit from technical advice and assistance in marketing arrangements than from the imposition of protective duties.

The Government, therefore, propose to make a grant for the benefit of cottage and small scale woolen industry amounting to Rs. 5 lakhs to be spread over 5 years and our intention is that it should be administered on lines somewhat similar to those adopted in the case of a corresponding grant for sericulture except that, as research is not likely to be involved, the States will not participate in the allocation of the funds. The actual execution of provincial schemes financed from this grant will be in the hands of Provincial Departments of Industries. Fourthly, a grant of Rs. 20 lakhs to the fund for the development of broadcasting. This fund is, of course, only available for capital expenditure.

The recurring expenditure is to be provided in the budget in the normal way. In my speech last year I emphasised that the expression "economic development and improvement of rural areas" was used "in a wide sense to cover any measures which will conduce to the amelioration of the conditions of the cultivators and rural classes." Broadcasting, which now provides instructional lectures on agriculture and health, has quite a legitimate claim on this fund and the additional grant will help to satisfy the demand for such information over a larger area. This allocation will bring the fund to Rs. 40 lakhs, although the expenditure so far incurred against the fund amounts to rather less than Rs. 4 lakhs (for the Delhi station). We have before us estimates for work costing Rs. 52 lakhs and the field for further development is extensive. It is obviously desirable—in fact essential—that we should have the best technical advice available before we embark on this further development. We have been fortunate in obtaining this, for the B. B. C. have very kindly lent us the head of their research department to advise us on our future programme and I hope it will be possible to place definite proposals before the Standing Finance Committee next time. After these grants there is still left in the fund Rs. 108 and a half lakhs. We shall in all probability allocate the bulk of this to the provinces on the rural population basis for expenditure on schemes to be approved by the Government of India, but before deciding upon this finally we shall review the results of last year's grant.

It will be remembered that I circulated to the House on September 6 last a full description of the schemes which have been approved by the Government of India in connection with grants amounting to Rs. ninety-two and half lakhs which have already been made to the provinces. We have called for full reports from the local Governments as to the actual progress and results of their schemes. We expect these to be available next month and in the light of them we shall decide whether any alterations are necessary in the conditions of our grants. It is needless to say that the Provincial Governments are more closely in touch with the local conditions and needs than we are, but at the same time the Government of India have their responsibilities in the matter and it will be for consideration whether we should define more closely the categories of the schemes which we are prepared to approve at all costs. We must guard against too much diffusion of effort and we must, moreover, be careful to see that our money is spent on most useful schemes. As soon as definite conclusions have been reached we shall take the House fully into our confidence both as regards the results of last two years. The Government of India have allotted nearly Rs. three and half crores in the way of special grants for rural purposes. I emphasise the word "special" for the leader of the Opposition waxed sarcastic over grants made last year as if they were only contributions which the Government of India had made to rural welfare. I dealt with that argument then and I have no doubt that I shall have to deal with it again. But at present my purpose is only to claim that we have shown and are showing, whenever resources are available, that we are prepared to supplement in no niggardly fashion the work that the Provincial Governments are doing on behalf of those in the villages.

Initial Building Equipment of Sind and Orissa : I now come to the surplu of Rs 2,42 lakhs which we expect to have on March 31 next. To begin with, I propose to allot Rs. 45 lakhs of it to the special fund for, assisting Sind and Orissa to meet their expenditure on adoption of the old provision of the new official buildings. It was originally intended to advance the amounts required for this purpose by way of interest bearing and repayable loans, but there are two reasons why we think that this would be ungenerous. First, because the needs of these two provinces look line being more than was supposed and, secondly, there is consideration of what has been done in the past in similar circumstances. In 1921 all the provinces were started off with the necessary buildings free of debt encumbrances. The N. W. F. P. was given at its inception not only the existing Government of India buildings in the provinces, but also a grant of Rs. 3 lakhs to adopt them. It might reasonably be held, then, that Sind and Orissa have corresponding claims on the Centre. Moreover, in assessing the subventions clearly the existence of liability for loan charges for such purpose would have been taken into account and it may, therefore, be said that for a good many years at any rate the Government of India would, if they insisted on payment of these loan charges, merely by taking away with one hand and giving back with another. I may perhaps add two things (a) that we propose to limit our liability strictly to Rs 45 lakhs and (b) that this amount should be divided so as to give Rs. seventeen and half lakhs to Sind and Rs. twenty-seven and half lakhs to Orissa. The reason for the apparent preference to Orissa is, of course, that Sind already has a considerable part of the buildings it will need.

After this grant there will remain available from 1935-36 a sum of Rs. 197 lakhs. Before I can deal with this we must not only look at the position as it is likely to be in 1936-37, but we must also cast forward and attempt to make some estimate of the position we shall be faced with in 1937-38 and the immediately succeeding year.

We now expect to have a non-recurring balance of Rs. 197 lakhs available from 1935-36 and an estimated surplus of Rs. 205 lakhs available for 1936-37. What does this imply for 1937-38, which we are assuming to be the first year of provincial autonomy ? If all goes well we may perhaps count upon certain reductions in interest charges and improvements of revenue which will produce what in the Government of India parlance is known as a betterment of some Rs. two and half crores over the figures for 1936-37. On the other hand the separation of Burma will cost us Rs. two and three-fourth crores in that year. While it would not be safe to assume the figure at least than Rs. two crores as the cost of initial adjustments which will emerge from the Niemeyer enquiry, i. e., on the existing basis of taxation, we can not expect in 1937-38 at best a bare balance. If this conclusion is right then it looks at first sight as if it would be unjustifiable to reduce taxation at all this year and, of course, it is always much more satisfactory to play for safety in financial affairs. I know, however, what feeling was aroused in commercial quarters by the postponement of their claim for a reduction of the emergency taxation in favour of the restoration of the pay cut and it behoves me, therefore, to look a little more closely into the possibilities. For this purpose it is necessary to look a'so at the year 1938-39. There ought in that year to be no major alterations in the expenditure while we may hope that if our affairs continue to go well there may be a further expansion of some Rs. 2 crores in revenue receipts. If this calculation is justified then it would perhaps be legitimate to reduce taxation in 1936-37 by something like Rs. 2 crores if we can find a non-recurring balance of about the same amount to fill up the consequent deficit in 1937-38. Here, then, is the significance of the Rs. 197 lakhs remaining over from 1935-36. I propose to ask the House to transfer this balance to the Revenue Reserve Fund available to help out the finances of the first year of provincial autonomy and in this way I can, with a fairly clear conscience, propose remissions of taxation in 1936-37 so long as they do not alienate the revenue to a greater extent than about Rs 2 crores yearly. What, then, shall the reductions be?

Reduction of Taxes on Income: The most insistent demand with which I am confronted is the claim for the abolition of the emergency taxes upon income and the House knows that there exist certain pledge upon the subject given by my predecessor. Complete removal of the present surcharge of one-sixth on the income tax and super tax would cost Rs. 276 lakhs per annum while the abolition of the tax on incomes between Rs. 1,000 and Rs. 2,000 which, as I said last year, must also be included in the emergency class, would cost Rs. 47 lakhs more Obviously if we are limited to surrendering no more than Rs. 2 crores yearly, we cannot meet the demand for abolition in full. But we can go a good way towards it and we propose to abolish the tax on lower incomes and to halve the present surcharge, leaving it in future at one-twelfth. In other words, we shall in the last two years have removed the emergency tax on lower incomes altogether and reduced the surcharges on income tax by two-thirds. The cost of the proposed reductions is Rs. 185 lakhs and the surplus for 1936-37 is reduced to Rs. 20 lakhs accordingly.

With no more than Rs. 20 lakhs left in hand we can clearly make no further substantial cut in taxation and we propose, therefore, to make a postal concession which, though inexpensive, will, we believe, be generally welcomed, if not gratefully received. This is an increase in the weight of the one-anna letter from half to one tola and the adoption of a scale of an additional half an anna for every additional tola. It will cost Rs. 13 lakhs yearly and it will absorb all but Rs. 2 lakhs of the expected surplus on the Posts and Telegraphs Budget and all but Rs. 7 lakhs of that on the General Budget.

Concluding, Sir James Grigg said, 'I have now completed my story. I cannot expect that everybody will find it agreeable. I do expect, however, that all fair-minded people will admit that it is reasonable to compromise between the claims of the agricultural producer and the claims of the direct tax-payer and the supreme necessity of preserving the credit of India. If I have erred I think it is in departing too much from the strict canons of financial orthodoxy which I put forward last year, viz., that non-recurrent resources should not be devoted to recurrent demands. The only justification for this departure is the fact that India's economic and political barometers are both rising. If they continue to rise all may be well. If they do not the rise will be proved unjustified. And perhaps I may end by saying that the economic barometer cannot rise if the political barometer falls and that the political barometer must fall, if economic barometer rises.

General Discussion of Budget

3rd. MARCH:—General discussion of the Budget commenced to-day. Sir *G. H. Hidayatullah* congratulated Sir James Grigg on the surplus and relief in taxation, but could not see eye to eye with Sir James Grigg regarding the economic conditions in the country. The Railway Member had said that the economic barometer was falling. Sir James Grigg had said that it was rising. Continuing Sir G. H. Hidayatullah said that it was clearly a deficit budget. A perusal of the finances of India over the last few years revealed that the revenues were not increasing while the expenditure was increasing. Unless the Finance Member put this House in order the speaker feared that provincial autonomy would be a failure everywhere. Finally, he asked the Government to pay greater attention to cottage industries and grant more subvention to Sind.

Mr. *A. C. Dutta* challenged the Finance Member's statement that India had passed over the depression for levels of prices remained where they were in 1929.

The purchasing power of the masses had not increased, the industries were not flourishing and unemployment was still acute. Whatever relief had been given it had affected the rich and middle classes, and not the poor. The budget was a political one in the sense that money was being spent on broadcasting for propaganda. Provision had been made for broadcasting in Midnapore District. He urged that the jute tax should be given to Bengal.

Mr. *T. S. S. Rajan* said that the poor in India were suffering just as a patient suffered by the attention of too many medical experts. Dr. Rajan said that Sir James Grigg had given no indication when gold drain might end, nor had he listened to the voice expressed in the House last year that Quetta reconstruction should be charged under Capital.

Dr. *Khan Saheb* said that among optimists and pessimists he wished to speak as a realist and hoped to convert others to the same view. Sir James Grigg had balanced the budget on paper and he congratulated him as a representative of foreign exploiter for his jugglery. After describing three sections of opinion which backed the Government, he said "Now I come to the point" Naming the case of Afridis he alleged that the Government were exercising pressure on the Afridis by a threat of stopping allowances given in view of the Khyber Road toll, thereby breaking solemn pledges of Sir Aubrey Metcalfe on whose information the Member had made that statement. Dr. Khan Saheb said that the Government were creating trouble between the various sections of Afridis and had recently imposed five rupees tax on bullock-carts entering Peshawar carrying firewood, thereby taking away all profit, which the Afridis made on that trade.

When Dr. Khan Saheb concluded, Sir *Aubrey Metcalfe* requested the President to expunge from the proceedings the remarks of Dr. Khan Saheb attacking a particular officer of the Government as having given a false certificate on payment of money.

The *President* said that the remarks which were relevant could not be expunged, but Sir Aubrey Metcalfe could give the necessary correction. (Opposition cheers). If he found after reading the report that the officer could be identified he would have the remarks expunged. (Official cheers).

Dr. Khan Saheb: "Whatever I said is absolutely true, and the Foreign Secretary knows it".

Mr. *Bagchand Soni* delivered his maiden speech detailing the needs of Ajmere-Marwara, where compulsory education had not been introduced, no provision had been made for technical profession, where water supply was unfit for human consumption and people suffered like dumb animals. In fact Ajmer-Marwara was treated like an excluded area. There was only one member for the Federal Assembly for Ajmere-Marwara while Delhi being half its area could send two. He urged the Government to satisfy aspirations for a hand in administration.

Mr. *Nauman* complimented the Finance Member for his skill and claimed as President of the Skin Merchant's Association, Calcutta that Sir James Griggs' action last year in reducing the duty on skins had pushed up exports to 169 lakhs which was the highest for twenty years. He urged reduction of duty on petrol and motor cars. He wished the Finance Member would help the industries and put an embargo on gold export.

Mr. *Basant Kumar Das* urged the claim of Assam for the petrol duty and characterised the budget as helping the British domination of India.

Mr *Suryakumar Som* said that at least a quarter of the rural grant allotted to Bengal must be reserved for meeting the danger of the hyacinth pest. Bureaucracy could not do any good thing with grace, he regretted, as the price of post cards which were really used by the cultivator had not been reduced.

The House at this stage adjourned.

4th. MRRCH :—Dr. *P. N. Banerjee* said that the surplus shown in the budget was really the after-effect of the heavy taxation between 1930 and 1934. Retrenchment of civil and military expenditure was the absolute necessity of the hour. Without this no progress was possible. India could not afford an expenditure of seven crores on Quetta. Three crores would have been sufficient. He expressed concern at the finances of the provinces and said that, unless the whole proceeds of the income-tax were distributed immediately to the provinces, and Bengal in addition received the jute tax, the carrying on of the administration in the provinces would become difficult. He opposed the proposal for a reduction in the surcharge and wanted a reduction in the salt tax

Sir Cowasji Jehangir observed that the picture drawn by the Finance Member was wanting in perspective for having underestimated the revenue of last year despite non-official advice. He had got a surplus, which was really recurring, but he treated it as non-recurring, and doled out as a benefactor, whereas that money ought to go towards the relief of the tax-payer. Then, again, Sir James Grigg was not right in forecasting what would happen two or three years hence as he had done, and ought to have confined himself to forecasting for the next twelve months only. "I have seen forecasts in times gone by. I had a little experience of making budgets myself. I have seen how forecasts break down, especially in conditions in which we are living to-day, with war clouds which appear to be gathering in the Far East. Let the Finance Member listen to our advice, and not repeat his attitude of last year and treat the tax-payer with greater liberality. I have no objection to being taxed, provided that I am sure that the money will go really for the benefit of the masses and agriculturists, and to no middlemen or others. I object to seventy-eight lakhs being allotted for Quetta reconstruction and charged to the Revenue Account, and not Capital Account as it should be, even as the Government did in the case of the Pusa Agricultural Institute. Mr. Haroon has indicated that there are fifty lakhs from the sugar excise duty. Let both these amounts be utilised for granting relief to the tax-payer. If the Assembly makes a reduction in taxation to this extent let not the Government recommend the Viceroy to certify the amount and say that the Assembly is unreasonable.

Pandit S. K. D. Palliwal pleaded for direct taxation instead of indirect taxation which fell with severity on the poor.

Mr. *G. Morgan* did not wish that his speech should be taken as remarks qualifying unduly the gratitude he felt for the Finance Member's budget. Sir James Grigg had, if not grossly, considerably underestimated the yield of revenue. What assurance was there that the actual surplus would not be greater than the revised estimates ? Sir James Grigg was persisting in bad estimates and he invited the Finance Member to show when non-recurring surplus which recurred yearly ceased to be non-recurring (Laughter). A case was made out for the entire removal of the surcharge if the revenues were properly estimated and Sir James Grigg had been maintaining the tax at a level unjustified by his own estimate of economic recovery.

U. Ba Si said that this would be the last time for a Burmese member to participate in the budget debate. Last year the Finance Member did not show the courtesy to their speeches. The economic condition of the Burmese people was very poor and he wished for a just adjustment between Burma and India of the financial relations. He asked why Burma had been neglected in the allocation of the rural grant and why, when Bengal, for instance, had been given half the jute duty, his province had been given no share of the rice duty. He urged that Indian Postal employees in Burma should be given an opportunity of transfer to India or voluntary retirement thereby meeting a legitimate Indian demand and also helping the Burmese to obtain employment. Concluding he urged Burmanisation of the Burmese army.

Mr. *Mangal Singh* looking at the budget from the point of view of the villagers, asked the Finance Member to reduce the price of post cards to six pies and issue instructions to the Provincial Governments to spend on rural reconstruction the grant of one or two selected items instead of spending a large number of items which was not very much beneficial to peasants. Concluding, Mr. Mangal Singh urged the Government to issue instructions to all local Governments not to impose restrictions on "kirpans."

Mr. *B. Das* said that it was particularly unlucky for Orissa for the Government gave large subventions to other provinces and too little to Orissa. The amount was particularly too meagre, as compared with the N. W. F. P. to make autonomy particularly real.

Pandit Govind Ballabh Pant, deputy leader of the Opposition, commenting on Sir James Grigg's practice in issuing his speech in two parts, said that this showed a distrust of Government subordinates and was the forerunner of a decay just as the Moghal Empire decayed when Aurangzeb became suspicious even of his own shadow. Referring to Sir James Grigg's references to Cassandra like prophecy, Mr. Pant recalled last year's budget debate in which the Opposition had told him of the underestimated revenue and said that it was a queer way of chastising the Opposition who warned him for his own folly of calculated determination to suppress the revenues. Last year the returns quite indicated the trend of the imports. Yet, Sir James Grigg underestimated the revenue. If he did so deliberately he should have frankly confessed like Sir Guy Fleetwood Wilson. The fact was that the Finance Member was neither a fool nor a knave, but quite sagacious, knowing his motive and intentions and imputing the worst intentions to others.

Sir James Grigg said that the Finance Department was devoting unremitting attention to the question of control over expenditure and he hoped to see improvement as years went on. Referring to the demand for reduction of the post card rate to half anna, he emphasised that the central budget should not be used for subsidising commercial departments. With regard to the lack of co-ordination in transport, Sir James Grigg remarked that unless the provinces realised and were prepared to co ordinate the various forms of transport and co-operated with the Central Government than some of them had been inclined so far, the revenues of the railways would suffer and correspondingly there would be delay in the provinces getting any share of the income tax revenue. The ratio of 1s. 6d. would certainly remain as compared to the present purchasing power: it was not overvalued but under-valued. Answering Sir Muhammad Yakub, the Finance Member informed the House that the question of restoring medical and educational grants was under consideration and the Government would come to a decision shortly regarding the money allotted for rural uplift. He also informed the House that the Government of India had called for reports from local Governments and before the allocation was made the whole question of the conditions on which the grants were to be made would be carefully considered, and it was possible that the Government of India would restrict the grant to certain narrower categories than at present. He contended that after a detailed examination of budget figures, there was no reason to suppose that there was anything very much in the way of margin as a result of any underestimate of revenue. His object had been to prepare the provinces for autonomy and look ahead. The House at this stage adjourned till the 6th.

Official Bills Introduced

6th. MARCH :—Sir *N. N. Sircar* introduced in the Assembly to-day the *Bill to remove doubts as to the validity of certain proceedings in High Courts* and Sir *G. S. Bajpai* introduced the *Bill amending the Indian Lac Cess Act* proposing to increase to seven and five annas per maund cess on lac and refuse to provide funds for improving and developing the cultivation, manufacture and marketing of Indian lac.

Hammond Committee Report

Sir *N. N. Sircar* then moved that those portions of the Indian Delimitation Committee's report which related to the Federal Legislature might be taken into consideration. Sir N. N. Sircar said that since the Government had not come to a conclusion as to what their recommendations were going to be, it would be difficult and embarrassing for any individual Government member to express his opinion on the report. Therefore, Government members would not participate in the debate, but all suggestions made by non-official members would be forwarded to proper quarters.

Pandit *G. B. Pant* moved that the report be referred to a committee with instructions to submit their report before March 18. The members of the committee would be Sir N. N. Sircar, who would be president, Sir Zafarfullah Khan, Mr. Desai, Mr. Satyamurti, Mr. Asaf Ali, Sir Cowasji Jehangir, Mr. Jinnah, Mr. Abdul Matin Chowdhury, Mr. Aney, Sardar Mangal Singh, Sir Leslie Hudson, Mr. Vassanji, Rao Bahadur M. C. Rajah, Mr. Joshi, Mr. A. C. Dutt, Pandit Nilkantha Das and the mover, the quorum being of seven members. Pandit Pant added that he did not mind what course the Government adopted for receiving the report of the committee, but personally he would prefer the report coming before the House and then going to the Government.

At *Sir Leslie Hudson's* suggestion the name of Sir Henry Gidney was added to the committee.

Sir N. N. Sircar said that he could not find another day in this session to discuss the report of the committee. He thought he would report on behalf of the House and that the Government would have these as the views of the House.

The *President* said that unless a clear precedent was shown that the House could delegate its function to the committee, he was not prepared to allow a motion of that character.

Sir N. N. Sircar said that Government members would be unable to participate in the proceedings of the committee as they would have no views to express.

Mr. *Joshi* wanted to move another amendment, but the *President* said that he could do so only after the previous amendment was disposed of.

Mr. *Joshi* thereupon, speaking on Sir N. N. Sircar's motion, complained that the Hammond report was unfair to Labour in several respects. He suggested an amendment of the report in order to ensure that all Labour seats would be filled through Trade Unions except in Assam where these unions did not exist. Secondly, a railwayman who had his union registered in a province other than where he resided should be enfranchised.

Dr. Banerjee said that the cumulative vote was against the spirit of the Poona Pact and would in effect constitute separate electorates. It was for this that Mr. Gandhi had fasted. He opposed the proposal that only registered graduates should vote for the university seat, and particularly objected to the Bengal Government fixing a registration fee which meant that, though Calcutta was the oldest University, the number on its roll was the smallest of all the universities. He also criticised the proposals relating to Labour and commercial constituencies for Bengal and Assam.

Mr. *M. C. Rajah*, representative of the depressed classes, quoted the views of various depressed class witnesses before the Hammond Committee the majority of whom either favoured the single non-transferrable vote or the distributive vote. The cumulative system meant that neither a caste candidate nor a depressed class candidate would try to seek others' vote, thereby causing the Hindu Community to split and disintegrate. Mr. Rajah thought that this remark was against democracy and was liable to damage the work of depressed class associations.

Pandit G. B. Pant's motion for the committee was passed without opposition.

Labour Convention

Sir Frank Noyce moved non-ratification of the Labour Convention for reduction of hours of work to forty hours a week. He said that India had hitherto ratified the fourteen conventions compared to United Kingdom's eighteen, which had ratified France's seventeen and Japan's twelve.

Mr. *Joshi* moved an amendment that the forty-hours week be accepted in principle and be gradually enforced as far as practicable.

Mr. Joshi's amendment was rejected by 42 to 48 votes and Sir Frank Noyce's motion was carried. The House then adjourned till the 9th.

Voting on Budget Demands

9th. MARCH :—Voting on budget demands for grants commenced to-day. The first discussion held was in respect of the Home Department's demand to which a cut was moved to reduce it by Rs. 100.

Mr. *Desai*, on behalf of the Congress party, moving the cut drew attention to "propagandist activities through the Director of Public Information, especially the publication of 'India in 1933-34.' This publicity department had been continuously growing, particularly during the last three years, and despite the Standing Finance Committee's refusal to any additional expenditure, the Government had included a total provision for this department with its "record of the Rake's Progress." In the last three years the activities of this Department in this respect had taken a serious and unjustifiable turn. If it was merely a question of expenditure, however unjustifiable and high, there might be some excuse, but the activities of the Department had exceeded the bounds of propriety and decency. The first chapter devoted to politics was written with a venomous directness, yet to be beaten by the party press without attributing a single honourable motive in any good thing that had been done by the people's organisations. Referring to the Harijan campaign the report stated: "There was resentment as to sudden calls for cash which paved the way to reaction and in the circumstances it was natural that certain observers saw in the campaign motives other than a purely altruistic desire to remove social disabilities." By ascribing these observations to observers the author did not escape the responsibility of publishing them. In the name of Congress and in the name of honest work in the country, Mr. Desai wished to repel with indignation, resentment and scorn the method and manner wherein the great work done in the country for reorganisation and solidarity of the Hindu community and for the good of public life in general, had been described under the cloak of coloured observers. Mr. Desai quoted from the language of Mr. Gandhi on the Harijan campaign and the Secretary of the Central Harijan Sevak Sangh and said that the statements attributed to Mr. Gandhi's campaign was entirely false. In fact Mr. Gandhi's tour of the country on behalf of Harijan uplift was marked by greater success and at the end there was contribution of two lakhs of rupees the accounts of which were audited. Where was the necessity of attributing wicked and impure motives in it. Mr. Desai referred to funds collected for relief of Bihar earthquake and how Mr. Gandhi advised workers not even to drink milk when earthquake sufferers' demands were great and therefore every pie should be spent on sufferers.

Sir *Henry Craik* expressed surprise at Mr. Desai working up indignation over the prefatory note attached to the book when the same prefatory note was attached to all previous publications of this character, the contents of which were based on the Press and public comments. Sir Henry made it absolutely clear that neither the present Director of Public Information nor any of his predecessors nor any of their staff had anything to do with this book except the purely mechanical part of issuing it. The responsibility for the book and its contents were his (Home Member's) and if there was any personal bias or unfairness that blame did not attach to the Director of Information. Sir Henry Craik was amused at finding that the Congress Party had led themselves to believe that there should be no opinion except their own. There were always more than one point of view on each question. The book itself was on the whole a colourless and dull account. Indeed his own criticism of the first chapter was that it was too much of the history of the Congress activities and not enough of the history of India. Sir Henry quoting from the "Tribune" said that the paper had approved of "fulness and vigour of expression which could not be surpassed by any Congress chronicler". Again the paper stated that it did not remember on any previous occasion when the views of the Indian Press were quoted so largely in the official report as in the present case and in fact the present report was a wholesome departure from the unhealthy practice of the past. The Government made no false statement when it stated in the report that it was in the opinion of some observers that the Harijan campaign was actuated by motives other than of purely altruistic desire to remove social disabilities. The Government themselves had not the slightest desire to throw any doubt on the character of Mahatma Gandhi's campaign.

Sir Henry Craik next dealt with the Bihar earthquake issue. He said that Pandit Jawaharlal's criticism of the local officials was rebutted in a public statement issued by eminent men of the province including Sir Sultan Ahmed, Mr. Sachchidanand Sinha who on the contrary paid a tribute to the officials' work. Continuing the Home Member said that there was co-operation between the Congress and the Government immediately after the earthquake. The meeting at which Mr. Gandhi was present offered respectful co-operation to the Government and chalked out a programme of relief from Congress fund with house construction and clearance of sand as top items. Shortly afterwards the Congressmen declared that these were beyond their capacity and though Babu Rajendra Prasad proposed handing over to the Government ten lakhs for house-making purposes through the Government agency, the Congress Relief Committee turned down the proposal. The unfortunate result was that there was lack of co-ordination between the Government and the Congress over the most important feature on relief and the year passed with more than half the Congress fund still unspent.

The motion was put and negatived. The Home Department grant was sanctioned.

FOREIGN AND POLITICAL DEPT. GRANT

Sir James Grigg next moved for the demand for grant on Foreign and Political Department.

Mr. *Asaf Ali* moved a cut motion to condemn the forward policy of the Government. He said that this forward policy was dictated by England in the interests not of India, but Imperial interests, the result was that there was more expenditure for Imperial purposes on the watch and ward staff alone. The House then adjourned.

10th MARCH :—*Sir Aubrey Metcalfe* emphasised that it was not at all based on Imperial considerations, but, solely on what was believed to be in the interest of India. It might not be a counsel of perfection, but it was the best and most economical solution of an exceedingly difficult question. The Government had no intention of pushing through a road in the Afridi territory by force. The Government were not entirely responsible for quickening the pace of the policy of peaceful penetration. The old belief in isolation had been affected and there was considerable awakening among the tribes. Any hesitation to inflict punishment for misdoings would bring the tribesmen down in storms into the plains. The Afridis and other tribes on this side of the Durand line were Indian subjects and it was the Government's duty to give them some of the benefits which they could not obtain elsewhere. Concluding Sir Aubery Metcalfe welcomed any criticism provided it was of a constructive kind.

The cut motion being pressed was carried by 72 against 47 votes.

Executive Council Demand

Mr. *Satyamurti* moved that the demand for the Executive Council should be reduced to one rupee. He said that this meant a refusal of supplies with a view to show that the House had no confidence in the Government, who had failed to discharge their duties honestly and efficiently. He detailed the numerous grievances such as non-committal answers to questions, monkeying with the policy of protection, lack of attempt to solve unemployment or uplift the masses or run the railways profitably. The Government always had imputed malice to the Opposition and if Congressmen said that two and two make four, the Government would say that it made three.

Mr. *James* (European Group) refused to accept the invitation of Mr. Satyamurti to refuse supplies to the Executive Council. If the Executive Council was refused supplies and members thereof resigned, were Congressmen prepared to accept office? Mr. Satyamurti had said that the members of the Executive Council served only British Imperialism? What was meant by British Imperialism? Could he define it? It was the language of the superficial critic. The members of the Government could not be blamed for sins of omission or dereliction of duty on the part of Ministers of provinces as Mr. Satyamurti had done. The members of the Government had given answers to questions in the House more fully than Mr. Satyamurti would be prepared to give when he became a Minister.

Mr. *L. K. Maitra*, supporting the motion, said that so numerous were the sins of omission and commission of the present Government that Mr. Satyamurti was justified in cataloguing them. Did Government accept any one of the twenty-eight motions passed by the House during the last year's budget sessions? No. Did Government think they were everytime more right than the collective wisdom of the House dictated. The fact wss that Mr. Amarendranath Chatterjee sought to be prevented from visiting Midnapore for the second time lest he should, by his activities, disturb the working of certain union boards started under the Government auspices. But the sense dawned at the nick of time and the arrest order was not given effect to.

Sir *N. N. Sircar*, replying to the debate, made a most humorous speech. He said that Mr. Satyamurti had mentioned numerous subjects and stated 'inter alia' that the Executive Council was not honest. It has been represented constantly that the Members of the Executive Council go on offering unprovoked insults. One of the front benches opposite, referring to the railway member, Sir Joseph Bhore, met Sir Zafrullah Khan who was supposed to be after all not half so bad as some of his other colleagues, (Laughter), said that he had not thought of 47,000 unemployed on the railway and nothing could be more stupid and irresponsible. Yet a storm raged the other day because an officer was supposed to have used the expression stupid to a subordinate (official cheer). (Mr. Aney had then interjected "callous". I am not complaining because the Congress and Congress Nationalists are one and the same. The only dispute among them was on a matter which was dead, cremated, and its ashes thrown into the Ganges (Laughter).

Another member had said 'callousness of the most brutal nature.' I have given these instances of parliamentary pleasantry practised by the other side. Mr. Sri Prakash, an amiable youngman outside, talked like a wild man inside the House. The idea of the opposite side of a fair fight is that they will use the bludgeon and we will fight with hands tied behind our back (laughter). If my speech is discursive, the only reason is that nothing coherent has been said by the other side. Sir N. N. Sircar continuing said that some one had remarked in the course of the debate that India had no enemy and never had any. Perhaps Darius and Alexander had met to investigate the caste system, and Mahmud of Gazni came to contemplate over the architecture of South Indian temples. (Laughter). Mr. Lalchand Navalrai had also talked of national solidarity and had with the same breath talked of the Punjabees as foreigners in Sind. (Laughter). I am now coming to one who talked seriously, namely, Mr. Jinnah, who wanted to know if any first class issue was there on which the Government accepted the views of the House, what about the factory and labour legislation of the past eight years, what about the discriminating protection, which, whatever the individual views of any Finance and Commerce Member, had been adopted in this country and what about taking off the income tax? Finally, someone said that the Executive Council is a subordinate body; if so, the grievance is not against the Executive Council but against this constitution, which everybody knows is unsatisfactory. I submit that no case had been made for the refusal of supplies to the Executive Council. (Applause).

The House divided on the Congress Party's cut motion which was carried by 68 votes to 62 amidst opposition cheers.

QUETTA RECONSTRUCTION

The next cut motion related to Baluchistan. Sir Cowasji, Deputy Leader of the Independents, moving the cut protested against spending on Quetta reconstruction from revenue instead of from capital. In Japan they had spent on reconstruction after the earthquake not from revenue but from loan. The same should have been done in India.

Dr. *P. N. Banerjee* supporting the motion quoted James, Mills, Adam Smith and other authorities and said that it was essential that the Central exchequer should not be burdened with expenditure on Quetta for eight years as was proposed.

Dr. *Ziauddin* thought that if the expenditure was to be charged to the capital, then the debt redemption fund should be increased correspondingly.

Sir *James Grigg* agreed with Dr. Ziauddin who had touched the crux of the question. The sinking fund stood at only three crores. If Japan had charged to capital, then let the House realise that Japan was borrowing sixty per cent of her present budget. Did the House want the Government of India to do the same? Sir Cowasji stated that India was a poor country so they must borrow. That had been the bane of Indian finance both in the provinces and the Centre to a large extent. All provinces except two were in deficits and were having very heavy debt charges. By adding to capital expenditure as suggested, they would be raiding on the sinking fund, leaving it quite inadequate for preservation of India's credit.

The cut motion was put and carried by 73 against 52 votes. The House adjourned.

ARMY DEPT. DEMAND

11th. MARCH :—Mr. *K. L. Gauba* moved on behalf of Independents that supplies for the Army Department should be reduced to one rupee. This refusal to supplies was, he said, based on several grievances, including retrenchment of Indian King's Commissioned officers under the War Block scheme, the late Commander-in-Chief's amazing revelation that the right material was not entering the Dehra Dun Academy, excessive military budget, employment of Indian troops overseas without consulting the legislature, refusal of the Army secretary to agree to Indianisation of Gurkha regiments, and use of troops against unarmed crowds.

Mr. *Tottenham*, interrupting, said that the Commander-in-Chief had never said that the material at Dehra Dun was unsatisfactory. What he said was that the competition was unsatisfactory.

Mr. *Gauba* replied that this was because the method of recruitment was bad and applicants were rejected for the political views of their fathers. He objected to the large percentage of cadets who were drawn from ranks totally unfit to become officers because of their lower status in life. The smaller salary of Indian commissioned officers also did not attract the proper type. He said that payments like ten lakhs to the Nepal Government should be included in the defence budget. He ended by warning the Government of clouds of war gathering and that a discontented India would give them no help.

Mr. *Gadgil* attacked the Army and police and said that frontier campaigns was always won by Indians and not British soldiers. It was a misnomer to call the Gurkha army Indian and felt that employment of Gurkhas and Pathans in preference to Indians showed that Government were afraid of another tragedy like 1857, if practically-conscious classes were recruited in the army. But the youth of India like that of Bengal showed the danger if kept out of the Army. The speaker had served in the war as an N. C. O. and was rejected for a commission on political grounds. He was glad that this had happened because he still remained an N. C. O. (non-co-operator) (laughter). He had not handled a rifle for fifteen years but could still shoot a Pathan member opposite straight like a bull's eye. (renewed laughter). He concluded by assuring that Mahrattas alone could produce an entire army and every university town in India could give an adequate number of right type of cadets.

Sardar Mangal Singh, supporting the cut, said it might sound strange at this juncture to ask for reduction in the army, but the conditions in India were quite different. The demand was due to the people's grievances against the Army remaining unredressed for a long time. The Government had recognised the principle of Indianisation, but at the rate at which they were proceeding they would replace the first British officer by an Indian officer only in 1942. The system of recruitment of Indian officers was also defective. Eighty per cent of those taken into Dehra Dun after obtaining commission tried to leave the army and join the Political Department.

Dr. Deshmukh explained how the Government cleverly whittled down India's demand for Indianisation from the Indianisation of the army to the Indianisation of officers and then Indianisation of units and declared that if a man was competent enough in competition, why he should not be good enough later.

Mr. *Jinnah* pointed out to the President that it was the previous practice that before the debate on army affairs proceeded much further the Commander-in-Chief gave the House an account of what the Government had done in the course of the year. That practice was later followed by the army secretaries and that practice helped the debate considerably.

Mr. *Tottenham* said that he was not aware of any such practice. Apparently there is only one Government member who is in a position to speak on army affairs. That is the army secretary, but at the same time it is desirable that other Government members should intervene.

Mr. *Jinnah* said that he wished to enter emphatically a protest as regards the attitude of the Government. It was this sort of attitude which made the legislature an absolute farce. "Just imagine speaker after speaker put forward the case from the Opposition. We are told that there is only one man on the Treasury benches who is the entire store of knowledge on army and nobody else". He suggested why could not the Army Secretary participate in the debate and if there were points made by the Opposition some member of the Government could reply. Continuing, Mr. Jinnah said that the Government considered the army as a garrison supporting British occupation and the Indian people wished it to be people's army. These views stood as poles apart. Whenever a popular demand was put forward the Government held out ultimate dominion status and Indianisation of the army.

Some argument took place between Mr. Jinnah and Mr. Tottenham regarding the number of officers' vacancies filled in yearly by Indians. Mr. Jinnah said that only a lunatic could say that India could not produce yearly 120 men to fill those vacancies. Regarding martial and non-martial races, the Government played the old game. If there was no class the Government created it. If there was class they kept them separate and made them fight each other. The Opposition too should search their own hearts. Mr. Gadgil talked of Mahrattas. Did Mr. Gadgil wish the Mahrattas to rule India? Let the Opposition also remove their own weakness and create sanction. Turning to the Treasury benches Mr. Jinnah said that they were making the great mistake by the present policy. They were told at the Round Table Conference that British troops would be withdrawn gradually. He was shocked to hear last year the Government saying that they could not reduce any. (Mr. Tottenham—Immediately). Mr. Jinnah—I understand you. My misfortune is that my countrymen do not understand your language. If you wish to Indianise the army there is no obstacle.

Mr. *Tottenham*, replying to the debate, said that the Government was working out a definite experimental policy for the Indianisation of the army on a fairly large scale, based on complete substitution of the Indian for British officers in the considerable part of the army. The present method of recruitment to the Dehra Dun Academy was definitely recommended by the Indian Military College Committee, which contained representatives of the Assembly. The Public Services Commission had assured them that the candidates were not refused admission on any grounds connected with the traditions of the family. As certain educational adjustments were being made, they would get the best men to fill the vacancies in the army and those passing out of Dehra Dun would also be the best advertisements of the present policy. Continuing, Mr. Tottenham said that the few Indian officers retrenched under the war block scheme were not retrenched out of political bias, but on grounds of efficiency of the army and would get the same terms as British officers. The pay fixed for Indian commissioned officers was the same if not slightly more than offered in England to British officers serving at home. There was a party in the House who criticised the general level of salaries even as they stood. The defence secretary asked the House to remember that India was the only important country in the world which had not increased her troops or defence experiment in recent years. Concluding, he assured the House that the army expenditure would be kept at a level which the defence authorities honestly considered necessary.

The Independent Party's cut motion was carried by 79 to 46 votes amidst Opposition cheers.

POLICY OF REPRESSION

Mr. *Aney* moved a token cut on the Home Department grant to protest against the policy of repression. He said that a similar motion had been carried last year and the Government had done nothing during 12 months. The Home member had not shown that any of the civil disobedience prisoners had been given substantial remission of sentence nor detenus released. Owing to substantial improvement in the Bengal position detenus could easily be released. Moreover, for the success of autonomy in Bengal and Federation at the Centre, the Government must create proper atmosphere by the release of these untried people. The speaker wanted repeal of repressive laws, removal of the ban on certain political organisations affiliated to the Congress and relaxation in rules with regard to the treatment of political prisoners. He particularly wanted such prisoners to be released, who during the civil disobedience movement had committed acts of violence under the sheer force of circumstances. (Sir Henry Craik—How many of them there are). (Mr. Aney :— There are five or six from Bengal and Chindwara districts.

Mr. *Maitra* supporting the motion spoke about the release of detenus. He said that in India even the freedom of thought was banned, which was not done anywhere else in the world and even religious meetings were also banned.

12th. MARCH :—*Sir A. H. Ghuznavi* said that the Government had revised the rules regarding political prisoners at the instance of Congressmen only in 1930. If the rules ought to be amended further, the Opposition should approach the Home Member who, he felt sure, would give adequate consideration provided the request was reasonable and just. Regarding detenus Sir A. H. Ghuznavi referred to the policy adopted by Sir John Anderson, Governor of Bengal, combating terrorism. Freedom was restored in suitable cases and work in industrial concerns was offered to detenus with a view to making them useful members of the society and every six months all cases of detenus were examined with a view to their release. He cited the cases of Mr. Sarat Bose who was given an allowance of Rs. 2,000 per mensem and Mr. Subhas Bose who was granted freedom to enable him to go to Europe for treatment. Speaking for himself Sir A. H. Ghuznavi said that in a number of cases he approached the Government and pleaded for those detenus whose parents felt that they had a strong case for release or for more liberal treatment and these were invariably considered by the Government.

Dr. Khare remarked that the Government were suffering from Indophobia, its predisposing cause being the desire for domination. If the Government had yielded at any time before, it was not due to constitutional agitation but other cases.

Mr. *Nirmal Chandra Chunder* said what the Opposition wanted was that these laws should be exercised humanely and not emasculate the entire youth of the country because of the sins of few misguided people. The tragedy of the situation was that the Government did not allow Congressmen enquire into the causes of terrorism and wean the terrorists away from it. The black and tan methods failed for a quarter of a century and it required Sir John Anderson with his experience of Ireland to try his new policy. But in carrying out this policy the popular leaders were not consulted and so he feared the experiment would fail. Instead of taking Sir A. H. Ghuznavi into confidence why should not the Government take Mr. Bhulabhai Desai into confidence ? That would at once alter the atmosphere. Why was Mr. Saxena prevented from visiting certain districts of Bengal ? Were Bengalis so cursed as not to see the well-meant efforts to wean away their children from the dangerous fold of terrorism ? The truth was that the Government knew if they were right in one case, they were wrong in nine cases.

Sir *Henry Craik*, replying, said that he had listened to the previous speakers' appeal with great attention. He wished the House not to pass a verdict on the past ten years, but on the record of last year. Since Mr. Aney moved a similar motion in March he would show that there was no element of repression in last year's policy. There were all over India only five persons in Jail in connection with Civil Disobedience, (Mr. Pant : Even now ?) and they had either committed acts of violence or committed an offence after the movement was withdrawn. Sir Henry said that so far as Civil Disobedience was concerned it was really out of the picture. There had been no sign of a revival of the movement and it was hoped that it would be unnecessary to start fresh measures in that connection. As regards detenus, the position in Bengal was that during 1935 no major outrage took place but there was plenty of terrorist activity in the shape of distribution of terrorist leaflets, posters and minor outrages, murder of suspected police agents and possession of unlicensed arms. Many absconders engaged in establishing a widespread organisation were arrested and put on trial, but there were other equally prominent absconders still at large and they had so far eluded police efforts to arrest them. The Home Member said that this showed that police vigilance could not be relaxed nor weapons to fight terrorism discarded. The recent discovery, after three days' search, of a most carefully concealed consignment of arms, which came on a vessel, revealed 40 automatic pistols and 8,000 rounds of ammunition. That was one of the greatest pieces of evidence that terrorism still existed.

Mr. *Malaviya*: How do you connect it ?

Sir *Henry Craik*: I quite agree that I am not in a position to say definitely that these arms were intended to be sold to the terrorists, but knowing the conditions in Bengal and knowing how arms have been smuggled in the past, it is not difficult to draw the conclusion that they were, as a matter of fact, intended to be sold to the terrorists. The above description of the state of affairs in Bengal was black, but there was the other side of the picture. There was a welcome improvement in public tone last year. The Government had released unconditionally 217 detenus, 101 of whom were placed in home domicile and 80 were being taught industrial work. There were still about 1,400 persons in detention. The number of arrests averaged in 1935 only 18 monthly, against 52 in 1934 and 44 in 1933.

Pandit *L. K. Moitra*: What about female detenus ?

Sir *Henry Craik*: The same applies to some of the worst crimes committed by females. I cannot accept the position that because a terrorist is a woman she is less dangerous. The Home Member next cleared certain misapprehensions and took the House into confidence, describing the method adopted before a detenue was arrested. He said that the Government engaged no professional spies or informers. An enquiry was almost invariably started with some kind of confessional statement by a person in the confidence of the offender. This was tested by the statement of another person in the inner circle, but those two persons were entirely unknown to each other. Then the statements were corroborated through intercepting documents or through cyphers discovered in the course of house searches, by the discovery of arms and by watching the movements of the accomplices.

Mr. *Asaf Ali*: Why not put them on trial ?

Sir *Henry Craik*: Then the source of information would dry up.

Resuming his narrative the Home Member said that all the above information was then checked by a very high police officer—not an officer on the spot, but an officer at the central organisation. Checking is so careful that I may tell the House that great many people pass through the net who never ought to. It will be within the recollection of the House that one of the three District Magistrates of Midnapur, who was murdered was Mr. Burge. Only a few weeks before his murder, complete dossiers and evidence against three persons came before the police. They were highly suspicious but the police did not consider that there was enough evidence to justify their internment.

"These three persons were subsequently convicted and hanged for the murder of Mr. Burge, and I think that shows that utmost care is taken to see that persons are not interned without due and careful scrutiny of their cases".

The Home Member next dealt with the plea for amnesty and said that amnesty granted always led to a recrudescence of the terrorist crime. Sir Henry Craik was glad at the testimony of admiration by Mr. Chunder to Sir John Anderson. "I think it is largely due to the Governor's efforts that a great improvement has occurred in public tone towards terrorism. (Hear, hear). I was glad to hear such a tribute to one who is a great and successful administrator and in whom all sober sections of opinion in Bengal repose real confidence. Continuing, the Home Member said that whereas every year motions of this kind were brought up in the Assembly it was curious that never was such a motion put forward in the Bengal Council. (Hear, hear). The Bengal Council passed an anti-terrorist Act in 1930 by 61 to 15 votes; in 1932 by 58 to 12; and in 1934 it passed a permanent law by 61 to 16. That was indicative of public opinion in Bengal whose people alone could feel the pinch of the position and realise the misery, suffering and economic loss involved in the movement. Sir Henry concluded: "I ask the House to pause very carefully before it passes a verdict of censure, not on us because we do not come into the picture, but on the Bengal Government, the Bengal Legislature and the public opinion behind that Legislature.' (Loud applause).

Mr. *Aney's* token cut motion was pressed to a division and passed by 63 to 62 votes. Mr. Jinnah and a number of other Independents remained neutral.

Emergency Taxation

Sir Leslie Hudson, on behalf of the European group, moved a token cut on the Finance Department grant as a protest against emergency taxation of 1931 and to emphasise the urgent necessity of its abolition. Sir Leslie recalled the promise given by Sir George Schuster in 1931 at the time of imposition of surcharge to the effect that relief must come first in resorting to emergency cuts of pay and secondly in off-taking the surcharge on income tax, and that special taxes would not in any case be extended beyond March 1933. The speaker said that Sir James Grigg had renewed the pledge in 1933 and then in 1934. So far as the income tax-payer is concerned, he, after four and a half years, has secured relief in two instalments, each of which reduced surcharge by one-third. The concession of one-third was based on the estimated surplus of 142 lakhs, whereas he now expects an out-turn of the year to give him 266 lakhs more, so that the actual amount before the budget surplus receipts he had for disposal last year was 408 lakhs—a sum of 64 lakhs in excess of the total cost of remission of the entire income tax surcharges. These calculations leave untouched his surplus of 500 lakhs in the previous year." In these circumstances retention of surcharges even last year was an unavoidable necessity. Relief could have been granted in the interests of sound budgetary position before the reforms are inaugurated and in common justice to the tax-payer.

Sir Hormusji Mody hoped that Sir James Grigg would not regard the motion as legislative perversity. Let the emergency taxations be removed in fulfilment of the solemn pledges.

Sir James Grigg replying thought that the debate was inaugurated as a campaign for relief of Harijans who lived in Bombay (laughter). He did not agree with the leader of the European group that by removing the surcharge on income tax and super tax there would be improvement in trade, which would result in an increase of income tax revenue. Experience in England did not support this view. He agreed that the general burden of taxation in India, taken all round, was very heavy, but considering the income tax by itself, it was not true to say that the burden in India in upper ranges was much heavier than they were in the United Kingdom. They should also remember the burden of taxation by protection tariff. Proceeding Sir James Grigg emphasised that specific pledges of the Government were confined to pay cut and surcharges on income tax. The pledge in relation to other taxes was only in so far as it was a pledge implicit in the use of the word "emergency'

The motion of the European leader was rejected by 43 against 17 votes. The House then adjourned.

Custom Employees' Grievances

13th. MARCH :— Mr. *N. M. Joshi* moved a token cut in order to voice the grievances of the employees of the Customs Department in Bombay His main suggestion was that the scales of pay of the clerks of the Customs Office should be brought to the same level as the clerks in other offices in Bombay under the Government of India. He also wanted to give the employees the option of joining the provident fund or pension or their dependents to demand gratuity in case of the premature death of an employee.

Mr. *A. H. Lloyd*, replying to the debate, said that the scale of pay of Customs clerks could not be raised as the nature of their work was quite different from that of other offices of the Government of India in Bombay.

After Mr. Lloyd had replied to minor individual grievances, the cut motion was rejected.

Postal Employees

Mr. *Joshi* moved a cut to ventilate the grievances of postal employees. He wanted that postmen should not be debarred from becoming clerks after the age of thirty and that Indian postmen in Burma should be given the option, after the separation of Burma, either of remaining in Burma, or returning to India to the same department or retiring with adequate pension.

Mr. *D. K. Lahiri Chaudhury* mentioned the difficulties of the Railway Mail Service Union. Dr. *P. N. Banerjee* supported the motion, while Mr. *Giri* detailed the grievances of lower paid clerks and postmen. Mr. *Anwar-ul-Azim* supported Mr. Joshi's motion and detailed the grievances of postal employees in his territory.

Mr. *Bewoor* spoke for forty-five minutes and replied in detail to the various points. He said that there were thirteen all-India Unions with branches who had access to the head office, or Circle or local officials and all questions were freely discussed and the relations between the department and the unions were excellent. As regards postmen he could not remove the five-year limit before promotion to clerical service for the reason that he wished to give a chance to better class of men to fill the higher posts. At present there was no age limit, but the Postal Enquiry Committee had suggested that no peon above the age of thirty should be promoted to clerk. The Government would examine this in the light of opinions by unions and the remarks of the members of the Assembly.

Mr. Joshi's cut motion was rejected.

Mr. *Bagh Chand Soni*, through the next cut motion, complained of the high telephone rates and particularly of trunk calls.

Mr. *Bajoria*, supporting, said that the Telephone Department was making too large a profit. In 1935-36 the profit was twenty-five per cent. He wanted the telephone system to be further extended in Bengal.

Mr. *Bewoor* said that in considering the profits, the whole of the Posts and Telegraphs Department must be considered. They were just meeting their expenses and therefore there would be no justification at the present juncture for reducing the charges incurring a heavy loss.

The cut was rejected.

Viceroy's Aeroplane

Since to-day's debates were confined only to few members, opportunities occurred for many demands for grants being passed, which hitherto had been passed only under guillotine. When the demand for allowances of the Governor General reached at 4-50 p. m., Mr. *Satyamurti* jumped up from his seat and expressed gratification that once at least this demand was reached. He wanted the Government to supply details of the sumptuary allowance of the Governor General. Why should such a large amount as Rs. 75,000 be spent annually on the maintenance of the Viceroy's aeroplane ? (Mr. Aney—What was the necessity of appointing a new Cabinet Secretary).

Sir Henry Craik said that not having been a Viceroy himself or a member of the Viceroy's staff he could not say what the various items of expenditure were made of. The sumptuary allowance covered the cost of entertainment. Sir Henry mentioned that the use of aeroplane by the Viceroy led to great economy, not only in the Central Government but to the provinces who made police arrangements for the Viceroy's train.

Sir Henry was speaking when the clock struck five and the House cheered and the President applied the guillotine and put the remaining demands one after other which took forty minutes. The House then adjourned till the 16th.

Factories Act Amend. Bill

16th. MARCH :—Having voted the supplies the House met to-day to devote to the consideration and passage of the Finance Bill in order to vote the necessary income to cover the expenditure voted last week.

Two bills were introduced. *Sir Frank Noyce* introduced the bill amending the Factories Act of 1934. The Act gives local Governments power to notify as factories the premises which have ten or more persons working in them or in their precincts, but not outside the precincts. The proposed amendment intends to ensure that the manufacture carried on elsewhere than inside the buildings can be regulated whenever necessary. Sir Frank explained that the Bill did not affect the position of factories which came under the present Act and was meant to deal with factories which employed less than twenty persons or escape the regulations because they did not use machinery.

Cochin Port Transference Bill

The other bill which Sir *Zafrullah Khan*, Railway Member, introduced provides following the declaration of Cochin Port as a Major port, for the transfer of statutory powers in respect of the port under the Indian Ports Act of 1908 and the Madras Outports Landing and Shipping Fees Act of 1885 from local government to the

Governor-General-in-Council. It is not intended to take over powers concerning the port health administration as a general question of port health administration is now under the consideration of the Government of India.

THE FINANCE BILL DEBATE

Mr. *Anugraha Narain Singha*, from the Congress benches, initiated the debate on the Finance Bill. Mr. Sinha criticised the increasing expenditure of the Government of India and its utilisation for non-nation-building departments. He gave a detailed account as to how the funds raised by the Congress were spent in Bihar in order to benefit exclusive sufferers and emphasised that the Congress President did not allow the workers to mix Congress work with relief work.

Dr. *Ziauddin Ahmed*, while congratulating Sir James Grigg on the way he had spent the surplus, said that the depression had not yet gone, for emergency taxes still remained intact and the Finance Member felt it necessary to export gold. Agriculturists needed more relief and continued peace. In olden days, when a Government changed, all old debts also automatically disappeared. He wanted centralisation of Customs. All ports whether in British India or Indian States should be under the control of the Central Government. The Tariff should be more simplified and protection to injustices should be given in the interests of the people, and not of capitalists. He asked the Government to spend more money for education and give part of the sugar excise duty to the U. P.

Mr. *K. K. Malariya* criticised the pace of Indianisation and the new Government of India Act. He wanted the Government to train more youths for commission in the Army and technical education and thus relieve unemployment among educated classes. Mr. Malaviya condemned the Communal Award as being anti-national, anti-rational and anti-democratic and particularly grossly unjust to Sikhs and Hindus. He opposed the motion of the Finance Member.

Pandit *G. B. Pant* said that he had not much to say this year as the Finance Member had taken away some parts of the Finance Bill which used to provide some ammunition to the Opposition. He, however, wished to say something about his statement in the course of the budget speech. Balancing of the budget was mechanical so far as a subject race was concerned. It indicated neither the progress nor the prosperity of the people. There was no advancement when the budget showed a surplus. On the other hand surpluses were dangerous for they led to extravagance. Substantial additions to the returning expenditure which survived in a country like India in the interests of the people were not the same as those of the Government. Sometimes they were opposed to each other. A case in point was the ratio. If the ratio was maintained at eighteen pence the Government gained, if lowered to sixteen pence the people gained.

Continuing, Pandit Pant said that when he had heard the Finance Member's remark about the marvellous capacity for economic recuperation it brought before the speaker's eye a panorama of sublime mountains, fertile valleys, extensive waterways and great crops plantations, but it also brought to his mind the millions of of skeletons of famishing people in inconceivable destitution. Why, he asked, India with such marvellous gifts of God was a country whose national income per head was half of the liquor bill of England per head and whose total budget was hardly equal to the customs and excise on liquor realised in England? The answer was provided by Italy's hunger for Abyssinia and Germany's hunger for raw materials. India possessed all raw materials and people whose habits of thrift and abstinence were the greatest asset was suffering in the grip of the octopus of aggrandisement of British Imperialists.

The real reason was England's policy. She gave peace to India to get the benefit of labour of the serfs, to use her raw materials and sell her manufactured goods. Sir James Grigg was teaching them canons of orthodoxy which were discarded in the United Kingdom. It was like a communist coming from Russia preaching Christianity in this country (laughter). The speaker quoted from Sir John Strachy's speech of 1873, when Sir John, as Finance Member, had declared that he owed a duty to India, but a higher duty to England. Pandit Pant did not know how far Sir James Grigg shared that view, whether he had no divided loyalty so long as he received his salary from India.

Continuing Pandit Pant reminded Sir James Grigg of the "buy British" campaign organised by the present King as Prince of Wales, how England had put tariffs on every conceivable thing which competed with British products and how even though the Green Committee had said that beet sugar industry would never flourish in England, Major Walter Elliott had decided to continue four crore of rupees subsidy on larger grounds, such as employment to forty thousand people. Sir James Grigg had told them that had decisions rested with him he would not have given protection to many industries in India.

Pandit Pant recalled the writings of the German Professor List in 1844 and the speeches of Burke to show that England prohibited the entry of Indian goods, because the country which sold agricultural produce must remain subservient. Was there, he asked, no way out of the present mess? Did it ever occur to the Government that India could have produced ages ago her own rails and wagons? Had Government ever enquired whether a single industry in India could be promoted? And even where protection was granted, the price paid was in preference for British products without any compensating advantage to India. It was because Great Britain was the political master. Had Sir James Grigg read the refreshing speech of Sir Gavin Jones?

Pandit Pant offering suggestions said that he wished Government to undertake industrial surveys through experts to mark out industries, invite capital, guarantee interests of three and a half, four or five per cent as they did in the case of railways and make condition that the State might take over the industry at the end of twenty or thirty years and the Directorate could have representatives of State and labour. It would have genuine co-operation. Let the Government, he said, adopt an active policy of industrialisation, mechanisation, agricultural co-operation and scientific planning, bringing about an equillibrium between agriculture and industry. This was State planning, State control and State regulation. It was not socialism, because except in the case of tea no industry at present was capable of being managed by the State. In the east men believe that they live not for bread alone and Christ gave life for others. Let Sir James Grigg become an economic messiah, and remember that the exports of India at the present, meant to pay for liabilities from which India derived no benefit, amounted to export of distress gold even if gold was not exported. He was personally not in favour of protection but he wanted economic reconstruction so that India could prosper.

India was one-fifth of the human race but did not consume one-fiftieth of the world's goods. United South America having a tenth of India's population produced four times more cotton and wheat, consumed all goods internally and exported only one-tenth of that. India could prosper in the same way. The barometer indicated a storm and the thermometer an unhealthy condition. Let Sir James Grigg forget both and make India grow as a healthy country, and then would India show that marvellous capacity for recovery which she possessed in the past and deserved to possess in future.

Mr. *Mathuradas Vissanji* quoted a large number of figures from the returns to show that depression had not gone. The position was better than 1931, but was worse than 1928. The main sources of taxation had already been touched, namely, sugar and matches, and he hoped that the Tariff Board would not impose new handicaps on the textile industry. In England numerous ways and means were adopted to come out of trade depression, such as deflation of the currency, trade agreements, subsidies and bounties. The speaker explained that in India these measures were either not resorted to or resorted to half-heartedly. Turning to the budget estimates Mr. Vissanji said that a surplus was shown only as a result of emergency taxation, and according to his calculation the surplus next year would be four crores. If taxes were added to this surplus from such sources as taxes on salaries, allowances and pensions paid outside India the Government could easily reduce the salt duty by annas four and postcard rates to six pies and also remove the surcharges on incomes. The House at this stage adjourned.

17th. MARCH :—*Sir H. P. Mody* said that the issue was no longer political. There was no fanatical free trader in India and Mr. Pant had done injustice to Sir James Grigg. The Finance Member had accepted loyally the policy of India. This country must industrialise if it was to solve the problem of unemployment. He wished to be whole-hogger even though the speech might not influence Sir James Grigg. He pleaded that the time had arrived for adopting a more definite policy of protection. Another Fiscal Commission should be appointed in order to investigate the question and also how far the scheme of protection in this country affected the consumer. Sir James Grigg was wrong in making the mathematical calculation that the consumer paid thirty-four crores yearly for protection to textiles and sugar. The speaker maintained, that the consumer paid no more than would be paid had there been no protection

Dr. T. S. S. Rajan said that the grant of ten lakhs to the Research Fund Association for anti-malarial work was miserably low. A hundred million people annually suffered from malaria, two million deaths were caused by malaria and seventy-five millions were indirectly incapacitated as a result of malaria. The direct economic loss to the country was calculated at 1,900 lakhs annually, while 7,425 lakhs were lost through the after-effects of malaria on efficiency. These were staggering figures. The Government seventy years ago started growing quinine as a philanthropic object. Now they had commercialised it and by sale through the Post Office made a hundred per cent profit.

Sardar Sant Singh referred to the communal Award which he described as unjust particularly to the Sikhs, and said that so long as the Nationalist Party in the Assembly was there, let the Government be sure that the issue was a live one though Sir N. N. Sircar had described it as dead and cremated and its ashes thrown into the Ganges. The whole country was against the Communal Award. Sardar Sant Singh referred to the discontent created in the Punjab by the Award and the situation that had arisen which required statesmanlike handling. Mr. Jinnah's efforts of Shahidganj were not in the right direction. The mentality of the Muslims not only in the Punjab but also in the Frontier was wrong as evidenced by the anti-Hindu Gurmukhi circular of the Frontier Government. Why should that Government be given a subvention from the Centre for pursuing this anti-minority campaign ?

Sir *Muhammad Yakub*, who spoke next, regretted that speeches like Mr. Sant Singh's were responsible for the prolongation of the British rule. The Sikhs were only fourteen lakhs in number. But in the conscious belief of support by thirty-eight crores of Hindus these handful of Sikhs, confined only to one province, were preventing the progress. The Muslims, he continued, at the Second Round Table Conference went to the extreme length of concessions on the basis of joint electorates but the Sikh community would not yield and the agreement failed. What was the use of raking ill-will by referring to the Shahidganj trouble ? Mr. Jinnah had gone to Lahore and made honest endeavours. Where was the response from the Sikhs ? The Muslims knew that the new Constitution was defective, but they were prepared to work it for taking the best of it provided that the majority community would satisfy the minority community in the same spirit as Zaglul Pasha had satisfied the Christian minority in Egypt. The House at this stage adjourned.

18th. MARCH :—Sir *G. S. Bajpai* was the first speaker to-day and replied to Dr. Rajan's remarks relating to malaria. He said that the policy of self-sufficiency regarding the supply of quinine in India was inaugurated by the late Mr. Montagu, but under the present Act public health was made a transferred subject so that whereas the Government of India had the control of production and distribution of quinine, they had no power to regulate consumption of quinine. There was no ground for the suggestion that the Government of India had changed their humanitarian policy to commercial profit. The Government of India sold last year 90,000 pounds quinine of which 7,000 pounds were sold to traders and the rest to local Governments without profits. The sale through the Post Office was the concern of the local Government whose explanation was that after meeting the cost of distribution, whatever profit they had made they utilized for free distribution of quinine. Under the new Act even the existing powers of the Government of India relating to production of quinine had disappeared so that it would have been madness on their part to go on developing the plantations without any guarantee about the purchase of their output. If the provinces wished centralization of production, they could approach the Government of India. He would examine the question and would forward Dr. Rajan's suggestion to local Governments.

As regards nutritional research the Government had spent four and a half lakhs in the last five years and the question of devising machinery for investigation and dissemination through the setting up of a nutrition board would be considered.

19th. MARCH :—*Mr. G. S. Gupta* resuming his speech to-day said that Lord Curzon had laid down progressive moderation as the land revenue policy of the Government of India, but subsequent events had proved that it was one of progressive exploitation. In a short period the land revenue had increased by three hundred per cent. He urged immediate reduction of land revenue and fixation of a minimum of 15 acres in C. P. and 10 acres in other provinces as the holding which should not be taxed just as incomes below two thousand were not taxed. In the interests of Lancashire, Bombay and Ahmedabad the Government were spending lakks and lakhs on cotton improvement, but nothing was done for rice which was the main crop of India. Finally, he urged reduction of freight on cattle imported into Chhatisgarh Division of the Central Provinces in order to help the peasantry.

Sir Frank Noyce assured Mr. Gupta that the Government were doing a lot for the improvement of rice. A rice committee under the Imperial Council of Agricultural Research was already working. The work that was done for cotton was financed by the cess raised by the cotton industry itself, and he asked whether the rice industry was prepared to raise a cess. Turning to the speech of Mr. Joshi, Sir Frank Noyce said that the Government were still engaged in considering those recommendations of the Whitley Commission which had not yet been given effect to. As regards the health insurance scheme, the Government of India had ascertained views of the local Governments and, although he had not minutely studied them, he feared that these views were not very encouraging. He cited the difficulties which the Provincial Governments were facing in the matter, which was mentioned in a recent speech of the Minister for Agriculture, Bengal. The Government of India had done a good deal in the matter. The policy of discriminate protection of stores purchase and the action taken after the trade negotiations with Japan and the Anglo-Japanese Trade Agreement were evidence of the desire of the Government to assist Indian industries in purchasing Indian stores. The Stores Department had given Indian manufacturers valuable advice. Continuing, Sir Frank asked the members who had not seen the Industrial Exhibition in Delhi to visit it and see the extent of the development of Swadeshi industries. The speaker himself was wearing Swadeshi shirt, socks and underwear and drank Swadeshi mineral water and his hat too was as swadeshi a headgear as any other member of the House and he also smoked swadeshi cigars. (Cheers). The Opposition members continued to think in terms of heavy industries like locomotives and motor cars and ignored the veay healthy development they had already taken place.

Dr. Khan Sahib said that economists and financiers had unnecessarily tried to complicate simple facts. What the country wanted was a just fair distribution of products of this country, but this could not be done under the present system of exploitation. The entire machinery must be changed, he urged. Continuing Dr. Khan Sahib complained that the Watch and Ward staff on the Frontier was officered exclusively by the British. The Frontier Government had wonderful ways of doing things. The military Secretary talked of civilising the tribes. Why did not he visit Chhotanagpur in the Central Provinces which was full of mineral wealth ? He would find there starved and ill-clad people. The tribes did not want any civilisation. The speaker expressed dissatisfaction with the new method of Indianisation of the Army, namely, by reservation of selected units for Indians. Thereby the Indians were made to accept the Colonial Commission with a much lower status than the King's commission. He cited the case of an Indian Viceroy's Commission holder who became a King's Commissioned officer. When this officer met a junior British King's Commissioned officer he saluted him. The speaker asked him why did he salute the junior officer. He replied : "We are brought up in discipline whereby whenever we see a hat our hand goes up." (Laughter).

Mr. *A. N. Chattopadhya* said that if the jute duty were refunded, Bengal would be able to show a balanced budget. The speaker narrated his experiences in Midnapore where he went twice with a view to hear the grievances of the people over re-starting of so-called union boards and the methods used by the police. An order to arrest him was issued on the second occasion, but the Bengal Government's intervention prevented him from going to jail. Externment orders had been passed on respectable persons in Midnapore, including a leader of the Bar, who had shifted himself to Calcutta. Curfew orders against youths had been in force for two years. The persecution of "innocents" was still proceeding. The people were poor and famine-stricken, still the police were employing harsh methods. Representatives of the people in the legislatures were helpless. What was the use of voting money for such a Government ?

Sir James Grigg, the Finance Member, referred to the remarks of Pandit G. B. Pant and other speakers suggesting that there was a golden age before the British rule and there were exploitation and misery after the British rule. There was a reply to this in some of the speeches of the Opposition members themselves. Sir H. P. Mody had spoken of this laud of poor soil and precarious rainfall and Dr. Ziauddin of 1,200 crores of private debt that did not show the richness of soil or of thrifty habits. However, the speaker wished to examine this oft-repeated charge and to show how untrue it was. There was reference in the Vedas to famine and to the subject of taxation including the salt tax (laughter). In Chandragupta's reign there was famine for twelve years. In 970 A. D. the condition in the Kashmir State was such that the Jhelum had swollen with corpses of the dead. During the Khilji and Tughlak kings 1470 A. D. a commercial traveller had remarked, "The land is over-stocked with people who are miserable. Few are extremely opulent and live in luxury." During Akbar's reign famine had resulted in men eating each other. In Sahjehan's time a loaf could not be bought in exchange of human life. (The Finance Member was often interrupted and now the interruption took the form of a chorus demand for the name of the book.

Sir James Grigg answered that these were collections by Dr. Finlay Shiraz. (Voice : Now we know).

Sir James Grigg said that there was no doubt that during the British rule famine had disappeared, and there was a far greater measure of security than ever known before. Sir James next read another quotation from Lord Curzon, who during his term of Viceroyalty had answered effectively to similar charges and proved how the British rule had given better prosperity, superior justice and a higher standard of material wealth than this great dependency had ever previously attained. (Voice : Your own propaganda).

Sir James Grigg : No one can deny that mistakes had been made, but on the whole we can claim that India has been governed in the interests of India and not in the interest of the United Kingdom (Voices : Question). Now the usual nationalist theory of fiscal exploitation has receded into the background on account of the fiscal autonomy convention, (Mr. M. S. Aney : It is a fiction) and now we hear much more of the drain of contributions to pensions, profit and remittances.

Proceeding, Sir James Grigg referred to passages from the External Capital Committee's report to show that it was British investments which had helped to develop India and that for a number of years in the beginning without profit.

Sir James Grigg was indeed surprised that Pandit G. B. Pant and Sir H. P. Mody had entered into an unholy combination. both asking for industrialisation and the latter asking for more and more protection given after less and less enquiry for longer and longer time (laughter). Two things had been overlooked by those who wanted protection that the industry protected should ultimately be self-supporting and secondly, they must consider the effect on the revenue of the protection given. Then again the process of making India self-contained in the manner suggested would lead not to increase of employment but considerably to a net decrease, and this was quite apart from budget difficulties arising from a prohibitive tariff. The motion for consideration of the Finance Bill was passed without a division. The House then adjourned.

Voting on the Finance Bill

20th. MARCH :—Voting on the Finance Bill commenced to-day. *Pandit Nilkantha Das* moved that in the Clause Two of the Bill relating to salt duty the following should be added "and the said provisions shall in so far as they enable the Governor-General-in-Council to remit any duty so imposed be construed as if with effect from April 1, 1936 they have remitted the duty to the extent of the said one rupee and four annas and such remission shall be deemed to have been made out of leviable duty by a rule made under that Section."

Dr. Bhagwandas supported the amendment, saying that for a people whose daily income had been calculated by the Central Banking Enquiry Committee at seven pice, a salt tax of four annas per year was a cruelty. He endrosed Pandit Nilkantha Das's remarks that barren lands which could produce salt should be allowed to be so used.

Sir James Grigg, opposing the amendment, said that he did not wish to go into the details of this question and emphasised that the surrendering of something like eight crores of rupees on a narrowly balanced budget was quite impossible.

Mr. M. A. Jinnah was not anxious to save this Government and if a revolution came, as Mr. Ranga had visualised, he would not stand in the way. The Opposition had failed to produce an alternative scheme for balancing the budget, nor would, in his opinion, a reduction of the salt duty give substantial relief to the poor. His party did not propose, therefore, to support the amendment, nor would they go into the Government lobby.

Mr. *Satyamurti* asked Mr. Jinnah to remember that the kind of poverty which existed in India would give the poor people real relief if the salt duty was abolished. As regards constructive suggestions, Mr. Jinnah had admitted that the Opposition was not bound to make them, but the speaker suggested a ten per cent cut in salaries, abolition of the revenue reserve fund and proper estimating of the revenues. All these would give eight crores. Let the Government at least promise that they would wipe out the tax in four or eight years.

The amendment of Pandit Nilakantha Das, proposing to abolish the salt tax, was carried amidst Congress and Nationalist applause by 52 to 41 votes. The Independents remained neutral.

Mr. *Sri Prakash* moved an amendment reducing the price of post-cards to six pies, reply-post-cards to an anna and retaining the nine pies post-cards for those carrying pictures. He said that the only department of the Government which was doing good to the country and which was honest was the Postal Department. His suggestion that half the space on the address side of a post-card should be given to writing had been accepted. He only wished the size of private and postal post-cards to be made the same. He liked picture post-cards and wished the Department to develop them.

Mr. *Jinnah* thereupon asked whether the amendment would be put in parts to enable those who wished to support reduction of ordinary and reply post-cards to vote for that portion.

The *President* said that he could not do that, thereupon Mr. *Sri Prakash* withdrew his amendment and *Dr. Banerjee* moved his, namely, that a single post-card should be charged six pies and reply one anna. *Dr. Banerjee* emphasised that the loss was estimated at only fifty lakhs and this should be possible if the Government would consider the interests of the poor and the convenience of the public.

Sir *Frank Noyce* made nearly an hour's speech, surveying the financial position of the Posts and Telegraphs and Telephone Departments. He pointed out the improvement in revenue last year in the department as a whole, due partly to the publicity campaign of Mr. G. V. Bewoor who was the live-wire of the Department. "For the first time during my tenure as member in charge of Posts and Telegraphs I have been able to present a balanced budget and the Department is emerging from the slough of despondency. Why should the Assembly desire to thrust it back into what might well prove to be a bottomless pit ? I have been able to bring the finances of the Department on an even keel after so many years' depression and anxiety. The Assembly is not willing to allow a convalescing patient to recover naturally, but apply a stimulus which might prove detrimental in the end. The House has very wisely adopted the principle that post offices should pay their way and not be a burden on the general tax-payer. It will be unwise to depart from that policy. We have allotted sums of money for expanding postal facilities in rural areas. Any reduction in the postal rate at the expense of general revenues will be opposed on all sound financial considerations." Sir Frank Noyce added that there was no guarantee that a surplus would accrue next year. Unless there was a certainty of a recurring surplus it would be unwise to reduce the postal rates as demanded by the Opposition. Sir Frank dwelt on the reductions made in the rates on letters this year which he held was a rational step. No other relief was possible as yet.

No decision was taken on the amendment of Dr. Banerjee and the House adjourned.

23rd. MARCH :—Discussion on the Finance Bill having been resumed, to-day, Mr. *Muthuranga Mudaliar* supported the motion for reduction in the cost of postcard.

Mr. *Bewoor* recalled that the pay bill of postmen and other subordinate staff had been increased largely owing to pressure by the Assembly. If the price of the post card was reduced to half anna the increase in consumption would be reduced. The increase in consumption could not go beyond 47 millions and this the Government had taken into calculation in telling the House that the Government would be still faced with a deficit of 50 lakhs in the Department. He pleaded to the House to show patience and perseverance for one year more. He informed Mr. Jinnah that the separation of Burma would not affect the revenues till 1937-38.

Dr. Bannerjee's motion reducing the single post card to half anna and reply post card to one anna was carried by 83 to 44 votes amidst non-official cheers.

Pandit Nilakantha Das next moved the motion regarding Mr. Subhas Chandra Bose. Pandit Das moving the adjournment motion said that Mr. Subhas Chandra Bose required no introduction and was one of the gifted sons of India, foremost among the Nationalists and Congressmen. He condemned the Government's action and said that if Mr. Bose was allowed to return to India and if he held office of Secretary of the Congress during the next years under Pandit Jawaharlal a desirable atmosphere would be created in the country both to the good of the people and the Government.

Mr. *Hallett*, Home Secretary, was cheered as he rose to make his maiden speech. The reason, he said, why he was in the House was to show that the Government did not wish to conceal facts nor conceal the reason why they had considered that the return of Mr. Bose to India as a freeman would be a menace not only to Bengal but to the whole of India.

He hoped to convince members that the Government had valid reasons for the action. He became a politician not merely of the left-wing but a revolutionary of the left-wing. The reason why Mr. Bose liked the non-co-operation movement was because it had converted the Congress from constitutional methods to a revolutionary organization. He was disgusted when the movement was called off after Chauri-Chaura. Then occurred in 1922 the revival of terrorism in a more drastic form and Mr. Bose was arrested under the Bengal Regulation 1924. Mr. Bose's record was examined with great care by two judges who held that there was reasonable ground for belief that Mr. Bose was a member of a revolutionary conspiracy and if allowed freedom would be a danger to the State, more particularly because of his public position and outstanding organizing ability. The speaker agreed with Pandit Nilkantha Das that Mr. Bose had a great influence with the youth and there lay the real danger.

Mr. Hallett said that Mr. Bose published in 1923 an article in "Atmasakti", one of the revolutionary papers of Bengal, wanting the youth to sacrifice their lives. Apart from his public activities, Mr. Bose was personally in touch with the terrorist party and was cognisant of many of the plots for assassination of Government servants. Mr. Bose was detained in Rangoon and later released for reasons of health. Soon after that Mr. Bose tried to get hold of the most inflammable material, namely, labour and students. He started the Bengal Students' Conference in 1928 and preached to them the message of communism. Mr. Bose participated in the labour strikes in Jamshedpur and Bombay. Mr. Bose made no secret of his disgust with the methods of the right-wing politicians and wished to take more drastic revolutionary steps. At the Lahore Congress in 1929 Mr. Bose pleaded for a parallel government and organised the peasants and youth for the purpose of putting it into practice. In plain words it was a revolutionary policy which Mr. Bose put before the Congress. Mr. Bose had also stated then that the message of independence without adopting a definite policy to attain the objective was useless. In January 1932 Mr. Bose was convicted for a seditious speech at a meeting where revolutionary placards were distributed? When Mr. Gandhi held conversation with the Government, Mr. Bose tried to persuade Mr. Gandhi to include prisoners accused of violence and gave up his claim only when the Government announced their view against mercy to Bhagat Singh and others. Throughout this period Mr. Bose was eager to help the terrorists in Bengal. When Mr. Bose was arrested in 1932 it was not because of civil disobedience but because he was closely associated with terrorism and his case was under consideration sometime before action was taken against civil disobedience.

Finally, Mr. Hallett recalled the letter of Mr. Krishna Das which the Law Member had read out textually on a previous occasion. That letter had remained unchallenged. In it there was a reference to one Mr. A. and Mr. B. Mr. Hallett now disclosed to the House that Mr. A. meant Mr. Subhas Chandra Bose. He did not disclose the identity of Mr. B. The letter showed that the Yugantar party of revolutionaries were supporters of Mr. Subhas Chandra Bose and this party was responsible for the Chittagong armoury raid, Pahartali outrage and other crimes. Mr. Bose was head of that party.

Mr. *Akhil Chandra Dutt* said that the case the Government had put forward for a long time was the alleged complicity of Mr. Sarat Chandra Bose in revolutionary conspiracy, and they had ultimately released him being convinced that he was not guilty of conspiracy. The British Empire had not come down after Mr. Sarat Chandra

Bose's release. What was true of Mr. Sarat Chandra Bose was also true about Mr. Subhas Chandra Bose. No one knew why Mr. Subhas Chandra Bose was arrested in 1932. One thing was significant that he was not arrested under the Criminal Law Amendment Act or any other law dealing with terrorism. Mr. Dutt asked the Government whether there was any allegation against Mr. Subhas Chandra Bose that while in Europe he had been breaking the law there. Mr. Bose was an outstanding personality and the speaker wondered if the Government were apprehensive of his alliance with Pandit Jawaharlal Nehru. Until the Government had placed their cards on the table, apart from his ancient history, as to what took place in 1936 for such action, they would not be satisfied that the Government had any ground for imposing the restriction on Mr. Bose.

VOTING ON THE FINANCE BILL (CONTD.)

24th. MARCH :—Resuming the Finance Bill discussion to-day, Mr. *F. F. James* moved that book, pattern and sample packet charges be as follows: For weight not exceeding two and a half tolas—six-pies; for weight exceeding two and a half, but not exceeding five tolas—nine-pies; for every additional five tolas or fraction of five tolas—six-pies. Mr. James said that this amendment was in the interest of small retail traders. He reminded Mr. Bewoor of his advertisement campaign that the "trade follows mail". Surely the Government did not help trade by enhancing the rates by 50 per cent.

Mr. *Bewoor* explained that since 1878 the charges for book, pattern and sample post remained stationary whereas the charges in respect of all other articles had increased. After making a cut in the finances of fifty lakhs in respect of the postcard, how could they make a further cut? The Government fully realised the advantage of the proposed reduction, but they could not afford it.

The motion was rejected by 36 to 30 votes, the Congress, Nationalist and Independent parties generally abstaining from voting.

Mr. *Palliwal* next moved that quarter anna postage should carry registered newspapers weighting up to ten tolas instead of eight as now.

Mr. *Bewoor*, opposing, said that the change would cost the Government approximately Rs. 74,000. The rate was already the smallest compared to other countries and had not been increased since 1898.

The motion was passed by 64 to 41 votes. The Assembly passed schedule 1, as amended.

Babu *Baijnath Bajoria* moved the next amendment proposing abolition of the remaining surcharge on the income-tax and super-tax.

Sir *James Grigg* replied that his arguments against the motion were the same as previously stated, and moreover the motion would unbalance the budget very materially. The motion was rejected.

Dr. P. N. Banerjee moved that the reduction in surcharge, prospected in the Bill, should not be made. He said that this motion was made with a view to helping the Government.

Sir *James Grigg* said that he was grateful to Dr. Banerjee for the kind assistance but on the whole he preferred the Government's own scheme of taxation and remission of taxes. The motion was rejected.

Mr. *Nilakantha Das's* amendment, opposing reduction of surcharge on supertax, was similarly rejected.

When all the clauses had been disposed of Sir James Grigg was asked by the President to move the third reading of the Finance Bill. Sir *James Grigg* replied that he did not wish to make the motion.

25th. MARCH :—The *President* read to-day the Governor-General's message that after a careful consideration of the amendments adopted by the Assembly on the Finance Bill he had arrived to the conclusion that he must use special powers and ask for the continuance of the salt duty and the postcard at the rates proposed in the bill as introduced. The recommended bill was attached.

Sir *James Grigg* said that the bill was available for the members and he asked the direction of the Chair when he should move the amendments. The Government was ready to have them taken up at once if that suited the convenience of the House. To complete the story he laid on the table the declaration by the Governor-General restoring the demands for grants in respect of the Executive Council and Defence department which were thrown out by the Assembly.

Mr. *Bhulabhai Desai* after consulting Mr. Jinnah said that having regard to the business before the House they were prepared to take up for consideration the recommended bill.

All the demands having been voted, Sir *James Grigg*, Finance Member, moved an amendment restoring the salt duty in the Finance Bill. He said that the position was that the Government were unable to accept the views of the Assembly relating to salt or the post card but accepted the vote regarding postage on newspapers. (Ironical cheer by Mr. Jinnah.) Sir James Grigg admitted that it meant a reversal of the major votes of the House and the acceptance of a minor one, and that raised the issue of the proper limits of responsiveness. Sir James Grigg recalled in this connection the speeches made during the Finance Bill debates by Sir Cowasji Jehangir and Mr. Jinnah. Mr. Jinnah had asked whether the Government had met them on any first class issue. Sir James Grigg read extracts from the Simon Report, vol. I, stating that the Government had given full effect to 37 resolutions of the Assembly, and partial effect to 36 resolutions, the corresponding figures for the Council of State being 32 and 24 and that in 32 cases in the Assembly and 19 in the Council of State the Government had been unable to accept the resolutions. The matters over which the Government had acted in accordance with the wishes of the Legislature were *inter alia* the policy of discriminating protection, statutory recognition of trade unions, repeal of the special laws and the Press Act, the Bar Council Act. the Indian Territorial Force, the Royal Military College, withdrawal of the cotton excise duty, restriction on the exports of food grains and the setting up of the standing committees attached to various departments, stores purchase rules, Indians overseas, overcrowding in railway carriages, martial law administration in the Punjab, the school of coal mines, and the administration of Aden. Besides the above, a committee was appointed to investigate matters and views forwarded by provincial Governments or the Secretary of State. Continuing, Sir James Grigg said that on the other hand it was not within the power of the Government to obliterate the distinction between votable and non-votable expenditure or accelerate the revision of the constitution or release certain prisoners whose release was undesirable.

Replying to an interruption regarding the relevancy of these long quotations, Sir James Grigg said that he must deal with the question of proper limits of responsiveness. (A voice.—What about Lord Willingdon's time ?) Sir James Grigg said that as regards the time after the Simon Commission's report instances of responsiveness were the appointment of an advisory committee and the committee to examine the working of the Ottawa Agreement, of the retrenchment and duty on broken rice and wheat. Sir James Grigg commented : 'It seems to me that so far from being totally unresponsive the executive in India in its desire to temper the full rigour of the approach of irremovability has allowed and even encouraged the legislature to encroach on its function to an extent which might very easily prove to be extremely embarrassing to the executive of the future Government.'

There are three eminent spheres where the executive must, broadly speaking, have the last word if the Government is to be carried on successfully, namely. defence, law and order, and finance. In these spheres policy and administration are inextricably mixed where the executive must in the nature of things observe a good deal of secrecy regarding future intentions and the executive must carry out its responsibility sincerely and not throw it at the head of the legislature. There is the inescapable obligation on the executive to take a long view in these spheres and use the powers the constitution has conferred on them. Sir James next quoted from the Selborne Committee's report, showing that the reason why special powers were conferred on the executive was because they did not wish to cancel the responsibility for those powers by giving an official majority in the Council of State, but that the Government of India must face the responsibility directly before the eyes of the world. Continuing, Sir James Grigg said that the question next arose as to what were major issues and issues of principle. He considered that expenditure such as on Quetta should not be thrown on posterity, if they could possibly help it and in this matter, Government adhered to the principle involved and exercised their constitutional right as the last word. Mr. Jinnah had declared that the post card question was not a major issue. Sir James Grigg said that it was and informed the House that in England no Chancellor of the Exchequer would consider a reduction of £5,000,000 in taxation which would be the corresponding vote in England. Was it not a major issue ? Sir *James Grigg* held that if there was a margin of Rs. 50 lakhs in the budget it was the duty of the Government to reduce tax on its own initiative and deal with that surplus and if there was no such surplus, Government must resist the amendment. Concluding, Sir James Grigg said: "I know that the executive is irremovable, but in a few years the situation will have completely changed. Indian Ministers will be subject to removal by the legislature and when that time comes it will make the legislature more careful about pressing amendments which will unbalance the budget and the vote would carry the implication that the Opposition is ready to take up the burden of office.'

Mr. *Bhulabhai Desai*, the leader of the Opposition, opposed the amendment. He was glad that Sir James Grigg had shown that the executive was more conscious of having to explain to the House its obdurate and irresponsive attitude, but he asked why Sir James Grigg had referred to his ancestors to expiate his own sins. Let him take the period during which both Sir James Grigg and the speaker had been members of the House. Had any of the votes of the House been accepted by the Government during the last two years? So far as the salt duty went, he conceded that it was a difficult matter to adjust, but the leader of the Nationalist party had offered that the Government should promise a progressive reduction of this unpopular and oppressive tax. They had not been conceded in any sense. In fact, the powers of the legislatures were the same as depicted by Dadabhoy Naoroji 37 years ago, namely, that they were a delusion and a farce. What else was it when every opinion of this House given in the last 18 months on any major issue was disregarded by the executive? Eighty crores of the budget was non-votable and in the remaining votable items the Assembly carried only a very few cuts. but all of them had been restored.

Mr. *M. A. Jinnah* commented on the subjects mentioned in the Simon report and said: 'I have been in this House since 1910 and have grown grey in pleading before the Government all these years. We asked for the protection of industries. We got discriminating protection and the British Government will decide what it is. You have played with that word and you have driven in the wedge of imperial preference. Then there was the Indo-British agreement which this House rejected and you restored it. Surely, that was not in the interests of India. You abolished after 30 years the excise duty which should never have been imposed. We wanted a territorial force as a second line of defence, but it is still a moribund, nebulous and worthless institution. Regarding the Royal Military College, I maintain that we have been deliberately deceived. However, I am prepared to accept the Governor-General's recommendation for the restoration of the salt duty. But will the Governor-General accept our recommendation for a half-anna post card? You cannot. This is the recommended Bill. Hence, I have no option but to refuse supplies.'

Sir *Cowasji Jehangir* warned the Government to appreciate the implications of Sir James Grigg's speech which indicated how the safeguards contained in the 1935 Act were going to be used. Let Sir Muhammad Zafarullah, who is now a member of the Executive Council, say whether Sir James Grigg's theory was right. Sir James Grigg had the makings of a great Finance Member. He was honest. But he must change his views on the constitution under which they now worked, for under it the Government of India must accept decisions wherever possible. Surely, Quetta could be financed out of capital. Did Sir James Grigg mean to say that the credit of India would be shaken if Quetta was financed out of capital?

Mr. *M. S. Aney* said he was considerably surprised at the audacity with which the Finance Member introduced his speech on the plea of responsiveness. If he had wanted the House to discuss the Bill he should have adopted a different tone. He asked whether the Government was prepared to accept the Assembly's recommendation regarding the postcard, if the Assembly accepted the Government's recommendation regarding salt. The Finance Member should have shown that in view of the coming reforms and bringing harmony to this country he had changed, and as an earnest of that desire the Government were prepared to accept a small cut of Rs. 50 lakhs (Sir *James Grigg*.—A small cut!) As even the most reasonable suggestion had been turned down, he hoped that every self-respecting member would vote against the Bill.

The House divided and rejected Sir James Grigg's amendment relating to the salt duty by 68 votes to 51 amidst Opposition cheers.

Sir *James Grigg* asked the President to certify that the House had failed to pass the Bill in the form recommended. This was done and the House adjourned.

The Ottawa Agreement Debate

26th. MARCH :—*Sir M. Zafarullah Khan* announced to-day that the Government would accept the verdict of the Assembly on the Ottawa Agreement, but pleaded that in view of the wide range of the Indian trade involved and the complexity of the issue, the best method of giving judgment was to have the matter examined by a Committee, which procedure the House had previously followed.

Thereafter Mr. B. Desai, Mr. K. L. Gauba, Mr. M. A. Jinnah and Mr. M. Vissanji moved their respective amendments, on which the debate then proceeded. All these amendments, with the exception of Mr. Gauba's, proposed that the agreement should be denounced.

Sir *Zafrullah* moved "that in accordance with the recommendation of the Committee referred to in the resolution adopted by this Assembly on December 6, 1932, a Committee of this Assembly be constituted to examine the working of the Trade Agreement concluded at Ottawa on August 20, 1932, between His Majesty's Government in the U. K. and the Government of India and to report to the House thereon." Sir Zafrullah mentioned the following members for his proposed committee : Sir Frank Noyce, Sir G. S. Bajpai, Mr. F. E. James, Sir H. P. Mody, Mr. K. L. Gauba, Sir A. H. Ghuznavi and the mover and added that Congress and Nationalist members had not been persuaded to give any names for it. In case the House decided to appoint that Committee he might add further names. The Commerce Member gave a brief history of the circumstances under which the Ottawa Agreement came into being. He said that the Imperial Conference proposed the Ottawa Conference, but before the Ottawa Conference assembled the National Government was established in England and passed the Import Duties Act for India and the Dominions were given a certain time limit within which to enjoy the free entry of certain commodities. The question arose whether India should enter a mutually beneficial agreement to keep aloof and lose the preferences she enjoyed, especially in respect of commodities in which the dominions were active competitors in the U. K. Market. He had come to the House to seek its verdict on the agreement on its three years' working. He added : "a complaint has been made that there is always a sense of unreality relating to the proceedings of this House that the final decision rests with an Executive which is not responsible to the House. With regard to this particular matter I may observe that, having regard to the undertakings given by the Government that the Government are responsible to the House with regard to this trade agreement in the sense that the Government have undertaken that, in case the House comes to a decision after reviewing the working of this agreement for three years in the interest of India, notice of termination will be given, the Government would be bound to give such notice. That being so, I would make an earnest appeal to the House that, having regard to the volume of trade which will be affected by any decision of the House, the House should consider all aspects of the question carefully before it gives its decision. I shall not put it higher than that and have no reason to doubt that the House will do that. Continuing, Sir Zafarullah further hoped that, in considering this question, the House would not be influenced by any consideration except of benefit to India and the Indian trade. There might be different methods of considering the question. The Government thought that the best method was to take the matter to a committee. He explained why the Government had not come forward with a more positive motion asking for continuance of the agreement seeking a modification. The reason for the Government method was that the working of the trade agreement covered abnormal times, that in dealing with mass material the procedure of the Committee was more appropriate and that in the Committee points could be reconciled and criticisms answered. The commodities covered were 55 on the Indian side and 163 on the U. K. The disparity was due to the fact that the Indian side dealt largely with primary produce and commodities in bulk, while U K. articles were manufactured goods.

Mr. *Bhulabhai Desai*, leading the opposition to the agreement, said that it was refreshing to be reminded of the measure of responsibility which lay on the House. It was almost ironical, considering the way in which responsibility had been discharged by the Government from time to time. The Commerce Member had told them to the stress of circumstances arising out of the U. K. Import Duty Act. The agreement had a clause under which either party could give notice of termination. So far the U. K. had not given such notice. That was a fact of fundamental importance to which no reference had been made in the Commerce Member's speech. Sir

Zafrullah had failed to put before the House the positive opinion of the Government as to the effect of the agreement on India. The Government should, instead of getting the two experts who were sworn in to-day for the debate, get them to examine the agreement and give a verdict on it. To say that there was a negative advantage in the nature of insurance was like a doctor saying to his patient, "But for my treatment you would have grown worse." (Laughter). The fact was that the Government were the agents of the Secretary of State and were carrying out the wishes of their master. The opinion of the Federation of Indian Chambers and other Indian Chambers had been given decisively against the agreement. Proceeding, Mr. Desai said that the agreement provided for six months' notice which option it was open to either party to exercise without any danger of losing the other's goodwill. In this case Britain being the gainer there was no need for her to give notice. It was, therefore, for India to give notice. Indeed, giving such notice would bring a negotiating mind and the six months' period could be utilised by India to secure a fairer deal. Hence the present agreement must be determined. Mr. Desai then took up the case of tea and other commodities, and concluded saying that if India was a debtor country to England then the British must learn the lesson of Germany under Versailles Treaty and see that debtor country was kept solvent. In any case there was sufficient justification to denounce the agreement and secure a better deal if necessary.

Mr. *M. Vissonji* moved that the Ottawa Agreement be terminated forthwith and that no such trade agreement be hearafter concluded with any country except on the basis of complete reciprocity and after previous consultation with the Assembly. Really, the agreement was intended to improve British trade and establish new markets in that country and this fully had been accomplished. The gain had been wholly of England and the loss exclusively of India. Therefore, nobody could support such an one-sided agreement and it was entirely useless further to examine the working of the agreement as proposed by Sir Zafarullah.

Seth Govindas declared that public opinion in India had always opposed imperial preference, and even at the time of protection given to the textile and steel industries, while agreeing to give preference to some articles from the U. K., had made it perfectly clear that they were not accepting the principle of Imperial preference. In this connection he quoted the opinion of the Fiscal Commission, which had said that India could not grant extensive preference without a serious loss to herself. While India's exports to the U. K. had increased only by three crores, her loss of trade in other countries was twenty crores. If the pact was terminated India would negotiate an agreement with other countries who would send cheaper articles for her consumers, and in return India would have a vaster market.

Dr. *P. N. Bannerjee* said that the Pact was the outcome of England's post-war efforts to rehabilitate her position in the world. The Ottawa Pact was the culmination of this policy. Dealing with official propaganda by series of inspired articles by the Director of Commercial Intelligence, Dr. Banerjee pointed out that even those articles had proved that the pact was more advantageous to the United Kingdom than to India. The increase in the preferred exports of India to the U. K. was due to cause other than preference.

Dr. Banerjee pointed out that India was becoming bankrupt by meeting her external obligations by unchecked gold export and the pact was inimical to her public finance and industrial development. In the case of India the preference related to raw materials, which was a definite discouragement to her manufactures and this fact the framers of the pact had ignored. What was needed was that India should be left free to enter bilateral treaties and for this the Ottawa Pact stood in their way. Official propaganda merely endeavoured to cloud the issue by throwing a smoke screen all around.

Dr. *Mathai*, Director-General of Commercial Intelligence, said that an enormous amount of highly emotional literature had been published on the subject showing misdirected enthusiasm. The only satisfactory way to deal with the question was to ascertain what precisely was the scope and purpose of the agreement. If tried to preserve and, if possible, stimulate trade within the empire at a time when world trade was entirely upset, and judged from that limited scope the agreement yielded a fair measure of success and the argument for denunciation vanished. He warned the House from his long experience on Tariff matters that a sudden change in tariff arrangement would cause a serious dislocation of the course of trade and business which would be particularly serious when the preferential articles covered a greater part of their external trade. Moreover, denunciation was not the method to retain goodwill and mutual friendship, so essential for negotiating a trade agreement. He suggested that the inference, to be drawn from the fact that the United Kingdom had not given notice of denunciation, was not that drawn by Mr. Desai, but that the British people had a better knowledge of what was required of business people in circumstances of this kind. There had been considerable dis satisfaction with the agreement in other parts of the Empire, but none had spoken of denunciation. The House at this stage adjourned.

27th. MARCH:—Mr. *F. E. James* said that the views of the European business community on the agreement had been expressed by the President of the Upper India Chamber of Commerce, Sir T. F. Gavin Jones, who expressed the opinion that the Ottawa Agreement should be revived, and certainly not terminated. Mr. James then gave his alternative proposal. The Upper India Chamber had stated that the note of the Federation of Indian Chambers had made out a good case for a revision of the preferences allowed by Great Britain for the raw products of India. Mr. James gave the following indication of the lines of revision. Export items : Increase in preference for coffee ; drawback in the U. K. on manufactured products containing linseed oil ; specific duty by weight on cigars ; duty on foreign fats, oil and oilseeds ; duty on non-Empire cotton seed ; removal of Russian hemp from free list. More defensive footing for Indian raw cotton—Import items : Examination of the import schedule with a view to safeguarding Indian industries and the possibility of freedom to negotiate treaties with other countries. There should be a close association with representatives of commerce and industry either before or during the negotiations. He quoted the opinion of Mr. Nalini Ranjan Sarker in favour of a revision of the trade agreement along similar lines. On the other hand, if the agreement was denounced India could stand isolated as all the dominions talked of revision, not termination. India would play into the hands of British manufacturers as the report of the Committee of British Chambers in London showed that they did not like free import of manufactured goods into the U. K. from India and the Dominions and once the preferences were lost they would never be restored. India would also play into the hands of the Japanese in the coming negotiations in India and India would lose the friendly backing of the U. K. which proved so helpful in the crucial moment in 1934. One could hear, added Mr. James, the Japanese sharpening their knives in preparation for the scalping of Indian industries. (Laughter). Denunciation would strengthen the position of the dominions at India's expense and unsettle trade and commerce.

Mr. *Satyamurti* said that Mr. James's thunder showed that he, at any rate, had made up his mind that the agreement was good and Mr. James was a member of the proposed committee which was to examine the matter with an open mind. The speaker knew Englishmen better than Mr. James. They would fall at the speaker's feet to get trade advantage. The country had given decisive verdict by the defeat of Sir Sanmukham Chetty. Preference on Indian goods in the U. K. was about four to five per cent., while British goods enjoyed preference in India of 40 per cent. India had got nothing out of it for the producer and the Mody-Lees Pact too had not helped India, through it had inmmortalised Mr. Mody.

Mr. *Joshi* said that the Ottawa Agreement was based on a wrong foundation. It was opposed to recovery, international co-operation and world trade and was designed mainly to keep within the Empire all raw materials produced within the Empire. It also created vested interests of British trade in India which would be difficult to remove at any time.

Mr. *Venkatachalam Chetty* addressing last said that he had no faith in experts. On the other hand he would rely on the experience of traders, and that clearly was that the agreement had not been to their advantage. This was the experience not only of Indian business men but also of European businessmen, but for reasons political the latter did not want to own it. The House at this stage adjourned.

The Hammond Committee Report

28th. MARCH :—*Pandit Govind Ballabh Pant* moved "that the report of the Committee appointed by the Assembly to examine the recommendations of the Indian Delimitation Committee be adopted.

Pandit Pant expressed gratification at the committee having produced an unanimous report which he hoped His Majesty's Government would not look upon its acceptance

The delimitation report had formulated proposals in order to exclude men of robust spirit and facilitate the election of docile and pliable people, especially in the U. P. The proposals of the Assembly Committee aimed at securing the freedom of vote and secrecy of ballot and they decided to replace the cumulative vote by distributive vote.

Eight amendments were then moved without any speeches.

Mr. *G. S. Gupta's* amendment wanted to lower the qualification of the landholders' constituency in C. P. Mr. *Vissanji* wanted the secretary of a commercial association to function as a registering and returning officer.

Pandit Nilakantha Das's amendment opposed nomination to any Legislative Assembly.

Mr. *Bagchand Soni's* amendment aimed at lowering the qualifications of Ajmer-Merwara electors for the Federal Assembly. Dr. D'Souza gave a plan of distribution of Christian seats in different areas.

Mr. *Bajoria's* amendment wanted to lower the qualification for an elector or candidate in the commerce constituency.

After the amendments were moved general discussion followed when *Sardar Sant Singh* wanted secrecy of ballot and freedom of voting in the Punjab.

Mr. *Nauman* gave various proposals for facilitating the return of more Muslims representing trade, commerce, industry and landholders.

Mr. *Witherington* voiced the needs of tea garden labourers, both as regards seats and qualifications.

Dr. Hutton pointed out that if the residential qualification was removed in respect of the tribes in Assam, it would prevent these tribes from getting necessary education and producing leaders. He also objected to the Committee's recommendations relating to labour in collieries and oilwells, and said that in some cases labour was altogether non-Indian, and finally opposed the splitting up of the Shillong constituency with Gauhati.

Sir *A. H. Ghuznavi* said that the Muslim Chamber of Commerce had no chance of securing a seat in the federal legislature and proposed the Muslim Chamber's votes being increased to six instead of three or adoption of one of the alternatives proposed by Mr. Nauman. Babu *Baijnath Bajoria* and Mr. *A. C. Dutt* pleaded the case of the Bengal Mahajan Sabha and declared that the Sabha represented important inland trade and indigenous banking interests and could easily be given a seat out of two seats each for the Tea Association or the Calcutta Trades Association.

Mr. *V. Chetty* considered that the income-tax condition for commercial seats was too high, especially for Madras, and proposed that income-tax qualification should be lowered from Rs. 10,000 to Rs. 2,500 and in case of registered companies the requirement of capital should be lowered from a lakh to twenty-five thousand.

Sir *Henry Gidney* wanted a seat for the Anglo-Indians in Karachi and suggested an arrangement in this respect with Europeans.

Mr. *Gadgil* spoke reading urban constituencies in Bombay Presidency and also suggested abolition of registration charges for University graduates.

Mr. *Joshi* suggested redistribution of seats both in the federal and provincial legislatures.

All amendments were withdrawn. The original motion was carried. The House then adjourned till the 30th.

THE OTTAWA AGREEMENT DEBATE

30th. MARCH :—Mr. *T. A. Stewart*, Commerce Secretary, replying to the speeches of Opposition members, on the Ottawa Agreement said that Dr. De Souza had complained that the Commissioner and Trade Commissioner for India in the U. K. were less solicitous of Indian interests than officials representing other dominions and colonies. Mr. Stewart remarked that, on the other hand, these officials of India were unfailing in their attempt to promote India's interests, but counsel could not act without a brief and if the coffee industry would make out its case these officers would do their best for it. Mr. Stewart, replying to Pandit Govind Das's argument, contended that the fact that there had been a substantial increase in the exports of non-preferential articles to foreign countries was strong proof that there had been no retaliation against India. The Commerce Secretary next illustrated the kind of difficulties which would confront an Indian negotiator or bilateral agreements which Mr. Jinnah's motion had suggested. The first handicap would be India's policy of industrial expansion and discriminating protection. Now, it was axiomatic that in such negotiations India must give way somewhere which the other country was prepared to accept. Supposing, India negotiated an agreement with France, that country's trade with

India in gold thread had come down from 65 lakhs to three quarter of a lakh. The restoration of this trade was France's foremost desire. Was India prepared to repeal the protective duty on gold thread ?

Dr. Deshmukh described the agreement not as a pact but as a plot conceived in an atmosphere in which the people were led to believe that with economic advantage there would be political status. After this Ottawa Agreement Britain had entered into separate treaty agreements with sixteen other countries. Goodwill was a word frequently used. There was goodwill if India was to receive six hundred million yards of yarn in return for two lakhs of bales of raw cotton while Japan took fifteen lakhs of bales of raw cotton for four hundred million yarns. Could Sir H. P. Mody deny that it was after the Ottawa Agreement that several textile mills in Bombay had closed down ? Again what was the need of having preference on tea if England was to be under the quota system ?

Mr. Aney advised the House to consider the agreement from the point of view of interests to India, and not the Empire as Sir John Mathai had suggested. The fact remained that the balance of trade in India had gone down from thirty-five to twenty-two crores at which figure it threatened to remain. India's export within the empire had not expanded ; on the other hand imports had increased by nine crores because Canada, Australia and New Zealand had produced some articles. Thus the agreement had failed to serve India's interests. As for the effects of the agreement on India's trade with non-Empire countries, Mr. Aney referred to Sir M. Visveswarayya's view that it had been jeopardised. Mr. Jinnah's amendment for rejection of the present agreement and negotiation for a new agreement offered the only solution.

Sir Frank Noyce emphatically stated that by the Ottawa agreement no additional burden had fallen on the Indian consumer. Let the House discuss the question with a business-mind. If the agreement was to be treated as a business proposition, the opinion of none else was better than that of the two hard-headed businessmen of the House, Sir H. P. Mody and Seth Haji Abdullah Haroon.

Mr. Govind Ballabh Pant said that Mr. Mody had admitted that, as it stood to-day, the agreement was not satisfactory. Mr. Pant held that there was little difference in substance between the two propositions. Dr. Mathai's speech indicated to the speaker that he (Dr Mathai), while justifying the agreement in the circumstances of the past, considered that in the present circumstances it was criminal to enter into an arrangement of this kind. Sir G. S. Bajpai had stated that bilateral agreements were most dangerous between a creditor and a debtor country, and the Ottawa agreement, being a bilateral agreement, it was, according to Sir G. S. Bajpai's own showing, contrary to India's interests. The House had been asked to examine the matter unemotionally. Did the United Kingdom not give India notice that within a certain period India must negotiate a trade agreement ? Mr. Jinnah's amendment simply followed in the footsteps of the United Kingdom. The sponsors of the agreement had admitted that India was helpless and had to enter into the agreement, which amounted to an agreement under coercion. The fact of the matter was that the agreement was entered into at a time when England had an unfavourable balance of trade and when the ground was slipping from under her feet and she fell upon those who could not resist her wishes. After examining and giving certain figures Mr. Pant contended that the only sphere where India benefited was in the matter of carpets and rugs. As for raw cotton, England bought in 1929-30 10 centum of the total exports. This was not so now. Mr. Pant held that during the ten years 1921-30, India had an unfavourable balance of trade of Rs. 450 crores in her trade with the United Kingdom, whereas with other foreign countries of the world India had a favourable balance of trade. France had imposed duties on linseed and groundnut entirely in a retaliatory spirit. The Indian Commissioner in Germany had disclosed a similar state of things. If England wished to trade with India, she must adopt an attitude of genuine friendship.

Mr. *Jinnah* was cheered by the Opposition when he rose to explain his amendment and sum up the case for the Opposition. His amendment was as follows :

'This Assembly recommends to the Governor-General in Council that the Ottawa agreement dated the 20th August, 1932, be termirated without delay and notice of its denunciation be given in terms of Article 14 thereof. The Assembly further recommends that the Government of India should immediately examine the trend of the trade of India with various other important countries and the United Kingdom and investigate the possibility of entering into such bilateral trade treaties with them whenever and wherever possible to bring about an expansion of the export trade of India in those markets and submit such treaty or treaties for the approval of the Assembly."

He said that the other day the Finance Member had got the Finance Bill certified and appeared in the role of rent collector and to-day they were told that the responsibility had been transferred by the Government to the House and they would respect its verdict. Would that responsibility end at 5 o'clock in the afternoon when the voting was over?

The Government's body was in Delhi, its heart in Downing Street and its head in Westminster. The speaker assured the House that he was open to conviction and would drop the amendment if he was convinced to the contrary. The purpose before them all was to see that an expansion of India's trade occurred. The question was in what manner this should be done. Dr. Mathai had made a clever speech, but he spoke as an expert with a brief and would make a more brilliant speech had he had the brief of the Opposition. (Laughter). Dr. Mathai had asked them to get into the psychology of those who entered into the agreement. This the speaker agreed to. England had gone off the gold standard and she linked the rupee to sterling. Was India consulted? The Government of India had picked up the delegation for Ottawa and this delegation did not have with them any responsible representative of commercial, industrial or agricultural opinion of this country. The delegation's report showed that the principle of trade preferences had already been decided, that the question was not whether India stood to gain but whether she stood to loose by keeping out. It was thus a negative insurance policy. It had been stated by Mr. Baldwin and by the report of the India's delegation that in the matter of agreement about iron and steel and cotton piecegoods it had been found that the interests of India and the United Kingdom were consistent. Mr. Jinnah repudiated that statement and said that preference for the British under the Textile Protection Act was secured from the House with a pistol to its head, that unless preference was granted the bill would be withdrawn, and in the matter of steel, too, the House had prejudiced the case of the industry by giving preference to the United Kingdom.

Proceeding, Mr. Jinnah contended that it was not a question of repair, major or minor, but one of rebuilding. Sir Frank Noyce had said that the agreement must be continued and a committee could discuss how the details could be improved. Assuming that in some matters modification was necessary, what had the Government done? Clause 14 of the agreement provided for such modifications. Nothing had been done. And supposing a committee was appointed and if that committee made changes, say, that the linseed preference should be 20 instead of 10, had the Government of India the right to enforce it before the British Government? The Government of India was only a post office. A committee of this House had sat on the working of the agreement 15 months after the agreement was entered into. The majority, including Sir H. P. Mody, had stated that 15 months were not sufficient to assess the results. The minority came to the conclusion that the agreement must be put an end to and that negotiations should be conducted with such countries as were necessary with a view to expansion of India's trade. Of course preference to India meant an increase in export. But England was not the only country with which Indian trade was connected. India's trade with the United Kingdom was only 31 per cent. What about the other 69 per cent? Britain, after the Ottawa agreement, had agreements with 19 countries. There was no world economic conference as Sir Frank Noyce suggested. Could India enter into an agreement with any foreign country? And with what was India to negotiate after having promised to Britain to buy her finished products? Why should, for instance, Germany take India's raw materials when she could not send her finished products? Taking the cumulative effect of the agreement and examining the entire list of imports, Mr. Jinnah was clearly convinced that it was detrimental to India's interests. India was losing under the agreement. Why should she tolerate any further loss? The best thing was to give six months' notice of its termination. It was stated recently in the House of Commons by the British Government that no alteration in respect of the details of the Ottawa Agreement could be made when the whole agreement was about to be reviewed. India would be prepared to negotiate with Britain. But the present agreement must go. A committee, if appointed, would last for two years, meaning further loss to India.

Sir Muhammed Zafrullah said that Mr. Desai had suggested that India should have waited and seen the effect of the Import Duty Act before entering into an agreement. The result would have been that India, which Mr. Desai described as the weakest unit at the conference, would have been in a hopeless position after the other Dominions had settled their respective agreements. The Government would not have carried out their undertaking to the House if it had come to them with specific proposals, for the Government wished to take the lead from the House in the matter. It was not true to say that the Government had not made any bilateral agreements since the conclusion of the Ottawa agreement. The Indo-Japanese agreement was an outstanding example of a bilateral agreement. As regards other countries, attempts had been made without success. Sir Mahomed Zafrullah asked the House to remember the advantage derived through the free entry of articles which if subject to a duty, might cause the United Kingdom to think of having cheaper substitutes. For instance, for cement, already paper bags were getting into use. India's exports to the United Kingdom had undoubtedly been stimulated by the agreement in respect of preferential, non-preferential and free entry items. India had also been able to secure a modification of the agreement in the matter of rice and oilseeds. The case of coffee was that the industry had not been able to organize itself and take full advantage of the present preference and the Government had, by the Coffee Cess Act, helped the industry in this matter. Sir Mahomed said that the balance of trade, which stood in favour of India at only Rs. 4 crores in 1932-33, increased last year to £22 crores and this year it was expected to be Rs. 28 crores. The speaker felt that political considerations had been imported into the debate. Mr. Joshi had said that whatever the agreement, India could never benefit, being a subordinate Government. Mr. Satymurti had said: 'Do not talk to us of goodwill'. The speaker maintained that this was not the right attitude to take. When England passed the Import Duty Act it was not meant to force India to come to an agreement. It applied to the Dominions and India equally and, on the other hand, while protecting England against foreign competition, it gave the dominions and India time to avoid disturbance to their trade by negotiating an agreement. If the House denounced the agreement he did not suggest that England would retaliate. but the preferences would disappear and the trade of India would suffer. Sir Mahomed next emphasised that England's in-take of cotton had doubled and the denunciation of the agreement might make the Lancashire committee slacken its efforts till they knew the result of the fresh agreement. This might make India lose a great deal of ground which had already been gained. The repercussions would be serious in many other directions. It would be far better for India to have one agreement with the largest customer and small supplementary agreements with others. He regretted that no one in the House had indicated the direction in which the Government should negotiate an agreement Mr. Jinnah had not told them on what kind of foundation he would build a fresh agreement. (Mr. Jinnah made some reply which was inaudible. Sir Mahomed Zafrullah commented : 'That could be done without terminating the agreement'. Why had the Government been told that they should consult commercial opinion ? In the past the Government had been told that such expert opinion was available in the House. Why had the House confessed its bankruptcy on this occasion ? Why was the House afraid of shouldering responsibility ? (Cheers). When the House had examined the Hammond Report through a special committee, why did it not wish to observe a similar procedure in this respect ? What harm would be done if they allowed five months for examination of the agreement and then give their opinion in the next Simla session ? The Government did not wish to hold the matter up till the agreements with the Dominions were taken up by the United Kingdom. Sir Mahomed Zafrullah concluded his 90 minute speech amidst applause, whereafter Mr Jinnah's amendment, being the most comprehensive, was put to the vote and carried by 70 to 65 votes amidst Opposition cheers and cries of 'Down with Ottawa'. The House then adjourned till April 6th.

Death of Mr. M. Rajan Baksh

6th. APRIL :—The Assembly had a short sitting to-day when the House reassembled after the Mohurrum recess. Before any items on the agenda were taken up *Sir Henry Craik* said that he proposed to make reference to the death of Mr. Makdum Rajan Bakhsh who was the father of the House, having being elected to all the Assemblies since the Reforms. He was a descendent of an ancient family and two of his ancestors were Governors of Multan under the reigns of Jehangir and Shah Jehan. He was for many years President of the Multan Municipality and in that position did useful public service.

RELEASE OF POLITICAL PRISONERS

7th. APRIL :—The House resumed discussion to-day on Mr. *Mohan Lal Saxena*'s solution, urging the release of all political prisoners, detained without trial.

Mr. *A. C. Dutt*, quoting the Bengal Administration Report, said that the Governent considered detenus as "potential terrorists," and not actual terrorists. The olice had been actually planting bombs in Bengal. He quoted two cases, one in Calcutta id the other in Midnapore, where police informers were prosecuted and convicted i a charge of planting bombs. The Government wanted people to change heart. ow could there be any satisfactory results from a change of heart only on one side ?

Mr. *Basanta Kumar Das* said that the so-called terrorist must have to be reased one time, but why embitter his mind by the continued detention. This ally was the proper time to release. Even the hardened criminal was given time reform. Why not a political prisoner ? The policy of continued detention was ot in the best interests of the country and the long rope to the police made the olice unscrupulous and vindictive.

Mr. *L. K. Maitra* said that despite the remarkable speech of the Home Member ı the last occasion, he still remained unconvinced as to why should the Government arve the nation-building departments to feed the police. The Government were asting a lot of money for round-up and detention of the so-called terrorists. He d not advocate leniency to the confirmed terrorist but wanted justice for those who ere not terrorists.

Dr. J. H. Hutton, an Assam Official, opposing the motion, said that prevention was etter than cure. Assam on the whole did not like the release of these prisoners. In ıct, the Legislative Council had decided by a large majority against referring to a elect committee the circulation of the Criminal Law Amendment Bill. Dr. Hutton said that the experience shown by the immediate detention of certain persons om public life had caused an improvement in political crime. Therefore, the release f political prisoners would automatically increase political crime.

Sir Henry Craik assured the House that there was a steady decline, the number f detentions being just over 1,400 as the Government had realised that there had een no serious terrorist outrages recently. He criticised the wording of the resoluion in which there was no mention of the condemnation of the crimes and said :—

"Unless we know definitely that the Congress as an organisation will oppose errorism to stamp it out, I say there will be no general amnesty. Gradual releases vill go on, but general amnesty and the risks such a policy involved will require a ar more revolutionary change in the policy of the Congress Party in Bengal."

Continuing Sir Henry Craik believed with the Opposition that detention without rial was "per se" odious in the eye of the law, but they could not shut their eyes gainst realities as only three days ago there was a desperate struggle between the olice and terrorists in which most dangerous terrorists were involved. The Government had tried amnesty three times since 1920. Every time the situation had leteriorated and there was recrudescence of outrages. The Home Member emphasised hat a great majority of the people of Bengal, though opposed to the terrorist movement, were frightened by the activities of terrorists and were afraid to go in he support of the law.

There was constant interruptions when Sir Henry Craik referred to the silence of the Congress in condemning terrorist activities and pointed out that the Bengal Council had passed anti-terrorist measures by a sweeping majority (several members —"It has no confidence of the people. It has an artificial life") and Sir Henry Craik declared that so far as terrorism was concerned, the Congress as a body had failed to give a definite lead. The only section of the community immune from terrorist outrages was the Congress. If, instead of constantly sympathising with potential or actual murderers, the Congress had acted boldly as they did a good many years ago, it would be far better for the country. The Congress had not only failed to give a definite lead, but its nebulous attitude had afforded justification for doubts about their motives in failing to do so. No Congress member could produce a resolution of the Congress as a whole condemning terrorism within the last five years. Whatever improvement there had been in Bengal, the Congress had played little part in bringing it about, and until they took a definite stand against this abominable form of crime, their arguments based only on non-violence would fail to carry conviction.

After Sir Henry Craik's reply to the debate, Mr. *Saksena* read a note, saying that, as a protest against the President not allowing more speeches on the resolution, the

Congress Party had decided not to take part in the proceedings of the Assembly on this resolution. Thereupon the resolution was put to the House and the President said, "Noes have it." Thus the resolution was rejected.

IMPORT DUTY ON RICE

Mr. *Nauman's* resolution recommending levy of import duty of Re. 1 per maund on unbroken rice and annas eight per maund on paddy was under discussion when the House adjourned.

H. E. THE VICEROY'S FAREWELL SPEECH

8th. APRIL :—H. E. Lord Willingdon, the Viceroy delivered his farewell address this morning to the members of the Indian Legislature. The Assembly Chamber was fully crowded, only members of the Congress party being absent. The public galleries were packed to their utmost.

One incident, His Excellency said, had caused him some distress. He regretted the calculated discourtesy which had been shown to him by the members of the Congress party when he came to the House as the King-Emperor's representative or had in that capacity sent messages to be read to the House. He was sure that this action had met with the disapproval of every loyal citizen of India.

The Viceroy reviewed the Government's frontier policy, which had ensured peace and security and established friendly relations with countries which lie across India's frontiers.

Referring to the overseas question, Lord Willingdon averred that if their success had not always been equal to their expectations it had not been for want of earnest and strenuous endeavour. The powerful support of the Secretary of State for India had throughout his Viceroyalty been unfailingly and whole-heartedly given to the advocacy of the Indian cause. That splendid political organization known as the British Commonwealth of Nations, in which they all took just pride and which could only endure if all its constituent parts had faith in one another (?).

Touching unemployment, the Viceroy said that the Sapru Committee's report had carried them nearer than any previous report. If they were to achieve anything they must begin by facing facts, however unpleasant, and must recognize that they had a supply of young men for whose services there was no effective demand. They should adjust, by equal attention, demand and supply. The Viceroy was in full sympathy with those who sought the development of industries, in which there was a tremendous advance. The growing evil of unemployment had to be tackled at its source and the entire educational system had to be adjusted to bear much closer relations to the needs of the country. A strong lead had been given by the revival of the Central Advisory Board on Education, which was examining this problem.

India was a predominantly agricultural country, and His Excellency was therefore anxious to do everything possible to develop the science of agriculture, and the Imperial Council of Agricultural Research had continued to forge ahead with its task of initiating, promoting and co-ordinating research, which aimed at the improvement of the efficiency of the cultivator and an increase in his earnings.

The Viceroy next referred to a particular sphere of administration which had been severely criticised and in connection with which he was personally attacked for pursuing the policy of maintaining law and order. He would ask honourable members not to merely repeat the catchword 'repression,' but to compare India as it was in 1931-32 and India as it was to-day. He claimed that it was more peaceful and, as a result of greater tranquillity, more prosperous and happy, than it had been for many years. When the Congress reopened the civil disobedience campaign the Government had to use the full resources of the State in fighting and defeating the movement, which would otherwise remain as a perpetual menace to orderly government and individual liberty. As soon as the movement was suspended the Government was not slow to relax their measures or remove the ban on associations which had been declared unlawful. This gave the Congress party an opportunity of entering the central legislature. Communist propaganda also became dangerous and the Government had to take action which was effective without being unduly drastic.

The Viceroy hoped that communal relations in the Punjab would improve and that the efforts of the leaders would succeed in restoring peace.

India, like other countries, continued Lord Willingdon, had a prolonged trade depression and suffered from acute economic strain. but owing to its inherent strength had weathered the storm without recourse to remedies of despair. India had seen the worst of the depression and the surplus had been used to redeem the pledge to restore the cut in pay, to provide means for provincial Governments, to undertake measures for rural development, to give direct relief to certain local Governments and to reduce direct taxation.

Lord Willingdon visualised self-reliant provinces receiving from the Crown great authority, equipped with wide powers, each under the Crown but master in its own house, managing its affairs, promoting and stimulating its own activities, to ends congenial to the tastes, sentiments and condition of its people. He saw, perhaps in less immediate focus, a central Government left in no uncertainty of its powers in its field by possessing a jurisdiction precedent to that of all Governments in India and an executive authority protected in its fullest sense against encroachment or challenged—a Government supported by the obligation laid on the provinces to avoid all impediment or prejudice to the exercise of its executive authority. He saw the developing jurisprudence based more and more firmly on the broadest philosophical conceptions of the nature of law. The Federal Court would interpret the new constitution, elucidate the true character of legislative power, adjudicate between disputing Governments, determine the legitimate scope of the various legislative organs in India and would open to legal thought in India a new range of juridical ideas and a more intimate search into the bases of public and private rights and liberties. (Cheers.)

Concluding, the Viceroy said :—'Other figures, too, loom upon my gaze, but I would leave you with a general picture of the great problems demanding solutions.

'Fortunate are they who will join with you in realising this inspiring future and my every good wish attends the distinguished statesman who will so soon assume the burdens of the great office which I, with many grateful memories, shall regretfully lay down.' (Loud applause.)

Tariff Act Amendment Bill

After the Viceroy's speech the House met again in the afternoon. Sir *M. Zafarullah* introduced a bill amending the Indian Tariff Act relating to wheat and rice. In the statement of objects and reasons Sir Mohd. Zafarullah Khan states that since the passing of the Indian Tariff Amendment Act 1935, the Government of India have maintained a careful watch on the position of rice and wheat in India and other world markets. They are satisfied in the interests of the Indian rice-grower that the existing duty of 12 annas per maund on broken rice should continue for a further period of one year. As regards wheat they have come to the conclusion that the continuance of the operation of import duty for another year is essential in the interests of the Indian wheat grower. The statistical position, however, has shown a further improvement and it is consequently proposed to continue the import duty on wheat and wheat flour at the reduced rate of one rupee per cwt. for another year. A proviso appended in the bill states: 'It is hereby declared that it is expendient in public interest that the provision of this bill shall have immediate effect under the provisional Collection of Taxes Act, 1931'.

Several Official Bills Introduced

Sir James Grigg introduced a *bill further to extend the operation of the Salt Additional Import Duty Act* for two years, that is till 1938.

Sir *Zafarullah* introduced another *bill amending the Indian Tea Cess Act* while *Sir G. S. Bajpai* introduced a *bill amending the Indian Aircraft Act.*

Indian Mines Act Amendment Bill

Sir Frank Noyce thereafter introduced and moved to a select committee the Indian Mines Act Amendment Bill.

On June 29 last an accident occurred at the Bagdigi colliery in the Jharia coalfield causing the death of 19 persons and injuries to seven other persons. This was due to an influx of inflammable gases into the workings of a seam of coal from a fire in an upper seam ; the gases were ignited and caused a violent explosion. On Jan. 30 last, an accident occurred at the Loyabad colliery in the same coalfield owing to the influx of noxious gases, while the management were attempting to control a fire in the mine by the usual method of erecting stoppings. 35 persons, including five officials, lost their lives. There are now 47 separate fires in 29 different collieries in this field alone, and the bed of a river, flowing above collieries which are on fire, is in danger of collapsing. The situation disclosed by these facts requires urgent action.

An informal conference was held by this department with the representatives of the Government of Bihar and Orissa and the leading organisations of mine-owners, managers and mining labour on Feb. 19 and 20 last. Certain measures proposed by the Chief Inspector of Mines, for preventing danger from fires were discussed at this conference and generally approved with certain modifications. The proposals, as so modified, were referred to the local Governments represented at the conference. Their views show that the proposed measures are generally acceptable subject to criticisms or objections on matters of detail. The appendix shows the amendments to the Indian Mines Act regarded as necessary to enable suitable measures to be carried into effect, together with the objects and reasons in each case.

The hon. Sir Frank Noyce immediately moved that the bill be referred to a select committee with instructions to report on or before April 14. He said that there were now about 47 fires in 29 different collieries in the Jharia coalfield. The chief cause of the fires with one or two exceptions has been spontaneous combustion that is, a process of oxidation of crushed coal which goes on increasing until the heat developed is sufficient to cause the coal to break out into active combustion. In one important case, which was not apparently due to spontaneous combustion, the fire—an extensive one—appears to have been caused by the dumping of hot rejections from the manufacture of soft coke into a quarry into which there were openings into a coal seam. The coal eventually caught fire and all efforts to restrict and isolate the fire were unsuccessful with the result that it spread to five contiguous collieries.

Fires being due to the oxidization of crushed coal, the next question is what causes the crushing of the coal ? The chief cause of this is the premature collapse of the strata above the coal seams due to the weak nature of the pillars of coal left in mine to suppport the roof. In the past it has unfortunately been too frequently the practice to form the pillars of too small a size in the first instance or to reduce them to too small dimensions afterwards. The weakness of the support afforded by the pillars has resulted in the premature collapse of the roof and the crushing and burying of the small pillars of coal in the process. In some instance, systematic extraction of the reduced pillars has been started but when the work reached a stage when the collapse of the roof took place, the collapse has extended over a larger area than that from which pillars have been extracted, crushing and burying pillars in the way I have already described. Underground fires also occur though less frequently than in the case of premature collapses in mines in which pillars of a resonable size have been formed. In the extraction of the pillars, owing to the great thickness of the seams in the Jharia coalfield—some of them are between 40 and 60 in thickness—it is usually impracticable to remove all the coal. Parts of pillars and occasionally whole pillars of coal are lost and the conditions which cause spontaneous combustion arise.

The motion referring the bill to a select committee was agreed to, and the House adjourned.

Repressive Laws' Repeal Bill (Contd.)

9th. APRIL :—Mr. *Satyamurti* resumed his unfinished speech to-day on the motion to refer his bill to repeal and amend certain repressive laws to a Select Committee.

Mr. Satyamurti quoted long extracts from the "Law Reporters" to show that the attributing of improper and dishonest motives to Government amounted to sedition. That being the case, he said, a representative form of government could not be maintained in India, for nobody would dare to attribute dishonest motives in the doings and actions of the ministry. In other words, in India, unlike other countries. having a representative form of government, one could, under law, only attribute good motives in the doings of the ministry and thus never be able to replace it.

Mr. Satyamurti copiously quoted from the 'Law Reports' and argued that it was not just, commonsense or honest to proceed against a person simply because the Executive suspected that he was acting with the intention of promoting physical force or violence or public disorder. If the seditious action in the Indian Penal Code were strictly administered there would not be a writer in the country. He challenged the Government to quote even a recent case in English jurisprudence where a person had been convicted on this plea. In India magistrates had become merely signing machines when a police statement was placed before them. He emphasised that majesterial orders must be based on proper evidence.

As for Section 144, Mr. Satyamurti contended that it was constantly abused. Even such innocent act as the wearing of Gandhi caps or Swadeshi propaganda had come to be dealt with under this section He quoted from the famous Guntur case where Section 144 had been promulgated banning Gandhi caps as a symbol of Mr. Gandhi's movement. He pointed out that even under the Gandhi-Irwin Pact the representative of the Crown in India, namely, Lord Irwin had accepted peaceful picketing as legal. He urged that exparte orders under Section 144 should not remain in force beyond 48 hours.

Mr. Satyamurti, proceeding, dealt with the repressive laws enacted since 1818 and declared that the Bengal, Madras and Bombay State Prisoners Regulations had no right to exist on the Statute Book. He mentioned the cases of Mr. Sarat Chandra Bose and the Maharaja of Nabha, who had been interned since eight years without legal sanction and also Mr. Subhas Chandra Bose's arrest yesterday. Quoting the preamble and section in the regulation, he asked, with what country foreign relations would be endangered if these persons were free ? Particularly, he asked why periodical visits to State prisoners were refused in the case of Madras regulation.

Referring to the Moplah Outrages Act of 1859, Mr. Satyamurti declared that it was a piece of enactment of which every civilised Government should be ashamed. Vicarious punishments under this enactment (that is, for the offence of one man the whole village or town being penalised), was a worst injustice. He declared that the Moplahs were a race of hard-working, proud and brave people and it was a blot that such an enactment has been kept in the Statute Book stigmatising the entire community of indulging in murderous outrages. The Government ought to take steps to make them law-abiding citizens by giving them proper education. He referred in similar terms to the Punjab Murderous Outrages Act of 1867, which was even wider. Mr. *Satyamurti*, continuing, said that the Repressive Laws Committee, which had on it Sir Tej Bahadur Sapru, unanimously recommended the repeal of the Madras, Bengal and Bombay regulations. The Government instead of repealing them had passed the Criminal Law Amendment Act.

As regards the Press Emergency Act, the protection provided by section 35 at the hands of the High Court to owners of presses was illusory. Sir Abdur Rahim, as Chief Justice of the Madras High Court, had made out a good case for its repeal in one of his judgments. In England a pressman was free and could be tried under the ordinary laws. The Government's argument was that in India they could not get at the real editor who was usually shielded by a dummy. Mr. Satyamurti said that he was prepared in the Select Committee to empower the courts to get at the real culprit. As regards the States Protection Act he pointed out sections 125 and 126 and asked on the face of these sections where was the necessity of enacting this Bill. If the coming Federation had any meaning at all, it certainly ought not to be disfigured at its very inception by the continuance of the Indian States Protection Act, which was against British Indians and not against State Indians.

Turning to a batch of Bengal laws which the Bill sought to repeal, Mr. Satyamurti said that all these laws were based on mistrust. He deplored the Home Member's attack on the Congress. Did he not know that in Karachi a resolution condemning these outrages had been passed ? Time after time, he added, Mr. Gandhi had condemned terrorism. So long as terrorism existed the speaker was prepared to convert terrorists to the Congress point of view, but how could he do it unless the terrorists were released. The Government, he said, did not take the trouble of understanding the Congress, but knew only to abuse it. Had not the Home Member heard that for condemning terrorism Mr. Gandhi was bombed at Poona ?

The House adjourned at this stage.

Salt Additional Duty Act

14th. APRIL :—The Assembly, after two hours' discussion to-day, passed Sir *James Grigg's* Bill extending by two years the operation of the Salt Additional Duty Act, 1931, subject to reduction of rate of duty to one and a half annas. Sir James Grigg pointed out that the Bill was a fair compromise between the two conflicting views, namely, the interests of the consumer and producer.

Though there were a few amendments, none of them were moved and the Bill was passed. Sir James Grigg, again emphasising the Government's proposal, held out an equitable compromise of steering through a middle course between the various conflicting interests.

Wheat and Rice Export Duty Bill

Sir *Zafrullah Khan* moved taking into consideration the Bill for continuing for a year the import duty on wheat, wheat flour and broken rice. He said that the level at which the wheat duty had been fixed, namely, Re. 1 per cwt., would neither cause fluctuation of prices nor reduction of the general price level, nor would it permit more imports into India. The imposition of the duty on broken rice had had a salutary effect in checking imports of broken rice to India and also bringing down the amount of imports of whole rice and paddy. Therefore the continuation of the duty on rice would mean further continuation of those good effects.

BILL PROHIBITING LOAN TO ITALY (CONTD.)

The Assembly started further consideration of the Bill prohibiting the making of certain loans and credits to Italy. At the outset, *Sir James Grigg* announced that Government had given an assurance in a communique that premia payments made to Italian insurance companies would not come within the purview of the provisions of the Bill. In order further to remove doubts the Government proposed to move an amendment to the effect that no prosecutions under this Bill be launched without the consent of the Governor-General in Council.

Mr. Ayyanger moving an amendment said that the premia paid in respect of endowment policies was returned when the policy matured. Therefore, it could be construed as loan and his amendment wanted to make clear in the Bill that such premia would not be loans. The amendment was rejected.

Mr. Ayyanger's next amendment prohibiting prosecutions except with the sanction of the local Government, was rejected by thirty votes against fifty.

Mr. Ayyanger then moved an amendment eliminating that portion of the Bill which empowered the Governor-General to repeal the Bill. He asked why should not the Assembly be asked to take such a decision. Sir James Grigg in reply said that the decision would be of the League as to when sanctions were to be withdrawn. The amendment was rejected.

Mr. Ayyanger moved another amendment empowering the Governor-General to suspend the operation of the Act by a notification in the gazette but subject to ratification of that decision by the Assembly.

Mr. *Lalchand Navalrai* supported the motion, but the House rejected it. All the clauses of the Bill were then passed. The House divided on Sir Grigg's motion and the Bill was passed by fifty-nine votes to twenty-five.

COMPANY LAW AMEND. BILL

15th. APRIL :—When the Assembly met to-day, Sir *N. N. Sircar* moved that the Bill amending Company Law be referred to a Select Committee. He traced the history of the Indian Companies Act and referred to the necessity felt in recent years to amend the law. In August, 1934 the Viceroy, addressing the House, intimated that the Government had decided to appoint Mr. Susil C. Sen, a practising solicitor in Calcutta, in order to examine and report as to what amendments were necessary. Mr. Sen entered upon his duties in September, 1934, and considered the suggestions from the local Governments, the Associated Chambers of Commerce and other associations and individuals. The Government had further implemented the promise given by Sir Joseph Bhore that before legislating commercial opinion should be consulted in the matter. Consequently Mr. Sen's report was examined by the Federation of Indian Chambers of Commerce, the Associated Chambers of Commerce, the Bombay shareholder's Association, the Bombay Jute Mills Association and the Imperial Bank of India. Most of the conclusions of the committee had been accepted by the Government in drafting the Bill. Sir N. N. Sircar made it clear, speaking generally, that these proposals did not represent any unchangeable view of the Government and further discussions in the Select Committee and in the House would be required in order to give the final shape to the Bill in making their provisional suggestions. In the Draft of the Bill the Government had tried to their best ability to arrive at a mean of the two extreme views.

Mr. *Bhulabhai Desai*, who analysed the working of law from the legal point of view, indicated the numerous scopes for improvement. He did not share the view that the much-abused managing agency system had been entirely a failure. He thought this system had served the country fairly well and that total condemnation of the system would be a set-back. After showing the defects in managing agencies as at present existed, Mr. Desai advocated that in future the fortunes of managing agents should be coupled with net profits earned by the company by nominees of managing agents as that would be detrimental to the public as well as to shareholders. He did not like the indemnity clause in its present form. It had been argued that this clause made directors irresponsible. The speaker agreed that it should be eliminated in its present form and some provision should be made for bona fide error of judgment on the part of the directors. He also suggested that restrain should be imposed on the borrowing power of directors and also there should be no lending by one company to another, not merely under the same managing agents and that auditors should be independent of the managing directors and should be the watch-dog of the interests of shareholders. Mr. Desai hoped his suggestions would be given due weight, while the Bill was discussed in the select committee.

The *President* wanted to put the motion to the House, but Mr. *Ayyengar* insisted on making a speech, whereupon the debate was postponed and the House adjourned.

Import Duty on Unbroken Rice

16th. APRIL :—The Assembly passed to-day, by 68 votes against 45, the resolution of Mr. *Nauman*, for levying an import duty of one rupee per maund on unbroken rice and eight annas per maund on paddy.

Sir *G. S. Bajpai*, opposing the resolution, stated that there had actually been a reduction in the imports of broken rice and paddy and that certain ports of Bengal and Madras wanted rice for consumers.

Protection to Cottage Industry

Sardar Mangal Singh moved that the Government should take "definite and effective steps to extend the policy of protection to the small and cottage industries of the country and with this object in view immediately appoint a committee to enquire into and report on the subject." He said that India being an agriculturist country small industries played an important part and if revived would spread social contentment. Thus the import duties on raw materials and other goods would be carefully examined to see that these did not adversely affect the cottage industries. The Government had helped bigger industries and killed cottage industry. He quoted a speech of Sir Gokulchand Narang to the effect that the industries could not be developed without protection but the Government of India controlled the policy of protection.

Sir *Frank Noyce* detailed the steps taken by Government to encourage small industries and maintained that they had done much more in recent years than before. Though the subject was really provincial and transferred the Government of India had done their best within the limits of the Constitution and had achieved a record which they could be proud of. What small industries wanted most was technical advice and assistance. And the Government of India, by reviving the Industries Conference and annually discussing the industrial problems, were exploring means whereby they could encourage industries. In framing the stores purchases rules they had taken steps to ensure that those articles manufactured by hand were encouraged. The Industrial Research Bureau established recently was engaged in investigation into industries like soap, vegetable oil and glass. Furthermore, they had given financial assistance to industries like silk and woollen goods and the exhibitions held at Patna and Delhi were given subsidies to the extent of Rs. 10,000 and Rs. 7,500 respectively.

Mr. *Satyamurti* asked the Government to take advantage of the opportunity to make a survey of cottage industries and make out a list. He also appealed to the Government to work with Mr. Gandhi in the All India Village Industries Association started last year. This Association under the leadership of Mr. Gandhi had done enormous work as was shown by the exhibits at the Lucknow Exhibition, illustrating the strength of the movement behind that great personality. By encouraging small industries they would be able to eliminate the middlemen and capitalists and bring producers and consumers nearer. By this he did not mean that big industries should be neglected. They should be allowed to develop and expand in order to make India self-sufficient in many ways. But their profits should be taxed sufficiently for the benefit of the poor. In the case of small industries, the Government should give encouragement.

Mr. *Ramsay Scott* urged the adoption in India of the Japanese cartel system which was established in Japan to meet business depression after the world war in order to save industries from unfair competition and lead them on healthy lines and which had proved beneficial to manufacturers. Proceeding the speaker pointed out that Australia and Japan were about to sign the agreement and hoped that Government would study it carefully. He had no details of the treaty but he understood that Japan would respect the special treaty privileges granted by Australia to Britain by virtue of the Ottawa Agreement. He deplored that the safeguarding of the Industries Act had been allowed to lapse and suggested Government to bring another Bill soon as it would be of great assistance in rendering quick help to any small industry and should be on the statute book again before negotiations started for a new treaty with Japan.

Sir *Muhamed Zafrullah*, replying, said that Government had started giving help recently and the immediate question was not the quantum of that help but whether it was being given on right lines. The present policy did include protection to small and cottage industries. Thus in regard to textile and hosiery both mill and cottage industries got equal protection. The help to sericulture was help to the cottage industry, while the protection of gold and silver thread was protection of small industry. What was wanted was technical schools and assistance with regard to methods of production and marketing. This the Government of India was trying to do. Seven lakhs of rupees have been allotted for experimental purposes and if this proved valuable, help would no doubt be extended. A majority of the provinces were giving financial aid to industries. He did not agree with the suggestion for a committee as all the material the committee would collect was already available. He answered various points raised by the speakers and concluded by expressing the assurance that the Government policy was being carried on right lines.

Sardar Mangal Singh accepted Pandit Nilakanta Das's amendment and the resolution as amended was put and carried and read as follows: "This Assembly recommends the Government to take definite and effective steps to extend the policy of protection to small and cottage industries by adopting such measures as protective tariff as well as bounty, subsidy and State purchases wherever necessary and with this object in view to appoint a committee to enquire into and report. The House then adjourned.

Repressive Laws Repeal Bill (Contd.)

17th. APRIL:—In the Assembly to-day, Mr. *Satyamurti* resumed amidst opposition cheers his speech on the bill to repeal the repressive laws. Mr. Satyamurti said, that even if this bill became law, the Government would still have power to keep the Bengal detenus as prisoners. So the bill could safely go to the Select Committee. He hoped he had made a 'prima facie' case for an examination of the whole question relating to the repressive laws. He wanted bare justice. His whole object was that the innocent should not be punished. Another object was to remove suspicion against the Evidence Act. That was why the Government always wanted to enact special legislation. Then there was distrust of the Cr. P. C. when the I. P. C. was enacted. The idea of punishment was quite primitive and was draconian in many respects. Even this was not good enough for the Government. They wanted special legislation. He was strongly opposed to arming the Executive with special powers. Mr. Satyamurti summed up his case and gave an outline of what his bill stood for. He maintained that under the new Government of India Act which, the Government said, granted responsible government to the provinces, it should be possible to have free public and Press criticism of the Government and the power to bring the ministry into contempt and turn it out. He warned the European group that their "cousins" would not remain in power for ever and would regret the day when they did not support him. He asked the House to give a straight vote in favour of the motion and have all repressive laws examined so that freedom of person and speech could be secured and injustices put right. He concluded, amidst cheers of the Opposition, having spoken about six and a quarter hours.

Other Non-Official Bills

The debate on the Bill was adjourned at this stage to enable other bills of social and other character to be taken up. Sir *Cowasji* moved that the Assembly might take into consideration the *Parsee Divorce Bill* as passed by the Council of State.

Sir Cowasji Jehangir said that reform embodied in the Bill was demanded by the entire Parsee community. The Bill was considered and passed without any discussion.

The House next circulated Dr. *Deshmukh's Bill regarding the Hindu women's right to Property*. He said that the Bill merely involved the point of law.

Mr. *B. Das's Bill amending the Sarda Act* was circulated for public opinion and so also Dr. *Bhagawandas's Hindu Marriage Validity Bill*.

Dr. *Khare* moved reference to the Select Committee of the *Arya Marriage Validation Bill*. The Law Member said that the reason why he did not insist on circulation was that a similar Bill had been circulated for opinion previously. The motion was agreed to.

Mr. *Abdullah* moved consideration of the *Muslim Personal Law (Shariat) Application Bill.* Sir Henry Craik moved circulation on the ground that the Bill proposed many revolutionary changes and it was advisable to ascertain the different views. The Home Member's motion was accepted.

Mr. *M. C. Raja* moved reference to a Select Committee of the *Removal of Civic Disabilities Bill.* Mr. *B. N. Bajoria* opposed what he called Irreligious Bill". Sir *N. N. Sircar* moved for circulation of opinion by July 31. Mr. *M. C. Rajah* had no objection. Sir *N. N. Sircar's* motion was accepted.

Dr. *Thein Maung* was cheered when he introduced the *Budha Gaya Temple Restoration Bill.* Mr. *B. N. Bajoria*, on a point of order, said that the temple was a private property. The Bill was introduced and the House Adjourned.

Company Law Amend. Bill (Contd.)

18th. APRIL :—After an hour's discussion, the Assembly referred the Bill amending Company Law to a select committee. Sir *Leslie Hudson* agreed that the tightening up of Company Law was necessary and welcomed the procedure of the Law Member in calling an unofficial conference of representatives of commercial bodies. While a revision was necessary in the law, he hoped it would not be so drastic as to hamper the healthy growth of commerce in this country.

The Tariff Act Amend. Bill

The Bill to amend the Indian Tariff Act relating to staple fibre fents, cotton-knitted apparel and spun silk yarn was taken up. Sir *Mahomed Zafrullah Khan* detailed the reasons for the measure and, referring to fents imported from Japan, pointed out that there was no reason to believe that the Japanese authorities were evading their obligations by encouraging this trade. On the other hand, this was coming in large quantities by reason of the activities of the Indian exporters in Japan and Indian importors in India. The duty on fents of non-British origin, therefore, had been raised with a view to protecting the cotton textile industry.

The Bill also sought to give effect to the Tariff Board's recommendations on the woolen textile industry by making the protective duty now applicable to cotton-knitted hosiery to all cotton-knitted apparel as well. Further, spun silk yarn was to be subjected to the same duty as pure silk yarn because the competitive value of spun silk was under-estimated when the protective duties on raw silk and silk manufactures were originally imposed. Lastly, the import duty on staple fibre would be put at five per cent. in the case of imports from the United Kingdom and fifteen in the case of imports from other countries. The preference was under the Ottawa Trade Agreement.

The motion for a Select Committee report by April 21 was agreed to.

Payment of Wages Bill (Contd.)

Sir *Frank Noyce* moved that the amendments made by the Council of State to the Bill regulating the payment of wages to certain classes of persons employed in the industry be taken into consideration. He explained the three amendments carried by the Council and expressed the hope that they would work in the interests of the employees. After Sir Frank Noyce's reply all the amendments made in the Council of State were adopted.

Further consideration of the Tariff Act Amendment Bill relating to rice and wheat was next taken up. The debate had not concluded when the House adjourned, till 20th.

High Court Proceedings Validity Bill

20th. APRIL :—Official bills were discussed in the Assembly to-day, the most contentious being the Bill intended to establish the Validity of certain Proceedings in High Court. Sir *N. N. Sircar*, speaking on the decrees and orders of the Validating Bill, referred to two judgments passed on August 26 and September 11 last year, by a Court of Judicial Commissioners in the Central Provinces, holding that certain decrees passed by the Bombay High Court in exercise of the jurisdiction which that court conceived and possessed under clause 12 of its Letters Patent, were made without jurisdiction. Hence, clause twelve of the Letters patent of the Bombay High Court, which was identical in terms with clause 12 of Madras and clause 10 of Calcutta, had been variously interpreted by several High Courts and the question of amending it was under consideration. Meanwhile, the Bill intended to obviate inconvenience to parties which would result if the decrees passed by one High Court proved infructuous in another court holding a different interpretation. Continuing, Sir N. N. Sircar said that a dilatory motion like reference to a Select Committee would be harmful.

Mr. *M.S. Aney* moved that the bill be circulated for eliciting opinion by July 31 and said that thereby the House would be able to know the views of the judgment-debtor who would also be mainly affected by the Bill, for in some cases he would be called upon to cover a distance of 300 to 400 miles in order to defend himself.

The Wheat Duty Bill

The debate was resumed on the Tariff Bill relating to the Wheat Duty. Mr. *Mangal Singh*, continuing his unfinished speech, alleged that the Government had reduced the duty for the sake of the millers in Bombay and Calcutta. He wished that for the sake of wheat-growers the Government might fix one duty for a number of years.

Sir *Mahomed Zafarullah Khan*, replying to the debate, said that it was erroneously believed by some members that reduction of the duty would lower the prices of Indian wheat. All that the import duty would do was to keep out foreign wheat which might be offered at a lower price than Indian wheat. If that would not be achieved by the proposed duty he said the Government would take further action in the matter. The motion for consideration was passed. The House adjourned.

Adjournment Motions

21st. APRIL :—Two adjournment motions were attempted in the Assembly to-day. Mr. *Anantasayanam* sought permission to discuss the situation in Berhampur, Bengal, where, according to a press report, famine conditions prevail, deaths from starvation have occurred, cholera is raging and scarcity of water is greatly felt in the rural areas.

Sir *N. N. Sircar* pointed out that statements in the Press could not be taken as 'prima facie' evidence of what was stated. Moreover the matter rested with the Provincial Government. He suggested that he might obtain the information telegraphically.

The next motion was by Mr. *Mohanlal Saksena*, who wanted to discuss the report of suicide by Nalini Kumar Chakravarti, a Bengali, detained in a village in Mymensingh district. He stated that he gave a short notice question bearing this report on Saturday and was told that only late last night it could not be accepted as a short notice.

The *President* ruled out the motion as there was no "prima facie" evidence that the suicide was due to detention in a village.

Wheat Import Duty Act

Sir *Zafrullah* moved the final reading of the Wheat Import Duty Act.

Mr. *Satyamurti* raised a point of privilege as to why the Government had adopted a procedure which deprived the House of the right of retaining the old duty by letting the old Act lapse and then bringing a new Bill four days afterwards.

Sir *Zafrullah* informed the House that no imports of wheat occurred during the three days that the law did not exist.

Cochin Port Transference Bill (Contd.)

Sir *Zafrullah* next moved consideration of the Cochin Port Bill, making Cochin a major port. He said that later on some more legislation would be necessary to give effect to the agreement about the Cochin Harbour. The Bill was passed.

Other Official Bills

Sir *Frank Noyce* moved consideration of the Bill amending the Factories Act.

The motion for consideration was passed and, as Mr. *Ayyangar's* amendment to clause 2 for ensuring that the provisions of the Bill did not affect cottage industries, was rejected on Sir Frank Noyce assuring the House that that was not the intention, the Bill was passed.

The House also passed the *Aircraft Act Amendment Bill* which aimed at stopping egress and ingress of diseases by aircraft.

Sir *Frank Noyce* next moved that the *Indian Mines Act* be taken into consideration. The motion for consideration was passed. Two amendments of Mr. Satyamurti were withdrawn and another minor official amendment was passed. Thereafter, the Bill as amended was passed.

Sir *Girija Sankar Bajpai* moved consideration of the *Lac Cess Bill.* The House rejected Mr. *Ramnarayan Singh's* amendment about representation of lac cultivators on the governing body by election. Sir *G. S. Bajpai* explained that the proposal was too expensive and that nomination by Ministers in the provinces concerned should be accepted as impartial.

The amendment of Mr. *K. Chaliha* was rejected and those of *Prof. Ranga* and Mr. *Morgan* were withdrawn on the basis of assurances given by Sir *G. S. Bajpai* and the the Lac Cess Bill was passed.

On the motion of Sir *Frank Noyce* the House passed resolutions recommending the Governor-General not to ratify Geneva's draft conventions concerning the reduction of hours of work in glass-bottle works and other limiting hours of work in coal mines. The House then adjourned.

THE TARIFF ACT AMEND. BILL (CONTD.)

22nd. APRIL :—To-day's debate mainly related to the Tariff Bill concerning fents. Sir *Muhammad Zafrullah Khan* moving consideration of the Bill explained the various changes made in the Bill by the Select Committee.

Mr. *B. Das*, opposing the motion for consideration, said that he was opposed to the handicapping of cottage industries. If, after ten years' protection, the textile industry could not stand on its own legs, it was time that the industry should die a natural death.

Pandit Nilakanta Das remarked that India had already given a good deal of preference to England which was against India's economic interest.

Mr. *Sataymurti* protested against the Government trying by back-door methods to upset the Assembly's verdict on the Ottawa Agreement. He was opposed to this alliance between the British capitalist and Indian capitalist at the expense of the consumers.

Sir *Mohd. Zafarullah Khan* accepted the amendment on behalf of the Government though it did not go far enough. He believed that the reduction of length of the fents would prove effective and hoped that further measures of protection might not be necessary. The House adopted Mr. Gauba's amendment whereafter it adjourned. The following is Mr. *Gauba's* amendment :—

"Cotton knitted apparel, including apparel made of cotton interlocking material, cotton undervests knitted or woven and cotton socks and stockings (A) of weight not exceeding four pounds per dozen; twenty-five per cent. ad valorem or twelve annas per pound, whichever is higher."

23rd. APRIL :—Discussion on the Bill was resumed to-day. Mr. *A. Ayyangar* moved an amendment that 10 p. c. preference provided in the Bill would cease to operate when the Ottawa Agreement terminated.

Sir *Mohd. Zafrullah* said that he had accepted yesterday's amendment on the understanding that the effect of the Ottawa Agreement would not be dealt piecemeal but as a whole. He assured that the matter would not be considered behind the back of the House.

Mr. *Satyamurti* wanted an assurance that irrespective of whether certain preference be retained on their own merits, the entire preference range be reviewed as the result of the termination of the agreement.

Sir *Mohd. Zafrullah* maintained that Mr. Ayyangar's amendment was out of order, because its effect would be that on the termination of the Ottawa Agreement duty on British goods would be raised by 10 p. c., and as that involved an increase in tax the amendment was unadmissible. He gave Mr. Satyamurti the assurance that the whole question of preferential duties must be considered as the result of the termination of the Ottawa Agreement.

Thereupon, Mr. Ayyangar withdrew his amendment.

Prof. Ranga opposed the Bill even as amended by the Select Committee. He confessed that his heart was not in it as the interests of the consumers were ignored by the Bill, which gave preferences to Britain. He repeatedly argued that there should have been a special investigation by the Tariff Board before Government had decided on the amount of protection which Indian industries deserved. On the other hand, the Government of India merely agreed to some figure which others had suggested and then began to higgle in the Select Committee. Proceedings had confirmed him in his opinion that the Bill was being dictated by a few rich and powerful men.

Sir *Mohd. Zafarullah* replied that the Bill introduced no new principle of protection and that is why no enquiry by the Tariff Board was conducted.' The idea was merely to continue the principle of protection suggested by the Tariff Board and accepted by the House. In fact it was because that protection had been found to be inadequate in face of the inrush of imports from non-U. K. countries, particularly from Japan, that the Bill was brought. As an illustration Sir Mohd. Zafarullah pointed out that in the case of cotton fents alone imports rose from one million yards in 1932 to 23 million yards in 1934-35. As regards artificial silk and fents imports rose from the negligible quantity of two years ago to sixteen million yards in eleven months of 1934-35. As regards hosiery (excluding socks and underwear) the figures showed an increase by thirty-two times during last three years. Thus the Bill merely attempted to stop the hole created in protective wall and there is no question of Ottawa preference in this. Higher scale duties was preferred against non-British goods merely because of the inrush of imports from these countries jeopardising the position of Indian industries. The motion for consideration of the Bill was passed.

The effect of Mr. *K. L. Gauba's* amendment, which was adopted unanimously, would be that the existing duty, namely, 25 per cent against United Kingdom and 35 per cent against non-U. K. goods will be maintained. No change will be made in co.ton fents but as for artificial silk fents the length has been reduced from four to two and a half year.

Mr. *Gauba* pleaded that his amendment was a via media. *Mr. Shaukat Ali*, who participated in the discussion leading to Mr. Gauba's formula, said that Indian hosiery manufacturers could not produce all India's requirements. Why then should people be compelled to purchase costlier goods made in India ? Mr. *Ramsay Scott*, the representative of the hosiery industry, said that in accepting Mr. Gauba's amendment, the industry was making a sacrifice and assured that the industry was doing the best use of Indian cotton.

Mr. *Satyamurti* objected to a compromise being reached behind the back of the Assembly, especially when that question was not discussed in the committee which had exhaustively gone into the matter.

Sir *Mohd. Zafarullah* replied that Mr. Ramsay Scott, representing the hosiery industry, had assured him that without the relief of two annas there would be real hardship and hence Government accepted Mr. K. L. Gauba's amendment which was then put to vote and carried.

Mr. *A. Ayyangar's* minor amendment for deletion of sub-clause 2 of clause 1 was carried.

At the third reading, Mr. *F. E. James* protested against hurrying the Tariff Bill of this kind at the fag end of the session and also incorporating three items of protection in one and the same bill and thereby making it difficult for members, supporting one item of protection going against the bill, though they disliked another item of protection.

Sir *Cowasji Jehangir* endorsed Mr. F. E. James's observations as to why the tariff bill was rushed through and remarked that the textile industry had come off worse.

Pandit *G. B. Pant* spoke on behalf of the Congress Party, complaining against the manner in which Mr. Gauba's amendment was reached and brought. Sir *Zafarullah* vigorously defended the Government against the criticism of Mr. James and Sir Cowasji Jehangir. He conceded that wherever feasible and practicable protective measures should deal with only one industry at a time.

The Tariff Bill was then passed. This concluded the business before the session and the House *adjourned 'sine die'* amidst cheers.

Assembly's Record Session

The Assembly held to-day the fifty-second sitting of the session, which was of a record length. The average attendance of members had also been a record one, namely, 120. The highest was on the Ottawa voting when 138 members attended, while the lowest was on April 6 when it dropped to 89.

The questions asked during the session numbered 1,840 for oral answers and 616 for written answers, besides a number of short-notice questions answered during the session. One unusual feature of the session was that of eight pending bills inherited from the last Simla session, only one relating to payment of wages had been passed and the rest put off to the next Simla session. Nine of the new Bills introduced this session by the Government were passed, while the Finance Bill was certified.

The Bengal Legislative Council

LIST OF MEMBERS

1. The Hon'ble Maharaja Sir Manmatha Nath Ray Chowdhury (*President*)
2. Mr. Razaur Rahaman Khan (*Dy. President*)

Members, Executive Council

3. The Hon'ble Sir John Woodhead
4. The Hon'ble Mr. R. N. Reid
5. The Hon'ble Sir. Brojendra Lal Mitter
6. The Hon'ble Khwaja Sir Nazimuddin

Ministers

7. The Hon'ble Nawab Sir K. G. M. Faroqui
8. The Hon'ble Sir Bijoy Prasad Singh Roy
9. The Hon'ble Khan Bahadur M. Azizul Haque

Officials—Nominated

10. Mr. G. P. Hogg
11. S. K. Haldar
12. Mr. D. Gladding
13. Mr. G. G. Hooper
14. Mr. H. P. V. Townend
15. Mr. H. S. E. Stevens
16. Mr. L. R. Fawcus
17. Mr. H. R. Wilkinson
18. Mr. T. J. Y. Roxburgh
19. Mr. S. Basu
20. Mr. R. N. Gilchrist
21. Mr. R. L. Walker
22. Mr. A. K. Chanda
23. Mr. S. C. Mitter

Non-Officials—Nominated

24. Rev. B. A. Nag
25. Babu Guruprosad Das
26. Mr. K. C. Ray Chowdhury
27. Maulvi Latafat Hussain
28. Mr. D. J. Cohen
29. Khan Bahadur Maulavi Hafizar Rahaman Chaudhury
30. P. N Guha
31. Mr. Mukunda Behary Mullick

Non-Official—Elected

32. Babu Jatindra Nath Basu
33. Mr. S. M. Bose
34. Seth Hunuman Prosad Poddar
35. Rai Dr. Haridhan Dutta Bahadur
36. Sir Hari Sanker Paul
37. Dr. Sir Nilratan Sircar
38. Munindra Deb Rai Mahasai
39. Dr. Amulya Ratan Ghose
40. Babu Prafulla Kumar Guha
41. Rai Jogesh Chandra Sen Bahadur
42. Rai Satyendra Kumar Das Bahadur
43. Mr. Saileswar Singh Roy
44. Babu Jitedralal Bannerjee
45. Mr. J. N. Gupta
46. Rai Satya Kinkar Sahana Bahadur
47. Babu Hoseni Rout
48. Mr. R. Maiti
49. Rai Sahib Sarat Chandra Mukhopadhaya
50. Rai Satish Chandra Mukherjee Bahadur
51. Babu Haribansa Roy
52. Babu Sarat Chandra Mittra
53. Mr. P. Banerji
54. Rai Debendra Nath Ballabh Bahadur
55. Mr. Narendra Kumar Basu
56. Srijut Taj Bahadur Singh
57. Babu Amulyadhan Ray
58. Babu Jitendra Nath Roy
59. Babu Suk Lal Nag
60. Rai Keshab Chandra Banerjee Bahadur
61. Dr. Naresh Chandra Sen Gupta
62. Babu Satish Chandra Ray Chowdhury
63. Rai Akshoy Kumar Sen Bahadur
64. Rai Sarat Chandra Bal Bahadur
65. Mr. B. C. Chatterjee
66. Babu Lalit Kumar Das
67. Rai Kamini Kumar Das Bahadur
68. Babu Khetter Mohan Ray
69. Babu Hem Chandra Roy Chaudhuri
70. Babu Kishori Mohan Chaudhuri
71. Babu Prem Hari Barma
72. Rai Sahib Panchanan Barma
73. Babu Nagendra Narayan Ray
74. Dr. Jogendra Chandra Chaudhuri
75. Mr. Shanti Shekhareswar Ray
76. Mr. Prosanna Deb Raikat
77. Mr. A. Raheem
78. Mr. H. S. Suhrawardy
79. Maulvi Shaik Rahim Baksh
80. Maulvi Muhammad Solaiman
81. Maulvi Muhammad Sadatullah
82. Nawabzada K. M. Afzal
83. Maulvi Abul Kasem
84. Maulvi Abdul Karim
85. Khan Bahaduk A. F. M. Abdur Rahaman
86. Maulvi Abdus Samad

87. Maulvi Syed Majid Baksh
88. Maulvi Syed Nausher Ali
89. Maulvi Abul Quasem
90. Maulvi Abdul Ghani Chowdhury
91. Maulvi Azizur Rahaman
92. Maulvi Nur Rahaman Khan Eusufji
93. Maulvi Abdul Hamid Khan
94. Maulvi Abdul Hakim
95. Khan Bahadur Maulvi Ali-muzzaman Chaudhury
96. Maulvi Tamizuddin Khan
97. Maulvi Muhammad Hossain
98. Khan Bahadur Maulvi Hashem-ali Khan
99. Maulvi Abi Abdulla Khan
100. Maulvi Nural Absar Choudhury
101. Haji Badi Ahmed Chowdhury
102. Maulvi Syed Osman Haidar Chaudhuri
103. Khan Bahadur Muhammad Abdul Momin
104. Maulvi Muhammad Fazlullah
105. Khan Sahib Maulvi Md. Basiruddin
106. Khan Bahadur Maulvi Emad-uddin Ahmad
107. Maulvi Hassan Ali
108. Mr. A. F. Rahaman
109. Kazi Emdadul Haque
110. Maulvi Rajibuddin Tarafder
111. Khan Bahadur Maulvi Muazzam Ali Khan
112. Nawab Musharruf Hosain
113. Mr. F. C. Guthrie
114. Mr. W. L. Armstrong
115. Mr. A. R. E. Lockhart
116. Mr. J. W. R. Steven
117. Mr. R. H. Ferguson
118. Mr. L. T. Maguire
119. Mr. E. T. McCluskie
120. Raja Bhupendra Narayan Sinha Bahadur
121. Mr. Sarat Kumar Roy
122. Mr. Arun Chandra Singha
123. Kumar Shib Shekhareswar Ray
124. Mr. Syamaprosad Mookerjee
125. Rai Sosanka Comar Ghose Bahadur
126. Mr. Thomas Lamb
127. Mr. F. T. Homan
128. Mr. W. H. Thompson
129. Sir Heny Birkmyre, Bart
130. Mr. G. W. Leeson
131. Mr. W. C. Wordsworth
132. Mr. J. R. Walker
133. Mr. G. G. Cooper
134. Mr. C. G. Arthur
195. Mr. J. B. Ross
136. Mr. H. R. Norton
137. Mr. Surendra Nath Law
138. Maharaja Sris Chandra Nandy
139. Rai Ram Dev Chokany Bahadur
140. Mr. Ananda Mohan Poddar
141. Rai Giris Chandra Sen Bahadur
142. Major-General D. P. Goil
143. Mr. F. A. Sachse
144. Rai S. N. Banerjee Bahadur

Proceedings of the Council

Budget Session—Calcutta—12th. February to 30th. March '36

The Budget Session of the Bengal Legislative Council commenced in the Council Hall, Calcutta on the **12th. February 1936**. After 45 minutes' sitting, the House was adjourned as a mark of respect to the memory of His late Majesty King George V of England and Emperor of India. The House also decided to send a message of condolence to His Majesty the King Emperor Edward the VIII through His Excellency the Governor of Bengal.

Non-official Resolutions

13th. FEBRUARY :—The consideration of a couple of resolutions, one aiming at the introduction of legislation fixing minimum prices for agricultural products and the other seeking to raise the grant for primary and secondary education for women occupied for more than three hours the attention of the members of the Council when they met to-day to transact non-official business.

The two resolutions however met different fate, the first moved by *Rai Bahadur Satyendra Kumar Das* was rejected by the House while the second was withdrawn by Mr. *S. M. Bose*, its mover.

It was very unfortunate that the enthusiasm of *Rai Bahadur Satyakinkar Sahana* got so much the better of his wisdom that he remarked "illiterate mothers produced terrorist sons."

But the snubbing came straight and quick from Mr. *N. K. Basu*, who said that it was not high or primary education that made a good mother. Good mothers were born and not made. No amount of education could make a good mother. The remark of Rai Bahadur Satyakinkar Sahana was a libel cast on the Bengalee mother by a Bengalee son.

Official Bills

14th. FEBRUARY :—The House passed two official bills, namely, *The Calcutta Municipal Amendment Bill*, 1936 introduced by Mr. *S. K. Haldar*, Secretary, Local Self-Government Department and the *Bengal Alluvion and Dilluvion (Amendment) Bill 1936* introduced by Sir *B. L. Mitter*.

The *Bengal Water Hyacinth Bill 1936* was referred to a Select Committee without a division with instruction to report as soon as possible.

The Bengal Whipping Bill

Communalism in its ugliest form revealed itself in the speeches of certain members when Sir *B. L. Mitter* introduced the Bengal Whipping Bill and moved that it be taken into consideration.

The Bill which sought to provide for whipping as an additional punishment in the case of some of the more serious offences against women met with strenuous and persistent opposition from the Muslim members.

Mr. *H. S. Surhawardy* and *Maulvi Hasan Ali* moved two amendments urging that the bill be circulated for the purpose of eliciting opinion by the 15th March next. Levelling bitter and violent invectives against his sister community, Mr. Suhrawardy declared that there was a regular conspiracy among the Hindus to implicate innocent Muslims in offences of this nature.

Refuting the charges made by Mr. Surhawardy, Mr. *S. M. Bose* characterised the speech of Mr. Surhawardy as a "scandalous one in more senses than one." It was quite irrelevant to drag in any question as to the religion of the woman or of the ruffian who attacked her.

Mr. *Santisekhareswar Roy* was the solitary figure among the Hindus who amid cheers from the Muslim Benches supported the motion. The House then adjourned till the 17th.

17th. FEBRUARY :—The speech of Mr. *Surhawardy* came in for scathing criticism at the hands of several prominent members to-day.

It was derogatory to the dignity of the House, said Sir *Brojendra*, and might be useful in street corners in winning cheap applause but absolutely out of place in the Legislative Council.

In rising to oppose the motion for circulation of the Bill, Mr. *N. K. Basu* said that he should confine himself in meeting the arguments advanced by Mr. Surhawardy. He would at this stage deal with his proposals so far as he could make out. The reasons advanced by the mover were that in the present condition of social, political and judicial atmosphere prevailing in the country, the bill was uncalled for. After making a sanctimonious profession of his dislike for the introduction of communal issue into that question, Mr. Surhawardy had gone to say that the hands of the Government had been forced by the communal papers which had spread the scandal that offences against women were committed more by the Musalmans than by the Hindus. Mr. Surhawardy had also suggested that there was a regular conspiracy among the Hindus to implicate innocent Muslims in offences of this nature. Mr. Surhawardy had also referred to the statistics compiled by a newspaper which stated that crimes against women were committed more by Hindus than by Mussalmans. But, remarked Mr. Basu, memory was short ; it was only three years ago that in answer to a question put into the House by Mr. Kishori Mohan Chowdhury with regard to the crimes against women a big sheet was laid on the table giving figures district by district of such cases occurring from 1926 to 1931. Mr. Basu had ventured to make a summary of that statement and a few of those figures would tell the House of the number of crimes committed. The number of cases between 1926 and 1931 were 838, 928, 1000, 910 and 284 respectively totalling 5673. All these victims were mostly Mahomedans. In 1926 women victims belonging to the Mahomedan community were 494 against 324 Hindu women. Next year 579 Muslims against 326 Hindu women. The provisions of this Bill, proceeded Mr. Basu, were more in the interests of the Muslim Community and the Muslim members opposing the measure were guilty not only of travesty of facts but of treason to their own community. It was a fact to be noted that in course of the last six years no less than 3525 Muslim women were outraged. The total number of abduction of women during the last six years had been 5673 but, asked Mr. Basu, what were the number of total convictions of Hindus and Muslims year by year? From 1926 to 1931 the number had been 95, 94, 112, 147, 156 and 125 thus varying from year to year.

It was no use to say that whipping was a barbarous sort of punishment and it ought not to be inflicted even on the worst criminals. Mr. Basu was sure that the House was aware that the British Parliament passed two Acts, one in 1885 and the other in 1912, in which additions were made to the offences where whipping could be inflicted with greater deterrent effect. They all knew and the proposer ought certainly to know that in 1926 the Right Hon'ble Justice Syed Ameer Ali proposed to the Government that penalty of death should be inflicted on offenders convicted of crimes against women which the Government had turned down. That was the opinion of one of the revered and honoured leaders of the Mahomedan community. It was more in the interest of the Mahomedan society itself than of anybody else that the Bill had been brought forward by the Government. To say that it was sponsored for the purpose of playing into the hands of the communally-minded Hindus as suggested by Mr. Suhrawardy was not only demonstrably false but also treason against the Mahomedan community. Mr. Surhawardy, the speaker went on, had deprecated in his speech the making over of abducted girls to the Hindu Mahasabha. If such girls were taken under protection by the Mahasabha they all ought to be proud of this organisation. It did not lie in the mouth of Mr. Suhrawardy to say that there was no public opinion in favour of this measure. If there was a bill to which Mr. Basu could give his unqualified support it was this. Everyone knew Mr. Suhrawardy's professed dislike for turning things into communal issue but this was absolutely a piece of eyewash. He had been doing this as long as Mr. Basu was here but he did not know for how many years. Mr. Basu compared Mr. Surhawardy to the South American lizard which wallowed in the mire but spat out venom against all who came near.

The motion for circulation of the bill was then put to the House and declared lost, but a poll being demanded by *Maulavi Abul Quasem* the House divided and the motion was rejected by 68 votes to 17. *Kazi Imdadul Huq*. *Maulavi Abdus Samad*, *Nawab Musharraf Hossein*, Dr. *N. C. Sen Gupta* and Mr. *Santisekhareswar Roy* remained neutral.

Babu *Kshetra Nath Singh* by an amendment sought to provide that the sentence of whipping should be awarded publicly. The amendment was lost. A few other amendments having been quickly disposed of the Bengal Whipping Bill was passed by the House.

The Bengal Municipal Amend. Bill

The *Bengal Municipal Amend. Bill* moved by Sir *Bijoy Prasad Singh Roy* was next taken into consideration. The clauses of the measure were being discussed when the Council adjourned till the 24th.

Financial Statement for 1936-37

24th. FEBRUARY :—In presenting the Budget for 1936-37, the Hon'ble Sir *John Woodhead*, Finance Member to the Government of Bengal, referred to the growing deficits in the provincial Budget since 1929-30 until the assignment in 1934-35 of the jute export duty to the Province and said that though Bengal had not yet attained the desirable position of a balanced budget, still there was a definite improvement in the financial position of the Bengal Government.

"Our financial position since 1934-35 was one of the utmost gravity; it is true to say that it is now much less grave, but it is equally true to say that it is still far from satisfactory. The standard in Bengal is one of the lowest in India; and our financial position will not be satisfactory until funds are available for a considerable improvement in that standard of expenditure, until, as I have so repeatedly said, we have obtained an equitable financial settlement which will render possible the development of the more beneficial activities of Government beyond the present inadequate standard."

The total revenue receipts for 1935-36 were placed in the budget estimates at Rs. 11 crores 2 and one-fourth lakhs. According to revised estimates the figure is Rs. 11 crores 42 and three-fourth lakhs, an increase of Rs. 40 and half lakhs. Taking both revenue and capital receipts together, the revised estimates provide for a total revenue of Rs. 12 crores and 28 and a half lakhs.

On the expenditure side the anticipations are that the total expenditure on revenue and capital account will be Rs. 12 crores and 33 and three-fourth lakhs, which is 7 and a half lakhs less than the budget figure. There is a resultant net deficit of 5 lakhs, which will be met out of the opening balance.

The position for 1936-37 is estimated as follows :—

Total receipts Rs. 12 crores and 48 and half lakhs.

Total expenditure—Rs. 13 crores.

Deficit—Rs. 51 and three-fourth lakhs.

Of this deficit, Rs. 12 and a half lakhs will be met out of the opening balance and Rs. 39 and one-fourth lakhs will be covered by an overdraft from the Government of India.

Provision of Rs. 2 lakhs has been made in the budget estimates for the construction of a Central Jail at Dum Dum. The total cost of the scheme will be Rs. 10 and one-fourth lakhs.

Under "Capital heads" the biggest expenditure is that of Rs. 12,98,000 for repairing and recommending the Anderson Weir at the head of the Damodar Canal system.

Motor Driving Restriction to Non-Bengalees

26th. FEBRUARY :—The Council deliberated over a resolution to-day recommending to the Government that no professional license for driving motor cars in Bengal should be granted to anyone who is not a Bengalee.

In the absence of Mr. *K. C. Ray Chowdhury* who gave notice of the resolution, Mr. *N. K. Basu* with the permission of the President moved it.

The time limit being reached no decision could be arrived at with regard to the resolution. As no other day was allotted for the consideration of non-official resolutions during the session, the resolution was taken as being 'talked out.'

In moving the resolution Mr. *N. K. Basu* said that he knew that the resolution had attracted a good deal of attention both inside and outside the House. He also knew of the many hard things that had been said about the proposals embodied in the resolution. It was known to everybody that the question of unemployment among the young men of the province was very acute and Government had been alive to the situation for sometime past. Mr. Basu was sure that members of the House would remember that three or four years ago the Hon'ble Minister in charge of Agriculture and Industries called a conference of all the members of the House in order to try and suggest means for combating this peril. Of the several members of the Council who attended that conference and made certain proposals one was Mr. Thompson, leader of the European group in the House. His suggestion was that motor and motor driving formed a very good avenue for young men of Bengal and Government should grant opportunities to them for being trained as motor drivers but the Government could not at that time take up the suggestion. Mr. Basu was sure that motor driving would form a very good avenue of employment for Bengalee young men. The number of motor cars, continued Mr. Basu, motor buses, taxis and lorries in the province was very very large. From a symposium of motor business published recently in the "Statesman" it appeared that the latest number of taxis, buses and lorries in the province were respectively 3669, 3671 and 2785 respectively. That would clearly show how many openings as taxi drivers and lorry drivers there were in the province. As for private cars, not owner driven, their number was enormous. Not less than 22551 professional driving licenses had been issued in Calcutta. If a good portion of these could be assured to the sons of Bengal, the speaker was sure, it would go a long way to the solution of the unemployment problem. It had been suggested, the speaker went on, that this resolution would foster race hatred. It had also been suggested that it was a question of aptitude and inclination. A further suggestion was also to the effect that if people from other provinces had come to Bengal and captured the profession the Bengalee people also could go to the other provinces and do the same. But, Mr. Basu submitted, the fallacy underlying all those suggestions was that his resolution did not seek to shut out other people from the province; on the contrary, the underlying idea was to find avenues of employment for thousands of young men in Bengal.

Replying to the debate Sir *Robert Reid* said that the Government were in sympathy to any scheme that might be formulated to fight the unemployment problem. But the resolution would not achieve the object which was in view.

There were a number of practical difficulties in putting the resolution into effect. The Government therefore could not accept it. He informed the House that no discrimination was made in other provinces in the matter of granting licenses. Referring to section 298 of the Government of India Act, Sir Robert said that although the resolution would not produce any legislation it would go against the the spirit of the measure.

Bengal Medical Amend. Bill

27th. FEBRUARY :—The Council dealt with half a dozen non-official bills to-day within the brief space of 90 minutes. One of them was rejected, another passed, two referred to Select Committees and two simply introduced.

Mr. *Mukunda Behari Mullick* moved that the Bengal Medical (Amendment) Bill, 1935, be referred to a select committee. The Bill sought to further amend the Bengal Medical Act VI of 1914 by adding the following proviso to section 17 of the Act which "provided that the Local Government may, after consulting the Council of Medical Registration, permit the registration of (a) any person who shall furnish to the Registrar, proof that he is possessed of a medical degree, diploma, or certificate of any medical institution approved by the Council other than those described in the Schedule, and is such as was practising in the Western (modern scientific system of Allopathic) medicine, before the enforcement of Bengal Medical Act VI of 1914 ; and (b) any person who shall furnish to the Registrar proof that he came out successfully after obtaining proper training from any medical institution approved by the Council of Medical Registration, and has joined the medical profession before the enforcement of the present amendment."

On behalf of the Government, the *Home Member* opposed the principle of the Bill. Mr. Mullick's motion for reference of the Bill to a select committee was rejected by 41 against 34 votes.

Calcutta Municipal Amendment Bills

The Council passed without much discussion the Bill put forward by *Dr. Naresh Chandra Sen Gupta* which sought to further amend the Calcutta Municipal Act of 1923 with respect to rule 1 in schedule VI of the Act.

Mr. *Narendra Kumar Basu's* Calcutta Municipal Amendment Bill, 1935 was referred to a Select Committee. The Bill aimed at giving the principal officers of the Calcutta Corporation security of tenure as well as freedom from needless interference in carrying on their duties.

Explaining the attitude of the Government towards the Bill, Sir *Bejoy Prasad Singh Roy* said that Government did not propose to express any opinion with regard to the measure at this stage. Government would like to decide their lines of action in the Select Committee or afterwards.

Other Non-official Bills

Mr. *Sarat Kumar Roy* and *Mr. Jitendra Lal Banerjee* introduced the Bengal Tenancy Amendment Bill, 1935 and the Bengal Medical Amendment Bill, 1936 respectively.

Raja Bhupendranarayan Singh Bahadur's Bengal Patni Taluks Regulation (Amendment) Bill, 1936 was referred to a Select Committee.

General Discussion of the Budget

28th. FEBRUARY :—General discussion on the Budget Estimates for 1936-37 commenced to-day. Criticising the Budget *Dr. Naresh Chandra Sen-Gupta* compared the budget figures under various heads in 1932-33 with that of 1936-37. Dr. Sen-Gupta pointed out that the Transferred department had been systematically starved while the Reserved department had been pampered. In 1932-33 expenditure under the head Police was 2 crores 19 lakhs. It went on increasing until they had in the year under review the huge amount of 2 crores 30 lakhs. Under the head Jails in the year 1932-33 the expenditure was 40 lakhs whereas in the present year it had mounted to 43 lakhs. The expenditure on general administration had likewise increased.

Referring to the question of education, Dr. Sen-Gupta pointed out that while the department of education on the transferred side was being starved, the department on the Reserved side of it had been receiving a far different treatment. They had not yet been told when the Primary Education Act which was passed a few years ago would come into force. The grant to the University of Calcutta had been reduced by means of an agreement which the speaker could not but describe as the agreement of a 'Baniya.'

The Government had passed the Agricultural Debtors' Bill but the Act had not yet been put into operation. If it had been immmediately carried into effect the whole country would have been saved. The Mahajans had been refusing to lend money to the agriculturists and the result of this had been the ruin of rural economic structure. The Government, said Dr. Sen-Gupta, were certainly responsible for the serious situation. Had they made arrangements for lending money through Co-operative Banks, the peasantry might have been spared the ruination that had come over them. The Government revenues had been enhanced by about two crores of rupees, which sum, according to the speaker, should have been devoted to the work of rural reconstruction. That sum if wisely spent, could have changed the face of the province. Out of rupees sixteen lakhs which the Government of India had granted for rural development, the Bengal Government had decided to spend only the sum of rupees five and half lakhs this year, reserving the rest for expenditure during the next year. This policy, according to Dr. Sen-Gupta, was similar to the one pursued by the clever jackal in the ancient fable, which decided to eat only the bow string of the hunter leaving the rich booty of animals to be consumed the next day. The Government for a long time had been pursuing this stingy and unimaginative policy which was devoid of sympathy for the people.

Mr. *Satish Chandra Ray Chowdhury* said that the budget as well as its predecessors, were not people's budget as they called it. It was not enough for meeting the both ends. Judged by the standards, political, moral and economic the Bengal Government had miserably failed in their duty. Thy had only managed to eke out an existence. If they took away the two crores of rupees received from the Government of India as share of the Jute export duty the picture would be altogether different. The Government budget was one thing and the people's budget was another. The speaker felt bound to say that the budget which did not bring about amelioration in the condition of the people was not worth the paper on which it was written. Mr. Roy Choudhury wanted the Hon'ble Member to go to a village in Bengal and witness for himself the piteous condition under which they were living. He regretted that after more than 150 years of British rule nearly ninety per cent of people were illiterate. He asked the Government what they had done to bring about the industrial regeneration of the province. The State Aid to Industries Act had been still a dead letter. Merely training a few detenus would not solve the intricate problem. A few other members spoke and the House adjourned till the 2nd.March.

2nd. MARCH :—Resuming the Budget discussion to-day, Mr. *W. H. Thompson* referred to the estimates in the Budget under the head "Stamps" which in his opinion was placed higher than the revised estimates of the current year. He was not also very hopeful about the excise revenue. It had been recently discovered that there existed a large number of factories for distilling illicit liquor. He requested Sir John to give them an idea of how much revenue the Government had lost on account of these illegal activities. He enquired whether that matter had been fairly investigated. He complained that the proceeds from the new taxation measures had practically come from the Calcutta people who had thus been seriously affected. The landowners in general and the rural population were not contributing much in that direction. Concluding Mr. Thompson claimed that the whole of the jute export duty and a fair share of the income tax should be allocated to the provincial exchequer. He also claimed an adjustment of Bengal's debts to the Government of India which had been due to the inequitous Meston Award. If that was not done there must be a readjustment between the Centre and other provinces which had been enjoying unfair advantages over Bengal during all these years.

Quoting facts and figures, Mr. *N. K. Basu* refuted the statement made by the Finance Member in his budget speech that expenditure in Bengal was one of the lowest. Mr. Basu pointed out that expenditure 'per capita' on education, medical help and public health in Bengal was less than those in many other provinces including U. P., Bombay and Madras. He also complained that the total expenditure on the Transferred subjects as estimated in the next year's budget was even less than that in 1929-30. This according to the speaker had been forced upon the Government of Bengal because of the three things, namely, deprivation of the jute export duty and a share of the income tax and the presence of the Meston Award. It was true that Sir John Woodhead had discussed the case of Bengal with Sir

Otto but Mr. Basu's grievance was that Sir John had not taken the Bengal Legislative Council into confidence. The province, continued Mr. Basu, was a moribund one; but the speaker asked what step they had taken to revivify the patient before making it over to the administrators of the new constitution. It was no use saying that under the new constitution Bengal would be handed over to popular representatives. He did not want to see the transition of Bengal's blood into other provinces, existent or non-existent. Bengal's money was not to be treated as money of everyone except of Bengal. If Bengal was to live she must have the money which rightfully was due to her.

Mr. *S. M. Bose* pointed out that Assam and the three new provinces created after the Simon Commission Report would to a large extent be financed by subvention from the Federation. All these subventions would necessarily mean that a great deal of the proceeds of the income tax and of the jute duty would be absorbed for the purpose leaving but little to be given to Bengal. These deficit provinces were bound to ask for a High Court and a University and if the Federal Government made them more grants for the purpose it would mean that the legitimate share of Bengal to a large portion of income tax and its claim to the whole of the jute duty would not be paid. That was a very real danger. The admitted claims of Bengal in respect of jute export duty and a large share of income tax should be strongly pressed upon the authorities and the people of Bengal.

Replying to the debate, *Sir John Woodhead*, Finance Member, repudiated the criticism put forward by certain members that the civil administration in Bengal was top-heavy and that the Government were lavish on the well-paid appointments but were niggardly in the case of their menial staff. He pointed out that in the year 1934-35 the actual pay of the former amounted to only rupees thirteen lakhs and a quarter while expenditure under the head Establishment reached the figure of seventy-seven and a half lakhs of rupees. Moreover, expenditure under that head was far less than it was in the year 1929-30 which was the pre-depression year. Referring to the charge levelled by some members that although the Primary Education Act had been passed years ago it had not been enforced, Sir John said that the enforcement of the Act meant increased taxation. The Government had spent several thousands of rupees for the introduction of Primary Education. Government expected that it would be possible to introduce the Act when additional taxation involved in the Act could be imposed. Explaining the question of education on the Reserved side he said that the budget estimates on that head did not only include European and Anglo-Indian Education but also that among the people in excluded areas and in industrial and reformatory schools. There was a provision on that head for 30 lakhs in the next year's budget but of that sum only 10 lakhs would be devoted to educate Europeans and Anglo-Indians. On the other hand, education on the Transferred side had not been starved: there has been an increased provision of one lakh of rupees on that account.

Replying to Mr. Thompson's enquiry why the estimates for 1936-37 under the head "land revenue" were less by ten lakhs than the revised estimates for 1935-36 Sir John pointed out that during the last two years the Government had been collecting a very large amount of arrears. The collections in the Khas Mahals were 90 lakhs of rupees this year. Before the depression set in the Government never collected more than 65 lakhs of rupees. Sir John did not know how long the collections would continue in that manner, but in view of the fact that they had collected during the last two years very large sums of arrears and also in view of the fact they were faced with partial failure of crops in Western Bengal the Government had thought it wise to reduce the estimate by ten lakhs below the figures of this year.

Speaking on the excise revenue the Hon'ble Member observed that he was much worried about it. It showed signs of recovery as they would like to see. The Government, however, hoped that the excise revenue would increase later on. Perhaps the first effect of any improvement in prices was reflected on land revenue and later on the excise. Owing to distress in Western Bengal the revenue had fallen very considerably. As regards the particular case to which Mr. Thompson had alluded that was sub judice and they could not talk about a case which was pending before a court of law. But Sir John would be correct in saying that so far as that case was concerned it was not likely that the Government had lost much revenue. The revenue that might have been decreased was in all probability the Customs revenue which however was the concern of the Central Government. Further, this year the Government of Bengal had provided more money than in the last year for the extension of the Central Detective Department. The Department had been created with a view to meeting the danger of illicit distillation. As regards increase in receipts from Electricity duty, Sir John said that although there had been an increase it would be extremely difficult for him to say what the expected revenue would be. Perhaps they had been too conservative. It might yield more revenue than was anticipated.

Speaking on the future constitution of the province, Sir John said that after all they were not very far away from the day when the new constitution would be introduced. The present budget was not of such importance as the budget of the future. He thought that it was most important that the members of the Council should have stressed to-day the need for an equitable financial settlement for Bengal in the new constitution. Mr. N. K. Basu had twitted him for not taking the House into confidence in regard to the case which they presented to Sir Otto. Perhaps Mr. Basu was not serious. That case was well known and had been presented time after time. It had been discussed in the House as well as outside. Everybody knew what it was.

This finished the Budget discussion and the Council adjourned till the 9th.

Bengal Water Hyacinth Bill

9th. MARCH :—Not one of the fifty amendments to the Bengal Water Hyacinth Bill, 1936 that were moved by the non-official members in the Council was carried and the Bill as reported by the Select Committee was passed without a division. Mr. *H. P. V. Townend*, Rural Development Commissioner, informed the House that the Bill would virtually work under the reformed constitution.

Certain members expressed the apprehension that unless something was done by the Government to keep their own waters such as mighty rivers, bils and khals clear of the pest, not only the object of the measure would be frustrated but also in the working of it a lot of injustice and hardship would be done to the agriculturists in the shape of punishment for offences for which they were not responsible.

Speaking in course of the final passage of the bill, *Nawab Sir Mohiuddin Faroqui*, sponsor of the measure, congratulated the members of the House for their support and said that the measure was one of the most urgent and needed legislation which would have a salutory effect on the economic condition of the country.

Objects and Reasons of the Bill

It was pointed out in the statement of objects and reasons to the Bill that in 1929 and 1930 it was proved in Orissa by the work of Mr. Peck, District Magistrate of Cuttack, that under certain conditions water hyacinth could be practically eliminated by concerted popular efforts under the directions of a district officer. In 1934 and during the present year it had been proved by the work done in the Brahmanbaria sub-division in the Tippera district, in three sub-divisions of Faridpur, in parts of Rajsahi and later, in other sub-divisions of Tippera that similar methods were effective in the vastly more difficult conditions which prevailed in the river districts of Bengal. It had been established that the people in affected districts would respond to a call for concerted action and that such concerted action directed and supported by the efforts of the district staff of the Government, could in one season so diminish the water hyacinth in a district as to allow it to be controlled with comparative ease by similar action in subsequent years. The great difficulty at the moment was the apathy, or the active opposition of a minority who were not prepared to further a mass movement against water hyacinth by clearing their lands voluntarily ; and it was to give power to coerce this minority in districts where there was a voluntary campaign against water hyacinth that the present bill was put forward.

According to the provisions of the measure the acts of the following nature would be deemed offences : Bringing of water hyacinth into Bengal, sale of water hyacinth, growing or cultivation of water hyacinth, removal of water hyacinth to any land, premises or water, failure to remove or destroy water hyacinth, failure to cut branches of trees or shrubs for the purpose of facilitating discovery or destruction of water hyacinth, removal or of damage of any fences or barriers for the purpose of checking or diverting the movement of water hyacinth, failure to repair 'als', and failure to grow hedges of 'dhaincha' or other plants for protection against the ingress of water hyacinth.

Anybody convicted of any of the offences mentioned above would, according to the Act, be liable to a fine not exceeding one hundred rupees or in default to imprisonment not exceeding one month and upon a second or subsequent conviction to a fine not exceeding two hundred rupees or in default to imprisonment not exeeding two months.

The Council at this stage adjourned till the 13th. instant.

VOTING ON BUDGET DEMANDS

13th. MARCH :—A lively discussion, although rather of an academic nature, on the merits and demerits of the Permanent Settlement, occupied for more than 2 hours and a half the attention of the members of the Council when it met to-day to consider the Budget grants of the Government of Bengal for 1936-37.

Both the opponents and protagonists of the system went to the extremes, the former declaring it a curse on the country while the latter characterised it as an unmitigated blessing.

Condemning the Settlement as a curse upon the country, Mr. *J. L. Banerjee* remarked that it had impoverished the Government as well as the people.

On the other hand, Mr. *Sarat Kumar Roy* pointed out that the Permanent Settlement had vastly helped the development of agricultural resources of Bengal.

At the end, however, Sir *B. L. Mitter* drew the attention of the House that a great deal of its time had been taken up by a discussion which was absolutely besides the point at issue.

The debate arose out of a cut motion put forward by *Maulvi Tamizuddin Khan.*

14th. MARCH :—The Council granted in toto to-day the demands for grants under the head Land Revenue, Excise and Stamps. All the cut motions to those demands that were put forward were either withdrawn by their movers or lost without division.

The Hon'ble Sir *Bijoy Prasad Singh Roy* moved that a sum of Rs. 17,75,000 be granted for expenditure under the head Excise. In making the demand Sir Bijoy referred to the increased activities in the city and outside of gangsters in manufacturing illicit liquor and smuggling excisable articles. Suggesting the creation of a Central Department for carrying on an intensive and co-ordinated campaign throughout the province he announced in the house a scheme which the Government has formed of reorganising the staff to cope with the increasing offences.

Several cut motions having been defeated or withdrawn, the entire demand of the Minister was acceded to.

On a motion by the Hon'ble Sir *John Woodhead*, the House granted a sum of Rs. 5,21,000 for expenditure under the head Stamps. The Council then adjourned till the 16th.

16th. MARCH :—The House acceded in toto to-day to the demand for grant of Rs. 8,36,000 under the head Forests, Rs. 18,78,000 under the head Registration and Rs. 8,000 under the head Scheduled taxes.

Mr. *Khawaja Sahabuddin*, Member in charge of Irrigation, in course of his speech, informed the House that Government was taking all necessary steps to bring the Bengal Development Act into operation. Referring to the proposed establishment of a Waterways Board under the Bengal Waterways Act of 1934, the Hon'ble Member said that the financial position of the province was preventing the formation of the Board. The House adjourned at this stage.

TRAINING OF DETENUS

17th. MARCH :—The arrangements which the Government of Bengal have made for the training of detenus in order to enable them to take up, when released, useful and independent vocations ' were explained by the Hon'ble Sir *Robert Reid* in the Council to-day. The Council acceded to the demands for grant under the heads Irrigation and Interest on other obligations.

Sir *Robert Reid* moved that a sum of Rs. 1,10,61,000 be granted for expenditure under the head General Administration. In moving the demand for grant Sir Robert Reid referred to the scheme for training the detenus. The general idea underlying the scheme, he said, was to give a carefully selected number of detenus a course of training which fit them to stand on their legs in life afterwards and at the same time, as His Excellency the Governor in one of his speeches indicated, that the scheme for the benefit of a limited number of persons might eventually lead to the benefit of the whole province.

Four units, proceeded Sir Robert, had been opened for industrial training and one for agricultural training. The industries selected were Pottery, Cutlery, Umbrella-making and Brass metalling work. In each of these industries fifteen men were receiving training. At the agricultural centre at present twenty-five persons were working. The work in the agricultural centre covered about 450 bighas of land. In connection with industrial centres a depot was being opened for providing raw materials, the idea being that raw materials should be made available at a much lower rate. His Excellency had hinted, the Home Member continued, that it was hoped that when these young men had finished their training they would be able to work on co-operative lines. These centres were virtually run in the way of a boarding house with minimum restriction and such freedom as was consistent with the safety of the State. The first batch that was sent to the centre had to be very carefully selected before they could be sent there. Unfortunately from one of the camps one detenue absconded at dawn and it was only sometime afterwards when he was run down that he was found not in Bengal but in another province. That showed that the detenus were not so innocent as some people would have the Government to believe. Proceeding, Sir Robert said that some of the detenus selected had to be sent back because they were not confronting to the rules of the centres while some others resumed their old activities. There had been some among the detenus who did not like that sort of training. It was no use keeping those people in training and the Government had filled up the present vacancies and the results had been distinctly hopeful. Sir Robert informed the House that arrangements had been made to open six more industrial centres which would absorb another ninety men under instruction. The Government would open another agricultural centre which would have under instruction as many as 45 men. The results were far from discouraging and besides the keenness which these young men had already shown the Government owed a great deal to Mr. S. N. Roy who had worked it out and to Mr. S. C. Mitter, Deputy Director of Industries, who had thrown himself into the task with good enthusiasm in order to make it a success.

MIDNAPUR ROUTE MARCHES

18th. MARCH :—With a view to raising a discussion on the route marches bf troops in the various districts of Bengal, Mr. *P. Banerjee* moved to-day that the demany of Rs. 12,000 under the head Executive Council be reduced by Rs. 100. Speaking id support of his motion, Mr. Banerjee referred to certain instances in the district on Midnapore where, it was alleged, several persons had been maltreated by the soldiers and compelled to salute the Union Jack. Route marches had also been carried on in the district of Faridpur. Mr. Banerjee also alleged that the inhabitants had to hold receptions to the soldiers and provide articles of consumption to them. These marches, according to the speaker, were held in localities which were politically advanced.

Supporting the motion, Mr. *N. K. Bose* said that he possessed no personal knowledge of the incidents to which Mr. Banerjee had referred. But his statements deserve strict examination and a swift remedy if possible. Proceeding, Mr. Basu submitted that the stories related by Mr. P. Banerjee did smack of something like an action taken on the people of Midnapore for participating in the last Civil Disobedience Movement and protesting against the establishment of Union Boards there. The people, said Mr. Basu, had enough of official reticence in matters of Midnapore and enough of banning of visits of public men like Mr. J. N. Basu and Mr. Amarendra Nath Chatterjee, to that place. This hush-hush policy had got to cease. This matter of route marches and incidents at Midnapore were fit subjects for immediate attention from the Government and the speaker hoped that the Government would not shirk its duty in that respect.

Replying *Sir Robert Reid* expressed his surprise that none of the other representatives of Midnapore in the Council had come forward to represent the grievances to which Mr. Banerjee had referred. The Hon'ble Member had absolute faith in the veracity of Mr. Carter, District Magistrate of Midnapore and he was completely satisfied that what Mr. Carter had stated with regard to the incidents was true. He would accept the version of a reliable man on the spot. The Government, continued Sir Robert, had no intention of compelling anyone to salute the Union Jack. But, in one particular case, to which Mr. Banerjee had referred, that man deliberately insulted the flag and soldiers could not brook that. The motion was lost.

As a protest against the conditions prevailing in the Calcutta Corporation, particularly in the matter of Muslim appointment, and for stressing on the necessity oj appointment of a Committee to enquire into the affairs of the Calcutta Corporation, Mr. *H. S. Suhrawardy* moved that the demand of Rs. 64,000 under the head—Ministers—Pay of Minister for Local Self-government—be reduced by Rs. 100.

Mr. *P. N. Guha* expressed surprise that Mr. H. S. Surhawardy, the Swarajist leader and the first Muslim Deputy Mayor should come with folded hands and bended knees before the Government praying humbly to interfere in the affairs of the Corporation of Calcutta. The administration of the body may or may not have been conducted on right lines but the Government had little justification to interfere into the matter.

Mr. Surhawardy's motion was lost without division and the House adjourned.

19th. MARCH :—The Hon'ble Sir *Robert Reid*, Home Member, declared that the Government of Bengal did not contemplate at present a general release of detenus. It would be an unwise step, said Sir Robert, and the Government would not be doing its duty to the province if they did so.

The Council acceded to the demand of Rs. 73,40,000 for expenditure under the head Administration of Justice. The House rose when the demand for grant for Jails and Convict Settlements was being considered.

20th. MARCH :—The Council sanctioned to-day Rs. 42,08,000, the entire demand for grant for expenditure under the head—Jails and Convict Settlements.

Moving the demand for grant under the head Police, Sir *Robert Reid* indicated the possibility of a reduction in the Police force of the country. The House then adjourned till 23rd.

23rd. MARCH :—The Council sanctioned in toto the demands made by the Government under the heads Police, Ports and Pilotage and Scientific departments, the respective amounts being Rs. 2,12,01,000 Rs. 3,60,000 and Rs. 26,000.

After the demand for grant under the Head Education (Reserved) amounting Rs. 10,65,000 was passed, the House took up the consideration of grant for expenditure for Education (Transferred).

Budget deficit was advanced as a plea by the *Education Minister*, in moving for Rs. 1,10,47,000 Education grant for the inability of the Government to undertake a revision of the financial arrangements arrived at with the Calcutta University in 1932.

The Government, however, are prepared to examine the question of 'Varsity's increased receipts (particularly in Fee Funds) and would be prepared not to stand on the strict terms of the financial arrangements of 1932, assured the Minister.

Announcing revision of service rules to have more Muslims in the Education service, the Minister said that they do not intend to appoint any Mussalman, who is not fully qualified and competent in every way.

The Minister announced that a system of college extension lectures with a view to improve the work of mufussil colleges would be introduced from next year, and the Government wished to introduce a scheme of adult education in villages through thesub-inspectorate staff.

The Rs. 2 lakh Rural Development Grant has enabled Government to organise libraries in 108 villages, 86 play-grounds in villages and play-grounds with sporting requisites in 151 schools and 53 agricultural farms attached to schools.

The eventual aim of his Department, said the Minister, was to secure the establishment of a good H. E. School for girls at each district headquarters and of a good M. E. School for girls in each sub-divisional headquarters. A Board of Women's Education will be appointed in the coming financial year to advise Government on its future policy. Necessary fund has been budgetted and appointment of a special officer is also contemplated.

24th. MARCH :—Allegations against the University of Calcutta that disregard of Muslim feelings and sentiments were shown by that body in the preparation of text books provided a subject for an animated and protracted debate in the Council to-day. The entire demand amounting to Rs. 1,10,47,000 was acceded to by the House.

The House rose when the demand for grant under the head "Medical" was being considered.

25th. MARCH :—The Hon'ble Sir *Bijoy Prasad Singh Roy*, Minister for Local Self-Government, pointed out that the menace to Calcutta from Anopheles Ludlowi had not disappeared and uttered a warning to the local bodies concernod that if they did not agree to make contributions towards the controlling measures it might be found necessary for the safety of Calcutta for the Government to undertake legislation for compelling them to make such contributions.

The Council sanctioned the demands for grant under the heads Public Health and Agriculture and then adjourned.

26th. MARCH :—The Council concluded to-day the consideration of grants for the year 1936-37.

It sanctioned the entire demand for grants for expenditure under the heads Industries, Miscellaneous Departments, Civil Works, Famine relief, Superannuation allowances and Pensions and Continued value of pensions not charged to revenue, Stationery and Printing and Depreciation (Reserved) for Government presses, Miscellaneous, Loans and advances and Expenditure in England, the respective sums granted being Rs. 13,87,000, Rs. 4,19,000, Rs. 95,76,000, Rs. Rs. 2.000,00 Rs. 82,33,000, Rs. 19,40,000, Rs. 18,53,000, Rs. 20,05,000 and Rs. 7,50,000. The Council then adjourned.

27th. MARCH :—The Council sanctioned supplementary grants for 1935-36 of Rs. 35,000, Rs. 1,40,000 and Rs. 3,10,000 demanded under the respective heads Ports and Pilotage, Famine Relief and Loans and Advances

BENGAL NON-AGRICULT. LANDS ASSESS. BILL

The Hon'ble Sir *Brojendralal Mitter* introduced the Bengal Non-agricultural Lands Assessment Bill, 1936 which was designed to provide for the adequate assessment of land revenue or rent of certain lands not used for agricultural purposes.

The Bill was referred to a Select Committee. consisting of fourteen members, with instructions to submit their report as soon as possible.

In explaining the aims and objects of the measure, Sir Brojendra observed that though the Bengal Regulation VII of 1822 gave sufficient authority for the settlement of revenue, the Regulation did not specifically distinguish between agricultural lands and non-agricultural lands. Furthermore, the Regulation contemplated the adjustment of relationship between landlord. and tenant at the time of settlement of the revenue with the object of equalising the public burdens.

Under the Bengal Tenancy Act, 1885, the speaker proceeded, though settlement of fair rent was provided for in agricultural lands, non-agricultural lands were specifically excluded from the operation of the sections dealing with settlement of fair rent. It had been found with the growth of towns that lands originally leased a agricultural holdings had wholly or partly ceased to be used for agricultural purposes. In order to secure the proper revenue on such lands without interfering with contracts made between parties, which, in so far as the rent was concerned, could not legally extend beyond the terms of the settlement made by the Government, it was desirable to make clear provisions for the assessment of revenue on such lands and to make such assessments legally binding on the Government's direct tenants either in a Government estate or in an estate held 'Khas' on account of recusancy of the proprietors. There had been numerons cases, where, on account of failure of the tenant to agree under the law of contract to the terms offered by the Government, costly litigation had ensued with the ejectment of the tenant as the ultimate result. It was intended, concluded Sir Brojendra, that this Bill should provide a means of securing the proper assessment on such lands without undue interference with the liberty of contract.

BENGAL LOCAL SELF-GOVT. AMEND. BILL

30th. MARCH :—The Council referred to a Select Committee the Bengal Local Self-Government (Amendment) Bill introduced by the Hon'ble Sir *Bejoy Prosad Singh Roy*, Minister for Local Self-Government.

In the statement of objects and reasons of the Local Self-Government (Amendment) Bill it was laid down, that with the gradual establishment of union boards over the greater part of the province it has for some time been felt that local boards in their present form and with their present powers are more or less a superfluity. Under the Bengal Local Self-Government Act of 1885 local boards have no corporate existence, but only derive their powers and duties as agents of the district board. The question of the abolition of the local boards has been under the consideration of Government from time to time since 1922.

The present Bill which has been framed after a careful consideration of the views of the local officers and chairmen of district boards provides that the Local Government may with the consent of the district board concerned abolish the local board in any area within the district. It is proposed that where a local board has been abolished the members of district boards from that area should be elected by persons having qualifications similar to those of union board electors under section 7 of the Bengal Village Self-Government Act, 1919, who may have their names enrolled on the electoral roll of the district. It is also proposed that in areas where local boards have been abolished persons qualified to vote at a district board election shall be eligible to stand as candidates for election as members of district boards.

As the adoption of the system of direct election will involve a substantial increase in the cost of election to district boards, it is proposed to extend the term of office of members of district boards from four to five years.

When a local Board has been abolished in any area, all its powers and duties including powers of supervision and control over union boards conferred by the Bengal Village Self-Government Act, 1919, wil be taken over and exercised or performed by the district boards.

The amendments proposed to be made in the Bengal Village Self-Government Act, 1919, are consequential on those in the Bengal Local Self-Government Act of 1885.

In moving that the bill be referred to a Select Committee consisting of seventeen members and to submit their report as soon as possible, *Sir Bijoy* said that the question of abolition of local boards had been pending before the Government and the public since 1922. The Ministry of Sir Surendranath Banerjee considered this question but did not come to any final conclusion. Since then the matter was referred on several occasions to the divisional commissioners, district officers and chairmen of district boards. Majority of them supported abolition but as regards the method of election there were considerable divergence of opinion. Government had carefully weighed the arguments both for and against the proposal and considered their advantages and disadvantages and had come to the conclusion that the local boards had outlived their utility.

Maulvi Abul Quasem moved by way of amendment that the bill be circulated for the purpose of eliciting public opinion thereon before 25th. June. In moving the amendment Moulvi Abul Quasem said the Local Boards had existed in Bengal since 1885. And during their existence they had served a definite purpose. The statement of the Hon'ble Minister that there was a strong public opinion in favour of the abolition of these institutions was, in the opinion of the speaker, not perfectly correct. Public opinion was not in favour of their abolition. Higher Government officials and chairmen of the District Boards had been consulted on the question of the abolition of the local boards but, Moulvi Abul Quasem submitted, that the chairmen had only given out their individual opinion and not the opinion of the Boards which they did represent. The *raison de'etre* of the abolition of the local boards, the speaker proceeded, was the establishment of Union Boards throughout the province. But Union Boards had not yet been established in all parts of Bengal. So if it was a fact then the time for the abolition had not yet arrived.

Dr. *N. C. Sen Gupta*, speaking in support of the motion, observed that something of the nature of reform should have been undertaken long ago. At present the local boards, he admitted, were not serving any useful purpose not because they were incapable but because their resources were limited and completely at the mercy of the District Boards. The right way of tackling the problem according to Dr. Sen Gupta was to constitute in bigger districts the local boards as the only instrument of local Self-Government. And in the case of smaller districts the existence of one local board with requisite resources and authority would obviate the necessity for the existence of a District Board.

Replying to the debate' *Sir Bijoy Prosad* said that the question of the abolition of local boards had been before the public since 1922. District Boards and local boards had been consulted. The chairmen of the District Boards who met at the conference considered the local boards an absolute superfluity. During the last two years the Minister had met representatives of rural areas and of Union Boards and they had expressed their opinion in favour of the abolition of Local Boards which were serving no useful purpose.

The amendment when pressed to division was declared lost by 53 to 12 votes.

The Council was then *prorogued*.

The Bombay Legislative Council

LIST OF MEMBERS

1. Abdul Latif Haji Hajrat Khan, Khan Bahadur
2. Abercrombie, Sir John Robertson
3. Achrekar, Mr. Atmaram Bhimaji
4. Advani Mr. P. B.
5. Allahbaksh *walad* Khan Saheb Haji Mahomed Umar, Khan Bahadur
6. Ambedkar, Dr. B. R.
7. Andrew, Mr. T. A.
8. Angadi, Rao Bahadur S. N.
9. Asavale, Rao Bahadur Ramchandra Santuram
10. Azimkhan Inayatalikhan, Khan Bahadur
11. Bakhale, Mr. R. R.
12. Bangi, Mr. Abdul Kadir Jamaluddin
13. Bhutto, The Hon'ble Sir Shah Nawaz Khan Ghulam Murtaza Khan (*Minister for Local Self-Govt.*)
14. Bijarani, Khan Bahadur Sher Muhammad Khan Karam Khan
15. Biradar, Sardar Mahaboobali Khan Mohd. Akbar Khan
16. Bole, Rao Bahadur Sitaram Keshav
17. Boyle, Mr. J. D,
18. Bramble, Mr. C. P.
19. Bullocke, Mr. Alfred Guy Greville
20. Chaudhari, Mr. T. M.
21. Chikodi, Mr. P. R.
22. Chitale, Rao Bahadur Ganesh Krishna
23. Clayton, Mr. H. B.
24. Collaco, Dr. J. A.
25. Daulatrao Jayaramrao Zunzarrao, Mr.
26. Dehlavi, the Honourable Sir Ali Mahomed Khan (*President*)
27. Desai, Rao Saheb Bhagwandas Girdhardas
28. Desai, Mr. Hanmantrao Ramrao.
29. Desai, Mr. Shankarappa Basalingappa
30. Dhalumal Lilaram. Mr.
31. Freke Mr. C. G.
32. Dixit, Dr. M. K.
33. D'Souza, Dr. Joseph Alban
34. Gangoli, Mr. Ganapati Subrao
35. Garrett. Mr. J. H.
36. Gazder, Mr. Mahomed Hashim
37. Ghulam Hyder Shah Sahibdino Shah Mr.
38. Ghulam Nabi Shah Moujali Shah (Saiyed), Khan Bahadur,.
39. Gilder, Dr. Manchershah Dhanjibhai.
40. Gokhale, Mr. Laxman Raghunath
41. Gover Rora, Mr.
42. Greaves, J. B.
43. Humphrey, Mr. John,
44. Iyengar, Mr. H. V. R.,
45. Isran, Khan Bahadur Ghulam Mahomed Abdulla Khan
46. Jam Jan Mahomedkhan *walad* Jam Mahomed Sharif, Sardar Bahadur
47. Jan Mahomed Khan *walad* Khan Bahadur Shah Passand Khan, Khan Bahadur
48. Jitekar, Mr. Haji Ibrahim
49. Jog, Mr. Vishwanathrao Narayan
50. Kalbhore, Rao Bahadur Gangajirao Mukundrao
51. Kamat, Mr. B. S.,
52. Kambli, the Honourable Dewan Bahadur Siddappa Totappa (*Minister far Agriculture*)
53. Karbhari, Mr. Manchershaw Manekji
54. Kennedy, Mr. T. S.
55. Khuhro, Khan Bahadur Muhammad Ayub Shah Muhammad
56. Kirpalani, Mr. H. K.
57. Irwin Mr. I. B.
58. Kulkarni, Rao Saheb Pandurang Dnyaneshwar
59. Mackie. Mr. A. W. W.
60. Madan, Mr. J. A.
61. Madhavsang Jorbhai, Mr.
62. Matcheswalla, Mr. Gulamhussen Ebrahim
63. Meherbaksh, Khan Bahadur S.
64. Mehta, Mr. Manilal Harilal
65. Mitha, Mr. Mahomed Suleman Cassum
66. Modak, Rev. R. S.
67. Modi, Sardar Davar Temuras Kavasji
68. More, Mr. Jayawant Ghanasham
69. Naik, Sardar Rao Bahadur Bhimbhai Ranchhodji
70. Namdeorao Budhajirao, Mr.
71. Navle, Rao Bahadur Namdev Eknath
72. Parulekar, Rao Bahadur Laxman Vishnu,

73. Patel, Khan Bahadur Alibhai Esabhai
74. Patel, Mr. Bhailal Sarabhai
75. Patel, Mr. Chaturbhai Narshibhai,
76. Patel. Khan Bahadur Wali Baksh Adambhai
77. Patil, Dewan Bahadur Dongarsing Ramji
78. Patil, Mr. Narayan Nagoo
79. Patil, Rao Bahadur Vaman Sampat
80. Patil, Mr. Vithal Nathu
81. Pradhan, Rao Bahadur Gopalrao Vaman
82. Prater, Mr. S. H.
83. Rafiuddin Ahmad, Moulvi Sir
84. Rahimtoola, Mr. Hoosenally Mahomed
85. Resaldar, Mr. Abdul Rahman Khan Karam Khan
86. Sahebsinhji Juvansinhji, Mr.
87. Sakarlal Baladhai, Mr.
88. Saklatvala, Mr. S. D.
89. Sen, Mr. K. C.
90. Servai, Mr. A. E.
91. Shah Rookh Yar Jung Bahadur Nawab
92. Shaikh Abdul Aziz Abdul Latif Mr.
93. Shaikh Abdul Majid Lilaram, Mr.
94. Shinde Mr. Ramchandrarao Bapurao
95. Solanki, Dr. Purushottam G.
96. Soman, Mr. R. G.
97. Surve, Mr. A. N.
98. Surve, Mr. Vyankat Anandrao
99. Syed Miran Mahommed Shah Zanulabdin Shah
100. Syed Muhammed Kamil Shah Kabul Muhammad Shah Khan Bahadur
101. Syed Munawar, Mr.
102. Tairsee, Mr. L. R.
103. Talpur, Sardar Bahadur Haji Mir Allahadad Khan Mir Imam Baksh Khan
104. Talpur, Mir Bandewali Khan
105. Thakor of Kerwada, Sardar Bhasaheb Dulabawa Raisingaji
106. Tolani, Mr. Satramdas Sakhawatrai
107. Turner, Mr. C. W. A.
108. Vishampayan, Dr. Vishnu Ganesh
109. Vakil. Pestanshah N. Mr.
110. Vanderker, Rao Bahadur Ramchandra Vithalrao
111. Wadke, Mr. Bholanath Purshottam
112. Vad, Mr. B. G.

Proceedings of the Council

Budget Session—Bombay—17th. February to 20th. March '36

The Budget Session of the Bombay Legislative Council commenced in Bombay on the **17th. February 1936** and adjourned after passing the following resolution touching the death of King George V :

"This Council places on record its great sorrow on the death of King George, Emperor of India, and its deep and sincere sympathy with King Edward VIII, Emperor of India and Her gracious Majesty Queen Mary in their great loss and do tender His Majesty loyal homage."

Sir Robert Bell, Leader of the House, moved the above resolution and leaders of the various groups and the President associated themselves with the sentiments expressed in the resolution. The House passed the resolution, all standing.

Cotton Ginning Prov. Act Amend. Bill

17th. FEBRUARY :—The Council to-day passed the third reading of the Bill amending the Cotton Ginning Provisions Act of 1925.

A meeting of the Ginners' Association held at Hyderabad, Sind, on the 16th. Feb. to consider the Cotton Ginning and Pressing Bill passed a resolution deciding not to enter into any contract for the new crop kapas. The contracts are usually entered into to examine sowings which have already started. The meeting was of opinion that the competent body to legislate on the subject was the Sind Legislative Assembly which was to come into being shortly. The recommendations of the Select Committee, according to the views of the meeting, were more reactionary and created greater handicaps from the point of view of ginners.

GAMBLING ACT AMEND. BILL

19th. FEBRUARY :—The Council to-day passed the second and third readings of the Bill to amend the Bombay Prevention of Gambling Act of 1887, as recommended by the Select Committee. Mr. *Saklatwala*, Bombay Millowner' representative, moved an amendment, seeking to restrict the powers of the police. The amendment was supported by some Members. The mover of the amendment, however, withdrew the same on the assurance by the Home Member that the powers given by the Act will be used only for the purpose of prevention of gambling and would not be misused.

DT. POLICE ACT AMEND. BILL

20th. FEBRUARY :—The Council to-day passed the third reading of the Bill to amend the Bombay District Police Act 1890, which empowers the District Magistrate of Ahmedabad to extern persons not born within Ahmedabad municipal limits, and who have been convicted more than twice of offences punishable under the Indian Penal Code Sections 12, 16 and 17.

BORSTAL SCHOOL AMEND. BILL

The Council also passed the Bill to amend the Bombay Borstal School Act, 1929, which empowers the Government to detain offenders in other Provinces in Borstal Schools of the Bombay Presidency and send Borstal inmates from this Province to schools elsewhere.

COTTON GINNING & PRESSING FACTORIES ACT

21st. FEBRUARY :—The Council passed the third reading of the Bill to amend the Cotton Ginning and Pressing Factories Act. The object of the Bill was to stop certain malpractices in the cotton trade, i.e., adulterating cotton, watering of cotton, etc.

DT. POLICE ACT AMEND. BILL

The Council next passed the third reading of the Bill to amend the Bombay District Police Act of 1890.

BORSTAL SCHOOL AMEND. BILL

The Council also passed a Bill to amend the Bombay Borstal Schools Act of 1929, and then adjourned.

THE GOVERNOR'S ADDRESS

24th. FEBRUARY :—His Excellency the Governor of Bombay addressed the Council to-day. In the course of his address, the Governor referred to the sad demise of King George and the separation of Sind. He said :—

"As you know, Parliament has requested His Majesty to pass an Order in Council under which Sind will be separated from Bombay in a few weeks' time. In order that the necessary arrangements may be completed and be in working order by the time that the reformed Provincial Constitution is introduced, and in order that the new province may become an autonomous province simultaneously with all other Governors' Province in India, it is proposed that an interim separate provincial administration should be set up in Sind during the interval between its separation from this Presidency and the inauguration of the new Provincial Constitution. The Order in Council under Section 289 (2) of the Government of India Act 1935, giving an outline of the form of Government during the period of transition has been published already, and, if it receives the royal Assent in the near future, Sind will become a Governor's Province on the 1st April, 1936. I am aware that this draft has evoked criticisms in the public and in the Press both in Sind and in the Presidency proper. I am sure you do not expect me to give a reply to these criticisms. I may, however, tell you this, that there seems to be considerable misapprehension as to the scope of the Order in Council, and, as I have stated already, it is a means to an end and not the end itself. Its object is merely to prepare Sind for Provincial Autonomy.

"This will, therefore, be the last session of this House at which the honourable members from Sind will attend, and I think it is only proper that I should take this opportunity of bidding them farewell. From me and my Government there is nothing but good wishes for the new Sind and its people. The connection of Sind with the Presidency of Bombay dates from 1843, and although the official relationship of the Presidency proper with Sind may cease, memories of their long historic connection will not fade. For my part I assured you, the representatives of Sind in this House, in my last year's address to this House, and I assure you again to-day, that I will always continue to take the same interest in the welfare of the new province as at present."

The Governor then made a survey of the progress of the Presidency during the past year, which, he noted with satisfaction, was on the whole free from disturbances due to communal feeling. "With the one exception of the outbreak in Karachi over the funeral of a condemned murderer, the great communities have lived in comparative peace and orderliness, and I hope that the spirit of mutual tolerance will continue and grow stronger."

Dealing with the coming year, His Excellency said: "As regards the general effect of the separation of Sind on the financial position of the Presidency, it cannot be denied that separation will bring a welcome easing of Bombay's financial position. This matter will be dealt with in detail by the honourable Finance Member. It will, however, not be out of place if I refer briefly to the betterment resulting from the separation of its utilisation. A year ago a budget was placed before you which had a true revenue deficit of 29 lakhs. From the White Book dealing with the Presidency's financial position in the current year, it will be seen that the revised estimates show an actual deficit of Rs. 53 lakhs after removing extraordinary items of revenue and expenditure. The benefits arising from the separation of Sind and the favourable conversion, last November, of the Development Loan, will, after clearing the recurrent revenue deficit, leave a margin of 45 lakhs which has been utilised on the items specified in the Introductory Note to the Budget Blue Book.

"Among these items the first is the cost of the Motor Vehicles Tax Bill which this House passed at its last session. This valuable measure, which I was very glad to see placed permanently, upon the Statute Book, will remove an important handicap upon the development of long distance motor transport by the abolition of all tolls except Municipal tolls and it will present a considerable benefit to agriculturists by the abolition of all Provincial and District Local Board tolls upon bullock carts. Both of these measures should bring to the primary producer, a larger share of the prices at which his goods are ultimately sold. The Act has thrown a permanent burden upon the Provincial revenues of Rs. 9 lakhs due to the abolition of tolls on bullock carts and a temporary burden for one year of Rs. 6 lakhs in rebates of the new taxation admissible in respect of carts of which the registrations would otherwise have remained in force for some months of the next year.

"Next in importance comes the additional educational provision of Rs. 7 lakhs. In the retrenchment campaigns of 1931 and 1932, Government were compelled to reduce the grants to local bodies for primary education. Rs. 6 and a half lakhs were restored in 1933-34, and Government are glad to be in a position to make additional provision for primary and secondary education in next year's budget amounting to a further Rs. 6 and a half lakhs, together with a grant of half a lakh for the Indian Women's University. This grant is to the Shrimati Nathibai Damodar Thackersy Indian Women's University, towards the purchase of a plot of land on Queen's Road in Bombay. The plot of land which is required for the construction of a building for the college and offices of the University is the property of the Government of India, who have been requested to sell it to the University at a concession rate. In view of the great public importance both from the political and social point of view of furthering the cause of women's education in this country, my Government have decided to ask you to give a grant-in-aid towards the purchase of the plot equal to one-third of the cost subject to a maximum of Rs. 50,000 and have requested the Government of India to make a similar grant.

"There is one other item in the Educational Budget to which I would draw particular attention, and that is the provision of half a lakh for the vocational training of middle class unemployed. Government are fully alive to the importance of this question and are now proposing to embark on a further step in connection therewith. Government will do what it can to solve this almost insoluble problem, though I feel that its full solution must rest largely with those who direct the higher education of this Presidency, particularly the University authorities, combined with the re-orientation of social thought and customs which will widen the field of activities to which educated young men will devote themselves.

"Sind Members may have been disappointed that we have been able to place before this House only the Bombay Budget and not the Budget of Separated Sind. This is the inevitable result of the Constitutional position, which is that, if separation takes place from April 1 next. the provincial revenues of 1936-37 with which this House will be concerned will be those of Bombay excluding Sind, and it would be unconstitutional for it now to pass votes authorising expenditure in the next year from revenues which are likely then to be the revenues of another province. There are, however, various legislative measures before the House which will be of great importance to Sind even after separation. We hope, therefore, that honourable members from Sind, will play their full part in this, which is likely to be their last session as members of the Bombay joint family.

"Honourable Members will see that next year's Budget has been framed on the assumption that they will agree to extend the life of the present Finance Act. I should like to make it clear to the House that the passing of this measure is of vital importance to the Presidency's finances. I shall not attempt to make any suggestion as to which provisions it will be necessary to omit or curtail if the Finance Act is not passed, beyond indicating that, whatever heads Government agree to cut, the cuts will certainly be unpopular. I feel confident that this contingency will not arise. This Presidency, despite the handicap of the inequitable settlement of 1929, has done its best to pursue the path of sound finance. Despite the difficulties which followed from that unsound settlement, which were much increased by the slump in prices, it has accepted the hardships which have been required to balance its budget. At the present time a financial enquiry is in progress, from which we hope that a more equitable settlement will emerge. I and my Government feel that, in view of the determination which Bombay has shown in the past to balance its budget, they have a strong case to present. Renewal of the Finance Act in this session is not only necessary if the Presidency's finances are to continue on sound lines, but it is an important part of the case which I and my Government are pressing at the present time. We have every confidence that every party in this House will realise the importance of full co-operation at this juncture. At the same time while counting upon your support in this matter. I do not desire to raise false hopes. You are aware that the new reforms, combined with the separation of Burma, Orissa and Sind, will impose fresh burdens upon the Central revenues, so that while we hope that the new settlement will be very much fairer to Bombay than that of 1926, it is wise only to expect that the benefit will accrue gradually and in the course of time. We hope for some benefit in the immediate future, but it should not be assumed that the immediate benefit will be large.

"I do not propose to speak to-day about the coming reforms as they affect the Presidency proper as I will be addressing you again before their introduction. I will content myself with saying that active preparations are being made to ensure that we in this Presidency are ready for this great change when the moment comes."

Financial Statement for 1936-37

After the Governor's speech, the Finance Member, Mr. *Cooper*, introduced the Budget. In the course of his speech, he dwelt on the injustice done to the Province by the Meston Financial Settlement and the Government of Bombay had made a strong plea to the Otto Niemeyer Committe to accord equitable treatment to Bombay by revision of the Meston settlement.

The Budget estimates for the year 1936-37 disclose a small surplus of Rs. 41,000. The revenue receipts for the year 1936-37, according to estimates are Rs. 12,03,58,000. Expenditure debitable to revenue is Rs. 12,03,17,003, leaving a surplus balance of Rs. 41,000. Bombay will be better off on account of the separation of Sind by Rs. 76 lakhs. The betterment from conversion of the Development Loan will be Rs. 22 lakhs, and the revenue deficit of the current year Rs. 53,00,000.

Mr. *C. G. Freke*, the Finance Secretary to the Government of Bombay, in the course of an introductory note explaining the Budget proposals and estimates, says :—

The Bombay Budget for 1936-37 has been framed provisionally on the assumption that the proposals of His Majesty's Government in the Draft Government of India (Constitution of Sind) Order 1936 now under consideration by Parliament will be approved and will take effect from the 1st April 1936. If that order does not receive approval, or if it is approved with amendments which have financial implication in relation to the Bombay Presidency, it will become necessary to submit supplementary budget proposals in the light of the Parliamentary decision.

The accounts figures of 1934-35 and the Budget estimates of the year are for the Bombay Presidency including Sind, and there are no official figures for the separate areas of Bombay excluding Sind. Careful analysis of the figures has been made and the expenditure of Bombay (excluding Sind) in 1934-35 and 1935-36, as accurately as it can be ascertained, has been shown under all heads excepting the debt heads, which are dealt with in the next paragraph.

The financial provisions for the separation of Sind from the Presidency of Bombay are stated in the second schedule to the Draft Order-in-Council, which has been published in the Press. It may be convenient if its main provisions are briefly summarised. All permanent assets will be the property of the province in which they are situated and outstanding debt linked with the assets will pass with them. Bombay Development debt will remain with Bombay. Barrage debt will pass to Sind, save that the debt of Nasirabad Section will be taken over by the Government of India, and debt borrowed for pensionary charges will be divided between the areas on the same basis as other pensionary liabilities, which is that the liability for pensions earned before the date of separation and for loan moneys applied to meet pensionary charges, including pension commutations, will be divided in the proportions in which the revenues of the Bombay Presidency including Sind have been collected in the two areas. The adjustment will throw an additional burden of 3 lakhs on next year's Bombay budget, as 34 lakhs of barrage borrowings for pensionary charges will remain with Bombay. Outstanding debt which is not connected with permanent assets will be similarly allocated. The reason for allocation on this basis is that pensionary charges and unallocated debt are at present the joint responsibility of the Presidency including Sind, their annual costs are a burden upon the two areas in proportion to the revenues which are collected in those areas. Accordingly these responsibilities have been divided in the revenue ratio which, from an analysis of revenues over the ten years 1922-23 to 1931-32 has been ascertained to be 15 per cent collected in Sind and 85 per cent collected in the Bombay Presidency excluding Sind. The balance in the Famine Relief Fund will be divided on the same basis. The outstanding credit of the provisional loans and Advance Account will pass to the areas in which the borrowers reside, together with equal amounts of debt to the Government of India outstanding against that account. Loans savings will be allocated according to the purposes for which they were borrowed. Substantial quantities of unissued stores of any class will be divided in proportion to the indents of the two years over the past three years. The balance at credit of the Road Development Fund will be divided in such a way that, after taking account of expenditure in the two areas, Sind will receive one-quarter of the total credits received by the Presidency up to the time of separation.

The closing balance of the Presidency, including Sind, at the end of the current year has been estimated at Rs. 1,51,70 lakhs. The opening balance of Bombay (excluding Sind) is estimated at Rs. 69,91 lakhs. The revenue budget estimates of Bombay for next year are as follows : revenue receipts Rs. 12,03,58 lakhs ; expenditure debitable to revenue Rs. 12,03,17 lakhs ; leaving a revenue surplus of Rs. 0,41 lakhs. These estimates take account of the renewal of the Finance Act, 1932, of which it is estimated that the revenue in Bombay. excluding Sind) amounts to about Rs. 25 lakhs.

The betterment to Bombay from Sind separation was estimated in the Irving-Harris report at 97 lakhs, on the basis of the figures of the three years 1927-28 to 1929-30, and by the Sind Conference of 1932 at 79 lakhs. Part of the Irving-Harris estimate has been absorbed by the subsequent fall in revenue receipts. A recent analysis of the figures of 1935-36 indicates that the deficit of the sub-province of Sind in the current year is about Rs. 85 lakhs of which Rs. 9 lakhs of expenditure of Sind canals was financed from the Famine Fund excess, a source which will no longer be available. As on April 1, 1936 the fund will stand at its statutory minimum of Rs. 63 lakhs and there are no appreciable further recoveries expected of past famine expenditure. The betterment available from Sind separation may therefore be estimated at about Rs. 76 lakhs to which may be added Rs. 22 lakhs betterment from the development loan conversion. On the other hand, as has been shown in the introductory note to the White Book on the current year's revised estimates, the true revenue deficit of the current year amounts to Rs. 53 lakhs. Rs. 3 lakhs of increased receipts in 1936-37 under the principal heads of revenue are balanced by three lakhs made up of two items which were utilised in 1935-36 and which will not be available in 1936-37. namely, two lakhs of famine fund excess and one lakh saving from the pay cut for one month.

General Discussion of Budget

25th. FEBRUARY :—The Council discussed to-day the Budget proposals. Mr. *M. H. Gazdar* (Karachi) moved an adjournment of the House to discuss a matter of urgent public importance, namely, "the conduct of Government in not supplying members copies of, and present to the Council, the budget estimates for Sind for 1936-37, involving many new items of expenditure and changes of far-reaching character, and thus depriving the Council of its legal and constitutional right to discuss the Budget proposals and the new changes sought to be introduced."

Mr. *Gazdar* pointed out that there was no legal difficulty in allowing the present Council to discuss the Sind Budget proposals and the Government by not giving an opportunity to the Council to discuss the Budget proposals had deprived the House and its members of their right. He saw no ground, despite the Orders-in-Council issued by British Parliament on which Government could deprive the House of its right to discuss and pass Budget proposals. Government's failure to enable them to discuss the Budget proposals was all the more regrettable, because when Sind was separated, there would be only an Advisory Council, which had no power to vote on the proposals. He had an apprehension that separated Sind would have a top-heavy administration and members of the Advisory Council would be helpless.

Several other members joined Mr. Gazdar in criticising and condemning the Government's failure to discuss Sind Budget proposals.

The *Home Member*, who was the last speaker of the day, maintained that the Bombay Government had no reason to bring the Budgets of the two Provinces, and as far as Sind was concerned, whatever the Bombay Government might do, they were not bound to abide by those conditions. The motion was thus talked out.

During the general discussion of the Budget members launched a general attack on Government's failure to reduce taxation.

26th. FEBRUARY ;—The Council devoted the whole day to the general discussion of the budget proposals. Members generally congratulated the Bombay Government and its Finance Member on the bold stand they had taken in the matter of demand for revision of the Meston Settlement, which had done immense harm to the Presidency's finances. They, however, pointed out that commercial and industrial interests should have been consulted by the Government before they submitted their memorandum to the Niemeyer Committee. Mr. *Angadi* strongly criticised the Government's educational policy and urged that more money should be spent on primary education.

29th. FEBRUARY :—The Council passed to-day the third reading of the Bill to amend the Bombay Finance Act, 1932. An amendment suggesting reduction of levy of electricity duty from six pies to three pies, was thrown out after heated debate. The Council also concluded general dissoussion on the budget.

Voting on Budget Demands

4th. MARCH :—The Council to-day after a heated debate, threw out a cut motion of Rs. 1,000 moved by Mr. *Archekar* regarding the grants to Local Boards for primary education by 53 to 19 votes.

In the course of the debate members complained of the frequent transfer of teachers under Local Boards and criticised the injection of the poison of communalism in the administration of School Boards. They demanded the restoration of the cut in the salary of primary school teachers.

Replying to the debate, Dewan Bahadur *S. T. Kambli*, Minister for Education, pointed out that the grant of Rs. 6 lakhs for the current year for primary education would reduce the cut to less than eight per cent.

Debate was also raised on the question of registration of medical practitioners with the Bombay Medical Council, when *Sir R. D. Bell*, Home Member, made a demand for grant of Rs. 10,000 under "Medical Reserved."

Dr. M. D. Gilder stressed the need to raise the minimum qualifications for licentiate candidates as in other Provinces.

Dr. *Vad* (Bombay University) complained that those who were not citizens competed with Indian medical practitioners, while Indians were not allowed to practise in foreign countries. Thus there was no reciprocity.

The *Home Member*, in reply, stated that in Great Britain there were 1,200 Indians practising. As to the question of prohibiting unregistered practitioners, he said that the issue was a large one and even in Great Britain, it had not been sloved fully.

The cut motion was withdrawn.

Members criticised the Government of Bombay for surrendering the right of appointing the Surgeon-General, in reply to which Sir Shah Nawaz Khan Bhutto pointed out that the Government did not surrender the right, but it was taken away by the Secretary of State and the Bombay Government has already protested without avail.

11th. MARCH :—The Administration of Public Health department was subjected to criticism by non-official Members of the Council to-day. *Dr. Gilder* asked why there should be two members of the Indian Medical Service in the Halfkins Institute instead of one Member only as agreed to by the Secretary of State for India. He wanted different varieties of vaccines should be manufactured there and supplied free to local bodies to combat epidemics instead of looking forward to the London institute of Tropical Medicine and Germany for guidance.

Mr. *K. H. Kripalani*, Secretary on behalf of the Government said that the Government was contemplating vaccines. Regarding the appointment of two I. M. S. men in the institute he said that according to the Devolution Rules, senior I. M. S. men must be provided somewhere and therefore the Government necessarily provided for this incumbent.

13th. MARCH :—The fact that no scheme to relieve unemployment amongst the educated middle class has been evolved by the Government was subjected to severe criticism by non-official members in the Council to-day.

Mr. *L. R. Tairsee* (Indian Merchants' Chamber) urged Government to study how other Governments had tackled the unemployment problem. At present Government appeared too shy even to approach the problem.

Mr. *S. H. Prater*, a nominated non-official, stressed the need of the Government for the establishment of an Employment Bureau. He asked the Government to closely study the Sapru Committee report on unemployment, which clearly shows that Provincial Governments can do a lot to relieve unemployment. The growing unemployment amongst the educated middle classes was a positive danger, since it fertilised the field for communism. The Government's measure against communism had little effect so long as unemployment was allowed to continue. He urged the Government to grant loans for small industries.

16th. MARCH :—The Government were criticized by non-official members in the Council to-day for lending their support to the proviso penalising lightning strikes in the Wages Payment Bill passed by the Legislative Assembly. The debate arose over a cut motion on a grant demanded by the Government.

Syed Munawar criticised the Government's failure to relieve distress among industrial workers. While the land mortgage banks were established to relieve indebtedness in the rural areas, he said, nothing had been done for the industrial worker.

Mr. *R. R. Bakhale* accused the Government of having been instrumental in passing Sir Homi Mody's amendment in the Assembly which penalised lightning strikes, but he complained that the amendment did not deal with lightning lock-outs by employers. Sir Homy Mody's amendment, which could not have been passed but for the Bombay Government's pressure, was based on a wrong analogy, namely, what was good for Bombay was good for the whole of India. There was no element of reciprocity in the proviso, and though it was supposed to deal with lightning strikes only it dealt with all strikes. The speaker expressed satisfaction at the work done by the Labour Office, which had published two important reports lately on the condition of work in printing presses and work in hotels. His grievance was the absence of machinery to deal with major issues, such as wage cuts, the payment of wages, etc.

The *Home Member*, justifying the Bombay Government's action, said the proviso would prevent workmen from going on lightning strikes unnecessarily and without previous notice and a reasonable cause. As the result of the Fawcett Committee's recommendation there was a standing order that the wages of those who stopped away without giving a fortnight's notice and without sufficient cause was to be deducted at the discretion of the head of the department concerned. In the amendment there was nothing new. The speaker assured the House that the Government would see that this proviso was not harshly used.

Farewell to Sind Members

20th. MARCH :—Impending changes in India's constitution were referred to in the Council to-day when a non-official resolution bidding farewell to members from Sind was passed. Mr. *G. S. Gangoli* (Kanara District) moved that "this Council, in bidding farewell to members from Sind on the occasion of the creation of the Province of Sind, places on record its regret at the termination of a long and harmonious association with them, its good wishes for the future happiness and prosperity of the new Province and its appreciation of the valuable services rendered to the Presidency of Bombay by Sir Ghulam Hussain Hidayatullah and Sir Shah Nawaz Khan Bhutto during their tenures of office." Mr. Gangoli said that what struck him about the Sind Group was the united front they always presented in the House. He paid a tribute to Mr. H. K. Kripalani who will occupy the office of Chief Secretary in the new Province. The greatest difficulty in Indian administration, said Mr. Gangoli, was communalism but it could be said of Sir Shah Nawaj that there was not a tinge of it in his administration. He had been both responsible and responsive.

Various other members supported the resolution. Sir *John Abercrombie* (Bombay Chamber of Commerce), on behalf of the European Group, associated himself wholeheartedly with the resolution and with the remarks of the previous speaker. "Sindhi members," he said, "have made an active and virile group." The House hoped that they would carry as kind recollections of the Bombay Council as the latter had of the Sind members. The separation of Sind, he added, meant to the European Group the loss of one member in Mr. J. Humphrey who had represented the Karachi Chamber of Commerce for a considerable number of years. He had helped the European Group very greatly by his advice.

After several other speeches by non-official members, Sir *Robert Bell*, leader of the House, in supporting the resolution said that within 12 days there would be one of the first two moves in a series of constitutional and administrative changes which are certain to go down in history as some of the greatest events of the twentieth century. On behalf of officials in the House he wished to endorse the remarks of members. Not all officials on the Treasury Benches had served in Sind. But even those who had not served in Sind were aware of the fact that those who started service in Sind had always great affection for that Province although as they grew older in service they perhaps preferred to come to the Presidency proper. Sind was the officials' paradise. The Sukkur Barrage was going to change not only the face of Sind but the entire problems of Sind. One did not know what would happen to Hindus who were generally known as the majority community bu who would be a minority in Sind. Moslems, who were now generally regarded as a minority community, would be in a majority in Sind. Which would be the happier of the two communities in Sind remained to be seen. He hoped that Sind would solve the communal problem for the whole of India. The resolution was passed with acclamation.

The Shop Assistants Bill

The Shop Assisants' Bill was then taken up and Mr. *R. R. Bakhale*, its author, moved that it be referred to a Select Committee.

23rd. MARCH :—The Council to-day rejected by 38 votes to 30 Mr. *R. R. Bakhale's* motion to refer his Shop Assistants' Bill to a Select Committee. The Bill sought to prohibit the employment of children below a certain age in shops and limit the number of hours of work of shop assistants.

Sir Robert Bell, Home Member, opposing the motion said that though he accepted the general principle underlying the Bill, he thought it an impracticable measure. He believed that nothing useful would be done by referring it to select committee as the Bill could not be reshaped so as to make it a workable one. Moreover, the cost of administering the provisions of the measure would be very high.

President to Become Minister

The President, *Sir Ali Mahammed Khan Dehlavi*, announced that he proposed to vacate the chair at 4 p. m. as he would shortly be taking over the duties of a Minister. *Sir Robert Bell*, Leader of the House, moved a resolution placing on record the Council's high appreciation of the valuable services of the President. Sir Robert in the course of his speech referred to the dignity and impartiality of the Chair.

The resolution was adopted unanimously.

27th. MARCH :—The Council adopted a resolution placing on record its appreciation of and gratitude for the services of Lord Willingdon first as Governor of Bombay and again as Viceroy. The resolution also wished the Viceroy and the Countess of Willingdon *bon voyage*. The council was then *prorogued*.

The Madras Legislative Council

LIST OF MEMBERS

The Hon'ble Mr. B. Ramchandra Reddi (*President*)
Diwan Bahadur C. Natesa Mudaliyar Avargal (*Deputy President*)
1. Abdul Hameed Khan
2. Ahmed Meeran, Maulvi Hafeez Anumanthakudi Mustapha
3. Alagannan Chettiyar, Rao Sahib A. S.
4. Alamelumanga Thayaramma, Mrs. K.
5. Annamalai Chettiyar, S. A. A.
6. Appadurai Pillai, Diwan Bahndur, A.
7. Arasu, V. T.
8. Ari Gowder, H. B.
9. Basheer Ahmed Sayeed
10. Basu Dev, C.
11. Beyabani, S. M. K.
12. Bhanoji Rao, Sri A. V.
13. Boag, G. T.
14. Barcken, The Hon. Mr. G. T. H.
15. Dalavoi, R.
16. Davis, J. A.
17. Devadasan, M.
18. Dharmalingam Pillai, Rao Sahib, V.
19. Duraiswami Reddiyar, K. M.
20. Ellappa Chettiyar, Diwan Bahadur S.
21. Foulkes, G. F. F.
22. Gopalaswami Mudaliyar, Diwan Bahadur M.
23. Harischandrudu Nayudu, A.
24. Indraiah, C.
25. Iswaran Pillai, I. C.
26. Jagannatha Raju, Rao Bahadur G.
27. Jagannatham, H. M.
28. Jayaram Nayudu, Rao Sahib C.
29. Jones, C. E.
30. Kesavaramamurti Nayudu, K.
31. Khaiif-ul-lah Sahib Bahadur, Khan Bahadur, P.
32. Kolanda Reddi, Rai Sahib C.
33. Koti Reddi, K.
34. Krishniah Choudary, P. V.
35. Krishnamurti, Rao Bahadur D.
36. Krishnaswami Ayyer, Diwan Bahadur Sir Alladi
37. Krishnan Avargal, C.
38. Raj Kumar Muthiah Chettiar of Chettinad
39. Raj Kumar of Venkatagiri (Raja Velugoti Sarvangnya Kumarkrishna Yachendrulu Varu)
40. Kumaraswami Reddiyar, The Hon. Diwan Bahadur S. (*Minister*)
41. Kuppuswami Choudari, J.
42. Langley, W. K. M.
43. Madanagopal Nayudu, R. (*Council Secretary*).
44. Maharaja of Parlakimedi (Maharaja Sri Krishna Chandra Gajapathi Narayana Deo, of Parlakimedi),
45. Maharaja of Venkatagiri (Lieutenant-Colonel Maharaja Sir Velugoti Sri Govinda Krishna Yachendrulu Varu, Panchhazari Mansubhdar, of Venkatagiri).
46. Mahboob Ali Baig
47. Manikkavelu Nayakar
48. Moidoo, Khan Bahadur T. M.
49. Moses, P. C.
50. Muhammad Meera Ravuttar, K. P. V. S.
51. Muniswami Pillai, Rao Sahib, I. I.
52. Murugappa Chettiyar, Diwan Bahadur, A. N. M.
53. Muthu Chettiyar, Rao Bahadur P. C.
54. Nachiyappa Gounder, K. A.
55. Nadimuthu Pillai, A. Pl. N. V.
56. Nanjappa, Rao Bahadur Subadar-Major S. A.
57. Narasa Reddi, T.
58. Narasimhaswami, Rao Sahib D. V.
59. Narayanan Nambiyar, V. P.
60. Natesa Mudaliyar, Diwan Bahadur C. (*Deputy President*).
61. Obi Reddi, C.
62. Palat, R. M.
63. Pannirselvam, The Hon ao Bahadur A. T.
64. Parthasarathi Ayyangar, C. R.
65. Patnaik Mahasayo, Sriman M. G.
66. Patro, Rao Bahadur Sir A. P.
67. Pattabhiramayya, K.
68. Pattagar of Palayakottai
69. Peddi Raju, P.
70. Pocker, B.
71. Premayya, G. R.
72. Rajagopala Pillai, P. V.
73. Raja of Bobbili (The Hon. Raja Sri Ravu Sir Swetachallapathi Ramakrishna Ranga Rao Bahadur, of Bobbili) (*Minister*).
74. Raja of Khalikote (Raja Sri Ramachandra Marda Raja Deo of Khalikote and Atagada).

75. RAJAN THE HON. MR. P. T. (*Minister*)
76. RAMACHANDRA PADAYACHI P. K.
77. RAMACHANDRA REDDI, THE HON. MR. B. (*President*).
78. RAMAKRISHNA REDDI, A.
79. RAMALINGAM CHETTIYAR, DIWAN BAHADUR T. A.
80. RAMALINGA REDDI, C.
81. RAMAMURTI, RAO SAHIB PANDIT GANALA.
82. RAMAN MENON, K. P.
83. RAMASWAMI AYYAR, T. S.
84. RAMASWAMI MUDALIYAR, V. M.
85. RAMESWARA RAO, G.
86. RANGANATHA MUDALIYAR, A.
87. RANGANATHA MUDALIYAR, G.
88. RANGANATHAN, N.
89. RANGASWAMI REDDI, M. B.
90. RATNASABHAPATI MUDALIYAR, DIWAN BAHADUR C. S.
91. RATNAVELU THEVAR, P.
92. REID, DOUGLAS MUIR
93. RUKMANI LAKSHIPATHI, MRS. A.
94. RUSSELL, T. B.
95. SAHAJANANDAM SWAMI, A. S.
96. SANDANA GOUNDER, I.
97. SCHAMNAD, KHAN BAHADUR MAHMUD
98. SCOTT BROWN, W.
99. SESHA REDDI, RAO BAHADUR B. P.
100. SHETTY, A. B.
101. SIMHACHALAM PANTALU, G.
102. SIVA RAJ, RAO SAHIB N.
103. SIVASUBRAHMANYA AYYAR, K. S.
104. SMITH, J. M.
105. SOUNDARA PANDIAN, W. P. A.
106. SOUTER, THE HON. SIR CHARLES.
107. SRESHTA, M. S.
108. SRINIVASA AYYANGAR, T. C.
109. SRINIVASAN, DIWAN BAHADUR R.
110. SRIRAMULU, G.
111. STANES, F. J.
112. SUBBARAYAN, DR. P.
113. SUBRAHMANYA BHATT. U. C.
114. SUNDARA RAO NAYUDU, T.
115. SYED TAJUDDIN, KHAN SAHIB
116 THANGAL, P. M.
117. THOMAS, DANIEL
118. UZIELLI, H. R.
119. VASUDEVA PILLAI, V. G.
120. VEDACHALA MUDALIYAR, RAO SAHIB M.
121. VENKATACHALA REDDIYAR, K. C. M.
122. VENKATARAMA AYYAR, K. R.
123. VENKATAREDDI NAYUDU. THE HON. RAI BAHADUR SIR K.
124. VENUGOPAL NAYUDU, RAO BAHADUR R. K.
125. WRIGHT, SIR WILLIAM.
126. YAHYA ALI, KHAN BAHADUR
127. YAKUB HASAN
128. ZAMINDAR OF BODINAYAKKANUR (T. V. K. KAMA RAJA PANDIA NAYAKAR).
129. ZAMINDAR OF CHEMUDU (SRI VYRICHERLA NARAYANA GAJAPATI RAJU)
130. ZAMINDAR OF KIRLAMPUDI (SRI RAJA RAVU RAMAKRISHNA RANGA RAO).
131. ZAMINDAR OF MIRZAPURAM (MIRZAPURAM RAJA alias VENKATARAMAYYA APPA RAO).
132. N. HALASYAM AYYAR
133. KRISHNASWAMI AYYAR, RAO BAHADUR K. V.
134. ERLAM SMITH, W.
135. SUBBIAH NAYUDU, RAO BAHADUR R.

Proceedings of the Council

Budget Session—Madras—25th. February to 27th. March '36

CITY MUNICIPAL ACT AMEND. BILL

The Budget session of the Madras Legislative Council commenced at Madras on the **25th. February 1936**. After formal business, the *Chief Minister* presented a Bill to amend the Madras City Municipal Act.

The Bill is modelled on the Calcutta Corporation Act and provides for extension of franchise, creation of a Deputy Mayor and Aldermen, abolition of the nomination system with safeguards to secure adequate representation of the minorities and special interests and also confers powers on the Corporation for slum clearance and control of noise in the city.

MOTOR VEHICLES TAXATION BILL

The *Chief Minister* next introduced the bill to amend the Madras Motor Vehicles Taxation Act which is designed to tax those private Motor Vehicles which enter this Presidency from outside and use the Madras roads for a short time and go scot-free.

The bill was referred to a Select Committee

FINANCIAL STATEMENT FOR 1936-37

26th. FEBRUARY :—The Hon. Mr. *G. T. H. Bracken*, Finance Member, presented to-day the Madras Government budget for 1936-37. Mr. Bracken said that so far as the revised estimates for 1935-36 were concerned, the year 1935 was a normal one politically and economically. Despite improvement in market prices the provincial revenues continued to lag behind the economic recovery while on the expenditure side the progress was normal. The net result was a deficit of 32 lakhs.

As regards the budget estimates for 1936-37, his general attitude was one of hesitant hope. The grounds for this lay mainly in the improvement in commodity prices. He said that the debt position was satisfactory. The amount of unproductive debt outstanding was comparatively small. He pointed out that 1934-35 had closed with a surplus of 10.93 lakhs. The revised estimates for the current year showed a deficit of 31.69 lakhs which after adjustment for the separation of Orissa would be reduced to 9.91 lakhs. In the current year the expenditure and revenue would just balance after providing for Part II of the schemes chargeable to revenue.

Before concluding, Mr. Bracken referred to the Niemeyer enquiry and said : "Our case rests mainly on the sound and prudential management of our finances. We cut our coat according to our cloth. We have retrenched when retrenchment was necessary. We have taxed when taxation became necessary. When Sir Otto Niemeyer has to assess what is most deserving of the provinces, he will have to consider whether the province of Madras which has always pursued the path of financial rectitude and has endeavoured to balance its budget is or is not the more deserving than the province which has left its budget unbalanced and hoped for a subvention from the Centre.

In recent years this province has sacrificed 69 lakhs in toll revenue, and 55 lakhs in land revenue remissions, not to mention the fifteen lakhs due to postponement of resettlement. These sacrifices have affected the finances of both the province and local bodies. If the concessions were to continue and to be extended, they must explore alternative sources of taxation.

The Finance Member said that in future the budget problem should be approached from a new angle by the new Government. They must first consider what expenditure was really necessary and adjust the taxation accordingly, by either increasing or decreasing the taxation or substituting one tax by another as it happened in England and as he thought would probably happen here.

GENERAL DISCUSSION OF THE BUDGET

28th. FEBRUARY :—The general discussion on the Budget began to-day. Mr. *T. A. Ramalingam Chetty* congratulated the Finance Member on presenting a balanced Budget, but complained that very large sums were being spent on capital expenditure. He wanted land revenue to be made permanent at a certain figure, and hoped that the new Council would deal with the question.

Sir William Wright, leader of the European group, also congratulated Mr. G. T. H. Bracken on his first, and possibly last, Budget. It should be a matter of considerable gratification to him that as the last official Finance Member he had been able to maintain a prudent policy and hand over to the new Government the Presidency's finances in a sound condition. Referring to retrenchment, he said that it must depend upon a proper standard of efficiency.

Mr. *Balasyam Iyer* (Congress) could not congratulate the Finance Member, as the balanced Budget could not afford comfort to anybody except the Government which had prepared it with considerable trouble.

29th. FEBRUARY :—Almost all the members who spoke to-day referred to the hopeless indebtedness of the ryot and asked the Government to relieve his distress. Mr. *Simhachala Pantulu*, a member representing one of the Northern Districts, charged the Government with "supreme indifference, masterly inactivity, and profound ignorance".

The *Mayor of Madras* stated that the finances of the province had been reduced to such a state that they were handing over the Province to the new Government in a position almost of bankruptcy. Regarding education, he said the Government had not succeeded in removing illiteracy from the Province to the extent it should have done. He complained that the Government had done nothing to improve the existing industries.

Mr. *Appadurai Pillai*, ex-Director of Industries, stated that technical education was kept in the background and emphasized the necessity for imparting it.

Mr. *Kolanda Reddy* said that the Budget was unsatisfactory, and referred to the hopeless indebtedness of the ryot. On the eve of the reforms, Government were marking time without doing anything.

2nd. MARCH :—Mrs. *Lakshmipathi* (Congress) sounded a note of warning that if the Government failed to bring about a radical change in the policy an agrarian revolution and crisis would follow.

The *Revenue Member* announced that in as much as the Finance Member proposed to have a comprehensive survey of the finances of the Presidency, the Government had decided not to introduce the Tobacco Bill at present.

The *Chief Minister* stated that he realised that the rate of taxation on motor vehicles was high in the Presidency, but unless they could find an alternative source of revenue he could not hold out any hope of relief.

This finished the Budget discussion and the Council adjourned till March 11.

Debate on Hammond Report

11th. MARCH :—The proceedings of the Council took a very lively turn to-day after Mr. *G. T. H. Bracken*, member in charge of reforms, had moved that the report of the Indian Delimitation Committee be taken into consideration. Two polls were taken, both resulting in a win for the Government by large majorities. Mr. Bracken at the outset regretted that the Government was unable to place copies of the report in the hands of hon. members as sufficient copies had not been received. Newspapers had published pretty fully the gists of the report and he thought the hon. members were aware of the main points to enable them to participate in the discussion on the recommendations of the committee. Referring to the report he said that with due respect to the Hammond Committee, the reasons given by the committee for digering with the recommendations of the local Government in the matter of single member constituencies were, he said, unconvincing. He was afraid that the committee was unduly influenced by Bombay and thought what was good for Bombay was also good for Madras. It was not so. The committee also thought that public opinion in Madras was in favour of multi-member constituencies. Mr. Bracken said that the Government did not attach much importance to the committee's recommendations regarding University and Indian commerce as there was only one seat for each. Mr. Bracken suggested that the debate be restricted to the main issues and votes be taken thereupon. At the eleventh hour, it was unlikely that Parliament would go into questions regarding individual seats or minor points. He added that in any voting the Executive Councillors and the official members would remain neutral. The result of the debate would be cabled to the Secretary of State to-day.

Mr. *Abdul Hamid Khan* moved an adjournment of the discussion on the ground that copies of the report were not supplied to all members.

Mr. *Bracken*, opposing, said that when the question of the discussion of the report was raised the other day, he informed the House that it might not be possible to supply the House with copies. If the debate was adjourned he was afraid it would be too late. The Secretary of State knew that the debate would be taking place in the House to-day and was awaiting the result thereof. If the debate was to be of any use, it should not be postponed.

Dr. *Subbaroyan* and Mr. *C. R. Reddi* supported the adjournment motion. The poll resulted in the adjournment motion being lost by 65 votes against 16. Government members voting against it.

Dr. *Subbaroyan* moved that no voting be taken and the House should only express its opinion when the first of the several amendments to Mr. Bracken's motion was taken up for discussion.

The motion was lost by 63 votes to 19.

The discussion then centred round the question whether single or multi-member constituencies was most suitable for the Presidency, The opinion of the House was divided. Several members of the Justice Party favoured the former, while members of the Opposition preferred multi-member constituencies.

Mr. *C. R. Reddi* (Congress) considered that a multi-member constituency with the distributive system was best. The cumulative system would accentuate the sub-communal feeling and would do incalculable harm to the spirit of the Poona Pact. He added that the vast majority of people in the presidency voted for a multi-member constituency as the only means of overcoming communalism.

Dr. *Subbaroyan* felt that the committee had carefully considered the question regarding single-member and multi-member constituencies and came to the conclusion that the latter was preferable.

Mr. *Bracken*, winding up the debate, said that the Hammond Committee sprang a surprise on the local Government by recommending multi-member constituencies. Until Mr. C. R. Reddi analysed the view of the Congress he did not knew what the Congress view was on the matter. He read in the papers that Mr. Satyamurti, a leading member of the Congress, stood for single-member constituencies.

The House carried by 53 votes to 24 the following amendment moved by Mr. *Appadurai Pillai* (Justice):

"The delimitation of general constituencies by the Hammond Committee is opposed to the terms of reference of his Majesty's Government which lay down that the constituencies should generally be single-member except where plural or multi-member constituencies are absolutely necessary, that multi-member constituencies with cumulative voting will instead of diminishing or eliminating communal strife, accentuate the same while single-member constituencies are best suited to achieve the object the Committee has in view; that the proposals of the Madras delimitation committee and the local Government are best suited for working the constitution on a party basis in this province and for the proper beneficial functioning of provincial autonomy, and that to help minorities which is the object of the Hammond Committee single non-transferable vote is preferable to cumulative vote; and that cumulative voting would generally lead to the spoiling of voting papers and a wastage of votes and on this ground alone single non-transferable vote is preferable.

House for Madras Legislature

12th. MARCH :— Members of the Council to-day were considerably exercised over the design of the building that will accommodate the two houses of the new provincial legislature.

Severely Dravidian, Swadeshi and Moghul were some of the suggestions made when the Finance Member moved a recommendatory resolution on the subject.

Mr. *G. T. H. Bracken*, at the outset, explained that temporary accommodation would be found for the two houses in the present Council Chamber and the University Senate Building.

The site under consideration was on the Marina and was known as Napier Battery. The cost would approximately be Rs. 15,00,000. However, to proceed with the matter immediately and to avoid undue delay, the main expenditure necessary at present was for the appointment of a special architect.

Mr. *C. R. Reddy*, who was for a severely Dravidian and swadeshi design, asked Mr. Bracken to show "sufficient imaginative sympathy with the new forces that would be in charge of the Government of the Presidency." The design must conform to public opinion and Dravidian art. He also urged the use of Indian materials. Other speakers urged that the architect's post should only be advertised in India and desired improved accommodation for the Press, women members, etc. A Moslem member suggested Moghul architecture while Dr. Subbaroyan wanted the design to be thrown open to competition.

Mr. *Bracken* said that the Government had originally thought of holding a competition but this would have involved delay. Regarding Dravidian architecture, he was not sure what was meant by it. All that he could say was that the building should be in keeping with neighbouring buildings and should be worthy of the new legislature and the presidency. The design would be placed in the library and would be accessible to members. Personally he was in sympathy with the idea of an oriental design, whether Dravidian or Moslem or any other. The motion was carried without division.

Voting on Budget Demands

13th. MARCH :—Voting on Budget demands commenced to-day. The Council voted the entire demand under the head 'Land Revenue.' The cut motion criticising the Government's land revenue policy was defeated by 48 votes to 26. The *Revenue Member*, replying, strongly opposed the suggestion for salary cuts in order to give further relief to the *ryots*.

14th. MARCH :—The Council passed to-day the entire Excise demand of Rs. 30,95,100 made by the Minister for Excise, a cut motion to criticize the Excise policy of the Government having been lost without a division. During the discussion the

Opposition attacked the Government for not undertaking large measures of prohibition. It was pointed out that even when partial prohibition was being tried, measures adopted were not given a reasonable chance of success.

The *Minister* in his reply said the Government had decided to increase fees on foreign liquor, which would yield an income of about two lakhs of rupees annually. Referring to prohibition, the Minister stated that any spectacular innovations at this time would not only be out of the question but also out of place.

The *Finance Member*, answering a question regarding the programme of elections under the reformed constitution said that no communication had been received as to the date on which the reforms would be inauguarated. He added that no decision had yet been made as to when elections should take place under the new reforms.

18th. MARCH :—During the discussion on a cut motion to reduce the allotment of the demand under head 'Legislative Bodies—Reserved', the *Finance Member* in charge of the Reforms informed the Council to-day that it was presumed that the new constitution would be inaugurated with effect from April 1, 1937, and on this basis an electoral programme was being arranged. He thought that it was not possible to hold elections before January next and in the opinion of the Government the middle of February was not suitable for holding elections. Until draft Orders in Council, which the Government were expecting everyday, relating to the Hammond Committee's recommendations and general elections were published, it was not possible to say more about the elections.

The cut motion having been withdrawn, the whole demand was voted.

19th. MARCH :—Want of confidence in the Ministry was expressed by Mrs. *Rukmani Lakshmipati* (Congress) by means of a cut motion to reduce the allotmont of Rs. 4,92,200 demanded by the Chief Minister under head 'Ministers, civil secretariats and miscellaneous—transferred'. The speaker contended that the present Council was unrepresentative and the Ministry had no justification to continue to be in office any longer, having lost the confidence of the electorate as was evidenced by the elections to the Assembly and local boards and the bye-elections to the Assembly and local boards and the bye-elections to the local Council.

The Hon'ble *Raja of Bobbili*, replying, refuted the various allegations made during the discussion. The Opposition in season and out of season demanded the ministers' resignation whenever a bye-election was lost. If the Congress was serious and their advice was to be accepted, they should implement their election pledges. The Chief Minister declared that it was easy to make all sorts of allegations, but the real test could be seen in the next elections.

Referring to his proposed visit to England, he said that it was true that he had applied to the Governor on medical advice for permission to leave the presidency for a short period. So far no orders had been received from the Governor and so he could not enlighten the House on the subject, however, much he might like it. Referring to the Reforms, he said that speaking from his experience of the administration of the transferred departments placed in his charge, he could say that however defective the Reforms were, there was an advance on the present one. The cut motion was lost by 65 votes to 23.

20th. MARCH :—The Council voted to-day the entire demand of Rs 2,24,99,800 under the head 'secretariat and headquarters establishments, district administration and miscellaneous—Reserved". The cut motions were being either rejected, or withdrawn.

Mrs. *Rukamani Lakshmipati* (Congress), whose cut motion was rejected, criticising the repressive policy of the Government, said that India to-day was smarting under the repressive policy followed either by the provincial Governments or the central Government, though not in such a form as existed in Bengal. The local Government was trying to put down the activities of the Congress, an organisation which was the representative of the nation. Instead of trying to suppress the Congress and those agitators in the country who were being incarcerated and put down as a danger to the society, the Government should try to follow a conciliatory policy by acceding to their legitimate demands. There should be mutual confidence between the Government and the governed. She condemned the Government's action demanding the forfeiting of securities from certain vernacular journals.

Referring to the police, she said that instead of doing their duty the police were tormenting and harassing the people. She quoted an instance of a police officer having roughly handled a prominent Congress worker, but further reference to this incident was stopped as the Home Member, intervening, stated that the matter was *sub-judice*.

The *Home Member*, referring to the security demanded from the *Express*, said that the securities were demanded only when the limits had been clearly transgressed and the Government had always acted in consultation with their legal advisers.

23rd. MARCH :—During the discussion on the Education demand to-day, some members charged the Government with inactivity in enforcing the Champion scheme with effective and coercive measures while some others said that the scheme had been enforced to the detriment of certain communities.

The *Education Minister*, replying, said that the Champion scheme was not of a revolutionary character. There was an enormous wastage of energy and money under the present system of elementary education. To eliminate this wastage the scheme had been placed before the public, from 1930, and all interested in education understood now the scheme fully well and it had gained popular support. Continuing; he said that the Madras Presidency was the first in India in the percentage of literacy. He did not mean that everything in the matter of education had been done. Referring to the demand for separate schools for the depressed classes, he said that the Government were not in favour of separate schools unless they were absolutely necessary. The latest report of the Director of Public Instruction showed that there was 8 per cent increase in the strength of depressed class students in general schools.

The cut motion was withdrawn and the entire demand was voted.

The House also voted the demand of Rs. 7,54,600 under the head Education Reserved (European) without a cut.

Mr. *Abdul Hameed Khan* moved an adjournment of the House to discuss the recent enhancement of the provincial tax on motor buses from Rs. 7-8 per seat to Rs. 8-12. The mover pointed out that the enhancement would effect a large class of people who were not in a position to bear it.

The *Chief Minister*, replying to the debate, assured the House that he would examine the various points raised during the discussion and if in actual working they found the rates heavy it would be open to the Government to modify the rates.

The motion was rejected.

25th. MARCH :—The Government's work in connexion with medical relief in Madras was described by the Minister of Public Health during discussions on token motions in the Council to-day. The Council voted in full the demand for grant under "medicine" made by the Minister of Public Health.

Replying to the debate, the *Minister* said that in the matter of leprosy relief it was a matter for gratification that work had been taken up in right earnest by the Government, and good work was being done under the Chief Leprosy Officer. As regards the complaint of inadequacy of provision for treatment of tuberculosis, the Minister said that the Government were prepared to construct an up-to-date hospital on the Spur tank, but though estimates were prepared, the Corporation objected to the location of the hospital in that place. Various proposals were considered by the Government, and the disagreement of the Corporation stood in the way of the Government's undertaking building the hospital. The Government were also considering the question of taking over the sanitorium of Dr. C. Mathu which was intended for patients in the very early stages of the disease, and which would provide for 40 patients.

Another complaint was that the Government were not very liberal in regard to subsidizing rural dispensaries.

The *Minister* promised that when financial conditions of the province improved more liberal subsidies would be extended to rural dispensaries than had been done during the past four years. Recently a committee was appointed to go into the question of extending the system of appointing honorary physicians and surgeons. On the recommendations of the committee, the Government decided that honorary officers could be appointed in hospitals and dispensaries either in the city or in mofussils where there was a daily average attendance of 100 or more patients. The Government were also considering whether honorary officers working in hospitals could also be be allowed to work in educational institutions as honorary officers, being paid only a small allowance.

During the discussion on token motions under "Public Health Department," several members pointed out that inadequate allotments had been made for rural water supply and village communications.

The Hon'ble the *Rajah of Bobbili*, Chief Minister, replying, said that the grants had not been reduced, on the other hand they had been increased. He assured the House that they were trying their best to provide as much as was possible under the present circumstances.

The *Minister for Public Health* said that the working of the Public Health Department was based on the principles enumerated by members of the Council. As regards anti-malarial measures, the Minister said that the Government had sanctioned a free supply of 4,000 pounds of quinine for free distribution within the Presideny. The Government were considering proposals as to how best they could distribute quinine further. They had sanctioned anti-malarial operations at a cost of Rs. 50,000 in a few selected areas.

The cut motion was withdrawn and the grant was voted.

The Agricultural Department came in for a good deal of criticism. One of the members observed that the Department had done next to nothing, and graduates were roaming about in search of employment.

The *Minister for Agriculture*, replying, said that recently a simpler course had been instituted for helping those who wished to take to agriculture so that after learning something in the College they could utilize their knowledge for their own purpose. That course was introduced about three years ago ; it was fairly popular, and if it was found that there was greater demand for it, steps would be taken to give the necessary facilities in that direction. As regards the remark that the number of applications for admission to the Agricultural College had fallen, the Minister said that it was due to the fact that the Government were not recruiting or employing graduates of that institute to the extent they had done hitherto. That was why there was unemployment among the graduates. As regards the suggestion that they should be given lands so that they might use their knowledge to their own benefit and to the benefit of labourers, the Minister said that this was tried but none would come forward. Unfortunately their students, whether they came from the arts colleges or from technical colleges, had no inclination to go back to villages, improve lands and make village life attractive. If only their students could bring themselves to go back to the villages and utilize their knowledge and experience, it would be extremely useful from the viewpoint of the nation. That they did not do so was regrettable. As regards the suggestion that the Department had done next to nothing, the Minister said that the statement had no basis.

The cut motion was withdrawn and the entire grant under "agriculture" voted.

26th. MARCH :—The *Finance Member* moved that Government be granted Rs. 1, 33, 500 for necessary additions and alterations in the Senate House to accommodate the new Legislative Assembly. Under the new Reforms the Madras legislature would consist of two chambers, the Legislative Council (upper house consisting of 56 members, and the Legislative Assembly consisting of 215 members. It would not be possible to accommodate both chambers in the secretariat and the existing Council Chamber. The question of providing temporary accommodation to the Assembly had been examined. The only building considered suitable for the purpose is the Senate House which the University agreed to lease temporarily to the Government until the new Parliament House was constructed. A rent of Rs. 500 would be paid to the University monthly for the Senate House and its premises, including outhouses.

The grant was made.

Corporation Markets Act Amend. Bill

The Council passed into law the Bill introduced by the *Minister for Public Works* to amend the Madras Corporation Markets Act to make it obligatory on the part of pressing and ginning factory owners to take out a licence. The House then adjourned till the next day, the **27th. March**, when it was *prorogued*.

The Punjab Legislative Council

LIST OF MEMBERS

Officers of the Council.

1. The Hon'ble Chaudhri Sir Sahab-ud-din, *President.*
2. Buta Singh, Sardar Bahadur Sardar, (*Deputy President*)
3. Abnasha Singh, Sardar Bahadur Sardar. (*Secretary*)
4. Ahmad Shuja, Khan Sahib Hakeem. (*Assistant Secretary*)

Executive Councillors and Ministers

1. The Hon'ble Sir Donald Boyd
2. The Hon'ble Nawab Muzaffar Khan
3. The Hon'ble Sardar Sir Jogendra Singh
4. The Hon'ble Malik Sir Firoze Khan Noon
5. The Hon'ble Dr. Sir Gokul Chand Narang

Official Members

1. Anderson, Mr. J. D.
2. Askwith, Mr. A. V.
3. Bradford. Mr. W. G.
4. Darling, Mr. M. L.
5. Fazl Ilahi, Khan Sahib Shaikh.
6. Latifi, Mr. A.
7. Parkinson, Mr. J. E.
8. Puckle, Mr. F. H.
9. Rahman, Khan Bahadur Dr. K. A.
10. Ram Chandra, Mr.
11. Salusbury, Mr. C. V.
12. Tate, Mr. T. B.

Non-official Members

1. Abdul Gani, Shaikh
2. Afzal Haq, Chaudhri
3. Ahmad Yar Khan, Daulatana, Khan Bahadur Mian.
4. Akbar Ali, Pir
5. Allah Dad Khan Chaudhri
6. Arjan Singh, Sardar
7. Assadullah Khan, Chaudhri
8. Bahadur Khan, Sardar
9. Balbir Singh, Rao Bahadur Captain Rao.
10. Bansi Lal, Chaudhri
11. Bhagat Ram, Lala
12. Bishan Singh, Sardar
13. Chetan Anand, Lala
14. Chotu Ram, Rao Bahadur Chaudhri
15. Chowdry, Mr. Sajan Kumar
16. Faqir Hussain Khan, Chaudhri
17. Fazl Ali, Khan Bahadur Nawab Chaudhri
18. Ghani, Mr. M. A.
19. Gopal Das, Rai Sahib Lala
20. Gurbachan Singh, Sardar Sahib Sardar
21. Habib Ullah, Khan Bahadur Sardar
22. Haibat Khan Daha, Khan
23. Jagadev Khan Kharal, Rai
24. Janmeja Singh, Captain, Sardar Bahadur Sardar
25. Jaswant Singh, Guru
26. Jawahar Singh Dhillon, Sardar
27. Jyoti Prasad, Lala
28. Kesar Singh, Rai Sahib Chaudhri
29. Lab Chand Mehra, Rai Sahib Lala
30. Labh Singh Mr. M. A.
31. Lekhwati Jain, Shrimati
32. Malak, Mr. Muhammad Din
33. Mamraj Singh Chohan, Kanwar
34. Mangal Singh Man, Sardar
35. Manohar Lal Mr.
36. Mayadas, Mr. E.
37. Mazhar Ali Azhar, Maulvi
38. Mohindar Singh, Sardar
39. Mubarak Ali Shah, Sayad
40. Muhammad Abdul Rahaman Khan, Chaudhri
41. Mohammad Amin Khan, Khan Bahadur Malik
42. Muhammd Eusoof, Khwaja
43. Muhammad Hayat Qureshi, Khan Bahadur Nawab
44. Muhammad Hasan, Khan Sahib Makhdum Shaikh
45. Muhammad Jamal Khan Legari, Khan Bahadur Nawab
46. Muhammad Raza Shah Gilani, Makhdumzada Sayad
47. Muhammad Sadiq, Shaikh
48. Muhammad Sarfaraz Ali Khan, Raja
49. Muhammad Yasin Khan, Chaudhri
50. Mukand Lal Puri, Rai Bahadur Mr.
51. Mukerji, Rai Bahadur Mr. P.
52. Mushtaq Ahmad Gurmani, Khan Bahadur Mian
53. Muzaffar Khan, Khan Bahadur Captain Malik
54. Narendra Nath, Diwan Bahadur Raja
55. Nathwa Singh, Chaudhri
56. Nihal Chand Aggarwal, Lala
57. Noor Ahmad Khan, Khan Sahib Mian
58. Nur Khan, Khan Sahib Risaldar Bahadur

59 NURULLAH, MIAN
60. PANCHAM CHAND, THAKUR
61. PANDIT, MR NANAK CHAND
62. RAGHBIR SINGH, HONORARY CAPTAIN SARDAR
63. RAMJI DAS, LALA
64. RAM SARUP, CHAUDHRI
65. RAM SINGH, 2ND-LIENT. SARDAR
66. RIASAT ALI, KHAN SAHIB CHAUDHRI
67. ROBERTS, PROFESSOR W.
68. SAMPURAN SINGH, SARDAR
69 SEWAK RAM, RAI BAHADUR LALA
70. SHAH NAWAZ KHAN, NAWAB KHAN
71. SHAVE, DR (MRS) M. C.
72. SHEO NARAIN SINGH, SARDAR
73. UJJAL SINGA, SARDAR SAHIB SARDAR
74. UMAR HAYAT, CHAUDHRI
75 ZAMAN MEHDI KHAN, KHAN BAHADUR MALIK

Budget Session—Lahore—24th. February to 31st. March 1936

TRIBUTE TO LATE KING

The Budget Session of the Punjab Legislative Council commenced at Lahore on the **24th. February 1936** and was devoted to the memory of King George V.

The *Finance Member*, Leader of the House, moved a resolution placi ng on record the Council's deep sorrow at the death of King George, its heartfelt sympathy with King Edward and Queen Mary in their loss and conveying loyal congratulations to his Majesty on his accession to the throne.

Tributes to the memory of the late King were paid by the leaders of different groups with which the Chair associated itself. The resolution was unanimously passed, all standing, after which the House adjourned.

"While it is much to be regretted that the last year of the present Constitution is likely to end with a deficit, I am quite satisfied that the present Government will hand over to their successor a thoroughly solvent estate, which provides amenities in the form of education, canals, road, hospitals, agricultural institutions, veterinary relief and co-operative credit on a scale that is unsurpassed in India."

FINANCIAL STATEMENT FOR 1936-37

25th. FEBRUARY :—Presenting the Budget estimates for 1836-37 in the Council to-day, *Sir Donald Boyd*, Finance Member said :—The estimates show a deficit of Rs. 16,38,000, revenue receipts being Rs. 10,44,20,000 and revenue expenditure Rs. 10,60,58,000, which are respectively 20 and 16 lakhs more than the corresponding revised estimates for the current year. If the extraordinary receipts of Rs. 36,17,000, which represent the sale proceeds of Crown lands and the capital expenditure met from these receipts of Rs. 17,27,000 is taken into account, the Budget estimates show a surplus of two and a half lakhs.

Sir Donald Boyd stated that the revised estimates for the current year have shown a revenue deficit of Rs. 61 and one-fourth lakhs, instead of a surplus of Rs. 56.000 budgeted for. Land revenue, stamps and civil works "let us down" to the extent of Rs. 30 lakhs, but Forests, Agriculture, Irrigation, and Hydro-electric schemes made up, leaving the total revenue income, for the current year at Rs. 15.2 lakhs worse than the Budget estimate.

Sir Donald Boyd, after explaining the revenue estimates for 1936-37, remarked that they appeared to him fair and reasonable. "The weakness of our Budget estimates, of course, is that they depend to such a great extent on seasonal conditions. Good monsoon and full rivers make prosperous the province and prosperous the Government but failure of rains or low supply of rivers may wreck our Budget prospects. In fact, the Finance Member is in much the same position as the Punjab agriculturist of whom Rudyard Kipling wrote 'his life in a long drawn question between crop and crop."

Referring to expenditure estimates, which were Rs. 18 and a half lakhs above the decennial average, he said that, apart from general factors, the particular factors, which had swollen the expenditure, were the holding of the elections to the future Legislature, which cost Rs. 5 and a half lakhs, of Rs. 4,81,000 would be spent in

1936-37 and the communal situation. "We have been driven to heavy extra expenditure by the communal disturbances. The disturbances are an expensive luxury for the province, though they may bring profit to some individuals, who are mainly instrumental in raising the trouble. Additional police cost us Rs. 1,67,200 and for that sum we could have effected considerable expansion of the beneficent activities of the Government."

Sir Donald Boyd admitted that the increase in expenditure was disturbing. While assuring that no means of economy would be overlooked, he proposed to have the increases fully analysed at leisure.

Referring to the future financial prospects, the Finance Member stated that the adverse factors included the loss, when Provincial Autonomy commenced, of the fixed assignment of Rs. 697 lakhs granted to the Province by the Government of India in respect of excise on liquors distilled in the Punjab and consumed in N. W F. and Delhi Provinces, the threatened stoppage of export of charas from Yarkand under orders of that Government, by which the Punjab stood to lose Rs. 11 lakhs per annum and the anticipated recurring increase in expenditure of Rs. 4 lakhs owing to the new system of Government. On the brighter side were the share they were likely to receive from the surplus income-tax from the Federal Government and the growing returns from the Hydro-Electric Project and increase of revenue from the Haveli Irrigation scheme.

Criminal Pr. Code Amend. Bill

After the presentation of the Budget the Council passed without discussion the official Bill amending the Criminal Procedure Code in its application in the Punjab in order to make the offence of personation at elections to legislature and local bodies cognizable. Explaining the necessity for legislation, ***Nawab Muzaffar Khan***, Revenue Member, the mover of the Bill, said the offence of personation at elections both for the legislature and for local bodies was becoming frequent and as the existing procedure of prosecuting suspects in such cases was slow, cumbrous and uncertain, it was considered desirable to make the procedure quicker and more effective. With a wide franchise in the new Constitution, such legislation was badly required.

Entertainment & Service Control Bills

The Punjab Entertainments Duty Bill and the Punjab Control of Public Utility Services Bill were referred to select committees.

The object of the first named Bill is to raise revenue by levying tax on entertainments and the second Bill aims at providing against public utility companies for one reason or another putting the public to grave inconvenience by refusing their services. This Bill is the result of the situation which arose in Lahore in 1934 when owing to a dispute between the Lahore Electric Supply Company and Municipal Committees, the former threatened to cut off the supply of energy necessary for lighting the streets of the town and for raising water from tube-wells which serve the Lahore Water Works.

The Council also passed 21 Government demands for supplementary additional and token grants for the year 1935-36 in respect of various heads.

Land Revenue Assessment

27th. FEBRUARY :—The Government suffered a defeat to-day when a non-official resolution regarding the appointment of a Committee to investigate certain factors relating to revenue assessment was passed by 38 votes to 25.

The resolution, which was moved by ***Mian Nurullah*** recommended to the Government to appoint a Committee composed of officials and non-officials to (a) fix the meaning of "net assets"; (b) investigate the extent to which the cost of production has fallen or risen with the prices of agricultural produce; (c) determine whether the lower rate assessment, based on variation of actual prices from scheduled prices (other factors remaining constant), would represent the same proportion of the net assets as assessment, according to standard rates based on scheduled prices; (d) investigate and suggest a formula which would give the Government its share of 25 per cent of assets as prices rise or fall; and (e) determine what percentage of net assets Government has actually been realising in Lyallpur District during the last few five years.

Government opposed it on the grounds that the proposed Committee of Enquiry would be a waste of public money and the factors mentioned in the resolution were already taken into consideration in assessment.

Chaudhri Alladad Khan, supporting the resolution, described the condition of the Zamindars and said that they were so hard hit that they could not pay the land revenue from the profits of cultivation, which were nothing. But they paid land revenue by selling their cattle and ornaments. Many zamindars were rotting in lock-ups for not being able to pay Government dues. The resolution being pressed to a division, was carried.

Irrigation Schemes

Another resolution was passed recommending to the Government to forthwith prepare the Sindsagar Doabs Irrigation Scheme, commonly known as the Lesser Thal Project, and submit the same to the Government of India and the Secretary of State in good time for sanction, with a view to beginning its construction along with the Haveli Project, or as soon as the Haveli Project was near completion, Government did not oppose the resolution.

Govt. Servants' Minimum Salary

Mr. *M. A. Ghani* (Labour Leader) moved a resolution urging Government that all petty and whole-time Government Servants be paid a minimum salary of not less than Rs. 30. Discussion was proceeding when the Council adjourned.

General Discussion of the Budget

2nd. MARCH :—The urgent need for solving the unemployment problem in the Province and development of industries were stressed by non-official members in the Council to-day during the general discussion on the Budget.

Khan Bahadur Habibullah congratulated the Finance Member on his budget proposals, which clearly set forth the financial position of the province. He urged Government to help the industrial development of the Province without which the Province could not prosper.

Shaik Mohammad Sadiq referred to the acute poverty of the masses and complained that nothing had been done to ameliorate their conditions. He compared the position of the budget with what it had been during the last five years and regretted that nothing had been done to tackle unemployment.

Mr. *Thakur Panchamchand*, speaking on the general situation in the Province, attributed the appearance of communalism to the Montagu Reforms.

Sardar Arjun Singh was afraid that the present Government was going to hand over to the new Reformed Government an insolvent estate. He urged Government to make substantial reduction in the salaries of Government servants in the higher grades. *Sardar Ujjal Singh* expressed the opinion that the unrest in the Province was, to a large extent, due to the acute unemployment. The beneficial departments were being progressively starved, and nothing was being done for the development of industries. *Chaudhri Chotu Ram* suggested that Government should tap new sources of revenue. Mr. *Nanakchand Pandit* urged the reduction in land revenue, so as to afford relief to the agriculturist. He also accused the Government of having done nothing to tackle the problem of unemployment. Mr. Nanakchand suggested that Government should grant land to educated men and settle them on land. Industries should be developed and the present educational system should be changed in favour of vocational and industrial education. Referring to the communal question, he emphasised that this could be solved only by the introduction of Joint Electorates.

Voting on Budget Grants

10th. MARCH :—The Government suffered a second defeat to-day, when a cut motion by *Choudhri Allah Dad Khan* to urge 50 per cent reduction of fees for inspection and copy of Patwaris' records was carried by 30 to 25 votes. The mover pointed out that this fee caused hardship to Zamindars. The Revenue Member explained that the fee was justified, as Government had to maintain the records and keep a check thereon.

Four more cut motions were discussed to-day. Three withdrawn, while the other was under discussion when the House adjourned. The speakers described the plight of the Punjab zamindar, who, with depleted income, had met a number of demands from Government in the form of land revenue, water rates, etc.

Mr. *Choudhri Choturam*, moving his cut motion to urge the abolition of acreage rates, pleaded that the acreage rates should be abolished in view of the fall in prices of agricultural commodities. The cut was withdrawn on the assurance of the *Revenue*

Member that the matter would be examined, and if there were genuine grievances, an attempt would be made to redress them.

Mr. *Choudhri Choturam* accused the Government on insisting on its pound of flesh like an ordinary Bania moving another cut urging that Malikana should be charged only on the area sown.

11th. MARCH :—The extent of damage done to the standing crops in the Punjab by unprecedented hailstroms in the course of the last few weeks was emphasised by members from rural constituencies to-day, when a cut motion urging reduction in land revenue for the *rabi* of 1936 was discussed. *Nawab Muhammad Hayat Quareshi*, the mover of the cut, urged that the calamity done by nature was the sufficient reason for a reduction in land revenue for the *rabi*.

Mr. *M. A. Latifi*, financial commissioner, replying to the debate, referred to the rules under which remissions were made and said that the general practice was that when there was a calamity by nature the Government did give some remission. The Government was watching the situation and rebates of damage had been called for. He assured the House that the Government would examine the question and would decide as to what remission should be granted.

The cut was withdrawn and the Government demand for grant relating to land revenue was carried.

12th. MARCH :—*Chaudhri Choturam*, leader of the Opposition, staged a walk-out in the Council to-day as a protest against the ruling of the President given during the discussion on his cut motion to urge greater representation for statutory Hindu agriculturists in the excise department. While replying to the previous speaker, Chaudhri Choturam wanted 'certain statistics' whereupon the President pointed out that the question of representation of communities and classes in the cadre of tashildars was not under discussion and requested Chaudhri Choturam not to speak on this aspect of the question. This was followed by a walk-out by Chaudhri Choturam. No other member of the party followed him. The discussion proceeded and the cut was defeated.

A lively discussion followed on the cut motion of *Malik Zaman Mehdi Khan* drawing attention to the under-representation of Muslims in the Excise department.

Choudhri Afzal Haq, supporting the motion, accused the Government for not allotting a fair share to each community in the services. They were complaining for the last ten years but no steps had been taken by the Government. But on the other hand the Government was laughing at the expense of different communities of the province.

Mr. Latifi, financial commissioner, replying to the debate, quoted figures to show that within the last two years the percentage of Muslims in the Excise department had increased by 2.5. He said that it was not possible to make a revolutionary change and progress must be slow. He also told the House by giving an instance that Muslims did not like to serve this department. The mover withdrew the cut.

Surdar Sampuran Singh moved a cut to urge on the Government that their excise policy in the province was wrong and to bring to their notice that great injustice was being done to innocent people in the measures adopted to stop illicit distilliation of spirits.

Replying to the debate on this cut, *Sir Joginder Singh*, Minister of Agriculture, repudiated the criticism levelled by Mr. Abdur Rehman that the evil of liquor appeared with the advent of Englishmen and said that there was mention of liquor in the *Vedas* and it was also prevalent in the Moghul period. The Minister added that every precaution was taken that guilty persons would be brought to book and finally appealed to the public to co-operate with the Excise Department in detecting cases of distilling illicit liquor. In concluding, he said that so long as there was a desire for liquor, the evil could not be eradicated. The cut was withdrawn.

The cut to urge reduction of the price of bottled country liquor was under discussion when the Council rose for the day.

13th. MARCH .—*Chaudhri Afzal Haq* moved a cut motion to-day urging total prohibition throughout the province. He referred to the Government's repeated statements that they advocated the policy of reduction of consumption of liquor in the province but said that facts did not bear out these statements. On the other hand, there had been an increase in the number of liquor shops.

Mr. *Nanak Chand Pandit* urged on the Government to undertake total prohibition, saying that all the three communities were agreed that there was an evil and should be eradicated. He admitted that the Government would have to forego a large revenue but he felt that this consideration should not weigh with the Government in view of the enormity of the evil.

Mr. *Puckle*, Chief Secretary, said that there was no country in the world where there was complete prohibition. The United States of America tried it but failed.

A closure was moved and carried.

The *President* gave a ruling disallowing the Minister to reply to the debate. The cut was moved and defeated by 43 votes to 17.

The council discussed earlier a cut motion urging reduction of the price of country liquor. Sir *Joginder Singh*, Minister in charge of the Excise department, pointed out that the Government was deriving over a crore of rupees from this source and suggested that temperance should be taken up seriously by reformers.

The cut was withdrawn and the whole Excise demand was carried.

16th. MARCH :—A discussion on the representation of different communities in the public services monopolized today's debate in the Council. Three separate cuts, urging respectively adequate representation of Muslims, Indian Christians and Sikhs, moved by the members belonging to the respective communities, were discussed.

Mr. *Nanak Chand Pandit*, while opposing the cuts, emphasized that appointments should be made purely on merit and not on a communal basis but if it was decided to have fixed percentages for different communities, he submitted that this formula should be made applicable to all the services and if it was based on a population basis, he would urge that it would be made applicable to the whole country and not to the Punjab alone.

Chaudhri Afzal Haq accused the Government of having not still evolved a suitable formula for communal representation.

After the Sikh members had urged the representation of Sikhs, *Prof. Roberts* suggested the appointment of a committee which should fix the percentage for each community in the public services.

Rai Bahadur *Mukand Lal Puri* emphasised that appointments should not be filled on a communal basis, but by competition.

Nawab Muzaffar Khan, Revenue Member, replying to the debate, referred to the policy laid down by Sir Geoffrey de Montmorency, ex-Governor of the Punjab, in 1927 regarding the public services and said that the Government had been following that policy. The Revenue Member, admitting the under-representation of Muslims in the Forest department, said that the Government's difficulty was that since long there was no fresh recruitment. Nawab Muzaffar Khan, referring to the demand for a common formula for fixing the percentage of each community, said that the Government would welcome any such formula evolved by the House.

The movers withdrew their cuts and the whole demand was passed. The House then adjourned.

Debate on Hammond Report

19th. MARCH :—On the motion of Nawab Muzaffar Khan, Revenue Member, the Council discussed the Delimitation Committee's Report to-day. The *Revenue Member* invited the House to make specific proposals on the Report.

Mr. *Nanakchand Pandit*, opposing the Government motion for taking the the Report into consideration, stated that it was useless to discuss the Report at this stage. He took serious exception to the allotment of seats on the basis of urban and rural divisions. He referred, in this connection, to the suggestion made by him as a witness before the Delimitation Committee that seats should be divided on the basis of agriculturists and non-agriculturists, but this suggestion had not been accepted, with the result that representation of urban interests was very meagre, according to the recommendations of the Committee. He also pointed out that the Unionist Party in the Council only was represented on the Provincial Delimitation Committee.

The House rejected Mr. Nanak Chand's motion opposing the Government motion, and proceeded to discuss the Report.

The House agreed to the motion of Mr. *M. A. Ghani* recommending that all duly registered Trade Unions of industrial workers registered at least six months before the prescribed date for the preparation of the electoral rolls, should be included in the Punjab Trade Union constituency and that the Chief Inspector of Factories should be the Returning Officer.

The mover protested against the non-inclusion in the Punjab Trade Union constituency of Unions other than the North-West Railway Union.

On the motion of *Chaudhury Afzal Haq*, the House agreed that one rural seat be allotted for a Muslim woman. He pointed out that no seat had been allotted according to the Delimitation Committee's recommendatons to a woman.

The House rejected the motion for lowering the franchise qualification for landholder's constituencies from Rs. 500 to Rs. 250 land revenue.

The mover pleaded for wider enfranchisement for the four landholder's constituencies.

Sir *Firoze Khan Noon*, Minister for Education, opposing the motion said that in the future Punjab Legislative Assembly, special representation had been given to various interests, one of which was landholders. By adopting the motion before the House, they would only be strengthening the hands of those who pleaded for an Upper House for the Punjab.

The motion was vigorously opposed by landholding interests in the House.

Professor Roberts moved that the European and Anglo-Indian community be allowed to use the postal system of voting, which, he said, would enable Europeans and Anglo-Indians to spread over the Province to exercise their franchise.

The House agreed to the motion.

The House also accepted *Pir Akbar Ali's* motion that graduates of all recognised Universities living in the Punjab be entitled to vote for the University Constituency.

Mr. *Manohar Lal* (University) opposed it on the ground that under its proposal, even graduates of non-Indian Universities would be entitled to vote. Apart from that, in no other Province was such a system prevalent.

Sir *Firoze Khan Noon* and Mr. *Mukundlal Puri* also opposed the motion.

Mr. *Nanakchand Pandit* moved that seats should be so framed as to give agriculturists and non-agriculturists equal representation. He deplored that there should be hardly 75 non-agriculturists out of 170 members in the future House. He warned Government that such preponderance of agricultural interests would result in a loss of revenue to Government, as agriculturists were sure to make the best use of their large representation to their advantage. The House rejected the motion and adjourned.

20th. MARCH :—The resumed discussion on the report in the Council this morning centred round the question of urban *versus* rural representation. The House accepted *Chaudhri Chatu Ram's* motion that one of the eight seats allotted to the general urban constituencies be taken out and given to the rural general, while Lala Jyoti Prasad's amendment to this motion seeking two more seats for the urban general constituencies was automatically talked out. Chaudhri Chotu Ram contended that the rural areas had much less representation than they were entitled to on the population basis, while Lala Jyoti Prasad felt that, compared with 26 seats allotted to the general rural constituencies, the 8 seats given to urban interests were meagre.

Pandit Nanak Chand moved that the recommendation of the Delimitation Committee relating to the division of constituencies as urban and rural be set aside and that only towns with a population of 50,000 and above be classified as urban. He argued that the present division adopted by the Committee was done at the dictation of the agriculturist members, who predominated on the provincial Delimitation Committee and was artificial.

Nawab Muzzaffar Khan, Revenue Member, explaining the position with regard to urban and rural seats, said, after the Poona Pact the Government had to give two seats to urban interests at the expense of rural seats. Appealing to the Rural party to be generons, he pointed out that the representation of rural interests according to the Delimitation Committee's proposals was nearly double the present representation.

Pandit Nanak Chand's motion was rejected.

Sremathi Lekhwati Jain's motion that only women voters should vote for women candidates was carried, as also Mr. *M. L. Puri's* motion that the system of voting at the final election in constituencies where members of scheduled castes were members of a scheduled caste were not cumulative.

A motion recommending that the franchise qualification of income-tax on an income of Rs. 10,000 for the commerce constituency be lowered to Rs. 5,000, was also adopted before the House concluded its discussion on the report.

VOTING ON BUDGET DEMANDS (CONTD.)

23rd. MARCH :—The Council rejected to-day *Choudhri Afzal Haq's* cut motion urging on the Government the necessity for separating Judicial and Executive functions. The supporters of the motion pointed out that there could not be justice to people so long as Judicial and Executive functions were not separated. They further reminded the Government of the promises made in the past.

Sir Donald Boyd, Finance Member, denied the charge that the Government had not done anything towards this demand. He said that civil work had been entirely taken from Magistrates. Deputy Commissioners were empowered under the Criminal Procedure Code to maintain Law and Order, to disperse unlawful assemblies, etc. and if they had no control over Magistrates, how could they carry on those functions ? Sir Donald thought that it would be extremely difficult and rather expensive to fulfil the demand. According to the committee appointed by the Government to enquire into this matter, there would be extra expenditure of Rs. 8 lakhs yearly, if the Judiciary were separated from Executive functions. Concluding, he said: "We are getting on very well and there is no justification for incurring extra expenditure of Rs. 8 lakhs."

A cut motion urging that recruitment to the Indian Civil Service be totally stopped was withdrawn. Mr. *Nanakchand Pandit*, opposing the cut, expressed the fear that Punjab Civil Service men would be influenced by communal pressure under the future constitution, while I. C. S. men recruited by open competition could be relied upon to discharge their duties impartially. He pointed out that while there were several complaints of corruption and favouritism against Punjab Civil Service men there was not a single complaint against I. C. S. men.

The *Chief Secretary*, replying to the debate on the cut motion urging that more senior officers be appointed as district officers, stated that it was wrong to assume that junior officers were not capable. He referred to Mr. Jawaharlal Nehru who, he said, had become President of the Congress while he was hardly 40 years old. He added that out of 29 Deputy Commissioners in the Punjab, 19 were Indians.

24th. MARCH :—The problem of unemployment in the Punjab formed the subject of a lively debate in the Council to-day. A discussion was raised by moving a cut motion, the object of which was to draw the attention of the Government to the growing problem of the unemployed in the province and to request the Government to find out ways and means to solve it.

Mr. *Joyti Pershad*, moving the cut motion, pointed out that unemployment was growing by leaps and bounds in the province. When an employed failed to secure a job, the speaker said, he either committed suicide or became a criminal. It was the duty of the Government to provide work for unemployed young men as was done in other countries of the world.

Mr. *M. A. Ghani*, labour member, referred to an incident when railway authorities had to summon a fire brigade which dispersed a big crowd of employed who had collected at the Mughalpura workshops for recruitment by throwing water on them and urged the Government that it was the primary duty of the State to see that pepole were employed. Mr. Ghani suggested the appointment of special officers, the opening of an appointment bureau to collect figures of unemployed and find employment for workers. and the establishing of a foreign labour department which should supply workers to foreign countries

Mr. *Nanakchand Pandit* charged the Government for not tackling the vital question and warned the Government that if nothing would be done towards this question the Government would be faced with an economic revolution. He suggested the development of industries.

Dr. *Sir Gokulchand Narang*, Minister of Local Self-Government thought that the causes of unemployment were the rapid increase of population and a rise in the standard of living. As regards the defect in the present system of education, he said that had he been given control of education, he would have fixed three hours a day for the students of the primary classes to attend school and the remaining three hours to sit either on shops or work in field. When a boy, passed the primary examinations he felt it below his dignity to sit at the shop of his father. After passing the matriculation examination he would allow only those students who had either means or were exceptionally intelligent, to join colleges. The rise in the standard of living was a curse. He would at the same time welcome a rise in the standard of villagers. The standard of living of the educated class had risen abnormally high, particularly in the Punjab. Educated persons wasted money in purchasing toilets,

They depended on the industries of foreign countries. Crores of rupees were sent to foreign countries every year.

The mover withdrew the cut motion. As to-day was the last day of Government demands for grants, the President applied the guillotine at 5 p. m. and all the remaining 31 demands were passed. The Council then adjourned till 26.

Duty on Imported Wheat

26th. MARCH :—The Council unanimously passed a non-official resolution recommending the Government to convey to the Government of India in view of prevailing low prices that the import duty on wheat be raised to Rs. two per hundredweight. *Nawab Muzzaffar Khan*, the Revenue Member, supporting the resolution, said that the Pvnjab Government had already strongly represented the matter to the Government of India, and promised further to convey the wish of the House to them.

Entertainment Duty Bill

30th. MARCH: —The Punjab Entertainment Duty Bill (official measure), as reported by the Select Committee, was discussed and passed to-day. Mr. *Nanakchand Pandit*, opposing the motion that the Bill, as reported by the Select Committee, be taken into consideration, said that Government was throttling the cinema industry in the Punjab which was still in its infancy, by such legislation. The motion for consideration was passed. *Professor Roberts* moved an amendment, which aimed at exempting from tax all payment for admission to entertainment up to one rupee. The amendment was, however, rejected without much discussion.

Prof. Roberts moved another amendment that horse racing under approved conditions be excluded from the provisions of this Act. He said that Government should encourage the horse-breeding industry in the Punjab by exempting horse races from the tax. Mr. *Sampuran Singh*, supporting the motion, urged that Government should encourage and patronize horse races, so that the horse-breeding industry in the Province might develop.

Mr. *Nanakchand Pundit*, opposing the amendment, thought that horse race was gambling pure and simple. There were other ways of encouraging the horse-breeding industry but not by races. Sir *Donald Boyd*, Finance Member, opposed the amendment, which was rejected. The remaining clauses of the Bill were passed without discussion.

Debtors' Protection Bill

A number of non-official amendments to the Punjab Debtors' Protection Bill, as recommended by the Governor, were rejected to-day by the Council and the bill in the recommended form was passed. It will be recalled that the Bill was passed last session rejecting certain Government amendments relating to exemption of ancestral property from attachment. The Bill, sent back to the House during the present session in recommended form, incorporated these amendments.

Non-official Resolutions

31st. MARCH: —The Council to-day passed a non-official resolution of *Prof. Roberts* recommending to Government that active steps be taken to found a provincial land mortgage bank in the Punjab.

Mr. *M. A. Ghani*, labour leader's resolution recommending to Government that the minimum salary paid to all Government servants should not be less than Rs. 30 per month was rejected by 47 votes to 8.

Sir *Donald Boyd*, Finance Member, opposing the resolution expressed sympathy with the mover but pointed out that it was a question of supply and demand. When private servants were available at less than Rs. 30 a month how could Government be justified in spending more public money ? The Finance Member pointed out the difficulties in finding minimum wages and told the House that there would be an annual increase of one crore of rupees if the Government would accept the resolution and put it into operation. Hence the proposition was impracticable.

Another resolution which was withdrawn on Government assurance recommended the sanctioning of a substantial grant for the maintenance of the Jubilee Red Cross Sanitorium at Sambli to benefit the tubercular patients of the province.

The House was discussing a resolution recommending to Government to place a limit on the number of licences granted annually to new entrants to the legal profession in the Punjab, when it adjourned *sine die.*

The U. P. Legislative Council

LIST OF MEMBERS

The Hon'ble Sir Sita Ram (*President*).

Nawabzada Muhammad Liaquat Ali Khan, (*Deputy President.*)

1. The Hon'ble Mr. J. M. Clay (*Finance Member*)
2. The Hon'ble Kunwar Sir Maharaj Singh (*Home Member*)
3. The Hon'ble Nawab Sir Muhammad Yusuf (*Minister for Local Self-Govt.*)
4. The Hon'ble Sir Jwala P. Srivastava (*Minister for Education*)
5. Mr. H. Bomford
6. Mr. J. L. Sathe
7. Mr. A. B. Reid
8. Mr. P. M. Kharegat
9. Mr. A. A. Waugh
10. Rai Bahadur Mr. Phul Chand Mogha
11. Mr. H. R. Harrop
12. Mr. H. J. Frampton
13. Babu Himmat Singh K. Maheshari
14. Babu Pratap Shankar
15. Rai Bahadur Pandit Brij Chand Sharma
16. Khan Bahadur Munshi Mushtaq Ali Khan
17. Rai Bahadur Ram Babu Saksena
18. Mr. D. L. Drake Brockman
19. Mr. C. S. Venkatachar
20. Mr. C. W. Gwynne
21. Lady Kailash Srivastava
22. Khan Bahadur Maulvi Fasi-ud-din
23. Captain K. O. Carleton
24. Mr. E. Ahmad Shah
25. Rai Sahib Babu Rama Charana
26. Mr. Perma
27. Rai Bahadur Babu Awadh Behari Lal
28. Rai Bahadur Babu Kamta Prasad Kakkar
29. Chaudhri Ram Dayal
30. Chaudhuri Jagarnath
31. The Hon'ble Sir Sita Ram
32. Chaudhri Baldeva
33. Rai Bahadur Sahu Jwala Saran Kothiwala
34. Mr. Tappu Ram
35. Pandit Moti Lal Bhargava
36. Raja Bahadur Kushal Pal Singh
37. Chaudhri Ram Chandra
38. Chaudhri Ghasita
39. Rai Bahadur Chaudhri Raghuraj Singh
40. Chaudhri Arjuna Singh
41. Rao Bahadur Thakur Pratap Bhan Singh
42. Rao Sahib Thakur Shiva Dhyan Singh
43. Rai Bahadur Kunwar Girwar Singh
44. Pandit Joti Prasad Upadhyaya
45. Chaudhri Dhirya Singh
46. Rao Krishna Pal Singh
47. Rai Bahadur Kunwar Dhakan Lal
48. Thakur Balwant Singh Gahlot
49. Rai Bahadur Brij Lal Badhwar
50. Rao Bahadur Kunwar Sardar Singh
51. Rai Bahadur Babu Manmohan Sahai
52. Babu Ram Bahadur Saksena
53. Lala Shyam Lal
54. Rai Sahib Babu Kamta Nath Saksena
55. Kunwar Jagbhan Singh
56. Thakur Keshava Chandra Singh
57. Mr. Brijnandan Lal
58. Rao Narsingh Rao
59. Rai Sahib Ram Adhin
60. Mr. Bhondu Ram
61. Raja Bhagwati Prasad Singh
62. Rai Govind Chandra
63. Pandit Shri Sadayatan Pande
64. Raja Sri Krishna Dutt Dube
65. Rai Bahadur Babu Jagadeva Roy
66. Mr. Dahari
67. Rai Sahib Rai Rajeshwari Prasad
68. Rai Sahib Babu Adya Prasad
69. Raja Shivapati Singh
70. Thakur Giriraj Singh
71. Pandit Prem Ballabh Belwal
72. Thakur Jang Bahadur Singh Bisht
73. Sardar Bahadur Thakur Narayan Singh Negi
74. Pandit Brahma Dutt Bajpai *alias* Bhaiya Sahib
75. Rai Bahadur Thakur Hanuman Singh
76. Rai Bahadur Lal Sheo Pratap Singh
77. Kunwar Diwakar Prakash Singh
78. Thakur Muneshwar Bakhsh Singh
79. Thakur Jaindra Bahadur Singh
80. Raja Jagdambika Pratap Narayan Singh

81. Raja Ambikeshwar Pratap Singh
82. Raja Birendra Bikram Singh
83. Rai Bahadur Kunwar Surendra Pratah Sahi
84. Mr. C. Y. Chintamani
85. Rai Rajeshwar Bali
86. Mr. Zahur Ahmad
87. Syed Ali Zaheer
88. Khan Sahib Sahibzada Haji Shaikh Muhammad Rashid-ud-din Ahmad
89. Syed Yusuf Ali
90. Khan Bahadur Muhammad Maqsud Ali Khan
91. Khan Bahadur Shah Nazar Husain
92. Captain Nawab Muhammad Jamshed Ali Khan
93. Nawabzada Muhammad Liaquat Ali Khan
94. Hafiz Muhammad Ibrahim
95. Mr. Muhammad Rahmat Khan
96. Khan Bahadur Haji Muhammad Obaidur Rahaman Khan
97. Khan Bahadur Muhammad Hadiyar Khan
98. Munshi Amir Hasan Khan
99. Khan Bahadur Maulvi Saiyid Habibullah
100. Khan Bahadur Haji M. Nasarullah
101. Khan Bahadur Saiyid Zahid Ali Sabzposh
102. Khan Bahadur Shaikh Ghulam Husain
103. Khan Bahadur Hafiz Ghazanfarullah
104. Khan Bahadur Saiyid Jamid Hosain
105. Khan Sahib Shaikh Afzal-ud-din Hyder
106. Khan Bahadur Maulvi Muhammad Fazal-ur Rahman Khan
107. Khan Bahadur Sirdar Muhammad Shakirdad Khan
108. Khan Sahib Muhammad Imtiaz Ahmad
109. Raja Saiyid Muhammad Sa'adat Ali Khan
110. Shaikh Muhammad Habibullah
111. Raja Saiyid Ahmad Ali Khan Alvi
112. Raja Sir Muhammad Ejaz Rasul Khan
113 Raja Saiyid Muhammud Mehdi
114. Mr. L. M. Medley
115. Rai Bahadur Lala Ananda Sarup
116. Rai Bahadur Lala Bihari Lal
117. Chaudhri Muhammad Ali
118. Rai Bahadur Lala Prag Narayan
119. Raja Bisheshwar Dayal Seth
120. Raja Jagannath Bakhsh Singh
121. Mr. E. M. Souter
122. Rai Bahadur Vikramjit Singh
123. Munshi Gajadhar Prasad

Proceedings of the Council

Budget Session—Lucknow—22nd. February to 28th. March '36

Tributes to Late King

The opening day of the United Provinces Legislative Council commenced its Budget session at Lucknow on the **22nd. February 1936** and was devoted to the condolence motion relating to King George's death. All sections of the House joined in paying tributes to the memory of the late King. The following resolution was passed after which the House adjourned till the 24th. :—

"This Council records its sincere grief on the occasion of the death of His late Majesty King George V, and its deep sympathy with His Majesty King Edward, Her Gracious Majesty Queen Mary and other Members of the Royal Family in their great bereavement. It desires to offer His Majesty its humble and hearty congratulations upon his accession and assures him of its loyal devotion to his Royal person."

Budget Estimates for 1936-37

24th. FEBRUARY :—The Budget estimates for 1936-37 was presented to-day in the Council by Mr. *J. M. Clay*, Finance Member. It showed that the Government hoped to obtain revenue amounting to Rs. 11,70,96,600, the expenditure being Rs. 12,44,66,000, thus leaving a revenue deficit of Rs. 73,70,000. With the help of a loan of Rs. 77,86,000, the receipts under debt heads are estimated to be Rs. 331,88,000 and disbursements under these heads amount to Rs. 2,58,17,000 resulting in a surplus of Rs. 73,71,000 which exactly cancels the revenue deficit.

The revised estimates for 1935-36 show that the anticipated deficit in the revenue budget would be reduced to Rs. 4,64,000, though the Government originally budgeted for a deficit of Rs. 30,39,000. The Government hoped to reduce this deficit by a half through two taxation measures, which the Council rejected. Orders were then issued to all departments to effect cuts in sanctioned expenditure, aggregating to Rs. 15 lakhs and owing to these cuts and certain other variations in income and expenditure, the deficit is expected to be reduced to the above figure.

Coming to the new budget, Mr. Clay observed that it was impossible to regard it with equanimity. Apart from the falling off in revenue, the main items of increased expenditure consisted in larger debt and pensionary charges which he feared would grow in the future. Another special charge will be the expense in the first election under the new Constitution. Definitely new expenditure, both recurring and non-recurring, amounted to only Rs. 1,20,000. There was no addition to the meagre provision of one lakh for rural development, and "it is hard to see how it will be possible to finance, in the present conditions, any measure which Government may desire to undertake in response to the recommendations of the Sapru Committee, urgent and vitally important though they may be."

Enumerating the measures of economy contemplated by Government, Mr. Clay explained that only two methods were possible for further amelioration of the position, namely new taxation and subvention from outside. In view of the clearly expressed intentions of the Council, the Government are making no proposals for fresh taxation, while the question of subvention is being investigated into by Sir Otto Niemeyer.

Hydro-Electric Scheme

25th. FEBRUARY :—The Council spent practically the whole day debating on the resolution moved by the Finance Member, Mr. *J. M. Clay*, recommending to the Government that the revised estimates of the Hydro-Electric Grid Scheme as amended by the Grid Enquiry Committee of 1935 may be approved and the scheme completed during the years 1936-37 and 1937-38.

It might be recalled that the revised scheme involving a total expenditure of Rs. 337 lakhs were examined by a Committee of Experts, which came to the conclusion that it was technically and economically sound, and should produce the results anticipated and recommended that it should be proceeded with in accordance with the programme outlined.

After tracing the origin and development of the scheme, and describing the growing popularity of tube wells among cultivators, Mr. Clay said: "In 1935, Sir William Stampe, Chief Engineer, came to the conclusion that the scheme originally sanctioned by the Secretary of State had undergone such large changes that he considered it necessary to recast it in its entirety, and the whole position, accordingly, was examined by a Committee of Experts in 1935, whose report was eminently satisfactory." The mover next detailed the scope of the scheme and dwelt on its financial aspects.

Mr. *C. Y. Chintamani*, Leader of the Opposition, moved an amendment, generally approving the revised estimate of the scheme, but recommending to the Government that progress in the execution of the scheme, should be made with due regard to the financial results so far obtained and the effects of the Grid Scheme on general irrigation. He urged that Government should not proceed with the scheme with undue haste. He also referred, in this connection, to the financial difficulties of the Government on account of which they were not in a position to give effect to the recommendations of the Sapru Committee Report.

Mr. *Clay* accepted the amendment on condition that the House would not cut down any budget provisions for advancement of the scheme.

Naik Girls' Protection Act

26th. FEBRUARY :—The first division of the Budget session took place to-day on an amendment by *Thakur Jung Bahadur Bisht* (Almora) to the proposed alteration in rule 13 under sec. 7 of the Naik Girls' Protection Act. He wanted that the two ladies and one member of the Legislature who would be chosen to serve on the Advisory Committee should be Hindus.

Sir *Jwala Prasad Srivastava*, Minister-in-charge, was over-ruled by the President when he raised a point of order that no amendment could be made to the proposed rule. Government members remained neutral like many Muslims. Of the Muslims who however voted, the majority supported the amendment while only a few were against the amendment which was carried by the House by 35 votes to four (Nawabzada Liaquat Ali Khan, Mr. Shah Nazir Hussain, Md. Rahmat Khan and Mr. E. Ahmad Shah).

Govt.'s Retrenchment Proposals

Proceedings were enlivened towards the fag end of the day when Mr. *J. M. Clay*, Finance Member initiated a discussion on the retrenchment scheme of the Government. After dwelling at length on the measures the Government had taken from time to time to minimise expenditure, Mr. Clay said that a small official committee was appointed last year to explore further avenues of retrenchment. Originally, the Government had intended to retrench expenditure to the extent of Rs. 30 lakhs, but when they came down to realities, they found it was extremely difficult to reach that figure and finally decided on Rs. 20 lakhs of which Rs. 12 lakhs were to be distributed over the Reserved Departments and Rs. 8 lakhs over the Transferred Departments.

He added that a fairly large proportion of Government expenditure was absorbed by salaries, it being roughly Rs. 5,08,000 out of a total expenditure of Rs. 13,50,000 and it was impossible to reduce it without a salary cut or abolition of some posts, but he would say no more about the salary cuts until he had heard the views of the members. He next proceeded to deal with various items of retrenchment contemplated by the Government. As regards the abolition of the Jhansi Division and four districts, the Finance Member declared that Government put forward these proposals with the utmost reluctance, and they would welcome any means, by which this could be avoided as they appeared to be unpopular. He further pointed out that the inquiry by the Inspector-General showed that there was room for reduction of Rs. 4 and one-fourth lakhs in the Police Department. There was also in the Budget of 1936-37 an item for Rs. 8 lakhs under the head "Excise", which Government hoped to obtain by change in the system of auctioning opium and other drugs shops, and if the House so desired, Government was prepared to consider the suggestion made by the Minister-in-charge that this expected income be set off against the proposed retrenchment in Transferred Departments.

Among the important proposals for retrenchment are the abolition of the Jhansi division and the districts of Pilibhit, Derha Dun, Ballia and Sultanpur or Partabgarh and reduction in the strength of the Chief Court of Oudh by one Judge, reduction in the cadres of Sub-Judges and Munsifs, appointment of retired judges to the High Court to clear off arrears and reductions in special pays, travelling allowances, house rents, etc.

The Governor's Address

27th. FEBRUARY :—Addressing the Council this morning, *H. E. the Governor* traversed the entire field of Provincial administration, making a comprehensive survey of the activities of various Government Departments during the last years.

At the outset, he referred to the death of King George V and said : "None in the British Empire is more ready to respond to such a conception of Royal character than the Indian people, and they knew well how deep was His Majesty's interest in all that concerned them." Proceeding, H. E. the Governor referred to the coming Constitution, which would probably be introduced in a little more than a year, and he would not have the opportunity of addressing the Council.

He next dwelt at length on the new movement for rural development made possible by a grant from the Government of India and stressed that the scheme of development had been applied to every district of the Province. The work of rural development no longer depended on the enthusiasm of a particular officer, but was now organised all over the Province, in which Commissioners and District Officers were doing their best to ensure the proper launching of the scheme, with the assistance of non-officials. In this connection, he made special reference to the impetus given to the scheme by landlords. The movement had already gained sufficient ground to create an impression, and it had engendered a new hope in the villages. The object of the movement lay in co-ordinating and making readily available to villagers the work of different departments, particularly Agriculture, Public Health and Education. "The method is to get villagers do things for themselves, with a clear realisation of the advantages of the new activities and ideals. It is necessary to gain the confidence of the corporate spirit of enterprise and co-operation."

Nine health units had been established all over the Province, each unit representing a compact area, covering some 150 villages with a population of 35,000. Other schemes of development included improved water-supply, construction of embankments, improvements of cattle and poultry breeding. In this connection, he referred to the work of the Rural Development Officer, Mr. Venkatachar and the special interest of the Minister in the project.

Prrceeding, Sir Harry Haig suggested the introduction of a new staple crop form of cotton in view of the dwindling returns of sugarcane, which would greatly benefit the economic position of the Province. Introduction of cheap electrical power was made possible under the new Hydro-Electric Scheme. The sugarcane industry of the Province would receive an impetus in connection with small-scale production of sugarcane. H. E. the Governor next referred to the Exhibition in the coming winter at Lucknow with a view to bringing the producer and the buyer in closer contact and benefit the resources of provincial income.

The Governor next dealt at length on the resources of the Province and pointed out that all such developments enumerated had been made possible by grants from the Government of India, but they faced the problem of deficit when the Province had to depend on her own resources. The problem of deficit, though not new, had been enlarged by the question of elections under the coming Constitution, and though the cost of elections will not recur yearly, the enhanced cost of administration under the new Constitution will amount to something like the cost of elections. The Land Revenue policy of the Povince will involve considerable expenditure for sometime, but bring return later. Examination of the present resources of the Province have proved that there will be a serious gap between income and expenditure for the next five years and it is impossible to expect the deficit to be covered fully. The entire case in this connection was laid before the Nimeyer Committee.

His Excellency referred to the excellent work of the Sapru Unemployment Committee, which was of vital interest to the country, but the scheme involved expenditure in which the Province faced a deficit. H. E. the Governor hoped that constructive proposals would be forthcoming from the debate on the subject in the House. The Province had been free from political agitation last year and though there were feelings between communities at present they had been localised.

Concluding, the Governor expressed the hope that under the new Constitution, there would be progressive conciliation of views in the interest of the two communities. "I trust, therefore, that in the new Government, we shall find Hindus and Muslims working together, not primarily regarding themselves as members of one community or other, but jointly pursuing a policy that is in their joint interests. If we keep in front the goal of common good and development of the Province, I feel sure that sectional interests will fall to their proper perspective."

GOVT'S. RETRENCHMENT SCHEME (CONTD.)

Discussion on the Government's retrenchment scheme was not concluded when the Council rose for the day to-day. There was again stiff opposition from the Opposition members who opposed the abolition of some Districts and Tashils. One member said that the people of the Districts and Tashils concerned would be willing to pay new taxes rather than agree to the abolition proposals. Another suggestion put forward in this connection was a permanent cut in the salaries of Government servants, it being ten centum in the case of those drawing salaries of Rs. 500 and below and 25 centum for the rest.

The Home Member, *Kunwar Sir Maharaj Singh* assured the House that Government did not propose to abolish the concession of free return tickets to their homes to prisoners on their release nor any relating to the supply of cheaper diet in jails. As a matter of fact, the Inspector-General of Prisons' proposals were designed to remove the monotony, in jail diet, which were under consideration.

28th. FEBRUARY :—The debate concluded to-day after a spirited and vigorous denunciation by Mr. *Chintamani*, leader of the Opposition of the I. C. S. guardianship of the provincial finances since the inauguration of the present Reforms, the result of which was writ large on every page of the financial reports of the United Provinces. Mr. Chintamani urged that the only remedy was to be found in the reconstruction of the entire system of administration from the point of view of the people administered and he was loudly cheered at the conclusion of his speech by the whole House.

The debate was wound up by Mr. *J. M. Clay*, Finance Member, who thought that it was 'definitely unfair' to accuse the Government of having pursued recklessly an extravagant course during the last 10 or 12 years. He declared that the proposed abolition of districts and tashils would be reconsidered if the House could find some new form of revenue to make up for the shortage and also to provide funds to implement the recommendations of the Sapru Committee..

The Council rejected Rai Bahadur *Thakur Hanuman Singh's* amendment to reduce the number of first class districts to the status of second class districts but carried unanimously Babu *Ram Bahadur Saskena's* amendment that effect should not be given to the proposed abolition of districts.

The *Finance Member* next moved a resolution extending concession to the Minister in the matter of house rents paid by them. After asking the Council to agree to their retrenchment proposals there seemed absolutely no justification for the Government to seek the Council's approval for concession to the Ministers who are neither ill-paid nor poverty-stricken. The resolution was opposed by *Rai Rajeshwar Bali* and Mr. *Chintamani*, though it was eventually carried by the House.

The *Education Minister* next invited a discussion on the report of the proceedings of the Muslim Education Conference, but the House accepted an amendment moved by *Nawabzada Liaqat Ali Khan* recommending the Government to publish the report in the *Gazette* with a view to eliciting public opinion within two months and then publish their own decisions after considering the opinions so far received. The Council then adjourned till the 2nd. March.

DEBATE ON UNEMPLOYMENT COMM. REPORT

2nd. MARCH :—The debate on the report of the Unemployment Committee commenced with a speech by the Education Minister, Sir *Jawala Prasad Srivastva*, who was responsible for the setting up of the Committee in 1934. The Minister on behalf of the Government expressed his deep sense of gratitude to the chairman of the Committee, the Rt. Hon. Sir Tej Bahadur Sapru, for the immense labour undertaken by him at great personal sacrifice. 'The Government can do very little without money,' said the Minister in appealing to the House 'to find a treasure somewhere' so that they might be able to implement the Committee's recommendations, which in his opinion were very useful and were being examined by an officer placed on special duty.

The Rt. Hon. Sir *Tej Bahadur Sapru*, whom the House gave an enthusistic ovation as he rose to speak, explained the main recommendations of the Committee in an hour's speech marked by eloquence, ability, lucidity, cogency, clearness and a masterly array of facts and figures. He spoke with utmost frankness when he said that he would have refused to look at the proposal when he was asked to undertake the duties of the chairmanship of the Unemployment Committee, had he been told that at the end of their labours the Government could find no money to implement their recommendations. After graphically describing the magnitude of the problem which none could characterize as a 'political stunt', the Rt. Hon. Sir Tej Bahadur Sapru dealt with the acute discontent and bitterness prevailing among the educated young men who were unable to secure employment and outlined measures required to alleviate them. He charged both the Government and the society with the neglect of the important responsibility towards the rising generation and protested against the policy of retrenchment followed by the Government which bred discontent among the lower ranks without touching men high up in Government service who enjoyed statutory protection. He wound up his remarkable speech with an earnest appeal for the provision of funds to tackle the problem of unemployment, not avoiding taxation if it was necessary and if it could be reserved for the purpose. The distinguished speaker was loudly cheered at the conclusion of his very able speech.

Nine members took part in to-day's discussion, most of whom dwelt on the paramount pressing necessity to tackle the unemployment problem on the lines suggested by the Sapru Committee to find the money needed for the purpose.

3rd. MARCH :—No less than 16 members took part in to-day's discussion including the Leader of the Opposition, Mr. C. Y. Chintamani, Nawabzada Liaqat Ali

Khan, of the leader of the Democratic party, and Rai Bahadur Babu Vikramjit Singh, leader of Constitutional party. From the official *bloc* there were four speeches by Mr. S. P. Shah, officer on special duty, who examined the Unemployment Committee's report, Mr. Kharegat, Education secretary, Mr. Harrop, Director of Public Instruction, and Mr. Clay, Finance Member.

Opinion was not unanimous as regards the need for taxation with a view to providing necessary funds for the purpose of implementing the committee's recommendations. Not unnaturally the Government was severely censured for its career of reckless extravagance in the past and its unpardonable reluctance to reduce the princely salaries paid to the top. *Nawabzada Liaqat Ali Khan* forcibly expressed this point of view and stoutly opposed the levy of fresh taxation, suggesting that it was the Government's primary responsibility to find money for the solution of the problem of unemployment. Mr. *Chintamani*, on the contrary, took a different view of the matter, having regard to the fact that educated middle class unemployment had become so acute as to constitute a grave public danger of to-day and an increasing menace to public safety in years to come. He, however, insisted that there must be a statutory guarantee that whatever additional revenue was placed at the Government's disposal should be exclusively applied to measures for relief of unemployment and should not be absorbed in the general revenues of the province.

Mr. *J. M. Clay*, Finance Member, speaking on behalf of the Government, said that it was intended to bring forward two measures of taxation : increasing stamp duties and court fees when the Council would re-assemble after the Holi and Id holidays and he gave an undertaking that if the Bills were passed the Government would earmark three lakhs this year and recurring sums in succeeding years for the purpose of implementing the committee's reconsiderations. He further announced that one lakh would be allotted for expansion or development in various transferred departments which in the result would have an effect to unemployment. In addition the Government undertook to abandon their idea regarding the abolition of five districts and six tahsils, the loss of possible saving from this latter undertaking amounting to four and half to five lakhs. He also promised to earmark the sum of four lakhs for the above mentioned purpose. He added : 'It is a perfectly fair offer and there is no loophole for wriggling out of the promise.' The undertaking given by Mr. Clay reassured the House that the Government were earnest on implementing the committee's recommendations and it is very likely that the coming taxation measures might not share the same fate as their predecessors of last year.

Sir Tej Bahadur Sapru in his second speech stressed that the Government of India could not divest themselves of their share of responsibility in tackling the unemployment problem and urged that wisdom, experience, expediency and self-interest counselled that they should frankly recognise that it was time for them to bestir themselves in the matter lest they might be overwhelmed by a deluge which, he could distinctly foresee, would overtake us if the elders of this generation refused to be interested in problems affecting the mind of the younger generation who were their future hop e. He concluded his speech amidst loud and prolonged applause and the Council adjourned till March 11.

General Discussion of Budget

11th. MARCH :—The general discussion on the budget which commenced to-day was quite dull and uninteresting. The non-official benches looked practically deserted. 'I have often noticed,' remarked the President, 'that the first day's reluctance is compensated for by next day's eagerness to catch the eye of the Chair. This is rather embarrassing and I hope that hon. members will not be reluctant to catch the eye of the Chair as quickly as possible'. The President's apprehensions proved true and none got up to speak at 3-30 p. m. as the result of which the Council was adjourned. The keynote of all speeches was a vigorous plea for a percentage cut in the salaries of the services, both imperial and provincial. Most of the speakers congratulated the Finance Member and Mr. Sathe, Finance Secretary, on the presentation of a 'lucid' budget.

Court Fees Act Amend. Bill

13th. MARCH :—By 66 votes against 23 the Council to-day carried the motion of the *Finance Member* to take into consideration the Bill amending the Court Fees Act. The Government majority was both astounding and unexpected for it was generally calculated that the division might be a close one in view of the fact that a similar Bill together with the Stamp Duties Bill had been unanimously rejected by the House at this time last year.

No party in the House made the question a party issue and the members belonging to the same party were ranged in hostile camps. Lobbying had been going on briskly for some time past, those who were primarily anxious to save certain districts from the threatened abolition being extraordinarily active.

The cat was out of the bag when *Sheikh Muhammad Habibullah* openly confessed that he was a signatory to an application to the Government agreeing to the new taxation if the Government would not carry out their threat to abolish the districts and tehsils. Asked by Rai Rajeshwar Bali who the sponsors of this unprecedented and novel move were, Sheikh Habibullah candidly said that he was one of them. Further light was thrown on this mysterious petition by the reference made to it by the Finance Member himself in his reply to the debate. He said that it was signed by 26 members and he was not going to betray their confidence by mentioning their names. Rai Rajeshwar Bali, Mr. Chintamani, Nawabzada Liaqat Ali Khan pressed that the secret document be read out but the Finance Member refused to comply.

14th. MARCH :—The House passed into law to-day both the Bills enhancing the court-fees and stamp duties whose life was limited to three years. The Finance Member, who was opposed to the amendment seeking to limit the duration of the Court-fees Bill which the Government intended to make permanent, claimed a division after the President had actually put the amendment to the House and declared it carried. The President ascertained that the Finance Member had not actualty get up in time.

The *Finance Member* resisted two amendments moved by the Leader of the Opposition seeking a statutory guarantee regarding money to be spent on implementing the Unemployment Committee's recommendations and the duration of the Court fees Bill being limited to two years. The House divided on both the amendments which were rejected.

Voting on Budget Demands

16th. MARCH :—The voting on demands for grants commenced to-day, the first of them being the budget for the jails and convict settlements. *Sir Maharaj Singh* made a brief speech at the outset, dwelling on the salient features of administration of jails and emphasizing that the financial stringency stood in the way of several reforms recommended by the All-India . Jails Committee of 1919 and the U. P. Jails Enquiry Committee of 1929 being carried into affect.

The *Home Member* and the first Indian inspector-General of prisons, *Major Salamatullah* were both complemented by the leader of the Opposition, Mr. *C. Y. Chintamani* and some other members .for a number of improvements effected in the jails. Many interesting points were raised on the cut motion in the entire demand as regards the method of recruitment of superintendents of jails, classification and treatment of prisoners, racial discrimination etc. by Mr. Chintamani and the Home Member gave a sympathetic reply. The Home Member acknowledged that the Government were indebted for reforms effected in the administration of jails to the Jail Enquiry Committee's report and public opinion and above all to hon. members of the House who from time to time made valuable suggestions. While a spirit of responsiveness was shown by all Indian Home Members during the reformed regime a great deal more could certainly have been achieved in the way of reform of jails, if the reserved half of the Government had been responsible instead of being merely responsive to public opinion as voiced in the Legislative Council.

17th. MARCH :—The land revenue demand was discussed in to-day's Council. Many token cut motions were made by landlord members on varied matters of interest pertaining to their order and not one of them was passed. The cause of small zemindars and small tenants in connection with the coming settlements found a sturdy champion in *Rao Krishna Pal Singh* whose plea for sympathy for them found an answering echo in Government benches. The revenue secretary, Mr. *A. A. Waugh*, in a sympathetic speech explained that the law, as it stood, showed considerable sympathy to petty zemindars and poor tenants.

Many zemindars and taluqdars not unnaturally voiced their serious apprehensions that the coming settlement operations might eventually result in large enhancement of their revenue assessment and these apprehensions were set at rest by a very reassuring reply by Mr. *J. M. Clay*, Finance Member, who declared, 'Government will most rigorously and scrupulously observe all undertakings which they have given in the communique and in public pronouncements.' The demands were still under discussion when the Council adjourned.

18th. MARCH :—The landlord members strongly supported the cut motion of *Rao Krishna Pal Singh* to-day and expressed once again their feelings of resentment against the antiquated, barbarous and thoroughly unpopular method of issuing coercive processes and warrants of arrest against defaulting zamindars who failed to pay their land revenue in time. Mr. *Clay*, Finance Member, explained that coercive processes had progressively declined in number in recent years while warrants of arrest were mostly issued for realisation of arrears due to co-operative banks which, under the law, had to be realized as land revenue.

Another motion which evoked an interesting debate was made by the same member advocating the abolition of the institution of village *patwaris* on the ground that they maintained incorrect land records with a monetary gain and not infrequently gave rise to disputes between zamindars and tenants. While there was nothing but downright condemnation for *patwaris* as a class, the opinion was, however, divided among the landlord members as regards the abolition of their posts. Government viewed the proposal with strong disfavour, holding that revenue administration would be impossible to carry on without the 28,000 *patwaris* working in the province.

The Education demand was next taken up. Only one motion was discussed drawing attention to the inadequate grants made to the Allahabad University. While supporting the motion, the leader of the Opposition, Mr. *C. Y. Chintamani* suggested the appointment of a committee of three members to investigate into the finances available for educational purposes and report upon the equitable distribution of money among the various branches of education. The Education Minister promised to consider Mr. Chintamani's suggestion. The guillotine fell and the entire demand was voted. The Council then adjourned.

19th. MARCH :—Practically for the whole day one token cut under general administration was discussed by the Council, its object being to call attention to the improper manner in which *Nawab Sir Mohammad Yusuf*, Minister for Local Self-Government, had exercised his power of nominations to the district and municipal boards after the recent elections.

Mr. *Chintamani*, the leader of the Nationalist party, who made the motion drew a graphic picture of the Minister's abuse of his patronage.

An animated and lively debate ensued and even those who opposed the cut motion had very little to put forward in defence of the Minister's exercise of patronage. The *Minister*, in his reply, asserted that he had exercised his discretion in a reasonable and just manner.

As the discussion had fulfilled the object with which the motion was made and sufficiently exposed the Minister for the abuse of his power of nominations, Mr. *Chintamani*, after a spirited reply, withdrew it.

21st. MARCH :—The Council voted to-day without any cut the budgets for the Industries and Irrigation departments. The need for the industrial regeneration of the province with a view to promote the prosperity of the people and at the same time to tackle the problem of unemployment was emphasized by several speakers. Many important suggestions were made by several members, including Mr. *C. Y. Chintamani*, who asked why Government should not co-operate with the All-India Spinners' Association in promoting the handloom industry and with the Village Industries Association in promoting the village industries. No convincing answer was forthcoming from Sir *J. P. Srivastava*, Minister for Industries, except that the suggestion was an interesting one and the Government did not know whether the other party was equally desirous of co-operation.

24th. MARCH :—The demands under irrigation and hydro-electric works outlay not charged to revenue and charges on the irrigation establishment were voted to-day, the former in full and the latter with a substantial reduction of Rs. 6,700:

A suggestion was made during the discussion of the latter demand that the Government should supply an aeroplane to Sir William Stampe, chief engineer-in-charge of the Hydro-electric projects to enable him to move about quickly from one part of the province to another in connectien with his work. There was a strong difference of opinion on the question and those opposed to the proposal, including the leader of the Opposition, Mr. *Chintamani* who urged that the advocates of the proposal were trying to be more royalist than the King and it was for the Finance Member and the chief engineer to have come forward with it if they felt the need of an aeroplane. Mr. *J. M. Clay* turned down the suggestion on the ground of its enormous expense and added that the Government would consider whether it would be worth while for Sir William Stampe to charter an aeroplane on special occasions.

While it was generally recognized that the hydro-electric projects afforded some relief for the unemployed, a very important point was raised in connection with the question of the recruitment of the staff by Mr. Chintamani, namely, that the residents of the United Provinces should be taken only when the Government made quite sure that men of requisite qualifications were not available in the province.

25th. MARCH :—A number of grievances against the police was voiced to-day. The Government were severely taken to task for getting the Secretary of State's sanction behind the back of the Council for making the post of the second assistant to the inspector-general of police permanent. The Council had previously agreed to the creation of this post on a temporary basis but was to-day confronted with the accomplished fact of its having been made permanent and added to the list of non-voted officers. A token cut was moved by *Haji Obaidur Rahman Khan* to protest against this unwanted post having been made permanent and it was supported almost unanimously by all sections of the House. The *Inspector-General* and the *Home Member* put up a stiff fight but failed to carry conviction with the House that the post was indispensable. The cut motion was carried in the teeth of official opposition.

That even such high police dignitaries as superintendents, and deputy superintendents were addicted to the pernicious habit of accepting *dalis* from their subordinates during their tours was stressed by *Pandit Prem Ballabh Belwal* who offered to give private information to the Home Member to enable him to institute an enquiry. Another noteworthy point raised in to-day's debates referred to the morale among the police and the need for its improvement. The *Home Member* agreed that there was room for such improvement and that the police should have as their motto service of the public. He appealed to the hon. members to give particulars of cases of bribery among the police officials whenever they got scent of them so that the inspector-general could institute a searching enquiry and bring the offenders to book.

A number of substantial reductions was sought to be made and the Council succeeded in effecting a reduction of Rs. 10,000 in the allotment of Rs. 50,000 for the establishment for registration of motor vehicles. Two motions to reduce the sum allotted for rewards by Rs. 50,000 and Rs. 15,000 on the ground of financial stringency did not find favour with the House and they were rejected without division.

Kunwar Sir Maharaj Singh at the outset made an interesting speech in which he deplored communal animosities and appealed to the press and public to promote communal harmony in the province.

26th. MARCH :—A number of motions under the police demand were discussed by the Council to-day and pointed attention was drawn to the astoundingly inadequate representation of the Hindus in the Police department and a certain Muslim member sought to lend communal colour to the grievance of the Hindus.

27th. MARCH :—A doleful tale was told by *Nawab Sir Muhammad Yusuf*, regarding the restricted activities of the Medical department due to financial stringency. He frankly admitted that a stage had been reached where the Medical department could show no improvement and as a matter of fact it was very difficult to carry on its normal activities very efficiently. The Minister's invariable reply to almost every suggestion made by the hon. members to increase the useful activities of the department was that nothing would have given him greater pleasure than to comply with the suggestions if funds had been available.

Several valuable suggestions were made in the course of discussions on the Medical demand which proved to be no more than a cry in the wilderness and met with no tangible response from the Minister beyond an expression of sympathy. The question of unjust reservation of certain districts for European I. M. S. officers was raised by the Leader of the Opposition Mr. *C. Y. Chintamani*, with a view to keep the question alive and not give rest to the Government until the wrong was righted. The cut motion was unanimously carried.

Three other cut motions were also carried by the Council, protesting against (1) the abolition of tuberculosis dispensaries at Agra, Cawnpore and Allahabad, (2) hopelessly inadequate medical relief in rural areas and (3) reduction in the grant for the development of the indigenous system of medicine. It was mentioned by *Nawabzada Liaqat Ali Khan* that the Government at present spent only 14 annas per annum on 100 persons in rural areas and he was loudly cheered when he spoke the bare truth that it was nothing but scandalous and callous neglect on the part of Government in the matter of medical relief.

28th. MARCH :—The utter helplessness of the Minister-in-charge of the medical portfolio in the matter of recruitment and postings of I. M. S. officers once again formed the subject of forceful and vigorous criticism on the floor of the Council to-day in connection with the discussions on the medical demand. The Secretary of State's autocratic control in the matter of appointment of I. M. S. officers leaving absolutely no discretion to the local Government even in the transferred departments was strongly resented by the House and two token cut motions were carried, (a) protesting against the appointment as Principal of the Agra Medical School of an I. M. S. officer brought from outside the United Provinces and (b) against the large grant of Rs. 57,290 from the provincial funds made to the Ranchi Mental Hospital for the treatment of 41 European and Anglo-Indian patients, while a comparatively far less amount was spent on Indian patients treated in the mental hospitals situated inside the province.

Two other cut motions were also carried urging (a) provision of funds for medical relief in rural areas from the four lakhs promised for the unemployment relief out of the proceeds of the new taxation and from the allotment for rural uplift, and (2) increased representation for *vaids* and *Hakims* in the Board of Indian Medicine.

A lively debate ensued on the amendment of the rules under the Poisons Act made by the Government sometime ago which was strongly condemned by Rai Bahadur Babu *Vikramjit Singh*, Mr. *Chintamani* and Nawabzada *Liaqat Ali Khan* on medical profession in the province. Fundamentally divergent views were expressed in the course of the debate by Mr. Reed, Local Self-Government secretary, and Sir *Muhammad Yusuf*, Minister, on the one side, and non-official spokesmen on the other as regards the demands put forward by the deputation which had waited on the Minister on behalf of the U. P. Medical Association. A suggestion, therefore, was thrown out by Sir *Sita Ram*, President, that the best way to arrive at a decision on the controversial subject would be for the Minister to call a conference of the representatives of the Medical Association and party leaders in the Council before the June session at Nainital to consider the whole question. The suggestion found ready acceptance with the House and the matter was accordingly dropped.

The budget under Agriculture, Veterinary and Co-operative departments was taken up a little before 5 p. m. when the guillotine fell and no less than 24 demands which remained undiscussed were put to the House and voted. Mr. Chintamani and some other members of the Opposition loudly shouted 'no' when the P. W. D. and Excise demands were put. The Council was then *prorogued*. (From the 'Leader').

Summer Session—Naini Tal—16th. to 30th. June 1936

Grant to U. P. Indian Christians

The Summer session of the Council commenced at Naini Tal on the **16th. June 1936** with *Sir Sita Ram* in the chair. At the outset the President referred in feeling terms to the demise of Dr. M. A. Ansari. The House authorised the President to send a message of condolence to the bereaved family.

The resolution of *Syed Ali Zaheer* recommending to the Council not to spend the grant of Rs. 10,000 allotted "for Indian Christians whose origin is from the Depressed Classes for education and for aiding missions working amongst them" was accepted by the House, the Minister for Education accepting the view of the House that the wording of the communique on the subject might be misconstrued as affording monetary ralief to members of the Depressed Classes by the mere fact of conversion or used as incentive for the purpose of conversion.

APPOINTMENT OF LIQUIDATORS

The *President* made a lengthy statement on the communique issued by the Registrar of the High Court, Allahabad, regarding the admissibility of certain questions regarding the appointment of liquidators by the High Court who made representations to the Local Government that the question concerning the High Court could not be allowed to be asked in local legislatures. On representation to the President by the Judicial Secretary to the Government, the President did not see his way to agree with the Government or the High Court as the Budget concerning the pay of liquidators was discussed in the Council. The Chair regretted that the press communique issued by the Registrar of the High Court should have contained reflections on the Chair and expressed the hope that the unfortunate incident would now be taken as closed. Later, some non-controversial and non-official resolutions were discussed.

OFFICIAL INTERFERENCE IN ELECTIONS

17th. JUNE :—The coming elections loomed large at to-day's meeting of the Council, when no less than five non-official resolutions were discussed. Mr. *J. M. Clay*, Finance Member, made an important statement on the result of the enquiries made by him into cases of official interference in district and municipal elections, over which, it would be remembered, a full dress debate took place during the budget session in March on a cut motion by Mr. Chintamani under the General Administration demand. While some complaints were found to be either baseless or exaggerated, there were yet others in which certain district magistrates had clearly transgressed the rules governing elections and openly favoured one candidate against another. The Finance Member unequivocally and unambiguously stated that in all such cases the Government would make it plain to the district magistrates concerned that they should not have acted in the way in which they did and that the Government servant's conduct rules must be strictly followed.

Mr. *Chintamani*, congratulated the Finance Member on the promptness and keenness with which he had carried out his undertaking in letter and spirit, and adversely criticised the manner in which inquiries had been conducted by certain divisional commissioners. If the Government took steps to guard against such transgressions of the election rules by their own officials, especially in the coming elections to the provincial legislatures, the purpose of the debates held in March and to-day would be amply fulfilled.

The Government accepted two resolutions urging that *patwaris* be present at polling stations to identify votes and that polling stations be so located that no voter need have to traverse more than five miles.

DEVELOPMENT OF RURAL AREAS

An important statement was then made by *Sir Jwala Prasad Srivastava*, Minister for Education, regarding what the U. P. Government was doing in connection with rural development.

The Minister said that rural development schemes in the province were divided into three parts, the main scheme, departmental schemes and the Kumaon scheme. Under the main scheme, 270 rural development centres had been established in the province. and an organisation had been set up in each district by means of which all local officials of the different departments of the Government could work together to effect improvement in rural areas. Another achievement had been that over a large area, local apathy add fatalistic resignation had given place to active interest. Demonstration plots were being opened in village centres, seed unions were being formed, cattle-breeding taken up with earnestness and concentrated drive was being made for improving rural sanitation and hygiene. Considerable zeal had been displayed everywhere in the development of village games and sports, opening of night schools and village libraries and training of adult scouts for social service. This had the effect of making village life more interesting and this in turn stimulated desire for improvement in other directions. It was proposed to sink 2,250 wells in connection with the agricultural scheme, fifty wells had been improved and work was now proceeding more briskly. Survey work was being done in Benares, Sultanpur, and Allahabad districts. Fruit plants seed had been supplied free to selected villages and actual planting had started and would be completed before August.

Health units were working in the districts of Meerut, Allahabad, Benares, Gorakhpur, Lucknow, Fyzabad, Moradabad and Jhansi and nine units cover about 450 villages. These units carried on intensive health propaganda and gave medical relief by means of a mobile dispensary. 1,315 indigenous *dais* were trained for attending to normal labour cases and 495 rural sanitary boards had been formed in the villages for maintaining activities on a permanent footing. Besides the Public Health Department had supplied 8,000 medicine chests to villages under the main scheme of rural development.

For providing facilities for marketing products of village cottage industries it was proposed to open 24 shops. Three shops had been fixed up and 10 more were expected to be established soon. A new section for marketing village products had been opened at Lucknow. This section participated in the Kumbha Mela Exhibition at Allahabad and attracted much attention.

Indianisation of Secretaries

18th. JUNE :—The Council voiced to-day its sense of dissatisfaction and disappointment at the refusal of the Government to concede its oft-repeated demand that half the number of secretaries should be Indian officer, by adopting *nem con* a resolution on the subject moved by the Nationalist leader, Mr. *Chintamani*, who in a vigorous and forceful speech pointed out that of late years there had been retrogression instead of progress and that since the beginning of the current official year an Indian Finance secretary had been replaced by an European I. C. S. officer, while no Indian had been appointed to the post of any other secretary, with the result that the number of Indian secretaries had been actually reduced from two to one. He pertinently enquired why the deputy secretary in the Finance department, Pandit Suraj Din Bajpai, to whose remarkable ability successive Finance Members had paid superlative tributes. had not been appointed Finance secretary in the face of the well-known precedent when a former deputy secretary, Mr. Teyen, had been so appointed. The speech of the official spokesman, Mr. *J. M. Clay*, had utterly failed to carry conviction with the House, and there was no justification for ignoring the just claims of Indian officers to appointments at the headquarters of the Government. The statement that secretaries were appointed by the Government consisting of a majority of Indian members was at once challenged by Mr. Chintamani, who in his second speech rightly pointed out that every member of the Government could not have a voice in the selection of every secretary, basing his statement on his direct inside knowledge in the past and observations from outside in the present.

Seeing the unmistakable expression of opinion in support of the resolution from all sides of the House, the *Finance Member* felt compelled to accept the resolution.

Homes for Disabled Beggars

Four other resolutions were discussed in the course of the day, among which mention may be made of the resolution moved by *Lady Kailash Srivastava* urging financial help to local boards to start homes for disabled and maimed beggars. She confronted Nawab Sir Muhammad Yusuf with a very sympathetic speech he had made in support of such a resolution in 1921 before he became Minister. The *Minister* expressed profuse sympathy but pleaded financial stringency and spoke of practical difficulties. The resolution was adopted and the Government dared not challenge a division.

Public Health Scheme

20th. JUNE :—Official business was transacted in to-day's Council. After a brief statement by the *Finance Member* regarding the probable cost of the proposed extension of the Council House at Lucknow to provide accommodation for the unwanted Upper House under the new constitution, the House commenced the consideration of demands for supplementary grants aggregating to Rs. 40,07,565.

Keen divergence of opinion on the utility of the public health scheme manifested itself on the proposal of the Minister, *Nawab Sir Mohd. Yusuf* to extend the scheme to four more districts in the province, primarily to provide employment to qualified people without employment. A number of members expressed the view that better equipped dispensaries and more travelling dispensaries would be more useful to the public. Another item which evoked a lively debate related to the permanent appointment of Mr. C. W. Casse, mechanical engineer for water works, on the new scale of pay demanded by him after the termination of his three years' contract at the beginning of the next year. Several members voiced the view that no official should be allowed to dictate his own terms to the Government while on the official side it was stated by Nawab Sir Muhammad Yusuf that the scale of salary proposed was by no means extravagant, considering the qualifications and experience of Mr. Casse. The motion for omission of the item was, however, not pressed to division.

SUPPLEMENTARY GRANTS

22nd. JUNE :—The Government sustained a heavy defeat in to-day's Council over the motion made by the Nationalist party leader, Mr. *Chintamani* for postponement of consideration of the supplementary estimate of Rs. 34,81,530 till after consideration of the Underground Waters Bill which sought to control the rate of the abstraction of water from sub-soil in the best interests of all concerned. Several hon. members had a shrewd suspicion that if the House gave its assent in advance to the acceleration of programme of tubewell construction costing several lakhs they might be faced with a *fait accompli* and have no freedom to throw out that Bill if they were so minded. This suspicion found vent in the numerous questions addressed to Sir William Stampe, chief engineer for a clear explanation of the position in relation to the Underground Waters Bill and the replies given by him and the Finance Member failed to set their apprehensions at rest with the result that the Opposition Leader's motion for postponement was carried by the House by 42 votes against 30. The result of the division was received with loud applause from non-official benches.

Sir Jwala Prasad Srivastava, Education Minister, Mr. Shah, special officer, Mr. Kharegat, Education Secretary, as well as Nawab Sir Mohammad Yusuf, Local Self-Government Minister, and his secretary Mr. A. B. Reid were congratulated by the Opposition leader on their promptness and earnestness in implementing some of the recommendations of the Unemployment Committee. The Education Minister said that he was deeply grateful to Mr. Chintamani for his very appreciative remarks and expressed that the Government were particularly lucky in having got the Rt. Hon. Sir Tej Bahadur Sapru to preside over the Unemployment Committee, another lucky stroke being his acceptance of membership of the Council for a brief space of two days when he succeeded in convincing the House that the problem with which they were confronted was a grave one, requiring drastic measures. The Education Minister's speech gave a clear indication of the Government's earnestness of purpose in tackling the growing menace of unemployment among the educated classes.

24th. JUNE :—What was aptly characterized by the leader of the Opposition during the budget session as a 'scandal of the first magnitude' became a *fait accompli* by the Council's vote to-day sanctioning the creation of a new post of a whole-time inspector-general of registration. Mr. *Chintamani* made a motion for the omission of the supplementary estimate making provision for this new appointment.

Those who voted against the motion did not participate in the debate and make out a case in support of making the top-heavy administration more top-heavy by the creation of a post which did not exist in these provinces for at least three-quarters of a century. As usual, arguments were on the side of the Opposition leader and votes on the side of the Government. The Hon'ble *Nawab Sir Mohd. Yusuf* said that all corruption and leakage in the Registration department would vanish with a separate head for the Registration department. The Opposition leader's motion was rejected by 63 votes against 10.

Some reactionary rules drawn up by the Government with reference to the creation of class I. U. P. Service of engineers in the buildings and roads branch of the Public Works department in charge of *Sir Mohd. Yusuf* were severely criticised by Mr. *Chintamani* in connection with another supplementary grant. The Minister said that the head master or principal was the best person to give a certificate of character to a candidate when his attention was drawn to the fact that the rules objected and required such a certificate from the district magistrate. These rules sought to provide for 20 per cent. recruitment in England for the U. P. Service of Engineers, passage allowances and overseas pay for such recruits, and the debate showed that they were not approved by the finance committee. The debate was adjourned.

Agra University Amend. Bill

25th. JUNE :—A non-official bill making some far-reaching changes in the Agra University Bill was on the legislative anvil to-day and the trend of the debate gave unmistakable proof of the fact that the bill wanted to reduce the strength of teachers in various university bodies and increase the number of public men'. Only four amendments were discussed during the whole day and there were no less than three divisions.

Despite the strong Government backing, the author of the Bill, Rai Bahadur Babu *Vikramjit Singh*, found that the Opposition carried the day on the first amendment which was adopted by the House by 39 against 33 votes. This amendment sought to provide for the election of teachers by registered graduates to the senate of the Agra University, even though they might happen to belong to the institutions not affiliated to the University. The select committee introduced a new provision that not more than half the number elected by registered graduates shall be persons employed in teaching. There was a stiff opposition from the Education Minister to the amendment and the defeat inflicted on the Government made the Government whip extremely alert for the rest of the day.

Not satisfied with unjustifiable restriction needlessly imposed on the choice of registered graduates, another amendment of a more reactionary nature was next brought forward that none of those elected by registered graduates shall be a teacher employed in an affiliated college. It came as the greatest surprise upon the House when the Minister extended the official support to this amendment. Brisk whipping on behalf of the Opposition against the retrograde change proved to be a mere cry in the wilderness. The amendment was carried by 52 against 30 votes.

26th. JUNE :—The Bill passed its third reading in to-day's Council by 57 votes against 24 after a very stiff and determined opposition. from a section of members who held that the measure was detrimental to the best interests of teachers and education.

Another onslaught was sought to be made on the teachers' existing rights and privileges which entitle them to take their disputes with the managing committees before the tribunal of the university for decision. The Agra University very wisely framed a statute in 1934 providing for an agreement between the managing committees and teachers employed in affiliated colleges and clause 4 sought to do away with this salutory statute or, in other words, deprive them of their security of tenure. It came as a pleasant surprise upon the House when the Minister for Education announced that the Government had decided to oppose this clause with a view to protect the interests of teachers employed in affiliated colleges. The clause was rejected without a division, which the promoter of the bill dared not challenge in view of the attitude of the Government. The Government were severely criticised by Nawabzada *Liaqat Ali Khan*, the Democratic party leader, for lending the weight of their support to a non-official bill which sought to deprive the teachers of their position and influence in the university bodies and for not leaving the decision to the non-official section of the House.

Non-official Bills

Two other non-official bills occupied the attention of the House for the rest of the day. One of them aimed at giving power to dismiss a sanitary inspector in the hands of the majority in a municipality, and this was passed without a discussion. The other bill dealt with no-confidence motions in district boards. Its cardinal objective was to increase the majority required for the passage of such a motion from one half to two-thirds and it did not find favour with the House.

Change of Sub-Judges' Designation

29th. JUNE :—The Council passed into law to-day the official Bill changing the designation of subordinate judges to civil judges in compliance with the oft-repeated request made by the provincial judicial officers' conference. A number of members congratulated *Sir Maharaj Singh*, Home Member, on bringing forward this bill and there was a consensus of opinion among them that the subordinate judges performed very responsible and onerous duties and deserved greater emoluments and better treatment in the matter of listed posts in the judicial service.

Underground Waters Bill

'Confiscation without compensation' was the description given by Mr. Chintamani, Leader of the Opposition, to the Underground Waters Bill in respect of which Sir Joseph Clay, Finance Member, made a motion for circulation in order to elicit opinion by Sept. 15. The provisions of the bill appeared to several members of the House to be too drastic and quite unjust to the landlords and the cultivators and the conversations which Sir Joseph Clay had with them showed that they were opposed to the measure and the principle underlying it. The Government, therefore, wisely abandoned their original intention of making a motion for reference of the bill to a select committee.

The *Finance Member* in his speech in connection with his motion for circulation clearly explained that the Government were ready to consider alternative suggestions with a view to regulate the tube-well construction in order to ensure the continuity of underground water supply.

The House expressed its appreciation of the changed attitude and intentions of Government in connection with the bill and agreed to the motion for circulation.

Cotton Pest Control Bill

Sir Jwala Prasad Srivastava then introduced the Cotton Pest Control Bill and moved its reference to a select committee. Strong dissatisfaction was expressed with the penal provisions of the bill and the Leader of the Opposition rightly voiced the view of the whole House when he said that the bill itself should not become a pest to cotton cultivators.

The Minister assured the House that he had an open mind and the select committee could make such changes as it liked in respect of the penal provisions as well.

The motion for select committee was agreed to and the House adjourned.

Meerut Rath Procession

30th. JUNE :—Following supplementary questions, Mr. Chintamani gave notice of his intention to move an adjournment of the House particularly to discuss the policy underlying the prosecutions launched by the district magistrate against certain Hindus in connection with the above affair. When an objection was raised by the Finance Member that the debate might trench on matters which were *sub judice*, Mr. Chintamani gave a definite guarantee that the question of even one solitary person who was being prosecuted would not be raised in the course of speeches by himself and his supporters.

The *President* pointed out that the only question before the House was the policy of launching the prosecutions and the policy of the executive Government in continuing them.

The *Home Member* gave an undertaking to the House that he would look into this question and added that he was quite willing to consult the district magistrate on this point. This undertaking failed to satisfy Mr. Chintamani who urged that if there was a clearly expressed wish of the House, the Government might pay nearly as much regard to their opinion as to the opinion of the district magistrate.

'If the hon. Home Member will be pleased to say one word more that our case shall not be prejudiced by the opinion of the district magistrate', said Mr. Chintamani, 'and that he will give full weight to the wishes of the House in consideration of the opinion that might be given by the district magistrate, I think there will be a good case for withdrawing the motion.'

The Home Member gave such an assurance whereupon Mr. Chintamani withdrew his motion for adjournment. The House then adjourned *sine die*. (From the 'Leader'.)

The C. P. Legislative Council

LIST OF MEMBERS

The Hon'ble Sir S. W. A. Rizvi (*President*)
The Hon'ble Mr. E. Raghavendra Rao (*Ex-Officio Member*)
The Hon'ble Mr. E. Gordon (*Ex-Officio Member*)
Mr. N. J. Roughton
Mr. A. L. Binney
Mr. C. R. Hemeon
Mr. R. N. Banerjee
Mr. M. Owen
Mr. G. S. Bhalja
Mr. H. A. Hyde
Mr. J. C. McDougall
Mr. Lalman Singh
The Revd. G. C. Rogers
Mr. G. A. Gavai
Mr. T. C. Sakhare
Mr. S. G. Naik
Guru Gosain Agamdass
Rao Sahib R. W. Fulay
Mrs. Ramabai Tambe
Mr. Balraj Jaiswara
Mr. Daduram
Rai Sahib Badri Prasad Pujari
Mr. Chunnu
Mr. C. B. Parakh
Rai Sahib Lala Jainarain
Mr. T. J. Kedar
Mr. Sheoprasad Pande
Mr. Kashi Prasad Pande
Mr. Jhunnilal Verma
Mr. Dulichand
Rai Bahadur Dadu Dwarkanath Singh
Choudhari Malthulal
Mr. Waman Yado Deshmukh
Mr. Anjore Rao Kirdutt
Rai Sahib Ramsanehi Gaurha
Khan Bahadur F. F. Tarapore
Rai Bahadur Gajadhar Prasad Jaiswal
Mr. Bhagwant Rao Anna Bhow Mandloi
Mr. Arjunlal
Seth Sheolal
Mr. Chandan Lal
Mr. Ganapat Rao Shankar Rao Deshmukh
Mr. Shivramprasad Sultanprasad Tiwari
The Hon'ble Rai Bahadur K. S. Nayudu (*Minister*)
Mr. R. S. Dube
Mr. Vinayak Damodar Kolte
Khan Bahadur M. M. Mullna
Mr. Iftikhar Ali
Khan Bahadur Syed Hifazat Ali
Mr. Mahomed Yusuf Shareef
Beohar Gulab Singh
Thakur Manmohan Singh
Mr. D. T. Mangalmoorti
Mr. L. H. Bartlett
Seth Thakurdas Goverdhandas
Mr. Vithal Bandhuji Chaobal
Mr. R. A. Kanitkar
Dr. Panjabrao Shamrao Deshmukh
Mr. Motirao Bajirao Tidake
Rao Sahib Uttamrao Sitaramji Patil
Mr. Shridhar Govind Sapkal
Mr. Umedsingh Narainsingh Thakur
Rao Sahib D. Y. Rajurkar
Mr. Yadab Madhav Kale
Mr. Tukaram Shankar Patil
Mr. Mahadeo Paikaji Kolhe
Mr. Ganapat Sitaram Malvi
Khan Sahib Syed Mobinur Rahaman
Khan Sahib Muzaffar Husain
Khan Bahadur Mirza Rahman Beg
The Hon'ble Mr. Balkrishna Ganesh Khaparde (*Minister*)
Rao Bahadur Gajanan Ramchandra Kothare.

Proceedings of the Council

January Session—Nagpur—22nd. to 30th. January '36

The January session of the C. P. Legislative Council commenced at Nagpur on the **22nd. January 1936** with the hon'ble *Sir S. W. A. Rizvi*, in the chair. Visitors' Galleries were practically deserted.

The honourable Mr. *E. Raghavendra Rao*, Home Member and Leader of the House made the following feeling reference to the death of His Majesty King George V and moved for adjournment of the House.

"I wish to express on behalf of this House in language not of exaggeration or of convention, but of simple truth the feelings that lie deep in the hearts of all of us. They are feelings of two-fold character, of sorrow at the death of our King and of our loyal and respectful homage to his successor, the new King.

Money-lenders' Amend. Bill

23rd. JANUARY:—The Council discussed to-day Government Bills. Of these, Mr. *E. Raghavendra Rao's* C. P. Money-lenders' (second amendment) Bill evoked a lively debate and was ultimately referred to a Select Committee. In moving reference of the Bill to the Select Committee, the Hon. Mr. Rao traced briefly the legislative history of usury in India and England. The present Bill, he said, went a step further than the C. P. Money-lenders' Act, which was put in operation on April 1, 1935, and aimed at exercising some measure of direct control over money-lenders with a view to keeping their transactions within conscionable and equitable limits by making registration compulsory on payment of registration fees. He added that the principle underlying the Bill had the support of the Royal Commission on Agriculture and such a provision is part of the Money-lenders' Act in many advanced countries, including England and the professions of Law and Medicine, Motor Driving, etc., which imposed licences on those practising them. The Royal Commission had also stated that measures of this character would not lead to so great a restriction of credit that the cultivator would be hampered in his ordinary agricultural operations. Proceeding, the Home Member said that according to the Provincial Banking Enquiry Committee, the agricultural debt amounted to Rs. 300 millions in 1929. Even at the very low rate of six percent, the Mahajans made a profit of Rs. 18 millions annually. The measure would probably cause hardship to the small money-lender, but the speaker did not think this would be an unmitigated evil. "It is the petty money-lender who often causes great hardship to the agriculturists. The House must be aware of the unconscionable and illegal methods adopted by certain class of money-lenders, who are fast spreading their activities in the villages".

Mr. *D. T. Mangalmurti* (University) opposing the Home Member's motion, moved that the Bill be circulated for eliciting public opinion thereon. He alleged that the Bill had been sponsored by the Government, not on account of their anxiety to save the borrower, but with a view to filling their coffer. The burden of taxation, he added, would eventually fall on the debtors and instead of relieving agricultural distress by providing cheap credit facilities, the Bill would create more hardship for the cultivators. A Government, whose officers were not prepared to surrender part of their salaries, had, in his opinion, no moral or legal right to tax any section of the population.

The motion for circulation of the Bill was pressed to a division and defeated by 38 votes to 20. The original motion for Select Committee reference was then carried.

Non-official Resolutions

24th. JANUARY:—Visitors' gallaries were crowded to-day mainly because 150 peasants from the Akola district, who had come down to seek redress for their agricultural distress and who were banned from demonstrating near or entering the Council premises, were under orders of the Home Member, permitted to enter and watch the proceedings.

The Council discussed in all four resolutions, two of which were defeated, one withdrawn and the fourth was undecided when the House rose.

The first resolution was by Mr. *Arjunlal* urging reconstitution of the Revenue Districts of Narshingpur, Seoni and Damoh, which was opposed by Mr. *N. J. Roughton*, Chief Secretary, on financial grounds. He also pointed out that these districts had been abolished three years back in response to the wishes of the House as a measure of economy. The resolution, being pressed to a division, was thrown out by 37 votes to 19.

The next resolution by Khan Bahadur *Mirza Rahman Beg* recommending to the Government to postpone auction sales of Jagir lands in Berar was lost without division. The Revenue Secretary, Mr. *R. N. Banerjee*, speaking on behalf of the Government, said that Jagirdars have to thank themselves for having brought about the conditions in which they find themselves. Their own discretion was largely responsible for the same and there was no reason why the property law of the land should not be put into operation.

Mr. *C. A. Kale* next moved a resolution recommending to the Government to introduce legislation to stop competition of cross-word puzzles and the like, which in his opinion were demoralising the educated public in the province to an alarming extent. Mr Kale said that such competitions developed the spirit of gambling amongst the educated people. There were sometimes five or six solutions to a given clue, with the result that it was a question of mere chance to hit upon the correct solution. They thus ceased to be a game.

Khan Bahadur Tarapore thought that the resolution itself was a puzzle. If the competitions were demoralising they were demoralising the educated public not only in C. P. and Berar, but throughout India. He was of the opinion that they sharpened the intellect.

Mr. *N. J. Roughton* pointed out the various difficulties in the way of passing a law on the matter. Personally, he was adverse to gambling, but he should consider it a serious interference of personal liberty if anyone would prohibit him from gambling should he like to. Even the Government of India could not stop competitions appearing in papers having an international circulation, and they might be compelled to have recourse to the League of Nations. He, therefore, appealed to Mr. Kale to withdraw the resolution. Mr. Kale withdrew the resolution.

Discussion on Khan Bahadur *Syed Hifazat Ali's* resolution in respect of remission of stamp duty payable by the first grade pleaders of J. C. S. Court of Judicature at Nagpur was not concluded when the Council adjourned.

Official Bills

25th. JANUARY :—Of the twelve official Bills that came up for discussion to-day, nine were referred to the Select Committees, one Bill effecting minor amendments in the University Act passed into law, one circulated for eliciting public opinion and one, viz., the Tobacco Taxation Bill, thrown out by two to one majority.

Tobacco Taxation Bill

In moving for reference of the Tobacco Bill to the Select Committee, the Honourable Mr. *Gordon*,, Finance Member, said that it was the third time that the Bill had been brought by the Government and he expected better treatment this time. On merits the Government had an incontrovertible case. They had held their hands to the last in the hope that the tide would turn, but crop failures and liberal remissions and suspensions of land revenue, coupled with expenditure incurred in the establishment of debt conciliation boards and the fall in stamps revenue due to debt conciliation, left them no choice. There was also another aspect to the question viz., the financial position of the Provinces under the new constitution. Sir Otto Niemeyer was at the moment investigating the question of subvention to the Provinces and refusal of the Council to vote for a fare share of taxation would greatly prejudice the case of the Central Provinces before the Niemeyer Committee.

Mr. *D. T. Mangalmurti*, opposing the Bill, said that nothing had happened since the Council last threw out the Bill to induce them to change the view that the Bill was unwarranted. He failed to see why the five per cent salary cut should not have been allowed to remain. Mr. *M. P. Kolhe* moved that the Bill be circulated for eliciting public opinion thereon.

Mr. *C. B. Parakh* said that the Government could retrieve the position by reducing overhead charges which absorbed 68 per cent of their revenues. He also felt that the imposition of licences on tobacco dealers would furnish another tool in the hands of the authorities to harass people.

Mr. *Kolhe's* motion was defeated without division, while Mr. *Gordon's* motion was defeated by 40 votes to 20.

Another Bill, which was moved by the *Home Member*, seeking to reduce the rate of interest payable by debtors to creditors was referred to the Select Committee.

The House circulated for eliciting public opinion the Finance Member's Bill seeking to establish a Board of Revenue in the Province after the introduction of Provincial Autonomy

Religious and Charitable Trusts Bill

27th. JANUARY :—The Council disposed of to-day two out of the six non-official Bills. Interest centred round the C. P. Religious and Charitable Trusts Bill, which was introduced by Dr. *Panjab Rao Deshmukh* with the object of ensuring better management of Hindu religious endowments in the province. The present administration of these trusts, he said, was far from satisfactory. Therefore, he urged the House to agree to the measure.

The non-official opinion as revealed in the discussion, was sharply divided regarding the advisability of enacting such a Bill at present, while the Government opposed the measure owing to the provision suggested by the mover.

The Education Minister, Mr. *B. G. Khaparde*, further informed the House that the Government had under consideration another measure on the subject and it would be introduced in the House as soon as the Governor-General's sanction was secured.

The House threw out the measure rejecting the motion to refer it to a select committee by 37 votes to 13.

Mr. *K. P. Pande* moved a Bill which sought the repeal of certain provisions of the C. P. Land Revenue Act which empowered the Government to recover arears of land revenue by the arrest and detention or by the imprisonment of defaulter in the civil jail. Despite the Government's opposition the House agreed to refer the Bill to a select committee.

29th. JANUARY :—The Council to-day voted supplementary demands under the head of education and agreed to restore 25 per cent cut in the grants to the local bodies and private institutions on the motions of Mr. *B. G. Khaparde*, Education Minister, and Mr. *E. Gordon*, Finance Member.

A token demand of one Rupee was moved by Rai Bahadur *K. S. Nayudu*, Minister for Public Works, asking the House to sanction the cost of the new High Court building which was expected to cost about Rs. 10,00,000, was lost by a narrow margin of one vote, the voting being 26 votes against 27. The members opposing this demand contended that the cost would be prohibitive in the present financial position of the province.

The Home Member, Mr. *Raghavendra Rao* stated that the income realized from enhanced court fees would be utilized for the purpose of constructing the new building.

The House then passed two Bills seeking to validate the contributions made by several municipal committees and local bodies to charitable funds outside their jurisdiction, such as the Bihar Earthquake Relief Fund and their Majesties' Silver Jubilee Fund.

Non-Official Resolutions

30th. JANUARY :—The Council discussed non-official resolutions. The *President* ruled out of order the adjournment motion tabled by Mr. *C. B. Parakh*, who wanted the House to discuss the incident alleged to have taken place in village Ambaghad, Bhandara district, on Jan. 22.

Mr. *Parakh* alleged that during the investigation into a theft case a Police Sub-Inspector assaulted five villagers at Ambaghad, resulting in the death of one Goma Dhibar and injuries to four others.

The *Home Member* stated that a magisterial enquiry had been instituted to inquire into certain acts alleged to have been committed by the police officer and if the allegations proved true, Law would take the normal course. The matter was still *sub judice* and should not be discussed by the House.

The House accepted by 29 votes to 18 the resolution recommending to the local Government to suggest to the Government of India to float a public loan and advance the money thus raised to the Court of Wards and big landholders at a slightly higher rate of interest to meet their liabilities and indebtedness.

The failure of crops in Berar formed the subject of another resolution. During the discussion several non-official members pleaded for complete remission of land revenue for the current year owing to widespread agricultural distress. The speakers complained against the use of coercive processes by revenue authorities in realizing the revenue demands.

Both the Revenue Member and the Revenue Secretary, speaking on behalf of the Government, pointed out that full remission would mean considerable loss to the provincial revenues. However, the Government was sympathetically considering the position and give a liberal remission where circumstances justified such a course and denied the use of coercive methods in the matter of realization of the revenue demand.

A resolution urging the Government that the land revenue for the year 1935-36 be remitted owing to the failure of crops in Berar was carried by the House, the Government not claiming a division. The Council then adjourned *sine die*.

Budget Session—Nagpur—20th. February to 4th. March 1936

Governor's Opening Speech

His Excellency the Governor, *Sir Hyde Gowan*, in his address to the Council which commenced its budget session at Nagpur on the **20th. February 1936** referred to the new constitution and the problem of C. P. versus Berar, and appealed to all classes and the political leaders to work together for the common good.

At the outset the Governor referred to the demise of his Majesty King George, who was not only a great man and a great gentleman but he was above all a very humane father of his family and to us in India his loss brings special sorrow.

The Governor then described the various measures taken regarding the agricultural problem, and said that the debt conciliation boards had brought relief and fresh hope to the countryside. Ten land mortgage banks were established in the province as an experimental measure and had succeeded in the objective of keeping down the general rates of interest. With the generous grant of five lakhs from the Government of India they had been able to bring many amenities to villages, such as roads, and water supply and to embark on various experiments of rural reconstruction.

Referring to the serious position of provincial finances, the Governor hoped that the councillors, while considering the proposals for fresh taxation which had been dictated by the dire needs of the situation, would keep in view the common good of the province.

Coming to the new constitution, the Governor said it had now become law and when the 'tumult and shouting' had died down and a calm and dispassionate verdict of history came to be pronounced those who were responsible for its structure were confident that it would vindicate alike the honesty of their purpose, the liberality of their intentions and the skill and wisdom of their craftsmanship. The Governor then referred to the danger of disunion which seemed to him to take two forms.

On the problem of the Central Provinces and Berar, the Governor said that under the new Act the C. P. and Berar were treated as one province with a joint legislature dealing with all its affairs, and emphasised that the two parts of the province should reach an agreement on the question of financial arrangement to avoid discontent.

Coming to the general form of disunion, which had been brought about by the action of those who for many years stood aloof from working the present constitution and who had not made up their mind as to the attitude they would adopt towards the new constitution, the Governor asked them to read the history of the past 15 years during which the present constitution had been worked and worked successfully. If one considerable section of the people stood aloof from their proper task the whole work of the community must suffer. The Governor, therefere, appealed to all political leaders of the province to accept the new constitution, seize the substance they had gained and work together for the common good.

Budget for 1936-37

22nd. FEBRUARY :—The Finance Member, *Mr. E. Gordon*, presented the budget for 1936-37 to the Council to-day which showed an estimated revenue of Rs. 481,24,060, expenditure of Rs. 489,76,000, leaving a deficit on revenue account of Rs. 8,52,000. Adding the debt and deposit heads but excluding the famine relief fund, the total loss on the year rises to Rs. 19,87,000.

The revised estimates for 1935-36 show that the Government expected to close the year with small revenue surplus of Rs. 38,000, which was converted to a deficit of Rs. 2,45,000 as a result of the restoration of cuts in pay in certain transferred departments in August last, but owing to a fall in revenue under heads Land Revenue, Stamps and Excise the current year would close with a deficit of Rs. 25,59,000, the reason for deterioration being adverse economic condition and the cotton yield which was far below normal for the fifth year in succession.

The Finance Member in the course of his budget speech said that a financial settlement between the provinces and the central authority was impending and he believed that they had a good case for receiving assistance. However, it was essential that they must meet difficulties and in order to reduce the deficit in revenues Government would introduce and ask the House to pass two measures, one the Entertainment Tax Bill and another the Financial Bill imposing higher fees for non-judicial stamps and for motor taxation both of which were expected to produce a revenue of about six lakhs of rupees which would go towards revenue reduction of the deficit. Concluding, the Finance Member claimed that while the picture of their financial progress since the inception of the present reforms was not a happpy one, his two predecessors and himself set themselves to spend only when funds were available to match their expenditure with their means.

GENERAL DISCUSSION OF BUDGET

24th. FEBRUARY :—The Council devoted whole day to the general discussion of the Budget. Mr. *C. B. Parekh*, opening the debate, said that much economy in expenditure could be effected by reorganisation and retrenchment in Government Departments. He also felt that Government revenues could be improved by the abolition of the Malguzari system and also revision of the excise policy. The policy, which had been followed for the last eleven years, had proved ruinous to excise revenue and it was necessary to revise the policy which would supplement the excise revenue by Rs. 40 to 60 lakhs.

Mr. *Pande* felt that the budget afforded no relief to the poorer classes. Local bodies were still suffering from cuts in general purposes and education grants with the result that employees in local bodies were, in turn, subjected to salary cuts. Restoration of cut by Government in the case of its own employees had caused much heartburning in employees of local bodies.

Rao Saheb *R. W. Fulay* referred to the economic condition of the people and urged revision of the land revenue policy. He alleged that police resorted to coercive tactics with regard to Burhanpur textile strikers, that employees in the Government Press were not given promotion for the last two years and that Judges of the newly constituted High Court hurried cases through.

Mr. *D. T. Mangalmurti* vigorously attacked the taxation proposals and Mr. *R. A. Kanitkar* (Nationalist) deplored the failure of Government to restore education and general purposes grants to local bodies. They would agree to taxation measures if Government agreed to restore cuts in grants.

Seth Thakurdas favoured chalking out a bold line of action containing a forward programme, on the lines of Kemal Pasha's or President Roosevelt's. Several other members also participated in the debate. Members also complained that Government was increasing expenditure under Reserved Heads and crippling Primary Education.

Mr. *A. L. Binney*, Financial Secretary, denied that Government's estimates were too optimistic. He welcomed the suggestion of augmenting Government's revenues.

The Hon. Mr. *B. G. Khaparde*, Minister for Education, replying to the criticism levelled against his department, said that the problem of primary education was examined by the Government. The Local Self-Government Committee had recommended that it should be managed by local bodies. With regard to land mortgage banks, they had established ten in this Province and the Banks had just started work.

The Hon. Mr. *Raghavendra Rao*, Home Member, said it was the duty of Government to hand over to the new Government as perfect an administrative machinery as possible and to this end it was necessary to increase the police force in certain districts. The increase proposed was a technical increase, since, the Council had since 1930 every year accorded sanction to expenditure for extra police force in Raipur District. If Councillors expected the police to be civil and courteous and protect their lives and property and maintain law and order, it was necessary that constables should be given the necessary training. So the expenditure for a training school for constables was necessary and overdue.

The Hon. Mr. *Gordon*, Finance Member, said that the policy which Government were faithfully following regarding excise was the policy laid down by the Council eleven years ago. The question was being examined by the Excise Committee, and he preferred not to anticipate their recommendation regarding the desirability or othewise of continuance of that policy. Abolition of the Malguzary system was a subject on which the present Government could not reach a decision in the last year of its regime. The subject was so important that without the fullest backing of public opinion, it could not be properly tackled. Mr. Gordon assured the House that Government had done everything in its power to give relief to local bodies and cuts would be fully restored as soon as the financial situation is improved. The Council then adjourned.

MONEYLENDERS' BILL (CONTD.)

25th. FEBRUARY :—The Council enacted into law to-day the C. P. Money-lenders (Second) Amendment Bill on the motion of the Home Member. The Bill which would remain in force for four years made the registration of the moneylenders in the province compulsory, thus enabling the Government to exercise the same control over them in the interests of the debtors.

ENTERTAINMENTS DUTY BILL

The C. P. Entertainments Duty Bill was referred to a select committee. The object of bringing forward the measure, as the Finance Member stated, was to enable the Government to levy duties on entertainments such as cinemas and remove a part of the existing deficit in the provincial revenues.

THE FINANCE BILL

The House next discussed the C. P. Finance Bill on the motion of the Finance Member that it should be referred to a select committee. The Bill proposed to enhance the rates of taxes on motor vehicles in the province and also the duty leviable on certain instruments under Indian Stamp Act, 1899.

The Finance Member said that the present taxes levied on the motor vehicles in the province were very low when compared to rates in other provinces and the Government proposed to increase them so that the additional revenue thus obtained might be utilised to strengthen the finances of the province by removing the present deficit.

The discussion of the Bill revealed non-official opposition to fresh taxation, some members declaring that the motor industry would be seriously affected by the increased taxation now proposed at a time of economic depression and keen competition like that of the present.

The Home Member, intervening in the debate, asked the House to accept the Bill which was brought forward owing to financial necessity so that the Government might remove the deficit.

The House, however, rejected the select committee motion by 37 to 16 votes and thus threw out the measure.

VOTING OF BUDGET DEMANDS

26th. FEBRUARY :—The Council carried a token cut moved by Mr. *V. B. Chaubal* recommending to the Government 10 per cent reduction in the pay of all Government servants with a view to improving the provincial finances.

Dr. *P. S. Deshmukh* by another cut motion urged the postponement of the construction of the new High Court building involving an expenditure of about Rs. 8,00,000. He said that it was inadvisable to incur a fresh expenditure at a time when the financial position of the province was far from satisfactory.

The House, however, rejected the cut motion by 37 to 8 votes and voted the grant.

It would be recalled that the House had refused to sanction this expenditure during the last January session when the item in the form of a supplementary demand was brought forward for the approval of the Council.

The necessity of affording adequate relief to the agriculturists of the province with the help of land mortgage banks was stressed by Mr. *C. B. Parakh* through a cut motion the discussion on which was adjourned.

ADJ. MOTION—POLICE ASSAULT

2nd. MARCH :—In the Council to-day, the President, Sir *S. W. A. Rizvi*, read three identical motions for the adjournment of the House to discuss a matter of urgent public importance, namely, 'assault with *lathis* and batons on and the arrest of 43 persons by the police at Khandwa on Feb. 27.

The *Home Member* pointed out that the Government had no objection to the motion. The debate continued for one and half hours, after which a closure was applied. The motion was declared carried only four or five voices from the Government benches crying 'no'.

Mr. *Kashi Prasad Pande* moving the motion detailing his version of the incident, said that a sub-inspector with three constables proceeded to the Ashram, which was managed by the disciples of the dead saint at Khandwa on Feb. 27 in search of some suspects when a police officer was wrongfully confined in the Ashram. Thereupon another sub-inspector with 40 constables entered the Ashram at a time when a large congregation was busy offering prayers at the Ashram temple, and assaulted the people mercilessly with *lathis*, resulting in 50 injured, four seriously, while the police escaped with minor injuries. The mover asked the Government what was the justification for the *lathi* charge and why a magistrate was not summoned before the police resorted to force. Mr. Pande added that the police arrested next day 60 men, including innocent persons, all of whom were marched to the court in handcuffs except one. Pointing out that even pleaders had been refused interviews with the prisoners, Mr. Pande urged the Government to enquire into the incident thoroughly and take necessary action against those whose object seemed to create terror in the locality.

Seven other members, supporting the motion, protested against the conduct of the police at Khandwa and demanded justice in the case, one speaker alleging that some women sustained injuries from the *lathi* charge by the police.

The Home Member, Mr. *E. Raghavendra Rao*, recalling the facts based on the official report received from Khandwa, said that a number of people had come from outside to visit the Ashram and that the place was one on which the police should keep an eye in view of the possibility of suspicious characters arriving there. When a police party, consisting of a sub-inspector and four constables visited the Ashram on Feb. 27, and noticed the motor driver of the manager of the Ashram without a license, the police party was assaulted and confined within the limits of the Ashram. Another police party armed with muskets and *lathis*, arrived at the place to secure the release of the first police party when the police party were attacked by 300 persons. The sub-inspector, armed with a *lathi*, charged and brought the situation under control. Forty-three men, including the men of the Ashram, had been arrested and about 30 rioters and 50 policemen were injured, but none seriously. The Home Member denied that the women were involved in the *laihi* charge and declared that the police had acted with self-control and succeeded in restoring order with the least possible use of force and infliction of serious injuries. The Home Member added that the conduct of those involved would in due course be judged by the judicial authority at Khandwa and asked the mover to withdraw the motion.

The motion was, however, carried. The House then adjourned.

4th. MARCH :—In the Council to-day, Mr. *K. P. Pande* moved a token cut in the demand for police urging economy in expenditure. He complained that expenditure under this head had, in recent years, risen by leaps and bounds. The present were peaceful times, since civil disobedience was neither being practised nor was there any possibility of its revival for some years to come. This increase in expenditure had resulted in crippling the activities of the transferred departments and he saw no reason why the question of increasing the police force should not be held over and funds diverted towards the transferred departments.

Mr. *N. J. Raughton*, Chief Secretary, pointed out that Mr. Pande's contention was not correct. The fact that expenditure under police in 1935-36 was Rs. 55 lakhs showed that not only had expenditure not risen but had curtailed.

Mr. *Raghavendra Rao* also opposed the motion.

Seth Sheolal said that just as military expenditure was the highest item with the India Government, police expenditure was the highest in the Provinces. He pointed out that a police constable received a more salary than a primary teacher, at the end of his career.

Two more cuts, one urging the postponement of the question of making the additinoal armed police in Raipur permanent, and the other censuring the District Superintendent of the Police, Nagpur, for passing a prohibitory order in respect of the Murtizafur peasants, who arrived here in January last and demonstrated in front of the Council Hall, were moved but the first was withdrawn and the second lost.

Opposing the second cut, the Chief Secretary said that they ought to be thankful to the District Superintendent of police, for enabling Councillors to work peacefully. He reminded the House that during the last two or three sessions, money-lenders, taxi-drivers, peasants and others were marching in procession to the Council Hall and demonstrating. Members were jeered at by the processionists and but for the preventive action of the police, peaceful work in the Council would have been impossible. The motion was lost by 25 votes to 18.

The police demand then came out unscathed.

The guillotine was applied at 5 p. m., and the remaining demands were passed. The Council then adjourned *sine die*.

The B. & O. Legislative Council

LIST OF MEMBERS

THE HON'BLE BABU RAJANDHARI SINHA (*President.*)

RAI BAHADUR LAKSHMIDHAR MAHANTI (*Deputy President*)

1. THE HON'BLE BABU NIRSU NARAYAN SINHA (*Member, Executive Council*)
2. THE HON'BLE MR. P. C. TALLENTS (*Member, Executive Council*)
3. THE HON'BLE DR. SIR GANESH DATTA SINGH (*Minister*)
4. THE HON'BLE MR. SAIYID ABDUL AZIZ (*Minister*)
5. MR. W. B. BRETT
6. MR. H. C. PRIOR
7. MR. J. W. HOULTON
8. MR. W. G. LACEY
9. MR. S. LALL
10. MR. A. C. DAVIES
11. MR. J. G. POWELL
12. MR. F. A. BETTERTON
13. MR. G. E. FAWCUS
14. MR. N. F. PECK
15. LT.-COL. P. S. MILLS
16. LT.-COL. A. E. J. C. MCDOWELL
17. MR. B. W. HAIGH
18. MR. W. H. MEYRICK
19. BABU MADANDHARI SINHA
20. MR. A. E. D'SILVA
21. REV. BRAJANANDA DAS
22. KUMAR AJIT PRASAD SINGH DEO
23. MR. R. CHANDRA
24. CHAUDHURI SHARAFAT HUSSAIN
25. BABU BIMALA CHARAN SINGH
26. BABU SHEONANDAN PRASAD
27. BABU RAM NARAYAN
28. RAI BAHADUR RAM RANVIJAYA SINGH
29. RAI BAHADUR HARENDRA NATH BANERJEE
30. RAI BAHADUR BIRENDRA NATH CHAKRAVARTTI
31. MR. SAGRAM HEMBROME
32. MR. GARBETT CAPTAIN MANKI
33. MAHANTH MANMOHAN DAS
34. MR. SAIYID MUHAMMAD MEHDI
35. MAULAVI SAIYID MUHAMMAD HAFEEZ
36. RAI BAHADUR DALIP NARAYAN SINGH
37. BABU CHANDRESHVAR PRASAD NARAYAN SINHA
38. BABU MAHESHVRI PRASHAD NARAYAN DEO
39. BABU JAGDEVA PRASAD SINGH
40. BABU SARDANANDA KUMAR
41. BABU RAMASRAY PRASHAD CHAUDHURI
42. BABU JAMUNA KARJEE
43. RAI BAHADUR SRI NARAYAN MAHTHA
44. BABU RAMESHVAR PRASHAD SINGH
45. KHAN BAHADUR SHAH MUHAMMAD YAHYA
46. MR. MUHAMMAD YUNUS
47. M. MUHAMMAD FAZLUR-RAHMAN
48. KHAN BAHADUR ABDUL WAHAB KHAN
49. KHAN BAHADUR HAJI MUHAMMAD BUX CHAUDHURI
50. MAULVI ABDUL AZIZ KHAN
51. BABU KALYAN SINGH
52. RAI BAHADUR HALDHAR PRASHAD SINGH
53. BHAIYA RUDRA PRATAP DEO
54. BABU SHYAM NARAYAN SINGH SHARMA
55. RAI BAHADUR SARAT CHANDRA RAY
56. RAI BAHADUR LAKSHMIDHAR MAHANTI
57. BABU HARIHAR DAS
58. RAI BAHADUR LOKNATH MISRA
59. BABU BRAJAMOHAN PANDA
60. BABU BIRAB R NARAYAN CHANDRA DHIR NARENDRA
61. BABU SHIB CHANDRA SINGHA
62. BABU DEVENDRA NATH SAMANTA
63. BABU RAMESHWAR PRATAP SAHI
64. BABU BADRI NARAYAN SINGH
65. BABU RUDRA PRATAP SINGH
66. BABU BISHUNDEO NARAYAN SINGH
67. MAULAVI KHALILUR RAHAMAN
68. MAULAVI MUHAMMAD ABDUL GHANI
69. MAULAVI SHAIKH MUHAMMAD SHAFI
70. KHAN BAHADUR HABIBUR RAHMAN
71. MAULAVI ABDUL WADOOD
72. MAULVI MUHAMMAD HASAN JAN
73. KHAN BAHADUR SAGHIR-UL HAQ
74. MR. SAIYID AKBARI
75. BABU RAMANUGRAH NARAYAN SINGH
76. BABU BHAGWATI SARAN SINGH
77. MAULAVI SHAIKH ABDUL JALIL
78. BABU GODAVARIS MISRA
79. RAI BAHADUR SATISH CHANDRA SINHA
80. MR. KAMALDHARI LALL

81. Rai Bahadur Lachhmi Prashad Sinha
82. Babu Jagannath Das
83. Babu Radharanjan Das
84. Babu Nikunja Kishore Das
85. Mr. Suruj Kumar Prashad Sinha
86. Babu Harmadeo Prashad Sinha
87. Chaudhuri Muhammad Nazirul Hasan
88. Babu Radha Mohan Sinha
89. Babu Kamjiwan Himat Singka
90. Mr. Sachchidananda Sinha
91. Raja Prithwi Chand Lall Chowdry
92. Rai Bahadur Dwarka Nath
93. Rai Bahadur Shyamnandan Sahay
94. Kumar Kalika Prashad Singh
95. Babu Jogendra Mohan Sinha
96. Babu Radha Prashad Sinha
97. Mr. Nanda Kumar Ghosh
98. Rai Bahadur Krishnadeva Narayan Mahtha
99. Babu Lalita Prashad Chaudhuri
100. Babu Kunja Bihari Chandra
101. Babu Manindra Nath Mukharji

Proceedings of the Council

January Session—Patna—9th. to 14th. January '36

Public Safety Amend. Bill.

The six-day session of the Behar and Orissa Legislative Council commenced at Patna on the **9th. January 1936** with thin non-official attendance when the Public Safety Amendment Bill was passed by 49 votes to 13. Introducing the Behar and Orissa Public Safety Extending and Amending Bill of 1936, seeking enactment in a permanent form of certain features of the Public Safety Act of 1933 and supplementing the legislation of Government of India, Mr. *P. C. Tallents*, Home Member, dwelt lengthily on the necessity of the measure with a view to enable the Government to cope with subversive and reactionary element in the province. Continuing, Mr. Tallents stated that the province of Bihar and Orissa was the next door neighbour of a province where there was terrorism and there was the possibility of the political agitators getting across into Bihar. He pointed out that the Civil Disobedience Movement was only under suspension and could break out any moment. In view of such facts he urged that Government felt it would be shirking in its duty if the measure were enacted for three years only.

Mr. *Sachchidanand Sinha*, leader of the opposition, moved an amendment extending the life of the 1933 bill for a further period of three years but withdrew in favour of the amendment standing in the name of R. B. *Shymnandan Sahai* exending it to five years.

Mr. *Jamuna Karjee* and *Kumar Kalika Prasad Singh*, both Congressites, vigorously opposed the bill, the former holding that the Home Member would have been the first man to introduce revolutionary activities in England if Englishmen had been in need of political freedom as Indians. Kumar Kalika Prasad said that the bill was a New Year's gift from the Government to the province and held that emergency for the the bill did not exist presently.

10th. JANUARY :—The Council discussed the motion of adjournment moved by *Moulvi Mohammed Hafeez* regarding the order of the Director of Public Instruction ordering a re-examination in the Patna division of the Middle English School Examination due to the leakage of question papers.

It was withdrawn after a long discussion on the assurance by the Minister of Education that the matter would be investigated and steps would be taken to prevent a recurrence of such incidents.

B. & O. Municipal Amend. Bill

Mr. *W. G. Lacey*, Secretary, Local Self-Government moved the Bihar and Orissa Municipal Amendment Bill with the chief object of investing the Government with the power of dissolution of the existing Municipal boards in cases of mismanagement and holding fresh election instead of complete supercession. The Bill was referred to a select committee.

B. & O. Village Administration Bill

The Council passed the Bihar and Orissa Village Administration Amendment Bill of 1936 for the dissolution of union boards for gross incompetence and investing the Government with similar power as stated above. This Bill was also introduced by Mr. Lacey.

B. & O. Moslem Wakf Bill

13th. JANUARY :—The Bihar and Orissa Moslem Wakf Bill, 1933, as reported by the select committee, was thrown out by 41 votes to 15. The bill was moved for consideration of the House by *Maulvi Hasan Jan.*

Sir *Sultan Ahmad*, opposing the measure, pointed out the opposition to the measure from Shias and the wide divergence of opinion among Sunnis regarding the provisions of the bill even as reported by the select committee.

Mr. *Abdul Aziz*, Minister for Education, stated that the Government opposed the consideration of the measure and emphasised the inadvisability of considering the bill in view of the wide and hopeless differences amongst Muslims themselves in respect of some important provisions.

Many other Moslem and non-Moslem members spoke on the bill.

Non-official Bills Introduced

Mr. *Ramanugrah Narayan Singh* introduced two private bills, namely, the Municipal Amendment Bill, 1936 and the Local Self-Government Bill, 1936, proposing to debar members of the legislative body constituted under the Government of India Act 1935, from becoming commissioners of municipalities and District local boards.

Bengal Land Revenue Sales Amend. Bill

14th. JANUARY :—The Government suffered their first defeat of the session on the motion of *Maulvi Mahammed Hafiz* for reference to a select committee of the Bengal Land Revenue Sales Amendment Bill, 1935, which was carried by 45 votes to 25. The measure was intended to provide for serving notices on recorded proprietors in the event of default of payment of revenue and putting up their property for sale. Maulvi Hafiz pointed out that public opinion was in favour of the meas ure.

The hon. Mr. *Tallents*, opposing the motion, said that the amending bi ll was inconsistent with the present Act and impracticable.

After a lively debate throughout the day the bill was referred to a select committee of 18 Members.

Muslim Representation in Local Bodies

15th. JANUARY :—The House assented to-day to *Maulvi Abdul Gani's* motion to make a special order for the continuance of the B. and O. Municipal Amendment Bill, 1935, and the B. and O. Local Self-Government Amendment Bill, 1935. Both the measures were intended to provide adequate representation to the Muslim community in local bodies. The House then adjourned *sine die.*

February Session—Patna—22nd. to 29th. February 1936

Tribute to Late King

The February session of the Council commenced on the **22nd. February** and the day was dedicated to the memory of King George. All sections of the House joined in paying tributes to the late King and the House adjourned as a mark of respect after adopting the condolence resolution.

Moving the resolution, Mr. *Nirsu Narayan Sinha*, Leader of the House, said: 'We of this province have a special reason to cherish with gratitude the memory of King George. It is well known that every Bihari in his heart desired to have a separate province of his own. This was done at Delhi when His Majesty came to India for coronation. The proclamation which had announced the separation of the province has fulfilled that ambition which had been cherished by every Bihari at that time. This royal province, therefore, will for ever remember with gratitude the visit of the first sovereign to this country'.

The members stood for two minutes, in silence, unanimously adopting the resolution and conveying the respectful homage and loyalty to the late King

Budget for 1936-37

24th. FEBRUARY :—Introducing to-day the budget estimates for the new Province of Bihar for 1936-37, Mr. *Nirsu Narayan Sinha*, Finance Member, at first referred to the separation of the new Province of Orissa and explained that the finances of that Province were not under consideration in that House.

He commented on the financial history of the Province and pointed out that though the Province was not in debt, this was only because, throughout its life, the Province's finances had been guided along paths of financial rectitude, partly by starving the Province even of the necessities and the present resources of both the new Provinces were wholly inadequate to meet the requirements when compared with the standards of other Provinces, until sums were available out of income-tax for distribution to the Province, and it was necessary that both the Provinces should receive immediate assistance by means of grants-in-aids.

On the separation of Orissa, Bihar loses Rs. 94 lakhs revenue and transfers to Orissa Rs. ninety and a half lakhs expenditure. The budget however provides for Rs. 11 lakhs contribution to be received from Orissa.

As a result Bihar is better off by about Rs. seven and a half lakhs after separation, contributions being for the High Court, joint Medical and Educational institutions, leave and pension charges of joint services, and Orissa's share of pensions has already been sanctioned for being paid from the Bihar revenue.

Next year the new Province of Bihar will have revenue of Rs. 4,70,00,000, which after taking into account the revenue transferred to Orissa, is Rs. 11 lakhs more than the revised estimates. This increase results mainly from accounting charges and separation of Orissa and does not indicate increased prosperity. The estimated expenditure next year is Rs. 4,81,73,000 which, after making allowance for Rs. 90 and half lakhs transferred to Orissa and contribution of Rs. 7,36,000 received from the new Province is Rs. 19 lakhs more than the revised estimates.

The Budget provides for Rs. 4,91,000 for recurring and Rs. 14,38,000 for non-recurring new schemes. Recurring schemes include many which had been previously in existence on a temporary basis, and actual new recurring commitments total Rs. 1,15,000.

The more important of the new schemes are increased discretionary grants, permanent restoration of primary education grant, extension of the Cottage Industries Institute, building grants for primary schools, creation of boiler inspectorate and increased augmentation grant.

Summarising earthquake expenditure, the Finance Member said that the Government of India will likely have to meet a total expenditure of Rs. 206 lakhs and the Local Government Rs. 69 lakhs.

Agriculturist Relief Bill

After the presentation of the Budget, Mr. *S. K. P. Singha* moved reference to select committee of the bill to provide relief to the agricuturists from indebtedness and emphasised the acute poverty of Bihar peasantry and emergent nature of the proposed legislation.

Mr. *P. C. Tallents*, on behalf of the Government, moved the circulation of the bill for public opinion, pointing out the difficulties inherent in enacting such legislation and explaining what other provinces had done in that connection. The proposed legislation touched only a fringe of the problem and it was desirable that public opinion be ascertained whether the problem would be tackled in detail or as suggested.

The Council agreed by 30 to 23 votes to circulate the Bill for public opinion.

Non-official Resolutions

26th. FEBRUARY :—The Council discussed to-day non-official resolutions.

The resolution of *Khan Bahadur Habibur Rahman*, recommending to the Government to appoint a lawyer in each district to conduct prosecutions on behalf of the Crown and abolish the system of such prosecutions being conducted by police officers, was withdrawn after an explanation by Government that modifications in the system would involve enormous expenditure.

Mr. *S. K. P. Sinha's* resolution, asking the Government to appoint a committee to undertake the programme of extension of the present Council Chamber to provide additional accommodation required for Bihar legislatures under the new reforms, was accepted.

THE NIEMEYER SCHEME

27th. FEBRUARY :—The House adopted unanimously to-day Mr. *Radha Prasad Sinha's* resolution recommending the Government to convey to Sir Otto Niemeyer that this Council urges for a satisfactory and equitable financial resettlement for Bihar and the new province of Orissa, as in the opinion of the Council provincial autonomy was not likely to succeed unless such re-settlement was made as to remove the financial disabilities attaching to this province under the previous arrangements. The mover said that poverty had been imposed on the province, while the rest of India derived the benefit of its resources.

The *Finance Member*, accepting the resolution, said that the position of Bihar was stronger than others for subvention. In fact they had the right to demand it. He assured the House that he would press the claims of the province before Sir Otto Niemeyer shortly.

Mr. *Sachchidananda Sinha*, leader of the Opposition, and several other non-official members supported the motion.

B. & O. CESS AMEND. BILL

28th. FEBRUARY :—In the Council to-day, discussion centred round Mr. *P. C. Tallent's* motion for reference of the Bihar and Orissa Cess Amendment Bill to a Select Committee. Mr. Tallents lengthily explained the Government policy in amending the existing Law, which aimed at remedying the desperate state of roads in colliery areas and ensuring that all collieries, which used roads, should contribute and all such collieries which were making profit should pay something more in future as they had done in the past.

Mr. *H. D. Townend* and Mr. M. N. Mukherji, representing colliery interests, vehemently opposed the Bill. Discussion had not concluded when the House adjourned.

29th. FEBRUARY :—Resuming discussion to-day Sir *Ganesh Dutt Singh* said that the main object of the Bill was to cover the nakedness of the District Boards. Services after services had been retrenched owing to lack of income. If the boards were to exist, some source of income had to be found out for them. In Hazaribagh and Manbhum there was no other source of income by which the resources of the Boards could be augmented except levying some sort of tax on coal. He said that cess should not be levied on profits as it was very uncertain. Therefore, the speaker said that cess should be levied on actual production. The coalfields were raising the same if not larger quantity of coal depression. The method of taxation suggested would bring an income of about Rs. 3 to 4 lakhs. The consumers, said the speaker, would not grudge paying eight pies per ton of coal used by them. Despite everything the market for coal will remain the same as the slight rise will not affect its demand in market.

Mr. *J. M. Sinha* opposed the Bill on the ground that if it was passed, it would prove ruinous to the coal industry.

Mr. *B. W. Heigh* (European) said that he was in full sympathy with the objects of the Bill. He complemented the Government on their method of handling the problem of low revenue of the District Boards in the coalfields area.

Mr. *S. K. P. Sinha* said that he was in agreement with much of what had been said for the Bill but he disagreed with the idea of levying a uniform rate of cess for all kinds of coals. He suggested a graded rate of taxation according to the quality of the coal.

Mr. *N. N. Sinha* said that the issue before the House was that the income of the District Boards has declined to such an extent that they were unable to look after the education, sanitation and roads in the area. The reason for the falling off in the price of coal was due to the fact that the trade was dull all over the world. The cess proposed to be levied was 8 pies to a ton which the speaker said was negligible in so far as it would not very much add to the difficulties of the coal trade. The measure was in the interest of everybody in the district and as such the House should pass the Bill.

After the Home Member had replied to the debate, the motion for reference to a Select Committee was carried by 44 votes against 19. The House then adjourned.

The Assam Legislative Council

LIST OF MEMBERS

THE HON'BLE MAULAVI FAIZNUR ALI (*President*)

THE HON'BLE MR. W. L. SCOTT

THE HON'BLE RAI BAHADUR PROMODE CHANDRA DATTA

1. MR. J. A. DAWSON
2. MR. E. P. BURKE
3. MR. H. M. PRICHARD
4. MR. H. G. DENNEHY
5. MR. G. A. SMALL
6. SREEJUKTA ATUL KRISHNA BHATTACHARYA
7. SRIJUT MAHENDRA LAL DAS
8. KHAN BAHADUR MAULVI MUHAMMAD MASHRAF
9. RAI SAHIB PYARI MOHAN DAS
10. REV. TANURAM SAIKIA
11. SUBADAR MAJOR SARDAR BAHADUR JANGBIR LAMA
12. KHAN BAHADUR MAULVI KERAMAT ALI
13. THE REV. JAMES JOY MOHAN NICHOLS-ROY
14. BABU SANAT KUMAR DAS
15. BABU HIRENDRA CHANDRA CHAKRABARTI
16. BABU BIRENDRA LAL DAS
17. BABU KALICHARAN MUCHI
18. BABU GOPENDRALAL DAS CHAUDHURY
19. BABU JITENDRA KUMAR PAL CHAUDHURI
20. BABU CHIRATAN MUCHI
21. MR. SASANKA MOHAN DAS
22. KUMAR PRAMATHESH CHANDRA BARUA
23. SRIJUT BEPIN CHANDRA GHOSH
24. SRIJUT ROHINI KUMAR CHAUDHURI
25. RAI BAHADUR RAJANI KANTA CHOUDHURY
26. RAI SAHIB DALIM CHANDRA BORA
27. KUMAR BHUPENDRA NARAIN DEB
28. RAI BAHADUR BRINDABAN CHANDRA GOSWAMI
29. SRIJUT JOGENDRA NATH GOHAIN
30. SRIJUT KASHI NATH SAIKIA
31. SRIJUT MAHENDRA NATH GOHAIN
32. RAI BAHADUR NILAMBAR DUTTA
33. SRIJUT SARVESWAR BARUA
34. HAJI IDRIS ALI BARLASKAR
35. THE HON'BLE MAULVI ABDUL HAMID
36. MAULVI ABDUR RASHID CHAUDHURI
37. MAULVI MUNAWWARALI
38. MAULVI ADDUR RAHIM CHAUDHURY
39. MAULVI SAIYID ABDUL MANNAN
40. MAULVI ABDUL KHALIQUE CHOUDHURY
41. KHAN SAHIB MAULVI MAHMUD ALI
42. MAULVI ABDUL MAJID ZIAOSHSHAMS
43. KHAN SAHIB MAULVI MIZANAR PAHMAN
44. KHAN BAHADUR MAULVI NURUDDIN AHMED
45. THE HON'BLE MAULVI FAIZNUR ALI
46. MR. L. J. GODWIN
47. MR. A. J. RICHARDSON
48. MR. F. W. HOCKENHULL
49. MR. G. E. RAYNER
50. MR. W. E. D. COOPER
51. THE HON'BLE RAI BAHADUR KANAK LAL BARUA

Proceedings of the Council

Budget Session—Shillong—10th. to 28th. March 1936

TRIBUTES TO LATE KING

The Budget Session of the Assam Legislative Council commenced at Shillong on the **10th. March 1936** under the presidency of Mr. *Faiznoor Ali*. The Hon'ble Rai Bahadur *P. C. Datta* moved the resolution of condolence on King George's death and of loyalty to the new King. Mr. Hockenhull, Khan Bahadur Nuruddin Ahmed, and Rai Bahadur Nilambar Datta spoke on the motion.

The Hon'ble *President* associated himself with the resolution. Thereafter the Council adjourned as a mark of respect to the memory of King George.

The Governor's Address

11th. MARCH :—His Excellency Sir *Michael Keane*, addressing the Council this morning, paid a tribute to the memory of the late King George and recalled the message recently broadcast by H. M. King Edward VIII making clear that His Majesty would follow in the footsteps of his illustrious father. Proceeding, the Governor said that this was the last Budget session which he would be addressing and, reviewing the political development in the Province, stated that his experience was that the moment opportunity was offered to Indians, they would work the system with a good sense of responsibility. The fact that people's minds had already been preoccupied with what the new Act would bring them, showed that all vague talk of not working the new Constitution had evaporated into thin atmosphere. Referring to the financial position of the Province, he pointed out that the gravest anxiety of the Government and the people of the Province, at the moment, was about the estimated deficit of Rs. 57 lakhs. His Excellency here adverted to the Niemyer Enquiry, and paid a tribute to Sir Otto Niemeyer who, with an open mind, gave a patient hearing to the case presented by their Province.

Budget for 1936-37

The Hon. Mr. *W. L. Scott*, Finance Member, then presented the budget for 1936-37 . Assam's total income estimated is Rs. 2,27,93,000 while the expenditure is Rs. 3,29,5000. A loan of 57 lakhs and 12 thousand from the Provincial Loans Funds will be required to balance the accounts.

The debt at the end of this month would be Rs. 192 lakhs and in March 1937 it would be Rs. 339 lakhs, a sum greater than the provincial revenues. Under "Excise" a decrease of Rs. 1 and half lakhs was expected owing to the opium restriction policy.

The Hon'ble Mr. Scott addressing said : "In 1936-37, we have to find Rs. 19 lakhs to pay our dues and this we can only do by borrowing more, a process vulgarly known in commercial circles as 'feeding the dog on his own tail' and recognised as a prelude to bankruptcy."

Bills Introduced

The following bills were next introduced : the Cattle Trespass (Assam Amendment) Bill, 1936, the Assam Criminal Law Amendment Bill, 1936, the Assam Land and Revenue (Amendment No. 1) Bill, 1936, the Assam Land and Revenue (Amendment No. 2) Bill, 1936, the Assam Motor Vehicles Taxation Bill, 1936, and the Assam Debt Conciliation Bill, 1936.

A motion for circulation of the Assam Criminal Law Amendment Bill, 1936, for eliciting public opinion, raised by *Maulvi Abdur Rashid Choudhury*, was declared carried by 25 votes against 19.

Maulvi Abdul Khalique Chaudhury's Bill, the Assam Land Revenue Re-assessment Bill, 1935, was referred to a Select Committee.

Maulvi Abdur Rashid Choudury's motion to refer his Assam State Aid to Industries Bill, 1935, to a Select Committee was opposed by the Government and eventually lost.

Maulvi Abdul Khalique Choudhury's motion to refer the Assam Embankment and Drainage Bill, 1935, to a Select Committee was supported by Mr. Rohini Kumar Choudhury, Khan Bahadur Keramat Ali, Khan Bahadur Md. Moshraff and others, but opposed by Rai Bahadur Brindaban Goswami Mr. E. P. Burke, Chief Engineer, and the Hon. Rai Bahadur P. C. Datta, Judicial Member and eventually lost when put to the vote.

Moneylenders' Amend. Bill

12th. MARCH :—The Council decided to-day to circulate the Assam Moneylenders' Amendment Bill of 1936 moved by *Maulavi Rashid Chaudhury* for eliciting public opinion before the 31st July, 1936. The Hon'ble *Rai Bahadur Promode Chandra Datta*, Judicial Member, pointed out the drastic nature of the Bill.

ASSAM MUNICIPAL AMEND. BILL

The Assam Municipal Amendment Bill of 1935 for getting public places of worship exempted from paying water and latrine taxes was also to be circulated for eliciting public opinion before the 31st August, 1936.

Mr. *Maulavi Abdul Khalique Chaudhuri's* Assam Disorderly Houses Bill of 1935, and Mr. Gopendra Lal Das Chowdhury's Bill, the Assam Land Revenue Amendment Bill of 1936 were sent to the Select Committee.

13th. MARCH :—Mr. *Abdul Khaleque's* Cruelty to Animals Bill and Money Lenders' Bill were withdrawn. Mr. *Abdul Khaleque's* Disorderly Houses Bill and Mr. *Abdur Rashid's* Money Lenders' Bill were circulated for eliciting public opinion.

HIGH COURT FOR ASSAM

Khan Bahadur *Keramatali's* resolution for high court in Assam was lost by 26 against 15 votes, the Tea Planters opposing the resolution. Assam Valley members supported the resolution while the Surma Valley members opposed it, only Messrs. Abdul Khaleque and Abdur Rashid (Surma Valley members) voting in favour of the resolution.

BUDGET DISCUSSION

16th. MARCH :—The Council concluded to-day the budget discussion. Mr. *F. W. Hockenhull* deplored borrowing by the Government to finance their needs and pressed for improvement of services.

Mr. *Gopendralal Das Chaudhury* regretted the absence of any programme for raising literacy, improving health and increasing the earning capacity of the masses.

Khan Bahadur Nuruddin Ahmed hoped that terrorism had left Assam for ever and the Assam Criminal Amendment Law would remain a dead letter.

Mr. *J. A. Dawson*, Chief Secretary, Assam Government, requested the members to make Assam a bigger and stronger province by working in unity.

Rai Bahadur Kanak Lal Barua, Minister, said that the Sylhet Medical School could not be started in the present financial condition.

Mr. *B. G. Dennehy*, Secretary to the Transferred Department, said that the question of distributing opium in pill forms in Assam could not be taken up in the present condition of provincial finances.

17th. MARCH :- The Council passed to-day the Assam Criminal Law Amendment Bill as also the Cattle Trespass (Assam) Amendment Bill. The former encountered some opposition.

The Assam Land Revenue Amendment Bill, as reported by the select committee, was taken into consideration, while the Assam Debt Conciliation Bill and the Assam Motor Vehicles Taxation Bill were sent to select committees. The Sylhet Tenancy Bill was introduced.

The adjourned motion of Mr. *Gopendra Lal Das Chaudhury* to discuss the recent decision of the Government to bring the Local Rates Amendment Act of 1932 into force from the 1st of April 1936 and to increase the rate from 1343 B. S. in north Sylhet sub-division, was defeated by 26 votes to 13.

VOTING ON BUDGET DEMANDS

19th. MARCH :—The Council passed to-day the demands under land revenue, forest, stamps and navigation. Cut motions moved were withdrawn or lost.

Mr. *Kasinath Salkia* urged for giving Mauzadars the right to appeal to the Government and Mr. Sarveswar Barua sought to raise their commission by 10 per cent. The Government did not agree.

Mr. *Kasinath Salkia* urged upon the Government the necessity of spending at least a portion of the grazing tax for growing grass for fodder.

The Hon'ble Mr. *W. L. Scott*, Finance Member, did not agree to earmark any portion of the revenue for any particular purpose as suggested.

20th. MARCH :—The Council passed to-day demands for grants under general Administration, Administration of Justice and Ports and Pilotage. A cut motion moved by Mr. *Sanat Kumar Das* for making appointments on merit alone to the extent of 20 or 25 per cent of appointments in certain services was opposed by Khan Bahadur Keramat Ali, Maulvi Abdur Rahim Chowdhury and others and eventually withdrawn.

Mr. *Rohini Kumar Chowdhury's* cut motion urging abolition of one of the posts of Commissioner of Division was carried.

24th. MARCH :—The Council passed to-day the demands under Excise, Education (reserved) and Education other than European. The House by 25 to 9 votes rejected Maulvi *Abdur Rashid Chaudhury's* cut motion raising a discussion about the appointment of more Muslims as professors and lecturers.

Mr. *G. A. Small*, Director of Public Instruction replied that these appointments were made by a selection board on which there were two Mahomedans to look after Mahomedan interests and the instructions of the Government were to appoint the best available men, preference being given to natives of the province.

On a cut motion moved by *Hazi Idris Ali Barlaskar* the Government were criticised for their excise policy.

Hon. *Maulvi Abdul Hamid*, Minister of Education, stood by the declared policy of the Government to reduce consumption of opium. The motion was withdrawn.

26th. MARCH :—On a cut motion raised yesterday in the Council by Maulvi Abdur Rashid Chaudhury, the House discussed to-day at considerable length as to what should be the principle of appointment in the grades of lecturers and professors in Assam and eventually decided by a majority of 25 to 9 votes that the principle should be one of merit, preference being given to the natives of Assam.

Assam Land Revenue Amend. Bill

27th. MARCH :—The Council passed to-day the Assam Land Revenue (Amendment No. 1) Bill, 1936, which made provision for setting aside the sale of an estate for non-payment of land revenue.

The Bill was introduced by the Hon'ble Mr. *W. L. Scott*, Revenue Member.

Sylhet Tenancy Bill

The Sylhet Tenancy Bill was referred to a select committee.

Reduction of Rent

28th. MARCH :—The Council passed to-day *Khan Sahib Maulvi Mizanar Rahman's* resolution for reduction of rent in Mechpara and Bijni Raj estates on account of their inability to pay rents due to various causes.

The Hon. *Maulvi Abdul Hamid*, Minister of Education, accepted the resolution moved by Mr. F. W. Hockenhull, Leader of the planting group in the House, for a further departmental investigation and report regarding the possibility of developing animal husbandry in the province.

Assam Dis-orderly Houses Bill

The House next adopted the Assam disorderly Houses Bill, 1936, which made provisions for discontinuance of disorderly houses in certain localities in Assam.

Mr. *Sarveshwar Barua's* motion for having a tuberculosis sanitarium was withdrawn on assurance being given that there was prospect of a small sanitarium shortly. The House then adjourned *sine die*.

The Burma Legislative Council

Budget Session—Rangoon—17th. February to 4th. March 1936

Burma Criminal Law Amend. Bill

The Budget Session of the Burma Legislative Council commenced at Rangoon on the 17th. February 1936 and after three hours' debate, rejected the Burma Criminal Law Amendment Act Bill by 44 votes to 33. Members of *U. Ba Maw's*, *U. Chit Hlaing's*, *Myat Paw's* and *People's Parties* and the Indians voted against the Bill, while the official bloc, including Ministers, Europeans and several Independents, voted in favour.

The *Home Member*, in moving that the Bill be passed into law, implored the House not to be prejudiced and biassed, but to be reasonable, as the Bill did not contain any objectionable provisions.

Mr. *S. A. S. Tyabji*, leading the attack, remarked that persons detained as terrorists were not terrorists but branded so by the C. I. D.

Mr. *Ganga Singh* held that the terrorists were Government's own making owing to unemployment.

Mr. *M. M. Rafi* criticising the principle of the measure, said that no attempt was made to give the accused persons opportunities to test the veracity of the prosecution statements collected by the authorities concerned.

Mr. *B. N. Das* and several Burman speakers condemned the Bill.

Bill Recommended by Governor

19th. FEBRUARY :—*H. E. the Governor* returned to the Council to-day, the Burma Criminal Law Amendment Bill, with a recommendation that the Bill be passed in the form in which it was originally introduced.

Council Rejects the Bill Again

22nd. FEBRUARY :—For the second time by 37 votes to 32, the Council rejected the Home Member's Criminal Law Amendment Bill when he asked for leave of the House to introduce the Bill in the form as recommended by H. E. the Governor.

Sir Maung Ba, Home Member, said that the Act was justified. It enabled Government to frustrate the attempts of Bengal terrorists. Prevention was better than cure.

Mr. *Ganga Singh* termed the measure as a lawless Bill.

The House then refused to grant leave on division.

Demands for Grants

24th. FEBRUARY :—The Council commenced the two-day debate on the Finance Member's demands for grants, and the whole day was occupied in discussing four cut motions, of which one was withdrawn and three were passed. *U. Ba Saw* moved a cut to discuss grievances of indigenous oil extractors, since the Burmese regime in Yenang-yaung oil-fields and maintained they were being exploited by the B. O. C. The Financial Commissioner, however, pointed out that the grievances were imaginary. The cut was passed by 41 to 24 votes.

Rangoon—Madras Mail Service

27th. FEBRUARY :—Mr. *M. M. Vellayan Chettiar*'s cut motion in the Home Member's demands for grant to discuss the action of the local Government in acquiescing in the discontinuance of the direct mail service between Madras and Rangoon were carried unanimously.

The *Home Member* said that he had no objection if the House wished to discuss the matter but he stated that the Government would not participate in the debate, but would forward the views expressed to the Government of India.

Several Indian members strongly resented this action of the Government of India and urged the local Government to make recommendations for the continuance of the service.

RELEASE OF POLITICAL PRISONERS

Release of political prisoners and detenus was discussed by way of cut motions under the Home Member's demands for grants which was voted with reduction of Rs. 101 by passing two cuts.

Mr. *Gangasingh's* cut urged the release of all political prisoners convicted under Sections 124-A and 153-A, I. P. C. and Burma Criminal Law Act (excepting those who had committed violence) simultaneously with the introduction of reforms. He argued that it was right and proper that under the new constitution, Burma should start with a clean slate by liberating all political· prisoners whose patriotic feelings had offended law. The speaker instanced the release of prisoners during the last Coronation.

Government speakers pointed out that only 18 persons were now in custody, of whom 16 were under the Burma Criminal Law Act. It would be dangerous to release them in the interests of public peace and tranquillity.

The motion was carried by 33 votes to 20.

Mr. *S. A. S. Tyabji* moved two cuts, one calling attention to the unsatisfactory method adopted for the release of detenus and the other to the desirability of sending detenus to Bengal or teaching them industry. After hearing Government views, both cuts were withdrawn.

As regards the first cut, the *Chief Secretary* assured the House that if any detenu gave an undertaking that he would not participate in any subversive act in future and his guardian gave a guarantee to that effect, Government would be normally satisfied and release him. Regarding the second cut, the Judicial Secretary stated that so far as the training of detenus locally was concerned Government would do its best to treat any case sympathetically.

28th. FEBRUARY :—Owing to want of quorum, the President adjourned the Council, when it met after luncheon recess to discuss the demands for grants under the charge of the Forest Minister. The warning bell was given for two minutes under the Standing Order but only 18 members, including the President, was found to be in their seats.

2nd. MARCH :—A lively debate was heard to-day when *Ramri U Maung Maung* (Independent Party) moved a cut to pass a vote of censure on Dr. *Ba Maw*, Education Minister, after the latter had moved his demands for grants.

Ramri Maung Maung was continually interrupted by members of Dr. *Ba Maw's* Party who questioned and cross-questioned him and made humorous remarks.

The mover supported by *U Kyaw Din*, ex-Education Minister, criticised the ministerial policy and asserted that Dr. Ba Maw had not acted according to his pledges.

Several members of Dr. *Ba Maw's* Party opposed the motion.

Dr. *Ba Maw* refuted the allegations.

The motion was lost, only six including Sir *J. A. Maung Gyi*, Leader of the Independent Party, standing up in favour of the motion, while the rest of the House opposed it.

Thereafter *Ramri Maung Maung* moved another cut to restrict the travelling of the Education Minister at public expense for his private propaganda work.

While the mover was speaking the Council was adjourned, owing to want of quorum.

THE GOVERNOR'S FAREWELL ADDRESS

4th. MARCH :—"The responsibilities of this Council under the new Constitution will be very vastly increased. Through the support which you give to or withhold from Ministers you will directly be responsible for the policy of Government and that responsibility will keep you very fully occupied", was the note of warning sounded by H. E. the Governor, in the course of his farewell address to-day to the Council.

His Excellency continued that under the new Constitution, the Executive agency would have no control over policy. That would rest with the Council, and they would enforce their control over policy through the Ministers and would see that to-day administration through the Executive agency was conducted in accordance with the general policy approved by the Council. It was no part of the duties of the Legislature to interfere with the details of daily administration.

Reviewing the past three years of his administration, H. E. the Governor said that financial equilibrium was restored, but it was attained by considerably retarding the progress of the Province. He, however, thought that the revenue position of Burma would be better after separation. As regards the political situation, His Excellency thought that the prospects of political progress were much better than they were three years ago.

RANGOON STUDENTS' STRIKE

A full dress debate on the University strike was held in the Council in the special night sitting, which commenced at 8-30. The debate lasted till about mid-night. *U Saw's* motion as amended by *U Kun* was passed without division. Two other amendments moved were withdrawn.

The motion recommended that a Committee be appointed, consisting of eight persons including seven M. L. C.'s to enquire into the recent strike of the University students and submit recommendations to the Local Government.

Several Burmese and Indian speakers, supporting the motion, criticised the Government's attitude as irresponsible detachment and emphasised that the Government and the Legislative Council were under a definite moral obligation to settle the issue.

The *Education Secretary*, explained that under the University Act the University Council was the supreme authority on internal matters, like strike. Therefore Government have no legal status in these matters and could have no attitude.

The *Education Minister*, replying to the debate, stated that by virtue of the Act, internal matters were within the competence of the University Council. As regards external affairs, he sympathised with the desirability to examine the working of the Act. Government, though prepared to convey to the Governor the full report of the debate, would not participate in voting. He also informed that the Governor, who was the Chancellor of the University, would consider the views of the House while selecting the personnel of the Committee that had been decided by the University Council to end the issue. The Council was at this stage *prorogued*.

The N. W. F. Legislative Council

LIST OF MEMBERS

1. THE HON'BLE KHAN BAHADUR ABDUR RAHIM KHAN (*President*)
2. THE HON'BLE MR. G. CUNNINGHAM (*Executive Member*)
3. THE HON'BLE KHAN BAHADUR NAWAB SIR ABDUL QAYUM KHAN (*Minister*)
4. THOMSON, MR. J. S.
5. ROSS, MR. G. M.
6. DELGALE, MR. H. O.
7. COLONEL, H. H. THORNBURN
8. S. RAJA SINGH
9. ALLAH NAWAZ KHAN, NAWABZADA
10. KHAN GHULAM RABBARI KHAN
11. HASSAN ALI KHAN, SULTAN KHAN SAHIB
12. KHAN MALIK-UR-RAHMAN KHAN, KAYANI
13. NARINJAN SINGH BEDI, BABA
14. KHAN ABDUL GHAFUR KHAN
13. ABDUL QAYUM KHAN, MR.
14. ABDUL RAHMAN KHAN ARBAB
15. KHAN ABDUL HAMID KHAN, KUNDI
16. BAZ MUHAMMAD KHAN, KHAN BAHADUR, NAWAB
17. GHULAM HAIDER KHAN, KHAN BAHADUR
20. GHULAM HASSAN ALI SHAH ALIAS HASSAN GUL PIR
21. KHAN SAHIB HIDAYTULLAH KHAN
22. KHAN HABIBULLAH KHAN
23. HAMIDULLAH KHAN, KHAN BAHADUR NAWAB
24. ISHER DAS, RAI BAHADUR LALA
25. KARAM CHAND, RAI BAHADUR
26. KHUDA BAKHSH KHAN, MALIK
27. LADHA RAM, LALA
28. MUHAMMAD ZAMAN KHAN, KHAN BAHADUR
29. KHAN MUHAMMAD ABBAS KHAN
30. MUHAMMAD SHARIF KHAN,
31. MUHAMMAD AYUB KHAN, MR.
32. MEHR CHAND KHANNA, RAI SAHIB, LALA
33. NAWABZADA NASRULLAH KHAN
34. PIR BAKHSH, MR
35. SARDAR JAGGAT SINGH
36. ROCHI RAM, RAI BAHADUR
37. SAMUNDAR KHAN, MR.
38. TAJ MUHAMMAD KHAN, KHAN BAHADUR

Proceedings of the Council

Budget Session—Peshawar—10th. to 28th. March 1936

The Budget session of the N. W. Frontier Legislative Council, which commenced at Peshawar on the **10th. March 1936**, adjourned after passing, all standing, *Sir George Cunningham's* motion on King George's death, expressing deep sorrow and heartfelt sympathy with His Majesty King Edward and Queen Mary and the Royal Family and reaffirming constant loyalty to the Emperor and the British Crown.

Sir George Cunningham said that the death had removed a true guide and friend, revered as a King and loved as a man, full of dignity and simplicity and ever faithful to his own supreme standards of duty and service.

Party leaders and the Minister, Sir *Abdul Qaiyum*, associating, paid tributes to the late King's personal interest in the people's welfare.

The President, *Khan Bahadur Abdul Rahim* said that he would convey the Council's feelings to King Edward and the Queen Mother.

All Hindu and Sikh members who were absent in the last session as a protest against issuing the language circular were present. They also attended to-morrow's sitting, when the condolence motion on the death of Khan Bahadur Abdul Gafer of Zaidae came before the Council. Thereafter, they proposed to leave the Council Hall in accordance with their constituents' mandate to abstain from attending till the circular was withdrawn.

BUDGET FOR 1936-37

11th. MARCH :—Sir *George Cunningham*, Finance Member, presented to the Council to-day the budget for 1936-37.

After taking stock of the present and past position, the Finance Member estimated receipts at Rs. 170 lakhs and expenditure at Rs. 180 lakhs, a deficit of Rs. 10 lakhs, to be met from the opening balance of Rs. 10 and one-fourth lakhs. Last year Sir George Cunningham opined, Rs. 7 and a half lakhs must be taken as standing deficit due to non-recurring expenditure of Rs. 1 and a half lakhs to the Council hall building and Rs. 50,000 on other items including election charges, leaving a net deficit of Rs. 8 lakhs. To increase revenue, the Government proposed to introduce the Motor Taxation Bill in the form recommended by H. E. the Governor as a result of which one lakh revenue was estimated, reducing the net deficit to Rs. 7 lakhs.

The Finance Member observed that "the future course of our administration must depend largely on the decision of the Government of India, regarding future subvention to the Province. Sir Otto Niemeyer is now enquiring into the question. Local Government have placed before him full account of the Province's needs. The verdict will anxiously be awaited by none more than myself."

TAXATION ON MOTOR VEHICLES

The *President* next read the Governor's message recommending the passage of the Motor Taxation Bill in a modified form, aiming at lower taxation of cheap vehicles, after which the Finance Member sought leave to introduce the Bill, which was granted by 19 votes to 13.

Referring to Motor dealers' representation regarding the fees and taxes charged by the local Government, the Finance Member assured the House of reduction after scrutiny. He impressed the urgent necessity of facing the moral and financial obligations to strengthen the case for increase of subvention.

Mr. *Khuda Baksh*, Leader of the Opposition, said that Government, at the expense of local bodies, wanted to fill the gap caused by unnecessary expenditure, not considered by the Haig Committee, while calculating the subvention.

UNIVERSITY FOR THE FRONTIER

12th. MARCH :—The Council carried a non-official resolution to-day recommending the establishment of a Unitary University at Peshawar.

Dr. Gill, Director of Education, said that the Local Government submitted a case for a grant to the Government of India, hoping it would include it in the subvention.

Sir Abdul Qaiyum, Minister, said that the new University would cater to the needs of the tribal area forming half the Province. It was not their intention to transmit to the tribal area ideas imported by mistake from South India.

VOTING ON BUDGET DEMANDS

26th. MARCH :—Mr. *Peer Baksh*, an Independent member, moved a token cut to-day in the demand for grant under General Administration : Reserved" "to condemn the Government for the misuse of the provisions of the Public Tranquility Act by unjustifiable restraining of the lawful activities of associations and individuals."

Mr. Peer Baksh urged the lifting of the ban of unlawfulness from the Frontier Congress Committee and restrictions on individuals in view of the changed political atmosphere.

The *Home Member*, Sir George Cunningham, said that Government's conscience was clear that they had not abused the Act. The restrictions on associations were under the Criminal Law Act. The tranquillity Act was applied on 13 persons, of whom at present, six are believed to be in sympathy with terrorism and five were members of the Naujawan Bharat Sabha. The 12th was Maulvi Ghulam Ghaus, President, Frontier Jamait-ululema, and the 13th, Inayatullah Mashraoui, founder of Kakshar movement. If there was any order directed against constitutional activity like seeking election to the Legislature, Government were prepared to relax it. The cut was rejected without division.

Proceedings of the

CONGRESS, MOSLEM, HINDU SABHA

and

Other Provincial Political Conferences

JANUARY—JUNE 1936

The Indian National Congress

Resolutions passed at the 49th. Session of the Congress held at *Lucknow on 12-14 April 1936*

1. Condolence

This Congress expresses its sense of sorrow and loss at the deaths of Sriyuts B. N. Sasmal, M. V. Abhyankar, A. T. Gidwani, T. A. K. Sherwani, Arif Hasvi, Deep Narayan Singh, Shapurji Saklatwala, Sir Dinshaw Wacha, Nabin Chandra Bardolai, Shrimati Kamla Nehru, Syts. Mohanlal Pandya, Seth Nathmal Choradia, Ganpatrao Tikekar, T. V. Venkataram Iyer, Aga Mohammad Safdar and Mahadeo Prasad Seth.

2. Greeting to Prisoners Etc.

The Congress sends its greeting to the thousands of Indians whom British imperialism keeps in prison, in detention and in exile, and who suffer in silence and with brave endurance in the cause of India's freedom. In particular, the Congress sends affectionate greeting to Khan Abdul Ghaffar Khan, a member of the Working Committee, and offers its earnest sympathy to the people of the North-West Frontier Province, and of Midnapore District, and other parts of Bengal, who have long had to endure the fiercest repression under a regime approximating to Martial Law.

3. Shri Subhas Chandra Bose's Arrest

The Congress has learnt with indignation of the Arrest under Regulation III of 1818 of Shri Subhas Bose on his return to India after long exile, when on his way to attend this session of the Congress. This Congress considers it a further and significant proof of how British imperialism continues to use its full apparatus of repression to prevent normal political and personal life in India. To Shri Subhas Chandra Bose the Congress sends its warm greeting and sympathy.

4. Suppression of Civil Liberties

The Congress draws public attention again to the widespread and intensive suppression of civil and, in many instances, personal liberties in India by the British Government, with the object of crushing the national and labour and peasant movements. In particular, to the banning of hundreds of Congress and other national organisations, and labour and peasant unions, and political and other groups; seizure and continued possession by the Government of many ashrams and other educational institutions; the continuance of the Ordinance regime by the certification and passage of the Criminal Law Amendment Act, even after its rejection twice by the Assembly, and the enactment of similar provincial Acts; the proscription and banning of books and periodicals; the numerous Press laws and censorship resulting in the suppression of 348 newspapers in recent years and the forfeiture of large sums deposited as securities; the detention of large number of people for indefinite periods without charge or trial, the numerous special and additional disabilities under which the people of the Frontier Province have to suffer; the many encroachments on personal liberty in parts of Bengal; the restriction by externment, internment and otherwise to the free movement of persons within the country, thus preventing them from carrying on their usual occupations and business, and even obstructing humanitarian and relief work; the application of measures like the Criminal Tribes Act and the Foreigners' Act to political workers; indiscriminate and widespread searches of houses; the difficulties placed in the way of Indians going abroad; and the barriers to the return home of many Indians in foreign countries, who have thus to live in exile far from their own people and their motherland. The Congress notes that at no period since the great Revolt of 1857 has the suppression of civil and personal liberties and the repression of the Indian people, which is the normal feature of British administration in India to-day, been so great as it is now. While recognising that this extraordinary suppression and repression are measures of the strength and success of India's struggle for freedom, the Congress desires to point out that such is the background to the Constitution Act in spite of the statements made by representatives of the British Government that constitutional progress is being made in India.

Further, the Congress deeply regrets that in the Indian States there is a similar suppression of civil and personal liberties, and, in many of them, conditions in this respect are even worse than in the rest of India and almost every kind of liberty is non-existent; that in some States even the Congress has been banned and normal peaceful work of organisation prevented, and insult offered to the National Flag. The Congress realises that the effective power behind the States is that of the British Government and many of the States are under the direct control of British Officers. Howsoever the responsibility for this deplorable state of affairs might be shared between the British Government and the Rulers of the States, the Congress declares that it can recognise no differentiation in personal, civil and democratic liberties as between the States and the rest of India.

The Congress expresses the determination of the Indian people that notwithstanding this attempt to paralyse national growth and activity they will continue to face the situation with courage and fortitude and will carry on the struggle for freedom till independence is achieved.

5. Foreign Department

The Congress authorises and directs the Working Committee to organise a foreign department of the A. I. C. C. office to work under the general superintendence of the Working General Secretary and with such special staff as may be necessary, with a view to create and maintain contacts with Indians overseas, and with international, national, labour and other organisations abroad with whom co-operation is possible and is likely to help in the cause of Indian freedom.

6. Romain Rolland's Invitation to the World Peace Congress

This Congress, having considered the invitation of Monsieur Romain Rolland, Honorary President of the World Committee of the struggle against War and Fascism, to participate in the World Congress for peace to be held in Geneva in September next, conveys its greetings to the organisers of the Peace Congress and its assurances of its full sympathy and co-operation in the great work of ensuring peace in the world based on national and social freedom. The Congress is convinced that such a peace can only be established on an enduring basis when the causes of war are removed and the domination and exploitation of nation by nation is ended.

7. War Danger

The Congress, at its sessions held in Madras in 1927, drew the attention of the country to the danger of imperialist war and the possibility of India being made a tool in such a conflict for imperialist purposes, and declared the right of the Indian people to refuse to participate in any such war without their express permission.

The danger has become more evident and urgent since then with the growth of fascist dictatorships, the Italian attack on Abyssinia, the continuing Japanese aggression in North China and Mongolia, the rivalries and conflicts of the great imperialist Powers, and the feverish growth of armaments, and vast and terrible war threatens the world. In such a war an attempt will inevitably be made to drag in and exploit India to her manifest and disadvantage and for the benefit of British imperialism. The Congress therefore reiterates its old resolve and warns the people of the country against this danger, and declares its opposition to the participation of India in any imperialist war.

8. Sympathy for Abyssinia

The Congress expresses the sympathy of the Indian nation for the Ethiopian people who are so heroically defending their country against imperialist aggression and considers Abyssinia's fight as part of the fight of all exploited nations for freedom.

The Congress condemns the great Powers and the League of Nations for their policy in regard to the Italo-Abyssinian war.

9. Government of India Act

Whereas the Government of India Act, 1935, which is based on the White Paper and the Joint Parliamentary Report and which is in many respects even worse than the proposals contained in them, in no way represents the will of nation, is designed to facilitate and perpetuate the domination and exploitation of the people of India and is imposed on the country to the accompaniment of widespread repression and the suppression of civil liberties, the Congress reiterates its rejection of the new constitution in its entirety.

The Congress, as representing the will of the Indian people for national freedom and a democratic state, declares that no constitution imposed by outside authority and no constitution which curtails the sovereignty of the people of India and does not recognise their right to shape and control fully their political and economic future can be accepted. In the opinion of the Congress such a constitution must be based on the independence of India as a nation and it can only be framed by a constituent Assembly elected on adult franchise or a franchise which approximates to it as nearly as possible. The Congress therefore reiterates and stresses the demand for a Constituent Assembly in the name of the Indian people and calls upon its representatives and members in legislatures and outside to work for the fulfilment of this demand.

In view of the fact that elections for the Provincial legislatures under the new Act may, according to official statements, take place before the next session of the Congress, this Congress resolves that in such an event candidates should be put forward on its behalf to contest such seats in accordance with the mandate of the Congress and in pursuance of its declared policy. Such candidates must be chosen from those who fully support the Congress objective of Indian Independence and pledge themselves to carry out its policy in regard to the legislatures.

The A. I. C. C. shall place before the country prior to the election, a manifesto explaining the political and economic policy and programme of the Congress in conformity with the resolutions passed by it from time to time. The Provincial Congress Committee may further supplement the manifesto by adding thereto specific items which have special application to their respective provinces. All Provincial manifestoes must be approved by the Working Committee of the A. I. C. C.

Resolved further that the functions of the Parliamentary Board be discharged in future by the Working Committee of the A. I. C. C. The Working Committee is authorised to apppoint such Boards or Committees as may be necessary to organise elections to legislatures as well as to guide, co-ordinate and control the activities of Congress members in Legislatures. Accordingly the Parliamentary Board need not be reconstituted hereafter.

The question of acceptance or non-acceptance of office by Congress members elected to the legislatures under the constitution having been agitated in the country the Congress, in view of the uncertainties of the situation as it may develop, considers it inadvisable to commit itself to any decision at this stage on the question and leaves it to be decided at the proper time by the A. I. C. C. after consulting the Provincial Congress Committees.

10. Indians Abroad

The Congress reiterates its sympathy for the Indian settlers in South Africa, East Africa, Zanzibar, and the Fizi Islands and deplores the continuing deterioration in their status and the privation of personal and property rights in spite of past agreements and declarations of Local and British Governments and assures them of its readiness to take such action as may be within its power to ameliorate their condition.

11. Congress and Mass Contacts

The Congress is of opinion that it is desirable to develop closer association between the masses and the Congress organisation, so that they may take greater share in the shaping of congress policy and in its activities, and the organisation might become even more responsive to their needs and desires. With a view to this, and further to bring about closer co-operation with other organisations, of peasants, workers and others, which aim at the freedom of the Indian people and to make the Congress a joint front of all the anti-imperialist elements in the country, this Congress appoints a committee consisting of Sriyuts Rajendra Prasad, Jairamdas Daulatram and Jayprakash Narayan to make recommendations in this behalf including proposals for such amendment of the constitution as may be considered necessary. The Committee shall report to the A. I. C. C. through the Working Committee by the end of July 1936 and its report shall be then circulated to provincial and district committees for opinion. The final recommendations of the A. I. C. C. on this report shall be placed before the next session of the Congress.

12. Agrarian Programme

This Congress is of opinion that the most important and urgent problem of the country is the appalling poverty, unemployment and indebtedness of the peasantry fundamentally due to antiquated and repressive land tenure and revenue systems and intensified in recent years by the great slump in prices of agricultural produce. The final solution of this problem inevitably involves the removal of British imperialistic exploitation, a thorough change of the land tenure and revenue systems and a recognition by the State of its duty to provide work for the rural unemployed masses.

In view, however, of the fact that agrarian conditions and land tenure and revenue systems differ in the various Provinces, it is desirable to consult the Provincial Congress Committees and such peasant organisations, as the Working Committee considers fit, in the drawing up of a full All India Agrarian Programme as well as a programme for each Province. This Congress, therefore, calls upon each Provincial Congress Committee to make recommendations in detail to the Working Committee by August 31, 1936, for being considered and placed before the All India Congress Committee having particular regard to the following matters :—

1. Freedom of organisation of agricultural labourers and peasants.
2. Safeguarding of the interests of peasants where there are intermediaries between the State and themselves.
3. Just and fair relief of agricultural indebtedness including arrears of rent and revenue.
4. Emancipation of the peasants from feudal and semi-feudal levies.
5. Substantial reduction in respect of rent and revenue demands.
6. A just allotment of the State expenditure for the social, economic and cultural amenities of villages.
7. Protection against harrassing restrictions on the utilisation of local natural facilities for their domestic and agricultural needs.
8. Freedom from oppression and harrassment at the hands of Government officials and landlords.
9. Fostering industries for relieving rural unemployment.

13. Indian States

This Congress while re-affirming the resolution regarding Indian States passed in the Calcutta Session of 1928, and expressing its approval of the policy laid down in the statement issued by the A. I. C. C. in Madras in October 1935, desires to make it clear that, in its opinion, the people of the States should have the same right of self-determination as those of the rest of India, and that the Congress stands for the same political, civil and democratic liberties for every part of India. The Congress, however, desires to point out that the struggle for liberty within the States has, in the very nature of things, to be carried on by the people of the States themselves.

14. Amendments to Constitution

A number of amendments to the Congress constitution were passed. The amended constitution is printed separately.

15. Next Congress

Resolved that the next session of the Congress be held in Maharashtra.

The All India Congress Committee

First Meeting—Lucknow· 9th. April 1936

A meeting of the A. I. C. C. was held in the Subjects Committee Pandal at [illegible] Nagar, Lucknow on April 9, 1936.

Shri Rajendra Prasad presided. The Committee consisted of new members elected for the coming year. The minutes of the last meeting held at Madras on October 17 and 18, 1935 were confirmed.

The audited accounts of the period extending from April 1, 1934 to March 31, 1935 and from April 1, 1935 to December 31, 1935 circulated along with the General Secretary's report were passed.

The General Secretary's report was placed before the meeting. Sri Sampuranand objected to the adoption of the same as the members who had just received it had no time to go through it. The adoption of the report was therefore postponed to allow members time to read it.

The President then thanked the members of the Committee and the country at large for the co-operation that he had received from them in his work and for their unfailing courtesy towards him throughout his term of office. He invited the President-elect Sri Jawaharlal Nehru to take the chair.

Maulana Abul Kalam Azad proposed a vote of thanks to the retiring President. He eulogized his great services to the country and said that Babu Rajendra Prasad had infused new life in the nation at a time of great depression. Srimati Sarojini Naidu spoke in support and paid a glowing tribute to the retiring President. Sri Sampuranand on behalf of the Socialists associated himself and his party with this vote of thanks.

Second Meeting —Lucknow—13th. April 1936

The adjourned meeting of the A. I. C. C. was again held on the 13th at Lucknow. Shri Jawharlal Nehru presided.

The General Secretary's report was adopted after a brief discussion. Some minor items were suggested for inclusion.

The treasurer's audited accounts placed before the Committee were passed.

Third Meeting—Lucknow—15th. April 1936

Another meeting of the A. I. C. C. was held immediately after the Congress on the morning of April 15. Sri Jawharlal Nehru presided.

Messrs. Dalal and Shah and Messrs Chottalal and Agarwal of Bombay were appointed as honorary auditors for the next year.

Dr. Pattabhi was thanked for the earnest zeal with which he had done his work as the historian of the Congress.

Babu Rajendra Prasad made a statement about the Bengal election disputes. He was authorised by the Committee to continue to deal with the Bengal disputes.

The President then made a statement reviewing the situation and pointing out his difficulties in the selection of the new Working Committee.

The New Working Committee

On *April 16* at Lucknow the President nominating the members of the new Working Committee issued the following statement to the press :

The constitution of the Congress directs the President to select the members of the Working Committee for his term of office. This duty and this burden thus devolve upon me and I have given this matter the most careful and earnest consideration. Inevitably, I have consulted many colleagues and sought their guidance in the matter. This became specially incumbent on me as I was placed in a somewhat peculiar position. As President, I was the chief executive of the Congress and was supposed to represent that great organisation. But in some major matters of policy I do not represent the majority viewpoint to which expression has been given in the resolutions of the Lucknow Congress. Thus the Working Committee could not, at the same time, represent, on these matters, my views as those of the majority. I have felt that it would be improper for me, under these circumstances, to select a committee entirely in consonance with my views and the views of the majority of Congressmen, as expressed in the open sessions of the Congress, must prevail. I was tempted to shift the burden of selection on the All India Congress Committee, so that this Committee might choose such persons to represent it as it thought fit and proper. But after much thought I have come to the conclusion that this would not be a proper course to adopt and I may not shirk the responsibility that has been cast on me. I have tried therefore to form a committee which represents mainly the majority viewpoint, but which also contains some representatives of the minority. Such a selection has its advantages. I have endeavoured, however, to make it a committee which, I hope, will pull together in the struggle against imperialism and serve the Congress and the country worthily in this great struggle. I trust that my colleagues of the All India Congress Committee and Congressmen in general will give this Committee their loyal co-operation and support and strengthen its hands in the great work before us, so that we can build up a joint and impregnable anti-imperialist front.

The Committee is limited, under the constitution, to fifteen members including the President. It is impossible to include all those whom I would like to have in it. I regret especially that some old and valued members, who have served on the Working Committee in past years, have been left out of it. I hope, however, that we shall continue to have their full co-operation and that we shall frequently avail ourselves of their advice.

I select the following fourteen members for the Working Committee :

Treasurer : Shri Jamnalal Bajaj.

General Secretary : Shri J. B. Kripalani, ***Members*** : Maulana Abul Kalam Azad, Shri Rajendra Prasad, Shri Vallabhbhai J. Patel, Khan Abdul Ghaffar Khan, Shri C. Rajagopalachari, Shri Subhas Chandra Bose, Shri Narendra Dev, Shri Jairamdas Doulatram, Shri S. D. Deo, Shri Jaya Prakash Narayan, Shri Bhulabhai Desai, Shri Achyut Patwardhan.

So long as Khan Abdul Ghaffar Khan is in prison, Dr. Khan Sahib will act for him.

Two of the persons above named, Shri C. Rajagopalchari and Shri Jayaprakash Narayan, are not at present members of the All India Congress Committee. The A. I. C. C. has, however, been enlarged by the decision of the Lucknow Congress and I trust that these two members will soon become members of this enlarged A. I. C. C.

The first meeting of the new Working Committee will take place at Wardha on April 27 at 3 p. m.

The Working Committee

A meeting of the Working Committee was held in the Harijan Colony, Delhi, on March 21-24, 1936. The meeting adjourned on March 24, to reassemble at Allahabad on April 6. It carried on deliberations at Anand Bhawan on the 6th and 7th and adjourned again to meet on the morning of 8th at Lucknow. Thereafter the committee met everyday till April 14. The members present were :—

Sri Rajendra Prasad ; Sri Jawharlal Nehru ; Sri Vallabhbhai Patel ; Sri Pattabhi Sitaramayya ; Sri Sarojini Devi ; Sri Jamnalal Bajaj ; Sri Gangadharrao Deshpande ; Sri Purshottam Das Tandon ; Sri K. F. Nariman ; Sri Surendra Mohan Moitra : Sri Syed Mahmud ; Sri Jairamdas Doulatram ; Sri J. B. Kripalani ; Maulana Abul Kalam Azad joined the deliberations at Allahabad and Lucknow.

Sri Bhulabhai Desai and Sri Govindballabh Pant attended the meeting by special invitation. Sjt. Rajagopalachari was invited to attend the meeting at Allahabad and Lucknow.

The following business was transacted :—

A. I. C. C. Elections in Bombay

In the opinion of the committee no substantial irregularity is disclosed in the elections of members to the All India Congress Committee from Bombay. The election therefore stands.

Election of Delegates of Utkal and Mahakoshal

Resolved that the President be authorised to condone the irregularity caused by non-payment of delegates' fees and the non-issue of certificates on payment of the prescribed fee for all the delegates present and participating in the meeting of January 20, 1936.

Bengal Election Dispute

"Considered the resolution of the Executive Committee of the Bengal Provincial Congress Committee dated March 15, 1936, and the ***ad interim*** report of Messrs. Surendra Mohan Moitra and Birendra Nath Majumdar, scrutinisers, and also heard Dr. Suresh Banerjee, Sjts. Biren Majumdar and Dhiresh Chakravorty.

"The Committee is of opinion that it is not possible to substitute the nomination of delegates for their election by primary members and it is necessary, in the opinion of this Committee, that election of delegates should be held by primary members.

"The Committee, accordingly, directs that the election of delegates should be held in those districts in which there is no dispute, and in the districts in respect of which the scrutinisers have been able to submit the final list of members as per statement given below, and the committee allots the number of delegates mentioned against each district or in the districts where more than one delegate is elected, the whole district should be treated as one multiple constituency. As regards the remaining districts, the scrutinisers are requested to expedite their scrutiny and the President is authorised to allot a number of delegates to them as soon as the scrutinisers' reports are received. The Executive Committee of the Bengal Provincial Congress Committee will announce in the press names of the Returning Officers and polling station for each district by March 28. The nomination of candidates should reach the Returning Officer by 7 p. m. on March 31, 1936, and the scrutiny of the nominations will take place on April 1. The polling of votes shall take place on April 4 next and the results shall be declared on April 6 at the latest.

"A meeting of delegates will be held at 10 a. m. at the Bengal Delegates' camp at Motinagar, Lucknow, on April 9, to elect one-twelfth of their number as members of the All India Congress Committee from Bengal.

The number of delegates to be elected from the districts is as follows :—

Bankura 3, Sylhet 5, Dacca 2, Nadia 2, Pabna 3, Dinajpur 6, Chittagong 1, Jessore 3, Khulna 3, Hooghly 2, Birbhum 1, Barisal 1, Jalpaiguri 2, Burdwan 2, Murshidabad 2, North Calcutta 4, South Calcutta 2, Central Calcutta 2, Burra Bazar 2, 24-Parganas 2, Noakhali 3, Faridpur 1, and Midnapur 7."

Babu Rajendra Prasad also issued the following statement :—

"In view of the power given to me by the Working Committee to nominate delegates and members of the All India Congress Committee to represent the district of Midnapore where the Congress organisation is still under a ban, I nominate the following gentlemen, viz., Sjt. Subhas Bose, Sjt. Mohim Chandra Das, Kumar D. L. Khan, Pramath Nath Banerjee of Contai, Sjt. Ramsundar Singh, Sjt. Manmatha Nath Das and Sjt. Lalit Mohan Sinha.

"It will be noticed that in the above list I have included the first-named two gentlemen who are not residents of Midnapur. I included Sjt. Subhas Chandra Bose for obvious reasons and I nominated Sjt. Mohim Chandra Das of Chittagong, where Congress work has become difficult if not impossible, and I think it desirable that this district should not go unrepresented. Another gentlemen of Chittagong should be elected as a delegate by the members of Dacca in combination with those of Chittagong to enable that district to get adequate representation.

"I record my appreciation of the Bengal Provincial Congress Committee and the scrutinisers and hope the rest of the work will be completed in time for the Congress.

"I hope this decision will give satisfaction to congressmen and Congresswomen in Bengal and I trust the election will be conducted with fairness and completed in time."

Fresh Election Disputes

"Resolved that the President be authorised to decide any election dispute that might arise before the ne-t session of the Congress at Lucknow."

Headquarters of Andhra P. C. C.

"As temporary measure the Andhra P. C. C. is allowed to keep Madras as its headquarters."

Enrolment of New Primary Members

The permission given by the President in February last for enrolment of Congress members from then onwards for the year beginning with April 1936, before the assembling of the next Congress at Lucknow in April 1936, was approved.

Repairs to Swaraj Bhawan

"Resolved that a sum of Rs. 750 be sanctioned for the next year for the repairs of Swaraj Bhawan."

The Committee drafted resolutions on the following subjects to be placed before the Subjects Committee of the Lucknow Congress :—

(1) Condolence ; (2) Greeting to Prisoners etc., (3) Shri Subhas Chandra Bose's arrest ; (4) Suppression of Civil Liberties ; (5) Foreign Department ; (6) Romain Rolland's invitation to the World Peace Congress ; (7) War danger ; (8) Government of India Act ; (9) Sympathy for Abyssinia ; (10) Indians Abroad ; (11) Congress and Mass Contacts ; (12) Agrarian Programme ; (13) Indian States ; (14) Amendments to the Constitution.

Resolutions of which due notice had been given by the members of the All India Congress Committee were discussed. Some of these were covered by the resolutions recommended by the Working Committee. Others were declared out of order. Only 6 resolutions remained for the ballot and these were to be placed before the Subjects Committee.

The New Working Committee

The first meeting of the new Working Committee was held at Wardha on April 27, 28 and 29, 1936. The following members were present :

Sri Jawaharlal Nehru (President) ; Sri Rajendra Prasad ; Sri Vallabhbhai Patel ; Sri Rajagopalachari ; Sri Jamnalal Bajaj ; Sri Jairamdas Doulatram ; Sri Bhulabhai Desai ; Sri Narendra Dev ; Sri Jaiprakash Narayan ; Sri Achyut Patwardhan. Sri J. B. Kripalani attended the meeting a couple of hours later.

Minutes

(1) The minutes of the last meeting held at Delhi, Allahabad and Lucknow were read and confirmed.

Donation of Rs. 10,000

The President informed the Committee that anonymous donation of Rs. 10,000 had been received earmarked for the organisation of a foreign department of the All India Congress Committee office.

Foreign Department

(2) In view of the Congress decision on the subject it was resolved that the President be authorized to organize a foreign department of the All India Congress Committee office and that Rs. 2,000 be sanctioned for this purpose out of the special donation for foreign work.

Political and Economic Department

(3) Resolved that a Political and Economic Information Department be created in the All India Congress Committee office in order to collect information in regard to political, economic and allied activities in the country. The President be authorised to organize such a department and Rs. 2,000 be sanctioned from the general fund of the All India Congress Committee for the purpose.

Karnatak P. C. C's Letters

(4) The Karnatak P. C. C's letter dated Dharwar, April 27, 1936 regarding the procedure to be followed for the election of A. I. C. C. members was considered. The Committee held that under the provisions of the Constitution it was essential for a meeting of the delegates to be held at one place for the purpose of electing A. I. C. C. members and that this could not be done by post.

Delhi Province

(5) The letter from Delhi D. C. C. about the city and the District of Delhi to be made into a separate province, was considered and it was decided that opinion on the matter be called for from the district and town Congress Committees of Delhi, Meerut and Muzaffarnagar, as well as the U. P. P. C. C.

Treasurer's Balance Sheet

(6) The following items in the accounts that were being carried on form year to year wear either written off or accounted :—

1. As the Congress pavilion is worn out and has no value, resolved that the amount of Rs. 9, 750 be written off.
2. Resolved that Rs. 600 advanced to Mr. Tendulker be written off.
3. Amount shown as advances against Pandit Jawaharlal Nehru advanced in December 1931 and in 1932, to him and to Srimati Kamala Nehru for work in U. P. and Behar, were amounts spent during the period. These must be accounted for as expenditure.

Deposit of Funds

(7) Resolved that the treasurer be authorized to deposit the funds in his hands in such banks or firms doing banking business as he may think fit.

Accounts

(8) Resolved that in future there should be only one account, the treasurer's account. The office accounts at Allahabad should be amalgamated with this. The

office should get money periodically from the Treasurer and send monthly accounts with the vouchers to the treasurer's office in Bombay.

Anomalies in the Amended Constitution

(9) Various anomalies being pointed out in the Constitution as amended at Lucknow, Messrs. Rajagopalachari, Jairamdas and Kripalani were requested to examine the transitory provision of the Constitution and to submit proposals on the day following for any consequential changes that might remove these anomalies.

On the recommendation of the Committee the following consequential Rule and transitory provision were made for removing the anomalies caused in the Constitution by the amendments introduced in it at the last Congress session at Lucknow.

Consequential Rule under Art. XVIII

(10) If any delegate elected to a Session of the Congress resigns after the session is over, the vacancy so created shall be filled in by the constituency concerned and such newly elected delegate shall exercise all the functions devolving on a delegate according to the constitution until the next session, including membership in the Provincial Congress Committee.

Transitory Provision Under Art. XVIII (d)

(11) It is hereby resolved that the next Congress Session having been advanced to December 1936, and the time allowed for enrolment of members being thereby considerably reduced, notwithstanding anything contained in Art. V(a) and the general time-table issued by the Working Committee any member enrolled this year on or before August 31 shall be entitled to exercise his vote at all Congress elections.

Labour Committee

(12) Resolved that a Labour Committee consisting of Srijuts Jairamdas Doulatram Shankerlal Banker, V. V. Giri, M. R. Masani and J. B. Kripalani be appointed to keep in touch with the labour movement and endeavour to co-operate with it, and advise the Working Committee thereon.

Parliamentary Committee

(13) Resolved that a Parliamentary Committee consisting of Srijuts (1) Rajendra Prasad, (2) Vallabhbhai Patel, (3) Abul Kalam Azad, (4) Rajagopalachari, (5) Bhulabhai Desai, (6) Narendra Dev and (7) Govind Ballabh Pant with the last named person as its Convenor, as well as the Presidents of all Provincial Congress Committees (excluding Burma) and Dr. Khan Sahib from the Frontier be constituted, to take such steps as may be necessary in connection with the organisation of elections to the legislatures. The Committee shall report to the Working Committee from time to time and shall be guided by the Working Committee's directions.

(14) The following time-table was sanctioned by the Committee to regulate the enrolment of primary members and the various elections for the next Congress :—

1. Congress to meet—*Last week of December*
2. Announcement of Presidential election—*10th December.*
3. Receipt in the A. I. C. C. office of results of the voting in the provinces of Presidential election—*8th. December.*
4. Meeting of delegates for electing the President—*6th December.*
5. Receipt of lists of delegates by the A. I. C. C. office from the Provincial Congress Committees—*1st December.*
6. Receipt of names of delegates by the Provincial Congress Committees from districts—*25th November.*
7. Election of delegates in Districts - *15th November.*
8. Receipt by provinces from A. I. C. C. office of figures of Provincial quotas of delegates—*31st October.*
9. Despatch of above quotas by the A. I. C. C. office—*25th. October.*
10. Receipt by the A. I. C. C. office from the Provincial Congress Committees of lists of qualified congress members for fixing provincial quotas of delegates—*18th. October.*
11. Receipt by the P. C. C.'s of above lists from primary committees—*10th. September.*
12. Despatch by the primary committees of above lists—*5th. September.*
13. Last date of enrolment this year (vide Resolution No. 11)— *31st. August.*

Next Meeting of the Working Committee

(15) It was decided that the next meeting of the Working Committee be held at Wardha in the second half of June next.

2. Important Circulars About Congress Work

The following Circular letter was addressed by the President to Congress organisations drawing their attention to some of the principal resolutions of the Lucknow Session and inviting them to take immediate steps to see that effect is given to them :

DEAR COMRADE,

Now that the Congress is over, I venture to address you and to draw your attention to some of its principal resolutions. These resolutions cast a responsibility on all of us and we have to take steps to give effect to them in so far as we can. I trust that you will immediately circularise your district and local committees on this subject and request them to hold committee meetings, as well as public meetings, in order to give full publicity to the Congress resolutions and plan out their future work in accordance with them.

Our office has already addressed you on the subject of the changes in the Congress constitution, and copies of the amended constitution and the Congress resolutions are being sent to you separately. Please study this constitution carefully and arrange to take early steps to give effect to the amendments and the transitory provisions. This will probably result in enlarging your committees and in adding to your A. I. C. C. members. This desirable change at the top should be accompanied by a livening up of the primary committees so that even our primary members might take more interest and greater part in our day-to-day activities. With a view to bring this about, as well as to broaden the mass basis of the Congress, a committee has been appointed. This committee proposes to issue a questionnaire to you in order to have the benefit of your experience and advice.

The long and comprehensive resolution on the suppression of civil liberties is one to which the fullest publicity should be given and it should be repeated at public meetings. Special point is given to this resolution by the arrest and detention of Sri Subbas Chandra Bose as he was on his way to attend the Congress. A suggestion has been made that all India demonstration should take place on a particular day to mark our indigation at this further outrage of public opinion and to send our greetings to our comrade Subhas Bose. I commend this suggestion to you and hope that such meetings will be held as wisely as possible on Sunday, May 10. At these meetings, besides the special resolution on Subhas Babu's detention, there should also be a repetition of the Congress resolution on the suppression of civil liberties.

Another Congress resolution which requires publicity is the one on War Danger. The importance and urgency of this should be stressed and the implications explained to our people. The fact that it is not merely an academic resolution but one which affects us, nationally and individually, and which is likely to have far-reaching consequences, should be made clear.

Every Congressman will realise the great importance of the resolution on the Agrarian Programme. This resolution is still incomplete and in order to fill in the gaps and make it a complete whole, the co-operation of Provincial Congress Committees, their local committees, and Kisan Sabhas is desired. May I suggest, therefore, that you should ask your local committees immediately to consider this problem and to confer with their primary committees, so that the widest possible discussion of this vital question takes place. Each Provincial Congress Committee should then make its own recommendations to the Working Committee.

As you are aware, the resolution which was debated most in the Congress was the one on the new Government of India Act. Whatever the differences in regard to this might have been, one fact stands clear : that the Act has to be combated and rejected. On that there is unanimity and it is desirable to stress this as well as to make this the plank of our anti-imperialist programme. The Congress stands firmly for independence and anti-imperialism and it is only with this back-ground that we can consider any question. The constructive side of our rejection is the Constituent Assembly and full publicity should be given to this in public meetings. The slogan of the Constituent Assembly must be popularised and explained to the masses.

3. Subhas Babu and Foreign Propaganda

The following statement was issued by the President in this connection from Wardha on April 28, 1936 :

"In the course of the discussions at the Subjects Committee meetings at Lucknow on April 14, my attention was drawn by a member to a public statement made by Srijut Subhas Chandra Bose, prior to his arrest, in which he had stated that the Working Committee had declined to vest him with a representative capacity on behalf of the Congress, for carrying on foreign work. I was asked if any communication asking for such authority had been received by the then President of the A. I. C. C. or by the Working Committee and whether the Committee had considered it.

As I had no personal knowledge, I asked Rajendra Babu and he told me that during his whole period of office, that is nearly a year and a half prior to the Lucknow Congress, he had received no communication from Sjt. Subhas Bose on the subject and thus the question of considering it by the Working Committee had not arisen.

It has now been pointed out to me that Sjt. Subhas Bose issued a statement to the press on this subject in July 1935 and various press agencies and newspapers, presuming that the Working Committee would consider the subject, made forecasts and commented on it in August 1935.

May I point out that these forecasts and unauthorised reports of proceedings of Working Committee meeting are wholly unreliable. I have been astonished at reading in the press during the last month about matters which had never been even touched upon during our committee meetings. It is quite clear that all the references in the press in August 1935 to an alleged letter from Sjt Subhas Bose being considered by the Working Committee were without foundation. No such letter was received by Rajendra Babu or the A. I. C. C. office, no such letter is to found in our office files, and there is no mention of any such discussion in the detailed minutes of the Working Committee meeting. Neither the then president nor the Secretary has any recollection of even an informal letter on the subject. It is difficult for them to remember now if they saw the press statement at the time, but in any event the Working Committee does not usually proceed on the basis of press statements as these might be incorrect.

I find no clear reference to a letter in any of Sjt. Bose's statements. It is possible that the misapprehension in the minds of the public has arisen owing to some part of Sj. Subhas Bose's statement being construed to refer to a letter. It is also possible that a letter he sent was intercepted by Government.

On the larger question of Foreign propaganda I do not wish to say anything in this statement. I have long been in favour of our developing foreign contracts and a world outlook. But when we come to the manner of doing so the subject is full of difficulty under present conditions in Europe and in India I doubt if it is desirable or possible to have official representatives of the Congress in foreign countries. This may come later. I imagine that well-known Congressmen can do good work in foreign countries even without a special authorisation. Personally I would prefer to be such an independent Congressman when I go abroad, than one whose words have to be weighed carefully lest they commit the Congress. Whenever I spoke in Europe during my last stay there I prefaced my remarks by saying that I did not speak officially in the name of the Congress and I could not commit it. I did so even after my election to the Lucknow Congress presidentship.

It is our misfortune that Subhas Babu is cut off from us at present. If he was available I am sure the misapprehension in the minds of some people would be removed.

4. Subhas Day

The following press statement was issued by the President on April 22, 1936 in connection with Subhas Day :

"It has been suggested that a special day should be fixed for an all India expression of our indignation and resentment against the arrest and detention of Sri Subhas Chandra Bose. I gladly commend this suggestion to all Congressmen and others and fix Sunday, May 10 for this purpose when public meetings should be held all over the country and resolutions passed on Subhas Babu's arrest conveying the greetings of the people to our comrade.

Subhas Babu's arrest is one of the latest and most significant instances of the wide-spread and intensive suppression of civil liberties in India. It is desirable therefore that this wider aspect is also stressed and the resolution passed by the Lucknow Congress on the suppression of civil liberties be placed before the public and endorsed by them at all public meetings. It should be remembered that the question of protecting civil liberty is one that affects all Indians to whatever political or other party or group they might belong, or whether they belong to none. It is not a matter that affects Congressmen only. Therefore on this question we should invite the co-operation of all who believe in civil liberty. and endeavour to build up a joint front on this issue."

The following cablegram was received by the President from the Irish Indian Independence League about the arrest of Sri Subhas Chandra Bose :

"Indian Irish Independence League express indignation at arrest of Subhas Bose. Repudiate British Government and all its Acts."

5. Abyssinia Day

The following statement was sent to the press on May 5, 1936 by the President for the observance throughout India of the Abyssinia Day on hearing the news about the fall of Addis Ababa :

"Addis Ababa lies at the foot of the conqueror. Ethiopia, in spite of her gallant defence of her independence, lies helpless and prostrate before the brutal might of fascist imperialism. Poison gas and liquid fire and all the modern engines of destruction have triumphed and in their triumph have not only exposed afresh the true nature of imperialism, but have also shown us the hypocrisy and duplicity of the Great Powers and the utter futility of that body which is known as the League of Nations. For the moment imperialism triumphs again in the long world struggle for freedom, but that struggle will go on in Ethiopia as elsewhere till freedom comes and puts an end to imperialism everywhere. We in India can do nothing to help our brethren in distress in Ethiopia for we also are the victims of imperialism. But we can at least send them our deep sympathy in this hour of their trial. We stand with them to-day in their sorrow as we hope to stand together when better days come. I appeal to the Indian people therefore to give a country wide expression to our sympathy and solidarity with Ethiopian people and our resolve not to submit to the fascist imperialist menace. I trust that demonstrations for this purpose will be held throughout the country on Saturday next May 9. The Sunday following, May 10, as I have previously appealed, will be observed as Subhas Day to register our indignation at the suppression of Civil Liberties in India."

In connection with the above, the Italian Consul General in Calcutta issued a statement protesting against the appeal.

The President's reply to the Italian Consul General is given below :

The Italian Consul-General in Calcutta has criticised and expressed his resentment at my issuing an appeal for the observance of an Abyssinia day to express our deep sympathy for the people of Ethiopia in their hour of trial and humiliation. He has protested against what he terms "empty talks" against Italy, a country which has always been friendly to India. Against Italy and the Italian people we have no grievance and for the friendliness they have shown to us in the past we are grateful. To me personally Italy has been dear from my childhood days. Her wonderful natural beauty and magnificent art have drawn me to her ; her history has fascinated me. The story of freedom struggle has been an inspiration of my youth. I have felt the majesty of Rome with its long and varied heritage, the mysterious charm of Florence, the beauty of Venice and Naples. But our love and admiration for Italy have nothing to do with our hostility to imperialism and fascism. The passionate love that we, who are the children of India, bear to our motherland does not mean approval of the imperialist machine that governs and crushes us. That very love calls upon us to combat this imperialism and to free our country. And whereever imperialism appears in whatever guise it might be, it is the opponent of the forces struggling for freedom and we have to oppose it.

What are the Ethiopian people, I am asked. They are the people who have been subjugated by the Italian forces by fire and sword. They are a backward people, I know, and they have many failings. They may lack unity, and imperialism, as in India, may spread disunity amongst them. But I repudiate utterly the suggestion that imperialism has gone to Abyssinia, or come to India, for humanitarian motives or the spread of civilization. Imperialism goes to exploit and remains to exploit and the people under its heel sink materially and spiritually. Its true messengers in Abyssinia have been poison gas and liquid fire and they reveal its nature more than any argument. That is the foretaste of the civilization that it brings, and we in India, who suffer humiliation enough in our land, cannot permit the additional spiritual degradation of remaining silent when imperialism spreads out its cruel wings and crushes other peoples.

I appeal therefore again to the Indian people to observe Saturday, May 9 as Abyssinia day and to send their heartfelt message of sympathy to the people of that unhappy country.

6. Civil Liberties Union

The President addressed the following letter on April 23, 1936 to prominent public men of all shades of opinion throughout India inviting them to co-operate in the formation of the above Union for the protection of Civil and Individual Liberties against arbitrary action by the State. The public may look forward to an early organisation of the Union:—

DEAR FRIEND,

I am taking the liberty of addressing you on the subject of the suppression of civil liberties in India. This suppression has been progressively getting more widespread and intensive and has now become the feature of the administration. As has been pointed out, at no time since the Revolt of 1857 have civil liberties in India been suppressed to the extent they are to-day. It is manifest that real political life, and even social and personal life, are very seriously interfered with by this suppression. Various political and other organisations have protested against this from time to time and it would be desirable for them to co-operate on this issue, even though they might differ on others, so that a joint fight might be put up on the vital question.

The existence of civil liberities is generally considered to be essential for the development of every kind of national activity—political, cultural, social, economic. With their suppression all these activities suffer. In countries with a democratic background the greatest value is therefore attached to civil liberty and people of the most diverse and mutually hostile opinions join together in a common attempt to protect this foundation of all liberty and activity. They consider it their duty to resist even the suppression of any opinion or activity to which they are personally opposed, for once the principle of such suppression is admitted it can be, and frequently has been, extended to all manner of other activities. In America, England and France powerful Civil Liberties Unions, of a purely non-party character, have been established to resist all such encroachments and their activities have borne substantial fruit. In India the necessity for a joint effort embracing all groups and individuals, who believe in civil liberties, is obviously even more necessary than elsewhere.

It is proposed, therefore, to start an Indian Civil Liberties Union the sole function of which will be the protection of civil liberties in all departments of national activity. It should be open to all individuals who believe in this fundamental proposition and it should avoid any enlargement on any other political or economic issues. Such a Union could have a national council with a whole time secretary, as well as local committee wherever possible. The first object of this Union would be to collect data and give publicity to it. Other activities, such as the organisation of public opinion to resist all encroachments on civil liberties, would follow.

I am addressing this letter to some friends who are not connected with the Congress organisation and I trust that it will be possible to build up, with their help and co-operation, a non-party and non-sectarian union of the kind I have out-lined above. The exact form that such a union might take and its future activities would naturally depend on the views of those interested in this subject who join it.

I hope that I may count on your co-operation in this important national work, Politicians and those who dabble in public work are naturally interested in this; equally so are educationists, lawyers and professional men, authors and journalists, printers and publishers, social reformers and those who work for the betterment of the peasantry and the industrial workers.

Could you kindly favour me with your views on this subject?

7. Late Dr. M. A. Ansari

On the morning of May 10, 1936, the whole of India was shocked and overwhelmed by the unexpected news of the sudden death of Dr. M. A. Ansari of heart failure in the train while he was returning to Delhi from Mussoori. The whole of the country was thrown into mourning. There were spontaneous hartals and meetings of condolence everywhere.

On receipt of the news the President announced May 17 as a day of universal mourning.

Proceedings of the Congress

49th. Session—Lucknow—12th. to 14th. April 1936

The forty-ninth session of the Indian National Congress opened at Lucknow on the **12th. April 1936**. Various enclosures intended to accommodate 50,000 persons were fast filling at the time the session opened. There was the Lucknow touch about the decorations. The various gates of Moti Nagar had been constructed on the Lucknow architectural model, so pleasing to the eye.

The main gate of the open arena where the session was held attracted most attention. Decorated in tricolour, it had on either wing a painting of village life and next to it, on either side, jail bars showing prisoners handcuffed within. At the top were painted the stages whereby the Congress had since 1885 progressed to where it had reached to-day and the picture of Dadabhoy Naoroji, who first talked of Swaraj as the ideal, the picture of Mr. Tilak who introduced the element of suffering and of Mr. Gandhi who put forward the policy of direct action, were exhibited there. It was further shown that the next march to the goal was the most steep. The goal was represented by a lotus holding the Congress flag.

Inside the enclosure, little flags were the only decoration except for mottos which lined the route through which the leaders' procession passed. Loudspeakers stood prominently reminding the audience of their importance, in serving the audience of this proportion.

The raised section of the enclosure represented the seat where the President would sit with his colleagues and guests. But as the President's seat was distant from the rostrum, three lights were installed, the white indicating that a speech is going on and the red hinting to speakers that the President has called him to order or wishes him to conclude his remarks. This control by lights which is so familiar to road traffic has been for the first time thought of as a means of controlling speeches.

Various mottos hung were extracts from speeches and writings of Congress leaders of the past, including those from the late Sir Dinshaw Wacha, late Mr. Gokhale, Mahatma Gandhi and Mr. Jawaharlal Nehru such as "United we stand, divided we fall", "Imperialism has always been synonymous with bureaucracy", "Success comes to those who dare and act."

When the hour struck for the Presidential procession to arrive and the band played, there was silence. A soft breeze, which is such a relief after the hot and terrible dust-storms during the day, was blowing. The procession which started from the President's camp nearby included Mahatma Gandhi, Dr. Ansari, Mr. Jawaharlal, Pandit Malaviya, Mrs. Naidu, Maulana Abul Kalam Azad, Babu Rajendra Prasad, Sardar Vallabhbhai Patel, Mr. Bhulabhai Desai, Mr. K. F. Nariman, Mr. Deshpande, Dr. Pattabi Sitaramayya, Mr. Kripalani, Mr. Moitra, Sardar Sardul Singh, Mr. Sri Prakash, Pandit Govind Ballabh Pant, Dr. Murarilal, Mr. Rafi Ahmed Kidwai and the Secretaries of the Reception Committee and of the Provincial Congress Committee.

Cries of "Jawaharlal-ki-Jai" and "Gandhi-ki-Jai" resounded from all sides of the pandal as the procession advanced towards the dais. As proceedings advanced into the evening and darkness supervened, the rostrum stood out in artistic glory, carrying overhead a "chhattar" in three flags representing the tri-colour symbol of the Congress Flag and indicating as "chhattars" do to the Indian mind the emblem of sovereignty.

Proceedings began with a National song and after Mr. Sri Prakash read his welcome address, Mr. Jawaharlal Nehru addressed the gathering in Hindi.

Prominent among those seated on the dais were Mahatma Gandhi, Dr. Ansari, Pandit Madan Mohan Malaviya, Mr. T. Prakasam, Mr. B. Sambamurti, Mr. S. Satyamurti, Dr. Khare, Mrs. Lakshmipathi, Mrs. Naidu, Mrs. Kamaladevi, Mr. Nageswara Rao Pantulu, Mr. R. S. Pandit, Sardar Vallabhbhai Patel, Mr. Bhulabhai Desai, Seth Jamnalal Bajaj, Dr. Syed Mahmud, Maulana Abul Kalam Azad, Mr. Jairamdas Daulatram, Mr. C. Rajagopalachari, Dr. Pattasitaramayya, Mr. Gangadhar Rao Deshpande, Mr. K. F. Nariman, Mr. and Mrs. Munshi, Mrs. Kasturibai Gandhi, Mr. Mohanlal Saxsena, Dr. Murarilal, Mr. Rafi Ahmed Kidwai, Dr. Satyapal, Mr. Nehru's sisters, Pandit Govind Ballabh Pant, Mr. Mahadev Desai, Mr. G. R. Gadgil, Mr. S. A. Brelvi,

Mr. Tushar Kanti Ghose, Dr. Khan Sahib, Sri Parvati Devi (Babu Rajendra Prasad's sister), Acharya Kirpalani, Babu Purshotamdas Tandon and Mr. Moitra.

Mr. Jawaharlal Nehru concluded his presidential address at 9-30 p. m., having taken two and a half hours to deliver it. He introduced some new points, including a reference to terrorism and federation and the debate in the Working Committee over the Government of India Act resolution.

The Welcome Speech

The following speech was delivered by Mr. *Sri Prakash*, Chairman, Reception Committee :—

On behalf of the United Provinces, I offer a most hearty welcome to all who have assembled here to-day at this officially the 49th—but really the 51st—session of the Indian National Congress. I will not indulge in the usual language of convention, and talk of the short-comings of our arrangements, obvious as they are : nor offer apologies, hypocritical as they must sound, for any discomforts that you might have to suffer. I will also not try to enter into any self-defence on the ground of our difficulties which are entirely of our own creation, and for which we fully deserve to be punished. One thing however needs must be mentioned. It has happened perhaps only once or twice before in the history of the Congress—and that too for the sake of very special personalities—that the Chairman of the Reception Committee should not himself belong to the town where the Congress is being held. I have a shrewd suspicion that a small man like myself has been forced into this position to-day so that no citizen of Lucknow itself might suffer direct criticism when it has not been possible for us to offer hospitality on that grand and lavish scale for which this town is traditionally famous. I fear the Chairman of the Reception Committee, as well as the head of the volunteer force, have been drafted from Benares—the ancient pilgrim centre of Kashi—not so much to prove the united nature of our United Provinces, as to enable us to say that though the arrangements here may not be worthy of those who are used to receive rajas and nawabs, they are good enough if made in the name of those who have only acted as hosts and chaperons to pious pilgrims. And I of Benares gladly welcome you knowing only too well that delegates and visitors to Congress come in the same spirit of reverent pilgrimage as do all those, rich and poor alike, who come to worship at the shrines of my city.

Our Great Losses

Many comrades, known and unknown, valiant fighters for the country's liberty, have left us since we met at Bombay. The Congress in its resolutions, will doubtless give expression to the nation's sorrow at the loss we have sustained. Two of these, however, I must single out as intimately affecting my own Province. In the passing away of Kamala Nehru, not only has our President lost a noble wife, but we have all lost our Kamalaji, who always made her home at Allahabad, a home to the least of us, and not only extended to us unstinted hospitality, but gave us cheer and hope in the darkest days of depression. We who have sat with her in the inmost counsels of the provincial Congress executive, will for ever miss the grace and dignity of her presence in our deliberations. Our hearts go out to Jawaharlal in his grievous bereavement ; and we may only hope that, brave as he is, his sorrow will be assuaged by the thought that it is being shared by countless men and women in the land ; and that his nearest fellow-workers feel it as their own. In the death of Tasadduq Sherwani, we have lost a great gentleman, a stout-hearted patriot and a true champion of nationalism overriding all petty considerations of class, creed, or community ; one who gave up all he possessed for the cause of the country's freedom which was so dear to his heart. To his brothers and other members of his family we send our heartfelt condolences to-day.

The Present—and the Future

It is no business of mine to review the present situation or to suggest any programme for the immediate future. But I cannot allow this opportunity to pass without putting on record the result of my little experience as a humble worker of the Congress, and referring to the chief difficulty that I find in the way of improving matters alike in the political as in other spheres of our national activity. I hope I shall not shock the susceptibilities of my friends present, when I say that individuals as such have ceased to interest me. The only person who I think matters, is that unknown but most important person—the common man in the field, factory, in the cottage and the street and on whom falls the heaviest load of life. I regard the sole end of all effort, to be his betterment; and to my thinking, the highest achievements and the noblest endeavours are in vain if they do not result in bringing any light to him or in enhancing his life in any way. We have had plenty of great men in our country in the past. We can claim some of the greatest men of to-day also as being of our land; but in the present as in the past, great men seem to come and go, leaving only their name and fame behind, while the mass goes on for ever in its own apathy, ignorance and destitution, moral and material. Something must be done to change this state of things. We have already innumerable gods who, I take it, were the great men and women of the past now enshrined in stone and marble, for passing generations to revere and worship. No one would object to it, no one would have any cause to complain, if this mentality had not given us the notion that the duty of the mass is only to honour the great from a distance and go its own way heedless of their teaching. We seem to think there is a separate caste of patriots, away and above the ordinary run of man, whose business it is to be patriotic, to win freedom or whatever public good may be their craze, by some mysterious methods which they must devise and practise, while the sole duty of the ordinary man is to adore these good people and do nothing himself to help in the task of nation-building. We do not seem to realise the simple truth that the activities of leaders are futile unless we ourselves respond to their call in our own lives.

As corrective to this mentality, I think the time has now come to put a complete stop to ovations, processions, addresses, and the like for those who are great; and at the same time we must also draw up a simple code of disciplined life, commensurate with the limitations of ordinary human nature, and insist on all to follow it enforcing it with a sanction. We must say that any one who lives according to that code, however humble his sphere may be, is as great a patriot as the greatest so recognised in the land, for true greatness resides in fulfilling the tasks one undertakes in a spirit of duty and responsibility. What we need are injunctions to tell us how a person worthy of Swaraj behaves, how he is considerate and accommodating to his fellowmen in the smallest things in life. There is much misunderstanding on the subject; and though it may appear a matter of small consequence, I personally regard it as of the greatest moment viewing the conditions of our life as they are. Thus alone, to my mind, can we infuse the spirit of hope in the hearts of our countless men and women and pour them to action on right lines; and thus alone can we harness to the country's service, the latent energies and the great possibilities of our human material, now remaining unutilised. Thus also I feel we can eliminate the unnecessary personal jealousies and bitterness and communal and political bickerings that are ruining public life in our land to-day.

Our Real Aim

I regard the so-called problems of council entry and office acceptance—so intensely exercising the minds of many—as of no importance whatsoever. These can be safely left to take care of themselves. So far as I can see, I have no doubt that we of the Congress to-day stand for a reconstruction of society. We are impatient of things as they are. It is no more possible to tolerate excessive wealth in the hands of a few on the one hand, and crushing poverty of the vast masses on the other; unlimited power for a handful and the condition of serfs and slaves for the rest. We definitely stand for an equitable distribution of work and wages, for a society of freedom and of love. The thousands of poor men and women who to-day are sacrificing their all for the cause that the Congress represents, are not doing so in order to continue the cruel and irresponsible oligarchy that is crushing us all. Let those who are better off than the rest of their brethren, or who to-day enjoy the monopoly of all position and power, wealth and leisure, not forget that the very things that they prize, are endangered when the many are wallowing in drift and in poverty, deprived of all the light that proper knowledge and adequate comfort can give them. Widespread poverty inevitably reacts on the well-to-do; and disease and death creep within their sheltered walls because the neighbourhood is unhappy and unclean. Viewed from the purely selfish standpoint too, enhancement of life in all its aspects, really depends upon a proper setting; and it is up to those who feel unnecessarily disturbed to-day by our ideals, to help actively instead, in bringing about a state of things where there will be, as a matter of fact, more real gain for themselves. It is time that we placed before the country our exact ideas about the society we are seeking to build. That will help all to know what we want and will eliminate all doubts and suspicions—and may be false hopes and ambitions as well—that so unnecessarily clog us at every step. We must now frame our own future constitution, not so much of the Government which is after all not very important, but the constitution of society itself for the well-being of which alone any Government can be allowed to exist.

Logical preciseness and intellectually correct programmes, however, can be of little value unless we have people to appreciate and follow them. What India needs are real men and women, sturdy and efficient citizens, who can be depended upon to perform their tasks in every sphere of activity with which they may be connected, humble or high; and so long as these are not forthcoming, we can achieve nothing, however perfect our resolutions on paper, however brave our voice on the platform. Let the story of the last 15 years of our earnest labours teach us a lesson. If we are really determined to be free we cannot afford to be oblivious of the underlying nature of the forces that are arrayed against us. The Government as it is, is a compact and efficient organisation, each part of which knows exactly its duty even in the most distant and isolated places, and fulfils its task properly and punctually for the strength and stability of the whole and in a spirit of mutual loyalty hard to equal. In order to meet this we have also to be organised in a similar manner, and our units have also to be of a character similar to the units of the opponents we are facing and fighting. Unless we are able to do that, our greatest efforts are bound to go in vain; and we shall always find ourselves at the end of every great movement, just where we started. The history of India from the earliest times has this sad tale to tell. Everytime we have to begin at the beginning. Let the Congress now devise methods by which we as a nation shall not be sliding back each time we make a move forwards, just leaving a few great names behind to illumine the pages of our history and to give us some fanciful satisfaction of our past greatness when darkness envelopes us in the present and we become a butt of ridicule for the sister nations of the world. Let us make sure that we are really out for the true freedom and greatness of a whole people and not merely to exploit or enhance the undoubted greatness of a few. It is not enough to do our little bit when there is something going. It is necessary to be always on the alert and working. It is the day-to-day work that tells in the long run, and not the work done merely in spurts. Organisation for peace is far more necessary than organisation for war. If the former is secured, the latter will probably never be needed; or if it ever is, it will be completed at a moment's notice.

The task before us is verily a mighty one. We are out to win Swaraj. Swaraj for us is the recovery of our lost soul and not merely the finding of our lost wealth. We want Swaraj because we desire to fashion our lives in our way, we want to get back our capacity to make our own contribution to world-thought and world-endeavour: and to feel and realise that the words 'India' and 'Indian', unlike the case to-day, stand for everything that is noble and good; and that we too can move about the world as a self-respecting people, as members of a race that is truly great and really free. Comrades, I welcome you all once again and earnestly hope that your deliberations here may lead us nearer to our cherished goal.

The Presidential Address

The following is the text of the Presidential Address of *Pandit Jawaharlal Nehru* :—

Comrades,—After many years I face you again from this tribune, many weary years of strife and turmoil and common suffering. It is good for me to see this great host of old comrades and friends, linked together by strong bonds that cannot break, to sense the old brave spirit yet again, to feel your overwhelming kindness and goodwill to one whose greatest privilege it is to have been a comrade and a soldier with all of you in a mighty struggle for freedom. I am heartened and strengthened by you, though even in this great gathering I feel a little lonely. Many a dear comrade and friend has left us, worn out, long before the normal length of our earthly days, by the stress and strain of conflict. One by one they go, leaving a void in our hearts and a dull misery in our minds. They find peace from this turmoil perhaps, and it is well, for they deserved it. They rest after their labours.

But what of us who remain behind with a heavier burden to carry? There is no rest for us or for those who languish in prison or in detention camp. We cannot rest, for rest is betrayal of those who have gone and in going handed the torch of freedom to us to keep alight; it is betrayal of the cause we have taken; it is betrayal of the millions who never rest.

"TIRED CHILD"

I am weary and I have come back like a tired child yearning for solace in the bosom of our common mother, India. That solace has come to me in overflowing measure; thousands of hands have been stretched out to me in love and sympathy; millions of silent voices have carried their message of affection to my heart. How can I thank you, men and women of India? How can I express in words feelings that are too deep for utterance?

For many years now I have been a distant looker-on on this Indian scene where once I was an actor, and many a thing has happened that has filled me with distress and anguish. I do not wish to survey this recent past of ours, which must be fresh in your memory, and which has left a sorry trail behind and many knots which are difficult to unravel. But we may not ignore it for out of that past as well as the present, we have to build our future. We have followed high ideals and we have taken pride in the fact that our means are worthy of those ideals. We have been witnesses of many a miracle in this old and battered land of ours, and yet our very success has been followed by failure and disillusion. Temporary failure has little significance when the aim is high and the struggle bound to be a long one; it is but incentive to further effort. Often it teaches us more than a victory easily won and becomes a prelude to a greater success. But we profit by it only if we learn its lesson and search our minds for an explanation of that failure. Only by constant self-questioning, individual and national, can we keep on the right path. An easy and unthinking confidence is almost as bad as a weak submission to helpless dejection. Real failure comes only when we forget our ideals and objectives and principles and to wander away from the road which leads to their realisation.

In this crisis of our history, therefore, let us look into ourselves and examine without pity or prejudice, what we have done and what others have done to us, and seek to find out where we stand to-day. We dare not delude ourselves or evade real issues for fear of offending others, even though some of these others are comrades whom we respect. That is the way of self-deception which none who seek great and vital changes can follow except at their peril.

Sixteen years ago, under the inspiration of our leader, we took a new and long step converting this Congress from an ineffective body, feebly functioning amongst the upper classes, into a powerful democratic organisation with its roots in the Indian soil and the vast masses who live on it. A handful of our old friends, representing an age and a class which had had its day, left us, fearful of this democratic upsurge, and preferring the shelter and protection of British Imperialism to joining hands with the new vital forces which convulsed the country and struggled for freedom. Historically, they lapsed into the past. But we heard the rumbling of those forces and, for the moment, lined up with them and played a not unworthy part in current history. We sensed the new spirit of mass release, of psychological escape from the cramping effects of long subjection; we gloried in the breaking of the mental bonds that encompassed us. And because our minds became free we felt that political freedom could not be far, for it is often harder to break the bonds of the spirit than physical bonds and chains of iron and steel. We represented the Spirit of the Age and were marching step by step with countless others in our country and outside. The exhilaration of being in tune with the masses and with world forces came upon us and the feeling that we were the agents of historic destiny.

We were engrossed in our national struggle and the turn it took bore the powerful impress of our great leader and of our national genius. We were hardly conscious then of what was happening outside. And yet our struggle was but part of a far wider struggle for freedom, and the forces that moved us were moving millions of people all over the world and driving them into action. All Asia was astir from the Mediterranean to the Far East, from the Islamic West to the Buddhist East; Africa responded to the new spirit; Europe, broken up by the war, was struggling to find a new equilibrium. And right across a vast area in Europe and Asia, in the Soviet territories, a new conception of human freedom and social equality fought desparately against a host of enemies. There were great differences in the many aspects of this freedom struggle all over the world and we were misled by them and did not see the common background. Yet, if we are to understand those varied phenomena, and derive a lesson from them for our own national struggle, we must try to see and understand the whole picture. And if we do so we cannot fail to observe an organic connection between them which endures through changing situations. If once we grasp this organic bond, the world situation becomes easier to understand and our own national problems take their proper places in the wider picture. We realise then that we cannot isolate India or the Indian problem from that of the rest of the world. To do so is to ignore the real forces that are shaping events and to cut ourselves adrift from the vital energy that flows from them. To do so, again, is to fail to understand the significance of our own problems, and if we do not understand this how can we solve them? We are apt to loose ourselves, as we have indeed done, in petty conflicts and minor questions, like the communal problem, and forget the major issues; we are apt to waste our energy (like our moderate friends do) in interminable discussions over legal quibbles and constitutional questions.

AFTERMATH OF WAR

During the troubled aftermath of the Great War came revolutionary changes in Europe and Asia, and the intensification of the struggle for social freedom in Europe, and a new aggressive nationalism in the countries of Asia. There were ups and downs, and sometimes it appeared as if the revolutionary urge had exhausted itself and things were settling down. But economic and political conditions were such that there could be no settling down, the existing structure could no longer cope with these new conditions, and all its efforts to do so were vain and fruitless. Everywhere conflicts grew and a great depression overwhelmed the world and there was a progressive deterioration everywhere except in the wide-flung Soviet territories of the U. S. S. R., where, in marked contrast with the rest of the world, astonishing progress was made in every direction. Two rival economic and political systems faced each other in the world and, though they tolerated each other for a while, there was an inherent antagonism between them, and they played for mastery on the stage of the world. One of them was the capitalist order which had inevitably developed into vast imperialisms, which having swallowed the colonial world, were intent on eating each other up. Powerful still and fearful of war, which might endanger their possessions, yet they came into inevitable conflict with each other and prepared feverishly for war. They were quite unable to solve the problems that threatened them and helplessly they submitted to slow decay. The other was the new socialist order of the U. S. S. R. which went from progress to progress, though often at terrible cost, and where the problems of the capitalist world had ceased to exist.

Capitalism, in its difficulties, took to Fascism with all its brutal suppression of what western civilisation had apparently stood for; it became, even in some of its homelands, what its Imperialist counterpart had long been in the subject colonial countries. Fascism and Imperialism thus stood out as the two faces of the new decaying Capitalism and though they varied in different countries according to national characteristics and economic and political conditions, they represented the same forces of reaction and supported each other, and at the same time came into conflict with each other, for such conflict was inherent in their very nature. Socialism in the West and the rising nationalisms of the eastern and the other dependent countries opposed this combination of Fascism and Imperialism. Nationalism in the East, it must be remembered, was essentially different from the new and terribly narrow nationalism of Fascist countries; the former was the historical urge to freedom, the latter the last refuge of reaction.

Thus we see the world divided up into two vast groups to-day—the Imperialist and Fascist on one side, the Socialist and Nationalist on the other. There is some overlapping of the two and the line between them is difficult to draw, for there is mutual conflict between the Fascist and Imperialist Powers, and the nationalism of subject countries has sometimes a tendency to Fascism. But the main division holds and if we keep it in mind, it will be easier for us to understand world conditions and our own place in them.

WHERE WE STAND

Where do we stand then, we who labour for a free India? Inevitably we take our stand with the progressive forces of the world which are ranged against Fascism and Imperialism. We have to deal with one imperialism in particular, the oldest and the most far-reaching of the modern world, but powerful as it is, it is but one aspect of world-imperialism. And that is the final argument for Indian independence and for the severance of our connection with the British Empire. Between Indian nationalism, Indian freedom and British imperialism there can be no common ground, and if we remain within the imperialist fold, whatever our name or status, whatever outward semblance of political power we might have, we remain cribbed and confined and allied to and dominated by the reactionary forces and the great financial vested interests of the capitalist world. The exploitation of our masses will still continue and all the vital social problems that face us will remain unsolved. Even real political freedom will be out of our reach, much more so radical social changes.

With the development of the great struggle all over the world we have seen the progressive deterioration of many of the capitalist-imperialist countries and an attempt at consolidation of the reactionary forces under Fascism or Naziism or so-called 'national governments. In India the same process has been evident to us during these past years, and the stronger the nationalist movement has grown the more have efforts been made by our imperialist rulers to break our ranks and to gather together under their banner the reactionary elements in the country. The Round Table Conferences were such attempts and, though they helped our rulers in some measure, they served a useful purpose by showing us clearly the division between the imperialist and the anti-imperialist forces in the country. Unhappily we did not fully profit by this lesson and we still imagine that we can win over some of these imperialist groups to the side of Indian freedom and anti-imperialism and in a vain attempt to do so, we suppress our ideals, blush for our objectives and tone down our activities.

Decay of British Imperialism

Meanwhile the decay of British imperialism in India becomes ever more apparent. It cannot, by its very nature, solve our economic problems and rid us of our terrible poverty, which it has largely itself created. It subsists on a normal fare of the fiercest repression and a denial of civil and even personal liberty. It surrounds us with a wide network of spies and, among the pillars of its administration, are the tribe of informers and agents provocateurs and the like. Its service try to seek comfort for their obvious deterioration and incompetence by perpetually singing songs of mutual adulation. Argument gives place to the policeman's baton and the soldier's bayonet and prison and detention camp, and even our extraordinary finances are justified by the methods of the bully. It is astonishing to find to what depths of vulgarity our rulers have descended in their ardent desire to hold on to what they have got, and it is depressing, though perhaps inevitable, that some of our own countrymen, more interested in British imperialism than the British themselves, should excel at this deplorable game. So wanting in mental equilibrium are they, so obsessed by fear of the Congress and the national movement it represents, that their wishes become thoughts, their thoughts inferences, and their inferences facts, solemnly stated in official publications, and on which the Majesty of the British Government rests in India, and people are kept in prison and detention camp without charge or trial. Being interested in psychology, I have watched this process of moral and intellectual decay and realised, even more than I did previously, how autocratic power corrupts and degrades and vulgarizes. I have read sometimes the reports of the recent Assembly meetings and noted the great difference in tone and content between them and the Assembly of ten years ago. I have observed the forced attempts made to discredit the Congress by a reference to the Tilak Swaraj Fund with which I was connected for many years as Secretary of the Congress. But prepared as I was for much, even I was surprised at the insinuations made against our much loved chief, Rajendra Babu, and the charges brought against the Behar Relief Fund. A mild criticism by me of official incompetence soon after the Behar earthquake was deeply resented probably because the truth of it was realised. Newspapers that criticized the official arrangements at a subsequent earthquake were heavily penalised or suppressed. All criticism hurts the sensitive skin of the Government and its reactions are quick and far-reaching. The more incompetent it grows the less it likes being told so. But this does not prevent it from indulging in reckless allegations about others.

This psychological aspect interests me even more than the more aggressive manifestations of British authority in India, for it throws light on much that has happened. It shows us how a clear and definite fascist mentality has developed among our rulers and how closely allied is imperialism to fascism. How this fascist mentality has functioned in the recent past and is functioning to-day, I shall not go into now. You know well the horror of these years and of the nightmare that we have all experienced. We shall not easily forget it and if there are some who have been cowed down by it, there are others who have steeled themselves to a greater resolve to end this infamy in India.

Deprivation of Civil Liberties

But of one thing I must say a few words for to me it is one of the most vital things that I value. That is the tremendous deprivation of civil liberties in India. A Government that has to rely on the Criminal Law Amendment Act and similar laws, that suppresses the press and literature, that bans hundreds of organisations, that keeps people in prisons without trial and that does so many other things that are happening in India to-day, is a government that has ceased to have even a shadow of a justification for its existence. I can never adjust myself to these conditions, I find them intolerable. And yet I find many of my own countrymen complacent about them, some even supporting them, some, who have made the practice of sitting on a fence into fine art, being neutral when such questions are discussed. And I have wondered what there was in common between them and me and those who think like I do. We in the Congress welcome all co-operations in the struggle for Indian freedom; our doors are ever open to all who stand for that freedom and are against imperialism. But they are not open to the supporters of repression and those who stand by the British Government in the suppression of civil liberty. We belong to opposite camps.

Recently, as you know, we have had a typical example of the way Government functions in India in the warning issued to a dear and valued comrade of ours, Subhas Chandra Bose. We who know him also know how frivolous are the charges brought against him. But even if there was substance in them we could not tolerate willingly the treatment to which he has long been subjected. He did me the honour to ask me for advice and I was puzzled and perplexed for it is no easy thing to advise another in such a matter, when such advice might mean prison. Subhas Bose has suffered enough at the cost of his health. Was I justified in adding to this mental and physical agony? I hesitated and at first suggested to him to postpone his departure. But this advice made me unhappy and I consulted other friends and then advised him differently. I suggested that he should return to his home-land as soon as he could. But, it appears, that even before my advice reached him, he had started on his journey back to India.

Terrorism

This instance leads us to think of the larger problem, of the way the bogey of terrorism has been exploited by the Government to crush political activity and to cripple physically and mentally the fair province of Bengal. You know that terrorism as such is practically non-existent now in Bengal or any part of India. Terrorism is always a sign of political immaturity in a people, just as so-called constitutionalism where there is no democratic constitution, is a sign of political senility. Our national movement has long outgrown immature stage, and even the odd individuals who have in the past indulged in terrorist acts have apparently given up that tragic and futile philosophy. The Congress, by its stress on peaceful and effective action, has drawn the youth of the country into its fold and all traces of terroristic activity would long have vanished but for the policy of the Government which feeds the roots out of which a helpless violence grows. But terrorism or no terrorism, a government which adopts the methods which have long prevailed in Midnapore and elsewhere in Bengal stands self-condemned. Similar methods have also long prevailed in the Frontier Province, although there is no hint of terroristic activities there, and that fine man and true, beloved of millions, Abdul Gaffar Khan, still lies in prison. Excuses differ, but the real reason is the ever-growing fascist mentality of our rulers.

That is one side of the picture. What of us? I have found a spirit of disunion spreading over the land, a strange 'malaise', and petty conflicts amongst old comrades growing ever bigger and interfering with all activity. We have forgotten for the moment the large ideals we stood for and we quarrel over petty issues. We have largely lost touch with the masses and, deprived of the life-giving energy that flows from them, we dry up and weaken and our organisation shrinks and loses the power it had. First things must always come first and because we have forgotten this and argue and dispute over secondary matters, we are in danger of losing our bearings.

Middle Class Leadership

Every great struggle has its ups and downs and temporary failure. When such a setback occurs there is a reaction when the fund of national energy is exhausted and has to be recharged. That happens again and again, and yet that is not an adequate explanation of all that has taken place. Our direct action struggles in the past were based on the masses, and especially the peasantry, but the backbone and leadership were always supplied by the middle classes, and this, under the circumstances, was inevitable. The middle classes are a vague group or groups; at the top, a handful of them are closely allied to British imperialism; at the bottom are the dispossessed and other groups who have been progressively crushed by economic circumstances and out of whose ranks come the advanced political workers and revolutionaries; in between are the centre groups, which tend often to side with the advanced elements, but which also have alliances with the upper groups and live in the hope of joining their superior ranks. A middle class leadership is thus often a distracted leadership' looking in two directions at the same time. In times of crisis and struggle, when unity of aim and activity is essential, this two-faced leadership is bound to injure the cause and to hold back when a forward move is called for. Being too much tied up with property and the goods of this world, it is fearful of losing them; and it is easier to bring pressure on it and to exhaust its stamina. And yet, paradoxically, it is only from the middle class intellectuals that revolutionary leadership comes, and we in India know that our bravest leaders and our stoutest comrades have come from the ranks of the middle classes. But by the very nature of our struggle, these front rank leaders are taken away and the others who took their place tire and are influenced more by the static element of their class. That has been very evident during our recent struggle when our propertied classes were hit hard by the Government's drastic policy of seizure and confiscation of monies and properties, and were thus induced to bring pressure for the suspension of the struggle.

How is this problem to be solved? Inevitably, we must have middle class leadership but this must look more and more towards the masses and draw strength and inspiration from them. The Congress must be not only for the masses, as it claims to be, but of the masses; only then will it really be for the masses. I have a feeling that our relative weakness to-day is due to a certain decay of our middle class elements and our divorce from the people at large. Our policies and ideals are governed far more by this middle class outlook than by a consideration of the needs of the great majority of the population. Even the problems that trouble us are essentially middle class problems, like the communal problem, which have no significance for the masses.

This is partly due, I think, to a certain historical growth during the last fifteen years to which we have failed to adapt ourselves, to a growing urgency of economic problems affecting the masses, and to a raising mass consciousness which does not find sufficient outlet through the Congress. This was not so in 1920 and later when there was an organic link between Congress and the masses, and their needs and desires, vague as they were, found expression in the Congress. But as those needs and desires have taken more definite shape, they have not been so welcome to other elements in the Congress and that organic connection has gone. That though regrettable, is really a sign of growth and, instead of lamenting it, we must find a new link and a new connection on a fresh basis which allows for growth of mass consciousness within the Congress. The middle class claim to represent the masses had some justification in 1920; it has much less to-day, though the lower middle classes have still a great deal in common with the masses.

Narrowness of Congress Constitution

Partly also our divorce from the people at large is due to a certain narrowness of our Congress constitution. The radical changes made in it fifteen years ago brought it in line with existing conditions then and it drew in large numbers and became an effective instrument of national activity. Though the control and background were essentially middle-class and city, it reached the remotest village and brought with it political and economic consciousness to the masses and there was wide-spread discussion of national issues in city and village alike. One could feel the new life pulsating through this vast land of ours and, as we were in harmony with it, we drew strength from it. The intense repression by the Government during later years broke many of our physical and outward bonds with our countryside. But something more than that happened. The vague appeal of earlier days no longer sufficed, and on the new economic issues that were forcing themselves on us, we hesitated to give a definite opinion. Worse even than the physical divorce, there was a mental divorce between the middle class elements and the mass elements. Our constitution no longer fitted in with changing conditions; it lost its roots in the soil and became a matter of small committees functioning in the air. It still had the mighty prestige of the Congress name behind it and this carried it a long way, but it lost the living democratic touch. It became a prey to authoritarianism and a battleground for rival cliques fighting for control, and in doing so, stooping to the lowest and most objectionable of tactics. Idealism disappeared and in its place there came opportunism and corruption. The constitutional structure of the Congress was unequal to facing the new situation; it could be shaken up anywhere almost by a handful of unscrupulous individuals. Only a broad democratic basis could have saved it and this was lacking.

Last year an attempt was made to revise the constitution in order to get rid of some of these evils. How far that attempt has succeeded or not I am not competent to judge. Perhaps it has made the organisation more efficient but efficiency means little if it has no strength behind it, and strength, for us can only come from the masses. The present constitution stresses still further the authoritarian side of the organisation, and in spite of stressing rural representation does not provide effective links with the masses.

REAL PROBLEM

The real problem for us is, how in our struggle for independence we can join together all the anti-imperialist forces in the country, how we can make a broad front of our mass elements with the great majority of the middle classes which stands for independence. There has been same talk of a joint front but, so far as I can gather, this refers to some alliance among the upper classes, probably at the expense of the masses, That surely can never be the idea of the Congress and if it favours it, it betrays the interests it has claimed to represent and loses the very reason for its existence. The essence of a joint popular front must be uncompromising opposition to imperialism, and the strength of it must inevitably come from the active participation of the peasantry and workers.

Perhaps you have wondered at the way I have dealt at some length with the background of international and national affairs and not touched so far the immediate problems that fill your minds. You may have grown impatient. But I am convinced that the only right way of looking at our own problems is to see them in their proper place in a world-setting. I am convinced that there is intimate connection between world events, and our national problem is but a part of the world problem of capitalist-imperialism. To look at each event apart from the others and without understanding the connection between them must lead us to the formation of erratic and erroneous views. Look at the vast panorama of world change to-day, where mighty forces are at grips with each other and dreadful war darkens the horizon. Subject peoples struggling for freedom and imperialism crushing them down; exploited classes facing their exploiters and seeking freedom and equality. Italian imperialism bombing and killing the brave Ethiopians; Japanese imperialism continuing its aggression in North China and Mongolia; British imperialism piously objecting to other countries misbehaving, yet carrying on in much the same way in India and the Frontier: and behind it all a decaying economic order which intensifies all these conflicts. Can we not see an organic connection in all these various phenomena? Let us try to develop the historic sense so that we can view current events in proper perspective and understand their real significance. Only then can we appreciate the march of history and keep step with it.

I realise that in this address I am going a little beyond the usual beat of the Congress president. But I do not want you to have me under any false pretences and we must have perfect frankness with each other. Most of you must know my views on social and economic matters for I have often given expression to them. Yet you chose me as president. I do not take that choice to mean an endorsement by you all, or by a majority, of those views, but I take it that this does mean that those views are spreading in India and that most of you will be indulgent in considering them at least.

Only Key to Solution

I am convinced that the only key to the solution of the world's problems and of India's problems lies in socialism, and when I use this word I do so not in a vague humanitarian way but in the scientific, economic sense. Socialism is, however, something even more than an economic doctrine ; it is a philosophy of life and as such also it appeals to me. I see no way of ending the poverty the vast unemployment, the degradation and the subjection of the Indian people except through socialism. That involves vast and revolutionary changes in our political and social structure, the ending of vested interests in land and industry, as well as the feudal and autocratic Indian States system. That means the ending of private property. except in a restricted sense, and the replacement of the present profit system by a higher ideal of co-operative service. It means ultimately a change in our instincts and habits and desires. In short, it means a new civilization, radically different from the present capitalist order. Some glimpse we can have of this new civilization in the territories of the U. S. S. R. Much has happened there which has pained me greatly and with which I disagree, but I look upon that great and fascinating unfolding of a new order and a new civilization as the most promising feature of our dismal age. If the future is full of hope it is largely because of Soviet Russia and what it has done, and I am convinced that, if some world catastrophe does not intervene, this new civilization will spread to other lands and put an end to the wars and conflicts which capitalism feeds.

I do not know how or when this new order will come to India. I imagine that every country will fashion it after its own way and fit it in with its national genius. But the essential basis of that order must remain and be a link in the world order that will emerge out of the present chaos,

Socialism is thus for me not merely an economic doctrine which I favour ; it is a vital creed which I hold with all my head and heart. I work for Indian independence because the nationalist in me cannot tolerate alien domination ! I work for it even more because for me it is the inevitable step to social and economic changes. I should like the Congress to become a socialist organisation and to join hands with the other forces in the world who are working for the new civilization. But I realise that the majority in the Congress, as it is constituted to-day, may not be prepared to go thus far. We are a nationalist organisation and we think and work on the nationalist plane. It is evident enough now that this is too narrow even for the limited objective of political independence, and so we talk of the masses and their economic needs. But still most of us hesitate, because of our nationalist backgrounds, to take a step which might frighten away some vested interests. Most of those interests are already ranged against us and we can expect little from them except opposition even in the political struggle.

Congress and Socialism

Much as I wish for the advancement of socialism in this country, I have no desire to force the issue in the Congress and thereby create difficulties in the way of our struggle for independence. I shall co-operate gladly and with all the strength in me with all those who work for independence even though they do not agree with the socialist solution. But I shall do so stating my position frankly and hoping in course of time to convert the Congress and the country to it, for only thus can I see it achieving independence. It should surely be possible for all of us who believe in independence to join our ranks together even though we might differ on the social issue. The Congress has been in the past a broad front representing various opinions joined together by that common bond. It must continue as such even though the difference of those opinions becomes more marked.

How does socialism fit in with the present ideology of the Congress ? I do not think it does. I believe in the rapid industrialisation of the country and only thus I think will the standards of the people rise substantially and poverty be combated. Yet I have co-operated whole-heartedly in the past with the khadi programme and I hope to do so in the future because I believe that khadi and village industries have a definite place in our present economy. They have a social, a political and an economic value which is difficult to measure but which is apparent enough to those who have studied their effects. But I look upon them more as temporary expedients of a transition stage rather than as solutions of our vital problems. That transition stage might be a long one, and in a country like India, village industries might well play an important, though subsidiary role even after the development of industrialism. But though I co-operate in the village industries programme my ideological approach to it differs considerably from that of many others in the Congress who are opposed to industrialisation and socialism.

The problem of untouchability and the Harijans again can be approached in different ways. For a socialist it presents no difficulty for under socialism there can be no such differentiation or victimisation. Economically speaking, the Harijans have constituted the landless proletariat and an economic solution removes the social barriers that custom and tradition have raised.

New India Act

I come now to a question which is probably occupying your minds—the new Act passed by the British Parliament and our policy in regard to it. This Act has come into being since the last Congress met, but even at that time we had had a foretaste of it in the shape of the White Paper, and I know of no abler analysis of those provisions than that contained in the presidential address of my predecessor in this high office. The Congress rejected that proposed constitution and resolved to have nothing to do with it. The new Act, as is well known, is an even more retrograde measure and has been condemned by even the most moderate and cautious of our politicians. If we rejected the White Paper, what then are we to do with this new charter of slavery to strengthen the bonds of imperialist domination and to intensify the exploitation of our masses? And even if we forget its content for a while, can we forget the insult and injury that have accompanied it, the contemtuous defiance of our wishes, the suppression of civil liberties and the wide-spread repression that has been our normal lot? If they had offered to us the crown of heaven with this accompaniment and with dishonour, would we not have spurned it as inconsistent with our national honour and self-respect? What then of this?

A charter of slavery is no law for the slave, and though we may perforce submit for a while to it and to the humiliation of ordinances and the like, inherent in that enforced submission is the right and the desire to rebel against it and to end it.

Our lawyers have examined this new constitution and have condemned it. But constitutions are something much more than legal documents. "The real constitution" said Ferdinand Lassalle, "consists of the actual relationships of power", and the working of this power we see even to-day, after the Act has been passed. That is the constitution we have to face, not the fine phrases which are sometimes presented to us, and we can only deal with it with the strength and power generated by the people of the country.

To this Act our attitude can only be one of uncompromising hostility and a constant endeavour to end it. How can we do this?

Since my return from Europe I have had the advantage of full and frank discussion with my colleagues of the Working Committee. All of us have agreed that the Act has to be rejected and combated, but all of us have not been able to agree to the manner of doing so. We have pulled together in the past and I earnestly hope that we shall do so in the future, but in order to do so effectively we must recognise that there are marked differences in our outlooks. I do not yet know, as I write, what the final recommendation of the Working Committee will be on this issue. I can only, therefore, venture to put before you my own personal view on the subject, not knowing how far they represent the views of Congressmen. I should like to make it clear, however, in fairness to my old colleagues of the Working Committee, that the majority of them do not agree with all the views I am going to express. But whether we agree or disagree, or whether we agree to differ, there is a strong desire on our part to continue to co-operate together, laying stress on our many points of agreement rather than on the differences. That is the right course for us and, as a democratic organisation, that is the only course open to us.

Constituent Assembly

I think that, under the circumstances, we have no choice but to contest the election to the new provincial legislatures, in the event of their taking place. We should seek election on the basis of a detailed political and economic programme, with our demand for a Constituent Assembly in the forefront. I am convinced that the only solution of our political and communal problems will come through such an Assembly, provided it is elected on an adult franchise and a mass basis. That Assembly will not come into existence till at least a semi-revolutionary situation has been created in this country and the actual relationships of power, and apart from paper constitutions, are such that the people of India can make their will felt. When that will hapen I cannot say, but the world is too much in the grip of dynamic forces to-day to admit of static conditions in India or elsewhere for long. We may thus have to face this issue sooner than we might expect. But obviously, a Constituent Assembly will not come through the new Act or the new legislatures. Yet we must press this demand and keep it before our country and the world, so that when the time comes we may be ripe for it.

A Constituent Assembly is the only proper and democratic method for the framing of our constitution, and for its delegates then to negotiate a treaty with the representatives of the British Government. But we cannot go to it with blank minds in the hope that something good will emerge out of it. Such an Assembly, in order to be fruitful, must have previovs thought behind it and a definite scheme put forward by an organised group. The actual details, as to how the Assembly is to be convened, must depend on the circumstances then existing and need not trouble us now. But it will be our function as the Congress to know exactly what we are after, to place this clearly and definitely before the Assembly, and to press for its acceptance.

One of the principal reasons for our seeking election will be to carry the message of the Congress to the millions of voters and to the scores of millions of the disfranchised, to acquaint them with our future programme and policy, to make the masses realise that we not only stand for them but that we are of them and seek to co-operate with them in removing their social and economic burdens. Our appeal and message will not be limited to the voters for we must remember that hundreds of millions are disfranchised and they need our help most for they are at the bottom of the social ladder and suffer most from exploitation. We have seen in the past widespread official interference in the elections; we shall have to face that, as well as the serried and monied ranks of the re-actionaries. But the real danger will come from our toning down our programme and policy in order to win over the hesitating and compromising groups and individuals. If we compromise on principles, we shall fall between two stools and deserve our fall. The only right way and the only safe way is to stand four-square on our own programme and to compromise with no one who has opposed the national struggle for freedom in the past, or who is in any way giving support to British imperialism.

Office Issue

When we have survived the election, what then are we to do? Office or no office? A secondary matter perhaps, and yet behind that issue lie deep questions of principle and vital differences of outlook, and a decision on that, either way, has far-reaching consequence. Behind it lies, somewhat hidden, the question of independence itself and whether we seek revolutionary changes in India or are working for petty reforms under the aegis of British imperialism. We go back again in thought to the clash of ideas which preceded the changes in the Congress in 1920. We made a choice then deliberately and with determination and discarded the old sterile creed of reformism. Are we to go back again to that blind and suffocating lane, after all these years of brave endeavour, and to wipe out the memory of what we have done and achieved and suffered? That is the issue and let none of us forget it when we have to give our decision. In this India, crying aloud for radical and fundamental change, in this world pregnant with revolutionary and dynamic possibility, are we to forget our mission and our historic destiny, and slide back to static futility? And if some of us feel tired and hunger for rest and quiet, do we imagine that India's masses will follow our lead, when elemental forces and economic necessity are driving them to their inevitable goal? If we enter the backwaters, others will take our place on the bosom of the flowing stream and will dare to take the rapids and ride the torrent.

How has this question arisen? If we express our hostility to the Act and reject the entire scheme, does it not follow logically that we should have nothing to do with the working of it and should prevent its functioning, in so far as we can? To accept office and industry, under the conditions of the Act, is to negative our rejection of it and to stand self-condemned. National honour and self-respect cannot accept this position, for it would inevitably mean our co-operation in some measure with the repressive apparatus of imperialism, and we would become partners in the repression and in this exploitation of our people. Of ocurse we would try to champion the rights of the people and would protest against repression, but as ministers under the Act, we could do very little to give relief, and we would have to share responsibility for the administration with the apparatus of imperialism, for the deficit budgets, for the suppression of labour and the peasantry. It is always dangerous to assume responsibility without power, even in democratic countries; it will be far worse with this undemocratic construction, hedged in with safeguards and reserved powers and mortgaged funds, where we have to follow the rules and regulations of our opponents' making. Imperialism sometimes talks of co-operation but the kind of co-operation it wants is usually known as surrender and the ministers who accept office will have to do so at the price of surrender of much that they might have stood for in public. That is a humiliating position which self-respect itself should prevent one from accepting. For our great national organisation to be party to it is to give up the very basis and back-ground of our existence.

Self-respect apart, common sense tells us that we can lose much and gain little by acceptance of office in terms of the Act. We cannot get much out of it, or else our criticism of the Act itself is wrong, and we know that it is not so. The big things for which we stand will fade into the background and petty issues will absorb our attention, and we shall lose ourselves in compromises and communal tangles, and disillusion with us will spread over the land. If we have a majority, and only then can the question of acceptance of office arise, we shall be in a position to dominate the situation and to prevent reactionaries and imperialists from profiting by it. Office will not add to our real strength, it will only weaken us by making us responsible for many things that we utterly dislike.

Again, if we are in a minority, the question of office does not arise. It may be, however, that we are on the verge of a majority and with the co-operation of other individuals and groups we can obtain office. There is nothing inherently wrong in our acting together with others on specific issues of civil liberty or economic or other demands, provided we do not compromise on any principle. But I can imagine few things more dangerous and more likely to injure us than the acceptance of office on the sufferance of others. That would be an intolerable position.

It is said that our chances at the elections would increase if we announced that we were prepared to accept offices and ministries. Perhaps that might be so, for all manner of other people, eager for the spoils and patronage that office gives, would then hurry to join us. Does any Congressman imagine that this would be a desirable development or that we would gain strength thereby? Again it is said that more voters would vote for us if they knew that we were going to form ministries. That might happen if we deluded them with false promises of what we might do for them within the Act, but a quick nemesis would follow our failure to give effect to those promises, and failure would be inevitable if the promises were worth while.

There is only one straight course open to us, to go to the people with our programme and make it clear to them that we cannot give effect to the major items in it under the present conditions, and therefore, while we use the platform of the legislatures to press that programme, we seek to end these imperialist bodies by creating deadlocks in them whenever we are in a position to do so. These deadlocks should preferably take place on those programmes so that the masses might learn how ineffective for their purposes are these legislatures.

One fact is sometimes forgotten—the provision for second chambers in many of the provinces. These chambers will be reactionary and will be exploited by the Governor to check any forward tendencies in the lower house. They will make the position of a minister, who seeks advance, even more difficult and unenviable.

Some people have suggested, though their voices are hushed now, that provincial autonomy might be given on this office issue and each Provincial Congress Committee should be empowered to decide it for its own province. An astonishing and fatal suggestion playing into the hands of our imperialist rulers. We who have laboured for Indian unity can never be parties to any proposal which tends to lessen that unity. That way lies disaster and a disruption of the forces working for freedom. If we agree to this, why then should we also not agree to the communal issue being decided provincially, or many other issues, where individual provinces might think differently? First issues will sink into the background, independence itself will fade away, and the narrowest provincialism raise its ugly head. Our policy must be uniform for the whole of India, and it must place first things first, and independence is the first thing of all.

So that I am convinced that for the Congress to favour the acceptance of office, or even to hesitate and waver about it, would be a vital error. It will be a pit from which it would be difficult for us to come out. Practical statesmanship is against it, as well as the traditions of the Congress and the mentality we have sought to develop in the people. Psychologically any such lead might have disastrous consequences. If we stand for revolutionary changes, as we do, we have to cultivate a revolutionary mentality among our people, and anything that goes against it is harmful to our cause.

Psychological Aspect

This psychological aspect is important. For we must never forget, and never delude our masses into imagining, that we can get any real power of real freedom through working these legislatures. We may use them certainly to advance our cause to some extent, but the burden of the struggle for freedom must fall on the masses, and primarily, therefore, our effective work must lie outside these legislatures. Strength will come from the masses and from our work among them and our organisation of them.

Of secondary importance though the work in the legislatures is, we may not treat it casually and allow it to become a hindrance to other work. Therefore it is necessary for the Congress, through its executive, to have direct control over the elections and the programme placed before the country, as well as the activity in the legislatures. Such control will inevitably be exercised through committees and boards appointed for the purpose, but the continued existence of semi-autonomous parliamentary boards seems to be undesirable. Provision should also be made for a periodical review of all such activities so that Congressmen in general and the country should keep in touch with them and should influence them.

We have considered the provincial elections which, it is said, may take place early next year. The time is far off yet and it is by no means impossible that these elections may not take place for a much longer time, or may not take place at all, and the new Act may take its rightful place in oblivion. Much may happen in the course of the next year, and war is ever on the horizon, to upset the schemes and time-tables of our rulers. But we cannot speculate on this and we have to make provision for contingencies. That decision might even have been delayed, but dangerous and compromising tendencies seek to influence Congress policy, and the Congress cannot remain silent when the issue is raised and its whole future is in the balance.

Indian States

The provincial legislatures may come, but few persons, I imagine, are confident about the coming of the federal part of this unholy structure. So far as we are concerned we shall fight against it to our utmost strength, and the primary object of our creating dead-locks in the provinces and making the new Act difficult of functioning, is to kill the Federation. With the Federation dead, the provincial end of the Act will also go and leave the slate clean for the people of India to write on. That writing, whatever it be, can never admit the right of the Indian States to continue as feudal and autocratic monarchies. They have long survived their day, to continue as feudal and autocratic monarchies. They have long survived their day, propped up by an alien Power, and have become the strangest anomalies in a changing world. The future has no place for autocracy or feudalism; a free India cannot tolerate the subjection of many of her children and their deprivation of human rights, nor can it ever agree to a dissection of its body and a cutting up of its limbs. If we stand for any human, political, social or economic rights for ourselves, we stand for those identical rights for the people of the States.

I have referred to the terrible suppression of civil liberties by the British Government in India. But in the States matters are even worse, and though we know that the real power behind those States is that of British imperialism, this tragic suppression of our brothers by their own countrymen is of painful significance. Indian rulers and their ministers have spoken and acted increasingly in the approved fascist manner, and their record during the past few years especially has been one of aggressive opposition to our national demands. States which are considered advanced ban the Congress organisation and offer insult to our national flag, and decree new laws to suppress the Press. What shall we say of the more backward and primitive States?

COMMUNAL QUESTION

There is one more matter concerning the Constitution Act which has given rise to much controversy. This is the communal decision. Many people have condemned it strongly and I think rightly; few have a good word for it. My own view-point is, however, somewhat different from that of others. I am not concerned so much with what it gives to this group or that but more so with the basic idea behind it. It seeks to divide India into numerous separate compartments, chiefly on a religious basis, and thus makes the development of democracy and economic policy very difficult. Indeed the communal decision and democracy can never go together. We have to admit that, under present circumstances, and so long as our politics are dominated by middle class elements, we cannot do away with communalism altogether. But to make a necessary exception in favour of our Muslim or Sikh friends is one thing, to spread this evil principle to numerous other groups and thus to divide up the electoral machinery and the legislature into many compartments, is a far more dangerous proposition. If we wish to function democratically the proposed communal arrangement will have to go and I have no doubt that it will go. But it will not go by the methods adopted by the aggressive opponents of the decision. These methods result inevitably in perpetuating the decision for they help in continuing a situation which prevents any reconsideration.

I have not been enamoured of the post Congress policy in regard to the communal question and its attempts to make pacts and compromises. Yet essentially I think it was based on a sound instinct. First of all the Congress always put independence first and other questions, including the communal one, second, and refused to allow any of those other questions to take pride of place. Secondly, it argued that the communal problem had arisen from a certain set of circumstances which enabled the third party to exploit the other two. In order to solve it, one had either to get rid of the third party (and that meant independence), or get rid of that set of circumstances, which meant a friendly approach by the parties concerned and an attempt to soften the prejudice and fear that filled them. Thirdly, that the majority community must show generosity in the matter to allay the fear and suspicion that minorities, even though unreasonably, might have.

ECONOMIC ISSUES

That analysis is, I think, perfectly sound. I would add that, in my opinion, real solution of the problem will only come when economic issues, affecting all religious groups and cutting across communal boundaries, arise. Apart from the upper middle classes, who live in hopes of office and patronage, the masses and the lower middle classes have to face identical political and economic problems. It is odd and significant that all the communal demands of any group, of which so much is heard, have nothing whatever to do with these problems of the masses and the lower middle classes.

It is also significant that the principal communal leaders, Hindu or Moslem or others, are political reactionaries, quite apart from the communal question. It is sad to think how they have sided with British imperialism in vital matters, how they have given their approval to the suppression of civil liberty, how during these years of agony they have sought to gain narrow profit for their group at the expense of the larger cause of freedom. With them there can be no co-operation, for that would mean co-operation with reaction. But I am sure that with the larger masses and the middle classes who may have temporarily been led away by the specious claims of their communal leaders, there must be the fullest co-operation, and out of that co-operation will come a fairer solution of this problem.

I am afraid I cannot get excited over this communal issue, important as it is temporarily. It is after all a side issue and it can have no real importance in the larger scheme of things. Those who think of it as the major issue, think in terms of British imperialism continuing permanently in this country. Without that basis of thought, they would not attach so much importance to one of its inevitable offshoots. I have no such fear and so my vision of a future India contains neither imperialism nor communalism.

Yet the present difficulty remains and has to be faced. Especially our sympathy must go to the people of Bengal who have suffered most from these communal decisions, as well as from the heavy hand of the Government. Whenever opportunity offers to improve their situation in a friendly way, we must seize it. But always the background of our action must be the national struggle for independence and the social freedom of the masses.

Contact With Masses

I have referred previously to the growing divorce between our organisation and the masses. Individually many of us still have influence with the masses and our word carries weight with them, and who can measure the love and reverence of India's millions for our leader, Gandhiji? And yet organisationally we have lost that intimate touch that we had. The social reform activities of the khadi and village industries and Harijan organisations keep large numbers of our comrades in touch with the masses and those contacts bear fruit. But they are essentially non-political and so, politically, we have largely lost touch. There are many reasons for this and some are beyond our control. Our present Congress constitution is, I feel, not helpful in developing these contacts or in encouraging enough the democratic spirit in its primary committees. These committees are practically rolls of voters who meet only to elect delegates or representatives, and take no part in discussion or the formation of policy.

It is interesting to read in that monumental and impressive record, the Webbs' new book on Russia, how the whole Soviet structure is based on a wide and living democratic foundation. Russia is not supposed to be a democratic country after the Western pattern, and yet we find the essentials of democracy present in far greater degree amongst the masses there than anywhere else. The six hundred thousand towns and villages there have a vast democratic organisation, each with its own soviet, constantly discussing, debating, criticising, helping in the formulation of policy, electing representatives to higher committees. This organisation as citizens covers the entire population over 18 years of age. There is yet another vast organization of the people as producers, and a third, equally vast, as consumers. And thus scores of millions of men and women are constantly taking part in the discussion of public affairs and actually in the administration of the country. There has been no such practical application of the democratic process in history.

All this is of course utterly beyond us, for it requires a change in the political and economic structure and much else before we can experiment that way. But we can profit by that example still and try in our own limited way to develop democracy in the lowest rungs of the Congress ladder and make the primary committee a living organisation.

An additional method for us to increase our contacts with the masses is to organise them as producers and then affiliate such organisations to the Congress or have full co-operation between the two. Such organization of producers as exist to-day, such as trade unions and peasant unions, as well as other anti-imperialist organizations could also be brought within this sphere of mutual co-operation for the good of the masses and for the struggle for national freedom. Thus Congress could have an individual as well as a corporate membership, and retaining its individual character, could influence, and be influenced by, other mass elements.

These are big changes that I have hinted at, and I am by no means sure how they can be brought about, or whether it is possible to go far in this direction in the near future. Still we must move to some extent at least if we are to have our roots in the soil of India and draw life and strength from its millions. The subject is fascinating but complicated and can only be tackled by an expert committee which I trust will be appointed on behalf of the Congress. The report of that committee must be freely discussed so as to get the widest backing for it.

Anomalies In Congress Constitution

All this will take us to the next Congress. Meanwhile perhaps some urgent changes are needed in our constitution to remove anomalies and avoid difficulties. Owing to my absence I have had little experience of the working of the new constitution and cannot make any concrete suggestion. The reduction in the numbers of delegates and A. I. C. C. members would be, to some extent, desirable if there was a background of widespread activity in the primary and secondary committees. Without it, it makes us even less responsive to mass opinion, and, therefore, an increase seems desirable. But the real solution is to increase the interest and day-to-day activity of the lower committees.

I have been told that the manual labour franchise has not been a success and has led to a great deal of evasion. If that is so a change is desirable for a constitution must be such as can be worked easily and without subterfuge.

The Congress is an all-inclusive body and represents many interests, but essentially it is a political organization with various subsidiary and allied organizations, like the Spinners' Association and the Village Industries Association. These allied organisations work in the economic field but they do not seek directly to remove the burdens of the peasantry under the present system of land tenure. Nor can the Congress, situated as it is, wholly function as a peasant organization, although in many provinces it has espoused the cause of the peasantry and brought them much relief. It seems to me necessary that the Congress should encourage the formation of peasant unions as well as workers' unions, and co-operate with such as already exist, so that the day-to-day struggle of the masses might be carried on on the basis of their economic demands and other grievances. This identification of the Congress with the economic struggle of the masses will bring it nearer to them and nearer to freedom than anything else. I would welcome also the organization of other special interests, like those of the women, in the general frame-work of our national struggle for freedom. The Congress would be in a position to co-ordinate all these vital activities and thus to base itself on the widest possible mass foundation.

"Get Ready For The Test"

There has been some talk of a militant programme and militant action. I do not know what exactly is meant, but if direct action on a national scale or civil disobedience are meant, then I would say that I see no near prospect of them. Let us not indulge in tall talk before we are ready for big action. Our business to-day is to put our house in order, to sweep away the defeatist mentality of some people, and to build up our organization with its mass affiliations, as well as to work amongst the masses. The time may come, and that sooner perhaps than we expect, when we might be put to the test. Let us get ready for that test. Civil disobedience and the like cannot be switched on and off when we feel like doing so. It depends on many things, some of which are beyond our control, but in these days of revolutionary change and constantly recurring cries in the world, events often move faster than we do. We shall not lack for opportunities.

The major problem of India to-day is that of the land—of rural poverty and unemployment and a thoroughly out-of-date land system. A curious combination of circumstances has held back India during the past few generations and the political and economic garments it wears no longer fit it and are torn and tattered. In some ways our agrarian conditions are not unlike those of France a hundred and fifty years ago, prior to the great revolution. They connot continue so for long. At the same time we have become parts of international capitalism and we suffer the pains and crises which afflict this decaying system. As a result of this elemental urges and conflicts of world forces what will emerge in India none can say. But we can say with confidence that the present order has reached the evening of its day, and it is up to us to try to mould the future as we would like it to be.

War Threat

The world is filled with rumours and alarms of war. In Abyssinia bloody and cruel war has already gone on for many months and we have watched anew how hungry and predatory imperialism behaves in its mad search for colonial domains. We have watched also with admiration the brave fight of the Ethiopians for their freedom against heavy odds. You will permit me, I feel sure, to greet them on your behalf and express our deep sympathy for them. Their struggle is something more than a local struggle. It is one of the first effective checks by an African people on an advancing imperialism and already it has had far-reaching consequences.

In the far East also war hovers on the horizon and we see an eastern imperialism advancing, methodically and pitilessly over ancient China and dreaming of world empire. Imperialism shows its claws wherever it may be, in the West or in the East.

In Europe an aggressive fascism or Nazism steps continuously on the brink of war and vast armed camps arise in preparation for what seems to be the inevitable end of all this. Nations join hands to fight other nations, and progressive forces in each country ally themselves to fight the fascist menace.

Where do we come in in this awful game? What part shall we play in this approaching tragedy? It is difficult to say. But we must not permit ourselves to be passive tools exploited for imperialist ends. It must be our right to say whether we join a war or not, and without that consent there should be no co-operation from us. When the time comes we may have little say in the matter and so it becomes necessary for the Congress to declare clearly how its opposition to India's participation in any imperialist war, and every war that will be waged by imperialist Powers will be an imperialist war, whatever the excuses put forward might be. Therefore we must keep out of it and not allow Indian lives and Indian money to be sacrificed.

To the progressive forces of the world, to those who stand for human freedom and the breaking of political and social bonds, we offer our full co-operation in their struggle against imperialism and fascist reaction, for we realise, that our struggle is a common one. Our grievance is not against any people or any country as such, and we know that even in imperialist England, which throttles us, there are many who do not love imperialism and who stand for freedom.

Tribute to Gandhiji

During this period of difficulty and storm and stress, inevitably our minds and hearts turn to our great leader who has guided us and inspired us by his dynamic personality these many years. Physical ill-health prevents him now from taking his full share in public activities. Our good wishes go out to him for his rapid and complete recovery, and with those wishes is the selfish desire to have him back again amongst us. We have differed from him in the past and we shall differ from him in the future about many things, and it is right that each one of us should act up to his convictions. But the bonds that hold us together are stronger and more vital than our differences, and the pledges we took together still ring in our ears. How many of us have that passionate desire for Indian independence and the raising of our poverty-stricken masses which consumes him? Many things he taught us long years ago it seems now—fearlessness and discipline and the will to sacrifice ourselves for the larger cause. That lesson may have grown dim but we have not forgotten it, nor can we ever forget him who has made us what we are and raised India again from the depths. The pledge of independence that we took together still remains to be redeemed, and we await again to guide us with his wise counsel.

But no leader, however great he be, can shoulder the burden singlehanded; we must all share it to the best of our ability and not seek helplessly to rely on others to perform miracles. Leaders come and go; many of our best-loved captains and comrades have left us all too soon, but India goes on and so does India's struggle for freedom. It may be that many of us must suffer still and die so that India may live and be free. The promised land may yet be far from us and we may have to march wearily through the deserts. but who will take away from us that deathless hope which has survived the scaffold and immesurable suffering and sorrow; who will dare to crush the spirit of India which has found rebirth again and again after so many crucifixions?

PROCEEDINGS & RESOLUTIONS

Second Day—Lucknow—13th. April 1936

Jallianwala Bagh Day

The Congress session was resumed to-day at 5-30 p. m.. half an hour earlier than yesterday. Attendance was as large as yesterday, visitors having been helped by reduction in the ticket fee. Another reason for good attendance was the decision of the Working Committee to give preference to the resolution on the Government of India Act and discuss it to-day, in order to help members of the Assembly to debate the matter and return to Delhi, from where urgent whips have been sent to them.

Proceedings began with two minutes' silence observed by all standing in celebration of the Jallianwala Bagh Day, Gandhiji did not attend the session to-day, as it was his silence day.

In asking the audience to observe the two minutes' silence, *Pt. Jawaharlal* said: "We have to observe the day of remembrance. To-day, 17 years ago in this country, about this time, in Jallianwalla Bagh, there was slaughter of innocent men. In their remembrance, let us join the names of those who have since suffered similarly, or are suffering in person, for in this country it seems a crime to think in terms of freedom of the country."

---

*For text of resolutions. See page 247.

Suppression of Civil Liberties

After silence had been observed, the *President* put from the Chair, the resolution regarding the suppression of civil liberties.

He said that it was quite appropriate that on Jallianwalla Bagh Day, they should begin with a resolution of this kind. The resolution was passed.

Congress Foreign Department

Thereafter, the *President* moved the resolution regarding the opening of the foreign Department of the A. I. C. C.

He emphasised that whereas the battle for freedom must be fought without outside help, they must establish contacts with foreign countries to educate themselves about world affairs and those countries about Indian affairs.

World Peace Conference

The resolution to M. Romain Rolland's invitation to the World Peace Conference was taken up.

Mr. Jawharlal explained that the resolution expressed sympathy with the objects of the Conference and was ambiguous about India's participation in it. He wished someone would go from India, but could not be sure. The resolution was passed.

War Danger

Mr. Jawharlal next moved the resolution relating to the war danger.

He said that its importance should not be minimised by the fact that it was moved from the Chair. The original idea was that Moulana Abul Kalam Azad should move it, but pressure on time made him put it from the Chair. The resolution was adopted.

Sympathy for Ethiopia

The next resolution was about sympathy for Ethiopia.

Mr. Nehru explained how gas was used in Ethiopia. The element of bravery associated with war in days of old was not there. But modern warfare was most barbarous. He did not know what would be the end of the war, but he thought it impossible that Italy should retain hold on Ethiopia. The English people had gone time and again up to Kabul, but the brave people there had regained their freedom.

The resolution was passed.

Sanatanist Demonstration

At this stage, there was some demonstration outside and referring to it, the *President* said that he had received a warning beforehand that some people wished to create trouble. He asked Congressmen to keep quiet and ignore the matter. He added that some Sanatanists had told him that they would march on the Lucknow Congress as Fascists had marched and conquered Rome (laughter). He said that those who were reactionaries were getting restless, and those who wished the country's progress to be stopped, financed from behind such disturbances. In India also such features might have to be faced, but they should remain undisturbed.

Govt. of India Act

All resolutions from the Chair having been adopted, Babu *Rajendra Prasad* moved the Working Committee's resolution as approved by the Subjects Committee on the Government of India Act.

Most speakers repeated the arguments used in the Subjects Committee. Mr. Jawharlal took his seat on the rostrum, so as to be able to watch and control the debate.

As soon as Babu *Rajendra Prasad* had finished reading the resolution, a delegate asked whether non-Congressmen, who had signed the election pledge, could be put up as Congress candidates.

Babu Rajendra Prasad replied that he could not think that any person who accepted the creed of Purna Swaraj would hesitate to pay four annas and become a member. However, there was an additional safeguard that candidates, if elected, would pledge themselves to obey the Congress mandate.

He explained the object of the resolution and reserved further remarks to the occasion when he would answer the debate on the amendments.

Mr. *Jawharlal* said that there were four amendments to the resolution. He wished a full dress debate on the subject, but must conclude the debate to-day. He appealed to the speakers to be brief. The debate would be conducted in Hindi, but a few speakers, who cannot speak Hindi, will address in English and should not be disturbed by the cry for speech in Hindi.

Mr. *T. Prakasam* said that the Congress was pledged to Independence and rejection of a Constitution. Therefore the question of acceptance of office did not arise in the ordinary accepted sense: "All we want is that our enemies should not occupy places of vantage to direct the rifle fire into our bosom, when we are engaged in our work for the country." Continuing, Mr. Prakasam said that Gandhiji had created a revolutionary outlook in the country.

Mr. *Jawharlal*: The resolution is not about Gandhiji.

Mr. *Prakasam* assured the President that they could establish Congress Committees in seven lakhs of villages only if they took office and gave strength to the terrorised people. The Russian revolution broke out in 1917 after 15 years of work among the masses. Let them not, like children, copy the Russian example when the masses were not ready yet, and were in a terrorised condition.

Socialist Amendments

Sardar Sardul Singh Cavasheer moved on behalf of Mrs. Kamaladevi, her amendment which had been rejected by the Subjects Committee.

He said that other parties in the field had disclosed their programme of work in the Legislatures. When would Congress do the same? It had been said that it was enough to declare that the Congress had set up candidates. The speaker doubted if this would be enough, especially with part of the electorate, which was not fully conversant with their politics. He asked why the final decision was being postponed. What changes did they anticipate? He admitted that the King and the Viceroy had changed (laughter), but that did not alter the Constitution. In any case they could alter the decision, if the situation altered later on. His suspicion had been roused against the open door policy by the fact that some of the supporters of the resolution made no secret of their belief in the usefulness of the policy of acceptance of offices.

Continuing, the Sardar said that it was possible for them to change the text books or hoist National Flags, or promote sanitation, but could that feed the hungry people or clothe the naked? (Cheers.) This was impossible under the Constitution, even if the Viceroy and the Governor had the best of goodwill, because Indian finances had been pawned away for the Services and the Army expenditure. To accept office and create deadlocks was the wrong way of proceeding about their business. They should refuse to accept office. The procedure suggested by the pro-office people to create deadlocks would surely catch them in the neck. (Applause.)

Mr. *Sampurnanand* moved the same amendment, as was rejected by the Subjects Committee. He recalled how the agrarian movement was suppressed in the United Provinces and how 'Liberal' Ministers like Mr. Chintamani and Mr. Jagat Narain had supported the special Act, to crush that movement. Indian Ministers would fight India's Nationalist Movement and English people would watch this process with delight

Mr. Sampurnanand asked the pro-office party to be honest and say what they meant. His amendment did not bar acceptance of Ministry; but directed that the purpose of all legislative activity was to create deadlocks and not try to secure small advantages.

Seth Govind Das then moved his amendment proposing that a decision on office acceptance should be taken before the General Election. He pleaded that the matter should be decided before the next election, otherwise they would be fair neither to the voters nor to the candidates. He was told that the Working Committee's intention was the same as his amendment, but he was disappointed to find that Babu Rajendra Prasad had not cleared the position. He feared that the history of 1923 might be repeated and unless pledges were taken beforehand, their own candidates might defy the mandate after the election.

Communal Award

Mr. *Dinesh Chandra Chakravarty* moved his amendment on the Communal Award which was not allowed in the Subjects Committee for want of notice in time.

The first para of the resolution, as amended by Mr. Chakravarty, read: "Whereas the Government of India Act, 1935, which was based on the White Paper and the Joint Parliamentary Committee Report and on anti-national, undemocratic separate communal electorate, which is in many respects even worse than the proposals contained in the White Paper and the J. P. C. Report in no way represents the will of the nation and is designed to facilitate and perpetuate domination and exploitation of the people of India and stereotype communal divisions is imposed on the country. The Congress reiterates the rejection of the new Constitution including the communal decision in its entirety".

He said that the Communal Award was an imperialist electoral device, designed to perpetuate and carry to perfection the policy of divide and rule and thereby perpetuate foreign domination. The Congress had throughout opposed Separate Electorates and worked for Joint Electorates. There was unanimity of opinion in the country that the Communal Award should be rejected lock, stock and barrel. Why then did the Congress adopt the illogical course neither to accept nor reject the Award ? Feeling in Bengal against it was reflected in cent per cent success of the Congress Nationalist candidates in the Assembly elections. Why then did the Congress under fear of possible Muslim defection support the anti-national decision of the British Government. Mr. Jawaharlal himself had said that the Communal Award and Nationalism could not go hand in hand.

Mr. *Govind Ballabh Pant* informed the delegates that about 30 speakers had participated in the debate in the Subjects Committee and the resolution had been passed by an overwhelming majority. Such a resolution should, therefore, carry conviction with them. The first three amendments were also moved in the Subjects Committee and members elected by the delegates had rejected them. Eight months ago, none could say that Italy could attack Ethiopia ; two moths ago, none could have dreamt that Germany would occupy the Rhineland ; two weeks ago none could have said that the Turks would disown the Laussanne Treaty. Thus none could say how the international and the Indian situation would change in eight months. Why then take the final decision on the matter now ? Mr Jawaharlal had told them that he could not anticipate when direct action would be possible. In the circumstances was it not wise for the Congress to act according to the needs of the situation ? Such adjustment was proof of a living organisation. He assured the House that no Congressmen wanted to work the Constitution and everybody had agreed to work for complete Independence and total destruction of the new Constitution.

Mr. *Meherally* said that if they did not listen to his warning, the Congress would convert itself into another Liberal organisation. Mr. Prakasam's speech was one of defeatism.

At this stage, Mr. *Jawaharlal* left the rostrum to look into the disturbance created outside by a small band of Sanatanists and Babu Rajendra Prasad took the chair. A small party of Sanatanists tried to rush the gates, but were held back by the volunteers.

Mr. *Meherally* said that the reason why a handful of Englishmen were ruling India was by paying well to the middle class, who provided the civil servants, the police and the Army. The offices under the Reforms would be a further bribe to the middle classes. Their real struggle was to break this middle class which kept Imperialism in power. The Working Committee had slackened in its struggle and its resolution would make a very poor impression on the world. He said that Socialists would remain neutral on the Communal Award amendment. They did not approve of the Award, but believed in a solution on economic and not religious lines.

Mr. *Jawaharlal Nehru* who returned to the rostrum said that he had come empty-handed, as the demonstrations had already melted away. (Laughter).

Mr. *Viswanath* asked whether it was statesmanlike to let the position of vantage to be exploited by reactionaries.

Mr. *Masani*, supporting Sardar Sardul Singh's amendment, was glad that there were men like Mr. Prakasam and Mr. Satyamurthi to say in public what others thought in private. In his opinion, nothing short of evacuation of India by the British forces would justify acceptance of office. What was meant by the uncertainties of the situation ? Did it include a gesture from Lord Linlithgow ? Mr. Satyamurthi had talked of Irish methods, but where was a De Valera in India with all the methods of his, and where was Mr. Satyamurthi with resignation in his pocket ?

Acharya Kripalani, supporting the official resolution, described the Socialists as self-constituted guardians of the revolutionary mentality and asked whether Sardar Vallabhbhai Patel, Babu Rajendra Prasad and Gandhiji were unofficial allies of the bureaucracy.

President : Nobody had said so.

Mr. *Kripalani* : I am referring to the agruments used in the past.

President: We are dealing with the present and the future and not the past. Such personal references are highly undesirable.

Mr. *Kripalani* contended that the Socialist Party had made a certain statement, and he wished to refer to them.

The *President* ruled him out of order on the point.

Proceeding, Mr. Kripalani contended that it was possible to maintain the revolutionary spirit in the legislature even with acceptance of office.

Mr. *Bhattacharya* (Bengal) supported Mr. *Chakravarty's* amendment.

Dr. *Khan Saheb*, supporting, said that they should abide by the decision of their Cabinet. Revolutionary speeches, without revolutionary action, would not cut much ice. They should prepare for the coming fight and trust their leaders.

Swami Saradananda (Bihar) spoke in favour of the resolution.

Mr. *Satyamurthi*, supporting, asked them to avoid mutual recriminations. He felt the country was with those who favoured acceptance of office, which was a wrong expression for capture of power from the enemy. There had been a lot of talk of revolutionary mentality, but the only revolution, during the last 15 years, was that led by Gandhiji and conducted magnificently by those who were members of the Working Committee (Cheers.) He asked if the delegates to the Congress included 50 Ministers, whether it would not add to their strength and importance. (Applause.)

A voice: What about Mr. Tambe and Mr. Raghavendra Rao ?

Mr. *Satyamurthi*: I do not know them. If you cannot have 50 honourable Congressmen as Ministers, then you had better shut up shop. The difference between Congress Ministers and others would be that the former would be like camels, with nose pins in the hands of the Congress. A wrong step to-day would make them lose ten years.

Closure war moved, but Mr. *Jawaharlal* said that he had, on his list, Pandit Malaviya and Sardar Vallabhbhai.

A voice: We want to hear them.

Mr. *Gopika Sen* supported Sardar Sardul Singh's amendment. He asked if any detenue could be released or repressive laws on Bengal could be repealed by acceptance of Ministry in Bengal. He answered no. Why then accept office ? Did they want Lord Willingdon to go home and tell England that he had crushed the Congress and made it accept the Constitution ? (Cheers.)

Pandit Madan Mohan Malaviya was cheered when he came to the rostrum. He said that he had been pained to hear the debate in the Subjects Committee and the open session. He wished to say what he felt on the occasion, particularly on the Bengal amendment regarding the Communal Award. He said that for 50 years the Congress had laid down demands for compulsory education, agricultural education, and banking developments. To-day they heard nothing of these, but only hoisting of flags. Would not the flag go by itself, if they developed sufficient strength ?

He knew the Working Committee decision was arrived at after long deliberation, but he opined that having rejected the Constitution, they could not accept office. He found that the condition was as wretched as 50 years ago, and he was so greatly grieved that he wished to die rather than bear witness to it. India wanted the same freedom for her own affairs as England had. Continuing, Pandit Malaviya said that the position of unemployment in India was worse than any part of the world. They should tell England that the Reforms Act was not acceptable. Never had, since the advent of the British people, the prestige and position of India been lowered more than by passing of this Act. While the law had been made in a manner that Indians might have no freedom to improve their own lot, the present position was worse than the existing reforms.

He did not suggest that the Legislatures should be boycotted, but that efforts should be made to get it amended. He did not rule out the resolution from the weapons to be used to win freedom, but it was criminal to adopt revolutionary methods till the country was prepared for it.

The need of the moment was to produce a united front which would make the Government amend the Act. There must be unity between the communities and also among the political parties. The Communal Award had intensified communal bitterness. Who said that it was a dead issue ? It was a daily spreading poison. The Government had given the Communal Award and not Self-Government. Mr. Jinnah and Sir Wazir Hasan had asked for unity, but they must be prepared to remove the chief obstacle in the way of that unity The speaker believed that so long as the Communal Award existed, there would never be self-government. He wished that the delegates would accept the Bengal amendment to the resolution relating to the Communal Award. The speaker had never approached the Government for a change of the Award. He always tried for mutual settlement. Next should come unity of political parties. Then would the Viceroy send for Gandhiji and Mr. Jawharlal and ask for a settlement. (Cheers.)

Mr. *Annapurnaya* (Andhra), opposing the resolution, advocated wrecking the Constitution immediately after the Congress entered the Legislatures. Any other action would be contrary to the spirit of rejection of the Constitution.

Sardar Vallabhbhai Patel, supporting the resolution, regretted that on the question of the Communal Award he had to oppose Malaviyaji. A Bengali delegate had put forward an amendment on the subject. He believed that acceptance of that amendment would not help the cause of Bengal but would worsen the communal situation. If they wished to oppose the award they must be prepared to fight with the Government and Muslims combined, and be ready to destroy the atmosphere created during the year. The only solution was either replacement of the Government, which gave the Award, or have an agreed settlement. He was surprised that Socialists, who talked of revolution and accused the Working Committee on their decision, had themselves declared neutrality on the matter. Would that attitude help the cause or was it vote-catching device ?

As regards the main resolution, he assured the House that the members of the Working Committee were not personally interested in Council-entry or acceptance of office. These men had ruined their careers with some fire of revolution in them. Were such men deceiving them ? He and Babu Rajendra Prasad were villagers, who did not know how to talk in terms of destruction. When they found their bones weak, they would retire into the jungles, but they hoped yet to participate in revolution. (Cheers). The council-entry decision was taken by Gandhiji in view of the changed atmosphere in the country. He felt some pain, as Mr. Jawaharlal felt to-day, but to-day he advised them in the best interests of the country. He and the President had worked together and would still bear common suffering. Mr. Jawaharlal had come out of jail recently, but Babu Rajendra Prasad had travelled 18 months in the country and knew its condition. Too much fetish had been made of the office issue. All he felt was that if office was to be accepted to strengthen the country, that might have to be considered.

Continuing, Sardar Vallabhbhai Patel said that the Constitution had been framed by the English people, keeping in view all possible steps Congress might take. Could they decide to fight such a Constitution without the fullest thought ? Could cheers for words bring about revolution ? When Gandhiji sanctioned individual civil disobedience, Pandit Malaviya did not turn up. (Laughter). The task was to re-vitalise the country, and if they quarrelled, they would lose seats, and the question of office would not arise. He appealed to them to stop their quarrels. He thought that there was plenty of time to decide the office question. The Congress must grow stronger, and they must not give up the fight for fear of black sheep. If all favoured non-acceptance, he would decide to-day against acceptance, but it was not the case.

Mr. *Patwardhan*, opposing the resolution, said that the country to-day had been divided into two groups, namely those who would be associated with the British and others who believed that there could be no compromise with the British.

Babu Rajenda Prasad, replying to the debate, said that 20 speeches including his, had been delivered. The Congress had criticised the Communal Award in stronger terms than any one else. The Congress did not accept the Award, but it had been forced on them. Proceeding, Babu Rajendra Prasad said that nothing had happened since the last Congress session to change this verdict on the Award. Efforts had been made for mutual settlement, but they had failed. Another attempt would be made, but how and in what form was not clear. He did not wish fresh obstacles to be created in the way of settlement by reversal of the Bombay attitude.

Regarding other amendments, he said that if the burden of decisions as to whether office be accepted or not was thrown on the A. I. C. C., they should also leave that body to decide as to when the time was ripe for such decision.

Babu Rajendra Prasad said that he did not belong to the school of thought who ruled out acceptance of office under any circumstances. "I believe such occasions can arise, when through acceptance of Ministerial responsibility, we may advance the cause of Swaraj." They should not believe that Congressmen would work the Act as Government wished them to work it. The masses of people had confidence in the Congress, while a premature decision, if found wrong afterwards, would affect the people's confidence in the Congress.

He concluded: "I do not believe people are down and out, or that the hunger for Swaraj is less. The only deficiency is that people are taking time. Let us keep courage and office or no office, let us go ahead. The flame of Swaraj will never be extinguished until freedom is achieved. (Applause). I believe that all Congressmen, both of the pro-office and anti-office view, have the same urge for freedom. Have confidence in yourself and your country, and pass the resolution of the Working Committee." The debate concluded at 0-15 hours.

Sardar Sardul Singh's amendment was put to vote and declared rejected by a majority, voting approximately being 250 to 450.

Mr. *Sampurnanand's* amendment was similarly declared rejected but as poll was demanded by Mr. Sampurnanand the President asked those who supported it to move to the left and those against it to the right. Members of the Working Committee and other leaders on the dais had already come down to the enclosure of delegates. The vast concourse watched with interest the novel departure in the Congress procedure.

Mr. *Satyamurthi* and Mr. *Pandit* were appointed tellers for one side and Mr. Patwardhan and Acharya *Kripalani* for the other.

The amendment was declared lost by 255 to 487 votes amidst cries of "Rajendra Prasad-Ki-Jai", as this division represented a victory over the Socialists.

Seth Govind Das's amendment and Mr. Chakravarty's amendment were lost without division.

Babu Rajendra Prasad's resolution was carried without division. The majority for the resolution of the Working Committee was contributed largely by delegates from Bihar, Gujerat, Andhra and Tamil Nad. The Congress adjourned at 1 A. M.

Third Day—Lucknow—14th. April 1936

After three day's session during which the session passed fifteen resolutions (some of which evoked heated debate), the 49th session of the Indian National Congress concluded at 2 a. m. amidst scenes of wild enthusiasm and shouts of "Inquilab Zindabad" and other slogans. Over 50 persons participated in the debates during the three days and the President, Mr. *Jawharlal Nehru,* conducted the proceedings in a remarkably able manner, giving opportunity to every section to have its say. Socialists scored their only victory of the session when *Sri Kamaladevi's* amendment to the official resolution seeking abolition of proportional representation was carried by a majority of 20 votes.

The Congress re-assembled to-day at 6 p. m. Attendance, both of delegates and visitoss, had dropped, but the proceedings were nonetheless lively, because of the resolution on Indian States, the proposed changes in the Congress Constitution and the agrarian programme.

The *President* and members of the Working Committee arrived, as usual, in procession, headed by the band.

Proceedings commenced with the singing of National songs and poems in praise of Mr. *Jawharlal Nehru.*

Indians Abroad

The first resolution to be moved for the day was the one regarding Indians abroad.

Mr. *Nehru*, moving it from the Chair, said that the real way of helping Indians abroad was by securing freedom for India. The resolution did not go into details, because so much had been said on it.

Swami Bhawani Dayal, representative of the South African Congress, then addressed the House.

The Swami said that the resolution first referred to South Africa, where Gandhiji had spent 21 years. Indians in the Union were facing a great danger. A deputation had come to the Cawnpore Congress, and pressure from India prevented laws from being enacted. Then came the Cape Town Agreement, but now that Agreement had been broken, and the Asiatic Land Tenure Act proposed to segregate Indians into what, in Indian parlance, might be called a Harijan colony. If any Indian homes in the town were found dirty, the Municipality could forfeit such houses. "We feel that until India is free, Indians abroad cannot improve their status, but it is apparent that we must fight for our rights of citizenship in the Empire." In East Africa and Zanzibar, Indians were suffering, while in Fizi it was a matter of shame, as Indian members had pleaded for nomination instead of election.

Continuing the *Swami* said that if the recommendations of the Feetham Commission Report for more lands for Indians were not accepted by the South African Government, then the Indian community there might have to revive Satyagraha in accordance with the resolution passed two years ago. Indians in South Africa looked to the Congress for guidance and help. Let not the Congress forget that the 25 lakhs of Indians who lived abroad looked to them for support. The resolution was passed.

Representation for Peasants

Mr. *Purshattomdas Tandon* moved a resolution proposing a Committee consisting of Babu *Rajendra Prasad*, Mr. *Jairamdas Daulatram* and Mr. *Jaiprakash Narain* to examine the question of bringing about closer contact between the Congress and the masses. Mr. *Tandon* said that this resolution showed that the Congress realised that it must move with the times if it was to live.

The Congress always had been popular with the people, but until 1920, it was not truly representative of the masses, as Congress leaders were intellectuals, who prided themselves on their western dress and about their English speeches. To-day the majority of speeches were in Hindustani and the Congress was coming into contact more and more with the masses. Government had started its rural programme, and various other political parties were also trying to sing in the same tune.

The Congress had yet a great deal of ground to cover regarding village organisation. The Government was carrying on false propaganda against the Congress in the villages. Speeches of Congress leaders had been torn from their context for anti-Congress purposes. He welcomed the present urge on the part of the masses to get representation in the Congress. The purpose of the resolution was to organise the masses. *Acharya Kripalani* seconded the resolution.

Socialist Amendment

Mr. *Sampurnanand* moved the same amendment, as in the Subjects Committee, namely, suggesting a method for direct representation of organised peasants and workers.

Mr. *Sampurnanand* said that the country could win freedom, not by the efforts of the educated few, but through the support of peasants and labourers. They must, therefore, rope them into the Congress. Bringing in such element into the Congress would force its hands to redress the grievances of the peasantry and labour.

Mr. *Tripadi* said that they were shirking the issue by merely proposing "greater share" to peasants and labourers in shaping the Congress policy.

Mr. *Jairamdas Daulatram*, opposing the amendment, said that Gandhiji had introduced the word "Swaraj" in terms of the masses. It represented all elements in the country. If it was to consist of class organisations, then it would bring about a clash of interests and result in loss of strength. Mr. Jairamdas said that there was no proper peasants' organisations and, perhaps, it might be possible to find a solution on the line that in village and Tehsil Congress bodies, they might insist that the percentage of peasant members be fixed at 70 per cent or thereabout. That would ensure for the peasants a proper voice in the Congress organisation.

Swami Sahajanand, supporting the amendment, said that peasants did not understand terms like "Swaraj". They understood only issues like land and living, but not political questions.

The amendment was lost by a large majority and the official resolution was carried.

Agrarian Programme

Mr. *Bhulabhai Desai* was cheered when he came to move the resolution on the agrarian programme. He spoke in English. The following is the resolution :—

"This Congress is of opinion that the most important and urgent problem of the country is the appalling poverty, unemployment and indebtedness of the peasantry, fundamentally due to the antiquated and repressive land revenue system and intensified in recent years by the great slump in the prices of agricultural produce.

"A final solution to this problem inevitably involves the removal of British Imperialism and exploitation, a thorough change of the land tenure and revenue systems, and recognition by the State of its duty to provide work for the rural and unemployed masses.

"In view, however, of the fact that the agrarian condition and land tenure and revenue systems differ in various Provinces, it is desirable to consult the Provincial Congress Committees and also such peasant organisations as the Working Committee considers fit, in the drawing up of a full All-India agrarian programme, as well as a programme for each Province.

"This Congress, therefore, calls upon each Provincial Congress Committee to make recommendations in detail to the Working Committee by August 1, 1926, for being considered and placed before the All-India Congress Committee, having particular regard to the following matters :—

(1) Freedom of organisation of agricultural labourers and peasants ;

(2) Safeguarding the interests of peasants where there are intermediaries between the State and themselves ;

(3) Just and fair relief of agricultural indebtedness, including arrears of rent and revenue ;

(4) Emancipation of peasants from feudal and semi-feudal levies ;

(5) Substantial reduction in respect of rent and revenue demands ;

(6) A just allotment of State expenditure for social, economic and cultural amenities of villages ;

(7) Protection against harassing restrictions on utilisation of local natural facilities for their domestic and agricultural needs ;

(8) Freedom from oppression and harassment at the hands of Government officials and landlords ; and

(9) Fostering industries for relieving rural unemployment.

Mr. *Desai* said that he had come to the Congress after several years. He stood for self-sufficiency in the realm of economic thought and action, for there was nothing India could not produce by way of natural produces or finished product for consumption, even if they were multiplied four or five times. The present factory labour, even if increased to the limits, which industrial expansion could allow, would not absorb beyond three millions more. Thus relief had to be provided for those dependent on agriculture, and the time had arrived when all political power that India might get should be utilised for the purpose of raising the standard of living of the people in the villages. The average income per head per annum was between Rs. 60 to Rs. 72, and even in the present capitalistic state of society, it had been recognised that Labour required more humane treatment, and every one should get food, clothing, shelter and also education. Hence the agrarian problem must engage the attention of Indian statesmen and Indian political workers. He himself was born in a village. He was aware of village life in India and how burdensome was the lot of the villager. True, legislation for agricultural relief and indebtedness had been attempted in the Punjab, Bengal, U. P., C. P., and in Bombay but these had not solved the question of agricultural indebtedness. Tillers of the soil still remained in the grip of the money-lenders, as there were no credit facilities and the steps outlined in the resolution were an indication of the direction in which the problem could be usefully tackled.

Dr. *Syed Mahmud* said that it was lucky that on the most important resolution, there was unity between the working Committee and the Socialists. The points raised in the resolution should have been taken up 50 years ago.

Dr. *Kassika* supported the resolution. Mr. *Nehru* explained its purpose in Hindi, and the resolution was carried.

States' Subjects

Babu Rajendra Prasad next moved the resolution relating to Indian States. He said that the Congress had full sympathy with Indian States' subjects, and wanted them to get the same rights and liberties as those in British India, but the main struggle must be carried on by the States' subjects. This resolution also made it clear that baseless hopes should not be raised of Congress helping any particular movement in any State. There were some Princes who were trying to move with the spirit of the times. There were others who did not do this. Such States were numerous, and many excesses took place there and it would be impossible for the Congress to take up all those cases. Even if the Congress did take up these matters, it would weaken the cause of States' subjects, who should really rely on their own strength. Until the two Indias are joined, there would remain some difference in their standard of development.

The chief cause of their backwardness was that the British Government would not let them advance to such an extent as to excel the British standard of administration. For example, Baroda excelled British India in the matter of education. In the same way, Mysore was industrially very very advanced. We believe that if we can make British India totally democratic, its influence on Indian States would be an effective step. At the moment, we do not wish to add to our problems, and therefore, do not wish to raise false hopes in the minds of Indian States subjects.

AMENDMENTS

Mr. *Amritlal Seth* moved the amendment which was rejected in the Subjects Committee. Mr. *Seth* reminded the House that the people of Indian States also fought for emancipation of the Motherland. When the Congress had declared in 1928 in favour of support of the cause of States' subjects, why did they want to lower that position? The A. I. C. C. at Madras in 1935 promised to exert friendly, moral influence with the States. What influence would they have with the States, after their President had declared for their abolition? The resolution before the House made the position worse by asking States' subjects to fight their own battles. The speaker said that the Congress claimed India as one country and nation. This resolution meant that their ideology had been lowered, and they did not want freedom for the country as a whole.

Mr. *Avadesh Pratap Singh* moved another amendment stating that the struggle be carried on mainly by the States' people.

If the Congress turned down even this request, then it must change its creed, and not speak for the "people of India", but only for the people of British India.

Seth Jamnalal Bajaj, supporting the official resolution, said that he was born in Sikar State, and this State was under the Jaipur State, its subjects were slaves fourfold. The British Government could prevent lots of mischief and misery if it wished, but it did not. If the Congress made empty promises and was not able to help, it would make itself the laughing stock. There was agitation in Sikar State. What could the Congress do in such a case? He warned them against passing any resolution impulsively.

Mr. *Gopal Singh Razmi* supported Mr. *Amritlal's* amendment. He instanced the Patiala State and conditions of the subjects there. He hoped the President would give up his neutral attitude and join them.

Mr. *Narasingham* said that in Federation the Princes would rule over the whole of India, and how were Indian States to be treated as foreign States, like Afganistan and Japan?

Mr. *Amritlal Seth*, replying to Mr. *Jamnalal Bajaj's* remarks, said: "We did not join the struggle for selfish ends. We are sons of India and even if disinherited and disowned, we would not leave the Congress." (Applause).

Sardar Vallabhbhai Patel, replying to the debate, claimed that few had experience of Indian States as he had. Mr. Amritlal had always belonged to the opposition camp in this matter. Mr. Amritlal, though born in an Indian State, lived in British India and the speaker did not think that Mr. Amritlal had authority to speak on behalf of all States. He asked the Sikh speaker and Mr. Amritlal whether the Congress had ever asked them not to defend the honour of their sisters and wives. What was the kirpan for? Captain Avadesh Prasad Singh had charged them at Jubbulpore for not keeping the promise.

The *Captain* protested he did not say that; he had been always a Congressman and taken interest in the matter as such, and was not a member of any States' Subjects Conference.

The chair asked the speaker to confine his remarks to the resolution.

Sardar Patel said that the fact of the matter was that the responsibility for the Madras decision was that of Mr. Avadesh Prasad and the Madras resolution was made by the Working Committee as a vote of confidence, because they could not take over a responsibility which they could not bear. Relief could not be obtained by hot speeches. The position was complicated and delicate. For centuries, this system has been prevailing, and if to-day States' subjects were vocal, that was a reflection of the Congress strength, and yet these people carried on anti-Congress propaganda in some States, just as some Kisan and Labour organisations, which sprang up because of Congress work, were trying to set up rival claims to represent the masses. He asked them to vote with a full sense of responsibility.

Both the amendments were put and negatived; one for deletion of reference to the Madras resolution was defeated by 70 to 250 votes approximately.

The amendment of Mr. *Avadesh* was then put to vote. The amendment proposed that the struggle be carried on 'mainly' by the subjects of Indian States in the respective States, the implication being that the Congress could also be expected to support them.

When vote was taken, someone complained that visitors had smuggled themselves into the delegates' enclosure. This, on inspection, was found to be so. The enclosure was cleared of such men, and tellers were appointed and the amendment was rejected by 218 to 176 votes and the main resolution, moved by Babu Rajendra Prasad, was carried without division.

Amendments to the Constitution

The *President* then called on Dr. Pattabi Sitaramiyya to move the various amendments to the Congress Constitution adopted by the Subjects Committee.

By agreement, *Dr. Pattabi* moved the amendments of a non-controversial nature, and they were adopted.

Mr. *Balakrishna Sarma* made an attempt to get the name of the United Provinces changed to Bubeya Hind, but this failed.

When *Dr. Pattabi* moved deletion of the Manual Labour clause, surprisingly a delegate moved an amendment demanding retention, and made a vigorous speech in support thereof, but the proposition was, however, carried when put to vote, the amendment being lost.

Election to A. I. C. C.

Mrs. *Kamaladevi Chattopadhyaya* then moved an amendment opposing abolition of proportional representation, regarding election to the All India Congress Committee.

She said that she was moving the amendment not because she happened to be a Socialist, but because she wanted to ensure representation of any minority on the A. I. C. C., and proportional representation was the only means to do it. The speaker, therefore, appealed to the House to accept her amendment.

Mr. *Sri Prakash* said that the system of single transferable vote was certainly unworkable for election of delegates, but it was necessary to retain it to secure representation of minority groups in the A. I. C. C.

Mr. *Kishori Prasad Singh* said that the system of proportional representation had the approval of Gandhiji during the Bombay session of the Congress, and should not be abandoned.

Acharya Kripalani explained his experience as General Secretary. Though the single transferable vote was good as a system, it has either not been understood, or has been wrongly applied. With one or two exceptions, all Provincial Committees had asked for election. A good thing could not be given into the hands of a monkey. In the same way, this system was not workable. The so-called minority consisted of men who had been there, even when there was no system of proportional representation. If the Socialists undertook to educate the people about its proper use, it could be reintroduced.

Mr. *Bhattacharya* was opposed to the amendment in principle. He warned that if proportional representation was abolished, splits and bitterness would be caused through failure of minorities.

Mr. *Meherally* said that there was no constitution free from corruption in its working. If Provincial Congress Committee members did not know how to work the system of single transferable vote, then they forfeited their claim to represent the nation.

Dr. *Pattabi* maintained that its retention would lead to corruption. Therefore, he said it should be abolished.

Amendments Carried

Before the House divided a delegate asked Mr. *Nehru* for his views. He replied that these had been expressed three days ago in the Subjects Committee.

The House divided by show of hands, the President declaring that those in favour of retention of proportional representation were 190 and those against 160.

The division was challenged, and tellers were appointed. Mrs. Kamaladevi's amendment seeking retention of proportional representation was carried by a majority of 20, voting being 227 for retention and 207 against.

Socialists thus recorded the first victory of the session, and the President's view in favour of retention was upheld.

The Socialists and others who voted for Mrs. Kamaladevi's amendment were happy that the last act of the session was a triumph not so much for their view as for the President's view, who stood vindicated by the delegates' verdict in favour of his view as against that of the Working Committee.

It may be recalled that Mr. Nehru had taken in the Subjects Committee the unprecedented course of stating his opposition to the abolition of proportional representation regarding elections to the A. I. C. C. on the ground that it embodied a principle for minority representation, which had a broader meaning.

Thereafter, the *President*, before bringing the session to a close, thanked the Reception Committee and said: "It is customary on such an occasion for some to indulge in a funeral oration, and who may be more fit for this task than Mrs. Naidu, who uninvited (laughter), proposed to tell you about this session and about the President of this Congress, who has sat on high eminence these three days and is now going back to oblivion." ? (Cheers.)

MRS. NAIDU'S TRIBUTE TO PRESIDENT

Mrs. *Naidu* said that she had come to deliver the funeral oration for old things that have taken long to die. "In this city of old tradition and old forgotten kings, which is now the scene of Mushaira and weeping for the dead, has been born a new vision. The President says that he is going into oblivion. He may be hidden in radiance of glory, but he will illumine the path to freedom. Only a few years ago, in this city, I saw the passing of a great man, who was the symbol of India's struggle for freedom, who, with his last breath spoke of the freedom of India, and his last charge to India was that they should never go back on their plighted word. To-day, his spirit must rejoice that his son is carrying out the mandate that was a legacy to him (cheers)

"It was long overdue that the Congress and India should realise that she was only a unit of the great world scheme and an indivisible part of a great world scheme. If it is the funeral oration for the dead of yesterday it is a welcome to the dawn, of which the President is the herald We look on him with his courage, with his great idealism, we think of him with his great international experience and vision. We are proud that he has been chosen unanimously by the nation as her guide to the dawn of freedom. His task has not been easy. It has been a task of trying to reconcile almost irreconcilable modes of thought, and yet he has managed so to harmonise these views that this idealist, this man so implacable for freedom, so insatiate in his desire for freedom, has sweetness, grace, wisdom, statesmanship and forbearance to be able to hold together in friendliness elements that might have been hostile to one another and irreconcilable with one another. Therefore, I end with adieu to yesterday and welcome to to-morrow, in which we do join together in a pilgrimage towards the dawn of liberty (applause)."

Mrs. *Naidu* next thanked the Reception Committee and volunteers.

The session ended at 1-15 a. m., with "Bandemataram" song and cheers for Mr. Jawharlal, Gandhiji, Mrs. Sarojini Naidu and "Bharatmata"

A REVIEW OF THE CONGRESS SESSION

Mr. *S. Satyamurti*, President of the Tamil Nad Congress Committee, addressed a well-attended meeting, on the **29th. April 1936**, at the 'Congress House,' Madras, on "The Lucknow Congress and the Work Before Us". Mr. *Satyamurti* said that the session of the Congress in Lucknow was unprecedented in three respects. For the first time in the history of the Congress, a person belonging to the province in which the Congress was held, was in the chair. Secondly, the session was held during the Easter holidays and thirdly Congress met under the Bombay constitution. They had the smallest All-India Congress Committee and they had a small number of delegates. Another feature was that the session was held in open air. He desired to tell the youth of the Presidency that if they wanted to take their place in national life and to play their part in all-India organisations, they should learn Hindustani Mr. Satyamurti paid a tribute to the women volunteers for the services rendered by them during the Congress session. Proceeding, the speaker said that Mahatma Gandhi was definitely out of the Congress. No doubt, he was available to those who wished to get his advice. Being a courteous man, he could not refuse to answer questions put to him by leaders. Beyond that, it was not correct to say that he played any part, directly or indirectly, in the Lucknow Congress and the decisions arrived thereat.

The Congress Cabinet

The Working Committee practically decided every question that came up before the Congress. The Subjects Committee and the open session of the Congress generally adopted the Working Committee's suggestion. There was one exception, and that was on the question of proportional representation by means of the single transferable vote for the election of members to the All-India Committee. On this, there was a difference of opinion. In the open session of the Congress the principle was accepted. But generally the Working Committee decided all issues. It had been contended that this was against democratic principles. In England, every decision was arrived at by the British Cabinet. The average number of the House of Commons voted to order. In India where they were fighting for freedom there was no room for difference of opinion among the soldiers, and those in high command had the right to give a lead to the country.

The Bombay constitution had been radically altered. The manual labour clause had gone, much to the relief of many. The number of delegates had been doubled. The All-India Congress Committee had been strengthened. The Congress session would be held hereafter in December every year.

One of the criticisms levelled was that the Lucknow Congress decided nothing. Lucknow decided nothing, in the views of those gentlemen to whom office acceptance was everything. The Congress, the speaker declared, decided many fundamental questions of profound national importance.

Resolutions offering greetings to the prisoners who were languishing in jail and especially the detenus, and condemning the imprisonment of Mr. *S. C. Bose* were adopted. The speaker would heartily endorse the appeal made by the Congress President for the observance of May 10 as the "Subhash Bose day," and he hoped that members of other parties would also participate in the observance.

Suppression of Civil Liberties

The next resolution passed related to suppression of civil liberties. Special attention was drawn in the resolution to the fact that the suppression was at its worst at present and an appeal was made for the carrying on of an agitation against the repressive laws. The aim of the powers-that-be was to demoralise the nation. There could not be any greater repression than in Abyssinia by Italy, the use of poison gas, bombing of cities and the massacre of women and children—and yet the Emperor and the Empress were fighting the Italians, with courage. It should be brought home to the Government that even the worst repression could not shake the resolve of a nation determined to achieve freedom.

India's Freedom

The next resolution pointed out that the question of India's freedom should be made an international one. India was an Original Member of the League of Nations. They should make it clear to the world that so long as Imperialism lasted, India could not be free and that only when India was free could there be permanent peace in this world. When India was admitted into the League as an original member Britain promised to give her freedom. That promise had not been kept. The existence of the war danger was pointed out by the Lucknow Congress, and a resolution was adopted stating that Indians had the right to refuse to participate in a war unless their express permission was given for launching on it. This right had been given to the Dominions. The war danger had become imminent because of the Italian attack on Ethiopia, the Japanese aggression and the occupation of the Rhineland by Germany, India had no interest in any imperialistic policy. She wanted to make the world safe for democracy and for humanity.

Congress and the Reforms

Mr. *Satyamurthi* next dealt with the resolution on the Government of India Act, and said that the decision of the Congress was an important one. Beginning with the Simon Commission, the Round Table Conferences, the White Paper, the Parliamentary Committee's report, the Act and the rules thereunder—there had been a progressive decline. The Congress therefore stated that the Act was designed to facilitate and perpetuate the domination of the British over the people of India and therefore reiterated its rejection of the new Constitution in its entirety. The Constitution could not be rejected by merely passing a resolution. The Congress wanted to bring about a state of affairs under which the Government would have to take back this constitution and replace it by an agreed one, consistent with the wishes and aspirations of the people of India. On this, he said, there was no difference between one school of Congressmen and another. The Congress also declared that an acceptable constitution should be based on the independence of India, and must be framed by a Constituent Assembly elected on adult franchise or the nearest approach to it.

Taking a practical view, the Congress also decided to set up candidates for the ensuing elections to the provincial legislatures, to set up candidates only in accordance with the mandate of the Congress, choose candidates only from those who fully supported its objective of independence and pledged themselves to carry out the Congress policy in regard to the Legislative Councils. Ten per cent of the people of this country had been enfranchised, and he appealed to all to co-operate in making the electoral rolls complete and accurate. He suggested that the Government should take the co-operation of all parties and individuals in this matter. In Madras Presidency alone there would, he thought, be at least about five million voters and they should endeavour to bring them all on the rolls. The prestige of the Congress and above all the highest interests of the country required that they should bring all voters on the rolls. Mahatma Gandhi claimed at the second Round Table Conference that he represented the people of India and no one else. It was up to them all to help the Congress to make good that claim. He appealed to every patriotic man and woman in this country to help in this work.

The All-India Congress Committee, he said, would, before the elections, issue a manifesto explaining the political and economic programme of the Congress in conformity with the resolutions passed from time to time, and the provincial committees might supplement the programme. There was one matter over which he might shed a tear, but he would not and that was the abolition of the Parliamentary Board. But as one of those who had cried hoarse since 1920 that the Congress should not boycott legislatures, he said. he was now immensely pleased that the Congress had decided to undertake the work in relation to the legislatures directly.

Office-Acceptance Issue

The speaker next referred to the discussion in the Congress on the question of acceptance of office, and said that Lucknow accepted a resolution which was the same as the one adopted by the Tamil Nadu Conference at Karaikudi early this year. He was strongly in favour of the resolution. He had not changed his views on office acceptance. He was still of the opinion that the Congress should capture power wherever it could. But to him it was a means to an end, the immediate end being the destruction of the new constitution, and the ultimate end being the independence of India. Therefore, to him a majority vote in the Congress would not suffice ; he wanted the vote of the entire Congress or the almost entire vote of the Congress. He did not want Pyrrhic victories He would wait till the Congress, to a man, accepted this resolution. Further, who knew, the situation might change at any time. A world war might break out or Lord Linlithgow might send for Gandhiji or the Reforms might be scrapped. If the Act became a scrap of paper, none would be happier than he. But if the Reforms were introduced, in spite of their efforts he wanted to 'seize the lion by its mane, put his hand into its mouth and choke it to death'. He wanted to make an appeal to all parties outside the Congress who were patriotic and nationalist to join forces with the Congress.

Appeal to Muslims

Paying a tribute to Mr. Jinnah's bold and patriotic stand in the Assembly, the speaker appealed to him to work in co-operation with the Congress, if he could not actually coalesce with it. The enemies were many, strong, resourceful and unscrupulous and they (Indians) should not divide their forces. He hoped the Muslim Parliamentary Board, if it materialised, would either coalesce with the Congress or work in close co-operation with it. He also appealed to the Congress Nationalists and the Nationalists of Bengal to co-operate with the Congress. Sooner or later, he knew, Hindus and Muslims would join together. There was now no room for too many parties in this land. He would make an appeal specially to his Liberal friends in Madras for whom he had great respect individually that there was no room for more than two parties, those working for India's freedom and those opposed to it. He would therefore appeal to the Liberals to join forces with the Congress.

The resolution on the Government of India Act was the *piece de resistance* of the Congress. If he had wanted a vote in favour of office acceptance, he was sure, he would have got the vote, but, as he said, he was content to wait.

As for the resolution of the Congress on Indians abroad, he said that their condition was becoming worse every day and he thought that till India became free, the position of her nationals abroad could not improve.

Contact With The Masses

Referring to the resolution of the Congress on promoting contact with the masses, and the 'dhwani' in the resolution that there should be functional or organisational representation, he said the Congress represented the masses and it should make good that claim by enrolling increasingly a large number of men and women as members by continued and disinterested service to the masses. It could not share the claim with others. It was open to every adult to join the Congress. He would be prepared to support a reduction in the enrolment fee, but to accept divided allegiance would be the undoing of the Congress. The Congress also rightly called attention to the appalling poverty and indebtedness of the peasantry. But until they had full power in their hands, they could never give relief to the people. But it might be useful to put their ideas on paper in order to educate themselves and the people as to the means of work.

Qualifications For Congress Candidates

The speaker, proceeding, said that he had heard from several gentlemen that there were persons who were waiting to join the Congress the instant it decided in favour of office acceptance. After Vellore, he did not want any of these gentlemen. He would rather be in a permanent minority with a small number of honest, self-sacrificing and disinterested Congressmen than have a miscellaneous luggage of traitors, possible, present and past.' If the so-called indecision of the Lucknow Congress would help to make these gentlemen decide not to join the Congress, it was good for them and the country. The Tamil Nad Congress Working Committee, he said, had decided that if any one wished to be set up as a Congress candidate, he should have been for six or at least three months a member of the Congress. He should be a habitual wearer of khaddar. There would be no room for title holders and each man should prove his loyalty to the Congress by continuous and propaganda work.

Mr. *Satyamurthi* appealed to all to carry the message of the Congress to all parts of the province during the ensuing months. He appealed to those who had not already done so to enrol themselves as members of the Congress and to wear only khaddar and use only Swadeshi. He appealed to them once again to help in the 'stupendous work' of preparing the electoral rolls accurately. The Tamil Nad Congress, he said, also desired to start a Summer School of Politics, and give a short course of training to about thirty young men in doing Congress work and impart to them some very necessary education in matters relating to public finance, general economics, Indian history, Indian tariff policy, khaddar, village industries, Harijan work. Hindi, Seva Dal and health work. Competent lecturers, he said, would be requested to participate in the work of the school, and instruction would be given free. He hoped the various District Congress Committees of the province would co-operate to make the School a success.

Other nations fighting for their freedom, he concluded, had paid the supreme penalty of their lives. He would appeal to all present to do something for their country. The situation in India and in the world to-day, he said, was very favourable—so favourable that they had only to know how to kick the ball, kick it straight and kick it as a team, and it would go straight into the goal, in spite of the British Imperialist goal-keeper. (Applause).

The Muslim Polity

The All India Muslim League

24th. Session—Bombay—11th. & 12th. April 1936

The 24th session of the All-India Muslim League opened at Bombay on the **11th. April 1936** in the specially constructed pandal under the presidency of Sir *Syed Wazir Hasan*, ex-Chief Judge of the Oudh Chief Court. There was a large gathering present, including about 200 delegates from outside. The proceedings commenced with recitation from the "Quoran", after which *Sir Currimbhoy Ebrahim*, Chairman of the Reception Committee, read his address.

Welcome Address

"Unity is the bedrock of nationhood, as it is also the essence of all religion. And no Constitution, however advantageous from our point of view, can work well or survive in the absence of inter-communal good-will and harmony. Unity is, therefore, the prime need of the hour", declared Sir *Currimbhoy Erahim*, in the course of his address. He appealed to the Hindus to take a large view of the efforts of the Muslims at self-realisation, emphasizing that their (Muslims') aim was not to secure more jobs or preferential treatment, but the general uplift of the 70 million of Indian Muslims, for which mainly the All-India Muslim League stood.

Referring to the momentous character of the present session, Sir *Currimbhoy* said that the first and foremost question facing them was the defining of their attitude with regard to the reformed Constitution. Whatever may be the criticism levelled against it, he considered that it had come to stay and all of them agreed that it must be worked in a spirit of co-operation. The reforms may not have gone far enough, but that was no reason for a counsel of despair and an attitude of negation. He hoped that their attitude towards the working of the reforms would be so framed and co-ordinated as to lay special stress in their efforts at improvement in the direction of bringing more education to the poor and better scope for the agricultural and industrial classes and the improvement of good relations between the various communities in the land.

Discussing the imperative need of mass education among Muslims, Sir Currimbhoy expressed gratification that, as a result of the efforts in the past, much headway had been made in the matter of Muslim education. He advocated that practical training for an industrial or commercial career should go hand in hand with general education. This would, he thought, relieve the stress of present unemployment and serve as an absorbing channel for youthful energy. It was also necessary to neglect the aspect of physical development of youths. A short course of military training at the right period would make the community strong, vigorous and self-reliant and would imbue Muslim youths with a feeling of fitness and confidence in the life's battle ahead. As regards female education, Sir Currimbhoy said that the conditions of modern life had rendered the education of women no less important than that of men, if the Society were to make all-round progress.

Describing Mr. *M. A. Jinnah* as "the fearless upholder of the Muslim cause" Sir Currimbhoy paid a glowing tribute to the life-long services of the permanent President of the League (Mr. Jinnah) in the cause of the Muslim community Though held in high esteem by all the communities in the country and by the Government, the Muslims should be particularly grateful to Mr. Jinnah for his championing their cause when the occasion called for it.

Sir Currimbhoy concluded with an impassioned appeal for communal unity and said, "For the sake of God, of our country and our community, let us make disagreement and discord a thing of the dead past, and let us invite others also to make it so. Let us approach our people and say that we cannot do without unity, and let us ask the Hindu leaders to say likewise to their people."

Mr. Jinnah's Speech

Mr. *M. A. Jinnah*, in inviting Sir Syed Wazir Hasan to occupy the chair, recalled the latter's services to the Muslim community and the country at large. He added that Sir Wazir Hasan was also prominently associated with the Lucknow Pact. In view of the vital importance of the present session, when they had to formulate their attitude towards the coming Constitution, when they had to evolve a policy and programme for work inside and outside the Legislatures and they had to chalk out a plan for the much desired communal unity, no one was more suitable than Sir Syed Wazir Hasan to give them the proper lead. Therefore, the eyes of Muslim India fell upon the "soldier and warrior," to guide its political destinies.

Presidential Address

Sir *Syed Wazir Hasan* then read his address. In the course of his lengthy presidential address, Sir Syed traced the position of Muslims from the time of the Indian Mutiny, the efforts of Sir Syed Ahmed and other leaders to raise them from the slough of despond and ignorance and their entry into politics. He traced the successive attempts made by the leaders of Hindus and Muslims to arrive at an understanding regarding the vexed questions of communal representation in the legislatures and the Government services and stressed the attitude of Muslims towards the Reforms. After analysing the defects in the new constitution, he observed :

A constitution is literally being forced on us by the British Parliament, which nobody likes, which no one approves of. After several years of Commissions, Reports, Conferences and Committees, a monstrosity has been invented and is being presented to India in the garb of this Constitution Act. It is anti-democratic, it will strengthen all the most reactionary elements in the country and instead of helping us to develop on progressive lines, it will enchain and crush the forces making for democracy and freedom. The Muslim classes, the Muslim masses will suffer from the new scheme as much as any other section of the Indian people.

We have no other choice left but to work on the lines of what is compendiously called constitutional agitation. It has one great advantage, it can be pursued both inside and outside the legislatures and should be pursued in both these spheres. But to be of any use it must be effective, almost compelling in its results, and it cannot be so unless and until it is the voice and the act of a united India. The existing political circumstances of our country present no obstacle in effecting unity. The object of all political organisations, Hindu, Muslim and Agriculturists, is avowedly the attainment of self-government for India. The question of separate and joint electorates has been set at rest and we shall be well advised to leave it there. In the higher interests of the country I appeal for unity not only between Hindus and Muslims as such but also between the various classes and different political organisations. Such unity will not only make an ideal a reality but it will also give opportunity for political adjustment amongst all concerned. Even in the past there was no difference on essentials and there is none now. The differences in details have also ceased to exist. Is there any moral justification left for perpetuating differences, when the supreme need of the country in its struggle for freedom is unity ? A united India will be a force to be reckoned with, not the helpless victim of callous and irresponsible government.

This unity should not merely be an abstract and distant ideal. We must give it a concrete shape by organising the broadest strata of the entire Indian people. Hindus, Muslims, Sikhs, Parsis and Christians, on the basis of a common programme of action. We should immediately set about, in co-operation with other progressive political parties in the country to find such minimum measure of agreement as would enable us to act together. I suggest for your consideration the following programme of our immediate aims :—

(1) A democratic responsible government, with adult franchise, to take the place of present system.

(2) Repeal of all exceptionally repressive laws and the granting of the right of free speech, freedom of the press and organisation.

(3) Immediate economic relief to the peasantry ; state provision for educated and uneducated unemployed ; and an eight-hour working day with fixed minimum wages for the workers.

(4) Introduction of free, compulsory primary education.

A programme of this nature will give us the opportunity to organise a nation-wide movement ; it will arouse the political consciousness of millions of our countrymen : it will bring together the various communities and create a spirit of mutual confidence and, finally, it will bring such a pressure on the Government that it cannot be ignored. Its inevitable consequence will be that we will be brought nearer to our goal of freedom. The salvation of the Indian people can only come through their own united efforts. And there is no other method of creating this unity than action on the lines of a programme that cuts through our communal divisions and has an appeal not only for the patriotic section of our upper classes but for millions of our poorer countrymen.

I suggest that in order to work out the details of this programme a letter should be issued over the signature of the Permanent President of the League and the Indian National Congress to all political organisations, consisting of Hindus, Muslims and Sikhs etc., alike to attend a meeting at the earliest opportunity. This meeting may be called upon,

(a) to settle an annual programme of action, to be worked both inside and outside of the new legislatures, and local boards.

(b) To draft a constitution for India.

This body should also elect a permanent committee, to see that agitation on the basis of the settled programme is carried through in the country as effectively as possible, to organise the electoral campaign, and generally to give a lead to the country on all important political issues which may arise from time to time. The session at this stage adjourned till the next day.

Subjects Committee Resolutions

The Subjects Committee of the League, after 4 hours' heated debate, passed the following resolutions which were placed on the next day at the open session :—

"The All-India Moslem League enters its emphatic protest against forcing a Constitution upon the people of India, as embodied in the Government of India Act, 1935, against their will inspite of the repeated disapproval and dissent expressed by various bodies and organisations in the country.

"The League considers that having regard to the conditions prevailing in the country, the provincial scheme of the constitution be utilised for what it is worth, in spite of the most objectionable features contained therein, which render real control, responsibility of Ministry and Legislature over the entire field of Government and administration nugatory.

"The League is clearly of the opinion that the All-India Federal Scheme of Central Government, embodied in the Government of India Act, is fundamentally bad. It is most reactionary, retrograde, injurious and fatal to the vital interests of British India *vis-a-vis* Indian States, and it is calculated to thwart and delay indefinitely the realization of India's most cherished goal of complete Responsible Government, and is totally unacceptable.

"The League considers that the British Parliament should still take the opportunity to review the whole situation afresh, regarding the Central Scheme, before it is inaugurated, as the League feels convinced that the present scheme will not bring peace and contentment to the people. If it is persisted and enforced upon the people, it will lead to disaster, because it is entirely unworkable in the interests of India."

The Subjects Committee also passed a resolution forming a Central Parliamentary Board, with Mr. M. A. Jinnah as Permanent President authorising him to appoint 35 members and also organise Provincial Parliamentary Boards for contesting the coming elections.

Another resolution suggesting four-anna membership for the League, instead of one rupee, was thrown out.

Resolutions—2nd. Day—12th. April 1936

The Second day's session of the League, which re-assembled this morning, passed five resolutions before it adjourned for lunch. The first offered respectful condolence to His Majesty King Edward VIII and Queen Mary on the sad demise of His late Majesty King George and its loyal congratulations to King Edward on his accession to the throne and assured him of the loyalty of the Muslims of India. Condolence resolutions were also passed on the deaths of Khan

Bahadur Hafiz Hidayat Hussain, Mr. Sharifdewji Canji, Syed Makdhum Rajan Baksh Shah and Sheikh Makbul Hossain.

The League offered its gratitude to Mr Jinnah for his valuable services rendered in connection with the Shahidganj Mosque question at a time when no other leader could venture to undertake the responsibility.

The resolution was moved by Haji Anisuddin and seconded by Nawab Ahmed Yarkhan Daulatana.

Mr. *Ali Bahadur* moved a resolution that a Committee be formed to revise and amend the constitution and rules in order to bring it to the present day requirements of the Muslims of India. The resolution was passed after heated discussion in which Sir Mahomed Yakub refuted the charges levelled against the authorities of the League by the mover that they had been indifferent to meet the wishes of the Muslims in general in this respect.

The annual report of the League presented by *Sir Mahomed Yakub* reviewing the activities of the League since the time of its last session, was also adopted. Sir Mahomed Yakub referred to "financial bankruptcy" of the League which impeded the expansion of its activities.

Sir Syed Wazir Husan, President of the session, stated that he had committed a mistake in fact when he said in his address yesterday that the League was prepared to work the constitution. It was not so, as the question was left to be decided by the open session

RESOLUTION ON INDIAN CONSTITUTION

In moving the resolution regarding the constitution, Mr. *M. A. Jinnah* traced its history and examined in detail what they got under it. He said that in this constitution there was only two per cent responsibility and 98 per cent safeguards and special responsibilities of the Governor-General. Even this two per cent of responsibility was hedged in by the constitution of two Houses of Federal Legislatures:

Referring to the efforts made at the Round Table Conferences, to bring about an agreement between Hindus and Muslims, Mr. Jinnah asserted that it was not religious or communal motives which actuated them as a minority community to ask for certain safeguards from Hindus before marching with them along the road to freedom but unfortunately their terms were not acceptable to the majority community. Proceeding, Mr. Jinnah asked if there was any largest common agreement in favour of the coming constitution. (Voices: "No, no".) He advised Indians to do with it what Germans did with the Treaty of Versailles which was forced upon them. He examined the ways and means to put pressure on the British Government to modify the constitution. Armed revolution was an impossibility, while non-co-operation had been tried and found a failure. There was left constitutional agitation which meant work inside and outside the Legislatures for releasing the forces which would make the British Government bend. But it could not be done by one community. It required all communities to stand shoulder to shoulder. He asserted that the Congress would never reach the goal which they all desired unless and until they approached the Muslims. But whether the Congress recognised their claims or not, they owed it not only to their own community but to their country at large to organise themselves and march along the road to freedom and ultimately attain their goal. If they succeeded in doing so, the Congress would be forced to them.

Raja Gaznafar Ali (the Punjab) supporting Mr. Jinnah's resolution, said that the Federal part of the constitutional scheme was yet incomplete as it involved the condition of the entry of Indian Princes into it which hitherto had not been fulfilled. Princes in their own interests as well as those of British India should refuse to enter the Federation until and unless there was complete unity between the various communities in British India and friendly understanding between the Government and the people of this country.

Syed Hossain Imam (Bihar) also supported the resolution. He said that there was only one political aim open to Indians and that was to secure freedom. It was time to unite for achieving this end and not for fighting among themselves. He thought that the present constitution was better than the coming one as the former contained seeds of growth.

Raja Gaznafar Ali Khan, moving the resolution, said that it was an essential part of Mr. Jinnah's resolution on the Constitution Act, as it was designed to give practical effect thereto. By this means they would be able to send their true representatives to the Legislatures and popularise and carry out the policy enunciated in Mr. Jinnah's resolution.

About a dozen speeches supporting the resolution were made, speakers including Haji Rashid Ahmed (Delhi), Nawabzada Liaqat Ali Khan, (U. P.), Mr. Abdul Hamid Khan, Mayor of Madras, Mr. Hossain Imam of Bihar and Maulana Irfan of Bombay. The resolution was unanimously carried.

ELECTION COMMITTEE

Before concluding, a resolution was passed asking the League to take steps to contest the approaching provincial elections and for this purpose authorised Mr. *M. A. Jinnah* to form a Central Election Board under his presidentship, consisting of not less than 35 members, with powers to constitute and affiliate provincial election boards.

Sir Wazir Hasan, in his concluding remarks, said that Mr. Jinnah's resolution extended the hand of friendship and co-operation not only to the Congress but to all political organisations. "We must remember we are a minority section of the great nation of India. We are prepared to co-operate with every other political organisation in the country on the great struggle for attaining freedom. It remains for the majority section to respond. The work we will have to do independent of any other organisation."

Referring to the Government of India Act. Sir *Wazir Hasan* said that they must make the best use of it. "Remember that success or failure of the experiment by utilising the reforms to the best of our abilities within the limits of the law for the benefit of our country depends on the character of representatives you send to Legislatures. Be very careful to secure the best men to represent you in the Legislatures", he concluded.

Nawabzada Liaqat Ali Khan, U. P., was elected Honorary Secretary of the League in place of Sir Mahomed Yakub, while elections of the Vice-Presidents and the Joint Secretary were postponed.

A REVIEW OF THE LEAGUE SESSION

Mr. *Abdul Hameed Khan*, Mayor of Madras, gave his impressions of the League Session at a meeting of the members of the Muslim Parliament, held in Madras on the **26th. April 1936.** In the course of his speech, Mr. Khan spoke on his impressions of the recent session of the All-India Muslim League. He said that the proceedings of the All-India Muslim League Session had not been reported in the Press in full. The League was accepted on all hands, particularly among Muslims, as the only organisation which truly represented Muslim opinion in the country. It was no doubt true that there was a period when it was not functioning in the manner in which it ought to have done as the accredited organisation of the Muslim community, and when other Muslim Community organisations came into existence. But the Muslim community was now veering round to the view that it should concentrate its attention on a single organisation for the community. The choice could not but fall on the All-India Muslim League. The session at Bombay was momentous. The President of the session, Sir *Syed Wazir Hasan*, ex-Chief Judge of the Oudh Chief Court, was an active politician before he entered service, and his address at the session was a master-piece. He made out a very strong case for freedom for India and also made suggestions for bringing about communal unity in this country in a practical manner. He urged the need for co-operation between the various political organisations. Mr. Mahomed Ali Jinnah, the permanent President of the League, also made an important speech. After the serious attempts that Mr. Jinnah made to bring about communal unity between Hindus and Muslims—particularly between the Congress and the Muslim League—on the basis of a joint electorate, had failed, and the Communal Award had been made by the Premier. Mr. Jinnah felt that it was not possible for him, either single-handed or with the community behind him, to bring about a lasting settlement between Hindus and Muslims on the basis of joint electorate. He thought therefore that the best thing for the Muslim community to do, under the circumstances, was to carry on the fight for the country's freedom under the auspices of the All-India Muslim League.

This year's session of the All-India Muslim League, Mr. *Abdul Hameed Khan* continuing said, was held, not so much for the sake of advancing the interests of the Muslim community as to give expression to the opinion of the advanced section of the community on the Constitution Act of 1935. The session showed that the Muslim community was prepared to go on with the fight for the country's freedom even without the help of other communities. Mr. Mahomed Ali Jinnah made this very clear in his speech. Nobody could, therefore, say that when there was the Indian National Congress, there was no need for an All-India Muslim League. The Hindu Mahasabha had been hampering the advance of the Congress towards the cherished goal and making it impossible for the Congress and especially for the Hindu Members of the Congress to join hands with the other communities. Therefore on the question of the Communal Award, the Congress had not been able to give any decided lead. Under such circumstances, the Muslim community had no other alternative but to fight the battle of the country under the auspices of the All-India Muslim League.

Office-Acceptance

The session this year was momentous on account also of the fact that the Constitution Act of 1935, in the words of Mr. Jinnah himself, had been forced upon this country against its will. There were two courses open. One was to non-co-operate entirely with the Constitution. But that was not the policy pursued even by the Congress. The Congress had decided to enter the Councils, but the question of office acceptance had not yet been settled. Anybody who knew the direction in which the minds of the Congressmen worked, however, would realise that there was a fairly large opinion in favour of acceptance of office. But after accepting office what Congressmen would do no body knew. The course of non-co-operating with the Constitution having thus been eliminated, there remained the course of working it willingly. This course they could not adopt, in so far as the entire country had more or less declared the Constitution as being totally unacceptable. The only thing they could do was to utilise the Provincial scheme of the Constitution for what it was worth. There was no use allowing the Constitution to be worked by those who would be mere tools in the hands of the Government. So the Congress as well as the Muslim League had decided to utilise the Provincial scheme for what it was worth. So far as the All-India Federation scheme was concerned, the League had clearly expressed the opinion that it was fundamentally bad and most reactionary.

The League and the Other Parties

Concluding, Mr. *Abdul Hameed Khan* said that the All-India Muslim League had thus decided on the setting up of a Central Election Board as well as Provincial Election Boards and of branches of the League at district centres in the provinces for the purpose of setting up candidates. It was not going to be a reactionary party, but one with an advanced and progressive programme and one which would co-operate with groups and parties with proximate aims and ideals. In this province, he did not think it would be possible for the Muslim Party to co-operate with any other than a party which had an advanced and progressive programme. He did not know what the Congress would do with regard to the question of office acceptance. He did not think that the Muslim League would, in any case, taboo office. If the Congress, by any chance, tabooed office acceptance altogether, then the Muslim Party in the Provincial Legislatures would have to consider the advisability of joining the most advanced party other than the Congress. There was in the air the possibility of the formation of another party called the People's Party. Whether it was advisable to have a communal party in the Legislatures or not, was a question one might ask. If a person entered the Council on a particular ticket he should remain in the Council only until such time as he adhered to the principles of the party on whose ticket he had been returned.

It was necessary that Muslims should have a common programme on the basis of which alone they should get into the Legislatures. This programme need not necessarily be a communal programme. He appealed to his Muslim brethren, therefore, to respond to the appeal of the All-India Muslim League and set about the formation of district leagues and a Provincial League. The League would not be a rival to any political organisation in the country. Its only object would be to take the entire community together and send representatives to the Legislatures on a definite ticket.

THE LEAGUE PARLIAMENTARY BOARD MANIFESTO

After discussion lasting over four days, the All-India Muslim League Parliamentary Board, under the presidentship of Mr. *M. A. Jinnah*, adopted the following manifesto and issued it from Lahore on the **11th. June 1936** :—

The advent and announcement of the Minto-Morley reforms brought home to leaders of Mussalmans the necessity of starting a Muslim political organisation and thus was founded the All-India Muslim League at Dacca in December, 1906. The League adopted its creed and ideal definitely in December, 1912, and altered its constitution, having for its aims and objects (1) full responsible government for India with adequate and effective safeguards for Mussalmans, (2) to protect and advance the political and religious and other rights and interests of Indian Mussalmans, (3) to promote friendship and union between Mussalmans and other communities in India, and (4) to maintain and strengthen brotherly relations between Mussalmans in India and those in other countries.

The League has been faithfully and loyally acting in accordance with these fundamental principles ever since. During the period of existence of the Minto-Morley constitution, it continued its development from time to time and represented and voiced the true feelings and opinions of Mussalmans. As time went on, the co-operation and help of prominent leaders of India and particularly of that great man, the late Maharaja of Mahmudabad, whose selfless devotion and patriotic fervour and single-mindedness of purpose gave the League such strength, power and support that it reached the zenith of its ascendency and accomplished what is one of the greatest beacon lights in the constitutional history of India, the Lucknow Pact, which is known as the "League Congress Pact" in 1916. This pact will go down in Indian history as a landmark in the political evolution of the country as signal proof of the identity of purpose, earnestness and co-operation between the two great sections of the people of India in the task of the attainment of responsible government.

But the Pact was not the last word on the question of adjustment of political differences between Hindus and Mussalmans. Nor was it even intended or could be so considered in the new circumstances that arose and developed since then. The national demand for complete responsible government after the Montagu-Chelmsford Reforms became more and more insistent from 1921 onward. Mussalmans stood shoulder to shoulder with sister communities and did not lag behind in their patriotic co-operation with Hindus. But as a minority they maintain the principle that this position in any future political constitutional structure should be protected and safeguarded. Here it might be stated that at first sight it may appear to an amateur politician that such demand savours of communalism but in reality to those who understand the political and constitutional history of the world, it must be evident that it is not only natural but is essential by insuring whole-hearted and willing co-operation of the minorities who must be made to feel that they can rely upon the majority with a complete sense of confidence and security.

INDIA'S GOAL

In the various steps that followed the deliberations and collaborations that took place, the League has always stood for full responsible Government for India and unflinchingly stands for the same ideal. It deplores that as a result of the Round Table Conference, the British Parliament has forced upon the people of India constitution embodied in the Government of India Act of 1935. Its attitude towards the constitution is defined by its resolution passed at the session of the All-India Muslim League to the following effect: "While it accepts the Communal Award till a substitute is agreed upon between the communities concerned, emphatically protests against the constitution embodied in the Government of India Act of 1935 being forced upon the people of India against their will and inspite of their repeated disapproval and dissent expressed by the various parties and bodies in the country. The League considers that having regard to the conditions prevailing at present in the country the provincial scheme of the constitution be utilised for what it is worth, in spite of the most objectionable features contained therein, which render real control and responsibility of the Ministry and Legislature over the entire field of Government and administration nugatory. The League is clearly of opinion that the All-India Federal scheme of Central Government, embodied in the Government of India Act of 1935 is fundamentally bad,

It is most reactionary, retrograde, injurious and fatal to the vital interests of British India *vis-a-vis* Indian States and it is calcutated to thwart and delay indefinitely the realisation of India's most cherised goal of complete responsible Government and is totally unacceptable. The League considers that the British Parliament should still take the earliest opportunity to review the whole situation afresh regarding the central scheme before it is inaugurated or else the League feels convinced that the present scheme will not bring peace and contentment to the people but on the contrary it will lead to disaster if forced upon and persisted in as it is entirely unworkable in the interests of India and her people."

Election Board

But as the provincial scheme embodied in the Government of India Act is going to be enforced in the course of next year, the League decided that having regard to the conditions prevailing at present in the country, the provincial scheme of constitution be utilised for what it is worth. In view of this decision, the League further decided that a Central Election Board be formed with power to constitute and affiliate provincial election boards in the various provinces and passed the following resolution: "Whereas the parliamentary system of government which is being introduced in this country with the inauguration of the new constitution pre-supposes the formation of parties with a well-defined policy and programme which facilitate the education of the electorate and co-operation between the groups with approximate aims and ideals and ensures the working of the constitution to the best advantage and whereas in order to strengthen the solidarity of the Muslim community and to secure for Muslims their proper and effective share in provincial governments it is essential that Muslims should organise themselves as one party with an advanced and progressive programme, it is hereby resolved that the All-India Muslim League do take steps to contest the approaching provincial elections and for this purpose appoint Mr. Jinnah to form a Central Election Board under his presidentship, consisting of not less than 35 members, with powers to constitute and affiliate provincial election boards in the various provinces, having regard to the condition in each province and devise ways and means for carrying out the aforesaid objects."

In pursuance of that resolution, the Central Board has now been formed and the policy and programme of the Central Board has to be defined. The inauguration of the Montague-Chelmsford scheme of constitution and the working thereof has developed and brought forth various forces and it appears that such power as was available under the scheme has been captured in the various provinces by the reactionary conservative elements in combination with a coterie of men whose sole aim and object is to secure offices and places for themselves wherever and whenever available. This has suited the Government and these two classes have received every encouragement and support with the result that they have not only been a hindrance and an obstacle in the way of the independent and progressive intelligentsia, but people generally have been exploited. Thus was created a double domination of reactionary forces and imperialistic power. Our aim is that this domination must cease.

Political Situation

The present political situation has been aptly described by the president of the last session of the All-India Muslim League in the following words: "New problems have arisen to-day. It is not only the question of educating the middle class of Muslims in India on western lines and providing them with jobs, it is only the question of infusing in them the ideals of Victorian Liberalism. On the contrary, present conditions compel one to go much deeper into the problems of the entire social regeneration of the seventy millions of Muslims, of extricating them from the terrible poverty, degradation and backwardness into which they have fallen and giving them at least the rudiments of civilised existence and making them free citizens of a free land. We must realize, as people of other countries have realised, that a change is necessary and that unless such change is soon made the whole of this social structure must come down with a crash which will involve the extinction of not only the educated section of our people but also of all privileged classes, whether they hold privileges by reason of caste, land or money. The foundations of the superstructure in which we are living to-day were laid centuries ago and it is but natural that those foundations have ceased to be stable now. It is the duty, if it is not only an obligation created by the motives of self-interest. of all of us educated classes. capitalists and land-holders to lay the foundations of the new structure. Of course, in order that this effort must fructify, sacrifices will have to be made on the part of all. Let me tell you that the building of such a social edifice will be more glorious, more human and more just that the building of an empire." But at the same time we must make it clear that the League is opposed to any movement that aims at expropriation of private property.

The main principles on which we expect our representatives in various legislatures to work will be (1) that the present provincial constitution and proposed central constitution should be replaced immediately by democratic full self-government; (2) and that in the meantime, representatives of the Muslim League in the various Legislatures will utilize the Legislatures in order to extract the maximum benefit out of the constitution for the uplift of the people in the various spheres of national life. The Muslim League Party must be formed as a corollary so long as separate electorates exist, but there would be free co-operation with any group or groups whose aims and ideals are approximately the same as those of the League party. The League appeals to Mussalmans that they should not permit themselves to be exploited on economic or any other grounds which will break up the solidarity of the community.

PROGRAMME FOR ELECTION

The manifesto lays down the following programme for the ensuing elections: To protect religious right of Mussalmans in which connection for all matters of purely religious character, due weight shall be given to opinions of the Jamiat-Ulema-i-Hind and Mujtahids, to make every effort to secure the repeal of all repressive laws; to reject all measures which are detrimental to the interest of India, which encroach upon the fundamental liberties of the people and lead to economic exploitation of the country, to reduce the heavy cost of administrative machinery, Central and Provincial, and allocate substantial funds for nation-building departments; to nationalise the Indian Army and reduce military expenditure; to encourage development of industries, including cottage industries; to regulate currency, exchange and prices in the interest of the economic development of the country; to stand for social, educational and economic uplift of the rural population; to sponsor measures for the relief of agricultural indebtedness; to make elementary education free and compulsory; to protect and promote the Urdu language and script; to devise measures for the amelioration of the general conditions of the Mussalmans; and to take steps to reduce the heavy burden of taxation and create healthy public opinion and general political consciousness throughout the country.

The All India Muslim Conference

Executive Board Meeting

To define the attitude which the Indian Muslims should adopt regarding their future in the Indian political world, a large number of Muslim leaders met under the chairmanship of H. H. the *Aga Khan* at the Executive Board of the All India Muslim Conference held at New Delhi on the **16th. February 1936**:—

His Highness the Aga Khan took the chair amidst cheers. The Aga Khan read out the following statement which was frequently punctuated with applause:—

The first half of the 19th century saw the sovereignty of India pass out from the Muslim hands into the British hands. The responsibility for the events of 1857 was laid at the door of the Muslims and this made the thoughtful section of them to think of their future position in India. It took Indian Muslims a quarter of a century to make up their minds and the result was great. The policy of Sir Syed Ahmad Khan of Aligarh was to concentrate on education and avoid political agitation of an acute kind. A few Muslims joined the Indian National Congress but the community as a whole stood apart.

As a reaction of 20 years' inactivity the All-India Muslim League came into being in 1906 and the co-operation between the Congress and the League culminated in their agreement of 1916 which was to form the basis of the Mont-Ford Reforms. Thus in the first decade of the 20th century the Muslim India reconsidered its policy and in the second decade formulated a new one. Had it not been for the World War things might have been different but the problem of political advance was pressing and the Indian Muslims decided that despite their being in a minority in India they would not stand in the way of their motherland, placing before itself the goal of self-Government. The Indian Muslims realised that most of them were of the same blood as their Hindu brethren, that many of them were of mixed blood and those who had come to India with the Muslim invaders had settled down in India for many centuries and had made India their home and had no home outside India, that they were natives of India just as their Hindu brethren were natives of India. The mere fact that they professed a religion which was professed by the inhabitants of other countries also made no difference. Just as the Afghan would not like the Arabian domination and the Arabs did not like the Turkish domination, there is no occasion to doubt the genuine feeling of the Indian Muslims for Indian nationalism. Our cultural and spiritual links with the Muslims of other countries do not and cannot prevent us from following considerably purely national programmes for self-Government. Having made their choice they were ready for political advance and the 1916 agreement between the League and the Congress was the result. The Hindu leaders assured the Muslim leaders of their religious and cultural integrity and readily agreed to separate representation through separate electorates and assured the Muslim leaders of adequate representation in future as the Muslim community took to politics. Unfortunately co-operation did not last long.

What would the Muslims do in the matter of further reforms? The Muslim leaders gave this matter their most careful consideration and came to the conclusion that they were in a minority and, at that, a weak minority. Though the attitude of their powerful sister community has been cold and distant, their patriotism and their sense of self-respect and honour did not permit their going back on their ideal of self-Government for their country. So they decided to ask for maximum reforms and to this object they have adhered all along. They knew that provincial autonomy in the Central Provinces, the United Provinces, Bihar and Orissa, Madras, Bombay and Assam would spell ruin for them if worked with communal spirit, but they hoped that better sense would prevail and all the communities would work for the betterment of their motherland instead of against each other and in return they only wanted to have the satisfaction of being a majority community in the Frontier Province, the Punjab, Sind and Bengal, knowing full well that their majority in the Punjab and Bengal was only nominal while the Frontier province on account of its geographical position and economic condition was not likely to have much of real provincial autonomy. Thus the Muslims were not improving their communal position in any way but still they were for political advance. Why? They are for this political advance solely from the National motive. Their objective, therefore, in matter of representations was to secure such a position as would enable them to have a majority in the legislatures of four provinces. They succeeded in the case of three provinces but failed in the case of Bengal.

In the case of Central legislature they retained their proportion to certain extent but with the extinction of official block from the communal point of view they were not going to be as strong in future as in the past. But here again their motive for political advance was national, not communal. They failed to secure the clear enunciation of their undoubted right to adequate representation in the services in the provinces but have been feeling that their case is so strong that no Government claiming to be civilized will be in a position to refuse their just demand. They are not elated by successes achieved nor are they too depressed by the failures suffered. The success and failure in life and particularly in political life is inevitable and regardless of them we should go on.

Plea for Economic Reorganisation

India is now entering a new phase of political life. The Indian Muslims are ready to take their due share in developing the political life in the best interests of the country. Their political goal is dominion status. They feel that India's most pressing needs are to secure recognition in other countries. The Indians are not fairly treated whether in the dominions or in the colonies. At home the Indians must have economic reorganization—there is a wide gulf between different sections of Indians. In the midst of extreme poverty, hunger and nakedness, emaciated and enfeebled body, ignorance, they are human beings by courtesy only. Add to his the economically depressed status and add to it that they are intellectually depressed.

With this denial of divinity in mankind there is a denial of human brotherhood and we have developed intolerance in matters religious and sectarian. The whole economic, social and religious fabric calls for an immediate relief—uplift of the weak—economically, intellectually and culturally that there may be left no one to be called down-trodden.

FAITH IS INDIVIDUAL CONVICTION

Faith is a matter of individual conviction and should not be allowed to create ill-will between the various communities of India. Islam teaches tolerance and the smallest and humblest should feel that in a self-governing India his faith and religion will be secure and also his culture.

FUTURE PROGRAMME TO BE OF 'UPLIFT'

I have so far referred to the past. What is the immediate future which is to be the object of the political changes that are coming ? What are we to strive for and pledge as a programme to our countrymen ? What is the real work to be accomplished ? The future programme is for the 'uplft' of the personal, spiritual, moral, intellectual and economic life, not only of individuals, not only of families but also of the poor masses, the needy and the backward. It is this noble work of uplift with which we should concern ourselves irrespective of considerations of caste, colour and creed. Thus the prescription which thoughtful Indians prescribe for the betterment of India is 'uplift' at home and securing for her people an honourable position abroad.

Proceedings and Resolutions

Sir Safaat Ahmed Khan moved a resolution that 'this meeting of the executive board of the All-India Muslim conference places on record its grateful thanks to His Highness the Aga Khan for the constructive lead he has given to the community at this juncture in his statement made at this meeting, adopts the policy there enunciated as an integral part of its programme and appeals to the Indian Muslims of all schools of thought to give effect to it."

Mr. Abdul Matin Chaudhury asked for a ruling whether the meeting was of all those invited or of the executive board. He had throughout been opposed to the Muslim conference and did not wish to participate in its proceedings.

The *Aga Khan* said that the meeting was of the board and others were invited as guests.

The above resolution was passed after a large number of speeches were made, paying glowing tributes to the services of the Aga Khan.

QUESTION OF LEAGUE AND CONFERENCE MERGER

The question of amalgamating the Muslim League with the Muslim Conference was not put forward in view of the Aga Khan's opinion that it would be left over for decision by the Muslims elected to the new provincial legislatures.

Sir Safaat Ahmed Khan moving his resolution said but for the Aga Khan's personality the Muslim community would not have achieved what it did and would have been exposed to imminent risks (Applause). He assured all the nationalists that his friends would ally themselves with the nationalists for the development of the country and the home rule. The Aga Khan was the leader of the entire delegation to the Round Table Conference and the fact the Muslims worked in accord with the rest of the delegates was borne out by the Hindu Mahasabha delegate to the conference.

Hon. *Syed Mohammad Padshah* supported the resolution and paid a tribute to the Aga Khan's services.

Raja Gazanfar Ali said that the success achieved by the Indian delegation in London was entirely due to the Aga Khan's personal influence. He felt, however, it was difficult to maintain two parallel Muslim organisations. The Aga Khan and Sir Fazl-i-Hossain were here and also Mr. Jinnah whose services to the community were unparalleled and unique (Cheers). Let three meet and bring about a merger.

The *Aga Khan* replying said that both he and Sir Fazl-i-Hossain had carefully considered the matter and felt as democrats that the question should not be decided just now.

When the Muslim conference was organized in 1929 the main idea was that it should be a conference of Muslims elected to the legislatures. Shortly, the provincial councils would be elected by a very wide franchise. Let those Muslim legislators who would be elected under the provincial autonomy decide the question. Had those elections been not imminent he and Sir Fazl-i-Hussain would have faced the responsibility of deciding the question. He reminded them that non-Muslims also had more than one body.

Raja Gaznafar Ali and *Mr. Azhar Ali* pointed out that it would cause confusion and trouble as happened at the last election if both the League and the Conference put up rival candidates.

Mr. *Hussain Imam* did not like the wording of the resolution.

The *Nawab of Chattari* said that the resolution had their unanimous support. As regards the question of merger this should be brought up, if necessary, as separate resolution.

Sir Mohammad Yakub deprecated any speech which would give the impression outside that the conference and the League were hostile organisations when in fact they had the same objective.

The resolution was declared carried unanimously.

Sir Abdul Halim Ghaznavi mentioned what the Aga Khan did for Bengal and how the Hindu-Muslim settlement about Bengal had been almost reached through the good offices of the Aga Khan. It was a lie to say that the Aga Khan was a communalist.

Maulana Shaukat Ali wished to be heard as he had been invited to the meeting and the agenda had been sent to him which should not have been done if the meeting was of the executive board only. He appealed to the Aga Khan not to lend his name to the resolution as his Highness did not know how some people had exploited his Highness' association with such resolutions. He said the Aga Khan was not a king but the Muslims treated him like one (appaluse) and wished him to be above party politics.

The *Aga Khan* asked what improvement Maulana Shukat Ali would suggest.

Maulana Shaukat Ali said that he wished the resolution to be confined to thanks to the Aga Khan.

Mr. *Habib* declared that the resolution had been already passed.

Maulana Shaukat Ali said that it was not so. They should not pass any such resolution in this meeting.

Thereafter Mr. *Hussain Imam* moved that a sub-committee be appointed to fix the date and the venue of the next Muslim conference session. This was agreed to and the meeting dissolved.

PROCEEDINGS OF THE SIXTH ANNUAL SESSION

The All-India Muslim Conference commenced its sixth annual session at Delhi on the **28th. March 1936** in singularly oriental atmosphere. Proceedings opened with recitation from the Holy Quran.

Khan Bahadur Haji Wajhiuddin, M. L. A., Chairman of the Reception Committee, in his address, eulogised the services of Haji Abdullah Haroon, President-elect of the Conference, and expressed the hope that under his patronising care and guidance, their new programme of economic and social uplift of Moslems would take long strides towards its ultimate glorification. He recounted the services of the Moslem Conference during the past years in the politics of India and claimed it was the only platform for Moslems of all shades of opinion. He gave the greater credit to H. H. the Aga Khan for his sincere and indefatigable efforts in bringing Moslems together on one platform at most critical time and in unifying the purpose of the different Moslem organisations. He closed with an appeal to Moslems of India to sink their differences and work to the greatest advantage the scheme of economic amelioration of the Moslem Conference. Haji Wajhiuddin then proposed Haji Abdullah Haroon for the Presidentship of the session.

Sir *Mahomed Yakub*, among others, supporting the proposal denied the existence of any dissensions among Moslems. He claimed that the unity of purpose among Moslems of India was unique.

Haji Abdullah Haroon was unanimously elected to the Presidential chair, among cheers.

PRESIDENTIAL ADDRESS

In the course of his presidential speech, *Haji Abdulla Haroon* said :—"Abolish all taxes on kerosene oil and matches. Tax the rich for the benefit of the poor. Save the agricultural-classes by providing from money-lending classes for their debts to be paid off through the agency of Panchayats instead of Law Courts"

Mr. Haroon quoted from the Aga Khan's address delivered in Delhi on February 16 last, outlining the programme of economic amelioration of the people and said that the Muslim Conference could adopt this programme as it had received the support of religious and national leaders. Generally speaking, the whole of India was in the grip of poverty and destitution and the plight of the Muslim community was particularly bad. The radio could be used for spreading knowledge on the latest methods of cultivation and, as a means to increase productivity. The radio could also be used for effecting moral uplift of the rural population. Let Muslims learn the lesson from the glorious life of the Prophet who reformed the morals and manners of his community in Arabia and gave them character.

Resolutions

The Conference reassembled on the next day, the **29th. March 1936**. About 700 persons were present, including Sir Mahomed Yakub, Messrs Gauba and Ghulam Bhik Nairang.

The Conference passed several resolutions, including one condoling the demise of the late King and several Moslem leaders: condemning the renewed attempts against the Communal Award; sympathising with Moslems of the Punjab in their agitation for restoration of Shahidgunj and praying for their success, and holding that all resources of the Conference should be utilised for the economic, social, moral and intellectual uplift of the masses till the next session of the Conference, when the programme would be reconsidered.

Other resolutions were: "That in view of the present plight of the masses, specially of Moslems, this session deems it imperative to adopt a programme for their moral, intellectual social and economic betterment, and accords welcome to the valuable suggestions made by the President of the Conference in his presidential address and to the solid and constructive programme laid down by him before the Indian masses, and particularly Mussalmans.

"This Conference authorises the Working Committee to execute and popularise the programme and frame definite lines of action at the earliest possible moment and devise effective measures most likely to reform and ameliorate the condition of the poor and unemployed cultivators and starving masses of India.

"In the opinion of the Conference this programme consists of two parts, one of which relates to the ever-increasing taxes levied by the Central and Provincial Governments and local bodies, which are making the position of the poor and the tiller of the ground worse day by day. It is proposed that the poor peasants should be relieved of such taxes."

The second part concerns the general public: "it is necessary that by vigorous propaganda in the public press and platform, the poor in general and the Moslems in particular, be induced to work it out. It shall be the duty of the Working Committee to keep both parts in view and take practical measures to make it a success.

"This Conference resolves that with a view to pursuing the programme adopted successfully, an office should be established in Delhi to collect and disseminate all relevant literature and take all possible means to carry out the economic, social, intellectual and moral programme."

The Khilafat Conference

Following are extracts from the presidential address of the Hon'ble Captain *Khwaja Habibullah*, Nawab Bahadur of Dacca, delivered at the Khilafat Conference held at Mahomed Ali Park, Calcutta, on the **4th January 1936** :—

"The question of Independence, in my opinion, is outside the pale of practical politics. I believe that Dominion Status will not only secure all that we wish to gain by independence but something more which India can never attain without the equal membership of that wonderful Commonwealth of Self-governing Nations which is the greatest contribution of the British to the civilization of the world.

"I wish to quote here the section of my Delhi speech entitled "The Political Ideal of Indian Muslims":

"We are not party to any bellicose creed of race hatred for the world is learning at great cost that narrow-visioned race workship and extreme forms of group egotism is the greatest curse from which humanity is suffering in this century. As Muslims, we do not, and cannot, subscribe to any of the current forms of political idolatory which is seriously threatening to upset the foundations of Modern Liberal Civilization of the world.

But we confess that we are "Indian Muslims." We refuse to believe that our being true and loyal "nationals" of an Indian "Nation-State" should be a bar to our being faithful members of the 'Commonwealth of Islam" which is the mightiest single power for world peace, social democracy and international brotherhood in the world. We accept India to be our only "Fatherhood." We look to no other country as our homeland. We have been born and bred up in India and we will live and die as Indian Muslims. In the past and present we have contributed our best "National-Self" to the making of Indian life and culture and in the future we want to be a free and progressive people in order to contribute our best to the building of a free, self-governing and progressive India.

We cannot accept extreme nationalism to be the final gospel of the salvation of humanity. We are fully conscious of the limitations of these political dogmas. As practical men we want to steer our bark clear of these rocks and shoals.

The fundamental political objective of the Indian Mussalmans is a Self-governing India in the Political Polity of which Islam must have a place as a free community of culture. We have no use for a system of 'Imperium-in-Imperio.' But equally we cannot allow the freedom and unity of India to mean in practice the political subjection, economic exploitation and cultural submersion of the 80 millions Indian Mussalmans who constitute what Sir Bijoy Chand Mahtab aptly terms "a community and race within a race, a sub-nation within a sub-continent." The political individuality of Indian Muslims must be recognized in many schemes of national self-government or Swaraj. That is our political ideal. There is no earthly reason why such an idea should be regarded as incompatible with that of a real creative and catholic Indian Nationalism.

If Indian Mussalmans are guaranteed that position we are ready to become the corner-stone of a free "Indian Nationality" and the frontier guards of a free "Indian Nation-State." As such we look upon India to be our first and last homeland. Islam has nothing to fear in the system of a real unity and liberty of this country. The freedom and welfare of India is our only political aim. But as Indians we claim that we must have an equal share in that freedom and welfare, otherwise these terms, in day to day practical life, degenerate into mere shibboleths empty of any content and devoid of all meaning to the man in the street. We do not think this demand of an adequate share in the administration of our country is in any way objectionable.

With the purest of intention and the sincerest of desire for Muslim solidarity in Bengal, last week, I took the initiative in holding an informal conference of Muslim leaders at my residence. Its report has already been published in the press. The provisional committee is engaged in drafting a constitution for the proposed All-Bengal Muslim United Party. The Federation will be the political organization of Muslims outside the Legislature and the United Party shall be its parliamentary wing inside the legislature. Our plan is, first, to prepare the draft constitution and then to place it before a bigger representative group of all the Muslim leaders of Bengal. The constitution which will emerge out of this second leaders' conference will be placed before All-Bengal Muslim Conference.

I hope all Muslims will agree with this procedure which seeks to do justice both to the principles of intellectual aristocracy and representative democracy.

The main object of the United Muslim Party will be to bring together the Muslims of Bengal for obtaining the greatest good from the coming new constitution which to a great extent will fulfil our desire for Provincial autonomy. The party will strive to achieve the greatest good of the greatest number. The good of the peasant and labour classes will be its sole purpose of existence.

There cannot be the slightest doubt that the interest of Bengal as a whole can never be served and advanced unless a party is formed for the betterment of the material and moral conditions of the teeming millions of the Presidency. The Muslims, and I hope, the Depressed Classes, as a group, will be absolutely prepared to identify themselves heart and soul with such a people's party. To speak clearly, the economic interests of the Muslims of Bengal are identical with those of all backward communities. Economically they form the one and the same class of the 'Proletariat.' No party can claim to represent Bengal which does not accept the good of this 95 p. c. of her population as its supreme purpose of existence.

The United Party, therefore, will not be a really communal party but a party based on the community of economic interests and the identity of political opinion. We shall keep our door open to other groups who are ready to work with us shoulder to shoulder.

The main line of action and policy of the party will be to follow the dictum of tho Prophet that 'the best of all things is the middle course.' It will, therefore, strive to find a 'via media' or a half-way-house between the extremes of soulless Communism and relentless Capitalism. That is the way of Liberal and Social Reform. As Muslims we can have no faith in an economic regime of 'laissez faire' which can only result in the exploitation of the weak by the strong. Our great social religion condemns usury and swearing, monopoly and cornerning, loot and greed, despotism and the tyranny of caste, colour and race. Our course of practical politics within the coming legislatures must be guided by these high principles of Islamic Social Economics which are now attracting the attention of the thinking minds of Moscow and Washington.

"The sovereign idea and purpose which has actuated me to work for the forming of such a United Party is my desire to give a decent burial to the politics of individualism. In the past Muslim Politics, at least in this Presidency, has been mainly guided by one or two commanding personalities. Times have now entirely changed. The irresponsible bureaucracy is giving place to the responsible cabinet system of democracy. The masses of Bengal, therefore, must be made the basis of a political party. The extension of the franchise and the vast increase in the number of voters presents a problem of organisation which can be solved only through the agency of a popular party enjoying the confidence of the generality of the people. Every measure of this party must have the sanction of the people's opinion behind it. In short, the greatest good of the greatest number and the sanction of general will shall be the guiding principles of this party. It will not be the means of the personal aggrandisement of a person or clique.

The problem of reforming the Calcutta University has been hanging fire for a long time. The Muslims of Bengal have legitimate grounds of complaint against this temple of learning which has been in practice converted into a citadel of class monopoly and narrow-visioned communalism. The Muslims as a class have a very poor or negligible representation on its teaching and executive departments. The University is practically ruled and administered by a very close hierachy of caste Hindus who are naturally very jealous of their vested interests and privileges. No one can deny that they have made very important contribution to the cause of culture and education but this does not mean that all other peoples, who collectively comprise the 80 p. c. population of Bengal, can be permanently deprived from either the benefits of culture for a share in the administration of the University. Yet precisely this has been the object of the hierachy ruling over the destiny of the University. Our most important demand, therefore, with regard to the Calcutta University, is that the Muslims should have adequate representation on its Senate and Syndicate and the executive and the teaching departments. Unless this is granted our grievances against the University will not be removed. The remedy against class monopoly can only be proportional representation of all groups. So that they may combine and comprise for the good of all.

I also agree with the recommendations of the Bengal Muslim Education Committee and the recently-published Government Resolution on the Education Reform in Bengal. This hue and cry against these proposals, I believe, is not based on any sincere desire for reform but on the conservatism of the class in power.

The resolution of the Port Trust has shown Government Resolutions and rules have been defeated and frustrated by the subordinate heads of the bureaucracy who are naturally anxious to preserve their privileges and vested interests. The Muslims have never asked for any favour. They want their rights. The monopoly of a class or caste in public administration in a continent like India is sure to become the hotbed of corruption, and class tyranny.

Human nature being what it is the only effective safeguard against this danger is the guarantee of securing fair representation of all classes in the public administration. This is a salutary check to the growth of graft and spoils systems as well as sectionalism.

Modern State is primarily concerned with the economic problem and politics in its final analysis resolves itself to economics. To cry down, therefore, the demand of representation in services as beggary for loaves and fishes is to show ignorance of the most fundamental factors of present day life. The question of the representation of classes in public administration is as old as the laws of Solon. The Modern State is fast becoming the economic leviathan charge with the performance of manifold industrial, social and cultural functions. With the growing socialization of industry and public utility services and the policy of protection is more and more bringing the economic life and livelihood of every individual and group completely under the control of the State. The exclusive group which controls the public administration of the State wields a great influence on the life of the entire people. The danger of leaving the State services in the virtual monopoly charge of a caste oligarchy constitutes under the conditions of modern capitalism an economic problem of first class importance.

"Amelioration of the lot of the Pariah." says H. H. the Aga Khan," is essential to the building of Indian nationhood." Every Indian community is entitled to contribute its part to the liquidation of this thorny problem.

The other important matter is the question of text books. The Muslims of Bengal have rightly voiced their resentment and indignation against the wilful slandering of Muslim heroes and kings and the propagation of anti-Islamic myths of Hinduism in the Bengal selections and text books. This has been doing great harm to our students who are taught to respect everything Hindu, howsoever grotesque or absurd it may be and hate everything Islamic whatever may be its significance and greatness.

It is a source of great satisfaction to me that all section of Bengali Muslims are now realizing the great danger of the cultural denationalization of our students. The anti-Islamic policy of the Calcutta University and the lack of contact with the more virile and vitalizing culture currents of the Muslims of nothern India is responsible for this situation. "At present," said Maulana Akram Khan, "Hinduism is the most overwhelming. dominating and deadening influence working over the minds of the Bengali Muslim students.'

The remedy lies firstly, in the conquest of the Bengali language and literature by Muslim men of letters, and secondly, in the cultivation and promotion of Urdu in Bengal. The Muslims of Bengal should be bilingual, in the sense that they should accept Bengali as their main medium of instruction and Urdu as their secondary classical language so that they may not lose all connections with their brethren in faith in the rest of the country.

The protection and advancement of Urdu is the national and patriotic duty of Indian Muslims for this is the greatest and noblest contribution of the Muslim Period of Indian history to Indian unity. It is our proud heritage from our glorious past.

The cultural movements of Aligarh, Deoband. Jamia Millia Islamia. Delhi, Nadwa : Lucknow, Shibli Academy, Azamgarh and the Osmania University of Hyderabad. Deccan, have all made Urdu to be their vehicle of expression. The Osmania University has accepted Urdu as the medium of instruction for all grades of University education. The Muslims of Bengal have unfortunately not benefitted from the fruits of these cultural activities although some of their monumental works have been translated from Urdu into Turkish, Arabic and Persian in Istambul, Cairo and Kabul. It is now imperative that we should do all that lies in our power to remedy this state of affair for unless we do something for the advancement of Urdu in Bengal the Hinduised Bengali is bound to undermine Islamic culture in Bengal.

The 'Maktab' is the traditional system of Islamic instruction in India. The recent attack on this Islamic institution by the Calcutta University and the Calcutta Corporation is simply intolerable. Muslims must unite to preserve and modernise the 'Maktab' system under all circumstances.

The treatment which has been meted out to Muslims by the authorities ruling over the Calcutta Corporation and the Calcutta Port Trust is my opinion a insult to the whole community of Islam in India. The charge that Muslims as a class are inefficient and efficiency is the monopoly virtue of a certain class or community is the most shameless plea for the defence of an indefensible system of caste monopoly Raj in public administration. The Muslims will not take this challenge lying down.

"Inequality," says Dr. *Ambedkar*, "is the very basis of Hinduism and its ethics are such that the Depressed Classes can never acquire their full manhood in it." This resolution has been supported by the Depressed Classes Leagues in Sind, Bombay, Madras, C. P. the Punjab and U. P.

It presents a great and golden opportunity for the Islamisation of Harijans. Unfortunately we have neglected this duty so far. But now that the Harijan leaders and leagues themselves are saying that the salvation of India lies in their Islamisation, we must seriously think over this problem and devise ways and means for the mass conversion of these peoples to Islam.

Among the prominent Muslim leaders H. H. the Aga Khan and the late Moulana Muhammed Ali of revered memory have advocated the Islamization of Harijans through Islamic missions.

Is it not a pity that the suggestion of organizing "Missionary Society on a large scale for the conversion of the suppressed classes" first put forward at the Cocanada Congress by Moulana Muhammad Ali has not been translated into action by Muslims as yet?

Recently I have come across a similar suggestion in the Muslim Press. Mr. *Raghib Ahsan*, M. A., one of the most promising of our youngmen has formulated a Fifty Year plan for the Islamization of Harijans. The sum and substance of it is that a great association by the name of Muslim Mission for the emancipation of the Depressed Classes of India should be organised. One lakh Muslims should become its life members, one thousand life-missioneries should devote at least 20 years of their lives in the service of the Mission. A basic fund of Rupees One Crore should be raised and consecrated into a Waqf foundation under the name of the Muslim Mission Foundation—a financial trust composed of prominent Muslims like H. H. the Aga Khan. The Mission should take no part in politics or sectarianism but work with a singleness of purpose for Islamizing the Harijans religiously, socially and culturally. I wholeheartedly support this plan and commend it to the serious consideration of all leaders, specially Muslim chiefs and nobles like H. H. the Aga Khan, who has been taking very keen interest in the upliftment of the Depressed Classes from a long time past.

Time has now come when Muslims should realize their duty towards their Harijan brethren and do something substantial for their good. They are ripe for mass conversion to Islam but this can be done only in a planned and organized way through a great mission equipped with immense resources of men and money.

This brings us to the problem of Hindu-Muslim relations. Whatever Muslims want to do with regard to the Harijans they want to do it in a straightforward manner. Under all circumstances, Muslims are bound by the dictates of Islamic Shariat to keep the goodliest of relations with their Hindu neighbours. Keeping of the rules of good morals, good behaviour, and fair dealings and the preservation of the rights of neighbourhood of the Hindus is among the great religious injunctions of Islam.

I have not yet lost my hopes of constructing a harmonious whole in India based on a system of diversity in unity. I suggested a programme of work for Unity and National Reconstruction in my Delhi address. Unfortunately it has not been received by the Hindus with the warmness of spirit with which it was presented. However, I again present the 10 points of the programme before the people for their calm consideration as a separate appendix.

There are fanatics in all religious communities. One such instance is supplied by one Dr. Kurakoti, president of the All-India Suddhi Conference, held on the 21st December 1935 at Poona as an adjunct to the Mahasabha session according to the 'Statesman', dated 1st January 1936. This man, emphasising the need of converting all non-Hindus to Hinduism, claimed that India was for the Hindus alone, other communities being merely 'Guests' who should be asked to behave as such. I hope the saner sections of the Hindus will not fail to condemn this mischievous and criminal idea.

The Hindu Sabha Polity

A. I. Sanatan Dharma Mahasabha Conference

Due to the efforts of ***Pandit Madan Mohan Malaviya***, unanimity was secured among the learned Sanatanists assembled at Allahabad Ardh Kumbh, from the **23rd.** to **26th. January 1936** in connection with the All India Sanatan Dharma Mahasabha conference, from different provinces and States. on the question of the uplift of the depressed classes, specially under the present conditions in the country.

The question was being discussed among the learned Pandits for the last several days and definite resolutions on the subject were recorded at the sitting of the All-India Sanatan Dharma Mahasabha held on Saturday night under the presidentship of *Mahrajadhirj of Darbhanga*.

The Mahasabha declared unanimously that the so-called untouchables were the followers of the Sanatan Dharma and, therefore, it was the duty of all Sanatanists to assist them in the enjoyment of all the privileges, to which the followers of Sanatan Dharma were entitled.

The Mahasabha also recorded the opinion that the so-called untouchables had got the inherent right of having *deva-darshan* by virtue of their being Sanatanists, which right they actually enjoyed in respect of many prominent temples in India, inasmuch as they were allowed *darshan* there, they also taking bath at the Tribeni Sangam together with the caste-Hindus.

The Mahasabha recorded that wherever they were not allowed *deva-darshan* they should be allowed to have it now from the door of the deity room of the temple; and it requested the managers of the temples to take necessary steps to enable the so-called *Achchuts* to have *deva-darshan* in their temples.

A resolution was also recorded expressing the opinion that the so-called untouchables should also be allowed the use of public wells, tanks, gardens, *sara s*, cremation *ghats* public schools. etc., without any let or hindrance.

The difference in the opinions with regard to the formula to be adopted in the initiation of the so-called untouchables was also composed. One view was that the *mantra* to be given should be 'Om Namah Shiva' as in their view this *mantra* was composed of five syllables : while the other view was that only Namah Shiva' would do as according to them *mantra* without 'Om' was composed of five syllables. The compromise effected wast hat '*Shiva mantra*' should be used, namely, wherever *Shiva mantra* without 'Om' was considered sufficient it could be used while those who attached importance to the *mantra* with 'Om' they could use in initiation the Shiva *mantra* with 'Om'. The Mahasabha enjoined upon its working committee to arrange for the giving of '*Shiva mantra*' of five syllables on the occasion of the coming Shiva Ratri (Feb. 21) to those Sanatanists, from Brahmans to the so-called untouchables, (males and females) who were not yet initiated and who had faith in initiation into that *mantra*. the initiation ceremony being performed according to the usage prevalent in a particular province.

Abduction of Hindu Women in Bengal

Earlier in the evening, on Saturday. the Mahasabha recorded several other resolutions. One of the resolutions condemned the evil of the abduction of Hindu women in Bengal and exhorted the Hindus in general, and the Bengal Hindus in particular, to realise their duty of organising themselves to check the evil and protect the women.

By another resolution. the Mahasabha urged the necessity of the protection of cows and improving their breed.

Other resolutions related to Hardwar and related to Har-ki-Pabri and other Hindu *ghats* etc.

Fishing at Hardwar

The Mahasabha also noted with regret that the U. P. Government had not yet issued any orders for the prohibition of fishing in the sacred Ganges at Hardwar, as requested by Shri Ganga-Sabha, Hardwar. and the conference earnestly urged upon Government to forbid fishing as in its opinion fishing amounted to 'hinsa' at the sacred pilgrimage of Hardwar.

All-India Mahabir Dal

The conference decided to form an All-India Mahabir Dal for the protection of Hindu *samaj* and *dharma* and *math* and *mandir*, and appointed a committee with Pandit Malaviya as chairman to draw up a constitution for the same.

Malerkotla Incident

Another resolution was passed about the Malerkotla incident. Pandit Malaviya, the president of the conference, was requested to intervene in the matter and take steps to remove the grievances of the Hindus of Malerkotla, by sending a deputation or by other means.

Sermons and Kathas on Sundays

By another resolution the Hindus were exhorted to hold sermons and *kathas* every Sunday in the morning—and if morning was not possible, in the evening,—in order to provide facilities to the Harijans to hear sermons on Gita for an hour at least.

The office-bearers of Sanatan Dharma Mahasabha were also elected to-day. Pandit Madhan Mohan Malaviya was elected president. Pandit Din Dayal Sharma, vice-president, Goswami Ganesh Dat, general secretary and Pandits Hari Dat Shastri and Radha Kant Malaviya, secretaries. A working committee was also formed, five representatives being elected from each province.

The U. P. Hindu Sabha Conference

The session of the United Provinces Hindu Sabha Conference opened in the Dharamshala of Raja Ramnarain Das at Agra on the **18th. April 1936**. It was in the fitness of things that a tried and respected Hindu leader like *Raja Sir Rampal Singh* was chosen for the chair.

Pandit Radha Kant Malaviya proposed his election. He regretted the Hindu mentality of indifference and condemned the communal 'award' which was unfair to the Hindus. It was the duty of the Hindus to protect their rights and interests. In the United Provinces the Government considered the Hindus inconvenient agitators and therefore granted a representation of 30 p. c. to the Muslims intead of their actual percentage of 14 in the population. He was pained that the Congressite Hindus entered the Legislatures with the votes of the Hindus but disowned them when they reached there; while there were others whom Government won over to serve their own purposes and those of the Muslims. At this juncture it was specially fortunate that Raja Sir Rampal Singh was there to give a lead, although he had fever. It was not possible to secure better guidance from any one else.

Rai Bahadur Babu Brijendra Swarup in seconding the proposal said that the Hindus were a dead people. Their voice reached neither the Government nor the Congress. This was due to the absence of unity in the Hindu ranks. It was desirable that the differences should be made up and true ideals placed before the community. The communal 'award' had strengthened the roots of imperialism. The present was a time of crisis for the Hindus. Raja Sir Rampal Singh was the pride of the Hindus and he actually felt for them. It was for this latter reason that in spite of his old age and infirmity that he had acceded to their request and come.

Dr. Dharam Prakash of Bareilly in further supporting said that along with Hindu interest it was necessary to protect Hinduism also. The Hindus were digging their own graves. The Hindu mentality was responsible for most of their ills. They were 86 per cent. of the population in these provinces yet they were low and humble because they were disunited. They had denied their natural rights to the depressed classes and their own rights were denied to them.

President's Observations

Raja Sir Rampal Singh was greeted with a vociferous ovation. After his written speech which was read out by his secretary because he could not get up, he made the following oral observations :—

'Although I have not been able to serve the Hindus much it seems you have some new meter by which you have measured my heart. In my mind there is no doubt an intense warmth for the Hindus. Disunion has ruined us. It is due to this that we are under foreign subjugation. Although we have braved many cataclysms, the devil of disunion is surely going to ruin the community. We should always avoid it. Our social conditions also are in a very bad way. A great portion of our community is depressed and separated from us. If we did not do our duty towards the depressed classes they will be separated from us for ever. In the political field our Government has been banning the Hindus and according to the *Satyayuga* standard of Pandit Radha Kant Malaviya it is dishonest, but in the *Kaliyuga* when every one is selfish we cannot call it dishonest. It governs in its interests. To get policy changed we should become strong and instead of helping it we should be prepared to oppose it. You should send such representatives to the legislatures as may have the heart and the will to protect Hindu rights and interests. Pandit Jawaharlal is my great friend. It may be that in some distant future his socialism may succeed but for the present it is not at all a useful remedy.'

After the speeches of the chairman of the reception committee and the president the Conference was adjourned.

Second Day's Proceedings

The second day's proceedings commenced with a *bhajan*. The first day's attendance was rather thin, but to-day the attendance was overflowing. There was great enthusiasm and the lively interest taken by the people clearly showed that the Hindus had begun to feel the grave injustice done to them in every matter and from every side. There were in all 17 resolutions passed. The proceedings terminated with scenes of great enthusiasm after 9 p. m

HINDU SABHA AND ELECTIONS

Great interest centred round resolution no. 6 which laid down that the Hindu Mahasabha should set up and support only such candidates for election to the Legislatures as may pledge themselves to protect and safeguard Hindu interests.

Rai Bahadur Thakur Hanuman Singh, moved a rider that in cases in which members of other parties gave a similar pledge to their own parties they should not be required to give it any more to the Hindu Sabha. The amendment was ruled out of order but an assurance was given by the President, and Messrs. Radha Kanta Malaviya, Raj Nath Kunzru and Bhai Paramanand that what Thakur Hanuman Singh wanted was included in the resolution and that, as was clearly explained in the subjects committee, especially by Pandit Madan Mohan Malaviya, the Hindu conference was at one with Rai Bahadur Thakur Hanuman Singh.

Pandit Madan Mohan Malaviya who had been very busy trying to bring about a compromise among the various parties regarding the elections to the Provincial Sabha of the Hindu Mahasabha thanked the President and said: 'It is very kind of you to appraise my humble services highly. I do not deserve the praise. On your behalf I thank the President. All his labours in this hot season, when he does not possess good health, are praise-worthy. Such jewels of men absorbed in the service of the Motherland are very few amongst us. I have known the Raja Saheb for about 20 years. He is a great patriot. I pray that he may yet live long and that the Hindus may derive benefit from his services.

The compromise arrived at by the Hindus and Muslims of Agra has given great satisfaction all over the country. You have shown perseverance and made sacrifices. You deserve praise. I congratulate you. The Hindus and the Muslims have to live together in the country. We work together in thousands of ways. We have the walls of our houses side by side and live together and yet there is no trouble—when we fight there is trouble. It is the duty of all of us here to promote unity. The Hindus may have their worship in the temples and the Muslims may say their prayers in the mosques. You did not get sufficient time for the pre-preparations for the conference. Yet you worked enthusiastically.

'Now I want to say something to my Hindu Brethren.

Some Jain brothers want to take out their Rath procession and some Vaishnavites put obstacles in their way. I am a Vaishnava. Vaishnavism is a fine religion. No religion in the world sanctions any trouble to be given to the followers of any other religion. (Here Panditji read a Sanskrit verse.) God is one. Therefore create no difficulty in their Rath being taken out. They may take it out and you may help them. Budhas, Jains, Sikhs are brothers. They should help one another.

The word untouchable fills me with shame. I hate it. They should never be called by this name. They are our brothers. The Sastras say that it is a sin to prevent any one from having access to wells and tanks. God is merciful. He is kind to all equally. Therefore, you should give them equal rights. The idols of gods can never be defiled by a *darshan*. Therefore, let them have *darshan*. Consider them as your brothers. The 'Panchaksar Mantra'' purifies the heart. It burns sins. I do not want to hear that the Hindus are weak. No one should say this to me. I am confident that the Hindu religion will progress. As science advances, non-Hindus will also accept our religion. Our religion is the purest. Those who have not taken any "Mantra" should do so.

'I repeat what I have said previously. Arrange "Kathas" in every village. Open Pathshalas everywhere. As soon as a child attains the age of five years put him in a Pathshala. No such child should remain unadmitted in a Pathshala. Teach them the Nagri Alphabet. No characters are more beautiful than the Nagri characters. This is the opinion of foreigners. Learn wrestling. Even if there be no school there must be a gymnasium. I am of the opinion that if a boy cannot wrestle he should not be married. Consume lot of milk. Keep cows. The milk of a cow is better than that of a buffalo. In western countries cow's milk is used. Why do you then use buffalo's milk? The use of buffalo's milk makes one' intelligence like that of a buffalo. Wherever there are Gaushalas they should be re-organised. Where there is none they should be established. As in Bombay pastures should be arranged everywhere. My brothers of the so-called depressed classes should keep cows and save the profit of the skin. I shall be very glad; when wells, temples, schools, meetings, roads and burning ghats all are thrown open to Harijans.

Babu Brijendra Swarup in seconding the resolution of thanks to the chair said that the best proof of respect to the President would be to see the resolutions passed by the Conference put into practice.

The Conference ended with cheers after the President thanked the various workers and helpers.

Text of Resolutions

The following are the texts of the resolutions passed by the Conference on the **19th. April** :—

I.—Death of H. M. King George V.

This Provincial Hindu Conference places on record its sense of deep regret at the death of H. M. King George V, Emperor of India, and offers its respectful condolence to his Majesty the King-Emperor, Queen Mary and other members of the Royal family.

II.—Accession of H. M. King Edward VIII

This Provincial Hindu Conference offers its dutiful and respectful homage to H. M. King Edward VIII on his accession to the Throne of England.

III.—Welcome to Lord Linlithgow

This Provincial Hindu Conference offers its respectful welcome to his Excellency Lord Linlithgow on his assuming the exalted office of Viceroy and earnestly hopes that during his regime justice will be done to the great Hindu community

IV.—Sympathy and Condolence

This Provincial Hindu Conference expresses its deep sense of sorrow at the sad death of Mr. Gopal Krishna Deodhar, Kunwar Ganesh Singh Bhadoria, Mrs. Kamala Nehru and Bhanu Vishwaram of Nasik, and conveys heartfelt sympathies to the members of the bereaved families.

V.—Government of India Act and Communal Award

(*a*) This Provincial Hindu Conference reaffirms its opinion that the Government of India Act is a highly unsatisfactory and retrograde measure and reiterates its condemnation of and opposition to the Communal Award which is detrimental to the interests of the country generally and is grossly unjust to the Hindus specially and makes the growth of responsible government in India impossible.

(b) This Provincial Hindu Conference calls upon Hindus in these provinces to carry on active agitation against the Communal Award until it is replaced by a national system of representation and to strive for a better constitution by all legitimate means.

VI—Hindus and Elections

In the opinion of this Provincial Conference unsatisfactory though the coming constitution is, the interests of the Hindu community require that the elections to the legislatures should be contested and only such candidates should be set up or supported by the Hindu Mahasabha as pledge themselves to protect and safeguard the interests of the Hindu community.

VII.—Restrictions of Hindu Celebrations

(a) This Provincial Hindu Conference expresses its strong protest against the restrictions imposed upon the celebration of Ram Lila at Allahabad and the action of the authorities in getting the Hindu flag removed and Hindu festivitities suspended on the occasion of the Ram Navami day at Allahabad and condemns the fanatical Muslim demands made at Etawah, Aligarh and other centres that during Moharram Hindus should be compelled to stop all their festivities.

(b) This Provincial Hindu Conference expresses its horror at the atrocities perpetrated at Aonla on the occasion of the last Holi, when two children were burnt to death and several persons injured and offers its heartfelt sympathy to the sufferers.

VIII.—Communal Trouble at Agra

This Provincial Hindu Mahasabha congratulates the Muslim and Hindu residents of Agra on the happy settlement arrived at by them that customary worship and prayer shall be performed in temples and mosques with mutual good-will and without interference from one side with the other and earnestly hopes that the same settlement will be adopted generally all over the country.

IX.—Equal Rights for all Hindus

The Provincial Hindu Conference is strongly of opinion that Hindus of all classes and castes should be given equal access to all public amenities and institutions such as schools, wells, tanks, ghats, places of water supply, hotels, roads, parks, Dharamsalas and public places of worship and burning ghats and the like.

X.—Hindi and Gurmukhi in Frontier Province

This Provincial Hindu Conference strongly condemns the action of the N. W. F. Province Government in laying an embargo on Hindi and Gurmukhi, the languages of the Hindu and Sikh minorities of the province, and requests it to withdraw the ban and allow equal facilities for the growth and cultivation of all local languages as a recognised right of linguistic minorities.

XI.—Hindus in U. P. Police

This Provincial Hindu Conference protests against the present glaring paucity of Hindus in the U. P. Police force and strongly urges the Government to remove this grave anomaly and appoint Hindus in the force according to the numerical strength of their population.

XII.—Hindu Volunteers

This Hindu Provincial Conference considers it necessary for the Sanghathan of Hindus to form an organized Volunteer Crops and open its branches in different districts. It may be called Mahabir Dal.

XIII.—Hindus of Bahawalpur

That this Provincial Hindu Conference places on record its heartfelt sympathy with the sufferings which the subjects of the Bahawalpur State have undergone during the last four months and expresses the earnest hope that his Highness the Nawab Saheb will soon redress all their just grievances.

XIV.—HINDUS OF MALERKOTLA

That this Provincial Hindu Conference expresses its heartfelt sympathy with the Hindus of the Malerkotla State in the sufferings which they have undergone for nearly a year, and expresses the earnest hope that his Highness the Nawab Saheb will soon remove their just grievances by ordering that *arti* should be performed in conformity with the ancient practice without interference by Mussalmans and such other steps be taken as may be necessary to restore confidence and contentment among his Hindu subjects.

XV.—CRIMINAL TRIBES

Inasmuch as the so-called criminal tribes section of the depressed classes, cannot make any improvement in their position nor can they retain their ancestral religion, on account of their being treated as criminal tribes, this Conference respectfully urges upon the Government the urgent necessity of discontinuing the practice of treating them as criminal tribes.

Bihar Provincial Hindu Conference

Presiding over the 4th. Bihar Provincial Hindu Conference held at Patna on the **29th. & 30th. March 1936**. *Kumar Ganganand Singh*, delivered his speech in Hindi. The following is a free English rendering of its important parts.

Ever since the Hindu Sabha movement was started there has been various criticisms against its objective and scope of work. It has been said that this movement stands for communalism and is prejudicial to nationalism and as such is against the interest of the country. How far such attacks are warranted and justified, will be amply borne out by a perusal of the aims and object of the Hindu Mahasabha.

I have not come across any single item in the object which can be characterised as anti-national. Hindus who constitute 75 per cent of the Indian population have their own complicated internal problems and if their attempts at self-preservation and defence be characterised as 'anti-national', in my opinion there could not possibly be a more glaring misapplication of the expression. Then among the stalwarts of the Hindu Sabha movement, you will come across a people who have played important parts in nation-building. The Hindu Sabha movement is primarily concerned with the solution of international problems of the Hindu society and its relation with politics extends only to this extent that whenever there is any injustice being perpetrated upon the community or there be any obstruction to its developments, the Hindu Sabha will do its best to counteract all such evil influences. If these are the instruments of encouraging 'communalism and are 'anti-national' in character I would not deem these expressions to be in any way objectionable, anything which may be ashamed of. There is no greater shame than passive submission to injustice. That there is no blacker sin than suicide, is no less true of individuals as it is of the communities. It will be clear from the proceedings of the various sessions of the Hindu Mahasabha that it has not, consistently with its aims, passed any resolution which may be against the best interests of Indian nationalism. Besides, I am not for a moment prepared to concede that the national cause can be furthered even by an inch by trampling upon the majority community and by crushing its natural aspirations and sacrificing its interests. What international goodwill is to universal brotherhood and what national unity and solidarity is to international concord exactly the same relation exists between communal fairness and national unity. Contentment and goodwill can be broadbased on fairness and it has been the purpose and object of the Mahasabha to contribute to that contentment and goodwill.

HINDUS IN BIHAR

With these ideals the Bihar Provincial Hindu Sabha has been rendering all possible service to you. You are a majority in Bihar, but your actual position is such as to provide no encouragement to you.

The total population of the province is 3,23,71,000 out of whom 28,75,000 are Hindus. Within this are included the scheduled castes who account for 44,91,000, the backward tribes 38,55,000 of which 2,96,000 have already embraced Christianity and as such are out of your fold and the balance is included in the Hindu population stated above. Muslims in Bihar number 41,40,000, Anglo-Indians 5,892, Europeans 5,390 and Indian Christians 3,20,000. Out of the total Hindu population if we take out, for the time being, the scheduled castes numbering 44,91,000 and backward tribes numbering 35,59,000, the total number of Hindus left is 2,01,45,000. This is no significant number. But what do we actually find? Hindus are so hopelessly divided among themselves and the considerations of narrow caste and sub-castes and personal likes and dislikes cast such a powerful influence that the very conception of Hinduism is set at naught. So long as such bitterness will be dividing us one from another, and so long as our breadth of vision is not widened, the assumption that the Hindus are a majority in Bihar will be a myth and it will have to be considered as to which caste or sub-caste is numerically uppermost. Even the Muslims have their own sectional division but it has been found that they merge all their differences when the call of their religion is raised and this accounts for their solidarity.

Therefore so long as the mentality of the Hindus will not change, it is difficult to imagine how poisonous and perverse the public life of the province will continue to be. History bears witness to the fact that the Hindus lost India because of their disunion. Even to-day although they have lost India, they have not lost disunity. I think, a solution has to be found for this undesirable problem. The various castes should contribute to strengthen the idea of common Hinduism instead of acting in a manner which may disintegrate it. It is only meet that the leading representatives of the districts should lay their heads together and devise some ways and means to evolve a formula which may give satisfaction to all and inspire confidence. Differences there may be and will be among individuals but they should not be allowed to corrupt the public life. In the absence of this, Hindus will be beset with innumerable difficulties.

Depressed Classes

The next problem before us is that of the depressed classes, which has assumed great importance. In my opinion this matter is not so much political as social and economic. With the aroused consciousness of the people, the depressed classes are also legitimately aspiring to better and more honourable life and their claim to humane treatment at the hands of the caste Hindus is natural. It is indeed fortunate that the attention of the Hindu leaders has been attracted towards this great problem. Institutions besides the Hindu Mahasabha, such as the Harijan Sevak Sangh, Arya Samaj and Anti-untouchability League etc., are doing good work in this behalf. In 1923 as well as recently in the Ardh-Kumbh fair at Allahabad, there was remarkable concourse of Sanatanist leaders and the all-India Sanatandharma Sabha under the presidentship of the Maharajadhiraj of Darbhanga decided to give the depressed classes their legitimate civic and religious rights. To put the resolution in a concrete shape, Pandit Madan Mohan Malaviya gave the holy 'Diksha' (initiation) to numerous members of the so-called depressed classes. The resolutions of the Sabha need wide publicity and effective propaganda throughout the country. Hindus should provide encouragement to the members of the depressed classes by giving them more facilities in economic and industrial spheres. The depressed classes should also try to imbibe the habits of cleanliness and better living.

'Shuddhi'

"Shuddhi" is another problem before the Hindus. We find that Muslim and Christian missionaries are exploiting our social evils and increasing their number by constant additions. If this proces of slicing away of the Hindu community continues, at no distant date the Hindus will be reduced to a minority even where they are in a majority. Sanatanists have also come round the idea of 'Suddhi'. The Hindu Sabha has already paid its attention to it, but financial stringency is standing in the way. It has also come to light that the Government officials have indirectly placed some impediments in the way of the Hindu missionary workers working among the backward tribes. This has naturally caused resentment in the Hindu mind. Hindus claim the same degree of freedom for the propagation of their own religion as are available to other religious missionaries in Bihar.

Female Education

Women in Bihar are educationally more backward than their sisters in other parts of India. This naturally operates as a handicap to the social life of the province. Awakening has set in but the speed of progress is slow. But I am not in favour of the same line of education for females as is imparted to males. Their spheres of activities are different. To make a heaven of the home by their domestic skill, sweetness of disposition and other feminine qualities is woman's work. But I am definitely of opinion that ideas imported from the west, are not suited to our womenfolk. Puraus and other religious books are full of noble ideals of chastity, bravery, erudition, self-sacrifice and love for religion, which should guide and inspire them, and I appeal to lady-workers to take up more earnestly the work of reform among the womanfolk within the frame-work of the Hindu Sabha organisation.

Military Training

For the defence of the country, Hindus need thorough military training. To demand Dominion Status without developing this capacity to defend the country has no meaning. Our thanks are due to the noble and untiring efforts of my esteemed friend Dr. B. S. Moonje who is going to organize a military school in India. He has received encouragement from the Commander-in-Chief and the Governor-General. I trust, that when he comes to Bihar for funds, he will meet with befitting response. Hindus are a martial race but the martial spirit has become dormant. Dr. Moonjee has indeed undertaken a splendid work of national reconstruction.

Need for Organisation

I have briefly put before you the present programme of the Hindu Sabha. But nothing will be possible unless there is a widespread and effective organisation in each village. Every village must have a Hindu Sabha, a gymnasium, a school and arrangement for keeping alive the religious spirit by means of religious discourses and holy recitations. Attempt should be made to enhance the importance of the temple as a religious and social centre and the Hindu festivals should be observed on a national scale. What we need is self-confidence, character and soul-force. Let the ideals of our fore-father inspire us and let our Sanskaras be our helping guide and let us be the masters of our destiny by own action.

Provincial Problems

Very soon the new Government of India Act will come into force. The Act satisfies no section. But it will be operative nonetheless. On the other hand, the Communal decision about which you have heard so much since the last election tends to hopelessly disintegrate the Hindu solidarity. Hindus are determined to put an end to it and they will not rest unless they have done so. It is rather curious that even the Muslims whose famous 14 demands have been substantially conceded. are making fresh demands and do not seem to be satisfied with what this constitution gives them. But there can be no non-coperation with it. Whatever the purpose every party is planning to capture the legislature. The Hindu Sabha in conformity with its ideal will like to see such Hindus returned to the legislatures who may have the spirit of the protections of the Hindu interests.

Hindus are in an overwhelming majority and contribute the largest quota to provincial revenues. But with reference to this population the representation of Muslims is by far excessive in almost all the departments. Since the province was created if one minister is a Hindu, another is a muslim ; if there are 2 Hindu High Court judges there are 2 Muslim judges as well, leave aside others. The portfolio of education has always been in the hands of a Minister. No Hindu has yet been the Vice-Chancellor of the Patna University. Is there no Hindu worthy of it ? Similiar hinge prevail in smaller spheres. Hindu youths go from pillar to post simply because they are not non-Hindus. To be a Muslim is an easy passport to public services. I am told that people in authority are reported to have suggested that Hindus should learn Urdu script and vice versa. That is to say, it should be made obligatory for 2 crores of Hindus to learn the script of 44 lacs and that too at the expense of the majority community. In local bodies provision for the teaching of Urdu is made even if there be a handful of Muslim pupils. If these things are talked of, one is accused of being 'anti-national'. If similar demands are put forward by the Hindus in provinces with Muslim majority they are characterised as unjust. What is unjust for the one is just for the other. The result is that even with a population of 75 per cent, Hindus have to live like a minority and if some one makes a grievance of it, he is taken to be quarrelsome and anti-national.

But the Hindu awakening is evident. Hindus cannot tolerate their interests being sacrificed by their own people or others and are bound to raise their voice of protest. They can never tolerate their own destruction. They want their legitimate rights according to their population. They want protection of their culture, property, art and literature. But the Hindus who want justice for themselves are prepared to do justice to others. As I have said before, Hindus want goodwill but now they have come to realize that this is not possible without the organisation of the Hindus. To-day we have assembled here to think of that organisation. May God bless our efforts with success.

Second Day—30th, March—Resolutions

Resolutions deploring the growing tendency of a section of Hindu Congressmen who are getting indifferent to the interests of the majority community under the influence of misguided ideas of nationalism, condemning the suicidal policy adopted by that section and emphasising that true nationalism cannot be promoted by ignoring the interests of the majority community and submitting to the demands of the minority community for the purpose of flattering it, were passed at the second day 's sitting of the Conference.

Another resolution adopted condemned the Communal Award most strongly as it struck at the very root of nationalism and was calculated to do utmost injury to Hindu interests.

The Conference further adopted that inasmuch as the policy adopted by the Congress towards the Communal Award is opposed to the principle of justice and nationalism,' it is hoped that Congress would even now give up its attitude of neutrality in relation to it and devise some practical and effective national solution for it.

The Conference also passed resolutions on the death of King George and Mrs. Kamala Nehru.

The Liberal Party Polity

The Madras Liberal League

Under the auspices of the Madras Liberal League, a public meeting was held, on the **5th. January 1936**, at the Ranade Hall, Madras with *Sir S. P. Sivaswami Aiyar* in the chair, when the Rt. Hon. V. S. Srinivasa Sastri, Mr. T. R. Venkatarama Sastri and Mr. Yakub Hassan spoke on "Nagpur and After". There was a large gathering.

The Chairman, *Sir Sivaswami Aiyar* said that various accounts had appeared in the Press regarding the happenings at the session of the Liberal Federation held at Nagpur. It had been stated that the motto of the Liberal Party had been changed by the President of the Liberal Federation. Their old watchword was "Co-operation where possible, and opposition where necessary." This, it had been stated, had been reversed and the one recommended by his friend, Mr. Venkatarama Sastri, the President of the Liberal Federation, was substituted : "Opposition where possible and co-operation where necessary." He doubted very much whether Mr. Venkatarama Sastri would have deliberately proposed such a change. When he read the presidential address and saw that passage he rubbed his eyes and wondered what his friend would have meant by that. He was not surprised that this passage in the speech had been misunderstood. There was, unfortunately, a certain amount of unintentional ambiguity. His friend could have given the opinions of different schools of politicians within inverted commas. He omitted to do so. Their critics rejoiced at the change in the watchword of their party. It had been said in one of the leading newspaper that in view of this change in the watchward of their party, the differences between the Liberal school of thought and the Congress school of thought might disappear. He was not, on that occasion, going to emphasise the differences. But he merely wished to point out the unfortunate way in which the passage had been printed in the address resulting in currency b ei ng given to the interpretation he had referred to. He did not think that was the inteution of Mr. Venkatarama Sastri.

Another matter he desired to refer to was the report in the newspapers of a 'breeze' in the Liberal Federation between Sir Cowasji Jehangir and Mr. C. Y. Chintamani. He believed the Press and exaggerated the 'breeze'. There was nothing like a passage-at-arms between the two. Sir Cowasji, he was told, was disposed to lay the responsibility for the unsatisfactory character of the Reforms upon their own shoulders. Mr. Chintamani seemed to have urged that the responsibility was not solely theirs. He did not think that Mr. Chintamani ever intended to assert that the disunion in their ranks had nothing to do with the unsatisfactory character of the Reforms. There was some amount of truth in what Sir Cowasji Jehangir stated, that to a very considerable extent, the absence of a united front on the part of Indians was responsible for the nature of the Reforms Act. It was also true that that responsibility could not rest entirely upon the shoulders of Indians. The Imperial Parliament, it could not be contended, had no share of responsibility whatever for the defects in the scheme. There were matters upon which possibly more light might be thrown by the Madras delegates who had returned from the Federation. For this part, he was not so much concerned with what happened in the past. The subject for to-day's meeting had been put down as 'Nagpur and After'. He was more interested in the 'after' than in 'Nagpur'. The question was what to happen after the introduction of the Reforms.

While the Reforms had to be properly worked, could they be worked in such a manner as to be advantageous to the country? The question, whether there should be council-entry or not and whether the Reforms should be worked or not, was fully examined by Mr. Venkatarama Sastri in his address to the Liberal Federation and it was also fully discussed at the Federation meeting. He had no doubt that the resolution which the Liberal Federation passed, would commend itself to all persons, belonging, at any rate, to the Liberal school of thought. Whether the resolution would commend itself to others or not, was a matter about which they need not trouble themselves. On the merits, he thought, the resolution ought to commend itself to every school of politicians. On this question, the Liberals could claim to be able to take a detached view. The Liberals were not office-seekers. At the same time, he desired to say that if, owing to any unforeseen causes or contingencies, which were altogether of a most remote nature, any Liberal was asked to work the Reforms, he would not shirk the responsibility. The Liberal Party had no wish to seek office nor did it desire to get into office. Any opinion that they expressed was thoroughly of a disinterested character. He would also say that they had not the ghost of, a chance in the next elections (laughter). Their party had immensely dwindled in strength. But let them not forget that the Liberal Party had a very distinguished record in India. They had not lost faith in Liberal principles. They had reaffirmed that faith and they flattered themselves in the belief that they would rather be in the right with two or three rather than be in the wrong with the many.

The question of great importance at the present moment was what the politicians of other schools of thought would do when the Reforms would come into force. They were anxious that the exponents of other schools of political thought should seek to enter the councils and they wished all success to those who wished to serve the country as a whole and not the interests of any particular class or community. What they desired most earnestly was, that whichever party came into power through the elections to work the Reforms, that party should have the single desire to extract the maximum possible benefit out of the Reforms, limited though the scope of the same might be, whenever opportunities were thrown open to them. He did not conceal from himself the fact that a great measure of responsibility was laid upon the Governors of the provinces in working the Reforms.

He could not imagine that there would be no opportunities, notwithstanding the Safeguards and Reservations, for the representatives of the people to take advantage of in the interests of the country. Even under the Montagu-Chelmsford Act, he had felt often that there were opportunities which were not seized. During Budget discussions in the Assembly he had found that almost all the time allowed was wasted in raising futile constitutional issues, which could lead to no tangible results. H desired to emphasise the point that their repr esentatives should take advantage of every possible opportunity that offered itself for doing useful work for the benefit of the people. He had read a statement in the papers, made a few days ago by a distinguished gentleman from the Punjab, on the financial difficulties under the Reforms. These financial limitations, he was afraid, were likely to prove the great rock on which the Reforms might split. He did not wish to stand any longer between them and the Rt. Hon. V. S. Srinivasa Sastri, and he would now ask Mr. Sastri to address them.

Rt. Hon. Sastri

The resolutions passed at the Nagpur Session of the Liberal Federation, the Rt. Hon'ble V. S. Srinivasa Sastri said, referred mainly to the need for the progressive political parties in the country, coming together in order first to keep the anti-national forces in check and secondly to derive whatever good was possible out of the new constitution. The generally worded appeal was applicable to the Indian National Congress also. "What we mean then by that resolution, stripped of generality is" Mr. Sastri continued, "that the Indian National Congress, being the organisation most prominent in the field of politics, influential and most powerful, it is its duty to gather together all forces in the country that they make for the further development of the constitution along healthy and proper lines." Expressing his own view, the speaker said "it would redound, in the end, to the good of the country in the present circumstances if the results of the forthcoming elections themselves were predominantly in favour of the Indian National Congress" (Cheers). "At the present moment" he continued, "owing to historic circumstances some of the powerful political parties in the land have taken to working on communal and sectarian lines. They are no good for our great purpose in the future. From them we may not expect anything but the prosecution of plans and schemes which may bring them and their particular sections some advantage at the expense of the general good of India. We have got to fight these people."

In the Central Government of the future, Mr. Sastri said, there was going to be a bitter and acrimonious fight between the various interests. His own personal fear was that on many an occasion, national interests were bound to go to the wall. It might be different, and he believed from the bottom of his heart it would be different in the provinces. In the provinces it would be possible to keep those forces in severe check and do a good thing or two to further their national scheme.

"It is therefore our duty" the speaker continued, "to find out whose success at the elections we have to wish for. Shall we wish for the success of the Justice Party (laughter), to take the example of Madras? Although we may ardently wish it, shall we expect the success of the Liberal Party? (Renewed laughter), The instance of Madras is a fair guide to the state of affairs all over the country. It is the Congress that has established itself in the position of primacy amongst the forces that make for the welfare of the future". (Cheers). Supposing the Congress was wobbling and forgot its own higher duty and lost either absolutely or relatively at the forthcoming elections, Mr. Sastri asked, what would happen? The pressure mainly constitutional and occasionally un-constitutional, which was now being exerted upon the authorities in England in order that they might be awake and vigilant to further India's interests, that force, that pressure, would disappear largely. They could not expect that to be exercised by any other party in the country. The parties that were to some extent powerful, were likely to exercise their influence for their own purposes. In that respect it was the success of the Indian National Congress in the coming elections in the provinces which all patriotic-minded people ought to pay for. (Hear, hear.)

In the Central Government, Mr. Sastri, proceeding, said, the Congress however triumphant it might be, might not get power, whereas in the provinces it was possible, and in some provinces highly probable, that it would win a position of power. But even so the forces of reaction were there. For there were tremendous powers of interference and arbitary action vested in the Governors. These forces of reaction would still be powerful. And it would be an act of wisdom on the parts of the Indian National Congress to summon to their aid every assistance that was available. A few days ago an article in a magazine contended that the Congress was not a mere party but that, it represented what was progressive in the entire nation. The speaker did not want to examine that proposition. He mentioned it because one thing was clear, namely, that even if the Congress was not representative of the nation to-day, it ought to become representative of the progressive part of the nation immediately. "And for that purpose". Mr. Sastri said, "the high command in Congress circles should bear in mind that outside their own sworn ranks there may be here and there, some persons, some institutions of value in their battle against arbitrary power. It will not do for them to say to themselves, 'Well' we are strong enough. We do not care for others. There may be similarly-minded, well-intentioned useful folk. Let them become Congressmen in name as well as in spirit. If they choose to stand outside, we will fight them too, if necessary'. An attitude of that kind seems to me, to be wrong, disadvantageous to the country and, in a certain sense, a betrayal of the high position which Providence has called upon this organisation to occupy. Having become so powerful, it should not neglect opportunities to become still more powerful. To fight the forces of reaction and British prejudice, every single element of power that they can bring under their banner, it is their duty as well as their privilege to gather. And that is the real meaning of the appeal we have made to the progressive parties in the country to put themselves together upon one platform in order to carry on what is likely to be, in the coming years, a war not merely of brains, but a war of hearts, a war which will on the one side, be characterised by bitterness, selfishness and greed and on the other side be inspired by all that there is in the land to which we can apply the name of patriotism, national spirit and sleepless vigilance on behalf of the future generations of India". (Cheers).

"Since we made this appeal, the Press in this country," the speaker said, "has naturally been exercised over it. A certain section has been somewhat critical, caustic and severe, as it usually is where we, poor Liberals, are concerned. I am not bothered about this uncharitable criticism. To-day, I would rather dwell on the well-meant and thoroughly friendly advice that has been given to us by more than one true representative of public opinion. That was, to the effect, that since the Liberals seem to have gone so far in their wish to co-operate with other progressive parties, why not they join the Indian National Congress ? In doing so, we are told they would be only restoring themselves to the place they once occupied as soldiers in the cause of India's freedom. Rightly or wrongly for a time the Liberals went and ranged themselves under a different flag. The time is now come, so we are told, for us to go back to the Indian National Congress. I appreciate and highly value the genuineness of this appeal that is made to us. We are not new to the Congress. Some of us have been in it longer than outside it. To ask us, therefore, to come back to the fold is not to give us any unwelcome advice. We should very much like to do so."

They found, Mr. Sastri continued, some difficulty in responsing to the appeal readily. First of all, there was the question of civil disobedience. Some of them believed that, taking the circumstances into account, civil disobedience was a mistake. What was necessary in that particular respect in inviting them back to the fold, was not a temporary suspension of the movement with the proclamation that it was always there to be taken up as soon as there was provocation, but an abandonment of the campaign. It was quite open to them to convince the speaker that what was for tactical purposes called "suspension" was for all intents and purposes, "abandonment."

The speaker, proceeding, said that he was obliged to remember in that connection that the words "Purna Swarajya or complete independence" had been chosen in order that they might satisfy two different sets of people. One set wished to interpret the goal, after the Mahatma, as the substance of independence although it might still be upon terms of complete equality with the members of the British Commonwealth. Another set wished to interpret it as complete severance of all connection with the common-wealth or Empire. "Liberals have, from the beginning and Congress people have at the beginning," Mr. Sastri said, "sworn to the doctrine that the political salvation of India must be found within the ambit of the British Commonwealth on a footing of equality and self-respect. To ask us now to adopt words which may also carry a different interpretation and are often construed in the contrary and blazoned forth as to carry a different interpretation is to asking us to perform a piece of somersault which is somewhat difficult, especially for elderly people (laughter). Even here, it may be possible to persuade me and others who are anxious to be persuaded that what is good enough for the Mahatma is good enough for us".

The speaker then examined the question of the habitual wearing of Khadi. Much as he appreciated and admired the spirit of Khadi, while he greatly valued those who, really believing in it, put themselves to hardships and expense in order to be "Khadarites" always, he would like to ask why everybody should be compelled to believe in it. After all, there must be a certain measure of individual freedom.

Even on economic propositions a person should be allowed to have his own specific view. Why should they compel every patriot who held progressive views in politics, why should they compel every one, dragoon every one, into this very specific Khaddar view? It did not seem to be justified by anything that was happening in any political organisation in the world, unless there was something in it which was in the nature of a triumphant scientific certitude which only a mad man could disbelieve. Everyone was shut out of the Congress who was unable to persuade his conscience that the Khaddar view was the only possible view in the realm of economics.

There was another doctrine of equally dubious import, one that involved manual labour. They were aware that there was a view of life which proclaimed to humanity that manual labour was dignified, that every human being was bound to render some service with his hands before he was entitled to eat his daily bread. The speaker would ask whether that was so universally accepted? Was it in the nature of a commandment like 'Thou shall not steal'? Was it in the nature of those mighty truths which were like guiding stars in their journey in the universe? The speaker did not do any manual service. Nevertheless, he did not think that he could be regarded as a burden to society. He considered deliberately that he was also rendering a service in working with his mind. There was a school of thought which held that mental work might be accepted as a substitute for manual labour. While it was possible for patriotic people to hold different views on that particular doctrine, he would ask again, was it right to so organise the biggest political organisation in the country as to exclude from it those who were not of a particular brand? Greatly honoured as those people who held such extreme views were, and revered as leaders and teachers of humanity, it was not right, even out of deference to their views, to impose on unwilling patriots and workers all over the country tests of that severe kind which might involve violation of their own conscience. Mr. Sastri considered that if people were willing to pay due deference to other people's susceptibilities, regulated the political organisations of the country, they would not find such drastic conditions imposed upon candidates for admission thereto. The Congress was a political organisation meant to achieve a political end in the political sphere by fighting against political obstacles, and it seemed to the speaker that the conditions imposed for admission to the organisation should be political in nature and ought not to be derived from any views on humanity or duties of human beings, which, however exalted they might be, however conclusive they might be from a certain point of view, were not still on the level of the accepted truths.

He had indicated, Mr. Sastri continued, one or two difficulties from his point of view in joining the Congress and he would venture to say that he felt it a disability, which he had not deserved at all by anything he had said or done, that he could not join the organisation. They wanted to impose Khaddar or manual labour upon people who with equal justification in their own eyes might feel that those were not requirements that came down to them from Heaven, or that could stand the tests of science. That was why the President of the Liberal Federation, in his speech pointed out that there might be difficulties in the way of their complete identification with that political school of thought, but that it was still their duty to find out ways to come together on one platform and work for the country while maintaining their own separate points of view. He was not so influential as to think he would be able to persuade the Congress to relax any rules in order to admit him. (Laughter). "I only ask" he said, "that we should be permitted, wherever possible, to join forces with this great organisation—though harshly narrow it has become in certain respects —that we should be permitted to work wherever possible along with it for those higher political purposes we have in view."

"When we seek to enter the Councils and when we have entered them", Mr. *Srinivasa Sastri* concluded. "I can think of a dozen ways in which it is possible for the Indian National Congress, although they may not remove these barriers, to throw their doors open in the outer court in order, as I said, before, that no element which may be useful in this severe battle against reaction may be lost. That is the appeal we have made at the Liberal Federation gathering. That is not too great a demand even from a small and non-vocal party. This is the point I wish to emphasise. The Indian National Congress has now come amongst the forces in the country to occupy such a high position that it has a burden cast upon it to discover ways and means of making everything easy for those who wish to co-operate with it from the Liberal Party. From the Liberal Party proposals cannot be put forward for them to consider. I say this on the doctrine that it is the powerful that must hold out the hand of fellowship to those who are not powerful. It is the duty of the high Command in the Congress organisation to think of ways in which they could guarantee the success of India's cause in the future—that is, by arraying against communalism, sectarianism and self-aggrandisement all progressive forces in the country. Single-handed their success may be doubtful, but if they gather all the strength they possibly can, success may be made not only possible, but highly probable". (Cheers.)

Mr. *T. R. Venkatarama Sastri* said that he had been misunderstood as already pointed out by the Chairman. He hardly expected that anybody would misunderstand the position. In the portion of his address adverted to, he was referring to the opinions of various schools of thought and he was merely stating the view that, according to the opinion of some of these schools of politicians, the old motto of the party ought to be reversed as stated therein. It would have been better if he had stated that it was the view of some people and not the opinion of the Liberals. That did not mean that there was no difference as suggested in the newspapers, between the Liberal Party and the Congress. For one thing, there was no invitation to them from the High Command of the Congress to join that organisation. But they could co-operate and work together in respect of those matters where there was no difference of opinion between the Congressmen and the Liberals. This he had made it clear in his address. The President of the Congress had also stated like that. The Congress had not yet decided the question whether it should contest the election and accept offices. The Liberals could co-operate with the Congress in the election campaign. There was no difficulty in the two parties working together in respect of those matters on which there was agreement, each preserving its own individuality.

Mr. *Yakub Hasan* said that the meeting had been organised to spread the message of the Liberal Party. Though he did not belong to that party, he had been invited to say a few words. He was very glad at being given an opportunity to address the gathering. The Congress, after the advent of Mahatmaji, had made the people of India politically awake. If India to-day could say that she knew what she wanted that was due to the lead given by Mahatmaji. It was Gandhiji who made the Congress the people's party. The power and influence of Congress organisation were derived from the people. History had taught them that tremendous political forces must be properly controlled, and not only generated. Otherwise the country, where such a force was generated, would suffer. The Indian National Congress had created a tremendous political force and so long the Mahatmaji lived and so long as non-violence was the creed of the Congress, the political farce would be well controlled. But Mahatmaji was only a mortal. Those people, who had the benefit of liberal education and who wanted earnestly that the political force generated by the Congress should be controlled and directed properly, should join the Congress and take part in its work. If anything untoward happened to the people on account of the political forces not being controlled properly, the blame will certainly lie with those who had a liberal education but who did not control the forces in the best interests of the country.

It was stated by the Rt. Hon. Sastri, the speaker proceeded, that what kept the Liberals away from the Congress was the the question of Civil Disobedience. Now everybody knew that Civil Disobedience had been suspended. Mr. Sastri urged that the Congress should resolve to abandon it. What they had to consider in this connection was this: The Congress was thoroughly a democratic institution and the rule of the majority was the principle by which it was guided. The minority, though it might not agree with the majority, should not go away from the democratic body. Let the Liberals rejoin the Congress and if they found Civil Disobedience being revived, much against the interests of the country, they could then come away. Mr. Sastri had also referred to the question of Dominion Status and Independence. When Mahatmaji was satisfied that independence meant also that India could remain within the Commonwealth of British nations, Mr. Sastri also could be satisfied. The speaker did not see any difficulty in respect of this matter at all. Khaddar and manual labour, in his opinion, were minor matters. The rules were there in the interests of the discipline of a big political party. After all politics was politics and not religion, where one should not act against his conviction. He was of the opinion that communalism must be fought and even the new constitution should be made an instrument for winning liberty by working it properly.

The *Chairman*, in bringing the proceedings to a close, said that the Rt. Hon. V. S. Srinivasa Sastri had explained the principles of t e Liberal Party and had stated how they were quite willing to co-operate with the Congress. The gesture was made years ago and they had repeated that gesture to-day. While they were quite willing to co-operate with the Congress,—and for the matter of that with any other political party—which would seek the welfare of the country, they did not wish to express any anxiety to be wedded to another party, if the step involved sacrifice of their self-respect and a change of their creed and principle. He would state on behalf of himself and his other Liberal colleagues that they would heartily rejoice at the success of the Congress and would welcome its advent into power. He would only hope that the Congress Party, when it was returned to the councils occupying a position of power and influence, would be guided by wisdom and would act with a due sense of its responsibility to the interests of the country at large and seek to do what was feasible under the circumstances. There was no use in wasting one's energy upon impracticable things. The best test of a person's character, strength, wisdom and courage would be when he enjoyed prosperity and power. He hoped the Congress would emerge successful from the ordeal of prosperity, as it had been from the ordeal of adversity.

The U. P. Liberal Conference

The Tenth Session of the United Provinces Liberal Conference opened at the Town Hall, Fyzabad on the **11th. April 1936** before a large and distinguished assemblage, including Raja Sir Rampal Singh, Mr. C. Y. Chintamani, Pandit Hirdayanath Kunzru and Dr. R. P. Paranjpye. *Rai Bahadur Thakur Hanumansingh* was formally proposed as president by Mr. Chintamani. The motion was seconded by *Dr. Paranjpye* and carried by acclamation.

The welcome address was read by Pandit *Parameshwar Nath Sapru*, Chairman of the Reception Committee, and the Presidential Address by Rai Bahadur Thakur Hanuman Singh.

Presidential Address

Rai Bahadur Thakur Hanuman Singh, delivering his presidential address, entered into a strong criticism of the Government of India Act, 1935. He said that from the time when the Simon Commission was appointed, till the final stage, Indians missed no opportunity to make comments on the different aspects of the problem and draw the attention of those in whose hands the decision rested, but all was disregarded by our masters who were seldom amenable to Indian views, whenever it was a question of substraction from the power which they had been wielding arbitrarily since the inception of the British Raj. Not only had they been disregarding Indian opinion but also the promise held out to India and due to the non-observance of pledges, Indians had come to believe that Britain's promises were only made to be broken.

Condemning the Reforms, he said that it had been the deliberate policy of Britain to withhold India's right to govern herself and to give with one hand and take away with the other had been its practice.

When the so-called autonomous Governments in the Provinces were inaugurated, each Province would have a sort of quasi-dictator to carry out his own policy or the policy dictated by the Governor-General under the Secretary of State. The new Constitution bristles with safeguards, special responsibilities and discretionary powers about which a Cabinet Minister in England said, 'The machinery of Government contains every safeguard that the wit of man could devise."

Examining the aspects of the security of the services, the Governor-General and Governors' powers, he remarked that British statesmen succeeded in getting those provisions inserted, which were advantageous to themselves. He opined that members from British India and nominated members from Indian States would have a conservative outlook, which would adversely affect the Reforms.

Indirect elections to Federal Legislatures and defence policy came in for strong criticism, the fictitious nature of Provincial Autonomy was emphasised, and the high cost of the Services and Second Chambers in Provinces were condemned.

Taking up the Communal Award, he said that the Communal Award, if not modified, would continue to be a stumbling block in the way of the healthy growth of Indian Nationalism. In effect, it had divided the Indian people into as many sections as possible, and joint action on a non-communal basis had been rendered extremly difficult. Hindus did not want any community to be denied its just due, but they could not acquiesce in anti-national devices. Indians of national outlook should continue to exert themselves to their utmost to get the Award amended in a way not to affect adversely the healthy growth of Nationalism.

He blamed the Government for neglecting rural development and said: "Government stands discredited for inaction and apathy in the discharge of this imperative duty." He appealed to non-official agencies to take up an intensive educative propaganda among the villagers.

Taking up the question of reconstruction of the Hindu society, he deplored the fissiparous tendencies in Hindu society and suggested unity and co-operation as the only remedies to restore the Hindu society to the position from which it had fallen. On the problem of reclamation of Harijans, he believed that the future of Harijans was very hopeful but prejudices die hard and the work of reformation takes time. He agreed with Malaviyaji that Harijans should be given "Diksha" and they being Hindus, their rights should be conceded.

Concluding, he criticised the Government's repressive policy and said that mass consciousness to the disadvantage of alien rule cannot be stifled through repression. He hoped that British statesmanship will rise equal to the occasion, and do the proper thing to remedy the situation. He appealed to the religious communities and political parties to co-operate and serve the cause of the nation, as Swaraj would bring to every citizen much more benefit than this or that concession.

Resolutions—2nd. Day—12th. April 1936

The Conference assembled again to-day and passed a number of important resolutions, after expressing its deep sense of sorrow at the death of the late King George V, Sir Dinshaw Wacha, Mr. G. K. Devadhar, Rao Bahadur R. R. Kale, Dewan Bahadur U. M. Kelkar, Mrs. Kamala Nehru and Mr. S. N. Mallick. The Conference also paid homage to King Edward VIII.

The revival of the auction system of disposal of excise licences and its extention to opium drug shops was "strongly" condemned, the Government being asked to abandon it and restore the reforms introduced on the recommendations of the Excise Committee in 1921.

Another resolution urged the establishment of a Land Mortgage Bank and the rapid development and extension of the co-operative movement to provide adequate finance at cheap rate of interest.

While expressing satisfaction at the Government's practical interest in rural development, the Conference opined that the work could be economically and efficiently carried on by the Co-operative Department and hoped that the official agency would not be used in the coming elections in the interest of candidates of any particular party.

The Conference reaffirmed its strong condemnation and opposition to new constitution as embodied in the Government of India Act of 1935, which, it was pointed out, was still more objectionable than the Bill originally introduced and on the whole was worse than the present constitution. It emphatically asserted that no constitution could satisfy Indian opinion which did not approximate as nearly as may be the Dominion constitutions and immediately concede to the people full rights of national self-government, with an irreducible minimum of reservations, for a short period fixed by statute and which did not make for national solidarity.

The resolution was moved by *Rao Raja Sham Behari Misra*, a retired District Magistrate, who said that the Act was so bad that India would not at all be sorry if the Act was withdrawn even at this stage.

Mr. *Bodhraj Sahney*, seconding, said that the Communal Award was a pernicious offspring of the new constitution, the sole object of which was to punish Hindus.

Other resolutions adopted by the Conference related to the Unemployment Committee's report, Overseas Indians question, Swadeshi and Untouchability.

Coming Reforms

Another resolution urged that despite the fact that the coming constitution was utterly unsatisfactory, it was still the duty of public-spirited persons to take part in the elections coming off early next year as experience had demonstrated that effective boycott was an impossibility in the present circumstances and that reactionaries and communalists should not be left free to capture the Legislature. The Conference urged Liberal candidates for either chamber of the United Provinces Legislature to appeal to the suffrage of the electorate on the programme of (1) active effort to secure early revision of the constitution, (2) utilisation of constitution for results it was capable of yielding for the good of the people, (3) economic development of rural and urban areas, (4) measures to deal with acute problem of unemployment, (5) agrarian legislation for the benefit of tenants, without infringement of legitimate rights of landlords, (6) improvement of the condition of the working classes, (7) expansion of facilities for the reform of the system of education, (8) removal of Untouchability and amelioration of the condition of Depressed Classes and (9) impartiality in all communal matters. Liberal candidates were authorised to make common cause with other candidates whose policy might be similar to that of the Liberal Party.

Mr. *C. Y. Chintamani*, in moving the resolution, did not disguise his own feeling in favour of boycott if it could be successfully organised but they were conscious of its impossibility in the existing circumstances. The National Congress had itself recognised that it made a profound mistake in boycotting the first reformed Legislature. Appealing to Liberals to fight hard in the coming elections and return a majority of men to whom membership of the Legislature was a solemn public obligation, Mr. Chintamani urged that no effort should be spared to keep out reactionaries. He added that Liberals were bound to meet with opposition from the side of the Government through reactionary organisations and candidates pledged to revolutionary policy. "If we reformers who stand by ordered progress are worth our salt, if we deserve to continue our existence in the public life of the country, duty clearly calls upon us to put forth the maximum effort at this time to win our way through to the extent our countrymen will enable us to do so, in spite of opposition of both revolutionaries and reactionaries".

The resolution was enthusiastically supported by Rai Saheb S. P. Sanyal of Benares, Dr. Paranjpye, Vice-Chancellor of the Lucknow University, and Pandit Hirdaynath Kunzru, President of the Servants of India Society.

All speakers emphasised that Liberals had played an important role in Indian politics and they should, as genuine nationalists, welcome the assistance of others who had the good of the country at heart and had a programme similar to theirs. They gave an assurance to all minorities to look after their interests as their own and approach the communal questions not as Hindus, Moslems or Christians, but as children of the same Motherland and as colleagues engaged in common task.

After all the resolutions were carried, Thakur Hanuman Singh, President, in his concluding speech, said that the Liberal Party had existed in the United Provinces for a very long time but its work had not been very satisfactory. He stressed the need of a substantial party fund and appealed to the delegates to popularise the Liberal Party by active sustained propaganda by starting Liberal Leagues in their respective districts on enrolling many members. The Conference terminated late in the evening amidst enthusiastic scenes.

The Shahidgunj Gurdwara

Origin and History of the Movcment

The following are excerpts from the History of the Gurdwara Shahidgunj, Lahore itten by Prof: *Ganda Singh of Amritsar* :—

The Gurdwara Reform Movement, which aimed at purifying the Sikh temples of un-Sikh-like deviations and practices and at protecting their endowed properties om the misappropriation of their self-aggrandising custodians, resulted in the issage of the Sikh Gurdwara Act, 1925, which placed all the Sikh historical Gurwaras under the management of a Sikh Central Board, called the Shiromani Gurwara Prabandhak Committee, with branches all over the province. The Act eclared the Shahidganj, a scheduled Sikh Gurdwara as per Punjab Government otification No. 292-G of 28th April 1926, and gave it for management to the Local urdwara Prabandhak Committee of Lahore, and a consolidated list of the properes belonging to the Gurdwara was published with the Punjab Government Notification No. 275-G of 22nd December 1927, in the manner required by Section 3, Subection (2) of the Act.

The old Mahant Bhai Harnam Singh, as we know, had converted the endowed property of the Shahidganj, and certain additions thereto, into his personal property. n suit No. 651 of 1885, Khem Kaur widow of Ganda Singh *versus* Asa Singh son f Ganda Singh, in the court of Lala Amolak Ram, Munsif, Lahore, the learned judge, as previously mentioned, had ordered :—

"After a careful consideration of the whole case, I am clearly of opinion that the whole of the property attached to Shahid Bunga inclusive of the mosque, mill, shops and stable, is of the nature of an endowed property belonging to a religious institution. No doubt a few shops and the stable had been built during the incumbency of Ganda Singh, but the site had admittedly belonged to the shrine, the materials too had come from buildings or ruins belonging to the shrine, and Ganda Singh's sole income consisted of the rents of lands endowed therefor. Ganda Singh was simply a manager or trustee, and any additions made to the estate by means of the income derived therefrom belongs to the shrine and no one else."

But Bhai Harnam Singh would not willingly transfer the property attached to the Shahidganj to the Committee, and protracted litigation ensued between the parties in the first Sikh Gurudwara Tribunal at Lahore.

The Anjuman-i-Islamia, a Muslim Association of Lahore, also now found an opportunity to rake up the old question and filed a petition in the Tribunal, through Chaudhri Abdul Ghani, Advocate, claiming properties Nos. 16, 17, 23, 23-1, 23-2, 24-2, 25. 26, and 27 of the consolidated list, comprising the so-called mosque—the Shahidging *Dharamsala*—and a few shops belonging to the Gurdwara. The same property was also claimed by Bhai Harnam Singh, the old Mahant, and his brother Giani Hari Singh, of Khalsa Collegiate School, Amritsar, as their personal property.

Sayyed Mushim Shah, Advocate High Court, Joint Secrotary Anjuman-i-Islamia, appeared before the Tribunal to present the claim of the Anjuman upon the building without any documentary evidence, not even knowing who was its original founder and when it was built, but simply because it was shaped like a mosque. The learned President of the Tribunal, Mr. Justice Hilton, dismissed the petition of the Anjuman-i-Islamia, No. 1282, and wrote in his judgment :—

"The learned counsel for the petitioners based his argument before us on the claim that the mosque having been built as a mosque by Mir Mannu in about 1750 must always remain a mosque and that property once dedicated to *wakf* can never be lost by adverse possession. He *did not*, however, *cite before us any authority to support his proposition*, and in my judgment there is not sufficient ground upon which we can depart from the view which was taken in the suits of 1852 and 1855 and 1883, which are relevant under section 42 of the Act. It is clear from the documents O-23 and O-19, to which reference has been frequently made in the judgment, that Ganda Singh and Asa Singh were in possession of this mosque and were receiving the rent which accrued from it and that *they regarded it as a part of the Gurdwara property. In my judgment the claim of the Anjuman-i-Islamia has no valid foundation and the mere fact that the building is shaped as a mosque does not justify us in granting them a decree.* I would therefore dismiss petition No. 1282."

Rai Bahadur Munna Lal, the second judge of the Tribunal, also agreed with and endorsed the judgment of the President, dismissing the claim of the Anjuman-i-Islamia, in the following words :—

"As regards case No. 1282 by the Anjuman-i-Islamia, I am of opinion that they have been evidently flogging a dead horse. *The mosque has since long ceased to serve as a sacred place.* Its conversion to private use was *established since before 1852* and has been abundantly proved by the evidence of Gian Singh (P. W. 15). The existence of Samadhs in the compound of the mosque is an additional eloquent fact against the Anjuman. This was a triangular contest. The onus lay upon the petitioners Both the objectors and the Anjuman have failed to discharge it."

Similarly the petition of Nizam Din and Feroz Din, claiming a small area of the grave together with a right of way from the southern road to this grave, was dismissed by Mr. Justice Hilton and was endorsed by Rai Bahadur Munna Lal, the second judge of the Tribunal.

The petition of the old Mahant, Bhai Harnam Singh and his brother Giani Hari Singh, claiming the property attached to the Shahidganj as their personal property, was also dismissed on the 20th January 1930, and the learned President of the Gurdwara Triubnal wrote in his judgment :—

"On the basis of these documents, I therefore, hold on the first issue that all the properties in dispute in all these petitions (with the exception of certain property in dispute, petitions 1317 and 1278, to be dealt with later) belonged originally to the notified Gurdwara and that Hari Singh and Haranam Singh do not own them, nor have ever owned them, in their private capacity. It follows from this finding that the petition of Harnam Singh and Hari Singh should fail on this main point... I would hold, therefore, that their petition is liable to dimissal in toto."

Harnam Sing, and Hari Singh, however, filed an appeal from this decree of the Tribunal in the High Court of Judicature at Lahore. Mr. Justice M. M. L. Carrie and Mr. Justice J. H. Monroe dismissed the appeal on the 19th October 1934, and maintained the decision of the Gurdwara Tribunal, and ordered :—

"It is clear that the *actual area described as Shahidganj in 1868, comprised the masque* and the adjacent land, and that the present Gurdwara is what was described as Mandir, lying to the north of the road. There can be no doubt that *originally the whole area, north and south of the road, was one plot, the humman being attached to the mosque.*

"It is, in my opinion, clear from these admissions, coupled with the history of the place, that the property in dispute was originally attached to the institution Shahidganj and that it was held by the petitioners and their predecessors-in-interest as managers of that institution. It is also almost certain that it was granted to them by the Bhangi Sardars when they ousted the Muhammadans from power in Lahore, and subsequently continued by Maharaja Ranjit Singh. The petition was, therefore, rightly dismissed.

"As regarding the question of compensation no argument has been addressed to us on this point, and it is clear that any improvements effected have been effected from the income of the institution and from the proceeds of the alienation, from time to time, of various plots, attached to it. The Tribunal was, therefore, right in refusing to grant any compensation.

"I would, therefore, dismiss the appeal with costs."

A small technical difficulty in the handing and taking over of the possession was overcome by a mutual compromise between the parties and, thus, all the property attached to the Shahidganj compromising the so-called Mosque—named the Shahidganj Dharmsala—the Khanqah, a few shops, etc., passed into the possession of the Local Gurdwara Prabandhak Committee, Lahore, with Jathedar Tara Singh of Thethar as its President, in March 1935.

The Muslim Agitation of 1935

With the transfer of the possession of the Shahidganj into their hands in March 1935, the Local Gurdwara Prabandhak Committeee, Lahore took in hand the improvement of this 'Shrine of Sikh Martyrs.' It was really a matter of great pain to every Sikh

visitor that a Sikh monument of so great an historical importance should have been in a neglected condition. The building of the Shahidganj *Dharmsala* or Gurdwara—the so-called mosque—being about one hundred and eighty five years old, had worn down with age, and was in a tottering condition. The other buildings in the precincts were in a still worse condition. As the Gurdwara Reform Movement itself aims at the improvement and better management of Sikh temples and the purifying them of un-Sikh-like deviations and non-Sikh usages, the Committee decided to clear the site of all old and dilapidated buildings and the rubbish and debris that had been collecting there for long, for a new and better building.

With this object in view, the clearance began on May 30, 1935. The northern bazar wall and the southern roadside wall were built in the first three days, and a small door connecting the *Samadhs* (since demolished for the site) and Gurdwara Shahidganj Singhanian was erected on the 3rd June. Most of the general clearance of the compound was finished by the evening of the 7th. The demolition of the dilapidated buildings in the precincts, including the Shahidganj *Dharamsala*—the so-called mosque—began on June 8. The work of demolition had been carried on for twenty days and all the buildings and the northern portion of the alleged mosque had been levelled with the ground, without the least of excitement, when all of a sudden, on Saturday the 29th June 1935, a large crowd of local Muhammadans, armed with sticks and hatchets, collected near the Shahidganj to attack the Sikhs in their temple and to take forcible possession of the building.

During the previous week, a rumour had been set afloat that the Sikhs had demolished some Muslim tomb in the Gurdwara property, but this had proved to be wrong and the Muslim agitation had subsided.

On the 28th June, a Sikh mason, Mela Singh by name, working on the northern portion of the dilapidated building, was accidently buried under the falling debris and died at about 6-15 p. m. As the news spread, the Muslims broadcast the death of Mela Singh as a miracle of Allah and an indication of His wrath against the Sikhs and inflamed the feelings of their co-religionists with fire-breathing speeches and exciting slogans, urging them to march upon the Shahidganj Gurdwara.

Throughout the afternoon of the following day, the 29th June 1935, parties of Muslims collected outside the Gurdwara, raising cries of 'Allah-u-Akbar' and other communal slogans, and at one time attempted to rush upon the northern gate to enter the precincts, but the Gurdwara was successfully defended by a few Sikhs present there. Fearing a communal riot and disturbance of peace, caused by this attitude of the Muslims, Mr. S. Partab, Deputy Commissioner Lahore, desired the Sikhs "to cease demolition of the mosque pending examination of relevant papers concerning the Gurdwara and the mosque," and the Sikhs, with remarkable patience, obeyed the order of the Deputy Commissioner to the very letter and discontinued their work.

But, "in spite of all precautions taken by the authorities by 10-30 p. m. on Saturday [the 29th], nearly 2,000 Muslims had collected outside the Gurdwara and cries of 'Allah-u-Akbar' were raised. The situation was threatening when the City Magistrate was informed by telephone. The Deputy Commissioner, the City Magistrate, the Senior Superintendent of police and an Assistant Superintendent of Police, accompanied by a strong contingent of police arrived on the scene......On Sunday [the 30th June, 1935] police precautions were continued in the city...At the Gurdwara the Muslims continued to collect but only in small numbers. However, by the evening, the crowd swelled and at 7 p. m. the City Magistrate had again to be called."
[*C. & M. Gazette*, Lahore, Tuesday, July 2, 1935]

Tuesday, the 2nd, was marked by some stray assaults by Muslims on Sikhs and the Deputy Commissioner was constrained to issue an order that "any attempt at rowdyism or hooliganism will be promptly and effectively suppressed." But this was of no avail. "At about 10-30 p. m., some 200 Muslims, carrying spades, appeared near the Gurdwara. They were marching in military formation and were accompanied by a crowd of nearly 3,000 Muslims." [*C. & M. Gazette*, July 3, 1935]

The Deputy Commissioner made every effort to create a calm atmosphere, but the situation remained unchanged on Wednesday the 3rd. "From time to time parties of Muslims—mostly irresponsible youths—marched shouting 'Allah-u-Akbar' in various parts of the city, particularly in the vicinity of the Gurdwara ... On the other hand nearly 3,000 Akalis from outside had arrived in Lahore by Wednesday noon for the purpose of defending Sikh rights against a show of force." [*C. & M. G.* July 4, 1935.]

Finding that there was no prospect of better counsels prevailing with the Muslims, a warning was issued by the City Magistrate to the Muslim leaders saying that "use of force has so far been avoided in the hope that better counsels would prevail and that responsible persons would use their influence to keep others in check, but the matters have not improved ... if responsible sections feel helpless in the matter. the District Magistrate would be constrained to permit the use of force." The Muslims defied these orders in the evening of the 3rd, when the authorities had to declare the Muslim crowds, marching towards the Sikh temple, unlawful assemblies and had to disperse them by baton charges,

The 4th passed in comparative peace, but "the situation created by the Muslim-Sikh tension in Lahore took a serious turn on Sunday afternoon [the 5th July, 1935], when a crowd of Muslims estimated at 3,000, armed with lathis and bricks, marched towards the Shahidganj Gurdwara from the Badshahi mosque after 'Juma' prayers. The crowd was assuming a very violent and lawless attitude, and the police had to disperse it with a lathi charge. "When the police made their charge, members of the crowd retaliated, throwing stones at the police and even using lathis against them. A Head-Constable was seriously injured and was profusely bleeding when he was removed to the City Kotwali. He is stated to have been struck several times by lathis and stones. The City Inspector, Mirza Muhammad Baqir, was hit with a stone in the chest. A Sub-Inspector and several constables were also hit." [*C. & M. Gazette*, July 6, 1935.]

With the increasing danger, a number of Sikhs from outside poured into Lahore to defend their Gurdwara, and in the words of Mr. D. J. Boyd in reply to Pir Akbar Ali's question in the Punjab Legislative Council on 4th November, 1935:

"The ingress of Sikhs into Lahore was a direct result of Muslim demonstrations outside the Shahidganj Gurdwara...Up to July 4, the number of outside Sikhs increased as Muslim demonstrations increased in size and violence. ...As regards the ingress of Sikhs into Lahore, the local Sikh leaders were advised to stop it. They took some action accordingly, but the position was made more difficult by continued Muslim demonstrations and exaggerated accounts of these demonstrations in the Muslim press. For instance, the *Zamindar* published in large headlines that on July 5, 100,000 Muslims demonstrated outside Sahidganj" and that the Gurdwara was besieged by them. [*Civil & Military Gazette*, November 5, 1935, P. 8, column 5.)

In view of the seriousness of the situation and imminence of danger to the peace of the province by this lawlessness of the Muslim agitators, His Excellency Sir Herbert Emerson, Governor of the Punjab, had to come down from Simla, arriving at Lahore on Saturday, the 6th. July. His Excellency received the deputations of both the Muslim and the Sikhs but, unfortunately, his efforts at an amicable settlement met with a failure.

"His Excellency explained to them [members of the Muslim deputation on Saturday, July 6] that the Punjab Government had carefully examined the legal aspect of the case and were bound by the decisions of the Civil Courts. These had been consistently in favour of the Sikhs and in particular the Gurdwara Tribunal had rejected the claim of the Anjuman-i-Islamia in connection with the mosque. It was clearly not possible for the executive Government to go behind those decisions. They had also considered action under Criminal Law, but had reached the conclusion that this also was not possible." [*Vide* Press Communique issued by the Punjab Government, dated July 10th, 1935, published in the *C. & M. Gazette*, July 11, 1935.]

But the Muslims would not abide by the decisions of the Courts of Justices and, the Sikhs could not relinquish their legal rights, as recognised by the law Courts over the building which they claimed to be sacred to the memory of their Martyrs.

The "relevent papers" had been examined in the meantime by the Government, and the Sikhs quietly decided on sunday night to continue the work of demolition, which began in the early hours of Monday, the 8th July. "The authorities received the information regarding the demolition soon after it had started and were confronted with the necessity of a prompt decision regarding their line of action. They decided that it was not possible to prevent the Sikhs from exercising their legal rights and that bloodshed should be avoided by preventing Muslims from approaching the scene of demolition." [*C. & M. Gazettee*, July 9, 1935.]

The position and attitude of the Government is further explained in the telegram of the Punjab Government dated 9th July, 1935, to all Commissioners and Deputy

Commissioners throughout the Province that "they had also considered action under the criminal law but had reached the conclusion that this also was not possible." The relevent portion of the telegram runs as follows :—

"As regards the legal position, the Government were definitely advised that Section 295 I. P. C. was not applicable and this opinion has been confirmed by the law officers of the Government of India." [*C. & M. Gazette*, July 10, 1935.]

The question of preserving the so called Shahidganj mosque under the provisions of the Ancient Monuments Preservation Act was also considered, but in the words Mr. Boyd, in reply to a question in the Punjab Legislative Council, on November 11, 1935 :

"This expedient was considered and rejected as impracticable in the circumstances." [The *Tribune*, November 12, 1935.]

To prevent Muslim crowds marching towards the Sikh temple and creating unpleasant situation, "cordons of British troops and the police were placed on the roads leading to Shahidganj Gurdwara and traffic along the roads completely stopped.

The Muslim excitement now manifested itself in stray assaults. A Sikh, named Ganda Singh, was attacked from behind by a Muslim Muhammad Rafiq by name and was brutally done to death at about 10-20 a. m. outside the Mochi Gate, near the Thandi Khuhi on the Circular Road. Another attack by a Muslim assailant Muhammad Ishaq was made on a Sikh constable Harnam Singh of the Railway Police at 1 p. m. while on duty at Akbari Gate. Two more stabbing cases were reported on the same evening, July 8, one proving fatal. A Sikh electrician named Sadhu Singh was stabbed on Fleming Road, and he died at 11 p. m. in the Hospital. "The other stabbing case occurred near the Railway station and here too a Sikh was the victim." "Two Hindus also complained of having been assaulted near Mochi Gate. Their injuries were minor." [*C. & M. Gazette*, July 9, 1935 ; and *Bulletin* issued by the Punjab C. I. D., at 5 p. m. on July 8]

"The Deputy Commissioner proclaimed by beat of drum in the City that any one seen committing a murderous assault or arson was liable to be shot dead. Latter a Curfew Order was proclaimed under Section 144 of the Criminal Procedure Code."

Finding that the Muslim Press was mostly responsible for the lawless state of affairs, "the Deputy Commissioner called Sayed Habib of the *Siyasat*, Maulana Zafar Ali and his son Maulana Akhtar Ali of the *Zamindar* to the City Kotwali and warned them against any attempt to instigate Muslims against Sikhs."] *C. & M. Gazette*, July 9, 1935.]

The Government stood for the protection of its law and of peace and order in the country, and the *Civil & Military Gazette*, Lahore, in its editorial of July 9, warned the Muslims "that Muslims gain nothing and stand to loss much by allowing passion to get the upper hand...... The law was on the side of the Sikhs, and Muslims will not improve their position by challenging the law with brute force. The Government cannot override the law, or arbitrarily set aside findings of a competent Court... As soon as the Sikhs declared their intention of enforcing what was legally been accepted as their right, there was no alternative left for the Government but to uphold law, nor is any alternative left for Muslim to bow to the authority of the law......"

"Thanks to the enforcement of Curfew Order, Monday [8th July]'s happenings in Lahore were followed by an eventless night and the Muslim excitement in the city had time to subside," and Tuesday the 9th passed without any serious incident. As usual the Government continued its efforts to bring the city to normal condition and the situation remained calm and peaceful on Wednesday the 10th. "It was not, however, yet considered safe to relax any of the special measures which enabled the authorities two days ago to bring a serious situation under control."

"The situation showed signs of improvement on the 11th, and, according to a communique, the Shromani Akali Dal issued telephonic instructions last night [of the 11th] to various places to stop Akali Jathas from coming to Lahore. The Akali Jathas in Lahore are being sent back." [The *Tribune*, July 13, '35, the *C. & M. Gazette*, July 12, 1935.]

Friday the 12th also passed in peace, and in view of the easier situtation, the Government considered it safe on Saturday the 13th to reduce by about one half the number of the troops stationed in the city.

To placate the agitating Muslims and to dissuade them from their lawless behavior, a Press Communique was issued on the 13th and published on the 14th that "the Punjab Government has decided to hand the Shah Chirag mosque [a large and very commodious building worth several lakhs, bought by the Government in

1860 from a person who was using it as a private residence, and now used as Sessions Court,] to the Muslim community through the Anjuman-i-Islamia. with as little delay as possible."

But the Muslims were not to be easily pleased. They mistook the generosity of the Government for weakness. The Government was disillusioned the same evening to find that in a meeting of about 10,000 persons, with 1000 blue shirts, where the chairman thanked the Government for this decision of handing over the Shah Chirag mosque to the Muslim community, "other speakers, however, expressed the view that the Government action, considerate and generous as it was, could not deflect Muslims from their demand for the site of the demolished Shahidganj mosque. People were asked to enrol themselves as volunteers under the Council of Action." the immediate programme of which was "to recruit volunteers—and dress them in blue shirts—for the purpose of carrying on agitation."

Owing to the "intemperate speeches" of the Muslim leaders, on the same day of promising the gift of the Shah Chirag mosque, and "other activities of a group of persons who are deliberately trying to create mischief," an official order banning the discussion of the Shahidganj mosque dispute at public meetings in Lahore, a decision to deport four Muslim leaders from the town and an order continuing the censorship of the Press for another week were among the week-end developments in the situation." On the third day, the 16th July, the unlawful processions of the Muslims had to be dispersed with lathi charge, and, on the seventh day, the 21st July, the Government was driven to the painful necessity of opening fire on the Muslim rioters of Lahore to keep them under "restraint," which, unfortunately—perhaps under some misapprehension in happened to appreciate on July 13 when—it promised to restore the Shah Chirag mosque to the Muslim community.

A press Communique, issued by the Director of Information Bureau of the Government of the Punjab on the 15th July 1935,, stated :—

"A Muslim meeting was held yesterday at Lahore attended by about 12,000 persons at which plans were announced for carrying on agitation with regard to the demolition of the Shahidganj mosque. Some of the speeches were very intemperate and contained deliberate repetition of false statements, which the speakers knew to be false, regarding the action of the Government. In consequence of this meeting and the other activities of a group of persons, who are deliberately trying to create mischief, the Punjab Government has externed from Lahore and confined to certain places the following persons :—

(1) Maulana Zafar Ali. (2) Sayyed Muhammad Habib. (3) Mr. Feroz-ud-Din Ahmad. (4) Malik Lal Khan."

And on the 16th, it appeared to the District Magistrate that the agitation of the Muslims was "likely to cause a breach of peace, and that immediate prevention or speedy remedy is necessary." He was, therefore, constrained to "strictly warn and enjoin the public not to take any part in such processions, within the limits of the Lahore District for a period of one month with effect from to-day the 16th July 19.5." *C. & M. Gazette*, July 17, 1935.]

His Excellency Sir Herbert Emerson, Governor of the Punjab, made a pathetic appeal for "a settlement, honourable to all, of this deplorable affair" at a conference of members of the Legislative Council held in Lahore on Wednesday, the 17th July 1935. to discuss the situation, and referred to the "deliberate dissemination of false statements by unscrupulous persons." He categorically refuted certain accusations levelled by Muslims against the Government, especially those ascribing to Government "a breach of faith." Currency had been given by the Muslim Press to a false statement that the Deputy Commissioner and the Governor had held out an assurance to the Muslim deputation that the so-called mosque would not be demolished in any circumstances. Referring to this, His Excellency said :—

"I, therefore, wish to make it clear in most unqualified terms, first that the Deputy Commissioner of Lahore (who throughout this crisis has shown great efficiency, tact and devotion to duty) did not give a promise that the building would not be demolished in any circumstances. He promised that he would prevent this until the Punjab Government had had time to examine the legal position. He carried out this promise.

"Second, I wish again to make it absolutely clear that neither the Punjab Government nor I myself made any such promise when we met the Muslim deputation on the 6th and 7th of July.

"We had previously most carefully considered what action was possible in the legal circumstances of the case, and we had reached the conclusion that it would be only raising false hopes to give any assurance of the kind now attributed to us. We left the deputation in no doubt on that point." [*C. & M. Gazette*, July 18, 1935.]

The non-official members of the Council also issued an appeal on the afternoon of the 17th, to restore harmony and good will'

But all efforts failed to produce any effect. "A Muslim meeting was again held in the Badshahi mosque on Wednesday (the 17th) afternoon to defy the orders of the District Magistrate banning meetings and processions. The meeting started at 5 p m. after prayers and lasted for an hour and a half. It was attended by about 1,000 Muslims."

After the meeting as the crowd came out "some members of the crowd also threw stones on the police but none is reported to have been hurt... Small parties of 100 or 200 men, however, marched off towards the city. Inside the city these small processions of the Muslims had to be dispersed by the Police who made lathi charges at two places—one in Bazaz Hatta and the other outside Delhi Gate." (*C. & M. Gazette*, July 18, 1935.)

On Thursday the 18th, the situation was well in hand, but the Friday of the 19th July brought with it its usual dread. According to the Press Communique issued on that day by the Director of Information Bureau, Punjab Goverment :—

"At Friday prayers to-day at the Badshahi Mosque some inflammatory speeches were made and while the main congregation dispersed; quietly to their homes a procession was formed in defiance of orders by an irresponsible element with the object of marching through the city to the Shahidganj Gurdwara. The Police made 36 arrests and the prisoners were successfully despatched to the jail. When the police attempted to make other arrests, a hostile crowd gathered and police were unable to effect their purpose. For some time the police were hemmed in a hostile crowd and reserves had to be used to extricate them. Three mild lathi charges were made, but as the people in the processien lay on the ground the police abstained from the use of further force. The situation at 10 p. m. was that the processionists were all insistent on their original intention of marching through the city to the Shahidganj Gurdwara but were being prevented by the Police from carrying out their purpose. The crowd did considerable damage to some police vans..."

"In view of the seriousness of the situation, the District Magistrate had to issue a new Curfew Order and to extend the Curfew hours ordering that 'no person within the limits of the Lahore Municipal Committee shall remain outdoor after 8-30 p. m. and before 5-30 a. m. till further notice.'

But despite all orders of the District Magistrate and "all efforts of the police, the Muslim crowd which had assembled on Friday afternoon failed to disperse during the night or on Saturday, the 20th July when its number was considerably swelled." According to the official Communique of July 20, issued by the Director of Information Bureau, Punjab Government :

"From about 7 a. m. a hostile crowd gathered in front of the Kotwali with the intention of going to Shahidganj Gurdwara. The crowd was from the beginning violent and *tried repeatedly to break through the police cordon*, *throwing bricks and missiles at the police.* The police carried out a number of charges with the object of dispersing the crowd. Mounted police was also used and several cavalry charges were made. Attempts to disperse the crowd continued for nearly two hours, the mob in the meantime *becoming more violent* and a number of injuries being caused to Police and to Cavalry. Apart from minor injuries, eight cases are in hospital. The crowd was very determined and very violent.

"All efforts to disperse having failed, order was given to fire. Six rounds were fired and the crowd then broke. After an hour later the crowd regathered and was again violent It was then necessary to fire again, two rounds only being fired. The number of casualties from the firing is not definitely known, but so far it has not been possible to trace more than three killed. The number of wounded is also not known but is very small."

Fire had again to be opened on the violent and hostile Muslim crowd on Sunday afternoon, the 21st, when all other efforts had failed to disperse or to keep it in check, and the police and troops were pelted with missiles and brickbats. It is not possible to give here full details of the circumstances under which firing had to be resorted to, and they can be had from the official Communique of that day, and from the official narratives by Mr. S. Partab, District Magistrate Lahore, Mr. J. T. M. Bennet, Deputy Inspector-General Police, Investigation Department, Punjab, Mr. J. P. Morton, Assistant Superintendent of Police, Lahore, and Mr. Abdul Hussain Khan, Magistrate 1st Class, Lahore, published in the Tribune of Lahore, dated

August 26, 1935. Though the situation was under control at night, yet "in view of the possibility of bands of Muslims from outside entering Lahore, the necessary steps have been taken heavily to reinforce the troops and the Police" by drafts from outside the Punjab, said the Government Communique.

It may be mentioned that as a result of the retaliations of members of the hostile and violent Muslim crowds on the 20th and 21st July 1935, the number of police and troops wounded and "under treatment in Government hospitals or treated at first-aid posts," as given in the Communique of 22nd, was as large as 124, as follows :—

(1)	Military Officers	3
(2)	Police Officers	7
(3)	Other ranks British troops	12
(4)	Other ranks Indian troops	22
(5)	Other ranks Indian police	80
	Total	124

Monday, the 22nd July, passed without any untoward happening, but the situation took a new turn on Tuesday, the 23rd, "when it was decided at a Muslim meeting in Wazir Khan's mosque to send *jathas* of five persons or more to defy District Magistrate's orders about unlawful assemblies." But this Civil Disobedience and defiance of law could not be continued for more than two days, and practically came to an end on the 25th, when some of the Muslim government officials came to the rescue of their community saying that the "Muslims cannot afford to forfeit the goodwill of the Government."

From the 26th July the situation improved day by day, and, to all appearances, Lahore settled down to normal conditions by the end of the month. Troops were withdrawn from the camp in the city on the 10th of August 1935.

Much of the latter trouble was created by the economic boycott of Hindus and Sikhs by Muslims suggested by Mr. K. L. Gauba in his letter published in the *C. &. M. Gazette* of August 27, 1935. Unfortunately for the Province, the Rawalpindi Conference of the Muslims held on the 31st August and 1st September 1935, appointed Pir Jamait Ali Shah as the first Amir-i-Shariat or Director of the community, to receive the Shahidganj agitation by Civil Disobedience.

Pir Jamait Ali Shah, however, dared not launch Civil Disobedience and diverted his energies to the economic boycott of Hindus and Sikhs, as he appears to have been made to realize that "no Government worth its salt can be cowed down by civil disobedience."

Besides, the Muslim agitators of the Punjab worked up a sudden disturbance on the North-Western Frontier of India, which at one time threatened to be of a very serious nature, involving the Government of India in a war on the Hazara border, for which troops had to be sent from down-country. A Government Communique dated Nathiagali, September 11, '35, regarding the Hazara Border Disturbances, states :—

"This sudden outbreak was not spontaneous. Besides other evidence in the possession of the Government, leaders of the Lashkar have themselves revealed in a letter to the Deputy Commissioner, Hazara, that the unrest was deliberately worked up by interested outside agitators from the Punjab to further their purposes in connection with the communal agitation in British India.

The declared object of the Lashkar was to murder non-Muslims and to desecrate their religious places."

This view is further supported by the proceedings of a public meeting of Muslims held at Rawalpindi in the Jumma mosque on Friday, the 6th September 1935, when a resolution "protesting against the Government's policy of bombing the trans-border tribes [in suppressing the above disturbances on the North-Western Frontier] was adopted." [*Tribune*, September 9, 1935.]

The effect of the Rawalpindi Muslim Conference and the activities of Pir Jamait Ali added fuel to the smouldering fire of the Muslim agitation, resulting in intemperate speeches by certain Muslim leaders and inflammatory articles in the Muslim press. The Punjab Government was compelled to place the agitators under restraint and to confiscate the securities of the offending newspapers in the middle of Sept.

The Secretary of the Shromani Akali Dal (of the Sikhs), Amritsar, in the statement of September 11, 1935, "regrets that certain Muslim papers are trying to fan communalism, which might tend to endanger peace of the country. In spite of such provocation, the Shromani Akali Dal has requested the Sikhs to *desist from being driven* into any communal upheaval but should show utmost self-restraint and self-control. The Shromani Akali Dal, nevertheless, wants to make it clear that under no circumstances will they tolerate any infringement of their inviolable right, and will defend by all possible means every inch of the sacred premises of Gurdwara Shahidganj." (The *Tribune*, September 14, 1935.)

The Shromani Gurdwara Prabandhak Committee, in particular, appealed to the Sikhs to do nothing on the coming Shahidganj day, "the 20th September, that might in any way tend to distrub the peace of the Province," and the Secretary wrote in his appeal dated 16th September "that the S. G. P. C. deems it necessary to request the Sikhs to make every effort to maintain peace. No counter-demonstrations should be held on that day." (The *Tribune*, September 13, 1935)

On the 20th September the Muslims observed "Shahidganj Day" which greatly helped to excite the feelings of the overzealous fanatics, whose bloodthirstiness occasionally manifested itself in murderous assaults on the lives of law-abiding and peaceful Sikhs.

It was really very unfortunate that, at a time when Muslim agitation was at its hightest, not only against the Sikhs but also against the Government, the Punjab Government decided to exempt swords from the provisions of the Arms Act, and the notification thereof was published in the Punjab Gazette on Friday the 20th Sept. '35 when the agitators were observing the "Shahidganj Day" throughout the country. (*C. & M. Gazette*, September 25, 1935.)

Reports of stray assaults by Muslims on Sikhs were "received from several villages including Meki Dhok and Adhwal, two important villages in the Attock District. A party of Muslims assaulted two Sikhs (Prem Singh and Bhagwan Singh) in village Meki Dhok, three miles of Kot Bhai Than Singh, resulting in serious injuries to one of them who was removed to the Fatehjang hospital." (The *Tribune*, September 27, 1935.)

It was during these days that the well-known Muslim leader Maulana Shaukat Ali wrote a letter to Master Tara Singh, one of the most influential Sikh leaders, with a view to opening "negotiations with the Sikh leaders regarding the Shahidganj questions." Master Tara Singh wrote back to Maulana Shaukat Ali :—

"As far as any question relating to the site of the so-called mosque is concerned, this must be regarded as closed. The so-called mosque and its site mean infinitely more to Sikhs than to Muslims and any Sikh leader who for a moment put this fact out of sight would be traitor to his religion and his community."

Referring to the Muslim agitation in the Punjab, Master Tara Singh said that :—

"It has been wantonly started for political ends. It is not Islam that is speaking. It is the Punjab neo-Muslim fired by crude political ambitions based on communal vanity generated by the Anglo-Muslim alliance which has developed a dangerous type of superiority complex.

"The Sikhs will not, therefore, countenance tactics which are being employed against them for their own undoing."

"If you still think that we should meet and that some useful purpose can be served thereby, I shall be at your disposal on October 1, 2, & 3.', (The *Tribune*, September 30, 1935)

Maulana Shaukat Ali, Sayyed Murtaza Sahib and Mr. K. L. Gauba, members of the Legislative Assembly, arrived at Amritsar on the morning of October 3, and accompanied by Mir Maqbul Mahmud, Khwaja Ahmed Sadiq and Shaikh Muhammad Sadiq, M. L. C., met eight Sikh Leaders including Master Tara Singh, Sardar Dalip Singh Doabia, Giani Gurmukh Singh Musafir, Sardar Kartar Singh, Sardar Harnam Singh and Sardar Pratap Singh, at 1-30 p. m. at the Shahid Sikh Missionary College.

The conversations were held in camera and continued for over five hours. "In the beginning Maulana Shaukat Ali is reported to have said that there had been a mosque on the site of Shahidganj in olden times. The Sikh leaders contended that it was a Gurdwara. Eventually it was pointed out that the discussion could only proceed if it were conducted on the assumption that the site of Sahidganj could not be restored to Muslims." The draft of the statement to be issued after the conversations "was discussed for a long time and many alterations were made" at the suggestion of the Muslims leaders who finally approved of and agreed upon the following statement issued by the Sikh leaders :—

"It has given us genuine pleasure to meet Maulana Shaukat Ali, Sayyed Murtaza Sahib, Mr. K. L. Gauba and other Muslim friends in connection with the Shahidganj affair. Maulana Shaukat Ali has provided an occasion for us to understand and appreciate each other's point of view and for that we are grateful to him. Though the Sikh community is not prepared to part with the site, *this does not preclude the possibility of further negotiations. This can only be possible if our Muslim brethren create a calm atmosphere.* The prospects at present are discouraging but *representatives of Sikh community would welcome a talk with representatives of Muslim community in changed circumstances.*" (*Civil & Military Gazette*, October 4, 1935.)

But unfortunately no calm atmosphere was created and there was no change in circumstances. Amir-i-Shariat Pir Jamait Ali Shah, dictator of the Muslim Community, as usual, toured about the country, preaching his doctrine of boycott, exciting the feelings of his people and disseminating the seed of hatred and intolerance with much greater enthusiasm. On October 15, a number of fresh suits were instituted against the Sikhs involving therein almost all important Akali leaders. The exemption of swords from the provisions of the Arms Act further encouraged the agitators who are now literally converted into armed terrorists for peaceful and law-abiding people, and the public confidence in "the safety of life and property in the British *Raj*" is liable to be rudely shaken by broad-day-light murders in the streets of the capital of the Province.

On the 23rd October 1935, one Hasan Muhammad of Haveli Pathranwali, Lahore, accompanied by five other Muslims, came armed with an axe, and attacked a Sikh, named Sant Singh, resident of a village in Lyallpur District, all of a sudden, when he (Sant Singh) was enjoying a musical treat between the Shah-almi and Mochi gates. Sant Singh was given two axe-blows, one on the neck and the other on the chest. Leaving his victim unconscious on the ground, Hassan Muhammad shouted that "he was out to kill Hindus and Sikhs" and advanced towa'ds Mochi Gate where he came across another Sikh, Ragbir Singh, of Kapurthala, whom he attacked with the same savagery and inflicted several injuries on him. The assailant then proceeded towards Kucha Moti Panda, inside the city, where he attacked one Bishan Singh, killing him instantaneously. One Hindu, Baldev Raj by name, who happened to be quite close to the scene of the occurrence, chased the murderer but the latter attacked and overpowered his captor with the axe, and tried to escape. He was, however, surrounded and apprehended by several Hindus of the locality when the Police arrived on the scene and arrested the culprit. (*C. & M. Gazette* & the *Tribune* October 24, 1935.)

The crime caused a great deal of horror in the city. The *Tribune*, Lahore, wrote in its editorial of Friday the 26th October, 1935 :—

"The heinous crime which was perpetrated at Lahore on Wednesday (the 23rd October, 1935), and as a result of which one Sikh was killed and two others seriously injured, and a Hindu, who tried to grapple with the assailant was wounded, will cause a thrill of horror and indignation among all humane and law-abiding people of all communities."

The crime was repeated after a fortnight and another Sikh Mangal Singh of Gageki, Sialkot, was stabbed in the neck by a Muslim, behind the Water Works of the Badami Bagh, Lahore, on Friday, the 8th November, when the Muslims of Lahore were observing the second 'Shahidganj Day."

On the afternoon of the 9th, "a joint conference of Muslim leaders and Ulemas was held......at the Barkat Ali Muhammadan Hall" Lahore, where "it was decided that ten lakhs of volunteers should be enlisted in the course of November and December and funds should be collected." (*Tribune*, November 10, 1935.)

"It was resolved that during the current lunar month and the next month of 'Ramzan' the work of enrolling volunteers should be pushed on in order to strenghthen the movement, so that the number of enrolment should reach a million by last Friday of the month of Ramzan. During this period a communal fund should be established." (*C. & M. Gazette*, November 10, 1935.)

In the words of Mr. C. S. Ranga Iyer in the *C. & M. Gazette*, November 24, 1935, "it is clear that the million volunteers are to break the constitution, to violate the law, and illegally to force the Government to surrender. Here then is openly and thoughtlessly a move to resort to shock tactics and desperate methods of political and communal warfare. Those who call for volunteers forget that their opponents among the Sikhs can also organize volunteers. The Government cannot watch a Muslim-Sikh War......No Government can......If the resolution was carried out in action, public life in the Punjab would be reduced to wearisome waste."

What are the real underlying intentions of these "Muslim leaders and Ulemas" in enlisting one million volunteers—the dreadful civil disobedience, or "a disaster by means of civil war, which some of the intemperate speakers of our community are provoking" as Mian Mohd. Abdullah of Rawalpindi wrote in the *C. & M. Gazette*, September 19, '35 —are still to been seen.

On the 10th of November 1935, the day following the conference, some Pathans dressed as Akali Sikhs were arrested, from the train for Nanakana Sahib on the birthday of Guru Nanak, for possession of 12 bombs, which, in all probability, they would have thrown on a crowd of several lakhs of Sikh pilgrims on the following day.

Efforts for an amicable settlement between the Sikhs and Muslims begun on Oct. 3, could not be renewed as "our Muslim brethern" failed to "create a calm atmosphere". It is very unfortunate that even some of the most responsible Muslim leaders have not made any serious attempt to dissuade their co-religionists from unconstitutional and lawless activities.

In the words of the *Tribune*, Lahore, October 30, 1935, "so far not a single responsible Muslim has condemned even the latest wanton and unprovoked crime, as a result of which one Sikh was killed, and two Sikhs and one Hindu were injured Maulana Shaukat Ali himself [who was the leader of the negotiators from the Muslim side] has not condemned it." And, it will not be less interesting to know that the meeting of the 9th November, called by Amir-i-Shariat Pir Jamiat Ali Shah, wherein such a dangerous resolution of enrolling one million volunteers and of establishing a communal fund was adopted, was attended by such prominent and responsible Muslim gentlemen as Maulana Shaukat Ali, Nawab Muhammad Shah Nawaz Khan of Mamdot, M. L. C., Khan Bahadur Haji Rahim Bakhsh, Sayyed Ghulam Bhik Nairang, M. L. A., Mian Abdul Aziz, Barrister of Lahore, Allama Inayat Ali Mashraqi, the founder of the "Khaksar" movement, Sayyed Hamid Riza of Bareilly, Makhdum Sadr-ud-Din Gilani, Dr. Khalifa Shuja-ud-Din, Barrister, and Prof. Abdul Qadir of the Islamia College, Lahore.

"The [Muslim] challenge of raising a million volunteers for unconstitutional purposes will kill every chance of a settlement," writes Mr. C. S. Ranga Iyer in the *Civil & Military Gazette*, November 24, 1935. In fact it has already done so. In view of the appeal of Amir-i-Shariat, Pir Jamait Ali Shah, Dictator of the Muslims [to "Muslims of the Punjab to spread a network of Majlis It had Millat in the province which should entrol volunteers"], subsequent crime resulting in the murder of S. Bishan Singh and serious injuries to two Sikhs, Sant Singh and Raghbir Singh, and a Hindu, Baldev Raj and other activities of the Muslims, the well-known Akali leader Master Tara Singh has thus given a finishing touch to this question in his statement to the press, dated November 4, 1935, that:—

"Under the circumstances it is cowardly to have any such talk with the Muslims. I, therefore, wish to declare that I, at least, shall not participate in any such talk... No Sikh leader, no Sikh organization and not even all the Sikh organizations combined have the power to agree to this (the Muslim) demand. Owing to Muslim threats and bullying, the Sikhs consider it an insult to the Panth and the Martyrs to yield an inch even." (The *Tribune*, November 5, 1935.)

This brings the history of the Shahidganj Lahore, including the current relevant events up to the 24th of November 1935. Reference to the criminal cases instituted, during the agitation, by Muslims regarding the alleged demolition of a tomb in the Gurdwara premises and property, and of the so-called mosque—in reality the *Shahidganj Dharamsala*—has been intentionally avoided, as they are still *sub-judice*

It is a matter for gratification that the Government has done and is doing its best, in its own way. to create a calm atmosphere and it is hoped that with its continuous efforts the Province, and particularly the city of Lahore, will soon be restored to normal conditions

THE SHAHIDGANJ CIVIL SUIT

Lahore Session Court Judgment

The Shahidganj judgment day dawned at Lahore on the **25th. May 1936** with batches of policemen moving out of the police stations to take up duties as pickets in the danger zones of the city. While the entire police force had been asked to stand by, only a small part had been sent on duty. A small detachment of Indian troops had also been summoned and was stationed near the kotwali to meet emergencies. The precincts of the sessions court where judgment was delivered were closely guarded by armed and lathi police. Despite the fact that admission was restricted the courtroom was crowded by members of the bar and prominent Sikhs and Muslims, while outside the police were kept busy engaged in controlling a large crowd of Sikhs and Muslims.

STORY OF THE CASE

The Shahidganj civil suit filed by Dr. Mohammad Alam was the outcome of the alleged demolition by the Sikhs on July 8, 1935 of a dilapidated old building standing in the compound of the Shahidganj Gurdwara, which was claimed by the Muslims as a mosque built during the Moghul rule and by the Sikhs as a place sacred to the memory of Sikh martyrs. The agitation arising out of the demolition of this building, which was kept up in a virulent form till recently, led to grave rioting and bloodshed of more than one occasion and to stray assaults intermittently and was responsible for estrangement of the relations between the sister communities in Lahore.

CIVIL SUIT

While agitation was going on outside, Dr. Mohammad Alam diverted the dispute to the judicial channel by filing a civil suit on behalf of 18 plaintiffs, including the Shahidganj 'mosque' itself, in the court of the district judge, Lahore, seeking a declaration for allowing Muslims to say prayers at the disputed site, which the plaintiffs claimed as a mosque.

The plaint *inter alia* stated that the building in dispute was a mosque dedicated to God and that it could not be used for any purpose other than that of a mosque and that the plaintiffs and also all the followers of Islam were entitled to use the mosque for purposes of worship without let or hindrance by any one, with consequential relief in the form of a perpetual and mandatory injunction against the defendants to the effect:

(a) that they should not use the site of the demolished mosque for any purpose which might be contrary to its '*sharai*' use and sanctity;

(b) that they should not interfere in the 'rights of worship' of the plaintiffs regarding the said mosque;

(c) that they should reconstruct that part of the mosque which they demolished or caused to be demolished in the same shape and form, on the *pucca* elevation with three domes, minarets and *mehrab* as it was before demolition, or in the alternative a decree be passed against the defendants for a sum which might be found equitable in the circumstances of the case and also costs of the suit might be awarded.

The plaintiffs added that the mosque in dispute was built for offering prayers and worship by Muslims in general and was dedicated as *wakf* to God for centuries since the time of the Moghul emperors and was in existence in a safe and sound condition up to the event of July 7, 1935, and was known as Masjid Shahidgunj. Long after the erection and existence of the mosque, during the Sikh regime, the Sikhs built in its neighbourhood the *samadh* of Bhai Taru Singh and a Gurdwara of the same denomination and the possessors and occupiers of the said *samadh* also held possession of the mosque, but it remained in its form, shape, status and character, distinguished as a separate entity and continued to remain so up to the day of its demolition. After the Sikh Gurdwaras Act was enforced in the Punjab on the application of the Sikh Gurdwara Prabandhak Committee, the Gurdwara Bhai Taru Singh, with the attached properties, including the mosque, was declared as a notified Sikh Gurdwara by the Government. Besides the occupiers of the Gurdwara, the Anjuman-i-Islamia filed applications before the tribunal with regard to their respective rights in the properties of the Gurdwara and the mosque, but the tribunal dismissed these applications. The plaint further stated that the mosque in dispute had a right to maintain its status as a mosque dedicated to God and to keep up its sanctity, and the other plaintiffs individually and collectively, along with other Mussalmans, had a right to maintain its sanctity and to say their prayers and worship in it and every Mussalman had a right to seek redress in a court of law against any person or persons who interfered in this right. The mosque being a *wakf* dedicated to God had never been the property of any one individual or individuals, nor could it ever be so, nor was it subject to adverse possession by any person and had in itself a separate juristic personality. The mosque had a right to maintain itself as it existed and the present plaintiffs were not bound by the act of any other Mussalman nor by any decision given against the latter.

DEFENDANTS' CONTENTION

The Sikh Gurdwara Prabandhak Committee, the defendants, in a written reply, stated that there was no legal entity known as the mosque. According to the averment in the plaint, it was apparent that the site in dispute was a vacant site and that no mosque stood at the disputed site in the shape of a building or otherwise. So the mosque was not competent to maintain the suit.

The property in suit was included in the consolidated list published under the Sikh Gurdwaras Act as property of Gurdwara Shahidganj Bhai Taru Singh as per notification of the Government. The property in dispute had been decided to be the property of the Gurdwara by the Gurdwara tribunal on January 20, 1930. The suit was not cognizable by the court.

The defendants added that the Anjuman-i-Islamia, Punjab on behalf of the Muslim community in general, made a petition under sec. 5 of the Gurdwara Act on the allegation that the property in dispute was a mosque. The petition was inquired into and dismissed. The decision of the Tribunal was binding on the Muslim community. In any case the property in dispute was the property of a Sikh Gurdwara and the defendants had been impleaded as defendants as the managers of the said Gurdwara. The jurisdiction of the court was barred according to the imperative provisions of the Sikh Gurdwara Act. Several cases had been brought in various courts on the allegation that the property in dispute was a mosque. All those suits failed. The defendants relied upon those decisions. Inasmuch as the Gurdwara Bhai Taru Singh had been in possession of the property in dispute for over 150 years, the present suit was time-barred.

The S. G. P. C. controverted the allegation of the plaintiffs on merits and contended that there was no mosque at any time at the site in dispute. It contended that at the site in dispute there was a building which was used for the forcible conversion to Islam of Sikh men and women, who on their refusal were executed on the spot. As the building was used for the propagation of Islam it had a sound structure. When the Sikhs came in power in the Punjab they took possession of this place and because numerous Sikhs, including Bhai Taru Singh, had been tortured and executed, they held the place as sacred. A memorial was erected to commemorate the martyrdom of Bhai Taru Singh. A road was subsequenty opened dividing Shahidgunj in two portions.

The court ordered that a copy of the above written statement be supplied to the plaintiffs' counsel and the plaintiffs would then file their written replication.

The suit was instituted on Oct. 30 1935 by Dr. Mohammad Alam against the Shiromani Gurdwara Parbandhak Committee, which was represented by Rai Bahadur Badri Dass, advocate, assisted by about half a dozen lawyers.

The actual hearing of the case commenced on March 23, 1936 and concluded towards the end of April. Forty-two witnesses, including a number of Ulemas and Mr. S. Partab, deputy commissioner of Lahore, were examined for the plaintiffs, while 25 witnesses appeared for the defence. Sixty-seven documentary exhibits were filed by the plaintiffs, while the defence filed 92 exhibits.

Dr. Mohammad Alam argued the case for the plaintiffs for full six days and the defence arguments occupied four days, while Dr. Alam's reply took another two days.

The Judgment

Summarizing the findings, the judge observed:—'The mosque Shahidgunj is a juristic person capable of suing through Maulana Mohammad Ahmad (Mutwali of Wazir Khan Mosque) as next friend. A suit for a declaration does lie. But the suit is barred (*a*) by the decision of the Sikh Gurdwara Tribunal dated Jan. 20, 1930, and (*b*) by the provisions of the Gurdwara Act though not by the decisions between 1850 and 1883. The notification under the Gurdwara Act was not secured by fraud and deceit. The subject matter of the suit was in its origin a *wakf*, that is, a mosque originally dedicated for prayer in 1722, but it has not been used as a Muslim place of worship since its possession and control passed to the Sikhs about 1762. The plaintiffs' suit is not within the limitation.' The sessions judge added:—'The plaintiffs are not entitled to the reliefs claimed. The result is that the plaintiffs' suit fails and is dismissed.

'As regards costs, I have, while holding all claims to be barred by the limitations by statute and judicial decision, found in favour of the plaintiffs in one important issue, namely, that the site in dispute in its origin was a *wakf* property dedicated as a mosque. The sudden and precipitate demolition of the mosque by the defendants on the night of July 7-8 last was no doubt in pure Islamic law an act desecration which gave the plaintiffs considerable justification for seeking a remedy in the civil court. I, therefore, leave the parties to bear their own cost.'

Tomb Case Appeal—Shahidganj offshoot

Judgment was also delivered on the **25th May 1936** in the Pir Kaku Shah tomb case appeal, an offshoot of the Shahidganj dispute.

The sessions judge accepted the appeal and acquitted all the accused.

The eleven Sikhs, including Jethadar Tara Singh and Kuldip Singh, president and secretary, respectively, of the local Gurdwara Parbandhak Committee, had been sentenced in this case to terms varying from six to 15 months' imprisonment on two charges relating to the alleged demolition of the tomb of Pir Kaku Shah, stated to have existed in the Shahidganj compound and which was held sacred by Muslims in general and Khojas in particular. Tara Singh, Kuldip Singh and five others were sentenced on both the counts to nine and six months' imprisonment respectively, the sentences to run consecutively, while two others were sentenced on the first count only to nine months' imprisonment and two more on the second count only to six months' imprisonment.

The defence plea in the lower court was that the tomb in question was not of Pir Kaku Shah and that the land whereon it stood was in the possession of the Sikhs who had a right to do with it what they liked. The lower court held that the oral as well as the documentary evidence showed that the tomb was of Pir Kaku Shah and the Sikhs had no right to demolish the tomb merely because it stood on the property which had passed into Sikh hands.

Judgment

In the course of his judgment, the sessions judge, after analysing the evidence, remarked :—'It is difficult, in the face of all this evidence to accept the oral evidence given now almost for the first time during a period of acute tension that the place in question is the burial place of Saint Pir Kaku Shah. I hold that there is considerable doubt as to who, if anyone, was buried at this place. It is not impossible that the site in question was a tomb, but it is not enough for the purposes of sec. 297 I. P. C. (trespass into a burial place), to hold that the site in question may have been a tomb. To sustain a conviction under sec. 297 it is necessary to find as a fact that the site in question was a place of sepulchre and I consider that the evidence given in this case is too indeterminate to enable me to reach any definite finding.' After discussing the subject further, the judge observed :—'It is difficult in these circumstances to hold that the appellants, even if they did demolish the structure, which the prosecution call a tomb and which Tara Singh, appellant calls a *thara* (platform), committed trespass within the meaning of sec. 297.' The judge further referred the decision of the Gurdwara Tribunal dismissing the application of two Muslims for ownership of the tomb and commented that the committee of management of the Gurdwara, in these circumstances, might reasonably presume that they were entitled to deal as they liked with their own property. The judge held, therefore, that the knowledge and intention required under sec. 297, I. P. C., cannot be presumed in the present case. In view of these findings the judge thought it immaterial whether the appellants actually demolished the mosque. He, therefore, accepted the appeal and acquitted the appellants.

THE EUROPEAN POLITY

EUROPEANS IN SOUTH INDIA

The first annual conference of the European Association in South India was held in Madras on the **24th. January 1936** in the premises of the Burmah Shell House, with Mr. D. M. Reid in the chair. Mr. *F. E. James* initiated a discussion on "Future Policy." In the course of his address, Mr. *James* said :

"Europeans in India have been recipients of a plethora of advice recently, most of which comes from Bombay. We certainly receive it in the spirit in which it is tendered though we may, perhaps, suggest that less credit than is justified has been given to the spirit of constructive co-operation which has been evidenced in European poli cy in the last fifteen years. A study of the proceedings of the various Provincial Councils and of the work of our European Group from the beginning of the present Reforms will substantiate this claim.

"Generally speaking, European policy in the country now and in the future must be based upon the principle of partnership between India and Britain and the advance of India to the position of a dominion within the Commonwealth. This, of course, involves the rejection of policies calling for rupture of all ties between the two countries and the separation of India from the Crown and the Empire. But within that framework, there are immense opportunities for co-operation with all communities in this country upon a large number of political and economic subjects.

"The European community is held together partly by race and tradition, partly by its special position in this country. Our European Groups have not developed as a result of agreement as to political programme ; they have been formed on communal and minority considerations. It has first been our duty to organise, educate and protect ourselves. In recent years, therefore, we have largely concentrated our energies upon securing a recognised position in the constitutional development of the future. That has meant strenuous and co-operative endeavour in which we have been reasonably successful. Now that the Government of India Act is on the Statute Book, however, all that is behind, and we have to take stock of what is before us.

"It has been suggested that we should join an All-India Party to work the Reforms. What are needed are parties which will take the Reforms for granted, and proceed to live a normal political life under them. The Reforms will be worked in different Provinces by different methods and from different motives. Once Provincial Autonomy begins to work, policies and parties based upon identity of economic interests and ideas will probably emerge. The Congress Socialist Party is an indication of this. Much of the present party division will disappear. In South India there are two parties—one which bases its programme mainly on future promises and the other mainly on past achievements. Neither of these is enough. It is possibly too much to expect that a party will emerge with a clear-cut social and economic programme free from the limitation of past policies, until the new Constitution is actually working. That being so, is it not difficult for us now to define clearly what our policy will be in the future ? At present, we are independent of all parties and are willing to co-operate with any in securing stability and solvency in the State and steady improvement in the conditions of the people. Those are general terms however. Our European groups will never be powerful enough to dominate, lead or be entirely independent of other groups and parties. We shall have to identify ourselves to the fullest extent with any and every group which is working on lines which we believe to be sound and in the interests of this country. The interests of India are our interests and her pride should be our pride. If she prospers we prosper ; if she suffers we suffer.

"Before policies can be laid down, it is necessary to consider some of the main problems with which we shall be confronted and on which our leaders may be expected to give some guidance.

"One, the municipal administration of Madras, is at our doors. The Corporation is not as efficiently run as it used to be. It will get worse under the new Act unless great changes take place in the present political atmosphere in which members of the Corporation do their work, and unless programmes take the place of personalities and politics. The administration of the city needs a thorough financial overhaul and a concentration of effort (the fashionable phrase is a 'united front') on the improvement and increase in the amenities for which its citizens pay. This is a matter which should be taken up by the new Madras Circle of the European Association. Take provincial matters—there is a problem which is at present before South India, on which all parties should be united—the position of Madras with regard to the Otto Niemeyer Enquiry. Madras has enemies who are envious of her solvency and would penalise her for her past financial prudence and high level of taxation. Nor has Madras a good 'press' in Delhi. No Finance Member of the Government of India has been in the Madras presidency for eight for nine years. It is therefore urgent that we should all unite in pressing that financial adjustment should do justice to the province. The present Government of Madras under the leadership of His Excellency the Governor deserve the support of every one in their fight for Madras interests.

"Then there is the land revenue system which will be a matter of increasing importance in the future. Are assessments too high? Is their basis just? These questions affect not only the planting community but all community in South India for they affect the prosperity of the province.

"Then there is Hydro-Electric and industrial development, and there are the problems of planned production; public health; agriculture, Local Self-Government and Education and provincial taxation. We are vitally interested in these problems. They will become claimant in the future, and we shall have to take sides and develop our own policy.

"Then there are All-India problems, quite apart from those intricate and difficult ones which will be involved in this question of Federation. There is the problem of overseas trade, Ottawa and Bilateral treaties. There is the general problem of fiscal policy. Is the principle of discriminating protection suitable to modern conditions? Should another fiscal enquiry be held? There is the problem of distribution of taxation, the removal of the emergency taxation, the revision of the income tax, loan and exchange policy. There is the difficult problem of railway finance in which everyone should take special interest just now. If the railways go bankrupt, it is the tax-payer who will have to pay. It is sometimes forgotten that the railways are our concern as much as the roads Federation is likely to make this problem more acute unless some system of co-ordination as to control and policy is devised. Where is the oft-promised Ministry of Communications?

"Then there are all the problems involved in what is known as 'Rural Uplift' including public health, debt relief, co-operation and broadcasting.

"There is the defence of India. Few people no much about our defence forces. They have been regarded in the past as something which is alien—for obvious reasons. Actually they are one of India's greatest assets. What is India's defence policy? What is our attitude to this question? We shall have to enunciate our own policy or join some group which has defined its attitude.

"There is the question of Labour legislation. The Federal Government controls trade, the units control production; both have to do with labour laws. There is endless room for conflict."

Proceeding, Mr. James said: "Provincial Autonomy will probably come into force on April the first, 1937, when elected Ministries will take the place of the present system. We have fifteen months for intensive preparation as far as organisation is concerned. As usual, Madras has given the lead to the whole of India in this regard. As far as education is concerned, we have our own monthly Bulletin. This began as an experiment, but I believe that it has been justified and that it may have to be developed and extended. We must have an organ like this. It is true that there are several competent English newspapers in the Presidency which have been generous in the past in giving our Association publicity: We are grateful for this help and I am sure it will continue to be given."

Mr. James then pointed out that there was need for the holding of periodic conferences and the fullest publicity for the work of their representatives in the Legislatures.

In conclusion, Mr. James said: "One word of warning. Though the Government of India Bill is on the Statute Book, we are by no means finished with the constitutional issues between Britain and India. The Act is not a final settlement of all these issues, though it settles a large number of them—particularly in the provincial sphere. There will be agitation for further advance—some of it constitutional, some of it extra-constitutional. With those who are constitutional we cannot but sympathise. That sympathies may be required to be translated into concrete and practical form in the future. It would be well, therefore, for us always to keep in mind those large questions involved in India's place in the Empire. There could be no surer guarantee of that good-will which we claim to be our best safeguard than a frank appreciation of India's case for self-government, and a willingness to work with our Indian friends in using the opportunities now coming to bring India nearer her goal."

Mr. *W. K. M. Langley* said that Mr. James had in his speech outlined for them a definite programme of work, which was, if he might say so, refreshing. He had great regard for the present Ministry in Madras when he joined the Legislative Council. He thought that he would find responsible Ministers going about the country with a definite programme. But so far from finding that, during the whole time that he had been in the Legislative Council—he had been there nearly three years now—he did not think that outside an occasional conference of the party which was usually held behind closed doors or more or less closed doors, he had ever heard any of the responsible Ministers, who represented an important section of the Madras Government, either going out into the mofussil and putting forward a programme before the people or defending themselves in the manner generally expected in political circles. Mr. James had given them a programme which they should think over seriously.

The question of the influence of Europeans in the Reformed Councils had already been referred to in gracious terms by His Excellency the Governor. Mr. James also had spoken of it in his speech. His own experience was—he thought those who were or had been members of the Legislative Council, would bear him out in this—that in proportion to their numbers, the influence of the Europeans was very great. Their influence, he believed, would become greater and not less under the Reformed constitution. The reason was very simple. Hitherto, rightly or wrongly, Europeans inevitably had been regarded really as a part of the Government, and secondly they were apt to get the kicks in connection with policies with which they really had nothing to do or with which on some occasions they were not really in agreement. Under the Reforms, he felt they would be in a freer position to express themselves, that they would be able to attack the Government of the day and ally themselves on suitable terms with any constitutional party with whom it might appear to them they could work in concert. Generally, he felt, in those circumstances their influence would be definitely greater than it had been in the past. He was speaking only from his experience of the Madras Council. It would be impossible, in his opinion, to have a Council with greater harmony between Indians and Europeans than there was in the Madras Legislative Council. He had been in the Council these last three years, and he never noticed or heard even the slightest hint of racialism in the Council during the whole period. (Cheers). He did not see any reason why that attitude should not continue in Madras and why Madras should not set an extremely good example to the rest of India.

As far as the general programme of Mr. James was concerned, Mr. Langley said he would express his own view that, generally speaking, under the reformed Councils, he expected first of all a very distinct cleavage between the 'capitalistic classes' and the socialistic classes. As the socialistic classes were not likely to err on the side of moderation, he thought there was very little doubt on which side Europeans would find themselves ranged. He thought that for some years to come they would find themselves fully occupied in supporting the constitutional and 'capitalistic' parties in that struggle, and that the two rival parties would be so busy with their own dissensions that they would have very little time to be bothering about 'a small section of the country' like the Europeans. He thought they would then get on to 'the great struggle which shall come between industrial interests and high protection on the one hand and on the other, agricultural interests.' In that struggle if he should be in Madras and still represent the planters in South India on the Council, then possibly he would find himself ranged on a different side of the House from that occupied by Mr. F. Birley ! (Laughter).

In bringing the proceedings to a close, Mr. *Reid*, the Chairman, said that they were about to take their full share in what was known as Provincial Autonomy. All the provincial subjects would be transferred. They would not have permanent officials in the Council to guide them as in the past. The laws of the provinces would be made by a fully elected legislature. The members of the European community would be called upon to elect seven members to the Lower and one to the Upper

House and they would be the only Europeans there. They had always prided themselves on the fact that they exerted an influence in keeping with the great interest they represented.

"We shall give our unstinted support to good government of this province under the new constitution," the chairman continued, "and we all should whole-heartedly give our assistance to the people of this province and to do so, we must identify ourselves with them. We are Madrassis. We are proud of the lead which this Presidency has given to all India in the successful working of self-government. We must be prepared to enter more and more into the life of the people and to share the burden in the fight against communalism and corruption. It is not enough for us to take interest only in what we think affects us. If we narrowly watch only immediate personal interests, we will be keeping up that unfortunate complex in which we visualise ourselves threatened. That is a wrong mental attitude. Have we not yet learned to appreciate the special characteristics of the people of Madras, in which generosity and good humour, besides mental ability, intelligence and capacity for hard work are so evident? I think we have. We are ready, willing, and anxious to co-operate with any party, group or groups who may find themselves entrusted with the Government of Madras, trusting that they will realise the great responsibility placed upon them and will govern for the good of all. The words I have just uttered are pointless unless they lead to deeds."

The Chairman next stressed the necessity of a sound preliminary training for European young men. He suggested that they should take a real and active interest in the Municipal Councils, District Boards and every local self-government body. It was not a small thing to be in a local council. Training and practical experience were needed if they were to play their part well.

He had been stressing the need for training because they must have a full team ready to represent them. It was to the credit of a number of firms in South India that they had been willing to allow, and even to encourage their men to take part in public affairs and it was to their enterprise that they owed the fact that at present in the Legislative Council, there were two experienced and able debators, Sir William Wright and Mr. W. K. M. Langley.

The Chairman concluded by saying: "We stand to-day at the beginning of a new era in Indian history. We in the Madras Presidency are confident of the future. We ask that every European shall do his duty for and by this province and this country."

All India Congress Socialist Conference

Second Session—Meerut—19th. & 20th. January 1936

Over 50 delegates, prominent local Congressmen and several hundreds of peasants and students were present when the Second All-India Congress Socialist Conference commenced at Meerut on the **19th. January 1936** on the public grounds which the Municipality only last month had refused to lend to the Congress for Jubilee celebrations.

Welcome Address

The Chairman of the Reception Committee, *Srimati Satyavati Devi* of Delhi, denounced the Council-entry programme and urged Socialists to free Congress from the domination of capitalists and make it in the true sense an organisation of the masses. Congress should take up the cause of the subjects of Indian States and see that in the future Congress struggles, the immediate as well as the ultimate benefactors were the masses and not the capitalists and millowners as hitherto. Her Utopia was a workmen's and peasants' Raj. She wanted the Congress to have that ideal.

Presidential Address

The Conference elected *Srimati Kamaladevi Chattopadhyaya* to the chair. Srimati Kamaladevi, reviewing the present situation, said that the alliance between Foreign and Indian vested interests was fast developing and was bound to take a more menacing form in the Provinces under the new constitution. That would bring the significance of socialist activities more into the forefront. She justified the existence of the Socialist Party within the Congress, objected to the working of the next reformed Constitution and urged Congress men to place before the country their immediate programme. There was pressing need for a suitable programme on immediate economic demands of peasants and workmen by which the fight on a class basis would be built out of their day to day struggle, with a view to ultimately linking with the larger struggle for freedom. The building up of a united front, along with other parties, amounted to betrayal of the masses.

Resolutions

The Conference passed a number of other resolutions, two of them being put from the chair, one expressing condolence on the death of Mr. Shapoorji Saklatwala and the second sending greetings to a former chairman of the Conference, Mr. Narendra Dev, now lying ill.

The Secretary of the Conference, Mr. *Jaiprakash Narayan* moved a resolution urging the election of Pandit Jawaharlal Nehru as President of the ensuing session of the Indian National Congress.

Mr. *Meherally* seconded the resolution which was unanimously carried.

Mr. *Mohanlal Gautam* moved a resolution characterising the demands of Mr. S. C. Chatterjee, prisoner on hunger-strike, as reasonsable. These demands were (1) concentration of political prisoners in central jail, (2) equal treatment and abolition of the system of classification, (3) abolition of cellular confinement, (4) free supply of daily newspaper, magazine and books, (5) return of Andaman prisoners to their respective provinces, (6) proper medical treatment, and (7) privilege of supplementing diet and clothing at prisoner's cost. The conference suggested observing February 2 as Chatterjee Day to draw the attention of the Government to the above demands. The resolution was carried.

A resolution appealing for funds for the party was moved from the Chair and carried.

The Reforms

Swami Sampurnanand moved the resolution on constitutional Reforms adopted by the Subjects Committee, rejecting the Reforms Act and urging the Congress to wreck the new constitution. This resolution also advised those who entered Councils to press for certain demands of the masses, such as the abolition of land revenue system, its replacement by a graduated income-tax on agricultural incomes of above

Rs. 500 per annum, abolition of landlordism and other forms of intermediaries between the State and cultivator, a minimum wage of not less than Rs. 30 for 40-hour week, freedom of speech and press, cancellation of all arrears of debt and revenue and provision of cheap credit.

Swami Sampurnanand said that the British Parliament had no right to frame India's constitution. It had been framed definitely to strengthen reactionary forces in the country, for example, States' subjects' had not been given any voice in the affairs of their Governments and big zamindars and landlords had been allowed to legitimate demands of the masses. The police and jail port-folios would be nominally in the hands of Ministers, who would have strong parties at their back to suppress all legitimate agitation. It would be really a case of Indians fighting Indians. Congress Socialists believed in making use of the Legislatures only for wrecking the constitution.

Mr. *R. A. Khedgikar*, General Secretary, All-India Trade Union Congress, said that workers had been all along opposing the framing of the constitution by Parliament. When the Simon Commission landed in Bombay, as a protest, workers went on strike and this was the first strike on a purely political issue. By the proposed constitution, the right of electing representatives by trade union was given, which in no other country existed. By giving this right, the Government proposed really to encourage the starting of new unions and thus divide workers into two groups, one in favour of working the constitution and the other against it. The All-India Trade Union Congress had made it very clear that workers stood for wrecking the constitution and of asserting their right to frame their own constitution. Workers were also against acceptance of office.

Mr. *R. K. Khadikar* of Poona, winding up the debate, said that once the Congress decided to go to the electorate with determination to accept Ministership under the constitution, it would make the most undesirable alliance with a view to secureing majorities. He said he knew that some Provincial Congress Committees had already made approaches to Rao Bahadurs who had kept aloof from the struggle, to turn them into good Congressmen for the purpose of election. It would be suicidal if the Socialist Party kept quiet, believing that the Working Committee of the Congress had not still made up its mind. It was the duty of the Party not to allow Congress ranks being demoralised and disrupted in this manner. The resolution was passed.

Messrs. Charles Mascarenhas, Paliwal, Kulkarni and Khedijkar supported the resolution strongly opposing the acceptance of office by the Congress. The resolution was adopted. The last resolution concerning Italo-Abyssinian War and objecting to India's participation in any war was moved by Mr. S. Banerji and passed.

Resolutions—Second Day—Meerut—20th. January 1936

The second and last sitting of the Conference opened this afternoon, with *Srimati Kamaladevi Chattopadhyaya* in the chair. The audience was slightly larger than yesterday, being about a thousand. The agenda contained 20 resolutions, which had been agreed to in the Subjects Committee after lengthy discussions.

Congress Work in Councils

Mr. *Meherally* moved the first resolution pointing out the line of action which the Congressites should take in Councils—a line of action which would force the Government to resort to Ordinance rule.

Mr. *Patwardhan* said that even Liberals in office would do as much an Congressites could do if they accepted the Ministry. The Congressmen in Councils should try to link the struggle of the masses outside with the struggle inside Councils. That was how mass action should be built up and not by satyagraha.

The resolution was adopted.

Greetings to Peasants' Organisations

On the motion of the President, resolutions were passed extending greetings to organisations of workers for peasants in India and abroad and declaring the Party's solidarity in their struggle.

Swami Sampurnanand moved that the Congress constitution be so amended as to include adequate representation of the exploited classes, such as workers and peasants, and so as to have as its objective complete independence.

Mr. *Charles Mascarenhas* said that not until peasants and workers participated in the struggle for freedom would freedom be achieved. The resolution was passed.

Mr. *Khedgikar* moved calling on members of the party to participate in the Labour Week.

Mr. *Mahajani* said it was by thus organising Labour they could over-throw Imperialism. The resolution was passed.

PROTECTION FOR THE UNEMPLOYED

Mr. *Rajaram Sastri* moved appealing to the unemployed middle class men to join hands with the unemployed workers and peasants to establish social ownership over means of production and as an immediate basis to agitate for an unemployed insurance of Rs. 15 per mensem, free supply of milk for children of the unemployed, free housing and other benefits to the unemployed. He cited extreme cases of poverty and suggested that strong measures should be devised, with a view to relieving economic distress. The resolution was passed.

Mr. *Chandobis* moved a resolution denouncing the formation of an alliance between Congress and reactionary and vested interests.

Mr. *Faridul Haq Ansari*, supporting, said that it was out of greed for high offices under Government that members of the Congress Parliamentary Board were considering an alliance with Liberals and others. The resolution was accepted.

On the motion of Mr. *Mohanlal Gautam*, a resolution was passed calling on parties to organise peasants in their territories and send delegates to the Lucknow Kisan Conference.

Several resolutions were put from the chair including one concerning the holding of an Independence Day and passing resolutions stating the minimum demands of the party, expressing sympathy with certain workers of the N. W. F. Province and Socialists in jail.

Dr. *Lohia* moved a resolution urging the party to sponsor a resolution at the next Congress session for democratisation of the Congress by introducing points already published, including the removal of the clause relating to manual labour and wearing of khaddar. Such obstacles, he said, did not help the Congress, but were liable to lead to corruption. The resolution was passed.

At the conclusion of the Conference, Mr. *Masani*, extending greetings to Socialists outside India, said there was considerable response from British Socialists, when the speaker toured in England last year.

The Conference ended amidst the shouting of revolutionary slogans.

The Kerala Congress Socialist Conference

Third Session—Tellicherry—14th. June 1936

The Third All-Kerala Congress Socialist Conference was held at Tellicherry on the **14th. June 1936**. More than thousand persons attended the Conference. *Babu Sampurnanand* of U. P. presided.

WELCOME SPEECH

Extending a cordial welcome to the delegates and visitors, Mr. *A. K. Pillai*, Chairman of the Reception Committee, referred to the emergence of the Socialist Party within the Congress and said it was not a show put up by certain individuals, socialistically inclined. The Socialist movement in the country was the expression of a necessary stage in the political and economic evolution. Constituted as the Indian National Congress was to-day, he feared that it would be difficult to convert the Congress into a Socialist body. However unpleasant it might be, Mr. Pillai continued, the truth was that the influence that prevailed within the counsels of the Congress to-day was predominantly conservative and even capitalistic. The interests of the Indian capitalist class and vested interests would be naturally to get bargains in their business as against their rivals in Britain. But this neutral conflict of interests was always subject to the more fundamental and instinctive desire of self-preservation. If the commercial and business communities in India supported the Congress in the last two fights, it was only because they saw in those movements possibilities to improve their business. Now that the working class movement was growing more and more vocal and militant and the Socialist Party had definitely stated that they stood for the abolition of private property, the vested interests had become frightened.

Under the circumstance, Mr. Pillai doubted whether it was not too sanguine to expect to turn the Congress into an essentially anti-imperialistic organisation without first freeing itself from capitalistic influence.

Mr. Pillai expressed his belief that socialism was the only salvation of India and in this connection animadverted on the suggestion that socialism was foreign.

Presidential Address

Mr. *Sampurnanand* then delivered his presidential address of which the following are extracts :—

"The Congress session is over and it is no use expressing any opinion about it. From the point of view of the Congress socialists' party it may appear to have been a success, but if it has been a success, the success has not so much been won by us as handed over to us by the group opposed to us, for reasons that suited it best. For example, they generously came forward to support our resolutions about war. In fact, the war resolution became a resolution of the Working Committee. They had made up their minds to concentrate on one or two resolutions, particularly, to the election resolution, turning down the rejection of office acceptance. On this resolution they were adamant, and proved to the hilt that they held the trump cards in their hands. While one may not say much about the Congress session itself, the tour of the Congress President is an important event. Throwing all precedent to the winds he has devoted himself to an exposition of socialism and thereby invited much criticism, on his devoted head. A great deal of the agitation that has been engineered against socialism, is mere election propaganda. Its mushroom existence will come to an end after the elections, but in the meantime it will have spread its pernicious purpose of misrepresenting socialism and injected a number of perfectly sensible people with the virus of anti-socialism. This is a fact which you must not forget. It behoves you and me to do our little bit.

Pandit Jawaharlal is trying to stress the anti-imperialistic issue and speaking socialism as an allied subject. But a concentrated attempt has been made to draw attention away from what he might have to say as an opponent of British imperialism and to concentrate it on his socialistic utterances.

"The second alarming fact is that the Congress Socialist Party seems to have gone into hibernation. We have left Pandit Jawaharlal to do our work for us. This will never do. He is not a member of our party aad cannot speak for us. It is no part of his business to strengthen our party organisation. As the President of the Congress, his hands are partially tied and he has probably to speak the language of compromise where his intellect would lead him otherwise. It is for us to strengthen our party and to speak where others cannot or will not.

"One of the things advocated by the President was the foundation of the "Civil Liberties' Union", a union, whose membership should be open to all political parties and whose function should be to resist the encroachments on civil liberties like the right of association, speech, writing and freedom of movement, unless, it has been proved in a competent court of law that such right has been abused. A vast volume of opinion has been expressed on the subject, but what is remarkable is the absolute unanimity not only of thought, but of languages as well, which has characterised the expression of liberal opinion. Pandit Jawharlal Nehru has made it perfectly clear that the proposed Union will function in a purely non-party manner. The most timid of liberals need not therefore lose his sleep over it. He may rest assured that if he joins it, his march towards Dominion Status will not be deflected by a step. I speak of Dominion Status. It is a goal unworthy of India, the Statute of Westminister notwithstanding. And the amount of suffering and sacrifice required to reach it are no less than what is necessary for the attainment of complete independence.

"This brings me to the subject of the united front. In the recent past we have heard a good deal about it. The main question is this, are you prepared to suffer and are you prepared to take the responsibility of making the country suffer all that the attempt to attain independence implies ? If you are not, then you are welcome to try to talk your way to Swaraj but little is to be gained by our standing shoulder to shoulder together. I have spoken in detail only about the Liberals, but what I have said will apply with much more equal force to those other bodies, many of them communal organisations, which seem to have no principles to guide them, but change their view from day to day to suit the changing views of this leader or that. There are genuinely anti-imperialist bodies in the country, inside and outside the Congress, which howsoever much they may differ as to their other objects and methods or details or ideals, are absolutely united in their objective of removing that incubus of imperialism which is eating into the very vitals of the country. It is with them that a united front is not only desirable but profitable.

"The Congress has decided that the elections shall be contested. We are not opposed to this decision. But the great question of office acceptance has been shelved. The Congress High Command which includes amongst itself some of our greatest diplomats—may I congratulate you, gentlemen, from the south for supplying some of the greatest masters in this line?—have so manoeuvred things that the question will not come up for discussion, at any rate for decision, till the time comes when only one decision is possible, and that, a decision in favour of office acceptance.

"In this situation our party has an important part to play. It is the herald of the new light and the new life. It has to wake up people from lethargy. Our great role lies in preaching to the people the message of a new life, in enthusing them for taking part in the great revolution in which all that is bad in law, religion and morals, in social organisation, property relations, and politics shall disappear. Much will have to go, but thus alone can a new life emerge. No tinkering reforms will serve our purpose."

RESOLUTIONS

The Conference adopted the following resolutions :—

The Conference congratulated *Pandit Jawaharlal Nehru* on having given a distinct and authoritative lead as President of the Indian National Congress and appealed to all radicals in the Congress to develop the anti-imperialist struggle by making the primary Congress organisations live cells of the wider nationalist struggle by bringing about closer contact between the radical elements and the masses by sternly resisting all suppression of civil liberties, by guarding against all attempts to hustle India into an Imperialist war and by carrying on a ceaseless campaign against the Government of India Act and for the right of self-determination.

The Conference held that Right Wing Congress leaders lay more emphasis in capturing the legislatures than in resisting the Government of India Act and that the demand for the constituent Assembly was entirely neglected.

The Conference appealed to the radicals to start forthwith a strong campaign to focus public attention on this vital issue.

The Conference drew the attention of the public to the suppression of civil liberties in Cochin and Travancore and appealed to the public workers to strengthen the movement for securing fundamental citizenship rights.

The Conference believed that it was the duty of the State to provide work and livelihood for every citizen of the State and welcomed the movement of the unemployed started in Malabar.

The Conference welcomed the move made recently at Lucknow to form an All-India Peasant movement and appealed to public workers in Kerala to develop a strong agrarian movement there.

Provincial Political Conferences

The Bihar Political Conference

19th. Session—Patna—15th. & 16th. January 1936

The 19th. Session of the Bihar Political Conference, convened for the first time since it was dispersed by the authorities six years back, commenced sitting at Patna on the **15th. January 1936** amidst scenes of unprecedented enthusiasm, heightened to a considerable extent by the presence of Babu Rajendra Prasad, President of the Indian National Congress. About 5,000 delegates, mostly Kisans and Sonthals, and an equal number of visitors attended.

Welcome Address

Welcoming the delegates, Sj. *Ramnarayan Singh*, Chairman of the Reception Committee, made a special appeal to take into consideration the question of the excluded areas in the new Constitution. He regretted that although Chhotanagpur was very rich in natural resources, its inhabitants were extremely poor due to systematic exploitation by outside agencies.

Presidential Address

Babu *Ramdayalu Singh*, President of the Conference, next delivered an illuminating address in the course of which he said that the Government of India Act was not at all based on popular opinion and as such did not deserve to get the support of the people of India. In the course of an incisive analysis of the proposed Indian Constitution, he declared that what is being sought to be foisted on India in the name of Responsible Government was nothing but autocracy pure and simple, and that in spite of the new Constitution, the Government of India would continue to be as irresponsible as before. They could have an idea of the spirit in which the Constitution was likely to be worked from what had been going on even before the introduction of the Reforms, as evidenced by the enactment of coercive laws, both in the Centre and in the Provinces. Their masters were out to arm themselves with sufficient powers by means of Public Safety Acts throughout the country, which constituted an encroachment on the elementary rights of the people. The speaker emphasised that India's interest lay in being able to frame her own Constitution and in creating such an atmosphere in the country that the situation might compel the British Government to accept that Constitution.

Mr. Sinha emphasised that the Congress creed of independence could not be achieved through the Councils. But he supported the Council programme because Congressmen's entry into the Legislatures would prevent the latter from being puppets in the hands of Governors and help in promoting the awakening in the country. For achievement of their aims, special attention would have to be paid to work outside the Councils and to the task of creating a powerful section by harnessing all scattered forces and removal of their own weaknesses. It was the bounden duty of all Congressmen—whenever the policy and programme to be decided hereafter in respect of Councils may be,—to apply themselves to the task of organising the people and making them strong and powerful.

The speaker pleaded for concentration on the Congress constructive programme to the need of strengthening the Congress organisation and making it more widespread. Although the cry of Independence reverberated in every village and respect for Congress was literally overflowing, as the Congress Golden Jubilee celebrations have demonstrated, he confessed that branches of the Congress had not sprung up in all places nor were those existing as strong or effective as they ought to be. The country lived mainly in the villages and the Congress workers should, therefore, take up their abode in the villages and work amongst the people.

Mr. *Sinha* put in a passionate plea for the amelioration of the lot of the Kisans, who had been hit disastrously by the prevailing economic depression and for whom no ameliorative measures had even been attempted in Bihar and from whom illegal exactions yet continued to be exacted by many landlords. Referring to the sugar industry, the speaker asserted that instead of being an instrument of point to the Kisans, it had become a means of exploiting them and narrated at length the various ways in which the Kisans are harassed and denied even the cost of production by sugar mill-owners.

Resolutions—2nd. Day—16th. January 1936

The conference concluded to-day. Eleven resolutions were adopted, four of which, put from the chair, were carried without discussion. One of the resolutions drew a spirited attack on the Government policy from Mr. *Srikrishna Singh* who criticised members of the local council for passing the public Safety Act and gave a warning that in future elections such people would not be allowed representation.

Two other resolutions for reduction of rents due to economic depression and the *zulum* of zamindars were also passed. The former resolution was sponsored by Mr. *Sahajananda* who warned the zamindars that if they did not improve the day was near when they would cease to exist. It also demanded the appointment of an enquiry committee of the Congress for the amelioration of the condition of the tenancy.

Business concluding, Babu *Rajendra Prasad*, Congress President, addressed the conference emphasizing the necessity of carrying out a constructive programme of the Congress which had effected great changes throughout the country and held that all political improvements were due to Congress efforts and said that the message of the Congress had reached the remotest parts of the country. Babu Rajendra Prasad appealed for Hindu-Muslim unity for the attainment of Swaraj and said disunity between communities was exploited by Governments. The speaker concluded by emphasizing the need of furthering rural uplift work and village industries. He said that it was the duty of the Government to reduce their expenditure budget.

The Tamil Nad Provincial Conference

37th. Session—Karaikudi—25th. & 26th. January 1936

The 37th. Session of the Tamil Nad Provincial Conference commenced at Karaikudi on the **25th. January 1936**. Mrs. *Rukmani Lakshmipati*, in the course of her presidential address, said :—

"In reviewing the work as between the last Conference and now and the results achieved thereby it is our proud privilege to state that we have carried on intensive work in Tamil Nadu with implicit confidence in the policy and programme of the Congress. Triumph after triumph has established the confidence of the people in the Congress Reactionary parties who have been routed in all the elections from the Legislative Assembly to the Local Boards and Municipalities.

"I would on this occasion humbly and respectfully invite all those who have held out so long from joining the Congress. It is high time we realised that it is wrong to divide forces when the objective is the same.

"In their recent public utterances liberal leaders have expressed much willingness to join the Congress but pointed out difficulties. Some ask the Congress to change its goal from one of complete Independence to one of Dominion Status and denounce the methods adopted by the Congress during the last 15 years. In short, they demand that the Congress should give up all that has secured for its present strength.

"I need hardly say that this is not practical politics. As regards Khadi clause and manual labour franchise, these provisions relate only to holders of office in the Congress organisation and not to candidates for legislatures. But I must plainly declare that Congress cannot benefit by mere addition of men and women who come in with mental reservation or open objections to the vital articles of the Congress programme, viz., Khadi, removal of untouchability, prohibition and nationalism as opposed to communalism. I must make it equally plain that everyone who comes in is welcome but he must accept the Congress discipline in the entirety.

"I need not say anything about the Socialist members of the Congress except that I hope that they will adhere to the timely advice of Pandit Jawaharlal Nehru not to set up dissensions in the Congress.

"The curse of untouchability is alienating the intelligentsia among the Harijans from the Hindu religion. I do hope and pray that this will be realised by the leaders of the Hindu community before it is too late. It is true that the Harijans will really gain nothing worth gaining by abandoning Hinduism and will probably lose much by isolating themselves permanently from the Hindu community. Both Harijans and the general body of the Hindus stand to lose much by a wrong step. It is true that the oppressor has no right to ask for patience on the part of the oppressed. Yet I plead for patience in view of the undoubted awakening of the Hindu community that is coming, if it has not already come.

"I would take this opportunity of congratulating the Harijan Sevak Sangha for their splendid record of work and I appeal to you to support them in every way.

"Yet another distressing problem to be tackled to-day is the condition of the agricultural population. The prosperity of the State depends upon the well-being of the ryots, for it is they that contribute the largest portion to the revenues of this province. With the fall in prices agriculture fell and with it fell trade. Bad seasons, bad harvests, the import of foreign rice, the ruinous land revenue policy of an unsympathetic Government, the indebtedness of ryots, the lack of proper irrigation facilities, prohibitive rates in railway freight, lack of proper credit facilities, and lack of proper communications have added to the distress of the ryots. Much worse are the conditions of the zamindari ryots to whom some kind of relief is sought to be brought through the Estate's Land Act Amending Bill of Mr. Patnaik. I hope it will receive the support of all those who sympathise with the cause of Zamin ryots. The first task of Swaraj Government will be to effect agrarian reforms.

"The policy of Justice Ministers in respect of District Boards and Municipality, particularly the bifurcation of Boards and misuse of nomination powers in this connection has created universal indignation as admitted even by the Anglo-Indian journal the "Madras Mail."

"The root cause of this and other evils is the unjustifiable extension of the life time of the legislature and a ministry on whom the electorate has passed the clearest voice of no-confidence on all possible occasions. It is scandalous that such a time-expired and openly-denounced ministry should have the power to nominate the members to bifurcated boards and that new legislation such as the Tobacco Bill should be sought to be passed through the present unrepresentative Council ignoring widespread protests.

"Let me also refer to another crying injustice viz., the Criminal Tribes Act, under which whole communities are presumed to be guilty and made to undergo indignities without proof of guilt. The act is a shame to the Indian Statute Book.

"Capture of Legislatures and Boards apart, the strength of the Congress depends on the amount of work we do in villages by way of propaganda as well as constructive work. If only we learn to have faith in ourselves, to understand one another in a good spirit, place the country's interests above personal considerations and cultivate the spirit of mutual toleration. I am sure it is not very difficult to see our goal within a measurable distance of time.

Resolutions—2nd. Day—26th. January 1936

Goal of Purna Swaraj

The following resolutions were passed at the open session of the Conference to-day. The resolution defining the goal of the Congress as Purna Swaraj to be attained by non-violent means was adopted unanimously.

The following are some of the important solutions which were passed at the Subjects Committee and passed in the open Conference.

"This Conference meeting on the Independence Day reiterates the determination of the people of this province as of the rest of India that their struggle shall not cease until the attainment of Purna Swaraj and that they are resolved on adopting every means decided upon from time to time by the Indian National Congress to that end in accordance with the creed of non-violence and prays that God may give the people of Tamil Nad the requisite determination and spirit of sacrifice to respond to the call of national self-respect."

"This Conference offers its grateful thanks to the people for showing their confidence in the Congress in all the elections recently held and tenders its congratulations to all Congress workers and sympathisers in the province for their zealous and patriotic service in this connection, which has been crowned with such marked success in spite of all odds and appeals to the voters to continue their support to Congress on every occasion and make it an irresistible power.

Propagation of Khaddar

The resolution regarding propagation of khaddar in spite of the high cost was subjected to severe criticism in which Mr. *C. Rajagopalachariar* took an active part. As many as ten delegates spoke on the subject, majority of them holding the view that the popularity and sale of khaddar would be seriously affected if the price was increased consequent on increased wages to spinners. They held that there had already been a setback in sales as a sequel to the Congress not insisting on its members to wear Khaddar and having given them an alternative in the use of Swadeshi mill-made cloths.

Mr. *Gopalkrishnan*, on behalf of the Socialist group, suggested retrenchment by putting an end to the Khaddar depots in various parts of the province on which they were incurring a good lot of expenditure running to several hundreds. He said Congress had been doing vigorous Khadi propaganda for the past thirteen years educating the people particularly on the economic aspect of the question and if the Khaddar movement had not come to stay, the Congress, he said, would do well to bid goodbye to the same and take up some other work which would pay better and relieve the starving millions in the country. He wanted the sale of Khaddar to be given to independent merchants instead of stocking them and selling them through depots kept up at enormous cost.

Mr. *Rajagopalachariar*, meeting the criticisms, made a fairly long speech in Tamil. The move to increase the wages of the spinners, he said, came last year when Mahatma Gandhi found that the wages paid to them were hardly sufficient to meet their bare cost of sustenance. The fundamental object underlying the Khaddar movement was to provide food for the foodless or half-fed, whose number in the country ran into millions. It ought to be the function of a civilised Government to provide means of occupation for the unemployed or provide funds to give them doles. Since the Government was not doing it, the Congress had taken up the duty and the Khaddar Movement was principally intended to solve to some extent the problem of finding food for the actually starving people.

He appealed to the delegates to view this matter in that aspect more than anything else and create a greater demand for khaddar by intensive propaganda in the country. The resolution was split into two parts, one asking for support to khadi movement and the other regarding wages to spinners. The latter raised a controversy and ultimately it was withdrawn by the permission of the house. The first part was put to vote and carried.

Harijan Uplift

The other resolutions were :—

"This Conference appeals to the people to show greater vigour and earnestness in carrying out the programme of removal of the religious and social disabilities of the Harijans in the Hindu community which anyone with a sense of justice or fairplay cannot tolerate any longer.

Support to Khaddar and Village Industries

"The Conference appeals to the people to give increased support to khaddar and all other village industries which are the sure instruments of rural reconstruction and put hope and life in the people of this country.

Extension of Council's Life

Regarding extension of the life of the Council, the resolution that was passed read :—

"The Conference records its emphatic condemnation of the extension of the lifetime of the Madras Legislative Council and of the ministry, on the plea that a fresh election under the new constitution may take place at some unknown date in future. That the electorate will be enlarged under the new constitution is no justification whatsoever for continuing the Council, and the Conference considers that the authority of the beauracracy is preferable to the continuance of wholly discredited Ministers, whose only concern will be how to circumvent the popular vote. The plea of the Chief Minister that he did not desire and was never even consulted about the extension, if true, exposes unfitness for the office he holds, as it was his plain duty to insist on being consulted and to advise a dissolution, which Government could not have overruled."

OTHER RESOLUTIONS

The Conference strongly condemned the land revenue policy of the Government and urged early codification of the law governing land revenue. The Conference further condemned the attitude of the Government in the matter of remission of kist and called upon the ryots to agitate for necessary reforms.

The Conference recommended to the Tamil Nad Congress Committee the suggestion to organise walking tours of Congress propagandists in villages in every district for carrying the Congress message and to fulfil the constructive programme.

The Conference further requested all Congress leaders to travel in third class while on Congress propaganda tour at Congress expense.

"This Conference expresses its sincere sympathy to Indians overseas in their present state and appeals to Congress members in the Assembly to take steps to remedy their grievances."

"This Conference strongly condemns the Tobacco Bill introduced by the Government in the Madras Legislative Council."

CONGRESS AND WHITE PAPER

Put from the Chair and carried unanimously, the Conference congratulated the Congress members of the Legislative Assembly on their work in the last two sessions but strongly condemned the attitude of the Government of India and of the Viceroy in having disregarded the verdict of the Assembly duly constituted, on many occasions.

Mr. *Ramamurthi* brought an amendment to be added as para three of the resolution and the same was seconded by Mr. Karuppiah. The amendment was almost on the same line as the resolution passed recently at the All-India Socialists' Conference at Meerut. The mover of the amendment criticised the action of the Congress representatives of the Assembly in not rejecting the White Paper in toto and for having formed a coalition with the Jinnah party and supported his resolution. He also said that the Congress Party had not taken any steps for the convening of a Constituent Assembly and that these were breaches of election pledges by Congressmen. The President observed that a similar amendment was moved at Jubbulpore before the All-India Congress Committee and it was defeated. He would, therefore, place the amendment for consideration of the House.

Mr. *Muthuranga Mudaliar*, M. L. A., contended that there was no breach of election pledges, that the mover had brought two charges against the Assembly Congressmen, that they did not reject the White Paper in toto and that they did not make any attempt for convening of the Constituent Assembly. Regarding the first charge he would say that the Congress Party brought forward a resolution for the rejection of the White Paper. There were communal differences in the Assembly also, but Mussalmans and Europeans voted against it. Mr. Aney's resolution did not come up before the Assembly at all. Mr. Jinnah's resolution was the only one, which came up before the Assembly and Government, they knew, would not support it. So Congressmen had to support the only resolution condemning the White Paper. The speaker could not see anything wrong in it, and would leave the matter to the judgment of the house.

As regards the second charge, the formation of a Constituent Assembly was not a day's task and was not an easy one. They were working in that direction. Besides, some support was necessary from Government also. When the Congress found that they could expect some help from Government, they would move in that direction. Failing that, they would try to unite and consolidate the other parties in their favour. For these reasons he would say there was no meaning in Mr. Ramamurthi saying that there was a breach of election pledges on the part of the Congress representatives in the Assembly.

The amendment was put to vote and defeated by an overwhelming majority and the original resolution was carried unanimously.

ELECTORAL ROLLS

The next resolution read :—

"This Conference draws the attention of all Congress workers in the Province to the importance of having electoral rolls under the Reforms Constitution prepared perfectly, and appeals to them to carefully watch the preparation by Government and to take steps to remove imperfections wherever they may occur". This was carried unanimously.

The Conference was of opinion that Congress should participate in labour movements for redress of grievances and that labourers should join the Congress and work for it and their uplift.

The following resolution regarding conditions for the adoption of Congress candidates evoked considerable discussion :

"The Conference, while welcoming into Congress organisation all those who have so far stood aloof, is of opinion that before new entrants may be set up as Congress candidates, their names should have been in Congress register for a period of at least six months and they should surrender any titles they may have received from Government. It calls upon Tamil Nad Congress Committee to make rules to this effect."

The Andhra Provincial Conference

15th. Session—Cocanada—9th. & 10th. February 1936

The Fifteenth Andhra Provincial Conference assembled at Cocanada on the **9th. February 1936** in the Conference Pandal under the presidentship of Mr. *C. Ramalinga Reddy*. A large number of delegates from all over the province, including ladies, attended. The Conference began with recitation of the Vedic hymns by pandits and prayer by lady volunteers.

Welcome Address

Dr. *Subrahmanyam*, Chairman of the Reception Committee, welcoming the President and delegates, commended the triple programme of boycott of councils, preparing the country for direct action and carrying on village reconstruction work.

Mr. *T. Prakasam*, declaring the Conference open, advocated council-entry and acceptance of office, as there was no suitable atmosphere in the country for direct action.

Presidential Address

The President, *Mr. C. R. Reddy* then delivered his address in Telugu extempore, which lasted an hour. The following is the English rendering of his speech :—

Irrespective of party, the country shares with the Empire and the world the grief felt for the death of the King-Emperor. The world's fever which started in 1914 has not yet quite subsided and, if anything, additional ailments have cropped up. It is therefore a universal misfortune that so good a physician as George V is not available to continue his healing touch.

Great is our concern at the continued ill-health of Mahatma Gandhi. He also is a personality of universal reach. His nationalism is an inference from his humanity and the gospel for human uplift which he has been preaching and practising. May the might of our universal good wishes help to restore him speedily to full health and strength.

So Babu Rajendra Prasad is laying down the Presidentship of the Congress soon. His reign over us has been a year of noble service and universal benevolence. It was a most auspicious hour of my life when he stopped with me as my guest in Chittoor. I confess I have become a slave to his personality. So sweet, so charming, so strenuous and soulful it is ! It is a pity that the Government of India should have attacked him in the way they have done in their annual publication. The attack is unfair and ill-conditioned and, I am sure, will be resented by Europeans as well as Indians. The Government are furious at his success and the idea of parallel Government by the Congress. If he has failed, they would have praised. Failures are the pets of Imperialism.

I congratulate Pandit Jawharlal Nehru on his election as President of the Congress. I ardently desire to extend to him all co-operation possible.

My present address should be read as a continuation of my Tuticorin speech. No doubt, as Lord Morley said, if a truth is worth stating it is worth repeating, but I would rather avoid repetitions, at any rate by myself, as I don't think that my truths are quite so precious as all that, and pass on to fresh woods and pastures new.

What is the Congress situation? Its present characteristics are as follows:—(a) Indefinite suspension of Civil Disobedience; and (b) capture of all statutory bodies and using them as far as possible as leverage for Indian Nationalism.

Civil Disobedience or any policy of a revolutionary nature, whether violent or non-violent, is not dependent on numbers but on equality, discipline, valour and organisation of the troops and their capacity to strike at the right moment and perseverance. Council-entry, on the other hand, is much more a function of numbers and therefore there is bound to be a deterioration of equality. Elections sometimes attract holiday patriots who won't be available on working days. This shows that the general level of character in the country is still below nationalistic par. Council politics not infrequently necessitate working with other groups and making necessary readjustments in our policies and methods. Allowance must be made for these contingencies and a less puritan spirit cultivated which, however, should not degenerate into latitudinarianism. My views on the relationship between Council-entry and lifting of the ban on office are well-known. If Council-entry, then no ban; if ban, then no Council-entry.

The new Constitution should be replaced by another in substantial conformity with the doctrine of self-determination proclaimed as one of the aims of the allies in the Great War. Hoare-archy is worse than dyarchy and indisputably so in the Centre. It intensifies the divisions amongst our people; is based on distrust; denies adequate political liberty and imposes economic fetters which render promotion of mass material prosperity impossible. Our parties also condemn it strongly. The Liberals are one with us in wanting this Constitution scrapped. The Justice Party also condemns the Central arrangements and would like to see them changed. The paradox of Indian politics are one in substance, parties are different. The reasons for this are:—(a) Lack of intense sincerity in the views publicly held and the maladjustment of profession and character; (b) Differences in the methods to be employed; for example, other parties have said that on account of Civil Disobedience they would not join the Congress: but now that Civil Disobedience has been given up for the present, they did not seem to be in a hurry to come in; (c) Scramble for positions and subordinating the country's interests for personal. In our public ethics we are nearer the Chinese than the Japanese.

An analysis will show Council-entry involves functioning at three different levels.

(a) Central or All-India: This is the field of national rights. Here we would like to see all our countrymen fight shoulder to shoulder together as one body.

(b) Provincial: It cannot be denied that some real power is given to the people, though the Constitution by its peculiar provisions respecting the composition of the local Councils, Upper Chambers, Communal electorates, interest electorates, etc., has not given us a democracy. Straight functioning seems difficult. But still we can make our policies prevail in substance. Land Revenue, Estates Land Act, spread of education, temperance, Swadeshi, etc., may all be dealt with in sufficiently radical fashion. Questions of finance and taxation will arise: also additions to the income of the Province as by State-enterprises, like compulsory insurance of officials, etc. A large majority functioning on a definite and fairly extensive programme may do much to alleviate the lot of the masses.

(c) Local: In the local bodies much may be done to promote Hindi, elementary education, Swadeshi, etc.

I would like to see a Central Stores especially for supplying on indent articles needed by local bodies. In this way we can impose and improve Swadeshi on a large scale. Rural reorganisation and rural finance should not be neglected. In this connection, I would emphasise the need for reserving a definite percentage of the yearly revenue collections from each village to the use of that village itself, so that each village may have a development fund which will grow automatically from year to year.

Though thus there are three levels, all should be nationalistic in tone and function under the Congress. The constructive programme which is more a prosperity programme than politics should be a common ground of all parties. It is a pity that Government scents politics in this field also and has insinuated in its attack on Babu Rajendra Prasad that the Congress has given a standing invitation to earthquakes in order to rehabilitate itself by consequential social service. Of course, it is now clear that after Quetta even earthquakes won't give us a chance of serving our people. I sincerely trust that Government will not continue this rigid policy of prophylactic measures to prevent the spread of Congressism amongst our countrymen.

The elections generally involve contests, though in a subject country sufficiently patriotic, they are neither necessary nor desirable ; however, these are and will be contested. The Congress contests as a national organisation, the rest either as local parties or vain-glorious individuals whose one ambition is to be the cocks on their own dunghills and to show how in their particular corners they are wonderfully supreme and invincible. In England, though there are parties, administrative integrity is never allowed to be vitiated. If administrative power is misused, the followers themselves will not tolerate it. Administrative honesty and integrity and patriotism are the common ground of all the parties in England. Their politics are clean and do not provoke the South American spirit of Civil War An enlightened and large-minded leader of the Justice Party once remarked to me that because England was free, therefore she was honourable. True, as far as it goes, but then it is not equally true to say the English race is honourable and therefore England is free ? In any case as freedom is a root of racial integrity, I hope all parties will work to achieve it.

A new reign in English History has commenced. The international situation is not without possible portents. Germany, heavily armed ; Russia a standing menace to Capitalism ; the Far East in turmoil with Japan functioning in China as England had done in India. The Italo-Abyssinian War and United Egyptian nationalism ; England cannot afford to alienate India and if India can speak with one voice British Imperialism will drop its pretended deafness.

The Rt. Hon. V. S. Srinivasa Sastri's call for unity is conceived in noble spirit to which we all respond. But the actual methods he suggests are likely to create more difficulties than they selve. What is the good of asking the Congress to change its creed ? And its methods by which it has gained the popularity it now enjoys ? Babu Rajendra Prasad's solution is better. He says fusion on these lines being impossible, the Liberal Party should co-operate i. e., on specific issues. I would like to make a remark or two.

Trying to co-operate on this or that isolated issue, as it arises, will reduce our Councils and Assemblies to shandies with their daily bargains. I would prefer a coalition on a large enough programme in which the main part of the Congress policy should be embodied. This would lead to a general co-operation not dependent on each day's temperature and lead to more intimate understanding and coalescence. In connection with the Karaikudi Conference much was published for and against coalitions. It goes without saying that fusion is better than coalition, provided of course it is the other parties that fuse with the Congress and are absorbed into the premier nationalistic organisation. Though logic favours fusion, historical antecedents may hinder its immediate adoption. And history is a karma which can only be liquidated gradually. Pre-election coalitions are obviously better than post-election coalitions, because they avoid expense and bitterness of contest. And furthermore they render the adoption of a comprehensive and radical programme easier. If, after the general election, when you are known to be in a minority or in a shaky position, you try to effect coalition, it will not be satisfactory. Coalitional comradeship in a general election would itself be a cementing influence. If hands are joined to-day, hearts may join to-morrow, which is the principle of orthodox Hindu marriages.

From an unexpected quarter there has been a response to the appeal I made recently in my Gokhale Hall speech for Party Federation on the basis of the primacy of the Congress and the Karachi programme. I allude to the speech of the Kumararaja of Venkatagiri who, speaking on behalf of his party, declared readiness to co-operate with other parties and alluded appreciatively to what I had said on the subject.

Recent developments in Egypt convey some valuable lessons. The constitution of Zaghlul Pasha, the leader of the Wafd or the Egyptian Congress Party, was abrogated by the King five years ago who imposed a new and restrictive constitution by Royal Decree and inaugurated an era of repression under Mahmud Pasha, Sidqui Pasha and others. The Wafd was not merely hounded out of office but was persecuted. And yet though it did not occupy ministerial positions, because it stood firm and the people unitedly stood by it, the King found that he could not carry on for ever, international dealings having become impossible because his Ministers were regarded as unpopular and unfit to speak in the name of the country. A year and a half ago, the King felt bound to dismiss his anti-Wafd ministers and install a neutral ministry under Nessim Pasha, the Wafd leader. This illustrates that offices are not essential to influence and a power for national good—a lesson which, I trust, all Indian parties will learn. When the Italo-Abyssinian War broke out, the Egyptian leaders were wise enough and patriotic enough to form a united front. And presecutors of Wafd are now its worshippers. Instead of losing caste thereby, they have gained honour and popularity. The essential terms of this united front appear to be the following: that a neutral Government be installed to carry on the routine until the general elections are over. Incidentally, it is to see that the election game is not played with loaded dice by any party. The delegation empowered to negotiate a treaty with England should be headed by Nahas Pasha, the Wakf leader.

Our Round Table Conference failed because it had no head and all did not have the same heart. A further lesson of pith and moment derivable from the Egyptian Constitution is this that the Wafd achieved this result without recourse to civil disobedience or other measures of passive resistance.

Council-entry has undoubtedly its uses, but its effectiveness depends on the masses' strength behind the representatives. The power of an Ambassador is proportional to the force of the country he represents. Similarly, with the Councillors. If the people are not behind a parliament, the parliament cannot last. The Czar was able to dissolve the Duma again and again until his autocracy came crushing to the earth during the war. Satyagraha is the moral, spiritual root of what poor India has achieved so far, and what honour she commands in the world at large. Patriotic spirit and patriotic service, contempt for all that is low and currupt even when it occupies positions of secular power and influence, devotion to duty, sympathy with the masses—these are the real life of a people and not the Boards and Councils. Institutions are the tools and the organs, life and soul are greater than institutions and cover a large sphere. The Gandhian Yuga is perhaps the brightest period in our history since the fur-flung glory of Asoka. Mahatmaji has re-discovered to us the lost world of woman-power in India, lost since the Vedic and Mahabharata times. Civil Disobedience is the application of Satyagraha in one particular manner or direction and is not the whole of Satyagraha. For Satyagraha is a spirit that must pervade all our activities. People may be unfit for one reason or another, to break laws, to court jail and carry on Civil Disobedience. But they should not therefore be regarded as unfit for other and minor functions in the great army of Nationalism. But honour first and foremost always to the soldiers and more especially Sri Gummididala Durgabai, Sri Vedantam Kamaladevi and other sisters of their type and quality. Nor should I forget Sri Vemuganti Papayamma, a resolute worker in the constructive field. Just as peace has its victories no less than war, so the constructive work has its heroism no less than Civil Disobedience. If we, Councilwallas, and others of our type shine at all to-day, it is by the reflected light of the heroes and heroines of Satyagraha.

We cannot rest content until Swaraj is achieved and by Swaraj, I mean the substance of Independence as Mahatmaji defined it in his imperative manner. We do not want the shadow of national status, such as membership of the League of Nations, by people selected by the Governments, or constitutions, drafted after consultation with people possessing no direct and visible authority from the franchise of the people. We have enough of ceremonial nationalism. Even the child that seemed satisfied with its toys yesterday, to-day feels too grown up to be satisfied with tinsel and tamasha. It is the smaller of the two truths to say that our strength will depend on our policies and ideals. It is the bigger of the two truths to say that our policies should rest on our strength. So let us look after our strength, our inner unity, our courage and character, and the policies will look after themselves. Be strong and united, the rest will follow.

Resolutions

After the presidential speech the following resolutions were passed. A resolution expressing sorrow over the deaths of Mr. Saklatwala and others moved from the chair, was carried.

Another resolution reaffirming that "the goal of India is the attainment of Purna Swaraj, i.e., complete independence," was passed.

Mr. *T. Prakasam* moved the following resolution on acceptance of office and Mr. *A. Kaleswar* Rao seconded it :

"This conference is of opinion that while rejecting the new constitution, the ban on acceptance of office should be lifted by the Lucknow Congress and definite instructions should be issued to Congress organisations to capture legislatures and

Cabinets and carry out the Congress programme and policy that would render the safeguards, reservations and communal barriers inoperative and ineffective. Congress ministries should also give effect to the Fundamental Rights and economic programme passed at the Karachi Congress and should be subject to the control of the All-India Congress Committee.

This Conference is further of opinion that freedom should be allowed to provinces if the above decision cannot be applied to all provinces."

Dr. Pattabhi Seetharamayya, Mr. M. Annapurnayya and others opposed the resolution, which was carried by 93 votes to 35. The Conference then adjourned.

Resolutions—Second Day—10th. February 1936

The following are the more important among the resolutions passed to-day :—

"This Conference recommends to the Lucknow Congress that it should definitely lay down that the Congress party should not enter into any coalition with any other party or parties either during the elections for the legislatures or in the formation of ministries."

A resolution inviting the attention of the Assembly members to the immediate necessity for modifying prison rules on the broad lines indicated in the demands of Mr. Jogesh Chandra Chatterjee (Kakori Conspiracy Case prisoner now on hunger-strike) to whom the conference extended its full sympathy in his fast, was passed. The resolution urged the abolition of the classification of political prisoners and the grant of amenities due to them as citizens and soldiers that struggled for their country's freedom. By another resolution the conference resolved to carry on constitutional agitation against the classification of political prisoners into A, B and C classes and to agitate for more amenities to political prisoners.

The Conference recommended to the All-India Congress Committee to advise Provincial and District Congress Committees to form separate committees within them for investigating into the grievances of the peasants and workers and taking steps to get them redressed.

The Conference expressed its sympathy with the famine stricken people of Nellore and Ganjam districts and appealed to the people to help in all ways to alleviate their misery.

The Conference condemned the continued detention of the Bengal detenues and State prisoners without trial and demanded their immediate release. The conference protested against the detention of some Sitaramaraju Fituri prisoners after they had served their term of sentence and demanded their immediate release.

The Conference congratulated Dr. B. Pattabhisitaramayya on his writing and presenting the history of the Indian National Congress at the time of the Congress Golden Jubilee.

The Conference condemned the Government's action in not releasing all political prisoners even after civil disobedience had been suspended.

The Conference condemned the action of the Government in prohibiting wholesale the right to prepare salt on the ground that at a few places some breaches were committed by some poor people and opined that this action of the Government was against the spirit and letter of the Gandhi-Irwin Pact and requested the Congress workers and Congress members of the Assembly to carry on agitation to get the right restored.

The Conference demanded the formation of a separate province for the Andhra districts in the Madras Presidency.

The Conference appealed to the people to give encouragement to cottage industries in general and khaddar in particular.

The Conference exhorted the people and District Congress Committees to root out the untouchability and to work for the economic and educational uplift of Harijans.

The Conference recommended to the All-India Congress Committee to advise all Provincial and District Committees to organise agricultural exhibitions in provincial and district conferences with a view to making such conferences more useful to the ryots and to enlightening them on the modern agricultural methods.

Another important resolution recommending the ensuing Lucknow Congress to change the Congress aim, constitution and programme to provide for the establishment of Sampurna Swaraj through social and economic reconstruction based on scientific Socialism, was moved by Mr. *T. Viswanadham* and supported by Messrs. Gopalareddi, B. Rangasayi and N. Satyanarayana and carried by overwhelming majority, only two or three voting against.

The Punjab Political Conference

Gujranwala—30th May 1936

The session of the Punjab Political Conference was held at Gujranwala on the **30th. May 1936** under the presidency of *Pandit Jawharlal Nehru*. In the course of his address Pandit Nehru said that they had assembled there to discuss not the old issues, but the new problems of poverty and starvation of millions of their countrymen.

The day had come, he added, when they should have to learn to think and ponder over the real issues, particularly in the case of the Punjab where the people in spite of enthusiasm were apt easily to be carried away by minor issues.

Turning to the Communal Award, Pandit Jawharlal Nehru said that he was aware of the agitation against the attitude of the Congress with regard to the Award which had been started by the Hindu Sabha and the Congress Nationalist Party. He emphasised that anyone who believed in the independence of the country could never accept the Communal Award. "I am for independence and so is the Congress, and neither I nor the Congress accept the Award."

Pandit Jawaharlal reiterated his faith in Socialism and said that it was the only remedy for all ills. He declared that they would not thrust it on the Congress, but they wanted to wait.

The Pandit regretted that on account of his presence the Conference had assumed the characteristics of a mela and instead of a conference where vital problems were to have been discussed, it had become a public meeting. They could not remain satisfied with hearing to loud speakers. They had to think and ponder over the vital issues before the country. The real strength of the Congress was not a few top leaders but the thousands who had suffered for the Congress.

Referring to the communal award he expressed surprise that even some of their own friends in the Punjab had their grievances against the attitude of the Congress on the award and desired a change in that. He declined to do anything without the Congress organisation as such agreeing to do so, but personally he was himself opposed to any change in the present attitude of the Congress towards the award, and for the sake of a few more seats for the Congress would receive hearty support even without a change.

He, however, remarked that if he had some hand in drafting the Congress resolution on the communal award, he might have worded it differently.

Referring to the manifesto of certain Bombay businessmen, he said that these people in Bombay were closely connected with all that was British and he declared that he would never welcome the co-operation of such men and would rather like them to remain on "the laps of their old 'mai baps' (meaning the British) lest they come to us and desert us in the hour of need."

Concluding, the Congress President stated that his repeated incarceration had prevented him from being in their midst often, but whether he came or not he exhorted them to do their duty and support the Congress.

Resolutions

After Pandit Jawharlal's address the Conference adopted fifteen resolutions. The conference reiterated that the new constitution was completely unacceptable to India, appealed to the people to support the Congress, hoping that the Punjab would complete the enrolment of 62,000 members, recommended the formation of a Provincial Volunteer Corps and appointed a sub-committee to devise ways and means to establish a closer contact with the working classes.

Among other resolutions one reiterated the faith of the conference in joint electorates and appealed to the people to create an atmosphere of mutual goodwill and confidence for its adoption and another advised the people not to be a party to any world war.

The U. P. Political Conference

28th Session—Unao—7th. & 8th. June 1936

The U. P. Political Conference held its 28th session at Unao on the **7th. June 1936** in the presence of a large gathering, a special feature being the attendance of peasants in large numbers. Mr. Jawaharlal Nehru and other U. P. leaders were present. Mr. *Rafi Ahmad Kidwai* in the course of his presidential address said :—

Friends, the Congress was started with very limited aims to secure representation of Indians in the superior judicial and executive services of the Government and in the Legislative Councils. As these questions affected only educated classes they began taking interest in Congress meetings in ever increasing numbers. Later on, when Congress started preaching Swadeshism and demanded protection of Indian industries, our industrialists also began to show interest in and express their sympathies with the Congress movement. But the motive behind all those demands was to obtain certain 'concessions' for Indians at the expense of Englishmen ; there was no question of any split amongst Congress, and every Indian considered it his patriotic duty to support these demands, and as the issues raised and discussed did not affect them in the least, they kept themselves aloof from the Congress activities, nor was any attempt made to enlist their sympathy. But with the widening of the Congress aims and with the advent of the Mahatma, the Congress constitution underwent a revolutionary change and the sympathy of the masses was enlisted in ever increasing measure with the Congress activities.

It will not be possible to retain their sympathy with, or to harness the strength of their number to the fight for the independence of the country unless Swarajya is defined in terms of mass interest ; and the very attempt of so defining Swarajya is resented by certain classes, for it adversely affects their vested interest. These friends should realise that the times have changed and they should adjust themselves to the changed circumstances. But unless the relations of exploiters and the exploited are readjusted on equitable basis, class conflict is bound to grow and the Congress representing the masses, as it claims to do, shall have to protect mass interest. Thus to-day is facing two problems, (1) external problem, *i. e.* struggle for the Independence of the country and (2) internal problem *i. e.* readjustment of relations between the exploiters and the exploited on equitable basis.

All Congressmen stand for complete independence. They are pledged not to accept any constitution, which does not give us complete control over both our external and internal affairs. We will not accept a constitution which though guaranteeing complete freedom both in external and internal matters, places us, even though only technically, under the subordination of the British. Our self-respect will not tolerate such an agreement. There can therefore be no question of our working the constitution to be introduced under the new Government of India Act. There can be no question of our examining its provisions. It is not, even in semblance, what we want. If anything, it is an attempt to govern the country through vested interests. I am sorry that the resolution of the Lucknow Congress is not what it should, in the circumstances, have been. It has left the office acceptance question to future decision.

Both at the Bombay and Lucknow sessions of the Congress, it has been declared that the constitution is unacceptable to us and we reject it. Now you cannot reject a constitution by working it. You can do so, either by keeping yourself aloof as we did in 1920-21 when the Mont-Ford Reforms were introduced or by capturing the legislatures and creating deadlocks and thus rendering its working impossible. These are the only two ways of rejecting the constitution. You cannot at one and the same time reject the constitution and also work it. Congressmen can accept offices only when they are in majority, and if they are in a majority they can wreck the constitution, there is no occasion of our applying for appointment as Ministers.

Congress can accept offices not to wreck, but to work the constitution. And when they are working the constitution for doing as much good to the people, as is in the circumstances possible, they will have to accept statutory limitations of the Government of India Act, otherwise they will not be allowed to function long as Ministers.

We are a subject race, striving for the liberation of our motherland. We can carry on this fight only so long as we are in opposition. Once we are snared into offices and ministries, we cease to be effective in our struggle. If Congress leaders are occupying ministerial chairs, it becomes the duty of every Congressman to defend their action in public. We become the Government party and it will not be open to us to criticise the Government or to strive for its destruction. In my opinion, acceptance of offices by Congress leaders; will change the character of our national organization.

Our internal problem in the U. P. is mainly agrarian. Our whole structure of economy is based on agricultural produce. Under the existing system most of what a peasant produces is taken away from him in payment of rent, etc., and unless revolutionary changes are introduced in the system the condition of the peasants will deteriorate.

The system prevailing in the province when the Britishers occupied it was quite different from that in force to-day. At that time the tiller of the soil was not required to pay any rent for the land leased out to him. But instead he was required to share his produce in fixed proportion (generally half) with the zamindar. Thus unless there had been a complete failure of crops, he would be left a half of his produce to maintain his family till the next crop season, and if there had been a complete failure of crops, he would not have to pay anything to the zamindar or the agent of the State. But to-day the case is quite different. A peasant has to pay a fixed rent for his holding. He will have to pay it irrespective of the price his produce will fetch, or even if there has been a total failure of crops. So long as the prices of agricultural produce maintained upwards tendency this system apparently worked well, but the prevalent economic depression has demonstrated its failure. The sale of the agricultural produce hardly fetches enough money to pay the rent. If he pays the rent, he does not save anything to maintain himself and his family till the next crops. If he does not pay the rent, he is ejected from his tenancy. In my opinion the old system must be reintroduced.

Friends, in dealing with agrarian problems, I have not said anything about the abolition or retention of the zemindari system for in my opinion it does not concern the agrarian problem. How does it affect the *kisan* whether he pays the rent to the zamindar or to some agent of the Government. It is the rent itself that affects him. But if he is not interested in the question as a rent-payer, surely the abolition of the zamindari affects him as it affects the mill-labourer, engine-driver or goldsmith *i. e.* as a member of the State. In every country there has grown up a school of politicians and economists who demand the abolition of private property and nationalisation of key-industries. The world opinion is veering round towards Socialism. In the Congress itself a party has been formed with the object of explaining socialism to the country and advocating nationalisation of land and other key-industries.

Friends, I don't think you expect me to say anything on the controversy that is going on in the country as to whether Congress should adopt socialist programme. I am the least competent to deal with it. I have never been a student of politics or sociology. I have not read Marx or Lenin, nor Trotsky, nor anything of them. I do not know what Marx has written about any particular issue, nor do I know what is meant by 'materialistic interpretation of history.' I have vague notions about capitalism, Fascism and Imperialism and Socialism, Syndicalism and Communism. I had joined the Congress to fight for the liberation of our Mother-land and am of opinion that so long as that is not achieved, we should avoid split amongst those who can otherwise combine to strive and struggle for the independence of Hindustan. But in spite of the desire to avoid split in our ranks when I am in a village and am brought face to face with the victims of the greed of profit, all zest for Swaraj vanishes. Unity in our ranks is essential, but still more essential is an assurance to the starved and naked producer of our wealth, the *kisan*, that under Swarajya we will not tolerate a system which deprives the worker and the producer of all that his labour produces simply to enable idlers to live a luxurious life. In our anxiety to maintain a united front we must not forget the misery of the millions without whose active co-operation it will not be possible to win Swarajya.

I will here draw your attention to the two resolutions of the Congress passed at its Lucknow session. It has appointed a committee to make recommendations including proposals for such amendments in the constitution of the Congress as may be considered necessary to develop closer association between the masses and the Congress organisation. By another resolution it has asked the Working Committee to prepare, in consultation with the different provincial Congress Committees and such peasant organizations as it considers fit, an All-India Agrarian programme for being considered and placed before the All-India Congress Committee. I am sure actions on the lines of these resolutions will enable our workers and peasants to take a more lively interest in Congress activities, and the Congress will become more alive to the problems affecting them.

The President of the Congress had recently approached Liberals and other non-Congress leaders to join Civil Liberties Union to protect the civil liberties of Indians. Some of the Liberal leaders have in their replies betrayed a very narrow outlook. They think because the Congress is not willing to act according to their advice, the Government is justified in behaving as it pleases. It can arrest and detain anybody, without giving him or her any opportunity to prove his or her innocence, but Liberals will not even raise their usual voice of protest because that particular individual had not conducted his or her activities on the lines approved by the Liberal party.

Friends, the Congress has decided to set up candidates for election to Provincial Legislatures. These elections will be fought on the basis of definite political and economic programme. Our election manifesto shall make it clear that no constitution shall be acceptable to us unless it is drawn by a Constituent Assembly elected on adult suffrage. Such a constituent Assembly can be constituted only when revolutionary conditions have created an atmosphere of Independence. The election campaign shall give us an opportunity to carry the message of the Congress to millions of our villagers. Mushroom parties will emerge with pretentions of protecting class or communal interests. Voters should be warned against these parties and the hollowness of their pretentions should be exposed.

All sorts of rumour are afloat about the preparations of Government to defeat the Congress candidates at the polls. From Governor downward everyone in official hierarchy is busy with the election work. In delimiting constituencies special care has been taken to provide safe seats for some 'desirable' persons. Districts with large populations suspected to be under the influence of the Congress have been allotted lesser number of seats than the one with smaller population but supposed to be under control of some safe man. District and subordinate officers supposed to wield special influence in any particular district are being posted there.

Gentlemen, the official spokesmen in the local Legislative Council have denied the charge of official interference in the last local boards elections. Those of us who were in charge of the election work in the different districts know what value to attach to such denials. Enrolment of Congressmen as electors was refused on the ground of their conviction, although according to the provision in the District Board Act, they were not disqualified. The Act fixes a day after which the district magistrate could not order the entry or removal of any name from the electoral roll, but the names of Congressmen, whose nomination papers had already been accepted and who were busy in conducting their election campaign, were removed from these rolls ; and consequently their nomination became invalid. There was no time to nominate another. All this can not be denied, for official records can be produced in support of these allegations. In most of the districts zamindars were warned by district or subordinate magistrates not to support Congress candidates and to ensure compliance with this warning renewal of license of arms was postponed to a date after the elections. At polling stations Congress supporters found it difficult to get admission to the polling booth to record their votes. At places where Congress supporters had gathered in large numbers the polling officers so regulated the admission to the both that only equal number of both sides were admitted and the surplus Congress supporters had either to leave the place without recording their votes or had to go to opposite camp and enter the compound as their supporters. At some polling stations an attempt was made to influence the voters by terrorising the Congress supporters. It will take long to refer to all the incidents of which reports have been received in the provincial Congress Committee office.

The antics of the Minister for Local Self-Government were no less atrocious. We have read of the nomination of a woman, of the Minister's statement in the Council of her resignation, and of her subsequent denial of having sent any ; we also know how he abused his power of nomination by nominating his friends even against the statutory provisions. We know of cases where, to ensure the defeat of Congress candidates for the chairmanship, partisans and dependents of the rival candidates were nominated. Exposure of these tactics would have caused the retirement of any one from public life, but such considerations cannot affect the conduct of a man of his moral calibre.

Friends, before I close, I would like to sound a note of warning against the activities of a few of our friends who are to-day in the Congress not because they believe in its ideals or agree with its general policy, but they realize that it is the only organization which can influence the country. They have no faith in our capacity or strength to win complete freedom. They are always on the lookout for an opportunity to take the Congress back to pre-non-co-operation days. At Poona they succeeded in persuading Mahatma Gandhi to withdraw mass civil disobedience. At Ranchi they secured his blessings to their 'parliamentary' programme. They are really constitutionalists striving for a form of government in which the authority to administer the country on behalf of the British Government shall be vested not in the alien bureaucracy, but in the elected representatives of the country. They dare not think of a situation in which they would be devoid of British protection. These friends are alarmed at the advocacy of socialism by the President of the Congress and are showing signs of restlessness. They are seeking allies in the Liberals and industrialists. Mr. Satyamurthi has gone even further and has appealed to Englishmen to join the Congress and thus strengthen men of his school. This shows what sort of Independence he and his friends are working for. We should take account of their tendencies in all our calculations and estimates of our strength. They are a source of our weakness.

Resolutions—War Danger

After the presidential address the war danger resolution as passed by the subjects committee was adopted by the conference.

'This conference draws the special attention of the people of the province to the war danger resolution of the Indian National Congress held at Lucknow and to the fact that even during the last two months the international situation has progessively deteriorated and brought the world nearer to war. The victory of imperialism in Abyssinia demonstrating the collapse of the League of Nations' system of collective security and the triumph of naked and unabashed imperialistic might, the support by the British Government of German Fascism which openly stands for war and conquest, the continuity of repression of Japanese imperialism in the Far East and the ever-growing rivalries of imperialist Powers have made the danger of vast imperialist world war imminent and threatening. This conference therefore stresses the Congress warning and resolves that in the event of such imperialistic war India should be no party to it and should not help it in any way."

Speaking on the resolution, Mr. *Jawaharlal Nehru* said : One view was that Indians had their own problems, why should they discuss about any war which might break out in Europe ? Mr. Nehru pointed out that the view could have been true in old times. At present war in any country was really a world war as it affected all countries. Another view was that if war broke out in Europe India would not be a loser. Mr. Nehru was not certain of what might happen. India might be a gainer. It was quite possible that India might be a loser and not a gainer.

Suppression of Civil Liberty

The resolution reiterating maintainance of civil liberty, freedom of thought and speech, and calling upon the people to combat the wide-spread suppression of civil liberties in India and to strive to prevent the encroachments by the executive on the few liberties that still remained was passed. This resolution further sent greetings to thousands of sufferers from this suppression, praticularly, Mr. Subhas Bose.

Resolutions—Second Day—8th June 1936—New Constitution

Resuming to-day the conference passed a condolence resolution on the death of Mr. Tasadduq Ahmed Khan Sherwani, Mrs. Kamala Nehru, Dr. M. A. Ansari and others.

The resolution on the new constitution of the Government of India passed by the subjects committee said that, "whereas the constitutional scheme embodied in the Government of India Act of 1935 is sought to be hoisted on the country in the teeth of opposition of the nation, the conference reaffirms the Congress decision for rejection of the new constitution and resolves to adopt effective measures to resist and wreck it. The conference declares that no constitution that is not based of the independence of India as a sovereign nation and framed by a democratic assembly constituted on the principle of adult suffrage can be acceptable to the people of India and reiterates the Congress demand for a constituent assembly.

CONGRESS CANDIDATES

Another resolution passed welcomed the decision of the Lucknow Congress to set up candidates on behalf of the Congress for the forth-coming elections to the provincial legislatures and appealing to the people of these provinces including every class and community to accord the Congress candidates their active support, concentrating on the supreme objective of political independence of India irrespective of any divergence of views in matters pertaining to social reconstruction or readjustment of relations between the various classes and interests.

MASS CONTACT

A resolution on mass contact was passed by the Subjects committee in view of the decision of the Lucknow Congress to develop even closer association between the masses and the Congress organisation. The resolution calls upon all communities and Congressmen generally in the province to further this policy by working among the masses and taking part in their day to day struggles, by making primary committees of Congress vital bodies which should take an active part in the Congress and help in shaping the Congress policy and developing closer co-operation between the Congress and other organisations of peasants and workers. In the opinion of the conference an effective and desirable method of bringing about this closer co-operation would be to give representations in the Congress organisation to organised groups of peasants and workers subject to their acceptance of the main political position of the Congress and its general policy.

UNEMPLOYMENT

'The Government should do its duty towards the unemployed by providing food and clothing as is done in the advanced countries or should get out so that wiser men may come and solve the problem', said Mr. *Jawaharlal Nehru* supporting the resolution on unemployment.

The resolution condemned the Government for not doing its duty towards the unemployed class. Babu *Sampurnanand* said that the Sapru report on unemployment was worth throwing into the waste paper basket. Both he and Mr. Nehru opined that the Government as constituted at present was incapable of solving the problem. The principles of socialism could alone be a lasting solution for the great problem of widespread unemployment in the country.

THE NEW CONSTITUTION

The resolution on the new constitution of the Government of India Act as adopted by the subjects committee was passed.

The resolution declared that the new scheme was a subtle device designed to tighten the stranglehold of British imperialism and facilitate the political domination and economic exploitation of the people. The resolution reaffirmed the rejection of the new constitution and further reiterated the demand for a constituent assembly.

The resolution appealing to the people to accord support to the Congress candidates at the forthcoming elections as adopted by the subjects committee was also passed.

Pandit *Govind Ballabh Pant* speaking declared that the Congress stood for complete independence of India. It worked for the good of Indians. It never declared itself against zamindars but it wanted to improve the condition of the poor and unemployed. He appealed to the people to vote in favour of Congress candidates.

OTHER RESOLUTIONS

The Conference welcomed the resolution of the Lucknow Congress calling upon the Provincial Congress Committees to frame an agrarian programme. The resolution stressed that the programme recommended should not only deal with the immediate grievances of the peasantry but the basic causes which undermine the present land system and created the vast problem of agrarian poverty, indebtedness and unemployment.

The subjects committee resolution recommending to the Indian Congress to give representation in the Congress organization to organized groups of peasants and workers and Mr. Jawaharlal's resolution sending greetings of good wishes to Arabs in Palestine in the brave struggle they were carrying against British imperialism for complete independence were also passed. The Conference then dispersed.

The International Women's Conference

Opening Day—Calcutta—30th. January 1936

Many problems facing the women of India were dwelt upon by Her Highness the *Maharani of Baroda* in her presidential address at the joint Conference of the International Council of Women and National Council of Women in India which met at the Town Hall, Calcutta, on the **30th. January 1936.**

· The gathering might well be described as unique of its kind in India. Many conferences of women take place now-a-days in this country but seldom are they attended by so many talented women of international fame as were to be seen at to-day's Conference. Many of them had travelled thousands of miles at great personal sacrifice and inconvenience to give the benefit of their counsel to their Indian sister.

The gathering was also symbolic of the progress Indian women have made in recent years in self-reliance and in taking counsel together on problems which affected their kind without the help of men.

At the outset, the entire assembly stood with the president · to pay silent homage to the memory of His late Majesty King George V and as an expression of sympathy with Queen Mary and other members of the Royal family.

Welcome Address

Welcoming the delegates *Lady Ezra*, Chairwoman of the National Council of Women in India, said that Bengal felt proud that the first International Conference of Women to be held in India should assemble in this province. This was not pre-arranged. It had just happened in the ordinary course of things. Proceeding, Lady Ezra gave a brief history of the Indian National Council and said that they had all along kept in close touch with the work that was being done Overseas.

What they most needed in India, she said, was social, educational and civic service. They had begun later than countries in the West; they had a great deal to catch up with, handicapped as they were by the customs of the country. But looking back on the 10 years of their existence, Lady Ezra claimed as the Chairman of the National Council of Women in India that the Council had given a good account of itself and had justified the generous faith of the International Council in admitting it to membership from the very beginning.

Messages were received from *Her Excellency Lady Willingdon* and the Marchioness of Aberdeen. Lady Willingdon expressed great pleasure in welcoming the delegates representing so many countries and such widely different parts of the world. She had great faith in the beliefs for which the International Council of Women stood, namely, that women had contributions of very real value to make towards the solution of the social and economic problems which were perplexing the world. It seemed to her that suspicion and distrust, creating barriers between countries lay at the root of most of their troubles and that for this sympathy and mutual understanding were the only solvents. This sympathetic understanding was pre-eminently the quality of women and it was for them to diffuse that spirit throughout the world and make it and recognise it as the guiding principle of their action whether as individuals or as communities.

The *Marchioness of Aberdeen* in her message expressed regret at her inability to be present at the conference. She was deeply sensible, she said, of the very important character of this gathering at which subjects of special interest to the women of India and of the Pacific coast would be considered, subjects which at the same time had a bearing on the position of women all over the world. This was the first time when representatives from European. Australian and New Zeland National Councils would have heard those subjects discussed in Asia by those who knew the difference in conditions.

Greetings from the National Council of Women, Great-Britain, and National Council of women, Belgium, China and Australia, were conveyed personally by their respective delegates. Messages were also received from the Indian Councils of Burma and Madras and the All-India Women's Conference (conveyed by Mrs. S. C. Mukherjee).

Dame Elizabeth Cadbury in a brief address thanked the organizers of the Conference on behalf of the Overseas delegates. "Every moment since their arrival," she said, "had been full of interest and they had received the greatest kindness everywhere." From the perusal of the reports of the different councils they had realised what an immense account of social work the National Council of India was doing. When they travelled round the world like globe-trotters they only saw monuments, buildings and other places of interest but here they would come into personal contact with each other and come to know each other better.

Miss Tyan, delegate from China, said that while sitting in her place at the Conference the feeling that passed through her mind was that a "League of hearts" was of much greater importance than a League of Nations. It was only through a league of hearts that the peace of the world would come.

Among the delegates at the Conference were Dame Elizabeth Cadbury. Lady Pentland. Hon. Margaret Sinclare. Mrs. Greaves. Miss Eluinid Lewis. Mrs. Montgomery (Great Britain). Miss Lousie Thompson (Ireland). Mlle de Buchere (Belgium). Princess Cantacuzane (Romania). Miss Zellweger. Miss Sartorious and Dr. Renne Girod (Switzerland). Madame Legrand and Mlle. Riviere (France). Miss Martha Malthe (Denmark). Mrs. Apostolides (Greece). Miss Van Veen (Holland). Mrs. A. G. Thomas and Miss Portia Greach (Australia). Miss Patterson (New Zeland). Miss Tyan (China). Miss C. Wood. Mrs. Mackenzie. Miss Anderson. Her Highness the Maharani of Cooch Behar. Princess Ila of Cooch Bihar. Rani of Nandgaon. Lady Maharaj Singh. Ladr Woodhead. Mrs. Margaret Sanger. Miss Muriel Lister. Lady Reed. Lady Mitter. Mrs. Latiff. Mrs. Sarala Devi Chaudhurani. Mrs. S. R. Das. Mrs. J. M. Sen Gupta, Mrs. Kumudini Bose. Mrs. S. N. Roy. Mrs. S. N. Mukherjee. Mrs. S. C. Roy. Mrs. K. Bose. Mrs. Forsyth. Mrs. F. S. Talyarkhan, Mrs. F. Low. Mrs. Summnd Shah. Miss Leah Hirad and Mrs. F. G. Currimbhoy (Bombay). Mrs. Sirrur (International Council of Women). Miss Pillai and Miss Shepherd (Delhi). Lady Imam. Mrs. Dhavle. Mrs. P. B. Ganguly. Mrs. S. K. Mitra. Mrs. Godbole. Miss Day and Miss Das (Bihar and Orissa). Dow Mia Shwe (Burma). Mrs. B. C. Dutta. Mrs. Remfry and Miss Peacock (Bengal). Mrs. H. Stanley and Mrs. J. Stanley and Mrs. J. N. Ghose.

Presidential Address

The *Maharani of Baroda*, in the course of her presidential address, expressed regret at the absence of Lady *Aberdeen* who was to have presided. She then stressed the advantage of having in their midst as delegates women who were specially qualified by their experience to indicate the various ways in which they thought women's councils in India could add to their already valuable achievements.

Her Highness found the education obtaining in schools, and particularly in universities, unsuited to the girls ; it was a waste of energy and did not lead to a cultural development. Nowhere was this lack felt more keenly than in the home where cultural influence was most useful. One of the best things they could do would be to establish schools where great importance should be attached to "social qualities", schools in which the knowledge which the pupils acquired was a really formative influence in their lives—a knowledge of themselves and of their duty to their fellows which would help them to realise themselves fully as women, and not lead them to think themselves superior because of their diplomas. Referring to another essential of good education Her Highness said : "The very fact that to-day we welcome representatives of various National Councils should remind us that the form of education we should aim to give our women should be such as to make them good citizens not only of India, but of the world."

The Maharani particularly referred to two questions—women's education and the position of women in the coming Constitution. Her Highness maintained that the education imparted to the girls was unsuited to their needs. "It is our duty to see," she said, "that they are given that training which will fit them to play their part in national affairs and at the same time, make them more efficient mothers."

As regards the second, Her Highness said that although their claims had not received full recognition, the position that had been accorded to them in the new Constitution made a good beginning which they should utilize to the fullest extent to achieve their objective.

Estimating the value of the new constitution Her Highness said : "Under the terms of the new Act we can at least claim that the rights of women to seat in the Legislature, and to the vote, have been reorganized to an extent which while it is still totally inadequate to the number of women in India, puts us in a stronger position than we were in before the Act was passed." It might well have been a still stronger position, she added, had the women been wise enough to present a united front at the time when their demands came before the Round Table Conference. Many more franchise qualifications had been added to those granted under the Reforms Act of 1919. The property qualification had been lowered, with the result that many women in rural areas now had the right to vote, and many among the poorer classes in the towns. The wives or widows of men with existing property qualifications would be entitled to vote. Then there was the educational qualification. Her Highness advised that universal franchise should be their aim.

Another question for consideration was the legal position of Indian women—their inequalities. They could not for instance inherit property. Considered in the light of one of their demands, the right to divorce, inheritance of property assumed a great importance for "the right to divorce must remain a dangerous one as long as a woman is denied the right to inherit the substance which alone can enable her to be economically independent of her husband."

In conclusion, the Maharani expressed the hope that as a result of this conference many new branches would be inaugurated throughout the country and that the National Council would become a strong and representative organization for the whole of India.

With a vote of thanks proposed by Mrs. *Kamala Devi Chattopadhya* and seconded by *Begum Shah Nawaz* the proceedings of the day came to a close.

Second Day—Calcutta—31st. January 1936

Women and Rural Work

The value and necessity of rural work in this country was emphasized at the morning session of the Conference to-day. The Conference unanimously appointed a sub-committee to examine and promote rural welfare.

Opening the session, *Lady Petland*, who presided, referred to the Country Women's Association, England, which embraced 54 Societies, and suggested that the National Council of Women in India might develop a similar organisation such as a Central Rural Organisation which would have a very useful scope.

Speaking on rural reconstruction, *Lady Nilkanth* (Ahmedabad) drew a vivid word picture of the plight of villagers in India which was largely due to ignorance. In Russia and Japan ignorance had been got rid of by compulsory education. It was the duty of the State to educate the masses, and unless the State helped nothing much could be done. The National Council of Women in India could use its influence to make the State alive to its duty.

Poverty in villages, she continued, was so great that a large amount of relief work was needed, and one way was by encouraging the manufacture and purchase of hand-made cloth. The Government had made a beginning but voluntary workers and a body like the N. C. W. I. could do much in this direction.

Dame Elizabeth Cadbury remarked that near where she came from there was a shop which sold Indian-made cloth and those who once bought it always went back for more as it wore so well.

Recently in England there were efforts to make village life more attractive, and one of those efforts was to reintroduce into village the habit of not listening to music on the wireless or gramophone but to take music themselves. Six Countries had taken up this idea and 80 small choirs had been formed among agricultural labourers. She suggested that is rural reconstruction in India, music should not be left out.

Confining herself entirely to villages in Bengal, Lady *Bose*, who spoke on education, urged that villages in this province should be made centres of activity as they were in a moribund condition, full of stagnation and had no schools worth the name. Everyone realized the great need for improvement for which two things were needed, education and the development of industries. Bengal, *Lady Bose* added, was backward in respect of primary education and should have primary education suited to the requirements of her women so as to make them useful members of society.

She suggested village societies and women teachers in every village. Bands of voluntary workers were trying to remove the existing disabilities but there must also be generous support by the State. Further, there was great need for the revival of village industries. These problems could not be solved without the wholehearted support and co-operation of educated village women.

In an address on village contitnuation school courses, Miss *M. Malthe* (Denmark) referred to education in Denmark which was free and compulsory, and said that no factor had been of greater importance in developing the industrial prosperity of that country than the high schools. She stressed the necessity of rural adult education in continuation of primary education.

Speaking on village school, Mrs. *K. Chattopadhgaya* (Mangalore) said that if they entered a village they were confronted with the tremendous problem of poverty and they could not cope with the problem of education unless a child was well nourished and lived in healthy surroundings.

Of India's 350 millions, Mrs. Chattopadhya continued, 75 per cent lived by agriculture, and if it was burdening the land it should be drawn away into industries. There was very heavy taxation, and wherever the peasants lived under landlords the rent they paid was 80 to 85 per cent of their income. Unless they created a better economic condition for the whole family it was not possible to deal only with children as if they were apart from the rest of the family.

Dame Elizabeth Cadbury inquired whether with instruction for agriculturists it would be possible for agriculturists to produce sufficient to support themselves as the Russians had done ?

Mrs. *K. Chattopadhya* replied that practically in every province the Government had got experimental farms which, however, did not meet the requirements of the millions of peasants working in the fields. Villages were so isolated that unless the result of all this research work was actually brought within the reach of the peasant, he did not get it. She suggested State-aided teachers who would carry these results to the villagers.

A discussion followed in which Mrs. Nadirshaw (Delhi), Mrs. Rustomji Faridoonji (Hyderabad), Begum Shah Nawaz, Mrs. Milford (Calcutta), Miss Peacock ((Bengal) and Miss P. Geach (Australia) took part.

On the motion of Begum Shah Nawaz, seconded by Mrs. K. Chattopadhya, the Conference adopted a resolution that a special sub-committee of the Council be appointed to examine and promote rural welfare.

Co-Education

A discussion took place on the question of special curriculum for girls' schools in the afternoon session presided over by Mrs. Faridoonji.

In the absence of Mrs. *P. K. Ray* a paper contributed by her on the subject was read by Miss M. Bose. The women's Education League in Calcutta, said Mrs. Ray, had been working for the last few years for furthering the cause of women's education in Bengal. They had been agitating for a special board for girls' education under the Education Department, and although they had suggested an equal number of non-official men and women in the constitution of the Board, it was their intention to qualify this membership with certain restrictions.

They must, she said, eschew politics altogether. Only those who were conducting girls' institutions or were connected with their governing bodies or were specially interested in girls' education should be eligible for membership of the Board.

The functions of the proposed Board, she said, should be to decide the syllabus and text books of all primary and secondary girls' schools, to suggest improvements, to conduct examinations of primary and secondary schools, to demand the provision of an equal sum of money for girls' education as for boys' and to recommend and insist on the appointment of a special woman officer to be in charge of girls' education.

Mrs. *A. N. Chaudhuri* remarked that when so much stress was being laid on internationalism and on the recognition of universal brotherhood it seemed strange that anyone should venture to suggest a further division between the two classes, sufficiently divided already. No nation could advance unless its men and women worked together in full sympathy and understanding. If at the very beginning boys and girls received an entirely different education, the cleavage already existing between them would be made sharper and more irrevocable.

Let boys and girls, she continued, have the same curriculum at school, which after all, they left at the age of 16. After that the ordinary girl could enter the "women's sphere", leaving the boy to go out into his wider world. The girl who must earn her own living or had dreams of a career would also find herself well-equipped. But the curriculum could be given a different treatment for girls. Take a subject like hygiene. It could be taught in girls' schools emphasizing those details that made for good house-keeping.

There also seemed to be a great insistence on the advisability of cooking being taught to girls at schools. As a rule that art was better learnt at home where a far wider range of dishes could be attempted and where treasured family recipes could play their part. Cooking taught at schools tended to degenerate into "mass" cooking. But much could be done in the way of training girls to cook invalid fare—a branch of cookery that did not always receive attention it deserved.

In the matter of handiwork two differences could be made. Where boys learnt carpentary, girls could specialize in sewing, painting and the decorative arts.

The *President* referred to the part played by the All-India Women's Conference in introducing reforms in women's education. The Conference, she said, came into existence to improve women's education. In the first year the Conference indicated the lines on which changes should be made and in the second year the All India Women's Education Fund was started.

This was followed by an inquiry by a commission of educationists, and considering the fact that for many years to come at least 80 per cent of Indian girls would be married, the Commission recommended that the girls should be given an education which would be useful for them in their homes. With that idea the Lady Irwin College was started in Delhi and she was glad to inform the House that practically every Province in India was represented there. The College, she said, laid special stress in the teaching of domestic sciences.

Begum Shah Nawaz also emphasized the necessity of including domestic sciences in the curriculum for girls' schools.

Delegates representing Belgium, Rumania and Burma described the special feature of the systems of girls' education prevailing in their respective countries after which the discussion was adjourned.

A plea for the establishment of nursery schools in Bengal was put forward by Mrs. *Roy* (Calcutta). Nursery Schools, she said, would save the country lakhs of rupees by preventing ill-health. These institutions aimed at providing opportunity for the healthy all-round development of the child of pre-school age thus raising the level of its physical, mental and moral growth.

After referring in detail to her scheme of infant and nursery schools, Mrs. Roy said that the curriculum was to be thought of in terms of activity and experience rather than of knowledge to be acquired and facts to be stored. The child should be put into a position to teach himself and the knowledge that he was to acquire should come not so much from the instructor as from the environments.

Dr. *Headwards* (Calcutta) welcomed the establishment of a nursery schools in Calcutta on the lines suggested by Mrs. Roy. The Conference then adjourned.

Third Day—Calcutta—1st. February 1936

Women and the Press

The conference discussed to-day the position of women and the Press.

Miss Zellweger of Switzerland, who presided, said that there were many women all over the world working on newspapers but few of them were real journalists. They were just dabbling in newspaper work, writing an occasional article or two. Many of them did not seem to know that for journalism one needed a special gift as in the case of painting and music. Most of the professional women journalists occupied very humble positions, working as reporters or "doing" women's "pages". There were, however, some women sub-editors on important newspapers.

But what they were really interested in was not the question of women journalists but newspaper publicity of topics concerning women. She wanted women to give greater attention to newspaper work and write competent articles on subjects affecting them.

Miss Lewis thought that women could do as well as men in journalism, except on the political side as they (women) were not very good at compromise. The old idea of the segregation of the sexes had to go as men and women were interested in the same subjects.

Mrs. K. Chattopadhya felt that women were not doing so well in journalism as they ought. Life, she said, would take a different aspect with Indian women entering journalism. She was opposed to the restrictions on the Press in India though she admitted that a certain amount of control was necessary.

Social Worker

Speaking on the "Training of the Social Worker," *Dame Elizabeth Cadbury* said that such training was of recent growth. After the Great war people began to ask for a definite course of training for social workers and a need was felt for a course of lectures on the right kind of social work. Great Britain had colleges where training was given in social work and diploma were granted. She stressed the need for voluntary workers as well as those who took social service as a profession. The work that specially appealed to women was work for children, tried mothers and girls.

Mrs. S. Permanand (Berar) said that the two main problems in India in finding suitable workers and giving them requisite training were illiteracy and the caste system. India being an agricultural country a great deal of work had to be done in villages where conditions were far from satisfactory. The system of voluntary workers did not generally obtain in this country. Since the Great War, there had been a great awakening of civic consciousness among the women of India but owing to their domestic duties they could not spare time for social work. There was no provision in Indian society for women who wanted to engage in social work. For the training of social workers they would have to go to the West.

Miss Wingate (Calcutta) dealt with one aspect of this big question, the facilities offered in India for social training and the need for social training—general social training—apart from specialized training such as child welfare. It must be already obvious to newcomers to India what a tremendous amount of voluntary social work was being done there such as rural reconstruction, village uplift, child welfare, work among the depressed classes and industrial workers. There was a growing demand, Miss Wingate stated, among students of both sexes to do social work and there was tremendous scope for untrained voluntary service. One condition necessary to make the untrained voluntary service effective was that it must be given under trained leaders. She had known cases where such untrained service without leaders had been of little use.

Social work needed two kinds of training, training of a university standard and, training of a high school or vernacular standard. Calcutta once had a training school for women. She suggested the establishment of a settlement suited to India in conditions where those who wanted to become social workers could go and get practical training. There should also be a residential centre in a city or a rural centre where workers could get first hand knowledge. With this should be combined a theoretical course. Practical work was of the utmost importance and this was not possible except at a centre under a trained leader. Lectures alone could not produce trained social workers.

Mrs. *Tyan* of China referred to social work in the slums of Sanghai and said that unless there was love for the souls of the poor one could not succeed in being a real social worker.

Mlle. de Busschere (Belgium) said that in Belgium, girls had a three years' training after which they were given diplomas for social work.

Initiating a discussion on "The League of Nations," *Begum Shah Nawaz* gave the impression of an Eastern woman who had been twice associated with that body. She referred particulalry to the work of the Fith Committee which, among other splendid things, had reduced the number of slaves from 25,000,000 to fewer than 5,000,000, restricted the production of narcotic drugs to legitimate consumption, helped small nations in reducing child mortality, substituted education in the place of punishment for delinquent minors and stressed the value of educational films for children.

In the beginning of 1937, an international Conference was to be held in the Dutch East Indies on traffic in women and children. The Government of India thought that there was hardly any traffic in women in India and that there was no need to send representatives but the women of India, who thought differently, would do their utmost to be represented there.

The discussion on this subject had not concluded when the Conference adjourned.

Fourth Day—Calcutta—3rd. February 1936

WOMEN AND PUBLIC HEALTH

Various Problems of public health were discussed to-day.

Speaking on the subject of medical inspection of schools, Dr. *Headwards* said that medical inspection of school children was only a part of the whole scheme for the care of a child. A few years ago the Vice-Chancellor of the Calcutta University together with others organised a students' welfare centre and the results of their examination were startling. Surely, the examination of students at University age—important though it was in its rightful sequence of events—was like putting the cart before the horse.' What was the history of medical inspections of school children in Calcutta? Those who were familiar with India knew that when financial stringency arose and cuts had to be made child welfare and kindred activities were the first to suffer. Some years ago there was functioning a scheme for the medical inspection of boys' and girls' schools in the city of Calcutta under the control of a medical woman for girls' schools and a medical man for boys' schools. The first post to be abolished was the medical woman, possibly because it was felt that the girls' health did not matter. The Public Health Department of Bengal were responsible for the health in boys' schools but the girls were left uncared for.

Continuing, Dr. *Headwards* said that at present there was not scheme in practice for any medical inspection of girls' schools in this province, except under private agencies and the school authorities themselves. Her point was that in such an important matter it was for the Government and the municipalities to take the lead. The authorities best suited to the purpose seemed to be the local municipalities, especially those already possessing health officers.

Miss *Jyotirmoyee Ganguly* reminded the Conference, particularly the delegates from overseas, that conditions and things in India were totally different. In every part of the world it was the State which took care of its children but not so in India.

The public in this country had for many many years made it a grievance that sufficient money was not spent on education and sanitation. This had been constantly dinned into the ears of the Government, but all these had been a cry in the wilderness. The Government was spending the larger part of the revenue for the maintenance of peace and order; but everyone in Bengal knew what was happening in the villages. Ruffians were kidnapping women from their peaceful homes. The myseries that followed in the wake knew no bounds.

India was still in the Middle ages, proceeded Miss Ganguly, she was forgetful of the fact that the world had progressed much, that new ideas and ideals had grown up. Indian women did not know how to demand from the Government money to have their children properly cared for by the Public Health Department. She did not think that anybody could blame India for that. For the last 150 years it had been dinned into her ears that she was inferior to everybody in the world, and she was unable to manage her own affairs.

She concluded with a stirring appeal to all mothers to rise equal to the occasion and learn to demand what was their legitimate right.

Miss *S. B. Gupta*, Inspectress of Schools, said that the foundations of national salvation must ultimately rest on the robust health and physical well-being of the citizens as a body. However glibly they talked of progress, freedom, advancement and power in high sounding phrases, yet how foolishly they neglected to take care of the very tender plant that required so judicious nursing that it might grow into a healthy tree. If India aspired to take her seat amongst the sister nations, the question of looking after her children was of vital interest. Every child born on Indian soil was a potential capacity and it would live to attain glory if only properly looked after. The question now before them was not of looking after all the children but what they wanted to emphasise was the question of the medical examination of the lower percentage of the children who went to the school.

Miss Gupta described at length the condition of the health of school-going children from her own experience and pointed out that a thorough and systematic examination of these children by competent doctors made it impossible to overlook any serious disturbances either physical or mental.

Besides, advanced knowledge of experimental psychology in these days enabled a doctor to estimate the mental calibre of the child. In many cases it was impossible to get a comprehensive idea of the special aptitudes of the wards, to help them to develop their body and mind accordingly and thus above all to prevent a good deal of time and money and energy from being wasted in wrong directions which was not infrequently the case with many young men of this country. She felt very strongly that as soon as possible every district and sub-divisional headquarter town in Bengal should have a child training centre where all the school children should have the facility of free treatment and in cases of necessity free medicine. But if the financial condition of the Government did not permit them to have these centres opened in the near future, let them at least have two women assistant surgeons, health visitors who would visit or tour from district to district being assisted by sub-assistant surgeons and medically examine school children if not twice at least once a year, and give such practical advice regarding food and clothing as could easily be observed by the parents.

She personally thought that medical inspection of children was perhaps more a necessity than the teaching of three R's in a primary school. The society was really responsible for the children whom they have brought in to this world and the society must take the trouble of looking after them.

Speaking on Housing and Health, Mrs. *Zarina Currimbhoy* (of Bombay) said that in large cities the housing conditions of working classes were not all that they should be. They had created in Bombay a consciousness among the women of the working classes for a better standard of cleanliness and health than what they had been used to in the past. They had secured amongst the large working class population of that city a nucleus of social opinion and a model on which other women could likewise manage to get their surroundings improved.

After giving an account of their visits to many of those houses it was her experience that what they should first do was to infuse in the minds of the working women in the urban area a desire for amelioration. Thereafter through the meditation of trained social workers they had to teach them how to organise opinion among themselves and how to make such opinion effective with those in whose power lay the means to secure conveniences and amenities which were the elementary requirements for modern existence and of civilised life. Increased earnings could come to the working classes only through an increased efficiency and let them hope that the efforts which they had been making through the Labour Committee of the Women's Council of Bombay during the last one year would lead to the improvement of health condttions widely. "Let us hope", she concluded, "that this example would be copied in urban areas throughout India and that the results will contribute to some extent to the improvement of their life and lot and of their efficiency in work through which a still higher standard of life may come within their reach."

Speaking on maternal mortality, *Dr. Girod* of Bombay said that the subject of maternal mortality had received special consideration in the West for some years past. The sum total of the investigations of various committees was that a large percentage (40 per cent) of deaths would be avoidable—about the third of the deaths were due to sepsis, fifty per cent of these being after a normal labour.

These figures coming from the west with its height of civilisation, advanced public opinion, improved sanitary conditions, facilities of transport etc. were to say the least staggering. What a tale of woe can we relate in this country! If we can but probe into the subject carefully we shall be aghast at the tremendous loss of young promising lives. As doctors had to play an important role in a maternity service it was essential that the training of the future doctor should be adequate and efficient. She emphasised the need for organised research into the causes of maternal mortality peculiar to India by a well represented committee.

Child Welfare

At the evening session the subjects of child welfare and after-care of tuberculosis patients were discussed. *Begum Shah Nawaz* presided.

Speaking on child welfare, *Princess Cantacuxene* (Roumania) deplored the practice of sending young persons to prison and suggested that steps should be taken to see that this was not done except in very exceptional cases. Certain countries had introduced desirable legislation to the effect that children under a certain age should not be sent to prison. She condemned the exhibition of undesirable posters outside cinemas which aroused the curiosity of children and which were harmful. So far as films were concerned, it was desirable to have pictures which were not sensational but largely educational.

Mrs. *S. Mehta* (Calcutta) said that the future of a nation depended on its children. This was recognized both by the State and the people. Those countries which looked to child-welfare had healthy children while infant mortality was very low.

Mrs. *Greeves* (Great Britain) described infant welfare centres in Northern Ireland. This work, she said, was started in 1919 and there were now 56 centres in operation in the six countries. A few of them were controlled and operated by local authorities, a few by a joint committee of the local authorities and the local nursing societies. Those two groups received Government grants. The majority were worked by the local nursing societies and received grants from the Government and local authorities.

TUBERCULOSIS CAMPAIGN

Lady Pentland read a paper by *Lady Aberdeen* on tuberculosis work in Great Britain. Mrs. *C.O.Remfry*, Honorary Secretary, Tuberculosis Association, Bengal, said that there were five tuber-culosis dispensaries in Calcutta, one in Howrah and two in the mofussil. It was an underestimate, she added, to say that there were 1,000,000 million people suffering from tuberculosis in Bengal alone. In Calcutta no less than 30,000 people suffered from the disease and there were 300 deaths here yearly. Five per cent of those who were definitely diagnosed as having tuberculosis were servants and hawkers, people who were constantly in contact with food. Three per cent were school teachers, and eight per cent were students of the Calcutta University. In Bengal there were something like 200,000 people who were what was called "open cases" spreading the disease every time they coughed or sneezed or spat. Those were the people who were the great danger at the moment. The accommodation for tuberculosis sufferers was hopelessly inadequate as in the whole of Bengal there were something like 284 beds for 1,000,000 patients. The Conference at this stage adjourned.

Fifth Day—Calcutta—4th. February 1936

TRAFFIC IN WOMEN & CHILDREN

The evil of the traffic in women and children and the steps that should be taken to cope with it, were emphasized at the morning session of the conference to-day.

The Conference adopted two resolutions. One urged the National Councils of Women to support the work undertaken by voluntary and official agencies in each country against the traffic in women and children. The other recommended the National Council of Women in India to urge upon the Government of India the necessity of India's representation in the conference to be held in the Far East (probably the Dutch East Indies) in 1937 in connexion with the question of the traffic in women and children.

Initiating the debate on the traffic in women and children, Miss Millicent Shephard (Delhi), representative of the Association for Moral and Social Hygiene, India, briefly sketched the outstanding feature of the Association's work and assured her hearers that the Association's efforts had always been undertaken with a real love for India and only with the desire to help Indian men and women to undertake the reforms which so many of them desired to see carried out.

Investigation. Miss *Shephard* continued, into the causes which led to the entry of girls into a life of shame disclosed that sometimes it was poverty but that was not the primary factor. The main cause in India, as elsewhere, was the demand which it was profitable to supply. Unless there was a revolution of thought, a real challenge against this cause of the traffic in women and children, all rescue work, all legislation, all medical work would be fruitless.

Therefore, she appealed to every woman of whatever nationality to consider her own deep responsibility for reducing the demand by the teaching of moral standards. Concluding, Miss Shephard said that since 1930 there had been a considerable advance in the number of women interesting themselves in rescue work. It was still true to say that the chief rescue agencies were the Salvation Army, the various Missionary Societies, the Brahmo Samaj, the Seva Sadan and the Servants of India Society.

Begum Shah Nawaz remarked that so far as India was concerned, in every province the Government were doing their best to strengthen the laws against this immoral traffic. Statistics before the League of Nations showed that India was one of the most moral countries in the world compared with other countries.

Dr. *S. Noronha* (Bombay) confined herself to the conditions prevailing in that City and what Bombay was doing to remedy this evil, and said that the Bombay Act as it stood at present was very inadequate.

Mrs. *L. Menon* (Lucknow) attributed the fundamental cause of this social evil to poverty. Mrs. *Tyan* (China) described the steps which the Chinese Government were taking to cope with the evil.

EDUCATION BY FILMS

Speaking on the cinema, Mrs. *Shamsun Nahar Mahmud* (Calcutta) characterized it as one of the greatest achievements of modern civilization and stressed the necessity of utilizing it to educate children.

Mrs. *Tyan* (China) said that the Chinese Government were now giving due attention to films with the result that the cinema was exercising a beneficial influence. Miss *Millicent Shephard* suggested that it would greatly help the Boards of Film Censors in India if those who disapproved any film which was being shown would write in expressing their disapproval, first, to the manager of the cinema in question and, secondly to the Secretary of the Boards of Film Censors.

Another way in which the Council of Women could help was to appoint a Film Appraising Board, as had been done in Madras, to see films when they came to a town and issue to the local Press a summary of the film whether it was class (a), (b) or (c). Class (a) was for everybody, class (b) for adults only, and class (c) was undesirable.

Legal Disabilities of Women

The next subject taken up was legal disabilities.

Mrs. *S. N. Ray* (Calcutta) pleaded for a wholesale revision of Hindu law and for remedies in the light of modern conditions. The policy of the Government of India of non-interference in religious and social matters had led them to perpetuate and uphold a system of law which should have no existence in a modern State. Indian women were deeply disappointed that in the new Constitution their legitimate demands had been ignored.

Miss *Zellweger* (Switzerland) said that there was a reactionary wave throughout Europe to take away from women the rights they have.

Child Marriage

The last matter taken up before lunch was the amendment to the Child Marriage Act. Mrs. *L. Menon* (Lucknow) said that since the introduction of the Act there had been an increase in the number of child marriages. There were defects in the law which made it a dead letter. What was needed was the issuing of prohibitory injunctions to stop contemplated marriages, doing away with the present security of Rs. 100 and safe custody of the child-wife after she had been married in contravention of the law. Dr. *Nowrungi* thought that the Act had failed to achieve its object.

Food and Health

After lunch, under the presidency of *Lady Maharaj Singh*, the subject of food and health was discussed. Dr. *Biggar* (Calcutta) stressed the inadequacy of the diet of the poorer classes of Indians whose food was very ill-balanced and lacking in animal proteins, vitamins, and mineral salts. This poor diet, she said, had a disastrous effect on the health and physique of the masses. The basic cause of this state of affairs was economic.

Lady *Ezra* briefly referred to the many subjects that had been covered, the count they had taken of one another and the large amount of excellent work accomplished. With cheers for Lady Ezra, the Conference closed.

The Tamil Nad Women's Conference

Over 600 ladies attended the Tamil Nad Women's Political Conference which was held on the **27th. January 1936** at Karaikudi (Ramnad district) under the presidency of Mrs. *Lakshmi Sankara Aiyar* of Kallidaikurichi. There was equal number of men also given seats at the rear of the hall. The proceedings commenced with the singing of national songs by girl pupils.

Sri Visalakshmi Ammal, Chairwoman of the Reception Committee, welcomed the guests. She referred in the course of her address to the status of women in Hindu household at present and their part in the national work and criticised the Indian constitution. She dwelt at length on the importance of education and the spread of literacy among women and the need for reforms in social customs and practices. She appealed to them to join the Congress and work for the country.

Mrs. *Lakshmi Sankar*, President, after thanking them for the honour conferred on her, pointed out to the importance and political character of their meeting since it was meeting along with the Provincial Congress Session, presided over by another lady, Mrs. *Lakshmipathi*. It was a sign of the times, she added, that women were progressing but they should still further advance and improve their condition in all aspect of life. During the last civil disobedience movement, women came forward boldly and their work heartened the workers a great deal. Their aim must be to do work to enable their country to be free, only then could the women in India advance and take their rightful place.

She then explained the franchise under the new reforms and advised the women to see that the names of eligible voters were included in it. They should also acquire a love of their country and the products of their country by which they could contribute largely to the Swadeshi movement. The Congress had changed its policy of work into one of capturing local boards and legislative councils and with the enhanced franchise among women it behoved them to come out courageously even to contest seats on these bodies with the help of the Congress.

Resolutions

The conference then passed a number of resolutions regarding women's uplift. The first two resolutions prayed for the speedy recovery of Mahatma Gandhi and Mrs. Kamala Nehru. The conference requested Mr. C. Rajagopalachariar to return to politics. These resolutions were moved from the chair and passed unanimously.

Moved by Sri *Alamelu Ammal* of Karaikudi and seconded by Sri *Kannaki Ammal* and supported by Sri *N. R. Visalakshmi*, a resolution was adopted that women themselves should work for their uplift.

The Conference requested women to exercise to the full the franchise given to them. Sri *Kalyani Ammal* moved the resolution and Sri *Visalakshmi* seconded it. The Conference requested the Government and the members of the Assembly to amend the Hindu law in such a way as to give the same rights of inheritance to daughters as the son. The Conference requested the Local Boards to appoint a majority of women teachers in elementary schools for boys of tender age. The Conference requested the community to permit the remarriage of young windows.

Another resolution urged that nunneries should be established in important towns all over the country and urged the women of the land to take active part in the removal of untouchability.

Resolutions over, the president appealed to women to join the Congress and support Swadeshi. The Conference terminated with a vote of thanks.

The Andhra Women's Conference

The Andhra Provincial Conference was held at Cocanada on the **11th. February 1936**. Srimathi *B. Kameswarama* presided.

"Our last conference," she said, "was held at Vizag and I propose briefly to review the principal events of the year since then. The country has since witnessed the passing of two constitutions, one by the Indian National Congress and the other by the Parliament. The one was passed by the people's chosen representatives, men and women who worked and suffered for the emancipation of our Motherland, while the other was adopted by those who want to hold us in subjection, I mean, the British Parliament. The one was an attempt, an honest endeavour to put our house in order so that we might become organised and disciplined fighters for freedom of our Motherland. The other was an organised and determined effort to crush the indomitable spirit of a rising nation struggling to break the shackles imposed on her from without. The Congress constitution has rightly abolished the reservation of seats for women in the elections to the various committees, while the Government of India Act has thrust upon the unwilling women of India, reservation of seats. I am proud—I hope all of you share my pride—that the representatives of the women of India were the solitary exceptions amidst a host of communalist and reactionary representatives that visited the Round Table Conference in London, who unequivocally and emphatically repudiated separate electorates and fought for the joint electorate system with no reservation of seats. Though the Congress boldly abolished the reservation of seats for women in their constitution, I am sorry to note that the Congress leaders are very tardy in their attempt to set up lady candidates for the general constituencies in the elections. No woman was returned to the Assembly and while we are glad that Mrs. R. Lakshmipathi was returned to the local Legislative Council, with a thumping majority, I venture to submit that many more women ought to come to the Provincial and the Indian Legislature. I am more sorry to note that the Andhras have for 81 seats returned only two women as delegates to the Indian National Congress this year. Is Andhra womanhood barren of ability or are Andhras so utterly lacking in a sense of proportion and in a sense of fair play and justice I do not say, of chivalry? We do not want chivalry. We want our rightful share in the public life of the country. I appeal to you, sisters, to fight out this injustice, fight relentlessly and success shall be ours."

Referring to the Government of India Act, she said, the tests by which it was to be judged were: "Is there power for the People's representatives to pass their own laws and enforce them? Have they the control of the purse? Have they got the elementary rights of free speech, free association and free press? Is the country's defence in the hands of the people? Judged from these four crucial tests, the Act is declared hopelessly unsatisfactory by persons of all shades of opinion. The whole Act is hedged in by safeguards which nullify the very substance of the Act. With the elementary rights of free press and free speech denied, with the purse practically under bureaucratic control, and with defence and foreign affairs under the control of the Governor-General, the Act becomes the very negation of self-government. I cannot resist the temptation of drawing your attention to one important particular regarding the distribution of seats in each province. Let me take up Madras first. Out of 215 seats in the Provincial Legislative Assembly, the general seats are only 116, the rest are all special seats, through separate electorate or through joint electorates with reservations of seats. I need not tell you how difficult it is for a subject nation divided into castes and creeds to return nationalist candidates through communal electorates. Reservation of seats through joint electorates is, of course, slightly better but is in no sense, a proper substitute for the general seats. There are restrictions on the candidates also, those convicted and sentenced to more than two years for political offences, not involving even violence or moral turpitude being debarred from standing as candidates except with the special permission of the powers-that-be. This deprives the legislatures of the best men and women in the country and is therefore a severe handicap for the Congress in the selection of candidates for the Legislatures. Thus every effort was made in the Act to weaken the back of the opposition.

"Further, only 14 per cent of the total population is enfranchised, whereas in other countries every man and woman above a certain age has a vote. The enfranchisement of women is still more deplorable. Only 5 per cent of the Indian women are enfranchised. The qualifications for a voter are literacy and property. Very few men in the country are literate and the law does not permit women to own property as men. The women in rural areas are at a greater disadvantage than the women of the urban areas. The clauses regarding the qualifications for the right to vote are largely operative only in the urban areas. Neither the independent property qualification nor the literary qualification will give franchise to many women in the rural areas. Besides, the women have to apply for being enlisted as voters, while not men. The lists are prepared by the authorities themselves. This injustice should be done away with immediately. The women all over India are protesting strongly against this as well as the reservation of seats for women on communal basis in the legislatures. Let me not be understood as striking a note of despair for the enthusiasts of council-entry. I am myself an advocate of council-entry. In my opinion the logical course to be followed when once council-entry is accepted is to proceed further and capture the offices as well. I do not, for a moment, believe that the millennium could be reached by accepting office under the coming constitution particularly in view of the special authority vested in the Governors and the Governor-General but I maintain that by accepting office it will be possible to demonstrate to the world at large how incongrous and impossible it is to work a constitution which is a quaint admixture of democracy and bureaucracy. Women in particular ought not to be indifferent about the legislatures] or even the local boards or, municipalities. It is my firm conviction that the emancipation of women and the emancipation of the Motherland go hand in hand. The women of Turkey under the valiant lead of Kemal Pasha had freed their country and themselves and so did the women of Russia. The women of India too have played their part nobly in the national movement. They braved lathis, suffered the hardship of jail life and subjected themselves to all sorts of humiliations for the sake of the Motherland. Desa Sevikas in robes of orange was a sight for the Gods to see in the heyday of Satyagraha. Woman, the incarnation of Shakti, has awakened. May that spirit of Shakti infect the whole nation and may we all one fine morning awake to find ourselves free, if not famous.

"I note with great pain that communalism is raising its ugly head again and again. We hear of communal riots in Northern India and we all deplore them very much. Even in our presidency we think in terms of our respective communities and in the local elections it is a pity that even some Congressmen betray their communal spirit. It is a tragic spectacle that we Congressmen and women freely participate in purely communal gatherings and functions. The All-India Independence League and the All-India Youth League enjoined on their members not to have anything to do with any communal organisation. The same is the case to-day with the Socialist Party. It is time that the Indian National Congress passed a resolution that members of communal organisations are inelligible to be returned as Congress delegates or members of District Congress Committees. All the communal associations, e. g., the Saiva Sabha, the Brahmin Mandali, the Arya Vysya Sangha, the Rasaputra Samaj, the Kamma Conference, the Telugu Association, the Reddi Samiti etc., must be banned and it is incumbent on every Congressman not to encourage communal uplift. All the energies of Congressmen should be expended for national and not communal uplift. In this connection, I am reminded of the noble example set by Srimati Bharati Devi of Nidubrolu, who declined the Presidentship of the Kamma Ladies' Conference some time ago. Personally, I hold that the caste system, whatever its utility might have been once upon a time, has long survived its usefulness and ought to go in the interests of the solidarity of the Hindu community. I also hold that one can be a Hindu without being a Brahmin, a Kshatriya, a Vysya, a Kamma or a Kapu or a Reddi or a Harijan. After all, birth is an accident and no one can claim superiority because of that accident.

"A word about the Harijan problem. It has of late assumed very serious proportions, thanks to the bombshell thrown by Dr. Ambedkar. He advised mass conversions of Harijans to some other religion. He described Hinduism not as a religion but as a contagious disease. If, by Hinduism, he means Hindu customs now in vogue I am in whole-hearted agreement with him. Our society to-day is rotten to the core, ignorance and superstition having dethroned religion and taken its place. To condemn six crores of our fellowmen to a perpetual state of untouchability is simply inhuman but we do it every moment of our lives. Religion, of course, is a matter of faith and each must decide for himself. It is, therefore, idle to talk of mass conversions. But we must not lightly brush aside the serious temper, rather the distemper of Dr. Ambedkar, especially when his proposal is gaining some support here and there. I can understand the impatience and indignation of Dr. Ambedkar. Let us now at least understand our degradation and try to throw it off. Woman, indeed, has a greater role to play in this matter. The biggest social reformer can do nothing to push on his reform if his wife or mother declares non-co-operation with him. And that is what happens in most of our homes. I therefore appeal to you, my sisters, to bestir yourselves and resolve once for all, to wipe out the blot of untouchability from our society.

"It would be presumtuous on my part, at this stage of our national life, to make a plea for Swadeshi, Khaddar or village industries and so I don't propose to waste your time by dilating on them. A vow of Swadeshi taken by the woman, will revolutionise our home-life in an instant, and gradually revolutionise our whole national life. We are here assembled to-day as delegates of the Andhra Women's Conference And let us, as Andhras, contribute our mite to the cause of the Andhra Province. We were the very first in India to agitate for a linguistic province. And what a pity that we seem to be the very last to get it. We have been agitating for the separate Andhra Province now for quarter of a century and it is a matter for deep regret, that while Sindh and Orissa got it almost in a trice, we are left behind. Let us bring about a mutual goodwill and understanding between the Circus and the Rayalaseema and unify the whole of Andhradesa into one indivisible whole. And let us in one voice demand a separate province for Andhra.

"Coming as I do from Mysore, which is beyond the Andhra borders, you expect me to speak a few words about the Andhras abroad. I confess I have not made a careful study of the problem. But I tell you that in the Mysore State, there are many Andhra families particularly in the Kolar District. I regret to say that our sweet mother-tongue is fast disappearing there. I make bold to say that it would have completely disappeared had it not been for the women—our sisters—who have saved Telugu from extinction. I am quite sure that the Mysore Government will, if duly approached, help the Telugus to preserve their mother-tongue. But we must agitate and agitate strongly. I appeal to the Andhra Mahasabha to take up the matter in right earnest and help us in solving this difficult question."

In conclusion, she said: "I appeal to you to stand unflinchingly by the Congress and like disciplined soldiers bravely march forward to the goal of freedom. Let us not think in terms of Brahmin, Kshatria, Vysya, Kamma, Kapu, or Reddi, Hindu Muslim, or Christian but as Indians in thought, word and deed."

Resolutions

The Conference then discussed and passed the following resolutions :—

A resolution expressing sorrow on the deaths of Messrs. Saklatwala, B. Ch. Yegnanarayana Sarma, T. K. Sherwani, A. Appalanarasimham, B. Venkataramma Reddi and Dip Narayan Singh was moved from the chair and carried.

The conference expressed its thankfulness to God for the improvement in the health of Mahatma Gandhi and Messrs. Kamala Nehru and wished them long life and sound health in order to enable them to coutinue their noble services to the country until Swaraj was achieved.

The conference opined that there was necessity for writing a history of the part played by Andhra women in the Satyagraha movement and congratulated Srimathis P. Kanakamma and D. Lakshmibayamma on their readiness to take up that work and appealed to the District and Firka Congress Committees to help them with the necessary information.

The conference expressed its thanks for the services being rendered by the Andhra Mahila Sabha, branch of the All-India Mahasabha, in the cause of women's education and their social uplift and approved the resolutions of the Andhra Mahila Sabha passed at its last session held at Guntur.

The conference appealed to all Women's Associations to give training to Desa Sevikas, and to start Women's Associations where they were not already started.

The conference opined that in the new voters' lists for the legislatures all women who were eligible should get themselves enrolled and cast them in favour of Congress candidates. Women should contest not only the reserved seats but also the general seats. The conference appealed to the Congress Civic Board to set up women candidates for the general seats also and thus give every encouragement to women.

This resolution was moved by Mrs. *Cousins*. who, in a forceful and impressive speech, pointed out at length the need for women entering the councils in large numbers.

Sri Syamalamba moved and Sri Balanthrapu Seshamma seconded a resolution appealing to Congressmen and Congress women to work for giving equal representation to women in the Congress Committees as the present representation was inadequate.

The conference opined that all marriages should be registered under the Act of 1887.

Sri Yamini Purna Tilakamma proposed and *Sri Duvvuri Subbamma* seconded a resolution appealing to the people to root out the institution of prostitution in the country and render every help to Deva Dasis.

A resolution reaffirming that Indians' goal was complete independence and appealing to men and women of India to carry on agitation incessantly for its attainment was unanimously carried.

The conference reiterated the resolution passed by the Andhra Provincial Conference on the previous day recommending to the All India Congress Committee to change the present Congress creed and base it on the principles of scientific Socialism for the attainment of complete independence.

With a vote of thanks to the President and delegates and to all others who contributed to the success of the conference, proposed by Sri V. Kamala Devi, the conference came to a close.

The Bombay Women's Conference

The Bombay Presidency Women's Conference met at the University Convocation Hall, Bombay, on the **22nd. January 1936**, and adopted the report of the Parliamentary Sub-Committee, which had to its credit the sustained agitation carried on in the province against Mr. H. R. Desai's "Bill to Amend the Law of Adoption", which was ultimately thrown out by the Legislative Council. The Committee also considered the "Bill to amend the Hindu Law of Inheritance", sponsored by Rao Bahadur R. R. Kale (since dead), and sent their recommendations.

Miss *M. K. Davis*, Superintendent of the Umerkhadi Children's Home, gave a pathetic account of the conditions of mental defectives among juveniles and pointed out that they required the greatest protection. It was estimated that out of the 2,560,000 mental defectives of all ages, there were nearly 284,000 children and their cases required special attention and treatment. Lunacy and mental defect were two different evils requiring different methods of treatment. At present there were only two homes for mental defectives in India, one at Kurseong near Darjeeling for European children and the other in Midnapore District for Indians. They charged prohibitive rates monthly for each case admitted and they could not be of any use to the Bombay Presidency. She suggested that a special Home with adequate equipment for the protection of the mental defectives among children be provided through charity by way of endowment. Miss Davis paid a tribute to the organisers of the only school for mentally defective children in Bombay Presidency at the Byramji Jeejeebhoy Home, Matunga, where a courageous experiment was being carried out.

Mrs. *R. P. Masani* gave a brief account of the working of the School at Matunga, and said that instead of waiting for help from others, the Women's Council should take the initiative and try to open some more institutions of the kind.

Mrs. *V. Inglis* then led a discussion on "Long-term Women prisoners." She said that suitable occupations for women prisoners had engaged the attention of the authorities. In Bombay Presidency, the women prisoners generally came from the lowest classes. Some of the prisoners were from rural areas, who were quite independent and industrious, but for some unfortunate act during a moment of passion, they were serving long terms. There was a suggestion that the Red Cross organisations might provide some work for these women.

Mrs. *Shufi Tyabji* said that formerly they were allowed to give brief lectures to women prisoners, but that practice was stopped after the Civil Disobedience movement. Formerly these prisoners were being supplied cloth for sewing but the Home Department of the Government informed them that the rules did not allow such work.

Mrs. *Sarojini Naidu*, who was the only speaker who had studied the conditions first-hand, having spent nearly two years in jail thus coming into close contact with the women prisoners, said that long-term prisoners were over-worked and they had too little energy or leisure left for learning or education. What they needed was the human touch while the Prison laws were quite inhuman and did not count the human equation. There were women who would have made good mothers and wives, but in a fit of rage, they had committed some offence unable to bear their misery and had been sent for long terms. It was not merely a question of providing them some comforts. It was a question of making the Jail Code more elastic and more human. All of the women prisoners were not criminals though they were condemned to imprisonment.

A resolution was passed by the conference "urging the Government to find ways and means for strict enforcement of the Child Marriage Restraint Act.

The promotion of home industries in Middle class families with a view to adding to the income of the families concerned, was the interesting topic on which discussion was initiated by Mrs. Rasikamani Desai. Several speakers pointed out that such institutions were already functioning in the city and the suburbs, imparting instruction to women in home crafts, so that they might supplement the family income.

Trade and Industry in India

Chambers of Commerce

Trade Union Congress

and

The Indian Economic Conference

India and the Ottawa Agreement

I.—CONDITIONS BEFORE OTTAWA

The following are a series of Press notes issued by the Director of Information, Delhi on the present tendencies of India's Foreign Trade and have an important bearing on the working of the Ottawa Agreement.

Critics of this Agreement, both friendly and hostile, have rightly insisted that in any study of its working the issues involved should be examined against the background of economic developments, which have influenced the course of international trade in recent years.

A bare comparison of the figures of India's foreign trade before and after Ottawa, which failed to take into account the economic forces which have convulsed world trade in the interval, would yield wholly misleading results.

Even in normal times the delicate mechanism of international trade is profoundly effected from year to year by a variety of disturbing causes. Failure or abundance of crops in the principal agricultural countries, price fluctuations, political disturbances, changes in fashion or taste in the consuming countries, industrial disputes, these are some of many such factors.

Since the autumn of 1929 the world has been deeply enmeshed in an economic depression of unparalleled severity. The economic structure of the world has been dislocated. The gold value or international trade has been steadily declining, and is now only about one-third of what it was in 1929. The volume of world trade, despite a slight recovery since 1932, is no more than 77.5 per cent of what it was in 1929.

As the crisis has proceeded, a number of countries have imposed ever fresh restrictions on imports by such means as higher tariff, quotas and clearing and compensation agreements, for the purpose of protecting home industries, for maintaining currency stability and an even balance of trade.

If we are to gain a due perspective in which to judge of the effects of the Ottawa preferences, it is essential to pass in review the salient features of world economic conditions, particularly in their relation to the trade and business of India, in the year immediately preceding and following the conclusion of the Ottawa Agreement.

The economic recuperation of the world after the crisis of 1920-21 though slow at first proceeded with surprising rapidity between the years 1925 and 1929. The total world trade in 1927 (recalculated at 1913 values) was 20 per cent greater than in 1913, while in India, although local production was being increasingly diverted to the satisfaction of local needs, both imports and exports in 1928 equalled in volume those of 1913.

With stable prices and an expanding trade there emerged the characteristic phenomena associated with an industrial boom, and looked as though, after the sore trials of the post-war period, the world was once again entering on an era of prosperity.

Yet, amid this scene of world-wide progress, a discerning observer might have discovered cause for uneasiness in the position of India as a great supplier of raw materials. The gradual tendency towards overproduction made the outlook for countries producing raw materials increasingly disturbing.

Of more ominous significance to India was the growing competition to which her export trade was being subjected in western markets. Virgin land in many parts of the world was being brought under cultivation, and, thanks to improved transport facilities, the resulting products were being introduced to markets where they were before unknown.

In other countries production was expanding, and export trades which before the war were of negligible proportions were proving to be serious competitors in the markets of the western world. Oil seeds, textile fibres, food-grains, dried and fresh fruit and timber might be cited as examples of products in respect of which India had to face increasingly keen competition.

The position was aggravated by the measures taken by many Continental countries and by the United States of America, to stimulate the demand for the product of their respective colonial territories.

France, Italy, Belgium, Spain and Portugal were pursuing a policy to stimulate imports of produce from their tropical and sub-tropical possessions. In other countries, with no tropical colonies, which could not themselves produce the natural products they required, considerable attention was being paid to the development of synthetic substitutes in direct competition with Indian goods.

Already, therefore, even before the onset of the present depression, it was becoming increasingly apparent that defensive measures would have to be taken to maintain the position India had attained in world markets.

The problem was rendered more acute by the crisis which began in 1929. As a producer of primary products India was one of the first countries to feel the full effects of the catastrophic fall in prices. By the end of 1930 the Calcutta index number of wholesale prices had fallen by 30 per cent from the level of September 1929, while fall in the price of exported articles during the same period amounted to 36 per cent against 17 per cent for imported articles. The strain on the price structure was equally severe in Australia and the Argentine, both of them debtor agricultural countries, and before the close of the year they were compelled to go off gold.

In 1931 the deflationary tendency in prices continued unchecked with disastrous consequences to countries producing primary commodities, such as India and the Dutch East Indies. The total value of world trade in that year in terms of sterling fell by 38 per cent as compared with 1929. and India's share in the total trade receded from 3.02 per cent to 2.54 per cent. This was partly due to the relatively greater fall in the prices of raw materials, and partly to the growing restrictions continually being placed on international trade by the importing countries.

In an endeavour to combat the growing menace of the depression, many countries, notably the newer economic units in Europe created by the war, embarked on a policy of economic isolationism by the election of higher tariff walls, the imposition of 'contingents' or quotas and the institution of stringent foreign exchange controls. The result was a steady decline in demand and a gradual restriction of the free markets of the world.

Such, in brief, was the position in 1931 when two events of outstanding importance to India occurred.

The first was Great Britain's abandonment of the gold standard in September 1931 and the linking of the currencies of most of the Empire countries, including that of India, to sterling. The departure of sterling from gold served to arrest the fall of the prices of India's staple exports for a time, but this was a purely temporary phase. In June 1932 rupee prices again began to show a distinctly downward trend..

The second notable event was Great Britain's formal renunciation of a Free Trade in favour of a Protectionist regime with the enactment of the Import Duties Act in March, 1932.

By that Act duties were imposed on a wide range of articles covering nearly two-thirds of the total imports into the United Kingdom. Provision was made, however, for the exemption of Empire products from these duties, pending negotiations with the Dominions and India for the conclusion of reciprocal tariff arrangements.

Accordingly, in July, 1932, an Imperial Economic Conference met at Ottawa for the discussion of the new policy of trade agreements between the constituent parts of the Empire.

It is only necessary to emphasise that refusal to negotiate would have meant for India forfeiture of her freedom of access to the world's most stable and largest open market.

II. FEATURE OF INDIA'S FOREIGN TRADE

The main features of India's export trade after the Ottawa Agreement are now examined.

After Ottawa the course of events suggest that the forces making for recovery or recession in international trade are about evenly balanced, with perhaps some

slight advantage to the former. On the one hand, commercial and monetary policies pursued by a number of countries continue to be restrictive of trade. In particular, the increasing number of clearing and compensation agreements that have been concluded have tended to reduce triangular trade and depress prices. In the League of Nations "Enquiry into Clearing Agreements" it is stated that reduction in purchases by debtor countries in Europe of "oversea raw materials, due to diversion of her demand to the countries with which she had concluded clearing agreements, naturally contributed to the fall in world market prices and thus affected adversely the economic situation of the world as a whole."

On the other hand, prices have generally risen, as a result in some cases of agreements to restrict output—tea, rubber and tin are examples of interest to India; production has increased, and there is evidence of increasing economic activity over a wide area, notably in U. K. and U. S. A.

Industrial Activity in India

It should be stated, however, that the rise in industrial activity is still confined in the main to capital equipment industries, especially the building industry, and that expansion in the textile industries and in consumers' goods trades generally is much less marked than in the heavy industries. At the same time, the trend of prices of raw materials and manufactured products indicates a further approach to the relationship which existed between them in pre-depression days.

Further, though the gold value of world trade has continued to decline, there has been a progressive increase in the quantum of trade since 1932, and as the following figures will indicate the pace of recovery has been greater in the case of India's foreign trade than in world trade as a whole.

Movement of Quantum Trade—(i) World Trade

1929	1930	1931	1932	1933	1934
100	93	86	74	75.5	77.5

(ii) India's Trade

1929	1930	1931	1932	1933	1934
30	31	32	33	34	35
100	87	76	75	78.5	86

These indications point to an upward tendency in internationl trade, but there are still so many elements of instability in the world economic situation that it seems justifiable to regard the recovery so far registered as "superficial rather than fundamental."

An examination may now be made of the figures of India's exports before and after Ottawa. The relevant figures are exhibited in the following table:

Total Exports from India

(In lakhs of rupees)

Total value.	1931-32	1932-33	1933-34	1934-35
To all countries	157,56	133,27	147,52	153,39
Index	100	84.6	93.6	96.7
To U. K.	42,88	36,82	47,21	48,07
Index	100	85.9	110.1	112.1
To other countries	114,68	96,45	100,31	104,32
Index	100	84.1	87.5	90.9

	Percentage increase in 1933-34 in comparison with 1932-33.	Percentage increase in 1934-35 in comparison with 1933-34.	Percentage increase in 1934-35 in comparison with 1932-33.
All countries	10.5	3.3	14
U. K.	28.2	1.8	30.5
Other countries	4	3.9	8

(These figures differ somewhat from those given in the Review of Trade 1934-35, and have been constructed on the basis of figures in Table II and third which are reproduced from the Second Report on the working of the Ottawa Agreement.

It will be observed that between 1932-33 and 1933-34, India's export trade to the United Kingdom increased by 28.2 per cent, while her trade with other countries advanced by only 4 per cent. It has been suggested in certain quarters that the remarkable improvement in the trade to the United Kingdom is due almost entirely to the increased business activity in that country and can in no way be attributed to the preferences granted to India.

It may at once be admitted that the increased demand for raw materials was partly responsible for this improvement; but, as has been pointed out, industrial recovery in the United Kingdom has not been uniform over the whole of the range of production. The decree of recovery was greatest in the heavy industries, the raw materials for which are not supplied by India on any large scale, and this factor therefore cannot wholly account for the increase in India's exports to the United Kingdom during the year.

This conclusion is borne out by an examination of the import trade figures of the United Kingdom for 1932 and 1933. Total imports in 1933 declined to £675 02 million from £701.67 million in 1932, while imports of raw materials and articles mainly unmanufactured rose from £164.61 million to £180.40 million, or by 10 per cent. At the same time, imports from India or articles other than tea (tea has been omitted as it is not a raw material of industry) advanced from £19.16 million to £23.33 million, or by 21 per cent, and India's share in the total import trade of the United Kingdom increased from 4.6 per cent to 5.5 per cent.

That is to say the increase in imports from India was more than in proportion to the increase in the total imports of raw materials. It may fairly be claimed therefore that the preferences must have contributed in no small measure to the expansion in India's exports in 1933-34.

Indo-British Trade Tends

The most striking feature of the figures for 1934-35 is the slowing-down in the rate of improvement in the trade with United Kingdom as compared with that with other countries. On this ground, it has been argued that the Ottawa Agreement has been of no substantial benefit to India. This view fails to take into account certain important consideration.

In the first place, it is only to be expected that extension of trade due to the stimulus of a preferential duty will normally be most marked in the first year; therefore, progress will be more gradual, the rate of development showing a progressive decline until the limit of expansion is reached. Secondly, the special factors at work during the year operated to put a definite check to the rate of increase in India's trade with the United Kingdom.

For instance, with the restriction of exports, tea has become for all practical purposes an inelastic item, any considerable increase in the value of the export being possible only in the event of a rise in prices above the level attained in 1933-34. Again, in contrast with the tendency observable in the previous year, the increase in the quantum of world trade in 1934 was accounted for not so much by raw materials as by iron and steel, building materials and semi-capital goods, such as motor cars.

In the United Kingdom, though the imports of raw materials increased from £180.40 million to £209.68 million, the improvement (except in the case of rubber of which India is not an important supplier) was confined to the raw materials of the engineering and building industries, the demand of agricultural raw materials showing no great variation from the previous year. While these causes led to a slackening in the rate of expansion in India's exports to the United Kidgdom, her exports to countries other than the United Kingdom were assisted by abnormal purchases of cotton by Japan to make up for the short purchases during the 1933 boycott.

Japanese Purchase

Japan's purchases in 1934-35 amounted in value to Rs. 21 crores against an average of Rs. 11 crores for the three years ending 1933-34. If her purchase in 1933-34 and 1934-35 are averaged out and India's total exports to countries other than the United Kingdom are adjusted accordingly, the percentage variation in each year will be found to be as follows:—

Percentage of variation in 1933-34 in comparison with 1932-33.—(9.2)
Percentage of variation in 1934-35 in comparison with 1933-34—(5.7)

But for the accident of Japan's having purchased less cotton in one year and more in the next, there would have been a decline of 5.7 per cent in India's exports to foreign countries in 1934-35. If any useful deduction could be drawn from this regarding the value of the Ottawa Agreement, it must surely be one in favour of the Agreement rather than adverse to it.

A better method would perhaps be to examine the results of the two years 1933-34 and 1934-35 as a whole, instead of separately, in order to secure the elimination of the effects of the abnormal features of each year.

A comparison of the figures on this basis still reveals a higher relative expansion in the exports to the United Kingdom, the percentage increase being 30.5 against 8 in the case of exports to foreign countries. (It may be objected that an adjustment should be made on account of the increase in the price of tea. If this is done, the percentage increase will be reduced to 22.5; but it is still considerably higher than the corresponding figure for foreign countries). Clearly, therefore, it would be unreasonable to base an indictment of Ottawa on these figures.

III. INDO-BRITISH TRADE

India's trade with the United Kingdom is compared with that with other countries in this, the third Press note on the tendencies of India's foreign trade.

When trade is separated into articles enjoying preferences and those which do not, a more detailed and vivid appreciation of the effect of all these preferences is obtained. These figures tell their own story :

Exports from India of articles enjoying preference.
(In lakhs of rupees.)

	1931-32.	1932-33.	1933-34.	1934-35.
Total exports ...	110,93	95,04	99,34	94,41
Index ...	100	85.7	89.6	85.1
To United Kingdom ...	33,30	29,73	36,48	36,71
Index ...	100	89.3	109.5	110.2
Percentage share of U. K. in total exports	30.0	31.3	36.7	38.9
To other countries ...	77,63	65,31	62,86	57,70
Index ...	100	84.1	81.0	74.3
Percentage share of other countries in total exports ...	70,0	68.7	63.3	61.1

	Percentage variation in 1933-34 in comparison with 1932-33.	Percentage variation in 1934-35 in comparison with 1933-34.	Percentage variation in 1934-35 in comparison with 1932-33.
United Kingdom...	+22.6	+.6	+23.4
Other countries...	—3.7	—8.3	—11.7
Total...	+4.5	—5	—.7

(The total value of our export trade was Rs. 152.4 crores in 1934-35. The preferential items accounted for 62 per cent of it.)

Exports of coir manufactures, spices, castor seed and ground-nuts from the Indian States enjoying preferences have been taken into account so far as statistics are available.

Exports from India of articles not enjoying preferences in the United Kingdom.
(In lakhs of rupees.)

	1931-32.	1932-23.	1933-34.	1934-35.
Total exports ...	46,63	38,23	48,18	57,98
Index ...	100	82.0	103.3	124.3
Exports to the U. K. ...	9,58	7,09	10,73	11,36
Index ...	100	74.0	112.0	118.6
Percentage share of U. K. ...	20.5	18.5	22.3	19.6
Exports to other countries ...	37,05	31,14	37,35	46,62
Index ...	100	84.0	101.1	125.8
Percentage share of other countries	79.5	81.5	77.7	80.4

	Percentage increase in 1933-34 in comparison with 1932-33.	Percentage increase in 1934-35 in comparison with 1933-34.	Percentage increase in 1934-35 in comparison with 1932-33.
United Kingdom ...	51.3	7.7	60.3
Other countries ...	20.4	24.4	49.7
Total ...	26.0	20.3	51.6

The enormous increase in the consumption of articles not on the preferential list has been interpreted by some critics as justifying the conclusion that the extension in the trade in the preferential items has been due, not so much to the Agreement as to the general increase in the demand for Indian goods in the United Kingdom.

In the view of these critics the conclusion to be drawn from these figures is two-fold. First, that the revival of industrial activity in the United Kingdom has stimulated a demand for such commodities. Second, that in regard to the preferential items the preferences granted by the United Kingdom have been of little benefit to India.

This view seems to be based on an insufficient appreciation of the facts. "Of the total increase of Rs. 364 lakhs under the non-preferential" head in 1933-34, Rs. 176 lakhs was accounted for by cotton and Rs. 45 lakhs by raw wool. The greater use of Indian cotton in the United Kingdom was due partly to the favourable price parity but more particularly to the propaganda conducted by the Lancashire Indian Cotton Committee.

In so far as the increased off-take was due to the price factor, it is clear that industrial revival was not the cause of the improvement; and in so far as it was due to the activities of the Lancashire Indian Cotton Committee it was a measure of the success that has attended the steps taken by his Majesty's Government to implement Article 8 of the Agreement.

The second item, namely, raw wool, is liable to wide fluctuations from year to year presumably in accordance with variations in the price parity and no valid general conclusion could be drawn from the volume of the trade in it in any particular year.

In 1934-35 there was a further advance of Rs. 63 lakhs in the non-preferential items owing mainly to increases in rubber (25 lakhs), metals and ores (18 lakhs), lac (14 lakhs), and cotton (4 lakhs).

The increase in rubber was due solely to the restriction scheme; that in metals and ores apparently to the renewed activity in the heavy industries; that in lac to speculate purchases by the London 'ring' which tried to operate a 'corner' in shellac and pepper; and that in cotton to the circumstances already explained.

There is thus little evidence to support the view that the improvement in the exports in the non-preferential items was due mainly industrial revival, and that the trade in the preferential items would on that account have in any case shown a sympathetic increase.

A study of the figures shows that the Ottawa preferences must have been of material advantage to India in improving her position in the United Kingdom market. In 1933-34 there was a net increase of Rs. 430 lakhs (+4.5 per cent) in her total exports of the articles enjoying preference, resulting from increase of Rs. 675 lakhs (+22.6 per cent) in the trade to the United Kingdom, partially off-set, however, by a decline of Rs. 245 lakhs (—3.7 per cent) in the trade to other countries.

Decline in Foreign Exports

In 1934-35 there was a further decline of Rs. 516 lakhs in the exports to foreign countries, but exports to the United Kingdom increased by Rs. 25 lakhs.

Between 1932-33 and 1934-35, therefore, there was a total decline of Rs. 761 lakhs in the exports to foreign countries and an advance of Rs. 698 lakhs in the exports to the United Kingdom. That is to say, at a time when India's competitive power in world markets outside the United Kingdom was failing off she made up nearly the whole of the loss in the United Kingdom.

IV. INCREASED EXPORTS TO UNITED KINGDOM

Is the contention of critics of the Ottawa Agreement correct that the recent increased exports to the United Kingdom are merely a diversion of trade?—In this fourth Press Note on India's foreign trade tendencies this contention is examined and shown to be inaccurate.

The principal decreases in 1933-34 in the total trade to countries other than the United Kingdom in the articles enjoying preference are tabulated below

The articles are arranged in two groups, Group A comprising those which registered a decline both to the United Kingdom and to other countries and Group B comprising all other. The figures in brackets indicate the percentage decreases as compared with 1932-33.

GROUP A

Articles		Total decrease in comparison with 1932-33. Rs. (in Lakhs)	
1. Rice	...	351	(26)
2. Castor Seed	...	25	(26)
3. Bran & Pollard	...	7	(46)
4. Coffee	...	4	(5)
	Total.	387	
GROUP B.			
5. Groundnuts	...	39	(6)
6. Tea	...	9	(4)
	Total.	48	

As the trade with U. K. in the articles included in Group A also showed a decline, it is clear that in the case of these articles the hypothesis of diversion is untenable.

It will nevertheless be of interest to examine the reasons for the abnormal decline in the trade in rice, the largest single item of decrease on the export side.

CAUSES FOR LOSS IN TRADE

The Review of Trade for 1933-34 attributes the loss in trade, firstly, to the "deliberate and intensive development of certain tracts which, instead of importing their requirements of rice from outside, endeavoured to grow the crop themselves," and, secondly, to the restrictions imposed on imports in some foreign countries by legislation and other measures.

As illustrative of these measures the Review gives the following instances :—

"In Netherlands Indies, for instance, where a drastic reduction in the cultivation of sugarcane was producing a steady change over to rice, it was found necessary to restrict imports of rice in order to conserve the home market for the local production. China and the Federated Malay States imposed an import duty on rice. Further Japan has inaugurated elaborate measures for rice control, and the change in her status from an importing to an exporting country is important to India.

Concurrently, China has decided to protect herself by the imposition of small import tariff on rice coming from abroad.

All these factors were bound to have considerable reactions on the rice export trade of Burma. Even in those markets where rice is capable of being sold on a strictly price basis in competition with other foodstuffs, the inability to provide in sufficient quantities the quality of rice demanded by the consumer, had had a restrictive effect on the export trade."

The articles included in Group B stand on a different footing in that smaller exports to foreign countries were accompanied by larger sales to the United Kingdom.

GROUND-NUT TRADE

In the case of ground-nuts, however, the fall in value does not indicate a diminution in the volume of exports. Actually, despite smaller despatches to France owing, it is said, to the imposition of an import duty on groundnuts other than those grown in the French Colonies, the quantum of trade with foreign countries rose from 31,600 tons to 52,800 tons.

As an instance of the difficulty of reconciling trade figures of different countries in regard to the same item it may be mentioned that according to the French official statistics India increased her exports from 2,595,000 quintals to 3,070,000 quintals, thus capturing a larger share of the French market.

On the other hand, in the case of tea, there was drop both in value and quantity. For this, however, the division of markets agreed upon by the parties to the international scheme for the restriction of exports was no doubt responsible.

It follows, therefore, that there is no foundation for the suggestion that the improvement in the United Kingdom market disclosed by the figures for 1933-34 was gained at the expense of the trade with other countries.

The figures for 1934-35 point to the same conclusion. The trade with foreign countries in the articles admitted to preference dropped by Rs. 516 lakhs, resulting in a net decrease of Rs. 493 lakhs in the total trade. The principal decreases during the year are shown below :

GROUP A.

Article		Total decrease in comparison with 1933-34. Rs. (lakhs).	
1. Linseed	...	85	(33)
2. Goat Skin (raw)	...	60	(30)
3. Paraffin Wax	...	29	(17)
4. Coffee	...	21	(30)
5. Cotton Yarn	...	18	(23)
6. Castor Seed	...	16	(23)
7. Coir Yarn	...	6	(7)
8. Miscellaneous	...	87	(9.5)
Total	...	322	
GROUP B.			
9. Groundnuts	...	167	(28)
10. Rice	...	67	(7)
11. Tea	...	29	(13)
Total	...	263	

Here again, as regards articles in Group A it is only necessary to point out that the reduced off-take by foreign countries is due to curtailment of demand (e. g., castor seed and goat skins) or to increased competition (e. g., linseed) and that the corresponding decline in each case in the demand from U. K. precludes the possibility of diversion.

In Group B, the principal item that calls for comment is groundnuts, the exports of which to France fell from 188,100 tons to 99,300 tons in the year as a result of reduction of demand to about half the usual volume and of the imposition of a quota system, limiting foreign imports to 50 per cent of the total imports.

RESTRICTION ON IMPORTS

The recession in rice exports was due mainly to the causes observed in the previous year, but partly to import restrictions introduced by Germany and certain other European countries.

Exports of tea during the year to foreign countries were regulated in accordance with marketing arrangements entered into by the producing countries ; they were also affected by a shift in demand from the higher grades to lower grades represented by Java growths, and, as a result, a larger quantity was shipped to the United Kingdom than would otherwise have been.

The diversion, therefore, was entirely caused by extraneous factors.

It is abundantly clear that the causes underlying the rapid expansion in the trade in non-preferential items, both with the United Kindom and foreign countries, are hardly such as would have led to a spontaneous improvement to the extent that has been achieved in the trade in the preferential items to the United Kingdom. Nor can it be contended that the trade has been artificially increased by the diversion of exports from foreign to inter-Imperial channels.

The advance that India has made in the British market in the last two years has resulted in a genuine expansion of trade in many, if not all, of the articles entitled to preference, and has been facilitated by the preferences granted, particularly on such commodities as rice, groundnuts and teak and other hardwoods.

COFFEE TRADE

Where India has lost ground to other parts of the Empire, as for instance to Kenya in the trade in coffee, it is easy to see that she would have fared worse had she been under a tariff handicap.

It is obviously necessary in such cases, in order to take the fullest possible advantage of the preferences, to improve our methods of marketing and publicity with special reference to the needs of the British market.

It is to be hoped that the labours of the newly constituted Coffee Cess Committee will bring about an early revival in our export trade in coffee. The gains secured by Kenya and other Colonies are a measure of the advantages accruing from the preferences. There is no reason why India, by suitable propaganda and other measures, should not participate in an increasing degree in the expanding British market for Empire products.

In the preferential section of our trade, it is true that the gains so far made in the United Kingdom market have not been sufficient to compensate for the losses in other markets, but as has already been shown the construction of demand in foreign markets has been due to the operation of special factors.

When international trade is so disorganised as at the present time it is idle to expect speedy or sensational results from any programme of recovery. Nor must it be forgotten that the year 1934 was on the whole unfavourable to debtor countries, particularly those producing raw materials.

In the great majority of deetor countries, the balance of trade in merchandise was less satisfactory than in the previous year (e. g.), Germany, Australia, New Zealand and Cuba).

TRADE BALANCES
(Merchandise only)

Country	In terms of U. S. gold dollars (000,000) (+) Surplus of exports ; 1933	(—) Surplus of imports. 1934.
India	+73.6	+52.2
Netherlands Indies	+56.7	+93.4
Argentine	+57	+66.4
Brazil	+37.3	+48.5
New Zealand	+38.1	+36.0
British Malaya	+8.1	+28.4
Germany	+159.1	—66.8
Roumania	+14.6	+3.1
Denmark	—9.2	—16.4
Australia	+113.1	+40.1
Cuba	+32.3	+5
South Africa	+139.5	+32.4

The main exceptions were countries which benefited from restriction schemes raising the prices of their exports (e. g. British Malaya and the Netherlands Indies), and those which depreciated their currencies further and also benefitted from restriction schemes brought into force in the other parts of the world (e. g. the Argentine and Brazil). India has, nevertheless, been able, despite the unfavourable conditions of the year, to record an appreciable expansion of her export trade.

The extent to which the preferences have contributed to this result is not capable of exact statistical assessment. No one examining the question with an unprejudiced mind, can fail to be convinced that the unrestricted right of entry obtained by India under the Agreement, ranks high amongst the factors which have enabled her to maintain and develop her position in the British market during a period of exceptional difficulty

V. RETALIATION CHARGE EXAMINED

One of the most persistent criticisms of the Ottawa Agreement in its application to India is that foreign countries have retaliated against this giving of tariff preferences. In this and the next following Press Notes that criticism is examined.

When the Ottawa Resolution was debated in the Legislative Assembly in 1932, it was pointed out that the fear of reprisals was greatly exaggerated. The necessity of obtaining raw materials in the cheapest market, and the obligation resting on most foreign countries under treaty engagements to accord to Indian goods most-favoured-nation treatment, were alone sufficient to restrain aggrieved foreign countries, should there be any such, from taking retaliatory action against India.

Critics of the Agreement were not disposed to agree with this view. They considered that India's dependence on foreign markets for the absorption of nearly two thirds of her exports made her position specially vulnerable, and that, even if foreign countries refrained from subjecting Indian goods to discriminatory treatment by way of retaliation, the inevitable result of a system of preferences in favour of the United Kingdom would be a decline of India's import trade with foreign countries and with a corresponding diminution in her exports to such countries.

In 1934, when a Committee of the Assembly was appointed to examine and report on the working of the Agreement, the suggestion was made that certain foreign countries had imposed restrictions on imports from India by-way of retaliation.

The Committee made a detailed review of the restrictive measures introduced by foreign countries since 1927, and, by a majority, recorded the finding that "in no case was the restrictive action retaliatory in nature or specially directed against India."

Nevertheless, the accusation has been freely made in recent months that the restrictions on imports imposed by a number of foreign countries since 1932 are a direct result of the Ottawa Agreement.

Here and there, it is true a voice has been raised in protest against so baseless a charge. The "Indian Finance", for instance, in its issue of September 28, 1935. remarked, "it must be admitted, too, that those, who condemn the Ottawa Pact for the restrictions on Indian imports in foreign markets, are guilty of either ignorance or intellectual dishonesty."

The majority of the opponents of the Agreement, however, are still obsessed with the idea that the Agreement is somehow responsible for the spate of emergency restrictions on trade, which have been so marked a feature of European Commercial policy since the deepening of the depression.

It is singular that there should be so much ill-informed criticism on a matter which is not one of opinion, but of fact.

It is pertinent to inquire in the first place whether there was any reason to suppose that the institution, on a reciprocal basis, of preferential tariff arrangements between the United Kingdom and India would be regarded by any foreign country as constituting a breach of any of the accepted canons of commercial policy.

In order to answer this queston it is necessary to examine briefly the inter-related questions of the exceptions to the "most-favoured-nation" principle and of the Colonial and-inter Imperial trade policies of the big Powers.

There have always been recognised certain customary exceptions to the unlimited and unconditional application of the most-favoured nation clause. One such exception permits countries bound by the clause to enter into a customs union providing complete free trade with each other, while continuing to impose tariffs against others. In virtue of another, certain groups of closely associated countries e. g., the 'Baltic', group comprising the Scandinavian countries and the 'Iberian' group covering Spain and Portugal and countries of Latin America, have been allowed to impose specially favourable duties *inter se* which are inapplicable to other countries.

Of this type, also are the preferential tariff arragements between U. S. A. and Cuba and U. S. A. and the Philippine Islands (since the enactment of the Act of Independence), the benefits of which are not available to third parties.

To these must be added the right of preferential treatment enjoyed as between members of the British Commonwealth of Nations, although the right is sometimes expressed as one arising from their common political sovereignty rather than as an exception to the clause.

The position that a general preferential scheme within the Empire is a matter of domestic concern, and can not be regarded as discriminatory by any foreign power was attained by stages, and has not been seriously challenged since the end of the tariff war between Canada and Germany in the early years of the present century. The first step in the direction of a system of inter-Imperial preferences was taken by Canada in 1897 when she reduced import duties by one-eighth on goods coming from the United Kingdom. The benefit of the lower duties was for a time extended to a number of foreign countries, but in 1907, a new Tariff Act was enacted containing three columns of duties, British preferential, intermediate and general. The example of Canada was followed by New Zealand and South Africa in 1903 and by Australia in 1907.

The war brought the question of inter-Imperial trade once again into prominence, and since 1920 the Dominions and Colonies have given further extensive preference to the United Kingdom.

By 1922 there were already preferential tariffs in operation in twenty-six British Colonies, the Mother country being the principal beneficiary.

For her part, the United Kingdom, in 1919, abandoned her opposition to preferences in favour of Empire countries and introduced preferential rates of duty on a limited number of articles of Empire origin.

From then on the policy of preference was consistently pursued within the framework of the British fiscal system and additions were made from year to year to the list of articles entitled to preference.

The nucleus of a preferential scheme within the Empire was thus already in existence at the time of the Ottawa Agreement. What was achieved at Ottawa was the general extension of the scheme throughout the Empire on the basis of reciprocity.

The adoption of this scheme by India no doubt meant a re-orientation of her tariff policy, but the right of Empire countries to establish a system of preferential tariffs to their mutual advantage was by them so well established that it was hardly likely that India's exercise of that right would involve serious reactions upon her commercial relations with foreign countries.

To the policy of inter-Empire preferences, moreover, none would be less justified in taking exception than the big Colonial Powers.

Officially the United State of America has no colonies, but it nevertheless possesses a Colonial Empire with a population of 14 millions. Its policy in respect of Hawaii and Porto Rico has been one of assimilation, that is to say, of extension to the Colonies of the tariff system of the Mother Country with mutual free trade amongst themselves, while as between the U. S. A. and the Philippine Islands there exists a preferential regime.

France, too, has extended the principle of assimilation to a number of her foreign possessions, e. g., Indo-China, Madagascar and Guadeloupe, and French goods enter these assimilated territories free of duty. Among the non-assimilated group of colonies, some maintain the Open Door while many accord preferential treatment to goods of French orign in return for tariff concessions in respect of their exports to France. The aim of French Colonial trade policy has been in fact to foster the closest trade relations between the Mother Country and the Colonies.

Since the War, various measures have been taken with a surprising degree of success to stimulate France-Colonial exchanges.

The Conference held in Paris at the beginning of this year to concert measures for the further encouragement of colonial trade was therefore hardly in the nature of a counterblast to Ottawa, but rather the logical outcome of the policy unswervingly pursued by France since the War.

But, it may be asked, when it is true that foreign countries could have no justifiable grievance against India's acceptance of the principle of inter-Empire preferences, is it still not possible that some of them, at any rate, through a feeling of irritation, may have discriminated against Indian goods ?

This is a valid objection, and which requires to be carefully considered.

VI. RETALIATION CHARGE

The sixth and last Press Note continues the examination of the suggestion that foreign countries have retaliated against India for giving preferences under the Ottawa Agreement.

Have foreign countries discriminated against India's exports because of a feeling of justifiable irritation ?

The Report of the Committee of the Legislative Assembly appointed to examine the working of the Agreement sets out in one of the Appendices a list of the restrictive measures taken by other countries which affect exports from India.

Since the issue of the Report further restrictions have been introduced by a number of countries.

It is significant that the foreign countries which are sometimes described as our "best customers" are not alone in applying quantitative restrictions to trade. A number of other countries with whom our trade exchanges are of negligible proportions, and even certain Empire countries, have adopted the use of quotas, licensing systems and similar weapons as instruments of commercial policy.

It is also significant that the restrictions apply to all countries alike, and that, in addition to raw materials, a number of commodities in the export of which India is not interested fall within their scope.

So universal an application of emergency trade restrictions suggests that the action of particular countries, even when it may be said to affect adversely the interests of India's export trade, cannot have been inspired by animus against India.

The fact is that the quantitative regulation of imports, in the various forms in which it is in operation in different parts of the world, has unfortunately come to be regarded by many countries as the most effective device in present conditions for maintaining their commercial and financial stability.

It follows that where foreign countries which compete with the United Kingdom for the Indian market have adopted restrictive measures they have done so for reasons of domestic policy, and not with the intention of retaliating against India.

Of the countries said to have vigorously pursued a policy of retaliation against India, the important are France, Germany and Italy in Europe and Turkey and Iran in Asia. The restrictive measures taken by these countries may therefore suitably form the subject of detailed examination.

France has the unenviable distinction of being the orginator of what has been described as the "pernicious system" of import quotas. Originally introduced in 1931 to restrict imports of manufactured goods into France, the quota system has been rapidly extended to cover imports of agricultural products and raw materials.

By 1933 quotas had been applied to no fewer than 1,200 tariff items, or about one-sixth of the whole, including many of the chief import groups.

The following commodities in which India is interested are now subject to import quotas, viz., coffee, dari, barley, maize, pulses, lentils, peas, tissues of jute, cotton manufactures, oil cakes, oil seeds, tanned hides and skins and sports goods. In the case of some of these commodities there is in existence a licensing system as an adjunct to the quota.

A tariff change of some importance to India is the imposition of a duty of groundnuts of other than colonial origin, which came into effect in August 1933.

As the following figures will indicate, the duty must have been imposed with the object of preserving a due share of the home market for the colonial product (mainly undecorticated) against the invasion of British West Africa.

IMPORTS OF GROUNDNUTS (DECORTICATED) INTO FRANCE

(In thousand quintals)

	1929	1930	1931	1932	1933 (Jan.-Oct.,
British India	2926	2542	2462	2695	2635
British West Africa	581	460	632	1175	1165
Total	3656	3417	3446	4532	4055

In 1934 a system of licensing was introduced in respect of imports of groundnuts, but the French trade statistics for the year show that, despite these handicaps, India continues to hold her own in the French market.

The measures referred to above were taken in the interests of French West Africa whose prosperity depends on the price of the groundnuts, the principal crop of the Colony, and were in no way directed against India.

If further proof were needed to show that the extension of the quota system to commodities in which India is interested was not actuated by a spirit of vindictiveness, it is supplied by the fact that the French Government are now being urged to impose a quota for Algerian and Tunisian wines in the interests of the French wine industry.

The quantitative control of imports was undertaken by Germany in 1932, partly with a view to safeguarding her financial stability and partly in pursuance of her policy of agricultural protection.

The import of a number of agricultural and dairy products was made subject to a quota syestem, while that of rice and rice products was severely restricted by reason of their inclusion in the Maize Monopoly. With the deterioration in her exchange position a system of licensing was introduced for the import of the important raw materials of industry such as cotton, jute, wool and hides and skins accompanied by a rigid system of 'rationing' of foreign exchange.

By September, 1934, the position had become so embarrassing that a new method of control was established, under which the total amount of exchange made available for the financing of imports was to be based from month to month on an estimate of the exchange likely to result from Germany's exports in the ensuing month.

All foreign exchange dealings and all imports are thus now subject to control in Germany, the avowed object of the German Government being to create an export surplus by establishing in the first instance equilibrium between foreign imports and the exchange obtained from export.

As further measures to this end, Germany has negotiated a number of clearing agreements, designed to secure (though seldom successfully) an even balance of trade with individual countries as well as compensation agreements, for the bartering of goods against goods, both with State organisations and with private individuals and firms. It is understood that much of the import business with India lately has been done on the basis of compensation arrangements with the larger exporters.

Under the new regime of exchange control introduced in September 1934, priority is to be given to essential food stuffs, raw materials and semi-manufactured goods.

India with other suppliers of raw materials is thus placed in a less unfavourable position than other exporting countries.

A further advantage to India has been secured by a clause in the Agreement between the United Kingdom and Germany concluded in November, 1934, providing that on the allocation of foreign exchange Germany will take no measures to reduce the customary proportions enjoyed by the United Kingdom and the British Colonies in the supply of raw materials and food stuffs which she has been accustomed to purchase, either through the United Kingdom or as re-exports from the United Kingdom. Notwithstanding these provisions, India's export trade with Germany, particularly in rice, hides and skins and oil-seeds, has fallen off considerably in the last two years. Indian trade figures indicate that the balance of trade has moved heavily against India, but, according to the German figures, which in view of the obvious limitations of the Indian statistics relating to trade with Germany may be accepted as the more reliable, there is still a small margin in favour of India.

The heavy export surpluses of the pre-depression period have, however, disappeared, and in certain of her main export staples India is apparently being displaced by countries with whom Germany has included clearing agreements. These are almost all of those countries which had an adverse balance with Germany and accordingly found it in their own interest to come to terms with her.

On the other hand, countries in a similar position to India which have favourable balance with Germany have nothing to gain and everything to lose by entering into an agreement of this nature. The only effect of so doing would be to areduce still further the balance in their favour.

Nor is India the only country whose trade with Germany has suffered by reason of the restrictions ; other countries have also been badly hit, particularly the United States of America, whose share in Germany's cotton purchases has fallen to a fifth of what it was two years ago. These facts are plainly irreconcilable with the theory of retaliation, except on the assumption that Germany, in her bitterness, has thought fit to penalise the trade not only of India but of innocent countries outside the British Empire !

The fact, of course, is that for India's declining trade with Germany, no blame can attach to the Ottawa Agreement. It is the direct consequence of the application by Germany of the new doctrine of regulated bilateral trade with a view to the maintenance of an even balance in the trade with each and every foreign country.

CRITICISM OF THE AGREEMENT'S WORKING

(1) Note by Federated Chamber of Commerce

The Committee of the Federation of Indian Chambers of Commerce in a very exhaustive note issued by them in **January 1936**, examined the report of the Government of India on the working of the Ottawa scheme of preferences.

After the termination of the Great War, every country of importance decided to follow the policy of intense economic nationalism and tried to become self-sufficient in its requirements with the result that international trade between countries received a severe setback and the supremacy of the British industries gradually began to diminish in the world markets. Successive attempts were made by the British Government at the Imperial Conferences of 1923, 1926 and 1930 to create an economic bloc within the Empire and thus to preserve the Empire markets, particularly for the manufactured goods of the United Kingdom, as the McKenna Duties of 1926 and the Safeguarding of Industries Act of 1922 failed to afford adequate protection to British industries. The Import Duties Act of 1932 was fully utilised at the Imperial Economic Conference of 1932 for concluding reciprocal trade treaties with the Dominions and India at Ottawa.

The commercial and industrial interests in India unequivocally maintained, while the deliberations were going on at Ottawa, that it would not be in the best interest of India if a reciprocal agreement was entered into with the United Kingdom at a time when her constitution was in the melting pot. Inspite of all these protests from all quarters in the country, the Government of India entered into a certain reciprocal trade agreement at Ottawa and claimed substantial benefits to agricultural produce of India in exchange for certain preferences for manufactured articles from the United Kingdom. They particularly claimed that in certain important commodities of export such as, vegetable oils, linseed, coffee, tea, hides and skins, jute, raw cotton, pig iron and tobacco, India would not only capture a substantial market from the foreign competitors in the United Kingdom but as a result of the preference, it would lead to greater acreage of some of the crops and the position of the agriculturists in India would improve.

An attempt is made in the note issued by the Committee of the Federation to show how these expectations held out by the Government of India at the time of the ratification of the Ottawa Pact failed to materialise. On the other hand, the working of the Ottawa trade treaty obstructed India's direct trade relations with a number of foreign countries, particularly with the European countries which initiated quota restrictions, import licences and exchange control to arrest their passivity of trade with India as the working of the Ottawa scheme and the depreciation of the £ increased the competitive power of United Kingdom industries, while that of countries like Germany, Italy, France, Czechoslovakia declined in the Indian market for manufactured goods. The European countries were, therefore, compelled to find means for balancing their international accounts and there has begun a period of sub-conscious retaliation by these countries towards India purely as a self-defensive measure. These new systems introduced by the European countries gave rise to clearing agreements and bilateral treaties between industrial and agricultural countries. As an illustration, the note refers to India's export trade in raw materials to Germany, which was to the extent of 26.6 crores in 1929-30 and which came down to 10.3 crores in 1931-32 and after the working of the Ottawa pact, dwindled to 7 crores in 1934-35. India's export trade to Germany suffered because the scope in the Indian market for German manufactured goods was restricted by the effective operation of the Ottawa scheme. The Government of India's contention that there was no discrimination aimed at India by these European countries in their resorting to licences, quota restrictions or exchange control, did not save this country from the same harmful effects as would result from an act of discrimination against India. As quotas have to be allotted as between countries, the danger of discrimination was inevitable and so is the case of foreign exchange control; the inevitable corollary of exchange regulations is the control of imports. These devices can be utilised in complete freedom either to placate a friendly nation or to annoy a country like India, and Germany has been fully utilising the power vested in her executive to so control the foreign exchange as to adjust her balances of trade with her foreign customers.

France and Italy have been following since the Ottawa agreement a policy of developing their colonial possessions on lines similar to the British scheme and France is now taking from French West Africa raw materials in greater quantities at the cost of her trade with India. The forces thus let loose as a result of the Ottawa scheme in the sphere of international trade are responsible for the coming into existence of import licences or quota restrictions or exchange control. The United States of America have already on hand negotiations with not less than 14 countries for bilateral treaties and every country of industrial importance is trying to arrive at a certain reciprocal trade understanding with another agricultural country for the adjustment of trade balances between them. Unfortunately under the Ottawa scheme, India's power to enter into bilateral treaties with her chief foreign customers was restricted and there was no scope left for offering a certain portion in the import trade of manufactured articles to non-Empire countries who happened to be the United Kingdom's competitor in the Indian markets.

If India is to be a willing party to a certain scheme of economic bloc within the British Empire she must secure sufficient freedom to adjust her import trade with such of her chief non-Empire customers which have been in the past and even continue to be at present her substantial customers in her export trade.

The Committee have tried to examine the results of the Ottawa scheme with an unbiassed mind free from all considerations other than those warranted by the necessities of India and would have welcomed any appreciable improvement as a result of the scheme in the trade relations between India and the United Kingdom, but even after giving the scheme a trial for over two years, the Committee have no hesitation in asserting that any impartial examination of the working of the agreement will arrive at the same conclusions to which the Committee have come, namely :—

(a) That India's export trade in agricultural product with the United Kingdom did not show any substantial advance owing to the fact that the British dominions securing similar preference gained a better and stronger footing in the United Kingdom market over India's produce ;

(b) That the intense economic nationalism initiated by the United Kingdom in creating an economic bloc within the Empire has restricted the growth of internationalism of trade instead of encouraging it and forced a number of manufacturing non-Empire countries to resort to import licenses, quota restrictions and exchange control to arrest the passivity of trade, which measures in case of India, affected her export trade to these non-Empire countries.

The Committee feel that in view of the facts and conclusions adduced above, they are justified in recommending to the Government of India the termination of the present trade agreement between the United Kingdom and India as it has resulted in no material benefit to India's agricultural produce and has unnecessarily called for retaliation—however subconscious from her other foreign customers. The Committee are not averse to any trade pact between India and any of her customers ; on the other hand, they would welcome such pacts on purely reciprocal basis. They, therefore, suggest that the Government of India should forthwith terminate the present trade treaty and should open up fresh negotiations not only with the United Kingdom but with all other foreign countries for trade treaties, in consultation with representatives of commerce, agriculture and industry in India.

(II) Report of the Federated Chambers of Commerce

'The working of the Ottawa schedule of preferences has obstructed India's direct trade relations with a number of foreign countries, particularly with the European countries which initiated quota restrictions, import licences and exchange control to arrest their passivity of trade with India as the working of the Ottawa scheme and the depreciation of the £ increased the competitive power of the United Kingdom industries, while that of countries like Germany, Italy, France and Czecho-slovakia declined in the Indian market for the manufactured goods'.—This view is expressed in the annual report for the year 1935-36 of the Federation of Indian Chambers of Commerce and Industry issued on the **4th. March 1936**. The Federation appointed a small sub-committee consisting of Lala Padampat Singhania, the president, Messrs. D. P. Khaitan, Kasturbhai Lalbhai, Shri Ram and N. R. Sarkar which examined the working of the Pact.

The reports adds, 'The Government of India's contention that there was no discrimination aimed at India by those European countries in their resorting to licences, quota restrictions or exchange control, did not save this country from the same harmful effects as would result from an act of discrimination against India. France and Italy have been following since the Ottawa Agreement a policy of developing colonial processions on lines similar to the British scheme and France is now taking from French West Africa raw materials in greater quantities at the cost of her trade with India. The forces thus let loose as a result of the scheme in the sphere of international trade are responsible for the coming into existence of import licences or quota restrictions or exchange control. The United States of America have already on hand negotiations with not less than 14 countries for bilateral treaties and every country of industrial importance is trying to arrive at a certain reciprocal trade understanding with another agricultural country for the adjustment of trade balances between them. Unfortunately, under the Ottawa scheme, India's power to enter into bilateral treaties with her chief foreign customers got restricted and there was no scope left for offering a certain portion in the import trade of manufactured articles to non-empire countries who happened to be the United Kingdom's competitor in the Indian markets.

'If India is to be a willing party to a certain scheme of economic block within the British empire, she must secure sufficient freedom to adjust her import trade with such of her chief non-empire customers which have been in the past and even continue to be at present her substantial customers in her export trade.

The Committee recommend to the Government of India the termination of the present trade agreement between the United Kingdom and India as it has resulted in no material benefit to India's agricultural produce and has unnecessarily called for retaliation—however sub-conscious—from her other foreign customers. The Committee are not averse to any trade pact between India and any of her customers ; on the other hand, they would welcome such pacts on purely reciprocal basis. They, therefore, suggest that the Government of India should forthwith terminate the present trade treaty and should open up fresh negotiations not only with the United Kingdom but with other foreign countries for trade treaties, in consultation with representatives of commerce, agriculture and industry in India.

During the year under review the Committee held six meetings and the total number of member-bodies affiliated to the Federation stood at 56 and eight organizations, three from Calcutta, two from Delhi, one from Tuticorin one from Calicut and one from Ahmedabad were admitted during the year.

On the question of operation of non-Indian concerns in India behind the protectionist policy of the Government of India in respect of certain indiganous industries, the Committee circulated to all member-bodies and some of them were able to indicate instances in which indigenous enterprises have suffered because of the presence of non-Indian concerns in India.

The Committee of the Federation represented to the Government of India in June 1935 with regard to the question of the disposal of surplus stock of quinine, and suggested that the surplus of 150,000 lbs. of quinine held by the Government should be utilised by them towards making it available at cheaper rates to provincial Governments for distribution amongst the agricultural masses instead of selling it to the Kina Bureau, at a ridiculously low price. The Committee suggested extending their plantations in Bengal and Madras to yield sufficient quantity of cinchona for the requirements of the country. With regard to the discontinuance of direct mail service between Rangoon and Madras, the Federation deplored that the Government of India took decision without even a reference to the mercantile community directly affected by the discontinuance.

As regards the admission of Indian students to German factories and workshops, the representative of the Federation in Germany reported that after some enquiries he was able to ascertain from the Federation of German Chambers that the German Federation would be agreeable to admit Indian students to German factories in proportion to, or even more than the extent of orders placed by India in Germany for German goods. All member-bodies were asked to furnish necessary information and the matter will be furtner pursued in the light of the information that would be received from the member-bodies.

As for sugar production rules, the Committee suggested a certain procedure for adequately safeguarding the confidential information and reiterated their view that the Government should not call for information relating to the cost of production as such information was bound to affect the industry in years to come. The Imperial Council of Agricultural Research replied that a fresh notification was being issued amending the rules in the light of the criticisms made to the extent possible.

(III) Mr. Satyamurti's Analysis

On the eve of the Ottawa debate in the Assembly, the Secretary of the Congress Party, Mr. *Satyamurthi*, issued to members of the Assembly what purports to be an analysis of the working of the Agreement and incidentally a reply to some of the points raised in the series of articles officially issued :—

Has the Ottawa Agreement resulted in an increase of India's export trade or at least prevented a fall which might have occurred but for it ? Exports have increased from Rs. 136 crores in 1932-33 (Pre-Ottawa Year) to 154 crores in 1934-35. Imports have remained the same, 132 crores in 1932-33 and in 1934-5. But the balance of trade which in 1933-34 was 34 crores has now fallen to 22 crores—a very serious state of affairs in view of our external obligations. But for gold exports, there would have been an exchange crisis. Not until there is a balance of merchandise trade in our favour to the tune of about 50 crores, can India be said to have reached economic equilibrium.

A more relevant test is to note the growth of exports in the commodities in which we get preference. What do we find there ? Our exports in preferred commodities which increased in 1933-34 from 95 crores in the pre-Ottawa year to 99 crores have fallen seriously to 94 crores—to less than the figure of the pre-Ottawa year. This was just what was anticipated by the critics of the Ottawa Agreement.

Diversion of trade to Great Britain was certainly to be expected; what was feared was that it would not bring about the slightest improvement in exports. The fears have turned out to be true. The quantum of the trade in preferred goods has shrunk. It is true that the United Kingdom's share is a larger percentage of the trade in preferred commodities but is no relief to India, since as against the contention of the Ottawa champions, the total trade in preferred goods has shurnk. (See Matthai's Report P. 344).

Has our share in Great Britain's trade increased more than Great Britain's share in our trade? Yes. Taking first articles enjoying preference, our percentage share in the total import trade of Great Britain has increased from 5.3 in 1932-33 to 6.4 in 1933-34 and continued to be the same in 1934-35: whereas Great Britain's share in imports into India of preferred articles increased from 40 per cent in 1932-33 to 46 per cent in 1933-34, but fell to 44 per cent in 1934-35.

In the case of non-preferred commodities, India's share increased from 3.0 to 3.8 and to 4.7 per cent. whereas Britain's share in India's trade increased from 35.8 to 39.4 to 39.3 per cent.

But the above answer cannot be understood as indicating the advantages of the Ottawa Agreement. The assumption underlying Dr. Matthai's argument is questionable. He says: "If India has improved her relative position in the United Kingdom imports, then, other things being equal, the preference must *prima facie* be deemed to be valuable. Whether India' other customers have taken more from her than the United Kingdom is not quite relevant to the issue." On the contrary, that is quite relevant. If it can be shown that with the best intentions of the United Kingdom her share in India's export trade in various goods is diminishing, it shows the relative futility of preferences. Great Britain's share of our exports increased from 28.0 to 32.2 per cent in 1933-34 but fell to 31.6 per cent in 1934-35. It is true that her share in our import trade increased from 36.8 to 41.3 in 1933-34 but fell slightly to 40.6 per cent in 1934-35. But what they both show is that in the case of India, she gains no advantage from preference whereas in the case of Britain owing to the high price of her goods, she has not been able to gain more substantial advantages out of preference and would have been very badly off without preferences.

This can be clearly seen if we consider British imports in cotton goods, hardware steel, machinery and mill work, motor car, etc. The loss to Great Britain, if preference were not given in these commodities, would have been serious and the damage which she can inflict on India's trade is very limited indeed. For, if we exclude tea, jute, hides and skins, teakwood, myrobalams and castor seed, in which either India holds a monopoly or Great Britain cannot discriminate in her own interests, the remaining exports will be only 18 crores out of a total of 48 crores.

What has been the reaction of foreign countries to the Ottawa Agreement? The fall in our exports to foreign countries has been 8 crores of rupees, i. e., from 64 crores in 1932-33 to 56 crores in 1934-35. i. e., 12 and half per cent. But the whole of this fall cannot be ascrib to the Ottawa Agreement: because of the general depression in Europe and elsewhere of the exchange restrictions, quota systems, tariff, etc. But there is no gainsaying the fact that on account of discrimination in India against foreign goods the ability of foreign countries to buy Indian goods has been reduced. India's dependence on Europe, Japan, U. S. A. has been clearly revealed in the continued stagnation of our export trade.

Exports to Great Britain and imports from Great Britain have decreased as from 1934-35. This shows that on either side there are handicaps which cannot be easily surmounted by preferences. The price element is the limiting factor of the import from Britain, while the quality of some of our exports is the limiting factor in British market. But the sacrifices involved are disproportionate. The preference on Indian goods extends to no more than 4 to 5 per cent of total British imports; whereas the preference on British goods affects 40 p. c. The sacrifice of India is necessarily greater.

It is necessary in estimating the relative sacrifices involved to realise the extent of the loss in mere revenue which preferences to Great Britain imply. A rough calculation made below shows that India annually loses to the extent of 4 crores in revenue, which means that the Indian tax-payer has to bear additional taxation to that extent. Even though our exports to Great Britain might have fallen in the the absence of preference, our belief in taxation would have been an important compensation.

Nobody says that there have been deliberate reprisal on the part of foreign countries, although no one can deny (*pace* the Government's press note) that Ottawa must have aggravated the feelings of various nations to retaliate and impose more trade restrictions. It is not necessary that foreign countries should deliberately embark upon retaliation for India's foreign trade to suffer. International trade being based on barter, no country can buy from other countries unless it is able to sell. Discrimination against foreign goods has had the result of reducing the capacity of foreign countries to buy, and this is one important factor (along with others, like exchange restrictions, quotas, etc.) that has diminished our export trade with foreign countries.

Again, the Government's Press Note seeks to prove that "the hypothesis of diversion is untenable" because, forsooth, the trade with the United Kingdom too in certain articles like rice, castor seed, bran and pollards and coffee has showed a decline. What a pointless argument! It would be some consolation if the total exports had remained stationary while the exports to the United Kingdom had increased. The position, on the contrary, is that the increase of trade with the United Kingdom has not even been sufficient to compensate for loss elsewhere. One wishes that there was at least diversion of trade. The fact, however, is that preference has not increased our total exports in preferred commodities.

The concern for the consumer is inconsistent with taxing foreign goods highly. It is taxing the poor man's goods. Taxing British goods is not so injurious to the Indian consumer; on the contrary it is taxing the richer and the comparatively better off classes in the country who buy British goods. From this point of view, the so-called concern of the Lancashire capitalists for the teeming consuming poor of India is a myth which ought to be exposed.

The poor Indian consumer will gain nothing by discrimination in favour of British goods; on the contrary, he will lose tremendously by discriminating against foreign and Japanese cheap goods, which he can afford to buy more, if they are not taxed highly. During a period of depression as in the last ten years, it was but right (and inevitable) that Great Britain must buy more from India. Her share in the total export trade of India was only 22.1 per cent for 1925-30 whereas her share in India's import trade was 46.8 in the quinquennium 1925-30. This by itself would enable India to persuade Great Britain to buy more from India and narrow the gulf. Add to this the fact that India's interest in the maintenance of a large export surplus is to pay the Britisher annually about 50 crores of rupees. Mere self-interest would compel Britain to buy more from India and she dare not inflict any injury on India's export trade.

The general position in 1934-35 was very much as it was in the preceding year. The percentage share of Britain in export trade and in import trade fell by .6 and by .7 respectively. With the exception of Japan, the percentage share of other countries either remained stationary or diminished. Taking imports into U. K. of articles enjoying preference, India's share continued to be the same, while that of other countries increased thus showing that India did not gain. The position was worse than last year.

Had Ottawa not been?

Another statement seeks to explain the position as it might have been if the Ottawa agreement had not come about. The trends in trade relations between India and England as revealed by figures (average) from 1925 to 1931 have been assumed to continue during the succeeding years: the percentage share of England in the export and import trade of India calculated on that basis, and the relative gains or losses calculated from the actual trade figures (total) on the basis of these percentage shares. These figures are then compared with the actual figures of India's exports to England and England's exports to India in 1934-35, and it is shown that while England improved her trade by about 12.5 crores, India did so only by 2.5 crores There is also the loss in revenue of about 4 crores directly due to Ottawa arrangements to be taken into account.

India's Foreign Trade Balance

India's foreign trade balance has been the subject of an unusual amount of comment and criticism, especially during the last few weeks. In this survey issued by the Director of Public Information, New Delhi in February 1936 the position is clarified and comments that have been made are examined with the help of the latest and most accurate figures available.

Of the many problems with which India is confronted as a result of the world economic depression, not the least important is that presented by the shrinkage of her trade balance in recent years. A conspicuous feature of India's foreign trade in normal times is a large surplus of exports over imports, part of which is utilized for the discharge of her external obligations, the remainder being liquidated by the importation of the precious metals.

India's average credit balance arising from commodity trade was Rs. 78 crores in the five pre-war years, but declined to Rs. 76 crores in the five war years and still further to Rs. 53 crores in the five post-war years ending 1923-24, owing to an excess of imports over exports in the year 1920-21 and 1921-22. During the next quinquennium the average rose to Rs. 113 crores, but with the onset of the depression the movement of the trade balance has again been reversed.

The figures for this period are as follows :

Year	Balance of trade in merchandise. Rr. (crores)
1929-30	... 78.98
1930-31	... 62.02
1931-32	... 34.83
1932-33	... 3.36
1933-34	... 34.76
1934-35	... 22.96

The balance, it will be noticed, has throughout remained in India's favour, but since 1930-31 has been insufficient to meet her remittance obligations. The problem created by the disequilibrium between fixed international obligations and commercial transactions is, however, not peculiar to India; it is a problem which, in its acutest form, affects all debtor agricultural countries alike and which, in its more general aspect of rigid indebtedness in a period of falling prices, affects in varying degree almost all trading countries of the world.

Nevertheless, in view of the importance to India of a large active balance of trade, it is hardly a matter for surprise that public concern should frequently have been expressed at India's inability to provide for her external obligations out of current surpluses resulting from her foreign trade.

The downward trend was arrested in 1932-33, and the prophets of evil were silenced for a time by the striking improvements disclosed by the trade figures for 1933-34. This improvement, however, was not maintained in 1934-35. The apparent deterioration in the position in that year in association with the fact that the trade exchanges between the United Kingdom and India during the year had resulted in a surplus of nearly Rs. 5 and a half crores in favour of the United Kingdom appears to have aroused a vague suspicion in the public mind that the Ottawa Agreement, and the reprisals which it is stated to have provoked in foreign countries, have together operated to hinder a process of recovery which was otherwise inevitable.

Suspicion dies hard, but a moment's reflection will show how insubstantial are the grounds on which the supposed connexion between Ottawa and the decline in the trade balance in 1934-35 is believed to rest.

A surplus in favour of the United Kingdom is a normal incident of the trade exchanges between that country and India, though the amount of the surplus has shown a steady contraction in recent years.

In 1931-32, however, there was an exact balance between the exports to and the imports from the United Kingdom; the following year witnessed a reversion to the normal position with a balance of nearly Rs. 11 crores against India: but in 1933-34, the first complete year after Ottawa, there was again an even balance between exports and imports.

Equally significant is the fact that, simultaneously with the growth in imports from the United Kingdom in 1934-35, there was an increase of imports from foreign countries to the extent of nearly Rs. 9 crores, pointing to an all-round recovery in India's import trade.

This recovery was not confined to India. In almost every debtor country, with some notable exceptions, imports gained rapidly on exports during 1934, causing a diminution in their active balances.

The countries which succeeded in increasing their export surpluses in 1934 may be divided into two grroups, first, those which benefited from restriction schemes raising the prices of their staple exports. and second, those which depreciated their currencies further and also benefited from the operation of restriction schemes in other countries. In the first category fall the Netherlands Indies and British Malayas and in the second the Argentine and Brazil.

With these exceptions, however, the agricultural countries. in particular, suffered a sharp contraction of their export surpluses owing to the relatively greater expansion of their imports.

The reasons for this development are not far to seek. In the first place, imports during the year were to some extent of the nature of deferred purchases, which could no longer be postponed in view of the shortage of supplies. Secondly, imports were stimulated by the increased purchasing capacity of the consuming countries as a result of heavy exports in the preceding year on a higher level of prices. Thirdly, the increased demand of raw materials in 1933 inevitably led to a moderate expansion in the exports of manufactured articles in 1934, although the increased production was for the most part absorbed by the domestic markets.

This brings us naturally to an analysis of the fundamental causes underlying the decline in India's active balance. Such an analysis may appropriately begin with a general consideration of the factors which affect a country's balance of trade namely, changes in the quantum of trade, changes in price-level or both operating at the same time.

If while prices remained constant, the volume of both imports and exports declined to the same extent, then the balance of trade would also be reduced in the same proportion. If, however, the variations in imports and exports were unequal, the shrinkage in the trade balance would be more or less than it would otherwise be according as the drop in exports was greater or smaller than the drop in imports.

Precisely similar results would follow if prices varied while the quantum of exports and imports remained unchanged.

The position, however, would be more complicated if both the volume of trade and the price level were to decline at the same time. In that event, the two factors would act and react upon each other; and the relative movements of the quantum and price indices would either exaggerate or conversely mitigate or even neutralise their separate effects.

The extent to which these several factors have influenced the decline in India's trade balance may now be examined. In order to do this, it is necessary in the first place to determine, taking the average price level during the years 1926-27 to 1928-29 as the base, the percentage decline in prices in each succeeding year.

The figures are as follows :—

Year	Decline in prices	
	Exports	Imports
	per cent.	per cent.
1929-30	10	10
1930-31	30	22
1931-32	41	28
1932-33	44	34
1933-34	45	36
1934-35	47	37

Having ascertained the extent of the fall in the price level, we may either scale up the values of the exports and imports for each year to the pre-depression price level (Method A) or scale down the corresponding figures for the base period to the price level of each subsequent year (Method B) and then work out the balance of trade in each case.

Figures obtained by both these methods are included in the following table which also shows the extent of changes in the quantum of trade from year to year.

(In crores of rupees)

Year	Balance of trade (Actuals)	Balance of trade (Recalculated) Method A	Method B.
1	2	3	4
		(a)	(b)
1926-27 to 1928-29	82.6	Base Period.	
1929-30	79.0	87.9	74.4
1930-31	62.0	112.6	38.5
1931-32	34.9	97.6	17.2
1932-33	3.2	41.5	22.0
1933-34	34.7	92.5	23.6
1934-35	23.0	82.8	19 5

DECLINE IN QUANTUM

Year	Exports per cent (c)	Imports per cent (c)
1929-30	9	9
1930-31	1	14
1931-32	16	28
1932-33	26	17
1933-34	16	26
1934-35	1C	14

(a) Figures in this column are to be compared with the balance for the base period. viz. 82 6 crores.

(b) Figures in this column are to be compared with the actuals in column 2.

(c) Increase.

In 1929-30, prices of both exports and imports fell by 10 per cent, but the trade balance did not decline to the same extent, owing to an increase in the volume of trade. Since then there has been a shrinkage in both volume and prices. In this respect the present crisis has differed from previous crises, in all of which the fall in prices was generally accompanied by a maintenance or even an increase of the volume of trade.

Moreover, the decline has been unequal in its incidence. While exports have fallen further in prices than imports, they have, except in 1932-33, diminished less in volume, and these divergent movements have on the whole exerted a steadying influence on the trade balance.

The result is that, if allowance is made for the fall in the price level, the balance of trade in each of the depression years, with the single exception of 1932-33. will be found to be relatively better than in the pre-depression period

It would be equally interesting to determine, on the basis of the reduced price-level of each depression year, the percentage increase in the quantum of trade which would be necessary in order to maintain the value of exports and imports, and consequently, the balance of trade at the pre-depression figures.

The calculation involved is simple. In 1929-30 there was a fall of 10 per cent in the price of both exports and imports. It is obvious that in order to counteract the effect of this decline on the value of trade there should be an increase in volume of

$$\frac{10 \times 100}{100-10} \text{ or } 11\text{-}1/9 \text{ per cent.}$$

Working on similar lines we find that the maintenance of the pre-depression values of exports and imports and, as a corollary, of the pre-depression balance of trade would involve, so far as the quantum of exports is concerned, the following percentage increase in succeeding years.

Year	Decline in price of export	Increase in quantum required
1930-31	30 per cent,	43 per cent.
1931-32	41 " "	70 " "
1932-33	44 " "	79 " "
1933-34	45 " "	82 " "
1934-35	47 " "	89 " "

These figures illustrate, as perhaps no others can, the extreme difficulty of ensuring the preservation of a normal trade balance in a period of rapidly falling prices.

A decline in prices may, if of no great magnitude, be corrected by an increase in volume of approximately the same extent. Thus a 10 per cent fall in prices may be offset by an increase of volume of 11.1 per cent. But the co-efficient of increase must necessarily be higher than the percentage decline in prices, and the greater the price decline the wider the disparity between the two.

In 1934-35, for instance, the fall in export prices was 47 per cent, but this could not be fully compensated for unless there was an increase of no less than 89 per cent in the volume of exports. Even if India, by some miracle, were able to find purchasers for so large a volume of Exports, it would obviously be impossible for her to increase the production of her export staples to the required level.

The conclusions suggested above may be summarised as follows :—

(i) Except in 1932-33, the decline in the balance of trade was caused solely by the fall in prices, and more particularly by the relatively greater fall in export prices. In 1932-33 the relatively greater decline of the volume of exports was a contributory cause.

(ii) The relative movement of the quantum indices has on the whole been in favour of exports, and this has helped to moderate the effect of the fall in prices. The year 1932-33 is again an exception.

Worst of the Depression Over

Indications, however, are not wanting that the worst of the depression is now over. The volume of exports which touched its lowest point in 1932-33 has since steadily increased and in 1934-35 stood at only 10 per cent below the pre-depression level. The recovery in the volume of imports though somewhat hesitant in the earliest years, was equally pronounced in 1934-35. Imports, in fact, made a more striking recovery during the year than did exports, thereby restoring the normal balance between the two. Though the immediate effect of the natural adjustment is to retard the expansion of the trade balance, it is by no means an unhealthy development, for no permanent improvement in exports could occur whilst the import trade remained stagnant.

At the same time, there has been a welcome and sustained recovery in prices. The improvement noticed in the latter half of 1933-34 was fully maintained in 1934-35, changes during the year being generally in an upward direction.

In January, 1935, there was a sharp increase in the Calcutta index number owing to a speculative rise in the price of cereals and oilseeds, followed automatically by an equally sharp set back. Since March, however, there has been a steady appreciation in the price level.

The following table compares, for the principal articles of export, the Calcutta index numbers of wholesale prices for October 1935 (the latest month for which figures are available) with those of October 1934.

Index numbers of wholesale prices.

(Prices in July, 1914=100)

		October 1934	October 1935
1. Food grains :			
Cereals	...	73	78
Pulses	...	85	84
2. Tea	...	117	121
3. Oilseeds	...	98	113
4. Jute, raw	...	38	51
5. Cotton, raw	...	74	83
6. Hides and skins	...	44	67

The declared values per unit of these articles also show a similar advance, and the decline in the index number of declared values has been reduced from 47 per cent in 1934-35 to 44 per cent in the current year. On the other hand. the prices of imported articles have, generally speaking, continued to decline, and the index number of the declared values of such articles has dropped to 39 per cent as compared with the pre-depression period, from 37 per cent in 1934-35.

MALADJUSTMENT IN PRICE

Further progress has thus been made in the direction of rectifying the maladjustment between the prices of primary products and manufactured goods, which has in the past been one of the chief obstacles to trade recovery.

Under the influence of these favourable factors, India's foreign trade has registered a further advance in the first eight months of this trade year. Exports has risen to Rs. 102.1 crores from Rs. 98.0 crores in the corresponding period of 1934-35, and imports to Rs. 89.4 crores from Rs. 86.0 crores in the same period.

The totals are distributed between the main groups in the following table :—

	April—Nov. 1934-35	April-Nov. 1935-36
Imports.	(In crores of rupees)	
1. Food, Drink and Tobacco	9.1	8.8
2. Raw Materials	10.5	13.3
3. Articles wholly or mainly manufactured	64.6	65.5
4. Others	1.8	1.8
Total—	86.0	89.4
Exports.		
1. Food, Drink and Tobacco	24.1	26.3
2. Raw Materials	47.1	46.1
3. Articles wholly or mainly manufactured	25.9	28 5
4. Others	.9	1.2
Total—	98.0	102.1
	Balance of Trade in merchandise.	
	14.3	15.6

To say that exports have increased by a little over Rs. 4 crores is to convey an inadequate idea of the magnitude of the improvement that has taken place.

Export figures for 1934-35 were swelled by abnormally heavy purchases of cotton by Japan, and if exports in the present year had no more than maintained the level reached in 1934-35, that by itself would have been sufficient evidence of continued prosperity.

For the six months April to September exports of raw cotton were down by nearly Rs. 4 crores on 1934-35. but owing to a marked improvement in the exports of rice, hides and skins, raw jute and jute manufactures (the principal item under the head "Articles wholly or mainly manufactured") the net decrease in exports amounted to Rs. 35 lakhs only. Since then, not only has the improvement in the commodities named been well-maintained. but there has been a striking recovery in the exports of tea, raw cotton and oil-seeds.

REVIVAL IN EXPORTS

The revival in export trade is thus not confined to a few article, but is distributed over practically the whole range of India's export staples. As a result, for the nine months ending the 30th November 1935. exports show an increase of Rs. 4 crores in comparison with the previous year, and if the present rate of improvement continues, exports for the complete year should reach a higher figure than at any time since 1930-31. It may be objected that the effect of the increased exports has been nullified by the equally well marked increase in imports. Apart from the consideration that an increase in both exports and imports is merely symptomatic of a general revival of trade, this objection overlooks the important fact that of the increase of Rs. 3.4 crores as much as Rs. 2.4 crores is accounted for by larger imports of raw cotton owing to a shortage in Indian production. If this item is excluded, it will be seen that exports have increased at a much faster rate than imports.

Current statistics, therefore, testify to the intrinsically sound position of India's foreign trade, and serve to dispel the vague fears that have been expressed as regards her ability to bear the continued strain imposed on her economic structure by the world depression.

India's Foreign Trade Policy

(I) TRADE WITH GERMANY

"Is India to abandon her traditional policy of universal most-favoured-nation treatment in favour of the new and popular theory of bilateral trade engagements?" In this and the subsequent notes issued by the Director of Public Information, New Delhi in February 1936, this question is examined in various aspects.

An outstanding feature of the history of commercial policy in the recent past has been the increasing activity displayed by a number of trading countries in the conclusion of short-term bilateral agreements.

The method of bilateral negotiations is not new. As long ago as 1927 the World Economic Conference advocated its use upon the basis of most-favoured-nation principles for the purpose of securing an all-round reduction of tariff barriers. The method has reminded, though in a different guise, but is seldom employed for furtherance of its original object.

It is still customary in many such agreements to insert the most-favoured-nation clause, but the operation of the clause is rendered nugatory by the simultaneous inclusion of provisions relating to financial and quota arrangements, industrial understandings or regional preferences, which inevitably introduce an element of discrimination against third parties.

Of the many types of such agreements the most common are clearing and compensation agreements. The latter provide for the direct exchange of goods against goods and thus obviate the necessity of devising means of payment. Clearing agreements, on the other hand, do not specify the particular commodities to be exchanged; they are designed mainly to regulate bilateral trade so as to decrease passive balances of trade and produce, as far as possible, an exact balance of exports and imports.

Since 1932 numerous agreements of this nature have been negotiated, mainly by European countries between themselves, or with the countries of Latin America, or less frequently with Asiatic countries.

It is noteworthy, however, that "Japan defying the prevailing tendencies to bilateral trade, has managed to increase her total exports and imports more successfully than any other country and has done so by the time-honoured methods of triangular trade" (World Economic Survey, 1934-35, page 176).

Nevertheless, inspired no doubt by the example of European countries, the opinion seems to have gained ground in India that bilateral engagements alone offer a certain remedy for her economic ills. The policy of *laissez-faire* has been the subject of attack, and Government are being urged to modify it with a view to the conclusion of bilateral agreements with all-important countries with which India has commercial relations, and particularly with Germany, Italy, Iran and Turkey, whose policy of regulated commercial exchanges has had serious repercussions on India's exports trade.

The issue may be thus stated :—Is India to abandon her traditional policy of universal most-favoured-nation treatment in favour of the new and popular theory of bilateral trade engagements ?

In the following paragraphs an endeavour will be made to examine this issue in all its aspects against the background of the restrictive measures taken by the countries mentioned above. As a preliminary, it may be convenient to set out a resume of the measures which have been taken by these countries with an estimate of the extent to which India's export trade has been affected thereby.

Germany :—As early as 1932, Germany had found it necessary to impose import restrictions in defence of her exchange position. These restrictions were first directed towards encouraging the production in Germany of foodstuffs in replacement of foreign supplies, and of the nature were the restrictions on the importation of rice and bran and oilseeds.

By the end of 1933, however, the position became more critical, owing to the large increase in Germany's adverse trade balance, and the first half of 1934 saw the amount of foreign exchanges available for the financing of imports reduced by progressive steps to 5 per cent of the average requirements of 1931.

At the same time steps had been taken to bring under licensing control imports of some of the more important raw materials of industry, such as cotton, jute, wool hides and skins.

Germany's import trade fell into a chaotic state since there was no relation between the right to import and the right to obtain foreign exchange to finance imports.

From 24th September, therefore, a new regime came into being. Under this new regime the total amount of exchange made available for the financing of imports was to be based from month to month on an estimate of the exchange likely to result from Germany's exports in the ensuing month. Imports licences were only granted to an extent that would be covered by the estimate of exchange available and the grant of an import licence carried with it the right to the necessary amount of exchange. Priority in respect of import licences was to be given to essential foodstuffs, raw materials and semi-manufactured materials.

Thus, the position of Indian rice, jute, oilseeds, cotton and hides and skins appeared to be fairly well secured.

A further safeguard for India's export trade appeared to be found in Article 2 of the Agreement of November 1, 1934, between the United Kingdom and Germany which ran as follows :—

"The German Government in allocating foreign exchange for purchases of raw materials and foodstuffs which Germany has been accustomed to purchase either through the United Kingdom or as re-exports from the United Kingdom or direct from the British Colonies will take no measures to reduce the customary proportions enjoyed by the United Kingdom and the British Colonies in the supply to Germany of these goods."

As much of India's rice and jute trade with Germany was arranged and financed through London this provision was *prima facie* of considerable benefit to India.

Germany, however, to a very great extent, has been able to avoid the necessity of allocating exchange to finance imports from India. She has done so by persuading many of our larger exporters to undertake compensation or barter business, and has in this way been enabled to secure a sufficiency of raw materials of industry to enable her to carry on without any too great expenditure of the exchange resulting from her exports to India.

Reports received from the Trade Commissioner in Hamburg confirm that, to a very great extent, import business in the commodities in which India is mainly interested has been of 'compensation' nature.

In attempting to estimate the effect of the German restrictions on India's export trade, we are faced with the initial difficulty that our export statistics do not give a true picture of our export trade with Germany. On the one hand, our figures do not in many cases include shipments "for orders" which may find their way ultimately to Germany, and, again cargoes declared for non-German ports, such as, Antwerp and Rotterdam, may be transhipped thereat for Germany. On the other hand, Bremen and Hamburg are free entrepot ports and goods thereto consigned do not necessarily find their way into Germany

It has not been possible to work out any correlation between the German trade statistics and our own, and it is proposed therefore to set out, as far as possible, the falling off in trade according to both sources of information. The total for 1934-35 is 1.6 crores less than that of 1932-33 and 2.85 crores less than that of 1933-34, the latter figure representing practically a 30 per cent decrease. The falling off is particularly marked in jute, rice and oilseeds.

The figures for the first eight months of the present trade year show that the downward trend has been arrested, but that there has, nevertheless, been a falling off of nearly 21 per cent compared with the corresponding period of 1933.

The balance of trade has moved against India, as will be seen from the following figures, which represent crores of rupees :—

		Exports to Germany.	Imports from Germany.
1932-33	...	8 50	10.39
1933-34	...	9 73	8.88
1934 35	...	6.98	10.12
1935-36 (8 months)	...	5.06	7.67

The pre-war average balance was as 2.1 in favour of India.

The German figures are somewhat more favourable to India. Over the calendar year 1934 India's exports to Germany were in excess of Germany's exports to India by 42.6 per cent of the latter, in spite of the fact that over the last quarter of the year the balance against India was 24 per cent.

For the first quarter of 1935 there was a practically even balance at 26 millions Reichsmarks each way. For the half year ending 30th June imports from India into Germany totalled 57 million Reichsmarks, whereas exports to India from Germany touched 50 millions only. During the third quarter there was a further increase in the margin in favour of India, imports from India for the first nine months advancing to 91.8 million Reichsmarks and exports to India less steeply to 78.5 millions. The second and third quarters of the year therefore have shown a marked improvement.

A more detailed examination of the German trade figures for 1934 shows that in 13 out of the 22 commodities dealt with, India has either maintained her position or has not suffered much worse than other countries. She has done definitely and badly in respect of eight commodities and is apparently being displaced by other countries with whom Germany has concluded clearing arrangements. This group of eight commodities includes rice, hides and skins and oilseeds which are of prime importance to India's export trade.

It would appear, therefore, that though the two sets of statistics differ in detail, they lead to very much the same conclusion. The only difference appears to be that whereas Indian figures show a considerable falling off in jute, German statistics show a fairly satisfactory position. The detailed figures for the eight months ending 30th of November 1935 support the foregoing conclusions.

There is, therefore, no doubt that India's trade has been severely affected by Germany's present trade policy. A recent report mentions that Germany's total import trade remains at a level approximately that of 1933. In June 1934, India's balance with Germany was as 150 : 100. It is now practically as 110 : 100. India has therefore lost one-fourth of her share of Germany's import trade, which has not of itself diminished.

Germany has, in fact, been calling upon alternative sources of supply for essential raw materials. Brazil, for example, has come forward as a supplier of cotton and Italy has, to a large extent, replaced India as a supplier of rice. Both of these countries have concluded clearing arrangements with Germany

II. TRADE WITH ITALY, IRAQ AND TURKEY

This is the second Press Note on India's foreign trade policy surveying developments in Italy, Iraq and Turkey.

Italy first of all imposed import restrictions on a considerable scale in 1934. Of particular interest to India was the imposition of quota restrictions on the import of oilseeds.

A global quota was prescribed which was made effective in two instalments. So successful was India in the Italian market that she supplied practically the whole of the first instalment, which represented more than her proportionate share of the whole as estimated from her previous contributions to the Italian market. She was therefore excluded from participating in the second instalment. To this measure of restriction it was difficult to take exception though her exclusion was perhaps symtomatic of what was later to come.

The Italian Government was concerned to cut down, as far as possible, her unfavourable balance of trade with India.

Early in 1935, however, Italy's exchange difficulties called for much more drastic measures of restriction. By the Decree of 16th February 1935, imports into Italy were cut down to practically a quarter of their volume in the previous year. The original quotas ranging from 10 to 30 per cent have from time to time been modified and in respect of two commodities, namely, jute and cotton, in which India is particularly interested, they are raised to 50 per cent.

The grant of import licences against the restricted quotas was at first automatic The Italian customs authorities permitted import on the prescribed scale of mere presentation of customs documents showing the extent of imports in the preceding year.

The Italian authorities believed that by virtue alone of these somewhat drastic import restrictions, they would solve their foreign exchange problem, and that there would be no necessity for so strict a control as existed, for example, in Germany.

The Italian exchange had been under nominal control prior to the crisis in February, but by the end of April the control had been tightened up and serious difficulties were being experienced by cotton importers. At the same time, so far as cotton was concerned, the automatic admission by the customs officials on the strength of the previous year's documents had ceased, and the distribution of import licenses had been placed in the hands of the Cotton Institute—a central committee representing cotton manufacturing interests.

This more arbitrary system, which was first applied to cotton, was later made applicable in an even more stringent form to practically every commodity in which India has a considerable interest,—that is to say, jute, cotton and hides and skins (oil seeds have for more than a year been under a similar regime). For these commodities licences were issued by the Finance Ministry on the recommendations of "Corporative Executive Committee" representative of the various industries concerned in the import of the individual raw materials.

The disabilities to which Indian trade were apparently subjected are therefore :

(a) the restriction of imports to a comparatively small fraction of their previous volume ;

(b) the possible loss of even a proportionate share in the reduced quota through the transfer of India's more important export staples from the automatic regime to a system under which an arbitrary allotment of import licence may be made ; and

(c) the possible discriminatory treatment in the matter of the allocation of exchange facilities to pay for imports from India.

These disabilities, however, are now overshadowed by the virtual prohibition of imports from sanctionist countries into Italy.

In view of these very drastic restrictions, which were apparently applicable to most of India's important export staples to Italy, it might have been expected that there would have been a sudden and marked effect upon our export trade. That effect, of course could not be expected to show itself before the end of the year 1934-35, and in confirmation of this expectation the trade statistics show that exports to Italy for the year 1934-35, are just above the total of 1933-34 and show nearly a crore of advance on 1932-33. For the first eight months of this trade year, exports to Italy are down by nearly 25 per cent on 1934.

The following table will show in crores the trade exchanges between India and Italy for the past few years :

	Exports to Italy.	Imports from Italy.
1931-32	5.41	3.59
1932-33	4.65	3.95
1933-34	5.74	2.91
1934-35	5.73	3.01
1935-36 (8 months).	2.71	1.75

It will be seen that the favourable balance enjoyed by India had not been seriously disturbed at the time of enforcement of economic sanctions against Italy.

Iran—Under the Persian Tariff Autonomy Treaty of 1928 the United Kingdom and India are entitled to enjoy during the currency of the Treaty the tariff rates in force when the Treaty was signed, as also the most-favoured-nation treatment in every other respect.

The Persian tariff rates have, however, been made subject to a sur-charge on account of the depreciation of the rial. The surcharge is intended to maintain the gold value of the duty collections. and, in theory, it is supposed to vary with the exchange value of the rial. At the present time it is somewhat too high, but of more serious concern to India are the issues arising from the Foreign Trade Monopoly Law.

This law was passed in 1932 and has been amended from time to time. It provides for the imposition of quotas upon imports, for the issue of licences for importation to finance such imports in such a manner as to encourage the export of Persian produce.

Under the provisions of this law more favourable quotas have been allotted to the Soviet Government than to the United Kingdom or India.

The question, however, has been further complicated by the declaration last year of the import of cotton piecegoods as a Government monopoly. This, though designed to balance imports and exports has the effect of increasing the duties payable on importation of cotton piecegoods by the levy of a monopoly tax and a monopoly commission.

This monopoly regime will be applicable only to goods imported from sources other than the U. S. S. R, the Soviets having been granted a separate quota which will not be subject to monopoly restrictions.

A further and most important restriction imposed by the Government of Iran is in respect of cotton yarns. In 1933 the importation of yarns below 20s. was prohibited with a view to the protection of the local yarn spinning industry.

India's most important exports to Iran in the past three years are cotton twist and yarn, cotton piecegoods and tea.

The case of tea may first be dealt with. There has apparently been a considerable falling off but this has much more than been made up by the growth of trans-frontier exports, which have increased from 2 million pounds to12 million pounds in the past three years.

India's exports of yarn have suffered a catastrophic decrease since 1932-33, when they were valued at 20 lakhs of rupees. In 1934-35 this figure had fallen to 8 and one-forth lakhs, and on the basis of figures for the first eight months of the present year it is unlikely to reach more than Rs. 6,000 in the present year. This decrease must be attributed to a great extent to the prohibition of the importation of yarns of under 20 counts, though it may be mentioned also that no quota for higher counts has notified in the present year on the ground that markets are already over-stocked.

In the case of cotton piecegoods, 1934-35 saw a marked fall from 18 lakhs in 1932-33 and 1933-34 to 12 and half lakhs only. This result cannot, however, be attributed to the operation of the latest monopoly measures since that applies equally to all imports other than those from Russia. It is more likely due to the inability of India to compete with Japan.

The following figures show how Japan has progressed in the Iranian market in the past few years in spite of Russia' privileged position :—

Percentage shares in the Iranian piecegoods market,

	Russia	India	Japan
1931-32	54	14.11	8.3
1932-33	42	7.6	19.5
1933-34	25.6	7.6	45.3

So far as the balance of trade is concerned *prima facie* it appears to have been in favour of Iran since 1927-28, but if one excludes from the account, exports of mineral oil, the balance comes out in India's favour, the figures for sea-borne trade in 1932-33, 1933-34 and 1934-35 being 29 lakhs, 34 lakhs and 8 lakhs respectively. (It is difficult to dispute the contention that oil exports must be excluded from the balance of trade. The Iranian Oil Company is the real beneficiary except to the extent of the royalties.)

Turkey :—Turkey has probably been as hard put to it to maintain her exchange position as any country in the western group. She was early in the field with a series of import restrictions and she has now combined with her quota system, a system of exchange control.

Her latest quota decree divides imports into four categories—(1) List S, the free list comprising items which may be imported into Turkey free of any quantitative import restrictions ; (2) List K L. comprising goods which may be imported free of quota restrictions, provided they are the produce or manufacture of countries (a) having a clearing agreement with Turkey or (b) whose commercial exchanges are in favour of Turkey and in which no restrictive measures are applied against imports from Turkey ; (3) List V, comprising goods which may be imported free of quota restrictions under the authorisation of the competent Ministry.

More stringent requirements are required in respect of imports from countries to whom conditions (a) and (b) above do not apply ; and (4) List K comprises commodities in respect of which global quotas have been fixed.

The principal items of India's export trade to Turkey in the past were rice, tea, raw hides, cotton yarn, gunny bags and gunny cloth. The import of rice is totally prohibited, tea falls in List K, raw hides and gunny bags and gunny cloth are in List S and cotton yarn in List K L.

It appears, however, that it makes little difference whether India's imports fall in one list or another since their import into Turkey is governed by the provisions of the exchange Decree of 23rd August, 1934, under Article 32 of which firms importing from countries which, while having favourable trade balance with Turkey have not concluded a treaty of commerce with her, must deposit the equivalent of the value of the goods imported with the Central Bank of Turkey, which will open on its books a separate account for each of these countries.

The amounts paid into these accounts are paid to the creditors in chronological order and in proportion to the demands made from those countries by creditors in Turkey. Firms desirous of making an importation in conformity with the above, who have not deposited the value of the goods with the Central Bank will be refused permission to import the goods.

It is obvious from the subjoined table that if this decree is rigidly enforced against India, which since the expiry of Indo-Turkish *modus vivendi* of 22nd. February last has no trade agreement with Turkey, it will be impossible for India to export to Turkey.

Year	Indian export to Turkey Rs. (000)	Turkish exports to India Rs. (000)
1930-31	31,64	41
1931-32	26,17	31
1932-33	35,13	59
1933-34	35,76	85
1934-35	30,98	Not yet available.

In 1934-35 India's exports to Turkey did not show as marked a decrease, in comparison with the two preceding years, as might have been expected, total exports falling from 35 to 30 lakhs only. In the first eight months of the present year, however, more definite signs of the decrease are apparent, the total being 12.18 lakhs as compared with 18.49 in 1933.

As will be seen from the table given above, the balance of trade has invariably been enormously in India's favour and will continue to be so unless Indian trade is practically wiped out.

(III) AGREEMENTS WITH OTHER COUNTRIES

The nature of bilateral trade agreements, with special reference to their suitability to the circumstances of India's foreign trade, is discussed in this third Press Note.

The various restrictive measures which have been described in preceding articles, were not of course specially directed against India, nor has restriction been confined to the particular countries mentioned.

In Appendix IV to the Report of the Committee of the Legislative Assembly which examined the working of the Ottawa Agreement for the year ending 31st March, 1934, will be found a list of the restrictions imposed from time to time by various countries which are applicable to exports from India. To this must be added the German import and exchange restrictions imposed since August 1934, the Italian quota regime which has been in force since February, 1935, and the exchange restrictions of a number of less important countries, such as Roumania and the Latin American countries of South America.

It is a common accusation that such restrictions are a direct consequence of the Ottawa preferences. Whatever the merits or demerits of the Ottawa Agreement, there is not one atom of evidence to show that Ottawa is responsible for a single restriction. Except in cases where the restrictions are justified on hygienic or similar grounds, they have come into existence as measures to safeguard commercial and financial stability The only argument against Ottawa is in fact *past hoc ergo propter hoc*.

It may be of value to consider what other countries have done to meet the situations which have arisen in the past two years. and, in the first place, reference may be made to the action taken by the United Kingdom. His Majesty's Government have concluded agreements with Germany, Italy, and Turkey, but the circumstances suggest that they afford no suitable precedent for similar action by India.

The Anglo-German Agreement of November 1, 1934, is generally regarded as a clearing arrangement, but it is in its nature something entirly different. It is based on the fact that the trade exchanges between Germany and the United Kingdom were on the average 100 : 55 in Germany's favour.

Under the Agreement, the United Kingdom exporters are in any one month allowed exchange equivalent to 55 per cent of the value of German exports to the United Kingdom in the preceding month. This gives Germany surplus exchange equivalent to the value of 45 per cent of her exports to the United Kingdom, out of which balance she has undertaken to devote 10 per cent to the liquidation of frozen British debts, leaving 35 per cent for the service of other international obligations.

There are other provisions in the Agreement, which promise no discrimination in regard to the provision of exchange to finance colonial and Indian trade usually conducted through London.

It is obvious that the November Agreement was only possible in virtue of Germany's very considerable active balance of trade with the United Kingdom.

With Italy no such Agreement was possible. The United Kingdom in the year 1934 had a favourable balance of trade *vis-a-vis* Italy amounting to ,171 million lire. His Majesty's Government, however, quickly negotiated a clearing arrangement under which the quotas applicable to the United Kingdom were raised to 80 per cent of the trade of 1934.

The right to import did not, however, carry with it any right to exchange. The 80 per cent quota was only granted in combination with an exchange clearing arrangement.

Under this arrangement payment for imports into Italy from the United Kingdom was made in lire into a special account in the Bank of Italy. Similarly importers from Italy into the United Kingdom paid sterling into a special account of the Bank of England. The two banks were in communication, and, as sterling became available in the special Bank of England account, United Kingdom exporters were paid from that account in chronological order the value of their exports to Italy.

The nature of clearing accounts will be later discussed, but it may be stated in the meantime that the United Kingdom exporters have avoided one of the dangers of such agreements, namely, the accumulation of frozen debts, only by refraining from utilizing the whole of their 80 per cent quota.

There is evidence that the United Kingdom exporter was by no means satisfied with the Agreement. There was at one time a serious danger that under the Fascist regime there would be grave interference with the ordinary course of trade, Italy importing only such commodities as she required for her own immediate purposes.

The Turkish Agreement of the 4th June is a combination of an ordinary Trade Convention with a clearing Agreement. The United Kingdom, on the one hand, guarantees conventional rates of duty on a few commodities on importation into the United Kingdom from Turkey. On the other hand, Turkey relaxes her quota restrictions in respect of much larger number of products of the United Kingdom.

The clearing arrangement is of the usual nature, but there is this special feature that only 70 per cent of the sterling realised in the Bank of England special account against imports of Turkish goods becomes available for the payment of United Kingdom exporters to Turkey, the balance of 30 per cent being placed at the disposal of the Central Bank of Turkey.

The Agreement also provides for the negotiation of barter arrangements between persons in Turkey and persons in the United Kingdom on the same basis. The value of the United Kingdom goods imported into Turkey under a barter transaction must not exceed 70 per cent of the value of the Turkish goods taken in return.

In the case of Iran, the United Kingdom is in very much the same circumstances as India.

The commonest method of meeting the difficulties arising from the exchange and monetary embarrassments of individual members of the international trading community has been the conclusion of clearing agreements. Most European countries to a greater or less extent have entered into such agreements, as have also certain of the Latin American republics of South America.

The Report of the Joint Committee of the League of Nations, which recently conducted an enquiry into the nature and operation of clearing agreements, gives a list of 77 such agreements. This is, therefore, a device which carries the sanction of usage.

The theory of the operation of a bilateral clearing system is as follows. In each of the contracting countries importers of goods from the other country, instead of paying the supplier direct, pay into special clearing office the value, in the national currency, of the goods imported. From the amounts so received the clearing office takes the sums necessary to pay national exporters for goods sent by them to the other contracting country.

In principle exporters are paid in chronological order as payments are made by importers to the clearing house in the other country. Direct relations between the exporters of one country and the importers in the other are replaced by triangular relationships (exporters-clearing house-importers) in each of the contracting countries and a direct relationship between the two clearing houses.

There is a third method in which exchange difficulties may be overcome, namely, by compensation or barter trade. This may be either of the nature of barter transactions between two contracting governments or by way of barter transactions between individual traders in these countries.

It does not appear that the first of these methods has been utilised to any great extent. There has been mention of a deal in which American cotton was exchanged for German machinery, but no details are available as to how the transaction was arranged, if at all.

There are of course manifest difficulties in carrying out barter business between two governments. For example, were India to do a deal in cotton against manufactured goods from Germany, though it might be possible for the German Government to allocate cotton supplies to German spinners, the Government of India would find it much more difficult to conduct the retail business of distributing in India miscellaneous German manufactures.

It is to be expected, therefore, that individual compensation arrangements should be more common.

Germany and Italy have both framed regulations governing barter transactions. In both cases these regulations are directed towards obtaining additional exports and additional foreign exchange. Unless such conditions were laid down compensation business would have no advantage over transactions conducted under an ordinary clearing arrangement.

Has the action taken by other countries any lessons for India?

Prima facie it is not to be expected that the example of the United Kingdom is one that could be followed by India. Whereas the former is an exporter of manufactured goods, India is mainly the supplier of the raw materials of industry.

Again, the normal trade balance of the United Kingdom is against her, while India's position is precisely the reverse.

It is obvious that India could not have negotiated with Germany the November Agreement, since in 1934 her trade balance with that country was favourable to the extent of 40 per cent of the German exports.

The Anglo-Italian Agreement is in effect merely an ordinary clearing agreement. The apparent advantage of 80 per cent quota was neutralised by a shortage of sterling exchange and until recently, India did comparatively better than the United Kingdom in regard to trade with Italy. The Agreement does not call for further examination at present; the value of clearing arrangements will be considered later.

So far as Iran is concerned, the circumstances of India and the United Kingdom are identical.

In the case of Turkey, however, where the trade balance was practically even, it was possible for the United Kingdom to retain a considerable portion of her export trade at the price of giving Turkey a free hand with 30 per cent of the exchange resulting from Turkish imports into the United Kingdom. India's balance is as 40 to 1 against Turkey and there is obviously no basis for an Indo-Turkish Agreement of the same character.

(IV.) CLEARING SCHEMES

The discussion of the appropriateness of a system of bilateral trade agreements to the circumstances of India is continued in this fourth Press Note.

Would it be to India's advantage to follow the example of so many other countries and conclude clearing arrangements with those of her customers who are for the time being in exchange difficulties?

The answer is clear: India stands to lose rather than to gain by adopting a policy which at the best would tend to reduce her foreign trade to a balance of exports and imports.

Support is lent to this view by the recently published Report of a Committee of the League of Nations on the nature and functioning of clearing agreements. It is impossible to condense this most interesting and instructive report, but the general purport of the Committee's conclusions is that the final result of clearing agreements is to reduce the total volume of world trade.

For a country in India's position, i. e., normally with a favourable balance of trade a clearing arrangement is positively harmful.

To quote the Report, "An unfavourable or adverse balance in a country with a sound currency is a *sine qua non* if the clearing system is to operate so as to further the interests of that country." Again, "To have a good clearing system you must have bad balance of trade."

It is possible by means of a few quotations to convey the arguments set out by this very authoritative Committee, but from what has been said about, it would appear that there is most excellent authority for holding that India should avoid a clearing arrangement with any country with whom she does not have an unfavourable balance of trade.

It does not follow, however, that even in case where the balance is unfavourable to India, it would pay her to enter into clearing agreements. The tendency of a bilateral clearing agreement is to reduce the trade exchange of the contracting countries at least to the level of the exports of the country with the passive balance. The result is a net diminution in the volume of world trade resulting in a loss of the total trading capacity of the world, which must ultimately re-act on every constituent member of the trading community.

In spite of the attempts which have been made under the stress of circumstances to bilateralise, trade is and must continue to be a series of exchanges between "communicating vessels," and any restrictions which affect any one of the vessels must ultimately affect them all.

It may be that Germany and Italy have their system of control seriously affected by India's export trade. It would help us little to follow their example and cut down the favourable balance which Russsia now enjoys *vis-a-vis* India.

Compensation business on a national basis is, as already indicated, an impossibility in India. On an individual basis it is a matter for private enterprise, but it has two disadvantages. In the first place, in its ideal (from the German point of view) form it would cover only "additional" exports from the country of restriction. Compensation business would, therefore, tend to wipe out an unfavourable balance and turn it into a favourable balance *vis-a-vis* India. Secondly, it tends to disturb the normal channels of trade since in India, except in the case of certain large firms, the exporter is not usually an importer and *vice uersa* and is therefore not in a position to negotiate compensation deals.

Clearing or compensation arrangements are, however, not the only devices which may be employed,

There is, for instance, the type of bilateral agreements represented by that between the United Kingdom and Denmark, whereby certain advantages are guaranteed to Danish bacon, while Denmark takes from the United Kingdom the gunny cloth in which the bacon is packed.

Then there is our own Convention with Japan, which has been acclaimed as the supreme example of such a trade bargain. It cannot be too strongly emphasised, however, that the Indo-Japanese Convention is not a barter arrangement of raw cotton against cotton textiles. The so-called exchange is no exchange at all. It is in effect a double safeguard to Indian interests, for while the textile industry is protected by the limitation of imports of cotton piecegoods from Japan, the cotton grower is safeguarded by the linking of the permissible imports to the amount of cotton purchased.

What Japan got out of the treaty was a guarantee of most-favoured-nation treatment and conventional rates of duty on cotton piecegoods at the high rate of 50 per cent ad valorem She gets no advantage over other countries from her export allotment. India has given no guarantee to buy a single yard of cloth.

Even if the Japanese treaty is no great argument in favour of bilateral negotiation, there are many other precedents.

The United Kingdom has concluded agreements with the Scandinavian countries, she is negotiating with Spain, the U. S. A. has done a deal with the U. S. S R., the Union of South Africa with Italy and so on.

But bilateral agreements of this class have definite limitations; the commodities covered by them are necessarily restricted to those in regard to which the requirements of one party to the agreement are ordinarily supplied either wholly or mainly by the other.

The Anglo-Danish Agreement provides an example in the provisions relating to British coal and Danish bacon. The United Kingdom obtains her foreign supplies of bacon mainly from Denmark; conversely, Denmark imports coal from very few countries other than the United Kingdom.

It is, however, unnecessary to consider the precise nature of these agreements since they are based upon the particular relationships of the contracing parties, and have not necessarily any bearing on Indian conditions. Their importance consists here and now merely in their existence as precedents.

In any consideration of the desirability of bilateral engagements, a distinction should be drawn between "distress" and "non-distress" countries.

In the former class may be placed countries like Germany and Italy, where measures of restriction are a vital necessity. In the latter class would fall countries like India if there are any such—which have imposed no restrictions, and countries like France and Holland, which have imposed a partial quota regime as a measure of precaution rather than of emergency.

So far as the first class is concerned, India has little to gain by a bilateral agreement.

Germany does not want to buy more Indian goods. She wants to sell more to India. In her necessity it is more important that she should buy in the way best calculated to preserve exchange than that she should buy cheap. She has no free internal market for primary commodities which is capable of natural expansion and capture by India under the stimulus of a tariff preference.

Tariff preference by itself would be as useless as the most-favoured-nation clause in the face of quota and exchange restrictions, and the most that could be sought from a 'distress' country would be a guarantee of a reasonable share in its imports and a guarantee for their payment.

International trade has, however, shown that beggars can be choosers, and that under a strictly controlled import regime, the 'distress' country is in a position to drive a hard bargain with would-be suppliers. Bilateral agreements with such countries, whatever they guaranteed to India, could only be secured by considerable sacrifices.

Is India, however, justified in adhering to her traditional policy of general all-round most-favoured-nation treatment in regard to other countries?

It is fashionable now-a-days to condemn this policy as a "creed out-worn", but it still has a certain amount of authority behind it. The Economic Committee of the League of Nations, reporting in 1929, re-affirmed the principle of the most-favoured-nation clause, and later at the London Conference of 1931 a Sub-Commission was in favour of its maintenance—"since it provides the basis of liberal commercial policy and since any general and substantial reduction of tariffs by bilateral negotiation is only possible in combination with the unrestricted clause."

This expression of opinion may be dismissed as a counsel of perfection, but what is most needed at the present time are counsels of perfection—not temporary make-shifts which solve one difficulty only to create another.

It is of interest to note in this connection that the programme of reciprocal trade treaties recently initiated by the U. S. A. "has been conducted upon the traditional lines of tariff bargaining, rejecting quotas and barter agreements, and reducing rather than increasing Government interference with trade." (World, Economic Survey, 1934-35.)

But India's adherence to the most-favoured-nation clause finds justification other than the opinion of the experts. India's export trade consists mainly of a comparatively few raw materials sent to the great world markets, and it is essential for her prosperity that, to the extent possible, she should have free and unrestricted access to these markets.

Except in the case of jute, she has no monopoly of supply, and an abandonment of the most-favoured-nation policy in favour of bilateralism would immediately leave her in a very vulnerable position.

It may be argued, however, that Ottawa marked a departure from most-favoured-nation practice. 'Prima facie' this is so, but the real significance of the Ottawa experiment is that it was an attempt to lower tariff barriers by bilateral negotiation and ultimately to restore most favoured-nation conditions within the Empire when the nexus of bilateral engagements was complete.

Most of the agreements provided for automatic extensions of preferences granted to other members of the commonwealth, and if the progress towards the ultimate goal has been slow within the Empire group, it is only evidence of the difficulty which would attend any world attempt to lower tariff barriers by bilateral negotiation without the fullest application of most-favoured-nation principles.

(V.) MOST-FAVOURED-NATION TREATMENT BEST

Reasons for believing that general most-favoured-nation treatment is still the best trade policy for a country like India are summarised in this the fifth and concluding Press Note.

Some critics, alarmed at the apparent deterioration in India's balance of trade in merchandise, have suggested restriction of imports in order to maintain or improve that balance. Restriction of imports may be a regrettable necessity in the case of 'distress' countries, resulting as it does in a net diminution in world trade; but the adoption of such measures by countries still reasonably prosperous is sheer defeatism. For the reasons set out in the following paragraphs, it may fairly be claimed that India is in the latter category.

India's remittance obligations make it essential for financial stability that she should have a favourable balance of trade.

Leaving out of account for the moment exports of gold, India's balance of trade over the past nine years is shown in the following table :—

1926-1927	1927-1928	1928-1929	1929-1930	1930-1931
79.47 Crores	81.97 Crores	87.47 Crores	78.98 Crores	62.02 Crores

1931-1932	1932-1933	1933-1934	1934-1935
34.83 Crores	3.36 Crores	34.76 Crores	23 Crores

The average of the three pre-depression years is just under 83 crores—a figure with which last year's total at 23 crores compares very unfavourably.

If, however, we take account of the fact that primary commodity, or export prices have fallen by 45.3 per cent, and import prices by 34.8 perc ent since pre-depression time, we could expect a balance of 19.7 crores only in our favour even if our export and import trade had in terms of quantity remained at the level of 1926-29.

Applying the same correction to the separate figures of exports and imports, we find that there has been again in quantity a shrinkage of 7 per cent in exports and 11 per cent. in imports.

The Review of World Trade for 1934, issued by the League of Nations shows a decrease of 22.5 per cent in the quantum of world trade between 1929 and 1934.

Thus, though India has not escaped the combined effects of the great depression and the new regime of restriction, her circumstances compare favourably with those of the world in general.

Moreover the improvement in export trade which set in in 1933-34 still continues. For the eight months April to November 1935, India's exports exceed those of 1933 by 5½ crores, and those of 1934 by 4 crores, despite the fact that Japan's purchases of cotton in 1934 were of an exceptional nature, making up for the short purchases during the 1933 boycott.

If the purchases by Japan in 1933 and 1934 are averaged out and the total exports for the period under consideration are adjusted accordingly, the figures become :—

April-November	1933	100.0	Crores
"	1934	94.5	"
"	1935	102.1	"

Thus whereas in 1934 there was a definite deterioration in the position as compared with 1933, the present year shows a well-marked advance.

The objection will no doubt be put forward that the improvement in exports is offset by an increase of nearly Rs. 3 and a half crores in imports, and that, on balance, India's position is little better than it was a year ago.

To this argument two rejoinders may be made. In the first place, of the total increase of Rs. 3 and a half crores as much as Rs. 2 and a half crores is largely accounted for by imports of long-staple cotton, owing to a deficiency in local production. Essential raw materials, rather than manufactured goods, are thus mainly responsible for the growth in imports. Secondly, an increase in exports with a parallel increase in imports is indicative of increasing prosperity and the increasing purchasing capacity of India.

These are some of the manifestations of a slow but progressive movement towards economic recovery which is no less marked in other diesctions.

The upward tend in the prices of primary products, first observed in the latter half of 1933-34, was well maintained in the following year, and has in recent months resulted in a striking appreciation of the price-level. At the same time the deflationary tendency in the price of imported goods has continued, causing a further narrowing of the gap between the prices of agricultural and manufactured commodities. With the emergence of a more normal price relationship between these classes of goods, one of the chief obstacles to a widespread revival of trade has tended to disappear.

The unusual combination of favourable factors suggests the possibility that the clouds on India's economic horizon are at last beginning to disperse. Although, therefore, she is yet a long way from complete recovery, her present circumstances are, in comparison with most, not unhappy.

To sum up the conclusions which may be drawn from the foregoing discussion :—

(a) India's trade position is far from being in such desperate straits as some observers would seek to establish. On the contrary, current statistics justify a certain measure of optimism, and given a rising tendency in world prices, prosperity would be in sight again. It does not however lie in the power of the Government of India to bring about that consummation.

(b) So far as Germany is concerned, India has undoubtedly suffered, but the statistics for the present year show a marked improvement, the balance in India's favour for the second and third quarters of the year being 25 per cent of Germany's exports to India in that period. In Italy we have done much better than could have been hoped for after the February Decree. In Iran also our trade has received a set-back, but there is good reason to believe that Japanese competition, rather than Iranian restriction, is responsible. In regard to Turkey, we must be prepared for a certain amount of loss.

(c) Except in the case of Iran, the circumstances of the United Kingdom and India differ so much that the agreements concluded by the former with distress and other countries provide no useful models for India.

(d) The system of bilateral clearing agreements which has been so popular in Europe could in present conditions only be harmful to India.

(e) Compensation or barter trade with the Government of India as a principal is impossible. Private compensation trade has its own dangers.

(f) Bilateral agreements with distress countries are unlikely to be of benefit to India. A country which is prepared to restrict its imports will always drive hard bargain with one who is anxious to sell.

(g) Any question of restriction of imports should at the present time be unthinkable.

(h) General most-favoured-nation treatment is still the best policy for a country like India.

(i) The circumstances of India's import and export trade are improving and her financial solvency is not in danger. A change in policy is not therefore essential.

Whether one takes a short view or a long view of the situation the conclusion is inescapable that the policy pursued by India is one for which there is every justification.

On a short view, it is clear that India's abstinence from international engagements has not been to her disadvantage during the present crisis. In fact it would in all probability have done more harm than good, had she entangled herself in a series of of negotiations in an attempt to solve problems the nature of which was imperfectly appreciated.

If a longer view is taken, it must be remembered that India cannot isolate herself from the world and retain her present importance as a commercial unit. She must seek an outlet for her surplus produce in world markets, and her ultimate prosperity is dependent on the general prosperity of world trading community.

Circumstanced as she is, essentially a supplier of food-stuffs and raw materials, it is to India's interest that as early as possible there should be restored the free and unrestricted flow of international trade on which world prosperity depends.

It is all against India's interest to enter upon the type of agreement which has been so common in the past few years. Not only do such agreements tend to an immediate diminution of the mutual trade of the contracting parties, but by a diversion of trade from its natural channels inflict serious damage on third parties.

The policy of placing a favourable balance above volume of trade must lead to the extinction of all balances and the permanent shrinkage of international trade, India should be the last country to contribute to this result.

The Chambers of Commerce

Federation of Indian Chambers of Commerce & Industry

Opening Day—New Delhi—4th. April 1936

The Federation of Indian Chambers of Commerce met in the old Assembly Chamber, New Delhi, on the **4th. April 1936** when over 100 delegate representing various Indian Chambers of Commerce of India and Burma were present. Several members of the Centeral Legislatnre were also present. After the presidential address, the House adopted the Annual Report and accounts for 1935-36.

Resolutions—Ottawa Denunciation Approved

At the outset a resolution condoling the death of King George V was passed all standing, whereafter Mr. *D. P. Khaitan* moved a resolution congratulating the Legislative Assembly on the passing of the resolution on the Ottawa agreement against which the Indian Commercial Community had all along protested and recording the Federation's appreciation of the patriotic action of all members of the Assembly, who voted for it.

Mr. Khaitan said that the Federation went into the question very fully and took the fullest responsibility for the view they held regarding the Ottawa Pact. He assured that India was not running any risk in terminating the Agreement and the fears and apprehensions expressed by the supporters of the Pact were unfounded and unbiassed. He felt that it was not in the interest of India to direct India's trade in one channel only, namely Empire markets.

Mr. *Kasturbhai Lalbhai*, supporting, pointed out that only 25 elected members voted with the Government, who were either Europeans or those who generally were not familiar with the business interests of India.

The resolution was adopted with acclamation.

Payment of Hundi

Three resolutions were moved from the Chair and passed. The first urged the Goverement to pass suitable legislation to provide that payment of Shah-Jog hundi to a bearer who is a person of substance and credit in the market discharges the liability of such drawee, irrespective of the manner and nature of endorsements on such hundi.

Purchase of Gold

The second urged the Government to stop export of gold and to purchase gold for the Reserve Bank on the basis of export parity.

Promotion of Free Trade

The third urged the removal of all barriers for promoting free trade within the country between the different Provinces and States and emphasised early settlement with maritime or internal States of all questions, with a view to promoting free trade and minimising diversion of trade from British Indian ports.

Economic Condition

Mr. *R. M. Chinoy* moved a resolution drawing attention to the continued depression and existing disproportionately high level of taxation, despite the scanty resources in the country, and urged the Government to consider ways and means for economic recovery of the country, relieving taxation, effecting reduction in the expenditure of military and civil, administration of railways and utilise the savings towards the speedy recovery of normal trade and development of nation-building departments. It also protested against policy of underestimating revenues and diverting resultant surpluses to non-recurring items of expenditure.

Mr. Chinoy quoted the returns of various foreign countries to show that in India, taxation as compared with the wealth of the country was high and defence expenditure comparatively also was too high.

Mr. *B. Das*, seconding, covered vast economic field to show that there was great need for a scientific taxation policy. He warned the Government against any writing off of capital of railways and wanted revision of taxation being conducted by cool-headed businessmen.

Mr. *Dastur* supported the resolution which was passed.

Fiscal Policy

Mr. *A. D. Shroff* moved that "the Federation records its considered opinion that an industry otherwise entitled to grant of protection need not be required to satisfy the condition regarding the abundant supplies of indigenous raw materials laid down in para 97 of the Fiscal Commission Report." Regretting Government's decision rejecting protection to glass and woollen industries, the resolution urged that the Government should place with their recommendations the Report of the Tariff Board within six months their submission before the Assembly.

In a lucid speech, Mr. Shroff traced the history of the fiscal policy followed in India during the last 50 years which, he declared, was nothing but an illustration of political domination by the United Kingdom for the economic exploitation of helpless Indian masses. The Fiscal Autonomy Convention was an eye-wash. There was too much of the convention and very little fiscal freedom and nothing of autonomy. Mr. Shroff protested against the Government's policy in withholding the Tariff Board's reports indefinitely and urged that reports should be brought without delay before the Legislature. He realised that mere management of currency and exchange would not ensure adequate development of the industry in this country but what they wanted was complete reorientation of the economic policy of India in line with other industrial countries of the world where fiscal policy would be only one unit.

Mr. *S. M. Bashir* vigorously supporting the resolution deplored Sir James Grigg's "tirade against industrialism and fiscal protection" and said if industrialism was a wrong cry, it was at least better than a harangue to silence every cry. In his opinion no development of agriculture was possible by making a fetish of Empire markets by importing marketing experts and by holding out pious expectations which could never be realised.

Mr. *Mohanlal Saxena* criticised the Government's action in rejecting protection to the woollen and glass industries. The resolution was adopted

Indian Shipping Traffic

The next resolution which was put from the chair was also passed. It urged the Government to take immediate steps to ensure that Indian shipping carries 60 per cent of the total cargo and passenger traffic in the coastal as well as in the overseas trade of India.

Insurance Law Revision

Mr. *K. Santanam* moved a resolution expressing satisfaction with the appointment by the Government of a special officer, Mr. Sen, to enquire and report in the matter of revision of insurance law, expressing the opinion that this was insufficient and suggesting the appointment of a committee of officials and non-officials to consider Mr. Sen's report, take evidence, if necessary, of insurance companies and other interests concerned and report to the Government.

Messrs. Santanam and J. C. Setalvad put forward the difficulties of Indian insurance companies in competing with foreign companies.

Mr. *J. J. Kapadia* mentioned the point of view of policy holders. He said that the enquiry should specially prohibit certain speculative activities of insurance companies, particularly regulate the unfettered discretion of the Directors, and stop taking of too much remuneration by Managing Agents.

Mr. *Roy*, supporting the motion, said that he would not mind placing Indian and foreign insurance companies on the same footing as long as the particular hardships operating against Indian companies were removed.

Mr. *R. Aiyar* wanted first publication of Mr. Sen's report and then its reference to committee. The resolution was passed unanimously.

Other Resolutions

The Federation adopted three more resolutions proposed from the Chair. The first urged the Government to give effect to the Drugs Enquiry Commitee Report by suitable legislation. The second urged substantial reduction in import duties on dye stuffs and sodium sulphates and the third endorsed the Assembly's decision recommending State control of M. and S. M. and B. N. W. Railways.

RAILWAY FINANCES

Mr. *Manu Subedar* moved a resolution deploring the financial condition of Indian railways which had been brought about despite frequent and grave warnings from the business community in the direction of rigid economy, Indianisation and businesslike management. The resolution urged upon the Government to institute an enquiry at the hands of Indian business representatives into financial condition of railways and suggest changes both in policy and systems of account in range, personal grouping system of rates and classification etc. The contemplated increase in the rates of freights to meet immediate situation, in the opinion of the Federation, was likely to lead to further deterioration. Until the finances of railways were put on a firm basis to the satisfaction of the Legislature it would be most unwise to install the proposed statutory railway authority which might lead to even more acute mismanagement of India's most valuable assets.

Mr. Manu Subedar referred to several important features of administration of railway finance particularly the crushing interest charges on valuable assets of over Rs. 700 crores and also to 55 per cent overhead expenditure, which was unbusinesslike. The Indian business community had emphasised Indianisation and inspite of an Indian being in charge of the Railways and Commerce Department, the position to-day was the same or even worse than what it was ten years ago. Unbusinesslike handling of the railway rates policy was another source of constant irritation to the commercial community and he would suggest the constitution of a Rates Tribunal so that this matter should be part of the larger economic policy of the country.

Mr. Manu Subedar declared that they were not trying to make political capital out of mistakes of the Railway Department but their main concern was that the enormous assets and hundreds of crores invested in the Railway should be managed in a manner as would bring prosperity to the country. He protested against using railways as a milch cow in British interests and opined that the institution of the Statutory Railway Authority was nothing but a device to take away railways from popular control and he asked, whose political influence— Indian or British ? Mr. Subedar concluded that the Government should take serious steps to put railway finance in order. Until then they should drop the institution of the Statutory Railway Authority.

Messrs. E. M. Gandhi, K. Basu, Sodhbans and Misra also supported the resolution which was carried. The Federation then adjourned.

SECOND DAY—NEW DELHI—5th. APRIL 1936

PORT TRUSTS

When the Federation resumed session to-day a resolution was moved from the Chair regarding the constitution of Port Trusts and adopted.

The Federation viewed with serious concern the present working policy of the Port Trust administration in regard to Indianisation of higher Port Trust charges, purchase of stores and general administration, and opined that the grievances in the above respects were due to their being a minority on the Boards of Port Trusts. The Federation, therefore, emphatically urged the Government to amend the constitutions of Port Trusts, so as to provide statutory Indian majority on the Board to enable them to carry on the administrations in the best interests of the country.

The next resolution, which was put from the Chair and adopted, impressed on the Government the necessity of collection and publication of complete methods of competition of non-Indian industrial enterprises and concerns operating in India to enable the country to comprehend problems relating to establishment and growth of Indian concerns behind the Tariff wall.

ANTI-INDIAN LAWS

Mr. *Sidhwa* moved that the Federation views with apprehension the lukewarm attitude of the Government of India in regard to Anti-Indian laws passed in foreign countries and British Colonies, the most recent cases being those of the Government of Zanzibar and Iraq.

The resolution wished to point out the extreme desirability of taking steps for protecting and safeguarding Indian Nationals and their interests abroad, in case any such discriminatory laws were passed by any foreign Government, the Government of India should immediately retaliate.

Mr. Sidhwa said that unless the Government of India takes drastic action in the matter, the position would gradually worsen. No amount of paper sympathy would serve the purpose.

Mr. *B. R. Gupta* said that owing to the disinterestedness of the Government of India in the past, there were now very few places under the sun where Indians were welcome, while foreigners found India the safest place to explcit. The resolution was passed.

Chettiars in Burma

On the motion of Mr. *N. G. Jasani*, the House also passed a resolution urging the Government of India to recommend to the Burma Government to drop the proceedings of eviction of Chettiars from the lands in Minbu district, Upper Burma.

Another resolution passed, urged the Government of India to undertake legislation to make registration of Lis Pendens compulsory.

Sugar Industry

Lala Sriram moved that the Government of India having imposed an excise duty of Rs. 1-5 per cwt. on sugar manufactured by factories operating vacuum pan process, the Federation opines that more rapid and intensive steps should be taken by the Central Government, through the Imperial Council of Agricultural Research and by the Provincial Governments, to raise the standard of cultivation of cane, both as to quality and quantity by the establishment of cane nurseries in all cane-growing Provinces, in which canes of high sucrose content and early and late ripening varieties would be propagated for wide distribution to ryots for seed, by dissemination of information as to the best methods of cultivation, manuring and irrigation by the extension of the canal system or assistance in well sinking, by research as to the methods of combating cane diseases and pests and by the provision of better roads so that cane cultivation costs may decrease and production increase for the benefit of the ryot and the sugar manufacturer, enabling the industry to compete effectively with foreign countries before the expiry of the period of protection to the industry.

The Federation considers that at least two annas per cwt. out of the proceeds of the excise duty should be allotted for the purposes, as recommended by the Imperial Council of Agricultural Research.

The Federation further suggests that Government should carry on an intensive research work for the proper utilisation of molasses.

Lala Shriram congratulated the Government on the efforts so far made with a view to improving the sugar industry and providing cheap sugar for consumers and mentioned the creation of a Technological Institute at Cawnpore for sugar research. He suggested model farms in various parts of the country to find out the best variety of cane suitable to the climatic and soil conditions in particular areas. He criticised the activities of the Directors of Agriculture who, in several cases, became the agents of profit-making concerns in the matter of manufacturing artificial manure, etc. He suggested the extraction of alcohol from molasses and hoped Government would not sleep over the matter, so that when the time came for the next Tariff Board Enquiry, it might be possible for the industry to stand any onslaught on the percentage of protection.

Messrs. *Dahanukar* and *Janatanam* further supported the resolution, which was passed.

Dufferin Cadets

Mr. *G. L. Mehta* moved :

(a) The Federation urges the Government of India to take immediate and effective steps in order to ensure that Shipping Companies plying in the coastal trade of India should be under obligation to take at least two "Dufferin" Cadets in each of their vessels as apprentices for training and also employ qualified officers and engineers trained in the "Dufferin" up to at least 50 per cent of the total number of officers and engineers employed in their ships, as recommended by the Indian Mercantile Marine Committee ;

(b) The Federation urges the Government that they should use their influence with Shipping Companies like the P. and O., which receive mail subsidies and patronage of the Government and the people of India to employ duly qualified Cadets of the "Dufferin" as Officers of their steamers in adequate number ;

(c) The Federation urges that whenever mail contracts to Shipping Companies are made or renewed, definite conditions should be attached to the grant of mail subsidies as to the appointment of Indian apprentices and officers in ships belonging to such companies.

Mr. Mehta, in a lengthy speech, declared that it was subsidy which these shipping companies were getting and not payment for services, as the Commerce Member said in the Assembly, as the word subsidy was even used in postal returns. He said the problem was becoming acute and must be tackled by the Government immediately.

Mr. S. H. Lulla and Mr. Mazumdar strongly supported the resolution, which was carried.

Mr. *Haridas Lalji* moved a resolution recording emphatic protest against the attitude of steamship companies in not accepting measurement of cargo by all registered Chambers of Commerce at every port and against the Government for not giving full effect to the resolution of the Federation in this connection passed in 1923 and suggesting the appointment of Boards for the purpose of carrying out measurement work at minimum charge.

Mr. Buch supported the resolution, which was carried.

Duty on Imported Coal

The last resolution was moved by Mr. *A. L. Ojha* regarding the coal industry.

The resolution stated that in view of the most unsatisfactory position of the coal industry due to (1) the burden of numerous local taxes, (2) the surcharge on railway freight and terminal charges, (3) the unhealthy competition on account of imported coal and oil fuel and (4) the recent changes in the coal purchase policy of the Government of India for railways which is more or less responsible for the wasteful methods of mining with the consequential result of frequent colliery disasters, this Federation strongly urges the Government of India to impose immediately an adequate duty on imported coal and oil fuel, appoint a committee of enquiry for examining the present position of this important basic industry, with a view to suggesting remedies for its rehabilitation.

Mr. *K. Dutt* supported the resolution and it was passed.

The Federation discussed, several members participating, the question of taking steps for strengthening the finances of the Federation, with a view to increasing its activities. The matter was deferred to a later date. In the meantime, the question would be considered by various bodies and individuals concerned.

Mr. *D. P. Khaitan* moved a vote of thanks, expressing warmest appreciation of services rendered by the President, Mr. Padampat Singhania, the youngest President of the Federation, being about 32 years.

Mr. *A. D. Shroff* and Mr. *Kasturbhai Lalbhai* joined therein to which Mr. Singhania made a suitable reply. Thereafter the Federation dispersed.

Executive Committee

The following is the complete Executive Committee for 1936-37 :—

President : D. P. Khaitan.

Vice-President : Kumararaja of Chettinad.

Members (elected): Messrs. A. D. Shroff, Manu Subedar, Mr. Kasturbhai Lalbhai, Lala Shriram, Mr G. D. Birla, Mr. P. Thakurdas, Mr. Santanam, Mr. Padampat Singhania, Mr. R. M. Chinoy, Mr. Dahanukar, Mr. Walchand Hirachand, Mr. Chunilal B. Mehta.

Members (co-opted) : Mr. N. R. Sarkar, Mr. S. M. Bashir, Mr. B. Das, Rai Bahadur Ramsarandas, Babu Gurucharanlal.

Treasurers : Messrs. A. L. Ojha and S. C. Law.

The Bombay Indian Merchants' Chamber

Presiding over the 28th. Annual General Meeting of the Indian Merchants Chamber, held in Bombay on the **31st. January 1936**, Mr. *Manu Subedar* dealt with the big changes that are taking place in the distribution of wealth in the country, whereby the poor in India are becoming poorer, while the growth of industries has created opportunities for the rich to become richer, the middle class bearing a relatively higher burden of taxes and being oppressed by the perpetual nightmare of lack of prospects and unemployment. He only hoped that India, as a result of these factors, would not suffer from the bitterness of class hatred, in addition to communal.

Referring to the export of gold in large quantities, he observed :—"India sold in 1932-33, 1933-34 and 1934-35, an average of Rs. 86 crores less of merchandise every year than the average of the previous three years. Elsewhere in the world such a situation is adjusted by a reduction in the exchange value, by stimulating exports in various ways and by a rigorous curtailment of imports. In India not only has the exchange to be maintained, but in official quarters there is great anxiety to secure an increase of imports to be paid for by the export of gold. In national economy it is not right that India should have purchased the various commodities of commerce and paid for them with solid gold. To fritter away this valuable reserve that was in the hands of the population, for the temporary maintenance of exchange was a dis-service to this country when every county in the world, including England, was adding to its gold resources, and most countries in the world were taking up all the gold that was available inside for the purposes of central reserve.

"Other countries in the world have managed to mantain their exchanges by stimulating exports and putting difficulties in the way of imports, either by higher duties, or by quotas, or by developing internal sources to substitute the imports. In India not only are the doors kept open, but the Finance Member, who is a zealous free trader, is talking of reducing duties all round with a view to stimulate imports, that is to say, with a view to further stimulate the export of gold from India."

He next referred to the prevailing agricultural distress in India, where the Indian agriculturist was receiving crores of rupees less for his crops than he used to in 1928-29. With reduced purchasing power in has to bear many of the taxes, which were inelastic. The freight rates had not been materially reduced. Interest and other charges payable by the agriculturist had not declined and the low bank rate, which they were told was the result of the plethora of money, did not reflect business conditions in vogue in India and did not touch the agriculturist who is in debt. His complaint against the Government was that, they had not during the last five years made any attempt to bring about a rise in the prices of agricultural commodities, though the need of such a rise has been acknowledged over and over again oven by the officials themselves.

"Government have always been unwilling to have either expansion of credit or that of currency in this country on an adequate scale," he continued, "because a rise in prices and a favourable balance of trade on merchandise would stop the export of gold and may actually turn the tide, inducing purchase by India of gold —a position that would clearly be embarrassing to the Exchange Control, the Bank of England and the London Money market. There is a conflict of interests, and in this conflict, those in whose hands the administration of India's finances are put, are not throwing their weight on the side of this country.

Mr. Subedar criticised at length the Ottawa Agreement which, he held, benefitted India, while in our trade relations with other countries it actually injured Indian interests by provoking retaliation. With regard to protective tariffs, conditions had changed since 1922, when the Fiscal Commission laid down the principles, even the United Kingdom having gone over to the policy of heavy protection ; but the Government still stuck to the old conditions and interpreted them with such strictness and severity as to disagree with the recommendations of the Tariff Board at times and refuse protection. They wanted, therefore, that Government should be brought to take more interest in the development of Indian industries and trade by defining their policy with regard to protection, and by negotiating bilateral trade agreements with other countries. Among the needs of the trade, he suggested the immediate appointment of a Trade Commissioner in Japan ;

regulation of Indian trade with Germany with the object of introducing a reciprocal arrangement, which would increase the volume of trade between the two countries, and laws to make up for the present deficiency in the present state of law with regard to the regulation of monopolies, trusts, cartels, pools, etc.

Finally, opposing the proposed Railway, he said :—"As a businessman, I would like the Railways to be managed on business lines and I would deprecate interference with the working of the Railways through political or any other pressure either from Indians or Britishers. But the general policy in connection with the Railways could not be divergent from, and must be part of, the general economic policy of the State in India, and the outlook of the Railways towards Indian industries as carriers, and towards Indian manufacturers and suppliers as purchasers of their equipment and stores, must be distinctly national. The device of the Statutory Board appears to us as part of the general programme for reservation of financial and economic matters into the hands of people other than responsible Ministers in India with the possibility that political influences, not Indian, but English, might interfere with the working of the Railways."

The Calcutta Chamber of Commerce

The following is the text of the Presidential speech delivered by Mr. *Kanailal Jatia* at the Annual General Meeting of the Indian Chamber of Commerce, Calcutta on the **26th. February 1936 :—**

It is my painful duty to refer with feelings of sincere regret to the death of His late Majesty, King George V. Througouht the length and breadth of his vast domains, and the world in general, his loss was greatly felt, and we in India particularly mourn his loss at a time when great constitutional changes are in sight. It was the constant desire of His late Majesty that his Indian subjects should occupy their rightful place in the British Commonwealth of Nations, and with that end in view, His Majesty's reign was one of benevolent care and affection towards his Indian subjects in whose betterment he was greatly interested. His Majesty also enjoyed unfailing proofs of the loyalty of his Indian Empire— a fact which was corroborated only in June last by the spontaneous rejoicings all over India on the occasion of His Majesty's Silver Jubilee. On behalf of the Chamber and myself, I offer our heart-felt condolences to her gracious Majesty the Queen, and the Members of the Royal Family in their great bereavement.

We are, however, fortunate to find that our new Sovereign King Edward VIII has personal experience of this country and we have no doubt that His Majesty will take a keen and sympathetic interest in India's welfare both politically and materially. I would now refer to the question of the revision of the Indian income-tax system. As you all know, the Government of India have appointed two experts from the Inland Board of Revenue of Great Britain to examine the entire system and the operation of the Income tax Law in India. They are now touring India collecting material and hearing oral evidence from all those interested in this question. Representatives of our Chamber also met them on the 10th February and discussed with them the hardships that the commercial community is at present experiencing as a result of the various anomalies that exist in the Indian income-tax system. Among the various difficulties experienced by the commercial community, I would like to refer to one or two cases which deserve the closest attention on the part of the Government of India and the experts. I need hardly say that the Income-tax Law as it exists at present is admittedly defective in more ways than one. I would like to draw the attention of the income-tax experts to the necessity of amending Rule No. 8 of the Indian Income-Tax Act so as to permit a double depreciation allowance on machinery employed in factories running day and night, because it is only just and equitable that where machinery has been running day and night for an extented period, depreciation at proportionately increased rates should be allowed. An objection may, however, be raised to this proposal on the ground that it would be difficult to get authentic proofs of hours of daily work in a factory and also that it would entail much work on the Income-Tax Department. I would suggest that the depreciation allowance may be based upon the average daily running hours of the financial year under assessment and that a certificate of the registered auditors may be accepted as regards the hours of work per day.

The practice of making a roving inspection of account books by reopening the case of the previous year in the matter of income-tax assessment after the assessee is assessed for the current year is another genuine grievance which affects very much the commercial community. During the period of assessment now-a-days all the items of the assessee are subjected to careful scrutiny in case account books are produced and examined. Yet by virtue of section 34 of the Income-Tax Act the Income-Tax Officer is empowered to reopen the assessment of the previous year and to call for books and accounts of any assessee who, the officer thinks, has escaped assessment under certain heads of income or is assessed at too low a rate. This Section 34, as you are all aware, gentlemen, cannot be construed as a detective section but only to rectify the assessment where income has escaped. It has been the practice of the Income Tax Department to call for account books on most frivolous grounds, or even on the basis of anonymous letters posted to an Income-Tax Officer instigated by jealousy or enmity only to harrass an assessee. and a roving inspection of account books is instituted. Recently the Calcutta High Court has held in similar circumstances that the items under which the Income-Tax Officer thinks that income has partially or wholly escaped assessment should be disclosed in the notice that is being served on the assessee ; but inspite of this observation of the Calcutta High Court and without disclosing in the notice the income which has escaped, I understand, that the practice of making roving inspection of account books is still continued by the Incoms-Tax Department. It may be assumed that an assessee can get relief if an appeal is preferred before the Commissioner or Asst. Commissioner because they are impartial judges to give relief where necessary, but, gentlemen, I am sorry to say that the assessee gets very little redress of his grievances. It has often happened that where a case before an income-tax officer reaches a stage where an appeal will be preferred by the assessee, the income-tax officer takes the trouble of consulting the Assistant Commissioner or the Commissioner, and this prejudices the mind of those higher authorities. One is inclined to feel that the separation of judicial and executive functions should be carried out more rigorously also in the realm of income-tax. I trust that the Expert Committee will carefully consider this anomaly and suggest a suitable remedy to present the harassment to the assessee at the hands of the income-tax authorities, and further recommend suitable methods where there will be no denial of justice to the assessee.

I would also commend to the attention of these experts the necessity of allowing business losses incurred in former years to be carried forward and set off against the profits earned in subsequent years. It is well known that in recent years owing to trade depression several firms have been unable to losses. It is therefore only fair and reasonable that such set-off should be allowed.

Gentlemen, let me now refer to another important question affecting the commercial community and the general public of Calcutta viz. the rates of electricity charged by the Calcutta Electric Supply Corporation. The Government of Bengal appointed an Advisory Committee in August last whose terms of reference were to advise the Government of Bengal on the question of the charges at present levied by the Calcutta Electric Supply Corporation Ltd. Representatives of our Chamber appeared also before the Committee to give oral evidence. I feel that a public utility concern like the Calcutta Electric Supply Corporation which enjoys a monopoly should consider its duty to charge its various customers as low a rate as it is possible to do. At present the charges are very high and they could be considerably reduced, while still distributing a reasonable dividend to the shareholders of the Company. A perusal of the balance sheets of the Calcutta Electric Supply Corporation would show that its reserves and dividends have been consistently increasing, and it has issued even bonus shares. It is well-known that the Calcutta Electric Supply Corporation has declared dividends at the high rate of 13 per cent for the last few years. Considering the present market conditions, I feel that for a public utility company like the Calcutta Electric Supply Corporation which does not meet with any serious competition and whose chances of incurring losses are negligible, a dividend of 13 per cent is far on the high side. If the present dividend is reduced to a lower level it will enable them to decrease the flat rate charged, at present, to the consumers. The representatives of our Chamber also pressed the view that the Advisory Committee should carefully investigate the items on which the Corporation charges depreciation and should also see as to whether block capital consists of obsolete machinery or other items for which provision for depreciation is necessary. I would also suggest that the Government of Bengal should make a careful investigation into the administration expenses of the Corporation as well as into the necessity of Indianisation of the superior staff of the Corporation as far as possible. I trust that the Advisory Committee have considered all these points which were placed before them and have made suitable recommendations to the Bengal Government in regard to the advisability of making a reduction in the charges at present levied by the Calcutta Electric Supply Corporation.

Gentlemen, turning from a public utility corporation to Government, it is not too great a step. As you all know Posts and Telegraphs are valuable means of communication in the life of a country and their charges in India are at present very high. The rates for post cards, stamps for envelopes etc. were all increased at a time when India was faced with deficit budgets. This crisis no longer exists, as revealed by the Report of the Indian Posts and Telegraphs Department for the year 1934-35 recently issued by the Government. The net result of working for 1934-35 was a surplus of over Rs. 37 lakhs as compared with a net deficiency of more than Rs. 51 lakhs during the year 1933-34. Of all the branches of the department, such as the Post Office, Telegraphs and Telephone and Radio, the Post Office earned the highest surplus to the extent of Rs. 24 lakhs as compared with a deficit of Rs. 11.5 lakhs during the previous year. When one sees such bright indications of revenue in the Posts and Telegraphs Department, it is but natural that an appeal for a general reduction in postal rates is being made, and I trust the Finance Member will give adequate relief from the burden of postal rates which were increased when an emergency arose but which to-day no longer exists.

Gentlemen, I shall not allow this occasion to pass without making some observations in regard to the finances of Bengal. I think a reference to this important question is all the more necessary because recently Sir Otto Niemeyer, who has been entrusted with an enquiry relating to the adjustment of Central and Provincial Finances of India, has collected all the facts for an equitable settlement of Bengal's just claims. We in Bengal are deeply indebted to His Excellency Sir *John Anderson* for his consistent and able advocacy of Bengal's case for financial readjustment, and his speech at St. Andrew's Day Dinner, a few months back, is a striking example of the earnestness of his desire for promoting the welfare of the people of the province and of securing a just treatment for Bengal at the hands of the Central Government. It is hardly necessary for me to refer here to the deplorable condition of Bengal's finances and the recurring deficits since the year 1930-31. The revenues derived from various sources of taxation such as excise, stamps, forest and registration have been reduced on an average of about two crores of rupees during the last five years, and this is mainly due to the deterioration in the economic condition of the people. Jute, which is the mainstay of Bengal's agricultural population, has failed to yield an adequate return to the ryots whose debts are increasing at alarming rates. Only year before last, the Central Government agreed to remit one half of the jute export duty to Bengal in recognition of the just claims put forward by the Bengal Government. Moreover, the Government of Bengal imposed last year, five new taxes in order to make up a portion of their huge deficits. Although the present financial position as revealed on Monday last by Sir John Woodhead shows signs of improvement, it is clear that for years to come Bengal cannot embark upon any ambitious programme of economic reconstruction if she is to continue in her present position which is the creation of the Meston Award. From the year 1919 when the Reforms Act was passed this province has been paying on an average of about four crores of rupees every year by way of Jute export duty, which is now reduced to one half. I am firmly of opinion that if full justice were done to Bengal by a total remission of the jute export duty, Bengal will have less reason for complaint on this important question. I trust that Sir Otto Niemeyer will give careful consideration to the case of Bengal for an equitable adjustment of her claims, and make suitable recommendations which will relieve the financial distress of Bengal.

In conclusien, Gentlemen, I wish to thank the Members of the Committee for their whole-hearted co-operation with me in the discharge of my rerponsibility, and I trust that the members of the Chamber will lend their support in the same courteous manner for the benefit of our Chamber as in the past.

The B. & O. Chamber of Commerce

Presiding over the annual meeting of the Bihar and Orissa Chamber of Commerce held at Patna on the **21st. March 1936**, Rao Bahadur *D. D. Thacker*, President of the Chamber, said :—

"The present worldwide depression which began in 1930 is responsible for the slow progress in the recovery of world trade, and several countries in the world are trying their might and main to improve their trade. The problem seems to be one calling for a fair adjustment between production and distribution all over the world. It is admitted on all hands that over production is one of the causes that contributes to the present depression, and that the surplus of goods in one country does not find a ready market in other countries, because each country is trying to become economically self-sufficient. To us in India, our export trade consists mainly of agricultural commodities and raw products whereas the import trade of India consists of articles wholly or mainly manufactured. The effects of the depression were felt by India more keenly owing to the greater fall in prices of agricultural products and raw materials as compared with manufactured articles, which will be evident from the fact that in 1928-29, the year preceding the commencment of the present depression, the value of some of the principal crops in Bihar and Orissa was estimated at Rs. 137 crores, whereas in 1933-34 it was Rs. 55 crores only ; i. e., a reduction of Rs. 82 crores. Such a disastrous fall in agricultural prices has been directly responsible for the reduced purchasing power of the masses who form the bulk of the population in India and who depend mainly on agriculture for their subsistence. It is indeed gratifying to note that during recent years the Government of India have taken various steps to improve the condition of the cultivators, by disseminating knowledge about improved methods of agriculture, farming and husbandry, by establishing demonstration farms, by appointing marketing officers to help the ryots to dispose of their agricultural products, etc. In spite of all these measures, however, agricultural prosperity still seems to be distant, and I am inclined to think that the Government of India should undertake an intensive programme of economic planning over a series of years, with a view to effect an all round improvement in the condition of the people.

"The development of the sugar industry in Bihar under the impetus of protection is indeed responsible for giving direct assistance to the cultivator's of sagarcane. Bihar at present stands second in point of importance in the production of sugar in India, and had it not been for such a rapid development in the sugar industry, the cultivators would have been in still greater distress for want of remunerative prices for their agricultural products. At a time when agricultural products failed to give an adequate return, the cultivation of sugarcane came in handy for the agriculturists who were assured of reasonable price of their sugarcane. There is every prospect of the sugar industry making still greater progress provided the necessary co-operation is forthcoming between the Government and the people.

"I am sorry to observe that its position at present is anything but satisfactory. In recent years, it can hardly be said to have received just treatment at the hands of the Government of India. As you all know, the coal industry submitted a scheme for the restriction of the output of coal in order that production might not outstrip demand and better prices might be realised for the coal raised. But the Government of India did not see their way to adopt this scheme even though this scheme was strongly supported by Your Excellency's Government. The coal industry is at present labouring under various handicaps, such as sur-charge on Railway freight and competition of foreign coal in distant markets like Bombay, Ahmedabad, Ceylon, etc. The total abolition of sur-charge on railway freight on coal is an immediate necessity as otherwise coal would find it difficult to move freely to distant markets in India and compete with foreign coal. The Government of India should also impose an increased duty on coal entering into India in order to protect the indigenous industry.

"Another matter which has of late created some amount of anxiety in the public minds is the question of conservation of the coal resources of the country, particularly of the better quality of the Jharia coal, suitable for metallurgical purposes. India has vast resources of iron and other ores and it would indeed be a very great national calamity if in the future, coal be not available for development of the iron and steel industry for which there is a bright future before the country. Sir Lewis Fermor, Kt., Ex-Director of the Geological Survey of India has, in his recent address before the Asiatic Society of Bengal, laid very great stress on this danger of coal-famine and it is to be hoped that the Government of India will take the matter up at an early date and with the co-operation of the industry, devise some measures which may prolong the life of the better class of Jharia coal for the development of metallurgical industry.

"Before I leave the subject of coal, I think I should say something particularly regarding the soft coke trade on which the bulk of collieries working second class coal are mainly dependent at present. Outside the domestic hearth there is at present very little custom for second class coal.

"I shall now refer to the mica industry in brief. Mica occupies the third place in the list of minerals raised in this province. I am happy to say that the industry is progressing fairly well, as will be evident from the increasing exports of mica during the recent years, in 1932-33 the shipment of mica amounted to 40,000 cwts. valued at Rs. 32 lacs, in 1933-34 this increased to 66,000 cwts. valued at Rs. 45 lacs: while in 1934-35, the figures were 105,000 cwts. valued at 69 lacs. The position of this industry, therefore, seems to be very encouraging, particularly when we remember that the pre-war average of export was only 49,000 cwts. I have every hope that the mica industry will continue to progress satisfactorily in view of its increasing use in various branches of industries.

"I may take the liberty of referring here to two important enquiries which are being conducted on behalf of the Government and the results of which may affect our destinies in a large measure.

"The first of these enquiries relates to the modification of Income Tax law and its administration in this country for the examination of which the Government of India have requisitioned the services of two Experts from the Board of Inland Revenue. This Chamber has already submitted its Memorandum before the Committee and our representatives have also been orally examined. The announcement made by the Finance Member in introducing the Government of India Budget, raising the minimum limit of income tax assessment from Rs. 1,000 to Rs. 2,000, is a happy augury. This will automatically remove some of the hardships under which small assessess have been labouring. There is no doubt, however, that the law and its administration as at present do require important modifications and it is to be earnestly hoped that while amending the law, Government will take full account of the feeling in the country in respect of the carrying forward of losses, suitable allowances for depreciation, particularly on machinery running double shift and on wasting assets like coal mine, the removal of difficulties in the way of recognising partitions of the members of a Joint Hindu family although they may under the Hindu Law be actually separate, some allowance for the dependent members of the family, and the formation of an independent Appellate Authority on questions of fact.

Dealing with the question of Sir Otto Niemeyer's enquiry the Rao Bahadur said: 'This Chamber has already submitted a Memorandum pointing out the financial disabilities under which this province has been labouring and has suggested certain remedies. It is to be earnestly hoped that the claims of this province will receive full consideration, and not only ample provision for suitable subvention will be made but that also when the time comes for a redistribution of Income tax receipts amongst the provinces, this re-distribution will be done on a basis which will not only take into account our large population but also make it possible for us to approach the standard of material advancement attained in the sister provinces like the U. P. and the Punjab. For the purpose of determining the standard of re-distribution this Chamber has suggested an admirable scheme which I earnestly commend to the consideration of Sir Otto Niemeyer.

"I should now, with your permission, deal with another question, that is in connection with the B. and N. W. Ry. since the time has now come when the Government must make up its mind whether or not to take over the management of this Railway under the terms of their contract, rather severe criticisms have late been directed against this railway service. The grievances of the travelling public have become almost classic and the representatives of the public on the Provincial and the Central Legislatures have vied with one another in condemning the present management of this railway. No doubt, the grievances do exist, but we must also recognise that improvements have been made and are under contemplation. For instance, it will be found that it has probably the second fastest passenger service on the meter guage system in India.

"I may say a word here about the Chamber's policy and faith. This Chamber has been consistently and continuously co-operating with the Government and has always stood for a policy of reform by constitutional means, and there is no reason to suppose that it will ever deviate from that policy. No distinction of community, caste, or colour is observed in extending its services and membership, and to-day it is composed of corporations, firms and individuals represented by persons, Indian and European, Hindu and Muslim alike. The Chamber is now a recognised body of experts and is consulted both by the Government and the public, on all important questions affecting the public particularly the commercial community. Its members are invited to sit on special committees and to tender evidence before them. It has secured representations on important public bodies, like the E. I. Ry. Advisory Committee, the B. & N. W. Ry. Advisory Committee, the Senate, the Board of Industries, etc., and not the least of them, the Bihar Legislative Assembly under the new Reforms. In this latter connection, our best thanks are due to the Bihar Government which championed our cause and to the Committee presided over by Sir Lawrie Hammond which recognised the strength behind our just demand.

"Before I proceed to request your Excellency to declare this session open, I may be permitted to refer to one need of the Chamber. This Chamber is in the eleventh year of its existence and has been achieving progressively increased importance and recognition. The need for a suitable building to house it has been keenly felt for some time past in order to centralise and co-ordinate its activities. It has, therefore, been proposed to approach the Government for allotting a suitable plot of land where the Chamber's building may be constructed, and I earnestly hope and trust that the Government will give a favourable consideration to our request in this behalf.

The S. I. Chamber of Commerce

The 26th. annual meeting of the Southern India Chamber of Commerce was held at Madras on the **30th. March 1936**, *Sowcar Abdul Hakim Sahib* presiding. In the course of his speech moving the adoption of the annual report, Sowcar Abdul Hakim, the outgoing chairman said :—

We are yet in the depths of depression and what ray of hope was visible during the closing months of 1935 has been fading away. Prices and the purchasing power of the masses still remain at a low ebb. In this mood of gloom merchants are apt to be too susceptible to any and every circumstance tending to improve the situation and plunge into speculative dealings in the expectation of a boom. Such sporadic and ill-regulated enthusiasm is bound to retard still further any chances of return to normal conditions. The plethora of exchange clearing agreements, import quotas, high tariffs and other effective barriers to international trade have complicated the economic policy of every country and every attempt by the League of Nations to reduce the barriers has so far proved futile. The orgy of economic nationalism rules the world and each country has of course been paying and will continue to pay a heavy price in purchasing such a policy.

The import and export trade of India, as of other countries, has been suffering very badly. Our chief exports have been losing the customary markets. Our groundnut is losing in France, Germany and Italy ; our castor-seed in the United States of America ; our cotton and tanned hides and skins are struggling hard to retain the old markets. India cannot hope to retain those markets without concluding separate trade agreements with those countries and appointing competent Indian trade commissioners in those countries who would bring buyers and sellers together, popularise our products and watch the interests of Indian exports. It is of course very important also that indigenous banks should be helped to open branches abroad, transact exchange business and handle Indian goods in those markets when necessary. At the same time serious attempts should be made to cultivate the home market by all possible means such as reduction of railway freight, organisation of markets and propaganda, establishment of public warehouses etc. Transport charges are the biggest stumbling bloc to the promotion of inland trade and I am unable to appreciate the irrational attitude of port trusts which are still levying the post-war high port charges and harbour dues and decrying the railways for making any freight reductions to obtain more traffic. The railway administrations must drastically revise their rating policy in order to encourage overland transport. The Railway Board should not be content with merely making annual raids on the depreciation fund to feed the unrepentent railways but must take in hand the question of drastic economies in expenditure and of writing down the rates. Similarly each port would be well advised in reducing harbour dues and effecting economies.

It would have been so wise on the part of Government if they had adopted the policy of reducing the tax burden more wholeheartedly. Emergency taxes are raised to void deficits and when they bring surpluses Government are not expected to fritter them away on new schemes instead of abolishing the temporary levy. The surcharges on the income-tax and supertax, and on customs duties still remain although funds have been available to write them down. Such a policy belies Government solicitude for the masses.

The indebtedness of the masses remains a huge problem : but I do not think that the country as a whole is going to be benefitted by debt conciliation schemes which seek to rob the creditor and feed the debtor. His Highness the Aga Khan has suggested the drastic step of reducing the rupee price to 1 sh. It cannot be denied that many advanced countries which reduced the exchange value of their currencies have been benefitted by it. It is also true that anticipating the Indian businessmen's prediliction for the 16 d. rupee, Parliament have banged the door on the question. But there is no gainsaying the fact that Indian economic interests demand at least the restoration of the old exchange value of 16 d. in order to enable Indian producers to realise better prices without disturbing the world level of the prices or the position of Indian commodities in the world markets. The present condition of our export trade leaves much to be desired since it does not produce enough to pay our annual foreign obligation and consequently depends upon the ceaseless export of gold when all the world over there is such a scramble for gold and every attempt is made to conserve gold resources. The surplus of exports over imports was Rs. 16 crores in 1935. As against Rs. 25 crores in 1934 and Rs. crores· in 1933 the export of gold was Rs. 44 crores, Rs. 60 crores and Rs. crores in those years respectively. That is why there is a public outcry that we are living on our capital resources. Neither have Government given any attention to the popular demand to reduce India's foreign obligations. Every year sterling loans are maturing; money is very cheap, sterling resources are available. It would have been so easy for Government to raise cheap rupee loans and pay off the sterling loans. I think that the Reserve Bank, being a shareholders' bank, ought to interest itself in these matters of financial conservation.

The Punjab Chamber of Commerce

Presiding over the 31st annual general meeting of the Punjab Chamber of Commerce, held at New Delhi, on the **14th. April 1936**, *Rai Bahadur P. Mukherjee*, its Chairman, warmly welcomed the Hon. J. N. G. Johnson, Chief Commissioner, Delhi, who had shown continued interest in the Chamber.

After referring to the loss to the Empire in the death of King Geroge, Mr. Mukherji briefly reviewed business conditions during the past year. He urged reorientation of the whole policy of railway rating and also paying of such loans whereon interest was high with a view to improve railway finance.

The progress of civil aviation, he thought, was very slow. To ensure complete success of the Empire development scheme which was expected to be inaugurated in 1938, it was essential that mails within India should be carried by air at considerable frequency. Mr. *Mukherjee* criticised the Assembly's decision terminating the Ottawa Agreement and went on to demonstrate the fallacy of the decisions by examining the working of the agreement in some detail. He emphasised that each country was following the policy of agrarian self-sufficiency and international trade had been bettered. It was regrettable that a question of such vast moment to Indian trade had been influenced by considerations other than strictly economic.

Mr. *Johnson*, addressing the meeting, referred to the late King's Silver Jubilee Fund and the benefits which accrued to the Delhi Province therefrom. He announced that her Excellency and her Committee had very kindly found it possible operating through the Central Association of Indian Red Cross to allot a further considerable sum for the establishment of King George V travelling dispensary to work continuously throughout rural areas in Delhi. The Chief Commissioner expressed gratitude to the Finance Member who found it possible, after lean years, to assign at least financial provision for removal of refuse and disposal of sewage, so vitally important to the residents of Delhi.

Turning to the Punjab State Aid to Industries Act, Mr. Johnson promised fullest examination of any representation on the matter submitted by the Chamber. The improvement and extension scheme for Delhi was now being investigated by a special officer and the question of special area for factories in Delhi would receive due consideration. Dealing with the Chamber's representation in the future legislature, he hoped that the opportunities offered to the representatives of the Chamber would be fully utilised. Concluding, Mr. Johnson joined in expressing grati·ude and goodwill to Lord and Lady Willingdon.

The Malabar Chamber of Commerce

The annual Conference of the Malabar Chamber of Commerce was held at Calicut on the **27th. June 1936.** Mr. *Sami Venkatachalam Chetti*, in the course of his presidential speech, said that the commercial and economic questions now engrossed the attention of the world and Indians should study these problems almost unceasingly. The Chambers of Commerce all over the country should be strengthened and businessmen should treat these as part of their business organisations. They were aware that in the Government of India Act, a part of which was to come into force by next April, there was only one seat allotted to the commerce of the Presidency in the local Assembly and that that was given to the Southern India Chamber of Commerce. On that matter they had no doubt a grievence but he was an optimist and think that every thing happened was for the best. Nothing great was ever achieved without a grievance and he thought that this grievance of their would demolish the hedge round that field and really representative character be infused into it. He hoped that every trade would organise itself. Every functional and territorial organisation should be affiliated as members of the Southern India Chamber of Commerce.

There was yet another handicap in the qualification of a voter for the commerce constituency. That was that every voter should be an Income-Tax assessee for any year in five preceding years on an income of Rs. 10,000. That high qualification had made the representation plutocratic and deprived of some really capable businessmen of representation. Whatever might be the possibilities and failings of the new constitution, he added, it was imperative that the tried and tested Nationalists must capture the legislatures and seats of power.

He had no doubt, the speaker continued, that they heard with great relief the verdict of the Assembly to terminate the Ottwa Pact. Their pleasure was shared he businessmen all over the country, if not by all the contracting parties. The basic idea of that agreement was not what India should gain but the fear what she might lose. Their President, in his address, in May 1934, had said that "Ottawa Agreement had only diverted trade and had not given any stimulus to India's exports."

With England, he proceeded, their terms should be slightly different this time, preference being on the side of India. India was a debtor country to England. She imported not only her goods but also her nationals. England must take their products at world prices in payment of their charges. She must not expect to be paid in gold. In the trade agreements with Lancashire and Japan they had not made sufficient provision for keeping in tact the hand-weaving industry.

Adverting to socialism the speaker continued, it was a thorny subject with which he hesitated to deal excepting to state that the subject had not been well studied by protagonists and antagonists. That observation of his was itself the outcome of confused and contradictory views of the belligerents of the wordy war-fare. Recently they had had an interesting skirmish between the President of the Congress and the President of the Tamil Nadu Congress Committee. Both of them were said to have given their views on socialism in their extra official capacities. But the views of these dignitaries had given much room for some searchings of the heart in political and commercial circles. The history of big industry in this country, Mr. Sami part of the consumer and Venkatachalam continued, was one of heavy sacrifices on the grower of raw produce They had willingly given their full co-operation in the hope that the industries would stand on their own legs in the near future and return the benefits to the country as a whole. Therefore proprietors of big business should look to the interests of the country first before they looked to their own profits.

In the impending renewal of the trade agreement with Japan unlike the last occasion, the whole range of competing Japanese imports must be taken into account such as hosiery, steel and cement and the favourable balance of trade.

Nearer home they were having pin pricks from Ceylon. The States of Travancore, Cochin and British Malabar were loudly complaining against Ceylonese dumping of cocoanuts and oil into India while Ceylon gnashed her teeth against what they called the ingratitude of the West Coast for the employment she was providing for many of her unwanted children. They had now a favourable trade balance with Ceylon and they should be chary of distributing it if only Ceylon had been mindful of proximity and affinity with the mainland. Being under a different constitution she had treated India almost as a foreign country, in fact a shade less favourable than the United Kingdom. Ceylon's import trade in goods manufactured in India was more with foreign countries than with India. She bought more hosiery, textiles and cement from foreign countries than from India. He hoped that storm in the tea pot would bring the two countries together and he had every hope that it would be so in that the President of the Ceylon Chamber of Commerce was a South Indian who might be expected to appreciate the Indian point of view.

He found that the West Coast people were very fond of Ceylon tobacco and he hoped they paid for it by their delicious bananas. There was an agonising cry of unemployment particularly in this part of the country. He would venture to ask them if the possibility of tobacco plantation had been examined. Many waterways were neglected on account of railways. Since then most of the railways had become State concerns. The two railway systems in their presidency were still private concerns. The Assembly had recently recommended to the Government to absorb them on the completion of their term which is within the next five years. Their interest in the profits of these systems could not be wholehearted and the country might not feel impelled to give any co-operation to the Government in combating the keen competition of the road transport. Coasting trade could be further developed as Bombay was a vast market for coir, copra, tea, pepper and other spices. Rubber factories had sprung up in Karachi, Calcutta and Trivandrum. With the advantage of the Kerala Soap Institute the export trade in cocoanut oil and fish oil ought to be re-established.

Their internal trade suffered from several other impediments which fortunately were capable for removal and adjustibility by the people themselves. Their information regarding each trade was hopelessly meagre and organisation of salesmanship was non-existent. Their credit facilities were simply archaic. He ventured to suggest that the Chambers of Commerce should depute committees and commissions to study the source of growth and possibilites of each trade and suggest methods of reconstruction and salesmanship in each trade. That reconstruction would, he thought, be able to absorb some thousands of intelligent young men.

Cochin Harbour had, though it affected Madras, brought them nearer Bombay and even the United Kingdom. Postal and Telegraph facilities had increased and he thought they must not be parsimonious in their praise of the Director-General and Sir Frank Noyce, despite their refusal to reduce the postage on cards, for the facilities they were providing the commercial community. They as members of Chambers of Commerce have a duty to their brethren to supply them with information on all commercial matters which in effect meant all matters, by means of trade journals. All Chambers of Commerce must combine to form a statistical research and publicity bureau, collect information, study and examine each trade and broadcast the result of their thinking and discovery.

The All-India Trade Union Congress

15th. Session—Bombay—17th. May 1936

The 15th Session of the All-India Trade Union Congress opened at Kamgar Maidan, Bombay on the **17th. May 1936** in the presence of a large gathering of workers and Trade Unions leaders. Mr. Jawharlal Nehru, Congress President, together with other local Congressites and Socialists were present.

Mrs. *Mulji Maniben Kara*, President, and Mr. *S. H. Jabawalla*, Chairman of the Reception Committee, in the course of their addresses, laid stress on the necessity for immediate unity in Labour ranks and forming an anti-Imperialist front of all elements in the country for fighting for independence. Both urged closer contact between Trade Unions and the Indian National Congress and welcomed Mr. Nehru's efforts in this direction. While Mr. *Jabawalla* wanted leaders of the National Trade Union Federation to give up their present attitude and go the whole hog for structural unity, Mrs. *Maniben Kara* was prepared to accept Mr. Giri's compromise proposal for a merger of the two wings of Labour for a year but urged Mr. Giri and his friends not to insist on three-fourths majority as regards a decision on political questions and suggested two-thirds majority instead. Both maintained that unity must be achieved as that alone would enable them to fight anti-working class forces.

Mr. *Jabawalla* drew attention to rationalisation and said that it was a serious menace to workers. What was needed in the circumstances was a national offensive of workers against offensive capitalists. The question of general strike of all industries had become a practical one. He regretted that at a time, when unity was essential, all efforts at Trade Union unity had failed. He blamed the leaders of the National Trade Union Federation for this failure and appealed to workers to bring pressure on their leaders. The immediate problem before them was how best to forge a powerful united front against Imperialism. This could be done only by co-operation with other organisations particularly the Indian National Congress. He advocated collective affiliation of Labour with the Indian National Congress and severely criticised the Congress for postponing a decision on the office question, which, in his opinion, should never have been considered at all, as the new constitution was not worth looking at.

Mrs. *Maniben Kara*, at the outset, referred to the incarceration of Messrs. Ruiker, Nimbkar and other Trade Union workers and then dealt at length with repression. She also devoted a considerable portion of her speech to the growth of Fascism in the world and indicated how it was a growing menace to the working class interests. She warned the Indian National Congress leaders that there were elements of Fascism within it which would show their heads if not checked in time. She next referred to war danger and welcomed Mr. Nehru's anti-war move and assured him of the co-operation of the All-India Trade Union Congress.

Mrs. Kara next dealt with the new constitution, characterised it as a "new charter of slavery" and said that it could be rejected only by mass action and not by creating constitutional deadlocks or much less by accepting ministerial offices. She advocated that a united front by all opposed to the new constitution must be built up immediately and the country's attention should be immediately focussed on the need for a Constituent Assembly which alone was competent to draw up a constitution for the country. The rejection of Reforms, she said, did not mean the boycott of councils, which should be used as propaganda platforms.

Regarding forthcoming elections she suggested the formation of a national democratic block consisting of all elements in the country opposed to new Reforms. It should be the endeavour of this bloc to enforce national, economic and political demands through the legislatures. If such a bloc was formed, she stated that the working classes would support the Congress candidates, provided they accepted the programme embodying the minimum demands of workers. She also urged the Congress to set up Labour candidates in predominantly labour areas. These preliminary activities would, however, have significance only if they reflected a far more rigorous mass movement outside and the immediate task in India to-day was the building up of most-broadbased and militant mass action. She had no doubt that the Indian National Congress was the best organisation to do this because of its wide ramifications. Here again Mr. Jawaharlal Nehru had given a correct lead and the All-India Trade Union Congress, as the central organisation of militant working class movement in India, should establish relations of close co-operation with the Indian National Congress.

The President next dealt with dissensions in Labour ranks and briefly referred to the Nagpur split and subsequent efforts to repair the breach. She regretted that the National Trade Union Federation was not prepared for unity. If they could not have immediate structural unity, as the next best thing she suggested that the Trade Union Congress should accept Mr. Giri's proposal but hoped Mr. Giri would give up insistence on three-fourths majority for a decision on political issues and substitute two-thirds majority instead. She also hoped that both groups would be allowed freedom to carry on political propaganda. With such modifications Mr. Giri's proposals might be accepted as a penultimate step towards structural unity. She was guided in striving at this conclusion by the supreme necessity to close up their ranks and give united resistance to the growing capitalist offensive.

Addressing the Congress, *Pt. Juwaharlal Nehru* appealed to the working classes and the Trade Union Congress to establish closer contact with the Congress. The Congress was the only organisation in the country, he said, which had attempted to bring about a revolution. "You claim to be revolutionaries and raise revolutionary slogans, but they will not bring freedom," he added. "Although there is fundamental difference in the ideology and methods of working of the Indian National Congress and the Trade Union Congress, I firmly believe these two bodies can still work in unision in regard to many matters." Therefore he emphassised the need for closer contact.

"The existence of a foreign Government eclipsed many other issues and I believe that only political freedom can solve our difficulties," Mr. Nehru emphasised. He urged the workers to influence policy of the leaders and not to be mere blind followers. He also urged them to close up their ranks and bring about unity without sacrificing principles.

As regard talk about class struggle, Mr. Nehru said that no one liked it but mere dislike would not alter the facts since class struggle was there. It was, therefore, wrong to deny its existence. If the National Congress had ignored their grievances in the past, they had the right to criticise it but he warned them against indulging in mutual recriminations and abuse which would not be conducive to harmony and co-operation.

Several messages received from the League against Imperialism and other Associations were read at the Congress.

After the Chairman of the Reception Committee, the President, Mr. Jawaharlal Nehru, Mr. Achut Pattwardhan add Mr. Indulal Zagnik had addressed, the Congress passed a condolence resolution regarding Dr. Ansari's death and adjourned.

Resolutions—2nd. Day 18th. May 1936

The Congress took up consideration of the resolutions adopted by the executive committee. There were on the agenda paper nearly 30 resolutions, only five or six of which were duly moved and seconded while the rest were put from the chair and passed.

New Constitution

The first resolution to be moved was one strongly condemning the Government of India Act, declaring the determination of the working classes to adopt an attitude of irreconcilable hostility to the new Act, demanding a constituent assembly and emphatically declaring against office acceptance. Several speakers, including Mr. *Jawharlal Nehru*, supporting the resolution, condemned the Government of India Act and emphasised the need for agitation for a constituent assembly.

Suppression of Civil Liberties

The second resolution condemned the civil liberties and accorded support to the Indian National Congress in its move to form a Civil Liberties Union.

The third resolution condemned the continued repression, while the fourth demanded the immediate release of Messrs. Subhas Bose, Ruikar, Nimbkar, M. N. Roy, Mukundalal Sircar and other labour leaders and detenus. The fifth sent greetings to the pesantry.

The seventh resolution condemned imperialist wars and called on the working classes to join hands with the Indian National Congress in conducting anti-war propaganda.

The eighth resolution sent greetings to the people of Abyssinia.

T. U. C. and Indian National Congress

The ninth resolution defined the relations of the working classes and the Trade Union Congress with the Indian National Congress. It emphatically declared that the working classes must actively participate in the national movement and establish relations of close co-operation with the Indian National Congress with the object of broadening and deepening the national struggle for independence. Such co-operation was possible only if the Indian National Congress supported the working classes' immediate economic and political demands and made suitable provision for the participation of workers in the Congress through their class organizations. It urged affiliated unions to develop common action with the local Congress organizations in order to (1) reject the new constitution (2) oppose imperialist war, (3) defend the Soviet Union (4) defend civil liberties and (5) safeguard and advance the working class interests.

The tenth resolution welcomed the formation of the rapid growth of the Congress Socialist party and thanked the party and Mr. Jawaharlal Nehru on the work done at Lucknow.

The eleventh resolution welcomed the Lucknow Congress resolution to establish closer relations between the National Congress and workers and peasants and urged the creation of a genuine anti-imperialist front.

The twelfth resolution demanded the collective representation of labour in the Indian National Congress through labour unions.

The thirteenth resolution defined the immediate programme and emphasised the need for structural unity in the trade union movement, the mobilisation and preparation of workers for a direct struggle on the basis of their vital political and economic demands, giving trade unions a live mass basis and training organizers to carry on trade union activity even under conditions of ruthless repression.

Threat of All-India Railway Strike

The next resolution protested against the railway administration's policy against workers and threatening an all-India railway strike.

Another resolution expressed the willingness of the Trade Union Congress to carry on electoral campaign with the National Congress provided the latter agreed to certain demands of the working classes such as setting up a labour candidate in a predominantly labour area and other labour and economic demands.

Question of Merger with N. T. U. F.

The next resolution expressed the unqualified preparedness of the All-India Trade Union Congress to accommodate in a spirit of conciliation the demands of the National Trade Union Federation on all such issues as would not hamper the growth of the struggle of the working classes and accepted Mr. Giri's compromise proposal for a merger as the basis of unity subject to the following provision, namely, the constitution of the National Trade Union Federation be accepted with such modification as may be necessary by the executive committee of the T. U. C. later on, provided that where it was not possible to take any decisions on a political issue or a strike for want of a three-fourth majority, the T. U. C. be free to act according to its bare majority opinions, in case the Federation insists on taking independent action in connection with such political questions or strike.

The session concluded amidst enthusiastic scenes late at night after all the resolutions had been passed.

Election of Office-bearers

On the conclusion of the Trade Union Congress session, the following office-bearers were elected for the coming year :—Mr. Shivanath Banerjee of Calcutta, president; Messrs. R. B. Khedigeker, R. S. Ruikar, Narayandas Bechar and Rajaram Shastri vice-presidents; Mrs. Maniben Mulji, general secretary; and Mr. V. B. Karnik, treasurer. Mr. R. B. Khedigeker to act as president instead of Mr. Shivanath Banerji, who was in jail.

The Indian Economic Conference

19th. Session—Dacca—2nd. January 1936

The nineteenth Session of the Indian Economic Conference was held at Dacca on the **2nd. January 1936,** under the presidentship of Mr. *Manohar Lal* of Lahore. In the course of his address Mr. Manohar Lal said :—

In the world to-day economic problems are of such growing imperiousness, and the situation of our great and unhappy, because divided and poor, country so grave that I venture to press on your attention a few reflections on the task of the economist in India.

The brilliant French social thinker, Siegfred, diagnoses the broad features of the crisis of 1929 and since, in this significant manner : "First there was the liquidation of the war, which, contrary to the general illusion, had not been already fully carried out. The main difficulty was to absorb an over-expanded industrial equipment. While Europe was fighting, the rest of the world feverishly equipped itself in order to supply the needs of the belligerents and to cope with their withdrawal from the international markets. After the war, however, Europe in turn wished to recapture what she had lost." And we are now watching Europe's intense struggle—made harder by tariff barriers, and currency confusion. In Japan, low wages exist with remarkable superiority of technique and that makes it all but impossible for the West to compete. The present conditions of world competition are frankly recognised by many in Europe as marks of defeat. A general depression has spread over the face of Europe and no sure indications of escape are visible. Admirable and certain diagnoses of the causes of economic disablement have been made in works of high authority and unquestioned disinterestedness but no trustworthy feasible cure is anywhere suggested because political conditions—the strains and stresses of the present European state system—make deliberate and concerted action extremely difficult.

In such world conditions our eyes turn with natural anxiety to the governing factors in our own Indian economy. We have not escaped from sharing fully in the evil effects of the world-wide depression, and the essential weakness of our position has become acutely apparent because of our inability to withstand the strain of the crisis. Our excessive dependence on agriculture, and our poor industrial development caused deplorable distress, and our exiguous finances made many of the usual escapes from economic hardship extremely difficult. The people and the Government were equally helpless. It may be confidently asserted that in no country in the world, certainly in no large country, has governmental endeavour to remedy depression and secure recovery been so utterly non-existent as in India,—for small efforts at improvement in our agricultural departments, and the grant of discriminating protection to some industries constitute no part of any special programme to beat down the swelling tide of depression.

Agricultural forces are determined by world conditions under the influence of these important prices ; and these world-determined prices have to be accepted by us here where holdings are small and economic conditions of production necessarily primitive. Our dependence on agriculture is increasing, and in the exchange of our agricultural products against the world's industrial products and transport services, our disadvantage as that of all agricultural countries is growing. This constitutes a grave and fundamental problem of Indian economics to-day. The great tragedy of our deteriorating economic position is our utter helplessness. We cannot offer any solution of the vast and universal problem of agricultural depression, for no one country or people can furnish any effective remedy where the causes of the evil are so wide-pread and deep-seated ; but we seem not to be doing anything even towards any long-sighted relief of our own troubles.

Prof. Brij Narain in his recent book "India Before the Crisis" in his study of our population problem has pointed out that "the problem of relieving the growing presure on the soil is *insoluble*," for "the modernisation of Indian agriculture is impossible unless it is preceded by a very great development of industries." That is obvious enough, but it may be doubted whether even if large development of industries could be achieved, a remote ideal towards which no substantial progress is being made, there would be much room for modernisation of agriculture with our small and fragmented holdings and system of land ownership. India must either restrict her population, or import food from abroad. Our increase of population during the last census decade was described by Dr. Hutton, the Census Commissioner, as "a cause of alarm." It has been often said by sober statisticians in official document that "for all practical purposes, it may be taken as proved that India as a whole is already overpopulated." *Major-General Megaw*, a most cautious and competent authority, in calling attention recently to the fact of our extremely low average duration of life in India and our low level of health and comfort observed: "There is some differences of opinion as to whether conditions of life have improved or deteriorated during the past fifty years, but even if some slight improvement may have taken place, the existing state of affairs is still so *profoundly unsatisfactory* that it demands investigation and redress," and uttered the warning that forecast for the future is even more disquieting ; there is "a prospect of a *steady deterioration* in the nutrition of the people.

Now it may be argued that over-population is a relative term, and that it refers to the system of economy as established at any particular time. Change the economy, and the threat of overpopulation disappears. But we must look to the existing circumstances, and what is in near prospect having regard to existing facts and likely changes. In this view, we are liable to all the nature's violent modes of restoring balance. For restriction by foresight is a remote, far too remote, means of relief, for a people steeped in ignorance and superstition. And apart from the danger of restriction proving dysgenic, the scope of its application seems to lie more in the relief possibly of middle-class difficulties than in furnishing a solution of our national economic difficulties.

The problem of population is not merely one of their being not enough to go round. It implies also all the misery and economic waste involved in futile child birth and infant and maternal mortality. And we cannot afford this waste. Final conclusions are difficult to propound. Theoretical speculations furnish no guidance for exact immediate prophecies but here in India there appears little doubt that (i) nature has to establish equilibrium by her painful and violent methods of disease, famine and pestilence, and (ii) man does the same by accepting a low level of life even if we may not say that the level is being steadily depressed. In this connection, the words of Professors Bowley and Robertson are most significant. "Evidence seems to be that population tends to grow up to improvements effected in environment so as to bring the standard of life again down to the old level." "Improvements in public health also result in increased population pressure for the future." What a sad conclusion ! In our poverty and the extreme pressure of population on the soil, even the beneficent activities of a human department are not an unmixed blessing. The professors on a broad view conclude that the population problem is the gravest of India's problems. They favour the view that "in India at all events the population problem is still a problem of writing sufficient subsistence from the soil, while in any case rapid industrialisation might stimulate a greater growth of population than it could absorb." and the supreme question disengages itself "whether economic or social forces making for a reasonable balance between population and production are working with sufficient strength."

In New Zealand, the evil is fully realised in an official publication where the necessity of diverting some of her population to new local industries is stressed, and baring the imports of all articles she can produce at home advocated.

In Japan, in spite of all the difficulties of industrialization in a country with no iron, no cotton and poor coal supplies, the policy is clearly defined, and it is recognized that the building up of trade and industry alone can furnish a solution of the population problem. She has learnt a sure lesson from the classical example of England that increasing population needs securing food from outside in exchange for the products of industry and transport and financial services. And Japan's example furnishes us a lesson.

In this connexion we should not forget one important fact. It is obvious that our trade policy is easily summed up in three words : a certain measure of Discriminating Protection, the Fiscal Autonomy Convention, the Ottawa Pact and its implications : and the question of forging a bold and comprehensive trade policy of building up industries has never been faced in India. It has, however, to be admitted that stress of circumstance has led to a significant change in the policy of the Indian Government regarding manufacturing industries. But it has been boldly asserted by a careful economist that "the industrial development of India is proceeding on wrong lines" in so much as "we have almost entirely neglected the manufacture of capital goods." And he has called attention to a matter that deserves particular reflection and close study. He says: "under the existing system, the proportion of the population dependent on industry tends to decline with the progress of factory industries. The introduction of machinery causes unemployment in India while it creates means of employment in other countries."

What is being achieved, if not actually achieved in Japan, should be possible for India. We have an immense population and therefore ready demand for manufactured goods. We have an immense market which the whole world is trying to secure, yet in spite of our unbounded resources we continue hapless victims of world's dumping.

On the vital issue nearly all necessary quantitative thinking has been done, the nature of evil analysed, and the possible remedies defined. But all this can form only a starting point, and the task of the economist is to study in detail the extent of relief in varying circumstances that can result from (i) improvements in agriculture, (ii) voluntary restriction on the growth of population, (iii) increase in industrialisation in full view of the situation in the West. These are three main factors which require close quantitative study under a large number of assumptions of possibilities. Round these would naturally group a considerable mass of subsidiary problems concerned with diet, nutrition, public health and disease. It is gratifying that detailed consideration of this vital problem will now have the advantage of an expert body of students in the newly organised Population Conference to be shortly held at Lucknow.

The approaching reforms have forced pointed attention to the rigidity of our revenues, and the narrowness of our finances, for reforms mean increased expenditure, and our provinces have not even now the means of making proper or adequate provision for beneficent or nation-building activities. Narrow exiguous finance is merely the reflection of the poverty of the country and its ill-balanced economic structure. Serious students of Indian economics have recently stressed with growing intensity the excessive nature of our land revenue burden, a main source of provincial income; while even with this burden, and without contemplating any relief in this regard, our Provincial Finance Members are in despair as to any fruitful schemes of improving their revenues. The resourcefulness of government experts, individual and in committees, is exhausted in merely canvassing adjustments; hardly a single additional or further source of revenue is suggested, while provincial governments press for a larger share of what the Central Government absorbs at present. The pessimistic tone of experts, and the frantic advocacy of individual provincial claims is a saddening fact—it is the rock on which plans of federation and realities of reform may easily split. No solution is in sight. The Central Government's sources of net income are just three-fold; Customs, Income-tax and Salt. and the pitch to which each has been carried in recent years, affords no prospect of substantial improvement in income by any large enhancement of rates.

In this a cynic may, perhaps, see a ray of hope, because as our trade policy underwent a considerable transformation under the necessities of the war, the exigencies of conducting government under reforms may further compel our rulers to think of and devise means to secure healthier economy for India. The limits of revenue from land have been long reached, growing pressure of rural opinion cannot fail to make itself felt on preventing any increase of burden on land, even if it does not succeed in securing reduction of various direct and indirect land revenue charges. All hope of improvement must therefore rest on Customs and Income-tax which depend directly on industry and trade. The development of industry and trade, then, is necessary to keep our finances in balance and absolutely essential if any even urgent programmes of national advance are to be carried out.

Here perhaps I may be permitted to say that in our steadfast gaze on the absolutely necessary ideal of vigorous and healthy modern industry, we ought not to allow our attention to be diverted by fanciful pictures of cottage industries as the solution of our economic ills. The cottage industries may have their legitimate place in our village economy,— on that I wish to say nothing. But they furnish no means of providing thirty-seven crores of people with an adequate standard of living.

In the past few years, the weakness of our position in foreign trade has become strikingly apparent, and the heavy exports of "distress gold" at a time when central banking institutions all over the world have been making determined, well-nigh frantic efforts to amass gold, raise vital questions of currency policy; they also constitute a sad comment on our economic position. With the deterioration in her international trade position, it can no longer be affirmed that India is able to meet her debt obligations abroad and her 'home charges'.

What will happen if the forecasts of scientific men come true? Professor J. B. S. Haldane recently remarked that "by 1944 prices of food will fall so much that large numbers of agricultural states would go to ruin." The course of events during the past twenty years warrants the general soundness of this prophecy. Do we realize the import of this fast approaching fate on unhappy India maintaining one of world's largest populations on her own agriculture and struggling to buy manufactured goods from abroad at growing disadvantage?

The economist in India to-day is worthily engaged in the close study of economic fact and theory. But I venture to think that his most urgent task now is more than ever before, to rouse the conscience of both the people and the government to a consciousness of the peril towards which we are drifting and to the necessity of straining every nerve to reconstruct our economic life. Events are marching with such swiftness, the rest of the world with their alert governments is taking such rapid action, that if we are not up and doing now, aware of the possible dangers ahead and determined on the one course of salvation, our doom may be irretrievably sealed. That is the supreme task of the Indian economist—he is faced by a call which if missed to-day may never come again.

Finance of the Federation

Several interesting papers concerning fiscal questions were read in the afternoon session. Mr. *S. V. Aiyar* (Dacca University) read a paper on "Some aspects of the new constitution for India". He said that he disagreed with the view that in regard to fiscal questions the position under the new constitution would be worse than now and examined the constitutional position in the matter of the fiscal convention.

In indicating the additional estimated burden on the people of India by bringing into force the new constitution Mr. Aiyar said: India requires at the present time a new orientation in matters of public policy towards the economic betterment of the citizens, to dimish unemployment, to stimulate production and trade, to develop schemes of social insurance even as many other nations are doing. We want a programme—comprehensive and practical—but increasing expenditure in duplicating unnecessary and mischievous political machinery without any real power to regulate freely income or expenditure to the advantage of India is an avoidable luxury. India must again look only to additional taxation for expenditure on the social services which are so urgently necessary in India to-day.

Mr. *B. N. Ganguly*, of the Hindu College, Delhi, in the course of his paper on "The Fiscal Autonomy Convention under the new Constitution", observed that although India's right to develop her own fiscal and economic policy and to negotiate trade agreements had been recognised, discriminatory or penal treatment of British goods had been defined so widely as to make this safeguard as effective as possible. As a result, the extent of India's Fiscal Autonomy would be very ill-defined and arbitrary.

In his paper on the "Fiscal Prospects of the Indian Federation," Mr. M. K. Muniswami observed *inter alia* that the financial provisions concerning the Native States seemed to err on the side of generosity. The Joint Parliamentary Committee itself recognised that it was difficult to reconcile the Treaties of the States with any practical scheme of Federal finance. The financial settlement under the Act of 1935 was wanting in uniformity not only between British India and the States as such but between one State and another Burdens and benefits were unequal under the proposed Federation. Besides giving an undue weight in Indian affairs to the States the proposed settlement would saddle the Federal Government with increased expediture to be financed by declining receipts of revenue. From the economic standpoint the States would gain immensely from their entry into the Federation.

Discussing the finances of the proposed Federation, Mr. *Muniswami* expressed the fear that it might split on the rock of finance.

He maintained that the position in regard to fiscal question would be, on the whole, worse under the new constitution than what it was to-day. The particular special responsibility conferred upon the Governor-General for the prevention of commercial discrimination against British imports into India constituted a menace to the Fiscal Autonomy Convention and was a definitely reactionary depature from the spirit of the report of the Joint Select Committee of 1919 and of the reply of the late Mr. Montagu, Secretary of State for India, to the Lancashire deputation of 1921. Although the scope of the Convention was rather indefinite it was undeniable that under this convention India had enjoyed a certain amount of freedom in respect of fiscal matters. The Fiscal Convention was now in danger as a result of the new Act.

Discussing the nature of legislative control over Federal expenditure he remarked that non-votable expenditure would constitute over 80 per cent of the total expenditure of the Federal Government. The bulk of federal expenditure would, therefore, be beyond the control of the Federal Legislature. In one respect it would be worse, for, under the present constitution the power of restoration in respect of rejected votable grants was exercisable by the Governor-General-in-Council, whereas under the proposed constitution it would be exercisable by the Governor-General alone in the exercise of the individual judgment.

Mr. *P. S. Lokanatham* (Madras), in his paper on "The Structure of Industry in India", suggested that in spite of the theoretical superiority of large-scale industries in practice it was found that many of the small industries had survived either due to some inherent defects in transport and marketing, or to the fact that in a land of small farming like India, cottage industries were supplementary occupations which did not have to bear full overhead charges or pay full wages, because they did not need any expensive capital and could be carried on during the off season. He thought that it would be possible for India to develop village industries with the aid of modern appliances and cheap electrical power.

Dr. *Radha Kamal Mukherjee* (Lucknow University), dealing with Indian handicrafts, classified them according to structure and organisations. In most of the cottage arts and crafts carried on as subsidiary to agriculture and village subsistence industries, he found that the artisan dealt directly with the consumer and worked with his own materials There was the piece wage system in which the artisan dealt with the consumer with material supplied by the latter as in the case of wood-work, gold and silver-work and dress-making. In pottery, wood-carving, silk, carpet and blanket weaving, Dr. Mukherjee had found a survival of the medieval guild system in some places.

Mr. *J. W. Thomas* (Lahore), in his "Note on Japanese Industry" said that the Japanese industrialists were ahead of Indian manufacturers in effective, collective organisations. Compulsory education in Japan had played an important part in the efficiency of the Japanese worker. He deplored the immense waste of human life and energy in this country and lack of proper help in the matter of economic development.

Prof. *Benoy Kumar Sarkar* (Calcutta University), in his paper on "The theory of wages in the light of social insurance and public finance", said that in view of the existence of widely prevalent measures of State interference to regulate the earnings of labour, the wages paid in the course of employment were far below the standard of 'fair wages', and that, therefore, economic factors were not only factors in the determination of wages in a modern community. He concluded that the existence of social insurance and other methods of transference of wealth from the rich to the poor was both a critique and a corrective of the system of wages. He also drew the further inference that economic theory alone could not explain the cause of fair wages, but that, for an adequate explanation, we must fall back upon moral factors, political considerations, social institutions and other non-economic forces.

Dr. H. L. Dey (Dacca), discussing "Low wages and unfair competition in International Trade", showed that only when the efficiency-wages ratio in a certain country was higher than the corresponding ratio of another country, then the first country could produce goods cheaper than the second, and that this could be done both by high-wage and low-wage countries. He admitted, however, that there were undoubtedly larger stretches of employment areas in what were called backward countries, where wages were abnormally low in the sense of being below the expenses of the customary standard of living, either because of the absence of mobility of labour between industry and industry or because of a rapid growth in the supply of unskilled labour through unrestricted growth of population as in Japan and India, for instance. But, he suggested that tariffs and other penal measures against such countries could not remove these abnormal conditions, but would only tend to aggravate them. The proper remedy, he suggested, was the promotion of indirect mobility and demand through international trade, international loans for economic development and international regulation of hours and conditions of work.

Dr. K. B. Saha (Dacca), in his paper on "Wages and Costs in International Trade", referred to the doctrine prevalent in certain quarters that low-wage countries should be prevented from underselling in high-wage countries. Dr. Saha said that though the influx of some cheaper goods from a low-wage country might compel a reorganisation of industries in the high-wage country through transfer of labour and capital and thus inflict a temporary loss and suffering on certain sections of its people, it would ultimately derive a net benefit by an enlargement of the national dividend.

Reports on

THE HAMMOND COMMITTEE

THE NEIMEYER COMMITTEE

and

The Sapru Unemployment Committee

The Hammond Committee Report

On the Delimitation of Constituencies

The Report of the Hammond Committee on Delimitation of Constituencies, which was a unanimous document, was published from New Delhi on the **2nd. March 1936.**

On the question of urban versus rural areas, the Committee have dealt with each Province individually, securing that the proposals, among other things, were so framed that rural areas would not be dominated by urban elements, and at the same time, ensuring that urban areas received the full representation to which they are entitled.

In all Provinces, except Bombay and Madras, single member constituencies have been accepted as a rule, save where the multi-member constituency is necessitated by reservation of seats for scheduled castes or backward tribes.

The method of voting recommended is cumulative voting in all multi-member territorial constituencies, except in certain specified constituencies.

Territorial Constituencies

Dealing with territorial constituencies, the Committee have assigned for Madras 15 general and 2 Mahomedan seats for urban areas, the basis for conclusion in urban areas being combination of not more than two towns of substantial size in the same district. As for Bombay, 14 general seats and 6 Mahomedan seats have been allotted to urban areas.

Only the biggest cities, which have genuinely urban characteristics, and whose problems and interests are different from, or likely to conflict with, those areas, classed as rural, have been included in the urban category.

In Bengal, 12 general and 6 Mohamedan seats have been assigned to urban representation.

In the Punjab, the problem of rural versus urban has been greatly to the fore.

The Committee have decided that all towns with a population of not less than 7,500 and Cantonments and District Headquarters and first class Municipalities are to be included in urban areas.

In Madras

The report on territorial constituencies relating to Madras is the following :

The Committee have assigned 15 general and 2 Mahomedan seats to urban areas, the basis for inclusion in urban being a combination of not more than two towns of substantial size in the same district. The Committee have recommended two multi-member urban constituencies and a certain number of multi-member rural constituencies, the constituencies ordinarily containing not more than two unreserved seats.

The following areas have been included in the general urban constituencies : Madras, Vizagapatam, Cocanada, Masulipatam, Bezwada, Guntur, Tenali, Tanjore, Kumbakonam, Madura, Tinnevelly, Palamcottah, Coimbatore, Salem and Trichinopoly. Srirangam, Madras City, Calicut, Cannanore and Tellicherry have been included in Mahomedan constituencies.

Scheduled Castes

As regards scheduled caste constituencies, the Committee recommend that except in Bengal, there is to be no restriction on a member of the scheduled castes from contesting in an unreserved seat in the constituency where there is a reserved seat. In Bengal, however, no member of the scheduled castes, not elected at the Primary Election, is to be qualified to hold a seat in a constituency, where there is a general seat reserved for the scheduled castes.

In Madras, out of 30 seats allotted for the scheduled castes, one has been reserved for a constituency in the City of Madras and the remaining 29 to rural areas ; in Bombay 2 to Bombay City and 13 to rural areas ; in Bengal all the 30 seats have been assigned to rural areas in the five constituencies of Khulna, Dinajpur, Jalpaiguri-cum-Siliguri, Rangpur and Faridpur. Two seats are reserved for the scheduled castes in United Provinces ; 4 out of 20 seats reserved for the scheduled castes have been allotted to Lucknow, Cawnpore, Agra and Allahabad Cities. The remaining 16 are allotted to rural areas, where scheduled castes preponderate.

In the Punjab, Bihar, Assam and Orissa all seats are reserved in rural constituencies (there are no urban constituencies in Assam and Orissa). In the Central Provinces the scheduled castes of Nagpur City have been allotted a seat.

Women Constituencies

As regards women, the Committee have recommended the formation of special constituencies in selected areas. Their constituencies are generally in urban areas, though in Madras, Bombay and United Provinces, a few seats have also been allotted in rural areas.

The Committee also recommend enfranchisement in University constituencies of members of the Senate or Court, and all registered graduates of not less than seven years' standing.

Regarding landholders, territorial constituencies have been formed for filling seats for them in all Provinces, except in the United Provinces where of six seats reserved for them 4 are to be filled by the British Indian Association and two by the Agra Zamindars' Association.

The Report deals next with Commerce constituencies. The main basis of delimitation recommended is membership of an Association as a more appropriate qualification, but in cases where membership of a single Chamber or of one or two more Chambers is qualification for vote in the Commerce constituency, then such members should, in addition, in case of incorporated companies possess a paid-up capital of not less than one lakh of rupees, and in the case of a firm or individuals have been, in any of the five income-tax years immediately preceding the preparation of electoral roll, assessed to an income-tax on income derived from trade, commerce or industry of not less than Rs. 10,000.

As regards seats for Commerce in Madras, four seats have been allotted to European Commerce and two to Indian Commerce. The Madras Chamber of Commerce and the Madras Trades Association will, between them, have three seats and the Madras Planters, Southern Indian Chamber of Commerce and the Nattukottai Nagarathars' Association, each one seat. The Andhra Chamber of Commerce will not be enfranchised.

Labour

As regards Labour the Committee have accepted the principle that constituencies for Labour seats should partly be in organised Labour constituencies and partly in unorganised Labour constituencies. The Committee have achieved this in all cases, except in Orissa and Sind. Thus Trade Unions have been given 2 seats in Madras, 6 in Bombay, 2 in Bengal and one each in the United Provinces, Punjab, Bihar and Central Provinces. The remaining 24 seats have been assigned to unorganised labour of which one seat in Bengal and all 4 seats in Assam have been assigned to Tea Garden Labour. In the case of Tea Garden Labour, the Committee have accepted the principle of rotation for the sake of obtaining direct election.

In Backward Areas

One chapter is devoted to backward areas and tribes. The Committee recommend that 4 out of 5 seats allotted to backward areas and tribes in Orissa are to be filled by nomination. Seats assigned in Bombay and Bihar and one seat in Orissa are to be filled by direct election from multi-member general constituencies with 1 seat reserved for backward tribes. Madras, Central Provinces and Assam are to have special constituencies for election to these seats. In Assam, there are to be 4 seats for backward tribes and five for backward areas.

The Committee have accepted the proposals of Local Governments in regard to delimitation of constituencies for Provincial Legislatures and Federal Council of State. As for Federal Commerce seats, the recommendations of Local Governments are accepted in the case of provincial seats. The Non-provincial seat is to be filled by an electorate comprising the Northern Indian Chamber of Commerce, Punjab Chamber and Upper Indian Chamber. Delhi will have one general and one Mahomedan seat, while Ajmere-Merwara will have one general seat.

Personation in election is to be made cognizable, otherwise there is no change in the law relating to corrupt practices.

Summary of Recommendations

The following is the summary of recommendations of each chapter beginning from the second.

Chapter II : In distinguishing urban from rural areas it was impracticable to secure uniformity. The only course open was to deal with each Province individually securing that the proposals put forward,

(I) had the support of the decided bulk of public opinion ;

(II) were so framed that rural areas would not be dominated by urban elements

(III) ensured that urban areas received the full representation to which they were entitled, and in any case, in which weightage was given to urban areas, that that weightage was not greater than was appropriate ; and

(IV) were void of conspicuous anomalies.

Single or Multi-Member Constituencies

Chapter III : In all Provinces, save Bombay and Madras, single member constituencies should be accepted as a rule, save where a multi-member constituency is necessary by reservation of seats for scheduled castes or backward tribes In Bombay, where the public demand for multi-member constituencies is really strong, the principle of multi-member constituencies may be accepted. A certain number of multi-member constituencies, containing not more than two unreserved seats, may also be created in Madras.

The method of voting will be, save as otherwise stated, cumulative voting in all multi-member territorial constituencies, single non-transferable vote in Bihar general constituencies, where a seat is reserved for backward tribes, also in the Behrampur constituency in Orissa and the Singbhum Constituency in Bihar.

Territorial Constituencies for Madras

Chapter IV : The Committee have assigned 15 General and 2 Mahomedan seats to urban areas, the basis for inclusion in urban areas being a combination of not more than two towns of substantial size in the same district. The Committee have recommended two multi-member urban constituencies, and a certain number of multi-member rural constituencies, the constituencies ordinarily containing not more than two unreserved seats.

The following areas have been included in General urban constituencies : Madras, Vizagapatam, Cocanada, Masulipatam, Bezwada, Guntur, Tenali, Tanjore, Kumbakonam, Madura, Tinnevelly, Palamcottah, Coimbatore, Salem and Trichinopoly. Srirangam, Madras City, Calicut, Cannanore and Tellicherry have been included in Mahomedan urban constituencies.

In Bombay, 14 General seats and 6 Mahomedan seats have been allotted to urban areas. only the biggest cities which have genuinely urban characteristics and whose problems and interests are different from or likely to conflict with those of the areas classed as rural have been included in the urban category. Areas included in the general urban constituencies are the Cities of Bombay, Ahmedabad, Surat and Rander, Poona and Sholapur. Mahomedan Urban areas are the Cities of Bombay, Ahmedabad, Surat and Randar. The Committee have given one Mahomedan urban seat to Surat and Rander cities.

Other Provinces

In Bengal, all Municipalities which are subjected to the provisions of the Bengal Municipal Act, the Calcutta Municipal Act, and the Cantonment of Barrackpore and Town of Kharagpore, which is not enjoying Municipal Self-Government, are included in the general urban area and only selected Municipalities. In Mahomedan urban constituencies, 12 General and 6 Mahomedan seats have been assigned to urban representation.

In the United Provinces, the number of seats allotted to urban areas being a town with a population of 25,000 and over.

In the Punjab the number of seats allotted to urban areas being all towns with a population of not less than 7,500 Cantonments, District Headquarters and First Class Municipalities.

In Bihar the number of seats allotted to urban areas is General 5, Mahomedan 5, the basis for inclusion in urban areas being all municipal notified and Government areas.

In the Central Provinces and Berar the number of seats allotted to urban areas is General 10, Mahomedan 2, the basis for inclusion in urban areas being all Municipalities and Towns with a population of 1,00,000 and over. The number of seats allotted to the Central Provinces, is General 64, Mahomedan 8.

The number of seats allotted to Berar is General 20, Mahomedan 6.

In Assam, the number of urban constituencies, in Assam Valley, General 32, Mahomedan 13, Surma Valley, General 15, Mahomedan 21. In the North-West Frontier Province, the number of seats allotted to urban constituencies is General 3, Mahomedan 3, Sikhs 3, general urban constituencies being Peshawar, Bannu and Dera Ismail Khan and Mahomedan constituencies being Peshawar City and Cantonment, Risalpur and Nowshera Cantonments, the Municipalities and Cantonments of Kohat, Bannu, Dera Ismail Khan, and Abbottabad, with the two Cantonments of Madran and Cherat.

The number of urban constituencies in Sind and the number of seats allotted to urban areas are General 3, Mahomedan 2. The General areas are Karachi and Hyderabad cities; and the Mahomedan area, Karachi.

Scheduled Castes

Chapter V:—The Poona Pact points are (i) The number 4 is to be neither a maximum, nor a minimum, but an optimum; (ii) Withdrawals cannot be prevented; (iii) Except in Bengal, there is to be no restriction on a member of the scheduled castes from contesting an unreserved seat in a constituency where there is a reserved seat. In Bengal, however, no member of the scheduled castes, not elected at the primary election, to be qualified to hold a seat in a constituency where there is a general seat reserved for scheduled castes.

The method of voting in general constituencies containing reserved seats for scheduled castes is to be cumulative. If two panel candidates head the poll at the final election the first is to be declared elected for the reserved seat and the second for the non-reserved seat.

Summary trials of petitions connected with primray election are to be tried by District Magistrates and disposed of summarily and the decision is not liable to be set aside either by any court or any higher executive authority. Disqualification of any person on account of corrupt practices is to be capable of removal by the Governor. The deposit, which will cover both primary and final scheduled caste candidates, is to be Rs. 50, the deposit for demanding summary trial Rs. 200, the deposit for questioning the validity of final election Rs. 1000. Scheduled caste candidates will have to file return of election expenses.

In Madras, out of 30 seats, 1 seat has been allotted to a constituency in the City of Madras and the remaining 29 seats to rural areas.

In Bombay 15 seats are reserved for scheduled castes. The Committee have allotted 2 to the City of Bombay and 13 to rural areas.

In Bengal all the 30 seats are assigned to rural areas in 5 constituencies, 2 seats are reserved for scheduled castes.

In the United Provinces. 4 out of 20 seats reserved for scheduled castes have been allotted to Lucknow, Cawnpore, Agra and Allahabad Cities, the remaining 16 reallotted to rural areas where the scheduled castes preponderate.

In the Punjab, Bihar, Assam and Orissa all the seats are reserved in rural constituencies. In Assam and Orissa, as stated above, there are no urban constituencies.

In the Central Provinces the scheduled castes of Nagpur City have been allotted a seat.

Women's Constituencies

Chapter VI:—The Committee have recommended the formation of special constituencies in selected areas. The constituencies are generally in urban areas, though in Madras, Bombay and the United Provinces, a few seats have also been allotted to rural areas.

The Committee have also made some suggestions regarding the facilities given for the registration of, and voting by women, qalifications of candidates being a woman who possesses the necessary franchise qualifications, which would entitle her to a vote in any constituency in the Province, the communal qualification and the qualifications prescribed in Para 1 of the Fifth Schedule to the Government of India Act.

University

Chapter VI:—The Committee have recommended enfranchisement in the university constituencies of members of the Senate or Court and all registered graduates of not less than seven years' standing.

LANDHOLDERS

Chapter VIII :—In all Provinces except the United Provinces, territorial constituencies have been formed for the filling of seats allotted to landholders. In the United Provinces, the 6 seats assigned to landholders' 4 will be filled by the British Indian Association and 2 by the Agra Zamindars' Association. For the purposes of election, membership will in the U. P. be confined to 'persons paying land revenue of not less than Rs. 10,000 per annum.

COMMERCE

Chapter IX :—**The main basis of delimitation recommended is that the membership of an Association should be deemed a more appropriate qualification, that out of a number of competing bodies such alone should be selected as truly represent substantial** commercial interests **and that a single authoritative body,** wherever possible, should be concentrated upon ; the combination of unrelated and dissimilar organisations should bo avoided. In cases where the membership of a single chamber or of one of two or more chambers is a qualification for a vote in a commerce constituency, then such members should, in addition (1) in the cases of incorporated companies possess a paid-up capital of not less than Rs. 1 lakh, and (2) in the case of a firm or individuals have been in any one of the five income-tax years immediately preceding the preparation of the electoral roll assessed to income-tax on an income derived from trade, commerce or industry of not less than Rs. 10,000.

No Association, affiliated to a Chamber, is to have more than one vote. The remedy to meet frequent changes in the personnel of firms or a firm or a Hindu joint family concern or a Corporation included in the electoral roll of a Commerce constituency may be to nominate representatives **not exceeding three who shall be** entered to vote for such a Hindu joint **faimly concern, incorporated company or** Corporation.

As a remedy to keep outsiders from representing Commerce constituencies, it is provided that such representatives shall be a person who would otherwise be eligible to sign on behalf of the individual or company in the ordinary course of business. Registering and returning officers should invariably be Government officers.

In Madras 4 seats have been allotted to the European Commerce and 2 to Indian Commerce, the Madras Chamber of Commerce and the Madras Trades Association will between them have 3 seats and the Madras Planters, the Southern Indian Chamber of Commerce and the Nattukottai Nagarathars' Association. each one seat. The Andhra Chamber of Commerce will not be enfranchised.

In Bombay, the existing arrangements will continue, and the East India Cotton Association will get the seventh seat. The Bombay Chamber of Commerce and the Bombay Trades Association will between them have a three member constituency **with one seat reserved for the Bombay Trades Association.**

Bengal will have 14 European and 5 Indian seats, 2 have been assigned to the Bengal National Chamber of Commerce and one each to the Indian Chamber of Commerce, the Marwari Association and the Muslim Chamber of Commerce.

The seat allotted to Indian Commerce in the United Provinces is to be shared by the U. P. Chamber of Commerce and the Merchants' Chamber.

The electorate for the Punjab Commerce seat is to be composed of the Northern **Indian Chamber of Commerce,** the Punjab Chamber of Commerce, the Punjab Trades **Association and the Indian Chamber of Commerce.**

In Bihar, the three existing constituencies are to continue ; the fourth seat will be filled by the Bihar Chamber of Commerce.

In the Central Provinces, Orissa and Sind, the Committee have recommended the formation of constituencies comprising companies, firms and individuals possessing certain qualifications

Of the 11 seats allotted to Assam, 9 (7 Europeans and 2 Indians) have been assigned to planting (Tea) and 2 (1 European and 1 Indian) to Commerce and Industry. Here again, the Committee recommended special constituencies consisting **of companies, firms and individuals.**

LABOUR CONSTITUENCIES

Chapter X :—The Committee have accepted the principle laid down by the Joint Select Committee that constituencies for the Labour seats shall partly be in organised **Labour constituencies and partly in unorganised Labour constituencies. The Committee have achieved this in all cases except in Orissa and Sind. Thus Trade Unions have been given 2 seats in Madras. 6 in Bombay, 2 in' Bengal, and 1 each in the**

United Provinces, the Punjab, Bihar and the Central Provinces. The remaining 14 seats have been assigned to unorganised Labour, of which one seat in Bengal and all the 4 seats in Assam have been assigned to tea garden labour. In the case of tea garden labour, the Committee have accepted the principle of rotation for the sake of obtaining direct election.

The other recommendations are that the existing Trade Union Law be so amended as to invest Local Governments with the power of inspecting the registers of the Trade Unions and to make Government or professional audit of their accounts compulsory Tribunals, as suggested by the Royal Commission on Labour and supported by the Indian Franchise Committee are to be constituted by the Governor acting in his discretion. This Tribunal is to make a yearly review of the Labour constituencies recommended.

The qualifications of a trade union for inclusion in the electorate for Trade Union constituencies are that : (1) it has been in existence for two years and registered for one year before the date fixed for the preparation of the electoral roll, (2) membership during the year preceding the preparation of the roll is not below 250, (3) it has complied with any rules under the Trade Union Act for inspection of books, (4) the preceding conditions have been attested to by a Tribunal.

The electoral registers for Trade Union constituencies are to be confined to the Province in which the Trade Union is registered. Where election is to be indirect the electoral roll is to be prepared by the employer.

The qualifications of the electors are : (1) That the elector has attained the age of 21, and is a British subject or subject of the prescribed Indian State.

(2) He has had a place of residence in the province for 6 months immediately preceding a date to be fixed by the Local Government (seamen to be exempted from this residential qualification).

(3) In the case of a Trade Union constituency, that on the date of the preparation of the electoral roll he has been a member of the Union, and in the case of an ordinary member has paid his subscription for the preceding twelve months. Member includes an honorary member or an official.

(4) In the case of a special Labour constituency, that he has been in continuous employment in a factory or a mine or a railway, a dockyard or harbour, or in any other industrial establishment registered under the Indian Factories Act or the Indian Mines Act for a period of not less than 180 days in the twelve months preceding the date of preparation of the electoral roll on a salary of not less than Rs. 10 and not more than Rs. 300 a month. This period, it may be necessary to vary in accordance with the conditions prevailing in different Provinces in which there are not Trade Union seats. A member of a registered Trade Union in the constituency is to be eligible for admission to the electoral roll of a special constituency.

(5) He is not employed in clerical, supervisory, recruiting or administrative capacities. Where a voter can vote in more than one Labour constituency enrolment is to be on application, save in certain Trade Union constituencies in Bombay and Bengal.

Election is to be direct in all Labour constituencies and to be uniform throughout India, the qualification of candidates being that they have attained the age of 25 years and possess the qualifications prescribed in the Fifth Schedule to the Government of of India Act and is an elector in the constituency or in any other Labour constituency. In the provinces in which there are no Trade Union seats. honorary members or officials of registered Trade Unions, who satisfy the requirements regarding electors, are also to be eligible to stand as candidates for special Labour seats. The deposit at elections for Trade Union candidates is Rs. 250, for manual worker Rs. 50 Supervisory and clerical staff are to be excluded from the electoral rolls for special Labour constituencies.

Backward Areas and Tribes

Chapter XIV :—Four out of the 5 seats allotted to backward areas and tribes in Orissa are to be filled by nomination. The seats assigned in Bombay and Bihar and the one seat in Orissa are to be filled by direct election from multi-member general constituencies, with one seat reserved for backward tribes. Madras, the Central Provinces and Assam are to have special constituencies for election. To these seats in Assam, there are to be 4 seats for backward tribes and 5 for backward areas.

Chapter XV :—For the Provincial Legislative Councils the proposals of Local Governments in regard to delimitation of constituencies are accepted. The method of voting to multi-member constituencies is cumulative, qualifications of candidates being that of an elector in constituency.

FEDERAL COMMERCE

Chapter XVI :—Non-Provincial seat electorate: For the seat alloted to the Northern Indian Commercial bodies, the electorates are Northern India Chamber of Commerce, Punjab Chamber of Commerce and Upper India Chamber of Commerce. For provincial seats, the recommendations of Local Governments are accepted.

FEDERAL LABOUR

Chapter XVII : The seat assigned to Assam Labour in the Federal Assembly is to be filled by direct election from a tea Garden constituency, to be chosen in rotation by the Governor in his direction from one of the tea garden constituencies. For the Labour seats in the Assam Legislative Assembly, the non-provincial seat is to be assigned to the National Trades Union Federation or such other organisation of workers as may be selected by the Government of India for the nomination of the workers' delegate to the International Labour Conference under the provisions of Article 389 (3) of the Treaty of Versailes.

Chapter XVIII : The seats allotted to the Chief Commissioner's Provinces in the Federal Assembly seats are to be filled by direct election, one General and one Muhammadan seat in Delhi and one Federal seat in Ajmer-Merwara ; the seat assigned to British Baluchistan is to be filled by nomination by the Governor-General.

FEDERAL COUNCIL OF STATES

Chapter XIX :—For the Federal Council of State the recommendations of Local Governments as to constituencies are accepted. Single non-transferable vote will be followed in the case of the Muhammadan multi-member constituency in Madras. The seat assigned to British Baluchistan is to be filled by nomination by the Governor-General.

CONDUCT OF ELECTIONS

Chapter XX :—In regard to the conduct of elections the Committee have recommended :

(1) Simplification of procedure for nomination and scrutiny by the returning officer.

(2) The returning officer or the presiding officer to be given powers to correct obvious and minor mistakes in the electoral roll.

An Elections Department is to be established for revision of the electoral roll at any time ; election manual rules are to be made to avoid unnecessary challenging of voters.

CORRUPT PRACTICES

Chapter XXI :—As regards corrupt practices personation is to be a cognisable offence.

The rule regarding hiring is to be abrogated and the expenditure on this account is to be included in the return of election expenses.

There will be no change in the existing law relating to treating.

The Niemeyer Report

On the Financial Condition of Provinces

Sir Otto Niemeyer's report on the financial condition of the Provinces issued from Simla on the **30th. April 1936**, states that the budgetary prospects of India, "given prudent management of her finances, justify the view that adequate arrangements can be made step by step to meet the financial implications of the new constitution."

Assistance costing the Centre about two crores of rupees annually is proposed for eight out of the eleven Provinces.

Sir Otto Niemeyer says : "His Majesty's Government may safely propose to Parliament that Part III of the Government of India Act 1935, should be brought into operation a year hence."

Income-tax amounting to six crores of rupees assignable to the Provinces will be retained by the Centre for the first five years, unless Railways resume substantial contributions. The Centre should begin relinquishing this revenue gradually during the second five years, so that within ten years of Provincial Autonomy, the Provinces may hope to enjoy their full share of this revenue head.

Assistance to Provinces

Sir Otto Niemeyer proposes to deal with the provinces in three stages. Immediate assistance from the beginning of provincial autonomy is recommended to certain provinces partly in the form of cash subventions, partly in the form of cancellation of the net (i. e. after offsetting certain balances) debt incurred prior to 1st April, 1936, and, partly in the form of the distribution of a further 12 and half per cent of the jute tax. In the cases of Bengal, Bihar, Assam, the N. W. F. P., and Orissa, the entire net debt is cancelled and in the case of the U. P. all pre-1936 deficit debt plus approximately two crores of pre-1921 debt.

Annual cash subventions will be as follows : U. P. 25 lakhs for 5 years only : Assam 30 lakhs : Orissa—40 lakhs ; N. W. F. P. 100 lakhs subject to reconsideration after 5 years ; Sind 105 lakhs to be reduced by stages after 10 years.

The total approximate annual relief in lakhs aimed at by Sir Otto Niemeyer is as follows : Bengal 75 ; Bihar 25 ; C. P. 15 ; Assam 45 ; N. W. F. P. 110 Orissa 50 ; Sind 105, U. P. 25. The extra recurrent cost to the centre is 192 lakhs.

Orissa is to get a further non-recurrent grant of 19 and Sind of 5

Provincial Share of Income-Tax

By six equal steps, beginning from the sixth year from the introduction of provincial autonomy, but subject to the proviso to Sec. 138 (2) of the Act, the Centre is to distribute income-tax to the provinces so that finally 50 per cent of the distributable total has been relinquished in the intermediate five years. There is no possible relinquishment of the income-tax so long as the portion of the distributable sum remaining with the Centre together with any contribution from railways aggregate to less than 10 crore.

The percentage division of the distributable portion of the income-tax between the provinces is as follows :

Madras, 15 ; Bombay, 20 ; Bengal. 20 ; U. P. 15 ; the Punjab, 8 ; Bihar, 10 ; C. P. 5 ; Assam, 2 ; N. W. F. P. 1 ; Orissa. 2 ; and Sind, 2.

Sir Otto Niemeyer states that substantial justice will be done by fixing the scale of distribution partly on residence and partly on population, paying to neither factor a rigidly pedantic deference for which the actual data provide insufficient justification

Principles of Settlement

The following are salient extracts from the Report : Throughout the discussions leading up to the Government of India Act, it has been recognised that at the inauguration of provincial autonomy, each of the provinces should be so equipped as to enjoy a reasonable prospect of maintaining financial equilibrium and, in particular, that the chronic state of deficit into which some of them had fallen should be brought to an end. My first object has accordingly been to examine the present and prospective financial position of the provinces and to determine the extent to which special assistance would be needed in order to achieve the above aim. Next, it is necessary to consider how far the Central Government is in a position to render such assistance without jeopardising its own solvency. Finally, I have to look further into the future and to suggest to what extent and when it may be possible for the Centre to place additional resources at the disposal of the provinces out of the proceeds of the taxes on income.

From the provincial point of view, the desirability of attaining this final result is undeniable and the only question (though in itself a difficult question) is to determine an equitable basis of distribution. From the central point of view, on the other hand, it is clear that the financial stability and credit India as a whole must remain the paramount consideration. Moreover, this is as essential to the provinces and to the success of provincial autonomy as it is to the Centre itself. Throughout my recommendations, I have kept the stability of the Central finances continuously in mind. Expenditure at the Centre cannot be expected, consistently with safety, to decrease much below the point to which it has now been reduced. There may be future savings on debt conversions, but so far as they remain with the general budget, they hardly seem likely to do more than assist in reinstating a more adequate contribution to debt redemption than the present reduced figure of 3 crores. It is, however, at least unnecessary to contemplate any serious increase in the total expenditure unless the railway budget, contrary to expectation, fails to improve.

Expenditure in the provinces could obviously be increased with advantage on many heads. This is a question of degree and opportunity. Some expansion in fact took place even with the existing provincial resources, especially in the years before the slump when many provinces were able, for instance, to increase substantially their expenditure on education. It may now be anticipated from the recovery of provincial revenues, not all of which are or need be static. Nevertheless, the allocation at an early date of a share in taxes on income under Section 138 of the Government of India Act constitutes, for many provinces, the main hope for the future expansion.

On a general review of the existing tendencies, I should conclude that the budgetary prospect of India, given prudent management of her finances, justify the view that adequate arrangements can be made step by step to meet the financial implications of the new constitution. A change of constitutional and administrative arrangements cannot of course in a movement alter the general financial position or enable all conceivable financial desires to be met, but I see no reason why a cautious but steady advance should not be achieved.

Claims of Provinces

I turn now more particularly to the prior question. The present position of the provinces and their contrasted positions *inter se*, both of which fall under the objective of starting the provinces on the occasion of autonomy on "an even keel". Various matters arise in this connection. How far in actual fact is each province now solvent and likely to remain solvent? This is a matter which cannot be judged on the position in the year only. How far, whatever may be its present position, has a province administered its affairs, whether in taxation or in expenditure, with adequate firmness and how far has this or that province, for whatever reason, been financially neglected in the past and thereby condemned to a lot from which others have escaped? It is obviously impossible to reconcile all the conflicting views and arguments on these issues. The recommendations I shall make represent, in my belief, an equitable settlement as between the various contestants and will, I hope, be accepted on that basis. I would only add here that in any country of the size of India there must inevitably be substantial differences in the standard of administrative needs and possibilities just as there are in other areas of the same size in the rest of the world or, for that matter, even in smallest units. The present position and the relative size of the provincial budgets are shewn in appendix (II). As regards the figures for 1936-37, it must be borne in mind that they are estimates and experience suggests that the deficits thus prognosticated will, in the actual result, be smaller. Apart from that, there are a number of adjustments to be made in either direction before these figures can be regarded as any necessary indication of the future nor can any settlement undertake to secure that no province shall at any time and, whatever the course of its administration, be freed from the ordinary risk of a casual budgetary deficit. Provincial autonomy necessarily implies autonomous responsibility in this direction. Also, it is obvious as the Percy Committee said, that special assistance to certain provinces which, whatever the precise form it takes, can only be given at the cost of the Central revenues and must operate to delay *pro tanto* the general transfer to all provinces of their share of the taxes or income. This consideration cannot be absent from the mind of anyone endeavouring to deal fairly with the whole problem and sets on limit to the amount of prior readjustment which can reasonably be admitted. At the same time, it is equally clear that some provinces are intrinsically better off than others and at the moment has urgently in need of additional resources and it is both desirable and inevitable that a certain measure of correction should be applied even if it means that provinces which have been able to attain higher standards of administration should now to some slight extent. have to progress more slowly.

Certain further general comments may be made. Bombay has just received an annual relief to the extent of approximately 90 lakhs from the separation of Sind; Madras and Bihar approximately 20 lakhs and 8 lakhs respectively from the separation of Orissa. Madras, Bombay and the Punjab have certainly not the lowest administrative standards in India. Bengal is clearly on a low standard, while Bihar and Orissa has been generally recognised as the poorest province in India. To a less extent, similar considerations apply to the Central Provinces. The position of the United Provinces is so far peculiar that while its ultimate future gives less reason for anxiety, its immediate difficulties are considerable.

SIND

Sind and Orissa as newly instituted provinces have special problems of their own. The future of Sind and of the subvention as part of Sind finances is inseparably bound up with the financial future of the Lloyd Barrage. In considering to what extent it is justifiable to continue this charge on the Centre, I must assume that the Barrage scheme will be administered on lines comparable with similar schemes elsewhere and that adequate rates. will be charged for the facilities it will provide. In all the circumstances and bearing in mind the necessarily conjectural nature of estimates for a period stretching so far into the future, I recommend that the Sind subvention should remain at 105 lakhs for a period of 10 years (i. e., till 1946-47 inclusive) and should then be diminished by 25 lakhs a year for 20 years, by 10 lakhs a year for the next 5 years, by 45 lakhs a year for the next succeeding 5 years, and thereafter until the whole barrage debt is repaid, i. e., in about 40 years from 1942. Any remaining portion of the subvention will, of course, in any event cease.

ORISSA

It is impossible to ignore the fact that the existing standard of expenditure in Orissa is extremely low and the scope for expansion in the province's own resources in the early future is unusually limited as against the provision of 40 and a half lakhs in 1936-37 for recurrent Orissa expenditure. It is therefore necessary to contemplate a somewhat higher normal scale of assistance and my conclusion is that the figure should be increased to approximately 50 lakhs. I recommend also, in order to ease the position in the earlier years, that the Government of India should make a further grant to the Orissa Famine Fund so as to raise the total in the latter to the figure of 10 lakhs prescribed in the Orissa Order in Council. Five lakhs have already been provided for this purpose and a contribution of 1 and one-fourth lakhs included in the 1936-37 Orissa Budget so that a further non-recurrent sum of about 4 lakhs would be needed. Finally, it is clear that the cost of providing the new province with such essential buildings as are required will be rather more than the sum of 27 and a half lakhs for headquarters alone which the Government of India are setting aside out of their anticipated surplus of 1935-36. In my view, a further sum of 15 lakhs should suffice if a reasonable standard is set and I recommend that assistance for this purpose, additional to what has been proposed in the two preceding sub-paragraphs, should be provided at the rate of 3 lakhs per annum in each of the first five years. The total assistance which I propose should be given to Orissa is thus about 57 lakhs in the first year, 63 lakhs a year in the next four years, and, thereafter, 50 lakhs a year.

ASSAM

Assam has been universally recognised as a deficit province and must undoubtedly receive assistance. The measure of the assistance depends partly on the prospective revenue of Assam allowing for a very moderate amount of continued recovery and partly on the degree to which the existing provincial deficit (47 lakhs in 1935-36) can be regarded as having been unavoidable (either as regards expenditure or taxation). Allowance has further to be made for the cost of provincial autonomy and for certain adjustments of expenditure with the centre, including the cost of the Asssam rifles, hitherto mainly borne by the Central Government. At present the Central Government pays 12 lakhs per annum towards the total cost of the Assam Rifles (15 lakhs). In future the Central Government will in any case pay the cost of the Manipur Battalion (approximately 3 lakhs). The Central Government now proposes to bear 7 lakhs of the cost of the remaining Assam force and to treat this payment separately from any assistance for provincial needs proper. I think this an equitable arrangement. The Assam Government put forward a special claim in connection with the proceeds of the excise duties on Assam oil. Though the incidence of the tax obviously does not fall on the producing province, I do not think there is any economic justification for this particular claim or that it presents any real analogy with the superficially similar claim which it may be alleged, have been recognised elsewhere. In any case having regard to the amount of the proposed assistance which such a receipt could only operate to reduce, it is necessary to pursue this matter further.

North-West Frontier

The North-West Frontier Province which has since 1932 received an annual subvention of 1 crore from the Central Government, is so far in a special position that Section 142 of the Government of India Act permits an increase in its subvention at any time without an address from the federal legislature. It is however desirable, both from the point of view of the Province and from that of the Central Government, that the subvention should be fixed for a certain period of years. After examining the past and prospective budgetary position of the Province (and also, incidentally, the various references made in the past to equivalence in certain respects with the neighbouring districts of the Punjab), my recommendation is that the existing subsidy of 1 crore should be supplemented by approximately 10 lakhs per annum. In so far as this assistance may take the form of a subvention under Section 142, it should be fixed for a period of five years which should be subject to revision in the light of the then existing circumstances. By revision I am far from implying a further increase. I contemplate merely that the position should then be reviewed in the light of the five years' further financial administration.

Central Government's Position

Can the Centre support such an additional demand apart from this sum of nearly two crores per annum? Concurrently with the inauguration of provincial autonomy Burma will be separated from India at a net loss to the Central revenues now estimated by the Government of India at about two and three-forth crores. These two items together clearly would present a budgetary problem of some magnitude if they had to be faced in 1937-38 at one blow and so soon from the normal resources of a single financial year. Thereafter, owing to the expansion in the central resources which may with confidence be anticipated, they need occasion no special difficulty. Thanks, however, to the Reserve Fund of about 2 crores which is being constituted out of the anticipated surplus of the year 1935-36, I see no reason why the grant of these additional resources to the Provinces should not commence in 937-38.

In so concluding, I should be lacking in frankness if I did not make it clear that the scope in the next few years for the relaxation of revenue burdens is likely to be extremely small unless economic improvement takes place at a rate well in excess of what can now safely be assumed. I have, however, felt it right to assume that the establishment of provincial autonomy mus be regarded as an objective to which the Government of India will give special consideration in assessing the relative order of its financial aims.

From the financial point of view, I conclude that His Majesty's Government may safely propose to Parliament that Part III of the Government of India Act 1919 should be brought into operation a year hence.

Claim of Jute Provinces

The claim of the jute-producing provinces to the whole or part of the jute export duty has already been recognised to the extent of 50 per cent by the Government of

India Act. In my opinion, it is doubtful whether the argument that the incidence of this particular duty falls wholly on the producer can be maintained. No concrete statistical proof of this contention has been produced and, even if such proof could be proved for a specific date, it may be doubted whether it would be valid in all the circumstances of a changing market. Further, even if the argument were completely substantial, it would not be conclusive on the question whether or not the community as a whole in India was entitled to tap this source of revenue as it must in fact tap other sources of revenue of unequal provenance among the different parts of India. No source of revenue, whether customs, excise or income-tax, can in fact in any country be derived equally from all parts of the country alike, rich and poor, agricultural or industrial. In so far as a claim may be put forward on the ground that the taxable capacity of Bengal is limited by the incidence of this duty, that is a claim not so much to this particular duty as to financial assistance generally. It is part in fact of the case for a share in taxes on income or for such prior special treatment as it is the object of my present recommendations to secure. It may be thought that whatever validity there may be in the economic argument has already been met by the surrender to the provinces concerned of 50 per cent of the net produce of the duty. It will, however, be convenient that part of the assistance I contemplate should take the form of an increase in this figure and therefore I recommend that the percentage should be increased under Section 140 (2) of the Act to 62 and half on the estimated gross yeld of the duty in 1936-37 at 380 lakhs. This increase of 12 and half per cent would mean in round figures the following additions to the resources of the provinces concerned at a corresponding cost to the Central Government: Bengal, 42 lakhs ; Bihar 2 and half lakhs ; Assam 2 and one-fourth lakhs ; and Orissa rather over "one-fourth" lakh.

Apart from the separation of Burma and the provision of 2 crores assistance for the provinces which I have already recommended, the additional cost of the new federal institutions (probably something over half a crore) may be imminent and provision may have to be made for financial adjustments in respect of the States under Section 147 of the Act at a net ultimate annual cost now estimated at rather more than half a crore though the full annual charge on this latter account will presumably not fall to meet in the early years. If, however, there is bound to be delay, the provinces will no doubt recollect that they will be receiving from the Centre the amounts proposed in para 17 above, in addition to what certain of them have already been receiving from the jute export duty and about Rs. 1 and half crores per annum for roads as well as certain grants (Rs 3 and half crores) for rural purposes. Some of them have also received substantial assistance through being relieved of deficit areas.

Burden of Income-Tax

I wish to add two comments on these recommendations. After the abolition of the tax on the smaller incomes and the two successive reductions in the rates imposed in 1931, the rate income-tax and super-tax in India, especially on the higher incomes are by no means excessive. The general scheme of Indian taxation (Central and Provincial) operates to relieve the wealthier commercial classes to an extent which is unusual in taxation schemes, and there would be no justifiable ground of complaint if a slight correction of this anomaly were maintained. The assignment of taxes on income is the main method of assisting provincial finances contemplated by the Government of India Act, and if the remaining surcharge were maintained, it would materially contribute to the early receipt by the provinces of additional resources.

Position of Raiways

The position of the Railways is frankly disquieting. It is not enough to contemplate that in five years' time, the Railways may merely cease to be in deficit. Such a result would also tend to prejudice or delay the relief which the provinces are entitled to expect. I believe that both the early establishment of effective co-ordination between the various modes of transport and the thorough-going overhaul of railway expenditure in itself are vital elements in the whole provincial problem.

Basis of Distribution of Income-Tax

Naturally each province advocates the basis of division (population, residence, etc.) which gives it the largest dividend. It cannot be said that any of the proposed bases have any particular scientific validity or satisfy in any appreciable degree the ideal, but practically unascertainable test of capacity to pay. The mere accident of place of collection as has frequently been pointed out in previous discussions of this subject is clearly an unsuitable guide. The residence of the individual, though it may be a convenient and practically dividing line for purposes of avoiding double taxation betwen separate political units, is not in itself a very scientific criterion, particularly in a Federation and in fact, in India gives results (of necessity partly estimated), too suspiciously near those of collection to inspire much confidence.

Finally, even supposing it were practicable to ascertain to what part of India particular fractions of income (and, therefore, the incidence of the taxation burden) properly adhere, it is still arguable that in a Federation other considerations also involved, particularly if the benefits and incidence of other forms of common taxation are unequally divided as between the various partners.

Text of the Official Correspondence

The following is the text of the correspondence between the local Governments, the Government of India and the Secretary of State on the recommendations of the Niemeyer Report issued from Simla on the **27th. May 1936** and copies of which had been presented to Parliament by the Secretary of State.

Briefly put, the Secretary of State has accepted the Niemeyer Report as a whole. The provincial Governments' protests are strongly worded, the only exception being the C. P. Government who have sent in the shortest telegram and accept the Niemeyer award without an elaborate criticism.

The longest representation is by the Punjab Government and the Secretary of State's reply deals with this province at greater length than with any other province.

The Madras Government after drawing a comparative picture between Bengal and Madras urges that the population factor should be given a greater weight.

The Bombay Government regrets *inter alia* that the distribution of income-tax relief should be made entirely dependent upon the successful running of railways and presses for cancellation of fictitious debt created in respect of unproductive irrigation works.

The Bengal Government is moderate in its representation and while accepting the award wants the jute duty to be recognized in future as a provincial source.

The U. P. Government admits that the Niemeyer Report is a carefully balanced scheme and suggests that after five years until receipts from income-tax amount to Rs. 15.00,000 a subvention be given sufficient to bring the income-tax receipts plus subvention to Rs. 15.00,000.

The Punjab Government feels that the province will have a permanent sense of injustice and wishes that at least their income-tax share should be fixed on the population percentage.

Bihar puts in its claim as the poorest province and wishes that the basis of distribution should be wholly population.

The Assam Government is divided. The Indian Members and Ministers are profoundly disappointed while their European colleagues do not admit that a deficit of Rs. 25.00,000 is involved.

The N. W. F. P. objects to the Niemeyer Report unnecessarily prejudging its position regarding subvention five years hence.

The Orissa Government protests that the proposals involve a great disparity in the treatment among assisted units giving to Orissa subvention far less per head of population than to other units who have already a far higher standard of expenditure per head.

The Sind Government presumes that the door would be left open for adjustment of subvention and debt repayment in case revenue expectations are not realised.

The Provincial Governments' views were sent by the first week of May except the Punjab, whose views were submitted on April 13. The Government of India telegraphed to the Secretary of State their views on May 14 and enunciated the position in clear terms. They pointed out the figures of the initial cost of assistance to the Provincial Governments were in excess of anything the Government of India had hitherto contemplated and thought that the divisible income-tax receipts to be permanently retained by the centre would be fixed at two-thirds instead of a half. However, recognizing that the Niemeyer Report is in the nature of a quasi-arbitral award, they hope that the Niemeyer programme is feasible. They declare, however, that unless railway solvency on the basis of a full commercial accounting system can be restored (and that before long) the latter stage of the programme envisaged by Sir Otto Neimeyer, relating to income-tax would be quite impossible of execution. The Government of India also consider that any material increase in customs tariff will endanger the practicability of the plan. They conceive, in fact, that in order to conserve the revenue yield it will be necessary from time to time to propose reductions of particular duties.

As regards surcharges, 'whether these are retained permanently or only temporarily, it seems to us indubitable that in recommending a settlement so generous to the provinces Sir Otto has rendered it difficult in the next ten years for the Government of India either to increase its exiguous provision for the sinking fund to a reasonable figure or to reduce the indirect taxes which are an undue burden either upon the consumer, except in cases where such action will be clearly advantageous to revenue.'

As regards the Niemeyer proposals for decentralization of the balances and consolidation of the pre-autonomy debt, the Government of India regard them as an integral part of the initial financial settlement. The Secretary of State has agreed with this view, as also with the view of the Government of India that when the railways show a surplus these should not be used for replacing the sums borrowed from the depreciation fund. He also approves of the proposals regarding improvement of the railway accounting procedure.

The Government of India make it clear that they see no chance of relinquishing any further part of the jute duty by 1942 or indeed by any specific date. On this the Secretary of State declares that, if on account of the reduction in the jute export duty the value to the growing provinces of their percentage were materially reduced it would be necessary to consider whether those provinces required additional assistance.

As regards the question of the remaining surcharges on income-tax, the Secretary of State says—'If the scheme of finance upon which the successful operation of provincial autonomy depends is found to necessitate the continuance for some time longer of this burden (either in the present or in any equivalent form) I shall accord my full support to the Government of India.'

The Secretary of State deals briefly with the cases put by the various provinces. Referring to the Punjab, he says :—'I have no doubt that a province so well endowed with natural resources and with so high a tradition of efficient administration as the Punjab will, in fact, without assistance be much more favourably situated than many of the other provinces even after allowing for the help which the latter will receive.' The point raised by the Punjab Government regarding the supply of excise liquor by one province to another would require further examination. The Secretary of State assures the N. W. F. Province that the intention is to reconsider the question of subvention at the end of five years.

Both the Government of India and the Secretary of State express great appreciation of the service rendered by Sir Otto Niemeyer and regard his report as a quasi-arbitral award.

Secretary of State's Telegram

The Secretary of State sent to the Government of India the following telegram on May 20, giving reasons why he has accepted the Niemeyer Report as a whole and indicating his views on certain points raised by the Government regarding the future policy :—

'I have now received the views of each of the provincial Governments and of your Excellency's Government upon Sir Otto Niemeyer's Report, and having carefully examined these communications, I have reached conclusions which are set forth below. In order that a full information of the considerations that I have had to weigh may be available, I propose to present to Parliament both the views of the Government of India and this reply.

'I cordially join in acknowledgments which are due to Sir Otto Niemeyer for undertaking the responsible and difficult task that was allotted to him and for the manner in which he has discharged it. No problem connected with the process of constitutional reform in India has given rise to greater conflict of views and interests than the matter of finance and it is, indeed, fortunate that one who combined such exceptional experience and authority with complete detachment from Indian controversies was able to assist in the final stages of its solution. There can be no more striking evidence of formidable complexities of issues upon which he has delivered so clear a judgment than the documents now under review.

Sir Otto's task had two aspects. On the one hand he was appointed to conduct an independent investigation of the present and prospective budgetary positions of the Government of India and of the Governments of provinces before the final decisions were taken by his Majesty's Government and Parliament as to the date for the introduction of new provincial constitutions. On the other hand he was required to make recommendations for completion by Order-in-Council of a scheme of financial relations between the centre and the provinces embodied in the Government of India Act of 1935, and for other adjustments ancillary to that scheme. The matters remaining to be determined by Order-in-Council were allocation between the centre and the provinces of the proceeds of income-tax and jute export duty and prescription of grants-in-aid of revenues of such provinces as were found to require assistance in this form. The two aspects of enquiry are connected by an objective inherent in the constitutional plan of equipping prices with at least sufficient minimum of resources at the outset, and of providing them with further resources in future, for questions at once arise both of ability of the Central Government to surrender a part of its present resources and of the manner in which the sums available should be distributed among the provinces.

Sir Otto's conclusions upon the general question of adequacy of financial resources is 'that the budgetary prospects of India given a prudent management of her finances, justify the view that adequate arrangements can be made, step by step, to meet the financial implications of the new constitution' (parapraph no. 8), and after making recommendations to meet the immediate needs of the provinces, he adds specifically, from financial point of view I conclude, that his Majesty's Government may safely propose to Parliament that part II of the Government of India Act, 1935, should be brought into operation a year hence'. (paragraph no. 18). These conclusions have been reached after an expert and exhaustive examination of the position in consultation with the financial authorities of each of the provinces and of the Government of India and must accordingly command the respect.

Comments of Provincial Govts.

It was perhaps inevitable that so long as the final decision had not been pronounced upon the extent of benefit that each province might expect to receive, comments of the provincial Governments should generally speaking have been designed mainly to emphasise their individual difficulties and natural desires for greater resources In any case, it was scarcely to be expected that where aspirations have considerably out-run the financial possibilities and expections have been high, and where the effects of a setback that accompained depression are still keenly felt, necessarily limitted proposals now under consideration would receive from this quarter an unqualified welcome. I fully realize, indeed, that the financial administration of all provinces will continue to demand great caution and that the budgetary problems of some provinces will present difficulties.

I see no reason, however, to believe that those problems need prove insoluble and I find confirmation for the view not only in Sir Otto Neimeyer's judgment, but also in fact that no provincial Government makes any suggestion that the introduction of provincial autonomy should be delayed on financial grounds.

On the other hand the problem of the Government of India in finding some five crores, partly to assist the provinces and partly in consequence of the separation of Burma, demands consideration. Sir Otto Niemeyer was far from ignoring the implications of this problem which are further emphasised by the Government of India. It is clear that the central Government, no less than provincial Governments, will have to direct its financial policy with special care. but I do not understand that the Government of India anticipate insuperable difficulties and I share this view.

Deficit in Provinces

In considering this question, it is well, I think, to appreciate the extent to which such practical difficulties as remain to be overcome are inherent in the existing situation independent of prospect of constitutional reform. The anxiety of provinces for a more liberal allotment of resources has been continuously manifested over a long period. Moreover, the problem of chronic deficit in the provinces could not have much longer been left unsolved. These are the major factors in the situation and would have to be faced even if no change in the existing form of Government was contemplated. Besides them, the cost of such changes as the enlarged electorates and the legislatures which are connected with the new constitution is relatively insignificant.

It is, of course, clear that the solution of all these problems might have been simpler, had they been under consideration in more propitious economic circumstances. Unless, however, completely unforeseenable setback occurs, the position will evidently be markedly better than could have been anticipated at a time when the framework of the new constitution was under discussion. It will be recalled that the joint committee gave special attention to the financial background of reforms and concluded that Parliament would at an appropriate time require assurance from his Majesty's Government that the new constitution could be inaugurated without thereby aggravating the financial difficulties to a dangerous extent. In my view the assurance that may now be given can be framed in appreciably more positive and hopeful terms. After full consideration I entirely accept Sir Otto Niemeyer's conclusions and I had no hesitation in proposing with the concurrence of your Excellency's Government that April 1st, 1937 should be appointed as the date for the commencement of provincial autonomy. A draft order in Council for this purpose (upon the technical of detail which the Government of India and the provincial Governments have been separately consulted) will shortly be submitted to Parliament.

In regard to the second aspect of Sir Otto Niemeyer's enquiry, it is evident that the past history of the discussion of financial relations between the centre and the provinces afforded no good reason to hope that his recommendations would be immediately acceptable to all parties concerned As the Joint Committee pointed out the problem of allocation of resources in the federal system has everywhere proved singularly impracticable, for the conflict of interest that arises is practically incapable of complete resolution (?) The assessment of the relative financial need of the centre and of the provinces collectively is a sufficiently difficult task but the other facet of the problem adjudication of rival claims of provinces gives rise to issues of even greater delicacy. I share the Government of India's view that in both respects Sir Otto's report must be regarded as in the nature of a quasi-arbitral award and it is accordingly clear that such a nicely balanced scheme could not properly be disturbed except for strongest reasons. I have examined the recommendations closely on this basis. So far as concern the aggregate assistance to be afforded to provinces, I am not prepared to dissent from the Government of India's view that it is out of question at the present moment for the Central Government to undertake greater commitments, immediate or prospective, than Sir Otto has recommended. In these circumstances it is, of course, clear that any material alteration in the treatment accorded to particular provinces can be made only at the expense of other province. How extensive is the field of controversy to which this would lead is readily apparent from the conflicting views of the provincial Governments that are before me. Each province is inevitably convinced of the strength of its own claims and is bound to experience difficulty in appreciating the significance of its case relatively to circumstances of other provinces. It cannot be overlooked that Sir Otto Niemeyer has brought independent judgment to bear on this subject and that he has had exceptional opportunity of appreciating the problem as a whole. It is my considered view that he has achieved as equitable a settlement between the various contestants as the case allows. I propose accordingly to accept his recommendations as a whole. Before accepting the recommendations as not only equitable but practicable I have paid attention to the special problems that are mentioned by the Government of India.

Financial Position of Railways

As regards the financial position of railways, I note with satisfaction that the Government of India have the matter actively under consideration and your Excellency's Government may count on my support in any measure that may be necessary for the improvement of the position.

Customs Revenue

I note the Government of India's view regarding the customs revenue which is a matter that will undoubtedly call for most careful consideration in the near future.

Surcharge on Income-Tax

The question of retaining surcharge on income-tax is, as the Government of India point out, one of some difficulty and although it is only one aspect of the general budgetary problem which will arise from time time, I feel bound to say at once with reference to their observations on the subject that if the scheme of finance upon which the successful operation of provincial autonomy depends is found to necessitate the continuance for some time longer of this burden (either in its present or in any equivalent form) I shall accord my full support to the Government of India.

I agree that in any case there is bound to be some uncertainty whether the programme for transfer of income-tax to provinces can be fully realized and in this connection I think it well to associate myself with the warning given by Sir Otto Niemeyer in paragraph 32 of his report.

While every effort will be made, so far as I am concerned, and also I have no doubt by the Government of India, to fulfil the hopes now extended to provinces, the scheme cannot be assumed by them to represent the final commitment. At the same time with reference to the Government of India's observations as regards the provincial percentage, I am bound to emphasize the importance that I attach to securing the maximum possible ultimate distribution to provinces for which reason I welcome both Sir Otto's proposal and the Government of India's view, which I share, that there is a fair reason to believe in its feasibility. It is relevant to remember that the mistake in fixing the percentage unduly low cannot be rectified since the percentage originally prescribed is incapable of increase by a subsequent Order-in-Council. Against any mistake in the contrary direction, however, there are safeguards both of the Governor-General's delaying power, to which attention has been drawn by Sir Otto and the Government of India, and in the last resort a possible reduction in percentage by an amending order.

In view of my general conclusions already indicated, it would serve no good purpose to attempt a detailed commentary on the views submitted by each individual province. There are, however, certain specific points upon which a brief comment is unavoidable, and in the first place I wish to express concurrence in the Government of India's observations in connection with representations of Assam, Sind, Bihar and Bengal. As regards Bengal, I would add that it cannot in my opinion properly be assumed that the power in respect of jute export duty placed by the Government of India Act in the Central Legislature will not be exercised with due reard to the economic interests of that province. On such assumption applied throughout the field of central legislation, which of necessity includes subjects that affect certain units more than others, the federal idea would be practically unworkable. In so far, however, as there may be a case for reducing sooner or later the rate of jute export duty, I think it necessary to say now that if on account of such reduction the value to the growing provinces of their percentages were materially reduced it would be necessary to consider whether in the circumstances those provinces required an additional assistance either in the form of a change in jute duty percentage or otherwise.

Problems Before U. P. Government

I appreciate the practical problems that confront the Government of the United Provinces. I have, however, not understood that Sir Otte Niemeyer's recommendation was related to the precise requirements of each particular year and am unable to accept the suggesion that in aggregate it need prove inadequate, having regard to the circumstances of the United Provinces and to the special problems that the central budget will present in the first year or two. It appears to me not unreasonable that the beneficiary should accept the assistance in even amounts and make budgetary dispositions accordingly.

Punjab Government

While I sympathize with much that the Punjab Government says, I cannot refrain from observing that the case of that province relatively to others, particularly Madras and Bombay, appears to have been somewhat exaggerated. Sir Otto Niemeyer has clearly had to consider cases of those provinces after allowing for separation of Orissa and Sind and I am not prepared to dispute the equity of his conclusions. Moreover from the practical point of view the benefits of creation of Sind and Orissa have been largely absorbed into the budgets of the parent provinces this year and though they will, of course, permanently strengthen the position of those provinces they will not represent the additional free resources at the disposal of the new Ministries. Again, such benefits as Madras and Bombay may derive from the decentralisation and consolidation scheme is, as the Government of India point out, temporary, while on the other hand it may be noted that as part of the debt scheme the Punjab is left with a large block of debt on exceptionally favourable terms.

I sympathize with the natural disappointment of the Punjab Government that that province alone of the provinces of India should receive no assistance, except to a trifling degree through debt scheme. But I am not satisfied that there are sufficient grounds for giving any special relief to that province which Sir Otto Niemeyer has not recommended. The central resources, especially at the outset, are not such that assistance can be given except when the need is imperative. I have no doubt that the province so well endowed with natural resources, and with so high tradition of efficient administration as the Punjab will in fact without assistance be much more favourably situated that many of other provinces, even after allowing for help which the latter will receive. The fact that one or two other provinces, whose economic strength is perhaps comparable with that of the Punjab, happen to receive relief owing to their territorial reorganizations and debt scheme, cannot afford justification for grant of some equivalent benefit to the Punjab. It has also to be remembered that additional resources will become available to the new Punjab Government when income-tax begins to be distributed. I note that the Punjab Government consider that they will be at some financial disadvantage on the introduction of provincial autonomy owing to the expected loss in connection with the supply of liquor by the province to other administrations Arrangements covering the supply of excise liquor by one province to another will have to be reviewed in the light of the new constitutional position and I consider that the points raised by the Punjab Government in this connection will require further examination.

Draft Order

I am submitting to Parliament the draft distribution of Revenues Order which deals with income-tax, jute export duty and grants-in-aid to certain provinces in strict accordance with Sir Otto Niemeyer's recommendations.

Fundamental Assumptions

Technical points in the Draft Order have been separately discussed with the Government of India but there are certain fundamental assumptions that I must set forth on the present occasion.

(a) The calculation to which Section 138 (1) of the Government of India Act gives rise involves certain assumption as to the interpretation of that section and Sir Otto Niemeyer has recorded assumptions that he has made in the annexed letter. The order has been drafted upon the basis of these assumptions and as the allocation of appreciable sums is involved it is necessary that I should make this clear.

(b) It has always been assumed that 'corporation tax' (which is allocated by the Act as a federal source of revenue) would mean a tax of the nature of the existing supertax on companies and definition in section 311 (2) of the Act was intended to have this result. I understand, however, that doubt has arisen whether the definition is entirely satisfactory. If such doubt is substantiated hereafter it may be necessary to ask Parliament to rectify the position.

(c) Sir Otto has recommended that for the purpose of the formula which governs the allocation of income-tax in the first five years' period the computation of railway contributions to the general revenues should be made on the basis provided by the present railway convention which was formulated in the resolution passed by the Legislative Assembly on September 24, 1924. In accepting this recommendation I agree with the Government of India that the method of application of that resolution to the present purpose should in respect of treatment of loans from depreciation fund, the treatment of arrears of contribution to general revenues (which are not specifically mentioned but are in (*pari materia*) and the improvement of the accounting procedure be on the lines suggested in paragraph 5 of their views. The relevant provision of the Draft Order in Council are intended to give effect to the above.

(d) The provisions of the Draft Order in respect of North-West Frontier Province grant-in-aid do not bear on the face of them qualifications that the case of this province is to be reconsidered in five years' time, which was what Sir Otto recommended. It would, in fact, be inconvenient to make such a provision in the Order, but I wish to make it clear that the intention is to reconsider the matter at the end of five years. In this connection I have noted the concluding comments in the views of this province and I think it desirable to state that so far as I am concerned there is no question of prejudging at the present time any decision that may have to be taken in the light of the circumstances of five years hence.

(c) The provisions of Sind assume that the Barrage Debt Funding Scheme will be on the lines recommended by Sir Otto Niemeyer and measures to this end are in contemplation.

The scope of the Draft Order in Council does not extend to decentralisation of balances and cancellation and consolidation of debt referred to in paras 19 to 21 and appendix III of the report. These are matters which will fall to be dealt with immediately before the commencement of provincial autonomy under the existing statutory powers (subject to certain amendments of the devolution rules). It is clear in any event that the grant of specified assistance to certain provinces by the cancellation of debt is an essential part of Sir Otto Niemeyer's scheme and I shall assure Parliament that necessary action in this regard will be taken. In addition, however, I entirely agree with the Government of India that the scheme for decentralisation of balances and consolidation of debt must be regarded as an integral part of the whole plan and on this basis I have decided to accept the scheme. Detailed arrangements for its execution will be discussed.

Government of India's Telegram

The Government of India sent to the Secretary of State the following telegram on May 14 summing up their views on the Niemeyer Report :—

We wish at the outset to express our great appreciation of the service which Sir Otto Niemeyer has rendered to India in making a survey of Indian finances contained in his report and in undertaking the task of trying to satisfy all provinces as well as the centre from resources which are not indefinitely expanding.

Sir Otto estimates the cost of his recommendations at about Rs. 2 crores a year, diminishing by a few lakhs as the special non-recurring grants to Orissa and Sind run off. To this figure must be added the cost of decentralising the balances and the cost of the debt consolidation scheme referred to in Appendix III. Altogether the Government of India calculate that the initial cost of these adjustments is about Rs. 2 1/2 crores a year, of which Rs. 2 crores will fall directly on the budget and Rs. 1/2 crore will be the diminution of capital repayments. The consolidation proposals also involve the spreading of repayment instalments, which will have the effect of increasing somewhat the interest charges in the central budget in the early years, though the increase will be counter-balanced by corresponding decreases later on.

The figures of initial cost are in excess of anything the Government of India have hitherto contemplated, but nevertheless having regard to the supreme importance which is attached to giving provincial autonomy a fair start, they are prepared to accept the conclusion reached by Sir Otto in paragraph 18 of his report (*viz.*, that his Majesty's Government may safely propose to Parliament that part III of the Government of India Act, 1935, should be brought into operation as from the 1st April next) provided that there is no question of increasing in any appreciable degree the total of initial assistance recommended, and provided that it is clearly understood that it may be necessary to retain the remainder of the surcharges on income-tax and super-tax, at any rate for some time after the 1st April, 1937, in order to maintain a balanced central budget. Incidentally, we desire to indicate that we attach very great importance to the general adoption of the arrangements which we have proposed for decentralisation of the balances and the consolidation of the pre-autonomy debt and to express earnest hope that these arrangements will have our full support. Indeed, we go so far as to say that we regard them as an integral part of the initial financial adjustments. In this connection we wish to correct a misapprehension which appears to exist that some provinces will get large uncovenanted benefits from these arrangements. The greater part of the gains shown in Appendix III represents merely the immediate budgetary effect of spreading debt repayments over a longer period. In later years, of course, the result of this spreading will be to prevent budgetary reductions which would otherwise have taken place.

The next question which arises out of the report is whether the central budget can continue to sustain the burden involved by these initial adjustments *plus* the cost of the separation of Burma (estimated at Rs. 2 and 3-4 crores per annum) and in addition, can forego in stages over the following 10 years a further sum of at least Rs. 6 crores. Naturally we have had to frame for the information of Sir Otto Niemeyer such forecasts as we could reasonably make of our position in the years to come. Inevitably these estimates are invested with great uncertainty. The factors which make for uncertainty are, with two exceptions, set out by Sir Otto. Those exceptions are the possibility of India's being involved in war and the possibility of internal political disturbances of such a magnitude as materially tc affect the prosperity of the country. The former possibility no calculation can take into account, the latter the Government of India think that they may safely reject. For rest, there fall to be considered the position of the railways and the possibility of the law of diminishing returns setting in in connection with the customs revenue.

As regards railways, the Government of India have no hesitation in saying that unless their solvency on the basis of a full commercial accounting system can be restored, and that before very long, the latter stages of the programme envisaged by Sir Otto Niemeyer will be quite impossible of execution. At present it is hoped that the deficits can be met without depleting the existing reserve of Rs. 9 or 10 crores, but in the not distant future the annual demand for renewals and replacements is bound to increase considerably, and unless in the meantime a position of complete solvency has been reached the reserve will rapidly become exhausted with the consequence of a call upon the central budget. The Government of India have under consideration the practical steps to be taken in this connection, and they hope to approach the Secretary of State shortly in the matter.

As regards customs, the general level of tariff is now so high that the maintenance of an aggregate yield which is by far the most important single factor in the whole revenue position has become a somewhat precarious task. There is plainly no further reserve which could now be drawn upon to meet an emergency, as was done twice in 1931, and any serious relapse in the value of India's import trade would inflict a damage which would be beyond the remedy of a mere increase of tariff. Even if we exclude, further, a deterioration in the conditions of international trade the present pitch even of revenue duties is itself liable to provoke regressive tendencies. The Government of India, therefore, consider that any material increase in tariff will endanger the practicability of the plan. They conceive, in fact, that in order to conserve the revenue yield it will be necessary from time to time to propose reductions of particular duties.

The question now is regarded by the Government of India as feasible and acceptable. On this the Government of India are bound to observe that they had hoped that in view of the initial assistance to the provinces recommended by Sir Otto being far greater than was originally contemplated, the proportion of divisible income-tax receipts to be permanently retained by the centre would be fixed at two-thirds and not a half. However, recognising that the report is in the nature of a quasi-arbitral award the Government of India content themselves with saying that they hope and have fair reason to believe that Sir Otto's programme is feasible. In making this statement they rely, of course, on the powers of the Governor General under the proviso to sec. 138 (2) of the Act, to which Sir Otto pointedly draws attention in the concluding words of paragraph 32 of his report, but they would obviously have felt consideraby more confident that the delaying powers would not need to be invoked if the percentage allocated to the provinces had been fixed at 33 and one-third.

In this connection the Government of India cannot refrain from referring to some of the implications of the report. Those which relate to the solvency of the railways and the general level of the customs tariff have already been dealt with. That relating to the remaining surcharges on income-tax and super-tax raises very difficult questions which cannot be fully discussed here, but we do say that, so far as we can estimate the adoption of the suggestion contained in paragraph 31 (1) of the report would not enable the centre appreciably to increase the scale of initial subventions, though it would obviously advance the date when the distribution of income-tax to the provinces commences and it would render more certain of the full programme within ten years. In any case, whether the surcharges are retained permanently or only temporarily it seems to us indubitable that in recommending a settlement so generous to the provinces Sir Otto has rendered it difficult in the next ten years for the Government of India either to increase its exiguous provision for the sinking fund to a reasonable figure or to reduce those indirect taxes which are an undue burden either upon enterprise or upon the consumer except in cases where such action would be clearly advantageous to revenue. Indeed, unless prosperity returns at a quicker pace than now it seems likely that both the present Government of India and its federal successor will find their freedom of action in the financial sphere uncomfortably limited.

Finally, the Government of India would wish to mention one point of detail in regard to the first period of 5 years after provincial autonomy. Sir Otto recommends that the provinces should during this period get any sums by which the divisible pool of income-tax exceeds Rs. 13 crores less any contribution to general revenues from the railways. He explains that this railway contribution is to be assessed in accordance with the present separation convention, but this is not in itself a precise basis of assessment and indeed it would be quite possible within the present convention to render Sir Otto's recommendation nugatory. For example, if surpluses are applied first to replacing the sums borrowed from the depreciation fund no contribution can possibly arise. The Government of India assume that the Secretary of State will provide in the Order in Council against a possibility such as this. On the other hand, they wish to point out that they have for some time been considering whether, and have now actually decided, to remedy the present accounting rules under which an excessive amount of expenditure upon renewals and replacements is charged to capital. The plan decided upon involves reducing the charges to capital and increasing the net charge both against revenue and against the depreciation fund. In a normal year it will mean an additional charge of something like Rs. 20 lakhs against railway revenue and they assume that there is no question of regarding it as inconsistent with the report, which clearly could not intend that the centre should make payments on revenue account to the provinces at the expense of an illicit expansion of the railway capital account.

So far we have thought fit to set out our own views without specific reference to the views expressed by the provincial Governments. For the most part these take the form of asking for more for themselves and of complaining that other provinces have been treated too well. The cost to the central budget of the various additional demands now put toward is nearly a crore a year as from the 1st. April next, while there is the further proposal that the centre should forego an additional crore or more a year by way of reduction of the jute duty not later than the 1st April 1942. We wish to make it clear beyond a preadventure that we see no prospect whatever of being able to undertake additional burdens of this magnitude or indeed, as we have previously tried to show, of any appreciable size at all. This means that, if concessions are to be made to individual provinces, it can only be done at the expense of other provinces and not of the centre and for our part we see great difficulties in any redistribution of relief, which may easily create more discontent than it alleviates.

Apart from these general observations there are a few specific points which require mention.

Assam—We are clear that Sir Otto deliberately limited the cancellation of debt to that incurred prior to the 1st April, 1936. There are obvious reasons for such a course, but, apart from that, the residual relief which he recommends is definitely assessed on that basis.

Sind.—The Government of India would point out that the subventions proposed are equivalent to a capital gift of something like Rs. 20 crores, so that in effect a very large part of the Barrage debt is being cancelled, but in our view it is important that Sind should retain an incentive to make the Barrage remunerative as a business proposition. On the basis of the present estimates the Barrage will ultimately yield a considerable net annual surplus after allowing for the complete cessation of the subvention.

Bihar—This arithmetical argument is clearly invalid. There can be no doubt that if the debt had first been made less onerous by being spread over a longer period, Sir Otto Niemeyer would have assessed the relief immediately required, not at Rs. 25 lakhs, but at some smaller figure.

Bengal—(a) The proposal that the datum-line of divisible income-tax receipts for the first 5 year period should be fixed at Rs. 12 and not 13 crores is unacceptable. The latter figure was doubtless fixed, after a review of the forecast of the central budgetary position year by year, at a minimum which would reasonably promise an equilibrium. At all events, that is definitely our view of the situation.

(b) As regards the distribution of income-tax between Bengal and Bombay, we clearly can have nothing to say except perhaps to point out that Sir Otto Niemeyer explains that his proposals are not based upon any uniform combination of population and residence.

(c) We have already made it clear that we see no chance of being able to relinquish any further part of the jute duty by 1942 or, indeed, by any specific date. In the circumstances we deem it unnecessary to argue on the merits of this proposition.

U. P. GOVERNMENT'S VIEW

The U. P. Government recognize that the Niemeyer Report presents a carefully balanced scheme which, in its main outline, stands or falls as a whole. Though there are certain important factors to which they would have wished a different value to be given they realize that it is not practical at this stage to suggest fundamental changes in the scheme and put forward for solution an extremely difficult and complicated problem. There is, however, one important point relating to the United Provinces which appears to the U. P. Government not to have been fully appreciated and which is likely to have such serious effect on the new constitution in the province that they feel bound to press it strongly on the attention of the Government of India and the Secretary of State. The U. P. Government accept the general conclusions of the Niemeyer Report that apart from the ultimate share in income-tax receipts a temporary relief only is necessary in this province. The reason for the peculiar position of the United Provinces noted by Sir Otto Niemeyer is that its revenues are at present depleted by no less than Rs. 112 lakhs annually by slump in agricultural prices. The land revenue remission carries with it the remission of annual rents to tenants, amounting to four crores and thus affecting vitally the whole of the agrarian position. The loss in land revenue can only be gradually reduced. A temporary relief is thus essential in the earlier stages of the process of recovery. The position for the first few years of provincial autonomy is, however, appreciably worse than it appears to have been realized. The policy for adjusting the land revenue demand which the Government with the unanimous approval of the legislatures have just embarked upon involves a somewhat slow and costly procedure for settlement and revision of land revenue on the basis of the existing prices and the expenditure thereon in the first two years will exceed, resulting in an increase in land revenue receipts by substantial sums. Drastic retrenchment in provincial expenditure have been effected since the slump and during the past year the Government have again scrutinized every item of expenditure with utmost care and have made and taken into account in the estimates further reductions, which in their judgment carry retrenchment to the extreme limit. They have, indeed, reduced the standard of administration in some cases to an unreasonably low level which cannot be maintained much longer.

In addition, the legislature in the last session passed two taxation measures, increasing the court fees and stamp duty but the effect of this will be largely discounted during the next few years by the depressing effect of the debt legislation on the receipts under this head, the depression being at present greater and is likely to be more sustained than formerly anticipated. A careful re-examination of the position reveals that there will be inevitably a revenue deficit of Rs. 53 lakhs in the first year of provincial autonomy which the proposed subvention of Rs. 25 lakhs would reduce to 28 lakhs. In the second year it is estimated that with a subvention of Rs. 25 lakhs there must still be a deficit of seven lakhs. This means that as a result of two years' working of the new constitution the Government, even if it provided no fresh expenditure for developments which were urgently required, would have incurred a deficit of Rs. 35 lakhs.

The Government feels confident that neither the Government of India nor the Secretary of State would consider it reasonable that the new Government should be faced at the outset with inevitable deficit on this scale. The effect of the working of the new constitution and on the public attitude to finance will be most harmful. As far as the Government of the United Provinces can judge it is not the intention of Sir Otto Niemeyer that any other province should be launched into the new constitution with an actual inevitable deficit.

The Government, therefore, strongly urges that sufficient assistance should be given at the outset to enable the province to start not in a submerged condition. They suggest that the subvention be raised by Rs. 15 lakhs to Rs. 40 lakhs for each of the first three years and be fixed at Rs. 25 lakhs as proposed in the report, for the remaining two years. This would still leave the new Government with a deficit of Rs. 13 lakhs in the first year, but the recovery would at least be in sight.

In connection with the distribution of income-tax receipts this Government wish to emphasise the very great importance they attach to Sir Otto Nieyemer's proposal for an early and thorough-going overhaul of the railway expenditure.

Lastly, if it is necessary for the Governor-General at the end of five years to exercise his delaying power under sec. 138 of the Government of India Act so that a province does rot at that time receive any appreciable amount of the income-tax the loss by the cession of subvention, would result in a serious budgetary difficulty.

The Government, therefore, suggest that after the first period of five years until the receipts from income-tax amount to Rs. 15 lakhs a subvention should be given, sufficient to bring the total income-tax receipts plus the subvention to Rs. 15 lakhs.

BOMBAY GOVERNMENT'S VIEW

The Bombay Government's telegram to the Government of India and the Secretary of State records an emphatic protest in regard to the recommendations of the Niemeyer Report, as no steps are proposad to correct the position in which Bombay province is involved by the inequity of the Meston Settlement at the cost of the city development schemes undertaken at the behest of the Secretary of State and the drain on the presidency owing to its association with Sind. The telegram referring to retrenchment and taxation measures says that public opinion is unanimous that if these sacrifices were not made Bombay would have shared the benefits now proposed for provinces which face their financial difficulties less resolutely. The Bombay Government deplores that the distribution of income-tax in the provinces is entirely dependent upon the successful running of railway, the position of which is frankly disquieting. It is practically certain that the provinces will receive no share in the income-tax during the first five years and will be fortunate if they receive a substantial share during the second five years.

The net results of the recommendations as far as Bombay Presidency is concerned are that the province is left with no expending source of revenue untill such time as a share in the income-tax proceeds is received, is faced with additional expenditure which must follow the introduction of provincial autonomy, and the prospect of being compelled to restore a considerable amount of retrenchment which will swallow up the bulk of the relief accruing from the separation of Sind and will be forced to abandon any hopes of expansion in such directions as education, public health, agriculture, animal husbandry and the like. The Bombay Government consider that the annual benefit from the separation of Sind for the next year to the presidency will not be more than 76 lakhs. Therefore, (the Bombay Government ?) strongly press for the cancellation of the fictitious debt created in respect of unproductive irrigation works.

SIND GOVERNMENT'S VIEW

It is a matter of some disappointment to the Government of Sind that it has not been found possible in the Niemeyer Report to give assistance to Sind in the form of substantial reduction of the Barrage debt, states a communique containing the Sind Government's views on the Niemeyer Report. In the absence of any reasons in the report why this course is considered inconvenient, the Government of Sind are unable to appreciate why such an arrangement should not be given effect to, but if this be found impossible the proposals in the report are accepted subject to the following remarks: proposals both as regards the annual subvention and the repayment of the Barrage debt to depend upon the forecast of increased revenue due to the barrage proving correct. This can only happen if the normal agricultural and economic condition obtain every year during the next 45 years, but it is impossible to say that this condition will be fulfilled, in particular, the forecast assumes an increase of Rs. 19 lakhs in the revenue in 1947-48 and of increasing amounts for the next 15 years owing to the levy of increased rates of land revenue assessment. The imposition of these rates will also depend upon the then prevailing agricultural and economic conditions. The Government of Sind, therefore, presume that the door will be left open for adjustment of subvention and debt repayment in case the revenue expectations are not realised. In any such readjustment Sind must be assured the minimum revenues required for its needs as a progressive province.

BENGAL GOVERNMENT'S VIEW

The Government of Bengal accept the proposals contained in paragraph 17 of the Report in regard to the assistance to be given to certain provinces on the introduction of provincial autonomy. They regard the proposals as in the nature of an award given after determination of the amonnt immediately available for distribution among the provinces and after examination of the budgetary position of the several claimants to that amount. Looked at in this light they cannot but accept them as fair and reasonable, though they are deeply disappointed that the immediate assistance to be given to Bengal, a province in which by reason of what is now admitted to have been an unfair distribution of resources the standard of administration is admittedly low, falls far short of their orininal expectation.

As regards the proposals relating to the distribution of taxes on income the Government of Bengal while accepting the general scheme desire to raise two points.

In paragraph 30 of the report it is recommended that during the initial period the prescribed sum which centre may in any year retain out of provincial share of the proceeds of the taxes on income shall be the whole or such amount as together with any general budget receipts from the railways will bring the Central Government's share in the divisible total up to 13 crores. At present the divisible total is approximately 12 crores and the Government of Bengal suggest that this is a more appropriate figure. The adoption of this figure will fortify the argument advanced in the report in favour of creating an interest in the provinces in securing improvement in revenue from income tax and railways.

Further the Government of Bengal attach great importance to early distribution of some share in the proceeds of the taxes on income among the provinces. It was recognized on the introduction of the present constitution (vide Devolution Rule 15) that the provinces, particularly industrial provinces, were entitled to a share in the taxes on income and during the last fifteen years the industrial provinces have had a legitimate grievance since that rule failed to give relief for which it was specially designed. In justice to the industrial provinces therefore it is essential that every endeavour should be made to expedite the allocation to the provinces of some share in the proceeds of the taxes on income.

In paragraph 34 of the report the conclusion reached is that substantial justice will be done by fixing the scale of distribution partly on residence and partly on population and in paragraph 35 it is recommended that division among the provinces should be according to the percentages give therein. The same percentage of 20 per cent. is proposed both for Bengal and Bombay. If residence alone had been taken as the determining factory, there would be little difficulty in accepting the parity between Bengal and Bombay, and each would then gain at the expense of other provinces, but the Government of Bengal find it difficult to understand how parity can be justified with population as one of bases for the population of Bengal is nearly three times that of Bombay.

The calculations made with reference to the figures given in table three of paragraph 74 of the report of the Federal Finance Committee (Percy Committee) produce percentages approximately closely to those recommended by Sir Otto Niemeyer in respect of all provinces, except Bengal, Bombay and Assam. As regards Bengal and Bombay the percentages given by these calculations are somewhat below 25 for Bengal, and somewhat above 15 for Bombay. The report does not indicate if weightage has been given to Bombay, but if weightage were to be given anywhere the Government of Bengal would have expected to find it given to Bengal and not to Bombay in view of the fact that

(I) Bombay has obtained fortuitous relief to the extent of ninety lakhs from the separation of Sind and

(II) For many years Bengal has through no fault of her own been compelled to submit to an administrative standard markedly inferior to that of Bombay.

It is possible that the incidence calculated by reference to residence alone was moved in favour of Bombay since the Federal Finance Committee had reported, but in the absence of more detailed information the Government of Bengal find themselves unable to accept the proposal that Bengal and Bombay should be given the same percentage.

As regards the jute export duty the Government of Bengal must reiterate their claim that this should on principle be treated as a provincial source of revenue. The jute export duty was imposed originally as an emergency measure during the war. After the war and up to the onset of the trade depression jute commanded high prices and the ad valorem incidence of duty was low. In 1924-25 the incidence was between four and five per cent. The position, however, has now changed. The price of jute has fallen enormously whereas the deadweight of duty has remained constant and at to-day's prices the ad valorem incidence is over thirteen per cent. Again the competition by substitutes has increased, for instance, paper bags are now largely used for the transport on cement and the adoption of bull handling of grain is extending. In these changed conditions the Government of Bengal consider it unlikely that the export duty is now passed on to the consumer and in their view it is more probable that it is borne for a greater part by the producer.

The Bengal case was not, however, by any means founded entirely on the present incidence of the duty. There are other cogent arguments, though of a political rather than economic and financial nature. In the first place Bengal can never rest content with a fiscal system which aims at protecting largely at her expense as a consumer the products of other provinces, while taxing per distinctive staple product for the benefit of the Centre, in other words for the benefit of those provinces. In the second place, the prosperity of Bengal is bound up with the prosperity of the jute trade. The Royal Commission on Agriculture of 1926-28 drew attention to the risk of substitutes. They were impressed with the danger to prosperity of Bengal if jute failed to retain its present position and stressed the fact that if jute is to retain that position every effort must be made to maintain the present relative cheapness of jute as compared with other fibres. The provincial Government share to the full these views and are of opinion that it is inherently unsound that the centre which for this purpose means the non-jute producing provinces that will command a majority in the Central Legislature should be financially interested in the taxation of a product with which the prosperity of a comparatively small area is so vitally linked.

The question of export duties was examined at considerable length by the Indian Fiscal Commission and one of the principles they recommended for adoption was that in every case the export duty should be moderate in amount Whatever the actual incidence may be, it seems clear that the jute export duty to the extent that it falls on the consumer must raise the world price of jute and thus put jute at a disadvantage with its competitors.

Similarly to the extent that it falls on the producer it must reduce the price which the producer would otherwise obtain. As long as the amount of the duty is moderate it does not have an appreciable effort in either of these directions, hence the insistence of the Fiscal Commission on the principle mentioned. Now the jute export duty up to the commencement of the trade depression was moderate in its incidence, but at the present day prices it certainly transgresses that sound principle—the export duty which works out at approximately 13 per cent ad valorem cannot be described as moderate. It appears unlikely that the jute prices will return to the predepression level and the Government of Bengal are therefore of opinion that a reduction of duty must be contemplated in a not distant future.

At present financial considerations do not permit of any reduction of duty and the terms and implications of the report definitely negative the possibility of reduction in future at the expense of the provincial Governments concerned. But unless the assumptions made in the report are entirely falsified, there will be a progressive improvement at the Centre and accordingly the proposal which the Bengal Government put forward for acceptance as part of the present scheme of financial adjustment between the Centre and the provinces is that at a date not later than the end of the first five year period the rate of the duty should be reduced to a figure necessary to produce the amounts not allocated to the provinces plus any sum required for research and that simultaneously the percentage of the proceeds of the duty to be assigned to the jute-producing provinces should be increased so as to give the provinces the whole amount of net proceeds except what is retained by the Centre for research.

The Government of Bengal press most strongly for adoption of the proposal put forward in the preceding paragraph. This does not involve any modification of the orders-in-Council now to be made nor any addition to the resources which the report recommends should be given to Bengal. At the same time it recognises the position as regards the rate of duty and possesses the great political advantage of removing once for all the sense of injustice under which this province has laboured for so many years and which if not now removed will continue to the prejudice of sound administration and to the exceeding detriment of relations between the Province of Bengal and other parts of India.

ASSAM GOVERNMENT'S VIEW

The Government of Assam have examined Sir Otto Niemeyer's proposals for decentralisation of the balances. It is proposed that all debts contracted prior to the 1st April, 1936, will be cancelled and the province granted an increase in jute export duty, a share at a future date in income tax receipts, and a subvention of 30 lakhs. The Government of Assam assume that the cancellation of previous debts results in the sum provided in the current year's budget for payment of interest and capital of such debts amounting to nearly 19 lakhs being saved and the current year's deficit of 63 lakhs reduced thereby. In the interests of the new constitution this Government would request that the remainder of the current year's deficit so far as it refers to strictly provincial expenditure may also be cancelled. Beyond this point the opinions of the local Government differ to some extent. The Indian member and ministers have read the report with profound disappointment. They were looking forward to the province being made as self-sufficient as possible so that provincial autonomy may have substance. It was with that intention that the Government of Assam presented before Sir Otto in addition to the estimates of normal receipts and expenditure the estimates for such institutions as a high court, a university and medical and technical (including agricultural) schools. They now find that there is not only no room for further progress in making up the essential deficiencies, but on the contrary even on the present scale of expenditure there will still be a deficit of about 25 lakhs to be covered either by taxation or retrenchment. They consider that the economic condition of the people, the bulk of whom are agriculturists, does not permit of additional taxation. Retrenchment on the other hand would entail curtailment of the services rendered at present to the public a prospect which they are confident no ministry under the new constitution will face with equanimity.

Considering all these factors and the slender hope of an early expansion of revenues they think that an additional subvention of 25 lakhs is essentially necessary to put the province on an even keel.

The minority of the local Government though agreeing with a great part of this are not able to accept the position that a deficit of 25 lakhs is involved in the proposals and think that they are such as with some retrenchment will just enable the province to balance its income and expenditure in the opening years of the new constitution, provided that no natural calamity occurs to necessitate heavy additional expenditure. There will be of course no margin for some years to come for any expansion or improvement in the standards of administration the necessity of which has been particulary stressed in the discussions. Especially it is regretted that it will be impossible to establish a university without which the Government cannot control the educational system and an agricultural institute to explore the agricultural needs of the province. The recurring cost of these institutions was estimated at 5 and a half lakhs in papers put before Sir Otto Niemeyer.

OIRSSA GOVERNMENT'S VIEW

The following is the full text of the telegram sent by the Orissa Government to the Secretary of State for India and to the India Government on the recommendations of Niemeyer report.

"The proposals require modification on various reasons. The draft budget for 1936-37, on which the Orissa Government is now working, was originally framed after normal budget procedure and scrutiny by parent provinces and further scrutinised by the Government of India. Savings of four and a half lakhs have still to be found to make that budget balance on a basis of subvention of forty and a half lakhs granted this year without encroaching on two lakhs' opening balance. The Government cannot foresee savings of more than one lakh in place of four and a half lakhs although all proposals for the improvement of the present retrenched standard have already been cut out. Even that saving can only be found by avoiding expenditure which is either obligatory, namely ministers, and bacteriological laboratory in future years. Therefore the revenue deficit of this year, excluding subvention even on low existing post-retrenchment basis, is forty and a half plus three and half lakhs i. e., forty four lakhs. In future years expenditure will rise due to legislative Assembly and other charges which are incidental in the new Constitution.

Moreover, this year's estimate is based on the lowest pay of the time scales of all new establishment which includes the whole Headquarters establishment and will inevitably increase as the new incumbents draw increments. This year's estimates also include only eleven months' salary instead of twelve of the whole new secretariat and other headquarters staff, whereas the future budget must provide for twelve months. There will also be inevitable increases in other directions, especially in maintenance charges for buildings constructed from the capital grant and roads from the central reserve of the road fund, while the expenditure postponed this year must be eventually incurred. The province is a composite one with different methods of administration in different parts and it is difficult and undesirable to level all parts down to the lowest standard. Therefore, revenue deficit in future years, even on the existing retrenchment basis, will be little less than fifty lakhs and if subvention is limited as proposed to fifty lakhs there will hardly remain any scope for improvement of the existing standard.

In particular, there will be no prospect for many years of improving education, agriculture and health services or of establishing a University. At present Orissa depends on two Universities with little voice in either. Scope for revenue expansion as Sir Otto Neimeyer says, is unusually limited. Two-thirds of the province are partially excluded areas and half of the province is more backward than any part of India except excluded areas. Orissa's special problems of floods and retrenchment of recent years has prevented even poorer maintenance of vital protective works, not to speak of the adoption of any measures recommended by the 1928 Flood Expert Committee. Even with the additional fifty lakhs now proposed, the provision for buildings necessitated by separation is still inadequate since the provincial headquarters, one district head-quarter and two sub-provincial head-quarters have to be built up besides the Central Jail and other necessary buildings. The opening balance of two lakhs given this year will have disappeared by the end of the year. No margin will be left for unforeseen expenditure capital or otherwise or for the working balance. Once it is admitted that certain provinces and centrally administered areas must receive help from Indian revenues, it is fair to aim at some common standard for those areas. But the proposals involve great disparity in treatment among the assisted units, giving to Orissa a subvention far less per head of the population than other units who have already a far higher standard of expenditure per head.

BIHAR GOVERNMENT'S VIEW

The following are the views of Bihar Government on Niemeyer Report contained in their Telegram to the Secretary of State :—

Paragraph 17—In paragraph II, Niemeyer Report admits as past Committees have admitted that Bihar and Orissa is the poorest province in India. Bihar itself has an extremley dense population. It contributes largely to the wealth of India from its minerals and agriculture but derives no financial advantage as it is not permitted to tax the minerals and is under the disability attaching to no other Provinces except Bengal owing to Permanent Settlement making any increase in land revenue impossible. The existence of mining and industrial areas is consequently an extra financial burden.

Local Government urge strongly that the figure of 45 lakhs askod for by them is the minimum immediate requirements as a grant-in-aid. This figure is fully justified by financial history of the Province which has been starved since it came into existence in 1912 and has had perforce to maintain a lower standard of administration than any other Province of India, which standard has been recently lowered by the policy of retrenchment which has been followed. While 25 lakhs will allow some increase over .expenditure in 1936-37 budget provided excise receipts remain stable, this figure takes insufficient account of the factor mentioned above. Assistance proposed is therefore inadequate to start the Province on an even keel as proposed in paragraph 9.

Paragraphs 19 to 21—Bihar debt contracted before 1st April 1936 outstanding on 1st April 1937 will amount to 471 lakhs, of this sum 341 lakhs is pre-reform undated debt carrying interest at the rate of 3 and half per cent, the balance of 130 lakhs is dated repayable in years between 1941 and 1966 of which 30 lakhc is bearing interest varying between 4 and half and 5 and half and balance at 3 and three-fourth or less. If debt were consolidated as Appendix III repayable in 45 years, interest should not exceed 3 and three-fourth per cent. giving an annual instalment of about

21 and three-fourth lakhs. If the debt were not consolidated, the annual budget saving resulting from concellation of debt would for a few years slightly exceed this figure but would rapidly decrease as loans are rapid and would drop to 12 lakhs in 1956. Not more than 22 lakhs should therefore be taken as maximum annual recurring budget benefit resulting from debt cancellation.

In these circumstances local Government assumed that figure of 22 lakhs in paragraph 21 implied that in case of Bihar no part of decentralised balances would be set off against debt cancellation and the whole of decentralised balances of about 3 crores would be available to local Government for ways and means and for utilisation to secure funds for payment of the new liability for the Provinces after decentralisation of balances, viz., interest of 6 and half lakhs on Provident Funds, which sum is approximately all that can be realised by investment of the balance after providing for ways and means.

The Government of India have, however, advised in response to reference that assumption is incorrect and that Bihar will receive only a single sum of 21 lakhs out of its provincial balances under the scheme of decentralisation, implying that rest of provincial balance will be retained by Government of India as a set off to debt cancellation.

If the Government of India's view is correct, Bihar will not only have to find 6 and half lakhs a year to meet interest on Provident Fund but will be deprived of capital by investment of which this sum might have been produced. Local Government claim that on this theory the benefits which it is intended they should receive will be reduced not only by 6 and half lakhs but by the annual value of the balance of 280 lakhs which will be appropriated by the Government of India. This figure they put at 10 and half lakhs that being the sum by payment of which a debt of 280 lakhs can be repaid in 45 years at 2 and half per cent. The approximate net annual budget saving resulting from debt cancellation is, therefore, if the Government of India's view is correct, reduced to 11 and half lakhs in place of 22 lakhs referred to in paragraph 21.

Local Government cannot believe that Government of India's interpretation is correct in the case of Bihar as on that interpretation the special assistance for Bihar becomes largely fictitious and local Government are convinced that Niemeyer recommendation for net improvement of Bihar finances was intended to be the equivalent of a genuine grant-in-aid of 25 lakhs and this at least the local Government claim should be given without any reduction of decentralised balances. To sum up on Government of India's interpretation the Niemeyer recommendation would only benefit Bihar to the extent of 11 and a half lakhs plus 2 and a half from jute tax in place of 25 lakhs which Sir Otto found necessary in the first instance and to reach Niemeyer figure of requisite assistance from debt cancellation and extra share in jute tax would have to be supplemented by a grant-in-aid of 10 and a half lakhs.

Local Government are more convinced of their interpretation of the intention because under the present proposals they are being deprived of an advantage which will accrue on decentralisation of balances to other provinces which are not held to be in need of immediate assistance. By the method proposed in Appendix III for consolidation of debt, Madras is shown as befitting to the extent of twenty-six lakhs and Bombay to the extent of fourteen and a half which benefit is lost by provinces whose debts are cancelled by paragraph 21. In fact if the assignment of 45 lakhs claimed by Bihar cannot be given local Government urge that in addition to 25 lakhs grant-in-aid they should be allowed in some way to share the advantage given to provinces on liquidation of their debts against outstanding balances.

Paragraph 35—Local Government's claim was that the basis of distribution should be wholly that of population and they still consider that as the distribution of income-tax is a balancing factor to equalise the opportunities of various provinces, a distribution entirely on this basis would be fair. They would therefore press for an increase to 12 in the percentage allotted to Bihar to compensate in future for past financial starvation of Bihar.

INDIAN COMMERCE CHAMBER'S VIEW

The Secretary, Indian Chamber of Commerce, Calcutta sent the following to the Secretary to the Government of India, Finance Department :—

I am directed by the Committee of the Indian Chamber of Commerce, Calcutta, to address you on the Indian Financial Enquiry Report submitted by Sir Otto

Neimeyer. The Committee have carefully considered the Report and have to make the following observations.

Sir Otto Niemeyer states in paragraph 3 of the Report that "from the Central point of view, it is clear that the financial stability and credit of India as a whole must remain the paramount consideration." While the Committee did not wish to object to this statement of the position, they desire to point out that the needs and requirements of the Central Government are comparatively limited whereas the functions of the Provinces are capable of indefinite expansion. Most of the services which are socially and economically beneficent to the people of the country are provincial in character, e. g. education, public health, agriculture and industries.

The Committee would, in this connection, recall the observations of Sir Walton Layton in his report on Indian finance embodied in the report of the Indian Statutory Commission presided over by Sir John Simon. Sir Walter Layton stated that "in time of peace military budget should be a stationary or diminishing burden and not an increasing one. National enterprises such as the Post Office and the Railways should feed and not be a charge upon the Central Exchequer ; and while the functions of the Central Government in Civil administration may be expected to grow, the expenditure involved is a very small affair indeed, compared with that required for a nation-wide development of education, for the improvement of public health and sanitation, for the services charged with the great task of increasing the economic productivity of India and many other functions which have been definitely placed within the sphere of the Provinces."

The Committee wish to emphasise this aspect of the question which should always be recognised in determining the financial relations between the Central and Provincial Governments in India. Moreover, it is well-known that Provincial sources of revenue are comparatively inelastic while an examination of the new sources of revenue by the Federal Finance Committee presided over by Lord Percy showed that the prospects of increase in the direction also were not encouraging.

It has been the considered view not only of Indian commercial bodies and Indian non-officials but of impartial committees and experts that India is incurring expenditure on the primary functions of Government such as defence and maintenance of law and order which is as high in proportion to her wealth as Western nations, while her expenditure on social services such as education, sanitation, industrial and agricultural improvement, etc., is far behind Western standards and is in many directions almost non-existent. If, therefore, the standard of life of the people as a whole is to be raised, the paramount importance of Provincial finance cannot be ignored.

The present allocation of resources between the Central and Provincial Governments has evoked strong criticism of every expert enquiry from that of Sir Walter Layton to the Percy Federal Finance Committee. The Joint Parliamentary Committee after reviewing such criticisms, stated in paragraph 245 that "from the point of view of expenditure, the essentials of the position are that the Provinces have an almost inexhaustible field for the development of social services while the demands upon the Centre, except in time of war or acute Frontier trouble, are almost constant in character. The Provinces rarely have the means adequate for a full development of their social needs. The resources of the Centre comprise those which should prove most capable of expansion in a period of normal progress." It is also essential to emphasise that the advent of the Indian States into Federal Government would render difficult any subsequent reallocation of fiscal resources and readjustment of financial relationship between the Centre and the Provinces or States.

The Committee also desire to draw attention to some large assumptions made by Sir Otto Niemeyer. which cannot be accepted by Indian public opinion and Indian commercial bodies. For instance, Sir Otto observes that "expenditure at the Centre cannot be expected, consistently with safety, to decrease much below the point to which it has now been reduced." The Committee cannot possibly agree to this proposition in regard to Central expenditure. For example, there is unanimity of opinion on the question that the current expenditure on defence is an unduly heavy item. Sir Walter Layton in his report on Indian Finance, referred to before, observes that the expenditure on defence in India bears to the total expenditure of the Central Government a higher proportion than in any other country of the world and that since the high "defence ratio" in Indian Government expenditure is partly due to the low level of other expenditure, "it remains a peculiarly burdensome one."

Sir Walter Layton also mentions that "a recent comparison of the military expenditure of the nations of the world shows that in this respect India is 7th in the list among the great Powers and that her expenditure on armaments is between two or three times as great as that of the whole of the rest of the Empire outside Great Britain. Again, the total is not only high in itself and as compared with other countries, but it has also greatly increased as compared with the pre-war situation."

But even apart from military expenditure, however, there is no doubt that the cost of general administation is high owing to the level of salaries which bears no proportion to the ability of the tax-payer. The Percy Committee also drew attention to the opinion widely held in India that the cost of Government already exceeds what can properly be borne by a predominantly agricultural country and Sir Walter Layton too recognised the justice of this common complaint about the cost of general administration.

There is no doubt that the entire expenditure of the Government, both Central and Provincial, including the scales of salaries, allowances, etc., needs to be readjusted on the basis of reduced price levels, depressed trade and shrinking revenues. Even apart from world conditions, the hard facts of Indian economy and low average income demand a far less costly administration. The main difficulty in regard to public finance in India arises from the fact that while the expenditure on primary and unproductive functions has been established at an unduly high level, the constructive services are thereby starved unless the people are prepared to tax themselves further even in order to maintain such services.

The Committee need hardly point out that under the New Constitution, nearly 80 per cent. of the Central revenues have been mortgaged to the maintenance of military and civil establishments and cannot be touched by the future Federal Legislature. Even railway expenditure will, after the establishment of the Statutory Railway Board, be outside the control of the Federal Legislature. The Committee can hardly feel enthusiastic about the recommendation of a Report whose underlying assumption is that the present exorbitantly high scale of Central expenditure cannot be reduced with the logical corollary that taxation also cannot be reduced. The Central budget has been balanced during the last few years only by making emergency taxation permanent and the credit of the Government and the surplus in the Central budget are hardly reflected in any improvement in the economic condition of the masses.

The Committee regret to point out that no co-ordinated plan of Federal Finance underlies the recommendations of Sir Otto Niemeyer, which are frankly formulated with a desire to placate and accommodate different interests and rival claimants according to their respective political "pull." The Committee are aware that the problem of financial adjustments between the Centre and the Provinces is a very complex and difficult one and has hitherto been dealt with in a somewhat haphazard manner by more than one Committee and expert in the past. It was, therefore, expected that Sir Otto Niemeyer would at least view the problem as a whole and deal with it in a comprehensive manner after determining the needs and capacities of different Provinces.

The Committee would now pass on to Sir Otto Niemeyer's recommendations about Bengal. The Committee are glad to observe that Sir Otto acknowledges that "Bengal is clearly on a low standard" so far as its standard of administration is concerned. He has, therefore, recommended the grant of relief to Bengal as under :—

		Lakhs. Per Annum.
Cancellation of debts leading to an annual saving of	...	Rs. 33
Allocation of additional 12 and half per cent jute export duty, yielding	...	" 42
Total	...	Rs. 75

Although these recommendations constitute some improvement on the inequitable Meston Settlement, the Committee regret to observe that full justice has not been done to the claims of Bengal and the unanimous demand of its public have not been adequately met. The Committee see no reason why the Government should not allot the balance of 37 and a half per cent of the jute export duty also to the Provincial Governments. While the general principles enunciated by Sir Otto Niemeyer in paragraph 22 of his Report might be valid, it is essential to point out that they have little application to the peculiar conditions of Bengal. Since Bengal's economy is directly dependent upon the production trade and manufacture of jute, any revenue derived from this commodity is an integral part of Provincial finance and should, in equality, be assigned to the Province itself. The conditions in this case are rather exceptional owing to jute being a monopoly of this Province.

Moreover, although the duty might and does require revision and reduction both in the interests of jute growers and jute manufacturers, the question cannot receive impartial consideration from the Central Government which would be mainly interested in realising revenue from the yield of such a duty. It is, therefore, essential that the Province which has a primary financial interest in jute, should be allotted the entire proceeds of the duty. The low revenue of Bengal as well as Bihar and Orissa in proportion to their population was also pointedly mentioned in Sir Walter Layton's Report and the public finance of this Province must not be deprived of the yield of a duty whose incidence is almost wholly borne by its people.

The Committee would next refer to the distribution of Income-tax. Before coming to this question, however, the Committee would record their strong protest against the observations of Sir Otto Niemeyer in regard to the stabilisation of the present surcharges on Income-tax and Super-tax. The Committee have to point out that these observations are in the nature of "obiter dicta" and do not constitute in any way a part of the Report nor are the recommendations based upon these remarks. Without going into the larger question of reform in the present system of taxation in the country, the Committee would point out that the Government are definitely committed to the removal of these surcharges which were levied owing to an emergency and were of a purely temporary nature. The Committee trust that the Government will not take advantage of the general observations in Sir Otto Niemeyer's Report to perpetuate these surcharges since it would be a breach of the undertaking given by the Government in regard to the removal of these surcharges.

The other general observation of Sir Otto Niemeyer relates to the problem of railway finance. In his Report Sir Otto has made the assignment of Income-tax to the Provinces dependent upon improvement in the condition of railway finance. Despite past investigations into the various aspects of this problem, the condition of railway finance is causing serious anxiety and requires immediate and substantial efforts to improve it effectively. The Committee trust that railway expenditure would be completely overhauled and economy effected in all possible directions along with efforts to attract traffic. In this connection the Committee would suggest that the losses on the strategic railways should be charged to the military budget and all waste and extravagance in the railway administration should be prevented. Efforts should also be made to attract traffic and enhance revenue by co-ordination with other means of transport.

As regards the distribution of taxes on income as between the Federation and Provinces as well as between the various Provinces 'inter se,' the Committee have to express disappointment at the recommendations in the Report. As regards the manner of distribution, the Committee cannot help observing that in trying to avoid rigid pendantry, Sir Otto Niemeyer has applied a mere rule-of-thumb method which is obviously hapazard. Sir Walter Layton in enunciating the general principles of financial relations stated that the only simple, intelligible and equitable basis of distribution of centrally collected taxes in accordance with the needs of the various Provinces is that of population. This basis has precedents in several Federations including those within the British Empire. The application of the rough-and-ready compromise made by Sir Otto Niemeyer between the principle of residence has been particularly unfortunate so far as Bengal is concerned. For while the Percy Committee recommended for allocation to Bengal the amount of Rs. 405 lakhs out of a total amount of Rs. 1,350 lakhs available for distribution to the Provinces, i. e. 30 per cent of the total amount, Sir Otto Niemeyer recommends the allocation of only 20 per cent to the Province of Bengal. Even taking into account the net total yield of Income-tax which was envisaged by the Percy Committee at Rs. 1,720 lakhs, the share of Bengal comes to about 24 per cent.

The Committee of the Chamber also desire to point out that while the percentage recommended in Sir Otto Niemeyer's Report for transfer to the provinces is the percentage ratio of only 50 per cent of the net yield of Rs. 6 crores only at the present figure, the percentage recommended by the Percy Report is the percentage of the total net yield of Income-tax, as shown above. Thus in addition to having been severely handicapped along with the other Provinces by Sir Otto Niemeyer's recommendations in regard to the distribution of Income-tax only to the extent of 50 per cent of the net yield. Bengal has been further hit adversely even as regards the allocation of the percentage of this 50 per cent to her.

So far as Bengal is concerned, therefore, the Committee think that the financial relief recommended in Sir Otto Niemeyer's Report would not enable her to expand her social services or pursue a constructive programme of national welfare and they trust that the question of the allocations of the whole of the jute export duty as well as the question of assignment of a really fair share of income-tax revenue would receive the favourable consideration of the Government of India and the Secretary of State before orders on this subject are finally placed on the table of the House of Parliament.

U. P. COMMERCE CHAMBER'S VIEW

The Committee of the United Provinces Chamber of Commerce addressed the following letter to the Secretary to Government of India, Finance Department, Simla, commenting on the report of Sir Otto Niemeyer that the maintenance of the stablility at the Centre should be the main criterion in any financial adjustments between the Centre and the Provinces. They are seriously disappointed to note that Sir Otto considers the present expenditure at the Centre as an irreducible minimum. The Committee have no doubt whatsoever that unless expenditure at the Centre and specially under the heads Army and Home Charges is reduced, the various provinces will never be able to develop the nation-building departments and the condition of the masses would remain as deplorable as it is to-day. The various enquiries which have been held during the past few years into the financial position of the Government have been merely patch-works without even an attempt to touch the main problem, and the enquiries of Sir Otto are no exception. The Committee think that his recommendations are mere palliatives designed to make somehow a start with the plan of the so-called Provincial Autonomy.

"In order to maintain the present expensive machinery at the Centre and possibly to find out additional means for the upkeep of the expensive future Federal Government, Sir Otto has suggested that the rates of income-tax and super-tax in India specially on the higher incomes are by no means excessive. In his opinion the general scheme of Indian taxation (Central and Provincial) operates to relieve the wealthier commercial classes to an extent which is unusual in taxation schemes, and there would be no justifiable ground of complaint if a slight correction of that anomaly were maintained. Although this view of Sir Otto is not apart of his recommendations, still it is likely to pre-judicially affect the interest of commercial classes. The Committee of the Chamber do not agree with the views of Sir Otto that the scheme of Indian taxation operates to relieve the wealthier commerial classes. In their opinion the commercial classes are made to contribute more than they can really afford to. The present surcharges on income and super-tax were imposed at a time when the economic depression was at its height, and it will be nothing less than a breach of faith if the Central Government agrees with the views of Sir Otto and tries to perpetuate the remaining surcharges, when the cut of service has been restored long ago. In order that the views of Sir Otto Niemeyer in this connection may not be taken for granted, the Committee strongly suggest that the present scheme of taxation in the country in general and the commercial classes in particular should be examined without further delay.

"With regard to the financial position of the Railways, the Committee are glad to note that Sir Otto has also taken a serious view of the position. The Chamber along with many important commercial bodies in the country has for a very long time been stressing the necessity for the co-ordination of the various forms of transport and the curtailment of heavy railway expenditure but without any result. The Committee are therefore strongly of the opinion that in the interest of the tax-payer, the existing position of Railway expenditure should be immediately examined, by an expert Committee with a majority of non-official members from the Legislature and the public life of the country. The Committee think that unless the position of the Railways is examined and waste is stopped the condition of the Central Budget can never be improved and the Railways may once again become a drain on the public purse.

"The Committee welcome the decentralisation and consolidation of debt charges and the annual subvention of Rupees 25 lakhs for five years granted to the United Provinces, but they are disappointed to find that the United Provinces has been recommended only 15 per cent share in the residue of income-tax whereas, other deficit provinces e. g., Bengal have been granted a bigger share in income-tax residue in addition to the Jute Tax. The committee hope that the Central Government would press for adequate relief to the United Provinces Government in the matter, and thereby enable it to keep up the higher standard of work in various department".

ORISSA COMMERCE CHAMBER'S VIEW

The Orissa Chamber of Commerce considered the recommendations of Sir Otto Niemeyer in regard to the subvention to Orissa and issued a statement in the course of which it regards to observe that Sir Otto did overlook the responsibilities devolved on the Governor to administer the partially excluded area in Orissa, a permanent deficit area, being 60 per cent of the total area of Orissa and incurring even now a deficit of Rs. 28 lakhs on the present low standard of administration.

'Thus', the statement continues, 'neither the Orissa Legislative Assembly is left with any expanding revenue to spend on nation-building departments nor the Governor is left with the option to draw any appreciable sum from the general receipt of Orissa to develop these partially excluded areas. On the other hand, any strict interpretation of his responsibilities, by the Governor, will create undesirable and constant friction between him and the legislature'.

The Chamber strongly disapproves 'the arbitrary and pedantic system of distribution of income-taxes to the provinces as suggested, and recommends that it should be on a purely population basis and apprehends "undesirable bickerings and complications when the Federal Legislature will distribute Federal excises to the provinces", if the system of distribution be accepted.

The Chamber in conclusion feels that the recommendations of Sir Otto Niemeyer in regard to the help from the centre is inadequate and condemns Orissa adequate subvention so as to ensure reasonable 'per capita' expenditure in the province to raise Orissa's economic and trade prosperity and provide reasonable minimum expansion to the particular excluded areas.

The U. P. Unemployment Committee Report

(SAPRU COMMITTEE REPORT)

The following is a summary of the main conclusions and recommendations of the U. P. Unemployment Committee, as given in the report itself and published in January 1936 :—

Civil Engineers

Unemployment amongst civil engineers has increased since the stoppage of recruitment to the Buildings and Roads Branch and has become much more acute since the stoppage of recruitment in the Irrigation Branch consequent on the financial depression since 1931. It is recommended—

(1) that the policy adopted in connection with Buildings and Roads in 1922 should be reconsidered and revised to secure adequate supervision to all Government buildings and roads ;

(2) that stringent rules and regulations should be laid down to make it compulsory for Municipal and District Boards to have qualified engineers and overseers to maintain the roads and buildings under their control in efficient condition :

(3) that in order to secure reliability and efficiency of execution of contract work it should be ruled that A and B class contractors must have qualified engineers as employers or partners and all C class contractors should similarly have overseers as partners or employers ;

(4) That to secure compliance with these recommendations the existing laws and rules may be amended, if necessary.

Mechanical and Electrical Engineers

Some arrangements should be made for affording opportunities to Mechanical and Electrical Engineering students for receiving practical training. For instance, while placing Government orders with firms it may be stipulated that subject to other terms and prices being the same, preference will be given to firms that will afford facilities for practical training of Indian engineers recommended by Government.

Graduates in Mining and Metallurgy

(1) The students trained at the Engineering College, Benares, have, hitherto, generally, been successful in securing employment somewhere or other in India ;

(2) There is scope, both in British India and in the Indian states, particularly in those where there are mines, for the employment of men, trained in mining and metallurgy, but unfortunately, young men belonging to the United Provinces have hitherto been slow in availing themselves of the educational facilities offered by that University ;

(3) It is necessary that some well-thought-out system for imparting such practical training to civil, mechanical and electrical engineers should be provided, and this may necessitate some consultation with, and co-operation on the part of some departments of the Government, factories and the big industries, in these provinces, and possibly outside. The preparation of such a scheme should be left to experts. Steps may also be taken to prepare a scheme to complete the practical side of the education of mechanical and electrical engineers so that they be fit for immediate employment by the Government and industrial concerns.

Chemist

While graduates in chemistry succeed more than others in getting employment they are not always fairly treated by their employers. The employers not unoften break their contracts with their employees. The remedy for these trained scientific employees is to organize themselves to enable them to deal effectively with unsatisfactory and unsympathetic employers.

Products of the Technological Institute

No recommendations regarding the products of the Technological Institute can be made, as the percentage of employment among them is high and very satisfactory.

BACHELORS OF COMMERCE

(1) The B. Com.'s of the Allahabad and Lucknow Universities have been particularly fortunate but this good luck has not attended the careers of those who have taken degrees in Commerce from the other provincial universities. The utility of the B. Com.'s is considerably discounted partly because of prejudice among Indian businessmen and partly because—and seems to us to be true—that their education is almost theoretical and does not fit in with what is required by commercial houses or business offices.

(2) All universities, which provide for instruction in the Bachelor of Commerce course, should make arrangements for some practical training being given to their B. Com. students, in consultation with the possible employers of such men, so that they may have some idea of work done in commercial houses or those departments of Government, where there may be scope for their employment.

MEDICINE

(1) There is a considerable amount of unemployment prevailing in the medical profession in these provinces due to the tendency of the medical practitioners to congregate in big towns and cities where the remuneration is higher than in the rural areas though precise figures are not available ;

(2) The system of medical relief in hospitals, maintained by Government or district boards or municipal boards, requires organisation and the strengthening of the staffs employed ;

(3) It is necessary that medical men should be persuaded to settle down in rural areas in large numbers and for this purpose, it is necessary to subsidize them on more generous scale than has hitherto been done ;

(4) Investigation should be made into the efficacy of the indigenous drugs according to the modern methods and after the recognition of such medicines by the medical profession and their standardization, industries for the manufacture of such and other drugs should be started, and, if necessary, subsidized at the initial stages. If this is done, it should provide employment for a sufficiently large number of qualified medical men ;

(5) There is room for the complaint that the system under which a single man is appointed to treat patients, for all sorts of diseases, cannot be treated as a very modern or an up-to-date system. The attachment of private practitioners to hospitals, maintained by Government or local boards, should be encouraged so as to give the private practitioners a chance of becoming more efficient.

PUBLIC HEALTH

(1) This department can provide scope for the employment of a fairly large number of educated men ;

(2) Posts of assistant superintendents of vaccination, which have, hitherto, been given to men who are not even Matriculates, should in future be given to men who possess some medical or scientific knowledge ;

(3) The number of medical officers employed in municipalities, admits of an increase and such municipalities as have not got medical officers of health of their own, should be asked to employ qualified men ;

(4) New schemes of sanitary improvement, both in the towns and the villages should be taken in hand, and qualified medical men, possessing some diploma or degree in Public Health, should be employed by district boards ;

(5) That more adequate provision should be made for medical inspection and treatment of school-going children in the province and for that purpose the strength of the medical staff should be increased ;

(6) If the district boards have not got sufficient funds to employ qualified medical officers, they should be helped, as far as possible, by Government with financial assistance, unless, by a re-arrangement of their budget, or by fresh taxation specially for this purpose, it is possible for the district boards to find the necessary funds.

SUBSIDIARY BRANCHES OF MEDICINE

(1) The system which has been in vogue, in these provinces, since January, 1928 for the training of compounders, appears to be wholly inadequate, and falls short of the standards suggested in Colonel Chopra's report ;

(2) Provision should be made for the training of men in pharmacy, and the necessary qualifications should be prescribed by the rules and regulations, for those,

who may seek suc h education, and after an examination, held by a duly constituted authority, the successful candidates should be granted a diploma ;

(3) In future, Government should employ exclusively, in their hospitals and dispensaries, such qualified men as pharmacists ;

(4) Suitable legislation should be passed, organizing this profession, examination, and the grant of diploma, and penalizing the employment by private agencies of unqualified men.

DENTISTRY

A school of dentistry should be established at King George's Medical College, Lucnow, and suitable legislation, modelled on the English Act of 1921, should be passed, prohibiting, in future, the practice of dentistry by persons, other than those on the dentists' register, kept by the Dental Board of these provinces, to be created by that Act.

LAW

(1) The legal profession, in these provinces, is far too crowded, with the consequence that there is a great deal of unemployment in it. It is, and out to be, a very honourable profession ; bnt it has lost a great deal of prestige, in these provinces, and, unless some measures are taken to recognise the profession, we are afraid that in a few years' time, tho conditions of the profession will be even worse.

(1) Lawyers practising in these provinces should be divided, at their option, into two classes, viz.

(a) those, who will restrict themselves, exclusively, to the proper function of a counsel, that is to say, who will appear, in courts of law, to examine witnesses, to argue cases, and to do all other work, which properly falls within the province of a counsel ;

(b) those, who will apply themselves, exclusively, to the drafting of legal documents, and doing all such other acts, as may be necessary, for the completion of a legal transaction, or the progress of a law suit or a legal proceeding in a court of law. In their case partnerships should not only be allowed but encouraged.

(2) A member of one class should not be allowed to encroach upon the province of the other, though it should be open to a member, who merely 'acts' to consult a person performing the function of a counsel.

(3) Arrangements should be made, by the universities and the Bar Council, for giving training to law students at the various universities, in conveyancing, drafting and pleadings.

(4) Legislation should be passed, in order to guard against the evils resulting from the employment of unqualified draftsman, and also to protect trained lawyers doing the work of draftsmanship. It is necessary that there should be some legislation, providing that no petition or application by a litigant, which he intends to present to a court of law, shall be drawn up, for him, by anyone, except a qualified lawyer ; and, further, that a registrable document shall not be received, for registration, by the Registration department, unless, on the face of it, it bears the certificate of a qualified lawyer that it has been drafted by him on instructions received from the executant, an exception being provided in the case of a testamentary document, which a person writes in his own hand, or where such a document is written, for him and at his instance, by any person, other than a qualified lawyer undercircumstances, in which it could not be written of drawn up by a qualified lawyer or draftsman.

(5) While a student may attend the chambers of a practising lawyer during the course of his studies, or even after taking his law degree, if that is considered to be necessary, the old rule which required, in the case of a vakil, that he should have put in some years of practice in a district court, before he applied for permission to practice at the High Court, should be restored.

(6) A senior bar should be created and there should be the institution of King's Counsel, which prevails not only in Self-Governing Dominions, but also in some of the Crown colonies, provided, of course, that those who shall accept the higher status, shall also accept all the obligations, which are accepted by King's Counsel in England.

(1) (a) The subject of legal education at the universities must receive greater attention than it has hitherto done, provision being made for adequate instruction in subjects, which have hitherto not received due attention.

(b) A Council of Legal education should be created consisting of the representatives of :—

(i) the teachers of Law and Civics;
(ii) some eminent lawyers whose function must be to promote higher legal education; (iii) some judges.

(2) The course of study for a Law degree should not be less than three years;

(3) There must be liaison established between the Faculty of Law and the Bar Council, and the work of teaching should be divided between the two;

(4) A larger number of teachers, more adequately paid than they are, at present, should be employed for legal education;

(5) Concerted action must be taken, by all the universities in these provinces; and

(6) If the lengthening of the course of study should affect the candidates for judicial service adversely, in respect of the age qualification, the rules should accordingly be changed.

Other Professions

(1) There is great need for creating and developing some new professions, so as to provide new careers for our young men.

(2) Apart from such professions, as pharmacy and dentistry, professions, such as accountancy, architecture, librarianship, insurance work, secretariat work, and journalism, can be, and should be created in these provinces. Instruction in accountancy, and insurance work, and secretariat work, should be provided for by the universities, along with, or in addition to, the course prescribed for the B. Com. Examination. They should institute separate diplomas in all these subjects. Possibly, some of the subjects could be taught, at an earliar stage, in the secondary schools or the intermediate colleges.

(3) The universities should arrange for a course of instruction in journalism and librarianship and should institute diplomas in these subjects.

(4) We think the very meagre instruction in architecture now given at Roorkee should be expanded into a separate diploma class in architecture, branching off from the main civil engineering class after the first year. We recommend this because the subject of architecture has considerable kinship with the subject of civil engineering for which the Roorkee College is the best institution in this country.

Government Service

(1) There are certain departments, which are admittedly overworked, and there are certain others, such as United Provinces Service of Engineers, class (ii), irrigation, Hydro-electric branch, which are waiting for development.

(2) There are other departments, such as Public Health, which are said to be overworked and there are certain other departments like Medical, in which recruitment, though, not wholly stopped, has been restricted. Apart from the fact that such restriction has caused unemployment, it has also affected the efficiency of these departments.

(3) A considerable amount of unemployment must be attributed to the retrenchment of about 2,000 to 3,000 employees, in the Settlement department.

(4) The United Provinces Civil Judicial Service appears to be particularly overworked, and in the interest of efficiency, and to avoid delays in disposing of judicial work, the strength of the cadre of the judicial service, and the staffs of civil courts, should be increased.

(5) It is impossible to make any definite recommendations, as to the restorations of posts in certain departments, or the new posts to be added as this is a matter for separate departmental inquiries but;

(a) Government should take in hand, either directly or through small departmental committees, the question of restoration of posts, which have been retrenched, or the addition of such posts as may be necessary, having regard to the nature of work in each department, and the arrears that there may be in it. Probably, such restoration could not take place, all at once, but there must be a graduated scheme of restoration, and plans for such development should be prepared by the departments concerned.

(b) Except in regard to those appointments, for which university education is necessary or useful, own standards for subordinate services and recruit new men, either through competitive examination, or by selection, according to the needs of each department.

(c) In regard to the subordinate services, which attract by far the largest number of our young men, the age-limit for entrance should be reduced. This will prevent a great deal of wastage at the universities, by enabling young men, after the completion of their secondary school education, to enter life, without the necessity of possessing university degrees.

(d) The Public Service Commission, which has been recommended under the new constitution for the provinces. should be created at an early date, and in future, the conduct of competitive examinations, and generally, the recruitment of candidates for such appointments, should be placed in the hands of Public Service Commission.

(e) There must be a Local Self-Government service created, and appointments, which are, at the present moment, made by municipal and district boards, and in regard to which there is very unhealthy canvassing, should, in future, be filled up, out of a waiting list of candidates, maintained by the Ministry of Local Government. When a board, municipal or district, desires to fill up a certain appointment, it must apply to the Ministry concerned, and the Ministry concerned, may, in the case of each appointment suggest three names, out of which the board may select any. Rules and regulations with regard to such service, employments, security of tenure, promotions, etc., should be framed, and in the event of dismissal, a member of such service should have a right of appeal to the Ministry of Self-Government, or the Public Service Commission.

(f) The rules, regarding the age of retirement, should be rigorously enforced, and with a view to give a fair chance to young men, no extension should be granted, to any public servant, after he has completed the 55th year of his age.

(g) Men, who have retired from Government service, should not be employed by local bodies, if and when, young men, possessing the necessary qualifications, are available for such appointments.

Agriculture—Agricultural Institutes and their Products

(1) There is appreciable unemployment among the students who have received training at the Agricultural College, Cawnpore, and such men do not appear to have been employed, in any appreciable numbers, by big zamindars, in these provinces.

(2) There is justification, for the complaint, that the education, which is given to the students of the Agricultural College, and also at the agricultural schools, is more theoretical than practical. Steps should be taken, to provide for some practical training in agricultural institutes, and where it is possible, they should be attached, for a certain period of time, to Government farms, or *zamindaris*, to enable them to acquire some practical knowledge of the working of agricultural operations, and the institution of *zamindari*. At the end of the practical training such students should receive a certificate of their fitness as practical farmers from some competent authority which may be prescribed by the Ministry of Agriculture.

(3) It is desirable that graduates and the diploma holders of the Government colleges and schools should be encouraged to follow scientific farming within the provinces as a means of earning their living and recruitment for Government service in the department should be made from among those graduates and diploma holders who have done practical farming for a certain number of years. In the case of such men the rules relating to age for recruitment should be amended accordingly. Further it is necessary, to strengthen the Government Agricultural department by the addition of its staff of scientifically trained farmers with practical experience.

Agriculture as a Profession

(1) It is extremely doubtful whether the schemes of colonization, which have been taken in hand, will make any appeal, to that section of the educated classes, which has no connection with land, though, it is likely, that such schemes may be helpful in removing unemployment, in the case of those among the educated classes, who belong to the agricultural community, or who have no connections with village life, or who have imbibed, in their early life, some agricultural tradition.

(2) It is very doubtful as to whether subsidiary industries, such as fruit-growing, dairy-farming, market gardening, floriculture, sericulture, poultry-farming, canning, pisciculture spinning and weaving, carpet-making, clay-modelling, roap-making, pottery, cattle-breeding, will attract a large number of our educated men, unless they are adequately trained and financed, or subsidized for such industries, though several of these industries, can be, and should be, developed, with advantage to the country.

(3) The development of dairy-farming is a possible avenue of progress provided, the law, relating to the adulteration of food-supplies is stiffened, and an adequate knowledge of the subject and funds are available, and the public are prepared to pay for unadulterated milk and products.

(4) There is scope, for the employment of educated men, as farm managers, and as estate managers, provided, proper training is given to young men, and arrangements

made for giving them opportunties, to acquire practical knowledge of these subjects. In this matter, it is necessary that the point of view, of the big zamindars, should also undergo a change.

(5) The provincial Government should press the Central Government to take steps to inaugurate some policy which will raise the price level of agricultural products in the country. *Vide* Mr. Mr. T. Gavin Jones' note on page 243 of this report which we commend to the careful consideration of the Government.

INDUSTRIES

(1) To supplement the result of the industrial survey made in the years 1921-22 and in view of the altered situation a detailed industrial and economic survey, of these provinces, should be made, with a view to find out what industries, big or small, can be developed.

(2) Industrial research workshops should be established, and, if possible, they should be located at different university centres, where there are good science laboratories, or at important industrial centres.

(3) The grid system under the control of Sir William Stampe, which has already found employment for a number of educated men, should be further developed and cheap electricity should be supplied, for the development of big industries, as can be run more effectively and cheaply, by the use of power.

(4) So far as small industries, in these provinces, are concerned, a special official should be deputed to Bengal, to study the working of the Bengal scheme, referred to, in our report; and, subject to adaptations to local needs and conditions, a scheme, for helping educaded young men, in starting small industries, should be prepared, and a beginning should be made, in this respect, in certain centres, in these provinces. Not only should the young men, adopting such careers, be subsidized, under rules framed by the local Government, but they should also be helped, by expert advice.

(5) For the proper organisation and development of small industries, Government should take steps to collect authoritative information in regard to the running of small industries in Japan and in European countries.

(6) The recommendations of the industries Reorganization Committee, in regard to sugar and oil, deserve support and the claims of the textile and leather industries may also be pressed, but if Government are called upon, by private capitalists, to give them any assistance in this matter, it must be on the distinct understanding, that they will employ a certain number of qualified educated men, for technical work, in their concerns, irrespective of any considerations of caste or creed.

(7) The glass industry is an industry, in which the provinces are more vitally interested, and, therefore, the decision of the Government, refusing to accept the recommendations of the Tariff Board, for the protection of glass industry, should be revised. If the glass industry receives any assistance from the Government, Government should demand, from those interested in it, that they shall employ a certain number of qualified educated young men, belonging to these provinces, in their concerns. So far as the recommendations of the Industries Reorganisation Committee include the development of glass industry they also deserve support.

(8) The recommendations of the Industries Re-organisation Committee that special attention should be paid to the marketing of the products of cottage industrialists, giving them expert advice, and carrying on experimental research work, should be given effect to.

(9) Steps should be taken—

(a) to bring qualified educated men into touch with commercial houses for employment; and

(b) to foster and encourage the organization of co-operative stores, wherever possible, employing educated men who have received proper training in salesmanship etc.

(10) Particulary, the recommendation of the Industrial Finance Committee that the minor industries and many of the cottage industries in the United Provinces require some better form of organisation, than that provided by the Arts and Crafts Emporium, to link the purchaser with the manufacturer, to improve the quality of work produced by artisans, to help them financially and to obtain for them more remunerative prices is supported.

For all these purposes, an institution working on joint stock lines bearing the title of the United Provinces Financing and Marketing Company, Limited, should be established at an early date. Such a company, by itself, should secure employment to a certain number of educated men, and if the work of marketing is developed, it may provide employment to a number of trained men.

(11) It is essential to the development of industries that the present system of the adjustment of railway goods freight rates should be considered by a competent committee appointed to examine into the incidence of railway freight charges on the industries of the country with a view to the encouragement and development of industries and the internal trade of the country, found advisable to appoint a permanent railway freight tribunal to fix railway freight throughout India in the interest of all concerned.

(12) (a) The Director of Industries department should be an expert in industrial matters and possess a larger number of experts for technical advice on such industries, major or cottage, as may be developed ; and that the head of the department should be a practically trained industrialist.

(b) The department shonld have a separate and well organized intelligence and publicity branch, which should furnish necessary information, to industrialists and persons, interested in industrial careers, by publishing leaflets, or pamphlets, on various industries and giving the necessary information, in regard to each one of them.

Technical, Industrial and Vocational Education

(1) There is a great and growing demand, for the expansion of industrial and vocational education in these provinces.

(2) The following recommendations of the Kharegat Committee are supported :—

(a) that there must be adequate facilities for industrial training ;

(b) that, in addition to fully staffed and well-equipped central schools and commercial extension courses, arrangements should be made, for giving an industaial bias to the training, imparted at general educational schools ;

(c) that arrangements should be made with firms, factories as master craftsmen for taking students as apprentices, suitable fees being paid to them, for the purpose.

(d) that elementry industrial schools for boys, and tutional classes for artisans, should be maintained ;

(3) The right course to follow would not be to diminish the existing facilities for technical education but to recognize and remodel them so as to make them more efficient.

(4) It is not enough to establish new industrial or vocational schools, or to remodel or re-organize the existing ones, without, at the same time, creating an agency, for placing the products of these technical schools, and for establishing them in new careers. Without this, the multiplication of the industrially and vocationally trained young men, who cannot settle down in life, may accentuate the problem of unemployment and may create fresh difficulties, both for Government and society.

(5) Regional vocational guidance authorities, consisting of teachers and representatives of other interests, such as, commerce and industry, should be created, by the Ministry of Industries, in these provinces. The vocational guidance authorities should not only take an interest in vocational education, but should also be under an obligation to establish contacts with educational institutions and actual industries of the locality or the neighbourhood and to help the products of such schools, in securing employment in such industries.

(6) Where there exists a large and well-defined industrial or commercial area, within the territory of a district or a group of districts, regional committees. to look after the educational interests of that area and to help qualified young men, should be created.

(7) The importance and necessity, of developing apprenticeship industries and crafts, should be emphasized. This will only revive a very old tradition in Indian industries and crafts.

(8) Government should undertake, through the Industries department, or any other department, the publication of pamphlets, regarding the careers, more or less, on the models of the pamphlets, issued by the Board of Education or the Ministry of Labour in England.

Advice to Parents and Boys as to Careers

(1) Some steps should be taken to afford advice to parents, in regard to the intellectual capacity of their boys, and their suitability for certain careers.

(2) Head masters assisted by other teachers in these provinces, should be asked to carefully watch the intellectual capacity of the boys from the very start of their school education.

(3) If there are no psycho-technical experts available among the head masters or school masters, who have made a study of modern psychological methods, in the

field of educational and vocational guidance, then one or two experts should be engaged, for a temporary period, from England, who would give the necessary training to our school masters, or, in the alternative, two or three school masters from India should be deputed to England, on other foreign countries, for the study of these methods, so that, on their return, they may help in the development of those methods in these provinces

(3) Arrangement should be made for the study of and research in experimental and educational psychology in various universities.

OUR RECOMMENDATIONS AS TO EDUCATION GENERALLY

(1) While it should be the aim of primary education to remove illiteracy, it should also be its principal aim to qualify boys, to become better agriculturists, and more useful members of village communities. Primary education, as it is given at present, is ineffective partly because it does not lay sufficient emphasis upon rural and agricultural needs, and partly because the age-limit is too low.

(2) Primary education should be brought more into line with rural needs and agricultural conditions, and enable boys, reading at primary schools, to become more efficient members of the agricultural community.

(3) The age-limit for the purpose of primary education, should be raised to 12 or 13 and every child should remain at school for at least six years. If this is done primary education will not only become more efficient, but also find employment for a number of teachers.

(4) We strongly recommend that the compulsory primary education be extended all over the province as in our opinion without it economic prosperity cannot be built up. In this connection for the spread of primary and adult education it is worthwhile considering how far the agency of broadcasting can be called in aid.

SECONDARY EDUCATION

(1) The underlying policy of the resolution of the local Government, in regard to the secondary education, dated Aug. 8, 1934, is sound, and the High School Examination should have two kinds of certificates—one certifying completion of the course of secondary education and qualifying for admission to industrial Commercial and agricultural schools and the other qualifying for admission to Arts and Science colleges.

(2) The intermediate course, if the high School course is curtailed by one year, should be extended to three years, and should be of four parallel types : (1) Industrial, (2) Commercial, (3) Agricultural and (4) Arts and Science.

(3) Secondary schools should provide much more diversified courses of study, care being taken to give more practical, than theoretical, education to the boys.

(4) The industrial courses in secondary schools should aim at giving technical training, of general character, designed to develop skill of hand and eye and cultivate practical aptitudes, so as to predispose them towards industrial life.

Proper agencies should be created, for advising boys, as to their careers.

UNIVERSITY EDUCATION

1. The number of students, seeking admission into the universities, has increased appreciably.

2. No arbitrary limit, for the admission of students into the universities, should be prescribed in view of the recommendations of (a) secondary education, (b) technical and vocational education (c) reduction of age-limit, for the appointment to subordinate Government service etc., which will have the effect of automatically reducing the number of students at the universities.

3. While no arbitrary limit to admission of students should be prescribed, there should be greater strictness exercised, in the matter of admission. The universities should be under no obligation, to take in men, who have passed their Intermediate Examination or School Leaving Examination, in third class, except in rare circumstances, when the Admission Committee is satisfied that the student has taken the third class, due to illness, or some other satisfactoy reason, but is likely to do well at the university.

4. While education, in what are called humanities, is concerned, universities should not be discouraged, greater stress should be laid on scientific and vocational education.

5. So far as research work, conducted at the universities is concerned, universities

should study the need of industries, and encourage such research, in particular, as may be of practical use to the industries.

6. There should be some system of co-ordination between different universities so as to secure the uniformity of standards and prevent unhealthy competition.

7. Steps should be taken to establish contacts between the science department of the universities and industrialists and businessmen, and such departments of the universities should devote themselves, not solely, or exclusively, to higher academic research in abstract branches of scientific knowledge, but also undertake research, which may prove to be helpful to the industries, or to the economic development of the country. If, for this purpose, it is necessary to give more funds to the science departments of the universities, such funds should be given to them.

8. An advisory committee should be constituted to advise the Ministry of Education, in regard to the grants, that are to be made to the universities for reasearch work, and that on such advisory committees not only the universities but also business, trade, industry and agriculture, should be represented. This may, ultimately, lead to the establishment of a Council of Research.

9. The problem of Indian students, in England, requires careful consideration, and both Government and Indian parents should exercise greater discrimination, in sending young men to foreign countries, merely for academic education, while those, who are likely to benefit by education at Oxford or Cambridge, or other British or foreign universities, or who go there, with the object of carrying on post-graduate research work, should certainly receive encouragement.

Boards of Employment

1. An Appointment Board, for the graduates of all the five universities, in these provinces, including the products of such institutions, as the Harcourt Butler Technological Institute, the Agricultural Colleges, Allahabad, Cawnpore, and the Engineering College at Roorkee should be established more or less, modelled on the Appointments Board at Cambridge.

2. The Appointments Board should consist of the vice-chancellors of the universities, certain heads of departments, such as education, industries and agriculture, and some public men, and a certain number of businessmen, European and Indian.

3. Power should be given to this board, to appoint a working committee.

4. This Board should be financed, partly by Government and, partly by the universities.

5. Similarly, there should be a board created, for the products of secondary schools, intermediate colleges, vocational schools, medical and agricultural schools and industrial schools, and this board should consist of the director of public instruction, directors of industries and agriculture, head masters, inspectors of schools, and a certain number of non-officials, zamindars and businessmen. This board should be financed by Government.

6. These boards should be required to collect statistics of employment among the graduates, of the universities, and the products of secondary schools and intermediate colleges, etc. and from the sources indicated in no (1)

The following were the signatories of the Report :-

Tej Bahadur Sapru, Ahmad Said, Jwala Prasad, Anand Sarup, A Siddiqui. T Gavin Jones. Sam Higginbottom Tara Chand. Sohan Lal Srivastava

Official Review of Indian Polity

The Bengal Administration Report 1934-35

The following extracts are taken from the Report on the Administration of Bengal 1934-35 :—

Unlike several of its immediate predecessors, the year 1935 was one of general calm. Civil disobedience defeated in 1932 and discredited in 1933, had been formally discontinued in 1934, and the number of civil disobedience convicts in the Provincial jails fell during the year from 20 to 8.

No alternative form of political agitation had been substituted for this movement; and the reforms effected by Mr. Gandhi at the Bombay session of the Congress in October, 1934, followed as they were by his own virtual retirement from the political arena, tended to weaken in Bengal the hold of an organisation, the leaders of which made little secret of their disgust at the Province's twin troubles of terrorism and party faction.

It was not therefore surprising that in the course of the year the cleavage between Bengal Congressmen and the Working Committee of Congressmen which contained but one representative of this Province, became more pronounced ; or that the Congress Socialist Party increased its influence at the expense of the more orthodox and conservative elements in the movement. Dissatisfaction with the attitude of neutrality adopted by the Working Committee towards the Communal Award, and discontent at its failure to arouse any organized public opinion against the approaching Reforms, found frequent expression in certain sections of the Nationalist Press.

There was little evidence of enthusiasm, and apathy and indifference prevailed. The celebrations of "Independence Day" in January were of so undistinguished a character that they do not merit further reference ; but it was significant that certain Congress newspapers frankly derided as moral formulæ, lacking the essential ingredients of political principles, the resolutions proposed by the Working Committee for repetition on this occasion.

In February certain sections of the Press expressed disgust at the failure of the Congress group in the Legislative Assembly to take a firm stand against the Communal Award. During the same month the tendency towards the acceptance of Socialist and Communist ideas found expression in virulent speeches delivered at a series of meetings held in Calcutta under the auspices of two allied Communist ideas found expression in virulent speeches delivered at a series of meetings held in Calcutta under the auspices of two allied Communist organizations, and in March Government found it necessary to prescribe, under the Criminal Law Amendment Act of 1908, thirteen associations of a subversive nature. Further violent speeches followed this action, and in consequence all meetings and demonstrations were banned in Calcutta for a period of three months.

This necessity for the measures adopted was established by the recovery of quantities of subversive literature from the premises of these organizations, and by the repeated demands for violent and massed action which issued from their platforms ; while the presence of Congressmen at the meetings concerned, and the attitude adopted by the Congress Press towards Government's measures, indicated a further attempt to bring the forces of Labour within the Congress fold.

In April the Bengal Provincial Congress Committee held its annual Conference at Dinajpur. The occasion excited comparatively little interest, several prominent Congress workers were absent, and less than 700 visitors attended the Agricultural and Industrial Exhibition.

There was a pronounced Socialist atmosphere about the Conference, the Congress Socialist group distributed a large number of leaflets, and "Workers and Peasants" were the theme of many speeches. Despite the protests of the Muhammadan delegates, who left the Conference in a body the rejection of the Communal Award was carried by large majority ; the resolutions were adopted eulogizing the services rendered by those who "suffered" during the civil disobedience campaign, and protesting against the repressive policy of Government.

Practical decisions, however, were conspicuous by their absence, and the attitude adopted towards terrorism was typical of that presented by Congress as a whole. The Chairman of the Reception Committee denounced the terrorists; the President of the Conference expressed disapproval of their activities, but was more emphatic in the condemnation of Government's methods of combating them; while a Member of the Legislative Assembly referred openly to the "martyrdom of death-defying youths," and praised their "patriotism, self-sacrifice, and heroism."

The Conference cannot be said to have made any appreciable contribution to current politics, and it merely demonstrated the extent to which the views of the Congress Socialists were obtaining a hold in Bengal, and the dissatisfaction of local leaders with the policy of the All-India Congress Committee.

The meeting of this Committee at Jubbalpore did little to heal the breach, for the question of Congress's attitude towards the new constitution was shelved, and a growing divergence of opinion became apparent between the supporters of the Left and the adherents of the Right. During the month of May several Nationalist newspapers awoke to these facts and leading articles referred to the "crisis before the Congress," to the necessity of either expelling or absorbing the Congress Socialists, and to the superiority of their definite proletarian objectives over the vague capitalist ideals of the Congress creed itself. An alliance between Congress and Trade Unionism was advocated as essential to the attainment of Purna Swaraj.

Few efforts, however, were made to put these theories into practice, and there was little noticeable Congress activity in the middle of the year. In a few districts recruitment of members was, indeed, intensified, but in the majority of instances the immediate object in view was the capture of seats on Local Boards. Even the All-India Village Industries Association, which had been set up at Mr. Gandhi's instance for the purpose of rural reconstruction, aroused remarkably little enthusiasm in Bengal, and a visit of one of its members to the district of Murshidabad in July, produced few practical results.

Throughout the year the Congress Press adopted an attitude of hostility towards the Report of the Joint Select Committee and the Government of India Bill, but the actual passage of tho Bill through Parliament excited an interest that was characterised mainly by its almost fatalistic acceptance of the inevitable; and when in July the Working Committee at Wardha again postponed a decision on the question of the acceptance of office by members of the Congress, one Nationalist newspaper in Calcutta published a trenchant "leader", advocating the capture of the Legislature and the Cabinets and the acceptance of office under the new constitution. It was repeatedly contended that Bengal had been "let down" by Congress Headquarters, and that the Province must be allowed freedom of action in respect of the Reforms.

Offence was taken in August at the Working Committee's refusal to take action upon the application of Mr. Subhas Bose, the absentee President of the Bengal Provincial Congress Committee for permission to carry on propaganda abroad in the name of the Congress, and the opinion expressed by Mr. Bhulabhai Desai, the leader of the Congress Party in the Legislative Assembly, that Congress should not interfere betweeen the Princes and their people, evoked the criticism that the Working Committee was anxious to placate the States by confining its activities to the Provinces. Dis-satisfaction and despondency increasingly characterised the attitude of Congress in Bengal. The appointment of the Marquesses of Zetland and Linlithgow as Secretary of State and Viceroy-designate aroused little save gloomy and some what captious criticism.

In connection with the Congress Socialist Conference in Calcutta in September, the Nationalist Press admitted that there was in Congress circles a veering round towards a new philosophy, and that while there could nev er be in Congress itself any open war between the classes and the masses, there were definite indications that majority opinion was inclining towards the Left.

In October considerable discontent was aroused by the action of the All-India Congress Committee at Madras in again shelving the question of the acceptance of office; and relations between the Congress leaders and their Provincial followers were not improved by a further failure on the part of the former to settle the differences between the two factions in the Provincial Congress Committee.

These differences, dating from the personal rivalry between Mr. Subhas Bose and Mr. J. M. Sen-Gupta, were accentuated by the refusal of a section of the Committee to accept certain of Mr. Bose's suggestion for a settlement, and resulted in an announcement made by the Provincial Secretary in November to the effect that 25 out of the 34 members of the Committee had resigned.

At the same time the poor opinion entertained at Congress Headquaters of the importance of the Province in the sphere of Congress activity was illustrated by the announcement of Mr. Rajendra Prasad, the Congress President, to the effect that the Working Committee had no present intention of attempting to interfere in the squabbles in Bengal. A meeting held in Calcutta to settle the quarrel was attended by the members of one faction only, who referred the matter to the arbitration of Mr. Sarat Bose. This gentleman, a brother of Mr. Subhas Bose, had been since 1932 a State Prisoner under Regulation III of 1818. He had been permitted to live under restrictions near Kurseong' and he was released at the end of July while in Calcutta on parole. His return was greeted with acclamation as an act of belated justice, and the Calcutta Corporation presented him with an address of welcome. Mr. Bose, however, showed little inclination to plunge into politics, and at the end of the year no further progress had been made towards a compromise, despite the publication of his "award."

The lack of a political programme and the absence of any effective central Congress organisation in Bengal was further illustrated by the want of interest shown throughout the Province in the arrangement made to celebrate the Golden Jubilee of the Congress on 28th December. Flag hoisting ceremonies, meetings and speeches were the principal items, but these functions were attended by comparatively small crowds, and the principal meeting at Sradhananda Park, Calcutta, attracted not more than 3,000 spectators.

The date of the celebrations coincided with the Muhammadan festival of Id-ul-fitr, but there was no diminution of the immense congregation of Moslems who participated in the annual religious ceremony upon the Calcutta Maidan. In fact the simultaneous gathering of Congress supporters and Muhammadan worshippers in separate assemblies and frequently in close juxtaposition merely emphasised the widening gulf between the two communities, and the alleged interference of Congress music with Muhammadan prayers resulted in a communal riot at Deshabandhu Park, Calcutta while another was narrowly averted in Wellington Square.

In general the response of Bengal to the Jubilee appeals of Congress leaders, most of whom were assembled in Bombay, must be described as poor ; and it indicated the extent to which the Congress has lost popular sympathy in this Province during recent years by the ineffectiveness of its programme and by its persistent refusal to face realities in respect of the political and economic problems of the country.

The report then refers at length to the remarkable interest evinced in Their Imperial Majesties' Silver Jubilee in May.

After dealing at length with the provisions of the India Act, the Report turns to the communal relations. It says relations between the two great communities in the Province showed few signs of improvement during the year, and although there was no major outbreak of communal violence, a succession of minor occurrences demonstrated the readiness of the flame of antagonism to flare up on the slightest provocation. The Report then enumerates certain incidents and continues thus .

In a speech at the St. Andrew's Day dinner in November His Excellency the Governor deplored the extent of communal bitterness, and expressed concern at the manner in which a large section of the Press was encouraging or pandering to the communal spirit. He pointed out the dangers which would ensue if rivalry based upon communal cleavage was exploited as a means of winning these prizes which under a democratic system, are believed to be the reward of the party which can establish itself in the majority ; and he appealed to the potential leaders of the various parties in Bengal to face these dangers squarely, and not to countenance any attempts by one community to weaken another by creating or exploiting split in its ranks.

The pertinency of His Excellency's advice was illustrated by the disorderly scenes witnessed in the Calcutta Corporation in December, during a debate on a motion to earmark 25 per cent of Corporation appointments for Muhammadans, and by the subsequent resignation of 15 Muhammadan Councillors and of the Mayor, Mr. Fazlul Huq.

In view of the state of communal relations in Bengal, the election of Mr. Fazlul Huq as the first Muhammadan Mayor of Calcutta was a development of some interest. It was only a split in the Muhammadan vote that prevented the success of a Muhammadan candidate in 1933, and Mr. Huq himself was actually elected by the Sen Gupta-cum-Muhammadan group at the disorderly meeting which disgraced the Corporation in May 1934 and necessitated intervention by the Local Government. The eventual upshot was that Mr. Nalini Ranjan Sarkar held office as Mayor during the financial year 1934-35 ; but in April 1935 Congress support enabled Mr. Huq to achieve the Mayoral chair.

Ever since the Congress party captured control of it, the Corporation has reacted strongly towards current politics, and its behaviour during the year under review proved no exception to rule. Mr. Huq obtained some prominence by the support which he gave to Trade Union and Workers' Associations, and in July he was elected President of the Bengal Mariners' Union.

In connection with the Reforms, the Corporation declined to favour Government with its views on the delimitation of Calcutta constituencies, on the ground that the new constitution was being "forced upon the country." The Corporation's misplaced sympathy with persons placed under restraint on account of their connection with terrorism found an unfortunate expression in November, when it decided by a majority of 30 votes to 13 to allocate a piece of its property for the erection of a memorial to detenus killed during the disturbance at the Hijli detention camp in 1931. Government decided that such an edifice would tend to excite sympathy with terrorism, and to secure adherents to the terrorist movements ; and the Memorial Committee was accordingly declared an unlawful association under the Indian Criminal Law Amendment Act of 1908.

On the other hand it is pleasant to be able to record that the Corporation celebrated Their Majesties' Silver Jubilee Number of the "Calcutta Municipal Gazette," while on the occasion of the death of the Royal Highness Princess Victoria in December, it unanimously offered its respected condolences to Their Majesties and the Royal Family, the sponsor of the resolution declaring that the Corporation's loyalty and devotion to the Royal house of England was proverbially deep and unimpeachable

Patriotism, however, is not enough. In the administration of public affairs it requires to be coupled with efficiency. Suggestions have frequently been made in recent years that the City Fathers of Calcutta would do well to devote less of their time to the expression of contentious political opinions, and more of it to the details of civic administration ; and this criticism was lent particular force during the year under review by a number of incidents which suggested that Congress control of the Corporation has not in fact proved so efficient as its supporters would have the public believe.

In June and July the Corporation Scavengers and Labour Union addressed several letters to Government complaining of the belated payment of wages, and in the latter month deputations from this Union and from the employees of the Palta Waterworks waited upon the Mayor and the Chief Executive Officer, to draw their attention to the alleged prevalence of bribery among the Corporation's subordinate staff and to the existence of corruption among its contractors. A strike which would have paralysed the conservancy arrangements of the city was only averted by the payment of arrear salaries and the appointment of an Enquiry Committee.

The failure of the Corporation authorities to provide an adequate supply of drinking water in certain wards during the summer provoked general dissatisfaction and many protests in the Press ; and reports that the water itself was subject to contamination necessitated a discussion of the problems of water-supply and drainage at a conference specially convened by the Hon'ble Minister-in-charge of Local Self-Government. The Report then dwells at length on certain Corporation irregularities.

While Congress continued to languish and the problems of the new constitution loomed larger and larger upon the political horizon, Bengal continued to wrestle with the demon of terrorism. The year 1935 witnessed no major terrorist outrage in the usually accepted sense of the term, but if the incidents which occurred demonstrated the partial degeneration of terrorism into gangsterism, they nevertheless constituted a reminder that the menace of this movement has merely been curbed and not eliminated.

A series of minor occurrences exemplified the prevalence of the terrorist mentality among the youths of Bengal. In January five young men extorted at the point of the revolver nearly Rs. 300 worth of ornaments from a goldsmith of Dinajpur, and terrorist leaflets were distributed in certain villages in the districts of Chittagong and Murshidabad. Revolutionary posters were affixed to the walls of the College and Zilla School at Pabna ; a revolutionary pamphlet was sent to the Principal of Dacca Islamia Intermediate College and the Additional Superintendent of Police at Dacca, as well as the Superintendent of Police at Patna received letters threatening them with death. Similar letters were sent in February to a Sub-Inspector of the District Intelligence Branch at Serajganj and to a prosecution witness in a conspiracy case at Hoogly.

During these two months quantities of terrorist literature were recovered as a result of searches carried out at various places in the districts of Midnapore, Rangpur, Dacca, Faridpur and Noakhali. In March two youths attempted to seize at the point of the revolver a mail bag from a train near Faridpur and three other young men armed with revolvers secured several bags of mail from a train between Chapai Nawabganj and Amnura. The Inspector of Police, District Intelligence Branch, Rajshahi, received a threatening letter from Benares, and further finds of revolutionary literature were made in Dacca and Midnapore districts.

In April, a mail runner in the district of Jessore was attacked by three 'bhadralock' youths, who robbed him of the bags which he was carrying; while in May three young men snatched a bag of mail from a runner in Faridpur district. It is satisfactory to note that two of the latter were chased and captured by local Muhammadan cultivators. In the same month a revolver and some catridges were stolen from an Assistant Sub-Inspector of Police. Revolutionary leaflets entitled "Be ready with your pistol" appeared in certain villages of Pabna district in May; the District Magistrate of Howrah received a letter threatening him with death if the Silver Jubilee celebrations were not stopped; and information was obtained of a meditated attempt upon the life of the District Magistrate of Murshidabad.

On June 4th a youth, who was apparently thought to be a Police spy, was stabbed to death in Faridpur district, while on June 15th the Sub-Inspector of Police in charge of Goalundo Ghat thana in the same district was murdered with a 'dao' by a detenu domiciled in the locality, who was arrested on the spot.

During the same month guns were stolen in Jessore and Chittagong districts, and threatening letters were sent to the District Magistrate of Dacca and to an Assistant Sub-Inspector of Police in Birbhum; while revolutionary leaflets appeared again in Chittagong, and searches revealed the presence of terrorist literature in the districts of Rajshahi, Faridpur and Noakhali.

On July 3rd a domiciled detenu was killed with knives in broad daylight near Government House at Dacca by two political suspects, who seemed to be under the impression that he was giving information to the Police. One was chased and caught by passers-by, and the other was captured shortly afterwards. Later in the same month leaflets exciting local students to kill the District Intelligence Branch Officer were found at the Zilla School at Pabna, and in August further leaflets entitled "Long live revolution" were discovered in the same institution as well as in the Technical School.

On August 2nd a revolver and 25 rounds of ammunition were stolen from the house of a European at Barrackpore. A few days later a terrorist poster appeared upon the noticeboard of the High English School at Bajitpur in Mymensingh district. On September 1st two leaflets, containing an impassioned and bloodthirsty appeal for revolution, and addressed respectively to students and to members of Anti-Terrorist Associations, were distributed in Chittagong by the "Surya Communist Party", while on September 3rd revolutionary posters appeared upon the gates of the Narail College, Jessore district, on the occasion of the visit of the Divisional Commissioner.

On the 9th September terrorist prisoners in the Midnapore Central Jail severely assaulted a warder, and the District Magistrates's enquiry established the fact that their behaviour was premeditated and unprovoked. It is satisfactory to record that nine of them were subsequently convicted. During the same month further threatening letters were received by the District Magistrate of Dacca while searches in Chittagong district in November brought to light a quantity of dynamite and ammunition.

The recovery of arms and ammunition, and the capture of a number of absconders and suspects, testified on the one hand to the continued existence of terrorist organizations and on the other to the vigilance and courage of the Police. In January an important absconder of the Anusilan Party was arrested with incriminating documents in the 24 Parganas district; and Purnananda Das Gupta with Sitanath De and Niranjan Ghosal had escaped from the Alipore Central Jail during the trial of the Inter-Provincial Conspiracy Case in July, 1934, was arrested with terrorists at Titagarh, and an automatic pistol, ammunition, revolutionary literature, chemicals and explosive formulæ were recovered at the same time. In the same month a muzzle-loading pistol was seized in Hooghly, a 6-chambered revolver was recovered by a chaukidar from a tank in the same district, and spare parts of fire-arms were found at Natore ; while a Chittagong Raid Case absconder was arrested at Canning as a result of the acumen of a 'bhadralok', constable.

In February two guns and other weapons were seized from a house in Mymensingh district. In March a revolver and an automatic pistol were recovered in Faridpur, two guns were found in each of the districts of Jessore and Bakarganj, a country-made pistol and some catridges were seized in Midnapore, a stolen gun was traced in Mymensingh, and some ammunition was located in Pabna. The absconder Niranjan Ghosal, mentioned above, was arrested in April; and in the same month some ammunition was discovered in Mymensingh, a 6-chambered revolver was found upon the person of a passenger in a train at Asansol, and 49 live and 36 fired catridges were recovered from a tank in Dinajpur district. In May 3 revolvers, a gun, and 21 catridges were seized in Dinajpur, and ammunition was discovered in the districts of Bankura and Faridpur.

On 5th June the premises of the Rajshahi City Bank were searched and some catridges and documents containing formulæ for the preparation of T. N. T. and cordite were seized. The month of June saw also the recovery of a revolver, some catridges and a detective warrant, which had been stolen from an Assistant Sub-Inspector of Police ; while a single barrelled rifle and some catridges were secured in Malda, a revolver and some catridges in Khulna, and a gun in Bakarganj.

In July an absconder was arrested in Chittagonj ; a pistol of Belgian make was recovered in Mymensingh ; and a 5-chambered revolver was seized at Asansol railway station from a passenger in the Bombay mail, who escaped while being interrogated, jumped from the platform, and was cut to pieces by a passing train. On August 3rd a 6 chambered revolver and 3 catridges were found in the pocket of a youth at Tollyganj ; on August 4th 3 bombs, some chemicals, and some explosive formulæ was seized at Dacca, and a gun was recovered in Mymensingh ; while on August 17th a regular battery of firearms, comprising a revolver, a pistol three guns and 32 rounds of ammunition, was discovered at Dinajpur.

In the latter part of August an important absconder was arrested in Pabna district and in September a revolver and a muzzle-loading pistol were seized in Noakhali. At the beginning of October another absconder was secured in Dinajpur, and two important arrests were effected in Chittagong. In November a process-server in the 24 Parganas district recovered a revolver while attaching some property in a house, and another revolver was seized from a house in Faridpur district.

The extent of terrorist conspiracies for the secretion of arms and the commission of outrages and the measure of Government's success in combating them, were further indicated by the large number of cases disposed of by Special Courts in the course of the year. In February Dhanesh Bhattacharji, a detenue who escaped from the Bankura Leper Asylum and was captured while in possession of a loaded revolver, was convicted by a Special Tribunal at Dacca. In the same month a Special Tribunal sitting at Dinajpur disposed of three connected terrorist dacoity cases, as a result of which 8 persons received sentences ranging from 10 to 4 years' rigorous imprisonment.

On 1st May the Inter-Provincial Conspiracy Case, which had been proceeding so many months before a Special Tribunal at Alipore, ended in the conviction of no less than 35 persons in respect of offences of a terrorist and revolutionary character. Six were sentenced to transportation for life, and the rest to varying terms of imprisonment. In July the detenue who murdered the Sub-Inspector of Police at Goalundo was sentenced to death by a Special Tribunal at Faridpur, and in September the two youths who stabbed a detenue at Dacca were likewise sentenced to death by a Special Tribunal sttting in that city. The latter sentence was subsequently reduced by the High Court to transportation for life.

At the close of the year a Special Tribunal at Alipore was engaged in trying 31 persons including a woman, in connection with the recoveries of arms consequent upon the arrest of Purnananda Das Gupta in January. Magistrates vested with special powers under the Bengal Suppression of Terrorist Outrages Act disposed of many somewhat similar cases, some of which are worth recording. Four youths were convicted in an Arms Act case at Rajshahi in January, two of whom, aged 15, pleaded guilty to the charge and were sent to the Borstal School at Bankura.

In a Conspiracy Case at Rangpur in February, thirteen persons received sentences ranging from 7 years' rigorous imprisonment to a fine of Rs. 50 and in March two young men were convicted of somewhat similar offences in the Garbetta Conspiracy Case At Bankura two 'bhadralok' youths were convicted of mail robbery, and in April a third was sentenced at Bishnupur to 5 years' rigorous imprisonment for possessing catridges and materials for the repair of revolvers. Two persons were convicted at Dacca for harbouring the absconder Dhanesh Bhattacharji, and in Birbhum seven persons were sentenced to various terms of imprisonment for conspiracy to commit robbery and dacoity. In the Gaibandha Arms Conspiracy Case in May a further batch of seven youths was convicted, while in the same month there was a conviction in Dinajpur for possession of letters inciting to violence, and another in Bakharganj for the possession of explosives. At Hooghly in a case of dacoity with double murder, eight persons received sentences ranging downwards from 7 years' rigorous imprisonment, and in August two youths were convicted in Nadia district for the unlawful possession of a revolver. A number of similar cases were disposed of during the remaining months of the year: and it is to be hoped that the sentences imposed by these Courts will go some way towards diminishing the number of criminal conspiracies and crimes of violence.

The policy adopted in 1932, of deporting terrorist convicts to the Andamans, was continued during 1935, and in the course of the year 91 convicts of the type were despatched to Port Blair from Bengal. Congress leaders continued to evince sympathy for these deportees, and in April Mr. Mohanlal Saxena, a member of the Congress group in the Legislative assembly, applied for permission to visit the Andamans. As his ostensible object was to enquire into the "alleged hardships" of the terrorist convicts in the Cellular Jail, it was perhaps hardly surprising that his request was refused by the Government of India.

In May the Hon'ble Dewan Bahadur Narayanaswami Chetty, Member of the Council of State, who had behind him 25 years of interest in prison reform, paid a private visit to the Islands, and on his return published two letters to Government commenting favourably upon the conditions in which he found the terrorist convicts living. In August a Congress member tabled a resolution in the Bengal Legislative Council recommending the retransfer of all such prisoners from the Andamans to Bengal. Want of time prevented discussion on this motion, but it afforded a regrettable example of the concern felt in certain quarters for persons convicted of terrorist crimes.

It cannot be too strongly emphasized that the Andamans have never been actually closed down as a penal settlement, and that in addition to terrorists, about 5,000 ordinary convicts are detained at Port Blair. The object of sending convicted terrorists to the place is to prevent them forming in Bengal the nucleus of plots and conspiracies, to reduce the chances of their escape, and to remove the source of danger to the discipline and security of Bengal Jails ; and in view of these facts it is regrettable that sympathy for this small band of dangerous criminals should continue to be shown by Congress organizations.

Throughout the year efforts of Government and its officers continued to be directed not merely to the breaking up of terrorist conspiracies, but also towards the eradication of the terrorist mentality in affected areas of the Province. The Military Intelligence Officers, who with the status of Superintendents of Police are assisting the civil administration have done most valuable work in this direction in the districts of Midnapore, Chittagong, Tipperah, Noakhali, Faridpur, Dacca, Mymensingh, Rangpur, Rajshahi and Murshidabad. Encouragement was given to the formation of local Anti-Terrorist Committees affiliated to the All-Bengal Anti-Terrorist Association, and in addition to those already formed a number of such committees were organized in Darjeeling, Jalpaiguri, Dinajpur, Rangpur, Jessore, and Faridpur districts.

Referring to the employment of troops the report says :—There can be little question that the presence of these military forces in the districts most affected by terrorism not merely provided assistance to the civil authorities, but also gave encouragement to the loyal element in the population and acted as a partial deterrent in respect of terrorist ploting and propaganda.

Preventive detention under the provisions of the Bengal Criminal Law Amendment Act continued, however, during the year to be the principal method employed to guard against the commission of terrorist outrages ; and the detention camps at Buxar and Hijli, the two camps at Berhampore, and the camp at Deoli in Ajmere Merwara all remained in commission. At the close of the year out of a total of 3,418 persons dealt with under the Act, 194 had been released before the expiration of two months, 472 had been released unconditionally or upon terms, 214 were in home domicile, 838 in village domicile, 35 had been externed from Bengal, 1,517 were detained in jails and camps, 21 had died, 21 were untraced, the orders against

2 had been allowed to lapse, and 104 had been convicted or were awaiting trial in respect of specific offences.

Despite the insistence of its leaders that Congress, being pledged to non-violence, could have no connection with or interest in terrorism, the All India Congress Committee felt it incumbent upon itself to champion the cause of the Bengal detenus. In February questions were asked in the Legislative Assembly regarding the number of persons detained in Jails and camps under the Bengal Criminal Law Amendment Act, while articles appeared in the Congress Press suggesting that the reduction in the number of terrorist outrages should be followed by a revision of Government's policy in respect of detention without trial, and that the occasion of the Silver Jubilee should be signalled by a general release of detenus.

It was arranged in April that May 19th should be celebrated throughout India as "Detenue Day" and a committee of Congress Members of the Legislative Assembly, with Mr. Mohanlal Saxena, as its Chairman, was appointed "to enquire and report upon the administration of repressive laws" in this Province. Whatever may have happened in other parts of India, the celebration of "Detenu Day" fell completely flat in Bengal. Recognizing the dangers inherent in an agitation of this nature, Government decided that any publicity given to the cause of persons detained because of their connection with terrorists, a connection established in each case after an independent and most careful examination of the fact, must inevitably stimulate and encourage the supporters of terrorism. It was felt, also, that any widely advertised expression of sympathy with the detenus, however genuine might be the feelings by which it was prompted, must react unfavourably upon the efforts being made to eradicate the disease of terrorism from the body politic. Accordingly an order was issued on 17th May under section 2A, Indian Press (Emergency Powers) Act, 1931, for bidding the publication of any information either regarding the observance of "Detenu Day" or regarding other similar attempts to excite sympathy for those detained under the Bengal State Prisoners Regulations of 1818 and the Bengal Criminal Law Amendment Act of 1930. On the same date a communique explaining the reasons for the order was issued to the Press.

The effect of this action was immediate; and although the holding of meetings had not been prohibited, the actual celebrations on May 19th were a complete fiasco throughout the Province. The principal gathering arranged at the Albert Hall, Calcutta, was poorly attended: Mr. Fazlul Haq, the Mayor, who was expected to preside, had urgent business at Krishnagar; the collections made were insignificant; and the meeting itself degenerated into a Communist rally, which broke up in confusion at the appearance of the Police. The Nationalist Press waxed indignant over the "high-handed" behaviour of Government in this connection, and indulged in the puerile gesture of suspending publication on May 21st by way of protest. The province, however, remained quite unexcited by these antics, and the sponsors of "Detenu Day" can look back upon it with little save discomfiture and mortification.

Mr. Saxena's Committee met with even less success. On April 22nd it issued a lengthy questionnaire to various organisations and persons in Bengal, asking for information concerning the administration of "repressive" laws. The very wording of this circular showed that the Committee had not approached the subject matter of the enquiry with an open mind. Correspondents were asked, among other questions, to suggest methods of alleviating "the present hardship of detenus and their families" to describe the "inconvenience and harrassment caused by searches", to enumerate any "humiliating orders requiring individuals to report at police-stations", and to "give instances of repression and hardship, if any, caused to the public" as a result of "Military marches."

The replies elicited would appear to have been inadequate and unsatisfactory, for the Committee decided to explore other avenues. On 13th June Mr. Saxena wrote to the Government of Bengal, inviting it to "place its case" before the Committee, which would welcome its co-operation. He was informed in reply that Government would not countenance proceedings which to all appearances were prompted by a spirit of antagonism, not to terrorism, but to itself. Mr. Saxena expressed surprise at this answer and a hope that it was not final. He was advised that his hopes were vain, and was permitted to publish the correspondence which had passed between himself and the Chief Secretary.

Having done so, he arrived almost along in Calcutta on 7th. July. His reception was poor, and the interest displayed in his enquiry was luke-warm. He arranged to commence his tour by a visit to Tipperah, but on reaching Chandpur on 12th July, he was served with an order prohibiting him from entering the district. He thereupon returned to Calcutta, and after ascertaining that he would not be permitted to visit certain other districts, he left Bengal on 14th July. The refusal of the Government of Bengal to submit its case to the scrutiny of a self-constituted Committee of Congress parliamentarians, not appointed by the Legislative Assembly and lacking any constitutional authority, needs no justification and the suggestion that Government should have recognized the right of a political party to investigate and sit in judgment upon official policy, was remarkable, not merely for its effrontery, but also for its curious ignorance of the first principles of constitutional practice.

While Congress politicians were indulging in these misguided efforts to secure a general release of all detenus and to excite sympathy on their behalf, irrespective of the merits or demerits of individuals, and cheerfully oblivious of the public danger involved by the proposal to flood the Province with potential anarchists, Government began to develop a policy calculated to wean the majority of those detained from their mistaken leanings towards terrorism and to convert them into useful members of the State.

The general tone of Press during the year was similar to that of 1934, and although the improvement noticed in last year's Report was maintained and there was a considerable hardening of opinion against terrorism, the attitude of hostility towards Government still persisted in a considerable degree. At the beginning of the year there was strong criticism of the Report of the Joint Select Committee on the India Bill, and the Bill itself came in for steady attack while passing through Parliament. The financial proposals of the Bengal Government were also condemned on the ground that new taxation could not be justified, and while the Development Bill was generally welcomed, it was suggested that the Government of India's grant of money for rural reconstruction only resulted from the activities of Mr. Gandih's Village Industries Association.

Communal Outlook

The reprieve granted to one of the would be assassins of his Excellency the Governor was welcomed with the suggestion that it would do more to check terrorism than any number of repressive laws; but the action taken by Government against various communal associations in Calcutta roused considerable hostile comment. Sarcastic reference were made in April to the publication by the 'Morning Post' of a confidential circular of the Bengal I. C. S. Association.

The unfortunate pandering of the Press to communal antagonism has already been referred to, and it was particularly noticeable in connection with the firing at Karachi and the rioting at Ferozabad. The attitude of the Nationalist newspapers towards the Silver Jubilee celebrations in May cannot be described as anything more than lukewarm, and although some of them published Jubilee issues and royal greetings, there was a tendency to indulge in somewhat undignified criticism of the various arrangements that were made. The demand of security from the newspaper 'Bande Mataram' as a result of a scurrilous writing against His Majesty, even evoked some sympathy, and comments were made upon the risks to which the Press was exposed under the present law.

It is satisfactory to note that 'Bande Mataram' subsequently repudiated the sentiments expressed in the offending article, and later wrote in appreciation of the place occupied by His Majesty in the constitution. Despite considerable interest and general appeals for funds in connection with the Quetta earthquake disaster, there was much grumbling over the restrictions imposed upon the entry of volunteers into the devastated area and the decision to refuse admission to non-officials was criticised as likely to create public suspicion and resentment. The interest aroused by the passage of the India Bill through the House of Lords was soon overshadowed by the communal feelings excited by the Shahidganj mosque dispute at Lahore; and bitter opposition was expressed against the renewal of the Public Security Act and the Criminal Law Amendment Act. The debates in the Legislative Assembly over the latter measure were fully reported and its certification by His Excellency the Viceroy was viewed with marked disfavour.

Much interest was evinced in the distress caused by the Damodar floods, and there was occasional appreciations of official relief measures. With the placing of the Government of India Act upon the statute book, interest in home politics centred on the question of the acceptance of office under the new constitution, and a considerable volume of opinion in unexpected quarters appeared to favour the working of the Reforms.

SYMPATHY FOR ABYSSINIA

The war in Abyssinia aroused much genuine sympathy for the Emperor Haile Selassie and his people, but it was freely suggested that the part played by Great Britain, in support of the League of Nations and in the enforcement of Sanctions against Italy, was dictated by considerations of selfish imperialism and not by philanthropic motives. There was a general tendency to decry the efforts of the League, but on the other hand the Franco-British proposals for a settlement of the dispute were severely censured and the subsequent resignation of Sir Samuel Hoare, the Foreign Secretary, was declared to have been inevitable.

At the close of the year the main topics of discussion were the communal dispute in the Calcutta Corporation, the question of acceptance of office by the Congress under the new constitution, the celebration of the Congress Golden Jubilee and the impending financial inquiry by Sir Otto Niemeyar; and the Bengal Press was unanimous in its support of His Excellency the Governor's appeal for financial justice to Bengal in the next settlement between the Centre and the Provinces.

During the year 47 warnings were conveyed to newspapers by the Press Officer and security was demanded from four presses and five papers, while the securities of one press and one newspaper were forfeited.

The B. & O. Administration Report

The following extracts are taken from the Report for the year 1935 :—

The year 1935 was, generally speaking, one of suspended political activity. The previous year had closed with the almost simultaneous Congress success in the Legislative Assembly elections in November and the publication of the Joint Select Committee's Report ; but the Congress found little cause for solace in the events of the year under review, whether in the matter of capturing the votes of the people, or of influencing the course of the New Reforms legislation.

That the extreme Congress programme found little support among the people is shown by the wide-spread apathy evinced by the public on the usual "Independence Day" celebrations staged by the Congress on January 26th. The lack of public interest on January 26th. contrasted vividly with the ripples of enthusiasm on December 28th, the day of the Congress Golden "Jubilee," when the Congress, in co-operation with most parties, managed, on a non-party basis successfully to imitate, at many important centres of the province, some features of His Majesty's Silver Jubilee Celebrations of the preceding May. The other parties made it clear that they were honouring by the participation the aspirations of India to autonomy and were in no way endorsing the disloyal creed of the present Congress. The Hindu Mahasabha indeed felt so natually the evasive attitude of the Congress towards the Communal Award that at their annual session at Poona, during Christmas week, they not only refused to felicitate the Congress on the occasion of its Golden Jubilee but also decided to contest the elections under the new constitution in opposition of the Congress.

ENROLMENT OF MEMBERS

Apart from elections and jubilations there was little in the activities of the official Congress party worthy of record. The first-half of the year was spent by Congressmen in recruiting members under the new Congress constitution, but in spite of postponements of the final date for recruitment, and the fact that Babu Rajendra Prasad, the Congress President, was a native of this province, the results, even according to a resolution passed by the Provincial Congress Working Committee on April 17th. was disappointing. Of the provincial quota of one hundred thousand members, the Congress in Bihar and Orissa managed to enrol only some seventy-eight thousand. Still it afforded considerable consolation in Bihar Congress circles to know that of all the provinces of India, Bihar and Orissa stood first in the matter of enrolment of Congress members.

The activities within the province of the All-India Village Industries Association, about which much had been promised earlier in the year, consisted in expensive experiments at gur-making from the toddy palm, in the opening of a night school here or a village library there, or a few shops here and there selling articles somewhat above the market rate. In fact, most Congressmen with their desire to see the industrialization of India on modern lines progress as rapidly as possible, were, from the start, half-hearted about a matter to which they were prepared to pay lip-service in deference to the dreams of Mr. Gandhi. Moreover, the ban by Mr. Gandhi on workers of the Village industries Association actively participating in political work effectively deprived the scheme of its political attraction.

Socialist Discontent

The real interest in Congress politics however, in this province as elsewhere, was not so much the activity of the Village Industries Association or the Golden Jubilee Celebration as the increasing dissension within the party, owing to the growing impatience of its Socialist wing with the policy of Congress officialdom. Already in April, at the meeting of the All-India Congress Committee at Jubbulpore, the Congress President found some difficulty in keeping the Socialist members under control. In May, matters were precipitated by the declaration of Mr. Satyamurti M. L. A., Secretary of the Congress Parliamentary Party and President of the Madras (Tamil) Congress Committee, in favour of acceptance of office under the new constitution.

This declaration took Congress orthodoxy by surprise and caused a marked stir in political circles in the country. The Satyamurti group was loud in favour of office and the Socialist group was as vociferous against ; while Congress officialdom observed a discreet silence. The country, however, at once demanded to know the mind of the Congress on this important question, but was told by the Congress Working Committee at Wardha in July to wait for an answer.

This procrastination was endorsed by the All-India Congress Committee at its meeting in Madras in October and the matter was left over to the open session of the Congress at Lucknow in April 1936, neither the Working Committee, nor the All-India Committee, daring to give a lead to a matter in which opinion within the Congress was so sharply divided as to promise a split whatever the decision.

Kisan Sabha Activities

While Congressmen in Orissa seemed united in their determination to work the new constitution in Bihar the cleavage between Congress officialdom and the Socialist wing was accentuated by the activities of the Kissan Sabha and their leader Swami Sahajanand. Ostensibly an organization to promote the welfare of the tenantry, the Kishan Sabha, under the inspiration of their Socialist allies, became increasingly a body aiming at the complete elimination of the ownership of property in land. Throughout the year the Swami and his followers toured the districts in North and South Bihar, addressing meetings, where they enlarged upon the misdeeds of the landlords and the iniquity of the Bihar Tenancy (Amendment) Act which came into force in June.

Naturally the Swami and his friends were considerably annoyed when Pandit Shiva Shankar Jha and Babu Gursahai Lal, who had been the tenants' representatives in the Legislative Council during the passage of the Bill, toured the same districts, with the active good-will of the local Government, informing large assemblies of eager tenants of the benefits secured to them by the Act. In a Presidential speech at Hajipur, in November, the Swami appears to have over-reached himself for he was openly attacked by the Congress vernacular organ, the Navashakti of Patna for his views expressed there. This, however, did not deter the Swami, who succeeded, in December, in organizing a boycott of the Bihta Sugar Mill by the local sugarcane growers.

India Bill Reaction

In the wider constitutional sphere the debates in Parliament on the India Bill were followed with the closest interest in the province as elsewhere There was widespread disappointment at the omission of any reference to Dominion Status in the Bill itself, which the subsequent explanatory statements of responsible Ministers in Parliament and the assurance that His Majesty's Government will stood by the Viceroy of India's famous pronouncement of 1929 did not entirely dispel. Many of the amendments carried during the progress of the Bill were subjected to hostile criticisms in the Press.

There was one amendment, however, which was universally applauded, namely the amendment of the House of Lords substituting direct election to the Upper

Chamber of the Federal Legislature for indirect election. In August, the Royal assent to the Government of India Act was the signal for further conventional criticism of the new constitution, which the leading Congress organ of the province described as "a monstrous infliction" and "an unparalleled affront".

That this ferocity of language did not represent its real views, however, and still less the views of the public, is proved by the intense interest which it constantly betrayed in the work of the Reforms Department. Indeed all sections of opinion showed the keenest interest in the impending advent of the new constitution, which was reflected in the debates of the Legislative Council and the reception, given in October to the Delimitation Committee, in whose Chairman, Sir Laurie Hammond, the province recalled with satisfaction, one of its distinguished former public servants.

Another outstanding event which had wide reactions in the province was the Italo-Abyssinian war. The course of the war and the attitude towards it of the League of Nations, and of Great Britain in particular, were watched with the closest interest. Like the rest of India the sympathies of Bihar and Orissa were entirely with Abyssinia; and the attempts of the Italian community in Calcutta to arouse sympathy for Italy, by the issue of letters and communiques to the Press, and the distribution, in September and October, of pamphlets within the province fell flat.

COMMUNAL RELATIONS

The year 1935 saw a steady deterioration in communal relations chiefly owing to repercussions among Moslems of the events in other provinces and the correspondingly increased activity of the Hindu religious organisations. The year began in Bihar with fair prospects, which were soon dimmed in February by the failure at Delhi of the Rajendra Prasad-Jinnah talks to effect any agreed communal settlement. The firing on a frenzied Moslem mob at Karachi on the 19th March agitated the Moslem mind all over India and induced a desire for martyrdom that was not calculated to make the already strained relations with the major community any easier. Although the Bakr-Id in March passed off without serious trouble, rioting was narrowly averted at Kharagpur, Tegra and Sheikhpura in Monghyr district, while the sacrilegious defilement, with a slaughtered calf's head, of a Deviasthan outside Phenhara in Champaran, was to bear its fruit of death five months later.

MUHARRAM CLASHES

In April, the 7th day of Muharram happened to concide with the Ram Navami, which was celebrated with even larger Mahabir Jhanda processions than usual; a class of procession which throughout its few years' vogue has tended intensely to annoy Moslems who regard it as a provocative substitute for their Muhharam procession, in which both communities used to join in happier years. The result was that the police and the magistracy almost everywhere had an anxious time; while several clashes between the communities took place at Hazaribagh and Ranchi. Although many persons, including policemen were injured at both these places, previously the envy of the province for their lack of communal trouble no one was actually killed.

The atrocities of the communal riots at Ferozabad in the Agra District, of the United Provinces, in April, in which, eleven Hindus were burnt to death in a barricaded house, sent a thrill of horror throughout the country, and aroused Hindu feeling as intensely as Moslem feelings had been aroused in March by the Karachi tragedy. Although the barbarities were condemned by all right-minded persons including several Moslem leaders, the incident left an ugly impression that kept communal ill-feeling vigorously alive throughout May.

In June there was a somewhat unexpected outburst of Moslem feeling in Bihar as elsewhere, against clause 304 of the Government of India Bill, then before the House of Commons, which provided for future amendments in the method of election to the Legislatures. A statement issued by the Government of India with the authority of the Secretary of State on July 3rd did much to allay Moslem apprehensions that the Communal Award might be altered without consulting the minorities, and the corresponding section 308 of the Act, as passed, has given satisfaction to all but extreme Moslem opinion. Later in July the communal situation in the Punjab over the Sahidganj affair necessitated the despatch of the Gurkha Military Police from Ranchi to Lahore.

In August the embitterment of communal relations brought tragedy in our province. On the 4th of the month, very large crowds of armed Hindus, who had not forgotten the defilement of their Devisthan some five months before, assembled at Phenhara in Champaran ostensibly for a Mahabir Jhanda procession, and broke the terms of a compromise regarding the road of procession arrived at with the Moslems only two days previously. They then defied the repeated orders of the Sadar Subdivisional Officer to disperse, attempted to invade the Moslem Idgah, and compelled the Subdivisional Officer to order the armed police to open fire, in the course of which 30 rounds were fired resulting in the death of six men and in injuries to seven more.

There were attempts in certain quarters to make communal and political capital out of the tragedy, but the prompt issue of two communiques by Government, the first based on a telegraphic report and the second on fuller material, including the recorded evidence of several non-official Hindu eye-witnesses fully enlightened the public regarding the occurrence. Although the Legislative Council met at Ranchi shortly after, in the same month, no attempt was made to censure the action of Government or its officers whether by a resolution or by a adjournment motion.

Again, on the 27th October there was a serious Hindu-Moslem clash over the old question of processions and music before mosques. This time the scene was at Jamalpur in Monghyr district where an apparently inoffensive Moslem stranger was killed in the fracas.

But, although the scene may shift, the features in most of these clashes are much the same ; and there is little prospect of permanent harmony unless both the great communities exercise forbearance and mutual toleration. A feature of the year symptomatic of the tension between the two communities was the number of Mahabir Jhanda processions taken out, apparently at all seasons of the year, and increasingly in areas where no one found it a necessary part of his religion so to proceed before.

It is a significant commentary on communal realations that on the day of the Phenhara firing, which was not the date of any major festival, no less than six Magistrates in Champaran alone had to leave their ordinary work and go on deputation, with police forces, to various places in the district, in order to keep the communities apart on the occasion of these Mahabir Jhanda demonstrations. The very heavy burden on the administration need not be emphasised, but unless the two great communities take the situation in hand in good time, the increased expenditure, that may become necessary in future in order to maintain law and order in the province, may make the administration, in return, a burden on the people.

In addition to Hindu-Moslem tension there was some local friction, erupting in criminal cases between Christians and Hindus, among the aboriginals of Chota Nagpur, owing to resentment at intensified Hindu missionary activity, chiefly in Palamau district.

Within the Hindu community itself although the declared intention of Dr. Ambedkar, in October, to lead the depressed classes out of the Hindu fold, caused a considerable stir in orthodox circles, it does not seem to have had effect on the depressed classes in this province.

The year saw a marked increase in crime. The figure of reported cases in 1935 as compared with the triennial average for the three preceding years are murder 362 cases against 355, dacoity 475 cases against 415, robbery 249 cases against 205, burglary 16,320 against 15,482, theft 9,664 against 9,260, cattle theft 843 cases against 593 and riot 780 against 762. The increase in dacoity is not as serious as the figures suggest since the figures for the 2nd quarter are swollen by 28 cases in Saran which were merely revivals of suppressed or minimized cases of previous years.

It is difficult to account for the increase in crime, but possibly the explanation be found in the fact that the previous three years' period was a period of slump in crime after the boom in crime during the Civil disobedience era. Perhaps insistence on better reporting and the pre-occupation of the policy, in some districts, with communal trouble were also responsible for the increase in the figures. It is interesting to note that the no-police tract in the Santhal Parganas likewise recorded an increase attributed to the economic depression.

To cope with the problem there was an energetic drive of bad livelihood cases of which no less than 919 cases against 1.695 persons came before the courts in the course of the year. In Champaran and Purnea where there had been successful prosecutions under sections 110 of the Criminal Procedure Code there was a sharp increase in dacoity, vanishing to none in the 3rd quarter in Champaran. Purnea also greatly benefited from the restriction under the Criminal Tribes Act, of 375 notorious North Bhagalpur criminals.

A disquieting feature was the continued occurrence of railway obstruction cases. There were 47 such cases during the year. Although none of these cases had fatal results, the persistence of a mentality among certain persons, who would derail trains by tampering with the line or signals, in order to express their grievance against society, is a source of ever-present danger to the public.

Terrorist activity during the year was not inconsiderable. On April 3rd a bomb exploded in a Sikh Gurdwara in Patna city. The occurrence apparently had no political significance. In June, four youths who had been preparing to commit a political dacoity in the Jharia Coalfields, were arrested by the police. One confused and the other three were sentenced to four years' rigorous imprisonment.

On the sixth of July, while six youths belonging to the Madhubani revolutionary party were manufacturing bombs at Gandhwar in the Madhubani subdivision of Darbhanga district, one bomb accidentally exploded killing one of them outright and injuring the others severely. One of the five survivors turned approver and the other four alleged survivors were being tried by the Court of Sessions at the end of the year.

Again, at the end of December, a train on the Fatwa-Islampur Light Railway ran over and exploded a bomb, which had evidently been placed on the line with sinister intent. No one was hurt and the event probably had no political complexion.

Nine more persons were interned and three (including an arms smuggler) were externed under the Bihar and Orissa Public Safety Act during the course of the year. This Act which was due to expire in March '36, proved a most effective weapon in dealing with terrorism and communism and the necessity was felt of the re-enactment of certain sections as a permanent measure. Just after the close of the year the Legislative Council extended the operation of these sections for five years more.

Of the papers that began publication during the course of the year mention may be made of the 'Sentinel', an English weekly published at Ranchi since March, the 'Istiqlal', an Urdu twice-weekly of Patna, published since November, and the Hindi 'Janak' a daily of Patna that appeared at the end of the year.

Security under the Indian Press (Emergency Powers) Act was demanded only from the 'Jamhoor', a Urdu weekly of Patna, for an article containing a thinly-veiled incitement to murder; at the time of declaration from the 'Istiqlal'; and from the 'Chandrakala Press' at Hazaribagh. The 'Jamhoor' ceased publication on demand of security. The securities deposited by the 'Yogi' and the 'Navashakti' in the course of the previous year remained intact at the end of the year.

As a mark of protest against the certification by the Governor-General, in September, of the Criminal Law Amendment Bill, which the Assembly had refused to consider, certain papers withheld publication for a day.

Nevertheless the press as a whole, even those papers which are, from policy, automatically hostile to Government, offered every facility to the Publicity Officer in the publication of Government material; and, as the year advanced, all but the most extreme papers evinced an increasing readiness to try to understand the Government point of view.

The year was fairly free of industrial disputes. The strikes that occurred were of a minor nature and hardly merit detailed record.

There was an increasing disposition among employers to consider sympathetically the legitimate grievances of workers. Thus the India General Navigation Company met to a great extent the demands of the workers at the Digha workshop, who struck work for a few days in December, owing to the discharge of 78 of their number; and the action, in July, of the Tata Iron and Steel Company in granting a bonus of one month's pay to all their employees at an estimated expenditure of about Rs. 10 lakhs had a settling effect among the workers in one of the most important labour areas of the province.

There was some increase in Trade Union activity, in Monghyr and Jamalpur, as elsewhere, under the inspiration of the All-India Trade Union Congress and the Socialist Party; but, in places, the workers resented the attempts of the Socialist Party to use them for political ends. On the other hand, the accredited leaders of the workers took a keen interest in the position of Labour under the New Constitution, and the Metal Workers Union of Jamshedpur in co-operation with unions from the coalfields appeared before the Hammond Committee at Ranchi in October to argue the Trade Union point of view. In the same month the Provincial Congress Committee at its meeting at Patna showed some interest in labour matters and appointed Mr. Abdul Bari to investigate the labour problem throughout the province, while Babu Rajendra Prasad himself proceeded straight from the Patna meeting to Jamshedpur in order to try to pach up some agreement between the Metal Workers Union, which wished to keep aloof from politics, and its moribund rival, the Labour Association, with its distinct Congress sympathies. At the end of the year the release, on the 27th November, of Manek Homi from the Seraikela Jail evoked considerable enthusiasm among workmen in the Jamshedpur area.

The latest of the monsoon in setting in and its early departure would suggest at first sight a year of drought rather than of flood. But the unevenness with which the rainfall was distributed between July and September was responsible for widespread floods in North and South Bihar. At the end of the first week in August heavy rain fell in Chota Nagpur and South Bihar causing floods in Gaya and Patna districts. The Punpun with its tributaries the Moraar and the Dardha inundated the countryside. The 'bhadai' crop was very seriously damaged in and around the Jehanabad subdivision of the Gaya district. The flood interrupted railway traffic on the Grand Chord line for about two days, a bridge at Akbarpur at the southern extremity of the Dehri-Rohatas Light Railway and another on the Fatwa-Islampur Light Railway were carried away ; while the Patna-Ranchi road was badly breached at several places. An alarming feature of the flood was the threat to Patna City itself where an iron shutter in a culvert near Gulzarbagh station was carried away overnight. The efforts of the staff of the Public Works Department and the District Board saved the city from serious damage. On the 23rd August the rise in the Lakhandegi and other small rivers breached the ring-embankment that surrounds Sitamarhi since the earthquake, and flooded the town Fortunately the water subsided on the 25th. In the Bhagalpur district the Kosi in flood, as was fully expected, washed away the embankment put up to protect Madhipura, and also interrupted the train service in Supaul.

In September the unfortunate Tirhut Division once more suffered the worst natural calamity of the year in the province. Within a week of the 16th September twenty-five inches and more of rain deluged the greater part of the Division. This excessive rainfall coincided with high flood in the Bur Gandak in Muzaffarpur and Darbhanga districts. Therefore, while parts of Champaran and Saran also suffered badly, the damage was greatest in the Sitamarhi and Sadar subdivisions of Muzaffarpur and in the Sadar and Samastipur subdivisions of Darbhanga district. Some idea of the floods can be gathered from the fact that the roads, which, of course, were badly breached in all the districts, were at some places as much as ten feet under water. The loss of life from drowning was insignificant, thanks to the prompt measures of relief undertaken by the officers of Government and local bodies, and also by non-official organisations but several persons lost their lives by the collapse of mud walls, and many thousands of mud houses and thousands of maunds grain were badly damaged in the affected areas.

To cope with the situation caused by the floods, Government gave whatever relief was necessary. For the August floods, Government had given Rs. 5,000 for the relief of distress in the Gaya and Patna districts and Rs. 6,000 for relief in Tirhut. The September floods necessitated relief on a more extensive scale. About a lakh of rupees was placed at the disposal of the Commissioner of the Tirhut Division for gratuitious relief in the form of grants for house-building, or, for 'rabi' seeds, to compensate the poorer classes for the extensive damage to houses and crops that the flood had caused. In addition a sum of Rs. 96,000 was allotted to the four districts of the Tirhut Division for the purpose of 'taccavi' loans and the Collectors in these districts were also authorized by Government to stay certificate cases at their discretion.

There was, on the whole, no marked improvement in the economic condition of the people, but the slight increase in the revenues of the province under several heads suggests that the worst of the economic depression is over. There might indeed have been a distinct amelioration in the condition of the masses had not the monsoon in 1935 been disappointing almost everywhere in the province except Purnea and parts of Orissa. In June and July there was a marked deficiency in the rainfall, while in August and September the rainfall was exceptionally heavy in certain areas causing floods in the Patna and Tirhut Divisions with considerable damage to the 'bhadai' and winter rice crops. In October the monsoon failed almost completely except in Orissa, with unfavourable results not only on the winter rice crops, at the time of seeding, but also on the germination and growth of the 'rabi' crop. Indeed, the all but entire absence of rain in the last quarter of the year did not give promise of a good 'rabi' harvest. The failure of the later rains gave the ground in December the hard aspect of February, and already at the end of the year the wells in the Ranchi district were beginning to dry up.

The effect of the unfavourable harvests, however, is not likely to make itself fully felt till the following April or May when a temporary set-back in the condition of the agriculturists is feared. The scanty harvests in the districts of Bengal bordering on the Bhagalpore Division reacted unfavourably on agricultural labourers in that division, who, in good years, secure employment during the harvest season across the borders.

To relieve distress among the agriculturists, caused by floods and failure of crops, Government gave a sum of just under two lakhs of rupees for free grants and just under four lakhs as 'taccavi' loans. In parts of Singhbhum district the partial failure of crops in the previous season gave cause for anxiety, and in addition to a sum of over Rs. 70,000 included in the 'taccavi' loans, already mentioned, a sum of Rs. 32,000 was spent on relief works for the benefit of the labouring classes in the Dhalbhum, Kolhan and Porahat areas of that district.

There were some bright features in the situation. The sugarcane season started in November with a slight rise in the minimum price of sugarcane which was at first fixed by Government at 5 and a half annas a maund, or half an anna more than the minimum price of the previous season. Unfortunately as the season advanced the price had to be reduced owing to the fall in the price of sugar and with the New Year it was at 5 annas once more. However, the increasing vigilance of the Sugarcane Inspectors appointed by Government to supervise the work of the Sugarcane Rules protected the sugarcane cultivators to a growing extent from the depredations of middlemen. The price of common rice continued to show a tendency to rise. In July the average price for the province was 11.97 seers to the rupee against 12.91 seers the year before, while at the close of the year it was 11.79 seers against 13.48 seers in the first week of 1935.

On the other hand the price of lac, which had almost doubled itself in the previous year owing to artificial manipulations of the market, fell back sharply to Rs. 25 per maund by the middle of the year. The daily wages of agricultural labour ranged between 1 anna 6 pies to 3 annas in Sambalpur district and 4 annas to 6 annas in Shahabad. The progress of earthquake and flood reconstruction work continued to furnish employment to labour, while the grants disbursed by Government and the Bihar Central Relief Committee, and the bonus of Rs. 10 lakhs awarded to their employees by the Tata Iron and steel Company put large sums into circulation.

Nevertheless in the districts of North and South Bihar there was a good deal of agitation organised by the Kishan Sabha against the burden of rents and canal rates. While much of the agitation was spurious there is no doubt that in some places, especially in the Gaya district, where produce rents had been commuted to cash rents during the period of high prices of agricultural produce, the great fall in the price of agricultural produce, estimated in 1934-35 to have fallen in this province by about 60 per cent as compared with the prices for 1928-29, made the burden of the cash rents very heavy on the tenants. On the other hand, owing to the Bihar Tenancy Act, 1934, which came into force in June and permitted the unrestricted transfer of 'rayati' land on payment of a fixed transfer fee of 8 per cent to the landlord, there was a distinct tendency, in the districts of Bihar proper for the price of agricultural land to rise and tenants were able to raise more money from the mortgage of their lands than before.

The average prices of cereals remained more or less at the same low level as before. There was a slight rise in the price of common rice which was selling at 12.18 seers a rupee in the second week of December as compared with 13.55 seers in the corresponding period of the previous year. On the other hand the price of maize in the same period fell from 17.64 seers per rupee in 1934 to 19.11 seers in 1935.

Agricultural conditions during the year were not satisfactory. The rains were neither well distributed nor sufficient in most places. The want of sufficient rain in June and July delayed the sowing of the *'bhadai'* crops, while excessive rainfall in August and September damaged the crops of the Tirhut and Patna Divisions. The complete failure of the rains in the last winter paddy crop not only adversely affected the outturn of the winter paddy crop but also the germination and growth of the *rabi* crops. Fortunately, there is reason to believe that the reclamation of agricultural lands affected by earthquakes was almost completed during the year.

The appointment, during the year, of a Marketting officer and the Assistant Marketting officers for the province, was greeted with public satisfaction, as the importance of the proper development of agricultural marketting was widely recognised. In collaboration with the Central Marketting staff the Provincial Marketting Staff was engaged in a comprehensive survey of the production and the marketing of various commodities throughout the province.

In November the local Government convened a small conference to review the working of the Sugarcane Act and Rules in the light of the previous year's experience. That the Sugarcane Act and Rules were widely appreciated by the people is shown by the popular satisfaction which marked the decision of Government to extend them to the Patna Division.

Agricultural Education was not neglected. Three of the four Government stipendiaries studying at Nagpur Agricultural College, who appeared at the last B. Agr. examination of the Nagpur University, were successful and were offered posts in the Subordinate Agricultural Service in the province. The Central Farms continued to train their own overseers and *kamdars* and an increasing desire among the public to benefit by the practical training offered in the Central Farms was manifest. At Sabour an M. Sc. in chemistry worked as an Honorary Research worker in the Chemical section.

Seven agricultural shows, exhibitions and fairs were held during the year. The Department of Agriculture not only encouraged these events by awarding prizes for agricultural exhibits to the extent of Rs. 900, but also itself participated in them by sending exhibits and holding demonstrations. The agricultural show at the Sonepur fair attracted large crowds as usual. At all these shows and exhibitions the department vigorously pursued its policy of impressing upon the agricultural classes the importance of good seeds, suitable manures and improved methods of cultivation. An interesting experiment was started at Ranchi in order to foster the growth of vegetables by the middle classes with the expert advice of the Agricultural Department.

Propaganda by means of the printed word was continued during the year. Three bulletins in English were issued, while the quarterly Hindi Journal "Kisan" published under the auspices of the Bihar and Orissa Provincial Association became increasingly popular.

The department lent the services of two of its overseers to the Publicity Officer for the purpose of the Silver Jubilee Magic Lantern lectures.

The Anglo-Indian colony at Lapra in the Ranchi district was in its third year, and continued to make slow progress. About 75 families have been settled and some 3,000 acres of land acquired. A dairy farm was opened. The experiment is being watched with sympathetic interest by all communities.

There was some slight lifting of the industrial depression during the year under review. Of the main industries in the province the sugar industry, in spite of the excise duty recently imposed, and the iron and steel industry continued to flourish under the protection of tariff walls. There was a welcome improvement in the mica industry and the exports of mica showed a substantial increase. The coal industry, however, did not show any marked signs of recovery, and the prevalence of extensive fires in the Jharia coalfield gravely menaced the well-being of one of the most important industrial areas in the province. The post-earthquake activity in the building and allied trades continued. For the fifth year in succession no Government grant was made under the State Aid to Industries Act, but provision was made in the budget for 1936-37 to assist small industrialists.

There was a slight set-back in the fish export trade. In 1935 the export of fresh fish totalled 77.110 maunds against 91,245 in 1934. This was, however, better than the figure for 1933, which was 69,980 maunds. In addition to the two previous fry-distribution centres at Patna and Cuttack, a third was established at Sambalpore. The total supply of fry from three centres was 331,500 against 320,000 in 1934. The figure for 1933, however, was 382,500. Possibly the vagaries of the monsoon with alternate periods of drought and flood over large areas accounts for much of the difference between the figures for 1933 and 1935 in spite of an additional distribution centre. There was a welcome increase in the demand for larvicidal fish from 1,586 in 1934 to 3,000 in 1935.

The U. P. Administration Report 1935

Socialistic influence in Congress politics in the United Provinces is reviewed at some length in the Administration report for 1935. There is an increasing preference on the part of Congressmen for work among the rural rather than among the urban population.

The political situation, it says, continued to cause no anxiety and there was a marked decrease in the more important forms of crime but communal relations unfortunately remained strained. The various departments of Government registered progress within the limits set by their restricted budget.

In view of the differences of opinion held by the various groups into which it was split during the preceding year, the Congress was naturally anxious to avoid and direct statement of its attitude towards many important questions of policy. To ensure obedience to its authority the Congress Working Committee at its meeting at Delhi in January 1935, found it necessary to make rules empowering it to take disciplinary action against any committee or member of the Congress who acted deliberately in opposition to the official programme and decisions of the Congress. The only other decision of importance reached there was that the Congress should occupy all places of power and vantage in its "struggle for freedom to assert the dominating will of the people". This decision was made public in a statement issued by Dr. Ansari and other Congress leaders in July 1935.

Congress Dissensions

From the moment the June meeting of the United Provinces Congress Committee decided on Lucknow as the venue for the forty-ninth session of the Indian National Congress, Lucknow was the scene of bickerings between the local rival parties in connection with the office of Chairman of the Reception Committee. The differences were ultimately patched up by the election of Pandit Jawaharlal Nehru to the post but a further dispute arose over the proportionate representation of parties on the Committee. Several Committee meetings at Lucknow which were marked by stormy scenes, having failed to come to an amicable settlement, a meeting of the Provincial Congress Committee held at Agra in November 1935 decided to form a board of five "dictators" with absolute power to control and carry on the work of the Congress in this province and to make all the arrangements for the holding of the next Congress session.

Personal rivalries and discord were not confined to Lucknow but were also a feature of several District Congress committees, and in a few cases culminated in assaults in connection with the local board elections. A number of opposition parties such as the "Congressmen's Party" in Allahabad, the "Independent Congress Party" in Jhansi and the "Congress Kisan Party" in Meerut had been constituted and so acute were the differences between the different sections of the Congress, that a Provincial Civic Board composed of five prominent Congressmen of this province was formed to nominate canditates and to conduct elections. The disagreements however which soon arose between the Civic Board and several district Congress committees, notably those at Allahabad and Cawnpore led to the resignation of some members of the Provincial Congress Committee and of the Provincial Civic Board. Some measure of harmony was ultimately restored after protracted negotiation of the Civic Board with additional powers. Although in some places successful, the Congress Party on the whole achieved little ; and in some districts notably lost ground.

Socialist Party

One of the important developments of the year was the growth of the Congress Socialist Party. This party gained in influence by the transfer of the office of the General Secretary of the All-India Congress Socialist Party from Patna to Benares. A meeting of the Executive Committee held in Benares in July passed several resolutions which affirmed that the policy of the party was to wreck the reforms, to organise the peasants and workers in one corporate mass to overthrow the forces of capitalism and to work for the cancellation of peasants, debts and the elimination of landlords and 'taluqdars'. Congress socialists took advantages of political conference held in villages and tahasils to organise unions for peasants and labourers and further their own propaganda. A circular issued by Mr. Jai Prakash Narain as General Secretary emphasised the Socialist party's opposition to the principles of those of "revolutionary unionism" as laid down by Marx and Lenin. As a result of disputes over the local board elections the Congress Socialists who preponderated in the old executive committee resigned almost in a body in October and were replaced by members of the right wing.

Reforms Reaction

Socialistic influence is resulting in an increasing preference on the part of Congressmen for work among the rural rather than among the urban population. Seeing in the peasantry a promising field propaganda the Congress is extending the sphere of its activities and a number of 'Kisan'; conferences were organised in tahasils, small towns and districts. The enrolment of Congress members was continued in order to complete the quota required of each district.

Branches of the All-India Village Industries Association were established in Muttra and Gorakhpur in February and later on, at Meerut. Subsequently a few weaving schools were started in Haldwani and the Agra district, an industrial school at Aligarh and a depot in Gonda. The Association, however, has met with little success in the province and the provincial organising centre at Parkham in the Muttra district had to close down chiefly for want of funds.

The Annual Session of the Hindu Mahasabha was held at Cawnpore in April under the presidentship of Rev. Ottama, a Budhhist Priest of Burma. Its resolutions approving of the action of the authorities in firing on the Muslim rioters in Karachi and condemning the Communal Award aroused the antagonism of the Muslims especially in Cawnpore. The Sabha also condemned the Government of India Bill. After the session the President toured the province delivering speeches condemning the separation of Burma from India and pleading for the formation of a Budhist-Hindu federation.

Constitutional reform was much discussed throughout the year and received particular attention during the passage of the Government of India Bill through Parliament whose amendments were alleged by the Congress and advanced Liberal organs to have intensified the already unsatisfactory and retrograde character of the Bill. For the rest, Press comments ranged from a strong condemnation to qualified approval but were little more than a repetition of those evoked by the publication of the Report of the Joint Select Committee. The features selected for particular attack were the increased cost of the administration involved in the proposals as likely to lead increased taxation, the commercial safeguards in favour of Britain as calculated to retard the development of national trade, and the communal award which would perpetuate and even accentuate communal tension.

While the Congress papers openly advocated the wrecking of the constitution, Liberal papers as a rule were in favour of working it with a view to securing the fullest representation of advanced and nationalist opinion. Muslim papers in general followed the Liberal press subject to some criticism of detail and the expression in some quarters of the necessity for countering the danger of Hindu domination in provinces like the United Provinces by returning to the legislature only representatives who could be relied upon to safeguard Muslim interests. Such papers as support Government together with certain important independent organs claimed that the Bill would provide a substantial improvement on the present constitution, defended the safeguards as necessary, and, deprecating a policy of obstruction, pleaded for genuine and wholehearted co-operation in working the new constitution.

The question whether Congressmen should or should not accept office under the New Constitution was much discussed, the more influential among the extremist papers ultimately arriving at the conclusion that the acceptance of office by Congressmen would be inconsitent with their creed of non-co-operation and their goal of complete independence.

Against Zamindari

There was a considerable increase in the volume and intensity of the propaganda in the extremist Hindi papers directed against the established order and in particular against the 'zamindari' system and Indian States. In their comments on the economic depression these papers attempted to prove that the poverty of the agricultural and labouring classes could be removed only by the reorganisation of the State in accordance with communistic principles. Communism was in fact extolled in some quarters as the panacea for all the ills from which society and the country suffer, The number of advocates of this creed was increased by the conversion of a number of the older papers and by the appearance of several new papers, two being in English, of Socialistic views. The propaganda was in some cases direct but was often cloaked in the guise of stories and biographies of Communists like Lenin. Stalin, and Karl Marx or took the form of reproducing their speches and writings. Several papers sought to represent Russia as a modern Utopia for peasants and labourers, published eulogistic accounts of Russian institutions and administration and of the part played by young men in establishing a communistic regime. The same papers denounced the Indian National Congress as a 'bourgeois' institution and urged that freedom could only be secured by class war and the organisation of peasants and workers. Indian Ruling Chiefs were denounced as enemies of nationalism and their existence as the negation of democracy.

Rural Development

The Government's rural development scheme was widely discussed. Fears were entertained that most of the money would be spent on the salaries of the staff rather than on ameliorating the condition of the rural population. Congress organs sought to represent the scheme as a counterblast to Mr. Gandhi's Village Industries Association and alleged that Government's main object on allotting one crore of rupees to this work was to re-establish and maintain their own hold over the rural area. Some influential Muslim papers on the other hand, looked upon Mr. Gandhi's scheme as a political device to further the interests of the Congress and commended the wisdom of Government in thwarting it by its own measures for rural uplift.

Comments on the Italo-Abyssinian War were marked by condemnation of Italy, sympathy with the Abyssinians and criticism of the attitude of France, Britain and the League of Nations.

EDUCATIONAL PROGRESS IN INDIA

JANUARY—JUNE 1936

Educational Progress in India

Education in India 1934-35

A glance at the provincial education reports of 20 years ago and a comparison of them with the reports for the years 1933-34 would show that provinces long recorded as backward have in many ways come up to the level of advanced provinces, says the report prepared by the Government of India on Education in India for the year April 31st 1933 to March 31st 1934. "Communities which scarcely ever recorded pupils above the primary stage now have considerable representation at the university stage. Untouchability has been definitely eradicated in several provinces in so far as the schools are concerned, and the progress of education amongst the depressed classes has been considerable. Women's education has spread with remarkable rapidity and the educationally backward communities amongst women, such as Muslim women, have shown immense improvement. Physical instruction and athletics have developed out of all recognition and movements like the Olympic organisations, the Boy Scouts movement, the Girl Guides movement, the Red Cross movement, etc., have taken firm root. Village life has widened and schemes for rural uplift, village club, thrift societies and even village broadcasting are no longer unknown.

"The necessity for the trained teacher has been recognised almost everywhere and the numbers of trained teachers have been more than doubled. Considerable advance has been made in scientific research and in Technology and in their application to industry. The need for caution in the quantitative expansion of mass education has been fully recognised and consolidation and concentration are being attempted in most provinces. The evil of waste, stagnation and wastage which were scarcely recognised or diagnosed 20 years ago have been tackled and are being tackled with signs of ultimate success in most parts of India. There is however, it is true, a general dissatisfaction with many of the existing conditions. Universities are overcrowded, secondary education is too stereotyped, primary education is still too little related to the surrounding conditions of life and unemployment presents a grave problem. But there has been very real progress. Education is much more widespread and India is not alone in having to face difficult problems in education arising out of world depression and financial stringency. "It is satisfactory" continues the report "at least that the whole of India is now considering very seriously educational reconstruction and that a machinery has been created for the co-operation of every part of India in an attempt to solve some of the outstanding problems."

During the year under review the total number of educational institutions increased by 1,377 against a fall of 2,445 in the previous year. "The mere increase in the number of institutions is no index of progress," opines the Educational Commissioner with the Government of India. The large fall in the previous year in Madras, for example, was mainly due to a deliberate policy of providing a better and more economic distribution of schools. There has been a further fall in the number of institutions in four provinces and the total number of institutions in India would have again declined but for an increase of 1,599 institutions in Bengal. Only one other province shows a considerable increse 179 in Bihar and Orissa which is entirely accounted for by a rise in the number of unrecognised schools. Although, leaving aside Bengal, there has been a decrease in the number of institutions, there has been a very satisfactory increase in the number of pupils, an increase of 319,358 as against an increase of only 86,995 in the previous year. Taking recognised institutions alone, the increase was 299,659 as against 69,671 in the previous year. In spite of a decrease of 457 institutions in Madras its total enrolment increased by 103,075 and Bombay with a decrease of 83 institutions increased its enrolment by 34,332."

Between the years 1932 and 1933 all provinces and administrations except Delhi, Coorg and the minor administrations, showed a heavy fall in total expenditure, but during the year 1933-34 all previnces and administrations showed a considerable increase in total expenditure except the United Provinces, Burma and Assam. In spite of the prevailing economic depression and decline in the revenue per head of the population there has been some considerable improvement in ability of provincial governments to provide additional funds for education.

EXPENDITURE

The following table shows for the years 1927 and 1934 the expenditure from government fund on education and the percentage of total revenue spent on education in the provinces :

1927

Province.	Total Govt. Expenditure.	Percentage of total revenue spent on education.
	Lakhs.	Per cent.
Madras	202	13.3
Bombay	199	13.6
Bengal	148	14.0
U. P.	196	17.2
Punjab	151	13.9
Burma	95	9.4
B. & O.	72	12.5
C. P.	72	14.2
Assam	25	10.2
N. W. F. P.	—	—

1934

Province.	Total Govt. expenditure.	Percentage of total revenue spent on education.
	Lakhs.	Per cent.
Madras	246	15.9
Bombay	176	12.1
Bengal	135	14.9
U. P.	198	17.6
Punjab	160	14.0
Burma	58	6.8
B & O.	55	11.1
C. P.	44	10.2
Assam	28	14.0
N. W. F. P.	19	11.0

Between 1933 and 1934 the largest increase of recent years in the enrolment to Universities has occurred and the total number of students in the universities has risen by 6851 to 113,328. The only falling off in numbers has occurred in Dacca, Delhi, the Osmania University, the Andhra University and the Annamalai University, and the total fall in these five universities amounted to only 363. On the other hand the Calcutta University alone showed an increase of 4,104 and the Punjab and Bombay Universities have each increased nearly 1,000. Fortunately expansion has been accompanied by the institution of new types of courses, including scientific and technological courses, which are to be welcomed as providing not only more variety but more practical courses related to research and industry.

UNEMPLOYMENT

The problem of the continued unemployment of large numbers of University products has continued to exercise the minds of all those responsible for the control of higher education. The time is coming, says the report, when the question of deliberate restriction must be seriously considered both in the interests of efficiency and in the interest of lessening educated unemployment. It is usually urged that such restriction will particularly adversely affect poor scholars and scholars coming from backward communities. Actually this objection is not a very valid one, since an expansion of the present system which exists in many colleges of reservations, free places and scholarships should meet any difficulties which stand in the way of clever but poor scholars and scholars from educationally backward communities.

A comparison of the figures for the year under consideratien with those for the last few years shows that the total number of male candidates for the university examination, excluding the matriculation, is more or less constant whereas the number of girls is showing an appreciable increase every year. In general, girls have shown better results than boys. The pass percentages for girls in the various university examinations are considerably better than those for boys.

INDIAN STUDENTS ABROAD

The Indian students studying in the United Kingdom during 1933-34 numbered 1,393 as against 1,478 in the previous year. The Indian students known to be studying in Europe increased from 111 to 115 and the number of Indian students in the United States of America increased from 101 to 152.

The number of primary schools for boys increased by 344 and their enrolment increased by 214,817. These increases compare favourably with a decrease of 2,299 in the number of schools in the previous year and with an increased enrolment of only 26,504. It is also satisfactory that the increase in enrolment of boys is not confined to the lowest classes but is shared by all the five primary classes.

The average number of pupils per school is abnormally low. For India as a whole it is only 50, white in Japan, for example, it is over 300. If the primary schools in the provinces were better organised and larger in size a great deal of waste in expenditure could be avoided. In Bengal, for example, if the primary schools had the same average in number as Bombay 1,700,000 more pupils would be under instruction without the provision of any additional schools. Similarly Bihar and Orissa would have more than double their present number of pupils at school if the province had the same average as Central Provinces.

As regards co-education, the report says that experience has shown that one special factor which militates against larger enrolments in the primary schools in both advanced and backward provinces is the attitude of teachers and the inspectorate towards separate boys' schools and separate girls' schools. Except in a very limited number of areas there is at the present time little prejudice against co-education in the lowest Primary classes but it is common to find that in rural areas in which there are only boys' primary schools no endeavour is being made to encourage the girls of school age to attend the boys' schools. Similarly, in rural areas in which there are only girls' primary schools no endeavour is made to encourage the boys of school age to attend the girls' schools.

The backward position of girls in education as compared with the position of boys has for many years occupied the attention of the Provinces. While unfortunately there still remains a wide discrepancy between the relative position of boys and girls there are encouraging signs that the attention paid to girls' education in recent years had not gone unrewarded. The rate of progress of girls' education has, in a number of provinces, become quicker than that of boys. The number of institutions for girls has largely increased. Co-education at the primary stage has become far more common and the number of women teachers has been largely augmented. The total amount expended on girls' education has risen in most provinces in spite of the financial stringency and provinces which a few years ago could show hardly any progress in the higher education of women are now sending out nearly as many women as the other more forward provinces. There are, in fact, definite signs that the women's movement in India in all its aspects has created an awakening of ideas which is overriding custom and prejudice and which is manifesting itself in the increased willingness of all classes of the community to have their girls and women educated.

Between 1933 and 1934 the total expenditure on institutions for girls has increased in all provinces except in the United Provinces. The total expenditure for British India shows an increase of Rs. 11.18 lakhs in 1934 as against a fall of nearly 13 lakhs in 1933. To this increase Bombay contributed Rs. 3.17 lakhs, Punjab Rs. 1.77 lakhs, Madras Rs. 1.29 lakhs and Bengal Rs. 0.79 lakhs.

MUSLIM EDUCATION

As regards the Muslim Education, the total enrolment has declined in Bombay, the Punjab, Burma, Bihar and Orissa, Assam and Delhi. The decrease in Bombay was almost entirely confined to unrecognised schools and to Mulla schools in Sind. The fall in the number of pupils in the Punjab is attributed to the general agricultural depression. The decrease in Burma was small and it was mainly confined to colleges and to unrecognised institutions. In 1917 there were only 5,212 Muslim scholars in arts colleges and university departments, while in 1934 as many as 12,158 Muslim boys were reading in arts colleges and 2,272 in professional colleges. The figures of Muslims girls are much more encouraging than those of Muslim boys. The enrolment in all the major provinces has considerably increased and the total number of Muslim girls under instruction in India increased between 1933 and 1934 by 38,181 and if unrecognised schools are excluded from the figures the total increase was over 4,000. The position in the Punjab is perhaps the most striking since the Punjab has for many years had the lowest percentage of Muslim girls under instruction to the total

Muslim population in India and yet in 1934 the Punjab had the largest number of Muslim ladies reading at the university stage and at the secondary stage.

There has been an increase of over 69.000 students belonging to depressed classes during the year as against an increase of under 13.000 in the previous year.

Education in Madras 1934-35

The Government of Madras, in their review of the report on educational progress in the Presidency between 1934-35, observe :—

In the year under review, a Bill to amend the Madras Elementary Education Act, 1920, was passed into law. The Amending Act which has recently been brought into force gives Government power to order in any specified area the introduction of a modified form of compulsion under which children who have attended school for a prescribed period should not be withdrawn from school before they complete their school-age. It is hoped in this way to check the appalling wastage in elementary education and to diminish the number of those who spend a year or two (or in some cases less) at an elementary school and then relapse in a few years' time and for the rest of their lives into a state of permanent illiteracy.

The number of students reading in Arts Colleges showed a decrease during the year. This may be attributed partly to the general financial depression and partly to the increasing realization on the part of parents that the possession of a University degree is not a sure road to employment and a successful career in life. In any case, the slight reduction in the number of students in the first grade Arts Colleges from 9,209 to 8,847 is not a matter for regret.

Substantial changes were made in the S. S. L. C. scheme and the modified scheme was put into operation in the fourth form of secondary schools during the year under review. Since the close of the year the S. S. L. C. Board has reported that the modified scheme is not altogether satisfactory and has recommended that it might be held in abeyance pending further consideration. The Government have accepted this recommendation. The number of pupils under instruction in secondary schools for boys decreased from 179,411 in 1933-34 to 177,220.

There was a further increase in the number of pupils attending elementary schools for boys. Compulsory elementary education for boys of school-age was newly introduced during the year in Bezwada municipality. The schemes prepared by the local officers of the Department for the consolidation and concentration of elementary schools in municipal areas were under examination by Government during the year under review. The Government are glad that several local bodies have realized the usefulness of schemes of consolidation of schools and are taking steps to give effect to them as is evidenced by the reduction in the number of elementary schools for boys from 43,976 to 43,787 accompanied by an increase in strength from 2,338,608 to 2,417,410.

The number of elementary schools for girls has similarly decreased from 5,464 to 5,336 but here again the strength has risen from 374,430 to 381,013. The girls attending these schools, however, constituted less than half of the total number of girls reading elementary schools in the Presidency, for there were as many as 458,853 girls reading in elementary schools for boys—an appreciable increase over the previous year's figure of 420,311. In this connection, the Govt. would very strongly commend to local bodies and private agencies maintaining schools the desirability of employing women teachers in the lower standards of boys' schools, more particularly where there is an appreciable number of girls reading in these standards. The practice of employing men teachers in girls' schools should be definitely discontinued and those men teachers who are at present teaching in girls' schools, of whom there are far too many, should be provided with posts in boys' schools.

The total number of girls reading in secondary schools was 26,337 as compared with 25,198 in 1933-34. The total number of girls under instruction in all grades of schools rose by about 5 per cent.

There was an increase in the number of Mohammedan pupils in elementary schools but the number in secondary schools showed a decrease.

It is gratifying to note that the number of pupils of the scheduled castes reading in schools not specially intended for them has again risen by about 8 per cent over last year's figure.

In the field of European Education the year was noteworthy for the admission of men teachers for the first time into the Doveton Training School, Madras.

The Provincial Board for Anglo-Indian and European Education met twice during the year.

Education in Travancore 1934-35

A marked increase in the strength of English Schools, the introduction of Hindi as a second language in certain schools, provisions of free medical treatment in hospitals and rapid progress in women's education are the important features of the report for 1934-35 of the Travancore Education Department which has been recorded by the Government.

During the year under review there was a heavy fall under receipts on account of the reduction of the rates of school fees as a temporary measure, due to the general financial depression. The concession involved not only loss in the receipts of Departmental Schools but also additional expenditure by way of compensation to private management for loss of fee income.

Collegiate Education

The number of students attending the Colleges affiliated to the Madras University was 2,792 at the end of 1110 against 2,815 at the end of 1109. There was thus a total fall of only 23. The principle of restricting admissions to the Junior Intermediate and Junior B. A. Classes of the Government Colleges by slightly raising the standard for admission was accepted by the Government for the first time. The restrictions were, however, very moderate in character as only those candidates who had failed more than twice in the S. S. L. C. or the Intermediate Examinations were refused admission into the Junior Inter. or the Junior B. A. Class. Even in applying the above restrictions exceptions were made mainly in the case of backward communities and women.

Medical inspection was conducted during the year in all the Colleges. The Veda Section of the Sanskrit College was transferred to the control of the Devaswom Department.

The total number of English Schools during 1110 M. E. (1934-35) was 275 and the total number of pupils under instruction in them 58,893 as against 272 institutions and 53,831 pupils in 1109. The number of English Schools thus increased by three and the strength in them by 5062 in 1934-35.

Receipts and Expenditures

The total expenditure of the Education Department amounted to Rs. 47,23,208 and the total receipts to Rs. 8,10,412 against Rs. 46,91,482 and Rs. 8,95,233 respectively in the previous year. The decrease in receipts is mainly accounted for by the reduction of fees in schools.

More attention was devoted to organised games in schools and there was an awakening in games and sports in schools and student competitors to the Olympic Meet at Madras won distinction.

Hindi was introduced as a second language in form IV of the S. M. V. School, Trivandrum, and encouragement was given for the opening of Hindi Classes in some private schools. A course of vacation lectures in geography were given by Miss K. S. Ranga Rao, Principal of the New College for Women, Nagpur.

A scheme for the medical inspection of children in primary schools providing for free medical treatment in the hospitals and dispensaries of the State was approved by the Government.

WOMEN'S EDUCATION

The number of girls under instruction during the year under review was 2,69,444 as against 2,57,003 in 1109 and 2,46,693 in 1108 showing a steady increase of well over 10,000 from year to year. Co-education was largely prevalent in all types of institutions. More attention was being paid to games and athletics in all girls' schools, especially English Schools, during the year.

There was an increase in the number of Mahomedans under instruction at all stages during the year. The number of Mahomedan girls under instruction in English Schools was 240 as against 99 in the previous year. The number of depressed and backward pupils reading in all stages of education also showed considerable increase.

The total number of recognised institutions in the State during the year was 3,699 and the number under instruction 6,74,317. There was thus a fall in the total number of institutions by 50, due mainly to the abolition of overlapping and incomplete vernacular schools but the total number of pupils under instruction increased by 24,949 over the figure for the previous year. The percentage of the total number of pupils to the total population in 1110 M. E. was 13.2 as against 12.7 in 1109.

Education in Mysore 1934-35

"The Government are aware of the need of the Department for more money for addition to staff, equipment and accommodation and are doing whatever is possible under the unfavourable financial conditions now prevailing. They are pleased to observe that with the resources available the Department has, under the guidance of the Director, Mr. N. S. Subba Rao, done efficient and satisfactory work during the year". This is the observation of the Government of Mysore in their review of the report on the working of the Department of Public Instruction during the year 1934-35, issued on the 16th. March 1936.

The Government also express their thanks to the members of the public who cooperated with the Department and supplemented the efforts of the Government in the cause of education.

PRIMARY SCHOOLS

The number of primary schools showed a slight fall by four from 6,254 to 6,250 but there was a noticeable increase in the strength by 3,305 pupils from 245,273 to 249,573. Of these, 5,735 schools were for boys (with a strength of 216,721) and 515 schools for girls (with a strength of 32,857). Classified according to languages, there were 5,096 Kannada schools, 622 Urdu, 7 Telugu, 9 Tamil and one Mahratti school. The percentage of boys in the primary schools to the total male population of school-going age, calculated at 15 per cent of the total population, was 43.93 as against 43.4 in the year previous.

The Government observe that the finances of some of the local Education Authorities, particularly of the Shimoga District which has a large minus balance, are not satisfactory. It has also not been possible for the Government, the review states, in the present conditions of finance to meet the entire cost of the scheme as desired by some of the Local Education Authorities. The Government point out that the Local Education Authorities have to augment their resources as contemplated in the Regulation. Proposals for a levy of education fees in the Municipal areas have been received from the Local Education Authorities of Chitaldrug, Hassan and Kolar Districts and these are under consideration.

In view, however, of the pressing demand for primary schools, a scheme prepared by the Director for opening as many new or grant-in-aid schools as possible in different areas in the State, aided schools being opened as departmental schools, has been sanctioned by the Government and a sum of Rs. 15,000 provided for the purpose in the budget for 1935-36.

The Government note with pleasure the large number of benefactions made by members of the public during the year to supply the need for school buildings,

EDUCATION OF GIRLS

There were 562 separate schools for girls of all grades of education with a total strength of 36,554 (of whom 919 were boys) as against 583 schools with a strength of 35,814 (including 829 boys) in the previous year. The fall in the number of girls' schools is due to the amalgamations of several girls' school with the boys' schools. The Government are glad to note that the number of girls seeking admission is increasing in all grades of institutions and that girls are freely entering into boys' schools in places where there are no separate institutions for them.

The total expenditure on education for women (including University education) was Rs. 6,98,185 (exclusive of indirect expenditure such as scholarships, buildings and equipment) as against Rs. 6,93,209 in the previous year.

A sum of Rs. 5,74,634 or 11.71 per cent of the total direct expenditure on education was spent on Muslim education.

The scout Movement, the Government observe, continued to be popular and was making good progress during the year. The Girl Guide movement which was organised in 1932 progressed remarkably well.

EXPENDITURE

The total expenditure both direct and indirect on Public Instruction (including that on University education) amounted to Rs. 63,80,131. On an average, there was one school for every 3.8 sq. miles in area and 832 persons of the total population. One out of every 3.3 of the population of school-going age was under instruction, and the proportion was 1 in 20.24 as against 20.59 in the previous year. The percentage of boys under instruction to the total male population was 7.6, that of females to the female population was 2.2 and that of boys and girls under instruction to the population was 4.9.

The average cost of education per head of population was Rs. 0-15-11 as against Re. 1-1-3 in the previous year. Of this amount a sum of Rs. 0-12-6 was met from State funds as against Rs. 0-13-7 in 1933-34.

In conclusion, the Government observe that they are glad to learn that the administration of Primary Education by the Local Education Authorities and School Boards was satisfactory and that there was hearty co-operation and harmonious relationship between the departmental officers and these bodies, and the members of the Local Education Authorities took keen interest in the discussions at meetings.

Educational Reconstruction in Burma

Suggestions of far-reaching importance touching practically every aspect of education, general and technical, in Burma are made in the Report of Vernacular and Vocational Educational Reorganisation Committee which was issued to the Press in June 1936.

The report lays considerable stress of the need for the development of vocational and technical education in agriculture and animal husbandry and other technical occupations in the province. It suggests the constitution of a central education authority with effective powers of control to reduce illiteracy and to relate education to life and occupation in Burma. It recommends the constitution of a special committee by Government to make plans for the development of wireless broadcasting as an economical and potent adjust to the education, service and the other social and technical services directed by Government.

The report proposes that, consistent with the Government of Burma Act, 1935, a Board of Education consisting of not less than half the number of Ministers constituting the Council of Ministers, with the Ministers of Education as President be constituted with effective powers of control, supervision and initiative and suggests the improvement of the Secretariat of the Board of Education to secure more continuity and consistency of educational policy. It reviews and examines the inspectorate and its functions and makes proposals to develop the efficiency of the inspectorate and the utility and efficiency of instruction in the schools.

The Committee proposes that the constitution and powers of local education authorities be adjusted so that appropriate and equitable representation of all public and private interests in education shall be achieved and to the end that the administration of education by local bodies shall be directed solely to the educational welfare of the children and be un-influenced by considerations which are irrelevant.

Educational provision in "excluded" areas and in backward areas which are outside the rural self-governing areas is examined and future policy is suggested. The Committee makes a thorough examination of the problems of illiteracy and of 'wastage' and wastefulness in the primary vernacular schools and suggests various proposals. They recommend ways and means that should be adopted by local authorities to complete an accurate survey of existing educational provision and deficiencies in their jurisdiction. Plans are formulated and measures are described which should be initiated immediately to attack illiteracy and stop 'wastage' and to commence development that will pave the way eventually, in progressive stages and during period of 5, 10, 15 and more years towards compulsory education for all. The first stage recommended is, under legislative authority, local option schemes of compulsory attendance for three years after voluntary enrolment. This is designed in the first place to consolidate the existing system of primary schools and to create a sound foundation for further development.

Different Stages of Education

The Committee makes detailed proposals to bring about co-ordination and re-organisation of the system of schools and reconstruction of curricula for the co-ordinated and re-organised system. The reconstruction visualises the diversification of the existing single-track book-lore curriculum of the Anglo-vernacular and English schools and the bringing of the pupil of the Vernacular school into the general and particular streams of a homogenous education system and to relate schooling more intimately to life and occupation and leisure in Burma. The reorganisation of the existing differentiated system of schools in a co-ordinated yet diversified system of primary schools for children aged 6 to 11 years, of post-primary schools for adolescents aged 11 to 15 years, and of vocational and pre-University schools for youths aged 15 to 18 and more years of age is suggested. The construction implies the separation of 'intermediate' education from University education proper and the conduct of 'intermediate' courses and the part of the existing high school ceurses in selected high schools throughout the province. The liberal and cultural subjects will remain the foundation of the curricula. The place of languages in the curricula is discussed and adjustments of existing courses are suggested. Science courses with appropriate content related to conditions in Burma, it is suggested, should become compulsory components of the curricula. Physical education, personal and public hygiene and practical instruction in a craft or an art, it is argued, should be part of the education of every pupil in primary and post-primary schools.

The training of teachers and the re-organisation of training to equip teachers to fulfil the role prescribed for them in the re-organised and re-constructed schools are discussed at length and comprehensive proposals are made touching not only the training of all grades of teachers in the public service of educations but also the many matters concerning the teaching profession.

Financial Policy

The report reviews the financial policy of Government in regard to vernacular education since the inception of local self-governing authorities and recommends that the principle that local authorities are responsible for the whole cost of vernacular education should be modified and that the finance of vernacular education should be based as it is based in other democratic systems of education, on a system of authoritative central and delegated local administration and financial responsibility. The committee propose that vernacular primary education should be based on a system of central taxes and local rates and that to imbue local authorities with the realities of their responsibilities as self-governing administrators of education, local authorities should be directly responsibie for the raising of their share of the cost of vernacular primary education.

The representatives of non-Burmese communities, namely European, Anglo-Indian and Indian, feel that if the recommendations of the Committee are put into effect, a great deal of the discontent now prevailing among minority groups in connection with education al provision and administration will disapear.

THE INDIAN SCIENCE CONGRESS

23rd. Session—Indore—2nd. January 1936

His Highness the Maharaja Holkar of Indore inaugurated on the **2nd. Janua.y 1936** the 23rd session of the Indian Science Congress in Indore before a gathering of scientists from all over the country and visitors, including Sir S. M. Bapna, the Prime Minister, other ministers, high officers and prominent citizens of Indore State.

Welcome Address

Dr. *P. Basu*, Vice-Chancellor of the Agra University, Chairman of the Reception Committee, welcoming the delegates gave a survey of the great scientific discoveries in various fields in recent years and their immense effect on practical life, changing the very face of the earth. But the final mystery eluded the scientist's grasp and the Pandora's Box remained closed. He added that they were not nearer the end of their perplexity when told that what they saw were probably in point of events, in geometrical configuration, mere depressions in the vortex of energy. Practically life was healthier, more efficient and more comfortable to-day, but the aspect of things had entirely changed and the old machinery of social life had been suddenly thrown out of gear, and there was maladjustment of human personality which had yet to find a level in the new environment.

Scientific methods, Said Dr. Basu, had demolished the old religion and moral ideas were dominated by personal god but religion had failed to develop and fill the gap left by Science, because scientific ideas had been isolated from religion by habit, tradition and inertia, weakening the strongest social force and leaving social expediency as the only guide to action and social decorum as the only restraint on emotional expression.

Another non adjustment, Dr. Basu pointed out, was in the balance of human personality. Here science was up against greater difficulty, battling with human passions and emotions but without such adjustment, leading to intellectual and emotional balance man might like Faust win the world and yet be damned. Therefore work co-ordinating and dovetailing conclusions of all sciences was necessary. But neither the scientist nor the philosopher had considered it his business and this work was left to private enterprise, working for personal profit, which was not only insufficient but dangerous to society. He hoped that experts would not take up this co-ordination for the benefit of humanity.

Presidential Address

In the course of his address *Sir Upendranath Brahmachari*, the President, referred at length to the progress of science in the different fields like Bio-Chemistry (in which he dealt with the present-day conception of dietatics). Physiology, Genetics, Chemistry, Physics, Geology, Psychology and Mathematics, tracing the latest development in each field and pointing out how they help the treatment of diseases.

Adverting to problem of nutrition and the problem of a perfect diet, he made a reference to Indian dietary and said:

"Nearly 90 years ago, Chevers taught that the dietary of the Hindus with a very moderate quantity of animal food was the fittest for a tropical climate. Thus he wrote: 'It is certain, that the law-givers, who prescribed for the people of India a diet consisting mainly of vegetables and water, the lighter kinds of animal food, such as fish, pigeon's and goat's flesh, being only occasionally introduced in moderate quantities, judged almost as physiologically as they could have done, had they studied at the feet of Liebig and Prout'. Similarly in a discussion on the dietary of man, the meatless diet of some of the finest soldiers of His Majesty's Indian Army who fought in the last great world war was highly extolled. This is an interesting subject for research in the quest of minimum animal protein required for human consumption and the future may show that it may be influenced by climatic conditions. Recent researches of Berg tend to show that apart from the nature of proteins, there are other factors which determine the minimum quantity of protein necessary to preserve nitrogenous equilibrium, such as, the particular protein the subject is accustomed to taking and the ratio of inorganic bases to inorganic acids available to or formed in the body of the subject.

This brings us to the question of animal versus vegetable protein. Investigators of the present-day hold that, in general, proteins of animal origin are superior to the vegetable proteins for the purposes of nutrition and that the testimony of human vegetarians is useless in determining the amount of animal protein requirement of man, because they were probably not vegetarians during the first part of their lives.

"In recent times some interesting work has been done with the balanced diets for Indians by Tilak and his assistants. The dietary worked out by them is the inclusion with the staple food grains in common use by the people of India, of soya-beans, dried skimmed milk, rice polishings, fresh ground-nut cake and preparation of sprouted seeds. Such dietaries, if confirmed, may help in solving the problem facing large masses of people in India, i.e., how to obtain a reasonably good diet for 5 to 7 rupees a month. Aykroyd has found that diets which, in paper at least, adequately fulfil human requirements can be bought in Madras for about Rs. 4 per month. Cheap balanced diets of this nature must, of course, be subjected to the test of practice.

"Perhaps millions of the people of India, especially among the poor classes, suffer from the various degrees of malnutrition which leads to lessened power of resistance to infection. McCarrison's work in this field is wellknown. Sanitation and nutrition must go hand in hand in all countries especially in India, where so many diseases, epidemic and endemic, prevail.

"In India where diabetes is common, the proper dietary of the disease is an important subject, and I shall very briefly refer to it. Since the epoch-making discovery of insulin in the treatment of diabetes, the pendulum is swinging from the fat diet of Newburgh and Marsh to 'high' and 'higher' carbo-hydrate diet of Sansum and others. Recently it has been observed that administration of carbo-hydrate stimulates the production of an unknown insulin-kinase, the insulin acting as a substrate in the metabolism of sugar (Himsworth). On the other hand large amounts of fat may inhibit the action of insulim. On this view a 'high' or 'higher' carbohydrate diet for diabetes aided by insulin finds a rational support and it is possible that, by the adoption of such a diet, the life of a diabetic may be more prolonged and death rate from diabetes more reduced than what has been achieved in the present day, in spite of the introduction of insulin.

Tracing the growth of Physiological knowledge he said :—

Recent researches have thrown light on the mechanism of the fundamental reflex reaction for the protection of the animals and have shown how with the evolution of an anti-gravity mechanism and of extended movement, the brain stem has become evolved to take over this increased responsibility. Magnus has analysed the various nervous stimuli from the periphery which are concerned in this very delicately co-ordinated mechanism. The new data have completely revolutionised our conception of the nervous system, and signs and symptoms of disease which hitherto could not be properly understood, have now become capable of analysis.

It has been held that the ductless glands are the 'glands of our destiny' and that 'these potent overlords of our bodies are dictators of our minds and personalities'. It may be possible that the future may reveal that genius, intelligence, beauty, character, morality, and other human characteristics are dependent upon diverse combinations of the secretions of these bodies, just as their deficiency or excess may give rise to disease.

Insulin has completely changed the prospect of the treatment of diabetes. The discovery that Parathyroid extract mobilizes the calcium of the bones has revolutionised the treatment of diseases due to calcium derangement.

Our knowledge of the interaction of endocrines has increased in recent times. I would just mention a remarkable fact that, as shown by Houssay and co-workes, there is no glycosuria when both the pituitary and the pancreas are removed, and further that the injection of extract of the anterior pituitary is followed by the appearance of glycosuria.

May I end this portion of my address by making a little more reference to the pituitary, which seems to have a multiplicity of functions. It may be regarded as the headquaters for the hormones or the chemical messengers which control most of the other endocrine glands and thereby probably almost every cell of the body. The chemistry of the pituitary is by no means closed and it may be that the most important discoveries in the pituitary chapter have yet to be written.

Herring very recently has referred to the functions attributed by the ancients to the pituitary. We may make here a reference to the remarkable claims made by the ancient Yogis of India who practised what is known as Khechari Mudra. They elongated the tongue slowly by practice and manipulation aided by cutting its fraenum, if necessary, and carefully introduced it into the nasopharynx. The Yogis claimed to have developed remarkable powers of their body and mind in this way. Did they conceive that the tongue mechanically stimulated the secretion of the grandular structures in the nasopharynx (pituitary) which might be subsequently absorbed into the system, in the same way as ardenalin is absorbed when put under the tongue, and interact with the secretions of other endocrine glands? Will some future investigator test the validity of the above claims?

The recent invention in the Rockefeller Institute for Medical Research jointly by Carrel and Lindbergh, of a 'Life Chamber', a sort of artificial body of 'heart, lungs and bloodstream' has enabled scientists for the first time to keep the organs alive, functioning and even growing for a long period outside the body. The method of Carrel-Lindbergh consists of the transplantation of an organ or of any part of the body into a sterile chamber and its artificial feeding with a nutrient fluid through the arteries. In this way the thyroids and ovaries of animals have been artificially cultured, and made to grow. The perfusion fluid consists of protein hydrolytic products, haemin, cysteine, insulin, thyroxin, glutathione, vitamins A and C, blood serum and other substances according to the necessities of the particular organ to be perfused. There is no doubt that tissue culture is likely to be of immense importance in the study of the human body and in the preventive and curative treatment of diseases.

He then briefly referred to recent activities in the field of genetics and observed:

The practical outcome of the application of the principles of genetics as demonstrated by the magnificent work in research laboratories such as those at Cambridge, Edinburgh, Aberystwyth and Aberdeen, has been of immense value in improving crops and livestock. The boundless possibilities in heredity revealed by the science of genetics have placed great power in the hands of breeders of plants and animals and they can now tell with approximate accuracy what to expect from matings. This knowledge has revolutionised breeding in all directions, and resulted in the production of bigger and better plants and animals used for food, clothing or pleasure. In the course of time man may be able to replace the natural selection of more fertile mediocrity and the artificial sterility of high-grade parents by human selection and the artificial fertility of high-grade parents. Sooner or later the frequency of the latter would increase in geometrical progression and control and guide the qualities of mankind in any way it desires for the good of man. The future trend of creative evolution, including man's own destiny, depends on his response to the new knowledge and on his intelligent application of genetical discoveries, in the near as well as distant future (Hurst). Genetics aided by better environments may also be able to prevent the transmission of hereditary weakness and hereditary diseases, some of which are sex-linked. In this way it may lead to the production of better type of men, free from diseases of the mind and body that are propagated from father or mother to their children and thus the difficult task of medicine for averting or curing hereditary diseases or diathesis will be reduced to a minimum.

The relation between chemical constitution of compounds and their varied physiological and therapeutic properties, though at present consisting mostly of a jumble of empirical facts may one day lead to generalization of vast importance. Therapeutics is moving to-day from merely qualitative to quantitative foundations. Some of you may live to see that remarkable results may be attained by chemistry in the treatment of diseases like tuberculosis or cancer for which chemical therapeutics has at the present day only a limited application in gold or selenium and lead respectively. Crystalline insulin free from impurities is now available. Newer treatments of epilepsy, of myasthenia gravis and of agranulocytic angina are coming in the field due to the triumphs of chemistry. You may see the synthesis of other and newer vitamins and internal secretions as well as extracts from different organs of the body synthesized or isolated in a pure state and used in medicine for the treatment of disease. We look forward to the day when endocrine preparations will [illegible]vailable for oral administration and the dread of the needle averted.

With regard to the contribution of physics to medical science its application is partly for the purpose of diagnosis of diseases and partly for their treatment. Further, physics is slowly evolving new conception of living matter by X-ray analysis, by improved methods of microscopy and by the advancing knowledge of the constitution of matter.

The Electro-cardiograph is a valuable apparatus for studying certain diseases of the heart. A portable apparatus which can be taken to the patient's house and which is constructed on the principle of the string galvanometer is now available. Another portable Electro-cardiograph based on the principle of the valve-amplifier is also available.

The Electro-cardiograph has shown that tracings taken of patients dying of various maladies can demonstrate that for some time after clinical death, some cardiac activity could be registered, the duration varying from six to twenty minutes. These observations show that in cases in which there is cardiac stand-still during anaesthesia or in the new born, resuscitation may be effected by timely cardiac injection or needle puncture. There may be other conditions that may be discovered in future in which the same may be possible.

X-ray methods of analysis may be applied one day in the study of the cancer cell and it is hoped that its application may increase our knowledge of cell construction and cell growth, which helped by our future knowledge of the colloidal state in living cells may one day strengthen our powers in combating the dreadful scourge of the malignant disease. The changes that take place in the tissues in cancer and other pathogenic conditions have been studied by this method by Clark and co-workers.

X-ray diagnosis has improved in the present day to an almost spectacular extent; and radiation therapy has now established its claim to an important place in the treatment of malignant disease. X-ray and radium therapy is bidding fair to displace the knife in the treatment of certain forms of cancer. The response of tumours to radiation demands wide study, each type of tumour having a different response, both clinically and histologically. By contrasting the sensitivity of growths with that of skin—in both cases using the minimum lethal dose as the standard—it has been possible to place tumours in different groups—radio-sensitive tumours, epitheliomata, adenocarcinomata and radio-resistant tumours.

When we survey the immense development in the use of light waves, visible, ultra-violet, X-rays, and others in the investigation of structures and the treatment of disease, with their future potentialities, it may be said without conceit—truly we are beginning to see through a glass less darkly.

Mental disease, before the advent of psychology in medicine, was a *terra incognita.* Recent researches in psychology have thrown a flood of light on the domain of psychiatry. The significance of a mental approach to the problems of psychology had long been misunderstood, but to-day not only we have a better understanding of mental diseases by means of psychological method but also we get extremely encouraging results in the treatment of such disorders.

To-day a firm alliance has been concluded between medicine and psychology, and medical men have more and more fully recognized the necessity of studying the mental history of their patients. Much work has been done in the study of the unconscious in many institutions, notably, the Nancy School. The aftermath of the great war was seen in many cases of nervous debility which are treated in famous clinics, e. g., of Hadfield and others. The power of the instincts and the inhibition of the latent forces, of their release, as well as the phenomena of fatigue, have been thoroughly studied to the great advantage of medical practice and efficiency. Modern psychologists and medical men are paying more and more attention to that aspect of psychological investigation of the body-mind known as sublimation of instincts and emotions. Many medical men at the present day devote themselves as specialists to the practice of psycho-therapy.

Thus the various sciences can be of great service to Medicine. Some of them have contributed very substantially to the relief of human suffering from disease. They can obtain valuable findings for the clinician in deceased conditions which may be helpful to him, but the responsibility finally rests with him as to how to act upon their findings. This shows the great importance of what is called to-day Clinical Science. Anatomy, the science of structure of the body, physiology, the science of function and the meeting ground of physics and chemistry in their application to problems of health and disease and bio-chemistry, the science concerned with the chemical processes underlying the activities of living matter, can be of great service to the clinician. In recent times, the need for increased application of physics and chemistry to medicine has grown with tremendous rapidity.

The contribution of medicine to civilization aided by the other sciences is great. A healthy body means a healthy mind and such minds are less likely to cause internal and external strife. There is no doubt that a large part of the greatly increased comfort and safety that we enjoy to-day is the result of the phenomenal advance that have been made in the medical sciences in recent times.

The body-mind of man is the finest product of the universe even when compared with the most magnificent of the stars and the nebulae. Man's appearance cannot be regarded purposeless or accidental or as a sign of disease. He has discovered the laws of motion and of relativity as well as of radio-telegraphy, radio-telephony, aviation and television. He unfolds the constitution of the stars and the nebulae, millions and millions of miles away from the earth. He calculates the weight and temperature of the stars and determines their ages. He finds out the constitution of the atoms and discovers the cosmic rays. He smashes the atoms and produces new radio-active elements. He transforms one element into another. He may, one day, be able to determine the mathematics of the atom by means of his calculator. He tries to find out when and how primordial life came into existence. He tells the story of the oldest man who existed in the earth a million years ago, and gives the history of his evolution. He discovers the chromosomes and finds out the structures that are responsible for heredity. He discovers and dissects the micro-organisms of disease, and finds the defensive mechanism against their attacks. He studies the specific carbohydrates and proteins, and tries to discover the structure of the viruses and the bacteriophage. He discovers the treatment of diseases once considered incurable. He records the electric changes of the brain cortex of man in various cerebral states, and may one day record human thoughts on a sensitive plate. He studies the endocrine glands, and synthesizes their secretions. He may one day be able to influence the sex of the embryo at his will. He cultures the organs of the body and studies their growth in vitro. Ponce de Leon did not perhaps search for the impossible and unattainable when he sought the fountain of eternal youth, for man one day will conquer old age, disease and death. Though I dare not say what the 'final secret' is likely to be yet the bodymind of man must be to-day the consummation of the work of the Great Design. In this most complicated machine in which, it may be said, 'matter, life and mind translate roughly into organisation, organism and organiser (Smuts)' Medicine tries to give the healing balm to act as a powerful agent for the maintenance of harmony and strength when disease sets in.

Second Day Indore— 4th January 1936

Development of Agriculture

Sectional meetings relating to Agricultural, Medical and Psychological sections were delivered to-day.

Mr. *A. K. Yegnanarayana Aiyar*, who presided over the Agricultural section, spoke on "Some aspects of scientific research as applied to Indian Agriculture". In the course of his address, he said :

One of the peculiar features of agricultural research has been the test by which its success is generally measured viz., the extent to which results of immediate practical value and application are attained and adopted by the agriculturists of the country. The test is bound to become more severe as the years go by under the new form of Government. But the record of the past 25 years is one of signal success both for research and propaganda more than justifying the expenditure on the various Departments of Agriculture and certainly encourages us to hope that in the future as in the past agricultural research can fully meet the test. The instance of Mysore is given in illustration, where improvements have taken place on an extensive scale. Improved ploughs, threshing appliances, sugarcane mills and pumping installations have largely displaced the traditional methods. Oilcakes and artificial manures have come into general use ; new crops, new and improved varieties of groundnut, ragi, paddy, cotton and sugarcane are grown on thousands of acres ; spraying against arecanut and coffee diseases have been extensively taken up ; the prickly pear has been exterminated ; inoculation of cattle agaist diseases made thoroughly popular ; serum and vaccines are manufactured locally and mortality from the deadly disease—Rinderpest—effectively kept down.

Encouraging as these results are, progress can be greatly speeded up if profitable and ready markets for produce can be assured preferably by means of local manufacturing industries which will furnish an outlet for these crops. This is strikingly demonstrated by the improvements which have taken place in the cultivation of sugarcane for the new factory at Mandya in the Mysore State, where the use of improved ploughs, artificial manures, growing of improved varieties of sugarcane and its cultivation by social methods have all come into vogue within less than a year in contrast with the period of several years which they have taken elsewhere in the absence of such stimulus. A measure of all-round prosperity has also been ushered in as the result of this ready outlet for all the cane grown by the ryots which augurs well for other improvements. The development of the cultivation of Cigarette Tobacco in the Madras Presidency has led to similar results in that part of the country, as like-wise the making of casein for the dairy farmers in parts of Bombay. The organisation of special Committees on the lines of the Indian Central Cotton Committee which will comprise growers, scientific workers, manufacturers and traders in respect of each important crop or group of crops in India is likely to lead efficiently not only to a solution of the many problems of crop improvement, but also to an exploration of their commercial utilisation by local manufacturing industries and to the kind of progress illustrated by the sugar industry described above.

The sugar industry has brought into prominence the question of the utilisation of molasses in a manner profitable to the industry and beneficial to agriculture. The manufacture of alcohol of all grades including absolute alcohol for use for various industrial purposes offers great promise and Mysore has already made a beginning which is worthy of all the support which the Government can give. Among its other uses, the making of cattle feed mixtures offers almost unlimited scope and will meet one of the crying needs of Indian Agriculture. Experiments in the making of products like molascuits with the addition of begasse dust, groundnut shells and haulms or shredded straw are suggested as promising methods of utilisation.

The utilisation of bye-products, which are at present mere waste products in respect of other crops also is a subject which needs greater attention, if only as a means of making the cultivation of these crops more profitable, leaving aside the question of industrial advantages. Arecanut husks, plantain stems, groundnut husks, paddy husk, cotton stalks, coffee pulp, are some of the materials that come in this category and the methods of one kind or another which have from time to time been suggested may with advantage be examined and work on alternative methods also undertaken for investigation.

The subject of 'Quality' in crops and the possibility of improving it by methods of manuring deserves to be taken up without further delay. So far all manurial experiments have had for their object only an increase in the 'Quantity' of the produce concerned and little or no attention has been paid to the effect on the composition of the commodity. Many factors to which the economic value of a crop is due such as the sugar in sugarcane, oil content in oil-seeds, starch in the potato, the burning quality and nicotine content of tobacco, staple in cotton, 'Quality' in rice, protein in wheat, keeping quality in fruits etc., are already known in a general way to be affected by soil constituents and manuring, but the matter has not so far formed the subject of serious investigation. What really constitutes 'Quality' in many crops like rice, or coffee for example, and to what constituent or constituents such 'Quality' is due will have also to be gone into as a preliminary, but in respect of sugar, starch, oil, proteins and known essential principles to which the other crops mentioned owe their quality, this difficulty does not exist and the problem is less complicated. So far the performance at the weigh bridge alone has been the test of the action of manures and judged by this test many a manurial experiment has yielded results either contradictory or inconclusive. It is not at all unlikely that if attention should be directed to the composition of the crop as well these experiments will tell a different and a very valuable tale.

The effect of soil constituents sometimes called catalysts, including even the rare elements is also worthy of study, as in addition to their reported increase of yields, it is possible that connection may be traced between them and some of the baffling plant diseases put down now to physiological disturbances, viruses and so on, much in the manner of the subtle effect of vitamins in the animal body. As a practical need of immediate importance is a strengthening of the staff for the investigation of plant diseases and pests and increased attention devoted to their investigation. The loss due to these in the aggregate is stupendous and for most of them cheap and simple remedies are extraordinarily difficult to suggest. Many, indeed, are most baffling and the problem is really one for more than one branch of science. A many-sided attack from the mycological, Entomological, Chemical, Botanical and agronomic sides has to be organised in regard to these with provision for proper co-ordination and co-operation. Among pests that have assumed special importance recently is the borer pest on sugarcane, which is a serious menace to the sugar industry. A large scale campaign of parasitic control is indicated as about the most feasible while the action of light of different kinds of irradiation and the newly patented Entorav light traps need to be tested extensively.

In the field of cattle improvement work has been somewhat halting and tentative owing to the conflict of views regarding methods, whether it should be by crossing with foreign breeds or by selection from local breeds. Matters, such as adequate fodder supplies and their conservation, the problem of the dead load of useless cattle have added to the difficulties. But, on the other hand, we are bringing diseases under control, popularising the castration of scrub bulls and the keeping of proper stud bulls and are thus removing some of the old obstacles; while the large demand for milk due to the growth of cities is acting as a powerful stimulus to cattle improvement. Conditions are thus favourable for some marked progress in the near future.

Among the many economic factors, which set effective limits to the spread of improvements is the lack of proper marketting organisations. The creation of the new department for agricultural marketting is, therefore, welcomed as a powerful ally to the scientific worker in his attempts to increase the profits of farming. Lines of work which will benefit the country as a whole, both grower and merchant alike, as the result of the present marketing surveys are indicated. The opinion that science has led to over-production and the present depression in agriculture is strongly controverted. As long as there are millions of people, who though able and willing to work have still to remain ill-fed and ill-clad, it is useless to talk of over-production or superfluity. What Indian agriculture wants on the other hand, is science and still more science to rescue it from the ills that beset it on all sides.

Psychology of Education

Mr. *J. M. Sen* delivered the presidential address at the meeting of the Psychological section. In the course of his address he said :

In all problems of education, two things, he said, were of fundamental importance, one was the child who was to be educated and the other the environment in which he grew up. But both were variables; no one could fully predict what a child was going to be, nor was it impossible to change the environment to a certain extent. Education was therefore a function of two real variables. No mathematician could, however, lay down any precise formula governing the relationship of these two variables.

All human beings, he continued, came into this world with certain possibilities and limitations. These must be regarded as things given to the child. The child began life as a sort of field of operations for two forces that sometimes worked in harmony, but frequently opposed each other; these forces were known as heredity and environment. Heredity was generally accepted as an ordinary principle of life. For the teacher, the problem of heredity was an enquiry into the question of the inheritance of acquired characteristics, viz., "Does the child inherit from his parents qualities that they have acquired for themselves during their life-time?" In education, the teachers were liable to the fallacy of apparent transmission. Characteristics acquired by the father might appear among the children not because they were transmitted but because they were again acquired by the children.

It was perfectly true that the children of parents who had received some education themselves could be taught more easily than the children of those who had not the opportunity of receiving any education. But all the same, the former group would have to be educated in almost the same way as the latter group. Hence it could be asserted that educability could be admitted but the results of education could not be transmitted. From the point of view of practical teacher the influence of the environment was the most important factor. The pupils' qualities must be taken as they were given. But in the matter of environment, the teacher could certainly manipulate it in such a way as to produce a definite effect upon the pupil.

The intelligence of an individual, he continued, increased (though differently in different individuals) from birth to sixteen or eighteen years of age and thereafter remained constant. This statement assumed a prominent position in regard to his education. Most part of this period he was at school and the teacher could help him in increasing not merely the pupil's knowledge but his native intelligence as well. It was therefore of utmost importance that the conditions of the school atmosphere should be such that it could help in increasing the Intelligence Quotient of each and every individual. The classification of pupils according to mental age therefore was a condition precedent to good teaching in class-rooms. With the growth of education in India, this problem was assuming a position of great importance in the administration of education by governments and local bodies. Mr. Sen then discussed about the various problems concerning the science and art of measurement in education.

Mr. Sen then discussed the problems concerning general intelligence tests, memory tests, ability tests, vocational tests (i. e. tests for determining skill for a particular vocation in life) in schools and colleges. But he said that these did not cover all types of pupils. There were patient plodders in all walks of life and it was worth while finding them out while they were in educational institutions. By means of a series of tests, Dr. E. Webb had determined that there was a second central factor in life known as "The persistence of motives (denoted by "W"). Even this could not explain all cases. Mr. Maxwell Garnett had brought to light a third independent factor, viz., "originality or cleaverness" (denoted by "C"). High values of "C" characterized men of genius and first-rate artists, poets and scientists. These fascinating researches enabled them to determine "the promise and potency of the individual so far as these depend on his endowment." These, however, proved that there could not be any clashing of interests of individual pupils in class-room and out side. All three factors 'G'. 'W' and 'C' could not be identical even in two cases, not to speak of three or more cases. Hence it was necessary to develop the potentialities of a pupil during his school age by creating for him an atmosphere of study and character congenial to all and not inimical to the best interest of the society as a whole.

Immunity Against Diseases

Lt.-Col. H. E. Shortt, who presided over the Medical section, spoke on "Immunity in protozoal diseases". The following is a summary of his address :—

It is a well known fact that after the attacks of many diseases caused by bacteria, such as enteric, and also after diseases caused by filterable viruses, such as small-pox and yellow fever, the individual affected is immune to further attack for a long period, possibly for the rest of his life.

It is only exceptionally that this happens after diseases caused by protozoa, such as malaria. In this case, the person affected seems to have no subsequent immunity and is liable to repeated attacks of the disease.

These facts would make it appear that the bodily mechanisms responsible for the production of immunity were acting differently in the two cases but evidence is brought forward to show that this difference is only apparent and that the probability is that the mechanisms concerned in immunity are the same whatever the invading organism may be.

A description is given of the course of events when animals are infected with various species of pathogenic and non-pathogenic trypanosomes and how immunity against these is sometimes attained and sometimes fails entirely to come into action.

A consideration, on general lines, of the various phenomena of immunity involved in the reactions between an invaded animal and the invading parasite lead to fascinating speculations as to how these mechanisms of immunity arose, why they appear to be so perfect in the case of some disease and so apparently ineffective in others.

These speculations are applied especially to the case of man and malaria. Why, when man has been exposed to malaria for hundreds of thousands and possibly millions of years, he has not acquired a greater immunity ?

It is suggested that, had man remained, as regards his social habits, in the primitive conditions obtaining when he was at the evolutionary level of the anthropoid apes, he would have acquired an efficient immunity against the local strains of malaria parasite. Man, however, decided to live in large communal aggregations and to wander far and wide in the world in the search for food. Each rung on the social ladder took him farther from the primitive conditions of his evolutionary ancestors and their possible immunity to the bad effects of malaria so that he finally achieved the sometimes questionable benefits of civilisation at the expense of relatively ineffective immunity to malaria.

Embryology and Evolution

Prof. *H. K. Mookherjee* of the Calcutta University, presiding over the Zoology Section meeting, in the course of his address dwelt on "The development of the vertebral column and its bearing on the study of organic evolution." The address was illustrated by diagrams of the vertebral column (or back-bone) and photomicrographs of sections of the vertebrae of fishes, frogs, lizards, snakes, birds, moles, etc.

Contrary to the opinion of the late Prof. Gadow and other embryologists, Prof. Mookherjee considered that all vertebrates followed the same course of development and exhibited a gradual evolution from one end of the series to the other. Each vertebra, he said, was composed of a centrum or body, an upper arch, and in some cases, a lower arch also. The centrum was formed from the perichordal tube which was converted into bony ring, distinct from the notochordal sheaths. The arches did not take part in the formation of the centrum as supposed by the previous workers. The perichordal tube was cut into pieces corresponding to vertebrae, by strands of migratory connective tissue cells. Various types of vertebrae were formed according to the direction followed by these migratory cells while passing within the tube. The course of the migratory cells, was, in turn, influenced by the movement of the embryo. The above explanation as to the cause of formation of different types of vertebrae was not given by previous authors. Prof. Mookerjee showed that the upper or neural arch which protected the spinal cord was composed of cartilaginous arches known as basidorsalia and connective tissue or membrane bone arches. The latter were not noted by previous authors. The lower arch was similarly formed. He also shewed how some vertebrate species deviated from the above fundamental plan of development as a result of adaptation. He traced the ossification and formation of articulating processes and ribs. He was of the opinion that the classification of vertebrae given by the late Prof. Gadow was untenable. He pointed out that the results of embryological studies were of great value to the evolutionists inasmuch as the lines of descent could be traced by following the developmental history, where anatomy or palaeontology failed to given a clue. Comparative embryology probed deeper into the mysteries of life and opened new fields of investigation on the embryonic life of animals.

Bicycle Terpenes

Dr. *P. C. Guha*, President of the Chemistry section in his address dealt with recent developments in the chemistry of bicyclic terpenes.

The bicyclic terpenes occur mostly in essential oils, like turpentine oil, camphor oil, etc., good many of them being known also through synthesis and Dr. Guha's address pertains to the discussion of the recent developments in this field. Amongst subjects that have tackled the ingenuity, experimental skills and imagination of chemists, bicyclic terpenes occupy a very high position. The uses to which these and allied compounds have been put are many and varied, and consequently they are of great industrial importance. The enthusiastic chemist to whom the joy in work is of greater importance than the ultimate material gain, finds in them substances of inexhaustible sources of fruitful experimental results. It being well known that the synthetic experiments of the pure chemist have proved to be the stepping stone to a large number of successful industrial developments, there cannot be any question of conflict between these two aspects of chemistry.

One finds that India has been singularly lagging behind in work on this particular subject while Germany, England and America have made and still continue to make signal contributions. The difficult nature of the problem rendered all the more difficult by the astonishingly rapid contributions by master-minds should not deter one in taking up research in this line.

The address which is highly academic and rather technical in its nature, describes the salient features of bicyclic ring systems as a class—occurring naturally or otherwise and their stereochemical aspect. The more important and recent advances in synthetic and degradative work alike, in Thujane, Carane, Pinane, Camphane-Fenchane, and Santane series of compounds are described. The theoretical aspects of two different peculiar phenomena exhibited by some of these compounds discovered by Wagner and Nametkin are discussed. The physiological activity of some compounds of this group in relation to their chemical constitution also finds a brief mention in the text. Problems still awaiting solution are discerned and methods of attack likely to be attended with success are pointed out. The results that have attended the experiments at the Indian Institute of Science are described in appropriate places in the body of the text. The address may be expected to give an additional stimulus to attract more workers in India to this very important branch of organic chemistry.

Medical Philosophy

Dr. W. Burridge, President of the Physiology Section, in the course of his address on "Some future lines of advance in Medical Philosophy," said :—

To see a muscle, which has been cut out of the body and lies inert and apparently lifeless, suddenly spring into activity when an electric current is passed through it, is to witness what has fascinated doctors for over a century. They saw in this the promise of solution of their fundamental problems. How does living substance react to its surrounding? What events take place when light, say, enters an eye to set up from its sensitive nerve-endings those nerve impulses which provide seeing after they reach the brain? Or what takes place in the nerve-cells of the brain when we think? To all such problems that apparently lifeless muscle, galvanised once again to active life, seemed able to supply the key.

When messages are sent from the brain along the nerves to set muscles in action, those muscles are said to be stimulated to activity. Similarly, light stimulates sensitive nerves in our eyes to give us vision, and the contact of objects with our skin stimulates its nerves to give us the sense of touch. A knowledge of the underlying nature of these stimulations is of the utmost importance to medical science because all its ideas or theories concerning how living organs do their work are ultimately based on the beliefs concerning what this is.

Now, doctors have firmly believed that the action of electric currents on a muscle which has been cut out of the body is essentially the same as the natural stimulation of living organs which takes place when light, say, stimulates sensations through the eye. Acting on this belief, numberless experiments have been performed on muscles with electricity to gain insight into the nature of natural stimulation.

The difference between the old and new medical ideas can be exemplified from petrol motors. For years, medical scientists in laboratories all over the world have been studying through muscles and electric currents a process that plays in organs of our bodies the same part that gas-sparking plays in a motor. They have investigated, as it were, the best type of sparking plug, the proper spark-gap, the time taken to explode the mixture, the rate at which the explosion travels in the cylinders, and so on. The motors on which they did their experiments, however, lacked throttles to vary the mixture, had hand-operated sparks, and stopped dead after each explosion.

Of the imperfections of their motors, they had no suspicion; instead, they firmly believed that there was nothing more to be learnt about motors generally than what they could learn from their own machines which give them the further idea that the running of a motor depended entirely on the spark.

The New Psychology is a welter of doctrines of new medical sects who have released themselves from the bonds of age-long tradition in which orthodox medicine is still held through holding fast to what are now demonstrably wrong beliefs concerning electric currents and muscle. Until these new discoveries had been made, however, it could be held doubtful whether the New Psychology was an advance of science or merely an excursion into the wilderness. The evidence now available shows that it was an advance, but of empirical type.

Until recently, then, necessary knowledge of the condition of living matter was lacking. In the absence of this knowledge doctrines have been built on a foundation presumption that living matter remains inert until excited to action by some external agency. The new facts show instead that this living matter is ever active, and that external agents do not initiate activity in it but many modify an activity already present. The ultimate difference between the two conceptions is as great as the difference between Creation and Evolution, because any explanation that is given of the behaviour of a living organ must accord with the conception of its fundamental inertness or activity. An explanation based on inertness must differ radically from one based on activity. If then there be this activity where previously inertness was presupposed, every explanation must change, and that means a new science.

Racial Classification of Indian Peoples

"Problems of racial classification of the Indian peoples" was the subject of the address, delivered on the **8th. January** by Mr. *H. C. Chakladar*, who presided over the meeting of the Anthropology section. In the course of his address, Mr. Chakladar said:

In India racial classification has so long proceeded on very scanty anthropometric data, and hence it has been quite unsatisfactory. Risley initiated anthropomorphic measurements in India, but the data obtained by him supplemented by those collected by others, are quite inadequate for such a vast country as India, especially as the Indian peoples are divided into innumerable independent groups that do not intermarry. Risley's classification of the Indian peoples, based upon this inadequate material, into seven racial types, has rightly been rejected by anthropologists. Risley gave, for example, the racial designation of Mongolo-Dravidian to the peoples of Bengal and Orissa, though they are not marked by Mongoloid features at all. Then again Risley's Dravidians fall at least into four racial types: (1) the dark, long-headed, wide-nosed type which has been given the unsatisfactory designation of 'Pre-Dravidian' by some and which has been called 'Proto-Australoid' by Dr. Hutton in the last census report of India although craniological measurements have shown clearly that the theory of a common racial stock for the jungle tribes of the Deccan and the aborigines of Australia is quite untenable; this type had better be called simply Vedaic. Hutton's theory of its migration from Asia Minor is also disproved by the great difference in the nasal index between the ancient Mesopotamian and Indian skulls; (2) the Mundakol group of Chota Nagpur which possesses a considerable affinity with the former, but has points of difference also; (3) the long-headed, fine-nosed type speaking Dravidian languages who on account of their Mediterranean affinity, had best be called 'Indo-Mediterranean', independently of any reference to the language they speak; (4) and lastly, the round-headed, fine-nosed type with Alpin affinity which claims numerous individuals amongst the Dravidian-speakers. The two latter types are not peculiar to the Dravidian-speaking area alone, but are of a much wider distribution in India. Intensive anthropometric work involving 60 measurements and 31 somatoscopic observations on each individual among the people of Bengal by the author, shows the presence, both among the high castes, such as the Radhi Brahmins, as well as the low castes like the Muchis, of a predominant round-headed type, and also of an appreciable number of Indo-Mediterranean type, this latter type being more numerous among the lower castes than among the higher. Anthropometric investigations in other parts of India would probably show a very wide distribution of these two types. Both of them are represented in the skulls excavated at Mohenjo Daro, and they appear to have been the earliest importers of advanced civilisation and culture into India.

The speakers of Aryan language are represented by two groups in India, one, the round-headed type and the other, a tall and long-headed type which has been called *Proto-Nordic*, and the dialect spoken by the two groups belong to two distinct branches of the same Aryan tongue. The present distribution of the round-heads in India in the marginal areas in the west, south and east, as also their presence at Adichanallur, shows that they must have entered the country earlier than the Proto-Nordics. As such they must have initiated the Vedic culture in India which the tall, long-heads, arriving later, absorbed from them. The Vedic culture was carried, even in the Rigvedic age, by long-haired, brown-robed Munis—pioneer missionaries of the Vedic religion—over a great part of India, from the Western to the Eastern Ocean, as the Rigveda (X. 136) puts it. The Brahmana portion of the Vedas speak of mighty empires established by the Vedic Aryans in eastern India. The charge of impurity brought against the peoples of Sind, Gujarat and Konkom in the west and Bengal and Orissa in the east, belongs to a much later literature, and is due to their trade and intercourse with foreigners by land and sea: this the purists in the midland where the latter Vedic literature flourished, condemned in severe terms, and prescribed the most distressful penances for them in the midland itself where the people were getting fossilized in their habits and customs with a narrow outlook towards life, and they began to think that the habitation of the pure Aryans was confined within very narrow limits—between the Ganges and the Jamuna. But the presence of tribes at a low stage of culture, but resembling the Indo-Aryans in their physical features over the wild area from the borders of Assam to the hills of Annam, amply proves that people with Indo-European features had traversed the whole of northern India from the western gates to the eastern frontier and passed through the forests and hills beyond, even up to the Pacific in every early times.

No sound and definite conclusions, however, about the racial composition of the Indian peoples, are possible without further anthropological material and therefore extensive measurements should be taken in all parts of India, preferably by local investigators with an efficient training in anthropological method, and possessing a knowledge of the language of the people among whom they work. In England, an appeal has recently been issued 'to set on foot a comprehensive survey of the past and present populations of Great Britain; the need for such a movement in India is much more urgent, as the anthropological work so far done is of the nature of a preliminary survey only.

Botanical Section Meeting

Dr. *S. R. Bose*, who presided over the meeting of the Botanical section on the

7th. January, dwelt, in the course of his address, on the various aspects of Bengal 'Polyporaceae' which he studied in the course of the last twenty years. He dealt with the geographical distribution of Bengal Polyporaceae, the conditions for their development in Bengal, the fossil records of Polyporaceae, cytology of reproduction and the chemical nature of fruit body of 'Ganoderma lucidum', their physiology and other uses.

When climatic conditions such as temperature, rainfall, humidity, etc., were analogous, he said, it was astonishing to find the repetition of the species in very distant parts of the globe. Recently in 1935 he recorded the occurrence in the high hills of Locra (Assam) in Bengal 8,000 to 10,000 feet elevation of six European Polypores (P. squamosus, P. Sulphureus, P. gilvus formalicnoides, Fomes fomentarius, F. pinicola, Amarodarma rugous), never found in the plains of Bengal. This was probably because most of the plants of the high hills harbouring these species of Polypores as parasites or saprophytes did not grow in the plains.

Dr. Bose opined that for the establishment of stable classification of Polyporaceæ morphological studies should be supplemented by detailed study of anatomical, cytological, chemical, physiological and biological, chemical and and other characters, and that the old classification, however imperfect, should not be changed till they had accumulated data from the completed study of these diverse aspects of Polyporaceæ.

The chemical analysis of the fruit body of Ganoderma lucidus with a strongly laccate upper surface, he said, showed that it contained resin, ergosterin, fatty acids, mannite, some polyfaccharides and a voluminous deep-brown amorphous substance much resembling humus acid. The biological peculiarities of Polypore showed that as saprophytes or parasites some species grew singly on logs or trunks and branches of forest trees, while others had a gregarious habit. The decays in wood according to the gross characters of the rot were known as white rots and brown rots, depending on the colour, in the former case the wood became lighter in colour and in the latter it acquired a dark-brown or reddish tinge. As soon as rain appeared, they set forth an advancing zone which was quite marked off from the old zone. Some Polypores began their lives as saprophytes attacking dead roots, stumps and branches, they then extended their hyphæ round the living cells in the adjoining portion and thus became converted into parasites. Others began their lives as parasites, their spores usually entering through a wound, then they killed the living portion and finally established themselves as saprophytes with a number of sporaphores on dead parts of the plants. In extreme cases the whole central cylinder (heart wood) was destroyed, converting the tree into hollow structure. Some, again, rarely continued their activity after the tree had been cut and converted into timber.

Interesting studies, he added, on spore-discharge from dried fruit-bodies of Polypores had been carried out. They showed that only those that had basidia revived under the moist condition and shed spores after varying period of desication (weeks, months or years). Specimens without basidia never shed spores. Brown and coloured Polypores did not survive desiccation long, when detached from the host; they had spores only for a short time in the fresh condition. In specimens of 'Ganoderma lucidus' and 'Ganoderma applanatus' the basidia were succeeded after the rains by hyphae projecting direct from the trama and bearing secondary spores at their tips, which are undistinguishable from the ordinary basidic spores in any way: probably these carried on spore-discharge in the dry season. It was a matter for future investigation whether basidia themselves were transformed into such tramal hyphae projections in the dry intervals. Complete life-history studies of about a dozen local Polypores from spore-germination to the final fructifying stage were carried out, and the details were published in the Journal of Linnean Society in 1930.

Continuing, Dr. Bose said that recent studies on the determination of sexual reactions of Polypores by means of monosporous cultures showed that most of them were heterothalliac and potentially bisexual. This theory of potential bisexuality first put forward by Ames in 1932, seemed to cover most of the facts in various groups of fungi, though in two local Polypores the author had shown two sexes were of a comparatively stable character and not easily interchangeable according to the varying conditions as was the case with various groups of lower fungi examined by different workers from time to time.

The Calcutta University Convocation

The following is the full text of the Convocation address delivered by Mr. *Syama Prasad Mukherjee*, the Vice-Chancellor, at the Calcutta University Convocation held on the **22nd. February 1936 :—**

Your Excellency, Fellow-Graduates, Ladies and Gentlemen :

In accordance with time-honoured usages, it is now my privilege to address the Convocation, and to accord to you all a sincere welcome on behalf of the University. I specially offer my congratulations and best wishes to the graduates who are assembled here and who have just been admitted to their respective degrees.

During the year under review we had to mourn the death of several distinguished members and scholars, all devoted to the welfare of the University. Before I pay my tribute of respect to their memory, let me first record at this Convocation our profound sense of sorrow at the sudden demise of His Majesty King George V. At a special meeting of the Senate, the University has already expressed its deep sympathy with the Royal Family and has conveyed to His Majesty King Edward VIII its loyalty and devotion on his accession to the throne.

Among members of the Senate and teachers, we mourn the loss of two great Islamic scholars, two life-long friends and colleagues, both imbued with courage and imagination, Sir Abdullah Suhrawardy and Aga Mahomed Kazim Shirazi ; of a former Vice-Chancellor, the first non-official to hold this office, a man of wide interests and an upholder of the best traditions of the University, Sir Deva Prasad Sarvadhikary ; of an eminent medical practitioner and a friend of the poor, Dr. Jatindra Nath Maitra ; and of a pioneer of the movement for the physical regeneration of our youths, Captain Jitendra Nath Banerjea. The departments of the Law, Mathematics and Sanskrit have been left distinctly the poorer by the death of three of our erudite teachers, Mr. Jyoti Prasad Sarvadhikary, Professor Ganesh Prasad and Professor Prabhat Chandra Chakravarti, the last being cut off in the prime of his life and in the midst of valuable work. In Rai Bahadur Narendra Nath Sen we have lost one of our devoted officers who, by dint of merit, rose from a subordinate position to an office of great trust and responsibility. We lament also the death two distinguished European scholars, Dr. Sylvan Levi and Sir John Woodroffe, both of whom were ardent well-wishers of the province and genuinely devoted to Indian culture and civilization, which by their life-long researches they raised in the estimation of the world.

It is customary for the Vice-Chancellor to review on this occasion the work of the University during the preceding year. So varied and numerous, however, have been the questions which have engaged our attention that I can only mention some of our important activities.

Last year I referred to the momentous changes made in connection with the Matriculation Examination, giving the vernacular language its rightful place in our scheme of studies. The regulations have since been approved by Government and I take this opportunity of thanking its representatives, particularly my friend, the Minister of Education, without whose energetic support they would not have been sanctioned even fourteen years after they were first formulated by the University. The task of collecting materials for the systematic preparation of text-books in Bengali in various subjects of study, specially in Science, has been successfully continued during the year by a number of scholars whose unselfish labours deserve our best thanks. Our experts are also exploring the possibilites of a standardised form of spelling in Bengali. The principles on which we desire to proceed and the difficulties that await solution have been stated in the form of a questionnaire and we have invited the criticisms of scholars and writers from all parts of the province. The Syndicate will now take steps for the preparation and selection of text-books which should be available towards the end of the year.

I referred last year to the urgent need for the supply of a large number of trained teachers for high schools. We have since made provision for short course of study in the University for the training of teachers. Out of 15,000 teachers in our schools only about 2,000 are trained and we realise what we have been able to do is hardly adequate. A beginning has however been made and, through the new department of

Teaching, we expect to be able to acquaint ourselves at first hand with many problems of secondary education, specially the difficulties under which the teachers perform their duties.

The new Library Hall has been completed and it now provides our teachers and students with increased facilities for work. We are remodelling the library and revising the system of cataloguing books so as to increase its usefulnes and efficiency.

We have partially reorganised the Biological laboratories, but these need further development. We have transferred to Ballygunge the department of Anthropology, a subject which is now also included in the syllabus for the intermediate examination. The work of constructing a new building for the department of Applied Chemistry and for providing increased accommodation for the department of Applied Physics is now in progress and the extended laboratories will be in full working order in less than six months. We are anxiously exploring the possibilities of expanding the activities of the Science College so that it may not only be an active centre of higher teaching and research but also a potent influence in raising the standard of work done in the affiliated institutions and in providing new courses of studies leading to industrial careers.

In the department of Applied Physics we have made provision for the study of communication engineering. We expect this will open a new avenue of employment for our trained youths. This activity of ours has already received the sympathetic attention of possible donors and I have every hope that within the next few months we shall be favoured with a special endowment for the equipment of this department. From Applied Physics let me turn for a moment to Chinese and Tibetan studies. The Consul-General of China has kindly offered us the honorary services of a teacher in Chinese and we have appointed a special instructor in Tibetan. A competent staff is now engaged in carrying on research in these subjects which will throw light on many a dark corner of ancient Indian civilization. The money we are spending on it may not be productive in any material sense, but it is expected to yield results of great academic and cultural importance.

The University has steadily carried on its duty of publication of the research activities of both teachers and advanced students. Some of them have attracted notice from different parts of the world and have been acclaimed as works of solid value. These publications and other contributions in numerous journals and bulletins of learned societies throughout the world testify to the spirit of investigation which the University has awakened in its alumni, a spirit which alone can keep the University alive and make it grow as an active centre of learning.

That such activities are not confined to a particular class of teachers is evident from the fact that this year we have conferred the degree of Doctorate on as many as eight graduates of the University, working in different places. Of these, four are in Arts, two in Science, one in Law and one in Medicine. The various research prizes and scholarships continue to attract a large number of brilliant young men whose investigations cover a wide field of studies. The total number of scholarships and prizes awarded during the year to fellows and advanced students for studies here and abroad amounted to 85 and their consolidated value was about one lac of rupees. Two special scholarships were awarded to two brilliant Bengali lady graduates for advanced studies in education and philosophy in Europe. Another was awarded to a Bengali graduate in aeronautics, who unfortunately met his death at a fatal air tragedy at Dum Dum last year. A special scholarship has been granted to another who has recently returned from Cambridge and is now attached to one of our medical colleges, to enable him to carry on research in epidemic dropsy under Sir Nilratan Sircar. Another scholar was attached to the de Terra Yale-Cambridge expedition, engaged in important work of exploration North-western India

We have adhered to the policy of inviting distinguished professors and well-known personalities to deliver special lectures for the benefit of our students. To mention a few, and we had amongst us Madam Halide Edib Adnan from Turkey, Prof. Noguchi from Japan, Professor Turner from America, and Dr. Kempers from Germany. Among others who have been similarly invited are Professors Zoltan De Takas from Hungary, Sir Manmathanath Mukherji, our new Tagore Professor, Professor Satyendranath Bose of Dacca and Sir S. Radhakrishnan who will speak on Comparative Religion as Stephanos Nirmalendu Ghosh Lecturer. I take this opportunity of congratulating Professor Radhakrishnan on his recent appointment at Oxford which is a fitting tribute to his remarkable scholarship and attainments in the furtherance of which Calcutta played no small part.

A reform of far-reaching importance which the Senate has recently sanctioned relates to the teaching of Science at the Intermediate standard: The Regulations provide that every scientific subject should be taught in colleges, both from the theoretical and practical standpoints. But at the University examination we are not called upon to hold any test in respect of the practical portion. We have now decided to make this provision. We have done so in the full conviction that this will not lead to an improvement of the work done at the Intermediate standard but will also reflect on the quality of teaching at the higher stages.

Another important scheme recently app roved by the Senate relates to the creation of a Fine Arts Gallery and Museum mainly in connection with post-graduate studies. It is our desire that the Museum, while it must represent the genius of Indian art, should also lay special stress on the contributions made in this domain by North-Eastern India, specially Bengal. The establishment of the Museum has already evoked the sympathy and support of many an eminent lover of art, official and non-official. I earnestly believe that will help the University in spreading amongst its students that essential knowledge of and respect for Indian culture, manifested through the realm of Indian Art, which has not only a supreme educative value but is also calculated to rouse the patriotic consciousness of our youths.

The building for the University Rowing Club, whose activities received favourable comments from Your Excellency the other day, will be completed within two months and will enable us to respond satisfactorily to the enthusiasm which the club has already evoked from the student community of Calcutta. The University Training Crops deserves our congratulations for the popularity and efficiency it has recently attained, which fill us with hopes for its future. The playground allotted to the University by the Department of Public Instruction this year will be of immense help to us. The activities of our students in games and sports, which have made satisfactory progress during the year, demand co-ordination and further expansion and also call for intensive training. The increased attention paid to the health and physique of our students will stimulate the growth of both body and mind and will endow them with discipline and capacity for corporate work. We must develop the habit of playing the game and remember that in sport, as in life, victory or defeat is not the supreme factor ; what is of paramount importance is that in every sphere we must bring into action our best and cleanest efforts, which should be unnceasing and unyielding in character.

During the year the University has received donations for specified purposes amounting to Rs. 40,000. To the donors we have already conveyed our grateful thanks. Special mention must here be made of an endowment of Rs. 30.000 created by Mr. Prafulla Chandra Ghosh, one of our distinguished teachers and now a member of the Senate, for a systematic publication of works of translation in Bengali from well-known treatises in oriental classical languages. This series will be associated with the honoured name of Mr. Isan Chandra Ghosh, the donor's father, whose death the University only recently mourned and whose contributions to the cause of development of Bengali literature have earned for him a permanent place in the affections of his countrymen.

This reference to endowments leads me to make a few observations on the financial position of the University. Our fee-income has increased in recent years. But unfortunately we have not yet been able to arrive at any satisfactory settlement with Government regarding the conditions of the State grant which covers only about 17 per cent of our total expenditure. The Government grant for a particular year is decreased by half of the excess income of the University during the previous year, if it goes beyond the standard figure of Rs. 11,72,000. I must emphasise in this connection that the recurring grant of Rs. 3,60,000 was not intended to include the various projects of reform on which Government and the University were both agreed, neither did it represent our average deficit. It is lamentable that although we have an increased revenue at present, we are not allowed to utilise it fully for improvement and extension and are thus hampered in our activities. During the current year our grant has been reduced by Rs. 1,55,000, only because last year we had a large fee-income. I would state with all the emphasis at my command that if the University is to pursue a progressive policy of reform and expansion, which is regarded as essential for the future welfare of the province both by Government and the people, the least that the State can do is to place the entire grant at our disposal without imposing restrictions and conditions.

Let me now turn to some aspects of our educational policy which has recently been the subject-matter of widespread discussion. A criticism with which we have become familiar in this country is that an alarmingly large number of students is receiving University education, and the Universities are responsible for wastage and unnecessary duplication of teaching arrangements. Let us examine the situation dispassionately and ask ourselves whether the criticism levelled against the Universities in India has any foundation at all.

Let me first take our own University. We serve the needs of Bengal and Assam with the exception of a limited area which is controlled by Dacca. We have thus practically one University for a population of about fifty million in Bengal and nine in Assam. The number of students reading in the Universities and the colleges is about thirty-one thousand and the total expenditure on higher education is eighty-six lacs of rupees, Assam spending about four. Take the whole of British India with a population of two hundred and sixty-three million. India has only sixteen Universities and the number of their students will be about one lac and twenty thousand. The total expenditure on higher education in India is less than four crores of rupees.

Let me now turn to other countries. The British Isles afford a good illustration for comparison from the point of view of population which is about forty-five million: but the number of Universities is as many as sixteen—what we have for the whole of India—and fifty-five thousand students receive instruction under their jurisdiction. About six crores and forty lacs of rupees are spent on higher education only in England and Wales. To universities alone within this area the State annually contributes two crores and twenty-seven lacs of rupees.

Let me take the figures for a British dominion. Canada, which has a population of ten million, has as many as twenty-three Universities and eighty-five thousand students pursue higher education. In Germany the population is sixty-six million with twenty-three Universities which have an enrolment of eighty-eight thousand students. In Italy which has a population of forty-one million, there are twenty-six Universities and fifty thousand students receive higher education. In Japan with a population of sixty-four million there are six Universties and seventy thousand students.

Let me now give some figures for secondary education. In Bengal the number of pupils in different grades of secondary schools is about four lacs and sixty thousand, of whom about three lacs belong to high schools recognised by the University. Assam has, in addition, an enrolment of seventy-seven thousand pupils in secondary schools. For every seventeen who receive secondary education, one proceeds to the higher stage. If we take the whole of India, there are about twenty-four lacs of students in schools, and for every twenty, one goes up to the University stage. But what about other countries? In the British Isles seven lacs of pupils read in secondary schools, and one in every twelve proceeds to higher education. In Canada one in every three joins the University. In Germany the proportion is one to nine; in Italy and in Japan it is one to ten.

The number of candidates at the matriculation examination of our University often disturbs the peace of mind of our critics. May I bring it to their notice that if about twenty-five thousand candidates will appear at our matriculation examination this year, four years ago fifty-seven thousand candidates sat for the Approved First Examination from secondary schools in England and Wales alone—an examination which has been adopted by the universities as a matriculation examination—and seventy-three per cent of them were successful?

Similar illustrations might be given in reference to educational opportunities existing in other civilised countries which allot enormous sums of money to education. We have not heard it stated that the number of students receiving instruction in universities, in colleges and in secondary schools in these countries is by any means excessive or that it displays an unhealthy mental development on the part of the people of these lands. Neither have we heard it stated that the large number of universities and educational institutions existing in each of these countries—which must necessarily make similar provision for teaching and research in many branches of study—are wasting national resources or are guilty of duplication of arrangements. Neither again have we heard any sweeping condemnation of their educational systems on the ground that the vast majority of the students is pursuing education, as indeed they must, not solely out of respect for learning for the sake of learning but also as a means to an end.

While I make these general observations, I do not ignore certain essential factors. I recognise that each country must have its own problems and nowhere is the educational system considered perfect. I recognise that in each one of these countries there is the amplest provision for elementary education. But surely, if in Bengal or in India primary education to-day is utterly inadequate, the fault does not rest with the university ; neither does it stand to reason that the educational opportunities offered at the higher stages should be curtailed or condemned. I do not ignore that in other countries education is of a varied type and affords facilities for the training of youths in diverse branches of knowledge, theoretical and practical. But surely, the remedy for the present state of things in this country would be to make provision for similar kinds of instruction in our schools and colleges and not to complain against the number of students reading in them. I do not ignore that in other countries, apart from the education which thousands of students receive through the medium of the universities, colleges and schools, there are other recognised institutes and bodies through which knowledge is spread for the benefit of the people, both young and old. In our country the number of such institutions is extremely limited. I do not ignore that in many other countries, although general unemployment is a disturbing element in national life, unemployment amongst educated people, though present, is not so distressing as in India. But let us not forget that national interests in those lands have secured among the different authorities—the State, the universities and other educational agencies and representatives of trade, industry and commerce—a better and more harmonius arrangement for the proper utilisation of the skilled services of trained men and women who are absorbed in diverse occupations and careers. In our country unfortunately such co-operation is not at present found in any appreciable measure.

I am moved to make these observations because in recent times there has been a marked tendency to throw a major portion of the blame for the existing state of affairs in this country on the universities and to minimise the importance of the work which has been done by them. There has often been a lamentable want of realisation of the scope for far greater service which the universities, if better equipped and organised, are capable of rendering for the advancement of national prosperity. Whatever reconstruction in the sphere of education might be made in future,—and we readily recognise the vital need of reforms,—it would be nothing short of a national disaster if the prestige and the authority of the university are sought to be curtailed or its influence minimised.

In recent years there have been numerous reports, resolutions and addresses on educational reforms. The criticisms and proposals which have appeared are so varied and formidable that it is often difficult to discover the correct path of action. This province presents for solution problems of educational reconstruction of an unusual complexity. Let us strive and do all that lies in our power to strengthen our foundation, to raise our standard, to revitalise the system and make it respond to the needs of the hour in full accordance with the genius of the people of this country. The time has come when we should sink our differences and inaugurate a new policy of education which will be for the highest good of the largest number of our people. Education offers a field of activity where it is possible for all parties to work in the fullest harmony and co-operation and all must work in that spirit if reforms are to be of any real significance. There must be no conflict of aims and ideals, no arbitrary exercise of authority, no domination of vested interests.

Our ideal is to provide extensive facilities for education from the lowest grade to the highest, to mould our system in such a way as to unify our educational purpose and to draw out the best qualities that lie hidden in our youths and to train them, intellectually, physically and morally, for devoted service in all spheres of national activity—in villages, in towns and in cities. Our ideal is to make the widest provision for a sound liberal education, to find the correct synthesis between cultural education and vocational and technical training, remembering always that no nation can achieve greatness by turning its youth into a mere machine-made product with nothing but a material end in view. Our ideal is to afford the amplest facilities and privileges to our teachers so that they may be endowed with learning, character, and freedom and may regard themselves as not only the torch-bearers and interpreters of knowledge and conquerors of new realms of thought but also as makers of men and women, of leaders and workers, true and brave, upright and patriotic. Our ideal is to link up education with the best elements of our culture and civilization, drawing strength, wherever necessary, from the fountain of Western skill and knowledge. Our ideal is to make our universities and educational institutions the home of liberty and sane and progressive thought,—generously assisted by the State and the public,—where teachers and students will meet and work in an atmosphere of harmony and mutual understanding, where none will suffer on grounds of caste, sex, creed, and religious or political belief.

I realise we cannot expect to attain this ideal in the immediate future. But what is essential is a searching and systematic examination of our educational needs and the formulation of our ideal. If Bengal is to take a leading part in the task of national reconstruction, the present atmosphere of distrust and suspicion must go for ever. Let us all,—the University, the State and the educated public belonging to all communities,—gather our forces together and combine resolutely, first, to determine the path of future reforms most suited to our environments and national development and, next, to agree to the means for carrying our project into execution.

If Your Excellency, as Chancellor of this University which has been the mouthpiece of the hopes and aspirations of generations of men and women, can help to discover and fulfil the conditions of this united action and lay the foundations for the gigantic task of educational reconstruction, you will be earning the everlasting gratitude of the people of Bengal. Let me conclude by saying that in the formulation of any scheme of reform which is calculated to enhance the well-being of the people and to raise the fame and prestige of our province, which has done so much for the advancement of Indian nationalism, you may always depend upon the ready and spontaneous co-operation not only of the University but of the entire educated public of Bengal.

The Delhi University Convocation

The following is the full text of the Convocation address delivered by Rai Bahadur Ram Kishore, the Vice Chancellor, at the 14th. Convocation of the University of Delhi, held on the **28th March 1936** :—

Mr. Pro-Chancellor, Members of the Court, Ladies and Gentlemen—

It is my duty and also my proud privilege to extend to you all a hearty welcome and particularly to you, Sir, whom the University has the honour to receive here at a Convocation for the first time as its Pro-Chancellor. Your distinguished public services, your long and varied experience as an administrator and statesman, and above all, your keen interest in every progressive movement in the country make us all confident that under your wise guidance and leadership as its Pro-Chancellor the University will rapidly develop its activities and grow to what it was intended to be, a University worthy of the Capital of India.

A few weeks ago we heard with the most profound regret of the death of Lord Reading, the first Chancellor of the University. It was during his regime as Viceroy and Governor-General of India that the idea of a University in this Imperial City was first conceived and as soon as it was established by an Act of the Central Legislature he saw it organised and completely constituted. The high ideal that he set for the University as its Chancellor and the hopes he infused in us by his keen interest in its affairs are recorded in glowing terms in the annals of this institution. I hope you will bear with me if I indulge myself, for a while, in the happy memory of the Convocation held in 1926 in this very hall at which many of you were present. Lord Reading who, as Chancellor of the University, presided on the occasion, was pleased to describe the position of the University and its future in these inspiring words:

"Let me invite you to reflect on the very special position occupied by this University of Imperial Capital of India. It is situated at the head-quarters of the Government of India and at the seat of the Central Legislature. It has an intimate connection with His Majesty the King-Emperor's representative in India, the Viceroy and Governor-General. It takes its name from a place famous in the annals of the past history of India and identified with great traditions of both Hindu and Moslem Empires. It is a link between the ancient lore and culture of India, of which many traces are to be found at Delhi, and the various activities of modern learning, science and research.

"What I hope, and what I believe you all hope, to see in Delhi is a University of which not only Delhi but India as a whole may be justly proud. And how, it may be asked, may this hope be attained? What characteristics should distinguish this

University to mark its special position? What particular aims should it hold before it? In view of its associations, the answer would seem to be that the Delhi University in the first place should give expression to the close concern of the Viceroy and the Governor-General for the moral and intellectual progress of India. It should further be a practical sign of the ultimate responsibility of his Government for the most complete realisation of the best educational ideals in India. It should likewise be a mirror to reflect the ardent desire of the representatives of India in the Central Legislature for the development of her people and the advancement of their capacity and culture to the highest plane. It should diffuse the most powerful influences for the improvement of mental qualities and the strengthening of character. It should be a field of ambition, in which all classes, parties and creeds may labour together in a labour of love, working in harmony in a great public cause."

Ten years have passed since Lord Reading expressed his high hopes about the University in the memorable words I have quoted. It may not be unprofitable, I, think, to review and estimate, as briefly as I can, the extent of the progress the University has made since then, and the measure in which it has been able to realise the educational ideal held before it by its first Chancellor. I do not wish to tire your patience by a recital of the visible achievements of the University—the reconstruction and the disposal of its buildings in the beautiful Viceregal Estate, the arrangements made for the housing and the equipment of its laboratories and library. For, important as they are, buildings and gardens do not make a University, far less do they represent the true educational ideal which it ought to pursue. I shall content myself with a few words about the recent endeavour of the University to formulate its academic policy and to shape its destiny. It is only during the last three years that the University has been able to turn its thoughts in these directions, the first ten years of its life having been spent in a severe struggle for existence which made self-determination practically impossible.

The deep interest now taken by the Government of India in the promotion of higher education in the Capital City of India and, as an earnest of that interest, the transfer of the Old Viceregal Lodge to the University as its permanent home have assured the University of a continued and useful existence. Thus encouraged, the University is now diligently engaged in studying its problems and requirements as well as making plans for its future development.

In these constructive activities, the advice and assistance of my esteemed friend, Sir George Anderson, the Educational Commissioner with the Government of India, have been invaluable. I desire here to make a public acknowledgment on behalf of the University and myself, of the debt of gratitude we owe him for the great services he has rendered to Indian education in general and to this University in particular. He has not only inspired and guided us in our endeavour, but created a better understanding between the Government of India and the University which has resulted in a happy and fruitful co-operation between the two in promoting the interests of higher education in the city of Delhi. It is to him chiefly that we owe the scheme of a federal university the general principles of which have now been adopted by this University. As early as 1933, in the illuminating Convocation address he gave to this University he suggested a solution of the perplexing problem of the relation between an Indian University and its Colleges. "There is, fortunately, a middle path", he said, "between the two extremes: the purely affiliating university, with separate, self-contained and largely autonomous colleges on the one hand, and the centralised unitary university on the other hand. This is the path which the University of Delhi is treading, but it is not easy to define the relations between the University and its colleges".

The idea of a federal university was discussed at some length by His Excellency the Viceroy in his epoch-making address when he opened the third Quinquennial Conference of Indian Universities held in Delhi in March 1934. "Only a University of the federal type", His Excellency said, "can guide and co-ordinate the development of existing colleges so that they shall make their most effective contribution towards the common weal. If only the colleges can be made to realise that this new type of University is intended to supplement, not to supplant their activities, to fulfil and not to destroy the purpose for which colleges exist, they would, I fill confident, be prepared to submit, in the large national interest, to the greater measure of control with which a federal university must be invested over its constituents so as to ensure the efficiency both of itself and its colleges".

A few weeks later my learned predecessor, Sir Abdur Rahman, tried to visualize in his Convocation address a federal university with all its implications and suggested a body of federal law defining, as far as possible, the rights and functions of the University and the colleges respectively. Further thought and frequent discussion by the University authorities on this important subject have not only clarified our ideas of the federal scheme but revealed many difficulties which must be faced before any measure of success can be expected. This scheme depends on two essential conditions. First, there should be complete co-operation between the University and its colleges in teaching and other activities, the colleges being prepared to forego some measure of their autonomy "in order to share in, and contribute to the life and goverment of the University as a whole". Secondly, in order to make such co-operation effective the colleges should be in close proximity to one another and to the University.

After long and earnest negotitations with the colleges the University has now been able to allay their fears and to persuade them to come to the University site so that they may participate fully in the life and activities of the University. But only one College has the necessary funds for the construction of the required buildings; the rest, unless they are able to dispose of their present buildings profit ably, will have to depend chiefly on Government grants which I trust will be available.

I have already referred to the suggestions made at a previous Convocation by my friend and predecessor Sir Abdur Rahman for the enactment of a special body of federal law regulating and controlling the activities of the colleges and the University. The basic federal law is now finally nearing its enactment. Statutes have been drafted defining the relations between the University and the colleges and providing among other things for the proper management of the colleges and their recognition. Recognising the fact the teachers of the University will play the most important role in the federal system, provision has also been made for better conditions of service and more attractive prospects for them. The draft statutes have met with the approval of the Academic and the Executive Council and have been submitted by the latter body to the Court, the supreme authority of the University, for consideration. If they are passed by that body and receive the assent of the Governor-General in Council, as it is hoped they will, the University will have on its Statute Book a body of federal law which will supply the constitutional and legal foundation of the scheme.

The propuosal to transfer the colleges to the University site in the Old Viceregal Estate has brought into prominence another problem of considerable difficulty. It has been in our view for some time; but few expected to be confronted with it so soon. For the last few weeks the general proposal for the reconstruction of the system of education in the country has engaged the special attention of the University. I need not here mention all the details of the proposal; but I should like to say a few words on one or two aspects which affect the University vitally. The question of strengthening the school foundations and the stage of admission to the University are inseparably connected. While we welcome the former as an essential condition of efficiency of teaching in the colleges and in the university, the latter seems to be complicated with numerous problems. At the present moment we admit to the University students who have passed the Matriculation or an equivalent examination. They go through a four-years corse in two stages of two years each—the Intermediate and the Degree—before they graduate. I am not considering here the post-graduate course of two years which leads to the Master's Degree. The problem before us is: What is going to happen to the Intermediate stage—the two junior classes—when the colleges move to the university site? Are these classes coming with the degree classes to the new site, or are they to be left behind and provided for separately? The opinion of the Government of India seems definitely against the inclusion of the Intermediate classes in the University. In a letter addressed to the Chief Commissioner, Delhi in April 1934 the Government of India expressed their views clearly on this important question. "The administration of the University," it was stated, "shou d not be overstrained by the imposition of functions which do not ordinarily come within the scope of a university; its teaching resources should not be diverted to the teaching of school children who are as yet unfitted to receive university teaching; the Estate, though spacious, is yet limited in extent and should be reserved as far as possible for university activities." The position of the intermediate classes seems very anomalous indeed. The majority of the students in these classes are immature, both physically and mentally, and ill-equipped and ill-prepared for university education. Their tender age and unformed character need a special treatment which a school ought to provide